MAP OF OLD TESTAMENT

MAP OF NEW TESTAMENT

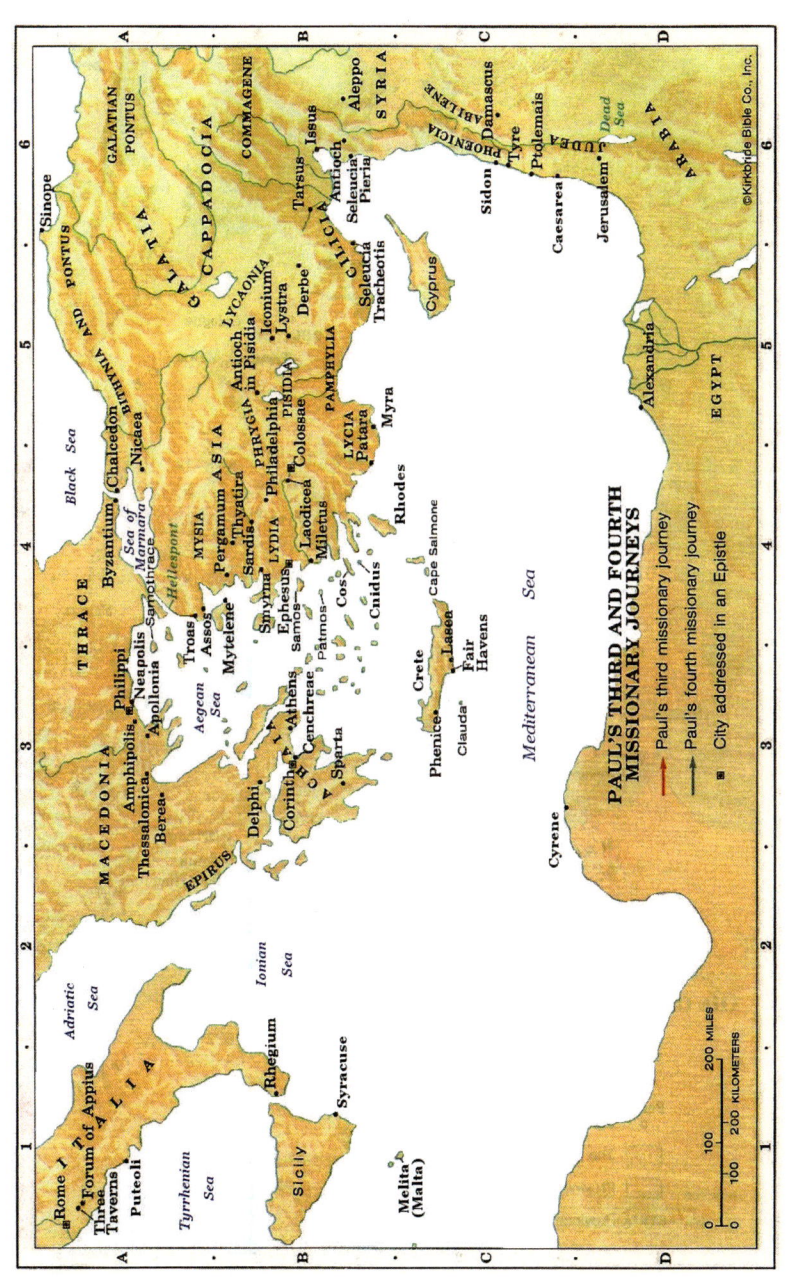

Gospel Dictionary
And Biblical Phrases

FIRST EDITION

Edited by
**Moses Bassey
and Mary Edwards**

English/Hebrew/Greek

HEHOM
Heavenly Home Press
LONDON

HEHOM
Heavenly Home Press
18 – 24 High Street
Edgware, Middlesex
HA8 7RP
United Kingdom

Hehom is a prefix for Heavenly Home Press, a division of Heavenly Home Ministries – a MBM Ministry with office in London. It furthers the objective of excellence in research, gospel teachings, Music and education by publishing the first ever Gospel Dictionary and Biblical Phrases to compliment Scriptural teachings throughout the universe. Hehom is a subsidiary of Womogu – Womogu is a registered trademark of the World Monetary Guide (Press) registered in France, the United Kingdom and Certain other Countries.

© Hehom in conjunction with World Monetary Guide Press 2014
Database right Heavenly Home Press (makers)

First Edition 2014
All rights reserved. No part of this publication may be reproduced, stored in a retrieval system, or transmitted in any form or by any means, without the prior permission in writing of Heavenly Home Press or as expressly permitted by Law or under terms agreed with the appropriate reprographic rights organization. Enquiries concerning reproduction outside the scope of the above should be sent to the Rights Department, Heavenly Home Press at the above address.

Accordingly, you must not circulate this book in any other binding cover and you must impose this same condition on any acquire.
A CIP record of this book is available at British Library Cataloging in Publication Data and Library of Congress Catalogue in Publication Data.

ISBN: 978-0-9542736-6-8
10 0 9 5 4 2 7 3 6 6 8
Printed and bound in London by Heavenly Home Press
Note: We have made every effort to mark as such all words which we believe to be trade marks. We should also like to make it clear that the presence of a word in this book, whether mark or unmarked in no way affects it Legal status as a trademark.

Again, every reasonable effort has been made by the publishers to trace the copyright holders of material quoted in this book. Any error or omission should be notified in writing to the publishers who will endeavor to rectify the situation and amend for any reprints and future editions

www. Womogu.com

www. Hehom.com

Contents

Gospel Map (Old and New Testament)

Preface   iv

Guide to the use of the dictionary   vi

Abbreviation used in the dictionary   xi

Gospel Dictionary and Biblical Phrases   16 -763

Gospel Notes   764- 771

PREFACE

This first edition of Gospel Dictionary and Biblical Phrases is the most valuable thing you can afford to inspire love of real Gospel of Christ Jesus into your life. It does not only prepare you for Salvation but also prepare you for your Heavenly Home. An inestimable treasure that excelled all the reaches of the earth – Gods word.... I derive spiritual inspiration to write the first ever Gospel Dictionary to strengthen the focus of Christians and Preachers of the Gospel extending from orthodox approach in understanding and interpreting the Gospel of God in the way and manner different bible writers present the texts of the Gospel and to provide both the apostolic and ecclesiastic direction to gospel words to enable readers forged understanding rather than dwell on deviations to unscriptural words in the canal dictionary as often is the case. Among other stream of values, the enhancement to the faith, the text and vigorous pursuits of accuracy combined with simplicity, beauty, interpretational legacy, philosophy, principles, style, basis and resources including specialize terms as well as dignity of expression in order to carry forward the correct order of the Gospel to God's Honour and Praise. It is very solid, biblically based and immediately helpful to Christians searching for insight of Gospel words, the new converts to the Gospel of Christ and all those eagerly to read the Gospel in order to discover the real and true meanings of words and phrases.

There is a supernatural source of power and energy in the Word of God (Gospel words) that can change your life 100%, as God's Holy Spirit is making the Words alive and powerful. You can be healed, saved and set free by reading, understanding and applying this Divine Word. The secret to Divine Revelations is to know the Word of God by your heart and through the Holy Spirit. Be ready for the end-times and what the book of revelation is talking about in prophecies and in (Matthew 24). Study the Word of God and do not be deceived on how to experience God's presence, when the bible makes it clear that "In the beginning was the Word, and the Word was with God, and the Word was God". (John 1:1). So, to get the word of God which is GOD into your spirit, you need a deeper understanding of each word – with which Preachers and Gospel actors developed into sentences forming the various inputs of the Gospel... So get into the heart of the word where... The full meaning to Gospel words, expressions, exegesis and synopsis are presented in a form reflecting diverse biblical presentations, parables, illustrations and idiomatic words and expressions, orderly explained or bang up to date to provide not only the divined inspiration but extraordinary interpretations and renditions to encourage or inspire

more readership to the Bible and set the mind of readers to much more focus to the living word of God that adds strength to your faith graciously in Christ Jesus.

Everyday thousands of examples of words are being collected in order to monitor scriptural words as being used by Christians everywhere. This body of language forms the Heavenly Home (Hehom) Gospel Dictionary, a unique database that makes it possible for us to see exactly how scripture is developing and to discover revealing facts about the Gospel of Christ. The predominant questions to the mind are;

What are the main scriptural words?
What are the commonest Gospel words?
What new words are entering into the body of Christ which create divisions or sometimes confusion?
Where do new words come from?
Why are people feeling reluctant from reading the bible?
What makes scriptural understanding today much more difficult?
How can Gospel words be used to make worshipers worship God in spirit and truth?

Now containing more than one billion words, Gospel dictionary and biblical phrases gives us the most up-to-date information available about how gospel words and meanings are directed to fulfil spiritual understanding than contemporary exegesis of the words by theological practitioners. This means that Gospel Dictionary and Biblical phrases offer the fullest, most accurate picture and divine means towards Christ faith today - profitable to all heavenly bound souls.

Guide to the Use of the dictionary

1 Structure of Entries

Gospel Dictionary and Biblical Phrases are designed to be as straight forward and easy to use in reference to gospel words and phrases. Below are the explanations of the main types of information in the dictionary. The main structure follows the English words and their correspondences in the Hebrew and Greek.

Narratives: Sometimes, narratives are given to through more lights into the impact of words and their effect to the gospel narratives as presented in the various forms of biblical or scriptural interpretations.

Quotations: Words quoted from King James Bible are left in their original forms such as the Old English forms like *(Abideth for abide, Speaketh for speak, Reigneth for reign etc)* While expressions in the (Amplified AMP, the New International Version NIV etc) are sometimes left in their original forms.

Referencing: In most cases and for the enhancement of oneness of mind in understanding the meaning of the gospel theme in the bible, referencing are limited to fulfill the aim of the dictionary in terms of focusing the mind to the insight or the in-depth understanding of the gospel words, expressions and exegeses .

VII

2 Spelling and forms of nouns and verbs

Gospel Dictionary and Biblical Phrases give's a great deal of advice and information on spelling, in particular for those words which do not follow regular patterns or which otherwise cause difficulty for English speakers in the various forms of Biblical translations. The main categories are given below and you will also find extra information on matters such as using hyphens in the effective English and the corresponding spellings in Hebrew and Greek.

Alternative spellings: Most words given in the dictionary are the accepted British spelling; the literal meaning of some of those words are already given in ordinary English forms. Although there is only one way that most words can be spelled, sometimes other spellings called (variants) are also accepted. Such spellings are given in other languages as Greek and Hebrew to show the origin of words which were translated into the English Bible – such words as Affection -Greek: *splagchnon* – [splangkh'-non], Hebrew: *agab* – [aw-gab'] etc. Some words are spelled directly in its Greek or Hebrew forms e.g Adonai , Adytum and so on. Most spellings in American base Bible are left in their sense or meaning of use, such as 'colour' in British English can be 'color' in American English. So the label US shows spellings that are used in American English.

Where verbs can be spelled with either an –ize or –ise ending the two spellings are given in the following way: apologize or (apologise), to show that either spelling can be used. The spelling -ise is far more common in British English, while –ize is usually found in American writing and in English in other part of the world - Although, these features are also found in the British English.

Hyphenation: Although standard spelling in English is fixed, the use of hyphens is not. There are a few general rules that should be followed as outlined below.

Noun compounds: There are no set rules as to whether a compound should be written as one word. For example, worldwide; world wide, and world-wide are all acceptable. However in modern Gospel English, people are tending to use hyphens less than before and are writing compounds either as one word worldwide or two words (whole world); like in preaching the Gospel to the 'whole-world' or whole world rather than with a hyphen. While you will find one-word and two-word compounds in both British and American English, there is a general preference to write compounds

VIII

as two words in British English and as one word in American English.

For the avoidance of complication and abstract terminologies, the dictionary gives only one of the three possible forms - the standard of British form. Nevertheless, this does not mean that other forms are not used or are incorrect.

Grammatical information: Hyphens are also used to show a Gospel word grammatical function. When a noun compound which is made up of two separate words (Example: Holy spirit) is placed before another noun, the rule is that the compound should have a hyphen, so that I invite the Holy Spirit but the Holy-spirit of truth. This is shown in the example sentences in the Gospel dictionary but it is not otherwise mentioned in the dictionary entries.

Accordingly, there is a similar rule with compound adjectives such as well known. When they are placed after the verb (in the predicative position) such adjectives are not written with a hyphen, but when they are placed before noun in the attributive position) they should have a hyphen, He is the Most High God but The Most-High God. The rule with verb compound is that, where a noun compound is two words – as in (**praise worship**) you should normally write any verb compound formed from it with a hyphen (to join **praise-worship**). Compound verbs of this type are always shown in the gospel dictionary.

Forms of nouns and verbs (inflections)

Plurals of nouns in the Gospel Dictionary

The plural of most nouns are formed by adding –s as in Pastors, or –es as in Churches or when they end in –s, -x, -z, -sh, or –ch (as in Church). These kinds of plurals are not shown in gospel dictionary unless they are extremely important. All other plural forms in the Scripture are spelled out in full, e.g. nouns ending in –i or –o like in some Greek and Hebrew word like Adonis, Dunamis,

Verbs: Most verbs change their form (inflect) by adding –s, -ing, and –ed to the infinitive (the basic unchanged part of the verb): pray – prays, praying, prayed. These kinds of verb forms are not shown in the dictionary.

Other verbs change their forms in the ways set out below and are shown in full.

IX

- Verb which change by doubting a consonant, e.g. promise – promises, promising, promised
- Verbs ending in –y to –I, e.g. try – tries, trying, tried
- Verb in which the past tense and or the past participle do not follow the regular –ed pattern, e.g. feel, -feels, feeling, felt, wake – wakes, waking, woke; past participle – woken.

Adjectives: Adjectives in the dictionary have three different forms that express the level or intensity of a particular quality. The basic level is called the positive, e.g. joy, the level expressing more of a quality is called comparative e.g. in the word sweet as sweeter, and the level expressing most of a quality is called the superlative, e.g. sweetest. Most adjectives from their comparatives and superlatives in the following ways, and these are not shown in the dictionary.

- Gospel words of one syllable adding -er and –est, e.g. great, greater greatest
- Gospel words of one syllable ending in silent (unspoken) –e, which drop the -e and add –er and –est, e.g. brave – brave (like in David with Goliath) –braver, bravest
- Gospel words which form the comparative and superlative by adding more and most.

The forms are however shown in the Gospel dictionary in all other cases – notably :

- Adjectives which form the comparative and superlative by doubling a final consonant, e.g. the word (hot) – hotter, hottest.
- Gospel words with two-syllable adjectives which form the comparative and superlative with –er and –est e.g.(the word happy) – happier, happiest

3. Gospel word Labels

The majority of gospel words and senses in this dictionary are all part of standard English application, which means that they are the kinds words used in every types of scriptural situation, whether in the Churches, Evangelism, outreaches, home, friendship Christian conversation. That being so, some words however, are suitable only for certain ministering situations or are found only in certain types of scriptural writing, and where this is the case a label (or a combination of labels) is used.

Register labels: These refers to the particular level of used in the language – indicated whether a term is informal, formal, historical and much more.

Formal Gospel words: Normally used only in writing, such as in official documents (e.g. abode)

Informal Gospel words: Normally used only in speaking, preaching or communicating to the multitude

Geographical labels: The Gospel is preach or is to be preached throughout the whole world, and while most of the words used in British English preaching style will be the same as those used in the American or Australian styles of preaching, there are some words which are only found in one type of English scriptural preaching. For example the normal word in American style of preaching for 'Honor' is Honour. These kinds of words are given in geographical label. The main regional differences word use in preaching are British, US, and Australian

Subject labels: These are used to show that a word or sense is associated with a particular scriptural word field or specialist activity such as Music, revival, outreach or drama.

4. Pronunciations

The Gospel dictionary and Biblical Phrases uses respelling system for pronouciations which is very easy to understand and to use. The dictionary gives pronounciation for any word native English preachers and readers might find difficult; it does not provide pronouciations for everyday words that are familiar to everyone, such as large or table. Foreign pronouciations are always shown in the way an English Christian would say of them in Greek or Hebrew, e.g. Greek: splagchnon – [splangkh'-non], Hebrew: agab – [aw-gab']

Pronounciations are divided into syllables by means of hyphens. The main stress is shown in thick dark type or broken syllable sometimes with punctuation. Occasionally, an apostrophe has been used instead of the sound in cases where there is a slight break beteen sounds, or where the sound is a consonant that is a whole syllable, as in /foh-k'l/ (focal) or /har k'n/ [hearken]

The sound of the word eye is shown in two ways notably as –I in the first part of words and in parts where it stands alone, as in I-ther as in [either]. However, a rhyming pronounciation is given where the alternative respelling would involve odd-looking word groups, as in aisle -et cetera.

List of respelling symbols

Vowels	Example	Vowels	Example	Consonants	Example	Consonants	Example
ah	as in calm	oi	as in join	d	as in day	p	as in pen
air	as in hair	oo	as in soon	g	as in get	s	as in sin
aw	as in law	or	as in corn	h	as in hat	t	as in top
ay	as in lay	u	as in cup	k	as in king	th	as in thin
I	as in eye	uh	as in 'a'	l	as in leg	th	as in this
ew	as in few	y	as in cry	m	as in man	w	as in will
oh	as in most	y	as in unit	n	as in not	zh	as in vision

5. Abbreviations used in the Gospel Dictionary

ABBREVIATIONS

- AMP – The Amplified Bible
- ASV - American Standard Version
- BOC – Body of Christ
- CSV - Contemporary Standard Version
- GNB - Good News Bible
- ISV - International Standard Version
- NKJV -New King James Version
- NIV - New International Version
- MSG - The Message Translation
- RSV - Revised Standard Version
- TANT - The Amplified New Translation
- TEV - Today's English Version
- TNLT -The New Living Translation
- NASB - New American Standard Bible
- PG - Peoples Group

Aaron

Aa

Aaron: Lofty, exalted, high mountain, Mountain of strength, or bearer of martyrs, a teacher (Keeper by Gods Command) The older brother of Moses and a prophet of God who represented the priestly functions of his tribe in Israel and thereby becoming the first High Priest of the Israelites. *(Exodus 6: 16-20) 2 At the time* when Moses was receiving his education at the Egyptian Royal Court and thereafter embarked on his exile among the Midianites, Aaron and sister Miriam were with their kinsmen in the eastern border land of Egypt (Goshen). At this time, Aaron progressed and gained accreditation for eloquent and persuasive speech so that when it was the time for Israelites freedom from captivity Aaron became his brother (Moses) Prophet to Pharaoh. 3 Aaron could be remembered in his miraculous blossoming of his staff or rod.

4. People with this name tend to form a powerful force to all lives they touch. Aaron, a true source of charismatic Leaders who often undertake large endeavours successfully. 'The Aarons' values truth, justice and discipline, and may be quick-tempered with those who do not. Often are rigid if potentials are not adequately developed.

Aaron's Beards: *(phr)* The popular name of the flowering plant – Rose of Sharon (Hypericum calycinum) looking like bright yellow, late spring.. It is like precious oil upon the head, coming down upon the beard, even Aaron's beard *(Psalm 133:2)* verses 2 and 3 repeat the Hebrew verb 'to go down' in three places: meaning running down Aarons's beard, running down Aarons collar, and falling dew. 2. Dwelling together in unity. Like good oil upon the head, descending upon the beard upon the beard of Aaron it descends, upon the mouth of his robes. 3 Like the dew of Hermon it descends, upon the mountains of Zion. For there YHWH – the Lord commands the blessing: Life forevermore (Psalm 133)

Aaron's Rod: A rod in the hand of Aaron the high priest was endowed with miraculous power particularly during the several plagues that preceded the Exodus. In this function the rod of Moses was equally potent. Aaron's rod in two occasions carried the singular virtue of spontaneous power, when not in the grasp of its possessor. At one occasion it swallowed the rods of the Egyptian magicians, and at another it blossomed and bore fruit in the Tabernacle, as an evidence of the exclusive right to the priesthood to the tribe of Levi.

2 In commemoration of this decision it was commanded that the rod be put again ""before the testimony"" (Number 17:10). Just like a later tradition exerts (Hebrew 11:4) that Aaron's rod was kept in the Ark of the Covenant. However, the main fact is thus confirmed, that a rod was preserved in the Tabernacle as a relic of the institution of the 'Aaronic' priesthood.

Abase: *(uh-bayss)* Behaviour that devalue ones integrity. Abasing oneself- Degrading yourself. Gospel wise, Negative thought often associated with lack of faith or believe in God or absolute lack of trust in God's word. Behave in a way that is demeaning or degrading. **(Derivative)** abasement. In short, to lower. In prayer, a number of Christians abase themselves to portray humility before God rather than speak the word of faith and inheritance of Christ heritage with him; such phrases as I am a Royal Priest, A chosen person, A Holy Nation is recommended. Why not take control of Psalm 23:1 - The Lord is my shepherd I shall not want rather than dwelling on 'I am poor and needy...

Abba: Aramaic word for father. Abba father. Expressing Jesus' awareness of his unique relationship to the father. Meaning, Jesus' self-revelation as the son of God is given a unique expression in the term Abba, Father. An Aramaic word which is preserved in the Greek text of Mark's Gospel (Mark 14:36). It appears precisely when Jesus addressed his Father. (God) Even though this word can be translated, yet on the lips of Jesus of Nazareth one can better understand its unique meaning. 2 A Prophecy fulfilled in messianic times. Abba expresses not only the traditional praise of God. "I bless you, Father, Lord of heaven and earth" (Mathew 11:25), but as used by Jesus (the son of God) it also indicates his awareness of the unique and exclusive relationship that exists between the father and himself. 3 It expresses the same reality to which Jesus alludes in such a simple and yet extraordinary way in the word preserved for us in the Gospels of (Mathew 11:27) and (Luke 10:22), thus "No one knows the son except the Father and no one knows the Father except the son and anyone to whom the Son chooses to reveal him. This demonstrates a dual revelation approach between the father and son and between the son and the father. 4 This is to say, the word Abba not only manifests the mystery of the

Abednego

reciprocal bond between Father and Son, but summarises in a certain way the whole truth about God's intimate life in the depths of the Trinity, that mutual knowledge of Father and Son which gives rise to the 'inspiration' of eternal Love, particularly the Agape love of God towards us. 5 *Abba*, taken from the vocabulary of family life and speaks of the personal communion between father and son and between the Son who loves the Father and is in turn loved by him. At the time when Jesus used this word to speak of God, his hearers must have wondered and even been scandalized. No one can and had ever used it in Israel even in prayer. Only the one who is recognized by God and who regarded himself as the son of God. Jesus Christ who "knows the Father" so profoundly came to manifest his name to the men whom the father had given him. Praise the Lord!

Abednego: Servant of Nebo in Akkadan, Nebo being the Babylonian god of wisdom. Abednego in the Babylonian context refers to the god of wisdom and it is the Babylonian name given to Azariah – one of the three men cast into a blazing furnace but saved by God. 2 Daniel's third companion who together with shadrach and Meshach was miraculously saved from destruction in Nebuchadnezzar's fiery furnace *(Daniel 3: 12 –30)*

3 In the Bible, a young man who with Meshach and Shadrach emerged unharmed from the fiery furnace of Babylon.

Abel: Commonly used in the old Testament-name of the younger son of Adam and Eve who was murdered out of jealousy by his brother Cain *(Genesis 4: 1-8)*. 2 Abel is regarded by the Christian Church as a pre-christian martyr and Jesus specifically spoke of him as righteous *(Mathew 23:25)*. 3 the Abel's murder is the first in the Bible which can scripturally or gospel wise be taken to imply that blood must be shed before peace can come. This name suggest that his life was cut short to this end or objective.

Abhor: To shudder at, recoil from, repelled by, have an aversion to, abominate, execrate regard with repugnance or horror- Saul was a man who did not abhor violence to Christians before his call. 2 As a Christian. You must abhor sin but love sinners. How difficult it is as Christians to separate our feelings towards a person's sinful behaviour and the person himself? As Christians trained by God through his word, we are commanded to abhor sin while loving the person committing sin. The word *abhor* goes directly to forewarn Christians not to commit sin because God hates sin.

Abiathar: (Hebrew - Ebyathar, Greek - Evyatar - meaning the (Divine) father is pre-eminent or father of plenty. Son of 'Abimelech' in the Old Testament. High - Priest at Nob. Considered the fourth in descent from Eli (He was the only survivor of a massacre carried out by Doeg). Having fled to David, he remained throughout his wonderings and his reign. He was loyal throughout the rebellion of Absalom but supported Adonijah. 2 Abiathar probably represents an early rival house to that of Zodak- the official priestly family of Jerusalem down to the exile *(1Samuel 22:20-23, 2 Samuel 15:24-37 and 1 Kings 2:26-27)* 2 *Abiathar* – The only one of Priests to escape from Saul's massacre. He fled to David at Keilah, taking with him the ephod and other priestly 'regalies'. He was of great service to David, especially at the time of the rebellion of Absalom. 3 *Abiathar* – A co-priest to 'Zadok' under Solomon. One of the supporters of 'Adonijah' who was later deposed by Solomon and banished to Anathoth.

Abide: To accept or obey a ruler or a decision. In the scriptural context to "abide in Christ" basically means "to remain". Every Christian remains inseparably linked to Christ in all areas of life. We depend on him for grace and power to obey, good health, liberty, long life, freedom, prosperity, victory. We look obediently to his word for instruction on how to live. We offer him our deepest adoration and Praise and we submit ourselves to His authority over our lives. In short, Christians gratefully know Jesus Christ is the source and 'sustainer's of their lives. People with genuine faith will remain - they won't defect, they won't deny Christ or abandon his truth. Jesus reiterated the importance of abiding as a sign of real faith when He said "If you abide in My Word, then you are truly disciples of Mine *(John 8:31)* 2 Abiding in Christ evidences genuine salvation. The Apostle John alluded to that when he referred to defected professors who " went out from us, but they were not really of us, for if they had been of us, they would have remained with us; but they went out, in order that it might be shown that they all are not of us" *(1 John 2:19)* Again *(Psalm 91: 1)* NKJV - imposes automatic qualification thus' He that 'dwelleth' in the secret place of the most High shall abide under the shadow of the Almighty. 3 Abide with me - A hymn by Henry Francis Lyte (1793-1847), probably written in 1847 which has been sung in FA Cup Finals since 1927. Since it was introduce at the suggestion of the FA Secretary, Frederick Wall. Earlier it was much parodied by soldiers in the First World War; one common version being 'we've had no beer, we've had no beer today'. The hymn gave much comfort to Edith Cavell (1865-1915), the British nurse imprisoned and condemned to death by the Germans for helping wounded soldiers to escaped and the night before she was executed

Abideth

as she sat in her cell singing it with a British chaplain. Generally the word abide appear 82 times in the bible. (NKJV)

Abideth: This is the archaic third person singular present tense suffix; meaning to stay in love, dwell, continue to tolerate, put up with, wait comply, submit, obey and conform. 2 Abideth – and now abideth faith, hope, charity. But, the greatest of these is charity. (*1 Corinthians 13:13*)

Abiding: (a-bi-ding) Something that is enduring, lasting or long-lasting, lifelong, remaining, standing fixed, durable, everlasting, perpetual, eternal, unending, constant, permanent, stable, unchanging, steadfast, immutable and much more. 2 abiding – lasting for a long time; the abiding love of God to the gentiles. The ever-ending love from God to us all.

Abiding in Christ: This is the mark of true salvation. Showing that our relationship to Christ is unlike anything else in the human realm. It can be described only by comparing it to relationships we are familiar with. In (John 15: 1-11)- He is the vine and we (Christians) are the branches. Thus, "I am the true vine and my Father is the vinedresser. Every branch in Me that does not bear fruit; He takes away; and every branch that bears fruit, He prunes it so that it may bear more fruit. You are already clean because of the word which I have spoken to you. Abide in Me, and I in you. As the branch cannot bear fruit of itself unless it abides in the vine, so neither you unless you abide in Me". 2. In the metaphor of (John 15), Christ is the vine and the Father is the vinedresser. He prunes the fruit bearing branches to make them bear more fruit. He removes the fruitless branches, and they are burned. Through the continual pruning, the faithfulness of the vine is increased. The branches that abides in the vine-Those who are truly in Christ- are blessed, they grow and bear fruit, and the father lovingly tends them. This represent the beautiful picture of Christian life, that magnifies the blessings associated with abiding in Christ: Salvation, fruitfulness, answered prayer, abundant life, full joy and divine security. 3 In (John 15:4), Jesus pleads with people who are superficial branches; 'Abide in Me'. This, He referred to people who are like Judas, "Be genuine; abide in Me and show that your faith is real; bear fruit; and remain on the vine. "It is like saying, "You superficial branches; be saved have a genuine relation to Christ".

Able: Simply capable or talented particularly on things which none is capable of doing (see God is able). 2 Having sufficient power to do, to sustain, to withstand, to act, to endure, to build or construct etc. 3 Christians should not misused this word by way of doubting the power of the Almighty God who rather is able, abundantly to do what he choose to do. Protracted problems turned a number of Christians to use the word in negativity which absolutely shows "lack of faith". For instance when a Christian or someone can say... 'the problem was able to tear me into pieces, or the problem was able to tear us apart'. Truly, it should be avoided when the subject does not have an ability as in sentences with passive constructions involving forms of the verb 'be' 4 Able is therefore considered as a 'word of faith' not alone but with the subject demonstrating the 'ability of able'. Jesus demonstrates this. When He tells the blind receive your sight and the blind see; He ordered the dump man to speak and he speaks, likewise the deaf hear, the lame walk and the dead ... and so forth were all able to do one action or the other through the word in the Gospel.

Able, God is... *(phr)* A term softened and Christianized to express the contentment which arises from the supply of all our needs by God. Otherwise understood as the divine capabilities of the Almighty God. 2 God is able – to make all grace overflow to you, make every blessing of yours overflow, for He is our shepherd (true Christians) shall not "want"(Psalm 23:1) 3 He gives us His constantly overflowing kindness, make all grace abound to us or make all grace abound towards you in particular and/or multiply every favour towards you, enabling you to always have whatever is sufficient for you in all things to enable you super-abound in every good work. 4 The power of God demonstrating the generously and enriching power of God. And God will generously provide all you need. Then you will always have everything you need and plenty and left over to share with others (see 2 Corinthians 9:8) 5 Indeed God is able to bestow all blessing on you in abundance so that richly enjoying all sufficiency at all times and to empower you to possess ample means for every good works. 6 God is able in order, words expresses the authority. Might, power, willingness to empower you for every good work through provision of substance wherewith you may abound in every good works that is sufficient even to enrich others.

Abner: (Hebrew - Avner) Meaning; "father of or is a light" First cousin to Saul and commander-in-chief of Sauls army. He is the son of Ner. Abner is incidentally referred to in Saul's history without a considerable mentioned in the disastrous battle of Gilboa when Saul's power was crushed and Abner seized the youngest but only surviving son of Saul's sons, Ishbosheth and move on to set him up as the King of Isreal at Mahanaim – east of the Jordan. *(1 Samuel 14:50, 20:25)*

Abominable: (adjective) denoting any unpleasant action causing disgust – an abominable crime. 2 Informal very bad and

Abomination

terrible. 3 Perpetual ungodly acts which unequivocally are detestable, loathsome, thoroughly unpleasant or disagreeable – the treatment of prisoners are sometimes abominable before God. 3 Something repulsive or divinely unlawful. 4 The gospel declares a number of things abominable, particularly as concerns unclean things, customs of pagans, sins of men, idol worship, lost souls, cheating. All in (Leviticus 7:21, 18:30, 2 Corinthians 15:8, 1 Peter 4:3, Micah 6:4), selected Chapters in (Proverbs 3 – 28) also mentioned a Froward-man (perverse; one who turns aside) a proud look, a lying tongue, Hands that shed innocent blood, A wicked scheming heart, Feet that are quick to sin, A false witness that speaks lies, A sower of discord, Wickedness, A false balance of scale, Sacrifices, thoughts and the ways of the wicked, A proud heart, justifying the wicked, condemning the just, divers dishonest weights, ignoring the law, prayers of the rebel. 5 Prejudice to Gay – Same sex acts are also added in Leviticus 18, 20:13 and Deuteronomy 23:18. Taking ornament from idols after destruction, eating flesh of peace offering, wearing clothes of the opposite sex, bringing the hire of a harlots or sodomite into Gods House, remarriage of former companions, cheating others, making images/idols- in form of idol of Ammon, Moab, Zidon, and even the incense offered by hypocrites and offering human sacrifices are all abominable in the sight of the Lord. 6 The worship of anti-Christ is narrated in Daniel 11:31 and 12:11, Mathew 24:15, and Revelation 13, Luke looks into things esteemed by man as abominable – Luke 16:15. While sins such as robbery, murder, adultery, violence breaking vows, lending with interest, Hardness of heart as well as lying with a monstrous woman and much more are opined as abominable in various chapters by Prophet Ezikiel from Chapter 18. It is abundantly clear from the scripture that all sin is considered abomination by God. So, as a Christian, you must gird against your acts for the purpose of geting to your Heavenly Home.

Abomination *(noun)* form of abominable. Things that causes disgust or hatred. Or a feeling of hatred or marginalised. Regarding the New Jerusalem the Gospel says; "But there shall by no means enter it anything that defiles, or causes an abomination or a lie, but only those who are written in the Lamb's book of life". Revelation 21:27 Also Revelation 21:8 says, "But the cowardly, unbelieving, [some text adds 'and sinners'], abominable, murderers, sexually immoral, sorcerers, idolaters, and all liars shall have their part in the lakes which burns with fire and brimstone, which is the second death". *See abominable*

Abound: Literally, this means to exist in large number or amounts. To be great in number, to be fully supplied, filled or teem. 2 To be plentiful, be abundant, be numerous, proliferate, or superabound. 3 Thrive, flourish, and be thick on the ground. 'And this I pray that your love may abound yet more and more in knowledge and in all judgement' Philippians 1:9 and in Chapter 4: 11-13 'Not that I speak in respect of want; for I have learned, in whatsoever state I am, therewith to be content. I know how to be abased, and I know how to be abound: everywhere and in all things I am instructed both to be full and to be hungry, both to abound on [or] to suffer need. I can do all things through Christ which 'strengtheneth' me KJV – to be firmed and prosperous with various skills to do all things –all through the abundant Grace of our dear Lord Jesus Christ filled in me.

Abraham, Abram: Father of multitude of nations. The first of the Jewish patriarchs who at the age of 75 entered into a covenant with God that his descendants should possess the land of Canaan *(Genesis 12:1-7).* 2 Abraham is the key figure in religious text of Christianity and other religions such as Judaism and Islam. As Christians, we are not so concerned with the last two. What we must concern is to understand Abraham as the first Patriarch of the Jews as first mentioned in the book of Genesis 11:26-25. His original name was Abram but this was changed at the covenant ceremony in Genesis 17. The two names are understood by many to have the same meaning except for dialectical variations on each other. However, the longer form the understanding in popular etymology to mean "father of multitudes". 3 Abraham's story relates [as] essentially to that of establishing a covenant with God. Afterwards, God calls Abraham to leave his land, family and household in Mesopotamia in return for a new land, new family and new inheritance in Canaan – the promised land. God established a covenant with Abraham after all threats such as lack of an heir, bondage in Egypt and absolute lack of the fear of God; but all these were overcome and the covenant was eventually established. 4 Abraham, husband of Sarah, father of Isaac.

Abrahamic Covenant: The promise given by God to Abraham because he left his father's house to live in strange land as God told him and interpreted to mean that the Messiah should spring from Abraham's seed. (Genesis 12:1-3 and 17

Abraham's bosom: The place where the just reposed in death.

Absalom: (Hebrew– *avshalom*) Father of peace; from a father and shalom, *'peace').* Being the son of *David remarkable* for his good looks and 2 He is the one who rose in rebellion against his father

Abstain

David and was aided or helped by Ahitophel. In his fleet (fleeing) after defeat, Absalom was trapped in the branches of a tree and slain by Joab, the Kings general. Note: As a result of Absalom's demission (demise), the father (David) expressed great sorrow in *(2 Samuel 18:33)* 3 Absalom – the one with whom the song –O my son Absalom, my son, my son Absalom! Would I had died for thee. O Absalom my son, my son!

Abstain: To restrain oneself from doing something, particularly what the word of God considers as sin or what the Word of God forbids. 2 Abstain from idol worship – as in Acts 15: 20 – But we write unto them, that they *abstain* from pollutions of idols and from fornication and from things strangled, and from blood. 3 In Acts 15:29 Apostle Paul warns "That ye abstain from meats offered to idols, and from things strangled, and from fornication: from which if ye keep yourselves, ye shall do well, Fare ye well; Accordingly, 1 Thessalonians 4:3 affirmed the will of God towards us, thus "For this is the will of God, even your sanctification, that ye should abstain from fornication". 4 As a Christian, you must abstain from every appearance of evil -1 Thessalonians 5:22

Abstinence: Ecclesiastically, Days of Abstinence are those when the eating of meat are not permitted, as distinct from Fast Days, when only one full meal is allowed in 24 hours. In modern Roman Catholic practice however, fasting generally means one main meal at midday and a small 'collation' in the morning and evening. The two obligatory Fast Days for Roman Catholics are ASH WEDNESDAY and Good FRIDAY

Abundance: This simply means to overflow. There are about 38 biblical verses about the word abundance

Abundant: (adjective) meaning, existing or available in large quantities

Abundantly: Available in large quantities, plentifully. 2 Extremely. Meaning, our God is more than sufficient. No wonder He is our Shepherd and we shall not want. Psalm 23:1. This Psalm portrays God as a good shepherd (GS), feeding (verse 1) and leading (verse 3) his flock. Thy "rod and staff" (verse 4) are also the implements of a shepherd. Some commentators see the shepherd imagery pervading the entire psalm. It is known that the shepherd is to know each sheep by name, thus when God is given the analogy of a shepherd, he is not only a protector but also the caretaker. God, as the caretaker, leads the sheep to green pasture (verse 2) and still waters (verse 2) because he knows that each of his sheep must be personally led to be fed with His abundant wealth. Thus, without its Shepherd, the sheep would die either by a predator or of starvation, since sheep are known for their stupidity. We are the sheep of his pasture. *(See phrases corresponding various verses inside)*

Accept: Agree to receive or do something offered. Christ offered to die on the cross for us. As Christians, what must we do? than accept Him as our only Lord and Saviour by believing, loving, trusting and obeying his commandment. As in *Romans 15:7* " Accept one another, then, just as Christ accepted you, in order to bring praise to God"(NIV). 2 Believe to be valid or correct. We must also trust in God to confirm the work of the cross by His only begotten son Jesus Christ. 3 Admit responsibility or blame for something. Why not admit responsibility? If a fellow brother or sister is hungry, or is in want then we show love as Christ commanded? NLT declares in the same *Romans 15:7* "Therefore accept each other just as Christ has accepted you so that God will be given glory. 4 Make someone welcome – Accept someone in good faith. 5 Come to terms with an unwelcome situation – Forgive someone as Christ also forgiven you.

Acceptable: *Well*-pleasing. Act in time; Receive in time; Answer of prayer in an acceptable time; Agreeing in time. The Acceptable year of the Lord. Acceptable unto God. Sacrifice – *Acceptable to God*

Acceptable Year of the Lord, The: *(phr)* Year of the Lord's favour, the Good News, *Luke 4 :19, Isaiah 61:2* To proclaim the acceptable year of the Lord. The spirit of the Lord God is upon me; because the LORD hath anointed me to preach good tidings unto... True. Stood on Sabbath... proclaimed acceptable year of the Lord...this day it is fulfilled. Christ proclaimed a day which fulfils the entire phrase. After 6000 years is the millennial Sabbath. Thus the year is also proclaimed. It means that this supports the so called "Gap Theory" as involved in (Luke 4) and (Isaiah 61: 1-2) The Day of Vengeance is not there yet. Probably that is partially why they were looking at Jesus. For Christians, prophecy fulfilled? Do you realize he cut short Isaiah's passage which is about the second coming? 3 To detest or hate something. (See hate) Gospel wise, the Revised Standard and the New Revised Standard use the word 'hate' as in (Romans 12:9.) Christians are relatively commanded to hate evil.

Acceptable Face, The: *(phr):* Gospel wise, this connotes the positive or reasonable side or aspect of the word or the truth in the word of God as characterised by certainty, acceptance, affirmation, forward moving, progress, explicitly, the presence

Acknowledge

of the special quality or character of Christ – in the spirit and in truth as opposed to the acceptable face of man or earthly laws. 2 Beholding the beautiful face of the Lord. When we behold His beautiful face, we accept it. We believe it and miracle signs and wonders happen through the word. 3 The beauty of his holiness is the acceptable face in which we worship, believe, trust, obey, 4 Phrase representing the fertile ground for conversation (from an orthodox perspective) because of the nature of Beauty itself. Orthodoxy holds that Beauty is a revelation and reflection of God within some of the Fathers, there is a Trinity of ideals Goodness, Truth and Beauty. Though there are treatments that use this to reflect on the persons of the Trinity, the only acceptable face in the Gospel of Christ still summarises the Christian belief that God alone is good and goodness only finds its meaning within God. Truth is acceptable face presented for our understanding while Beauty is what Truth looks like. 5 **The acceptable face** of something is its positive or reasonable side as distinct from what is being regarded as its negative or unpopular aspects.

Acknowledge: To accept that something exist or is true in it form, appearance, nature, word, quality, content, or action. Example, someone who acknowledges his error. Gospel wise, we must always acknowledge our mistakes before God in our prayer of forgiveness and/or supplication. 2 To confirm that one is grateful or pleased. 3 *Acknowledge* God by noticing his presence in your life or situation and show a spiritual gesture to thank Him. Acknowledge God by seeing him seated on the throne or His Holy Temple. By so doing 'let all the earth in your body' keep silence before Him or praise Him and adore Him. 4 *Acknowledge...* One most important praise input to move God. *Mathew 10:32* declares... Whoever acknowledges me before others, I will also acknowledge before my Father in heaven. (NIV) Or "Everyone who acknowledges me before men, I will also *acknowledge* before my Father in heaven. 5 *Acknowledge* – KJV Applied it differently but same objective –Whosoever therefore shall confess me before men, him will I confess also before my father who is in heaven. In GWT, "So I will acknowledge in front of my Father in heaven that person who acknowledges me in front of others". By getting into the real exposition of the word acknowledge in the Gospel of Christ, the recapping meaning of 'Whosoever therefore shall confess me before men,... The confession of Christ here, more especially designed, does not so much intend, though it may include, that which is less public and is necessary to be made in every believer in Christ: Howbeit, not enough to believe in him with the heart without confession of him which must also be made with the mouth. Through the ascribing of the whole salvation to him by way of: -Giving him the glory, declaring your faith in him to others as well as what he has done to your soul; Not leaving out the subjection of your very soul to his ordinances as it ought to be by words and deeds. As well as joining in fellowship with his church and people Remaining hearty and sincere, visible, open, before all men. All these are the ingredients in the sense of acknowledging. Above all what it is chiefly relates to is the confession of Christ by his ministers, for instance in the public preaching of the Gospel where the ministers ought openly, and boldly, faithfully bound to acknowledge and declare that Christ is truly and properly, without reduction of any of His divine value or quality, the only true Son of God; the eternal Son of God. 6 Furthermore, you could acknowledge Him as the only mediator between God and man, the Saviour and Redeemer of lost sinners through whose blood alone is the forgiveness of sins according to the riches of Grace; and by whose righteousness only can men be justified before God, and by whose sacrifice and satisfaction could sin be expiated; that he died for, and in the room and stead of us, rose again with power for our justification, ascended to heaven in our name and sat down at the right hand of God, and ever live to make intercession for us and will come again to judge both quick and dead. This free and open confession of Christ ought to be made by all his ministers before men as oppose to all the rage and opposition of earth and hell which shall not fail to be taken notice of and requited by Christ. There are various commentaries concerning the word 'acknowledge' by various commentators in the scripture, but the word itself need to be attached an ingredient of confession to fulfil the true meaning in the Gospel.

Acknowledgement: (noun) The action of acknowledging something or somebody. To acknowledge something or somebody or something given to express gratitude, for example to give thanks or gratitude to God for giving us life, hope, inspiration, protection and love. 'For God so love the world that he gave His only begotten son that whosoever believeth in Him should not perish but have everlasting life'. 'For God sent His Son into the world not to condemn the world but that the world through him might be saved (John 3: 16-17)

Act: In the context of the Gospel, this simply mean to take action with the word of God, use the word to do something or what the word say we should do. 2 Make the word to take effect – (act of faith). 3 Behave with the word as if you own or possesses

Act

it. (Trust the word) If you trust the word, you trust or attract God's attention to your situation. 4 To fulfil the assigned function. To all Christians, God has an assigned function for you to accomplish as in the case of Simon Peter and Paul of Tarsus in the Lucan Gospel as presented by Evangelist Luke and with where the history of the Apostolic age was outlined in (Luke 1:3-4) Thus:' With this in mind, since I myself have carefully investigated everything from the beginning, I too decided to write an orderly account for you, most excellent Theophilus, so that you may know the certainty of the things you have been taught'.

Act of Pilate, the: An Apocryphal work of the 4th century, recounting the trial, death and resurrection of Christ. 2 The combination of this work with another treatise on the Descent of Christ into Hades by which the two texts are known as the 'Gospel of Nicodemus'.

Adam: The first human created by God- (according to the creation myth of the Abrahamic religions) The first man created by ("Yahweh-God", (the God of Israel). 2 The first individual person and the general creation of humankind. 3 Symbolically, Adam stands for the first human error against God desire. Gospel wise, Adam weakness resulted in the downfall of what Christians often refers to the fall of the first man for committing sin

That later trunked to the birth of the messiah and redemption that follow through the sacrifice of Jesus Christ. 2 Most faith considers Adam to be the first prophet. 3 Adam is considered as the first human person who started the sin of the world through his subtlety to temptation by snake through his wife (Eve the first woman) while Jesus Christ is the first and last man through which salvation and redemption from the sin of Adam emanates. 4 Adam – the root cause *of the Bible.* It is translated in English as 'Lord' as in (Isaiah 6 v 1) of sin and death as oppose to Christ the only source of eternal life.

Add: To say or do something that increases the emotion of a person. In this context, God is the person. But we must not forget that God is not a person nor the son of man that He should lie. The bible warned Christians not to add to God's word. Why? What it means is that we should not add or man should not add his own word to what God says or gave. 2 Each one is a specific book that was completed, and that man was not to add or subtract from. The bible is a collection of all 66 books that are of the Old and New Testament. *Deuteronomy 4:2* "You shall not add to the word which I commanded you nor take anything from it. (Also *Deuteronomy 12:32*). The reason God is so adamant on this is because "the entirety of your word –God's word is truth" *(Psalms 119:160)*. Add thou not unto His words, lest He reprove thee, and thou be found a liar. (Proverbs 30:6). Adding does not only mean additional words but can also mean changing them to mean what they do not. When you add new word as equal to the Scripture you are really taking away from Scripture. This is why Gospel Dictionary remains an important book in the Life of any Heavenly bound Christian. 3 Add – In the book of Revelation which is prophecy completes in the Bible, just as Genesis began the Bible, it states " For I testify unto every man that 'heareth' the words of the prophecy of this book If any man shall add unto these things, God shall add unto him the plagues that are written in this book. (Revelation 22:18)

Adder: A poisonous snake with a dark zigzag pattern on it back. A serpent or a cobra. (Psalm 91:13) – "Thou shall tread upon the lion **and** adder: the young lion and the dragon shall thou trample under feet" (KJB) 2 As deaf as an adder. Like the deaf adder that stopped her ear which will not hearken to the voice of charmers. Charming never so wisely' (Psalm 58: 4-5)

Adonai: (Hebrew *adonay, plural of adon; 'lord')* A Hebraic name of God used instead of Yahweh (Jehovah) 'the ineffable name', wherever it occurs. *In Latin and Greek versions*

Adonists: Commonly referred to those Hebraists who maintain that the vowel of the word 'Adonai' are not those necessary to make the TETRAGRAMATON J H V H into the name of Jehovah.

Adonia: Conventionally, an eight-day feast of Adonis celebrated in Assyria, Alexandra, Egypt, Judea, Persia, Cyprus, Greece and Rome. 2 The women first lamented the death of Adonis, then widely rejoice at his resurrection. The custom is referred to in the Bible in Ezekiel 8:14 where Adonis appears under the Phoenician name of Tammuz.

Adonis: (Phoenician and Hebrew adon. Lord). In classical mythology this beautiful youth was the Myrrea (Symma). Born from a myrrh tree, loved by Aphrodite (Venus) and died young, killed by a boar while hunting. 2 The name sometimes is applied to any handsome young man. Both John and Leigh Hunt were sent to prison by libelling the Prince Regent by calling him 'a corpulent Adonis.

Adoption: The most important spiritual blessing. Formally approve or accept someone or something to oneself. Ephesians 1:5-6 declared: "just as He chose us in Him before the foundation of the world, that we would be holy and blameless before Him. In love. He predestined us to *adoption* as sons through

Adoption

Jesus Christ to Himself, according to the kind intention of His will, to the praise of the glory of His grace, which He freely bestowed on us in the Beloved...." 2 Chose an option or course of action. All Christians have been adopted as children of God and freed from the law. To adopt a child is to follow the lead of God who has adopted so many. 3 There are several *adoption* in the Bible, including Moses. There is no better way to welcome a child in than to adopt him or her. 4 With Christ, Christians needs to be inter-adoptive. Christ is in us as we are in Him. 5 There are about ten adoption Gospel to alit the Gospel of Christ in our lives- All who believed are adopted as Children of God- John:1:12,

Adoption by arms: An ancient custom of giving arms to a person of merit which put them under the obligation of being ones champion or defender.

Adoption of children: In English Law, adoption is effected by a court order that vests parental responsibility for a child to the adopter or adopters and extinguishes parental responsibility of the birth parents. The effect of adoptive order is that the child is treated as if born as a child of the marriage (not biologically delivered). The requirements for making adoption orders are set out in the adoption Act. 2 While adoption of children by earthly adoptive parents are in this form, true Christians are divinely adopted by Christ Jesus through the power of Holy Spirit. *See adoption*

Adrammelech: (Babylonian *Adar-malik*, 'Adar is prince') An Assyrian deity to whom infants were burned in sacrifice (2 Kings 17:31) This must have been a sun-god worshipped at Sippar (Sepharvaim)

Adulterer: (noun) Literally, a person who has committed adultery.

Adultery: (noun) Act of sexual intercourse between a married person and a person who is not their husband or wife. 2 The seventh of the ten commandments. (Exodus 20:14) "Thou shall not commit *adultery*".

Adversary, The: Satan or the Devil from (1 Peter 5:8) 2 An opponent in contest, conflict or dispute. Often times, when Satan or the devil planed evil against the children of God, God in His anger sends or orders a divine adversary (His angel) to defend His children, like what He did to Balaam when Balak send his servant to him as in (Numbers 22:22) 'And God's anger was kindled because he went: and the angel of the LORD stood in the way for an adversary against him. Now he was riding upon his ass, and his two servants *were* with him'.

Advertise

Adversity: (Plural –adversities) Hard or Difficult times or an unpleasant situation. Sometimes you must go through the valley to reach the top of the mountain. Figuratively, the valley is what we call the times of adversity. 2 These are those times when you may have some questions for your Heavenly Father. The hard times are when you should draw nigh unto God; He wants to hear from you (Hebrews 9:19). 3. In adversity, Christians often calls to mind a memory verse. One of our favorite memory verses especially when we are in the prayer mountain or the valley is one that was written by the weeping prophet, Jeremiah: "It is of the LORD's mercies that we are not consumed, because his compassions *fail* not. They are new every morning: great is thy faithfulness. The LORD is my portion, saith my soul; therefore will I hope in him. (Lamentations 3:22-24 KJV)

Advertise: (verb-ad'-ver-tiz:) In ordinary usage, this means to present or describe a product, service or someone. In the gospel, the goodness of the Lord or the good news must be declared 2 To publicize information about a person or event. – Talk about Christ and His wondrous works to mankind – this is the first commission in the Gospel as in Mark 16:7, 14-18 when Mary Magdalene, Mary the mother of James and Salome were told by the angel at the grave where Jesus was laid "Do not be amazed; you are looking for Jesus the Nazarene, who has been crucified. He has risen; He is not here; behold, here is the place where they laid Him. "But go, tell (or announce to) His disciples and Peter, 'He is going ahead of you to Galilee; there you will see Him, just as He told you.'" " Afterward he appeared to the eleven themselves as they were reclining at table, and he rebuked them for their unbelief and hardness of heart, because they had not believed those who saw him after he had risen. [15] And he said to them, "Go into all the world and proclaim – announce) the gospel to the whole creation. Whoever believes and is baptized will be saved, but whoever does not believe will be condemned. And these signs will accompany those who believe: in my name they will cast out demons; they will speak in new tongues; they will pick up serpents with their hands; and if they drink any deadly poison, it will not hurt them; they will lay their hands on the sick, and they will recover." In view of the above narration, all Christians should see the fruit of advertising Christ as the missionary journey progresses (see Mark 16:17 above) 3 Make a quality or fact known – Testify or Testimonies   Since Christianity is no other thing but by speaking, thinking and acting Christ, advertising is be the way the children of God preach and make known the name of God to everyone, including those who are not

Advocate

yet in the body of Christ. When Jesus healed the Leper, He said This word is found twice in the Old Testament: In Numbers 24:14 (from Hebrew, ya`ats, "to advise") Balsam advises Balak of the future of Israel and its influence upon his kingdom ("I will advertise thee"). In the King James Version Ruth 4:4 (from galah 'ozen, "to uncover the ear," - "to reveal") Boaz in speaking to the nearer kinsman of Ruth: "I thought to advertise thee" (the Revised Version, margin "uncover thine ear"). And now, behold, I go unto my people: come therefore, and I will **ADVERTISE** thee what this people shall do to thy people in the latter days. (Numbers 24:14)

Advocate: (noun) (Greek- 'Parakletos' or paravklhto) Ordinary meaning - Person who pleads a case on someone's behalf. In the gospel, this refers to Jesus Christ - the first advocate to all Christians. 1 John 2:1. Advocate appears five times in the Old Testament. 2 'One who speaks in our defence' – Jesus told the father to send another comforter - the Holy Spirit – (Parakletos) In John 14:26 Jesus said "These things I have spoken to you while abiding with you. "But the Helper, the Holy Spirit, whom the Father will send in My name, He will teach you all things, and bring to your remembrance all that I said to you. Here, the Gospel – explain the Man – Holy Spirit who is sent in the name of Jesus – Name in whom every other name must identify from because it is the Name above every other name. So that the advocacy, counselling, comforting, pleading of our causes, helping, anchoring, must be done on His name before our adversary could be defeated in court. 3 The Spirit-man (Holy Spirit) is

Advowson: (Latin – advocatino, 'summoning) In ecclesiastical law, the right of presentation to a church Benefice. It is so named because the patron was the advocate or the defender of the living and of the claim of his candidate. There are two kinds of advowson – collative 'advowson' – when the bishop of the diocese is the patron, and presentative 'advowson' when the patron is some other person's patron'.

Adytum: (Greek – aduton 'Not to be entered') The Holy of Holies in Greek and Roman temples, into which the public was not admitted. 2 Any sanctum.

3 ad'-i-tum (Latin from Greek aduton, adjective adutos, "not to be entered"): Applied to the innermost sanctuary or chambers in ancient temples, and to secret places which were open only to priests: hence, also to the Holy of Holies in the Jewish temple.

4 Adytum is a Greek word, signifying inaccessible, by which is understood the most retired

Affection

and secret place of the Heathen temples, into which, none but the priests were allowed to enter. The adytum of the Greeks and Romans answered to the sanctum sanctorum of the Jews, and was the place from whence oracles were delivered.

Affection: (noun, Greek: *splagchnon* – [splangkh'-non], Hebrew: *agab* – [aw-gab'] meaning - lusted, bowels, compassion, pity, the inward parts; the heart, affections, seat of the feelings. A gentle feeling of fondness or liking. "she felt affection for her neighbour" Synonyms: fondness, love, liking, endearment, feeling, sentiment, tenderness, warmth, warmness, devotion, care; and much more. 2 archaic- the action or process of affecting or being affected. Christians should have a feeling of fondness or liking to the Gospel of Christ because of the proof of love and *affection* there-in. In (Philippians 4:10) Paul was overwhelmed with the love of Christ in the Gospel that he became very passionate to declare to the Romans that "we should be sincere in our love. We should love each other with *affection*, not out of duty. We should also cling to what is good and let go of what is evil" as Paul's stated during his hardship and God grace in (2 Corinthians 6:12) "We are not withholding our *affection* from you, but you are withholding yours

from us". Just look at Christ advice to Ephesians in (Revelation 2:4-7) "Nevertheless I have somewhat against thee, because thou hast left thy first love. Remember therefore from whence thou art fallen, and repent, and do the first works; or else I will come unto thee quickly, and will remove thy candlestick out of his place, except thou repent. But this thou hast, that thou hatest the deeds of the Nicolaitanes, which I also hate. He that hath an ear, let him hear what the Spirit saith unto the churches; To him that overcometh will I give to eat of the tree of life, which is in the midst of the paradise of God". He says, "Renew your devotion to Me. Go back to the first works. You have left your first love. Renew your earlier devotion to Me." – Understand as a Christian that devotion is the sense in which the word "love" (agape) is being used. Devotion literally means "to vow completely." Baptism is the outward show that one has vowed to give his life to God, and so "devotion" implies complete dedication, total surrender. This hints at the Ephesians' problem: Their devotion—their complete dedication—was slipping away.

2 Again, devotion could be seen as a deep and ardent *affection*, a feeling. Its synonyms are "attentiveness," "dedication," "commitment," "earnestness," but all with a feeling of *affection*.

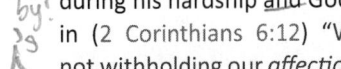

Affection

Devotion is not given out of a sense of obligation only, but with a warm feeling or a passionate desire. Jesus' charge to the Ephesians to return to their earlier devotion is not something that He is asking to be done merely as a duty. Some antonyms of "devotion" can help us see it from another angle: indifference, negligent, unconcerned, disregard, infidelity, and faithlessness. So, today in our Churches or in the body of Christ, there are people who are indifference, negligent, unconcerned – Don't practice tithing, praying, not supportive to the Ministerial works in which they were called, disregards instructions for fasting and praying, associate with unbelievers to criticize the (BOC) rather than join brothers and sisters in Christ to do the works of Grace and Charity, show love and kindness to emulate Christ. What you should do to maintain a feel of affection at all times is to abide by the words in (Philippians 4:8) "Finally, brethren, whatsoever things are true, whatsoever things [are] honest, whatsoever things [are] just, whatsoever things [are] pure, whatsoever things [are] lovely, whatsoever things [are] of good report; if [there be] any virtue, and if [there be] any praise, think on these things". Because, as Paul's pointed out in (2 Corinthians 6:12) "We are not withholding our *affection* from you, but you are withholding yours from us". But above all see (1 Corinthians 7:2) – "Nevertheless, [to avoid] fornication, let every man have his own wife, and let every woman have her own husband". Note: there are so many verses in the Scripture concerning affection, read up and equip your faith in Jesus Name! Amen!

Affliction, The source of:
God is the first source of affliction. The Hebrew mind did not dwell on secondary causes, but attributed everything, even afflictions, directly to the great First Cause and Author of all things: "Shall evil befall a city, and Yahweh hath not done it?" (Amos 3:6); "I form the light, and create darkness; I make peace, and create evil (i.e. calamity); I am Yahweh, that doeth all these things" (Isaiah 45:7) Thus, all things, including calamity, were referred to the Divine operation. The Hebrew when afflicted did not doubt the universal sovereignty of God; yet, while assuming this sovereignty, he was sometimes tempted to accuse Him of indifference, neglect or forgetfulness. Compare Job passim; Isaiah 40:27; 49:14; Ezekiel 8:12; 9:9. Christians should search the bible to know exactly what to do in times of affliction. The best thing to do is to keep your faith in the gospel of Christ alive and remain steadfast in prayers and Thanks Giving, Sacrifice of worship and love everyone.

Afraid:
Always followed by phrases 'thou shall not be' nor be afraid',

'do not be...',. 1 Not afraid with any amazement. Not distracted or tempted aside ...from doing God's bidding). The phrase occurs as the final words of the marriage in the Book of Common Prayer as quotation from (1 Peter 3:6) In (Deuteronomy 31:6) Christians are encourage to "Be strong and courageous. 'Do not be afraid or terrified because of them, for the Lord your God goes with you; he will never leave you nor forsake you." 2 Again Moses encourage the Israelite; "The LORD will deliver them up before you, and you shall do to them according to all the commandments which I have commanded you. "Be strong and courageous, *do not be afraid* or tremble at them, for the LORD your God is the one who goes with you. He will not fail you or forsake you."

Agape: (Greek *agape* – meaning 'love') A love feast. The early Christians held a love feast in conjunction with the Lord's Supper at which the rich provided food for the poor. Eventually they became a scandal and were condemned by the Council of Carthage (in AD 397) There has however been some interest in restoring, the agape in recent times, and in 1949 it was revived in the Norfolk parish of Hilgay in an attempt to bring Anglican and Methodists together. Agape was also the mother of Priamond, Diamond and Triamond in Edmund Spencer's – The Faerie Queen (IV.ii (1596). Agape is pronounced in three syllables.

Agape, Love of: The love of Christ towards us all. Christ 'giveth' His live as a ransom for all. 2 Selfless love of one person for another without sexual implications (especially love that is spiritual in nature) Having a divine emotion- a strong positive emotion of regard and affection; "his love for his work"; "children need a lot of love. 3 Qualification is not required in this type of love. (1 John 4:8) – "He that loveth not knoweth not God; for God is love". NKJV. 4 In (Mark 12:30), 'love of agape' start from the love of God which is the first commandment– Thus 'And thou shallt love the Lord thy God with all thy heart, and with all thy soul, and with all thy mind, and with all thy strength'. As agape is not from man's competent, but divinely release or given by God. So for us to freely love one another we must love God first.

Age of reason: The Roman catholic believe, the end of the seventh year, when a child is old enough to distinguish between right and wrong and to assume moral responsibility for his or her actions. The 18th century is also called the Age of Reason as a period of enlightenment when philosophy was in vogue throughout Europe.

Agree: Have the same opinion as that of another person. 2

Agreement

Accept someone else's opinion. 3 Allow your thoughts or actions to agree with the word of God as in (Mathew 18:19) "Again I say unto you, That if two of you shall agree on earth as touching anything that they shall ask, it shall be done for them of my Father which is in heaven". KJV. 3 In Amos 3:3 "Do two walk together unless they have agreed to do so"?

Agreement: The act of agreeing with the word or the state of being agreed. Most Christians failed to reach agreement with the word.

Alive: (alive – *adjective*) Living; not dead 2 Continuing in existence or use. Keeping hope alive – as in (Romans 6:11-15) "In the same way, count yourselves dead to sin but *alive* to God in Christ Jesus. Therefore do not let sin reign in your mortal body so that you obey its evil desires. Do not offer any part of yourself to sin as an instrument of wickedness, but rather offer yourselves to God as those who have been brought from death to life; and offer every part of yourself to him as an instrument of righteousness. For sin shall no longer be your master, because you are not under the law, but under grace." (NIV)

3 Alert and active with God's word. 4 Alive to – Jesus is very alive to the challenges we face. 5 Alive with – I am alive with Christ – see (Ephesians 2:4-6) "But God, being rich in mercy, because of His great love with which He loved us, even when we were dead in our transgressions, made us alive together with Christ (by grace you have been saved), and raised us up with Him, and seated us with Him in the heavenly places in Christ Jesus,… Steadfastness. Keeping the faith together. Doing God's will.

Agrippa, King: The King who tried Paul in Jerusalem after the Lord had revealed Himself and change his name from Saul to Paul. Act 26:1-29 "I consider myself fortunate to stand before you today as I make my defence against all the accusations of the Jews, and especially so because you are well acquainted with all the Jewish customs and controversies. Therefore, I beg you to listen to me patiently":

Ahab: The husband of Jezebel and a king of Israel who displayed more wickedness before God than any other King. He harassed the prophets especially Elijah and when he was finally killed in battle at Samaria 'the dogs licked up, his blood (1King 22:38) see also Naboth's Vineyard

Alleluia: Estimation variant - spelling of Hallelujah (see Hallelujah)

Alms: (Old English *almysee*, from late Latin *eleemosyna*, 'pity') Gift to the poor. It is a singular word, which, like 'riches (from French richesse), has by usage become

plural. The Bible has (he) asked an for of all its representative arts...
'alms are but vehicles of prayer'.

Almighty: The God.

Alpha and Omega: The first letter of the Greek Alphabet is (A) which is popularly known as Alpha and the last letter in the Greek alphabet is (o). In (Revelation 1:11) the uniqueness and the divine nature of God is shown when he declared I am first and the last (Alpha and Omega) otherwise maintained as The beginning and the End.

Altar: *(noun)* Origin from Latin word *(altus)* The table in a Christian church at which the bread and wine are consecrated in communion services. 2 A table or other structure on which religious offerings are made. 3 **Altar-** *(Phrase)* I go into the Muslim mosque and the Jewish synagogue and the Christian Church and I see one *altar*. Meaning in the spirit of goodwill, Muslims can start praying in Churches en masse, fraternity with Christianity! Share the bread! Skip the wine! (Haram!), Pay no attention to the holy rap especially when it gets intense at collection time. In the Church instead of the mosque? The Church with all its lights and paraphernalia incorporating the mortal flesh cast in marble, the holy water, the holy Eucharist etc, surely comrade, the Muslim must feel il-at-ease with all the heavily loaded symbolism to the full glory

am: First person. Singular present of being (God)

Am I my brother's keeper? Cain's rhetorical question to God, when following Cain's murder of Abel, the lord asked him where his brother Abel was (Genesis 4:9). The response has a modern ring and is typical of a person who resents any responsibility for the safety or welfare of another.

Ananias: In the New Testament (Act 5:1-11). A Christian convert who with his wife Sapphira sold his possessions but gave only part of the proceeds to the Apostle In collusion with his wife, Ananias kept back part of the money for himself. (Literally, he embezzled from the sale price) upon being rebuked by Peter fell down dead . Ignorantly of his deception, Sapphira came home three hours later and practiced the same deception and fell down dead also.

Anchor: (Greek – *ankura*) In the gospel, anchor is to fix something in a firm position like in a rock, particularly to be steadfast with Christ as the only Rock of our salvation. The only author and finisher of our faith. 2 A Christian symbolism and sign of hope, in allusion to (Hebrews 6:39) 'which hope we have in anchor of the soul'. Anchor also symbolises security. In art it is an attribute of St. Clement. Pope Clement 1

Anon

was said to have been martyred by being tied to anchor and cast into the sea in the 1st century AD. Again, St. Nicholas of Bari the patron saint of sailors. The emblem of anchor well entwined with a dolphin was used by the venetian printer Aldus Manutius

Anon: (Old English, 'on one, literally in one) The present meaning of the word as 'soon', 'in a little while'. Is a misuse of the earlier meaning. 'immediately', 'straight away' as in (Mark 1:30) –Authorise version, gives an instance of the old meaning 'Thus' But Simon's wife's mother lay sick of a fever an anon they tell him of her. While the Revised version used 'straightaway'. 2 William Wordsworth in the white Doe of Rylstone (i.31 (1815) exemplifies the later meaning –Fast the churchyard fills-anon; Lock again and they are all gone'.

Ancient of Days: A scriptural or gospel name given to God as contained in (Daniel 7:9) familiar from the first verse of Robert Grant's hymn (1833) paraphrasing Psalm 104 thus

"Oh worship the king all glorious above.

O gratefully sing the power and his love.

Our Shield and Defender. *The Ancient of Days*.

Pavilion in splendour, and girded with praise. The grandiloquent name is in fact a rendering of the Hebrew phrase 'old man' - creator of self when nothing else was created.

Andrew, St: The saint who was a fisherman and brother of St Peter, depicted in Christian art as an old man with long, white hair and beard holding the Gospel in his right hand and leaning on a St Andrew's cross. He is remarkable on 30 November. It is said that he was crucified in Patrae (c70 AD) on a *crux decussate*. 2 He is also the patron saint of Russia and Scotland.

Angel: Spiritual being acting as an attendant or a messenger of God represented as being of human form with wings. 2 A very beautiful, kind or good person. 3 In post-canonical and apocalyptic literature, angels are grouped in different orders. The commonly used hierarchy of nine orders is that popularized by the pseudo-Areopagite or pseudo-Dionysius (early 5th century AD) in his *De Herarchia Celesti* which arranges them in three triads: Seraphim: cherubim and Thrones in the first circle, Dominions, Virtues and Powers in the second circle; Principalities, Archangels and Angels in the third circle. The names are taken from the Old Testament and (Colossians 1:16). The seven holy angels or archangels are, Michael, Gabriel, Raphael, Uriel, Chamuel, Jophiel

Anoint

and Zadkiel. Michael and Gabriel are mentioned in the Bible, Raphael in the Apocalypha and all appear in the non-canonical first book of Enoch. There are several other angels including fallen angels including Moloch as Milton accounted for in 'The Lost Paradise'.

Angelic Hymn, The: The hymn also known as the Gloria in 'Excelsis', beginning 'Glory to God in the highest' (Luke 2:14) It is so called because the first part of it was sung by the angel host that appeared to the shepherds of Bethlehem.

Angel visits: Delightful encounter of short duration and rare occurrence.

Anoint: (Verb) To smear or rob someone with oil especially setting aside for a divine will of God or a divine assignment or as part of a religious right or ceremony. 2 In (Psalm 105:15), the Lord warned saying, "Touch not my anointed ones, do my prophets no harm!" the anointed ones here are those who have been set aside or anointed to do the work of God. They include; true Pastors, Evangelist, The Prophets of God, The Shepherds...

Anointed: (Past tense) Someone benefiting from anointing. (see anoint)

Anointed Water, the: Unlike Holy water, the anointing water came to be through a revelation from God to the man of God, Prophet TB Joshua. Prophet TB Joshua is the Senior Pastor and founder of The Synagogue, Church of All Nations in Lagos, Nigeria. Miracles, signs, and wonders have been operating through this ministry for many years. Unfortunately, the man of God cannot be in every country, or visit many places, so God instructed him to pray for bottles of water and distribute this water to people all over, for healing, deliverance, and breakthrough. Within the Scriptures, we see clear proof that God is able to use any medium to express Himself. For example, God used Paul's handkerchief as well as Peter's shadow to heal the sick. God also used the medium of Moses' staff to split the Red Sea and a dirty river to heal Naaman. And as the case during the time of Jerusalem's or the Israelites' unfaithfulness (Ezekiel 16:9) "Then I passed by you and saw you, and behold, you were at the time for love; so I spread My skirt over you and covered your nakedness. I also swore to you and entered into a covenant with you so that you became Mine," declares the Lord GOD. "Then I bathed you with water, washed off your blood from you and anointed you with oil. "I also clothed you with embroidered cloth and put sandals of porpoise skin on your

Answer

feet; and I wrapped you with fine linen and covered you with silk...."

2 By praying with *the anointing water*, you are setting yourself apart for God's special attention as you pray in faith. You are positioned for mercy, favour, healing, deliverance, blessing, prosperity, and fruitfulness. It is important to remember that it is NOT *the anointing water* that heals the sick, but Jesus Christ Himself. There must be faith in both the person praying and the person being prayed for. Prayer must proceed from and be accompanied with a lively faith. It is this that brings about the healing, not *the anointing water*. Therefore the anointing water is just a point of contact with the Lord for His rule over your situation to manifest just like the woman with the issue of blood who touched His garment and was ill.

3 *Anointing water* - God has been using the medium of the anointing water for quite a period of time now, and we thank God for this special grace. Many people have received a touch from God by praying, or being prayed for, with the anointing water. In recent times, we have seen countless miracles take place after praying for people with the anointing water on our Sunday services. A woman from western Washington was completely healed of colon cancer, two men on different occasions were delivered of alcoholism instantly, and another woman was completely healed of a bladder infection that doctors were unable to help her with. These evidences are only a small portion of what we have seen God doing this summer through prayer with the anointing water.

4 *Anointing water* - God is busy at work and we are privileged to be part of what He is doing everywhere. It is important to note that Christians, everywhere, have been specifically instructed by the man of God, Prophet TB Joshua, to pray for people with the anointing water every day on various Church services the world over. Please be mindful of the steps that need to be taken and come in faith, believing that Jesus Christ will meet you at the point of your need. Remember also that, right from creation the Spirit of the Most High God was on top of water as in (Genesis 1:2) "Now the earth was formless and empty, darkness was over the surface of the deep, and the Spirit of God was hovering over the waters". So water is a great carrier of God's Spirit. Hence, "better is not good enough, the BEST is yet to come! Be blessed in Jesus name! Amen!!

Answer: Response or something said or written in reaction to question or statement. 2 A solution to a problem –Under a cruelty world, you are the answer to the problems of the earth- as it is written, 'O let not the oppressed return ashamed: Let the poor and the needy praise thy name' *(Psalm 74:20-21).* 3 Satisfy a need. 4 Be responsible to someone. 5 Defend oneself against accusation. 6 Answer for – be responsible or to blame for; You are to be blamed for your lack of faith or trust.

Answer, We are the: *(Phr)-* This means that we are the solution to His word (Psalm 107:20), in the person of Jesus – the Christ as stated in John 1:14 that the word became flesh, and dwelt amongst us. 2 God first gives the solution in the package of a man- Christ Jesus who came as the Saviour of the world. We were the answer after the crucifixion, burial and the resurrection, He ascended to heaven; but not without commissioning us – the Church, to continue the work that He started. As pinpointed in (Isaiah 53:10)...*he shall see his seed, he shall prolong his days, and the pleasure of the Lord shall prosper in his hand'.* 3 Truly we are the answer, so long as we are the seed of Jesus Christ; His reproduction; and through us, the ministry that he started continues. 4 We are the answer because he has given us the power of attorney to use his name, and his word to live by. Now, we are God's light to the dark regions of the world today. That is why, when Jesus came he said "...I am the light of the world: he that 'followeth' me shall not work in darkness, but shall have the light of life" *(John 8:12).* Of course in *(Mathew 5:14),* His believers are paraphrased thus 'Ye are the light of the world...' Note: the dark places of the earth are found the habitations of cruelty, but Christians are the ones to do something about it. How? Preach the Gospel and shine the light of God's word into the dark regions of the earth through real life solutions divinely manifested through Grace.

Answer, God's: The divine response to prayers or our request that comes unconditionally through the love of God and His Grace. God often answers prayer in the following ways: "Yes, you may have it." "No, that is not good for you." "Wait, I have something better for you." "My grace is sufficient for you" (2 Corinthians 12:9) We should be ready to thank God in all circumstances whether He say "yes" to our prayer now or "no". Sometimes we don't take "no" for an answer and we persist in prayer. Let us not forget that God is sovereign, He does according to His desire and infinite wisdom purposefully for our protection. 2 Before God answers our prayer, He provides us with the spiritual blessing where with we will be able to keep His divine gift in our life. Often times we are not praying for this one. That is the interval of delay. He may have been waiting for you to grow spiritually in some area so that you could fully experienced the blessings to come (Ephesians 1:3) . "No wonder God's time

Ant

is the best" When God seems unresponsive and heaven is silent and we yield in praying more and more, God is up to something much bigger than our expectation. He is overjoyed when we keep on trusting Him Sometimes, God answers our prayer at His appointed time as in (Daniel 9:21). Don't forget, the way God answers Job's prayer is not the same way He answer Daniel. So God's answer to our prayers varies according to His purpose fitted to our situation – His desire and God's will for us.

Ant: (noun) A small insects, usually wingless, living with others in a highly organized group. 2 Ants are wise and are very independent and orderly as they keep to the seasonal order of nature in their survival. See (Proverbs 6: 6-8) "Go to the ant, O sluggard; consider her ways, and be wise. Without having any chief, officer, or ruler, she prepares her bread in summer and gathers her food in harvest". (ESV). As Christians we should take steps of faith in time, and act with the word to attain the result - what the word says.

Antichrist: Against Jesus Christ, His teachings and followership. The man of sin due to appear at the end of time, is mentioned in 1 John 2:18-22 and is derived from Hebrew teachings. The believe that the arrival of antichrist was to precede the second advent is clearly stated in 2 Thessalonians 23:12 and Revelation 13. 2 In the early Christian church, the Roman Empire and its rulers were frequently referred to as the Antichrist, and later the title was bestowed on the Emperor Frederick 11 and various Popes with the reformation. Following the Reformation, the Protestant conception of the papacy as Antichrist became expounded and its later use then became as an abusive term. 3 It has been use even to Napoleon Bonaparte and William 1 Germany. 4 Antichrist has a common legendary to other Religions that Christ will slay the Antichrist with all the beast at the gate of the Church at Lydda, in Palestine. 5 Apart from above stated account, there are many opposition groups around the world today that makes many suspects Antichrist is rising gradually.

Antioch: (Hebrew – Antiyokhya) An *ancient Greek* city on the eastern side of the Orontes River. Its ruins lie near the modern city of Antakya, Turkey, and lends the modern city its name. Founded near the end of the 4th century BC by Seleucus I Nicator, one of Alexander the Great's generals, Antioch's geographic, military and economic location, particularly the spice trade, the Silk Road, the Persian Royal Road, benefited its occupants, and eventually it rivaled Alexandria as the chief city of the Near East and as the main center of Hellenistic Judaism at the end of the Second

Temple period. As a result of its longevity and the pivotal role it played in the emergence of both Hellenistic Judaism and Early Christianity, Antioch was called "the cradle of Christianity. "It was one of the four cities of the Syrian tetrapolis. Its residents are known as *Antiochenes*. Once a great metropolis of half a million people, it declined to insignificance during the Middle Ages because of warfare, repeated earthquakes and a change in trade routes following the Mongol conquests, which then no longer passed through Antioch from the far east.

Antioch, The Church of: This is one of the five major churches that composed the Christian Church before the East-West Schism. The Church traces its origins to the Christian community founded in Antioch by people of the period known by a variety of names, including "Followers of the Way," and later recognized by the Apostle St. Peter. St. Paul (see Early centres of Christianity) was one of its leading members. It later became one of the five major patriarchates or Pentarchy of the state church of the Roman Empire. According to Acts 11:19-26, the Christian community at Antioch began when Christians who were scattered from Jerusalem because of persecution fled to Antioch. They were joined by Christians from Cyprus and Cyrene who migrated to Antioch. It was in Antioch that the followers of Jesus were first referred to as Christians.

Apocalypse: (noun) An event involving great and widespread or massive destruction. Normally an act of God. 2 The final destruction of the world as contained or described in the biblical book of Revelation.

Apocalyptic Number: The mysterious number 666 described in (Revelation (13:15) and the associated number of the beast.

Apocrypha: (*Apocrypta*) Are statements or claims that are of dubious authenticity. The word's origin is the Medieval Latin adjective *apocryphus*, "secret, or non-canonical", from the Greek adjective - (*apocryphos*), "obscure", from verb (*apocryptein*), meaning "to hide away" 2 It is commonly applied in Christian religious contexts involving certain disagreements about biblical canonicity. The pre-Christian-era Jewish translation (into Greek) of holy scriptures known as the Septuagint included the writings in dispute. However, the Jewish canon was not finalized until at least 100–200 years into the A.D., at which time considerations of Greek language and beginnings of Christian acceptance of the Septuagint weighed against some of the texts. Some were not accepted by the Jews as part of the Hebrew Bible canon. Over several centuries of

Apostle

consideration, the books of the Septuagint were finally accepted into the Christian Old Testament, by A.D. 405 in the west, and by the end of the fifth century in the east. The Christian canon thus established was retained for over 1,000 years, even after the 11th-century schism that separated the church into the branches known as the Roman Catholic and Eastern Orthodox churches. 3 Those canons were not challenged until the Protestant Reformation (16th century), when both the Roman Catholic and Eastern Orthodox Churches reaffirmed them. The reformers rejected the parts of the canon that were not part of the Hebrew Bible and established a revised Protestant canon. Thus, concerning the Old Testament books, what is thought of as the "Protestant canon" is actually the final Hebrew canon. The differences can be found by looking here or by comparing the contents of the "Protestant" and Catholic Bibles, and they represent the narrowest Christian application of the term *Apocrypha*. 4 Among some Protestants, *apocryphal* began to take on extra or altered connotations: not just *of dubious authenticity*, but *having spurious or false content*, not just *obscure* but *having hidden or suspect motives*. Protestants were (and are) not unanimous in adopting those meanings. The Church of England agreed, and that view continues today throughout the Lutheran Church, the worldwide Anglican Communion, and many other denominations. Whichever implied meaning is intended, *Apocrypha* was (and is) used primarily by Protestants, in reference to the books of questioned canonicity. Catholics and Orthodox sometimes avoid using the term in contexts where it might be considered disputatious or be misconstrued as yielding on the point of canonicity. Very few Protestant published Bibles include the apocryphal books in a separate sections

Apostle: (Greek – *apostolos* – meaning 'messenger' formed from *'apostellein'*). A special word applied to the 12 Disciples of Christ sent forth to preach the gospel in order listed in Mathew 10:1-4, Mark3: 14 – 19, Luke 6: 13 – 16 and Acts 1:13) 2 An apostle is someone sent with a special message or commission. **Jesus** is called the apostle and high Priest of our confession in Hebrews 3:1. The twelve apostles of Jesus were Simon Peter, Andrew, James the son of Zebedee, John, Philip, Bartholomew, Thomas, Matthew, James the son of Alphaeus, Thaddaeus, Simon the Zealot, and Judas Iscariot who was replaced by Mathias (Acts 1:26). Paul became an apostle after Jesus' resurrection (2Corinthians. 1:1), along with Barnabas (Acts 14:14), and others. Apostles established churches (Rom. 15:17-20), exposed error (Galatians. 1:6-9),

Apostle

and defended the truth of the gospel (Phil. 1:7, 17). Some were empowered by the Holy Spirit to perform Miracles (Matthew. 10:1, 8), and they were to preach the gospel (Matthew. 28:19, 20). 3 A quick look at how the word is used in the Scripture shows several categories that arise: There are apostles who were only among the 12. They performed miracles. Some wrote scripture. (Acts 1:21-22) 5 Paul was an apostle (unique?) specifically commissioned by Christ. He performed miracles and wrote scriptures. (Acts 14:14; 1 Cor. 9:1; Gal. 1:1) 6 Barnabas is an apostle. He performed no miracles and wrote no scripture 7 Jesus is called an apostle. He performed miracles . (Acts 14:14, 8-18) (Heb. 3:1) 8 There are apostles in the sense of simply being sent. They are messengers. They perform no miracles.(2 Cor. 8:23; Phil. 2:25; John 20:21) 9 It could be possible that anyone who was involved in Christ's ministry before his death and saw him after his resurrection could be referred to as apostles. (Acts 1:21-22) 10 There are false apostles.(2 Cor. 11:13; Rev. 2:2)

Appoint (*passive* – **Appointed**, *noun* – **appointment**, *derivatives* – **appointee**)) Literally, To give a role or a job to someone. 2 Decide on time or place. The appointed time of God or 'God's time is the best'. 3 *In the Old Testament*. The basic meaning of "appoint" is either "visit" or "establish or set in authority." The extension of visit carries the idea of appointment, meaning to set in place (as a time, place, or event). The theological importance focuses on the appointing, consecrating, or commissioning of persons for special service to the Lord and his people. It can also carry implications for God's providence or the establishment of laws or principles. 4 *Consecration for Service* - Consecration is a special type of appointment. Four examples can be noted: (1) the consecration of Aaron and his sons (Exodus. 28-29); (2) the appointment of Levites as servants of God (Numbers. 3-8); (3) the naming of seventy elders to assist Moses (Num. 11, 24-25); and (4) the commissioning of Moses' successor (Num. 27). 5 The appointment of the seventy to assist Moses was at God's initiative. Their ordination involved standing with Moses to receive the Spirit that rested upon Moses (Numbers 11:17-25). Joshua's ordination consisted of receiving commissioning while standing before the priest and the congregation (Numbers 27:18-23). Moses laid his hand on Joshua as a symbol of the transference of authority. 6 Of primary significance is the ordination of Aaron and the Levites. Aaron and his sons alone were to serve as priests (Exodus 28:1), to offer sacrifices (Number 8:1-7), and to bless the people (Number 6:22-27). Aaron was anointed (Leviticus 8:12) and

Apple

the special vestments previewed those worn by preexilic monarchs (see Exodus 28). Because it marked the beginning of the priesthood in Israel, the consecration of Aaron to this office was of special significance. The entire event and its accompanying instructions were completely detailed. 7 As an extension of the appointment of Aaron and his sons, they were to bless the people (Number 6:22-27). In reality, it is God's own blessing of his people. God himself commanded Aaron and his sons to place the Lord's name on the Israelites (Number 6:27) 8 *The Synoptic Gospels* Foundational to the understanding of "appoint" in the New Testament is Jesus' statement about the kingdom that he has appointed to his followers (Luke 9-10). The New Testament practice is often associated with the laying on of hands.

Jesus appointed twelve disciples to be with him and that he could send out to preach (Mark 3:14). The Great Commission was given on the basis of Jesus' authority (Matthew 28:18-20). The One who appointed the kingdom to Jesus, who granted him authority, was God the Father Almighty. 9 *Acts* - Matthias was appointed by the casting of lots to replace Judas among the Twelve (Acts 1:12-26). Most significant is the reference to Barnabas and Paul and their appointment of elders in every church after prayer and fasting (Acts 14:23). 10 At the conclusion of the first missionary journey Paul and Barnabas established leadership in the new congregations. There remains a question in Acts 14:23 regarding who *appointed* the elders the apostles or the congregation. The most natural reading of the passage suggests that Paul and Barnabas did. Perhaps in these settings the apostles' wisdom was necessary to establish leadership, though the apostles' selection may have been confirmed by vote of the congregations (see also Titus 1:5). 11 In (Acts 26:16) Paul recounts his experience with the risen Christ. God appointed or placed Paul into service. The statement is extremely forceful, offering the mental picture of God picking up Paul and pointing him in the divinely intended direction 12 **This also contains in Christ redemption through His blood as in** (Hebrew 9:27-28) "And inasmuch as it is *appointed* for men to die once and after this comes judgment, so Christ also, having been offered once to bear the sins of many, will appear a second time for salvation without reference to sin, to those who eagerly await Him".

Apple: The apple appear more than once in the Greek Legend – see Adam's apple. However, there is no mention of Apple in the bible – story of Eve's temptation. "She took the fruit of the tree which is in the midst of the Garden" (Genesis 3:3)

Apple of God's or one's eye, The: The pupil, because it was formerly believed to be a round, solid ball like an apple. The phrase came to apply generally to any very precious or much loved person or thing. A true Christian should always say " I am the apple of God's eye" as in (Deuteronomy 32:10) Thus 'He kept him as the apple of his eye'.

Apples of Paradise:. According to tradition, apples in the Garden of Eden had a bite on one side to commemorate that taken by Eve.

Arabia: (or Arab) A member of Semitic people inhabiting much of the middle east and North Africa. 2 A breed of horse originating in Arabia. 3 It was Ptolemy who devised the threefold division of the land into Arabia 'Petraea' otherwise known as Rocky Arabia – for the northwestern part, including the Sinai Peninsula, Arabia Felix – otherwise known as Fruitful Arabia, for the main part of the Arabian Peninsula, and Arabia 'Desertta' – Desert Arabia - for the northern part between Syria and Mesopotemia. Whichever section of Arabia was of unique important to the Gospel of Paul. Particularly as he said Sinai was Saudi Arabia (Galatians 4:25) thus "And now Jerusalem is just like Mount Sinai in Arabia, because she and her children live in slavery to the law".

Arabian: adjective relating to Arabian. The people of Arabian. (noun) Historical on Arab. Person born and sharing the culture and traditions of Arabian people.

Arameans: Small scattered nations. The Aramaeans were not a single nation, but a widespread branch of the Semitic race. In the King James Version they are generally called Syrians. According to (Genesis. 10: 22) Aram was son of Shem, but in (Genesis. 22: 21) he is called son of Kenuel and grandson of Nahor. The Aramaeans therefore had kingship with the Hebrews. Their oldest seats were in Mesopotamia (Aram-Naharaim or Aram of the Two Rivers). 2 From an early date there were many *Aramaeans* in Assyria and Babylonia, and in these countries the Aramaic language finally prevailed over the old Assyrian and was only displaced by the Arab conquest. On the other hand, the *Aramaeans* crossed the Euphrates and, pushing aside the old inhabitants of the Orontes valley, were settled in the time of David as far south as Damascus and Beth-Rehob on the southern skirts of Hermon (2 Samuel. 8: 3 and 2 Samuel. 10: 6). These immigrants were not yet strong enough to resist David, who reduced them to subjection, but Damascus regained its independence under Solomon and soon became the center of a powerful kingdom, which pressed hard on Israel from the days of Ahab downward, and reduced the house of Jehu to the last extremity. When the Assyrians advanced on Canaan the first brunt of their attack fell on the Syrians, and the relief thus given

Ararat

to Israel seems to be alluded to in (2 Kings. 13: 5). At length, in 733 B.C., Damascus fell before Tiglath-pileser II and the *Aramaeans* lost their political independence. But 3 Their language, which was already that of a great part of the empire of Nineveh, continued to spread in the train of Assyrian and Persian conquest. Aramaic was the diplomatic speech of Palestine in the time of Hezekiah (2 Kings 18: 26). There is evidence that after the return from exile the Jews themselves gradually adopted Aramaic as the language of common life. The dialect called Hebrew in the New Testament Scripture is not the language of David and Isaiah, but a form of Aramaic. 4 In (2 Samuel 8:4-6) "David captured from him 1,700 horsemen and 20,000 foot soldiers; and David hamstrung the chariot horses, but reserved enough of them for 100 chariots. 5 When the *Arameans* of Damascus came to help Hadadezer, king of Zobah, David killed 22,000 Arameans. Then David put garrisons among the Arameans of Damascus, and the Arameans became servants to David, bringing tribute. And the LORD helped David wherever he went...."

Ararat: The Sacred land or high land, the name of a country on one of the mountains of which the ark rested after the Flood subsided (Genesis 8:4). The "mountains" mentioned were probably the Kurdish range of South Armenia. In 2 Kings 19:37 , Isaiah 37:38 , the word is rendered "Armenia" in the Authorized Version, but in the Revised Version, "Land of Ararat." 2 In (Jeremiah 51:27) , the name denotes the central or southern portion of Armenia. It is, however, generally applied to a high and almost inaccessible mountain which rises majestically from the plain of the Araxes. It has two conical peaks, about 7 miles apart, the one 14,300 feet and the other 10,300 feet above the level of the plain. Three thousand feet of the summit of the higher of these peaks is covered with perpetual snow. It is called *Kuh-i-nuh*, i.e., "Noah's mountain", by the Persians. This part of Armenia was inhabited by a people who spoke a language unlike any other now known, though it may have been related to the modern Georgian. About B.C. 900 they borrowed the cuneiform characters of Nineveh, and from this time we have inscriptions of a line of kings who at times contended with Assyria. At the close of the seventh century B.C. the kingdom of Ararat came to an end, and the country was occupied by a people who are ancestors of the Armenians of the present day.3 Otherwise it is known to be "the curse reversed: precipitation of curse" a mountainous region of eastern Armenia, between the river Araxes and the lakes Van and Oroomiah, the site where Noah's ark came to rest. Or, the mountain where Noah's ark came to rest

Archangel: In gospel stories, the title is often given to Michael – the chief opponent of Satan and his angels and to Gabriel, Raphael, Uriel, Chamuel, Jophiel, and Zadkiel.

Ark: (noun) In the gospel, this refers to the ship built by Noah to save his family and pairs of every kind of animal from the flood. 2 (There is also - Holy Ark) – A chest or cupboard housing the Torah scrolls in a synagogue. 3 (Ark of Covenant) – the chest which contained the law of ancient Israelites. – see the Ark of Covenant below

Ark of Covenant, The: The sacred box made of 'Shittim' wood covered with gold that was borne by the Hebrews in their journey in the desert. Its lid, the 'MERCY SEAT', was of solid gold and had two cherubs with out-stretch wings that contains the tablet of the Law (Deuteronomy 10:2), a pot of Manna and Aarons Rod- (Hebrews 9:4) and was the vocal point of the power of God. It was kept at Shiloh until it was captured by the Philistines and set up in their temple at Ashdod were it found a resting place in the Temple of Solomon, where it remained until the fall of Jerusalem. Jeremiah hid it in a cave until God should gather his people again.

Arise: (*passive* – arose, *past participle* – arisen) Come into being, New difficulty has arisen. Old thing has past away. Arise for everything become new – Like in 'Arise and go your way – your faith has made you well' as in (Luke 17:19) Then he said to him, "Rise and go; your faith has made you well." NIV; Meaning there is a transformation because old things, your old situation has passed away. In this case your 'old state' which could also be poverty, sickness, tribulation, all kinds of diseases – your former state is no more because your faith has made you well or normal. 2 Or arise in a form of vision to Daniel about the emergence of Michael as in (Daniel 12: 1) "At that time Michael, the great prince who protects your people, will **arise**. There will be a time of distress such as has not happened from the beginning of nations until then. But at that time your people – everyone whose name is found written in the book – will be delivered." NIV 3 Arise can be use as a form of instruction or order – Get up O' sleepers as in (Isaiah 60:1) "Arise, shine, for your light has come, and the glory of the LORD rises upon you." 4 Arise could also be used as a form of warning as in (Matthew 2424) For false messiahs and false prophets will appear (or will arise) and perform great signs and wonders to deceive, if possible, even the elect. Throughout the Gospel of Christ, arise is used in different aspect suitable to the fulfilment of the purpose in God's word according to His Grace and Glory.

Ararat

Armageddon: *(Hebrew: har meggidon)* Actually, this is the 'mountain district of Megido') 2 The name given in the Apocalypse as stated in *(Revelation 16:16)* to the site of the last great 'battle of that great day of the almighty God between the forces of good and evil. Megido, in northern Palestine, is the site of various battles described in the Old Testament. 3 Armagaddon is any great battle or scene of slaughter.

Armour: A tough metal plate worn to protect the body from the enemy attack like the one to protect the body from the enemy bullet, bow or arrow. But in this context this imply making spiritual preparation for the warfare or encounter with the enemies as stated in (Proverbs 20:18 - NIV) - Make plans by seeking advice; if you wage war, obtain guidance. That is, as a Christian, you should consider and meditate on the Scriptural meaning of **each piece** of the *armour* of God, so that we might stand firm in the battles of life. In (Ephesians 6:10-17) ...Be strong in the Lord and in his mighty power. Put on *the full armour of God* so that you can take your stand against the devil's schemes. For our struggle is not against flesh and blood, but against the rulers, against the authorities, against the powers of this dark world and against the spiritual forces of evil in the heavenly realms. Therefore put on the full *armour* of God, so that when the day of evil comes, you may be able to *stand your ground,* and after you have done everything, to stand. Stand firm then, with **the belt of truth** buckled round your waist, with **the breastplate of righteousness** in place, and with your feet fitted with the readiness that comes from **the gospel of peace.** In addition to all this, take up **the shield of faith,** with which you can extinguish all the flaming arrows of the evil one. Take **the helmet of salvation** and the **sword of the Spirit,** which is the word of God.

Artaxerxes: (An old Persian word – meaning, 'powerful ruler' a term captivated from *arta,* 'powerful and 'khshtra' ruler. 'king) The younger son of Xerxes and king of the Persians (465-425 BC). He was called the long-handed (Long – imanus) because his right hand was longer than his left. He is mentioned sometimes in the gospel in connection with his part in the restoration of Jerusalem after the captivity. (See Ezra 4, 6, 7 and Nehemiah 2,5,8)

Ascend: (Synonyms – rise) 1 To go or move upward; rise. As in (Exodus 19:18) And mount Sinai was altogether on a smoke, because the LORD descended upon it in fire: and the smoke thereof ascended as the smoke of a furnace, and the whole mount quaked greatly. **2.** To slope upward.

Arise

Like when Christ ascended up into heaven see Proverbs 30:4 Who hath ascended up into heaven, or descended? who hath gathered the wind in his fists? who hath bound the waters in a garment? who hath established all the ends of the earth? what *is* his name, and what *is* his son's name, if thou canst tell? **3.** To rise from a lower level or station; this could take the form of nature or act of God like when 'He causeth the vapours to ascend from the ends of the earth; he 'maketh' lightings for the rain; he bringeth the wind out of his treasuries'. (Psalm 135:7) 4 To advance: ascended from poverty to great wealth; ascend to the throne or Heaven – See Psalms 139:8 'If I ascend up into heaven, thou *art* there: if I make my bed in hell, behold, thou *art there*' 5 *Take over in haste or at the Lord's command as* In (Joshua 6: 5) "And it shall come to pass, that when they make a long *blast* with the ram's horn, *and* when ye hear the sound of the trumpet, all the people shall shout with a great shout; and the wall of the city shall fall down flat, and the people shall *ascend* up every man straight before him" **6** To go back in time or upward in genealogical succession.

Ascension: The ascent of Jesus Christ into Heaven after the Resurrection. 2 The act of rising in status - promotion. 3 Acts 1:9-11 is the Christian teaching found in the New Testament that the resurrected Jesus was taken up to Heaven in his resurrected body, in the presence of eleven of his apostles, occurring 40 days after the resurrection. In the gospel narrative from the bible, an angel tells the watching disciples that Jesus' second coming will take place in the same manner as his *ascension*. 4 The canonical gospels include two brief descriptions of the ascension of Jesus in (Luke 24:50-53) and (Mark 16:19). A more detailed account of Jesus' bodily *Ascension* into the clouds is then given in (Acts 1:6-11). "So when the apostles were with Jesus, they kept asking him, "Lord, has the time come for you to free Israel and restore our kingdom?" He replied, "The Father alone has the authority to set those dates and times, and they are not for you to know. But you will receive power when the Holy Spirit comes upon you. And you will be my witnesses, telling people about me everywhere—in Jerusalem, throughout Judea, in Samaria, and to the ends of the earth." After saying this, he was taken up into a cloud *(Ascension)* while they were watching, and they could no longer see him. As they strained to see him rising into heaven, two white-robed men suddenly stood among them. "Men of Galilee," they said, "why are you standing here staring into heaven? Jesus has been taken from you into heaven, but someday he will return from heaven in the same

Ascension Day

way you saw him go!" This return could reversely be qualified during the Rapture.

5 The ascension of Jesus is professed in the Nicene Creed and in the Apostles' Creed. The ascension implies Jesus' humanity being taken into Heaven The Feast of the Ascension, celebrated on the 40th day of Easter (always a Thursday), is one of the chief feasts of the Christian year The feast dates back at least to the later 4th century, as is widely attested The ascension is one of the five major milestones in the gospel narrative of the life of Jesus, the others being baptism, transfiguration, crucifixion, and resurrection. 6 By the 6th century the iconography of the ascension in Christian art had been established and by the 9th century ascension scenes were being depicted on domes of churches—Many ascension scenes have two parts, an upper (Heavenly) part and a lower (earthly) part. Note: The ascending Jesus is often shown blessing with his right hand - directed towards the earthly group below him and signifying that he is blessing the entire church

Ascension Day: According to Christian Calendar, the day set apart by the Christian Churches to commemorate the ascent of Christ from earth to heaven. The Feast of the Ascension, celebrated on the 40th day of Easter (always a Thursday), is one of the chief feasts of the Christian year The feast dates back at least to the later 4th century, as is widely attested The ascension is one of the five major milestones in the gospel narrative of the life of Jesus. 2 It is popularly known as the HOLY THURSDAY. (Beat the Bounds)

Ashamed: abashed, confused, confounded; they looked unto him and were lightened and their faces were not *ashamed* (*Psalm 34:5)* and their faces will never be *ashamed.* Let your eyes be turned to him and you will have light, and your faces will not be *ashamed.* (BEB) 2 They looked unto him and were radiant their faces shall never be confounded

Ashes to ashes, Dust to dust: A phrase from the English burial service, used sometimes to denote total finality. It is based on scriptural texts such as "Dust thou art and unto dust thou shall return" based on (Genesis 3:39) and I will bring thee to ashes upon the earth in the sight of all them that behold thee' (Ezekiel 27:18) – Ashes to ashes and dust to dust; In other word, 'If God we have him the Devil must'.

Ash Wednesday: The first day of LENT, so called from the Roman Catholic custom of sprinkling on the head of penitents the consecrated ashes of palms remaining from the previous Palm Sunday. The custom is of uncertain date but is commonly held to have been introduced during the pontificate of Gregory The Great between 604 – 1590.

Asia: This is the Earth's largest and most populous continent, located primarily in the eastern and northern hemispheres. It covers 8.7% of the Earth's total surface area and comprises 30% of its land area. With approximately 4.3 billion people, it hosts 60% of the world's current human population. Out of which about 35% are Christians. Like most of the world, *Asia* has a high growth rate in the modern era. For instance, during the 20th century, *Asia's* population nearly quadrupled, as did the world population. The boundaries of Asia are culturally determined, as there is no clear geographical separation between it and Europe, which together form one continuous landmass called Eurasia. The most commonly accepted boundaries place Asia to the east of the Suez Canal, the Ural River, and the Ural Mountains, and south of the Caucasus Mountains (or the Kuma–Manych Depression) and the Caspian and Black Seas It is bounded on the east by the Pacific Ocean, on the south by the Indian Ocean and on the north by the Arctic Ocean. Given its size and diversity, the concept of Asia — a name dating back to classical antiquity - may actually have more to do with human geography than physical geography Asia varies greatly across and within its regions with regard to ethnic groups, cultures, environments, economics, historical ties and government systems — All which affect or influences the spread of the gospel of Christ greatly.

Ask: Simply to say something in order to get an answer. *Ask* God through prayer. Inquire about something. 2 Say that one wants someone to do, give or allow - The pastor *ask* him to pray... 3 Ask for – request to speak to someone. 4 Expect or demand something from God or someone. 5 Invite Jesus (Holy Spirit) into your gospel or any gathering. Ask Jesus to lead you or the way (ask Jesus or someone out). 6 Ask after – To ask or make polite enquiries about a fellow Christian's health or wellbeing. Christians are familiar with the most popular request or method of asking taken from the book of (Mathew 7:7-8) thus' "Ask, and it will be given to you; seek, and you will find; knock, and it will be opened to you. "For everyone who asks receives, and he who seeks finds, and to him who knocks it will be opened"....

Astraea: (Latin, starry maiden: as ultimate from ultimate from Greek aster star); a Roman goddess associated with justice. During the Golden Age, she dwell on earth but when sin began to prevail she reluctantly left it and was metamorphosed into the constellation then Virgo her name was used as an epithar by Elizabeth 11 of England.

Astral body

Astral body: (The Greek astron. 'star') in theosophical parlance the phantasmal or spiritual appearance of the physical human form which exist both before and after the death of the material body, although during life it is not usually separated from it. To certain gifted individuals, a person's astral body is discernible if not actually visible, as an aura. 2 Astral ...body of stars or relating to stars.

Astral Spirits: The spirits from where stars are animated. The occultists indicate that each star had its spirit. While the Paracelsus maintained that every man had it attendant star, particularly that which receive him at death and took charge of him until the great resurrection. 2 Christians are empowered with the divine spiritual power as opposed to the astral spirits in their belief.

Asshur or Assur Originally, the local god of Asshur–the capital of Assyria. He later became the chief god of the kingdom. His symbol was the winged sun disc enclosing a male figure wearing horned cap, often with a bow in his hand. His name was frequently link with the goddess Ishtar of Nineveh.

Assumption, the: Taking-up of body eg into Heaven This signifies the assumption of the blessed virgin Mary. One of the 'Feast of Obligation' in the Roman Catholic Church. It is celebrated on 15 August and commemorates the death of the Virgin Mary and the assumption - taking up of her body into Heaven when it was reunited to her soul. It can be trace back to 6th century as declared by Pius X11 as a matter of divinely revealed dogma that the Virgin Mary having completed the earthly course was in body and soul assumed into Heavenly Glory.

Assurance: Full of conviction, a protestant Christian doctrine. Always have assurance with God's word. *Assurance* of understanding. In much *assurance*, Full *assurance*- Completely convinced. Assurance of faith. Worth of Trust- Assurance of Gods promises Worth of hope, trust, believe. Christ *assurance* of Heavenly dwelling – In my fathers House, there are many Mansions...

Assurance of Eternal Life – Gods promise,

Assurance, Blessed- A well – known Christian hymn. The lyrics written in 1873 by blind Hymn writer Fanny J. Crosby to the music written in 1873 by Phoebe P. Knapp. The Knapp home was having a large pipe organ installed. As the organ was incomplete, Mrs Knapp used the Piano and played a new melody she had composed. Then asked Crosby "what do you think the time says?"", Crosby replied, ""Blessed Assurance, Jesus is mine" The hymn appeared in the July 1873 issue of Palmer's Guide to Holiness and Revival Miscellany – A magazine printed by Dr. And Mrs. W. C. Palmer. The full text appeared on page

36 which was more-the-less, the last page with complete text and Piano score indicating it had been copyrighted by Crosby that year. Though no one can tell if this was the first printing of the hymn, but it certainly helped to popularized what became one of the most beloved hymns in mankind history. The Crosby's lyrics now then make the tune to be called "Assurance" till the present day. See Hebrews 10:22 for verses 1-3 with all the references – all composed to uplift the our spirit.

Assyria: An ancient land located in what is now north-eastern Irag and taking its name from the small settlement of Asshur, on the west bank of River Tigris. It grew into the greatest empire in the world, becoming independent of Babylon in the 17th century BC. It capital was Nineveh, and one of best known ruler was Sennacherib. On the death of its ruler Essarhaddon, in the 7th century BC, the empire was divided and an alliance of Medes and Babylonians stormed and destroyed Nineveh, finally overthrowing the Assyrian Empire in 612 BC. The key episodes of its rise and fall are clearly accounted for in the chronicle of the Old Testament.

Ate: Goddess of vengeance and mischief cast down by zeus. That comprising with Caesar's spirit ramping for revenge. Most writers as Edmund Spencer attached this name to a lying and slanderous hag. Christians are warned not to use this word when the word of the living God is to have a way in their lives.

Atonement: (at-one-ment) Reconciliation; expiation; i.e the making of amends. In Christian usage, atonement denotes the reconciliation God and man through the life, sufferings and crucifixion of Jesus Christ. It presupposes man's alienation from God through sin. 2

Atonement, Day of: (phr) Day of coverings, or Yom Kippur (Hebrew; yom- 'day' and kipur – atonement) This connotes the great Jewish fast day held on the tenth day of Tishri, the seventh month (September – October). The events of this day includes prayer, confession and repentance, and the closing service of this most sacred day ends with the sounding of the 'Shofar'. The ceremonies are described in (Leviticus 16:29). And this shall be a statute for ever unto you that in the seventh month on the tenth day of the month, ye shall afflict your souls, and do not work at all, whether it be one of your own country, or a stranger that 'sojourneth' among you.

Authority: (noun) Simply, the power to give order to other people or forces and enforce their obedience. 2 Jesus was given the power to take *authority* in *heaven,* in the sea and the earth and all creation was commanded to be subjects to His *authority.* 3 Jesus gave true Christians the power over every demons, principalities and forces of darkness - a solid understanding of spiritual *authority* is vital to build your faith when casting out demons, healing the sick, and exercising your *authority* over the powers of darkness. 4 When we have been given *authority* to cast out demons, but instead we pray that God brings the demon out instead, we are basically asking God to do something that He gave US the tools to do ourselves! Jesus told US to cast out demons! Nowhere in the Scripture or the Bible does it tell us to ask God to cast out demons! (Mark 13:34), "For the Son of man is as a man taking a far journey, who left his house, and gave *authority* to his servants, and to every man his work, and commanded the porter to do the work. 5 *Authority* doesn't beg; *authority* doesn't ask; *authority* commands! We are not told to ask God to cast out demons, we are told to do it ourselves! We are not told to beg demons to come out, we are told to CAST them out! In (Matthew 8:8-9, 13), "The centurion answered and said, Lord, I am not worthy that thou 'shouldest' come under my roof: but speak the word only, and my servant shall be healed. For I am a man under *authority,* having soldiers under me: and I say to this man, Go, and he 'goeth'; and to another, Come, and he 'cometh'; and to my servant, Do this, and he doeth it... And Jesus said unto the centurion, Go thy way; and as thou hast believed, so be it done unto thee. And his servant was healed in the selfsame hour." 6 *Authority* is exercised through our spoken word. The power of life and death are in the spoken word: (Proverbs 18:21), "Death and life are in the power of the tongue: and they that love it shall eat the fruit thereof." (NKJV)

Ave Maria: (Medeval Latin 'Hail Mary') The first two words of the Latin prayer to the Virgin Mary used in the Roman Catholic Church (Luke 1:28). The phrase is applied to the smaller beads of a Rosary, the larger ones being termed Paternosters.

Awake: (verb) Stop sleeping. 2 Make or become active or functional again. A word of caution to Christians to persevere in prayers, thanksgiving and the word of God as in (Ephesians 5:13-15) "But all things become visible when they are exposed by the light, for everything that becomes visible is light. For this reason it says, "Awake, sleeper, And arise from the dead, And Christ will shine on you." Therefore be careful how you walk, not as unwise men but as wise,...

Azazel: (Hebrew 'azazel, perhaps 'power of God) In (Leviticus 16:8) tells how Aaron, as an atonement, was cast lots on two goats 'one lot for the Lord, and the other for the 'scapegoat' 2 Here 'scapegoat' is a mistranslation of Azazel, who was actually the demonic being to whom the scapegoat was to be sent.

Bb

Baal: This means the chief Semitic fertility god and in Phoenician mythology – the sun god and the supreme national deity. 2 There were also local Baals such as those establish in Canaan when the Israelite arrived. The later adopted many rites of the Canaanites and crafted same t their own worship of Jehovah who then after tended to become merely the national Ball. It was this form of worship that Hosea and other Prophet denounced as heathen gods or heathenism. also rendered 3 Baʿal (Biblical Hebrew, is a North-West Semitic title and honorific meaning "master" or "lord that is used for various gods who were patrons of cities in the Levant and Asia Minor, cognate to Akkadian A **Baal**ist or **Baalite** means a worshipper of Baal.4 "Baal" may refer to any god and even to human officials. In some texts it is used for Hadad, a god of thunderstorms, fertility and agriculture, and the lord of Heaven. Since only priests were allowed to utter his divine name, Hadad, Baʿal was commonly used. Nevertheless, few if any biblical uses of "Baal" refer to Hadad, the lord over the assembly of gods on the holy mount of Heaven; most refer to a variety of local spirit-deities worshipped as cult images, each called *baal* and regarded in the Hebrew Bible in that context as a false god.

Babel: (noun) This simply means the 'gate of God' – A confusion of noises or voices, a hubbub. Resulting in the allusion to the confusion of Tongues during the building of the Tower of Babel as in (Genesis 11:1-9) "Now the whole world had one language and a common speech. As people moved eastward they found a plain in Shinar and settled there. They said to each other, "Come, let's make bricks and bake them thoroughly." They used brick instead of stone, and tar for mortar. Then they said, "Come, let us build ourselves a city, with a tower that reaches to the heavens, so that we may make a name for ourselves; otherwise we will be scattered over the face of the whole earth." *But the lord came down to see the city and the tower the people were building. The lord*

Babes

said, *"if as one people speaking the same language they have begun to do this, then nothing they plan to do will be impossible for them. Come, let us go down and confuse their language so they will not understand each other. So the lord scattered them from there over all the earth, and they stopped building the city. That is why it was called babel because there the lord confused the language of the whole world. From there the lord scattered them over the face of the whole earth".*2 Otherwise and based on the above fact, babel meant a confused noise made by a number of voices originated from the tower of babel in the bible where god confused the language of the builders.

Babes: Literally babes, or singular (a baby), informal affectionate form of address for a lover. 2 An attractive young woman. In terms of the new convert to Christianity, they word address the new-born in Christ. A person where Christ love and cherishes, affectionately or divinely through Grace. 3 This word appears nine times in the Christian gospel or bible- meaning as in (Psalm 17: 12-17) "Like as a lion [that] is greedy of his prey, and as it were a young lion lurking in secret places. Arise, O LORD, disappoint him, cast him down: deliver my soul from the wicked, [which is] thy sword: From men [which are] thy hand, O LORD, from men of the world, [which have] their portion in [this] life, and whose belly thou 'fillest' with thy hid [treasure]: they are full of children, and leave the rest of their [substance] to their *babes*. As for me, I will behold thy face in righteousness: I shall be satisfied, when I awake, with thy likeness.

Babylon: This is the chief city of Mesopotamia first settled about 3000 BC. Founded in classical times for its luxury and its name came to be applied figuratively to any city thought of as decadent and materialistic. 2 Name often used by Rastafarians to designate western civilization viewed as oppressive and ungodly. 3 *Babylon* occurs in the Christian New Testament both with a literal and a figurative meaning. The famous ancient city, located near Baghdad, was a complete unpopulated ruin by 275 BC, well before the time of the New Testament. In the Book of Revelation, the *city of Babylon* seems to be the symbol of every kind of evil. 4 *Babylon* was later the *nominal* seat of Latin archbishop, of an Assyrian patriarch and of a Syrian archbishop. But according to the *International Standard Bible Encyclopedia*: "Babylon" there was probably no Christian community in the actual city of *Babylon* during the time when the New Testament books were completed (roughly, the second half of the first century). There are passing references to the historical Babylon of the Jewish past in (Matthew 1:11 - 17) "And Josias begat Jechonias and his brethren, about the time they were carried away to *Babylon:* And after they were brought to Babylon, Jechonias begat Salathiel; and Salathiel begat Zorobabel; And Zorobabel begat Abiud; and Abiud begat Eliakim; and Eliakim begat Azor;And Azor begat Sadoc; and Sadoc begat Achim; and Achim begat Eliud; And Eliud begat Eleazar; and Eleazar begat Matthan; and Matthan begat Jacob;And Jacob begat Joseph the husband of Mary, of whom was born Jesus, who is called Christ. "So all the generations from Abraham to David *are* fourteen generations; and from David until the carrying away into *Babylon* *are* fourteen generations; and from the carrying away into *Babylon* unto Christ *are* fourteen generations Also in (Acts 7:42-43), "But God turned away and delivered them up to serve the host of heaven; as it is written in the book of the prophets, 'it was not to me that you offered victims and sacrifices forty years in the wilderness, was it, o house of israel? 'You also took along the tabernacle of moloch and the star of the god rompha, the images which you made to worship. I also will remove you beyond babylon.' but these are literary. 4 Babylon is also used in Benediction and final greetings as in (1 Peter 5:13) where *Babylon* is designated as the place from which that Epistle was written, Thus "Through Silvanus, our faithful brother (for so I regard him), I have written to you briefly, exhorting and testifying that this is the true grace of God. Stand firm in it! She who is in Babylon, chosen together with you, sends you greetings, and so does my son, Mark. Greet one another with a kiss of love. Peace be to you all who are in Christ". but this has traditionally been interpreted as an example of the figurative sense of *"Babylon",* as a metaphor for Rome. Peter is believed to have spent the last years of his life in Rome. Nevertheless, In the Book of Revelation, the destruction of '*Babylon*', a city which seems to be a symbol of every kind of evil, is foretold. The connection with the actual historical city of *Babylon* is usually held to be metaphorical. It may be that "Babylon" is used here as a metaphor, dysphemism, or 'code word' for the power of the Roman Empire which was oppressing the nascent church much as the Babylonian empire had oppressed the Jewish people in Old Testament times; with the reason given usually being that it was not considered safe or prudent to speak openly against Rome.

5 Elsewhere in the Book of Revelation, Babylon is the name of a whore who rules over the kings of the earth and rides upon a seven-headed beast. In one of the Bible's most famous cases of numerology, the beast is commonly believed to have the identifying number 666, which has been linked with Nero Whom or what **Babylon** refers to in the Book of Revelation has been the subject of much speculation over the centuries: As noted above, the standard scholarly interpretation is that Babylon symbolizes

Rome and the "Whore of Babylon" therefore either refers to the Roman emperor, or personified the power of the Roman Empire under whom many early Christians and Jews were persecuted, tortured, and martyred for their beliefs because they would not submit to the Roman Emperor as a god. Many scholars[who?] believe that the early Christians used "Babylon" as a euphemism for pagan Rome, so that their small community wouldn't be found out and persecuted even more.

Some Fundamentalist Protestant commentaries on the Book of Revelation treat the references to the city Babylon in Revelation as both the City of Rome and the Roman Catholic Church personified in the institution of the papacy. Some Protestant denominations today do not give credence to such arguments however. Jehovah's Witnesses believe that Babylon represents all false religion (i.e.: that thought to be disapproved of or condemned by God). A modern interpretation is that the Whore of Babylon refers to the institution of multinational corporations. (*whore* - one whose loyalty can be bought; *rules over the kings of the earth* - is more powerful than any individual secular government.) 7 In the Rastafari movement, *Babylon* is a key theological concept referring to any oppressive power structure that adherents believe has been responsible for stealing and oppressing them for generations and still today. However it also refers to the literal Tower of Babel, which 'Haile Selassie' sometimes referred to in his speeches, seen as an act of human rebellion against JAH. 8 Some end-time prophets (Dumitru Duduman, Tom Deckard, Steven Crowder and others) assert that Babylon refers to America or to decadent western society in general. The considered opinions as to the identity of Babylon in the New Testament need also factor in gospel bible references to a geographical feature that is close-by to the historical site of *Babylon*; that is the "great river Euphrates", as mentioned specifically in (Revelation 9: 13-15) Then the sixth angel sounded, and I heard a voice from the four horns of the golden altar which is before God, one saying to the sixth angel who had the trumpet, "Release the four angels who are bound at the great river Euphrates." And the four angels, who had been prepared for the hour and day and month and year, were released, so that they would kill a third of mankind and (Revelation 16:11-13) particularly refer to the 'First Six Bowls of Wrath' thus... and they blasphemed the God of heaven because of their pains and their sores; and they did not repent of their deeds. The sixth angel poured out his bowl on the great river, the Euphrates; and its water was dried up, so that the way would be prepared for the kings from the east. And I saw coming out of the mouth of the dragon and out of the mouth of the beast and out of the mouth of the false prophet, three unclean spirits like frogs

Babylonia: (balbilahnia) An ancient Akkadian-speaking Semitic nation state and cultural region based in central-southern Mesopotamia (present-day Iraq). It emerged as an independent state c. 1894 BC, with the city of Babylon as its capital. It was often involved in rivalry with its fellow Akkadian state of Assyria in northern Mesopotamia. *Babylonia* became the major power in the region after Hammurabi (.1792 - 1752 BC middle chronology, or (1696 – 1654 BC), short chronology) created an empire out of many of the territories of the former Akkadian Empire Babylon is Akkadian "babilani" which means "the Gate of God(s)" and it became the capital of the land of *Babylonia*. The etymology of the name Babel in the Bible means "confused" as recorded in (Gen 11:9) "Therefore its name was called Babel, because there the LORD confused the language of all the earth. And from there the LORD dispersed them over the face of all the earth". and throughout the gospel in Old Testament, , Babylonia was a symbol of the confusion caused by godlessness. The name Babylon is the Greek form of the Hebrew name Babel. The Bible reveals that all false systems of religion began in the land of Babylon and will have their consummation from the spirit of Babylon in the last days. It is interesting to note that every organized system of religion in the world today has traces of ancient Babylon. The Bible records in (Genesis 10:10), that, after the great flood, all men spoke one common language and a man named Nimrod built a city and established a common religion. Nimrod was a descendant of Noah's son, Ham. (Genesis 11:1-9) describes the building of the city and its famous tower *"whose top may reach unto heaven."* It also records how God came down and punished the people's arrogance by creating a confusion of different languages and possibly their racial distinctions. This way man would be forced to obey God's original command to "be fruitful and fill the whole earth." It is interesting that the materials used to build the Tower of Babel were the same as those employed for the construction of the great ziggurat of Babylon and similar ziggurats, according to ancient building inscriptions. There is evidence that man has lived in this area of Mesopotamia – called Babylonia since the beginning of civilization. Before this it was a provincial capital ruled by the kings of the city of Ur. Then came the migration of the Amorites. 2 Babylonia (pronounced – 'babilahnia') was an ancient empire that existed in the Near East in southern Mesopotamia between the Tigris and the Euphrates Rivers. Throughout much of their his-

Babylonia

tory their main rival for supremacy were their neighbours, the Assyrians. It was the Babylonians, under King Nebuchadnezzar II, who destroyed Jerusalem, the capital of the Kingdom of Judah, and carried God's covenant people into captivity in 587 BC. The Bible reveals much about the Babylonians all the way back from the time of Hammurapi (2000 BC) to the fall of Babylon – the capital city in about 500 BC) Throughout the Old Testament there are references to the Babylonians, their people, culture, religion, military power, etc.

Further facts are that, Babylonia was a long, narrow country about 40 miles wide at its widest point and having an area of about 8,000 square miles. It was bordered on the north by Assyria, on the east by Elam, on the south and west by the Arabian Desert, and on the southeast by the Persian Gulf The earliest known inhabitants of Mesopotamia were the Babylonians who were the Sumerians, whom the Bible refers to as the people of the "land of Shinar" (Gen 10:10). "And the beginning of his kingdom was Babel, and Erech, and Accad, and Calneh, in the land of Shinar". Sargon, from one of the Sumerian cities, united the people of Babylonia under his rule about 2300 B.C. Many scholars believe that Sargon might have been the same person as Nimrod as in (Gen 10:8 -9 "Now Cush became the father of Nimrod; he became a mighty one on the earth He was a mighty hunter before the LORD; therefore it is said, "Like Nimrod a mighty hunter before the LORD."...

Backslider: A person or one who backslides (see backsliding below)

Backsliding: (back - **slides,** -**sliding,** -**slid,** - **slid** *or* – **slidden**) To revert to sin or wrongdoing, especially in religious practice. 2 To lapse into bad habits or vices from a state of virtue, religious faith, etc. 3 To relapse into bad habits, sinful behaviour, or undesirable activities. 4 An instance of backsliding 5 Backslide means to lapse or fall backwards in your relationship with Christ. To lose interest in following and serving the Lord. Some Christians use terms like "lukewarm" or "faith that's grown cold" to describe a person who is spiritually backsliding. 6 A believer who is "no longer on fire for the Lord" is another typical description of someone who is in a *backslidden* state. Follow the scripture in (Hebrew 6: 4-6) to guide you against backsliding. Thus: "For [it is] impossible for those who were once enlightened, and have tasted of the heavenly gift, and were made partakers of the Holy Ghost, And have tasted the good word of God, and the powers of the world to come, If they shall fall away, to renew them again unto repentance; seeing they crucify to themselves the Son of God afresh, and put [him] to an open shame".

Balm of Gilead: Jesus signifies the *Balm of Gilead*. In ordinary usage, this is a rare perfume used medicinally, that was mentioned in the Bible, and named for the region of Gilead where it was produced. The expression stems from William Tyndale's language in the King James Bible of 1611, and has come to signify a universal cure in figurative speech. The tree or shrub producing the balm is commonly identified as Commiphora gileadensis, which is the plant that bleeds the Balsam of Mecca. Some botanical scholars have concluded that the actual source was an unrelated plant, a Terebinth tree in the genus Pistacia. In three different places the Old Testament mentions the "balm" or healing ointment that comes from Gilead, the mountainous region east of the Jordan River. When Joseph's brothers conspired against him in (Genesis 37:25), they sold him to a caravan of Ishmaelite's from the region of Gilead carrying a load of gum, balm, and myrrh. Also, (Jeremiah 46:11) mentions the healing balm of Gilead and (Jeremiah 8:22) poses a question to the sinning people of Judah: "Is there no balm in Gilead? Is there no physician there?

2 Note the (noun) Balm is a fragrant cream or liquid used to heal or soothe the skin. "a skin balm for use after shaving" synonyms: ointment, lotion, cream, salve, liniment, embrocation, rub, gel, emollient, unguent, balsam, moisturizer; antonyms: astringent, irritant something that has a soothing or restorative effect. "the murmur of the water can provide balm for troubled spirits or sickness" Like when Jesus met the impotent man in (John 5:7)"The impotent man answered him, Sir, I have no man, when the water is troubled, to put me into the pool: but while I am coming, another steppeth down before me".

synonyms: relief, comfort, ease, consolation, cheer, solace; More 2 a tree which yields a fragrant resinous substance, especially one used in medicine. 3 A well-known African-American spiritual applies the words of the text this way: There is a *balm in Gilead* to make the wounded whole; There is a balm in Gilead To heal the sin sick soul. Jesus is truly the "balm of Gilead" for all the hurting people of the world. When J. C. Philpot preached on (Jeremiah 8:22) in 1852, he pointed out that God's grace is always greater than our sin: "There is more in the balm to heal than there is in guilt to wound; for there is more in grace to save than there is in sin to destroy." As Christians, if we truly know Jesus, we're going to heaven because his grace is far greater than our sin. His blood is the balm that heals the deepest wounds of sin. When we have fallen hard, he lifts us up and restores our soul. Is there no Balm in Gilead? Yes, there

Baptize

is. Jesus is the name that makes the wounded whole. When you are sick, be in despair, confused, confound, poor, disappointed, say, Blessed Lord, you specialize in healing the broken places of life. Speak your healing word today for me and I will be made whole. Hallelujah!

Baptize: (or Baptise –verb) Simply, this is the Sacrament of the Christian Church dates back in one form or another to pre-apostolic times. Also means to admit someone or a member to the Christian Church by the right of baptism.. Popularly to immerse or baptize in the water.

Baptize of the Holy Spirit:

Baptism of the Holy Spirit is a term used to describe a movement of the Spirit upon and or within a believer usually sometime after the person is saved. There is controversy surrounding this phenomenon as to whether it is legitimate or not. Some people believe that once a person is saved, the Holy Spirit is in the person; and there is no subsequent "baptism in the Holy Spirit." In other words, they maintain that this Baptism of the Spirit occurs at salvation. Others believe that it is possible for the Christian to experience an additional movement of the Holy Spirit sometime after salvation. Generally speaking, it is the charismatic movement that supports the Baptism of the Holy Spirit.

We need to know, first that all, Christians receive the Spirit upon their conversion; and in this sense all Christians have been baptized in the Holy Spirit. This means that they are saved and that they have all they need at that time to be able to live godly and holy lives. (1 Cor. 12:13) says, "For by one Spirit we were all baptized into one body, whether Jews or Greeks, whether slaves or free, and we were all made to drink of one Spirit." However, there are many Christians who claim to have had this "secondary" experience of the Spirit. 2 They say that it has brought great blessing and comfort to them. Furthermore, they say that the results of the experience is a renewed dedication and appreciation for God, a stronger desire to read the Bible, a stronger desire to fellowship with Christians, and a deeper sense of worship of God. Millions of Christians who claim to have had this experience force us to deal with the issue. Is it real or not? Let's look at the Scripture to find out.

The term **"baptize with the Holy Spirit"** occurs several times in scripture: (Mathew 3:11), "As for me, I baptize you with water for repentance, but He who is coming after me is mightier than I, and I am not fit to remove His sandals; He will baptize you with the Holy Spirit and fire." Mark 1:8, "I baptized you with water; but He will baptize you with the Holy Spirit." Luke 3:16, "John answered and said to them all, 'As for me, I baptize you

Baptized

with water; but One is coming who is mightier than I, and I am not fit to untie the thong of His sandals; He will **baptize you with the Holy Spirit** and fire." (John 1:33), "And I did not recognize Him, but He who sent me to baptize in water said to me, "He upon whom you see the Spirit descending and remaining upon Him, this is the one who baptizes in the Holy Spirit." Acts 1:5, "for John baptized with water, but you shall be baptized with the Holy Spirit not many days from now." (Acts 11:16), "And I remembered the word of the Lord, how He used to say, 'John baptized with water, but you shall be baptized with the Holy Spirit." We can clearly see that the phrase is used in the Bible. But, we do not find a clear teaching in the Bible of what the phrase means. Nevertheless, we can conclude that when a person is baptized in the Holy Spirit, he has power bestowed upon him. This power is for the purpose of the preaching of the gospel (Acts 4:31), living a purer life, and having a deeper devotion to God. Also, it is frequently accompanied by **speaking in tongues.** (Acts 2:4), "And they were all filled with the Holy Spirit and began to speak with other tongues, as the Spirit was giving them utterance." At this point, I would recommend the reader to examine (Acts 1-2) to see the movement of the Holy Spirit upon the early church **at Pentecost.** The issue now seems to be whether or not Baptism of/in/with the Holy Spirit is a subsequent event occurring after salvation. It would seem that this is the case. In (John 20:22) Jesus commanded that the disciples receive the Holy Spirit, "And when He had said this, He breathed on them, and said to them, "Receive the Holy Spirit." This means that they were saved since the Holy Spirit is not received by the unregenerate. Then, later in (Acts 1:4-5) we read, "And gathering them together, He commanded them not to leave Jerusalem, but to wait for what the Father had promised, "Which," He said, "you heard of from Me; for John baptized with water, but you shall be baptized with the Holy Spirit not many days from now."

Baptized: Having been baptised. Baptism is a cornerstone to our Christian beliefs. John the Baptist was ordained by God to be the predecessor of Jesus - he preached about His coming and even baptized Jesus. Being baptized is an important part of Christianity and although not everyone gets baptized, it's an important part of our beliefs that you should be knowledgeable about. That's why the following Bible verses on baptism is essential - so that you could learn more about this important part of Christianity!

(*John 1:33*) "And I knew him not: but he that sent me to baptize with water, the same said to me, On whom you shall see the Spirit descending, and remaining on him, the same is he which baptizes with the Holy Ghost". (*John 3:5*) "Jesus answered, Truly, truly, I say to you, Except a man be born of water and of the Spirit, he

Baptizing

cannot enter into the kingdom of God". (John 3:23) And John also was baptizing in Aenon near to Salim, because there was much water there: and they came, and were baptized. (Acts 1:5) For John truly baptized with water; but you shall be baptized with the Holy Ghost not many days hence. (Acts 1:22) Beginning from the baptism of John, to that same day that he was taken up from us, must one be ordained to be a witness with us of his resurrection.

Baptizing: In the process of Baptism.

Baptism: (noun) This is the Sacrament of the Christian Church dates back in one form or another to the pre-apostolic times which entails; 2 The Christian rite of sprinkling a person with water or dipping them in it, as a sign that they have been cleansed of sin and have entered the Church. 3 It is the Christian tradition of adoption to the Christendom.

Baptism with the Holy Spirit:

(alternatively Baptism in the Holy Spirit or Holy Ghost) in Christian theology is a term describing baptism (washing or immersion) in or with the Spirit of God and is frequently associated with the bestowal of spiritual gifts and empowerment for Christian ministry. While the phrase "*baptism with the Holy Spirit*" is found in the New Testament and all Christian traditions accept it as a theological concept, each has interpreted it in a way consistent with their own beliefs on ecclesiology and Christian initiation. One view holds that the term refers only to Pentecost, the "once-for-all" event for the whole Church described in the second chapter of the Book of Acts. 2 Another view holds that the term also refers to an experience of the individual believer distinct from salvation and initiation into the Church. 2 Before the emergence of the holiness movement in the mid-19th century and Pentecostalism in the early 20th century, most denominations believed that Christians received the baptism with the Holy Spirit either upon conversion and regeneration or through rites of Christian initiation. Since the growth and spread of Pentecostal and charismatic churches, however, the belief that the baptism with the Holy Spirit is an experience distinct from regeneration has come into increasing prominent

Barabbas: Simply means 'son of the father' – a title of Jesus. 2 At the trial of Jesus, the crowd were asked to choose between Him and Barabbas who was a robber under sentence of death for murder. And as a prisoner to whom Pilate will grant amnesty in honour of the Passover. The crowd choose Barabbas (John 18:40) - "Then they all cried again, saying, "Not this Man, but **Barabbas**!" therefore obliging Pilate to release a guilty man and condemn an innocent. The episode is regarded by some gospel scholars as a fabrication. Note: It might not be a coincidence that the name of Barabbas means son of the father'. A title of Jesus. If it does, this goes to the humiliation Jesus was subjected for us Christians that He was so named with sinners when He did not commit any sin – all for the sake of mankind.

Barbarian: The Greeks and Romans called all foreigners 'Barbarians' since they were babblers – speaking a language not understood by them. The word is imitative of speech that is unintelligible. In other word this implies 'uncivilized' or 'uncultured' is a natural consequence as stated in (1 Corinthians 14:11) – "Therefore if I know not the meaning of the voice I shall be unto him that speaketh *barbarian,* and he that 'speaketh' shall be a barbarian unto me".

Barnabas: (**Barnaby** - *son of consolation or comfort or encouragement*) a name given by the apostles, (Acts 4:36) While his real name was Joseph (or Jose), a Levite of the island of Cyprus, who sold all his property and laid the price or the proceeds at the apostle's feet. an early disciple of Christ. 2 *Banabbas* was a native of the isle of CYPRUS In (Acts 9:27) we find him introducing the newly-converted Saul to the apostles at Jerusalem. *Barnabas* was sent to Jerusalem, and is said to have sold all his property, and laid the price of it at the apostles' feet, (Acts 4:36,37). When Paul came to Jerusalem, three years after his conversion, about A. D. 38, *Barnabas* introduced him to the other apostles, (Acts 9:26,27). Five years afterwards, the church at Jerusalem, being informed of the progress of the gospel at Antioch, sent *Barnabas* thithes, who beheld with great joy the wonders of the grace of God, (Acts 11:20-24). He afterwards went to Tarsus, to seek Paul and bring him to Antioch, where they dwelt together two years, and great numbers were converted. 3 They left Antioch A. D. 45, to convey alms from this church to that at Jerusalem, and soon returned, bringing with them John Mark, (Acts 11:28-30) 12:25). While they were at Antioch, the holy Ghost directed that they should be set apart for those labours to which he had appointed them, the planting of new churches among the Gentiles. They visited Cyprus and some cities of Asia Minor, (Acts 13:2-14), and after three years returned to Antioch. In A. D. 50, he and Paul were appointed delegates from the Syrian churches to consult the apostles and elders at Jerusalem respecting certain questions raised by Jewish zealots; and having obtained the judgment of the brethren at Jerusalem, they returned with it, accompanied by Silas and *Barnabas*. At Antioch he was led into dissimulation by Peter, and was, in consequence, reproved by Paul.

Barreness

While preparing for a second missionary tour, Paul and *Barnabas* having a dispute relative to Mark, *Barnabas'* nephew, they separated, Paul going to Asia, and *Barnabas* with Mark to Cyprus, (Acts 13:1-15) (Galatians 2:13). Nothing is known of his subsequent history. There is a spurious gospel, but evidently written by some other hand. The name of Barnabas stands high in the annals of the early church. When he gave all his estates to Christ, he gave himself also, as his life of generous self-devotion and missionary toil clearly shows. He was a beloved fellow-labourer with Paul, somewhat as Melancthon was with Luther, and a true "son of consolation" to the church.

Barreness: Noun, Greek: steira [sti'-ros], (Adjective), Hebrew: aqar - [aw-kawr'], barren.

"uprooted," in the sense of being torn away from the family stock, and left to wither without progeny or successors. A similar import attaches to the word "'ariri" (from), "bared," "stripped," translated "childless"

References: (Psalm 113:9) He gives the barren woman a home, making her the joyous mother of children. Praise the Lord! (Isaiah 54:1-17) "Sing, O barren one, who did not bear; break forth into singing and cry aloud, you who have not been in labor! For the children of the desolate one will be more than the children of her who is married," says the Lord. "Enlarge the place of your tent, and let the curtains of your habitations be stretched out; do not hold back; lengthen your cords and strengthen your stakes. For you will spread abroad to the right and to the left, and your offspring will possess the nations and will people the desolate cities. "Fear not, for you will not be ashamed; be not confounded, for you will not be disgraced; for you will forget the shame of your youth, and the reproach of your widowhood you will remember no more. For your Maker is your husband, the Lord of hosts is his name; and the Holy One of Israel is your Redeemer, the God of the whole earth he is called. ... (Psalm 127:3-5) Behold, children are a heritage from the Lord, the fruit of the womb a reward. Like arrows in the hand of a warrior are the children of one's youth. Blessed is the man who fills his quiver with them! He shall not be put to shame when he speaks with his enemies in the gate. (Genesis 18:14) Is anything too hard for the Lord? At the appointed time I will return to you, about this time next year, and Sarah shall have a son." (Psalm 128:3-6) Your wife will be like a fruitful vine within your house; your children will be like olive shoots around your table. Behold, thus shall the man be blessed who fears the Lord. The Lord bless you from Zion! May you see the prosperity of Jerusalem all the days of your life! May you see your children's children! Peace be upon Israel! (Genesis 30:22) Then God remembered Rachel, and God listened to her and opened her womb.

Bartholomew: (Aramic-bat-talmay, 'son of Talmay) One of the saint. The symbol of this saint is a knife, in allusion to the one with which he was flayed alive reputedly in AD 44. His feast day is 24 August.

Baruch: According to the Old Testament, Baruch is the faithful secretary of Jeremiah who wrote his masters prophesies on a scroll and took it to the temple, where it was confiscated and taken to King Jehoiakim, who destroyed it as it was read out to him. 2 Baruch name has been attached to a number of works, one which is included in the Apocrypha. His book is a hotchpotch of a letter supposedly written by Prophet Jeremiah himself, a prophecy of a return to Jerusalem from the captivity in Babylon and an assortment of prophecies and pearls of wisdom. 3 Baruch as a name represent the Hebrew word for 'blessed', and it is the Hebrew phrase *barruk habba* (blessed be he that 'commeth' (in the name of the Lord) - (Psalm 18:26), occurring frequently in the Jewish liturgy, that gave modern French and 'brouhaha'. 4 Baruch is also the name of an angel who helps the boy – 'Will' in Pullman's trilogy 'His Dark Materials'.

Bath: (noun) Literally, a bath is a large tube that is filled with water for washing one's body 2 The act of exposing the body, or part of the body, for purposes of cleanliness, comfort, health, 3 To water, vapour, hot air, or the like; as, a cold or a hot bath; a medicated bath; a steam bath; a hip bath. While the above definitions depict the physical or bodily bath, Christians should concern with the bath by the power of Holy Ghost. As in (Psalm 51:10) "And renew a right spirit within me". (KJV). Also the gospel declare in (Hebrew 10:22) "Let us draw near to God with a sincere heart in full assurance of faith, having our hearts sprinkled to cleanse us from a guilty conscience and having our bodies washed with pure water". (NIV) While, (Luke 6:45) "The good man brings good things out of the good stored up in his heart, and the evil man brings evil things out of the evil stored up in his heart. For out of the overflow of his heart his mouth speaks. (NIV) (Psalm 51:7) We must not forget (Romans 12:2) that states: "Purify me with hyssop, and I shall be clean; Wash me, and I shall be whiter than snow". (NIV) and (Hebrews 12:1) warned "Do not conform any longer to the pattern of this world, but be transformed by the renewing of your mind. Then you will be able to test and

Bathe

approve what God's will is—his good, pleasing and perfect will. (NIV) Therefore ... let us strip off every weight that slows us down, especially the sin that so easily hinders our progress... (NLT).

Bathe: Wash by immersing one's body in water 2 To take a swim. Chiefly brit. 3 To soak or wipe something To wash by immersion, as in a bath; to subject to a bath. 4 To lave; to wet. 5 To moisten or suffuse with a liquid. 6 To apply water or some liquid medicament to; as, to bathe the eye with warm water or with sea water; to bathe one's forehead with camphor. 7 To surround, or envelop, as water surrounds a person immersed. 8 To bathe one's self; to take a bath or baths. 9 To immerse or cover one's self, as in a bath. 10 To bask in the sun. 11 The immersion of the body in water; as to take one's usual bathe gently with liquid to clean or soothe it as in (Leviticus 15:7) "And he that toucheth the flesh of him that hath the flux shall wash his garments, and *bathe* in water, and be unclean until the even".

Bear: (verb, bore – past, borne – past participle): To carry someone or something. 2 Have something as a quality or a visible mark. 3 Manage to tolerate – the grieve was more than He could bear. Referred to Christ suffering for our sake. So Christ bear guilt in grief. When He was facing His own death, it was a difficult time for all. The tensions were high and the prospects were low. All the disciples were jockeying for position of power and there was a lot to be guilty about concerning their behaviour. There were two disciples in particular that stood in contrast to each other concerning guilt in grieving circumstances, Judas and Peter. Both had much reason to carry guilt in their hearts concerning the death of Jesus, but the end results could not have been more opposite.

4 Bear could be used when guilt gone wrong as in the case of Judas and the Guilt of Betrayal (Matthew 27:3-5) Then when Judas, who had betrayed Him, saw that He had been condemned, he felt remorse and returned the thirty pieces of silver to the chief priests and elders, saying, "I have sinned by betraying innocent blood." But they said, "What is that to us? See to that yourself!" And he threw the pieces of silver into the temple sanctuary and departed; and he went away and hanged himself. (Acts 1:17-18) "For he was counted among us and received his share in this ministry." NOTE: (Now this man acquired a field with the price of his wickedness, and falling headlong, he burst open in the middle and all his intestines gushed out.

Bear, "God will never give you more than you can... Partially unscriptural. This is a common phrase that people tell one another in the name of Jesus (or maybe just in the name of any god).

> There have been many who have received comfort with this thought... and others who have experienced guilt from thinking that if this is true, then they should be handling their situation better than they are. Sadly, though, one might think, there is some serious error in the sentiment. First, it is not scriptural.

"God will never give you more than you can bear" does not appear in the Christian or Hebrew Holy books. (in truth, there are many things people think are there but aren't. Check it out. The closest passage, and the one that most people go to in defence of this statement is (1 Corinthians 10:13). Thus: "No temptation has overtaken you that is not common to man. God is faithful, and he will not let you be tempted beyond your ability, but with the temptation he will also provide the way of escape, that you may be able to endure it." (ESV)

Here we have a passage that is about idolatry, and in particular, temptation. What God promises is to never allow anyone to be tempted beyond their ability to resist the temptation. It does *not* say that God will never allow us to face more than we can bear in regards to grief, pain, abuse, debt, hurt etc... (for a much deeper look into the grief side of things, check out this series on grief)...

Further, check out Jesus' words about the early Christian life in (Matthew 24:9-10): "Then they will deliver you up to tribulation and put you to death, and you will be hated by all nations for my name's sake. And then many will fall away and betray one another and hate one another." (ESV)Or even better... "They will put you out of the synagogues. Indeed, the hour is coming when whoever kills you will think he is offering service to God." (John 16:2) Apparently, God never given us more than we can bear would not include being hated, betrayed, persecuted, and killed... sometimes in God's own name! Suffering to the point of death must not be considered "more than we can bear" since God allows and even sometimes brings all kinds of suffering into His people's lives. So, as another example of God giving someone more than they can at least *survive*...

John the Baptist suffers in prison until he is beheaded. (Mathew 14: 25-27) Jesus was beaten and crucified. Job was crushed in every way but physical, and always though his survival might have been the worst of all the pain he was given to face. I think my favourite person to ask this question would be Paul... listen to this that God allowed in His life! "...

Beard

Five times I received at the hands of the Jews the forty lashes less one. Three times I was beaten with rods. Once I was stoned. Three times I was shipwrecked; a night and a day I was adrift at sea; on frequent journeys, in danger from rivers, danger from robbers, danger from my own people, danger from Gentiles, danger in the city, danger in the wilderness, danger at sea, danger from false brothers; in toil and hardship, through many a sleepless night, in hunger and thirst, often without food, in cold and exposure. (2 C6 11:24-27) Eventually, church history says that Paul was also beheaded. So, not "more than we can *bear*" must not include things that actually kill us.

Apparently, life is more than we can *bear*, since we all leave it someday. But would God bring us to suffer – to give us so much that we bleed? The writer of Hebrews chastises his or her audience because they "have not yet resisted to the point of shedding blood!" (Romans 8:17) tells us that we suffer with Him so we can be glorified with Him!

Also Paul makes clear in (Philippians 3:10-11) that he rejoices in sharing in the sufferings of Christ to the point of death so that he can share in the resurrection with Him too! Maybe, then, the phrase would be meant to make us feel guilty for seeking help from others? After all, if God doesn't give us more than we can bear, then we should be able to bear, alone, whatever He sends our way… right? I think we will start not the above as important.

Beard: (noun) Growth of hair on the chin and lower cheeks of a man's face. 2 Boldly confront or challenge someone in form of daunting – Like when God issued decrees to the Israelites in (Leviticus 19:27-28) –Thus' "You shall not round off the side-growth of your heads nor harm the edges of your *beard*. 'You shall not make any cuts in your body for the dead nor make any tattoo marks on yourselves: I am the LORD". 3 *Beards* appear almost 26 times in the in the gospel opposing certain indoctrination in other gospels which are not Christianity. In (Deuteronomy-ESV) the bible warns: "You are the sons of the Lord your God. You shall not cut yourselves or make any baldness on your foreheads for the dead. For you are a people holy to the Lord your God, and the Lord has chosen you to be a people for his treasured possession, out of all the peoples who are on the face of the earth. "You shall not eat any abomination. These are the animals you may eat: the ox, the sheep, the goat, the deer, the gazelle, the roebuck, the wild goat, the ibex, the antelope, and the mountain sheep". More so, in (Leviticus 14:9) And on the seventh day he shall shave off all hair from his head, his *beard,* and his eyebrows. He shall shave off all his hair, and then he shall wash his clothes and bathe his body in water, and he shall be clean'. Note:

This is ceremonial law similar to the laws about circumcision, clothing fabric and animal sacrifices it was done away with when Christ died on the cross. Again, you are not saved by how well you keep the law but, by your faith in that Jesus) took your sins upon himself that you could stand blameless on the day of judgement.

(Romans 11). If you were not born Hebrew and you come to Jesus you are grafted into the olive tree (Israel) because you were formerly a wild branch. In (Acts 15), you can see where the apostles discussed what to do with the gentiles who were coming to the faith. To be a child of Israel one had to be circumcised according to the law so this is undoubtedly what Pauls opposition brought up. Apparently they missed this as Paul used in his debates (Numbers 15:16)" One law and one manner shall be for you, and for the stranger that sojourns with you." as far as *beards* are concerned they are a clear sign between the sexes as Paul also addresses the Corinthians men no having long hair which is feminine. God gave men *beards* and no matter how many times you cut it off it will keep coming back. As for the common separation of the laws there is no such thing in the gospel nor is following the law the hypocritical refrence that Jesus is asking again and again. (1 John 5:3)" "For this is the love of God, that we keep His commandments. And His commandments are not burdensome." Praise God!

Beards, Aaron (See Aaron)

Bear one's cross, To: To carry one's own burden or troubles. The allusion is to the practice of the person condemned to crucifixion being made to carry his cross to the place of execution. This was what our dear Lord Jesus Christ did for our sake. Then Jesus said to His disciples, "If anyone wishes to come after Me, he must deny himself, and take up his cross and follow Me. Jesus in the Gospel of (Matthew 16:24) **Beast:** (noun) an animal – large or dangerous mammal or bird. 2 A very cruel or wicked person. A merciless individual who discards righteousness and make others to sin in their ordinary ways of life. Agent of antichrist.

Beast, the: (Greek: - *Therion*) refers to two beasts described in the Book of Revelation. The first beast comes from "out of the sea" and is given authority and power by the dragon. This first beast is initially mentioned in (Revelation 11:7 -8) Thus: "When they have finished their testimony, the beast that comes up out of the abyss will make war with them, and overcome them and kill them. And their dead bodies will lie in the street of the great city which mystically is called Sodom and Egypt, where also their Lord was crucified...." This is described in detail in (Revelation 13:1-10), Thus:"**The dragon** stood on the shore of the sea. And I saw a ***beast*** coming out of the sea. It had ten horns and seven heads,

Beast, the

with ten crowns on its horns, and on each head a blasphemous name. The beast I saw resembled a leopard, but had feet like those of a bear and a mouth like that of a lion. **The dragon** gave **the beast** his power and his throne and great authority. One of the heads of **the beast** seemed to have had a fatal wound, but the fatal wound had been healed. The whole world was filled with wonder and followed **the beast**. ⁴ People worshiped **the dragon** because he had given authority to **the beast**, and they also worshiped **the beast** and asked, "Who is like **the beast?** Who can wage war against it?" **The beast** was given a mouth to utter proud words and blasphemies and to exercise its authority for forty-two months. ⁶ It opened its mouth to blaspheme God, and to slander his name and his dwelling place and those who live in heaven. It was given power to wage war against God's holy people and to conquer them. And it was given authority over every tribe, people, language and nation. All inhabitants of the earth will worship **the beast**—all whose names have not been written in the Lamb's book of life, the Lamb who was slain from the creation of the world Whoever has ears, let them hear. "If anyone is to go into captivity, they will go. If anyone is to be killed with the sword, with the sword they will be killed". ("This calls for patient endurance and faithfulness on the part of God's people).

2 And some of the mystery behind his appearance is revealed in (Revelation 17:7-18) which says: "One of the seven angels who had the seven bowls came and said to me, "Come, I will show you the punishment of the great prostitute, who sits by many waters. With her the kings of the earth committed adultery, and the inhabitants of the earth were intoxicated with the wine of her adulteries."

Then the angel carried me away in the Spirit into a wilderness. There I saw a woman sitting on a scarlet beast that was covered with blasphemous names and had seven heads and ten horns. The woman was dressed in purple and scarlet, and was glittering with gold, precious stones and pearls. She held a golden cup in her hand, filled with abominable things and the filth of her adulteries. ⁵ The name written on her forehead was a mystery: BABYLON THE GREAT! THE MOTHER OF PROSTITUTES!! AND OF THE ABOMINATIONS OF THE EARTH!!!

I saw that the woman was drunk with the blood of God's holy people, the blood of those who bore testimony to Jesus. When I saw her, I was greatly astonished. Then the angel said to me: "Why are you astonished? I will explain to you the mystery of the woman and of the beast she rides, which has the seven heads and ten horns. The beast, which you saw, once was, now is not, and yet will come up out of the Abyss and go to its destruction. The inhabitants of the earth whose names have not been written in the book of life from the creation of the world will be astonished when they see the beast, because it once was, now is not, and yet will come.

"This calls for a mind with wisdom. The seven heads are seven hills on which the woman sits. They are also seven kings. Five have fallen, one is, the other has not yet come; but when he does come, he must remain for only a little while. The beast who once was, and now is not, is an eighth king. He belongs to the seven and is going to his destruction.

"The ten horns you saw are ten kings who have not yet received a kingdom, but who for one hour will receive authority as kings along with the beast. They have one purpose and will give their power and authority to the beast. They will wage war against the Lamb, but the Lamb will triumph over them because he is Lord of lords and King of kings—and with him will be his called, chosen and faithful followers."

Then the angel said to me, "The waters you saw, where the prostitute sits, are peoples, multitudes, nations and languages. The beast and the ten horns you saw will hate the prostitute. They will bring her to ruin and leave her naked; they will eat her flesh and burn her with fire. For God has put it into their hearts to accomplish his purpose by agreeing to hand over to the beast their royal authority, until God's words are fulfilled. The woman you saw is the great city that rules over the kings of the earth."(NIV). **Cross References:** (Revelation 16:6; 17:7-20, Mathew 22:14, Jeremiah 47:2, Isaiah 8:7, Ezekiel 16:37-39, 2 Corinthians 8:16)

The second beast comes from "out of the earth" and directs all peoples of the earth to worship the first beast. The second beast is described in Revelation 13:11-18 – "Then I saw a second beast, coming out of the earth. It had two horns like a lamb, but it spoke like a dragon. [12] It exercised all the authority of the first beast on its behalf, and made the earth and its inhabitants worship the first beast, whose fatal wound had been healed. [13] And it performed great signs, even causing fire to come down from heaven to the earth in full view of the people. [14] Because of the signs it was given power to perform on behalf of the first beast, it deceived the inhabitants of the earth. It ordered them to set up an image in honor of the beast who was wounded by the sword and yet lived. The second beast was given power to give breath to the image of the first beast, so that the image could speak and cause all who refused to worship the image to be killed. [16] It also forced all people, great and small, rich and poor, free and slave, to receive a mark on their right hands or on their foreheads, so that they could not buy or sell unless they had the mark, which is the name of the beast or the number of its name.

Beatification

This calls for wisdom. Let the person who has insight calculate the number of the beast, for it is the number of a man That number is 666. (NIV) and is also referred to as the false prophet. The two *beasts* are aligned with the dragon in opposition to God. They persecute the "saints" and those who do "not worship the image of the beast [of the sea]" and influence the kings of the earth to gather for the battle of Armageddon The two beasts are defeated by Christ and are thrown into the lake of fire mentioned in Revelation 19:18-20 thus : "so that you may eat the flesh of kings, generals, and the mighty, of horses and their riders, and the flesh of all people, free and slave, great and small." Then I saw *the beast* and the kings of the earth and their armies gathered together to wage war against the rider on the horse and his army. But *the beast* was captured, and with it the false prophet who had performed the signs on its behalf. With these signs he had deluded those who had received the mark of the beast and worshiped its image. The two of them were thrown alive into the fiery lake of burning sulphur"(NIV).

Beatification: Commonly in the Roman Catholic Church, a solemn act by which a deceased person is formerly declared by the Pope to be one of the blessed departed and therefore a proper subject for a Mass and office in honour to the deceased, often times with some local restrictions. 2 Beatification is usually, though not necessarily a step forward to Canonization.

Beatific vision: The sight of God or of the blessed in the realms of Heaven, especially, that granted to the Soul at the instant of death as in (Isaiah 6: 1-3) Thus' "In the year that King Uzziah died, I saw the Lord, high and exalted, seated on a throne; and the train of his robe filled the temple. Above him were seraphim, each with six wings: With two wings they covered their faces, with two they covered their feet, and with two they were flying. And they were calling to one another: "Holy, holy, holy is the LORD ALMIGHTY; the whole earth is full of his glory (NIV) also in: (Acts 7:55-56) "But he, being full of the Holy Spirit, gazed into heaven and saw the glory of God, and Jesus standing at the right hand of God, and said, "Look! I see the heavens opened and the Son of Man standing at the right hand of God!" (NKJV)

Beatitude: (Greek: *makarios*; Blessedness. Perfect felicity. (blessed are the meek , for they shall inherit the earth; blessed are the merciful , for they shall be shown mercy et cetera), spoken by (or at least credited to) Jesus the Galilean.

2 The beatitudes have a similar rhetorical style to ancient songs of praise & ancient wisdom literature. in their hortatory aspect &

Beatitude

their two-part parallelism but (for their era) these beatitudes have a very strange twist to them - (like setting up a question, pausing & reversing the answer offering a biting little surprise, unsupported by commonsense)

supposedly arising from the (speculated) "Q-source" (a source alongside the Book of Mark) for gospel writers Matthew & Luke - the beatitudes would have been spoken in Aramaic; (the language Jesus the Galilean preached in, to his rural audiences) but (in these two gospels) the beatitudes have (of course) been recorded in Greek "makarios" is the Greek word which anchors the beatitudes. It means "blessed", but (a rich word), it also is a congratulatory word, a word which means happy or fortunate, (happy are the poor in spirit, ...fortunate are you who weep, ...) which makes the first half of these passages even stranger (people must have gasped & said "how can this be?" during the brief rhetorical pause, before the "answering" second half to each beatitude then becomes canted), but makarios is the Greek transcription of what Aramaic word? (& what are the nuances of this Aramaic word ?what links to rural Levantine cultural life are inferred from this word ?)

3 in the ancient (polytheistic) Temple religions the typical (perhaps sole) form of prayer is very public & very noisy remonstrations & incantations in praise of the local deity.The deepest form of life's meaning to polytheistic peoples (testimony of prayer being answered), is prosperity (being "blessed" by their favorite deity, and becoming rich ostentatiously well-off, nice clothes & nice home & exotic foods and all the cosmopolitan comforts which donkey-caravans can bring) but (2500 years ago) during the Axial Age, (across the globe), this common sense "meaning of life" begins to be questioned (considered pretty shallow, not nearly deep enough) "the rich", who can offer the biggest "sacrifices" at the Temple get the most attention of the Temple priests, where "the poor" are shrugged off, are sent to minor temples of less-powerful gods and this is true in Judea, as well and is (at core) what got the "prophets" so fired up (shaming Judaism for becoming just another Temple religion) and Jesus the Galilean (centuries later) walks in this same prophetic line.

4 To him, genuine "prosperity" is not the "blessing" of economic prosperity but something more abstract, a "prosperity" at the core of your being proclaiming that prayer is not a noisy & public remonstration but a quiet & private thing, an inner thing and that the life-rewards are inner rewards, an inner prosperity (prosperous are you who are hungry, for you shall be satisfied)

5 The Aramaic word which is translated in Greek as "makarios"

Beatitudes, The

(blessed or happy or fortunate) is, in its Aramaic original a word which means "prosperity" a word which has rich connotations in the ancient world regarding what is meaningful in life, a word which Jesus the Galilean so effectively undermines & reverses in the thought-processes of those to whom he is speaking saying (like the prophets) that the mark of being blessed comes, not from ostentatious wealth (not from a concrete "earthly" reward, but rather) the meaning of life comes from somewhere else entirely – Heaven – the kingdom of God! Praise the Lord!

Beatitudes, The: The eight blessings pronounced by Christ at the opening of the SERMON ON THE MOUNT. Cited by (Mathew 5:3-10) Thus: 1 Blessed are the poor in spirit, for theirs is the kingdom of heaven. 2 Blessed are those who mourn, for they will be comforted. 3 Blessed are the meek, for they will inherit the earth. 4 Blessed are those who hunger and thirst for righteousness, for they will be filled. 5 Blessed are the merciful, for they will be shown mercy. 6 Blessed are the pure in heart, for they will see God. 7 Blessed are the peacemakers, for they will be called children of God. 8 Blessed are those who are persecuted because of righteousness, for theirs is the kingdom of heaven"

Beginning: (noun) An act or circumstance of entering upon an action or state: the beginning of hostilities.2.the point of time or space at which anything begins: the beginning of the Christian era; the beginning of the route. You can match this with faith – The beginning of Heavenly journey – Early time when one decides to follow Jesus or be born –again.3.the first part: the beginning of the book; the beginning of the month.4.Often, beginnings. the initial stage or part of anything: the beginnings of science 5 The beginning of the World. (Genesis 1:1 - 2) In the beginning God created the heavens and the earth. The earth was formless and void, and darkness was over the surface of the deep, and the Spirit of God was moving over the surface of the waters....

Begotten: (Adjective, Greek: monogenés [mon-og-en-ace'] Hebrew: monogené [mon-og-en-ace'] only, only-begotten; unique. (begot, begotten begot, begetting) (esp. of a male parent) to generate (offspring).2 to produce as an effect: a belief that power begets power.3 of offspring) generated by procreation; "naturally begotten child" Jesus Christ – related by unseen condition but by Holy Ghost biologically – Having the same makes, As God is Spirit, so, Jesus is Spirit though He was born by a woman, Virgin MARY, was under the commandment from the father –God as no sexual intercourse took place before He was conceived. Similarly, if God was a biological father, He should have been of parents and children; related by blood; "biological child" But in this case He was conceived by the Holy Ghost to take the likeness of the father – Spirit who was not conceived at all. The phrase "only begotten Son" occurs in (John 3:16), which reads in the King James Version as, "For God so loved the world, that He gave His only begotten Son, that whosoever believeth in Him should not perish, but have everlasting life." The phrase "only begotten" translates the Greek word monogenes. This word is variously translated into English as "only," "one and only," and "only begotten."

It's this last phrase ("only begotten" used in the KJV, NASB and the NKJV) that causes problems.

False teachers have latched onto this phrase to try to prove their false teaching that Jesus Christ isn't God; i.e., that Jesus isn't equal in essence to God as the Second Person of the Trinity. They see the word "begotten" and say that Jesus is a created being because only someone who had a beginning in time can be "begotten." What this fails to note is that "begotten" is an English translation of a Greek word. As such, we have to look at the original meaning of the Greek word, not transfer English meanings into the text. So what does *monogenes* mean? According to the *Greek-English Lexicon of the New Testament and Other Early Christian Literature* ,*monogenes* has two primary definitions. The first definition is "pertaining to being the only one of its kind within a specific relationship." This is its meaning in (Hebrews 11:17) when the writer refers to Isaac as Abraham's "only begotten son" (KJV). Abraham had more than one son, but Isaac was the only son he had by Sarah and the only son of the covenant. Therefore, it is the uniqueness of Isaac among the other sons that allows for the use of monogenes in that context.

The second definition is "pertaining to being the only one of its kind or class, unique in kind." This is the meaning that is implied in (John 3:16) (see also (John 1:14) thus' "The Word became flesh and made his dwelling among us. We have seen his glory, the glory of the one and only Son, who came from the Father, full of grace and truth". Again in (John 18:3) "Whoever believes in him is not condemned, but whoever does not believe stands condemned already because they have not believed in the name of God's one and only Son".(1 John 4:9). "This is how God showed his love among us: He sent his one and only Son into the world that we might live through him". John was primarily concerned with demonstrating that Jesus is the Son of God (John 20:31), and he uses *monogenes* to

Believe

highlight Jesus as uniquely God's Son—sharing the same divine nature as God—as opposed to believers who are God's sons and daughters by adoption (Ephesians 1:5). Jesus is God's "one and only" Son.

The bottom line is that terms such as "Father" and "Son," descriptive of God and Jesus, are human terms that help us understand the relationship between the different Persons of the Trinity. If you can understand the relationship between a human father and a human son, then you can understand, in part, the relationship between the First and Second Persons of the Trinity. The analogy breaks down if you try to take it too far and teach, as some Christian cults (such as the Jehovah's Witnesses), that Jesus was literally "begotten" as in "produced" or "created" by God the Father.

Believe, Believed, Believeth, Believing: (verb used without object believing) -To have confidence in the truth, the existence, or The reliability of something, although without absolute proof that one is right in doing so: Only if one believes in something can one act purposefully. verb (used with object), be·lieved, be·liev·ing.

2.to have confidence or faith in the truth of (a positive assertion, story, etc.); give credence to. 3To have confidence in the assertions of (a person)4To have a conviction that (a person or thing) is, has been, or will be engaged in a given action or involved in a given situation: 5to suppose or assume; understand (usually followed by a noun clause): I believe that he has given his life to Christ (Mathew21:21-22) ...And Jesus answered and said to them, "Truly I say to you, if you have faith and do not doubt, you will not only do what was done to the fig tree, but even if you say to this mountain, 'Be taken up and cast into the sea,' it will happen. "And all things you ask in prayer, believing, you will receive.

Bell, book and candle: The popular phrase for ceremonial Excommunication in the Roman Catholic Church. The ceremony traditionally concluded with the words 'Doe to the book, quench the candle and ring the bell'. Whereupon the officiating cleric closed his book, quench the candle by throwing it to the ground and tolled the bell as for one who has died. The book symbolizes the 'Book of Life' and the candle that the soul is removed from the sight of God as the candle is from the sight of man.

Bells and Smells: Used in the Anglo-Catholic or High Church. The allusion is to the use of alter bells and incense in the service of the Eucharist, in the Roman Catholic Church.

Bells and Smells

Benediction: Literally, this is the speaking of a blessing or the state of being blessed. From the earliest church, Christians adopted ceremonial *benedictions* into their liturgical worship, particularly at the end of a service. Such benedictions have been regularly practiced both in the Christian East and West. At the time of the Reformation, Protestants abandoned many of the *benedictions* of the Roman Catholic Church, including the Apostolic Benediction made by the Pope and his delegates, the "last blessing" of the dying, and virtually all benedictions of inanimate objects. However, the Anglican church retained the principle of benediction, and a benediction or blessing ends most Anglican services. 2 A common form of *benediction* in Baptist and liturgical Protestant churches is for the worship leader to raise his hands and recite the words of the biblical Priestly Blessing (Numbers 6:23-27). Thus' "Speak to Aaron and his sons, saying, Thus you shall bless the people of Israel: you shall say to them; The LORD BLESS YOU AND KEEP YOU; the LORD MAKE HIS FACE TO SHINE UPON YOU AND BE GRACIOUS TO YOU; the LORD LIFT UP HIS COUNTENANCE upon you and give you peace. So shall they put my name upon the people of Israel, and I will bless them."

This addition to the mass was made by Martin Luther in his 'Deutsche Messe' and remains traditional in Lutheran Churches Some Protestant churches have recently started to reincorporate the use of benedictions in the closing of their church services. Such benedictions may be taken from Scripture, written by a church member, or a combination of the two. An often complex and lengthy blessing before communion took place in the mass of the 'Gallican' Rite and in some French sees survived until the 'Gallican' rites controversy when they were suppressed. Pope John Paul II, however, gave permission for these sees to restore this traditional element of their local rite. 3 In the Orthodox Church, benedictions will occur at both the beginning and the end of each service, and there may be other benedictions during the course of the service. The final benediction (the dismissal) is the most important, and will often entail mention of the feast or saint being commemorated that day. The priest will bless with his right hand, and the bishop will bless with both hands. In both cases, the hand is held so that the fingers form the initials IC XC (the abbreviation for "Jesus Christ" in Greek), and he traces the Sign of the Cross in the air with his hand. If a bishop or abbot is holding his crozier while making the benediction, he will raise his right hand and trace the Sign of the Cross with both his crozier and right hand, crossing the one in front of the other.

Benediction of the Blessed Sacrament

More solemn benedictions, such as that which comes at the end of the Divine Liturgy, will be made with a blessing cross rather than the hand.

Benediction of the Blessed Sacrament: One of the most generally popular services in the Roman Catholic Church is Benediction of the Blessed Sacrament, commonly referred to as Benediction and known in France as 'Salut' and in Germany as 'Segen' It is also the custom of some high-church Anglican churches to hold this service. It is ordinarily an afternoon or evening devotion and consists in the singing of certain hymns, or litanies, or canticles, before the Blessed Sacrament, which is exposed upon the altar in a monstrance and is surrounded with candles. At the end, the priest or deacon, his shoulders enveloped in a humeral veil, takes the monstrance into his hands and with it makes the sign of the cross in silence over the kneeling congregation. Benediction is often employed as a conclusion to other services, e.g. Vespers, Compline, the Stations of the Cross, etc., but it is also still more generally treated as a rite complete in itself. There is a good deal of diversity of usage in different countries with regard to details, but some of the elements are constant. The use of incense and wax candles, the singing of the "Tantum ergo" with its versicle and prayer, and the blessing given with the Blessed Sacrament are obligatory everywhere. In Rome the principle obtains that the only portion of the service which is to be regarded as strictly liturgical is the singing of the "Tantum ergo" and the giving of the Benediction which immediately follows. This idea is emphasized by the fact that in many Roman churches the celebrant, vested in cope and preceded by thurfier, acolytes, etc., only makes his entry into the sanctuary just before the "Tantum ergo" is begun. Previously to this the Blessed Sacrament is exposed, informally, by a priest in cotta and stole; and then choir and congregation are left to sing litanies and canticles, or to say prayers and devotions as the occasion may demand. 2 In English-speaking countries the service generally begins with the entry of the priest and his assistants in procession and with the singing of the "O Salutaris Hostia" as soon as the Blessed Sacrament is taken out of the tabernacle. Indeed in England the singing of the "O Salutaris" is enjoined in the "Ritus servandus", the code of procedure approved by a former synod of the Province of Westminster. On the other hand, the Litany of Our Lady, though usually printed after the "O Salutaris" and very generally sung at Benediction, is nowhere of obligation. It may be added that further solemnity is often given to the service by the presence of deacon and sub deacon in dalmatics. When the bishop of the diocese officiates he uses 'mitre' and crosier in the procession to the altar, and makes the sign of the cross over the people three times in giving the benediction. On the other hand, a very informal sort of service is permitted, where the means for carrying out a more elaborate rite are not available. The priest, wearing cotta and stole, simply opens the tabernacle door. Prayers and devotions are said or sung, and then the priest blesses those present with the veiled ciborium before the tabernacle door is again closed. The permission, general or special, of the bishop of the diocese is necessary for services where Benediction is given with the monstrance

'Benedicite' or 'Benedictus': (Latin, - 'bless ye' A grace or a blessing many of which began with this word. In the 'Book of the Common Prayer' it is the name of the canticle beginning 'O all ye works of the Lord, bless the Lord' (ERV) or 'Bless the Lord, all you works of the Lord; sing praise to him and highly exalt him for ever'. (Daniel 3:57)

Benjamin: The last-born of Jacob's twelve sons, and the second and last son of Rachel in Jewish, Christian and Islamic tradition. He was the progenitor of the Israelite Tribe of Benjamin. In the Biblical account, unlike Rachel's first son, Joseph, Benjamin was born in Canaan. In the Samaritan Pentateuch, Benjamin's name appears as "Binyaamem" (Hebrew: ***"Son of my days"***). In the Qur'an, Benjamin is referred to as righteous young child, who remained with Jacob when the older brothers plotted against Joseph. 2 According to the Torah, Benjamin's name arose when Jacob deliberately corrupted the name *Benoni*, the original name of *Benjamin*, since *Benoni* was an allusion to Rachel's dying just after she had given birth, as it means *son of my pain*. (Genesis 35: 18 – 19) "When she was in severe labour the midwife said to her, "Do not fear, for now you have another son." It came about as her soul was departing (for she died), that she named him Benoni; but his father called him Benjamin. So Rachel died and was buried on the way to Ephrath (that is, Bethlehem)....!

Bethany: This, in the gospel, was the name of a village near Jerusalem—see Bethany (Biblical village)—mentioned in the New Testament as the home of the siblings Mary, Martha, and Lazarus, and, according to the Gospel of John, the site of a miracle in which Jesus raises Lazarus from the dead. This village is commonly identified with the present-day West Bank city of **al-Eizariya** ("place of Lazarus"), located

Bethany, Jesus is anointed at

about 1.5 miles (2.4 km) east of Jerusalem on the south-eastern slope of the Mount of Olives. During the Crusades, al-Eizariya was still referred to as Bethany by Christians. The Raising of Lazarus episode, shortly before Jesus enters Jerusalem for the last time, takes place in Bethany. Bethany near the River Jordan (John 1:28) "It is He who comes after me, the thong of whose sandal I am not worthy to untie." These things took place in Bethany beyond the Jordan, where John was baptizing. It might refer to a town further north in Perea, i.e. Bethabara; or it might refer to the more northerly territory of Batanaea

Bethany, Jesus is anointed at: It was almost time for Passover, and people were going to Jerusalem to prepare for the feast by undergoing ritual purification. They were standing in the temple, speculating whether or not Jesus will come to the feast, aware that the chief priests and Pharisees are seeking his arrest. Again we see the interested crowd and the antagonistic authorities. But Jesus has already departed from the temple and will not be standing where they are standing as they ask such questions. He will come up to this feast, but he will not be coming to the temple. Rather, the one true sacrifice is about to take place in the temple of his body. This description of Jesus' danger adds a dramatic touch to the fact that he returns to Bethany again (John 12:1- 8). "Six days before the Passover, Jesus came to Bethany, where Lazarus lived, whom Jesus had raised from the dead. Here a dinner was given in Jesus' honour. Martha served, while Lazarus was among those reclining at the table with him. Then Mary took about a pint of pure nard, an expensive perfume; she poured it on Jesus' feet and wiped his feet with her hair. And the house was filled with the fragrance of the perfume. But one of his disciples, Judas Iscariot, who was later to betray him, objected "Why wasn't this perfume sold and the money given to the poor? It was worth a year's wages!" He did not say this because he cared about the poor but because he was a thief; as keeper of the money bag, he used to help himself to what was put into it. "Leave her alone," Jesus replied. "It was intended that she should save this perfume for the day of my burial. You will always have the poor among you but you will not always have me." Christians note; As we can see ... He was back with Lazarus and his sisters in a relatively private setting. There was a party in his honour *six days before the Passover* probably on Saturday night after the conclusion of Sabbath. It is not said where the party takes place, but from the account in Matthew and Mark it would be at the house of Simon the leper (Mathew 26:6 and Mark 14:3). Lazarus is also an honoured guest, while Martha helps with the serving (v. 2), true to the picture of her elsewhere (Luke 10:38-42). The picture of Mary is also true to that in (Luke 10:38-42); that is, she is a devoted disciple who ignores the taboos of her society in her commitment to Jesus. Sitting at his feet as a disciple (Luke 10:39) was not the place for a woman, but she is commended by Jesus (Luke 10:42). "Now she acts in an even more scandalous manner in anointing Jesus' feet with extremely expensive perfume and then wiping them with her hair (John 12:3). "Then Mary took about a pint of pure nard, an expensive perfume; she poured it on Jesus' feet and wiped his feet with her hair. And the house was filled with the fragrance of the perfume. Both aspects of her action--the extravagance and the method--were disturbing. The *pure nard* she uses was imported from northern India (Brown 1966:448). Judas says, no doubt correctly, that it was *worth a year's wages* (v. 5). The text literally reads "three hundred denarii" Note: Since a denarius was a day's pay for a day labourer, the NIV paraphrase is accurate, taking into account feast days and Sabbaths when one would not work. A rough equivalent would be something over $10,000, the gross pay for someone working at minimum wage for a year. No wonder the disciples (Mathew 26:8-9), a woman came to Him with an alabaster vial of very costly perfume, and she poured it on His head as He reclined at the table. But the disciples were indignant when they saw this, and said, "Why this waste? "For this perfume might have been sold for a high price and the money given to the poor."... Judas in particular, respond with dismay at such a waste. In the accounts in Matthew and Mark, she anoints Jesus' head, while in John it is his feet. Obviously, it could have been both, and with twelve ounces to work with (not a full pint, as in the NIV) she could have anointed his whole body. Indeed, since he interprets this as an anointing for his burial (v. 7) it seems she did anoint more than his head and feet, as Matthew and Mark suggest (Mathew 26:12 "For you always have the poor with you; but you do not always have Me. "For when she poured this perfume on My body, she did it to prepare Me for burial. "Truly I say to you, wherever this gospel is preached in the whole world, what this woman has done will also be spoken of in memory of her." Mark 14:8; For you always have the poor with you, and whenever you wish you can do good to them; but you do not always have Me. "She has done what she could; she has anointed My body beforehand for the burial. "Truly I say to you, wherever the gospel is preached in the whole world, what this woman has done will also be spoken of in memory of her."

Betray: *(betrayed - passive)* This is synonymous to breaking one's promise, to be disloyal to, be unfaithful to, break faith with, play someone false, fail, let down, expose (one's country, a

Better

group, or a person) to danger by treacherously giving information to an enemy like Judas betrayed Jesus Christ as in (Luke 22 :1 – 6) – "Now the Festival of Unleavened Bread, called the Passover, was approaching, and the chief priests and the teachers of the law were looking for some way to get rid of Jesus, for they were afraid of the people. Then Satan entered Judas, called Iscariot,one of the Twelve. And Judas went to the chief priests and the officers of the temple guard and discussed with them how he might betray Jesus. They were delighted and agreed to give him money. He consented, and watched for an opportunity to hand Jesus over to them when no crowd was present. and finishing the act of betrayal in (Luke 22: 47 - 48) thus' "While he was still speaking a crowd came up, and the man who was called Judas, one of the Twelve, was leading them. He approached Jesus to kiss him, but Jesus asked him, "Judas, are you betraying the Son of Man with a kiss?" 2 "she drew a deep breath that betrayed the Pastor" Ensure you don't practice this i the body of Christ so as to avoid Christ being crucified a second time. Don't betray anyone.

Better: This connotes comparative of good. Greater in excellence or higher in quality. As in (Ecclesiates 7 : 1) A good name is **better** than fine perfume – meaning- Who we are is more important than what we have or do not

have!"and the day of death better than the day of birth in that there are two days in our lives when our name is prominent: the day we receive our name, at birth, and the day our name appears in the obituary column. What happens between those two days determines whether our name is a lovely ointment or a foul stench Solomon is not buying into the philosophy of despair. If that were true, he wouldn't tell us eight times in his book to enjoy life. Ecclesiastes says that we must neither be hesitant to talk about death, nor scoff at it. Rather, we should talk about it forthrightly, for it is the inevitable prospect we all face, and its effects are devastating if we are unprepared. Have you ever noticed the way we mark a person's life span? We will write a person's name, and below it will put something like this: 1920–2013. We list the year of birth and a year of death. Between the two is what? *A dash*. Solomon might agree that this life is a quick dash between birth and death—just a vapur. All we will ever do on earth, all the influence we will ever garner, all the reputation we will ever build is summarized in a simple line between one year and another. It's not much time to serve God, but plenty of time for making a huge mess of things. *Adversity is better than prosperity.*

More useful, suitable, or desirable: found a better way to go;

(Ecclesiates 7 : 2) "It is better to go to a house of mourning than to go to a house of feasting, for death is the destiny of everyone; the living should take this to heart". 3 More highly skilled or adept: I am better at my present Church 4 Greater or larger, argued for the better part of an hour. As in (Ecclesiates 7:3) 5. More advantageous or favorable; improved: a better chance of success. adv. Comparative of well.

(Ecclesiastes 7 : 4-6) The heart of the wise is in the house of mourning, but the heart of fools is in the house of pleasure. It is better to heed the rebuke of a wise person than to listen to the song offools. Like the crackling of thorns under the pot, so is the laughter of fools. This too is meaningless. Extortion turns a wise person into a fool, and a bribe corrupts the heart.

Adversity cultivates godly character (Ecclesiastes 7:5-14). a short hot burn. If you needed to heat up something quickly instead of preparing a fire for slow cooking, you would throw This second section reminds us that God loves us too much to let us remain as we are. In 7:5-6 Solomon writes, "It is better to listen to the rebuke of a wise man than for one to listen to the song of fools. For as the crackling of thorn bushes under a pot, so is the laughter of the fool; and this too is futility." Solomon likens the meaningless praise and laughter of fools to "the crackling of thorn bushes under a pot." This was a culturally relevant comparison that we don't readily understand. Branches of a thorn bush thrown on a fire will flame up with rapid intensity, providing thorn branches on the fire. Solomon uses this illustration to say that the praise of fools is quick, hot, showy—but gone quickly. It flames up, dies out, and you need something else to stoke the fire. The rebuke of a wise man, however, can change your life forever.

Between: (*bihtween*) Preposition) In the space separating (two points, objects, etc.): between HeavenandEarth2intermediate to, in time, quantity, or degree:betweentenandtwoo'clock;between 500 and 600; pounds-between pink and red.3linking; connecting: air service between cities.4in portions for each of (two people): splitting the profits between them.5Among: sharing the responsibilities between the five of us. (Galaatians 3:28) There is neither Jew nor Greek, there is neither slave nor free, there is no male and female, for you are all one in Christ Jesus.

(Deuteronomy 7:3-4) "You shall not intermarry with them, giving your daughters to their sons or taking their daughters for your sons, for they would turn away your sons from following me, to serve other gods. Then the anger of the Lord would be kindled against you, and he would destroy you quickly". In the Old Testament there was differences between marriage such that people were warned not to marry a foreign woman but in the New Testament - after the death and resurrection of Christ there existed no more difference between men from joining anyone in marriage since as Christians we are save by Grace as we are one in Christ Jesus. Hallelujah!

Bethel: (*Hebrew:* House of God) A hallowed place where God is worshipped (Genesis 28: 18-19) – Early in the morning Jacob took the stone that was near his head and set it up as a marker. He poured oil on top of it and named the place **Bethel** though previously the city was named Luz". The name has frequently been given to nonconformist chapels especially Wales, and also to religious meeting houses for seamen. They were sometimes referred to by Anglicans, somewhat disparagingly, as 'little Bethels'.

Bethesda: This is a town on the River Ogwen and the A5 road on the edge of Snowdonia, in Gwynedd, north-west Wales, colloquially called *Pesda* by the locals. In the New Testament – the pool at the Sheep's Gate of Jerusalem whose water heals the sick–(John 5) Also Christ restored the sight of a blind man there. (see full text below

Bethesda, The Healing at the Pool of: House of mercy, a reservoir (Gr. kolumbethra, "a swimming bath") with five porches, close to the sheep-gate or market (Nehemiah 3:1 ; John 5:2). Eusebius the historian (A.D. 330) calls it "the sheep-pool." It is also called "Bethsaida" and "Beth-zatha" (John 5:2) ,. Under these "porches" or colonnades were usually a large number of infirm people waiting for the "troubling of the water." It is usually identified with the modern so-called Fountain of the Virgin, in the valley of the Kidron, and not far from the Pool of Siloam and also with the Birket Israel, a pool near the mouth of the valley which runs into the Kidron south of "St. Stephen's Gate." Others again identify it with the twin pools called the "Souter rains," under the convent of the Sisters of Zion, situated in what must have been the rock-hewn ditch between Bezetha and the fortress of Antonia. But quite recently Schick has discovered a large tank, as sketched here, situated about 100 feet northwest of St. Anne's Church, which is, as he contends, very probably the Pool of Bethesda. No certainty as to its identification, however, has as yet been arrived at. (John 5: 1- 15) "Some time later, Jesus went up to Jerusalem for one of the Jewish festivals. Now there is in Jerusalem near the Sheep Gate a pool, which in Aramaic is called Bethesda and which is surrounded by five covered colonnades. Here a great number of disabled people used to lie—the blind, the lame, the paralyzed. One who was there had been an invalid for thirty-eight years. When Jesus saw him lying there and learned that he had been in this condition for a long time, he asked him, "Do you want to get well?"

"Sir," the invalid replied, "I have no one to help me into the pool when the water is stirred. While I am trying to get in, someone else goes down ahead of me."

Then Jesus said to him, "Get up! Pick up your mat and walk." At once the man was cured; he picked up his mat and walked.

The day on which this took place was a Sabbath, and so the Jewish leaders said to the man who had been healed, "It is the Sabbath; the law forbids you to carry your mat."

But he replied, "The man who made me well said to me, 'Pick up your mat and walk.'"

So they asked him, "Who is this fellow who told you to pick it up and walk?"

The man who was healed had no idea who it was, for Jesus had slipped away into the crowd that was there. after Jesus found him at the temple and said to him, "See, you are well again. Stop sinning or something worse may happen to you." The man went away and told the Jewish leaders that it was Jesus who had made him well. (See FOUNTAIN; GIHON .)

Bethlehem: (Modern-Hebrew: ***Bethlehem*** "House of Bread"; Ancient Greek) "House of Meat" – "House of Bread" is a Palestinian city located in the central West Bank, about six miles south of Jerusalem. Its population is approximately 25,000 people. It is the capital of the Bethlehem Governorate. The economy is primarily tourist-driven. It is thought the original name was Beit Lachama, from the Canaanite god Lachama. The earliest mention of the city is in the Amarna correspondence c.1350-1330 BCE as "Bit-Lahmi". The Hebrew Bible identifies it as the city David was from and where he was crowned as the king of Israel. The New Testament identifies Bethlehem as the birthplace of Jesus. The city is inhabited by one of the oldest Christian communities in the worldalthough the size of the community has shrunk due to emigration. Bethlehem was destroyed by the Emperor Hadrian during the second-century Bar Kokhba revolt; its rebuilding was promoted by the Empress Helena, mother of Constantine the Great, who commissioned the building of its great Church of the Nativity in 327 CE. The Church was badly damaged by the Samaritans, who sacked it during the Samaritan Revolution in 529, but was rebuilt a century later by the emperor Justinian I, in very much its present form. Bethlehem was seized by the Arab Caliphate of 'Umar

Bethlehem

ibn al-Khaṭṭāb during the Arab conquest in 637, seized again by Egypt and then the Seljuks, and, in 1099, by Crusaders, who replaced its Greek Orthodox clergy with a Latin one. In the mid-13th century, invading Mamluks demolished the city's walls, which were subsequently rebuilt in the early 16th century, after Bethlehem became part of the Ottoman Empire.

Control of Bethlehem passed from the Ottoman Empire to the British Empire at the end of World War I. Pursuant to the proposed United Nations Partition Plan for Palestine of November 1947, Bethlehem was to be included in an international zone, controlled by Britain. The Arab states rejected the Partition Plan, and during the ensuing 1948 Arab-Israeli War, also known as the "First Arab-Israeli War", launched by the Arab League states to prevent the creation of a Jewish state and a second Arab state in Palestine, Jordan forcibly seized Bethlehem and formally annexed it in 1950. It was captured by Israel in the 1967 Six-Day War. Since 1995, when Israel ceded it to the PLO, Bethlehem has been governed by the Palestinian National Authority. Bethlehem has a Muslim majority, but is also home to one of the largest Palestinian Christian communities Originally, Bethlehem was a lodging point for Jewish pilgrims to Jerusalem during the three holiest days of the Jewish year. Bethlehem's chief economic sector is tourism which peaks during the Christmas season when Christians make pilgrimage to the Church of the Nativity, as they have done for almost two millennia. Bethlehem has over thirty hotels and three hundred handicraft workshops. Rachel's Tomb, an important Jewish holy site, is located at the northern entrance of Bethlehem.

The city of Bethlehem, located about six miles southwest of Jerusalem, is the birthplace of our Savior Jesus Christ. Meaning "house of bread," Bethlehem was also the renowned City of David. It was there in young David's hometown that the prophet Samuel anointed him to be king over Israel (1 Samuel 16:1-13). *"The* LORD *said to Samuel, "How long will you mourn for Saul, since I have rejectedhim as king over Israel? Fill your horn with oil and be on your way; I am sending you to Jesse of Bethlehem. I have chosen one of his sons to be king."*

But Samuel said, "How can I go? If Saul hears about it, he will kill me."

The LORD *said, "Take a heifer with you and say, 'I have come to sacrifice to the* LORD. Invite Jesse to the sacrifice, and I will show you what to do. You are to anoint for me the one I indicate."

Samuel did what the LORD *said. When he arrived at Bethlehem, the elders of the* town trembled when they met him. They asked, "Do you come in peace?"

Samuel replied, "Yes, in peace; I have come to sacrifice to the LORD. Consecrate yourselves and come to the sacrifice with me." Then he consecrated Jesse and his sons and invited them to the sacrifice.

When they arrived, Samuel saw Eliab and thought, "Surely the LORD's anointed stands here before the LORD."

But the LORD **said to Samuel, "Do not consider his appearance or his height, for I have rejected him. The** LORD **does not look at the things people look at. People look at the outward appearance, but the** LORD **looks at the heart."**

Then Jesse called Abinadab and had him pass in front of Samuel. But Samuel said, "The LORD **has not chosen this one either."** Jesse then had Shammah pass by, but Samuel said, "Nor has the LORD **chosen this one."** Jesse had seven of his sons pass before Samuel, but Samuel said to him, "The LORD **has not chosen these."** So he asked Jesse, "Are these all the sons you have?"

"There is still the youngest," Jesse answered. "He is tending the sheep." Samuel said, "Send for him; we will not sit down until he arrives." So he sent for him and had him brought in. He was glowing with health and had a fine appearance and handsome features. Then the LORD **said, "Rise and anoint him; this is the one."** So Samuel took the horn of oil and anointed him in the presence of his brothers, and from that day on the Spirit of the LORD **came powerfully upon David. Samuel then went to Ramah**". And in Micah 5, the prophet foretold that Messiah would come from the small and seemingly insignificant town of Bethlehem: **(Micah 5:2–5)** *But you, O Bethlehem Ephrathah, are only a small village among all the people of Judah. Yet a ruler of Israel will come from you, one whose origins are from the distant past. The people of Israel will be abandoned to their enemies until the woman in labor gives birth... And he will stand to lead his flock with the LORD's strength, in the majesty of the name of the LORD his God. Then his people will live there undisturbed, for he will be highly honoured around the world. And he will be the source of peace".*

Beulah: *(bolar)* Originated from Hebrew; meaning-'bride', 'married'-a name symbolic of Heavenly Zion-used to refer to Israel, the Land of Peace. A female given name in Hebrew- meaning married. Biblically, thou shall be called Heph-zi-bah and thy land *Beu-lah*: for the Lord delighted in thee and thy Land shall be married. (Isaiah 62:4 NKJ)

Beware

Beware: Christians need to be cautious and alert to risks or dangers of not praying at all time as Jesus Christ warned in (Philippines 3:2) which says –" Be on the watch against dogs, against the workers of evil, against those of the circumcision":be on your guard, watch out, look out, mind out, be wary, be careful, be cautious, be on the lookout because falls prophets may arise as in (Mathew 7:15-16) **Beware** of the false prophets, who come to you in sheep's clothing, but inwardly are ravenous wolves. "You will know them by their fruits. Grapes are not gathered from thorn bushes nor figs from thistles, are they? 2 Be on the alert, keep your eyes open - keep a sharp lookout, be on the 'qui vive'; take care, take heed, have a care, take it easy read (Jeremiah23:16) This is what the LORD Almighty says: "Do not listen to what the prophets are prophesying to you; they fill you with false hopes. They speak visions from their own minds, not from the mouth of the LORD". Also, (Ezekiel 22:27) encourage thus' "Her officials within her are like wolves tearing their prey; they shed blood and kill people to make unjust gain. And (Daniel 11:34) When they fall, they will receive a little help, and many who are not sincere will join them. So beware, Most importantly, remember (Matthew7:14) "But small is the gate and narrow the road that leads to life, and only a few find it. lowly, look where you're going, tread carefully, proceed with caution; Also 3 *informal* - watch your step, keep an eye out, keep your eyes peeled/skinned, look before you leap, think twice;

"there are loose rocks in the area or the world so *beware!*"

Bible: Greek – **Biblio** (noun) The Christian scripture book consisting of the Old and New Testament 2 The Jewish scriptures. 3 In informal terms, the book regarded as giving comprehensive and reliable information about something including the creation story like in (Genesis 1 – Old Testament) 2 The bible is the hub of the word of God – A must get book by all Christians. 4 The Bible is the true source of spiritual words from God to all Christians or Believers in Jesus Christ Gospel.

Bible, The Holy: The Holy Bible (from Koine Greek , biblía, "the books") is a canonical collection of texts that are considered sacred. The term "Bible" is shared between Judaism and Christianity, but the collection of texts each considers canonical is not the same. Different religious groups include different sub-sets of books within their Biblical canons, in different orders, and sometimes divide or combine books, or incorporate additional material into canonical books 2 The Hebrew Bible, or *Tanakh*, contains twenty-four books divided into three parts: the five books of the **Torah** ("teaching" or "law"), the **Nevi'im** ("prophets"), and the **Ketuvim** ("writings"). 3 Christian Bibles range from the sixty-six books of the Protestant canon to the eighty-one books of the Ethiopian Orthodox Church canon. The first part of Christian Bibles is the Old Testament, which contains, at minimum, the twenty-four books of the Hebrew Bible divided into thirty-nine books and ordered differently from the Hebrew Bible. The Catholic Church and Eastern Christian churches also hold certain deutero-canonical books and passages to be part of the Old Testament canon. The second part is the New Testament, containing twenty-seven books: the four Canonical gospels, Acts of the Apostles, twenty-one Epistles or letters, and the Book of Revelation. By the 2nd century BCE Jewish groups had called the Bible books "holy," and Christians now commonly call the Old and New Testaments of the Christian Bible "The Holy Bible" or "the Holy Scriptures" (Greek - *e Agía Graph*?). The oldest surviving complete Christian Bibles are Greek manuscripts from the 4th century. The oldest Tanakh manuscript in Hebrew and Aramaic dates to the 10th century CE but an early 4th-century Septuagint translation is found in the Codex Vaticanus. The Bible was divided into chapters in the 13th century by Stephen Langton and into verses in the 16th century by French printer Robert Estienne and is now usually cited by book, chapter, and verse. 4 The Holy Bible is widely considered to be the best selling book of all time, has estimated annual sales of 100 million copies and has been a major influence on literature and history, especially in the West where it was the first mass-printed book. The Gutenberg Bible was the first Bible ever printed using movable type.

Biblical: (adjective) Relating to or found in the bible.

Bible Belt: (noun) The areas of the southern and middle western US and western Canada where many Protestants believe in the literally translation of the Bible.

Bibliomancy: Divination by means of the bible. You love being bibliomancy in your presentation or in your speech.

Birthright: A right or privilege that you are entitle to at birth;For instance,»free public education is the birthright of every American child»heritage, inheritance any attribute or immaterial possession that is inherited from ancestors; «my only inheritance was my mother›s blessing»; «the world›s heritage of knowledge» an inheritance coming by right of birth (especially by primogeniture)patrimony inheritance, heritage that which is inherited; a title or property or estate that passes by law to

Bishop

the heir on the death of the elderly. 2 The birthright is emphasized in the gospel because it honoured the rights or privileges of the family's firstborn son. After the father died, or in the father's absence, the firstborn son assumed the father's authority and responsibilities. However, the Bible also shows that the father could rescind the birthright and pass it on to a younger son. A good example of this is the case of Jacob and his twelve sons. Reuben was the eldest, but the birthright was given to Joseph's sons. Even then, Jacob blessed the younger son, Ephraim, above the elder, Manasseh (Genesis 37:19-22; Genesis 49:1-4;Genesis 49:22-26). In addition to assuming the leadership role in the family, the recipient of the birth right inherited twice that received by the other sons. In cases where a husband might have more than one wife, the birthright always went to the firstborn son of the father and could not be awarded to the son of a favorite wife without proper justification (Deuteronomy 21:15-17) or if the firstborn son's mother was a concubine or a slave (Genesis 21:9-13;Judges 11:1-2). The birthright of a king's firstborn son included his succession to the throne (2 Chronicles 21:1-3). King Rehoboam of Judah violated this tradition by passing the birthright to Abijah, his favorite son. However, to avoid trouble with the older sons, the king paid them off (2 Chronicles 11:18-23).

As New Testament Christians, we have an inherited "birthright" status through Jesus Christ as the firstborn Son of God (Romans 8:2); (Colossians 1:15); (Revelation 1:5). As God's only begotten Son, Jesus received the kingdom from His Father and is Lord of all (Acts 2:36;Philippians 2:9-11;Revelation 19:16). Christ promises to share with us His kingdom and inheritance (Romans 4:13;Galatians 3:29;Ephesians 1:18;Hebrews 11:16). Christians are warned not to imitate Esau who, on impulse, gave away his birthright for a bowl of stew (Hebrews 12:16-17;Genesis 25:19-34). Because of his foolishness, Esau lost his birthright and the blessings of his father (Genesis 27). The lesson for us is to respect what is holy. We should never throw away what is important, godly, or honourable for the sake of temporary pleasure.

Our focus is to remain on Jesus, the appointed heir of all things (Hebrews 1:2;Psalm 2:7-8;Matthew 28:18). And we, through His grace and our faith in Him, are counted as joint heirs (Romans 8:17;Galatians 3:29; Titus 3:7

Bishop: (From the New Testament Greek , *epískopos*,"overseer","guardian") is an ordained or consecrated member of the Christian clergy who is generally entrusted with a position of authority and oversight. Within the Roman Catholic, Eastern Orthodox, Oriental Orthodox, Anglican, Old Catholic and Independent Catholic churches and in the Assyrian Church of the East, bishops claim apostolic succession, a direct historical lineage dating back to the original Twelve Apostles. Within these churches, bishops are seen as those who possess the full priesthood and can ordain clergy – including other bishops. Some Protestant churches including the Lutheran and Methodist churches have bishops serving similar functions as well, though not always understood to be within apostolic succession in the same way. 2 One who has been ordained deacon, priest, and then bishop is understood to hold the fullness of the (ministerial) priesthood, given responsibility by Christ to govern, teach and sanctify the Body of Christ, members of the Faithful. Priests, deacons and lay ministers cooperate and assist their bishop(s) in shepherding a flock. 3 A high ranking Christian Priest who has Spiritual and administrative power over a diocese.

Bishop, To: Formerly, to confirm, to admit into the church.

Blood: A bodily fluid in animals that delivers necessary substances such as nutrients and oxygen to the cells and transports metabolic waste products away from those same cells. In vertebrates, it is composed of blood cells suspended in blood plasma. Plasma, which constitutes 55% of blood fluid, is mostly water (92% by volume and contains dissipated proteins, glucose, mineral ions, hormones, carbon dioxide (plasma being the main medium for excretory product transportation), and blood cells themselves. Albumin is the main protein in plasma, and it functions to regulate the colloidal osmotic pressure of blood. The blood cells are mainly red blood cells (also called RBCs or erythrocytes) and white blood cells, including leukocytes and platelets. The most abundant cells in vertebrate blood are red blood cells. These contain hemoglobin, an iron-containing protein, which facilitates transportation of oxygen by reversibly binding to this respiratory gas and greatly increasing its solubility in blood. In contrast, carbon dioxide is almost entirely transported extracellularly dissolved in plasma as bicarbonate ion. Vertebrate blood is bright red when its hemoglobin is oxygenated. Some animals, such as crustaceans and mollusks, use hemocyanin to carry oxygen, instead of hemoglobin. Insects and some mollusks use a fluid called hemolymph instead of blood, the difference being that hemolymph is not contained in a closed circulatory system. In most insects, this "blood" does not contain oxygen-carrying molecules such as hemoglobin because their bodies are small enough for their tracheal system to suffice for supplying oxygen.

Blood, Life, Justice and

Jawed vertebrates have an adaptive immune system, based largely on white blood cells. White blood cells help to resist infections and parasites. Platelets are important in the clotting of blood. Arthropods, using hemolymph, have hemocytes as part of their immune system.

2 Blood is circulated around the body through blood vessels by the pumping action of the heart. In animals with lungs, arterial blood carries oxygen from inhaled air to the tissues of the body, and venous blood carries carbon dioxide, a waste product of metabolism produced by cells, from the tissues to the lungs to be exhaled.

Medical terms related to blood often begin with **hemo** - or **hemato-** (also spelled **haemo-** and **haemato-**) from the Greek word αἷμα (*haima*) for "blood". In terms of anatomy and histology, blood is considered a specialized form of connective tissue, given its origin in the bones and the presence of potential molecular fibers in the form of fibrinogen.

2 Christians are forbidden from eating any animal with blood. (Leviticus17:13–15)..."So when any man from the sons of Israel, or from the aliens who sojourn among them, in hunting catches a beast or a bird which may be eaten, he shall pour out its blood and cover it with earth. "For as for the life of all flesh, its blood is identified with its life. Therefore I said to the sons of Israel, 'You are not to eat the blood of any flesh, for the life of all flesh is its blood; whoever eats it shall be cut off.' "When any person eats an animal which dies or is torn by beasts, whether he is a native or an alien, he shall wash his clothes and bathe in water, and remain unclean until evening; then he will become clean....

Jesus Christ knew that He was the Messiah, the "Lamb of God" (John 1:29), see also John The Baptist). And yet, knowing what awaited Him in a few hours, since He was as *human* as anyone else, before or since (Hebrews 2:17, 4:15), He asked The Father to relieve Him of the need to actually go through with it. Ironically, He prayed so hard that "His sweat was as it were great drops of blood falling down to the ground" (Luke 22:44). He asked three times, in deep and sorrowful prayer, but God's answer was that it *must* be carried through. Why? Why did Jesus have to actually shed His blood as a sacrifice for humanity?

Blood, Life, Justice and: Right from the earliest times, *as God decreed* (God doesn't care what any differing human definition may be), blood was equated with life:"For the life of every creature is the blood of it" (Leviticus 17:14)

Again, "Whoever sheds the blood of man, by man shall his blood be shed; for God made man in His own image." (Genesis 9:6) The Penalty of Sin Is Death - When humans became sinners, they became subject to the penalty of sin, which is death: "Behold, the man has become like one of Us, knowing good and evil; and now, lest he put forth his hand and take also of the tree of life, and eat, and live for ever, therefore The Lord God sent him forth from the garden of Eden" (Genesis 3:22-23) "you are dust, and to dust you shall return" (Genesis 3:19) "For the wages of sin is death" (Romans 6:23)

Blood, Jesus Christ Paid The Death Penalty For us by His: "with the precious blood of Christ, like that of a lamb without blemish or spot. He was destined before the foundation of the world but was made manifest at the end of the times for your sake" (1 Peter 1:19-20) "for this is My blood of the covenant, which is poured out for many for the forgiveness of sins" (Matthew 26:28)"But one of the soldiers pierced his side with a spear, and at once there came out blood and water" (John 19:34 RSV) (see How Did Jesus Christ Die?)

Blood of Jesus – the 'Messiah', Old Testament Sacrifices Were Symbolic Of The: "But when Christ appeared as a High Priest of the good things that have come, then through the greater and more perfect tent, not made with hands, that is, not of this creation, He entered once for all into the Holy Place, taking not the blood of goats and calves but His own blood, thus securing an eternal redemption. For if the sprinkling of defiled persons with the blood of goats and bulls and with the ashes of a heifer sanctifies for the purification of the flesh, how much more shall the ***blood of Christ,*** Who through the eternal Spirit offered Himself without blemish to God, purify your conscience from dead works to serve the living God." "Therefore He is the mediator of a new covenant, so that those who are called may receive the promised eternal inheritance, since a death has occurred which redeems them from the transgressions under the first covenant."

"For where a will is involved, the death of the one who made it must be established. For a will takes effect only at death, since it is not in force as long as the one who made it is alive. Hence even the first covenant was not ratified without ***blood.*** For when every commandment of the law had been declared by Moses to all the people, he took the ***blood*** of calves and goats, with water and scarlet wool and hyssop, and sprinkled both the book itself and all the people, saying, "This is the blood of the covenant which God commanded you." And in the same way he sprinkled with

Blaspheme

the blood both the tent and all the vessels used in worship. Indeed, under the law almost everything is purified with blood, and without the shedding of **blood** there is no forgiveness of sins."

"Thus it was necessary for the copies of the heavenly things to be purified with these rites, but the heavenly things themselves with better sacrifices than these. For Christ has entered, not into a sanctuary made with hands, a copy of the true one, but into heaven itself, now to appear in the Presence of God on our behalf. Nor was it to offer Himself repeatedly, as the high priest enters the Holy Place yearly with **blood** not his own [see The Day Of Atonement]; for then He would have had to suffer repeatedly since the foundation of the world. But as it is, He has appeared once for all at the end of the age to put away sin by the sacrifice of Himself. And just as it is appointed for men to die once, and after that comes judgment, so Christ, having been offered once to bear the sins of many, will appear a second time [see The Return Of Jesus Christ], not to deal with sin but to save those who are eagerly waiting for Him." (Hebrews 9:11-28 RSV)

Blaspheme: (Greek –Blasphemein, Blasphemed passive,Blaspheming)To speak of (God or a sacred entity) in an irreveren impious manner.To revile; execrate. To speak blasphemy.To show contempt or disrespect for (God, a divine being, or sacred things), especially in speechTo utter profanities, curses, or impious expressions 2 Blaspheme is insult or contempt or lack irreverence for a God, religious or holy persons. The gospel according to (1 John 1:9), says "If we confess our sins, he is faithful and just and will forgive us our sins and purify us from all unrighteousness." This verse, and many others that speak of God's forgiveness, seem to be in contrast with Mark 3:29 and this concept of an unforgivable sin. So, how can one *blaspheme* against the Holy Spirit, - the eternal sin that can never be forgiven?

The only unforgivable sin is the rejection of Jesus Christ›s offer of salvation, his free gift of eternal life, and thus, his forgiveness from sin. If you don›t accept his gift, you cannot be forgiven. If you deny the Holy Spirit›s entrance into your life, to work his sanctification in you, you cannot be cleansed from unrighteousness. Perhaps this is too simple an explanation, but it is the one that makes the most sense to me in light of the Scriptures. Therefore, to "blaspheme" against the Holy Ghost" can be understood as a continued and persistently stubborn rejection of the gospel of salvation. This would be an "unpardonable sin" because as long as a person remains in unbelief, he voluntarily excludes himself from forgiveness of sin. *(Read more on Blasphemy below)*

Blasphemy: (blass-fuh-mi – noun, blasphemies –plural) Act of talking about God – the Supreme or to Christians – our Eternal King disrespectfully. 2 It is the act of insulting or showing contempt or lack of reverence for a God, to religious or holy persons or things, or toward something considered sacred or inviolable. Some countries have laws to punish religious *blasphemy*, while others have laws that allow those who are offended by *blasphemy* to punish blasphemers. Those laws may condone penalties or retaliation for *blasphemy* under the labels of blasphemous libel, expression of opposition, or "villification," of religion or of some religious practices, religious insult, or hate speech. 2 Christian theology condemns *blasphemy*. It is spoken of in (Mark 3:28-29), "Truly I say to you, all sins shall be forgiven the sons of men, and whatever blasphemies they utter; but whoever blasphemes against the Holy Spirit never has forgiveness, but is guilty of an eternal sin "-- here *blaspheming* the Holy Spirit is spoken of as unforgivable— the eternal sin. However, there is dispute over what form this *blasphemy* may take and whether it qualifies as *blasphemy* in the conventional sense; and over the meaning of "unforgivable". In (2 Kings 18: 31-35), "Do not listen to Hezekiah. This is what the king of Assyria says: Make peace with me and come out to me. Then each of you will eat fruit from your own vine and fig treeand drink water from your own cistern, until I come and take you to a land like your own—a land of grain and new wine, a land of bread and vineyards, a land of olive trees and honey. Choose life and not death! "Do not listen to Hezekiah, for he is misleading you when he says, 'The LORD will deliver us.' Has the god of any nation ever delivered his land from the hand of the king of Assyria? Where are the gods of Hamath and Arpad? Where are the gods of Sepharvaim, Hena and Ivvah? Have they rescued Samaria from my hand? Who of all the gods of these countries has been able to save his land from me? How then can the LORD deliver Jerusalem from my hand?" the Rabshakeh gave the word from the king of Assyria, dissuading trust in the Lord, asserting that God is no more able to deliver than all the gods of the land.

In (Matthew 9:, Jesus spoke the words "Your sins are forgiven you"; He was accused of *blasphemy,* since only God can forgive sins against Himself *Blasphemy* has been condemned as a serious, or even the most serious, sin by the major creeds and Church theologians (apostasy and infidelity unbelief were generally considered to be the gravest sins, with heresy a greater sin than *blasphemy,*

Bless: *(noun)* – Blessed (passive) – Blessing (continuous) This

Blessed

word appear (41 times in the Bible). Bless is a pronounce words in a religious rite in order to confer or invoke divine favour upon; ask God to look favourably on - *he blessed the dying man and anointed him* 2 (**bless someone with**) (Of God or some notional higher power) endow someone with (a particular cherished thing or attribute):*we have been blessed with a beautiful baby boy. God has blessed the city with huge sandy beaches* **Blessed:** "But blessed is the one who trusts in the Lord, whose confidence is in him. They will be like a tree planted by the water that sends out its roots by the stream. It does not fear when heat comes; its leaves are always green. It has no worries in a year of drought and never fails to bear fruit." (Jeremiah 17:7-8) NIV Blessing can confer assurances of God's protection and assurances " Worship the Lord your God, and his blessing will be on your food and water. I will take away sickness from among you,(Exodus 23:25) NIV **Blessing:** A **blessing** (also used to refer to bestowing of such) is the infusion of something with holiness, spiritual redemption, divine will, or one's hope or approval.

Blind: (noun) Something serving to conceal the truth. The metaphor is from window blinds which prevent outsiders from seeing in. 2 A *blind* person - is someone who is visually impaired or suffer the sickness of blindness. This aspect form a greater aspect of Jesus ministry as in (Isaiah 42:16) "I will lead the blind by a way they do not know, In paths they do not know I will guide them. I will make darkness into light before them And rugged places into plains. These are the things I will do, And I will not leave them undone." (John 9:39) Jesus said, "For judgment I came into this world, that those who do not see may see, and those who see may become blind." Because Jesus – the word and Holy Spirit is light. Light is not meant for light but light is to shine in darkness so that those who are in darkness can see the way since the god's of this world already has blinded the minds of unbelievers (2 Corinthians 4:4) 'In their case the god of this world has blinded the minds of the unbelievers, to keep them from seeing the light of the gospel of the glory of Christ, who is the image of God' (**Romans 11:8**) As it is written, "God gave them a spirit of stupor, eyes that would not see and ears that would not hear, down to this very day."

Blind leading the Blind, The:
The biblical allusion for those who give advice to others or take the lead but are unfitted to do so (Mathew 15:14) "Let them alone; they are blind guides of the blind. And if a blind man guides a blind man, both will fall into a pit."

Blindness
The complete lack of form and visual light perception and is clinically recorded as NLP, an abbreviation for "no light perception." Blindness is frequently

Blindness, The Spiritual

used to describe severe visual impairment with some remaining vision. Those described as having only light perception have no more sight than the ability to tell light from dark and the general direction of a light source. The World Health Organization defines *low vision* as visual acuity of less than 20/60 (6/18), but equal to or better than 20/200 (6/60), or visual field loss to less than 20 degrees, in the better eye with best possible correction. *Blindness* is defined as visual acuity of less than 20/400 (6/120), or a visual field loss to less than 10 degrees, in the better eye with best possible correction. But we are concern about blindness in the light of the Gospel. Wherefore, the scripture warns in (**Romans 11:25**) – "For I would not, brethren, that ye should be ignorant of this mystery, lest ye should be wise in your own conceits; that blindness in part is happened to Israel, until the fullness of the Gentiles be come in. In (John 9:1-41) "As he passed by, he saw a man *blind* from birth. And his disciples asked him, "Rabbi, who sinned, this man or his parents, that he was born blind?" Jesus answered, "It was not that this man sinned, or his parents, but that the works of God might be displayed in him. We must work the works of him who sent me while it is day; night is coming, when no one can work. As long as I am in the world, I am the light of the world." This shows the true light Jesus Christ who came as a true alternative or a complete opposite to darkness – blindness wherefore through him and in him the blind – the world will see. As also is recorded in (Isaiah 42:14-22) For a long time I have held my peace; I have kept still and restrained myself; now I will cry out like a woman in labour; I will gasp and pant. I will lay waste mountains and hills, and dry up all their vegetation; I will turn the rivers into islands, and dry up the pools. And I will lead the *blind* in a way that they do not know, in paths that they have not known I will guide them. I will turn the darkness before them into light, the rough places into level ground. These are the things I do, and I do not forsake them. They are turned back and utterly put to shame, who trust in carved idols, who say to metal images, "You are our gods." Hear, you deaf, and look, you *blind,* that you may see!

Blindness, The Spiritual: A grievous condition experienced by those who do not believe in God, Jesus Christ, and His Word (Romans 2:8;2 Thessalonians 2:12). Those who reject Christ are the lost (John 6:68-69). Being spiritually blind, they are perishing (2 Corinthians 4:3-4;Revelation 3:17). They choose not to accept the teachings of Christ and His authority in their lives (Matthew 28:18). They are blind to the manifestations of God as revealed throughout His Word and Jesus Christ (John 1:1;Acts 28:26-27). They are described as those who

Blindness, The Spiritual

"do not accept the things of the Spirit of God, for they are folly to him, and he is not able to understand them because they are spiritually discerned" (1 Corinthians 2:14). Peter spoke of such people as "scoffers [who] will come in the last days with scoffing, following their own sinful desires" (2 Peter 3:3;Proverbs 21:24;Jude 1:18). Those who reject Christ and His Word are spiritually blind and cannot understand the truth of the Scriptures. The truth sounds foolish to them (Isaiah 5:25;Isaiah 37:23). The Bible describes those denying God as fools (Psalm 14:1;Matthew 7:26). Because of their blindness and rejection of God and His Word, they are in a perilous, unsaved condition (John 12:48;Hebrews 2:2-4). **The spiritually blind** are simply unable to understand His Word (Matthew 13:13;Deuteronomy 29:4). Jesus said, "If you love Me, you will keep My commandments. And I will ask the Father, and He will give you another Helper, to be with you forever, even the Spirit of truth, whom the world cannot receive, because it neither sees Him nor knows Him. You know Him, for He dwells with you and will be in you" (John 14:15-17). Paul echoed this when he told the believers in Rome, "Those who are in the flesh cannot please God. You, however, are not in the flesh but in the Spirit, if in fact the Spirit of God dwells in you. Anyone who does not have the Spirit of Christ does not belong to Him" (Romans 8:8-9). Those outside of Christ are not of God because their lives are steeped in the things of the world with all its passions, their eyes blind to the Spirit of God. The Apostle John said, "If anyone loves the world, the love of the Father is not in him" but that person's love "is from the world" (1 John 2:15-16). The cause of **spiritual blindness** is made quite clear in the Scriptures: "In their case the god of this world has blinded the minds of the unbelievers, to keep them from seeing the light of the gospel of the glory of Christ, who is the image of God" (2 Corinthians 4:4). Paul refers to Satan as the "god of this world." Extraordinarily evil (John 8:44), Satan destroys the flesh (1 Corinthians 5:5), masquerades as an angel of light (2 Corinthians 11:14), and is the cause of all temptations (Luke 4:2;Hebrews 4:15;1 Corinthians 7:5). He revels in scheming against and trapping the unbelievers (2 Corinthians 2:11;Ephesians 6:11;2 Timothy 2:26). Satan's goal is to devour the weak who fall prey to temptation, fear, loneliness, worry, depression, and persecution (1 Peter 5:8-9). Without God and left to ourselves, we easily succumb to the devil's schemes. We can become so mired in the affairs of this world and its moral darkness that, in the end, God turns us over to **spiritual blindness** and eternal condemnation (John 12:40;Romans 1:24-32). As believers, we have the Spirit of God reigning in our lives to ward off the debilitating effects of Satan's power and the world's influence (1 John 4:13). John tells us, "Whoever confesses that Jesus is the Son of God, God abides in Him, and he in God" (1 John 4:15). Satan wars within and without us. His weapons are deceitful and crafty schemes to make us doubt and stumble (2 Corinthians 2:11;Ephesians 4:14). Yet God has provided us with powerful weapons ward off his flaming arrows (Ephesians 6:10-18). As believers we can overcome the evil one and remain in the Light and never become spiritually blind. For, in truth, Jesus has given us His wonderful promise: "I am the light of the world. Whoever follows Me will not walk in darkness, but will have the light of life" (John 8:12). To be spiritually blind is not to see Christ, and not to see Christ is not to see God (Colossians 1:15-16;2 Corinthians 4:6)

Boaz: Son of Rachab and Salmon mentioned 24 times in the Bible. Boaz was a wealthy landowner of Bethlehem, and kinsman of Elimelech, Naomi's late husband. He noticed Ruth, the widowed Moabite daughter-in-law of Naomi, a relative of his (see family tree), gleaning grain in his fields. He soon learns of the difficult circumstances her family is in and Ruth's loyalty to Naomi. In response, Boaz invites her to eat with him and his workers, as well as deliberately leaving grain for her to claim while keeping a protective eye on her. Ruth approaches Boaz and asks him to exercise his right of kinship and marry her. Boaz accepts, provided that another with a superior claim declines. Since the first son of Ruth and a kinsman of her late husband would be deemed the legal offspring of the decedent and heir to Elimelech, the other kinsman defers to Boaz. In marrying Ruth, Boaz revives Elimelech's lineage, and the patrimony is secured to Naomi's family. For those substituting, redeeming factors, Ruth's husband is considered by Christians to be a type of Jesus of Nazareth Their son was Obed, father of Jesse, and grandfather of David. Boaz is mentioned in both the Gospels of Matthew and Luke as an ancestor of Jesus 2 Boaz" was the name of the left one of The Two frontal Columns of Solomon's Temple. 3 Other meaning relates to the swiftness or quickness of the Horse.

Body, The: The physical I (metaphysics), physical matter subject to the whims of volition **2** Dead *body* or cadaver, a dead human body **3** Human *body*, the entire structure of a human organism **4** Physical *body*, an object in physics **5** *Body* plan, the physical features shared by a group of animals. The body in the context of the gospel relate directly with the Holy Spirit. It is the living House of God. The temple of the Holy Spirit. (1 Corinthians 6:19-20) " Do you not know that your bodies are temples of the Holy Spirit, who

Body of Christ

is in you, whom you have received from God? You are not your own; you were bought at a price. Therefore honour God with your bodies". In honouring God with our bodies, we must not ascribed to any man made creation, tattoos, Gastric bands, ascription to gods or idols etc.

Body of Christ: This is the unity of the entire faithful functions spelled out by the divine power of Christ to the Church. In Christian theology, the term Body of Christ has two separate connotations: it may refer to Jesus's statement about the Eucharist at the Last Supper that "This is my body" in (Luke 22:19-20), or the explicit usage of the term by the Apostle Paul in I Corinthians to refer to the Christian Church. Although in general usage the term "Body of Christ" may refer to Christ's body in the spiritual realm, the other two distinct usages are prominent theological issues. For some Christians, such as Roman Catholics, the term may refer to the Real Presence of Christ in the Eucharist. For a larger segment of Christians, including Catholics and some Protestants, it may instead or also refer to the Christian Church as a group of believers, as used in the Pauline epistles. 2 The body of Christ has to do with the Church and the Church refers to Christians in different places of worship. (1 Corinthians 12: 27 – 30) "Now you are the body of Christ, and each one of you is a part of it. And God has placed in the church first of all apostles, second prophets, third teachers, then miracles, then gifts of healing, of helping, of guidance, and of different kinds of tongues. Are all apostles? Are all prophets? Are all teachers? Do all work miracles? Do all have gifts of healing? Do all speak in tongues[d]? Do all interpret? The church will receive a fresh revelation of Jesus, especially though the book of Revelation. That revelation will launch the church into a transformation unlike any experienced in a previous age. As we see Him, we become like Him! The coming increase in the revelation of Jesus will be measurable through new dimensions of worship – corporate throne room experiences. 3 *Body of Christ* listed about the powerful combination of gifts brought to it's full potential through discipline. That is the picture of the Church becoming a mature man. It is singular, meaning we all function together as one – unity of faith. All its members will work in perfect coordination and harmony, complementing each other's function and gift, according to the directions given by the head - Jesus Christ. This was not a promise to be fulfilled in eternity. While this is not speaking of human perfection, but a maturity of function, without jealousy, that will develop as His presence becomes more manifest. As Christians, we need to embrace this as possible because He said it.

Booths: A hut, (Hebrew – Cukkah, synonymous to pavilion, tabernacle, cottage)made of the branches of a tree or wood. In such tabernacles Jacob sojourned for a season at a place named from this circumstance Succoth as in (Genesis 33:17). "Jacob journeyed to Succoth, and built for himself a house and made *booths* for his livestock; therefore the place is named Succoth". Booths were erected also at the feast of Tabernacles (Leviticus 23:42 - 43), "so your descendants will know that I had the Israelites live in temporary shelters when I brought them out of Egypt. I am the Lord your God." -"Live in temporary shelters for seven days: All native-born Israelites are to live in such shelters" which commemorated the abode of the Israelites in the wilderness.

2 Booth - The Hebrew word cukkah (rendered in the King James Version "booth" or "booths," eleven times; "tabernacle" or "tabernacles," ten times; "pavilion" or "pavilions," five times; "cottage" once) means a hut made of wattled twigs or branches (Nehemiah 8:15) "So they proclaimed and circulated a proclamation in all their cities and in Jerusalem, saying, "Go out to the hills, and bring olive branches and wild olive branches, myrtle branches, palm branches and branches of other leafy trees, to make booths, as it is written."

In countries where trees are abundant such wattle structures are common as temporary buildings as they can be constructed in a very short time. Cattle were probably housed in them Such hurriedly-made huts were use d by soldiers (2 Samuel 11:11; 1 Kings 20:12) and by harvesters--hence, the name feast of "booths" or "tabernacles" (see TABERNACLES, FEAST OF). (Job 27:18) uses booth (parallel moth's house) as a symbol of impermanence. Similar huts were erected in vineyards, etc., to protect them from robbers and beasts of prey. The isolated condition of Jerusalem in the time of the prophet Isaiah is compared to a "booth in a vineyard" mentioned in (Isaiah 18). 3 *Booths* are still being used in modern times in remote Christianised part of the world particularly for accommodating temporary worshippers and shorter conventional Church meetings.

Booths, feast of: *See feast of the Tabernacle.*

Book: A set of written, printed, illustrated materials fastened together in an edited or coded form. The bible is a form of a book with 66 books from Genesis to Revelation. 2 Different religious groups include different books in their Biblical canons, in varying orders, and sometimes divide or combine books, or incorporate additional material into canonical books. Christian Bibles range from the sixty-six books of the Protestant canon to the eighty-one books of the Ethiopian Orthodox Tewahedo Church canon. The Tanakh or T-N-K canon contains twenty-four books divided into three parts: the five books of the Torah ("teach-

Book

ing"); the Nevi'im ("prophets"); and the Ketuvim ("writings"). The first part of Christian Bibles is called the Old Testament, which contains, at minimum, the above twenty-four books but divided into thirty-nine books and ordered differently, sometimes also called the Hebrew Bible.The Catholic Church and Eastern Christian churches also hold that certain deuterocanonical books and passages are part of the Old Testament canon. The second part is the New Testament, containing twenty-seven books; the four Canonical gospels, Acts of the Apostles, twenty-one Epistles or letters and the Book of Revelation. The Eastern Orthodox, Oriental Orthodox and Eastern Catholic churches may have minor differences in their lists of accepted books. The list given here for these churches is the most inclusive: if at least one Eastern church accepts the book it is included here. 3 A *book* is a set of written, printed, illustrated, or blank sheets, made of ink, paper, parchment, or other materials, usually fastened together to hinge at one side. A single sheet within a book is called a leaf, and each side of a leaf is called a page. A set of text-filled or illustrated pages produced in electronic format is known as an electronic book, or e-book. Books may also refer to works of literature, or a main division of such a work. In library and information science, a book is called a monograph, to distinguish it from serial periodicals such as magazines, journals or newspapers. The body of all written works including books is literature. In novels and sometimes other types of books (for example, biographies), a book may be divided into several large sections, also called books (Book 1, Book 2, Book 3, and so on). An avid reader of books is a bibliophile or colloquially, bookworm.

Book of Life, The: Popularly known as the book that contains the list of the elects to Heavenly Home (Kingdom) and in Christianity and Judaism, the Book of Life (Hebrew- Sefer HaChaim); Greek: (Biblíon- tēs Zōēs) is the book in which God records the names of every person who is destined for Heaven or the World to Come. According to the Talmud it is open on Rosh Hashanah, as is its analogue for the wicked, the Book of the Dead. For this reason extra mention is made for the Book of Life during Amidah recitations during the Days of Awe, the ten days between Rosh Hashanah, the Jewish new year, and Yom Kippur, the day of atonement (the two High Holidays, particularly in the prayer (Unetaneh Tokef). 2 In the Old Testament the Book of Life - the book or muster-roll of God - records forever all people considered righteous before God. God has such a book, and to be blotted out of it signifies death It is with reference to the Book of Life that the holy remnant is spo-

Born of the Spirit

ken of as being written unto life in Jerusalem; compare also (Ezekiel 9. 4), where one of the six heavenly envoys "who had the scribe's inkhorn upon his loins" is told to mark the righteous for life, while the remainder of the inhabitants of Jerusalem are doomed. 3 The Psalmist likewise speaks of the Book of Life in which only the names of the righteous are written "and from which the unrighteous are blotted out".4 Even the tears of men are recorded in this Book of God.[5] "Every one that shall be found written in the book . . . shall awake to everlasting life"

6 This book is probably identical with the "Book of Remembrance" in which are recorded the deeds of those that fear the Lord.

Born: To begin to exist as a new creation. Brought into life by birth and or Brought into existence; created: 2 A new nation was born with the revolution. 3. Having from birth a particular quality or talent: - a born artist. 3 Destined, or seemingly destined, from birth: a person born to lead. 4. Resulting or arising: wisdom born of experience. 5. Native to a particular country, region, or place. 6 *Born by the Spirit* (Isaiah 9:6) "For a child will be born to us, a son will be given to us; And the government will rest on His shoulders; And His name will be called Wonderful Counsellor, Mighty God, Eternal Father, Prince of Peace".

Born again: In Christianity, to be born again is to undergo a "spiritual rebirth" (regeneration) of the human soul or spirit from the Holy Spirit, contrasted with the physical birth everyone experiences. The origin of the term "born again" is the New Testament: "Jesus replied, 'Very truly I tell you, no one can see the kingdom of God without being born again.'"[John 3:3) It is a term associated with salvation in Christianity. Individuals who profess to be born again often state that they have a personal relationship with Jesus Christ. "Truly, truly, I say to you, unless one is born again he cannot see the kingdom of God."

Born of the Spirit: To be born of a new living hope full with love, power, sound mind, freedom, fullness of life, peace, Joy of salvation – possessing gracious benefit and provisions - all by the spirit through Jesus Christ. (John 3: 6 -7) Jesus answered, "Truly, truly, I say to you, unless one born of water and the Spirit he cannot enter into the kingdom of God. "That which is born of the flesh is flesh, and that which is born of the Spirit is spirit. "Do not be amazed that I said to you, 'You must be born again.' Notice how Jesus cuts right across that with a sharp and penetrating sentence that must have gone like a sword thrust right into Nicodemus' heart. He said to him, "Truly, truly I say to you, unless one is born again he cannot see the kingdom of God." Observe what Jesus is saying in this startling word to Nicodemus. He introduces his words with this little phrase, "truly, truly." I have come to understand that that term is a sign our Lord gives that what he is about to say is extremely important and should not be missed. It is a revelation of a fundamental reality about life; a basic, elementary fact that we need desperately to understand if we are going to live realistically in this world. In a recent , billboards and newspaper advertisements, a hand with the index finger pointing was frequently used to highlight the important words. When I see these words, "truly, truly," I always see it in that light: a finger pointing at the important words that follow.

These then are the words which Jesus highlighted: "Unless one is born again he cannot see the kingdom of God." A new birth is absolutely essential to enter the kingdom. John uses a very interesting word here that is translated "a new," or "again." It is the Greek word, anothen, which has three meanings: It means again to do it a second time; it also means to begin radically, completely, a new beginning; and it also means from above, and it is used in that sense in other places in Scripture. It signifies God must do this. The Christian understanding of this word includes all three of those meanings. It is speaking of something radical, a new beginning. It is a second birth, but it comes from above. It is God that does it, not man; and it results in a new creation, a new beginning.

This idea appears many times in the New Testament. Paul speaks of "babes in Christ," (1 Corinthians 3:1). Peter says, "as new-born babes desire the sincere milk of the word that you may grow," (1 Peter 2:2). Again Peter says we are "born again, not of corruptible seed, but of incorruptible," (1 Peter 1:23). And he speaks of being "born to a living hope," (1 Peter 1:3). Paul speaks not only of being new creatures in Christ but of a new creation; of passing from death unto life, of a new, radical start. Jesus makes clear that this is the only way to enter the kingdom of God. If you do not come this way you cannot enter. There is no way you can even see the kingdom of God without this. To be in "the kingdom of God," of course, is to belong to God; it is to be a part of his rule, his reign, his domain. Paul speaks of being transferred from "the kingdom of darkness, ruled by the god of this world, into the kingdom of the Son of his love," (Colossians 1:13). Thus, Jesus was referring to a transfer of citizenship, a radical departure from what we once were.

Jesus sensed in Nicodemus a deep hunger, an emptiness. Here was a man who was doing his level best to obey what he thought God wanted, yet he had an empty and

Bought

unsatisfied heart that led him to seek out Jesus by night, at the risk of the displeasure of his peers, to talk with him about the kingdom of God. Sensing this, our Lord immediately puts him on the right track, saying to him, in effect, "You are wasting your time if you think you can enter the kingdom of God the way you are. You cannot do it. You must be born again."

Bought: Simple past tense and past participle of buy. Synonymous to purchase in the gospel context – That Christians have been redeemed, or recovered to God; (1 Corinthians 6: 19 - 20) "Or do you not know that your body is a temple of the Holy Spirit who is in you, whom you have from God, and that you are not your own? For you have been bought with a price: therefore glorify God in your body. (1 Corinthians 7:23-24) "You were bought with a price; do not become slaves of men. Brethren, each one is to remain with God in that condition in which he was called" 2 that this has been done by a "valuable consideration," or that which, in his view, was a full equivalent for the sufferings that they would have endured if they had suffered the penalty of the law;3 That this valuable consideration was the blood of Jesus, as an atoning sacrifice, an offering, a ransom, which "would accomplish the same great ends in maintaining the truth and honour of God, and the majesty of his law, as the eternal condemnation of the sinner would have done;" and which, therefore, may be called, figuratively, the price which was paid. For if the same ends of justice could be accomplished by his atonement which would have been by the death of the sinner himself, then it was consistent for God to pardon him. 4 Nothing else could or would have done this. There was no price which the sinner could pay, no atonement which he could make; and consequently, if Christ had not died, the sinner would have been the slave of sin, and the servant of the devil forever. 5 As the Christian is thus purchased, ransomed, redeemed, he is bound to devote himself to God only, and to keep his commands, and to flee from a licentious life. Glorify God - Honour God; live to him; (Matthew 5:16); "In the same way, let your light shine before others, that they may see your good deeds and glorify your Father in heaven". Also in (John 12:28); "Father, glorify Your name." Then a voice came out of heaven: "I have both glorified it, and will glorify it again." The perfections of his nature, particularly his justice and holiness, meaning in himself; by his sufferings and death; intimating hereby, that his Father's glory was what he had in view, and that the securing of that would give him an infinite pleasure amidst all his sorrows. The Arabic version, and Nonnus, read "glorify thy Son", as in (John 17:1) , and the Ethiopic version takes

Bound

in both, "glorify thy name, and thy Son": and indeed, what glorifies the one, glorifies the other;

> Then came there a voice from heaven as at his baptism and transfiguration, and which came from the Father, and was an articulate one, and what the Jews call "Bath Kol", or "the daughter of the voice": (saying], I have both, glorified it; - meaning in the incarnation, ministry, obedience and miracles of Christ; and particularly in that late one in raising Lazarus from the dead:

Bound: (bound·ed, bound·ing, bounds) - To leap forward or upward; spring. To progress by forward leaps or springs. 3 To bounce; rebound. A leap; a jump. A rebound; a bounce. In a simple meaning this implies dependency in the gospel where with every gospel is given, spoken, and must be adopted or applied by the inspiration of the Holy Spirit to make the gospel to manifest correctly according to the precept of righteousness in God and faith toward Christ Jesus. (2 Timothy 3:16): "All scripture is given by inspiration of God, and is profitable (or to be used) for doctrine, (well, doctrine isn't popular today) reproof, for correction"— We scarcely hear of reproof for correction because righteousness is not being preach in the television these days. So if the basic ingredient of the gospel is removed or is abased, does the teachings bound by the Spirit? This shows that the Spirit is the giver through God Grace, then for what is given to be effective it must be receive in the spirit and must be used through the spirit to make fulfil the bound in the gospel – Hallelujah!

Bound by the Spirit: The phrase *bound by the Spirit,* signifies the abiding in the gospel through righteousness since He has made us the Righteousness of God through Christ Jesus. (Acts 20:21). "Testifying both to the Jews, and also to the Greeks, repentance toward God, and faith toward our Lord Jesus Christ." repentance toward God makes us righteous through Christ Jesus who shaded His blood for us as a ransom. If we don't know Him, we are definitely of our own mind and not bound by the Spirit. and we are in rebellion against God, so we need to turn, we need to turn back to God.

Bread: Bread simply means food. Bread is a staple food prepared from a dough of flour and water, usually by baking. Throughout recorded history it has been popular around the world and is one of humanity's oldest foods, having been of importance since the dawn of agriculture. There are very many combinations and proportions of types of flour and other ingredients, and also of different traditional recipes and modes of preparation of bread. As a result, there are a wide varieties of types, shapes, sizes, and textures of breads in various regions. Bread may be leavened by many different processes ranging from the use of naturally occurring microbes (for example in sourdough recipes) to high-pressure artificial aeration methods during preparation or baking. However, some products are left unleavened, either for preference, or for traditional or religious reasons. Many non-cereal ingredients may be included, ranging from fruits and nuts to various fats. Commercial bread in particular, commonly contains additives, some of them non-nutritional, to improve flavour, texture, colour, or shelf life. Depending on local custom and convenience, bread may be served in various forms at any meal of the day. It also is eaten as a snack, or used as an ingredient in other culinary preparations, such as fried items coated in crumbs to prevent sticking, or the bland main component of a bread pudding, or stuffing's designed to fill cavities or retain juices that otherwise might drip away. Partly because of its importance as a basic foodstuff bread has a social and emotional significance beyond its importance in nutrition; it plays essential roles in religious rituals and secular culture. Its prominence in daily life is reflected in language, where it appears in proverbs, colloquial expressions ("He stole the bread from my mouth"), in prayer ("Give us this day our daily bread") as in (John 6:50-71) This is the bread that comes down from heaven, so that one may eat of it and not die. I am the living bread that came down from heaven. If anyone eats of this bread, he will live forever. And the bread that I will give for the life of the world is my flesh." The Jews then disputed among themselves, saying, "How can this man give us his flesh to eat?" So Jesus said to them, "Truly, truly, I say to you, unless you eat the flesh of the Son of Man and drink his blood, you have no life in you. Whoever feeds on my flesh and drinks my blood has eternal life, and I will raise him up on the last day. Here we can see the true gospel meaning of bread – the flesh of the 'Son of Man' eternal life and even in the etymology of words such as "companion" and "company" (literally those who eat/share bread with you like in Eucharist and Communion) as is the practice in many Christian Churches.

Bread of Life: (phrase denoting) An episode in the life of Jesus Christ that appears in the Gospel of John. Bread is the staff of life. A 17th century proverbs. Bread has long been important in religion and the Gospel of Christ. It has been mentioned in many contexts in the bible. And Jesus said unto them, I am the *bread of life* he that cometh to me shall never hunger: (John 6 v 35). Bread of life; divine-

Bread Breaking

ly essential and supernaturally important that true Christians seek the bread of life – Christ by keeping and doing the word of God and obeying his commandment. 2 The title Bread of Life for Jesus is based on the Biblical episode which takes place in the Gospel of John shortly after the feeding of the multitude (in which Jesus feeds the crowds with five loaves of bread and two fishes) after which the crowds follow Jesus to the other side of lake after Jesus walk on water. In the Gospel of John – Jesus said to them "Very truly, I tell you it was not Moses who gave you the bread from heaven, but it is my Father who gives you the true bread from heaven. For the bread of God is that which comes down from heaven and gives life to the world" They said to him "Sir give us this bread always." Jesus said to them "I am the bread of life. Whoever comes to me will never be hungry, and whoever believes in me will never be thirsty (John 6: 32-35)

Bread Breaking: Physically tearing a loaf of bread open, or breaking dry bread apart – traditionally method of separating bread, rather than cutting with a knife. Metaphorically, having a meal together, in communion or starting a meal. The Christian Eucharist. (Luke 22:19) And he took bread, and gave thanks, and brake [it], and gave unto them, saying, This is my body which is given for you: this do in remembrance me. (**Acts 2:42**) - And they continued steadfastly in the apostles' doctrine and fellowship, and in breaking of bread, and in prayers. (Acts 2:44-47) - And all that believed were together, and had all things common; (1 Corinthians 11:23-26) – For I have received of the Lord that which also I delivered unto you, That the Lord Jesus the [same] night in which he was betrayed took bread: And when he had given thanks, he brake [it], and said, Take, eat: this is my body, which is broken for you: this do in remembrance of me. After the same manner also [he took] the cup, when he had supped, saying, This cup is the new testament in my blood: this do ye, as oft as ye drink [it], in remembrance of me. For as often as ye eat this bread, and drink this cup, ye do show the Lord's death till he come. (**Acts 20:7**) - And upon the first [day] of the week, when the disciples came together to *break bread*, Paul preached unto them, ready to depart on the morrow; and continued his speech until midnight.

Bread from Heaven: Simply food from Heaven. Bread itself means something that can connote food in general. In the banquet given to his brethren by Joseph, He commanded the servants to set bread on the table – (Genesis 43:31 – 32)…Joseph hurried out for he was deeply stirred over his brother, and he sought a place to weep; and he entered his chamber and wept there. Then he washed his face and came out; and he controlled himself and said, "Serve the meal." So they served him by himself, and them by themselves, and the Egyptians who ate with him by themselves, because the Egyptians could not eat bread with the Hebrews, for that is loathsome to the Egyptians.... In this context, Bread from Heaven is the leaving bread that when one eateth will never die but have eternal life. Jesus is the leaving bread that comet from Heaven as in John 6:50 – 52 "This is the bread which comes down out of heaven, so that one may eat of it and not die. "I am the living bread that came down out of heaven; if anyone eats of this bread, he will live forever; and the bread also which I will give for the life of the world is My flesh." Then the Jews began to argue with one another, saying, "How can this man give us His flesh to eat?" The true meaning of the frsh here is the word of God.

Breastplate: Literally, a piece of armour covering the chest. Gospel wise, this remind us – Christians to prepare and alert, remaining steadfast in prayer and staying constantly in the word. As Paul put it in (1 Thessalonians 5:8), But let us who are of the day be sober, putting on the *breastplate* of faith and love, and as a helmet the hope of Salvation. Faith and love also protect our hearts. It's interesting to study how faith and love relate to righteousness. Faith works "through love" (Galatians 5:6) and Abraham's faith (which was shown by his doing what God said to do) was "accounted to him for righteousness" (Romans 4:3; Genesis 26:5). As many inspired commentators puts it: "'Faith,' as the motive within, and 'love,' exhibited in outward acts, constitute the perfection of righteousness" (note on (1 Thessalonians 5:8) 2 Facing the hordes of Satan, you brace yourself and pray. The hosts of your enemy share a collective, malicious grin, waiting for the command to do their worst. The battle cry sounds. They begin their charge; you tighten your grip on your sword and raise your shield. Weapons begin swinging with unrivalled fury; you do your best to parry the onslaught, but there are too many weapons to block. Eventually, you watch as one of your opponent's swords begins making a clean arc that continues right past your shield and toward your chest. 3 Breastplate -You brace yourself, preparing for the worst and expecting your quick demise, watching the weapon move ever closer to you as time slows to a maddening crawl—waiting, waiting, when *Clang!* The reverberating noise of the sword striking your breastplate pierces the air. 4 Shaking your head in disbelief, you look down to find that the breastplate of righteousness stopped the deadly blow in its tracks. Delivered by righteousness and with renewed vigour, you plunge back into the fight. The breastplate was a central part of the Roman soldier's armour—it provided protection for the torso, which contains vital organs like the heart,

Breath

lungs and so on. Without a breastplate, a soldier would be asking for death, as any attack could instantly become fatal. With a sturdy *breastplate*, the very same attacks become ineffective and useless, as blows glance off the armour. (Proverbs 11:4) "Riches do not profit in the day of wrath, but righteousness delivers from death. Without righteousness, we leave ourselves open to almost certain death. With righteousness—just as with a *breastplate*—the otherwise fatal attacks of our enemy are thwarted. (Psalm 119:172) "My tongue shall speak of Your word, for all Your commandments are righteousness". (1 John 3:4) Whoever commits sin also commits lawlessness, and sin is lawlessness "1 Corinthians 15:34 Awake to righteousness, and do not sin; for some do not have the knowledge of God"

Breath: (noun) The air taken into or expelled from the lungs."I was gasping for breath" synonymous to wind; informal puff synonyms to the: gulp of air, inhalation, inspiration; More archaic the power of breathing; life. synonyms: life, life force, animation, vital force - "there was no *breath* left in him" 2 A divine source of life and power. *Breath* is the unique and the limited creation of God – No one else can create *breath* but God. (Genesis 2:7) "Then the LORD God formed man of dust from the ground, and *breathed* into his nostrils the breath of life; and man became a living being".

"By His breath the heavens are cleared; His hand has pierced the fleeing serpent.

(Job 33:4) "The Spirit of God has made me, And the breath of the Almighty gives me life".

Breathing: The process that moves air in and out of the lungs or oxygen through other breathing organs such as gills. For organisms with lungs, breathing is also called ventilation, and it includes both inhalation and exhalation. Breathing is one part of physiological respiration and is required to sustain life. Aerobic organisms of these types—such as birds, mammals, and reptiles—require oxygen to release energy via cellular respiration, in the form of the metabolism of energy-rich molecules such as glucose. Breathing is only one process that delivers oxygen to where it is needed in the body and removes carbon dioxide. Another important process involves the movement of blood by the circulatory system. Gas exchange occurs in the pulmonary alveoli by passive diffusion of gases between the alveolar gas and the blood in lung capillaries. Once these dissolved gases are in the blood, the heart powers their flow around the body (via the circulatory system). The medical term for normal relaxed breathing is eupnea.

Breath of God: The eventful and living force from a supernatural being – God. In other word a divine power at work. The Holy Spirit through which deadly things must turn around and live. Spiritual action that normalise a deadly or stagnant condition. (John 20:21-22) So Jesus said to them again, "Peace be with you; as the Father has sent Me, I also send you." And when He had said this, He breathed on them and said to them, "Receive the Holy Spirit.

Breath of Life: The wind, the wave or storm. All lively acts from God that makes a deadly thing or situation to live. (Ezekiel 37: 1-2) God grabbed me. God's Spirit took me up and set me down in the middle of an open plain strewn with bones. He led me around and among them—a lot of bones! There were bones all over the plain—dry bones, bleached by the sun. 3 He said to me, "Son of man, can these bones live?"

I said, "Master God, only you know that." 4 He said to me, "Prophesy over these bones: 'Dry bones, listen to the Message of God!'" 5-6 God, the Master, told the dry bones, "Watch this: I'm bringing the breath of life to you and you'll come to life. I'll attach sinews to you, put meat on your bones, cover you with skin, and breathe life into you. You'll come alive and you'll realize that I am God!" 7-8 I prophesied just as I'd been commanded. As I prophesied, there was a sound and, oh, rustling! The bones moved and came together, bone to bone. I kept watching. Sinews formed, then muscles on the bones, then skin stretched over them. But they had no breath in them. 9 He said to me, "Prophesy to the breath. Prophesy, son of man. Tell the breath, 'God, the Master, says, Come from the four winds. Come, breath. Breathe on these slain bodies. Breathe life!'" 10 So I prophesied, just as he commanded me. The breath entered them and they came alive! They stood up on their feet, a huge army. 11 Then God said to me, "Son of man, these bones are the whole house of Israel. Listen to what they're saying: 'Our bones are dried up, our hope is gone, there's nothing left of us.'

Brimstone: This is used often in the gospel as expression of damnation or God's punishment particularly to the heathen. 2 Fire and *brimstone*, an idiomatic expression of signs of God's wrath in the Bible, or a style of Christian preaching that uses vivid descriptions of judgment and eternal damnation to encourage repentance. Brimstone (man now calls it "sulfur/sulphur") is a lemon-yellow colored stone. Brimstone means, "burning stone" or, "the stone that burns." At left is a picture of *brimstones* and powdered *brimstone*. When a plain *brimstone* (like those to the left) is exposed to the air, nothing happens--but if a match is put to it, it will burn in a peculiar way, like a liquid fire, and it emits noxious fumes. The stone melts like wax but the dripping is a peculiar

Breath

thick fire, like a piece of wax on fire. As it burns, it has a rich, fluorescent-type deep cobalt bluish colour (see below right). It is an interesting, sticky, "acidy"-type burning fire. The little drops burn for some time. Ancient peoples sometimes used *brimstone* as a type of match.

3 A burning match held under brimstone causes it to catch on fire. It then melts and drips like wax and gives off fumes that do something to your nostrils--I know because I burned some (the brimstones that I have are about one and a half inches long and maybe about an inch wide). The fumes should not be breathed in, it is dangerous. I read on the internet that: The fumes from burning sulphur...are "toxic and dangerously irritating..."

4 *Brimstone* starts out in the molten rock under the earth's surface. It spews out in the lava of volcanoes and often comes to the surface of the earth from volcanoes and hot springs. Sulphur deposits have been found on the Italian island of Sicily where it lay near the surface of the earth and also Louisiana (USA) deep underground near the Gulf of Mexico. One quote from the internet said, "a hundred years ago, people used to make a suspension of sulphur powder in molasses and drink it as a health tonic." I don't know anything about this type of usage and have not tried it and do not intend to try it in the absence of further pertinent information--and I do not suggest that anyone else try it.

5 *Brimstone* or sulphur has many commercial/industrial applications. It is often converted to sulphuric acid which is so widely used that it is known as the "king of chemicals." Brimstone/sulphur is used for things such as fertilizer, car batteries, chemical/petroleum refining, paper, rayon, film, automobile tires, paint, detergents, explosives, matches, food processing (sulphur dioxide in food preservation can be harmful), drugs, and dyes. It is said that sulphur is used at some stage of almost everything we eat, wear, or use. It is used to bleach fabrics. Too much sulphur dioxide in the air can kill people when they breathe it in--it causes choking and suffocation. It causes the throat and breathing passages to become irritated and closed up. Hell and death and all the wicked are going to be cast into the lake of fire that burned with fire and brimstone (Revelation 21:8). This is the second death. We all have to die the first time--sin requires that--but if a person dies without the Lord Jesus Christ, he will die a second time-but he will not die to go to sleep, he will continually be burning and tormented for ever--when unrepentant sinners die now, they go to hell, but at the end, when the Lord judges the world, hell and death and the wicked shall be cast into the lake of fire. Sin is when people break

God's commands--like when they lie, steal, rob, covet, etc. All of us have sinned and come short of the glory of God but God does not want to cast us in hell--that is why he sent his Son, the Lord Jesus Christ, to shed his blood to pay for our sins. The Lord Jesus Christ did not remain dead, he rose from the dead on the third day and if we put our trust in him and obey his word, we will be saved and will go to heaven when we die.

Hell is real and one day, hell and death are going to be cast into the lake of fire that burned with fire and *brimstone*. Now, while you are alive, is the time to get your testimony for the Lord Jesus Christ. The Lord Jesus Christ is the author of eternal salvation unto all them that OBEY him (Hebrews 5:9). Heaven is not for the disobedient and unrighteous. It is not for liars, whoremongers, murderers, sodomites, thieves, etc. It is for God and his people. I'm not trying to put anybody down, we have all sinned and come short of the glory of God. All saved people used to be unsaved. We were the liars, whoremongers, sodomites, thieves, etc. but we repented and believed in the blood of Jesus that he shed for our sins so that we could be forgiven. Then the Lord Jesus Christ gave us a whole new life, a clean one, and we purpose to keep his commandments which are found in his holy word. There is rejoicing in heaven over one sinner that repented. Jesus Christ is the ONLY way to God. If you continue in his word then are you his disciple indeed (John 8:31). "As the days go by, evil men and seducers are waxing worse and worse deceiving and being deceived. The end of time is near". The Lord Jesus Christ is coming back again to judge the world. (Don't be burnt in *brimstone.)*

Bring (Brought –passive): Cause to happen. Take or go with (someone or something) to a place. "she brought Luke home from the Church" synonyms: conduct, escort, guide, lead, usher, show, show someone the way, lead the way, pilot, accompany; More antonyms: follow cause (someone or something) to come to a place. "what brings you here?" synonyms: carry, fetch, bear, take; More involve (someone) in a particular activity. "he has brought in a new life in Christ Jesus" synonyms: involve, include, count in, take in "it was nice of him to bring me in on it" cause someone to receive (an amount of money) as income or profit "two important Chippendale lots brought (synonyms): earn, make, bring in, fetch, yield, net, gross; More cause (someone or something) to move in a particular direction. "he brought his hands out of his pockets" cause (something). "the bad weather brought famine" (synonymous): cause, make happen, bring about/on, give rise to, create, produce, result in,

Broken

wreak, effect, engender, occasion, generate, lead to, precipitate, kindle, trigger (off), spark (off), touch off, stir up, whip up, promote, contribute to; as in (Isaiah 66:9) " Do I bring to the moment of birth and not give delivery?" says the LORD. "Do I close up the womb when I bring to delivery?" says your Gods'. 2 Cause (someone or something) to be in a particular state or condition. As in (Genesis 1:20) "And God said, Let the waters bring forth abundantly the moving creature that hath life, and fowl that may fly above the earth in the open firmament of heaven".) Also, "He fail to do the prayer that would have brought the country to financial freedom" initiate (fast and pray session) against a bad situation. (synonyms): put forward, prefer, propose, present, submit, lay, initiate, introduce, institute, moot antonyms: 4 force oneself to do something unpleasant "she could not bring her child to dedication in early. "synonyms: force oneself to, make oneself, bear to "he couldn't bring himself to the Christ when he was alive"

Broken: The past participle of break, present – broke) (Psalm 51:17-18) "The sacrifices of God are a *broken* spirit; A broken and a contrite heart, O God, You will not despise. By Your favour do good to Zion; Build the walls of Jerusalem." Adjective -2. fractured, smashed, or splintered: a broken vase. 3 imperfect or incomplete; fragmentary: a broken set of books. 4 interrupted; disturbed; disconnected: broken sleep. . intermittent or discontinuous: broken sunshine. 6. (Music, other) varying in direction or intensity, as of pitch: a broken note; a broken run.

7. not functioning: a broken radio. 8 spoilt or ruined by divorce (especially in the phrases broken home, broken marriage) 9 (of a trust, promise, contract, etc) violated; infringed 10 overcome with grief or disappointment: a broken heart. (Psalms 51:17) "The sacrifices of God are a *broken* spirit; A broken and a contrite heart, O God, You will not despise". 11 (Grammar) (of the speech of a foreigner) imperfect in grammar, vocabulary, and pronunciation: broken English 12 Also: broken-in made tame or disciplined by training: a broken horse; a broken recruit. 13 exhausted or weakened as through ill-health or misfortune 14 confused or disorganized: broken ranks of soldiers. 15 breached or opened: broken defensive lines. 16 irregular or rough; uneven: broken ground. 17 bankrupt or out of money: a broken industry. 18 (Colours) (of colour) having a multi-coloured decorative effect, as by stippling paint onto a surface. Remember "The LORD is near to the broken hearted And saves those who are crushed in spirit" – (Psalm 34:18).

Brooks: (noun) (1 Kings 17:3) "Get thee hence, and turn thee eastward, and hide thyself by the brook Cherith, that is before Jordan".

Brooks

A brook is a small stream. "The Lake District boasts lovely lakes and babbling brooks" synonyms: stream, small river, streamlet, rivulet, rill, brooklet, runnel, runlet, freshet, gill; (verb: brook; 3rd person present: brooks; past tense: brooked; past participle: brooked; gerund or present participle: brooking) Other meanings are to tolerate or allow (something, typically dissent or opposition). "Nathalie would brook no criticism of Andrew" synonyms: tolerate, allow, stand, bear, abide, stomach, swallow, put up with, go along with, endure, suffer, withstand, cope with;

2 A torrent - Applied to small streams, as the Arnon, Jabbok, etc. (Isaiah 15:7) speaks of the "book of the willows," probably the Wady-el-Asha.

It is also applied to winter torrents (Job 6:15 ; Numbers 34:5 ; Joshua 15:4 Joshua 15:47), and to the torrent-bed or wady as well as to the torrent itself (Numbers 13:23 ; 1 Kings 17:3). One thing to note about a *brook* in the gospel is that it is the beginning of glories from grace. When Elijah was in the *brook* of Cherith as commanded by God he was under grace; but when the *brook* at Cherith dried up, by still maintaining the faith or his Faith in the Lord, he was moved to another grace in Seraphath. Was Elijah backsliding when the *brook* dried up on him? No, he was growing spiritually. Zarephath was many times more wonderful than Cherith. But please take note that God closed up Cherith before He revealed Zarephath. Faith had to be tested. There is always the time when everything looks absolutely hopeless. It happened with Elijah, Job, Joseph, Paul and it will happen to us as followers of Christ.

2 Many Christians stand with people beside their dried-up *brooks* trying to help them in daily basis trying to see that their world has not come to an end. In fact one of the hardest questions for Pastors or Ministers of the gospel are always "Why's?" Why did my baby die? Why did I lose my job, Children? Why are my children so unconcerned about spiritual things? Why did my companion abandon me for another? Lord, why didn't you answer my prayer and make miracle, signs and wonders to happen in my Church, so that multitude of people can throng in and pay tithes and offerings for the Church growth? With Elijah's example, *Brook* can be defined as the first stage of grace enjoyed after every temptation or God favourable act of grace in favour of an undeserved person. For the favour from God to abound, water flowing from brook can dried up after sometimes like the case of Elijah, or flowing to supply the needs according to His sufficient grace. Note the waters falling from brooks sometimes don't flow, oftentimes, the water is still; Whether a brook is still or flowing, depends on what the Lord want to

accomplish. For example, if God want to provide security for a city or a country, He can cause the running water falling from the brooks to settled and surround the city or country and He can empty it, make it dried up as in the afforded protection to a country in (Isaiah 19:6) "And they shall turn the rivers far away; and the brooks of defence shall be emptied and dried up: the reeds and flags shall wither". About eight brooks are mentioned as important in the gospel. As Christians, we must understand the manifestation of God's power in each of them – starting from the brooks of Arnon, Besor, Gaash, Cherith, Eshcol, Kidron, Kishon, Zered and of the Willows. Praise the Lord!

3 Read more about brooks in the following biblical verses (2 Samuel 17:20) And when Absalom's servants came to the woman to the house, they said, Where is Ahimaaz and Jonathan? And the woman said unto them, They be gone over the *brook* of water. And when they had sought and could not find them, they returned to Jerusalem. (2 Samuel 23:30) Benaiah the Pirathonite, Hiddai of the *brooks* of Gaash, (1 Kings 2:37) For it shall be, that on the day thou goest out, and passest over the *brook* Kidron, thou shalt know for certain that thou shalt surely die: thy blood shall be upon thine own head. (1 Kings 15:13) And also Maachah his mother, even her he removed from being queen, because she had made an idol in a grove; and Asa destroyed her idol, and burnt it by the *brook* Kidron. (1 Kings 18:40) And Elijah said unto them, Take the prophets of Baal; let not one of them escape. And they took them: and Elijah brought them down to the *brook* Kishon, and slew them there. (2 Kings 23:6) the LORD, without Jerusalem, unto the *brook* Kidron, and burned it at the *brook* Kidron, and stamped it small to powder, and cast the powder thereof upon the graves of the children of the people. (2 Kings 23:12) And the altars that were on the top of the upper chamber of Ahaz, which the kings of Judah had made, and the altars which Manasseh had made in the two courts of the house of the LORD, did the king beat down, and brake them down from thence, and cast the dust of them into the *brook* Kidron.

Brook, Favours at: This means an unrequested favour from God to His Love ones, Children or Servant as in Grass. (1 Kings 18:5) "And Ahab said unto Obadiah, Go into the land, unto all fountains of water, and unto all brooks: peradventure we may find grass to save the horses and mules alive, that we lose not all the beasts. Willows (Leviticus 23:40) And ye shall take you on the first day the boughs of goodly trees, branches of palm trees, and the boughs of thick trees, and willows of the brook; and ye shall rejoice before the LORD your God seven days. Also, (Job 40:22) the shady trees cover him with their shadow; the willows of the brook compass him about. Reeds; (Isaiah 19:7) The paper reeds by the brooks, by the mouth of the brooks, and everything sown by the brooks, shall wither, be driven away, and be no more. Abounded with fish; (Isaiah 19:8) the fishers also shall mourn, and all they that cast angle into the brooks shall lament, and they that spread nets upon the waters shall languish. Afforded protection to a country; (Isaiah 19:6) "And they shall turn the rivers far away; and the brooks of defence shall be emptied and dried up: the reeds and flags shall wither".

Brook, Flowing: "This has to do with wisdom as in (Proverbs 18:4) "The words of a man's mouth are as deep waters, and the wellspring of wisdom as a *flowing brook*".

Brook of Honey, The: This has to do with temporal abundance as in (Job 20:17) "He shall not see the rivers, the floods, *the brooks of honey* and butter".

Brook, Stream of: (Deceptive) This has to do with false friends as in (Job 6:15) "My brethren have dealt deceitfully as a brook, and as the *stream of brooks* they pass away";

Brook, Drink of the: Otherwise, phrased in the way of drinking. Meaning to render help in distress as in (Psalms 110:7) "He shall drink of the brook in the way: therefore shall he lift up the head".

Brother: A male born by the same mother or father or by both to another in biological relationship. 2 A good and True friend like Jesus. A good friend is better than bad brother - But the rich man answers roughly. A man of too many friends comes to ruin, But there is a friend who sticks closer than a brother.– (Proverbs 18:24) and (Proverbs 17:17) A friend loves at all times, and a brother is born for adversity.2 There have been many cases where brothers have given much for each other. Brothers have died for one another... Brothers have given organs to one another.. Brothers have taken the hit for one another... Brothers have gone to jail for one another... Brothers have rescued one another during perilous situations...

Brother, There is friend that sticks closer than a...: In this world, there are numerous types of friendships. There is a faucet friendship that people turn on and off. There is fake friendship wherein folk will fake you out when you need them most. There is a fair weather friend that will remain so long as the weather is fair. There are get-over and get under friends. These are all worldly friendships. But in our text today, Solomon introduces us to a unique friend, that will stick closer than a broth-

Burden

er. Let us consider the meaning of a genuine friendship. Friendship is the covenantal binding together of two people. Friendship is always preceded by self-giving. The first friend in the bible was God Himself. The first gift of the first friend was another friend. It was God who determined from the beginning that "it was not good for man to be alone." He then made woman to be a friend of man, from man. Friendship is based on the agape' or what is more aptly called the biblical love. It is the love of God that is shed abroad in the believer's heart. Love is a desire for and a delight in the well-being of the one loved; leading to an active and a self-sacrificing effort of on their behalf. God Himself is the very essence of friendship. The God-head is a perfect unity, wherein God is in relationship with Himself. A friend is someone you can be yourself with. A friend is someone who knows your weakness and respect your strenght. Abraham Lincoln said: "The better part of one's life consists of his friendships." "The only way to have a friend is to be one." A brother-friend is one who is a source of sunshine when you are under the weather. A brother-friend is one who believes in you, when you cease to believe in yourself. A brother-friend is a source of celebration when you feel that there is nothing to celebrate. A brother- friend is one who answers your call before you call. Friendship is of two categories. It is first vertical or God-ward and second horizontal or a reaching outward. Friendship thrives upon sacrifice. You can give without love but you cannot love without giving. True friendship is when two friends can wak in opposite directions, and yet remain side by side. A friend is one who walks in when the rest of the world walks out. A friendship with Jesus is truly the only unsinkable-ship. First the text teaches us something about highest measure of human friendship. To that end Solomon uses not a mother, not a father or a sister but a brother.

Burden. (noun a load, typically a heavy one. synonyms: l o a d , cargo, freight, weight; More a duty or misfortune that causes worry, hardship, or distress. "the tax burden on low-wage earners" synonyms: responsibility, onus, charge, duty, obligation, liability; More the main responsibility for achieving a specified aim or task. "the burden of establishing that the authority had misused its powers rests upon the prosecution" a ship's carrying capacity; tonnage. "the schooner Wyoming, of about 6,000 tons burden" 2. the main theme or gist of a speech, book, or argument. synonyms: gist, substance, drift, implication, intention, thrust, meaning, significance, signification, sense, essence, thesis, import, purport, tenor, message, spirit "the burden of his message" 3. archaic the refrain or chorus of a song .verb: burden; 3rd person present: burdens; past tense: burdened; past participle: burdened; gerund or present participle: burdening load heavily. "she walked forwards burdened with a wooden box" synonyms: load, weight, charge; More

Burden, Bear one another's: Take others load to provide solution. Provide solution and care to others as if they were yours. Jesus is the best friend who cares about all our situations and redeemed us by His blood on the cross. (Galatians 6: 1-3) "Brethren, even if anyone is caught in any trespass, you who are spiritual, restore such a one in a spirit of gentleness; each one looking to yourself, so that you too will not be tempted. Bear one another's burdens, and thereby fulfil the law of Christ. For if anyone thinks he is something when he is nothing, he deceives himself...."

Burnt Offering: (Greek: *Holocaustos*, Hebrew: *Koban alah*) The burnt offering is one of the oldest and most common offerings in history. It's entirely possible that Abel's offering in (Genesis 4:4) was a burnt offering, although the first recorded instance is in (Genesis 8:20) when Noah offers burnt offerings after the flood. God ordered Abraham to offer his son, Isaac, in a burnt offering in (Genesis 22), and then provided a ram as a replacement. After suffering through nine of the ten plagues, Pharaoh decided to let the people go from bondage in Egypt, but his refusal to allow the Israelites to take their livestock with them in order to offer *burnt offerings* brought about the final plague that led to the Israelites' delivery (Exodus 10:24-29). The Hebrew word for "burnt offering" actually means to "ascend," literally to "go up in smoke." The smoke from the sacrifice ascended to God, "a soothing aroma to the LORD" (Leviticus 1:9). Technically, any offering burned over an altar was a burnt offering, but in more specific terms, a burnt offering was the complete destruction of the animal (except for the hide) in an effort to renew the relationship between Holy God and sinful man. With the development of the law, God gave the Israelites specific instructions as to the types of burnt offerings and what they symbolized. (Leviticus 1) and (Leviticus 6:8-13) describe the traditional burnt offering. The Israelites brought a bull, sheep, or goat, a male with no defect, and killed it at the entrance to the tabernacle. The animal's blood was drained, and the priest sprinkled blood around the altar. The animal was skinned and cut it into pieces, the intestines and legs washed, and the priest burned the pieces over the altar all night. The priest received the skin as a fee for his help. A turtledove or pigeon could also be sacrificed, although they weren't skinned. 3 A person could give a *burnt offering* at any time. It was a sacrifice of

Bushel

general atonement—an acknowledgement of the sinful nature of man and a request for renewed relationship with God. God also set times for the priests to give a *burnt offering* for the benefit of the Israelites as a whole, although the animals required for each sacrifice varied: Every morning and evening (Exodus 29:38-42;(Numbers28:2) Each Sabbath (Numbers 28:9-10) The beginning of each month (Numbers 28:11) At Passover (Numbers28:19) With the new grain/first fruits offering at the Feast of Weeks (Numbers28:27) At the Feast of Trumpets/Rosh Hashanah (Numbers29:1) At the new moon (Numbers 29:6) The ultimate fulfilment of the physical life was completely consumed, He ascended to God, and His covering (that is, His garment) was distributed to those who officiated over His sacrifice (Matthew 27:35). But most importantly, His sacrifice, once for all time, atoned for our sins and restored our relationship with God.

Bushel: (noun – Bushelful, Bushelfuls -plural): A measure of capacity equal to 8 gallons (equivalent to 36.4 litres), used for corn, fruit, liquids, Jesus Christ used salt and light to express the extent of our faith by showing that we cannot receive the gospel – 'light' and cover it with worldly fleshly or earthly things. If that is done the gospel we receive will lose its taste like salt that wash off of original taste. (Mathew 5:15) "Neither do men light a candle, and put it under a bushel, but on a candlestick; and it giveth light unto all that are in the house". (Mathew 5:14-16)... "You are the light of the world. A city set on a hill cannot be hidden; nor does anyone light a lamp and put it under a basket, but on the lampstand, and it gives light to all who are in the house. "Let your light shine before men in such a way that they may see your good works, and glorify your Father who is in heaven. Here the gospel explains the good works that are abound in the word we received as Christians, Nevertheless, if we as the 'light of the world' receives the gospel and apply it correctly, we become a city that cannot be hidden, but progress to fulfil the purpose of God to us – A Royal priesthood, A Holy Nation that cannot be hidden but allow our light to shine before all men – with Good works through His Grace, Salvation, Favour, Redemption, fill with Holy Ghost as the Spirit direct. 2 Bushel, therefore is use in this context to stand for the measure of our faith. Firstly, if we can have faith like the little seed of the mustard, the gospel declare, we can tell this mountain be ye move and it will move. The seed of the mustard is a measure. Mustard is a grain like corn, rice and other cereals. Then when our light shine by keeping and doing the word accordingly we shall grow, multiply and move from faith to faith – meaning from one measure to another, the essence being from Glory to Glory according to the 'Glory of the New Covenant' as in

(2 Corinthians 3:17-18) "Now the Lord is the Spirit, and where the Spirit of the Lord is, there is liberty. But we all, with unveiled face, beholding as in a mirror the glory of the Lord, are being transformed into the same image from glory to glory, just as from the Lord, the Spirit" .**Note**: with unveil face not in a *bushel*, but allowing the spirit of light – the very Glory of God are transformed into the same image of God as He also created us in His own image! His first will to us all (Genesis 1:26) "Let us make man in our image", Hallelujah!

Bushel, Hide one's light under a: To avoid letting people know that you are good at something, usually because you are shy (often in continuous tenses) I didn't realize you could preach the gospel - you've been *hiding your light under a bushel.* Hide, cover a multitude of sins, haven't seen hide nor hair of to conceal one's good ideas or talents. (A biblical theme.) Babbra has some good ideas, but she doesn't speak very often. She hides her light under a bushel. Don't hide your light under a bushel. This is to say, you must share your thoughts with other people and be the light of the world. Once you have been sanctified, redeemed and be filled with Holy Ghost, preach the gospel and declare Christ to other people. "Don't hide your light under a bushel!" is the sort of thing you might say to someone who's being a bit bashful about their obvious talents. 2 The saying goes back to a rather comical word-picture of Jesus, where he pictures someone lighting a candle and then sticking it under a big measuring jar, and hoping it will still light up a dark room. He said it to encourage his followers to let their light shine out, so that other people could find the way back to God. Here are his original words, in the old King James version in the gospel...Ye are the light of the world. A city that is set on an hill cannot be hid. Neither do men light a candle, and put it under a bushel, but on a candlestick; and it giveth light unto all that are in the house. Let your light so shine before men, that they may see your good works, and glorify your Father which is in heaven. (Matthew 5:14-16). Glory to God!

By and By: "Face to Face" "... I should see Him By and By." As in the hymn! a future time or occasion. 2 Herodias`s daughter asked by and by John the Baptist`s head in a charger.. Time to escape the situation was given (by-and-by) But Herod's Pride lost him the way of escape - He liked John (1Cor 10:13) and immediately Herod sent for the executioner. .Note: John did not belong to Harrods Kingdom but 'Gods'. And John had let a little doubt drop his guard a little, in that when he sent to 'Jesus' from prison the message asking: "Are You `the One` or should we look for another.? KJV bible.

Call

Cc

Call: (calling – present continuous) call or calling has diverse meanings in everyday life and huge importance usage in the gospel. cry out to (someone) in order to summon them or attract their attention. Call someone to be disciple or discipleship, steward or stewardship. This prominent gospel term is used with particular theological significance in three ways: in connection with worship, with election, and with vocation and the general usage in our everyday life. Study it and put it different usage in your spirit.

Call to Worship: To "call on" God or the Lord is a frequent gospel or biblical expression: it occurs fifty-six times in total (Old Testament, 45; New Testament, 11); on four occasions it is applied to other gods. It often appears in the fuller form, "*call* on the name of" (31 times). The highest concentration is in the psalms (16 times). Across the range of its occurrences this expression acquires several nuances. The basic meaning, always present, is simply to utter the name of God (Psalm 116:4 ; Zechariah 13:9). But it can mean more broadly to pray (Psalm 17:6 ; John 1:6 ; Mathew 26:53), and indeed can signify a whole act of cultic worship (Genesis 12:8 ; 1 Chronicle 21:26). More particularly, to call on God's name can mean to appeal to his mercy and power from a situation of weakness and need (2 Kings 5:11 ; Psalm 116:4 ; Lamentation 3:55 ; Mathew 26:53), but more often it connotes a basic commitment to the Lord as opposed to other gods (1 Kings 18:24 ; Psalm 79:6 ; Zechariah 13:9 ; Acts 9:14), sometimes an initial commitment (Genesis 4:26 ; Acts 22:16). With this thought of commitment prominent, calling on the Lord can even have a 'proclamatory flavor': "Give thanks to the Lord, call on his name; make known among the nations what he has done" (1 Chronicle 16:8 ; . Psalm 116:13 ; Isa 12:4). The New Testament use of this expression is remarkable for the way in which it is applied to Jesus. Joel 2:32 is quoted in both Acts 2:21 and Romans 10:13, but in both places "the Lord" is then identified as Jesus (Acts 2:36) ; (Romance 10:14). The dramatic conviction of the first (Jewish) Christians was that

Israel's worship needed to be redirected: people could no longer be saved by calling on Yahweh/Jehovah, the Old Testament name of God, but only on that of Jesus: "there is no other name under heaven given to men by which we must be saved" (Acts 4:12). To "call on the name of our Lord Jesus Christ" (1Corinthians 1:2) therefore means worshiping him with divine honours.

Call to Election: "Call" is one of the biblical words associated with the theme of election. In both Hebrew and Greek, "call" can be used in the sense of "naming" (Genesis 2:19 ; Luke 1:13), and in gospel thought to give a name to something or someone was to bestow an identity. Names often encapsulated a message about the person concerned (Ruth 1:20-21 ; John 1:42 ; . Mathew 16:18). When God is the one who bestows names, the action is almost equivalent to creation: "Who created all these? He who brings out the starry host one by one, and calls them each by name. Because of his great power and mighty strength, not one of them is missing" (Isaiah 40:26). This theme is developed particularly in (Isaiah 40-55), which forms an important background to the New Testament use of the term. The creative "calling" of the stars is matched by the "calling" of Abraham, which meant both the summons to leave Ur and the call to be the father of Israel: "When I called him he was but one, and I blessed him and made him many" (Isaiah 51:2). Similarly Israel the nation has been called-"I took you from the ends of the earth, from its farthest corners I called you" (Isaiah 41:9,. 48:12)-and this means that they are "called by my name ... created for my glory" (Isaiah:43:7;.Hosea 1:10). God has bestowed his own name upon Israel as part of the creative act that made Israel his own elect people. Now also the Servant of the Lord has been "called" to be the Saviour of the world (Isaiah 42:6 ; 49:1); and so has Cyrus, to be the instrument of judgment of Babylon (Isaiah 48:15). Thus in Isaiah "call" brings together the ideas of naming, election, ownership, and appointment, as the word is used with different nuances in different contexts. It connotes the creative word of God, by which he Acts effectively within the world. So, the New Testament picks up all these ideas and takes them further. The influence of Isaiah is seen particularly in the writings of Paul and Peter, who use "call" as a semi-technical term denoting God's effective summons of people to faith in Christ; verb and noun together are used approximately forty-three times with this general denotation. However, within this overall usage various shades of meaning of and nuances may be discerned:

Call to Initiation: "Were you a slave when you were called?" (1 Corinthians 7:21). In this verse and many other places "called" is almost equivalent to "converted, " pointing to the moment of ini-

Call to Naming

tiation when faith was born. But it means more than "converted, " for it points beyond a change of mind and heart to the action of God. This theological hinterland comes out clearly in (Romans 8:30): "those he predestined, he also called; those he called, he also justified." Here the creative word of God is clearly visible. This is not a *"call"* that can be ignored: It comes from one who "gives life to the dead and *calls* things that are not as though they were" (Romance 4:17). By such a creative act God, says Peter, has "called you out of darkness into his wonderful light" and thus formed "a chosen people, a royal priesthood, a holy nation, a people belonging to God" (1 Peter 2:9). Hallelujah!

Call to Naming: This is to be "called" by God which means to be "called" something different: the new name "sons of living God" is given to those whom God has called, both Jews and Gentiles (Romance 9:24-26). Here the notion that God's people bear his own name receives a new shape. In baptism converts were washed, sanctified, justified in the name of the Lord Jesus Christ (1Corinthians 6:11), so that his is "the noble name of him to whom you belong" (James 2:7). Because they bear his name, Paul prays that "the name of our Lord Jesus may be glorified in you" (2 Thess 1:12).

Call to Destiny: In a string of references "call" and "calling" connote the ultimate destiny of believers. The moment at which they were called points ahead to the final goal to which they are called by God (1Corinthians 1:9 ; Ephesians 4:4 ; Philipians 3:14 ; 1 Thessalonica 5:24 ; 1 Tmothy 6:12 ; Hebrew 3:1 ; 1 Peter 5:10).

Call to Holiness: "We constantly pray for you, that our God may count you worthy of his calling" (2 Thesalonica 1:11). The fact of God's call, and the destiny it involves, has moral consequences now. Believers are called to be holy (Romance 1:7 ; 1 Corinthians 1:2), and must walk worthy of their calling (Ephesians 4:1). Peter twice uses the phrase "to this you were called" with reference to the meekness Christians must show their opponents, following the example of Jesus (1 Peter 2:21 ; 3:9).

Call to Apostleship: Apostleship is the only spiritual gift in connection with which the word "call" is used, and it may be that this reflects the uniqueness of the office in Paul's mind. However, from another perspective he regards all spiritual gifts as equally "the work of one and the same Spirit, and he gives them to each one, just as he determines" (1 Corinthians 12:11), and therefore it would probably not be biblically inappropriate to extend the idea of vocation to all ministries within the church. The exercise of whatever gifts we possess is a "call" from God (vocation is not just to the "ordained" ministry!). May we extend the idea of vocation also to cover secular employment? Luther took this step, radically teaching that any work may be a "calling" from God. Some have argued that Paul uses the word "calling" in something like this sense in (1 Corinthians 1:26 and 7:17, 20): "each one should remain in the situation which he was in when God called him" (7:20). Here "called" clearly refers to conversion, but "calling" could refer to the socioeconomic state of the convert (here, slave or freed). Since Paul is happy for this state to be changed, if opportunity presents (1 Corinthians 7:21), it seems unlikely that he would regard it alone as a full "calling" from God. Probably he is using the word in a broad sense: "Let everyone remain loyal to God's call, which means living as a Christian in whatever situation you find yourself."

Call in general Usage:

"she heard Rufus calling her" synonyms: cry out, cry, shout, yell, sing out, whoop, bellow, roar, halloo, bawl, scream, shriek, screech; More cry out (a word or words). "he heard an insistent voice calling his name" synonyms: cry out, cry, shout, yell, sing out, whoop, bellow, roar, halloo, bawl, scream, shriek, screech; More (of an animal, especially a bird) make its characteristic cry. "the mother bird was calling from the twig" shout out or chant (the steps and figures) to people performing a square dance or country dance. telephone (a person or telephone number). "could I call you back?" synonyms: phone, telephone, get on the phone to, get someone on the phone, dial, make/place a call to, get, reach; More summon (an emergency service, taxi, etc.) by telephone. "if you are suspicious, call the police" synonyms: summon, send for, ask for; More bring (a witness) into court to give evidence. "four expert witnesses were called" archaic inspire or urge (someone) to do something. "I am *called* to preach the Gospel" fix a date or time for (a meeting, strike, or election). "she intends to call a meeting of the committee early next week" synonyms: convene, summon, call together, order, assemble; More BRIDGE make (a particular bid) during the auction. "her partner called" guess the outcome of tossing a coin." 'You call,' he said. 'Heads or tails?'" predict the result of (a future event, especially an election or a vote). "in the Midlands the race remains too close to call" CRICKET (of an umpire) no-ball (a bowler) for throwing. "the umpire never called him in a first-class match, only in a festival game" COMPUTING cause the execution of (a subroutine). "one subroutine may call another subroutine (or itself)" 2. give (an infant or animal) a specified name. "they called their daughter Hannah" synonyms: name; More have a specified name. "her companion was called Ethel" address or refer to (someone) by a specified name, title, etc. "please call me Lucy"

Call to Vocation

refer to or consider (someone or something) as being. "he's the only person I would call a friend" synonyms: describe as, regard as, look on as, consider to be, judge to be, think of as, class as, categorize as "he's the only person I would call a friend" (of an umpire or other official in a game) pronounce (a ball, stroke, etc.) to be the thing specified. "the linesman called the ball wide"

3. British (of a person) pay a brief visit. "I've got to call at the bank to get some cash" synonyms: pay a visit to, pay a brief visit to, visit, pay a call on, call in on, look in on; More stop to collect (someone) at the place where they are living or working. "I'll call for you around seven" synonyms: p i c k up, collect, fetch, go/come to get, come for "I'll call for you around seven"(of a train or coach) stop at (a specified station or stations) on a particular route." the 8.15 service to Paddington, calling at Reading" noun: call; plural noun: calls 1. a cry made as a summons or to attract someone's attention. "in response to the call, a figure appeared" synonyms: c r y , shout, yell, whoop, roar, scream, shriek; Morea series of notes sounded on a brass instrument as a signal to do something. "a bugle call to rise at 10.30" a telephone communication or conversation. "I'll give you a call at around five" synonyms: phone call, telephone call; More an appeal or demand for. "the call for action was welcomed" synonyms: appeal, request, plea, entreaty; More a summons. "a messenger arrived bringing news of his call to the throne" synonyms: summons, request "the last call for passengers on flight BA701" a vocation. "his call to be a disciple"a powerful force of attraction. "walkers can't resist the call of the Cairngorms" synonyms: attraction, appeal, lure, allure, allurement, fascination, seductiveness; More demand or need for (goods or services). "there is little call for antique furniture" synonyms: need, necessity, occasion, reason, justification, grounds, excuse, pretext; More a shout by an official in a game indicating that the ball has gone out of play or that a rule has been breached. BRIDGE a bid, response, or double. "the alternative call of 2 would be quite unsound" a direction in a square dance given by the caller. a demand for payment of lent or unpaid capital. STOCK EXCHANGE short for call option. 2. the characteristic cry of a bird or other animal. "it is best distinguished by its call, a loud 'pwit'" synonyms: cry, song, sound "the call of the water rail"

Call to Vocation: Signifies the notion of appointment to office, which we observed in Isaiah, is also taken up in the New Testament. When Paul was "called by grace, " it meant not just his conversion but also his appointment as apostle to the Gentiles (Galatians 1:15). He is therefore "called to be an apostle" (Roman 1:1, 1 Corinthians 1:1).

Cain: (Hebrew - Qayin,) According to the gospel in Book of Genesis, A brother of Abel, (two sons of Adam and Eve). Cain is described as a crop farmer and his younger brother Abel as a shepherd. Cain was the first human born and Abel was the first human to die. Cain committed the first murder by killing his brother. Interpretations of Genesis 4 by ancient and modern commentators have typically assumed that the motives were jealousy and anger. In the Cain and Abel story found in the Quran, the text refers to them simply as the sons of Adam (Arabic). Adam knew his wife Eve intimately, and she conceived and bore Cain. She said, "I have had a male child with the LORD's help.

Camel: An even-toed ungulate within the genus Camelus, bearing distinctive fatty deposits known as "humps" on its back used mostly since the Abrahamic times (Genesis 12:16) "And he entreated Abram well for her sake: and he had sheep, and oxen, and he asses, and menservants, and maidservants, and she asses, and *camels*. Also recorded in (Genesis 24:10) "And the servant took ten *camels* of the *camels* of his master, and departed; for all the goods of his master were in his hand: and he arose, and went to Mesopotamia, unto the city of Nahor.

Once upon a time, Abraham owned a camel. According to the Book of Genesis, he probably owned lots of camels. The Bible says that Abraham, along with other patriarchs of Judaism and Christianity, used domesticated camels — as well as donkeys, sheep, oxen and slaves — in his various travels and trade agreements. Or did he?

The two surviving species of camel are the dromedary, or one-humped camel (dromedarius), which inhabits the Middle East and the Horn of Africa; and the Bactrian, or two-humped camel (bactrianus), which inhabits Central Asia. Both species have been domesticated; they provide milk, meat, hair for textiles or goods such as felted pouches, and are working animals with tasks ranging from human transport to bearing loads. 2 The term "camel" is derived via Latin and Greek (camelus and kamēlos respectively) from Hebrew or Phoenician 'gāmāl'. The Hebrew meaning of the word gāmāl is derived from the verb root meaning (1) stopping, weaning, going without; or (2) repaying in kind. This refers to its ability to go without food or water, as well as the increased ability of service the animal provides when being properly cared for. 3 "Camel" is also used more broadly to describe any of the six camel-like mammals in the family 'Camelidae': the two true camels: the dromedary and bactrian, and the four South

Canaan

American camelids: the llama and alpaca are called "New World camels", while the guanaco and vicuña are called "South American *camels:* 5 Understanding the Case of the Phantom *Camel* as a fight between archaeological evidence and biblical narrative misses the entire spiritual point of the text, as far as scholars are concerned. Anachronisms and apocryphal elements do not mean the story is invalid, but instead give insight into the spiritual community in a given time and place. In this case, *camels* were a sign of wealth and developing trade routes, so it is likely that the biblical writer used the camel as a narrative device to point out power and status. "We needn't understand these accounts as literally true, but they are very rich in meaning and interpretive power," The study is going to ruffle the feathers of people who believe in gospel or biblical inerrancy, a doctrine popular among evangelical and other right-orthodoxy movements that says every word in the Bible is literally true.

Canaan: The fourth son of Ham, (Genesis 10:6; 1 Chronicles 1:8) the progenitor of the Phoenicians [ZIDON, OR SIDON], and of the various nations who before the Israelite conquest people the seacoast of Palestine, and generally the while of the country westward of the Jordan. (Genesis 10:13; 1 Chronicles 1:13) (B.C. 2347.) The name "Canaan" is sometimes employed for the country itself. A region in the Ancient Near East, which as described in the Bible roughly corresponds to the Levant, i.e. modern-day Lebanon, Israel, the western part of Jordan and south-western Syria.

The name is used commonly in the Hebrew Bible, with particular definition in references (Genesis 10) and (Numbers 34), where the "Land of Canaan" extends from Lebanon southward to the "Brook of Egypt" and eastward to the Jordan River Valley. References to Canaan in the Christian gospel are usually backward looking, referring to a region that had become something else (e.g. the Land of Israel), and references to Canaanites commonly describe them as a people who had been annihilated.

2 Archaeological attestation of the name Canaan in Ancient-Near-Eastern sources is almost exclusively during the period in which the region was a colony of the New Kingdom of Egypt, with usage of the name almost disappearing following the Late Bronze Age collapse. The references suggest that during this period the term was familiar to the region's neighbours on all sides, although it has been disputed to what extent such references provide a coherent description of its location and boundaries, and regarding whether the inhabitants used the term to describe themselves. The Amana Letters and other cuneiform

documents use 'Kinahhu', while other sources of the Egyptian New Kingdom mention numerous military campaigns conducted in 'Kana-na'.

3 Canaan was of significant geopolitical importance in the Late Bronze Age Amarna period as the area where the spheres of interest of the Egyptian, Hittite, and Assyrian Empires converged. Much of the modern knowledge about Canaan stems from archaeological excavation in this area at sites such as Tel Hazor, Tel Megiddo and Gezer. Canaanite culture apparently developed in situ from the Circum-Arabian Nomadic Pastoral Complex, which in turn developed from a fusion of Near Eastern Harifian hunter gatherers with Pre-Pottery Neolithic farming cultures, practicing animal domestication, during the 6200 BC climatic crisis. The Late Bronze Age state of Ugarit (at Ras Shamra in Syria) is considered quintessentially Canaanite archaeologically, even though its Ugaritic language does not belong to the Canaanite group proper. Linguistically, the Canaanite languages form a group within the Northwest Semitic languages; its best-known member today is the Hebrew language, being mostly known from Iron Age epigraphy. Other Canaanite languages are Phoenician, Ammonite, Edomite, and Moabite.

Canaanite: A person or a national of Canaan. The name "Canaanite or (Canaanites – plural)" is attested, many centuries later, as the antonym of the people later known to the Ancient Greeks from c.500 BC as Phoenicians, and following the emigration of *Canaanite* speakers to Carthage, was also used as a self-designation by the Punic. This mirrors later usage in later books of the Hebrew Bible, such as at the end of the Book of Zechariah, where it is thought to refer to a class of merchants or to non-monotheistic worshippers in Israel or neighbouring Sidon and Tyre, as well as in its single independent usage in the New Testament, where it is used as a synonym for Syro-phoenician.

Candle: A solid block of wax with an embedded wick which is ignited to provide light, and sometimes heat, and historically was used as a method of keeping time.. For a candle to burn, a heat source (commonly a naked flame) is used to light the *candle's* wick, which melts and vaporizes a small amount of fuel, the wax. Once vaporized, the fuel combines with oxygen in the atmosphere to ignite and form a constant flame. This flame provides sufficient heat to keep the candle burning via a self-sustaining chain of events: the heat of the flame melts the top of the mass of solid fuel; the liquefied fuel then moves upward through the wick via capillary action; the liquefied fuel finally vaporizes to burn within the candle's flame. As the mass of solid fuel is melted and consumed, the candle grows shorter. Portions of the wick

Candle of the Lord

that are not emitting vaporized fuel are consumed in the flame. The incineration of the wick limits the exposed length of the wick, thus maintaining a constant burning temperature and rate of fuel consumption. Some wicks require regular trimming with scissors (or a specialized wick trimmer), usually to about one-quarter inch (~0.7 cm), to promote slower, steady burning, and also to prevent smoking. In early times, the wick needed to be trimmed quite frequently and special candle-scissors, referred to as "snuffers" until the 20th century, were produced for this purpose, and often combined with an extinguisher. In modern candles, the wick is constructed so that it curves over as it burns, so that the end of the wick gets oxygen and is then consumed by fire—a self-trimming wick. As in (Proverbs 20:27) "The spirit of man is the *candle* of the Lord, searching all the inward parts of the belly". Also in ((Luke 11:33) "No man, when he hath lighted a *candle*, putteth it in a secret place, neither under a bushel, but on a candlestick, that they which come in may see the light". And (Luke 11:36) "If thy whole body therefore be full of light, having no part dark, the whole shall be full of light, as when the bright shining of a *candle* doth give thee light". Note candle light can only be used on earth – meaning where darkness abound. It cannot be used in Heaven as described or explained in (Revelation 22:5) "And there shall be no night there; and they need no *candle*, neither light of the sun; for the Lord God giveth them light: and they shall reign for ever and ever". There are about 16 usage of candle in the gospel stories in the bible, read up to discover more.

Candle of the Lord, The spirit of man is the:

If a candle is not lighted, it is standing in darkness until someone comes to light it. To light it means He takes a force and the candle yields to it. When that candle yields to that force, it burns, gives light, and fulfils the purpose for its existence. Unlighted, the candle is not fulfilling its purpose! Lighted, it becomes that for which it was made; it performs the duty for which it was made; and it has fulfilment in its purpose in life. Don't forget, the Bible says, "The spirit of man is the candle of the Lord." God is light and God is fire. When God would manifest Himself on earth, He would do it by sending fire from Heaven. God was a pillar of fire by night. When Jesus spoke to the disciples going to Emmaus, they said, "Did not our heart burn within us?" So when the spirit of man yields itself to the fire of God, only then does he fulfil the purpose for his existence. We'll say several things about the candle and the fire. 1. When two things are made for each other, neither is complete alone. The fire was made for the *candle*, and the *candle* was made for the fire. The *candle* is not complete, for it is alone; and the fire is not complete, for it is alone. Until the fire comes in contact with the *candle*, the fire is not complete and the *candle* is not complete.

The *candle* is a symbol of the spirit of man. Until man's spirit comes in contact with the Lord, his Creator and comes in perfect union with that Creator, it is not complete and man is not fulfilling his purpose in life. Man is not complete without God. The Christian is made to yield himself to the Holy Spirit. 2. Fulfilment comes only when the weaker substance renders itself submissive to the stronger substance. When these two get together, the fire doesn't become a *candle*; the *candle* becomes a fire. Nothing is ever happy or complete in life until that something yields itself to the superior force for which it was made. Every problem that man has comes from this one error: The weaker does not yield him-self to the stronger. The wax must acknowledge that the flame is superior. Hence, it yields to that which is superior and in so doing becomes the best candle it can become and fulfils the purpose for its existence.

In every relationship this is true. A child gets in trouble when he doesn't yield himself to his parents. A human gets in trouble when he doesn't yield himself to his God. A Christian gets in trouble when he doesn't yield himself to the Holy Spirit. A citizen gets in trouble when he doesn't yield himself to his government. A church gets in trouble when she doesn't yield herself to her Christ who is the Head. pastor. A wife gets in trouble when she doesn't yield herself to her husband. Every human problem is caused originally because that which is inferior and that which is subordinate refuses to yield itself to that which is the stronger or the superior. By refusing to yield, nothing will succeed. No progress, no prosperity, instead confusion, chaos, hatred, divorce, no light, as the candle is not lighted it does not shine. You and your household or congregation will not be the light of the world as you have fallen short of Gods image which forms the first purpose of God to mankind as in (Genesis 1:26) "Let Us make man in Our image, according to Our likeness; and let them rule over the fish of the sea and over the birds of the sky and over the cattle and over all the earth, and over every creeping thing that creeps on the earth."

Candlestick (Exodus 25:3) And thou shalt make a *candlestick* of pure gold: of beaten work shall the *candlestick* be made: his shaft, and his branches, his bowls, his knops, and his flowers, shall be of the same. *Candlestick* is used about 40 times in the Christian gospel.

Canon: (Greek – Rule or measuring stick) sometimes duped a Jewish ideal word. The term "canon" is used to describe the books that are divinely inspired and therefore belong in the Bible. The difficulty in determining the biblical canon is that the Bible does not give us a list of the books that belong in the Bible. Determining the canon was a process conducted first by Jewish rabbis and scholars and later by early Christians. Ultimately, it was God who decided what books belonged in the biblical canon. A book of the gospel in the Scripture belonged in the canon from the moment God inspired its writing. It was simply a matter of God's convincing His human followers which books should be included in the Bible.

Canon, A biblical: A biblical canon, or canon of the gospel or scripture is a list of books considered to be authoritative scripture by a particular religious community. The word "canon" was first coined in reference to scripture by Christians, but the idea is said to be Jewish. The textual basis of the canon can also be specified. For example, the Hebrew and Aramaic text as vocalized and pointed in the medieval era by the Masoretes, the Masoretic Text, is the canonical text for Judaism. A modern example of this closing of a textual basis, in a process analogous to the closing of the canon itself, is the King James Only movement, which takes either the actual English text of various redactions of the actual King James Bible itself, or alternately, the textual basis of the King James Version—Bomberg's Masoretic text for the Old Testament and the Textus Receptus in various editions, those of Erasmus, Beza, and Stephanus, alongside the Complutensian polyglot, for the New Testament—as the specified, correct, and inspired textual tradition. Similarly, certain groups specify their particular self-published version or translation of the gospel word from the bible claiming theirs to be the most reliable. Most of the canons listed below are considered "closed" (i.e., books cannot be added or removed), reflecting a belief that public revelation has ended and thus the inspired texts may be gathered into a complete and authoritative *canon*, which scholar Bruce Metzger defines as "an authoritative collection of books." 3 In contrast, an "open canon", which permits the addition of books through the process of continuous revelation, Metzger defines as "a collection of authoritative books." (A table of gospel word in Biblical scripture for both New and Old Testaments, with regard to canonical acceptance in Christendom's various major traditions, appears as follows - These canons have been developed through debate and agreement by the religious authorities of their respective faiths). Believers consider canonical books to be inspired by God or to express the authoritative history of the relationship between God and his people. Books, such as the Jewish-Christian gospels, have been excluded from the *canon* altogether, but many disputed books considered non-canonical or even apocryphal by some are considered to be Biblical Apocrypha or Deuterocanonical or fully canonical by others. There are differences between the Jewish Tanakh and Christian gospel in the biblical canons, and between the canons of different Christian denominations. The differing criteria and processes of canonization dictate what the various communities regard as inspired scripture. In some cases where there are varying strata of scriptural inspiration, it becomes prudent even to discuss texts that only have an elevated status within a particular tradition. This becomes even more complex when considering the open canons of the various Latter Day Saint sects—which may be viewed as extensions of both Christianity and thus Judaism—and the scriptural revelations purportedly given to several leaders over the years within that movement. For the New Testament, the process of the recognition and collection began in the first centuries of the Christian church. Very early on, some of the New Testament books were being recognized. Paul considered Luke's writings to be as authoritative as the Old Testament (1 Timothy 5:18; see also Deuteronomy 25:4 and Luke 10:7). Peter recognized Paul's writings as Scripture (2 Peter 3:15-16). Some of the books of the New Testament were being circulated among the churches (Colossians 4:16; 1 Thessalonians 5:27). Clement of Rome mentioned at least eight New Testament books (A.D. 95). Ignatius of Antioch acknowledged about seven books (A.D. 115). Polycarp, a disciple of John the apostle, acknowledged 15 books (A.D. 108). Later, Irenaeus mentioned 21 books (A.D. 185). Hippolytus recognized 22 books (A.D. 170-235). The New Testament books receiving the most controversy were Hebrews, James, 2 Peter, 2 John, and 3 John.

Capernaum: (Greek: ke-pur-nee-m or Cap-er-nah-oom; Hebrew: Kfar Nahum, "Nahum's village") was a fishing village in the time of the Hasmoneans. Located on the northern shore of the Sea of Galilee. It had a population of about 1,500. Archaeological excavations have revealed two ancient synagogues built one over the other. A church near Capernaum is said to be the home of Saint Peter. 2 The town is cited in the Gospel of Luke and the Gospel of John where it was reported to have been near the hometown of the apostles Simon Peter, Andrew, James and John, as well as the tax collector Matthew. One Sabbath, Jesus taught in the synagogue in Capernaum and healed a man who had the spirit of an unclean devil. (This story is notable for being the only one common between the Gospel of Mark and the Gospel of Luke but not contained in the Gospel of Matthew. See - Synoptic Gospels for more literary comparison between the Gospels. Afterwards, he healed fever in Simon Peter's mother-in-law. According to (Luke 7:1–10), it is also the place where a Roman Centurion asked Jesus to heal his servant. Capernaum is also mentioned in the Gospel of (Mark 2:1), it is the location of the famous healing of the paralytic lowered through the roof to reach Jesus. According to the Synoptic Gospels, Jesus selected this town as the center of his public ministry in the Galilee after he left the small mountainous hamlet of Nazareth (Matthew 4:12–17). He also formally cursed the city, saying "You shall be brought down to Hades," (Matthew 11:23) because of their lack of response to his teaching.

Captivity: (Verb, Greek: *aichmalótizó* - [aheekh-mal-o-tid'-zo], Hebrew: *shabah* - [shaw-baw']; taken, take captive (in war); subdue, ensnare

2 The state of being imprisoned; "he was held in captivity until he died"; "the imprisonment of captured soldiers"; "his ignominious incarceration in the local jail"; "he practiced the immurement of his enemies in the castle dungeon" immurement, incarceration, imprisonment confinement - the state of being confined; "he was held in confinement" durance - imprisonment (especially for a long time), life imprisonment - a sentence of imprisonment until death, internment - confinement during wartime, 3   Captivity - the state of being a slave; "So every bondman in his own hand bears the power to cancel his captivity"—Shakespeare, enslavement, subjection, subjugation - forced submission to control by others

4 Captivity in the general usage means to take captive, or confined to imprisonment, but as related to the Hebrews it has come to mean expatriation. In the Biblical sense the terms captive and captivity were practically synonymous with exile, except the exile was mandatory; the people were in a dependent or oppressed condition. In ancient history, such violent removal of entire populations was not uncommon, and much more humane than selling the captives into slavery. There were reasons for expatriation of populations: the desire of rapidly populating new cities, to increase pride or policy, or to destroy hostile organizations. Most such expatriation not only broke national existence, but, even more seriously, caused bitterness from being separated from the sanctity of special places and the attachment of the local deity. Removal was thought to severe people from the care and protection of their god, thus implying a defeat of that deity.

Captivity, the Babylonian: The Babylonian captivity or exile refers to the time period in Israel's history when Jews were taken captive by King Nebuchadnezzar II of Babylon. It is an important period of biblical history because both the captivity or exile and the return and restoration of the Jewish nation were fulfillments of Old Testament prophecies. God used Babylon as His agent of judgment against Israel for their sins of idolatry and rebellion against Him.

There were actually several different times during this period (607-586 B.C.) when the Jews were taken captive by Babylon. With each successive rebellion against Babylonian rule, Nebuchadnezzar would lead his armies against Judah until they laid siege to Jerusalem for over a year, killing many people and destroying the Jewish temple, taking captive many thousands of Jews, and leaving Jerusalem in ruins.

2 *The Babylonian captivity* as prophesied in Scripture, - the Jewish people would be allowed to return to Jerusalem after 70 years of exile. That prophecy was fulfilled in 537 B.C., and the Jews were allowed by King Cyrus of Persia to return to Israel and begin rebuilding the city and temple. The return under the direction of Ezra led to a revival among the Jewish people and the rebuilding of the temple. Under the reign of King Nebuchadnezzar II, the Babylonian Empire spread throughout the Middle East, and around 607 B.C., King Jehoiakim of Judah was forced into submission, becoming a vassal to Nebuchadnezzar as in (2 Kings 24:1). It was during this time that Nebuchadnezzar took many of the finest and brightest young men from each city in Judah captive, including Daniel, Hananiah (Shadrach), Mishael (Meshach) and Azariah (Abednego). After three years of serving Nebuchadnezzar, Jehoiakim of Judah rebelled against Babylonian rule and once again turned to Egypt for support. After sending his army to deal with Judah's revolt, Nebuchadnezzar himself left Babylon in 598 B.C. to deal with the problem. Arriving in Jerusalem around March of 597 B.C., Nebuchadnezzar laid siege to Jerusalem, taking control of the area, looting it, and taking captive with him Jehoikim's son, Jehoiachin, his family, and almost all of the population of Judah, leaving only the poorest people of the land (2 Kings 24:8-16). At that time Nebuchadnezzar appointed King Zedekiah to rule as his representative over Judah, but after nine years and still not having learned their lesson, Zedekiah led Judah in rebellion against Babylon one final time (2 Kings 24–25). Influenced by false prophets and ignoring Jeremiah's warnings, Zedekiah decided to join a coalition that was being formed by Edom, Moab, Ammon and Phoenicia in rebellion against Nebuchadnezzar (Jeremiah 27:1-3). This resulted in Nebuchadnezzar again laying siege to Jerusalem. Jerusalem fell in July 586 B.C., and Zedekiah was taken captive to Babylon after seeing his sons killed before him and then having his eyes plucked out (2 Kings 25). At this time Jerusalem was laid to waste, the temple destroyed and all the houses burned. The majority of the Jewish people were taken captive, but, again, Nebuchadnezzar left a remnant of poor people to serve as farmers and vinedressers (2 Kings 25:12). In (2 Chronicles and 2 Kings) deal with much of the time leading up to fall of both the Northern King-

Careful

dom and Judah. They also cover the destruction of Jerusalem by Nebuchadnezzar and the beginning of the Babylonian captivity. Jeremiah was one of the prophets during the time leading up to the fall of Jerusalem and the exile, and Ezekiel and Daniel were written while the Jews were in exile. Ezra deals with the return of the Jews as promised over 70 years before by God through the prophets Jeremiah and Isaiah. The book of Nehemiah also covers the return and rebuilding of Jerusalem after the exile was over.

3 The Babylonian captivity had one very significant impact on the nation of Israel when it returned to the land—it would never again be corrupted by the idolatry and false gods of the surrounding nations. A revival among Jews took place after the return of the Jews to Israel and the rebuilding of the temple. We see those accounts in Ezra and Nehemiah as the nation would once again return to the God who had delivered them from their enemies. Just as God had promised through the prophet Jeremiah, God judged the Babylonians for their sins, and the Babylonian Empire fell to the armies of Persia in 539 B.C., once again proving God's promises to be true. The seventy-year period of the *Babylonian captivity* is an important part of Israel's history, and Christians should be familiar with it. Like many other Old Testament events, this historical account demonstrates God's faithfulness to His people, His judgment of sin, and the surety of His promises. Praise the Lord!

Careful: (adjective - Ephesians 5:15-16) "Therefore be *careful* how you walk, not as unwise men but as wise, making the most of your time, because the days are evil...." Making sure of avoiding potential danger, mishap, or harm; cautious. "I begged him to be more careful with the word of wisdom" synonyms: cautious, heedful, alert, aware, attentive, watchful, vigilant, wary, on guard, chary, circumspect, prudent, mindful, guarded; More antonyms: careless anxious to protect (something) from harm or loss; solicitous. "the Pastor was very careful of his reputation" synonyms: mindful, heedful, protective, watchful "Christians must be *careful* of their reputation" prudent in the use of something, especially money. "his mother had always been careful with money" synonyms: prudent, thrifty, economical, economic, economizing, sparing, frugal, scrimping, abstemious, canny, sensible, cautious; etc. 2. Also in (1 John 4:1) – "Beloved, believe not every spirit, but try the spirits whether they are of God: because many false prophets are gone out into the world". Done with or showing thought and attention. "a careful consideration of the facts" synonyms: Discern the spirit to see if it's from God. Attentive, conscientious, painstaking, meticulous, diligent, assiduous, sedulous, scrupulous, punctilious, fastidious, methodical, orderly, deliberate, judicious, perfectionist. (Colossians 2:8) – "Beware lest any man spoil you through philosophy and vain deceit, after the tradition of men, after the rudiments of the world, and not after Christ". Christians should search the gospels diligently to notes every verses that has to do with care in other not to abuse and or provoke the spirit of God.

Carmel: Carmel (biblical settlement), an ancient Israelite town in Judea. (Hebrew language: means "fresh" (planted), or "vineyard" (planted) and Karmiel (Hebrew: is a portmanteau meaning "God's Vineyard". 2 The term used to refer to a monastery of the monks and convent of the nuns of the Carmelite religious order.3 Otherwise it is a prominent headland of Central Palestine, consisting of several connected hills extending from the plain of Esdraelon to the sea, a distance of some 12 miles or more. At the east end, in its highest part, it is 1,728 feet high, and at the west end it forms a promontory to the bay of Acre about 600 feet above the sea. It lay within the tribe of Asher. It was here, at the east end of the ridge, at a place called el-Mukhrakah (i.e., the place of burning), that Elijah brought back the people to their allegiance to God, and slew the prophets of Baal (1Kings 18). Here were consumed the "fifties" of the royal guard; and here also Elisha received the visit of the bereaved mother whose son was restored by him to life (2 Kings 4:25-37). "No mountain in or around Palestine retains its ancient beauty so much as Carmel. Two or three villages and some scattered cottages are found on it; its groves are few but luxuriant; it is no place for crags and precipices or rocks of wild goats; but its surface is covered with a rich and constant verdure." "The whole mountain-side is dressed with blossom, and flowering shrubs, and fragrant herbs." The western extremity of the ridge is, however, more rocky and bleak than the eastern. It is ranked with Bashan on account of its rich pastures (Isaiah 33:9 ; Jeremiah 50:19 ; Amos 1:2). The whole ridge is deeply furrowed with rocky ravines filled with dense jungle. There are many caves in its sides, which at one time were inhabited by swarms of monks. These caves are referred to in (Amos 9:3) . To them Elijah and Elisha often resorted (1 Kings 18:19 1 Kings 18:42 ; 2 Kings 2:25). On its north-west summit there is an ancient establishment of Carmelite monks. Vineyards have recently been planted on the mount by the German colonists of Haifa. The modern Arabic name of the mount is Kurmul, but more commonly Jebel Mar Elyas, i.e., Mount St. Elias, from the Convent of Elias. It is a town in the hill country of Judah (Joshua 15:55), the residence of Nabal (1 Samuel 25:2 1 Samuel 25:5 1 Samuel 25:7 1 Samuel 25:40), and the native place of Abigail, who became David's wife (1 Samuel 27:3). Here king Uzzi-

Carmel

ah had his vineyards (2 Chronicles 26:10). The ruins of this town still remain under the name of Kurmul, about 10 miles south-southeast of Hebron, close to those of Maon. There are several references to Carmel in the Bible. Carmel is mentioned as a city of Judah in (1 Samuel 15:12) and also in (Joshua 15:55). It is mentioned as the place where Saul erects a monument after the expedition against the Amalekites (1 Samuel 15:12)..

Carmel, Mount: A coastal mountain range in Israel overlooking the Mediterranean Sea.

Cast abroad, the rage of thy wrath: Pour forth, scatter abroad, brought forth the overflowing of 'thine' anger; and look upon every one that is proud, and abase him.

Catholic or Catholics (Plural): A person practising Catholicism.

Catholic Church: The Catholic Church, also known as the Roman Catholic Church, is the largest Christian church, with more than 1.2 billion members worldwide. It is among the oldest religious institutions in the world and has played a prominent role in the history of Western civilisation. The Catholic hierarchy is headed by the Bishop of Rome, known as the Pope. The Catholic Church teaches that it is the one true Church founded by Jesus Christ,] that its bishops are the successors of Christ's apostles and that the Pope is the sole successor to Saint Peter who has apostolic primacy. The Church maintains that the doctrine on faith and morals that it presents as definitive is infallible. The Catholic Church is Trinitarian and defines its mission as spreading the Gospel of Jesus Christ, administering the sacraments and exercising charity. Catholic worship is highly liturgical, focusing on the Mass or Divine Liturgy in which the sacrament of the Eucharist is celebrated and, the Church teaches, bread and wine become the body and blood of Christ through transubstantiation. The Catholic Church practises closed communion and only baptised members of the Church deemed to be in a state of grace are ordinarily permitted to receive the Eucharist. The Latin Church, the autonomous Eastern Catholic Churches and religious communities such as the Jesuits, Mendicant orders and enclosed monastic orders reflect the variety of theological emphases within the Church. The Church venerates and holds in special regard Mary, the mother of Jesus Christ, and teaches that through divine intervention she gave birth to him while still a virgin. It has defined four specific Marian dogmatic teachings: her Immaculate Conception without original sin, her status as the Mother of God, her perpetual virginity and her bodily Assumption into Heaven at the end of her earthly life. Numerous Marian devotions are also practised. Catholic social teaching emphasises support for the sick, the poor and the afflicted through the corporal works of mercy. The Catholic Church is the largest non-government provider of education and medical services in the world. Catholic spiritual teaching emphasises spread of the Gospel message and spiritual works of mercy. In recent decades, the Church has been criticised for its doctrines concerning sexual issues and the ordination of women as well as for its handling of sexual abuse cases.

Catholicism: A broad term for describing specific traditions in the Christian churches in theology, doctrine, liturgy, ethics, and spirituality. In this sense, it is to be distinguished from the sense in which it denotes Christians and churches, western and eastern, that are in full communion with the Holy See, and that are commonly called the Catholic Church or Roman Catholic Church. In the sense of indicating historical continuity of faith and practice from the first millennium, the term "Catholicism" is at times employed to mark a contrast to Protestantism, which tends to look solely to the Bible as interpreted on the principles of the 16th-century Protestant Reformation as its ultimate standard. It was thus used by the Oxford Movement to qualify the practice therein.

Caul: (Exodus 29:13) "And thou shalt take all the fat that covereth the inwards, and the *caul* that is above the liver, and the two kidneys, and the fat that is upon them, and burn them upon the altar" Caul - Of an animal, the Liver–net or stomach-net which commences at the division between the right and left lobes of the liver, and stretches on the one side across the stomach, and on the other to the regions of the kidney."

Caul above the liver: "The fatty lobe attached to the liver above the kidneys" (Leviticus. 3:4). In (Leviticus 3:17), God specifically commanded the Israelites not to eat the fat of any animal. Notice: "It shall be a perpetual statute for your generations throughout all your dwellings, that you eat neither fat nor blood." Also, "You shall eat no manner of fat, of ox, or of sheep, or of goat" (Leviticus 7:23). When performing a sacrifice, the 'Levitica'l priests removed the fat, kidneys, and "caul above the liver" and burned them on the altar (Leviticus. 9:10).

Chanukah: (Tiberian: ⬚anukkah, usually spelled pronounced as (χanu⬚ka) in Modern Hebrew; a transliteration also romanised as Chanukah or Chanukkah), also known as the Festival of Lights, Feast of Dedication, is an eight-day Jewish holiday commemorating the rededication of the Holy Temple (the Second Temple) in Jerusalem at the time of the Maccabean Revolt against the Seleucid Empire of the 2nd century BCE. Hanukkah is observed for eight nights and days, starting on the 25th day of

Cheek

Kislev according to the Hebrew calendar, which may occur at any time from late November to late December in the Gregorian calendar. The festival is observed by the kindling of the lights of a unique candelabrum, the nine-branched menorah or hanukiah, one additional light on each night of the holiday, progressing to eight on the final night. The typical menorah consists of eight branches with an additional raised branch. The extra light is called a shamash (Hebrew: "attendant") and is given a distinct location, usually above or below the rest. The purpose of the shamash is to have a light available for practical use, as using the Hanukkah lights themselves for purposes other than publicizing and meditating upon Hanukkah is forbidden.

Cheek: (noun) (Luke 6:29) "Whoever hits you on the *cheek*, offer him the other also; and whoever takes away your coat, do not withhold your shirt from him either". *Cheek* - Either side of the face below the eye. "tears rolled down her cheeks" 2. Either of the buttocks. 3.Either of two side pieces or parts arranged in lateral pairs in a structure. 4. Talk or behaviour regarded as rude or lacking in respect. "he had the cheek to complain" synonyms: impudence, impertinence, insolence, cheekiness, audacity, temerity, brazenness, presumption, effrontery, nerve, gall, pertness, boldness, shamelessness, impoliteness, disrespect, bad manners, unmannerliness, overfamiliarity; More antonyms: politeness verb: *cheek;* 3rd person present: *cheeks*; past tense: cheeked; past participle: cheeked; gerund or present participle: cheeking speak impertinently to. "Frankie always got away with cheeking his elders" synonyms: answer back to, talk back to, be cheeky to, be impertinent to; (Matthew 5:38-39) "You have heard the law that says the punishment must match the injury: 'An eye for an eye, and a tooth for a tooth.' But I say, do not resist an evil person! If someone slaps you on the right *cheek,* offer the other *cheek* also".

Cherubim: (Hebrew – 'Cherub' – singular) A winged angelic being who is considered to attend on the Abrahamic God in biblical tradition. The concept is represented in ancient Middle Eastern art as a lion or bull with eagles' wings and a human face, and regarded in traditional Christian angelology as an angel of the second highest order of the nine fold celestial hierarchy. Cherubim are mentioned throughout the Hebrew Bible and once in the New Testament in reference to the mercy seat of the Ark of the Covenant as recorded in (Hebrews 9:5) "and above it were the cherubim of glory overshadowing the mercy seat; but of these things we cannot now speak in detail".

Clean: (adjective - clean·er, clean·est, cleanness) (Hebrews 10:22) "Let us draw near with a true heart in full assurance of faith, with our hearts sprinkled *clean* from an evil conscience and our bodies washed with pure water". Clean here means 1. Free from dirt, stain, or impurities; unsoiled. 2. Free from foreign matter or pollution; unadulterated: other meanings - clean air; clean drinking water. b. Not infected: a clean wound. 3(a) Producing relatively little pollution: a clean fuel; a cleaner, more efficient engine. b. Producing relatively little radioactive fallout or contamination: a clean nuclear bomb. 4. Having no imperfections or blemishes; regular or even: a clean edge; a smooth, clean joint. When we leave the Old Testament and come to the New Testament, we once again find that the definition of clean and unclean is critical to our understanding. We find these issues discussed and debated heatedly between the scribes and the Pharisees, and our Lord had to do with cleanness and uncleanness—particularly the area of ceremonial uncleanness as defined by Jewish tradition, not so much as defined by Old Testament revelation. If we are going to understand how our Lord differed from the scribes and the Pharisees, if we are going to understand how Judaism "went to seed" on the area of clean and unclean, we must first understand the backdrop teaching of cleanness and uncleanness as it is introduced in (Leviticus 11). We must also observe that cleanness and uncleanness is related to holiness. Certainly, this is so in Leviticus. And if that is so, then if you and I are committed to the concept of holiness in general, and to the reality of holiness in specific in our lives, then we must understand the role which cleanness plays in regard to holiness. All of this says to us that these chapters are important. We must understand what we are dealing with as we come to our study because clean and unclean is one of the great issues of the gospel.

Cleanness

In (Leviticus 11) Cleanness is somehow related to holiness. We say that "Cleanliness is next to godliness,". Now that has some earthly wisdom to it! But in Leviticus, cleanliness is next to holiness. When we get down to the basic reason why an Israelite is to make these distinctions between clean and unclean, it is because God says, "You are to be holy, for I am holy." For the first time in history—for the first time in the Old Testament—men and women are to observe these distinctions because God has made them. Therefore cleanliness is related to God's holiness, and Israel is to observe it because of the holiness of God. Twice it is repeated in this chapter. Therefore there is a direct relationship between what is clean and what is holy in Scripture. What is unclean can never be holy. Some things that are clean may be consecrated and set apart as holy, but nothing which is holy is unclean; only that which is clean can become holy.

Child: (Plural – Children): Generally a human between the stages of birth and puberty. The legal definition of child generally refers to a minor, otherwise known as a person younger than the age of majority. God give child or children as a heritage as in (Psalm 127:3-5) "Behold, children are a heritage from the Lord, the fruit of the womb a reward. Like arrows in the hand of a warrior are the children of one's youth. Blessed is the man who fills his quiver with them! He shall not be put to shame when he speaks with his enemies in the gate". 2 Child may also describe a relationship with a parent (such as sons and daughters of any age) or, metaphorically, an authority figure, or signify group membership in a clan, tribe, or religion; Or with God, a yardstick in measuring humility thus (Matthew 18:4) – "Whosoever therefore shall humble himself as this little child, the same is greatest in the kingdom of heaven". 3 It can also signify being strongly affected by a specific time, place, or circumstance, as in "a child of nature" or "a child of the Sixties". Many social issues affect children, such as childhood education, bullying, child poverty, dysfunctional families and in developing countries, hunger. Children can be raised by parents, in a foster care or similar supervised arrangement, guardians or partially raised in a day care centre and care for as Jesus Blesses the Children in the bible and used them as yardstick for the Kingdom of Heaven (Mathew 19: 14-15) - Then some children were brought to Him so that He might lay His hands on them and pray; and the disciples rebuked them. But Jesus said, "Let the children alone, and do not hinder them from coming to Me; for the kingdom of heaven belongs to such as these." After laying His hands on them, He departed from there.

Chicken: Actually a chicken is mentioned only once and only in the King James version of the Bible at (Mathew 23:37). 'O Jerusalem, Jerusalem, that killeth the prophets, and stoneth them that are sent unto her! How often would I have gathered thy children together, even as a hen gathereth her CHICKEN'S under her wings, and ye would not!"

Christian: (noun) A follower of Christ. According to the gospel of Christ, Christians were first so called at Antioch – (Act 11:26). 2 Christian is also the hero of Bunyan's Pilgrim's Progress (1678 and 1684) who fled from the City of Destruction and journeyed to the Celestial City. He started with a heavy burden on his back, which fell off when he stood at the foot of the cross. Christians *(plural)*

Christendom: A collective term of all Christians, that stands as a synonym for Christianity.

Christmas: In the Christian Calender, 25 December – Christmas day marking the day Christ was born although certainly not the day on which Christ was born as is popularly supposed. The date was eventually fixed by the Church in AD 440. And is the day of the winter Solstice which had anciently been a time of festival among heathen people. In Anglo-Saxon England, it began on 25 December, having started from late 12th century until the adoption of the Gregorian Calendar in 1752, the year began on Lady Day, 25 March, Christmas Day has the advantage of being exactly nine months after Lady Day, the traditional length of human pregnancy.

Church: A building used for religious activities, particularly worship services. The term in its architectural sense is most often used by Christians to refer to their religious buildings but can be used by other religions or any term synonymous in other religious context. In traditional Christian architecture, the church is often arranged in the shape of a Christian cross. When viewed from plan view the longest part of a cross is represented by the aisle and the junction of the cross is located at the altar area. Towers or domes are often added with the intention of directing the eye of the viewer towards the heavens and inspiring church visitors. Modern church buildings have a variety of architectural styles and layouts; many buildings that were designed for other purposes have now been converted for church use; and, similarly, many original church buildings have been put to other uses.2 The dwelling place of God's Spirit to a multitude of worshippers and or followers of Christ Jesus. (Ephesians 2:20-22) "Built on the foundation of the apostles and prophets, Christ Jesus himself being the cornerstone, in whom the whole structure, being joined together, grows into a holy temple in the Lord. In him you also are being built together into a dwelling place for God by the Spirit".

Cistern: (Middle English cisterne, from Latin *cisterna*, from *cista*, "box", from Greek, *kistê*, "basket") is a waterproof receptacle for holding liquids, usually water. Cisterns are often built to catch and store rainwater. Cisterns are distinguished from wells by their waterproof linings. Modern cisterns range in capacity from a few litres to thousands of cubic metres, effectively forming covered reservoirs. 2 The rendering of a Hebrew word 'bor' , which means a receptacle for water conveyed to it; distinguished from beer , which denotes a place where water rises on the spot (Jeremiah 2:13 ;

"For My people have committed two evils: they have forsaken Me, the Fountain of living waters, and they have hewn for themselves *cisterns*, broken *cisterns* which cannot hold water". 3 Again in (Proverbs 5:15-21) ; Thus "Drink water from your own *cistern*, running water from your own well. Should your springs overflow in the streets, your streams of water

Cistern

in the public squares? Let them be yours alone, never to be shared with strangers. May your fountain be blessed, and may you rejoice in the wife of your youth. A loving doe, a graceful deer— may her breasts satisfy you always, may you ever be intoxicated with her love. Why, my son, be intoxicated with another man's wife? Why embrace the bosom of a wayward woman? For your ways are in full view of the Lord, and he examines all your paths." 4 Cistern was mentioned again when Sennacherib invades Judah in (Isaiah 36:16-17), 'nor let Hezekiah make you trust in the LORD, saying, "The LORD will surely deliver us, this city will not be given into the hand of the king of Assyria." 'Do not listen to Hezekiah,' for thus says the king of Assyria, 'Make your peace with me and come out to me, and eat each of his vine and each of his fig tree and drink each of the waters of his own *cistern*, until I come and take you away to a land like your own land, a land of grain and new wine, a land of bread and vineyards....a fountain. *Cisterns* are frequently mentioned in the gospel. 5 The scarcity of springs in Palestine made it necessary to collect rain-water in reservoirs and *cisterns* (Numbers 21:22). "Let me pass through thy land: we will not turn into the fields, or into the vineyards; we will not drink of the waters of the well: but we will go along by the king's high way, until we be past thy borders". 6 Empty *cisterns* were sometimes used as prisons (Jeremiah 38:6; Lamentations 3:53 ; (Psalms 40:2). "He brought me up out of the pit of destruction, out of the miry clay, And He set my feet upon a rock making my footsteps firm". (Psalm 69:15) "Do not let the floodwaters engulf me or the depths *(Cistern)* swallow me up or the pit *(cistern)* close its mouth over me". 7 The "pit" into which Joseph was cast (Genesis 37:24) "and they took him and threw him into the cistern. The cistern was empty; there was no water in it". This was a beer or dry well.

There are numerous remains of ancient *cisterns* in all parts of Palestine and diverse places around the world today.

Clouds: (Psalms 97:2) '*Clouds* and thick darkness surround Him; Righteousness and justice are the foundation of His throne'. **Cloud** - A visible mass of liquid droplets or frozen crystals made of water or various chemicals suspended in the atmosphere above the surface of a planetary body. These suspended particles are also known as aerosols and are studied in the cloud physics branch of meteorology. Terrestrial cloud formation is the result of air in Earth's atmosphere becoming saturated due to either or both of two processes: cooling of the air and adding water vapour. With sufficient saturation, precipitation will fall to the surface; an exception is virga, which evaporates before reaching the surface. Clouds in the troposphere, the atmospheric layer closest to Earth's surface, have

Clouds

Latin names due to the universal adaptation of Luke Howard's nomenclature. It was introduced in December 1802 and became the basis of a modern international system that classifies these tropospheric aerosols into several physical forms, then cross-classifies them as low-, middle- and high-étage according to cloud-base altitude range above Earth's surface. Clouds with significant vertical extent occupying more than one étage are often considered a distinct group or sub-group. One physical form shows free-convective upward growth into low or vertical heaps of cumulus (cumuliform). Other forms appear as non-convective layered sheets like low stratus (strati-form), and as limited-convective rolls or ripples as with stratocumulus (stratocumuli-form). Both of these layered forms have middle- and high-étage variants identified respectively by the prefixes alto- and cirri-. Thin fibrous wisps of cirrus are a physical form found only at high altitudes of the troposphere (cirri-form). In the case of *clouds* with vertical extent, prefixes are used whenever necessary to express variations or complexities in their physical structures. These include cumuli- for complex highly convective vertical nimbus storm clouds (cumulonimbi - form), and nimbi- for thick strati-form layers with sufficient vertical depth to produce moderate to heavy precipitation. This process of cross-classification produces ten basic genus-types or genera, most of which can be sub-divided into species and varieties. Synoptic surface weather observations use code numbers to record and report any type of tropospheric cloud visible at scheduled observation times based on its height and physical appearance. While a majority of clouds form in Earth's troposphere, there are occasions when they can be observed at much higher altitudes in the stratosphere and mesosphere. Clouds that form above the troposphere have common names for their main types, but are sub-classified alpha-numerically rather than with the elaborate system of Latin names given to cloud types in the troposphere. These three main atmospheric layers that can produce clouds, along with the lowest part of the cloudless thermosphere, are collectively known as the 'homosphere'. Above this lies the 'heterosphere' (which includes the rest of the thermosphere and the exosphere) that marks the transition to outer space. Clouds have been observed on other planets and moons within the Solar System, but, due to their different temperature characteristics, they are often composed of other substances such as methane, ammonia, and sulphuric acid as well as water. God establishes the cloud and keep it (Job 37:15-16) "Do you know how God establishes them, And makes the lightning of His *cloud* to shine? "Do you know about the layers of the thick *clouds*, The wonders of one perfect in knowledge, (Job 22:14) '*Clouds* are a hiding place for Him, so that He cannot see; And He walks on the vault of heaven.' (Job 26:9) "He obscures the face of the full moon And spreads His *cloud* over it. 2 Cloud also mean multitude of people, followers as in (Hebrews 12:1) "Therefore, since we are surrounded by such a great *cloud* of witnesses, let us throw off everything that hinders and the sin that so easily entangles".

Cloud, God's Presence in the: The firmament atmosphere where the wonders of God's present is transmitted to the whole earth through the provisions in His Covenant; the rainbow, air atmosphere, cloudy pillars, the waters, astral creations - moon, stars, etc. His Spirit and the Supreme forces of divinity that makes people like Moses and Aaron, Elijah, Elisha and all true Christian worshipers to see Him in spiritual realm making His presence strongly felt by anyone who is able to discern in spirit as in (Genesis 9:13) "I set My bow (rainbow) in the *cloud*, and it shall be a token or sign of a covenant or solemn pledge between Me and the earth.

"I do now, and have just for the first-time set the rainbow in the sky, that mankind may hereafter have a token of the covenant between us."

At the heart of the idea of a Temple is the abiding presence of God. Although God is omnipresent, He has chosen to manifest His presence in certain locations and at certain times within history. This physical manifestation of God has come to be called the Shekinah. The Shekinah Glory is the visible manifestation of the presence of God. It is the majestic presence or manifestation of God in which He descends to dwell among men. Whenever the invisible God becomes visible, and whenever the omnipresence of God is localized, this is the Shekinah Glory. The usual title found in Scriptures for the Shekinah Glory is the glory of Jehovah, or the glory of the Lord. The Hebrew form is Kvod Adonai, which means 'the glory of Jehovah' and describes what the Shekinah Glory is. The Greek title, Doxa Kurion, is translated as 'the glory of the Lord.' Doxa means 'brightness,' 'brilliance,' or 'splendor,' and it depicts how the Shechinah Glory appears. Other titles give it the sense of 'dwelling,' which portrays what the Shechinah Glory does. The Hebrew word Shechinah, from the root shachan, means 'to dwell.' The Greek word skeinei, which is similar in sound as the Hebrew Shechinah (Greek has no 'sh' sound), means 'to tabernacle.'. . . In the Old Testament, most of these visible manifestations took the form of light, fire, or *cloud*, or a combination of these. A new form appears in the New Testament: the Incarnate Word (John John) Also see (1 Kings 8:10-12) "It happened that when the priests came from the holy place, the cloud filled the house of the LORD, so that the priests could not stand to minister because of the *cloud*, for the glory of the LORD filled the house of the LORD. Then Solomon said, "The LORD has said that He *would dwell in the thick cloud.*

Coat: An outer garment with sleeves, worn outdoors and typically extending below the hips: provide with a layer or covering of something. "His right leg was coated in plaster". 2 synonyms: cover, overlay, paint, glaze, varnish, wash, surface, veneer, inlay, laminate, plate, blanket, mantle, daub, smear, bedaub, cake, plaster, overspread, encrust, face; literary besmear (See the story of Joseph in (Genesis 37)

Coat of many colours: (Hebrew: *kethoneth passim)* is the name for the garment that Joseph owned. The translation and the actual nature of the garment is subject to dispute. It is possible that the idea of the coat being "of many colours" may mean that it was in fact a patchwork coat of different materials which may have been of different colours or merely different shades of a single colour.

Coil: A form of heilisso; to coil, rolled up or getting self together, organised or wrap -- fold up as in (Hebrew 1: 12) "And as clothing shall you fold them up, and they shall be changed: but you are the same, and your years shall not fail". Again in (Revelation 6:14) "And the heaven departed as a scroll when it is rolled together; and every mountain and island were moved out of their places".2 An affirmation of perfection (Hebrews 13:8) "Jesus Christ the same yesterday, and to day, and for ever". (Exodus 3:14) "And God said to Moses, I AM THAT I AM: and he said, Thus shall you say to the children of Israel, I AM has sent me to you". (John 8:58) "Jesus said to them, Truly, truly, I say to you, Before Abraham was, I am".

Colossi: (Plural – Colossus) Pauls letter to Colossians. The Epistle of Paul to the Colossians, usually referred to simply as Colossians, is the twelfth book of the New Testament. It was written, according to the text, by Paul the Apostle and Timothy to the Church in Colossae, a small Phrygian city near Laodicea and approximately 100 miles from Ephesus in Asia Minor. Scholars have increasingly questioned Paul's authorship and attributed the letter to an early follower instead. The authenticity of the letter, however, has been defended with equal strength.

Colossians: *(See Colossi above)*

Comforter: One that comforts: the nurse as comforter of the sick. Comforter - Christianity. 2 The Holy Spirit. 3 A quilted bedcover. 4 A person that provides comforts or consolation the Holy Spirit in

Companion of Jehu

(John 14:26) " But the Comforter, which is the Holy Ghost, whom the Father will send in my name, he shall teach you all things, and bring all things to your remembrance, whatsoever I have said unto you". Also Jesus – one of the comforter from the Trinity said "And I will pray the Father and He shall give you another comforter that He may abide with you for ever" (John 14:16). Here Christ speaks as Mediator, and promises his disciples, that he would intercede for them with the Father; which is designed as an encouragement to them to ask for what they want, in his name, and to comfort their hearts, which were troubled at the news of his departure from them; and he shall give you another Comforter. This is no inconsiderable proof of a trinity of persons in the Godhead; here is the Father prayed unto, the Son in human nature praying, and the Holy Ghost the Comforter prayed for; who is the gift of the Father, through the prevalent mediation of the Son, and is another "Comforter"; distinct from the Messiah, to whom reference is here had! One of the names of the Messiah, with the Jews, is , "a Comforter"; such an one Jesus had been to his disciples; and now he was about to leave them, and for their support under their sorrows, he promises to use his interest with his Father, that he would give them another Comforter, meaning the Spirit, who performs this his work and office, by taking of the things of Christ, and showing them to his people; by shedding abroad the love of the Father, and of the Son, into their hearts; by opening and applying the precious promises of the Gospel to them; by being a spirit of adoption in them; and by abiding with them as the seal, earnest, and pledge of their future glory; and with this view Christ promises to pray for him,

Companion of Jehu: The companions of Jehu are fellow students who were trained under Elisha. Jehu meaning "Jehovah is He"; Latin: Hieu) was the tenth king of Israel since Jeroboam I, as was directed by God in (1 Kings 19:16) "And Jehu the son of Nimshi shalt thou anoint to be king over Israel: and Elisha the son of Shaphat of Abelmeholah shalt thou anoint to be prophet in thy room". Jehu is noted for exterminating the house of Ahab at the instruction of God (Yahweh) He was the son of Jehoshaphat and grandson of Nimshi. His companions were fellow students who were trained under Elisha. One of Elisha's students led Jehu away from the others, anointed him king in an inner chamber, and then departed (2 Kings 9:5-6). "And when he came, behold, the captains of the host were sitting; and he said, I have an errand to thee, O captain. And Jehu said, Unto which of all us? And he said, To thee, O captain. And he arose, and went into the house; and he poured the oil on his head, and said unto him, Thus saith the Lord God of Israel, I have anointed thee king over the people of the Lord, even over Israel". Afterwards, the companions of Jehu asked where he had been. When told, they enthusiastically blew their trumpets and proclaimed him their king.

Commandment: Specific or divine rule given by God especially one of the ten commandment. *(see the ten commandment)*

Commandment, The ten: The divine rules of conduct given by God to Moses on Mount Sinai as recounted in the Bible in Exodus 20 and in Deuteronomy 5. The commandment are generally enumerated as have no other gods, do not make or worship idol, do not take the name of the Lord in vain, keep the Sabbath holy, honour one's father and mother, do not kill, do not commit adultery, do not steal, do not give false evidence, do not covet another's property or wife.

Commander of the faithful: This does not only refers to the past but has to do with the way you can maintain your faithfulness to please God till Christ come. Yet being faithful means making conscious choices to follow God. It means standing up when people disrespect your faith to explain why you're a Christian. It means doing what you can to become stronger in your faith and evangelize in a way that works for you. Noah was probably not accepted by his fellow man, because he chose to follow God rather than commit great sins. Yet, he found the strength to remain faithful - which is why we are all still here. Noah was a God-fearing man who lived in a time of great sin and turmoil. People around the world were worshipping other gods and idols, and sinfulness abounded. God was so upset with his creation that He considered wiping them off the face of the Earth completely. However, the prayers of one faithful man saved humanity. Noah asked God to have mercy on man, and so God asked Noah to build an ark. He placed representative animals on the ark and allowed Noah and his family to join them. Then God brought forth a great flood, wiping out all the other living things. God then promised Noah that He would never again bring a judgement such as this on humanity.

Faithfulness leads to obedience, and obedience brings about rich blessings from the Lord. (Proverbs 28:20) tells us that a faithful man will be richly blessed. Yet being faithful is not always easy. Temptations abound, and as Christian teens your lives are busy. It is easy to become distracted by the movies, magazines, telephone calls, Internet, homework, school activities, and even youth group events. God is always faithful to

Communicant

us, even when we are not faithful to Him. He is there by our side, even when we do not seek Him or even notice He is there. He keeps his promises, and we are called to do the same. Remember, God promised Noah that He would never again wipe out His people on the earth as He did in the flood. If we trust in God to be faithful, then He becomes our rock. We can trust in all He has to offer. We will know that there is no trial too great for us to bear, and thus become a light to the world around us. As God appointed Hanani and brother – Commander of the faithful in (Nehemiah 7:1 -3) Now when the wall was rebuilt and I had set up the doors, and the gatekeepers and the singers and the Levites were appointed, then I put Hanani my brother, and Hananiah the commander of the fortress, in charge of Jerusalem, for he was a faithful man and feared God more than many. Then I said to them, "Do not let the gates of Jerusalem be opened until the sun is hot, and while they are standing guard, let them shut and bolt the doors. Also appoint guards from the inhabitants of Jerusalem, each at his post, and each in front of his own house."

Communicant: *(noun)* In the Christianity ecclesiastical terms, this simply means a person who receives communion. 2 A member of a church who entitled to partake of the Eucharist.

Communion: A practice charged by Christ to his followers in order to pave a way for oneness or a divine spiritual intercourse with the Father – The Supreme in the God head. 2 Act of commune dialogue with God. Also, act of worship or fellowship, or sharing in oneness a solemn sacrifice by brethren of the same faith. 3 Greek – Koinonia *(koivwvia) Communion sharing or fellowship.* In the Christian Gospel, the basic meaning of the term communion *is* simply an especial close relationship of Christians as individual or as aq Church with God and with fellow Christians. 4 Communion in secular Greek for instance predates its more specific Christian usage. In ancient Greek, Koinonia very often is applied to a business partnership, to fellowship of life in marriage, to a spiritual relationship with divinity up to comradely fellowship between friends in a community or a society. Though the Greek translation Koinonia appears in the New Testament, it does not seems to appear in the Ancient Greek Translation – the Septuagint. But its noun or adjectival form is found in about 43 verses

Confide: (verb) Simply to tell someone about a secret or private matter while trusting them not to repeat it to others. There are several meanings of confide but looking at it in the gospel usage, one can aptly affirm that "Christians confide their fears or problems to God." synonyms: reveal, disclose, divulge, leak, lay bare, make known, betray, impart, pass on, proclaim, announce, report, declare, intimate, uncover, unmask, expose, bring out into the open, unfold, vouchsafe, tell; More antonyms: keep from trust (someone) enough to tell them of a secret or private matter. "he confided his planned projects to the Lord. " synonyms: o p e n one's heart to, unburden oneself to, embosom oneself to, confess to, tell all to, tell one's all to, commune with "I really need him to confide in" dated entrust something to (God) in order for Him to look after it. Act of confidence in God. (see confidence) as in (1 Peter 5:7) "Casting all your care upon him; for he careth for you". Trusting without doubt, reposing all your confidence, looking unto the rock in which ye were hewn. No wavering, nor undaunted. He is your only saviour as in (Isaiah 51:1) "Hearken to me, ye that follow after righteousness, ye that seek the LORD: look unto the rock whence ye are hewn, and to the hole of the pit whence ye are dogged".

Confidence: (*noun*) The general belief that one can have faith or rely on someone or something in order to achieve certain objective. 2 Self assurance based on ones own ability to achieve things. Scripturally, David relied on his previous record 'how he used to kill animals like lion when he was shepherding the flocks in the farm. That turned his confidence on when he was preparing to fight Goliath. Faith wise, you ought to know that God has confidence in you. Just like every good inventor brags about his product. God also boost of us simply because we are his offspring or his special crafted masterpiece. So He has confidence in his creation. Thus for we are his workmanship created in Christ Jesus unto good works, which God hath before ordained that we should work in them.' (Ephesians 2:10) 3 A feeling of trust that someone will not reveal or disclose private information to others. Things you were told in confidence need not be exposed or disclosed to others. 4 A private matter told to someone under the understanding of secrecy. The practice by members of the inner caucus of a church to keep issues of the church secret from non caucus members.

Confidence in God: *(phrase)* Simply in a position of trust with God. If your trust in other things fail, why not trust in God?. In the US currency, confidence of American citizens is boost when they enshrined, "In God we Trust."

Confident: Feeling certain about the word of God. 2 Assurance through faith in God's word as in (Philippians 1:6) thus Being ConfidentBeing A Perfect ChristianThe Completion Of RedemptionCertaintyConfidence, Based

Confidential

On Achievement end God, Goodness Of Completion Beginning Of Salvation The Final Days Of Time God, Immutability Of Acknowledging God Unceasing Abraham Security, Day of the LORD, Beginning ethics, and grace God Always Working Accepting Christ Goals Reliability Growth"For I am confident of this very thing, that He who began a good work in you will perfect it until the day of Christ Jesus" and in Acts 28:31 Christ conceptualize as in this narration thus Christian Teachers Herald Boldness, Proclaiming Gospel Preaching, Content of evangelism, nature of Importunity, Towards People Teaching Kingdom Of God, Coming Of"For whoever does the will of My Father who is in heaven, he is My brother and sister and mother." "However, so that we do not offend them, go to the sea and throw in a hook, and take the first fish that comes up; and when you open its mouth, you will find a shekel. Take that and give it to them for you and Me." "My heavenly Father will also do the same to you, if each of you does not forgive his brother from your heart." "For I say to you, from now on you will not see Me until you say, `BLESSED IS HE WHO COMES IN THE NAME OF THE LORD!'" They were utterly astonished, saying, (according to the confident in them based on what Christ has done) "He has done all things well; He makes even the deaf to hear and the mute to speak." "For everyone will be salted with fire. "Salt is good; but if the salt becomes un-salty, with what will you make it salty again? Have salt in yourselves, and be at peace with one another." Answering Jesus, they *said, "We do not know." And Jesus *said to them, "Nor will I tell you by what authority I do these things." Mary Magdalene and Mary the mother of Joses were looking on to see where He was laid. And answering they *said to Him, "Where, Lord?" And He said to them, "Where the body is, there also the vultures will be gathered." Then they returned and prepared spices and perfumes. And on the Sabbath they rested according to the commandment. "But if you do not believe his writings, how will you believe My words?" But Philip found himself at Azotus, and as he passed through he kept preaching the gospel to all the cities until he came to Caesarea. And he was travelling through Syria and Cilicia, strengthening the churches. But after two years had passed, Felix was succeeded by Porcius Festus, and wishing to do the Jews a favor, Felix left Paul imprisoned. preaching the kingdom of God and teaching concerning the Lord Jesus Christ with all openness, unhindered. ROMANS to the only wise God, through Jesus Christ, be the glory forever. Amen.1 CORINTHIANS

Confidential: (confidentiality – noun, confidentially – adverb) Intended to be kept secret. Confidential information. Christians ought to keep what may be termed as ' Faithful Secret' confi-

Confess

dentially. Faithful secrets are the habit of covering common mistakes and or sins of a fellow Christian and or members in the body of Christ secret or with confidence as the words of caution in (Proverbs 11:13) (ESV)" "Whoever goes about slandering reveals secrets, but he who is trustworthy in spirit keeps a thing covered".**Also (Proverbs 25:9)** advised "Argue your case with your neighbour himself, and do not reveal another's secret, **(Proverbs 17:9)** "Whoever covers an offense seeks love, but he who repeats a matter separates close friends. More so, in (James 5:16) "Therefore, confess your sins to one another and pray for one another, that you may be healed. The prayer of a righteous person has great power as it is working". And (1 Peter 5:1-14) So I exhort the elders among you, as a fellow elder and a witness of the sufferings of Christ, as well as a partaker in the glory that is going to be revealed: shepherd the flock of God that is among you, exercising oversight, not under compulsion, but willingly, as God would have you; not for shameful gain, but eagerly; not domineering over those in your charge, but being examples to the flock. And when the chief Shepherd appears, you will receive the unfading crown of glory. Likewise, you who are younger, be subject to the elders. Clothe yourselves, all of you, with humility toward one another, for "God opposes the proud but gives grace to the humble."

Confess: Confirmation, Congregation admit that one has committed a crime or done something wrong. "he confessed that he had attacked the old man" synonyms: admit, acknowledge, reveal, make known, disclose, divulge, make public, avow, declare, blurt out, profess, own up to, tell all about, bring into the open, bring to light; More antonyms: conceal, deny, acknowledge something reluctantly, typically because one feels slightly ashamed or embarrassed. "I must confess that I half believed you"synonyms: acknowledge, admit, concede, grant, allow, own, say, declare, affirm, accept, recognize, be aware of/that, realize, be conscious of/that "I confess I don't know" declare (one's religious faith)."The multitude of people confessed their faith in Christ" (James 5:16) Confess to one another therefore your faults (your slips, your false steps, your offenses, your sins) and pray [also] for one another, that you may be healed and restored [to a spiritual tone of mind and heart]. The earnest (heartfelt, continued) prayer of a righteous man makes tremendous power available (dynamic in its working). (Romans 10:9-10) But what does it say? "THE WORD IS NEAR YOU, IN YOUR MOUTH AND IN YOUR HEART "-- that is, the word of faith which we are preaching, that if you confess with your mouth Jesus as Lord, and believe in your heart that God raised Him from the dead, you will be saved; for with the heart a person believes, resulting in righteousness,

Confession

and with the mouth he confesses, resulting in salvation.... Hallelujah

Confession: A statement made by a person or a group of person acknowledging some personal fact that the person (or the group) would ostensibly prefer to keep hidden. The term presumes that the speaker is providing information that he believes the other party is not already aware of, and is frequently associated with an admission of a moral or legal wrong: In one sense it is the acknowledgment of having done something wrong, whether on purpose or not. Thus confessional texts usually provide information of a private nature previously unavailable. What a sinner tells a priest in the confessional, the documents criminals sign acknowledging what they have done, an autobiography in which the author acknowledges mistakes, and so on, are all examples of confessional texts. As in Psalm David to the Choirmaster when Nathan the prophet went to him, after he had gone in to Bathsheba. (Psalm 51:1-5) "Have mercy on me, O God, according to your steadfast love; according to your abundant mercy blot out my transgressions. Wash me thoroughly from my iniquity, and cleanse me from my sin! For I know my transgressions, and my sin is ever before me. Against you, you only, have I sinned and done what is evil in your sight, so that you may be justified in your words and blameless in your judgment. Behold, I was brought forth in iniquity, and in sin did my mother conceive me". There are several conversions in the bible to alight your Spirit and Faith.

Convert: (past tense – converted, Conversion - passive): (1 Timothy 3:6) "He must not be a recent *convert*, or he may become conceited and fall under the same judgment as the devil". Convert means to change one's religious faith or other belief. "at twenty he *converted* from Islam to Catholic. Although the term "conversion" is common in theological and gospel discussion today, it is a relatively rare term in the Bible. In its current popular usage it refers to someone who has come to Christ or become a Christian. The biblical roots of the concept involve the use of two terms that mean "to turn" (Hebrew. epistrepho). However, the New Testament usage is more like the common theological meaning. Examples of conversion, outside the New Testament, emerge when one looks at the Greek term "proselyte, " the convert from a Gentile way of life to Judaism. Such an example pictures in everyday Greek terminology what a convert looked like. Examples of *converts* appear throughout the Book of Acts, although the technical terminology is not present. Among such examples are Paul's change of direction at the Damascus road, Cornelius, the instant response of the Philippian jailer, and the picture of Lydia. 2 In the New Testament conversion seems to summarize the call of

Convert

the church in response to Jesus' commission to preach repentance for the forgiveness of sins to all the nations, as the Old Testament called for (Luke 24:43-47). In sum, conversion is a turning to embrace God. So on a few key occasions the concepts of repentance and turning appear together in (Acts 3:19 ; 26:20). Repentance reflects the attitude one brings into conversion, while turning pictures the change of orientation and direction that comes as a part of it (Acts 9:35) turned to the Lord; (Acts 11:21) alongside a reference to belief; (Acts 14:15) turn from worthless things; (Acts 15:19) turn to God; (Acts 26:18) turn from darkness to light). This is often Luke's way of describing what Paul refers to as faith, although Paul can speak of "turning to God from idols" as well (1 Thessalonica 1:9-10). (1 Peter 2:25) uses the picture of coming to the great shepherd to express this idea. As one can see, the term can describe what one has turned from or can indicate to whom one turns.

2 The concept of conversion is actually very rare in the Old Testament. The key term for "turning" is used in a variety of ways that really do not describe conversion. (1) It can refer to nations turning to God in the future (Isaiah 19:22). (2) It can describe an Israelite returning to God or, negatively, failing to do so (Isaiah 6:10 ; 31:6 ; Jeremiah 3:10 Jeremiah 3:12 Jeremiah 3:14 Jeremiah 3:22 ; Amos 4:6 Amos 4:8 Amos 4:10 ; Zech 1:2-4). A good illustration of this force is (Jeremiah 4:1-2), where the call is to return to God by letting go of idols. (3) Sometimes God is said to return to his people (Isaiah 63:17 ; Amos 9:14). In the Old Testament the passage that comes closest to meaning "convert" is (Isaiah 55:7). Here the wicked are called upon to turn to God for mercy and pardon of sin. Those who thirst are to come.

3 Other meaning of convert or conversion includes transformation, - change the form, character, or function of something. "Christianity has converted the country from a primitive society to a near-religious and civilised one" :
change, turn, transform, metamorphose, transfigure, transmute, translate; Be able to change from one form to another. "the seating converts to a double or two single beds" synonyms: change into, be able to be changed into, adapt "the sofa converts to a bed" change (money, stocks, or units in which a quantity is expressed) into others of a different kind. "the figures have been converted at $0.545 to the Dutch guilder" synonyms: change, turn; More adapt (a building) to make it suitable for a new purpose. "the company converted a disused cinema to house twelve machinists" synonyms: adapt, turn, rebuild, reconstruct, redevelop, remake, make over, refashion, redesign, restyle, revamp; LOGIC - transpose the subject and

Convince

predicate of (a proposition) according to certain rules to form a new proposition by inference.

Convince (Convinced, convincing, convinces): (verb) cause (someone) to believe firmly in the truth of something. "Robert's expression had obviously convinced her of his innocence" synonyms: persuade, satisfy, prove

To evince; to prove. To overpower; to surmount; to vanquish. Persuaded in mind; satisfied with evidence; convicted, to cause to feel certain; More persuade (someone) to do something. "she convinced my father to branch out on his own" synonyms: induce, prevail on, get, talk round, bring around, win over, sway; as in (Job 32:12 "Yea, I attended unto you, and, behold, there was none of you that *convinced* Job, or that answered his words": To persuade or satisfy the mind by evidence; to subdue the opposition of the mind to truth, or to what is alleged, and compel it to yield its assent; as, to convince a man of his errors; or to convince him of the truth. For he mightily convinced the Jews--showing by the scriptures that Jesus was the Christ. (Acts 18). Also see (Jude 1:15) " T o execute judgment upon all, and to *convince* all that are ungodly among them of all their ungodly deeds which they have ungodly committed, and of all their hard speeches which ungodly sinners have spoken against him".

Convict: To prove guilty; to constrain one to admit or acknowledge himself to be guilty. As in James 2 "If ye have respect to persons, ye commit sin, and are convinced of by the law as transgressors". To convince all that are ungodly among them of all their ungodly deeds. Jude 15.

Convincement:, (noun). Conviction. Little used.

Convincer: (noun). He or that which convinces; that which makes manifest.

Convincible: (adverb)1. Capable of conviction. 2. Capable of being disproved or refuted. Little used.

Convincing: (ppr) 1. Persuading the mind by evidence; convicting. 2. a. Persuading the mind by evidence; capable of subduing the opposition of the mind and compelling its assent. We have convincing proof of the truth of the scriptures, and of Gods moral government of the world.

Convincingly: (adverb). In a convincing manner; in a manner to leave no room to doubts, or to compel assent.

Corinth: A city and former municipality in Corinthia, Peloponnese, Greece. Since the 2011 local government reform it is part of the municipality Corinth, of which it is the seat and a municipal unit. It is the capital of Corinthia. It was founded as Nea Korinthos or New Corinth in 1858 after an earthquake destroyed the existing settlement of *Corinth*, which had developed in and around the site of ancient Corinth. 2 The place of Paul's Second Missionary Journey – the troubled Church as in (1 Corinthians 1:2-3) thus 'To the church of God in *Corinth*, to those sanctified in Christ Jesus and called to be his holy people, together with all those everywhere who call on the name of our Lord Jesus Christ— their Lord and ours: Grace and peace to you from God our Father and the Lord Jesus Christ'.

Corinthians: Actually referred to the people of Corinth. A Corinthian is an indigene of Corinth. 2 The First Epistle to the Corinthians (Ancient Greek:), often referred to as First Corinthians (and written as 1 Corinthians), is the seventh book of the New Testament gospel of the Bible. Paul the Apostle and "Sosthenes our brother" wrote this epistle to "the church of God which is at Corinth", in Greece. (1Corinthians.1:1–2) This epistle contains some well-known phrases, including (depending on the translation) "all things to all men" (1 Corinthians 9:22), "without love, I am nothing" (1 Corinthians 13:2), "through a glass, darkly" (1 Corinthians 13:12), and "when I was a child, I spoke as a child, I felt as a child, I thought as a child" (I Corinthians 13:11).

Corpus Christi, The Feast of:

(The Christi Domini) The Feast of Corpus Christi (Latin for Body of Christ), also known as Corpus Domini, is a Latin Rite liturgical solemnity celebrating the tradition and belief in the body and blood of Jesus Christ and his Real Presence in the Eucharist. It emphasizes the joy of the institution of the Eucharist, which was observed on Holy Thursday in the sombre atmosphere of the nearness of Good Friday. In the present Roman Missal, the feast is designated the solemnity of The Most Holy Body and Blood of Christ. It is also celebrated in some Anglican, Lutheran, and Old Catholic Churches that hold similar beliefs regarding the Real Presence.

The feast is liturgically celebrated on the Thursday after Trinity Sunday or, "where the Solemnity of the Most Holy Body and Blood of Christ is not a holy day of obligation, it is assigned to the Sunday after the Most Holy Trinity as its proper day". At the end of Holy Mass, there is often a procession of the Blessed Sacrament, generally displayed in a monstrance. The procession is followed by Benediction of the Blessed Sacrament. 2 A typical Eucharistic procession is that presided over by the Pope each year in Rome, where it begins at the Arch basilica of St. John Lateran and makes its way to the Basilica of Saint Mary Major, where it concludes with Benediction of the

Corpus Christi's - Gospel

Blessed Sacrament. A typical Corpus Christi proclamation is found in Moses words to the Children of Israel in (Deuteronomy 8:2-3) thus: "Remember how for forty years now the LORD, your God, has directed all your journeying in the desert, so as to test you by affliction and find out whether or not it was your intention to keep his commandments. He therefore let you be afflicted with hunger, and then fed you with manna, a food unknown to you and your fathers, in order to show you that not by bread alone does one live, but by every word that comes forth from the mouth of the LORD. "Do not forget the LORD, your God, who brought you out of the land of Egypt, that place of slavery; who guided you through the vast and terrible desert with its seraph serpents and scorpions, its parched and waterless ground; who brought forth water for you from the flinty rock and fed you in the desert with manna, a food unknown to your fathers." Again, there are responsorial Psalms in supports of Corpus Christi. Notably (Psalm 147:12-13), Glorify the LORD, O Jerusalem; praise your God, O Zion. For he has strengthened the bars of your gates; he has blessed your children within you. Praise the Lord, Jerusalem Hallelujah (Psalm 147 14-15), He has granted peace in your borders; with the best of wheat he fills you. He sends forth his command to the earth; swiftly runs his word! Praise the Lord Jerusalem. Alleluia! (Psalm 147: 19-20) He has proclaimed his word to Jacob, his statutes and his ordinances to Israel. He has not done thus for any other nation; his ordinances he has not made known to them. Hallelujah! Praise the Lord Jerusalem. Hallelujah!

3 Corpus Christi also connotes the one body of Christ through the breaking of the bread and drinking of wine – the blood of Christ. As in one body of Christ meaning that all Christly souls are one in Him - (1 Corinthians 10:16-17) "Brothers and sisters: The cup of blessing that we bless, is it not a participation in the blood of Christ? The bread that we break, is it not a participation in the body of Christ? Because the loaf of bread is one, we, though, many are one body, for we all partake of the one loaf".

Corpus Christi's - Gospel:

(John 6:51-5) Jesus said to the Jewish crowds: "I am the living bread that came down from heaven; whoever eats this bread will live forever; and the bread that I will give is my flesh for the life of the world." The Jews quarrelled among themselves, saying, "How can this man give us his flesh to eat?" Jesus said to them, "Amen, amen, I say to you, unless you eat the flesh of the Son of Man and drink his blood, you do not have life within you. Whoever eats my flesh and drinks my blood has eternal life, and I will raise him on

Counsellor

the last day. For my flesh is true food, and my blood is true drink. Whoever eats my flesh and drinks my blood remains in me and I in him. Just as the living Father sent me and I have life because of the Father, so also the one who feeds on me will have life because of me. This is the bread that came down from heaven. Unlike your ancestors who ate and still died, whoever eats this bread will live forever." Bread here means food.

Counsellor: (noun) In the gospel or Scripture, a Counsellor is a Man of God, a pastor, while Christians popularly recognise Jesus as a Saviour and Counsellor. The Holy Spirit is the one who comforts, advises and strengthens Christians, drawing them closer to Jesus Christ. The Holy Spirit is Counsellor in addition to Jesus Christ. Indeed Jesus Christ is a Counsellor (1 John 2:1) One Greek word "Parakletos" underlies this phrase which is primarily a legal term. It can also bear the meaning "comforter". The Spirit is another Counsellor (John 14:16-17). The word "another" means "another of the same kind". After the ascension, the Spirit is to assume the ministry of Jesus Christ. The Counsellor is the gift of the exalted Christ (John 16:7) and (John 7:38-39; Acts 2:33). The Counsellor comforts and reassures believers. (John 14:16-18; Act 11:12) Peter is reassured about going to the house of Cornelius; (Roman 8:16) Believers are reassured that they are God's children. God so endowed Jesus Christ with divine power and wisdom through the Holy Ghost to teach or counsel even the Pharisees in the temple. In that case, the definition of Counsellor is seen as: A person trained to give guidance on personal or religious, life, psychological problems. "a religious counsellor" synonyms: adviser, consultant, guide, mentor, confidant, confidante; a person who gives advice on a specified subject. "a debt counsellor like Jesus who paid our debt with His blood". The Counsellor strengthens and equips the church. (Ephesians 3:16) and (Act 4:31) The Jerusalem church is strengthened in the face of opposition; (Acts 9:31 the church in Judea, Galilee and Samaria; "Then the church throughout Judea, Galilee and Samaria enjoyed a time of peace and was strengthened. Living in the fear of the Lord and encouraged by the Holy Spirit, it increased in numbers". In (Romans 8:26) "In the same way, the Spirit helps us in our weakness. We do not know what we ought to pray for, but the Spirit himself intercedes for us through wordless groans". That means - The Counsellor teaches and instructs believers. Other meanings are: 2 A senior officer in the diplomatic service. "a counsellor at the Russian embassy" 3 A person who gives counsel; adviser 4 (Social Welfare) a person, such as a social worker, who is involved in counselling. 5 (Law) Also called:

Counsellor-ship

counsellor-at-law US a lawyer, especially one who conducts cases in court; attorney. 6 (Government, Politics & Diplomacy) a senior British diplomatic officer. 7 (Government, Politics & Diplomacy) a US diplomatic officer ranking just below an ambassador or minister. 8 (Education) a person who advises students or others on personal problems or academic and occupational choice

Counsellor-ship: (noun) Act of counselling or The entire process of counselling.

Covenant: Covenant (law), a promise to engage in or refrain from a specified action. 2 Restrictive covenant, a restriction on the use of property Religion. 3 Covenant (religion), a formal alliance or agreement made by God with a religious community or with humanity in general 4 Covenant (biblical) 5 Covenant (Latter Day Saints), in the Church of Jesus Christ of Latter Day Saints, a sacred agreement between God and a person or group of people.

6 A *covenant* is a contract or agreement between two or more parties. *Covenant* is how God has chosen to communicate to us, to redeem us, and to guarantee us eternal life in Jesus. These truths, revealed in the gospel, are the basis of Christianity. The Bible is a *covenant* document. The Old and New Testaments are really Old and New *Covenants*. The word "testament" is Latin for *Covenant*.

There is a pattern to the *covenants* found in the gospel. Basically, it is as follows. The initiating party describes himself and what He has done, then there is a list of obligations between the two (or more) parties. What follows is the section dealing with rewards and punishments that govern the keeping and breaking of the *covenant*. The Ten Commandments fit this pattern and are a *covenant* document. 7 *Covenant* is how God first decided to deal with mankind. We know this from studying the Eternal *Covenant* mentioned in (Hebrew. 13:20), "May the God of peace, who through the blood of the eternal *covenant* brought back from the dead our Lord Jesus, that great Shepherd of the sheep" . In this *covenant*, God the Father and the Son made an agreement regarding the elect. This *covenant* was made before the universe was created, and it consisted of the Father promising to bring to the Son all whom the Father had given Him (John 6:39; 17:9, 24). The Son would become man (Colossian. 2:9; 1 Timothy. 2:5), become for a while lower than the angels (Hebrew. 2:7), and be found under the Law (Galatian. 4:4-5). The Son would die for the sins of the world (1 John 2:2; 1 Peter. 2:24), and the Father would raise the Son from the Dead (Psalm 2).

The Eternal Covenant, then, leads to the *Covenant* of Grace. Where the Eternal *Covenant* was made between the Father and the Son, the *Covenant* of Grace is made between God and man. This latter *covenant* is where God promises to man eternal salvation based upon the sacrifice of Jesus on the cross. The manifestation of that *covenant* occurs in our world in a sequence of additional *covenants* that God made with individuals: Adam (Genesis 2:15-17), Noah (Genesis. 9:12-16), Abraham (Genesis. 17), the Israelites at Mount Sinai (Exodus 34:28), believers in the New *Covenant* (Jeremiah. 31:31-37), etc. I present the view that there are two main covenants. However, there is disagreement as to the number of *Covenants*. Some say there is really only one, the Eternal *Covenant*, with all others falling under it. Some say two, some say three, and others four, etc. There really is no absolute answer.

9 Understanding *Covenant* is important for several reasons: We learn that God deals with man covenant-ally. Since a *Covenant* is an agreement, it is a promise made by God. Because we can rely on God's word for eternity, we can take great comfort in His *covenant* promising us eternal life in His Son.

It helps us to see the Bible as a covenant document. The Old and New Testaments are Old and New *Covenants*. With *Covenant* understood as a framework through which the Bible was written, we can better understand it, God's dealings with us through it, and our responsibilities to God as well as His to us. We can better understand the symbols used by God in *covenant* ratification: The Lord's Supper and Baptism. Whatever covenant we understands in the gospel of Christ, we must not forget those that deals directly with good – through righteousness that leads to eternal life through Christ Jesus and refrain from the devilish covenant that leads to eternal condemnation.

Confirmation: One of the Seven Sacraments. A rite of initiation in several Christian denominations, normally carried out through anointing, the laying on of hands, and prayer, for the purpose of bestowing the Gift of the Holy Spirit. In Christianity, confirmation is seen as the sealing of the covenant created in Holy Baptism. In some denominations, confirmation also bestows full membership in a local congregation upon the recipient. In others, such as the Roman Catholic Church, confirmation "renders the bond with the Church more perfect", because, while a baptized person is already a member, "reception of the sacrament of *Confirmation* is necessary for the completion of baptismal grace".

Roman Catholics, Eastern Orthodox, Oriental Orthodox Churches, and many Anglicans view *Confirmation* as a sacrament. In the East it is conferred immediately after baptism. In the West, this practice is followed when adults are bap-

Covet

tized, but in the case of infants not in danger of death it is administered, ordinarily by a bishop, only when the child reaches the age of reason or early adolescence. Among those Catholics who practice teen-aged confirmation, the practice may be perceived, secondarily, as a "coming of age" rite.

In Protestant churches, the rite tends to be seen rather as a mature statement of faith by an already baptised person. It is also required by most Protestant denominations for membership in the respective church, in particular for traditional Protestant churches. In traditional Protestant churches (Presbyterian, Methodist, Lutheran etc.) it is recognized by a coming of age ceremony. Confirmation is not practised in Baptist, Anabaptist and other groups that teach believer's baptism. 2 Completes Baptism by a new outpouring of the Holy Spirit and enables the Christian for mission. This was seen at Pentecost with respect to the apostles. In the early Church it was often accompanied by charismatic signs, though these are not intrinsic to the sacrament. Conferred by the laying on of hands. In Acts 19:3-6, especially, it is clear that John's baptism, Christian baptism and Confirmation are all distinct realities. Also, in (Hebrews 6:2) baptizing and laying on of hands are distinguished. (Isaiah 44:3; Ezekiel 39:29; Joel 2:28; John 14:16; Acts 2:4; Acts 8:14-17; Acts 19:3-6; Hebrews 6:2).

Covet, (Covetousness): Yearn to possess (something, especially something belonging to another). Often used as covetousness. On the surface, covetousness may not seem to be related to the subject of goals. However, that what we covet becomes our goal. If we covet the wrong things, we will have the wrong goals, and we may thus sacrifice things of great value in our effort to attain what has little ultimate and eternal value. 2 Coveting is a desire. It is a matter of the heart, an attitude, a matter of strong emotion. As such, coveting is somewhat unique among the evils condemned by the commandments. The evils prohibited by the other commandments were such that one could be tried and found guilty of committing a certain act. This act was based upon attitudes, of course, but a society cannot convict people for what they are thinking and feeling. The final commandment is a forbidden feeling, as it were, not a forbidden act. 3 Coveting is a strong desire. Coveting is a desire, a motivation so strong that the one who covets something will have it if there is any way possible to do so, even if it involves evil. Coveting is a consuming desire, which is highly competitive. It is an evil attitude, which will likely lead to an evil act. Coveting is a kind of conspiracy in one's soul to commit evil. 4 The coveting which the Tenth Commandment condemns is the desire to have something which one does not have, or which one does not have, or which one does not think he or she has enough of. In brief, coveting wants more. It is not content with what it already has, no matter how much that might be. As (Habakkuk 2:5) put it, "He enlarges his appetite like Sheol, And he is like death, never satisfied"

Creation: This is the creation myth of both Judaism and Christianity. Thus in (Genesis 1:1) "In the beginning, God created the heavens and the earth. 2 The earth was without form and void, and darkness was over the face of the deep. And the Spirit of God was hovering over the face of the waters" It is made up of two parts, roughly equivalent to the first two chapters of the Book of Genesis. In the first part, (Genesis 1:1) through (Genesis 2:3), Elohim, the Hebrew generic word for God, creates the world in six days, starting with light and darkness on the first day, and ending with the creation of mankind on the sixth day. God then rests on, blesses and sanctifies the seventh day. 2 In the second part, (Genesis 2:4-24) God, now referred to by the personal name "Yahweh", creates the first man from dust and breathes a soul into him. God then places him in the Garden of Eden and creates the first woman from his rib as a companion. A common hypothesis among biblical scholars is that the first major comprehensive draft of the Pentateuch (the series of five books which begins with Genesis and ends with Deuteronomy) was composed in the late 7th or the 6th century BC (the Yahwist source) and that this was later expanded by other authors (the Priestly source) into a work very like the one we have today. (In the creation narrative the two sources appear in reverse order: (Genesis 1:1–2:30) is Priestly and (Genesis 2:4–24) is Yahwistic). Borrowing themes from Mesopotamian mythology, but adapting them to Israel's belief in one God, the combined narrative is a critique of theology of *creation*: Genesis affirms monotheism and denies polytheism. The two stories are complementary rather than overlapping, with the first (the Priestly story) concerned with the cosmic plan of creation, while the second (the Yahwist story) focuses on man as cultivator of his environment and as a moral agent. There are significant parallels between the two stories, but also significant differences: the second account, in contrast to the regimented seven-day scheme of Genesis 1, uses a simple flowing narrative style that proceeds from God's forming the first man through the Garden of Eden to the *creation* of the first woman and the institution of marriage; in contrast to the omnipotent God of genesis 1, creating a god-like humanity, the God of Genesis 2 can fail as well as succeed; the humanity he creates is not god-like, but is punished for acts which would lead to their becoming god-like (Genesis 3:1-24); and the order and method of creation itself differs.["Together,

Creator

this combination of parallel character and contrasting profile point to the different origin of materials in Genesis 1:1–2:3) and (Genesis 2:4b–3:23), however elegantly they have now been combined."

Creator: One that creates: 2. Creator – God - An epithet of God. Blessed Trinity, Holy Trinity, Sacred Trinity, Trinity - the union of the Father and Son and Holy Ghost in one Godhead hypostasis of Christ, hypostasis - any of the three persons of the Godhead constituting the Trinity especially the person of Christ in which divine and human natures are united as in (Nehemiah 9:6) "You alone are the LORD You have made the heavens, The heaven of heavens with all their host, The earth and all that is on it, The seas and all that is in them You give life to all of them And the heavenly host bows down before You".Hallelujah! Also in (Isaiah 45:7) God affirms He is the Creator thus "The One forming light and creating darkness, Causing well-being and creating calamity; I am the LORD who does all these".

Creature: (Kre'-tur) Referred to the content of Heaven, Earth, Seen and Unseen. Something created. 2 A living being, especially an animal: land creatures; microscopic creatures in a drop of water. A human. An imaginary or fantastical being: mythological creatures; a creature from outer space .3 One dependent on or subservient to another. 4 "creature," as it occurs in the New Testament, is the translation and also the exact English equivalent of the Greek ktisis, or ktisma, from ktizo, "to create." In the Old Testament, on the other hand, it stands for words which have in the original no reference to creation, but which come from other roots. Nephesh, "living creature" (literally, "a breathing thing"), occurs in the accounts of the Creation and the Flood and at the close of the lists of clean and unclean animals in (Leviticus 11:46). Chai, "living creature" (literally, "a living thing"), occurs 13 times in Ezekiel 1; 3 and 10 (see CREATURE, LIVING). Sherbets, "moving creature" (literally, "a swarming thing," generally rendered "creeping thing," which see), occurs once in (Genesis 1:20). 'Ochim, "doleful creatures," occurs once only in (Isaiah 13:21). It appears to be an onomatopoetic word referring to the mournful sounds emitted by the animals in question. From the context it is fair to suppose that owls may be the animals referred to.

Creature, Living: Existing and having the ability to grow, act, move, sense, shake etc. "Living creature" (Hebrew - chayyah) is the designation of each of the composite figures in Ezekiel's visions (Ezekiel 1:5, 13; Ezekiel 3:13; Ezekiel 10:15, 17, 20), of the similar beings in the visions of the Apocalypse, instead of the extremely unfortunate translation of zoon in the King James Version by "beasts" (Revelation 4:6; Revelation 5:6; 6:1; 7:11; 14:03; 15:07;

19:4), the low meaning which "beast," "beastly" have with us; are translated in (1Corinthians 15:44), the "beasts" that came up, the notable "beast" that men worshipped, represent the Greek therion, "a wild beast." 4a - The "living creatures" in Ezekiel's vision (Ezekiel 1:5) were four in number, "with the general appearance of a man, but each with four faces and four wings, and straight legs with the feet of an ox. Under their wings are human hands, and these wings are so joined that they never require to turn. The front face is that of a man; right and left of this are the faces of a lion and (of) an ox, and behind, that of an eagle. out of the midst of them gleam fire, torches, lightning's, and connected with them are four wheels that can turn in every direction, called whirling wheels (Ezekiel 10:12, 13). Like the creatures, these are alive, covered with eyes, the sign of intelligence; the spirit of the living creatures is in them. They are afterward discovered by the prophet to be cherubim". In Ezekiel's vision they seem to be the bearers of the throne and glory of God; the bearers of His presence and of His revelation (Ezekiel 9:3; Ezekiel 10:3). They also sound forth His praise (Ezekiel 3:12; Ezekiel 10:2). The four living creatures in (Revelation 4:6) are not under the throne but "in the midst of the throne" see (Revelation 7:17); compare (Revelation 5:6) and "round about the throne." They are also cherubim, and seems to represent the four beings that stand at the head of the four divisions of the creation; among the untamed animals the lion; among cattle the calf or ox; among birds the eagle; among all created beings the man. It gives "a perfect picture of true service, which should be as brave as the lion, patient as the ox, aspiring as the eagle, intelligent as man" 4b - Again, they represent the powers of Nature-of the creation, "full of eyes" as denoting its permeation with the Divine Reason, the wings signifying its constant, ready service, and the unceasing praise the constant doing of God's will. The imagery is founded on Ezekiel as that had been modified in apocalyptic writings and as it was exalted in the mind of the Seer of Patmos - According to (Revelation 1:3) Thus "Blessed is he that readeth, and they that hear the words of this prophecy, and keep those things which are written therein; for the time is at hand."

Creed: This is a statement of the shared beliefs of a religious community in the form of a fixed formula summarizing core tenets. One of the most widely used creeds in Christianity is the Nicene Creed, first formulated in AD 325 at the First Council of Nicaea. It was based on Christian understanding of the Canonical Gospels, the letters of the New Testament and to a lesser extent the Old Testament. Affirmation of this creed, which describes the Trinity, is generally taken as a fundamental test of orthodoxy for most Christian

Creeping things

denominations. 2 The Apostles' Creed is also broadly accepted. Some Christian denominations and other groups have rejected the authority of those creeds. 3 Creed simply means the Statements of faith.

Examples of creeds or declarations of faith in the gospels are as follows: (Deuteronomy. 6:4): " Hear O Israel, the LORD is our God, the LOR alone". (1 Kings. 18:39): "And when all the people saw it, they fell on their faces; and they said, "The LORD, he is God; the LORD, he is God." (Matthew. 16:16): Simon Peter replied, "You are the Christ, the Son of the living God." (Matthew. 28:19): "Go therefore and make disciples of all nations, baptizing them in the name of the Father and of the Son and of the Holy Spirit". "John 1:49": Nathan'a-el answered him, "Rabbi, you are the Son of God! You are the King of Israel! (John 6:68-69): Simon Peter answered him, "Lord to whom shall we go? You have the words of eternal life; and we have believed, and have come to know, that you are the Holy One of God." (John 20:28): Thomas answered him, "My Lord and my God!" (Acts 8:36-37): And as they went along the road they came to some water, and the eunuch said, "See, her is water! What is to prevent my being baptized?" And Philip said, "If you believe with all your heart, you may." And he replied, "I believe that Jesus Christ is the Son of God". And much more.

Creeping things: Moving things, the creature of God on the six day as in (Genesis 1:24 - 25) "Then God said, "Let the earth bring forth living creatures after their kind: cattle and creeping things and beasts of the earth after their kind"; and it was so. God made the beasts of the earth after their kind, and the cattle after their kind, and everything that creeps on the ground after its kind; and God saw that it was good...."

Cross: (*noun*) A geometrical figure consisting of two lines or bars perpendicular to each other, dividing one or two of the lines in half. The lines usually run vertically and horizontally; if they run obliquely, the design is technically termed a saltire, although the arms of a saltire need not meet at right angles. The cross is one of the most ancient human symbols, and has been used by many religions, most notably Christianity. It may be seen as a division of the world into four elements (Chevalier, 1997) or cardinal points, or alternately as the union of the concepts of divinity, the vertical line, and the world, the horizontal line. 2 Cross signifies the human sinful body. For anyone to follow Christ, must deny himself all the yearnings of life that may lead to sin and follow Christ. Note: the wages of sin is death. As Christians, when we deny the yearnings of life, we deny sin and submit ourselves to Christ who was nailed on the cross so that as He has resurrected into eternal life those who have abandoned the yearnings and worries of life and follow Him might reign with Him in Glory as in (Mark 8:34-38) "And He summoned the multitude with His disciples, and said to them, "If anyone wishes to come after Me, let him deny himself, and take up his cross, and follow Me. For whoever wishes to save his life shall lose it; but whoever loses his life for My sake and the gospel's shall save it. For what does it profit a man to gain the whole world, and forfeit his soul? For what shall a man give in exchange for his soul? For whoever is ashamed of Me and My words in this adulterous and sinful generation, the Son of Man will also be ashamed of him when He comes in the glory of His Father with the holy angels."

Cross of Christ: This is the centre of Christianity. After Communion the Lord explained to the disciples in very convincing words that His suffering on the *Cross* was necessary for believers to receive the gifts of the Holy Spirit: (John 16:7) "Nevertheless I tell you the truth. It is to your advantage that I go away; for if I do not go away, the Helper will not come to you; but if I depart I will send Him to you" A few days before His crucifixion, the Lord Jesus Christ again spoke of the great task that awaited Him, explaining to His Apostles that He had come to the earth precisely to accomplish this: "Now My soul is troubled, and what shall I say? `Father save Me from this hour'? but for this purpose I came to this hour" (John 12:27). Then the Lord explained that His death would be beneficial to mankind: "The hour has come that the Son of Man should be glorified ... Amen I say unto you, unless a grain of wheat falls into the ground and dies, it remains alone; but if it dies, it brings forth much grain ... Now is the judgment of this world; now will the ruler of this world [the devil] be cast out. And I, if I am lifted up ([the Cross) I will draw all peoples to Myself." "This, He said," adds the evangelist, "signifying by what death He should die" (John 12:23–34). Only at the Last Supper, during the farewell conversation, did the Saviour shed more light about the benefits of His suffering and death. In particular, the Lord explained that He must suffer for: the expulsion of the devil, the drawing of people to salvation, the remission of sins, the sending down of the Spirit Comforter, and the preparation of heavenly abodes. We are taught by the Scriptures that His voluntary sufferings and death were absolutely necessary for our salvation. In other words, His death on the Cross did not occur as a result of unfavourable circumstances, nor did He accept it only to admonish us, as some explain in a simplified manner: it was the main and most important event of His redemptive mission. The Lord came to earth specifically to save us by means of His suffering! Paul Apostle declare in (Galatians 6:14) "Far be it from me to boast, except in the *cross of our Lord Jesus*

Cross, The Christian

Christ, through which the world has been crucified to me, and I to the world."

Cross, The Christian: The Christian Cross, seen as a representation of the instrument of the crucifixion of Jesus, is the best-known symbol of Christianity. It is related to the crucifix (a cross that includes a usually three-dimensional representation of Jesus' body) and to the more general family of cross symbols.

Cross for sacrificial Service: Christ stated on more than one occasion, "And he who does not take his cross and follow after Me is not worthy of Me. He who finds his life will lose it, and he who loses his life for My sake will find it" (Matthew 10:38-39; also 16:24-25; Mark 8:34-35; Luke 9:23-24; 14:27). The cross represents our duty to follow in Christ's footsteps. There are three aspects to this. First, we must mortify our fleshly desires in obedience to God. For in times past, when heresies prevailed, many chose death through martyrdom and various tortures. Now, when we through the grace of Christ live in a time of profound and perfect peace, we learn for sure that the cross and death consist in nothing else than the complete mortification of self-will. He who pursues his own will, however slightly, will never be able to observe the precepts of Christ the Saviour. 2 The cross represents the standard by which we endeavour to persevere when we are being persecuted for our faith: As in Hebrew 12:2-3) "looking unto Jesus, the author and finisher of our faith, who for the joy that was set before Him endured the *cross*. For consider Him who endured such hostility from sinners against Himself, lest you become weary and discouraged in your souls". Also, the cross reminds us of what God was willing to bear in order to communicate His love to us, and therefore it is our example of what we should be willing to undergo for others: (John 15:13) "Greater love has no one than this, than to lay down one's life for his friends"

Cross for Reconciliation: There are many events in the Old Testament that foreshadow the *cross*: the blood of a lamb placed on lintels and doorposts during Passover (Exodus 12:23); Moses lifting his staff and parting the Red Sea (Exodus 14:16); Moses' arms outstretched in prayer for victory over Israel's enemies (Exodus 17:8-15); and Israel being saved from poisoning by looking at a bronze serpent on a pole (Numbers 21:6-9). There are also prophetic allusions to the cross: the curse of being hung on a tree (Deuteronomy 21:23); the predicted passion of the Messiah (Psalm 22); and the saving mark on the forehead (Ezekiel 9:3-6). These references attest that the cross was always part of God's plan for salvation. God *reconciles* His people by delivering us from the consequences of sin, and the means God uses to rescue us is the cross. Isaiah stated that the

Messiah "poured out His soul unto death and He was numbered with the transgressors. He bore the sin of many and made intercession for the transgressors" (Isaiah 53:12). The apostle Paul confirmed this prophecy when he wrote, "For it pleased the Father that in Him all the fullness should dwell, and by Him to reconcile all things to Himself, by Him, whether things on earth or things in heaven, having made peace through the blood of His cross" (Colossians 1:19-20; see also 2:13-15). The cross represents God's victory over sin: For the cross destroyed the enmity of God towards man, brought about *reconciliation*, made the earth heaven, associated men with angels, pulled down the citadel of death, unstrung the force of the devil, extinguished the power of sin, delivered the world from error, brought back the truth, expelled the demons, destroyed temples, implanted virtue, (and) grounded the churches.

Cross as a Shield: The cross is "the shield of faith with which you will be able to quench all the fiery darts of the wicked one" (Ephesians 6:16). From the very beginning of Christianity, believers were using the sign of the cross as a means of protection against evil. Crosses were commonly placed on walls, over doorways, and above beds in Christian homes to safeguard the family. Of course, it is not the piece of wood, nor the gesture of making the sign of the cross with our hands, that has supernatural powers; rather it is our faith that saves us (Luke 7:50; 17:19; 18:42). The cross is a powerful reminder to depend on God when we are being tempted. Having a cross doesn't necessarily mean we will be rescued from the hands of men-as the twelfth-century crusaders found out when they marched into battle with a portion of the true cross but still lost to Saladin's army. Nevertheless, the cross is a powerful ally against the demonic forces trying to rob us of our salvation: Learn how great is the power of the cross; how many good things it hath achieved, and doth still; how it is the safety of our life.... If we are on journeys, if we are at home, wherever we are, the cross is a great good, the armour of salvation, a shield which cannot be beaten down, a weapon to oppose the devil; thou bearest the cross when thou art an enmity with him, not simply when thou sealest thyself by it, but when thou sufferest the things belonging to the cross.

Cross as a sign of gathering: The prophet Jeremiah proclaimed, "Thus says the LORD: 'Stand in the ways (or "at the crossroads") and see, And ask for the old paths, where the good way is, And walk in it; Then you will find rest for your souls'" (Jeremiah 6:16). The most common architectural shape for a church building is that of a cross (cruciform). Churches have crosses on the apex of their roofs, on top of their steeples, or crowning their domes. There is a cross on

Cross as a Benediction

the wall of the sanctuary, on the altar, or hanging from the ceiling. The cross is central to the Church not because it merely symbolizes the Christian faith, but because all churches stand at the "crossroads." The church is the meeting place where people learn about the "old paths, where the good way is," are instructed how to "walk in it," and "find rest for (their) souls." In other words, the church-and the cross-is where we determine the course of our lives and are reminded of the commitments we've already made. The Orthodox Church also believes that the cross will be the sign in the sky heralding the Second Advent as (Isaiah 11:10 -12) "And in that day there shall be a Root of Jesse, Who shall stand as a banner to the people; For the Gentiles shall seek Him, And His resting place shall be glorious . . . He will set up a banner for the nations, And will assemble the outcasts of Israel, And gather together the dispersed of Judah From the four corners of the earth". Christ said in (Mathew 24:30) "Then the sign of the Son of Man will appear in heaven, and then all the tribes of the earth will mourn, and they will see the Son of Man coming on the clouds of heaven with power and great glory".

Cross as a Benediction: The cross is also used as an expression of blessing. Throughout the Bible, people prayed using various physical gestures: uplifted hands, laying hands on another, prostrations, and more. Today, many people fold their hands when they pray-although it is not a posture found in the Bible for prayer. Similarly, making the sign of the cross with one's hand is not found in the Bible, but it has traditionally been used as a gesture to ask for God's grace upon oneself, to give a blessing to another, or to consecrate something or someone for a sacred purpose. In the third century, the great Christian apologist Tertullian wrote: In every successful undertaking, at every arrival and departure, while dressing, putting on one's shoes, in bath or at table, at lamp lighting, in bed or on seats, in a word: in all our activities, we trace the sign of the cross upon ourselves, according to the tradition of the Apostles who inspired their first disciples, and through them, all the faithful, as a sign of their confession, always to place the sign of the cross over their face and chest. By the sign of the cross we are brought into the Church through baptism. The cross is the new circumcision that identifies us as part of God's people (Galatians 5:11; 6:14). By the cross we are sanctified to serve within the Church, and to receive what the Church imparts-most importantly, the Sacraments themselves.

Cross as The Tree of Life: The cross is symbolic of God's promise to us of eternal life. Orthodox hymnographies' often connects the tree of life found in the Garden of Eden (Genesis 2:9; 3:22-24) with the cross. For example: O wondrous miracle! Today, the Cross is beheld raised above the earth as a Jerusalem oak teeming with life, which held the Most High. By the Cross, we have all been drawn to God, and death is swallowed up. O undefiled tree! Through you we delight in the immortal food in Eden, glorifying Christ. (Praises, Outros, Sunday after the Elevation of the Precious Cross) This fruit from *the tree of life* is only granted to those who overcome trials and maintain their devotion to God (Revelation 21:7). Yet it is by clinging to the cross that we are able to do both. In fact, St. Basil the Great affirms that Christians will, metaphorically, become the cross/tree of life as was described in the first psalm: Thanks to the redemption wrought by the *Tree of Life*, that is by the passion of the Lord, all that happens to us is eternal and eternally conscious of happiness in virtue of our future likeness to that *Tree of Life*. For all their doings shall prosper being wrought no longer amid shift and change nor in human weakness, for corruption will be swallowed up in corruption, weakness in endless life, the form of earthly flesh in the form of God. This tree, then, planted and yielding its fruit in its own season, shall that happy man resemble, himself being planted in the garden, that what God has planted may abide, never to be rooted up, in the garden where all things done by God shall be guided to a prosperous issue.

Cross as a Ladder: Finally, the cross represents the totality of the Christian message. Our Lord was suspended between heaven and earth when He was crucified, and thus St. Paul reminds us, "there is . . . one Mediator between God and man, the Man Christ Jesus" (1 Timothy 2:5); see also (Hebrews 8:6; 9:15; 12:24). Christ symbolically becomes a type of "ladder" between this temporal world and the eternal realm beyond. St. Augustine stated, "For the Son of Man is above as our Head, being Himself the Saviour, and He is below in His body, the Church. He is the Ladder, for He says, 'I am the way.'" So, looking at the cross, we should be reminded of the entire life and ministry of Jesus Christ, who taught the way into God's Kingdom. The cross also stands for the whole history of the Church from the Old Testament to the present-all God has done to reach down to us as we struggle to climb up towards Him (James 4:8-10). As St. Jerome explained, "The Christian life is the true Jacob's Ladder on which angels ascend and descend." However, the cross not only informs us. It also transforms us. Crosses are placed on graves not just to indicate that the deceased was a Christian, but to express the hope that by the cross the loved one will "cross over" from this life to the next. There can be no resurrection without the cross. There can be no joyful entry into heaven without the cross: O wondrous miracle! The length and breadth of the Cross equals that of heaven, for by divine grace it sanctifies the universe. Barbarian nations are vanquished by it; sceptres of kings are made firm

Crown

by it. O divine ladder, by which we ascend to heaven, exalting Christ the Lord in song. (Praises, Outros, Sunday after the Elevation of the Precious Cross) The cross is more than a pretty piece of jewellery to wear around our necks; it is more than an attractive decoration to hang on the walls of our homes; it is more than a sign that defines a particular building as being a church. Canon 73 of the Council of Trullo stated, "Since the life-giving cross has shown to us salvation, we should be careful that we render due honour to that by which we were saved from the ancient fall. Wherefore, in mind, in word, in feeling giving veneration to it." If we are to have any hope of reclaiming the cross; if we are to illumine our the cross with the light of Christ; if we are to restore it to its place as the crux of our salvation-we must understand in our own hearts the relationship we are called to have with it. In the words of St. Gregory Palamas: You should venerate not only the icon of Christ, but also the similitude of His cross. For the cross is Christ's great sign and trophy of victory over the devil and all his hostile hosts; for this reason they tremble and flee when they see the figuration of the cross. This figure, even prior to crucifixion, was greatly glorified by the prophets and wrought wonders; and when He who was hung upon it, our Lord Jesus Christ, comes again to judge the living and the dead, this His great and terrible sign will precede Him, full of power and glory.

So glorify the cross now, so that you may boldly look upon it then and be glorified with it.

Crown: A circular ornamental headdress worn by a monarch as a symbol of authority, usually made of or decorated with precious metals and jewels. synonyms: coronet, diadem, tiara, circlet, chaplet, fillet, wreath, garland, headband; More the monarchy or reigning monarch. noun: Crown; noun: the Crown "their loyalty to the Church came before their loyalty to the Crown" synonyms: monarch, sovereign, king, queen, emperor, empress, tsar, tsarina, prince, princess, potentate, head of state, leader, chief, ruler, lord, overlord; More an ornament, emblem, or badge shaped like a crown. "shiny covers embossed with gold crowns. "a wreath of leaves or flowers, especially that worn as an emblem of victory in ancient Greece or Rome. 2 an award or distinction gained by a victory or achievement, especially in sport. "the world heavyweight crown" synonyms: title, award, accolade, honour, distinction, glory, kudos; etc. 3 The top or highest part of something. "the crown of the hill" synonyms: top, crest, summit, peak, pinnacle, tip, head, brow, cap, brink, highest point, zenith, apex, ridge; More antonyms: bottom the top part of a person's head or a hat. "his hair was swept straight back over his crown" the part of a plant just above and below the ground from which the roots and shoots branch out."

mulch should be mounded around the crowns of the shrubs" the upper branching or spreading part of a tree or other plant. "an erect evergreen tree with a dense crown" the upper part of a cut gem, above the girdle. 4 the part of a tooth projecting from the gum a thin layer of enamel covers the crown" an artificial replacement or covering for the upper part of a tooth. "emergency treatment for loose crowns" 5 a British coin with a face value of five shillings or 25 pence, now minted only for commemorative purposes .a foreign coin with a name meaning 'crown', especially the krona or krone. 6.a paper size, 384 × 504 mm. a book size, 186 × 123 mm. noun: crown octavo; plural noun: crown octavos a book size, 246 × 189 mm.noun: crown quarto; plural noun: crown quartos verb: crown; 3rd person present: crowns; past tense: crowned; past participle: crowned; gerund or present participle: crowning 1 ceremonially place a crown on the head of (someone) in order to invest them as a monarch "he went to Rome to be crowned" synonyms: invest, induct, install, instate, ordain, initiate, inaugurate, enthrone, swear in "David II was crowned at Scone in 1331"declare or acknowledge (someone) as the best, especially at a sport. "he was crowned world champion last September" (in draughts) promote (a piece) to king by placing another on top of it. "with his crowned piece he jumped them all" 2 rest on or form the top of. "the distant knoll was crowned with trees" synonyms: top, cap, tip, head, surmount, over top "the steeple is crowned by a gilded weathercock" 7 A type of dental restoration which completely caps or encircles a tooth or dental implant. Crowns are often needed when a large cavity threatens the on-going health of a tooth. They are typically bonded to the tooth using a dental cement. Crowns can be made from many materials, which are usually fabricated using indirect methods. Crowns are often used to improve the strength or appearance of teeth. While inarguably beneficial to dental health, the procedure and materials can be relatively expensive. The most common method of crowning a tooth involves using a dental impression of a prepared tooth by a dentist to fabricate the crown outside of the mouth. The crown can then be inserted at a subsequent dental appointment. Using this indirect method of tooth restoration allows use of strong restorative materials requiring time consuming fabrication methods requiring intense heat, such as casting metal or firing porcelain which would not be possible to complete inside the mouth. Because of the expansion properties, the relatively similar material costs, and the aesthetic benefits, many patients choose to have their crown fabricated with gold. There are five glorious crowns that will be given to believers according to the scriptures.

Crown, The Incorruptible

Crown, The Incorruptible: (1 Corinthians. 9:24,25). "Do you not know that those who run in a race all run, but one receives the prize? Run in such a way that you may obtain it. And everyone who competes for the prize is temperate in all things. Now they do it to obtain a perishable crown, but we for an imperishable crown.

This is also called the imperishable crown. This crown is given to believers who faithfully run the race, who crucify every selfish desire in the flesh and point men to Jesus.

Crown of Rejoicing, The: (1 Thessalonica. 2:19, 20).and (Daniel 12:3) "For what is our hope, or joy, or crown of rejoicing? Is it not even you in the presence of our Lord Jesus Christ at His coming? For you are our glory and joy". To those who faithfully are witnesses to the saving grace of God and leads souls to Jesus. This crown has also been named the soul winner's crown.

Crown of Life, The: (James 1:12). "Blessed is the man who endures temptation; for when he has been approved, he will receive *the crown of life* which the Lord has promised to those who love Him". For those believers who endure trials, tribulations, and severe suffering, even unto death (Revelation. 2:8-11). This crown is also referred to as the martyr's crown.

Crown of Righteousness, The: (2 Timothy. 4:8). "Finally, there is laid up for me *the crown of righteousness*, which the Lord, the righteous Judge, will give to me on that Day, and not to me only but also to all who have loved His appearing. To those who love the appearing of Christ, who anxiously wait and look forward to the day when He will return for His saints. This crown is given to those who have lived a good and righteous life for God while living down here on earth.

Crown of Glory, The: (1 Peter. 5:1-4). "The elders who are among you I exhort, I who am a fellow elder and a witness of the sufferings of Christ, and also a partaker of the glory that will be revealed: Shepherd the flock of God which is among you, serving as overseers, not by compulsion but willingly, not for dishonest gain but eagerly; nor as being lords over those entrusted to you, but being examples to the flock; and when the Chief Shepherd appears, you will receive *the crown of glory* that does not fade away". This is the pastor's crown and will be given to the ministers who faithfully feed the flock of God. . This probably could also include preachers, teachers, Sunday School teachers, missionaries and all those who teach the Word of God in their respective ministries.

Crucifixion: A form of slow and painful execution in which the victim is tied or nailed to a large wooden cross and left to hang until dead. It is principally known from antiquity, but remains in occasional use in some countries. The crucifixion of Jesus is a central event in Christianity and the crucifix is the main religious symbol for many churches.

Crucifixion, The: The New Testament account, presents Jesus, whom Christians believe to be the Son of God as well as the Messiah, was arrested, tried, and sentenced by Pontius Pilate to be scourged, and finally crucified. Collectively referred to as the Passion, Jesus' suffering and redemptive death by crucifixion are the central aspects of Christian theology concerning the doctrines of salvation and atonement. Jesus' crucifixion is described in the four canonical gospels, referred to in the New Testament Epistles, attested to by other ancient sources, and is established as a historical event confirmed by non-Christian sources, though there is no consensus on the precise details of what exactly occurred.

Crucify: (crucified, crucifying, crucifies): To put (a person) to death by nailing or binding to a cross. 2 To mortify or subdue (the flesh 3 To treat cruelly; torment: crucified the awkward child with teasing. 4 To criticize harshly; pillory: The media crucified the politician for breaking a campaign pledge. 5 To put to death by crucifixion 6 To defeat, ridicule, etc, totally: the critics crucified his performance. 7 To treat very cruelly; torment 8 To subdue (passion, lust, etc); Just as Pilate Delivers Jesus to Be Crucified as in (Mark 15: 12-14)

"Answering again, Pilate said to them, "Then what shall I do with Him whom you call the King of the Jews?" They shouted back, "*Crucify* Him!" But Pilate said to them, "Why, what evil has He done?" But they shouted all the more, "*Crucify* Him!" Also in (Matthew 23:34) the gospel declare "Wherefore, behold, I send unto you prophets, and wise men, and scribes: and some of them ye shall kill and *crucify*; and some of them shall ye scourge in your synagogues, and persecute them from city to city": because of the words of Grace to be preached to the poor, needy and sinners in order to transform them unto salvation and eternal life in Christ Jesus.

Cubit: (Hebrew – ammah – mother of the arm)An ancient unit of length based on the length of the forearm from the elbow to the tip of the middle finger. Cubits of various lengths were employed in many parts of the world in antiquity, during the Middle Ages and as recently as Early Modern Times. The term is still used in hedge laying, the length of the forearm being frequently used to determine the interval between stakes placed within the hedge. 2 Other units of measure based on the length of the forearm include some kinds of ell, the Indian Hasta 3 Cubit "mother of the arm," the

Cup

fore-arm, is a word derived from the Latin cubitus, the lower arm. It is difficult to determine the exact length of this measure, from the uncertainty whether it included the entire length from the elbow to the tip of the longest finger, or only from the elbow to the root of the hand at the wrist. The probability is that the longer was the original cubit. The common computation as to the length of the cubit makes it 20.24 inches for the ordinary cubit, and 21.888 inches for the sacred one. This is the same as the Egyptian measurements. A rod or staff the measure of a cubit is called in (Judges 3:16) "Now Ehud had made a double-edged sword about a cubit[a] long, which he strapped to his right thigh under his clothing". This is called Go-med , which literally means a "cut," something "cut off."

Cup: A unit of measurement for volume, used in cooking to measure liquids (fluid measurement) and bulk foods such as granulated sugar (dry measurement). It is principally used in the United States and Liberia where it is a legally defined unit of measurement. Actual cups used in a household in any country may differ from the cup size used for recipes; standard measuring cups, often calibrated in fluid measure and weights of usual dry ingredients as well as in cups, are available.

2 *Cups* of the Jews, The:, whether of metal or earthenware, were possibly borrowed, in point of shape and design, from Egypt and from the Phoenicians, who were celebrated in that branch of workmanship. Egyptian cups were of various shapes, either with handles or without them. In Solomon's time all his drinking vessels were of gold, none of silver. (1 Kings 10:21) Babylon is compared to a golden cup. (Jeremiah 51:7) The great laver, or "sea," was made with a rim like the rim of a cup (cos), with flowers of lilies," (1 Kings 7:26) a form which the Persepolitan cups resemble. The cups of the New Testament were often no doubt formed on Greek and Roman models. They were sometimes of gold. (Revelation 17:4)

Cup of Common's, The: Taken in Scripture both in a proper and in a figurative sense. In a proper sense, it signifies a common cup, of horn, or some precious metal,(Genesis 40:13, 44:2) (1King 7:26), such as is used for drinking out of at meals; or a cup of ceremony, used at solemn and religious meals-as at the Passover, when the father of the family pronounced certain blessings over the cup, and having tasted it, passed it round to the company and his whole family, who partook of it, (1Corinthians 10:16). In a figurative sense, a cup is spoken of as filled with the portion given to one by divine providence, (Psalm 11:6 16:5); with the blessings of life and of grace, (Psalm 23:5); with a thank-offering to God, (Exodus 29:40) (Psalm 116:13); with liquor used at idolatrous feasts, (1Corinthians 10:21); with love-potions, (Revelation 17:4); with sore afflictions, (Psalm 65:8 Isaiah 51:17); and with the bitter draught of death, which was often caused by a cup of hemlock or some other poison, (Psalm 75:8). Also See (Matthew 16:28) (Luke 22:42) (John 18:11).

Cup of wine, The: Otherwise known as special or ceremonial vessels. (Genesis 40:11, 21), various forms of which are found on Assyrian and Egyptian monuments. All Solomon's drinking vessels were of gold (1 Kings 10: 21). The cups mentioned in the New Testament were made after Roman and Greek models, and were sometimes of gold (Revelation 17:4). The art of divining by means of a cup was practiced in Egypt (Genesis 44:2-17), and in the East generally.

"Cup of salvation", The: (Psalm 116:13-14) is the cup of thanksgiving for the great salvation thus "What shall I render to the LORD For all His benefits toward me? I shall lift up the cup of salvation And call upon the name of the LORD. I shall pay my vows to the LORD, Oh may it be in the presence of all His people....2

"Cup of consolation" The: (Jeremiah 16:7) refers to the custom of friends sending viands and wine to console relatives in mourning (Proverbs 31:6). In (1 Corinthians 10:16),

"Cup of blessing," The: Is contrasted with the "cup of devils" (1Corinthians 10:21). The sacramental cup is the "cup of blessing," because of blessing pronounced over it (Matthew 26:27; Luke 22:17). The "portion of the cup" (Psalm 11:6; 16:5) denotes one's condition of life, prosperous or adverse. A "cup" is also a type of sensual allurement (Jeremiah 51:7; Proverbs 23:31; Revelation 17:4).

Cup of astonishment, The: Cup of Trembling, The: Cup of God's Wrath, The: All found in (Psalm 75:8; Isaiah 51:17; Jeremiah 25:15; Lamentations 4:21; Ezek. 23:32; Revelation 16:19; Comp. Matthew 26:39, 42; John 18:11). The cup is also the symbol of death (Matthew 16:28; Mark 9:1; Hebrews 2:9).

Curse: (also called a jinx, hex or execration) is any expressed wish that some form of adversity or misfortune will befall or attach to some other entity—one or more persons, a place, or an object. In particular, "curse" may refer to a wish that harm or hurt will be inflicted by any supernatural powers, such as a spell, a prayer, an imprecation, an execration, magic, witchcraft, God, a natural force, or a spirit. In many belief systems, the curse itself (or accompanying ritual) is considered to have some causative force in the result. To reverse or eliminate a curse is called removal or breaking, and is often believed to require equally elab-

Curses, breaking generational

orate rituals or prayers.. 2 "curse" may also refer to the resulting adversity; for example, menstruation has been described as the "curse of Eve". The bible warns in (James 3:8-10) "but no human being can tame the tongue. It is a restless evil, full of deadly poison. With it we bless our Lord and Father, and with it we *curse* people who are made in the likeness of God. From the same mouth come blessing and *cursing*. My brothers,[a] these things ought not to be so".

Curses, breaking generational:
Generational curses are mentioned in several places in the bible as in (Exodus 20:5; 34:7; Numbers 14:18; Deuteronomy 5:9). God warns that He is "a jealous God, punishing the children for the sin of the fathers to the third and fourth generation of those who hate Him." It sounds unfair for God to punish children for the sins of their fathers. However, there is more to it than that. The effects of sin are naturally passed down from one generation to the next. When a father has a sinful lifestyle, his children are likely to practice the same sinful lifestyle. Implied in the warning of (Exodus 20:5) is the fact that the children will choose to repeat the sins of their fathers. A Jewish Targum specifies that this passage refers to "ungodly fathers" and "rebellious children." So, it is not unjust for God to punish sin to the third or fourth generation – those generations are committing the same sins their ancestors did. There is a trend in the church today to try to blame every sin and problem on some sort of generational curse. This is not biblical. God's warning to visit iniquity on future generations is part of the Old Testament Law. A generational curse was a consequence for a specific nation (Israel) for a specific sin (idolatry). The history books of the Old Testament (especially Judges) contain the record of this divine punishment meted out.

2 The cure for a generational curse has always been repentance. When Israel turned from idols to serve the living God, the "curse" was broken and God saved them (Judges 3:9, 15; 1 Samuel 12:10-11). Yes, God promised to visit Israel's sin upon the third and fourth generations, but in the very next verse He promised that He would show "love to a thousand (generations) of those who love Him and keep His commandments" (Exodus 20:6). In other words, God's grace lasts a thousand times longer than His wrath. For the Christian who is worried about a generational curse, the answer is salvation through Jesus Christ. A Christian is a new creation (2 Corinthians 5:17). How can a child of God still be under God's curse (Romans 8:1)? The cure for a "generational curse" is repentance of the sin in question, faith in Christ, and a life consecrated to the Lord (Romans 12:1-2).

Curse of the Law:
Simply punishment by Law. This means each

separate antecedent of an event in human life before or without Christ; Starting from the sinful nature from Adam who was the victim of the first human curse. This is easily explained from the law itself. (Galatians:3:10) merely paraphrases an Old Testament passage: "Cursed is he who does not confirm the words of this law by doing them" (Deuteronomy:27:26, NASB). The curse is not the law—it is clearly the penalty imposed for not keeping the law. In the case of Adam, Before curse, there must be cause, the antecedent – they includes human lust, sin, poverty, fleshy yearnings, worldliness, sickness, discomfort, death or any other thing revealed by Law which without Law would not have known and imputed upon the the guilty one . Something that precedes and brings about an effect or a negative result - purnishment. A reason for an action or condition. A ground of a legal action is a cause, while the resultant sentencing is a curse. 2 An agent that brings something about. That which in some manner is accountable for a condition that brings about an effect or that produces a cause for the resultant action or state. "What shall we say, then? Is the law sinful?" (verse 7). If the law causes our desire for sin to increase, is the law bad? "Certainly not! Nevertheless, I would not have known what sin was had it not been for the law." The law reveals what sin is (Romans 3:20) — and that is a dangerous bit of knowledge. For example Paul illustrates the problem with the tenth commandment: "For I would not have known what coveting really was if the law had not said, 'Do not covet.' But sin, seizing the opportunity afforded by the commandment, produced in me every kind of coveting" (Romans 7: 7-8). Paul, like everyone else, had covetous desires, and the law told him that his desires, although normal, were sinful. Paul could keep the external rules of Judaism, but he couldn't prevent himself from coveting, and he learned from the law that this was sin. In Christ, the curse of the Law was removed. That ends the reign of Law. Since our sin was imputed on Christ. That is why anyone who is in Christ Jesus is free, old things have passed away all things become new through Grace in Christ Jesus as in (2 Corinthians 5:17 NKJV) "Therefore, if anyone is in Christ, he is a new creation; old things have passed away; behold, all things have become new". The restriction between Jews and Gentiles was also remove at the end of Law. This does not mean that Law is bad or there is no more Law, but what this imply is that there is virtually no responsibility for believers in Christ to ponder the burden of the sin, sickness, poverty, tribulation and so forth, - all which are cause that crime could be committed in their effort to help themselves, then triggering the curse of Law – punishment by Law. In Christ, there is no barrier anymore because "There is neither Jew nor Greek, there is neither slave nor

Cyprus

free, there is no male and female, for you are all one in Christ Jesus." (Galatians 3:28)

Cyprus: An island country in the Eastern Mediterranean Sea. *Cyprus* is the third largest and third most populous island in the Mediterranean, and a member state of the European Union. It is located south of Turkey, west of Syria and Lebanon, northwest of Israel, north of Egypt and east of Greece. 2 *Cyprus* played an integral part in early Christian History, although the events of the first 400 years are often overlooked. Few people know that Christianity reached Cyprus well before Barnabas and Paul arrived or that both Barnabas and Lazarus are buried on the island. Paul performed his first miracle and received his name in Paphos. Eustolios of Kourion was one of the first to openly dedicate his home to Christ, and one of the most ancient pieces of Christian jewellery ever publicly worn was found in Cyprus. 3 Cyprus play an important role for the spread of the Gospel and early Church. Most importantly, Lazarus left Bethany in fear of his life sometime around the time of the crucifixion, because "...the chief priests made plans to kill Lazarus as well for on account of him many of the Jews were going over to Jesus and putting their faith in him." (John 12:10-11) But where did Lazarus go and what became of him? He went to Cyprus where he was later ordained as the Bishop of Kition by Barnabas and Paul on their First Missionary Journey. 4 After the Holy Spirit commanded Barnabas and Paul to go forth from Antioch and spread the Faith, they set sail for Cyprus. There, they landed at Salamis and began to proclaim the Word of God, preaching the Good News, working wondrous signs and miracles in the island's synagogues on their way to Paphos. There they were confronted with Elymas, a Jewish civic leader and attendant to the Proconsul Sergius Paulus, who was the island's governor, appointed by the Senate of Rome. 5 At *Cyprus*, Elymas actively tried to prevent the pair from reaching the Proconsul. According to a strong local tradition, he even had Saul dragged to the synagogue, tied to a pillar, and whipped. Probably, that is why Paul testified "Five times I received from the Jews the forty lashes minus one, Three times I was beaten with rods, once I was pelted with stones, three times I was shipwrecked, I spent a night and a day in the open sea, I have been constantly on the move. I have been in danger from rivers, in danger from bandits, in danger from my fellow Jews, in danger from Gentiles; in danger in the city, in danger in the country, in danger at sea; and in danger from false believers. (2 Corinthians 11:24-26). Then there were the convert known as the Christians Cyprus. "Some of them, however, men from *Cyprus* and Cyrene, went to Antioch and began to speak to the Greeks also telling them the good news about the Lord Jesus." (Acts 11:20)

Dd

Damascus: This is the capital and the second largest city of Syria after Aleppo. Commonly known in Syria as *ash-Sham* (Arabic: ‎ash-Shām) and nicknamed as the *City of Jasmine* (Arabic: *Madīnat al-Yāsmīn*). In addition to being one of the oldest continuously inhabited cities in the world, Damascus is a major cultural and religious center of the Levant. The city has an estimated population of 1,711,000 (2009 est) Located in south western Syria, Damascus is the center of a large metropolitan area of 2.6 million people (2004) Geographically embedded on the eastern foothills of the Anti-Lebanon mountain range 80 kilometres (50 mi) inland from the eastern shore of the Mediterranean on a plateau 680 metres (2,230 ft) above sea-level, Damascus experiences a semi-arid climate due to the rain shadow effect. The Barada River flows through Damascus. First settled in the second millennium BC, it was chosen as the capital of the Umayyad Caliphate from 661 to 750. After the victory of the Abbasid dynasty, the seat of Islamic power was moved to Baghdad. Damascus saw a political decline throughout the Abbasid era, only to regain significant importance in the Ayyubid and Mamluk periods. During Ottoman rule, the city decayed completely while maintaining a certain cultural prestige. Today, it is the seat of the central government and all of the government ministries. Churches and other religious worship places. 2 Since our concern is about the Christian gospel significant and meaning of Damascus, the following provides deeper ingredients as Prophet Isaiah in Chapter 17 lamented earlier on: In the last days, the Bible tells us, a horrible series of events will take place in the lands of Israel and Syria – *Damascus is the Capital of Syria*. One of these events is the disappearance of *Damascus* as one of the premiere cities in the world. The oldest continuously inhabited city on the planet, *Damascus* has witnessed at least five thousand years of human history, and some historians believe the city actually dates back to the seventh millennium BC. In fact, Paul was on the road to Damascus when Christ first appeared to Him, an event that transformed not only

Damascus

his life, but the course of human history. 3 In the very near future, Damascus will once again play a major role in human events. The prophet Isaiah provides us with God›s commentary on a future conflict between Damascus and Israel, and in so doing, He reveals certain prophecies that have been partially fulfilled in the past. However, the ultimate fulfillment of Isaiah 17 remains in the future.

Damascus, The End time event in: The current existence of *Damascus,* which will one day cease to be a city, as well as the historical absence of the coalition of nations prophesied to attack Israel and be destroyed by God, is proof that Isaiah 17 prophesies events yet future. Now take a look at the gospel according to (Isaiah 17: 1-3)

"This message came to me concerning Damascus: ~Look, Damascus will disappear! It will become a heap of ruins. The cities of Aroer will be deserted. Sheep will graze in the streets and lie down unafraid. There will be no one to chase them away. The fortified cities of Israel will also be destroyed, and the power of Damascus will end. The few left in Aram will share the fate of Israel's departed glory,' says the Lord Almighty" (Isaiah 17:1-3)

These opening verses paint a bleak picture. The city of Damascus will become a heap of ruins, utterly destroyed. Few, if any, buildings will be left standing. The once great city will be devoid of human life and will become home to all manner of wildlife in the absence of humans to chase them away. According to these verses, the cities of Aroer, which are located on the northern bank of the Arnon River just east of the Dead Sea, will also be deserted. However, the passage doesn't say they will be destroyed in the same manner as Damascus, just that they will be deserted. It may be that people simply flee these cities out of fear.

In addition, many of the fortified cities in northern Israel will also be destroyed. The few who remain in Aram, thirty-eight miles south southeast of Damascus, will share the fate of these northern Israeli cities. ~In that day the glory of Israel will be very dim, for poverty will stalk the land. Israel will be abandoned like the grain fields in the valley of Rephaim after the harvest. Only a few of its people will be left, like the stray olives left on the tree after the harvest. Only two or three remain in the highest branches, four or five out on the tips of the limbs. Yes, Israel will be stripped bare of people,' says the Lord, the God of Israel" (Isaiah 17:4-6).

The breadth and scope of destruction is clearly illustrated as God describes the Israeli landscape as stripped bare of people. Only a small fraction of people either choose to stay in the land or else survive what is a massive holocaust, leaving only a few inhabitants who struggle in poverty. "Then at last the people will think of their Creator and have respect for the Holy One of Israel. They will no longer ask their idols for help or worship what their own hands have made. They will never again bow down to their Asherah poles or burn incense on the altars they built" (Isaiah 17:7-8,). As a result of this event, the people of Israel will once again turn to God Almighty. Currently, the nation of Israel is predominantly secular in nature. Other gospel passages infer that this will change as the prophesied rebuilding of the Temple in the last days indicates a spiritual resurgence among the Jews of Israel. Nevertheless, this passage clearly indicates the people of Israel will turn away from all false idols and gods.

Knowing that this will happen, we must ask: Why does it happen? "Their largest cities will be as deserted as overgrown thickets. They will become like the cities the Amorites abandoned when the Israelites came here so long ago. Why? Because you have turned from the God who can save "the Rock who can hide you. You may plant the finest imported grapevines, and they may grow so well that they blossom on the very morning you plant them, but you will never pick any grapes from them. Your only harvest will be a load of grief and incurable pain" (Isaiah 17:9-11). The devastation that overshadows Israel will come about because Israel has "turned from the God who can save them." All the hard work performed prior to this event will be lost. Those who have been distracted by the things of this world will be disappointed, for they have forgotten God, and by putting faith in the things of this world, they will ultimately be disappointed. Their only harvest will be "a load of grief and incurable pain." This grief will be brought to a climax when, in the midst of their suffering, the nation of Israel faces an imminent invasion:

"Look! The armies rush forward like waves thundering toward the shore. But though they roar like breakers on a beach, God will silence them. They will flee like chaff scattered by the wind or like dust whirling before a storm. In the evening Israel waits in terror, but by dawn its enemies are dead. This is the just reward of those who plunder and destroy the people of God" (Isaiah 17:12-14).

While Syria and Israel lie in ruin, the enemies of Israel will view her suffering as an opportunity to invade, their ultimate goal to destroy her forever. However, God has a different plan in mind, and He will destroy these invaders Himself. A more in-depth illustration of this attack is foreseen in (Psalms

Damascus

83): Thus; "O God, don't sit idly by, silent and inactive! Don't you hear the tumult of your enemies? Don't you see what your arrogant enemies are doing? They devise crafty schemes against your people, laying plans against your precious ones. Come,' they say, let us wipe out Israel as a nation. We will destroy the very memory of its existence.' This was their unanimous decision. They signed a treaty as allies against "these Edomites and Ishmaelites, Moabites and Hagrites, Gebalites, Ammonites, and Amalekites, and people from Philistia and Tyre. Assyria has joined them, too, and is allied with the descendants of Lot. Do to them as you did to the Midianites or as you did to Sisera and Jabin at the Kishon River. They were destroyed at Endor, and their decaying corpses fertilized the soil. Let their mighty nobles die as Oreb and Zeeb did. Let all their princes die like Zebah and Zalmunna, for they said, Let us seize for our own use these pasturelands of God!' O my God, blow them away like whirling dust, like chaff before the wind! As a fire roars through a forest and as a flame sets mountains ablaze, chase them with your fierce storms; terrify them with your tempests. Utterly disgrace them until they submit to your name, O Lord. Let them be ashamed and terrified forever. Make them failures in everything they do, until they learn that you alone are called the Lord, that you alone are the Most High, supreme over all the earth" (Psalms 83, NLT).

So how do we know that Psalms 83 describes the same scene envisioned in Isaiah 17? Let's compare the two. Here's how the intentions of Israel's enemies are described: There will be 'Plunder & Destruction' - "This is the just reward of those who plunder and destroy the people of God" (Isaiah 17:14,NLT). Destruction - "They devise crafty schemes against your people, laying plans against your precious ones. ~Come,' they say, ~let us wipe out Israel as a nation. We will destroy the very memory of its existence.' This was their unanimous decision" (Psalms 83:3-5, NLT). To plunder "For they said, Let us seize for our own use these pasturelands of God!'" (Psalms 83:12, NLT). Here's how the fate of Israel's enemies is described:

"They will flee like chaff scattered by the wind or like dust whirling before a storm" (Isaiah 17:13, NLT). "O my God, blow them away like whirling dust, like chaff before the wind!" (Psalms 83:13, NLT). From the description of their fate alone, it is reasonable to conclude that the armies of (Isaiah 17:12) are the same nations that sign a treaty against the Lord in (Psalms 83:5-8). Below is a list of those nations and their modern geographical equivalents:

Edomites = Jordan / Parts of the West Bank
Ishmaelites = The Arab people
Moabites = Jordan / Parts of the West Bank
Hagrites = Jordan / The Arab people
Gebalites = Lebanon
Ammonites = Jordan

Damascus

Amalekites = Southern Israel / Gaza
Philistia = Gaza
Tyre = Lebanon
Assyria = Syria / Parts of Turkey and Iraq
The Descendants of Lot = Jordan

By studying the geographical history of these ancient people and places, we can uncover which nations they currently compose. According to Psalms 83, in the aftermath of the destruction of northern Israel and Damascus, Israel will be invaded by armies from Jordan, the West Bank, Lebanon, Syria, and Gaza. All of these locations are heavily populated by the enemies of Israel today. An Expanding War? But are the nations cited in Psalms 83 the only nations involved in this attack? It's quite possible that additional conspirators are named in the book of Ezekiel. Isaiah 17 and Psalms 83 might well foreshadow the war of Gog and Magog.

In Ezekiel 38-39, an enormous coalition of nations, "a vast and awesome horde" will roll down on Israel "like a storm and cover the land like a cloud" (Ezekiel 38:9). This prophesied future war in Ezekiel has many similarities to (Isaiah 17:12-14). Both prophets foresee a time when enemy armies rush toward Israel while she awaits unprepared. Both prophets foresee God's instantaneous destruction of Israel's enemies. And in both scenarios, the marching armies intend to plunder and destroy the people of Israel: As a destruction, "You will say, Israel is an unprotected land filled with walless villages! I will march against her and destroy these people who live in such confidence!'" (Ezekiel 38:11,).

Another plunder - *"But Sheba and Dedan and the merchants of Tarshish will ask, Who are you to rob them of silver and gold? Who are you to drive away their cattle and seize their goods and make them poor?'"* (Ezekiel 38:13). More plunder and destruction thus "This is the just reward of those who plunder and destroy the people of God" (Isaiah 17:14,). In any case, could the events predicted in Isaiah 17 and Psalms 83 be a catalyst for the war of Gog and Magog prophesied in Ezekiel 38-39? Although it is not a certainty, the possibility cannot be completely ruled out. for her enemies. The surrounding Muslim nations will see an opportunity to destroy her, while Russia will see an opportunity to seize the upper hand in the oil-rich Middle East.

Today, the most virulent enemies of Israel reside in the very places named in Psalms 83--Hamas in Gaza, the Palestinians in the West Bank and Jordan, Hezbollah in Lebanon, and the Syria leadership and its Axis of Evil partners in the city of Damascus. As of this writing, the conditions are ripe for the fulfilment of Isaiah 17 and Psalms

Daily

83, paving the way for the Rapture of the church and the beginning of the Tribulation. In light of such developments, we should zealously preach the gospel of Christ to all who will listen, for the hour is late, and the return of Christ is near.

Daily: *(Adjective)* Happening every day or every weekday. Done every day (except Sunday). As in (Mathew 6:1 -12) Your kingdom come. Your will be done, On earth as it is in heaven. 'Give us this day our *daily* bread. 'And forgive us our debts, as we also have forgiven our debtors.... Here bread is attached to daily – showing Our fathers responsibility and care that we must live for him every day without problem as He is feeding us with bread – the good things of life through His Grace and Salvation is with Him and from Him alone to us ward. How do we get this from Him – through His Word. When His word abide in us Christians because His word is the 'bread of life' Halelujah! When He gives us, we must Chew, Swallow it, be fill with it, and owned it, so that Jesus can be in us and we in Him. Amen!

Dan: Gospel wise, one of the 12 sons of Jacob and thus a progenitor of one of the 12 tribes of Israel. His mother was Bilhah – the servant of Rachel. His tribal territory was in the extreme north of the Promise land, hence the expression from Dan to Beersheba.

Dance: (Dancing – continuous) A type of art that generally involves movement of the body, often rhythmic and to music. It is performed in many cultures as a form of emotional expression, social interaction, or exercise, in a spiritual or performance setting, and is sometimes used to express ideas or tell a story.Christians must always dance in praise to God as in (Psalm 149:3) "Let them praise his name with dancing, making melody to him with tambourine and lyre!" Dance may also be regarded as a form of nonverbal communication between humans or other animals, as in bee dances and behaviour patterns such as a mating dances. 2 Definitions of what constitutes dance can depend on social and cultural norms and aesthetic, artistic and moral sensibilities. (Psalm 150:4) also indicate "Praise him with tambourine and dance; praise him with strings and pipe! 3 Meanings may range from functional movement (such as folk dance) to virtuoso techniques such as ballet. Martial arts kata are often compared to dances, and sports such as gymnastics, figure skating and synchronized swimming are generally thought to incorporate dance.

There are many styles and genres of dance. African dance is interpretative. Ballet, ballroom and tango are classical dance styles. Square dance and electric slide are forms of step dance, and breakdancing is a type of street dance. Dance can be participatory, social, or performed for an audience. It can also be ceremonial, competitive or erotic. Dance movements may be without significance in themselves, as in ballet or European folk dance, or have a gestural vocabulary or symbolic meaning as in some Asian dances. Choreography is the art of creating dances. The person who creates (i.e., choreographs) a dance is known as the choreographer. such simple activity as the expression of feelings of joy and enthusiasm, or the more involved routing and movement of one skilled in interpreting and arousing powerful emotions. Numerous Old Testament instances of dancing being approved can be cited; however, a study of these accounts will reveal that each involved an expression of rejoicing or religious enthusiasm because of some victory or accomplishment. Such is the situation as Miriam led the women "with tumbrels and dances" (Exodus 15:20), after the deliverance from Egyptian bondage, or Jepthah's daughter greeting him with "tumbrels and dances" after a great victory (Judges 11:34). David's thanksgiving for the safe return of the ark of God was evidenced as he "danced before Jehovah with all his might" (II Samuel 6:14). Similar use of the term "dancing" is made by the Psalmist to express joy and praise unto Jehovah God.

Since the term "dancing" is capable of expressing a broad range of man's thoughts, Christians must be careful as it may also portray that which is lewd and sinful. Moses, having received the law from God, returned from the mount to find the people *dancing* naked around the golden calf which they had formed (Exodus 32:19-26). The dancing of the daughter of Herodias had such appeal to the base human passion that Herod promised to give her anything she might desire, a rash promise which led to the murder of John the baptizer (Matthew 14:3-10). sOur "modern dancing", a phrase used to include both ballroom dancing in which there is continuous body contact between partners and such dancing as that which commonly accompanies modern rock music, differs greatly from the dancing mentioned in the Bible, for such present-day dancing has no trace of religious significance, nor is it solo in nature, but involves men and women dancing together.

"Dance" in the sense used today does not appear in the New Testament; however, the idea it represents is mentioned and clearly condemned. The Apostle Paul lists -the works of the flesh and notes that "they who practice such things shall not inherit the kingdom of God" (Galatians 5:19-21). Appearing in this list of traits eternally destructive are two terms closely related to modern dancing, namely, "lasciviousness" and "revelling's".
Note - "Lasciviousness", according to reliable Greek-English lexicons or even an English dictionary is akin to sexual excesses, having reference to "filthy words, indecent

Dance, David

bodily movement, unchaste handling of males and females". "Revelling" basically refers to excessive feasting and carousing, but has a close relationship with "music and dancing". Who can deny that the body contact between the sexes and the bodily movements associated with dances to modern rock music lead to sexual arousal? In fact, some advocates of dancing stress such to be an outlet for sexual urges. The whole range of the modern dance is designed to express or convey a message, namely, "love-making" and is calculated to be sexually stimulating. It is understood, of course, that the sex urge is God-given and is not sinful per se. Yet, God-given desires must have God-appointed boundaries; the righteous fulfilment of the sex urge is limited to the marriage relationship (I Corinthians 7:1-9). To engage in any activity which produces lewd emotions or excites unlawful sexual desire is "lasciviousness" and stands condemned by God. (Galatians 5:19-21). Let none be deceived; the basic appeal of the modern dance, as admitted even by its proponents, has its foundation in human passion, Obviously, not every person who engages in dancing ends up a prostitute or fornicator, yet many who have come to immoral ends began their journey by way of the dance. Let none be deceived, the fruit of the modern dance has never increased purity and spirituality, but the destruction of all that relates to human happiness and eternal salvation.

Dance, David: (2 Samuel 6:16) "And as the ark of the covenant of the Lord came to the city of David, Michal the daughter of Saul looked out of the window and saw King David dancing and rejoicing, and she despised him in her heart". (2 Samuel 6:14) "And David was angry, because Jehovah had made a rent on Uzzah, and called the place Perez-uzzah" (rent of Uzzah). to tear a rent, is here applied to a sudden tearing away from life and is understood by many in the sense of "he troubled himself;" However, this meaning cannot be grammatically sustained, whilst it is quite possible to become angry, or fall into a state of violent excitement, at an unexpected calamity. The burning of David's anger was not directed against God, but referred to the calamity which had befallen Uzzah, or speaking more correctly, to the cause of this calamity, which David attributed to himself or to his undertaking. As he had not only resolved upon the removal of the ark, but had also planned the way in which it should be taken to Jerusalem, he could not trace the occasion of Uzzah's death to any other cause than his own plans. He was therefore angry that such misfortune had attended his undertaking. In his first excitement and dismay, David may not have perceived the real and deeper ground of this divine judgment. Uzzah's offence consisted in the fact that he had touched the ark with profane feelings, although with good intentions, namely to prevent its rolling over and falling from the cart. Touching the ark, the throne of the divine glory and visible pledge of the invisible presence of the Lord, was a violation of the majesty of the holy God. "Uzzah was therefore a type of all who with good intentions, humanly speaking, yet with unsanctified minds, interfere in the affairs of the kingdom of God, from the notion that they are in danger, and with the hope of saving them" (O. v. Gerlach). On further reflection, David could not fail to discover where the cause of Uzzah's offence, which he had atoned for with his life, really had lain, and that it had actually arisen from the fact that he (David) and those about him had decided to disregard the distinct instructions of the law with regard to the handling of the ark. According to Numbers 4 the ark was not only to be moved by none but Levites, but it was to be carried on the shoulders, not in a carriage; and in (Numbers 4:15) , even the Levites were expressly forbidden to touch it on pain of death. But instead of taking these instructions as their rule, they had followed the example of the Philistines when they sent back the ark (1 Samuel 6:7.), and had placed it upon a new cart, and directed Uzzah to drive it, whilst, as his conduct on the occasion clearly shows, he had no idea of the unapproachable holiness of the ark of God, and had to expiate his offence with his life, as a warning to all the Israelites.

Dance, Praise: (Psalm 150:1-6) "Praise the Lord. Praise God in his sanctuary; praise him in his mighty heavens. Praise him for his acts of power; praise him for his surpassing greatness. Praise him with the sounding of the trumpet, praise him with the harp and lyre, praise him with tumbrel and dancing, praise him with the strings and pipe, praise him with the clash of cymbals, praise him with resounding cymbals. Let everything that has breath praise the Lord. Praise the Lord".

2 We are here stirred up to praise God. Praise God for his sanctuary, and the privileges we enjoy by having it among us; praise him because of his power and glory in the firmament. Those who praise the Lord in heaven, behold displays of his power and glory which we cannot now conceive. But the greatest of all his mighty acts is known in his earthly sanctuary. The holiness and the love of our God are more displayed in man's redemption, than in all his other works. Let us praise our God and Saviour for it. We need not care to know what instruments of music are mentioned. Hereby is meant that in serving God we should spare no cost or pains. Praise God with strong faith; praise him with holy love and delight; praise him with entire confidence in Christ; praise him with believing triumph over the powers of darkness; praise him by universal respect to all his commands; praise him by cheerful submission to all his disposals;

Dance, Prophetic

praise him by rejoicing in his love, and comforting ourselves in his goodness; praise him by promoting the interests of the kingdom of his grace; praise him by lively hope and expectation of the kingdom of his glory. Since we must shortly breathe our last, while we have breath let us praise the Lord; then we shall breathe our last with comfort. Let everything that hath breath praise the Lord. Praise ye the Lord. Such is the very suitable end of a book inspired by the Spirit of God, written for the work of praise; a book which has supplied the songs of the church for more than three thousand years; a book which is quoted more frequently than any other by Christ and his apostles; a book which presents the loftiest ideas of God and his government, which is fitted to every state of human life, which sets forth every state of religious experience, and which bears simple and clear marks of its Divine origin. As a Christians we need to recite the Psalm of His Praise, Sing and dance it, rejoice in God our Saviour and shout for Joy – all to His Praise and Glory! Hallelujah!

Dance, Prophetic: (Exodus 15:20-21) "Then Miriam the prophetess, the sister of Aaron, took a tambourine in her hand, and all the women went out after her with tambourines and dancing. And Miriam sang to them: "Sing to the Lord, for he has triumphed gloriously; the horse and his rider he has thrown into the sea." This song is the most ancient we know of. It is a holy song, to the honour of God, to exalt his name, and celebrate his praise, and his only, not in the least to magnify any man. Holiness to the Lord is in every part of it. It may be considered as typical, and prophetical of the final destruction of the enemies of the church. Happy the people whose God is the Lord. They have work to do, temptations to grapple with, and afflictions to bear, and are weak in themselves; but his grace is their strength. They are often in sorrow, but in him they have comfort; he is their song. Sin, and death, and hell threaten them, but he is, and will be their salvation. The Lord is a God of almighty power, and woe to those that strive with their Maker! He is a God of matchless perfection; he is glorious in holiness; his holiness is his glory. His holiness appears in the hatred of sin, and his wrath against obstinate sinners. It appears in the deliverance of Israel, and his faithfulness to his own promise. He is fearful in praises; that which is matter of praise to the servants of God, is very dreadful to his enemies. He is doing wonders, things out of the common course of nature; wondrous to those in whose favour they are wrought, who are so unworthy, that they had no reason to expect them. There were wonders of power and wonders of grace; in both, God was to be humbly adored. So, Glorify His name. Hallelujah

Daniel: Daniel was one of several children taken into Babylonian captivity where they were educated in Chaldean thought. However, he never converted to Neo-Babylonian ways. Through instruction from "the God of Heaven" (Daniel.2:18), he interpreted dreams and visions of kings, thus becoming a prominent figure in the court of Babylon. He also had apocalyptic visions concerning the four monarchies. Some of the most famous events in Daniel's life are: Shadrach, Meshach, and Abednego, the writing on the wall and Daniel in the lions' den.

Dark: Dark is the "absence of light" redirect here. For other uses, see Dark (disambiguation) and Absence of light (disambiguation). *This statement makes it to be the opposite* of light. For other uses, see Darkness (disambiguation). In the Christian believe, it is a complete lack of the knowledge of the presence of Holy Spirit in one's life - see darkness

Darkened: To Turn light off thereby putting the place in total darkness – see darkness

Darkness, the polar opposite to brightness, is understood to be an absence of visible light. It is also the appearance of black in a coloured space.

Humans are unable to distinguish colour when either light or darkness predominate. In conditions of insufficient light, perception is achromatic and ultimately, black. The emotional response to darkness has generated metaphorical usages of the term in many cultures. Many Christians have forgotten about their divine quality as 'the light of the world' (Mathew 5:14) "You are the light of the world. A city set on a hill cannot be hidden"; In a Christian dwells a Spiritual brightness that is shinning to show the way through revelation as manifestation from the word of God. When a Christian falls from Grace, the light dims and darkness engulfs him or takes place. Then the Christian will not shine anymore, God will not hear his prayer anymore as there is no praying power, no ability to read the word of God, no communication with the Almighty because the bond of love with Christ is broken but Grace will still be sufficient for a while to lead the way for repentance. If there will be no repentance, the sinner could be consume with death or perish.

Darkly: adverb of dark. *See dark.*

David: (*Dawid*; Arabic: *Dāwūd*; Syriac: *Dawid*; Strong's: *Daveed*) Was, according to the gospel/Scripture, the second king of the United Kingdom of Israel and Judah, and according to the New Testament Gospels of Matthew and Luke, an ancestor of Jesus. His life is conventionally dated to c. 1040–970 BC, his reign over Judah c. 1010–1002 BC, and his reign over the United Kingdom c. 1002–970 BC. The Books of Samuel, 1 Kings, and 1 Chronicles are the only sources of information on David, although the Tel Dan Stele (dated c. 850–835 BC) contains the phrase בית דוד (*Beit David*), read as "House of David", which most scholars take as confirmation of the existence in the mid-9th century BC of a Judean royal dynasty called the House of David. 2 He is depicted as a righteous king, although not without faults, as well as an acclaimed warrior, musician, and poet, traditionally credited for composing many of the psalms contained in the Book of Psalms. David is an important figure to members of the Jewish, Christian and Islamic faiths. Biblical tradition maintains the Messiah's direct descent from the line of David. In most religions, he is considered a prophet.

David, The city of: Jerusalem, so called in compliment to King David.

Day: (noun) A period of twenty four hours reckoned from midnight to midnight corresponding to a rotation of the earth on its axis 2 The time between sunrise and sunset. 3 Days – usually, a particular period of the past. 4 The day – the present time or the time in question. 5 One's day – the youthful or successful period of one's life. 6 Done during the day – adjective – working or done during the day. 7 Day in, day out – continuously or repeatedly over a long period. 9 Day by day – gradually and steadily. 10 day-to-day – happening on a daily basis, involving the usual task or routines of everyday. The day to day prayer. That will be the day for the fast. These days – referring to the present. As (Ecclesiastes 12: 1-2) reminds us –Christians "Remember also your Creator in the *days* of your youth, before the evil days come and the years draw near when you will say, "I have no delight in them"; before the sun and the light, the moon and the stars are darkened, and clouds return after the rain;…"

The word for *"day"* in Genesis one is the Hebrew word (yomo. It can mean either a day (in the ordinary 24-our sense), the daylight portion (say about 12 hours) of an ordinary 24-hour day (i.e., day as distinct from night), or, occasionally, an indefinite period of time (e.g.. "In the time of the Judges" or "In the *day* of the Lord"). Without exception, in the Hebrew Old Testament the word (yom) is never used to refer to a definite long period of time with specific beginning and end points. Furthermore, it is important to note that even when the word (*yom)* is used in the indefinite sense, it is clearly indicated by the context that the literal meaning of the word *day* is not intended.

Day of the Lord, The: This phrase relies on military images to describe the Lord as a "divine warrior" who will conquer his enemies. In certain prophetic texts of the Old Testament, the enemies of the Lord are 'Israel's enemies' and in these visions the day of the Lord brings victory for the people of ancient Israel. Other prophets use the imagery as a warning to Israel or its leaders and for them, the day of the Lord will mean destruction for the biblical nation of Israel. This concept develops throughout Jewish and Christian gospel into a day of divine, apocalyptic judgment at the end of the world. 2 *The Day of the Lord* is a gospel term and theme used in both the Hebrew Bible (Old Testament) and the New Testament. A related expression is the Great Day as in "The sun shall be turned into darkness, and the moon into blood, before the great and the terrible *day of the LORD* come." which appears in both Old and New Testaments.

3 The meaning of the phrases may sometimes refer to temporal events such as the invasion of a foreign army and capture of a city but it may also be related to predicted events in a later age of earth's history including the final judgment and World to Come. The expression may also have an extended meaning in referring to both the first and second comings of Jesus Christ. This appears much in the first chapter of Isaiah. This promise is also picked up in the New Testament, when (Joel 2:28-32) – "And afterward, I will pour out my Spirit on all people. Your sons and daughters will prophesy, your old men will dream dreams, your young men will see visions". This is also quoted in (Acts 2:17-21). The phrase is also used in (1 Thessalonians 5:2) to refer either to the rapture or to the return of Jesus The phrase alludes to a judgment for eternal rewards in (2 Corinthians 1:14) where it says "we are your rejoicing, even as ye also are ours in the day of the Lord Jesus". Hallelujah!

4 The Book of Revelation describes *the day of the Lord* as an apocalyptic time of God's almighty wrath, which comes upon those who are deemed wicked. The text pictures every man hiding in the rocks of the mountains during a major earthquake to attempt to hide from God's wrath, while celestial phenomena turn the moon blood red and the sun dark as in (Revelation 6: 12 -17) ˙ "And I beheld when he had opened the sixth seal, and, lo, there was a great earthquake; and the sun became black as sackcloth of hair, and the moon became as blood. And the stars of heaven fell unto the earth, even as a fig tree 'casteth' her untimely figs, when she is shaken of a mighty wind. And the heaven departed as a scroll when it is rolled together; and every mountain and island were moved out of their places. And the kings of the earth, and the great men, and the rich men, and the chief captains, and the mighty men, and every bondman, and every free man, hid themselves in the dens

Deacon

and in the rocks of the mountains; And said to the mountains and rocks, Fall on us, and hide us from the face of him that sitteth on the throne, and from the wrath of the Lamb: For the great day of his wrath is come; and who shall be able to stand"? These celestial phenomena are also mentioned in (Joel 2:31), which foretells the same precise order of events mentioned in Revelation: The moon turns blood red and the sun turns dark before the great day of the Lord. Matthew 24:29-31 mentions the same event, yet it places the celestial phenomenon as occurring after the "tribulation of those days" as in (Mathew 24: 29 -31) – "Immediately after the tribulation of those days shall the sun be darkened, and the moon shall not give her light, and the stars shall fall from heaven, and the powers of the heavens shall be shaken: And then shall appear the sign of the Son of man in heaven: and then shall all the tribes of the earth mourn, and they shall see the Son of man coming in the clouds of heaven with power and great glory. And he shall send his angels with a great sound of a trumpet, and they shall gather together his elect from the four winds, from one end of heaven to the other". According to these passages, it then seems that *the day of the Lord* is an event closely tied with the coming of the Messiah to judge the world. (2 Peter 3:8-10 8) But, beloved, do not forget this one thing, that with the Lord one day (is) as a thousand years, and a thousand years as one day. The Lord is not slack concerning His promise, as some count slackness, but is long suffering toward us, not willing that any should perish but that all should come to repentance. But *the day of the Lord* will come as a thief in the night, in which the heavens will pass away with a great noise, and the elements will melt with fervent heat; both the earth and the works that are in it will be burned up.

Since, most Christians believe that the day of the Lord is a reference to a time of catastrophe and judgement for the wicked or a time of glorious renewal and salvation for believers, it is advisable to watch therefore and pray to avoid temptation. Praise God!

Deacon: This is a ministry in the Christian Church that is generally associated with service of some kind, but which varies among theological and denominational traditions. In many traditions the "diaconate", the term for a deacon's office, is a clerical office; in others it is for laity. The word "deacon" is derived from the Greek word *diákonos* which is a standard ancient Greek word meaning "servant", "waiting-man", "minister", or "messenger" .One commonly promulgated speculation as to its etymology is that it literally means "through the dust", referring to the dust raised by the busy servant or messenger.

Dead: Previously living, no longer living; deprived of life: dead people; dead flowers; dead animals. 2 brain-dead. 3 not endowed with life; inanimate: dead stones. 4 resembling death; deathlike: *a dead sleep; a dead faint.* 5.bereft of sensation; numb: *He was half dead with fright. My leg feels dead.*(noun)*the period of greatest darkness, coldness, etc.: the dead of night; the dead of winter.the dead, dead persons collectively: Prayers were recited for the dead. Adverb absolutely; completely: dead right; dead tired.* with sudden and total stoppage of motion, action, or the like: He stopped dead. As in (Revelation 14:13) Then I heard a voice from heaven say, "Write: Blessed are the dead who die in the Lord from now on." "Yes," says the Spirit, "they will rest from their labour, for their deeds will follow them." Take notice that as a Christian you shall not be proclaimed dead because you will be sleeping in the lord – watch out this biblical verse in support of this. (1Thessalonica 13:14) "Brothers, we do not want you to be ignorant about those who fall asleep, or to grieve like the rest of men, who have no hope. We believe that Jesus died and rose again and so we believe that God will bring with Jesus those who have fallen asleep in him". Again in (1 Corinthians 15: 42 – 44) the gospel declare ..."So will it be with the resurrection of the dead. The body that is sown is perishable, it is raised imperishable; it is sown in dishonour, it is raised in glory; it is sown in weakness, it is raised in power; it is sown a natural body, it is raised a spiritual body. If there is a natural body, there is also a spiritual body". There are several other biblical chapters about the word dead for your referencing and wider knowledge of the word.

Dead sea, The: (Hebrew: "Sea of Salt", also Hebrew: , "The Sea of Death"; Arabic: *al-Baḥr al-Mayyit* (help·info), also called the **Salt Sea**, is a salt lake bordering Jordan to the east, and Palestine and Israel to the west. Its surface and shores are 427 metres (1,401 ft) below sea level, Earth's lowest elevation on land. The Dead Sea is 306 m (1,004 ft) deep, the deepest hyperspace line lake in the world. With 34.2% salinity (in 2011), it is also one of the world's saltiest bodies of water, though Lake Vanda in Antarctica (35%), Lake Assal (Djibouti) (34.8%), Lagoon Garabogazköl in the Caspian Sea (up to 35%) and some hypersaline ponds and lakes of the McMurdo Dry Valleys in Antarctica (such as Don Juan Pond (44%)) have reported higher salinities. It is 9.6 times as salty as the ocean.[1] This salinity makes for a harsh environment in which animals cannot flourish, hence its name. The Dead Sea is 50 kilometres (31 mi) long and 15 kilometres (9 mi) wide at its widest point. It lies in the Jordan Rift Valley, and its main tributary's the Jordan River. *The Dead Sea* has attracted visitors from

Death

around the Mediterranean basin for thousands of years. Biblically, it was a place of refuge for King David. It was one of the world's first health resorts (for Herod the Great), and it has been the supplier of a wide variety of products, from balms for Egyptian mummification to potash for fertilizers. People also use the salt and the minerals from the Dead Sea to create cosmetics and herbal sachets. *The Dead Sea* seawater has a density of 1.240 kg/L, which makes swimming similar to floating

Death: This is the cessation of all biological functions that sustain a living organism. Phenomena which commonly bring about death include biological aging (senescence), predation, malnutrition, disease, suicide, homicide and accidents or trauma resulting in terminal injury. Bodies of living organisms begin to decompose shortly after death.In society, the nature of death and humanity's awareness of its own mortality has for millennia been a concern of the world's religious traditions and of philosophical inquiry. This includes belief in resurrection (associated with Abrahamic religions), reincarnation or rebirth (associated with Dharmic religions), or that consciousness permanently ceases to exist, known as eternal oblivion (often associated with atheism). Commemoration ceremonies after death may include various mourning, funeral practices and ceremonies of honouring the deceased. The physical remains of a person, commonly known as a *corpse* or *body*, are usually interred whole or cremated, though among the world's cultures there are a variety of other methods of mortuary disposal. In the English language, blessings directed towards a dead person include *rest in peace*, or its initialism RIP. The most common cause of human deaths in the world is heart disease, followed by stroke and other cerebro-vascular diseases, and in the third place lower respiratory infections.

Death do us part (or separate), Till!" Husband lives; but if her husband is dead, she is free to be married to whom she wishes, only in the Lord. (1 Corinthians 7:39) "A woman is bound to her husband as long as he lives. But if her husband dies, she is free to marry anyone she wishes, but he must belong to the Lord".

Deborah: (Hebrew: Modern – Dvora - Tiberian Deborah) was a prophet of the God of the Israelites, the fourth Judge of pre-monarchic Israel, counsellor, warrior, and the wife of Lapidoth according to the Book of Judges (chapters 4 and 5). The only female judge mentioned in the Bible. 2 Deborah led a successful counter attack against the forces of Jabin king of Canaan and his military commander Sisera, the narrative is recounted in chapter 4. Judges chapter 5 gives the same story in poetic form. This passage, often called The Song of *Deborah,* may date to as early as the 12th century BC [1] and is perhaps the earliest sample of Hebrew poetry. It is also significant because it is one of the oldest passages that portrays fighting women, the account being that of Jael, the wife of Heber, a Kenite tent maker. Jael killed Sisera by driving a tent peg through his temple as he slept. Both *Deborah* and Jael are portrayed as strong independent women. The poem may have been included in the Book of the Wars of the Lord mentioned in (Numbers 21:14). 'That is why the Book of the Wars of the Lord says:". . . Zahab[a] in Suphah and the ravines, the Arnon'

Debts: A debt is an obligation owed by one party (the debtor) to a second party, the creditor; usually this refers to assets granted by the creditor to the debtor, but the term can also be used metaphorically to cover moral obligations and other interactions not based on economic value. In (Romans 13: 7-8) "Pay to all what is owed to them: taxes to whom taxes are owed, revenue to whom revenue is owed, respect to whom respect is owed, honour to whom honour is owed. Owe no one anything, except to love each other, for the one who loves another has fulfilled the law". Christians need not borrow and not paying back as in (Psalm 37:21) "The wicked borrows but does not pay back, but the righteous is generous and gives; Again, Children of God, need not withhold the Grace of God that supposed to extend to others (Proverbs 3:27-28) "Do not withhold good from those to whom it is due, when it is in your power to do it. Do not say to your neighbour, "Go, and come again, tomorrow I will give it"—when you have it with you". 2 Debt is created when a creditor agrees to lend a sum of assets to a debtor. Debt is usually granted with expected repayment; in modern society, in most cases, this includes repayment of the original sum, plus interest.

> Debt is usually granted with expected repayment; in modern society, in most cases, this includes repayment of the original sum, plus interest.

But Christ has paid the debt over the head of every Christly Soul with His blood on the cross so that we might be free and owe no one as Paul warned "Owe no man anything, but to love one another." What has Paul been dealing with in this passage? He has been dealing with the error of some believers who feel no need to pay their taxes because they are not of this world. Paul's answer is, "Render therefore to all their dues." Whether tribute, custom, fear or honour; if you owe it to them, then give it as they require. In other words, if

Dedication

anyone has a proper expectation of us; if we owe them–then we should pay it. This matches the teaching of (Proverbs 3:27-28) "Withhold not good from them to who it is due, when it is in the power of 'thine' hand to do it. Say not unto thy neighbour, Go, and come again, and tomorrow I will give; when thou hast it by thee." Do not put someone off when it is their right and they claim it. Give them what you owe them to the best of your ability.

Dedication: This is the act of consecrating an altar, temple, church, or other sacred building. It also refers to the inscription of books or other artefacts when these are specifically addressed or presented to a particular person. This practice, which once was used to gain the patronage and support of the person so addressed, is now only a mark of affection or regard. In law, the word is used of the setting apart by a private owner of something to other users. There are many dedications in the Christian gospel, (Deuteronomy 6:4-7) "Hear, O Israel! The LORD is our God, the LORD is one! "You shall love the LORD your God with all your heart and with all your soul and with all your might. "These words, which I am commanding you today, shall be on your heart. As Christians, we must dedicate ourselves to God's commandment as Moses instructed the Israelites. 2 Dedication is also a divine duty or covenant between true Christians and God like in fulfilment of a vow (1 Samuel 1:26-28) "She said, "Oh, my lord! As your soul lives, my lord, I am the woman who stood here beside you, praying to the LORD. "For this boy I prayed, and the LORD has given me my petition which I asked of Him. "So I have also dedicated him to the LORD; as long as he lives he is dedicated to the LORD " And he worshiped the LORD there. Also, (Proverbs 22:6) – where dedication is regarded as a duty or responsibility "Train up a child in the way he should go, Even when he is old he will not depart from it. In (Ephesians 6:4) dedication is seen as commitment "Fathers, do not provoke your children to anger, but bring them up in the discipline and instruction of the Lord". (Luke 2:22) And when the days for their purification according to the law of Moses were completed, they brought Him up to Jerusalem to present Him to the Lord. In (1 Samuel 1:11) Sarah made a vow and promised to dedicate Samuel to the Lord as she said, "O LORD of hosts, if You will indeed look on the affliction of Your maidservant and remember me, and not forget Your maidservant, but will give Your maidservant a son, then I will give him to the LORD all the days of his life, and a razor shall never come on his head."

Dedication, The Feast of: The Feast of Dedication, or (Hebrew - Hanukkah), is a Jewish holiday. It is also known as the Festival of

Dedication, The Feast of

Lights. We will look at the Feast of Dedication from a Christian perspective, explaining its biblical basis, traditional observances, seasons, facts, and an interesting section revealing the fulfilment of the Messiah, Jesus Christ through the feast. Prior to the year 165 BC, the Jewish people who dwelled in Judea where living under the rule of the Greek kings of Damascus. During this time Seleucid King Antiochus Epiphanies, the Greco-Syrian king, took control of the Temple in Jerusalem and forced the Jewish people to abandon their worship of God, their holy customs and reading of the Torah, and he made them bow down to the Greek gods. According to the records, this King Antiochus IV defiled the Temple by sacrificing a pig on the altar and spilling its blood on the holy scrolls of Scripture. As a result of the severe persecution and pagan oppression, a group of four Jewish brothers, led by Judah Mccabeus, decided to raise up an army of religious freedom fighters. These men of fierce faith and loyalty to God became known as the Maccabeus. The small band of warriors fought for three years with "strength from heaven" until achieving a miraculous victory and deliverance from the Greco-Syrian control. After regaining the Temple, it was cleansed by the Maccabeus, cleared of all Greek idolatry, and readied for rededicated. The rededication of the Temple to the Lord took place in the year 165 BC, on the 25th day of the Hebrew month called Kislev. So Hanukkah received its name, the Feast of Dedication, because it celebrates the Maccabeus' victory over Greek oppression and the rededication of the Temple. But Hanukkah is also known as the Festival of Lights, and this is because immediately following the miraculous deliverance, God provided another miracle of provision.

In the Temple, the eternal flame of God was to be lit at all time as a symbol of God's presence. But according to tradition, when the Temple was rededicated, there was only enough oil left in the Temple to burn the flame for one day. The rest of the oil had been defiled by the Greeks during their invasion, and it would take a week for new oil to be processed and purified. But at the rededication, the Maccabeus went ahead and lit the eternal flame with the remaining supply of oil, and God's Holy presence caused it to burn miraculously for eight days, until the new sacred oil was ready.

This is why the feast is also called the Festival of Lights, and why the Hanukkah Menorah is lit for eight consecutive nights of celebration. Jews also commemorate this miracle of oil provision by making oil-rich foods, such as **Latkes**, an important part of Hanukkah celebrations. A typical example is Jesus and the Feast of Dedication: (John 10: 22-23 records, "Then came the Feast of Dedication at Jerusalem. It was winter, and Jesus was in the Temple area walking in

Deceive

Solomon's Colonnade." As a Jew, Jesus most certainly would have participated in the Feast of Dedication.

The same courageous spirit of the Maccabeus who remained faithful to God during intense **persecution** was passed on to Jesus' disciples who would all face severe trails because of their faithfulness to Christ. And like the miracle of God's presence expressed through the eternal flame of God burning for the Maccabees, Jesus became the incarnate, physical expression of God's presence, the **Light of the World**, who came to dwell among us and give us the eternal light of God's life.

Deceive: (past tense – deceived): Deliberately cause (someone) to believe something that is not true, especially for personal gain. "I didn't intend to deceive people into thinking was not a prophet" synonyms: s w i n d l e , defraud, cheat, trick, hoodwink, hoax, dupe, take in, mislead, delude, fool, outwit, misguide, lead on, inveigle, seduce, ensnare, entrap, beguile, double-cross, gull; More (of a thing) give (someone) a mistaken impression. "the area may seem to offer nothing of interest, but don't be deceived" fail to admit to oneself that something is true. "it was no use deceiving herself any longer—she loved him with all her heart" In the gospel context, the bible warned the Children of God not to be vigilant, not to allow themselves to be deceived by the great dragon who deceived people of God until it was thrown down . (Revelation 12:9) "And the great dragon was thrown down, the serpent of old who is called the devil and Satan, who deceives the whole world; he was thrown down to the earth, and his angels were thrown down with him" - Also, there are deceivers in form of false prophet who do not teach the truth and the bible warned also in (1 John 4:1) "Beloved, do not believe every spirit, but test the spirits to see whether they are from God, because many false prophets have gone out into the world".

Deceiver: He who deceived like the, Pharisee, Joseph Surface, snake in the grass, dissembler, Jesuit, Tartuffe, cockatrice, hypocrite, Maw worm, Janus, Judas, sophist, Peck sniff, serpent, wolf in sheep's clothing. 2 As a deceiver, satan is evil, liar, devious, scheming, slanderer in its deceitful work. He deceives individuals (1Titus 2:1) Eve was deceived by Satan the serpent. See also (Daniel 8:25; 2 Titus 3:13; Revelation 12:9; Revelation 20:3-10) He works counterfeit miracles (Timothy 2:9-10), He appoints false prophets (Mathew 7:15) He misuses Scripture (Mathew 4:6, Luke 4:10), He blinds unbelievers 2 (Corinthians 4:4)

Declare: (verb) Say something in a solemn and emphatic manner. (Romans 10:9) "If you declare with your mouth, "Jesus is Lord," and believe in your heart that God raised him from the dead, you will be saved". To proclaim, announce, make known, state, communicate, reveal, divulge, mention, talk about, raise, moot, air, bring into the open, voice, articulate, pronounce, express, vent, set forth, make public, publicize, disseminate, circulate, publish, broadcast, promulgate, trumpet, blazon; More formally announce the beginning of (a state or condition). 2 Speaking things into existence. (Mark 11:22-24) "And Jesus answered them, "Have faith in God. Truly, I say to you, whoever says to this mountain, 'Be taken up and thrown into the sea,' and does not doubt in his heart, but believes that what he says will come to pass, it will be done for him. Therefore I tell you, whatever you ask in prayer, believe that you have received it, and it will be yours". God Himself *declare* in (Genesis 1:3-4) "Let there be light"; and there was light. God saw that the light was good; and God separated the light from the darkness.... -Declare word of faith. Words of wisdom, Liberty and so forth in prayers.

Defile: (verb) damage the purity or appearance of; mar or spoil. "the land was defiled by a previous owner" synonyms:
spoil, sully, mar, impair, debase, degrade; More antonyms: p u r i f y desecrate or profane (something sacred) "the tomb had been defiled and looted" synonyms: desecrate, profane, violate, treat sacrilegiously; More archaic rape or sexually assault (a woman). "and the Babylonians came to her into the bed of love, and they defiled her with their whoredom" As Christians, we should keep ourselves undefiled. In (Hebrew 13) No marital couples should defile the marital bed. Marital bed could be defile through adultery and many immoral acts. The chapter contains a variety of admonitions by the apostle Paul. In (Hebrew 13: 4) he admonishes that marriage be considered honourable by all people and that "the marital union be undefiled" (the KJV has "and the bed undefiled"). The Greek word translated "undefiled" is "amiantos", Strong's Concordance, which literally means unsoiled or pure. The last part of (Hebrew 13: 4) is a warning that those who do "defile their bed," like adulterers, will be judged by God. To understand what it means to have an undefiled martial relationship, we need to know what can defile it. The Old Testament has plenty to say regarding how a person can pollute themselves through sex. God tells us NOT to commit adultery with another person's mate (Exodus 20:14, Leviticus 18:20). We are also commanded not to have intercourse with animals (Leviticus 18:23). Sex between those of the same gender are also expressly forbidden (Leviticus 18: 22). Avoiding these practices would not only save a person from experiencing the negative consequences they bring, they would keep (for those

Degrees

who are married) the "marriage bed" or sexual relationship with their partner pure.

The New Testament book of (1 Corinthians), the seventh chapter, gives us a principle or two regarding the proper sexual relationship within marriage. Both the husband and the wife need to seriously consider their mate's sexual needs and their capabilities. Each person should regard their bodies as belonging to their mate and not under their own total control to do with it whatever they please. Sex should be refrained from only by mutual agreement for the purpose of fasting and prayer, after which time the couple should come together sexually so that they are not tempted to fulfil their needs elsewhere (1Corinthians 7: 1 - 5). This spells out the 'Principles for Marriage' thus' "Now concerning the matters about which you wrote: "It is good for a man not to have sexual relations with a woman." But because of the temptation to sexual immorality, each man should have his own wife and each woman her own husband. The husband should give to his wife her conjugal rights, and likewise the wife to her husband. For the wife does not have authority over her own body, but the husband does. Likewise the husband does not have authority over his own body, but the wife does. Do not deprive one another, except perhaps by agreement for a limited time, that you may devote yourselves to prayer; but then come together again, so that Satan may not tempt you because of your lack of self-control"..

Degrees: A measurement of plane angle, representing 1⁄360 of a full rotation. It is not an SI unit, as the SI unit for angles is radian, but it is mentioned in the SI brochure as an accepted unit. Because a full rotation equals 2π radians, one degree is equivalent to $\pi/180$ radians. In the gospel our Heavenly father's wishes for us all is enablement for us to prosper. When we lived with our Heavenly Father, He explained a plan for our progression. We could become like Him, an exalted being. The plan required that we be separated from Him and come to earth. This separation was necessary to prove whether we would obey our Father's commandments even though we were no longer in His presence. The plan provided that when earth life ended, we would be judged and rewarded according to the degree of our faith and obedience.

From the scriptures we learn that there are three kingdoms of glory in heaven. The Apostle Paul mentioned that he knew a man who was "caught up to the third heaven" (2 Corinthians 12:2). Paul named two of the kingdoms in heaven: the celestial and the terrestrial (1 Corinthians 15:40–42). The celestial is the highest, and the terrestrial is second. Through latter-day revelation we learn that the third kingdom is the celestial kingdom We also learn that there are three heavens or degrees within the celestial kingdom). Exaltation is eternal life, the kind of life God lives. He lives in great glory. He is perfect. He possesses all knowledge and all wisdom. He is the Father of spirit children. He is a creator. We can become like our Heavenly Father. This is exaltation. When we leave righteous life, we are promoted to another degree or from previous glory to a higher glory i.e from Glory to Glory (If we prove faithful to the Lord, we will live in the highest degree of the celestial kingdom of heaven. We will become exalted, to live with our Heavenly Father in eternal families. Exaltation is the greatest gift that Heavenly Father can give His children

Degrees, Songs of or (Songs of Ascents in Hebrew): This is a title given to fifteen of the Psalms, (Psalm 120–134 (Psalm 119–133) in the Septuagint and the Vulgate), that each starts with the ascription Shir Hama'aloth (Hebrew: meaning "Song of Ascents"). They are also variously called Gradual Psalms, Songs of Degrees, Songs of Steps or Pilgrim Songs. Four of them (Psalms 122, 124, 131) and Psalm 133) are linked in their ascriptions to David, and one (Psalm 127) to Solomon. Many scholars believe these psalms were sung by the worshippers as they ascended the road to Jerusalem to attend the three pilgrim festivals (Deuteronomy 16:16) or by the kohanim (priests) as they ascended the fifteen steps to minister at the Temple in Jerusalem. They were well suited for being sung, by their poetic form and the sentiments they express. "They are characterized by brevity, by a key-word, by anaphora [i.e., repetition], and by their epigrammatic style.... More than half of them are cheerful, and all of them hopeful. As, Then, by the Higher Mystical Ascent from Matters that Concern ... they are so called because they speak of the going up from Babylon, according to history; but the fifteen degrees of going up out of the valley of weeping to the presence of God to be affliction, looking to God, joy in communion, invocation, thanksgiving, confidence, patient waiting for deliverance, God's grace and favour, fear of the Lord, martyrdom, hatred of sins, humility, desire for the coming of Christ, concord and charity, constant blessing of God.

Delilah: (Hebrew: - meaning "She who weakened")) is a character in the Hebrew bible Book of Judges, where she is the "woman in the valley of Sorek" whom Samson loved, and who was his downfall. Her figure, one of several dangerous temptresses in the Hebrew bible, has become emblematic: "Samson loved Delilah, she betrayed him, and, what is worse, she did it for money," Madlyn Kahr begins her study of the Delilah motif in European painting.[2] The

Deliver

story of Samson in (Judges 13-16) portrays a man who was given great strength by God but who ultimately loses his strength when Delilah allows the Philistines to shave his hair during his slumber. Suddenly, Delilah discovered Samson's secret (Judges 16:18-20). "When Delilah saw that he had told her all that was in his heart, she sent and called the lords of the Philistines, saying, "Come up once more, for he has told me all that is in his heart." Then the lords of the Philistines came up to her and brought the money in their hands. She made him sleep on her knees, and called for a man and had him shave off the seven locks of his hair. Then she began to afflict him, and his strength left him. She said, "The Philistines are upon you, Samson!" And he awoke from his sleep and said, "I will go out as at other times and shake myself free." But he did not know that the LORD had departed from him...." Samson was born into an Israelite family, the son of Manoah and his wife who is never named. Both are visited by the Angel of the Lord and told that their child will be a Nazi-rite from birth.

Deliver: To redeem, aid in time of difficulty Defend to play guardian angel role, heroic role liberate, protector salvage, conserve guard star preserve, rescue, friendliness. Play the Good Samaritan role, Shepherding etc. **as in** (Judges 3:9) "When the sons of Israel cried to the LORD, the LORD raised up a deliverer for the sons of Israel to *deliver* them, Othniel the son of Kenaz, Caleb's younger brother".

Deliverer, the: (noun) A Person who redeems, aids in time of difficulty Defender star guardian angel star hero star liberator star protector star salvation star conservator star guardian star preserver star rescuer star salvager star friend in need star Good Samaritan etc. as in (Judges 3:9) "When the sons of Israel cried to the LORD, the LORD raised up a deliverer for the sons of Israel to deliver them, Othniel the son of Kenaz, Caleb's younger brother". Even as God delivers the Israelites from the hands of the Egyptians - (Exodus 6: 1-8) "I am the Lord, and I will bring you out from under the burdens of the Egyptians, and I will *deliver* you from slavery to them, and I will redeem you with an outstretched arm and with great acts of judgment" As in the final exile, from which no escape is possible, our Creator has made a way for fallen men and women to be rescued from these lesser exiles, a way that also guarantees that they will enjoy blessing in the new heaven and earth. This way of escape is simple, and it has been essentially the same throughout history. All that it takes to be saved from exile and restored to a full, blessed relationship with the Lord is to embrace Him as the great *Deliverer*. Casting off all attempts to rescue ourselves, we can be freed from the state into which we were born — traitors who refuse to bow to God as King and instead serve another as our sovereign.

Dean: In a church context, is a cleric holding certain positions of authority within a religious hierarchy. The title is used mainly in the Anglican Communion, the Roman Catholic Church, and the Lutheran Church. A dean's deputy is called a sub dean.

Devil: (Greek: - diabolos - slanderer or accuser) believed in many religions, myths and cultures to be a supernatural entity that is the personification of evil and the enemy of God and humankind. The nature of the role varies greatly, ranging from being an effective opposite force to the creator god, locked in an eons long struggle for human souls on what may seem even terms (to the point of dualistic ditheism/bitheism), to being a comical figure of fun or an abstract aspect of the individual human condition. While mainstream Judaism contains no overt concept of a devil, Christianity and Islam have variously regarded the Devil as a rebellious fallen angel or jinn that tempts humans to sin, if not committing evil deeds himself. In these religions – particularly during periods of division or external threat – the Devil has assumed more of a dualistic status commonly associated with heretics, infidels, and other unbelievers. As such, the Devil is seen as an allegory that represents a crisis of faith, individualism, free will, wisdom and enlightenment. In mainstream Christianity and other religions, God and the Devil are usually portrayed as fighting over the souls of humans. The Devil rules Hell, where he and his demons punish the damned. The Devil commands a force of evil spirits, commonly known as demons.[2] The Hebrew Bible (or Old Testament) describes the Adversary (ha-satan) as an angel who instigates tests upon humankind.[3][4] Many other religions have a trickster or tempter figure that is similar to the Devil. Modern conceptions of the Devil include the concept that it symbolizes humans' own lower nature or sinfulness.

Die: (past-tense – died, dead, death) Cessation of life. To cease living; become dead; expire. 2. To cease existing, especially by degrees; fade: The sunlight died in the west. 3 To experience an agony or suffering suggestive of that of death: nearly died of embarrassment. 4 Informal To desire something greatly: For the purpose of Gospel Dictionary and biblical phrases we will look at die in the perspective of the gospel as in (John 11:2) "Jesus said to her, "I am the resurrection and the life. Whoever believes in me, though he *die*, yet shall he live", Again, Jesus said (1 Corinthians 15:51-54) "Behold! I tell you a mystery. We shall not all sleep, but we shall all be changed, in a moment, in the twinkling of an eye, at the last trumpet. For the trumpet will sound, and the dead will be raised imperishable, and we shall be

Disciples

changed. For this perishable body must put on the imperishable, and this mortal body must put on immortality. When the perishable puts on the imperishable, and the mortal puts on immortality, then shall come to pass the saying that is written: "Death is swallowed up in victory."

Disciples: (noun) Simply the follower of Jesus during his life especially one of the twelve Apostles 2 a follower or pupil of a teacher, leader or philosopher. (See the itemise list of Jesus disciples, their meanings and origin below.

Actually the Greek word for Disciple is *'mathetes'* meaning 'learner' or 'follower'. The word means accepting and following the views and practices of a teacher. Apart from having a large following of people, Jesus chose twelve disciples during his earthly ministry. The list is mentioned in (Matthew 10:2-4), (Mark 3:16-19), (Luke 6:13-16) and (Acts 1:13). The original twelve disciples are also called the 'apostles' (Greek – *'apostolos'* meaning 'one who is sent out with a special commission as a fully authorized representative of the sender, like an ambassador). This article lists the names and meaning of these apostles and their occupations.

Peter: (Greek: *Petros* meaning 'Rock') – Peter was one of the most prominent of the 12 disciples. He was a natural spokesperson and also the leader of the early Christian church. His original Hebrew name was Simon, a common popular Hebrew name. Jesus gave him a name *'Kephas'*, an Aramaic name. John translated into it Greek *'Petros'* meaning Rock. (John 1:42 – "you will be called *Cephas*.") Peter was a native of Bethsaida (John 1:44), was the brother of Andrew, lived in a fishing town- Capernaum. (Mark 1:29) He was a fisherman by occupation on the Sea of Galilee. He was a married man. (Mark 1:30, 1 Corinthians 9:5)

John: (Meaning – God is gracious) John was originally the disciple of John the Baptist (John 1:35), and was introduced to Jesus (in John 1:35-39). He was the brother of James and the son of Zebedee. He lived in Capernaum in Galilee, but most probably a native of Bethsaida. He was a fisherman on the Sea of Galilee along with his brother and father. (Mark 1:19-20). He was one of the three disciples, closest to Jesus, the others being Peter and James.

James: (Greek *Iakobos*- the English word for Jacob meaning Israel or he who supplants his Brother). James was the son of Zebedee (Mark 4:21), the older brother of John (Mat 17:1), by occupation a fisherman along with his brother and father at the Sea of Galilee, in partnership with Peter and Andrew. (Luke 5:10). He was the first disciple (apostle) to be martyred. (Acts 12:2)

Andrew: (Greek -*Andreas*, meaning 'Manly', man), was the brother of Simon Peter, the son of Jonas, lived in Capernaum like his brother, , and was a fisherman by occupation. He brought Peter, his brother, to Jesus. (John 1:25-42)

Philip: (Greek – *Philippos*, meaning 'Lover of horses'). He was a close friend of Andrew and Peter, and a native of Bethsaida (John 1:44). Jesus called Philip near Bethany where John the Baptist was preaching (John 1:43). He was the one who persuaded and brought Nathaniel to Jesus. (John 1:45-51)

Bartholomew: (Greek -*bartholomaios* meaning Son of Talmai). He is mentioned in all the four lists of the apostles in the New Testament. There is no other reference to him in the New Testament. Nothing much is known about him.

Thomas: (Greek -*Thomas* from Aramaic -*te'oma* meaning 'twin') He is also called 'Didymus' or 'the Twin' (John 11:16, 20:24, 21:2). When Jesus appeared to the apostles after His resurrection, Thomas was not present with them. Later on, when the disciples told him about Jesus' appearance, he would not believe them, until Jesus showed Himself a week later. (John 20:24-29). His occupation is unknown.

Matthew: (Greek -*maththaios*- meaning 'gift of Yahweh') is also called 'Levi' (Mark 2:14), (Luke 5:27). He was a tax collector by occupation. Jesus called him to be one of his disciples, when He was at the tax office (Mat 9:9, Mark 2:14). He is ascribed to be the author of the Gospel according to Matthew.

James:, He was one of the apostles of Christ. He was the son of Alphaeus.. Nothing much is known about him.

Thaddaeus: He is mentioned in two of the four lists of Jesus' disciples. (Mat 10:3, Mark 3:18). In the other two lists he is variously called as Jude of James, Jude Thaddaeus, Judas Thaddaeus or Lebbaeus. Nothing else is known about him apart from the mention of his names in the two lists.

Simon the Zealot: He is another disciple of Jesus. He was a member of a party later called as the 'Zealots' (Matthew 10:4, Mark 3:18)

Judas Iscariot: He is the disciple who betrayed Jesus. His last name 'Iscariot' is from the Hebrew word '*Ish Kerioth*' meaning 'a man from Kerioth', a place in the south of Judah (Joshua 15:25). He was a treasurer of the group. (John 12:6,13:29). After his betrayal of Jesus, he grieved for his actions and committed suicide. (Matthew 27:5). He is always mentioned last in the list of apostles.

Matthias: After Judas committed suicide after his betrayal of Jesus (Matthew 27:3–10), the eleven

Matthias

disciples selected Matthias as the twelfth disciple.

(Acts 1: 23-26) – So they nominated two men: Joseph called Barsabbas (also known as Justus) and Matthias. Then they prayed, "Lord, you know everyone's heart. Show us which of these two you have chosen to take over this apostolic ministry, which Judas left to go where he belongs." Then they cast lots, and the lot fell to Matthias; so he was added to the eleven apostles.

Dispensation: The system that God chooses to establish or dispense between himself and man. The dispensation of Adam was between Adam and God. The dispensation of Abraham and that of Moses were those imparted to these men. While the "Gospel of dispensation" is the one explained in each dispensatory era.

Dispersion: The action of dispersing people or things or the state of being dispersed. The state of being dispersed.particularly the Diaspora of the Jews or simply THE DISPERSION, was the general title applied to those Jews who remained settled in foreign countries after the return from the Babylonian exile, and during the period of the second temple. At the beginning of the Christian era the Dispersion was divided into three great sections, the Babylonian, the Syrian, the Egyptian. From Babylon the Jews spread throughout Persia, Media and Parthia. Large settlements of Jews were established in Cyprus, in the islands of the AEgean, and on the western coast of Asia Minor. Jewish settlements were also established at Alexandria by Alexander and Ptolemy I. The Jewish settlements in Rome, were consequent upon the occupation of Jerusalem by Pompey, B.C. 63. The influence of the Dispersion on the rapid promulgation of Christianity can scarcely be overrated. The course of the apostolic preaching followed in a regular progress the line of Jewish settlements. The mixed assembly from which the first converts were gathered on the day of Pentecost represented each division of the Dispersion. (Acts 2:9-11) thus "Parthians, Medes and Elamites; residents of Mesopotamia, Judea and Cappadocia, Pontus and Asia Phrygia and Pamphylia, Egypt and the parts of Libya near Cyrene; visitors from Rome (both Jews and converts to Judaism); Cretans and Arabs— Egypt...Greece; Romans...,we hear them declaring the wonders of God in our own tongues!" and these converts naturally prepared the way for the apostles in the interval which preceded the beginning of the separate apostolic missions. St. James and St. Peter wrote to the Jews of the Dispersion. (James 1:1) thus' "James, a servant of God and of the Lord Jesus Christ, To the twelve tribes scattered among the nations: Greetings".

Also (Peter1:1-3) added thus: "Peter, an apostle of Jesus Christ, to the strangers scattered throughout Pontus, Galatia, Cappadocia, Asia, and Bithynia, Elect according to the foreknowledge of God the Father, through sanctification of the Spirit, unto obedience and sprinkling of the blood of Jesus Christ: Grace unto you, and peace, be multiplied. Blessed *be* the God and Father of our Lord Jesus Christ, which according to his abundant mercy hath begotten us again unto a lively hope by the resurrection of Jesus Christ from the dead", 2.*Statistics.* The degree of scatter of people, data, usually about an average value, such as the median 3 The word is common in *Physics such as the*separation of a complex wave into its component parts according to a given characteristic, such as frequency or wave length and the Separation of visible light into colors by refraction or diffraction. It could also be used in Biology, *Chemistry* such as the disperse system and many other relevant field of study. In the case of the Gospel usage, this may be referred to the dispersion of the Jews or the Israelites in various places accounted by James and Peter in their Gospel.

Divine nature: Derives from the Greek phrase; *"theias phuseos"* – An association of the God –kind . Gospel wise, if you are born again, you are an associate of God-kind. You are in fraternity with divinity which is in the Holy Trinity – the God Head. True Christians have to be in the *divine nature* of Christ.

Divine, The: One who talks about God. One relating to, from or like God or a god. 2 Informal, excellent, dated a priest, religious leader or a theologian (the divine) providence or God.

Divinity: (plural-divinities) In gospel terms, divinity is the state of things that comes from a supernatural power or deity, such as a god or spirit beings that are being regarded as sacred or holy. The state or quality of being divine. 2 A god or goddess. 3 The divinity – God. 4 The study of religion; theology.

Divine-will: The will of God, divine will, or God's plan is the concept of God having a plan for humanity, and desiring to see this plan fulfilled...

Divine – Power: This simply means the force, strength, dominion, might of might of the supernatural being-God bestowed upon the Children of His love – True Christians. It is beyond human knowledge and imagination As recorded in 2 Peter 1:3-4 "seeing that His divine power has granted to us everything pertaining to life and godliness, through the true knowledge of Him who called us by His own glory and excellence. For by these He has granted to us His precious and magnificent promises, so that by them you may become partakers of the divine nature, having escaped the corruption that is in the world by lust...."

Divine Office, The: The obligatory prayer of the church, said by priest and the religious. The divine office *(horse canonical)* of the Roman Catholic is contained in the Breviary.

Doctrine: A codification of beliefs or a body of teachings or instructions, taught principles or positions, as the essence of teachings in a given branch of knowledge or belief system. The Greek analogue is the etymology of catechism.

Often doctrine specifically suggests a body of religious principles as it is promulgated by a church, but not necessarily; 2 *doctrine* is also used to refer to a principle of law, in the common law traditions, established through a history of past decisions, such as the *doctrine* of self-defence, or the principle of fair use, or the more narrowly applicable first-sale doctrine. In some organizations, doctrine is simply defined as "that which is taught", in other words the basis for institutional teaching of its personnel internal ways of doing business. 3 For the purpose of the gospel dictionary and biblical phrases, our focus point dwells on the gospel according to (2 Timothy 4:2-4) regarding the preaching of the word. Thus' "preach the word; be ready in season and out of season; reprove, rebuke, exhort, with great patience and instruction. 3For the time will come when they will not endure sound *doctrine*; but wanting to have their ears tickled, they will accumulate for themselves teachers in accordance to their own desires, 4and will turn away their ears from the truth and will turn aside to myths". And also as regarding the teaching of sound doctrine as in (Titus 2:1-6) "But as for you, teach what accords with sound *doctrine*. Older men are to be sober-minded, dignified, self-controlled, sound in faith, in love, and in steadfastness. Older women likewise are to be reverent in behaviour, not slanderers or slaves to much wine. They are to teach what is good, and so train the young women to love their husbands and children, to be self-controlled, pure, working at home, kind, and submissive to their own husbands, that the word of God may not be reviled. Likewise, urge the younger men to be self-controlled..."

Doctrine, Sound: This implied the truth. Sound doctrine is important because our faith is based on a specific message. The overall teaching of the church contains many elements, but the primary message is explicitly defined: "Christ died for our sins according to the Scriptures (and) . . . he was raised on the third day according to the Christian gospel" (1Corinthians 15:3-4). "For what I received I passed on to you as of first importance[a]: that Christ died for our sins according to the Scriptures, that he was buried, that he was raised on the third day according to the Scriptures", This is the unambiguous good news, and it is "of first importance." Change that message and the basis of faith shifts from Christ to something else. Our eternal destiny depends upon hearing "the word of truth, the gospel of your salvation" (Ephesians 1:3; see also 2 Thessalonians 2:13-14).

Doctrine, Sound (As a Sacred Trust): Sound doctrine is important because the gospel is a sacred trust, and we dare not tamper with God's communication to the world. Our duty is to deliver the message, not to change it. Jude conveys urgency in guarding the trust: "I felt I had to write and urge you to contend for the faith that was once for all entrusted to the saints" (Jude 1:3; Philippians 1:27). To "contend" carries the idea of strenuously fighting for something, to give it everything you've got. The Bible includes a warning neither to add to nor subtract from God's Word (Revelation 22:18-19). Rather than alter the apostles' *doctrine*, we receive what has been passed down to us and keep it "as the pattern of sound teaching, with faith and love in Christ Jesus" (2 Timothy 1:13).

Doctrine, Sound: (As guidance to our Actions) Sound doctrine is important because what we believe affects what we do. Behaviour is an extension of theology, and there is a direct correlation between what we think and how we act. For example, two people stand on top of a bridge; one believes he can fly, and the other believes he cannot fly. Their next actions will be quite dissimilar. In the same way, a man who believes that there is no such thing as right and wrong will naturally behave differently from a man who believes in well-defined moral standards. In one of the Bible's lists of sins, things like rebellion, murder, lying, and slave trading are mentioned. The list concludes with "whatever else is contrary to the sound doctrine" (1 Timothy 1:9-10). In other words, true teaching promotes righteousness; sin flourishes where "the sound doctrine" is opposed.

Doctrine, Sound: (As a Revealing Truth) - Sound doctrine is important because we must ascertain truth in a world of falsehood. "Many false prophets have gone out into the world" (1 John 4:1). There are tares among the wheat and wolves among the flock (Matthew 13:25; Acts 20:29). The best way to distinguish truth from falsehood is to know what the truth is.

Doctrine, Sound: (As ending in Life) Sound doctrine is important because the end of sound doctrine is life. "Watch your life and doctrine closely. Persevere in them, because if you do, you will save both yourself and your hearers" (1 Timothy 4:16). Conversely,

Doctrine, Sound

the end of unsound doctrine is destruction. "Certain men whose condemnation was written about long ago have secretly slipped in among you. They are godless men, who change the grace of our God into a license for immorality and deny Jesus Christ our only sovereign and Lord" (Jude 1:4). Changing God's message of grace is a "godless" thing to do, and the condemnation for such a deed is severe. Preaching another gospel ("which is really no gospel at all") carries an anathema: "let him be eternally condemned!" (Galatians 1:6-9).

Doctrine, Sound: (As courage to Believers)

- Sound doctrine is important because it encourages believers. A love of God's Word brings "great peace" (Psalm 119:165), and those "who proclaim peace . . . who proclaim salvation" are truly "beautiful" (Isaiah 52:7). A pastor "must hold firmly to the trustworthy message as it has been taught, so that he can encourage others by sound doctrine and refute those who oppose it" (Titus 1:9). The word of wisdom is "Do not remove the ancient landmark which your fathers have set" (Proverbs 22:28). If we can apply this to sound doctrine, the lesson is that we must preserve it intact. May we never stray from "the simplicity that is in Christ" (2 Corinthians 11:3).

Door: (noun)

(Revelation 3:7-8) "And to the angel of the church in Philadelphia write: He who is holy, who is true, who has the key of David, who opens and no one will shut, and who shuts and no one opens, says this: 'I know your deeds Behold, I have put before you an open *door* which no one can shut, because you have a little power, and have kept My word, and have not denied My name. Door can have several meanings and many forms of usage. The simple meaning is a hinged, sliding, or revolving barrier at the entrance to a building, room, or vehicle, or in the framework of a cupboard. "she looked for her key and opened the door" a doorway. "she walked through the door" synonyms: doorway, portal, opening, hatch, entrance, entry, exit, egress "she disappeared through a door" used to refer to the distance from one building in a row to another. "he lives just a few doors away from the Strong's. What concerns us in the context of the dictionary is as used in the gospel as in the passage according to Revelation above and many other useful passages in the bible as Jesus Christ opined in (Revelation 3:20) "Here I am! I stand at the *door* and knock. If anyone hears my voice and opens the door, I will come in and eat with that person, and they with me".

Doxology:

(Greek – doxologos 'uttering praise i.e to God) The greater Doxology is the hymn Gloria in Excelsis Deo (Glory to God in the Highest) at the Euchrist. The lesser Doxology is the Gloria Patri (Glory be to the Father) sung and said at the end of each psalm in the liturgy. 2 There is also Bishop Ken's Hymn – 'Praise God from whom all blessings flow'.

Dreadful: (adjective) Causing or involving great suffering, fear, or unhappiness; extremely bad or serious. "there's been a dreadful accident" synonyms: terrible, frightful, horrible, grim, awful, dire; More antonyms: mild extremely disagreeable. "the weather was dreadful" synonyms: unpleasant, disagreeable, nasty; (of a person) unwell or troubled. "I feel dreadful—I hate myself" (Genesis 28:17) And he was afraid, and said, How dreadful is this place! this is none other but the house of God, and this is the gate of heaven. Also (Job 15:21) A dreadful sound is in his ears: in prosperity the destroyer shall come upon him. 2 *Dreadful* sometimes used to emphasize the degree to which something is the case, especially something regarded with sadness or disapproval. "this was all a dreadful mistake"synonyms: outrageous, shocking; More

Drink: *(drunk – past tenses, drunkenness)* Take (a liquid) into the mouth and swallow. "we sat by the fire, drinking our tea" synonyms: swallow, gulp down, quaff, swill, guzzle, sup;

Consume or be in the habit of consuming alcohol. "she doesn't drink or smoke" synonyms: drink alcohol, take alcohol, tipple, indulge; quickly consume the rest of a drink. Informal (of a plant or a porous substance) absorb (moisture). "the seedlings apparently drink much more water than we had realized" (of wine) have a specified flavour or character when drunk. "this wine is really drinking beautifully" 2 watch or listen to something with eager pleasure or interest. "she strolled to the window to drink in the view" synonyms: absorb, assimilate, digest, ingest, take in, be absorbed in, be immersed in, be rapt in, be lost in, be fascinated by, pay close attention to "he drank in the details of the crime" noun: drink; plural noun: drinks - a liquid that can be swallowed as refreshment or nourishment. "fizzy drinks" synonyms: beverage, drinkable/potable liquid, liquid refreshment, thirst quencher; 3 Drinks (or beverages) are liquids specifically prepared for human consumption. In addition to basic needs, beverages form part of the culture of human society. Although most beverages, including juice, soft drinks, and carbonated drinks, have some form of water in them, water itself is often not classified as a beverage, and the word beverage has been recurrently defined as not referring to water. An alcoholic beverage is a drink containing ethanol, commonly known as alcohol, although in chemistry the definition of an alcohol includes many other compounds. Alcoholic beverages, such as wine, beer, and liquor, have been part of human culture and development for 8,000 years. Non-alcoholic drinks/beverages often signify drinks that

Drink

would normally contain alcohol, such as beer and wine but are made with less than .5 per cent alcohol by volume. The category includes drinks that have undergone an alcohol removal process such as non-alcoholic beers and de-alcoholised wines. While the above description of drinks is essential, the gospel dictionary concern focuses on the significant of drinks in the Gospel of Jesus Christ as it affect our Christian lives or Christianity as a whole. In the Old Testament, Aaron and his sons, the priests, were strictly forbidden to drink either wine or strong drink when they went into the tabernacle to minister before the Lord (Leviticus 10:9). Nasserites were likewise forbidden to use wine while under their vow (Numbers 6:1-3, 20; Judges 13:4-7). The Rechabites lived as noteworthy examples of permanent abstinence from wine, adhering strictly to the command of their ancestor, Jonadab, to refrain from it (Jeremiah 35:1-8, 14). The Bible book of Proverbs is filled with warnings against indulging in wine and strong drink (Proverbs 20:1; 21:17; 23:29-35; 31:4). Wine mocks those who use it as in (Proverbs 20:1) and rewards them with woe, sorrow, strife, and wounds without cause as in (Proverbs 23:29, 30). "In the end it (wine) bites like a snake and poisons like a viper" (Proverbs 23:32,). The prophet Isaiah declared, "Woe to those who are heroes at drinking wine and champions at mixing drinks" (Isaiah 5:22). Daniel and his companions set a worthy example by refusing to drink the king's wine as in (Daniel 1:5-16). When fasting later in life, Daniel abstained from wine (Daniel 10:3). However, in the New Testament, the usual word for wine, whether alcoholic or non-alcoholic, is (oinos - Hebrew). Jesus likened His revolutionary teaching to new wine, which would burst the old bottles of tradition (Matthew 9:17). Paul warned believers against drunkenness (Ephesians 5:18), and declares that deacons should not be "addicted to much wine" (1 Timothy 3:8). He counselled Titus that the older women should not be "slaves to drink" (Titus 2:3). Yet, Paul did recommend that his friend Timothy should "use a little wine" for relief from a digestive ailment (1 Timothy 5:23). A close look at this counsel shows that in those days, physical ailments, such as dysentery, were common occurrences—often due to contaminated water. Consequently, other ways of quenching thirst were often recommended. Some Bible students believe that in this verse Paul was advocating the temperate use of fermented wine for medicinal purposes. They call attention to the fact that through the centuries wine has been used in this way. Other Gospel/Bible Presenters say that Paul is referring to unfermented grape juice. Since the Greek word translated "wine" can mean either fermented wine or unfermented grape juice, they believe Paul would not give advice inconsistent with the rest of Scripture, which warns strongly against the use of intoxicating beverages—

and that he is, therefore, advising Timothy to drink pure, unfermented grape juice, moderate to the Glory of God. Hallelujah!

With the above enumerations about drink and whereas Christians have as many views about drinking alcohol as there are denominations, but the Bible is abundantly clear on one thing: Drunkenness is a serious sin.

Dust: Particles in the atmosphere that come from various sources such as soil, dust lifted by weather (an Aeolian process), volcanic eruptions, and pollution. Dust in homes, offices, and other human environments contains small amounts of plant pollen, human and animal hairs, textile fibres, paper fibres, minerals from outdoor soil, human skin cells, burnt meteorite particles, and many other materials which may be found in the local environment. In the context of the gospel dictionary, dust is seen in the perspective of its scriptural significance. In (Joshua7:6). 2 Dust or ashes put upon the head was a sign of mourning; sitting in the *dust*, a sign of affliction, (Lamentation 3:29 Isaiah 47:1). "Dust" is also put for the grave, (Genesis 3:19 Job 7:21). It signifies a multitude, (Genesis 13:16), and a low and mean condition, (1 Samuel 2:8). We have two remarkable instances of casting dust recorded in the gospel, and they seem to illustrate a practice common in Asia: those who demanded justice against a criminal were accustomed to throw *dust* upon him, signifying that he deserved to be cast into the grave. Shimei cast *dust* upon David when he fled from Jerusalem, 2 Samuel 16:13. The Jews treated the apostle Paul in a similar manner in the same city: "They cried out,? Away with such a fellow from the earth; for it is not fit that he should live.- And as they cried out, and cast off their clothes, and threw dust into the air, the chief captain commanded him to be brought into the castle," (Acts 22:22-24). To shake off the *dust* of the feet against another was expressive of entire renunciation, (Matthew 10:14 Mark 6:11 Acts 13:51). The threatening of God, recorded in (Deuteronomy 28:24), "The Lord shall make the rain of thy land powder and *dust*: from heaven shall it come down upon thee, until thou be destroyed," means that instead of fertilizing rains, clouds of fine *dust*, raised from the parched ground and driven by fierce and burning winds, shall fill the air. Of such a rain of *dust*, famine and disease would be the natural attendants. 4 Also, in (Genesis 3:19) God use dust to banish Adam and Eve - the first parent in the Garden of Eden "By the sweat of your face you shall eat bread, till you return to the ground, for out of it you were taken; for you are *dust*, and to *dust* you shall return -" which forms the common committal saying at every Burial around the world. Thus' Dust to dust, ashes to ashes! Note: this phrase does not exist anywhere in the bible.

Dunamis: (doo'-nam-is – Greek word) - meaning might, power, marvellous works used over 120 times in the New Testament gos-

Dunamis

pels – 2 Dynamic power, physical power, force, might, ability, efficacy, energy, 3 Plural: powerful deeds, deeds showing (physical) power, marvellous works. Powerful works of Grace.

4 "Able, having ability") – properly, "ability to perform" for the believer, power to achieve by applying the Lord's inherent abilities. "Power through God's ability" is needed in every scene of life to really grow in sanctification and prepare for heaven (glorification).

5 *Dunamis* - , "inherent power, power residing in a thing by virtue of its nature, or which a person or thing exerts and puts forth": (Luke 1:17; Acts 4:7; 1 Corinthians 4:20; 2 Corinthians 4:7; 2 Corinthians 12:9)

6 *Dunamis*, Overwhelming power, the power of God: (Matthew 22:29); "Jesus replied, "You are in error because you do not know the Scriptures or the power of God". Also (Mark 12:24; Luke 22:69; Acts 8:10; Romans 1:20; Romans 9:17; 1 Corinthians 6:14; Luke 1:35); especially in doxologies, the kingly power of God, Matthew 6:13 Revelation 4:11; Revelation 7:12; Revelation 11:17; Revelation 12:10; Revelation 15:8; Revelation 19:1; Hebrews 11:34; Revelation 1:16; Revelation 17:13; Acts 3:12; Acts 4:33; Matthew 25:15; beyond our power, 2 Corinthians 1:8; endued with power, Luke 4:36; 1 Corinthians 15:43; so in the phrase, Mark 9:1; powerfully, Colossians 1:29; 2 Thessalonians 1:11; contextually, equivalent to evidently, Romans 1:4; through the power which I exerted upon their souls by performing miracles, Romans 15:19; Hebrews 11:11; , Luke 9:1; sin exercises its power (upon the soul) through the law, i. e. through the abuse of the law, (1 Corinthians 15:56); the power which the resurrection of Christ has, for instructing, reforming, elevating, tranquilizing, the soul, Philippians 3:10; inhering in godliness and operating upon souls, 2 Timothy 3:5; Hebrews 6:5; 1 Peter 4:14 ; 2 Timothy 1:7; is used of the power of angels: Ephesians 1:21 2 Peter 2:11; of the power of the devil and evil spirits as in, (1 Corinthians 15:24-25) "then comes the end, when He hands over the kingdom to the God and Father, when He has abolished all rule and all authority and power. For He must reign until He has put all His enemies under His feet...."; i. e. of the devil, Luke 10:19 "Heal the sick who are there and tell them, 'The kingdom of God has come near to you". Revelation 13:2; angels, as excelling in power, are called Lightfoot on (Colossians 1:16; Romans 8:38; 1 Peter 3:22). Overwhelmingly, the power of God: Matthew 22:29; Mark 12:24; Luke 22:69; Acts 8:10; Romans 1:20; Romans 9:17; 1 Corinthians 6:14; , Luke 1:35; especially in doxologies, the kingly power of God, (Matthew 6:13 Rec.; Revelation 4:11; Revelation 7:12; Revelation 11:17; Revelation 12:10; Miracle power, Sign and wonders are all *dunamis*.

Ee

Earnest: (*adjective*) resulting from or showing sincere and intense conviction. "an earnest student" synonyms: serious, serious-minded, solemn, grave, sober, humourless, staid, steady, intense; This has to do with the trustworthiness in God's promise through Christ Jesus of another comforter – even the Spirit of truth. So, the Spirit is the *earnest* of the believer's destined inheritance (2 Corinthians 1:22) ; (2 Corinthians 5:5) ; (Ephesians 1:14). The word thus rendered is the same as that rendered "pledge" in (Genesis 38:17-20) ; "indeed, the Hebrew word has simply passed into the Greek and Latin languages, probably through commercial dealings with the Phoenicians, the great trading people of ancient days. Originally it meant no more than a pledge; but in common usage it came to denote that particular kind of pledge which is a part of the full price of an article paid in advance; and as it is joined with the figure of a seal when applied to the Spirit, it seems to be used by Paul in this specific sense." The Spirit's gracious presence and working in believers is a foretaste to them of the blessedness of heaven. God is graciously pleased to give not only pledges but foretastes of future blessedness. Hallelujah!

Earring: (1 Timothy 2:9-10) - In like manner also, that women adorn themselves in modest apparel, with shamefacedness and sobriety; not with braided hair, or gold, or pearls, or costly array; Also (Numbers 31:50) asserts – "We have therefore brought an oblation for the LORD, what every man hath gotten, of jewels of gold, chains, and bracelets, rings, *earrings*, and tablets, to make an atonement for our souls before the LORD". *Earring* A piece of jewellery attached to the ear via a piercing in the earlobe or another external part of the ear (except in the case of clip *earrings*, which clip onto the lobe). Earrings are worn by both sexes, although more common among women, and have been used by different civilizations in different times. Locations for piercings other than the earlobe include the rook, tragus, and across the helix. The simple term "ear piercing" usually refers to an earlobe piercing, whereas piercings in the upper part of the external ear are often referred to as "cartilage piercings". Cartilage piercings are more complex to perform than earlobe piercings and take longer to heal. *Earring* components may be made of any number of materials, including metal, plastic, glass, precious stone, beads, wood, bone, and other materials. Designs range from small loops and studs to large plates and dangling items. The size is ultimately limited by the physical capacity of the earlobe to hold the earring without tearing. However, heavy earrings worn over extended periods of time may lead to stretching of the earlobe and the piercing. Base on the meaning of Earring above, we should focus our attention to the ingredients attached to it in the gospel as men and women of old used to do as in (Exodus 35:22) – *"And they came, both men and women, as many as were willing hearted, (and) brought bracelets, and earrings, and rings, and tablets, all jewels of gold: and every man that offered [offered] an offering of gold unto the LORD".*

However, the Bible does show that people did wear earrings (the Hebrew word nexem, Strong's Concordance - means nose ring, *earring* or jewel), bracelets, jewels around the neck, rings and other adornments (Isaiah 3:18 - 22).

Interestingly, God HIMSELF stated he gave this jewellery as a gift! When God made a covenant with Israel he considered it like entering into a marriage covenant. After God "married" Israel he stated in the book of (Ezekiel 16: 10-12) "I dressed you in embroidered gowns and gave you shoes of the best leather, a linen headband, and a silk cloak. I put jewels on you - bracelets and necklaces. I gave you a nose ring and *earrings* and a beautiful crown to wear. Regardless of the expense or beauty of our rings, *earrings*, jewels, clothes and alike, the apostle Peter reminds us what truly is the MOST important adornment that can be possessed.

Earth: (Genesis 1:1-31) "In the beginning, God created the heavens and the earth. The earth was without form and void, and darkness was over the face of the deep. And the Spirit of God was hovering over the face of the waters. And God said, "Let there be light," and there was light. And God saw that the light was good. And God separated the light from the darkness. God called the light Day, and the darkness he called Night. And there was evening and there was morning, the first day". 2 *Earth* - also known as the world, Terra, or Gaia, is the third planet from the Sun, the densest planet in the Solar System, the largest of the Solar System's four terrestrial planets, and the only celestial body known to accommodate life. It is home to about 8.74 million species. There

Earth

are billions of humans who depend upon its biosphere and minerals. 3 The *Earth's* human population is divided among about two hundred independent states that interact through diplomacy, conflict, travel, trade, and media. According to evidence from sources such as radiometric dating, Earth was formed around four and a half billion years ago. Within its first billion years, life appeared in its oceans and began to affect its atmosphere and surface, promoting the proliferation of aerobic as well as anaerobic organisms and causing the formation of the atmosphere's ozone layer. This layer and Earth's magnetic field block the most life-threatening parts of the Sun's radiation, so life was able to flourish on land as well as in water. Since then, Earth's position in the Solar System, its physical properties and its geological history have allowed life to persist.

3 *Earth's* lithosphere is divided into several rigid segments, or tectonic plates, that migrate across the surface over periods of many millions of years. Over 70% per cent of Earth's surface is covered with water, with the remainder consisting of continents and islands which together have many lakes and other sources of water that contribute to the hydrosphere. Earth's poles are mostly covered with ice that is the solid ice of the Antarctic ice sheet and the sea ice that is the polar ice packs. The planet's interior remains active, with a solid iron inner core, a liquid outer core that generates the magnetic field, and a thick layer of relatively solid mantle.

4 Earth gravitationally interacts with other objects in space, especially the Sun and the Moon. During one orbit around the Sun, the Earth rotates about its own axis 366.26 times, creating 365.26 solar days, or one sidereal year.[n 6] The Earth's axis of rotation is tilted 23.4° away from the perpendicular of its orbital plane, producing seasonal variations on the planet's surface with a period of one tropical year (365.24 solar days). The Moon is *Earth's* only natural satellite. It began orbiting the Earth about 4.53 billion years ago (bya). The Moon's gravitational interaction with Earth stimulates ocean tides, stabilizes the axial tilt, and gradually slows the planet's rotation as in (Psalm 104:5) He set the earth on its foundations, so that it should never be moved. (Hebrews 1:10) And, "You, Lord, laid the foundation of the earth in the beginning, and the heavens are the work of your hands; (Job 26:7) He stretches out the north over the void and hangs the earth on nothing. Also, (Colossians 1:16-17) – "For by him all things were created: things in heaven and on *earth*, visible and invisible, whether thrones or powers or rulers or authorities; all things were created by him and for him. He is before all things, and in him all things hold together". See also (Nehemiah 9:6) - You alone are the LORD. You made the heavens, even the highest heavens, and all their starry host, the *earth* and all

that is on it, the seas and all that is in them. You give life to everything, and the multitudes of heaven worship you.

Earth, New Heaven and new: Significantly, there will be no sea in the new earth and new Heaven unlike those in the first earth as in (Revelation 21:1) Then I saw a new heaven and a new earth, for the first heaven and the first earth had passed away, and the sea was no more.

Earth beneath, The: (Acts 2:19) And I will show wonders in heaven above, and signs in the earth beneath; blood, and fire, and vapour of smoke: This is the earth's crust, extending down about 1,800 miles (2,900 kilometres), is a thick layer called the mantle. The mantle is not perfectly stiff but can flow slowly. Earth's crust floats on the mantle much as a board floats in water. Just as a thick board would rise above the water higher than a thin one, the thick continental crust rises higher than the thin oceanic crust. The slow motion of rock in the mantle moves the continents around and cause earthquakes, volcanoes, and the formation of mountain ranges. At the centre of Earth is the core. The core is made mostly of iron and nickel and possibly smaller amounts of lighter elements, including sulfur and oxygen. The core is about 4,400 miles (7,100 kilometers) in diameter, slightly larger than half the diameter of Earth and about the size of Mars. The outermost 1,400 miles (2,250 kilometers) of the core are liquid. Currents flowing in the core are thought to generate Earth's magnetic field. Geologists believe the innermost part of the core, about 1,600 miles (2,600 kilometers) in diameter, is made of a similar material as the outer core, but it is solid. The inner core is about four-fifths as big as Earth's moon.

2 Earth gets hotter toward the centre. At the bottom of the continental crust, the temperature is about 1800 degrees F (1000 degrees C). The temperature increases about 3 degrees F per mile (1 degree C per kilometer) below the crust. Geologists believe the temperature of Earth's outer core is about 6700 to 7800 degrees F (3700 to 4300 degrees C). The inner core may be as hot as 12,600 degrees F (7000 degrees C)--hotter than the surface of the sun. But, because it is under great pressures, the rock in the centre of Earth remains solid. It is believe, Hell locate in earth beneath. There are some of the verses sceptics cite to "prove" their point that the Bible says hell refers to a place under the earth:

It is as high as heaven; what canst thou do? deeper than hell; what canst thou know? (Job 11:8 KJV) For great is thy mercy toward me: and thou hast delivered my soul from the lowest hell. (Psalm 86:13 KJV) But he knoweth not that the dead are there; and that her guests are in the depths of hell. (Proverbs 9:18 KJV)

Easter

The way of life is above to the wise, that he may depart from hell beneath. (Proverbs 15:24 KJV) Yet thou shalt be brought down to hell, to the sides of the pit. (Isaiah 14:15 KJV) I made the nations to shake at the sound of his fall, when I cast him down to hell with them that descend into the pit: and all the trees of Eden, the choice and best of Lebanon, all that drink water, shall be comforted in the nether parts of the earth. (Ezekiel 31:16 KJV)

Though they dig into hell, thence shall mine hand take them; though they climb up to heaven, thence will I bring them down: (Amos 9:2 KJV) If I ascend up into heaven, thou art there: if I make my bed in hell, behold, thou art there. (Psalm 139:8 KJV) The Hebrew word - Sheol refers to the grave

Even though the verses above seem to imply that "hell" is under the earth, some of the verses are difficult to reconcile, given the context. First, one would have to ask why God would be in both heaven and hell (Psalm 139:8)? Isn't God supposed to be in heaven? And why is hell described as a "pit?" Unless it were a really big pit, it would be difficult to fit all the damned into such a "pit." The mystery is solved when one looks at the Hebrew word translated in the KJV Bible as "hell." The Hebrew word common to all these verses is 'sheol', which actually refers to the grave.

Easter: A festival and holiday celebrating the Resurrection of Jesus Christ from the dead, described in the New Testament as having occurred three days after his crucifixion by Romans at Calvary. It is the culmination of the Passion of Christ, preceded by Lent (or Great Lent), a forty-day period of fasting, prayer, and penance.

The week before Easter is called Holy Week, and it contains the days of the Easter Tritium, including Maundy Thursday (also known as Holy Thursday), commemorating the Last Supper and its preceding foot washing, as well as Good Friday, commemorating the crucifixion and death of Jesus. In western Christianity, Eastertide, the Easter Season, begins on Easter Sunday and lasts seven weeks, ending with the coming of the fiftieth day, Pentecost Sunday. In Orthodoxy, the season of Paschal begins on Paschal and ends with the coming of the fortieth day, the Feast of the Ascension. 2 Easter is a moveable feast, meaning it is not fixed in relation to the civil calendar. The First Council of Nicaea established the date of Easter as the first Sunday after the full moon (the Paschal Full Moon) following the March equinox. Ecclesiastically, the equinox is reckoned to be on 21 March (although the astronomical equinox occurs on 20 March in most years), and the "Full Moon" is not necessarily on the astronomically correct date. The date of Easter therefore varies from 22 March to 25 April inclu-

Easter Eggs

sive. Eastern Christianity bases its calculations on the Julian calendar, whose 21 March corresponds, during the 21st century, to 3 April in the Gregorian calendar, and in which therefore the celebration of Easter varies between 4 April and 8 May. Easter is linked to the Jewish Passover by much of its symbolism, as well as by its position in the calendar. In many languages, the words for "Easter" and "Passover" are identical or very similar. 3 *Easter* customs vary across the Christian world, and include sunrise services, exclaiming the Paschal greeting, clipping the church, and decorating Easter eggs, a symbol of the empty tomb.

Easter Eggs: (Noun) An artificial chocolate egg or decorated hard-boiled egg given at Easter. Also known as Pasch egg or Passover egg.2 The egg is a symbol of fertility and renewal of life derives from ancient world as did the practice of colouring and eating eggs at the spring festival. It represents the custom of eating egg on Easter Sunday and of making gift of Easter eggs to Children.

Easter Lilly, The: A symbol of the resurrection, traditionally decorates the chancel area of churches on this day and for the rest of Eastertide. Additional customs that have become associated with Easter and are observed by both Christians and some non-Christians include egg hunting, the Easter Bunny, and Easter parades. There are also various traditional Easter foods that vary regionally.

Eat: (verb, Plural Eats, passive – ate,) There are various meanings to the word 'eat' but the gospel meaning is our concern in this passage. Ordinarily, eat means to put (food) into the mouth and chew and swallow it. "he was eating a hot dog" synonyms: consume, devour, ingest, partake of, gobble (up and down), gulp (down), bolt (down), wolf (down), cram down, finish (off); antonyms: starve, fast have (a meal). "we ate the communion" synonyms: have a meal, partake of spiritual food, take food, consume food, feed; have a meal in a restaurant. "there were plenty of places to eat out in the city centre" have a meal at home. US vulgar slang perform fellatio or cunnilingus on (someone). noun informal, plural noun: eats; noun: eat light food or snacks. "these make great party eats". To Christians, whether eating or drinking, should be done to the Glory of God as in (1 Corinthians 10:31) – "Whether therefore ye *eat*, or drink, or whatsoever ye do, do all to the glory of God".

Eden, Garden of: In the gospel, this is the biblical "garden of God", described most notably in the Book of Genesis chapters 2 and 3, and also in the Book of Ezekiel. The "garden of God", not called Eden, is mentioned in Genesis 14, and the "trees of the garden" are mentioned in Ezekiel 31. The Book of Zechariah and the Book of Psalms also refer to trees and water in relation to the temple without explicitly mentioning Eden. Traditionally, the favoured derivation of the name "Eden" was from the Akkadian edinnu, derived from a Sumerian word meaning "plain" or "steppe". Eden is now believed to be more closely related to an Aramaic root word meaning "fruitful, well-watered." The Hebrew term is translated "pleasure" in Sarah's secret saying in (Genesis 18:11) The story of Eden echoes the Mesopotamian myth of a king, as a primordial man, who is placed in a divine garden to guard the tree of life. In the Hebrew Bible, Adam and Eve are depicted as walking around the Garden of Eden naked due to their innocence. Eden and its rivers may signify the real Jerusalem, the Temple of Solomon, or the Promised Land. It may also represent the divine garden on Zion, and the mountain of God, which was also Jerusalem. nehushtan, and guardian cherubs.

Edom: A Semite-inhabited historical region of the Southern Levant located south of Judea and the Dead Sea mostly in the Negev. It is mentioned in biblical records as a 1st millennium BC Iron Age kingdom of Edom and in classical antiquity the cognate name Idumea was used to refer to a smaller area in the same region. The name Edom means "red" in Hebrew, and was given to Esau, the elder son of the Hebrew patriarch Isaac, once he ate the "red pottage", which the Bible used in irony at the fact he was born "red all over". The Torah, Tanakh and New Testament thus describe the Edomites as descendants of Esau. 3 A nation consisting of the descendants of Esau, twin brother of Jacob and son of Isaac and Rebekah, was located to the southeast of Judah, in a rugged, mountainous region which is now the south-western part of the kingdom of Jordan. 4 Edom is sometimes referred to as Esau (Malachi 1:3), Idumea (Isaiah 34:5) and Mount Seir (Ezekiel 35:3). All of these names are interchangeable, referring to the same nation, Edom. Genesis 36 describes the rapid growth of Edom. (Deuteronomy 2:5) informs us that Edom's territory was not part of the land promised to Israel and never would be: "Meddle not with them; for I will not give you of their land, no, not so much as a foot breadth; because I have given mount Seir unto Esau for a possession." (Ezekiel 35:5) condemned the nation of Edom, saying, "Thou hast had a perpetual hatred, and hast shed the blood of the children of Israel by the force of the sword in the time of their calamity . . ."

Edomites, The: Were the descendants of Esau, the firstborn son of Isaac and the twin brother of Jacob. In the womb, Esau and Jacob struggled together, and God told their mother, Rebekah, that they would become two nations, with the older one serving the younger (Genesis 25:23). As

Effulgence, The

an adult, Esau rashly sold his inheritance to Jacob for a bowl of red soup (Genesis 25:30-34), and he hated his brother afterward. Esau became the father of the Edomites and Jacob became the father of the Israelites, and the two nations continued to struggle through most of their history. In the Bible, "Seir" (Joshua 24:4), "Bozrah" (Isaiah 63:1) and "Sela" (2 Kings 14:7) are references to Edom's land and capital. Selah is better known today as Petra.

Effulgence, The: (noun) The quality of being bright and sending out rays of light. Or the location of visual perception along a continuum from bright to white or dark to shine brightness, or appearance of reflected light – gleam, lambency, gleaming, glow i.e appearance of reflected light. Or the visual property of something that shines with reflected light –sheen, shininess, luster, lustre or the property of being smooth and shiny as in burnish, glossiness, polish gloss. In short, of a person or their expression emanating for goodness, shinning brightly; radiant. 2 The quality of being bright and sending out rays of light like in the Glory of GOD. Or the effulgence of his Glory. Just like the Lord Jesus is the Glory of God, you too are the effulgence of the Father's glory. And the glory which thou 'gavest' me I have given them that they may be me, even as we are one.

Eagle, Thy youth is renewed like the: (phr) This is biblical words from (Psalm 103:5) which referred to the ancient superstition that every ten years the eagle soars into the 'fiery region' and plunges into the sea, where, by moulting its feathers, it acquires new life.

Egypt: This is a transcontinental country spanning the northeast corner of Africa and southwest corner of Asia, via a land bridge formed by the Sinai Peninsula. Most of its territory of 1,010,000 square kilometres (390,000 sq mi) lies within the Nile Valley of North Africa and is bordered by the Mediterranean Sea to the north, the Gaza Strip and Israel to the northeast, the Gulf of Aqaba to the east, the Red Sea to the east and south, Sudan to the south and Libya to the west. 2 Egypt, a country where Abraham moves and dwell to escape a period of famine in Canaan.

3 In the gospel, Egypt, is noted for her role to keep the Israelites into captivity, the worship of Idol and the enslavement of the Israelites following the death of Joseph which suddenly provoked the anger of God as He spoke in (Isaiah 19:1-25) over an oracle concerning Egypt thus' "Behold, the Lord is riding on a swift cloud and comes to *Egypt*; and the idols of *Egypt* will tremble at his presence, and the heart of the Egyptians will melt within them. And I will stir up Egyptians against Egyptians, and they will fight, each

against another and each against his neighbour, city against city, kingdom against kingdom; and the spirit of the Egyptians within them will be emptied out, and I will confound their counsel; and they will inquire of the idols and the sorcerers, and the mediums and the necromancers; and I will give over the Egyptians into the hand of a hard master, and a fierce king will rule over them, declares the Lord God of hosts. And the waters of the sea will be dried up, and the river will be dry and parched... , (ESV)

Elder(s), An: (Acts 14:23) "And when they had appointed *elders* for them in every church, with prayer and fasting they committed them to the Lord in whom they had believed". 2 An elder in Christianity is a person valued for his wisdom who accordingly holds a particular position of responsibility in a Christian group or Church. In some Christian traditions (e.g., Eastern Orthodoxy, Roman Catholicism, Anglicanism, Methodism) an elder is a clergy person who usually serves a local church or churches and who has been ordained to a ministry of Word, Sacrament and Order, filling the preaching and pastoral offices. In other Christian traditions (e.g. Presbyterianism, Baptists), an elder may be a lay person charged with serving as an administrator in a local church, or be ordained to such an office, also serving in the preaching (in this case referring to teaching done during church gatherings) and/or pastoral roles. Though there is technically a distinction between the idea of clergy elders and lay elders, often the two concepts are conflated in everyday conversation (for example, a lay-elder in the Baptist tradition may still be referred to as "clergy," especially in America). Particularly in reference to age and experience, elders exist throughout world cultures, and the Christian sense of elder is partially related to this. In the gospel, the quality and or the qualification for eldership are those outlined in (Titus 1:6-9) thus "If anyone is above reproach, the husband of one wife, and his children are believers and not open to the charge of debauchery or insubordination. For an overseer, as God's steward, must be above reproach. He must not be arrogant or quick-tempered or a drunkard or violent or greedy for gain, but hospitable, a lover of good, self-controlled, upright, holy, and disciplined. He must hold firm to the trustworthy word as taught, so that he may be able to give instruction in sound doctrine and also to rebuke those who contradict it".

3 In short an Elder is a Church overseer. (1 Timothy 3:1-16) "The saying is trustworthy: If anyone aspires to the office of overseer, he desires a noble task. Therefore an overseer must be above reproach, the husband of one wife, sober-minded, self-controlled, respectable, hospitable, able to teach, not a drunkard, not violent

Elijah

but gentle, not quarrelsome, not a lover of money. He must manage his own household well, with all dignity keeping his children submissive, for if someone does not know how to manage his own household, how will he care for God's church?"

Elijah: (Hebrew: Eliyahu, meaning "My God is Yahweh") or Elias Greek: Elías;) was a prophet and a wonder-worker in the northern kingdom of Israel during the reign of Ahab (9th century BC), according to the biblical Books of Kings. According to the Books of Kings, Elijah defended the worship of Yahweh – the true God over that of the Canaanite god Baal (which was considered as idol worship); he raised the dead, brought fire down from the sky, and was taken up "by a whirlwind." (This means or mechanism of being taken up by a whirlwind is said plainly in (2 Kings 2:1-2) "When the Lord was about to take Elijah up to heaven in a whirlwind, Elijah and Elisha were on their way from Gilgal. Elijah said to Elisha, "Stay here; the Lord has sent me to Bethel."

and (2 King 2:11), first in while the chariot and horses separated "the two of them," that is, Elijah and Elisha.) In the Book of Malachi, Elijah's return is prophesied "before the coming of the great and terrible day of the Lord," making him a harbinger of the Messiah and the eschaton in various faiths that revere the Hebrew Bible. In Christianity the New Testament gospels describes how both Jesus and John the Baptist are compared with Elijah and on some occasions thought by some to be manifestations of Elijah, and Elijah appears with Moses during the Transfiguration of Jesus. Elijah is also a figure in various Christian folk traditions,

> In Christianity and certain Islamic traditions, Elijah is described as a great and righteous man of God and one who powerfully preached against the worship of Ba'al

often identified with earlier pagan thunder or sky gods.

Elas: Greece, officially the Hellenic Republic and known since ancient times as Hellas, is a country in Southeast Europe. According to the 2011 census, Greece's population is around 11 million. Athens is the nation's capital and largest city, with its urban area including Piraeus. Greece is very significant in the historical spread of the gospel to the whole universe.

Ella: She was the daughter of Athamas and Nephele. The name may be a cognate with Hellas (Greek:), the Greek name for Greece, which said to have been originally the name of the region round Dodona. Another source indicates the name is a Norman version of the Germanic short name Alia, which was short for a variety of German names with the element ali-, meaning "other."[3] It is also a common short name for names starting with El-, such as Eleanor, Elizabeth, Elle, Ellen, Ellie, or Eloise. Hebrew Ella has two meanings. 1 A tree indigenous to the middle east, Pistacia Terebinth, from the pistaccio family. As written in (Isaiah 6-13): And though a tenth remains in the land, it will again be laid waste. But as the terebinth and oak leave stumps when they are cut down, so the holy seed will be the stump in the land." 2 Ella means goddess in Modern Hebrew. Ella became used again during the Victorian era in English-speaking countries and has been revived in the last decade, becoming a popular given name for baby girls born in Australia, Canada, Ireland, New Zealand, the United Kingdom, the United States and other English-speaking countries.

Elisha: Meaning "My God is salvation", Greek: Elissaios or Elisaié, Arabic: Al-yasa◻) is a prophet and a wonder-worker mentioned in the Hebrew Bible, His name is commonly transliterated into English as Elisha via Hebrew, Eliseus via Greek and Latin and many other languages. He was a disciple and after Elijah was taken up into the whirlwind, Elisha was accepted as the leader of the sons of the prophets.

2 *Elisha* was a prophet and a wonder-worker of the Northern Kingdom of Israel who was active during the reign of Joram, Jehu, Jehoahaz, and Jehoash (Joash).[3] Elisha was the son of Shaphat, a wealthy land-owner of Abel-meholah; he became the attendant and disciple of Elijah. His name first occurs in the command given to Elijah to anoint him as his successor. After learning in the cave on Mount Horeb, that Elisha, the son of Shaphat, had been selected by Yahweh as his successor in the prophetic office, Elijah set out to find him. On his way from Sinai to Damascus, Elijah found Elisha "one of them that were ploughing with twelve yoke of oxen". Elisha delayed only long enough to kill the yoke of oxen, whose flesh he boiled with the wood of his plough. He went over to him, threw his mantle over Elisha's shoulders, and at once adopted him as a son, investing him with the prophetic office. Elisha accepted this call about four years before the death of Israel's King Ahab. For the next seven or eight years Elisha became Elijah's close attendant until Elijah was taken up into heaven. During all these years we hear nothing of *Elisha* except in connection with the closing scenes of Elijah's life. 3 *Elisha* first appears in (1 Kings 19:19-21.) When Elijah was taken up into heaven in a fiery chariot, Elisha picked up Elijah's mantle, struck it on the waters of the Jordan River

Elizabeth

and said, "Where is the Lord the Yahweh of Elijah?" (2 Kings 2:14). The water then parted and *Elisha* crossed over, thus beginning his service as a prophet of Yahweh. 4 *Elisha*, like Elijah, performed some extraordinary miracles as a prophet of Yahweh. He brought back to life the dead son of a Shunammite woman; he cured Naaman a general from Damascus, of leprosy; he multiplied loaves of barley and ears of grain to feed a crowd of people; he caused a metal ax head to float on water; he caused an attacking Aramean army to go blind and then returned their sight; and, among other miracles, he filled large empty vessels with oil.

5 *Elisha* is also bald, looking at 2 Kings 2:23-25. Elisha had a member of his company of prophets anoint Jehu to be king of Israel, and to strike down Jezebel and members of Ahab's household, which Jehu completed.

Elizabeth: This the Greek transliteration (Elisábet) of the Hebrew name Elisheba, meaning "Oath of my God". Elizabeth or Elisabeth have given rise to the nicknames of Libby, Lisa, Liza, Lilly, Liz, Lily, Beth, Ella, Elisa, Elise, and many others. Eliza, Elspeth, Elsa, Isabel, and Isabella, are among the many etymologically related names. In the gospel Elizabeth was the wife of Zechariah.

Just as the angel foretold, Elizabeth conceived. While she was pregnant, Mary, the expectant mother of Jesus, visited her. The baby in Elizabeth's womb leaped for joy on hearing Mary's voice. Elizabeth gave birth to a son. They named him John, as the angel had commanded, and at that moment Zechariah's power of speech returned. He praised God for his mercy and goodness. Their son became John the Baptist, the prophet who foretold the coming of the Messiah, Jesus Christ. Both Elizabeth and Zechariah were holy people: "Both of them were righteous in the sight of God, observing all the Lord's commands and decrees blamelessly." (Luke 1:6) "And they were both righteous before God, walking in all the commandments and ordinances of the Lord blameless".

Emmanuel: "God is with us"; A Romanized name from the Hebrew name Imanu'el) a symbolic name which appears in chapters 7 and 8 of the Book of Isaiah as part of a prophecy assuring king Ahaz of Judah of God's protection against enemy kings; it is quoted in the Gospel of Matthew as a sign verifying the divine status of Jesus Christ.

Enemies: An individual or a group that is seen as forcefully adverse or threatening. The concept of an enemy has been observed to be "basic for both individuals and communities". The term "enemy" serves the social function of designating a particular entity as a threat, thereby invoking an intense emotional response to that entity. 2 The state of being or having an *enemy* is enmity, foe-hood or foe-ship. While there are several ways we can define the word *'enemy'*, our focus points dwells on the gospel perception of the enemy. The Book of (Exodus 23: 4) states: "If thou meet thine enemy's ox or his ass going astray, thou shalt surely bring it back to him again. If thou see the ass of him that hateth thee lying under his burden, and thou wouldest forbear to help him, thou shalt surely help with him." The Book of Proverbs similarly states: "Rejoice not when thine *enemy* falleth and let not thy heart be glad when he stumbleth", and: "If thine *enemy* be hungry give him bread to eat, and if he be thirsty give him water to drink. For thus shalt thou heap coals of fire upon his head, and the Lord shall reward thee". Virtually all major religions have "similar ideals of love, the same goal of benefiting humanity through spiritual practice, and the same effect of making their followers into better human beings". It is therefore widely expressed in world religions that enemies should be treated with love, kindness, compassion, and forgiveness

3 The Jewish Encyclopedia contends that the opinion that the Old Testament commanded hatred of the enemy derives from a misunderstanding of the Sermon on the Mount, wherein Jesus said: "Ye have heard that it hath been said, Thou shalt love thy neighbour and hate thine enemy. But I say unto you, Love your enemies and pray for them that persecute you".

The Jewish Encyclopedia also cites passages in the Talmud stating: "If a man finds both a friend and an enemy requiring assistance he should assist his enemy first in order to subdue his evil inclination", and: "Who is strong? He who converts an enemy into a friend" That is why Jesus Christ command Christians to love their enemies in (Mathew 5:43-45) "You have heard that it was said, 'YOU SHALL LOVE YOUR NEIGHBOUR and hate your enemy.' "But I say to you, love your enemies and pray for those who persecute you, so that you may be sons of your Father who is in heaven; for He causes His sun to rise on the evil and the good, and sends rain on the righteous and the unrighteous....

Enemy of the Church: The greatest *Enemy of the Church* is the Christians themselves. They are the ones that pick and choose what they want from the Bible and refuse to hear about the rest of what God has to say. They are wilfully ignorant and it is seen as a rebellion against God. They claim that they get a "bad feeling" from certain subjects then say that it is the Holy Spirit telling them to run away. "It doesn't feel right in my spirit." If it makes the unsaved feel bad, that is excellent! How can people come to Christ if they feel good all the time? Also, so what if a Christian has a bad feeling about certain subjects? Since when is

Enemy of the Church, False Teaching as

our faith based on feelings? Our faith is supposed to be based on scripture, but how can we grow in faith if we pick and choose what we want to believe and ignore the rest? Jesus Christ is building His Church (Matthew 16:18), and the devil is seeking to tear it down and destroy it (1 Peter 5:8-9) "Be alert and of sober mind. Your enemy the devil prowls around like a roaring lion looking for someone to devour. Resist him, standing firm in the faith, because you know that the family of believers throughout the world is undergoing the same kind of sufferings." Those who are members of Christ's Church need to be alert and wide awake. As Christian soldiers we need to understand the enemy so that we can win the battles. Christ has already won the war (John 16:33) and we are overcomers in Him.

In (Acts 20:28-31. Why was Paul in tears (verse 31)? Why did Paul need to warn these believers? Was Paul concerned about the flock (the Church)? There are two ways that sheep can be killed. If the Shepherd does not feed the sheep they will die of starvation (verse 28). Bible teaching is needed. If the Shepherd does not protect the sheep from the Wolves (verse 29) "I know that after I leave, savage wolves will come in among you and will not spare the flock". Then they will be slaughtered. A warning ministry is needed. The Church must be alert and wide awake! Ten Enemies of the Church have been identified. There are more than ten, but these ten enemies are certainly some of the most dangerous ones.

Enemy of the Church, False Teaching as:

Peter spoke of the danger of false teaching: "But there were false prophets also among the people, as in (2 Peter 2:1) "But there were also false prophets among the people, just as there will be false teachers among you. They will secretly introduce destructive heresies, even denying the sovereign Lord who bought them—bringing swift destruction on themselves" A false teacher is a person who teaches what is false. A true teacher is one who speaks the truth in the love of Christ as in (Ephesians 4:15) "Instead, speaking the truth in love, we will grow to become in every respect the mature body of him who is the head, that is, Christ".

Unfortunately there are some teachers who are SPEAKING LIES (1 Timothy 4:2) and see verse 1). Most people are very careful about what they eat. Great harm can come to a person who eats or drinks the wrong things. Would you drink a glass of gasoline? Would you eat a box of rat poison? Once a wicked person put poison in some pills were later bought at a store. Some people swallowed these pills, unaware that they had been laced with poison. Some died because of this. The man who did this was a killer! Did you know that there are people today going around and poisoning men's souls? Just as the body needs to be fed with healthy food, so the soul needs to be fed with healthy teaching. The Bible calls healthy teaching sound doctrine (Titus 2:1). A good Pastor and a good teacher will feed believers with healthy teaching (good, wholesome food from the Word of God). A false teacher will feed people with false teaching (poison). 3 Where and how do false teachers do their work? Some speak on the radio or appear on television. Some write articles in magazines, in books, or on the Internet. Some false teachers stand behind pulpits and teach people in churches. Some false teachers go from house to house and from door to door trying to talk to people and spread their lies. Some false teachers are sincere and they really think that they are helping people, but they are sincerely wrong. They are deceived (2 Timothy. 3:13). Doctors once believed that sick people could be helped by putting leeches (blood suckers) on them. This was done to George Washington and it probably shortened his life. These doctors were sincere but they were sincerely wrong.

Here are some examples of false teaching which you can discuss in class: 1) All men will someday be saved and will be allowed to enter heaven. 2) A loving God would never punish people in hell. 3) Jesus Christ is the greatest angel that God ever created. 4) To be saved a person must keep the Ten Commandments. 5) It is possible for a person to fall into sin and lose his salvation and much more. Believers need to be alert. What should we do when we hear something taught (even by our own Pastor and Sunday School teachers and parents)? The answer is found in (Acts 17:11) "Now the Berean Jews were of more noble character than those in Thessalonica, for they received the message with great eagerness and examined the Scriptures every day to see if what Paul said was true" What ever is taught, must be examined in the light of the Gospel to see the truth in it. When you are taught something, you should go to the Bible and see for yourself whether or not it is really what the Bible teaches. A fair question is always: "Where does it say that in the Bible?" If you are taught that a person is saved by believing in Jesus Christ, then you can search the Scriptures to see if this is really true. Is it true or false (Acts 16:30-31; John 3:16)? Go away from the danger: Do not be poisoned by false teaching! Beware of anything that is contrary to what is taught in God's Word, the Bible.

Enemy of the Church, Worldliness as the: Believers are not of the world (John 17:16-19) "They are not of the world, even as I am not of it. Sanctify them by[d] the truth; your word is truth. As you sent me into the world, I have sent them into the world. For them I sanctify myself, that they too may

be truly sanctified" because they belong to the Saviour's kingdom. Unsaved people are of the world because they belong to Satan's system. The devil wants to draw believers away from the Saviour, and to draw them close to the world. In (Romans 12:2). Jesus wants to transform us (change us by working in our hearts), but Satan wants to conform us (squeeze us into the world's mole). For example, think about the kind of language that many of your classmates may use at school or on the playground. They may use bad language, swear, make fun of others, and tell dirty jokes. As a believer and as a member of the Church, you do not want to conform your language to theirs by allowing the same kind of filth to come out of your mouth. Instead you want the Saviour to transform your language so that you can enjoy the healthy use of your mind. Then unbelievers will be able to see that the language a Christian uses is good and wholesome and different. "Let no corrupt (filthy) communication proceed out of your mouth" (Ephesians. 4:29). Don't let garbage come out of your mouth. Rather, speak the kind of language that will encourage and build up others (end of verse 29). 2 The worldly person is the person who ignores God and who leaves God out of his thinking. He does not consider God in his thoughts, and in his plans and in his actions. He lives as if there were no God in heaven. The average person does not give God very much thought during the day. The Christian believer must be different! God is the very centre of His life, and he must include God in all of his thinking and plans and actions. When we live this way we are being a good witness, because we are causing others to realize that there is a God in heaven.

Let us see what God think about worldliness in (1 John 2:15-17) and (James 4:4) The more the Church becomes like the world, the more it will lose its witness and its power. Unsaved people will say, "Why do I need to become a Christian? The Christians that I know are no different than my other friends. They act like non-Christians, they talk like non-Christians, they think like non-Christians and I can't tell much of a difference. If Christians are no different than non-Christians, then why should I become a Christian?" Or another unsaved person might think in this way: "I see nothing wrong with being a Christian because all of my Christian friends live the same way I do. I can be a Christian and still live and speak and think the same way I always do." Does this person really understand what it means to be a Christian? The danger and duty here is for you not to be conformed to this world but be transformed by Christ into the kind of person He wants you to be. Don't let the world conform you; let Christ transform you.

Enemy of the Church, Legalism as the: Legalism is a special

kind of false teaching. In (Acts 15:1) "Certain people came down from Judea to Antioch and were teaching the believers: "Unless you are circumcised, according to the custom taught by Moses, you cannot be saved." we see that legalism crept into the early church: "And certain men which came down from Judaea taught the brethren. When you think of the word "legalism" you should think of the word "law." These people were saying that a person cannot be saved without keeping the law (being circumcised). Is this really true? To be saved, does a person need to be circumcised? According to (Acts 16:30-31), what is the one and only thing that a person must do to be saved? "He then brought them out and asked, "Sirs, what must I do to be saved?" They replied, "Believe in the Lord Jesus, and you will be saved—you and your household." As we can see, the simple answer here is "Believe in the Lord Jesus". Legalism is dangerous because it gets a person to look away from what Jesus Christ has done on the cross. The person starts looking at what he can do. Legalism says that man must do something to get God's blessing and God's salvation. The Bible says that Christ has already done it all (John 19:30). It is not what I do that counts; it is what Christ has done! Legalism says, "What Christ did on the cross is not enough. There are certain things which I must do also." The believer says, "Jesus died for me! What He did is enough. It is not my anything that saves me; it is God's everything!" There are people today who say, "You cannot be saved unless you are baptized in water." Is this legalism? Why? There are people who say, "You cannot be saved unless you live a good life and try to keep the Ten Commandments." Is this trusting what Christ has done, or is this man trusting what he can do? No one has ever been saved by keeping the law, but multitudes have been saved by trusting Jesus Christ and Him alone. Flee away from the danger of Legalism: Do not let anyone get you to take your eyes off Jesus Christ and what He did for you on the cross.

Enemy of the Church, Formalism as the: This connotes something that has outward form but no inward content. Formalism is like having a peanut shell without any peanut inside it. It looks like a peanut. It feels like a peanut, but something very important is missing. What good is a peanut shell without a nut inside? The peanut shell which has no nut may fool people as it has no peanut ingredients nor the chemical contents to do the work or the purpose of peanut in the body and therefore will never satisfy people. The same thing would be true of a banana peel without the banana. It may look like a banana but it is lacking the most important thing of all: the real and good part of the banana that you can eat! There are people who are like the peanut shell and like the banana peel: "Having a form of godliness but denying its power. Have nothing to do with such people". (2 Timothy 3:5). These people have an outward form that looks good and even fools many people, but they are missing the most important thing: the inner life and power that only God can provide. Think about what Paul said in (Romans 2:28-29). A person may be a Jew outwardly, but if he is not a Jew inwardly, then he is not really a true Jew. The same thing is true for a Christian. It is possible to be a Christian outwardly-to go to church, to carry a Bible, to bow the head in prayer, to open the hymnbook and sing, and to go through all the outward motions. This person could be just like the peanut shell-it looks good but there is no nut on the inside. Do you think that God wants more than just a "Christian shell"? If people could "open you up" and look on the inside, what would they see? Would they find a true Christian on the inside also? Would they find a heart that loves the Saviour? Would they find that when you sing you sing from the heart, and when you pray you pray from the heart with meaning and reality? It is not the shell that is important but the inside! God is concerned about the heart. "Yet you desired faithfulness even in the womb; you taught me wisdom in that secret place. (Psalm 51:6) "But the Lord said to Samuel, "Do not consider his appearance or his height, for I have rejected him. The Lord does not look at the things people look at. People look at the outward appearance, but the Lord looks at the heart." (1 Samuel 16:7). Did these people honour God outwardly? Did they give God "lip service"? In (Mark 7:6) He replied, "Isaiah was right when he prophesied about you hypocrites; as it is written: "These people honor me with their lips, but their hearts are far from me. As a Christian, avoid the danger: Beware of an outward form of religion without the inner power and reality that only God can give. Don't just go through the outward motions of being a Christian. Make sure your heart is right with the Lord. Make sure you are a real Christian, not just an outward Christian. Glory to Jesus!

Enemy of the Church, Emotionalism as the: This is a problem when people are led by their feelings and emotions (being glad, sad, mad, gossips etc.) instead of being led by God's Word. Most people are led and controlled by their feelings and emotions. When asked, "Why did you do that?" the common answer is, "Because I felt like it!" Feelings do not do very well in the driver's seat. Feelings come and feelings go. Feelings change and fluctuate. Bad feelings should point to the true problem, which is what causes the feelings. Usually the real problem has to do with the way a person lives. Bad feelings are usually the result of bad living or bad thinking. When the warning light flashes on your car's dashboard, it is telling you that there is a problem under the hood. Our feelings are like this flashing light. Martin Luther once said: "For feelings come and feelings go, and feelings are deceiving. My warrant is the Word of God, naught else is worth believing." God's unchanging Word must lead us and guide us. How I feel is not important. The important thing is this: What has God said? God always have something to say. In every situation. There are many churches today that are swept up in emotionalism. Really, this is part of walking in the flesh. If you were to walk into one of these churches you would see some very strange things: arms waving in the air, people making strange sounds which do not make any sense, different people speaking at the same time, people clapping because the teacher or the pastor speaks big grammar or setting canal analogy, Many don't clap as led by Holy Spirits and all kinds of movement and excitement. But in the middle of all this movement and excitement the Bible stays closed. The people do not stay quiet and still long enough for the Lord to speak to their hearts through His Word which can come as a little whisper as in (1 Kings 19:11-12)."The Lord said, "Go out and stand on the mountain in the presence of the Lord, for the Lord is about to pass by." Then a great and powerful wind tore the mountains apart and shattered the rocks before the Lord, but the Lord was not in the wind. After the wind there was an earthquake, but the Lord was not in the earthquake. After the earthquake came a fire, but the Lord was not in the fire. And after the fire came a gentle whisper" Again, avoid the danger: do not let your feelings control you but give God's Word control in all your endeavours? Do not go by your feelings but be guided by what God has told you to do in His Word.

Enemy of the Church, Diversion as the:
In (Mark 16:15) "He said to them, "Go into all the world and preach the gospel to all creation. 16 Whoever believes and is baptized will be saved, but whoever does not believe will be condemned". But take notice here, because there is that part of the gospel that emphasises love and affection, Charity and other hospitalities. But this has to operate within the framework of the gospel preached. But if you concentrate on Charity alone leaving the gospel, it is diversion. When you divert or deviate, you are a loss soul and only by His Grace and Salvation can you be save. Many churches have turned aside from doing this and they have done other things instead. Instead of preaching the good news about Christ and His salvation, they have concentrated on other things such as feeding the hungry, giving clothes to the poor, providing for those who are sick, helping those who are in need, etc. These are good things to do, but this is not the main thing that Christ told the Church to do. Food, clothes and good health are fine, but will these things get a person to heaven? Suppose your Mom gives you £10.00 and tells you to buy some groceries for her at the

store. On the way to the store you see an ice cream store, so you turn in there an buy ice cream for yourself and for your friends. This is Diversion! You were diverted (turned aside) from doing what you were told to do and you failed to accomplish your mission.

Another good example, - When the Salvation Army first started their ministry, they preached the gospel and also tried to help those who were poor and needy. As the years went by the Salvation Army helped the poor and needy more and more and preached the gospel less and less. Today the Salvation Army does very little preaching of the gospel. The main thing they are known for is not the preaching of the gospel, but rather the collection of money for the benefit of those in need (to provide clothing, food, Christmas gifts, etc.). They allowed themselves to become diverted from the main thing that Christ told them to do. Even deviating completely from William Booth concepts of Salvation Army. The man (William Booth had strong convictions about preaching the gospel: William Booth, the first general of the Salvation Army, say, when explaining his "Darkest England" scheme, that its real objective was, not just the amelioration of social conditions, but first and foremost the bringing of men to repentance that their souls might be saved. I can recall the flash in his eye, and the noble bearing of his commanding figure as he exclaimed, "Take a man from the filth and squalor of the slums, exchange his rags for decent clothing, move him from the stifling stench of the city tenement to a neat little cottage in the pure air of the country, put him on his feet economically where he can make a decent living for himself and his family, and then let him die in his sins, unsaved, and be lost forever at last—really it is not worthwhile, and I, for one, would not attempt it." (Cited by Harry Ironside, Except Ye Repent, pages 181-182.) Again, The YMCA started out as a Christian organization (The Young Men's Christian Association). But as time went on the people in this organization gave more importance to other things and less importance to preaching the gospel. Today, if you want to swim or play basketball or get some good exercise and healthy activity, the YMCA is a great place to go. However, if you want to learn how to be saved and how to go to heaven, do not go to the YMCA. They have been diverted.

Again, avoid the danger: Do not fail to do the main thing that Christ has commanded His Church to do. The Church must not forget why she is in the world. We must clearly point to Christ and His wonderful salvation. We must not get involved with things that Christ never told us to get involved with. Get involved in sharing the good news with others and exhort His name, Singing songs of praise to His Glory in your hear to Him at all times and get the Church onward matching on.

Enemy of the Church, Coldness as the:
In Revelation 2 we learn about a church which was about to have its light snuffed out (Revelation 2:5). What was the problem? What did these believers do wrong? Jesus said, in (Revelation 2:4) "Yet I hold this against you: You have forsaken the love you had at first". Something terrible happened to these people. Something happened that cooled their love for the Saviour. They no longer loved Him as they once did. Their love for the Saviour had grown cold. Their relationship with Christ had slowly and gradually lost its warmth and beauty and freshness. When a person is saved he enters into a love relationship with Christ Jesus: in (1 John 4:19). "We love because he first loved us". Once we are saved we need to keep our love for the Saviour burning bright and hot. It is possible for other loves to come in and crowd out one's first love. Some people are "lovers of selves as (2 Timothy. 3:4). "treacherous, rash, conceited, lovers of pleasure rather than lovers of God". They would rather lie at the beach than sit in church. They would rather play than pray. They would rather read comics than read Corinthians. Think of a husband and wife. If they never talked to each other and never did anything for each other and never spent time with each other, would they have a very good love relationship? Christ must be honoured to have supremacy in our lives as in (Colossians. 1:18). "And he is the head of the body, the church; he is the beginning and the firstborn from among the dead, so that in everything he might have the supremacy" Avoid the danger: Do not allow your love for the Saviour to grow cold. You must remember a time in your Christian life when you were walking closer to the Lord than you are now. In some church buildings you will find an organ, a piano, a choir, people in the pews, a pastor, but the Lord is missing. The Lord does not commend but He condemns a church where He is unloved and where the hearts of the people have grown cold towards Him. Remember, obedience is better than Sacrifice.

Enemy of the Church, Toleration as the:
In (Revelation 2:2) "I know your deeds, your hard work and your perseverance. I know that you cannot tolerate wicked people, that you have tested those who claim to be apostles but are not, and have found them false". There are some things that we must not tolerate. Suppose a rattlesnake were to be found in a yard where small children often play. Should this snake be tolerated and allowed to remain in this yard? Suppose you were to learn that there was cancer in your body. Would you tolerate this cancer and let it stay there and grow there? They were false apostles. Did these Christians tolerate these liars and allow them to continue to fool people and mislead people? Today there are churches that tolerate many things. There

are churches that tolerate sin. If someone has a serious problem with sin, should not believers seek to help the person deal with the problem God's way? Instead they often ignore the problem and pretend that everything is all right. This is like ignoring the rattlesnake and pretending that there is no danger. In (1 Corinthians 5) where Paul told the Corinthians that they needed to deal with a man who had fallen into deep sin. Some churches allow unsaved people to be church members. Some allow unsaved people to preach from the pulpit. This is a very dangerous thing to do. This would be like a shepherd telling the wolf to watch the sheep for him while goes for a long walk. This is a fast way to destroy the flock! Avoid the danger of toleration and keep the Church system free from filthiness: The church must never tolerate that which is wrong. The church that fails to deal with sin in the right way will be the church that is destroyed by sin. The cancer that is not removed from the body is the cancer that destroys the body.

Enemy of the Church, Division as the:

This was the case in the Corinthian Church. Was the Corinthian church a 'Divided church? (1 Corinthians.1:10-12) "I appeal to you, brothers and sisters,[a] in the name of our Lord Jesus Christ, that all of you agree with one another in what you say and that there be no divisions among you, but that you be perfectly united in mind and thought. My brothers and sisters, some from Chloe's household have informed me that there are quarrels among you. What I mean is this: One of you says, "I follow Paul"; another, "I follow Apollos"; another, "I follow Cephas[b]"; still another, "I follow Christ." These Christians were getting together and forming different groups within the church and each group thought they were better than the other group! It is a terrible thing to see family warfare within the church. It is a terrible thing to see gossip, jealousy, pride, failure to love the brethren, etc. Such things cause division and harm. Christians sometimes are so busy fighting each other that they have little time or energy left to battle the real enemies: the world, the flesh and the devil! How are Christians supposed to live with each other? Know your course in (Ephesians 4:2-3; 31-32)? It is a great danger If a person is a fellow Christian then he is supposed to be on the same team that you are on! Be alert! Love the brethren (1 John 3:14). Don't be one who sows discord and division among brethren. God hates this kind of thing (Proverbs 6:16-19) thus' " There are six things the Lord hates, seven that are detestable to, haughty eyes, a lying tongue, hands that shed innocent blood, a heart that devises wicked schemes, feet that are quick to rush into evil, a false witness who pours out lies, and a person who stirs up conflict in the community.

Enemy of the Church, Closed Bible as the:
One of the great enemies that the Church faces today is the closed Bible. There are many churches where the Bible is used very little. The next time you see people walking to church see if they are carrying their Bibles. There are many people today who do not even bring a Bible to church. There are many Pastors who never encourage their people to open their Bibles and use them (by turning to different passages). In many churches the Bible is a closed Book. According to (2 Timothy 4:2-5), "Preach the word; be prepared in season and out of season; correct, rebuke and encourage—with great patience and careful instruction. For the time will come when people will not put up with sound doctrine. Instead, to suit their own desires, they will gather around them a great number of teachers to say what their itching ears want to hear. They will turn their ears away from the truth and turn aside to myths. But you, keep your head in all situations, endure hardship, do the work of an evangelist, and discharge all the duties of your ministry" The danger is, is the Bible a closed Book in your church? Is the Bible a closed Book in your home? Is your Bible a closed Book or is it opened frequently? When do you use your Bible? When do you open your Bible? Do you open it only in church or at other times also? May God help us to have an 'Open Bible' and an Open Heart and open the eyes of our faith in Jesus Name?

Enemy of God:
Satan is the enemy of God (Job 2:1-7) "Again there was a day when the sons of God came to present themselves before the LORD, and Satan also came among them to present himself before the LORD. The LORD said to Satan, "Where have you come from?" Then Satan answered the LORD and said, "From roaming about on the earth and walking around on it." The LORD said to Satan, "Have you considered My servant Job? For there is no one like him on the earth, a blameless and upright man fearing God and turning away from evil. And he still holds fast his integrity, although you incited Me against him to ruin him without cause." Again in (Mathew 12:17-21) "This was to fulfill what was spoken through the prophet Isaiah: "Here is my servant whom I have chosen, the one I love, in whom I delight; I will put my Spirit on him, and he will proclaim justice to the nations. He will not quarrel or cry out; no one will hear his voice in the streets. A bruised reed he will not break, and a smoldering wick he will not snuff out, till he has brought justice through to victory. In his name the nations will put their hope".

Since men became enemies to God, they have been very ready to be enemies one to another. And those that embrace gospel must expect to meet with enemies in a world whose smiles seldom agree with Christ's. Recompense to no man evil for evil. That is a brutish recompense, befitting only animals, which are not conscious of any being above them, or of any existence hereafter. And not only do, but study and take care to do, that which is amiable and creditable, and recommends religion to all with whom you converse. Study the things that make for peace; if it be possible, without offending God and wounding conscience. Avenge not yourselves. This is a hard lesson to corrupt nature; therefore a remedy against it is added. Give place unto wrath. When a man's passion is up, and the stream is strong, let it pass off; lest it be made to rage the more against us. The line of our duty is clearly marked out, and if our enemies are not melted by persevering kindness, we are not to seek vengeance; they will be consumed by the fiery wrath of that God to whom vengeance belongeth. The last verse suggests what is not easily understood by the world; that in all strife and contention, those that revenge are conquered, and those that forgive are conquerors. Be not overcome of evil. Learn to defeat ill designs against you, either to change them, or to preserve your own peace. He that has this rule over his spirit, is better than the mighty. God's children may be asked whether it is not more sweet unto them than all earthly good, that God so enables them by his Spirit, thus to feel and act.

Enosh: Son of Seth and Grandson of Adam,

Ephah: Was one of Midian's five sons as listed in the Hebrew Bible. 2 The son of Abraham, Midian's five sons were *Ephah*, Epher, Enoch, Abida, and Eldaah. These five were the progenitors of the Midianites. 2 ("ephah" - Hebrew word means a particular measure for grain, and "measure" in general. The measurement for an *ephah* is about 36.4 litres, or ten omers, A dry measure of about one bushel capacity. It corresponds to the bath in liquid measure and was the standard for measuring grain and similar articles since it is classed with balances and weights (Leviticus 19:36 Amos 8:5) in the injunctions regarding just dealing in trade. In (Zechariah 5:6 - 5:10) it is used for the utensil itself. Ephphata: Greek: [ef-a'-tha], Hebrew: Pathach

Ephphata: This is an Aramaic word used by Christ (Mark 7:34), the 'ethpa`al imperative of Aramaic pethach translated, "Be (thou) opened"; compare (Isaiah 35:5). The Aramaic was the sole popular language of Palestine (Shurer, History of the Jewish People in the Time of Jesus Christ,) and its use shows that we have here the graphic report of an eyewitness, upon whom the dialectic form employed made a deep impression. This and the corresponding act of the touch with the moistened finger is the foundation of a corresponding ceremony in the Roman Catholic formula for baptism.

2 It is the Greek form of a Syro-Chaldaic or Aramaic word, meaning "Be opened," uttered by Christ when healing the man who was deaf and dumb (Mark 7:34). It is one of the characteristics of Mark that he uses the very Aramaic words which fell from our Lord's lips as in (Mark 3:17; 5:41; 7:11; 14:36; 15:34.)

Ephesus: An ancient Greek city on the coast of Ionia, three kilometers southwest of present-day Selçuk in İzmir Province, Turkey. It was built in the 10th century BC on the site of the former Arzawan capital Attic and Ionian Greek colonists. During the Classical Greek era it was one of the twelve cities of the Ionian League. The city flourished after it came under the control of the Roman Republic in 129 BC. According to estimates Ephesus had a population of 33,600 to 56,000 people in the Roman period, making it the third largest city of Roman Asia Minor after Sardis and Alexandria Troas. The city was famed for the Temple of Artemis (completed around 550 BC), one of the Seven Wonders of the Ancient World. In 268 AD, the Temple was destroyed or damaged in a raid by the Goths. It may have been rebuilt or repaired but this is uncertain, as its later history is not clear. Emperor Constantine I rebuilt much of the city and erected new public baths. Following the Edict of Thessalonica from emperor Theodosius I, what remained of the temple was destroyed in 401 AD by a mob led by St. John Chrysostom. The town was partially destroyed by an earthquake in 614 AD. The city's importance as a commercial centre declined as the harbour was slowly silted up by the Cayster River.

2 Ephesus was one of the seven churches of Asia that are cited in the Book of Revelation. The Gospel of John may have been written here. The city was the site of several 5th century Christian Councils (see Council of Ephesus). It is also the site of a large gladiators' graveyard. 3 The ruins of *Ephesus* are a favourite international and local tourist attraction and pilgrimage, partly owing to their easy access from Adnan Menderes Airport.

4 *Ephesus* - In the ancient world, Ephesus was a centre of travel and commerce. Situated on the Aegean Sea at the mouth of the Cayster River, the city was one of the greatest seaports of the ancient world. Three major roads led from the seaport: one road went east towards Babylon via Laodicea, another to the north via Smyrna and a third south to the Meander Valley.

Ephesians: The tenth book of the New Testament. Its authorship has traditionally been credited to Paul the Apostle but, starting in 1792, this has been challenged as Deutero-Pauline, that is, written in Paul's name by a later author strongly influenced by Paul's thought.

Ephraim

Ephraim: The second son of Joseph and Asenath. Asenath was an Egyptian woman whom Pharaoh gave to Joseph as wife, and the daughter of Potipherah, a priest of On. (Genesis 41:50-52) Ephraim was born in Egypt before the arrival of the children of Israel from Canaan. (Genesis 48:5) Ephraim had sons: Shuthelah, Beker, and Tahan. However, (1 Chronicles 7) claims that he also had two more sons, Ezer and Elead, who were killed by local men who came to rob him of his cattle. He then had another son, Beriah, who carried on his name. (1Chronicles 7:20-23) From him was descended Joshua, son of Nun, who in time became the leader of the Israelite tribes in the conquest of Canaan. (1 Chronicles 7:20-27) According to the biblical narrative, Jeroboam, who became the first king of the Northern Kingdom of Israel, was also from the house of Ephraim. (1 Kings 11:26)

Epiphany: (noun) The manifestation of Christ to the Gentiles as represented by the Magi (Matthew 2:1–12). a moment of sudden and great manifestation on realisation 2 A Christian feast celebrating the manifestation of the divine nature of Jesus to the Gentiles as represented by the Magi. January 6, on which this feast is traditionally observed. 3 A revelatory manifestation of a divine being. 4 A sudden manifestation of the essence or meaning of something. A comprehension or perception of reality by means of a sudden intuitive realization: "I experienced an epiphany, a spiritual flash that would change the way I viewed myself" - (Frank Maier). 5 A sudden realization about the nature or meaning of something. An epiphany can often come about due to some experience that may trigger the sudden realization. An epiphany may happen when one receive Christ as the only Lord and Saviour. New experience after one born again. A sudden encounter with Christ either in the dream or vision. Old things have past away. All things become new.

Episcopal: Bishop, an overseer in the Christian church, Episcopate, the see of a bishop – a diocese,

Episcopal Church: (disambiguation), any church with "Episcopal" in its name.

Episcopal Conference: An official assembly of bishops in a territory of the Roman Catholic Church.

Episcopal polity: The church united under the oversight of bishops

Episcopal Seat: The official seat of a bishop, often applied to the area over which he exercises authority.

Episcopate, Historical: Dioceses established according to apostolic succession.

Epistle: (Noun) forma I humorous a letter. "activists firing off angry epistles" synonyms: letter, missive, communication, written message, written communication, dispatch, report, bulletin, note, line; More a poem or other literary work in the form of a letter or series of letters. a book of the New Testament in the form of a letter from an Apostle. noun: Epistle; plural noun: Epistles "St Paul's Epistle to the Romans"

Esau: (Standard Hebrew - *Esav*; Greek - 'Ησαυ or "Rough"), *Esau* was the older son of Isaac mentioned in the Book of Genesis, and by the prophets, Obadiah and Malachi. (Genesis 25:25) , "Now the first came forth, red all over like a hairy garment; and they named him *Esau*." In Hebrew, the name *Esau* means "hairy" (Hebrew - se'ir) a wordplay on Seir, the region he settled in Edom after being 40 years of age where he became the progenitor of the Edomites. The name Edom is also attributed to *Esau*, meaning "red" (Hebrew: `admoni)] the same colour describing Esau's skintone (Genesis 25:25). Genesis parallels his redness to the "red lentil pottage" that he sold his birthright for (Genesis 25:30) The New Testament of the Christian Bible alludes to him in St Paul's Letter to the Romans and in the Letter to the Hebrews as the progenitor of the Edomites and the elder twin brother of Jacob, the patriarch of the Israelites. Esau and Jacob were the sons of Isaac and Rebekah, and the grandsons of Abraham and Sarah. Of the twins, Esau was the first to be born with Jacob following, holding his heel (the Hebrew name Yaacov meaning "Heel-holder"). Isaac was sixty years old and Rebekah is believed to have been younger when the boys were born.

The grandfather Abraham was still alive, being 160 years old at that time. The name of Edom, "red", was also given to him from his conduct in connection with the red lentil "pottage" for which he sold his birth right. The circumstances connected with his birth foreshadowed the enmity which afterwards subsisted between the twin brothers and the nations they founded (Genesis 25:22 Genesis 25:23 Genesis 25:26). In course of time Jacob, following his natural bent, became a shepherd; while Esau, a "son of the desert," devoted himself to the perilous and toilsome life of a huntsman. On a certain occasion, on returning from the chase, urged by the cravings of hunger, Esau sold his birth right to his brother, Jacob, who thereby obtained the covenant blessing (Genesis 27:28 Genesis 27:29 Genesis 27:36 ; Hebrews 12:16 Hebrews 12:17). He afterwards tried to regain what he had so recklessly parted with, but was defeated in his attempts through the stealth of his brother (Genesis 27:4) (Genesis 27:34) thus' "When Esau heard his father's words, he burst out with a loud and bitter cry and said to his father, "Bless me—me too, my father!"

Esau Birth-right

2 Also, *Esau*, a "man of the field" became a hunter who had "rough" qualities that distinguished him from his twin brother. Jacob was a shy or simple man, depending on the translation of the Hebrew word "Tam" (which also means "relatively perfect man"). Throughout Genesis, *Esau* is frequently shown as being supplanted by his younger twin Jacob (Israel).

> **Note:**
>
> Red & Hairy: That is a sign that he will be a person who sheds blood. he was completely like a coat of hair: full of hair like a woollen cloak, which is full of hair, 'flochede' in Old French and they named him Esau: They all called him this because he was complete (lit., made, and fully developed with hair, like one many years old.
> Born: Canaan, Died: Cave of the Patriarchs, Hebron, Jordan, Parents: Isaac, Rebecca, Children: Eliphaz, Siblings: Jacob

Esau Birth-right: The right to be recognised as first born with authority over the family. One day, Esau returned to his twin brother Jacob, famished from the fields. He begs Jacob to give him some "red pottage" (a play on his nickname, Hebrew -`Edom, meaning "red".) Jacob offers Esau a bowl of stew in exchange for Esau's birth right (the right to be recognized as firstborn with authority over the family), and Esau agrees. Thus Jacob bought/exchanged Esau's birth right. This is believed to be the origin of the English phrase "for a mess of pottage". In (Genesis 27:1– 40), Jacob uses deception, motivated by his mother Rebekah, (Because Rebekah loved Jacob more than Esau) to lay claim to his blind father Isaac's blessing that was inherently due to the firstborn, *Esau*. In (Genesis 27:5–7), Rebekah is listening while Isaac speaks to his son Esau. So when *Esau* goes to the field to hunt for venison to bring home, Rebekah says to her son Jacob, "Behold, I heard thy father speak to thy brother *Esau*, saying: 'Bring me venison and prepare a savoury food, that I may eat, and bless thee before the Lord before my death.'" Rebekah then instructs Jacob in an elaborate deception through which Jacob pretends to be Esau, in order to steal from *Esau* his blessing from Isaac and his inheritance — which in theory *Esau* had already agreed to give to Jacob. As a result, Jacob becomes the spiritual leader of the family after Isaac's death and the heir of the promises of Abraham (Genesis 27:37) "But Isaac replied to *Esau*, "Behold, I have made him your master, and all his relatives I have given to him as servants; and with grain and

Esau Birth-right

new wine I have sustained him. Now as for you then, what can I do, my son?" *Esau* is furious and vows to kill Jacob (Genesis 27:41). Once again Rebekah intervenes to save her younger son from being murdered by his elder twin brother, *Esau*.

Therefore, at Rebekah's urging, Jacob flees to a distant land to work for his uncle Laban (Genesis 28:5). Jacob does not immediately receive his father's inheritance after the impersonation aimed at taking it from *Esau*. Having fled for his life, Jacob has left the wealth of Isaac's flocks, land and tents in *Esau*'s hands. Jacob is forced to sleep out on the open ground and then work for wages as a servant in Laban's household. Jacob, who had deceived and cheated his brother, is in turn deceived and cheated by his uncle. Jacob asks to marry Laban's daughter Rachel, whom he has met at the well, and Laban agrees, if Jacob will give him seven years of service. Jacob does so, but after the wedding finds that beneath the veil is not Rachel but Leah, Laban's elder daughter. He agrees to work another seven years and Jacob and Rachel are finally wed. However, despite Laban, Jacob eventually becomes so rich as to incite the envy of Laban and Laban's sons.

The gospel implication of Esau's action is periled as he falls away from the Grace of Abrahamic covenant blessings of inheritance. Making the dissension of God promise to skip him. i.e rather than Gods promise flowing from Abraham, Isaac to Esau, he allow the promise to skip him to Jacob. And now become, Abraham, Isaac and Jacob. Fancy this! Today many Children including Christians or Children of God in Christendom have allowed the promise of inheritance or joint inheritance in Christ Jesus as in (Romans 8:17) "And since we are his children, we are his heirs. In fact, together with Christ we are heirs of God's glory. But if we are to share his glory, we must also share his suffering" to skip them having surrendered their birth right to deities or heathen God's. Especially in times of affliction and troubles. They fail to consider their position as joint heritage with Christ Jesus. They forgot that God so exalted and gave Him name above every other name that in the name of Jesus, every knee shall bow. One of the sacred trust God has committed upon His Children. One word to children. God has committed to you a great and sacred trust. Have you despised your birth-right? Have you made light of these blessings and vilely cast them off? If so, the day will come when you will see your folly in bitter anguish. Like Esau you may wail out with a great and bitter cry--"Oh! is there no forgiveness for me? is there none? As in (Hebrew 12:15-17) "Looking diligently, lest any man fail of the grace of God; lest any root of bitterness springing up trouble you, and thereby many be defiled: Lest there be any fornicator, or profane person, as Esau, who for one morsel of meat sold his birth right. For ye know how that afterward, when he would have inherited the blessing, he was rejected, for he found no place of repentance, though he sought it carefully with tears."

Now it can not be doubted that *Esau* understood all the important points involved in this legacy of promised blessings. He knew what his birth-right included; he must have known the promises made and renewed so solemnly to his grandfather Abraham and his father Isaac. He also doubtless understood the tenor on which these promises were to descend to him in connection with his birth right. And yet the history shows us how he took a course which forfeited them all. Returning at one time from the hunting field, faint with fatigue and hunger, he said to Jacob--"Feed me I pray thee, with that red pottage." Jacob said, "Sell me this day thy birth right." Esau said, "Behold I am at the point to die, and what profit shall this birth right be to me? A complete lack of understanding where the bible says in (Hosea 4:6) "my people are destroyed from lack of knowledge. "Because you have rejected knowledge, I also reject you as my priests; because you have ignored the law of your God, I also will ignore your children" And Jacob said, swear unto me this day; and he swear unto him: and he sold his birth right unto Jacob." Such is the simple record given us of the circumstances of this transaction. They serve to show how little Esau valued the blessings which came down to him from his godly ancestors. The appropriate reflection to be made on reading the narrative is, not this-See how strong the temptation was, and how much to be pitied was the unfortunate Esau who stood at the point of death and bartered away an intangible and valueless ideality for what which was the very stay of his life; but rather this--"Thus Esau despised his birth right." There is Esau "that profane person, who for one morsel of meat sold his birth right."

God set his seal to this act of Esau's. He took him at his word. Esau said--I sell it to Jacob. God confirmed the deed and it was henceforth Esau's no more. It passed from his hands forever. The Lord suffered another train of circumstances to transpire in which the solemn affirmation of the father transferred the birthright and the blessing to Jacob. There is no need at this time that I should fully detail all the circumstances--much less, that we should attempt to justify in all points the scheme of deception by which the mother effected this end. It may however be not amiss to remark that even before the birth of these two sons, the Lord had clearly predicted that the law of primogeniture in their case should be reversed so that the elder should serve the younger. She might therefore have felt that as the time drew near when a father's blessing was to single out the favoured son, it was important that the purpose of God in respect to the younger of the two should stand.

Essenes, The: (Modern Hebrew - Isiyim; Greek -, Essenoi, Essaíoi, Ossaíoi) Were a sect of Second Temple Judaism that flourished from the 2nd century BCE to the 1st century CE which some scholars claim seceded from the Zadokite priests. Being much fewer in number than the Pharisees and the Sadducees (the other two major sects at the time), the Essenes lived in various cities but congregated in communal life dedicated to asceticism (some groups practiced celibacy), voluntary poverty, and daily immersion. Many separate but related religious groups of that era shared similar mystic, eschatological, messianic, and ascetic beliefs. These groups are collectively referred to by various scholars as the "Essenes." Josephus records that Essenes existed in large numbers and thousands lived throughout Roman Judaea. 2 The Essenes have gained fame in modern times as a result of the discovery of an extensive group of religious documents known as the Dead Sea Scrolls, which are commonly believed to be Essenes' library—although there is no proof that the Essenes wrote them. These documents include preserved multiple copies of parts of the Hebrew Bible untouched from possibly as early as 300 BCE until their discovery in 1946. Some scholars, however, dispute the notion that the Essenes wrote the Dead Sea Scrolls.

2 The Essenes were a Jewish mystical sect somewhat resembling the Pharisees. They lived lives of ritual purity and separation. They originated about 100 B.C., and disappeared from history after the destruction of Jerusalem in A.D. 70. 3 The Essenes are not directly mentioned in Scripture, although some believe they may be referred to in (Matthew 19:11, 12) and in (Colossians 2:8, 18), and (Colossian 23). Interest in the Essenes was renewed with the discovery of the Dead Sea Scrolls, which were likely recorded and stored by the Essenes. It has been popular among some scholars to claim that John the Baptist was an Essene. There are some similarities between John and the Essenes: 1. John was in the desert (Luke 1:80). The Essenes were in the desert. 2. Both John and the Essenes used (Isaiah 40:3) to describe themselves as the voice in the wilderness. 3. The baptism (or washing) practiced by John and the Essenes required a change of heart. At the same time, there are significant differences between John the Baptist and the Essenes: 1. *The Essenes* hid themselves away from society in the wilderness. John was a very public figure. 2. John had a much stricter diet *(Luke 7:33)* than did the Essenes. 3. John preached Jesus as the Messiah. The Essenes did not recognize Jesus as Messiah, but they thought that the Teacher of Righteousness would himself be

Esther

an *Essene*. 4. There was a strong organization among the Essenes that was missing among John the Baptist's disciples. So, was John the Baptist an *Essene*? While it is possible, it cannot be explicitly proven either biblically or historically. The replica of the Essenes today is the Jehovah's witness.

Esther: A Jewish girl in Persia, born as Hadassah but known as Esther, who becomes queen of Persia and thwarts genocide of her people.

Esther, The Book of: Also known in Hebrew as "the Scroll" (Megillah), is a book in the third section (Ketuvim, "Writings") of the Jewish Tanakh (the Hebrew Bible) and in the Christian Old Testament. It relates the story of a Jewish girl in Persia, born as Hadassah but known as Esther, who becomes queen of Persia and thwarts a genocide of her people. The story forms the core of the Jewish festival of Purim, during which it is read aloud twice: once in the evening and again the following morning. Other than the Song of Songs, Esther is the only book in the Bible that does not explicitly mention God. Traditionally, unlike other Tanakh scrolls, a scroll of Esther is given only one roller, fixed to its left-hand side, rather than the customary two rollers (one fixed to the right-hand side as well as the one fixed to the left-hand side)

Eternal: Without beginning or end; lasting forever; always existing (opposed to temporal), eternal life. 2 perpetual; ceaseless; endless: eternal quarrelling; eternal chatter. 3 enduring; immutable: eternal principles. 4 Metaphysics. existing outside all relations of time; not subject to change. (Noun) 5 something that is eternal. 6 the Eternal, God.

This means that God is eternal He is self-existent, the only being who does not owe His existence to somebody else. He is independent of any other being or cause. He is over and above the whole chain of causes and effects. He is uncreated, un-originated, without beginning, owing His existence to no one outside Himself. He has life in and of Himself. As Jesus put it, "For just as the Father has life in Himself, even so He gave to the Son also to have life in Himself" (John 5:26). Were it any other way He would not be God. An eternal being must be self-existent.

Eternal Life: Continued life after death, as outlined in Christian eschatology. The Apostles' Creed testifies: "I believe... the resurrection of the body, and life everlasting." In this view, eternal life commences after the second coming of Jesus and the resurrection of the dead,

2 According to mainstream Christian theology, after death but before the Second Coming, the

Eternity

saved live with God in an intermediate state, but after the Second Coming, experience the physical resurrection of the dead and the physical recreation of a New Earth. The Catechism of the Catholic Church states, "By death the soul is separated from the body, but in the resurrection God will give incorruptible life to our body, transformed by reunion with our soul. Just as Christ is risen and lives for ever, so all of us will rise at the last day." N.T. Wright argues that "God's plan is not to abandon this world... Rather, he intends to remake it. And when he does, he will raise all people to new bodily life to live in it. That is the promise of the Christian gospel"

3 In the Synoptic Gospels and the Pauline Letters, eternal life is generally regarded as a future experience, but the Gospel of John differs from them in its emphasis on eternal life as a "present possession". In the synoptic gospels eternal life is something received at the final judgment, or a future age (Mark 10:30, Matthew 18:8-9) but the Gospel of John positions eternal life as a present possibility, as in (John 5:24) Thus, unlike the synoptic, in the Gospel of John eternal life is not only futuristic, but also pertains to the present. In John, those who accept Christ can possess life "here and now" as well as in eternity, for they have "passed from death to life", as in (John 5:24): "He who hears my word, and believes him that sent me, has *eternal life*, and comes not into judgment, but has passed out of death into life." In John, the purpose for the incarnation, death, resurrection and glorification of The Word was to provide *eternal life* to humanity.

Eternity: (Ecclesiastes 3:11) "He has made everything beautiful in its time. Also, he has put *eternity* into man's heart, yet so that he cannot find out what God has done from the beginning to the end". *Eternity* means endless time. In philosophy and mathematics, an infinite duration is also called 'sempiternity', or everlasting. *Eternity* is an important concept in many religions and the gospel of Christ, where the immortality of God or the gods is said to endure eternally. Some, such as Aristotle, would say the same about the natural cosmos in regard to both past and future eternal duration, and like the eternal Platonic Forms, immutability was considered essential.

2 But *eternity* is not such good news for the unbeliever. The eternal God who made people with no end also made places with no end. One of them was prepared especially for the devil and his angels, a place of "eternal fire" (Matthew 25:41), a place of "torment day and night for ever and ever" (Revelation 20:10). While God did not make this place for people, unbelieving people who reject His gracious offer of salvation will spend eternity there. "And if anyone's name was not found written

in the book of life, he was thrown into the lake of fire" (Revelation 20:15). There is no way to escape it other than by bowing before the eternal, self-existent God, admitting that we are unworthy of His favour, acknowledging our sin and our need for His forgiveness, and accepting the salvation He provided when He sent His Son to the cross. We are totally dependent on Him, totally at His mercy. It cannot be otherwise with a God who has no beginning or end.

Eucharist's: Also called Holy Communion, the Lord's Supper, and other names, is a sacrament accepted by almost all Christians. It is re-enacted in accordance with Jesus' instruction at the Last Supper, as recorded in several books of the New Testament, that his followers do in remembrance of him as when he gave his disciples bread, saying, "This is my body", and gave them wine saying, "This is my blood." 2 Christians generally recognize a special presence of Christ in this rite, though they differ about exactly how, where, and when Christ is present. While all agree that there is no perceptible change in the elements, some believe that they actually become the body and blood of Christ, others believe in a "real" but merely spiritual presence of Christ in the Eucharist, and still others take the act to be only a symbolic re-enactment of the Last Supper. A minority of Protestants view the Eucharist as an ordinance in which the ceremony is seen not as a specific channel of divine grace, but as an expression of faith and of obedience to Christ. In spite of differences between Christians about various aspects of the Eucharist, there is, "more of a consensus among Christians about the meaning of the Eucharist than would appear from the confessional debates over the sacramental presence, the effects of the Eucharist, and the proper auspices under which it may be celebrated."

2 The word Eucharist may refer not only to the rite but also to the consecrated bread (leavened or unleavened) and wine (or grape juice) used in the rite. In this sense, communicants (that is, those who partake of the communion elements) may speak of "receiving the Eucharist", as well as "celebrating the Eucharist".

Euphrates: (Genesis 2:10-14) A river flowed out of Eden to water the garden, and there it divided and became four rivers. The name of the first is the Pishon. It is the one that flowed around the whole land of Havilah, where there is gold. And the gold of that land is good; bdellium and onyx stone are there. The name of the second river is the Gihon. It is the one that flowed around the whole land of Cush. And the name of the third river is the Tigris, which flows east of Assyria. And the fourth river is the *Euphrates*. 2 *Euphrates* (Hebrew: Prat) This is the longest and one of the most historically important rivers of Western Asia.

Together with the Tigris, it is one of the two defining rivers of Mesopotamia. Originating from eastern Turkey, the Euphrates flows through Syria and Iraq and join the Tigris in the Shatt al-Arab, which empties into the Persian Gulf. Euphrates played an important role in the gospel story starting from the time of the Garden of Eden in Genesis up to the expected coming of Christ as stated in many gospels including (Revelation 16:12-15) The sixth angel poured out his bowl on the great river Euphrates, and its water was dried up, to prepare the way for the kings from the east. And I saw, coming out of the mouth of the dragon and out of the mouth of the beast and out of the mouth of the false prophet, three unclean spirits like frogs. For they are demonic spirits, performing signs, who go abroad to the kings of the whole world, to assemble them for battle on the great day of God the Almighty. ("Behold, I am coming like a thief! Blessed is the one who stays awake, keeping his garments on, that he may not go about naked and be seen exposed!")

Eve: Eve is known as Adam's wife. According to the creation myth of Abrahamic religions, she is the first woman created by God (Yahweh, the god of Israel). Her husband was Adam, from whose rib God created her to be his companion. She succumbs to the serpent's temptation via the suggestion that to eat the forbidden fruit from the tree of the knowledge of good and evil would improve on the way God had made her, and that she would not die, and she, believing the lie of the serpent rather than the earlier instruction from God, shares the fruit with Adam. As a result, the first humans are expelled from the Garden of Eden and are cursed. Though Eve is not a saint's name, the traditional name day of Adam and Eve has been celebrated on December 24 since the Middle Ages in many European countries such as Germany, Hungary, Scandinavia, Estonia, and Lithuania.

Everlasting: (adjective) Many definition emerge for the word everlasting. The commonest one being - lasting forever or a very long time. The Godly will enjoy everlasting life, while "the sinner will suffer everlasting torment" synonyms: eternal, never-ending, endless, without end, perpetual, undying, immortal, deathless, indestructible, immutable, abiding, enduring, infinite, boundless, timeless; antonyms: transient, occasional noun: everlasting; noun: the everlasting; plural noun: everlastings; noun: everlasting flower; plural noun: everlasting flowers, literary -eternity. 2 A flower of the daisy family with a papery texture, retaining its shape and colour after being dried, especially a helichrysum. Many gospels associate with the word everlasting as in (Genesis 9:16) "And the bow shall be in the cloud; and I will look upon it, that I may remember the *everlasting* covenant between God and every

Everlasting, From Everlasting to

living creature of all flesh that is upon the earth". The Word of God assures us that all who believe in the Lord Jesus Christ will have *everlasting* life (John 3:16; 6:47; 1 John 5:13). The Greek word translated *"everlasting"* means "perpetual, eternal, forever." Perhaps the word perpetual best explains the biblical concept of *everlasting* life; it is life that, once begun, continues perpetually into eternity. This speaks to the idea that man's life is not merely physical. Rather, the true life of human beings is spiritual, and while the physical life ends, the spiritual continues throughout eternity. It is perpetual.

Everlasting, From Everlasting to:

(Psalm 90:1-2) "LORD, Thou hast been our dwelling place in all generations. Before the mountains were born, Or Thou didst give birth to the earth and the world, Even *from everlasting to everlasting*, Thou art God." Also in (Psalm 103:17) "But the lovingkindness of the LORD is *from everlasting to everlasting* on those who fear Him, And His righteousness to children's children", Him- this simply means that in God, no one else begin for Him, in Him no one else will end for Him since no one started for Him to follow. Everything comes from someplace. Every physical object has a maker. Every effect has a cause. Somebody made my watch. Somebody built our houses. Humanly speaking, somebody was even responsible for bringing us into existence, a man and a woman we call father and mother. We teach our children from their earliest days of understanding that the ultimate builder and maker of all things is God. He created the universe, of which every other tangible thing we know about is a part. The next question is a natural one. We set them up for it. They are surely going to ask it. They really cannot help themselves. "Who made God?" No one! God is a Rising Spirit with the fullness of all creation as the Rising Spirit commanded. From everlasting to everlasting therefore means eternity to eternity. He always was. The Bible never tries to prove His existence or explain where He came from. It merely assumes that He is there and that He has always been there. He had no beg inning. If something is not made or created, it means it is rising to create and by creation other things are made. Since no one created Him, no one will end Him. Therefore Rising God will continue to Rise eternally, endlessly, infinitely – for ever and ever. He is the Lord. He always was. The Bible never tries to prove His existence or explain where He came from. It merely assumes that He is there and that He has always been there. He had no beginning.

What this imply is that because God is eternal He is self - existent, the only being who does not owe His existence to somebody else. He is independent of any other being or cause. He is over and above the whole chain of causes and effects. He is uncreated, un-originated, without beginning, owing His existence to no one outside Himself. He has life in and of Himself. As Jesus put it, "For just as the Father has life in Himself, even so He gave to the Son also to have life in Himself" (John 5:26). Were it any other way He would not be God. An eternal being must be self-existent.

Because He was Rising and Shining with light, He see the way to create other things and most of all He Created man in His own image and adorn him with His Glory. That is why He advise man be bold, arise as I was rising and shine for thy light has come as a remark to His future Glory to Zion promise from everlasting to everlasting (Isaiah 60:1-2) "Arise, shine; for your light has come, And the glory of the LORD has risen upon you. "For behold, darkness will cover the earth And deep darkness the peoples; But the LORD will rise upon you And His glory will appear upon you...." Praise the Lord! Hallelujah! Amen!!

The following gospels clearly show the impact of God as everlasting father in the Bible. And Abraham planted a grove in Beersheba, and called there on the name of the LORD, the everlasting God. (Genesis 21:33) Blessed be the LORD God of Israel from everlasting, and to everlasting. Amen, and Amen. (Psalms 41:13) Before the mountains were brought forth, or ever thou hadst formed the earth and the world, even from everlasting to everlasting, thou art God. (Psalms 90:2) Thy throne is established of old: thou art from everlasting. (Psalms 93:2) For the LORD is good; his mercy is everlasting; and his truth endureth to all generations. (Psalms 100:5) But the mercy of the LORD is from everlasting to everlasting upon them that fear him, and his righteousness unto children's children; (Psalms 103:17) The righteousness of thy testimonies is everlasting: give me understanding, and I shall live. (Psalms 119:144) Thy kingdom is an everlasting kingdom, and thy dominion endureth throughout all generations. (Psalms 145:13) I was set up from everlasting, from the beginning, or ever the earth was. (Proverbs 8:23) For unto us a child is born, unto us a son is given: and the government shall be upon his shoulder: and his name shall be called Wonderful, Counsellor, The mighty God, The everlasting Father, The Prince of Peace. (Isaiah 9:6) Trust ye in the LORD for ever: for in the LORD JEHOVAH is everlasting strength (Isaiah 26:4) Hast thou not known? hast thou not heard, that the everlasting God, the LORD, the Creator of the ends of the earth, fainteth not,

neither is weary? there is no searching of his understanding. (Isaiah 40:28) The sun shall be no more thy light by day; neither for brightness shall the moon give light unto thee: but the LORD shall be unto thee an everlasting light, and thy God thy glory. Thy sun shall no more go down; neither

Evil

shall thy moon withdraw itself: for the LORD shall be thine everlasting light, and the days of thy mourning shall be ended. (Isaiah 60:19,20) Doubtless thou art our father, though Abraham be ignorant of us, and Israel acknowledge us not: thou, O LORD, art our father, our redeemer; thy name is from everlasting. (Isaiah 63:16) But the LORD is the true God, he is the living God, and an everlasting king: at his wrath the earth shall tremble, and the nations shall not be able to abide his indignation. (Jeremiah 10:10) But thou, Bethlehem Ephrata, though thou be little among the thousands of Judah, yet out of thee shall he come forth unto me that is to be ruler in Israel; whose goings forth have been from of old, from everlasting. (Micah 5:2) (Art thou not from everlasting, O LORD my God, mine Holy One? we shall not die. O LORD, thou hast ordained them for judgment; and, O mighty God, thou hast established them for correction. (Habakkuk 1:12) But now is made manifest, and by the scriptures of the prophets, according to the commandment of the everlasting God, made known to all nations for the obedience of faith: (Romans 16:26)

Evil: (adjective) profoundly immoral and wicked. (1 Thessalonica 5:21-3222) But examine everything carefully; hold fast to that which is good; abstain from every form of *evil*. The word evil is has so many meanings. Whatever meaning is attached to it, will be looked at in the light of the gospel. Understand the various meanings of the word evil before the gospel meanings. "his *evil* deeds" synonyms: wicked, bad, wrong, morally wrong, wrongful, immoral, sinful, ungodly, unholy, foul, vile, base, ignoble, dishonorable, corrupt, iniquitous, depraved, degenerate, villainous, nefarious, sinister, vicious, malicious, malevolent, demonic, devilish, diabolic, diabolical, fiendish, dark, black-hearted; More antonyms: good, virtuous (of a force or spirit) embodying or associated with the forces of the devil. "we were driven out of the house by an evil spirit" harmful or tending to harm. "the evil effects of high taxes" synonyms: harmful, hurtful, injurious, detrimental, deleterious, inimical, bad, mischievous, pernicious, malignant, malign, baleful, venomous, noxious, poisonous; 2 (of a smell or sight) extremely unpleasant. "a bathroom with an ineradicably evil smell" synonyms: unpleasant, disagreeable, nasty, horrible, foul, filthy, vile; antonyms: pleasant, fine noun noun: evil, profound immorality and wickedness, especially when regarded as a supernatural force "his struggle against the forces of evil" synonyms: wickedness, bad, badness, wrong, wrongdoing, sin, sinfulness, ungodliness, immorality, vice, iniquity, turpitude, degeneracy, vileness, baseness, perversion, corruption, depravity, villainy, nefariousness, atrocity, malevolence, devilishness;

Note: In (Hebrew 12: 12-17) "Therefore, strengthen your feeble arms and weak knees. "Make level paths for your feet," so that the lame may not be disabled, but rather healed. As a word of warning and encouragement, (verse 14) states "Make every effort to live in peace with everyone and to be holy; without holiness no one will see the Lord". See to it that no one falls short of the grace of God and that no bitter root grows up to cause trouble and defile many. See that no one is sexually immoral, or is godless like Esau, who for a single meal sold his inheritance rights as the oldest son. Afterward, as you know, when he wanted to inherit this blessing, he was rejected. Even though he sought the blessing with tears, he could not change what he had done. There is a proneness in believers to grow weary, and to faint under trials and afflictions; this is from the imperfection of grace and the remains of corruption. Christians should not faint under their trials. Though their enemies and persecutors may be instruments to inflict sufferings, yet they are Divine chastisements; our heavenly Father has his hand in all, and his wise end to answer by all. They must not make light of afflictions, and be without feeling under them, for they are the hand and rod of God, and are his rebukes for sin. They must not despond and sink under trials, nor fret and repine, but bear up with faith and patience. God may let others alone in their sins, but he will correct sin in his own children. In this he acts as becomes a father. Our earthly parents sometimes may chasten us, to gratify their passion, rather than to reform our manners. But the Father of our souls never willingly grieves nor afflicts his children. It is always for our profit. Our whole life here is a state of childhood, and imperfect as to spiritual things; therefore we must submit to the discipline of such a state. When we come to a perfect state, we shall be fully reconciled to all God's chastisement of us now. God's correction is not condemnation; the chastening may be borne with patience, and greatly promote holiness. Let us then learn to consider the afflictions brought on us by the malice of men, as corrections sent by our wise and gracious Father, for our spiritual good. Avoid illicit sex, religious heresy - witchcraft, idolatry, social conflicts and Drunkenness. Indeed, all the evils from man revolved on the above Sins.

Evil, illicit Sex as: (Galatians 5:19) "The acts of the flesh are obvious: sexual immorality, impurity and debauchery"; This is evil against ones body which affect soul and Spirit due to the state of impurity created.

2 In (Hosea 4:6)"My people perish for lack of knowledge". Demonic transference of spirits via sex is the transference of evil or unholy spirits via sexual intercourse activities.

Evil, illicit Sex as

There is a very powerful transference of spirits via sex and it is the easiest ways through which evil spirits are transferred easily from one person to another. In every 100 per-cent of negative or unholy transference of spirits; over 85 per=cent are traceable from or to someone past very rough sexual activities. The Gospel tells us in (1Corinthians .6:16) that if you are jointed sexually with a harlot ; you both become one, so, if you have sexual relationship with a highly demonized persons or occultist agents, witchcraft agents, fetish priests, marine human agents; this would easily bring unholy transference of spirits from such a person to anyone involved. The under-listed are some of the ways in which demons can be transferred easily via unholy sexual activities such as :

1a Illicit sexual involvement: (not yet married but having illicit sexual affairs of fornication) can delay someone not to get married in time; because, demons can easily pass through such an express avenue to delay or block someone marriage.

1b Illicit Sexual Intercourse through Infidelity: Immoral act by either on the side of a man or woman within any instituted marriage life can easily open door for demons transferring or invading the party involved. (Deuteronomy22:22); (Leviticus.20:10);(Matt.5:27-28).

1c Illicit Sexual Intercourse through Homosexuality: (lesbianism/Gay) sexual activities undertakings (Leviticus.20:13).

1d Illicit Sexual intercourse through Bestiality: This is sexual involvement with animals (man having sex with an animal/woman having sex with an animal) (Exodus 22:19; Leveticus 20:15-16. 5)

1d Illicit Sexual Intercourse through Incest sexual activities or involvements: An act of having sexual intercourse with someone that is very close to oneself (abomination): It could be in form of Unholy sexual activities with one's parent (man or woman):(Leviticus 18:7). b.Unholy sexual activities withones'Stepmother:(Leviticus.20:11);(Leviticus.18:8)   c. Unholy sexual activities with one's sister: (Deuteronomy 27:22) ;(Leviticus.20:17). d. Unholy sexual activities with one's aunt: (Leviticus 18:12-13); (Leviticus.20:19). e. Unholy sexual activities with one's uncle (Leviticus.18:14). f. Unholy sexual activities with one's daughter - in - law:(Leviticus.18:15;Leviticus.20.12). g. Unholy sexual activities with one's brother's wife (Leviticus.18:15;Leviticus.20:21). h. Unholy sexual activities with a mother and grand daughter:(Leviticus 18:17). i. Unholy sexual activities with two sisters (Leviticus.18:18). j. Unholy sexual activities with one's sister - in - law (Leviticus.20:21). k. Unholy sexual activities with one's grandchild.

2 Illicit Sexual intercourse undertakings during one'smenstruation:(Leviticus.20:18;Leviticus.18:19) 3 Anal sex practices. 4.Oral sex practices. 5.Harlotry promotions, practices and visitations (1Corinthians.6:9). 6 Nude beaches promotions, practices and visitations "nude beaches are existing presently in some western countries". 7 It can also led to someone having demonic spiritual husband/wife and children. NOTE: point 1-7 can easily led to any of the following: 1.Curse or curses from God as a result of immorality/sexual perversion practices (Leviticus.18:1-30); (Leviticus.20:13);(Leviticus.18:22);(Romans 1:26-27) *Illicit sexual intercourse* is bad because if God decides to delay by cursing someone. Definitely Satan and cohorts would rush in speedily by laying their own curses/problems upon someone (Satan has no free gifts) he is also very vest in the scripture. His main purpose is to: steal, kill and destroy. 3.It can also led to (Hidden Form Covenant):Hidden form covenant is a covenant that is hidden or unknown to someone and that is making someone to suffer greatly. 4.It can also led to (Inherited Form Covenant):cross transferring or sharing of demons together. 5.Occultist Form Covenant: if anyone had sex with an occultist human agent. Then an occultist form covenant would definitely take place or transferred. 6.For those involved in the after mentioned 1-7 points above. If not married; it can led to delay or prevention of someone not marrying in time. 7.For those that are married: it can easily led to marriage separation/divorce; as a result of demonic manipulations. Satan has no free gift. He came purposely to steal, kill and destroy. And he hates marriage union greatly (no wonder he tempted Adam and Eve in the Bible; shortly after God jointed them together within marriage union). 8 It can led to sex starvation for the married persons. Because, the party involved is having it unholy ways with someone else at the back of one's door (unholy soul-ties in taking place). 9 It can led to: bareness/infertility problems in women/miscarriage problems in women. Or, impotency/infertility problem in men of any party involved, because of presence of demonic spiritual husband/wife and children. 10 It can led to physical fight or murder from the side of the person that consider himself or herself being cheated. 11.It can led to children not being well trained in fear of the Lord as a result of instability within any given married home(because of Satan's penetrations). 12 It can lead to shock, mental break down, hypertension, stroke, heart attack as a result of excessive thinking of the person injured. 13 It can give rise to very strong unholy soul-ties. 14 It can also led to backwardness in life endeavours as a result of very powerful demonic manipulations. 15 It can also led to someone contacting sexual transmitted disease easily. Solutions, .Repent/stop every rough sexual activities, Go for counselling. 3 Go for comprehensive deliverance, Embrace God fully by re-dedicating oneself back unto God.

Evil, Religious Heresy as: A concern in Christian communities at least since the writing of 2 Peter: "even as there shall be false teachers among you, who privily shall bring in damnable heresies, even denying the Lord that bought them"(2Peter. 2:1). While in the first two or three centuries of the early Church heresy and schism were not clearly distinguished and a similar overlapping occurred in medieval scholastic thought, heresy is understood today to mean the denial of revealed truth as taught by the Church.

3 Schleiermacher, writing in 1821 and 1822 defined it as "that which preserved the appearance of Christianity, and yet contradicted its essence"

4 The Catholic Church makes a distinction between 'material' and 'formal' heresy. Material heresy means in effect "holding erroneous doctrines through no fault of one´s own" as occurs with people brought up in non-Catholic communities and "is neither a crime nor a sin" since the individual has never accepted the doctrine. Formal heresy is "the wilful and persistent adherence to an error in matters of faith" on the part of a baptised member of the Catholic Church. As such it is a grave sin and involves ipso facto excommunication. Here "matters of faith" means dogmas which have been proposed by the infallible Magisterium of the Church and, in addition to this intellectual error, "pertinacity in the will" in maintaining it in opposition to the teaching of the Church must be present.

While individual Protestant churches have also used the concept in proceedings against individuals and groups deemed to be heretical by those churches, the lack of a central doctrinal authority has meant that beliefs can often not be unanimously considered heretical from the Protestant perspective. Likewise the Eastern Orthodox Church officially declares a heresy only at an ecumenical council, and currently only accepts the First seven Ecumenical Councils as ecumenical. All heresies add up to diminished the basic ingredients to the Gospel of Christ and therefore an evil.

Evil, Witchcraft as: (voodoo, black or white magic), any charms for protection or destruction all are bad no matter what and no matter how the witches represent it to deceive the people. Christian people do not need any protection from Satan's side. God is greater than the defeated Satan, also God's angel are stronger than Satan's army (evil spirits). According to (Psalms 34:7) God's angel guards those who honour the Lord and rescues them from danger. We should not follow those people that disobey the Lord, no matter how nice they are or claim they are Christian or have a gift from mother or ancestor. Those kind of the gift directly comes from Satan not God. Some of the witches claim they are Christians but they are not, they are wolves in sheep skin. According to the Bible Christians should never get involved with witchcraft of any kind even for the good purposes like white magic.

2 Witchcraft practices involves any of the followings: little Mexican sun gods, idols, incense, Buddha, hand carved objects from Africa or the Orient, Ouija boards, anything connected with astrology, horoscopes, fortune telling, and so on. Books or objects associated with witchcraft, good luck charms (mood rings, four leaf clovers, rabbit's foot, horse shoes), Cult religions, Eastern religion or any teaching such as Zen, Tao, Buddha, Hare Krishna, Transcendental meditation, I Ching, Reincarnation, Karma, Yoga, Kabala, Metaphysics, Christians Science, Jehovah's Witnesses, Mormonism, New age, any philosophy that denies deity of the Lord Jesus, rock and roll records and tapes all fall in the category of things which have been often loaded with evil spiritual power.

3 As a Christian and one dwelling in the Gospel of Christ Jesus, you must verbally denounce Satan and his power and all of his demon hosts and claim authority as a believer-priest, because of the name of Jesus Christ and authority of His shed blood. After prayer, let the believers alternate reading Scriptures preferably in every room of the house or apartment and claim the cleansing of the area by demanding in Jesus name that the angels of the Lord be in charge to capture the evil spirits and imprison them until the Judgement day. Some Scripture which has proven useful in this include: (Isaiah 8:9,10; Colossians 2:14, 15; Philippians 2:9-11; Galatians 3:13; Revelation 12:11; Revelation 22:3; Deuteronomy 21:23; Deuteronomy 32:5; Numbers 23:8; II Samuel 7:29; Psalm 124; Psalm 148; Psalm 150; Psalm 91; Psalm 149: 5-9). According to James 5:14 you may call for the elders of the church or those whom have experience in Deliverance Ministry and let them pray over the house or apartment and anoint it with oil in the name of Jesus. The door lintel and window sills must be anointed by touching them with olive oil which is symbol of the Holy Spirit. Other things such as statues, second-hand cars or things bought from garage sale or other places should be anointed in Jesus name too. Each thing and area should be claimed as ground for the Lord and taken back from Satan and his demons. Any known sins or occult connections should be renounced and confessed as sin and put away. Any specific areas of demonic activity or influence of which you are aware should be denounced by name (Proverbs 3:33).

Evil, Idolatry as: Simply, this is worshipping another god other than Jehovah – the Lord of Host. (Leviticus 26:1)" 'do not make idols or set up an image or a sacred stone for yourselves, and do not place a carved stone in your land to bow down before it. I am the Lord your God. (Numbers 33:52) drive out all the inhabitants of the land before you. Destroy all-their carved images and their cast idols (Deuteronomy 4:16)… do not become corrupt and make for yourselves an idol, an image of any shape, whether formed like a man or a woman (Deuteronomy 7:25)… the images of their gods you are to burn in the fire…or you will be ensnared by it, for it is detestable to the Lord your God. (Deuteronomy 27:15) cursed is the man who carves an image or casts an idol-a thing detestable to the Lord.

2 As Christians, when we look to anything else- the economy, the stock market, government, a political party or leader, our country, nationality or ethnicity, science, technology, a "cause" of any kind, formal education (Degrees and Credentials)- to give us security, protection, strength, life, purpose and meaning instead of God, we have an idols. That makes such Christians practicing Pagans. We must repent and rip these idols from our hearts. (Ezekiel 14:2-6) The word of the Lord came to me: "Son of Man, these men have set up idols in their hearts ... Should I let them inquire of me at all? therefore speak to them and tell them, 'this is what the sovereign Lord says: when any Israelite sets up idols in his heart and puts a wicked stumbling block before his face and then goes to a prophet, I the Lord will answer him myself in keeping with his great idolatry. I will do this to recapture the hearts of the people of Israel, who have all deserted me for their idols.' "therefore say to the house of Israel, 'this is what the sovereign Lord says: Repent! Turn from your idols and renounce all your detestable practices!

But Ezekiel is quoting God as saying that men bring their idols into their hearts. The idols do not originate there, but become rooted there. Idols become loved. Idols take over a man's heart- his devotion- even while that man seeks the Lord, remaining a believer in God. These idols are stumbling blocks- they lead to sin, not simply to trouble or misery for the idolater. Idolatry is the root and cause of all evil in society. Romans 1, (Colossians 3:5) eg- Idolatry is the major cause of the oppression of the Poor. 3 Idolatry, devotion to false gods in the heart, makes prayer (devotion) to the true God impossible. God hates this. He demands His people repent of the idols in their hearts and forsake them.

Evil, Social Conflicts as:
Issues that influences and is opposed by a considerable number of individuals within a society. It is often the consequence of factors extending beyond an individual's control and local geographical en-

vironment. In some cases, a social issue is the source of a conflicting opinion on the grounds of what is perceives as a morally just personal life or societal order. Different societies have different perceptions, and "normal" behaviour in one society may be a significant social issue in another society. Social issues are distinguished from economic issues; however, some issues (such as immigration) have both social and economic aspects. There are also issues that don't fall into either category, such as wars. Man's inability to "allow the same rights to others as we allow ourselves" causes the birth of a social conflicts and this can lead to wars and killings and endemic evil going around the diverse places in the world at all times.

2 Most Christians are misguided. For instance, the Christians who supported and engaged in slavery were amply supported by the Bible, in which slavery is accepted as a given, as simply a part of the social landscape. There are numerous biblical passages that implicitly or explicitly endorse slavery, such as (Exodus 21:20–21): "And if a man smite his servant, or his maid with a rod, and he die under his hand; he shall be surely punished. Notwithstanding, if he continues a day or two, he shall not be punished: for he is his money." Other passages that support slavery include (Ephesians 6:5), Colossians 3:22, Titus 2:9–10, Exodus 21:2–6, Leviticus 25:44–46, 1 Peter 2:18), and (1 Timothy 6:1). Christian slave owners in colonial America were well acquainted with these passages.

Evil, Drunkenness as: (1 Peter 4:3) "For you have spent enough time in the past doing what pagans choose to do--living in debauchery, lust, drunkenness, orgies, carousing and detestable idolatry". Drunkenness have various meanings - Delirious with or as if with strong drink; intoxicated. 2. Habitually drunk.3. Of, involving, or occurring during intoxication: a drunken brawl. It is a world temptation.

4. Cooked with wine or another alcoholic beverage: "Noah planted a vineyard; and he drank of the wine and was drunken." (Genesis 9:20-21) This Noah did the best thing and the worst thing for the world. He built an ark against that deluge of water, but introduced a deluge against which the human race has ever since been trying to build an ark-the deluge of drunkenness. In my text we hear his staggering steps. Shem and Japheth tried to cover up the disgrace, but there he is, drunk on wine at a time in the history of the world, when, to say the least, there was no lack of water. Inebriation, having entered the world, has not retreated. Abigail, the fair and heroic wife, who saved the flocks of Nabal, her husband, from confiscation by invaders, goes home at night and finds him so intoxicated, she cannot tell him the story of his narrow escape. Uriah came

Excommunication

to see David, and David got him drunk and paved the way for the despoliation of a household. Even the church bishops needed to be charged to be sober and not given to too much wine, and so familiar were people of Bible times with the staggering and falling motion of the inebriate that, Isaiah, when he comes to describe the final dislocation of worlds, says;" The earth shall reel to and fro like a drunkard." Ever since apples and grapes and wheat grew, the world has been tempted to unhealthful stimulants. But the intoxicants of the olden time were an innocent beverage, a harmless orangeade, a quiet syrup, a peaceful soda water as compared with the liquids of modern inebriation, into which a madness and a fury, and a gloom, and a fire, and a suicide, and a retribution have mixed and mingled. Fermentation was always known, but it was not until a thousand years after Christ that distillation was invented. While we must confess that some of the ancient arts have been lost, the Christian era is superior to all others in the bad eminence of whisky and rum and gin. The modern drunk is a hundredfold worse than the ancient drunk. Noah in his intoxication became imbecile, but the victims of modern day alcoholism have to struggle with whole menageries of wild beasts, and jungles of hissing serpents, and perditions of blaspheming demons.

Excommunication: This is a disciplinary tool adopted in most Christian Churches to maintain sanity and possibly Holiness in the church and the body of Christ in general. It is an institutional act of religious censure used to deprive, suspend, or limit membership in a religious community or (as in the present discipline of the Catholic Church) to restrict certain rights within it, such as the reception to Holy Communion. Some Protestants use the term disfellowship instead.

2 *Excommunication* means putting a specific individual or group on check, sometimes out of communion. The practice very common in the Apostolic Church. Also in some religions, excommunication includes spiritual condemnation of the member or group. Excommunication may involve banishment, shunning, and shaming, depending on the religion, the offense that caused excommunication, or the rules or norms of the religious community. The grave act is often remedied by sincere penance, public recantation, sometimes through the Sacrament of Confession, piety, and or through mortification of the flesh.

In (Matthew 18:15-17) Jesus says that an offended person should first draw the offender's fault to the offender's attention privately; then, if the offender refuses to listen, bring one or two others, that there may be more than a single witness to the charge; next, if the offender still refuses to listen, bring the matter before the church, and if the offender refuses to listen to the church, treat the offender as "a Gentile and a tax collector". Also, (1 Corinthians 5:1-8) directs the church at Corinth to excommunicate a man for sexual immorality (incest). In (2 Corinthians 2:5-11), the man, having repented and suffered the "punishment by the majority" is restored to the church. Fornication is not the only ground for excommunication, according to the apostle: in 5:11, Paul says, "I am writing to you not to associate with anyone who bears the name of brother if he is guilty of sexual immorality or greed, or is an idolater, revile, drunkard, or swindler - not even to eat with such a one." In (Romans 16:17), Paul writes to "mark those who cause divisions contrary to the doctrine which ye have learned and avoid them." Also, in (2 John 1:10-11), the writer advises believers that "whosoever transgresseth, and abideth not in the doctrine of Christ, hath not God. He that abideth in the doctrine of Christ, he hath both the Father and the Son. If there come any unto you, and bring not this doctrine, receive him not into your house, residence or abode, or "inmates of the house" (family)], neither bid him God speed: for he that bidet him God speed is partaker of his evil deeds."

The following gospel passages from the bible adds more ingredients to understanding of excommunication. (Matthew 18:15-20) - Moreover if thy brother shall trespass against thee, go and tell him his fault between thee and him alone: if he shall hear thee, thou hast gained thy brother. (Romans 16:17) - Now I beseech you, brethren, mark them which cause divisions and offences contrary to the doctrine which ye have learned; and avoid them. (Proverbs 25:26) - A righteous man falling down before the wicked [is as] a troubled fountain, and a corrupt spring. (2 John 1:10) - If there come any unto you, and bring not this doctrine, receive him not into [your] house, neither bid him God speed: (Matthew 4:1-25) - Then was Jesus led up of the Spirit into the wilderness to be tempted of the devil. (2 Chronicles 17:1-19) - And Jehoshaphat his son reigned in his stead, and strengthened himself against Israel.

Exile, The: (noun) "the exile" in the sense of the gospel is a watershed in the history of the Old Testament. For instance, literature after the exile (post-exilic) is very different from that addressed to the period of the monarchy (pre-exilic). The word exile is the state of being barred from one's native country, typically for political or punitive reasons. "he knew now that he would die in exile" synonyms: banishment, expulsion, expatriation, deportation, eviction; More antonyms: return a person who lives away from their native country, either from choice or compulsion. plural noun: exiles" the return of political exiles" synonyms: émigré, expatriate; present: expel and bar (someone) from their na-

Exile, The

tive country, typically for political or punitive reasons. "a corrupt dictator who had been exiled from his country" synonyms: expel, banish, expatriate, deport, ban, bar; A corrupt generation or race like the Israelites. Most exiles declared by God through the mouth of the prophets were for punitive reasons due to some arbitrary actions by the Kings or political rulers of each era. The deportation of leaders was a common feature of both Assyrian and Babylonian imperial policy. In biblical studies the term "the exile" or "captivity" refers to the deportation of Judah's leaders from Jerusalem in the 6th century. Earlier the leaders of the Northern Kingdom (Israel) had been deported by the Assyrians, following the fall of Samaria in 722BC. The main core of the word is in (Genesis 3:21-23) during the expulsion of Adam and Eve from Paradise "The LORD God made garments of skin for Adam and his wife, and clothed them. Then the LORD God said, "Behold, the man has become like one of Us, knowing good and evil; and now, he might stretch out his hand, and take also from the tree of life, and eat, and live forever "-- therefore the LORD God sent him out from the garden of Eden, to cultivate the ground from which he was taken...."

2 *Exile* is a form of punishment that God has used from the very beginning. Here in Genesis 3, in the book of beginnings, we have the first instance of exile imposed by God Himself. It was exile from the Garden of Eden, from all that was wonderful and good that God had created, the perfect environment in which He had placed Adam and Eve. They could never go back. God placed an angel with a flaming sword that would turn whichever way any man juked to get back. If it were still there, it would deny us "paradise" even now.

Contextually this shows three reasons we can glean to determine why God uses *exile*. The first one is evident—it was punishment for their sins. Adam and Eve took of the tree of the knowledge of good and evil when God said they should not take of it. That is sin, breaking a direct command of God. Exile was the punishment. What else can Christians glean? What did their exile do? It separated them from access to Him. 2 Exile separates man from God. He does not want to be separated from us, but because of sin, it happens. It must happen because He does not like sin in the least. So this is a kind of corollary to the first point. Sin brings exile, and sin causes separation from God.

3 God imposes exile to spur repentance because it should be the natural inclination of men who have known God and all the glorious things that we can have in His presence to return to His good graces. Sin, Separation from God and repentance forms the reason a great numbers of Israelites where in exile- see instances in 4 below.

4 The estimates of numbers deported vary (Jerimiah 52:28-30) lists three deportations and gives 4,600 as the total exiled from Judah; while (2 Kings 24:14) claims

10,000 in the first deportation alone). Whatever the exact figure, only a proportion of the population was directly affected. Yet since these were the leaders and skilled craft workers (2 Kings 24:14,16) and since, at the same time, the Lord's temple and the city of Jerusalem were destroyed, the effect on the nation was traumatic. Like Psalm 137 and the quotations from exiles in the prophets as in (Psalm 49:14) give a feel of the extent to which the foundations of faith and nation were shaken. While it was the deportation of Judah's leaders which marked the Old Testament texts most, when Amos speaks of *exile* it is deportation from the North by Assyria of which he warns. Amos fears that the coming punishment may be final, for God's patience is near its end. (Amos 5:3) warns of military decimation, while in (Amos 5:14-15) (one of the few places where the disaster is not spoken of as total) notice that the possibility of "grace" is opened only for the "remnant" of Joseph, thus after the destruction. ("Joseph" is here Northern Israel personified.) In fact, although we know of Judean exiles who returned (2 Chronicles 36:22).; Ezra, Nehemiah etc.) there is no indication in the Bible or other sources of the fate of the Northern *exiles*. While the above constitute physical exile, there is also Spiritual Exile.

Exile, Spiritual: Spiritual exile is that moment in a Christian life, where a person – a Christian who were once safe falls away from Grace and embrace the work of Satan or sinful nature, not praying anymore, not listening to Gods word nor keep them, defiant in listening, hearing and acting with the word. No more vision, no more revelation, no more prophesy etc. Indeed, this trend can extend to the whole Church if many members are affected. When there is no more communication between a Christian and the Heavenly father the trend will be like the trend between the Jews and the Gentiles. The terms "Jew" and "Gentile" do not relate to this or that individual, but express two spiritual situations in the same person. The word - Jewish (Hebrew: Yehudi) comes from the word – unification (Yechud), connection with the Creator, the inner essence of man's soul and a Gentile is its outer essence. Our freedom of choice is in choosing to develop the inner part, called Jewish, and overcome the outer part, called Gentile... (Genesis 46:1-7) By their own choice, the family of Israel went into a self-imposed exile, from Canaan to Egypt. We see in verse 3 that God Himself wanted this to occur. He had plans for Israel, and the Israelites had to go through this period of Egypt as part of that plan. They did not realize at the time that this voluntary sojourn in Egypt would lead to their forced slavery. Several generations would pass until the time they would be put under bitter bondage, when the Pharaoh would go so far as to call for all the sons of Israel to be killed after their birth. It was only by God's mighty power in the Exodus that they were ever able to leave Egypt; they could not have done it on their own. In their minds, they were half-Egyptian by that time,

Exodus

perhaps even more. They really did not want to leave. Sure, they loved the idea of freedom, but as soon as they left Egypt, they wanted to go back. Probably they were temporary separated from God during this time. Because they have separated from the Spirit and probably adopted another god- worship of deities in the land of Egypt. It is ironic how hard it was for them to return to Canaan because they had forgotten that their real homeland was in the land of Canaan which God who is Spirit gave to them through Abraham, not in Egypt. They had taken the place of their exile as home. They had become so enmeshed in the culture of Egypt that they considered it their own. We see this when, only a month out, they forced Aaron to bring some of that culture back into their lives in the form of a Golden Calf.

2 In (Deuteronomy 28:62-68) however, that is low—not even good enough to be sold as slaves. This is how far God is willing to go to make the lessons of exile sink in. Because of sin, He has to do this as punishment. He has to separate us away from Him for a time. The purpose is to get us to repent, to bring us back to Him in the end. If this is what it takes, He is willing to do it. It is very ironic that He says that He would rejoice in bringing Israel—or the church in type—low. This is not a fiendish type of joy in which a person gets his jollies out of making others hurt. God will rejoice because He can see the end and know that at least another step in His plan has been accomplished. He will put His whole heart into it to make sure that we come out of it as His people—in far better shape—on the other.

3 In the Church and the entire body of Christ today, a number of Christians who once were saved have fallen short of the Grace of God and went to *exile* through sin in the bondage of Satan. But God in His infinite mercy send His only begotten son Jesus Christ to die and bring redemption in order to bring us back to the Father (who is Spirit). When the lost or exile souls return back to God, through sanctification, they will worship God in Spirit and in truth and set themselves aside for His Heavenly Home. Hallelujah!

Exodus: (noun) A mass departure of people. synonyms: mass departure, withdrawal, evacuation, leaving, exit; antonyms: arrival the departure of the Israelites from Egypt noun: Exodus; plural noun: the Exodus "the Passover festival celebrates the Exodus" 2 A going out; a departure or emigration, usually of a large number of people: the summer exodus to the country and shore. the Exodus, the departure of the Israelites from Egypt under Moses. (initial capital letter) the second book of the Bible, containing an account of the Exodus.

Exodus, Book of: This is the second book of the Hebrew Bible, and of the five books of the Torah (the Pentateuch) The book tells how the Israelites leave slavery in Egypt through the strength of Yahweh, the God who has chosen Israel as his people. Led by their prophet

Moses they journey through the wilderness to Mount Sinai, where Yahweh promises them the land of Canaan (the "Promised Land") in return for their faithfulness. Israel enters into a covenant with Yahweh who gives them their laws and instructions for the Tabernacle, the means by which he will dwell with them and lead them to the land, and give them peace.

Traditionally ascribed to Moses himself, modern scholarship sees the book as initially a product of the Babylonian exile (6th century), with final revisions in the Persian post-exilic period (5th century. It is arguably the most important book in the Bible, as it presents the defining features of Israel's identity: memories of a past marked by hardship and escape, a binding covenant with the god who chooses Israel, and the establishment of the life of the community and the guidelines for sustaining it. Exodus shows the entire life of the Israelites under oppression, listing out the names of the Children of Israel whose remnant also suffered in the hands of Pharaoh. (Exodus 1: 1 - 5) "These are the names of the sons of Israel who went to Egypt with Jacob, each with his family: Reuben, Simeon, Levi and Judah; Issachar, Zebulun and Benjamin; Dan and Naphtali; Gad and Asher. The descendants of Jacob numbered seventy[a] in all; Joseph was already in Egypt.

Eye: (Mathew 6:22 -23) "The eye is the lamp of the body; so then if your eye is clear, your whole body will be full of light. "But if your eye is bad, your whole body will be full of darkness. If then the light that is in you is darkness, how great is the darkness!...While the above definition provides us with the gospel importance of light, the biological meaning of light must well be understood in order to have in-depth knowledge of the importance of light in the gospel. 2 Eye is the organs of vision. They detect light and convert it into electro-chemical impulses in neurons. The simplest photoreceptor cells in conscious vision connect light to movement. In higher organisms the eye is a complex optical system which collects light from the surrounding environment, regulates its intensity through a diaphragm, focuses it through an adjustable assembly of lenses to form an image, converts this image into a set of electrical signals, and transmits these signals to the brain through complex neural pathways that connect the eye via the optic nerve to the visual cortex and other areas of the brain. Eyes with resolving power have come in ten fundamentally different forms, and 96% of animal species possess a complex optical system.[1] Image-resolving eyes are present in molluscs, chordates and arthropods. The simplest "eyes", such as those in microorganisms, do nothing but detect whether the surroundings are light or dark, which is sufficient for the entrainment of circadian rhythms. From more complex eyes, retinal photosensitive ganglion cells send signals along the retinohypothalamic tract to the suprachiasmatic nuclei to effect circadian adjustment. Base on the above definition, eye play

Ezra

predominant role in the gospel of redemption and grace. (Matthew 7:3-5) "Why do you look at the speck that is in your brother's *eye*, but do not notice the log that is in your own *eye*? "Or how can you say to your brother, 'Let me take the speck out of your eye,' and behold, the log is in your own *eye*? "You hypocrite, first take the log out of your own *eye*, and then you will see clearly to take the speck out of your brother's *eye*. Are you clean enough to be saved so that you can from there see the dirt in your brothers eye? Have you given your life to Christ? Rid yourself from your sinful nature?, Accept Jesus Christ as your only Lord and Saviour? The following Gospels will give you true insight on the Gospel of light which is lamp of the body:

(1 Corinthians 2:9) but just as it is written, "THINGS WHICH EYE HAS NOT SEEN AND EAR HAS NOT HEARD, AND which HAVE NOT ENTERED THE HEART OF MAN, ALL THAT GOD HAS PREPARED FOR THOSE WHO LOVE HIM." (Ephesians 1:18) I pray that the eyes of your heart may be enlightened, so that you will know what is the hope of His calling, what are the riches of the glory of His inheritance in the saints, (Ephesians 6:6) not by way of *eye* service, as men-pleasers, but as slaves of Christ, doing the will of God from the heart. (1 John 2:16) For all that is in the world, the lust of the flesh and the lust of the *eyes* and the boastful pride of life, is not from the Father, but is from the world.

Ezekiel: Simply means "May God strengthen him" and : Hazqiyal, in Arabic meaning "God will strengthen" (from literally "to fasten upon", figuratively "strong", and literally "God", and so figuratively "The Almighty") is the central protagonist of the Book of Ezekiel in the Hebrew Bible. In Christianity, and other Faith, Ezekiel is acknowledged as a Hebrew prophet. In Judaism and Christianity, he is also viewed as the author of the Book of Ezekiel that reveals prophecies regarding the destruction of Jerusalem, the restoration to the land of Israel and the Millennial Temple visions, or the Third Temple.

Ezra: Also called Ezra the Scribe (Hebrew: Ezra ha-Sofer) and Ezra the Priest in the Book of Ezra. According to the Hebrew Bible he returned from the Babylonian exile and reintroduced the Torah in Jerusalem (Ezra 7-10) and (Nehemiah 8). According to First Ezra's, a non-canonical Greek translation of the Book of Esdras, he was also a high priest. His name may be an abbreviation of Azaryahu, "God-helps". In the Greek Septuagint the name is rendered Esdras (Greek:), from which Latin: Esdras. The Book of Ezra describes how he led a group of Judean exiles living in Babylon to their home city of Jerusalem (Ezra 8.2-14) where he is said to have enforced observance of the Torah and to have cleansed the community of mixed marriages. Ezra, known as "Ezra the scribe" in Chazalic literature, is a highly respected figure in Judaism.

Ff

Face: (noun) Several meanings emerged to the word face. You will not understand the gospel meaning without its ordinary meaning. In ordinary usage, it is the front part of a person's head from the forehead to the chin, or the corresponding part in an animal. "she was scarlet in the face and perspiring profusely", Again, "Let us behold the glory of Christ", as in (2 Corinthians 3:18) " And we all, with unveiled face, beholding the glory of the Lord,[a] are being transformed into the same image from one degree of glory to another. For this comes from the Lord who is the Spirit" This word is synonym with countenance, physiognomy, profile, features; More an expression shown on the face. "the happy faces of these children" synonyms: expression, facial expression, look, appearance, air, manner, bearing, countenance, guise, cast, aspect, impression; More an aspect of something. "the unacceptable face of social drinking" synonyms:(outward) appearance, aspect, air, nature, image. In the gospel usage, face is applied according to individual believe and faith. For instance you cannot see the face of the Lord without you humbling yourself and being attentive in obedience to His word. *Face* simply means presence, as when it is recorded that Adam and Eve hid themselves from the "face of the Lord God" because of sin. They disobey God. (Genesis 3:8) ; "Then the man and his wife heard the sound of the Lord God as he was walking in the garden in the cool of the day, and they hid from the Lord God among the trees of the garden". Here, iniquity, forbids man to see the *face* of the Lord. Compare Exodus 33:14 Exodus 33:15, where the same Hebrew word is rendered "presence"). The "light of God's countenance" is his favour (Psalms 44:3 ; Daniel 9:17). "Face" signifies also anger, justice, severity (Genesis 16:6 Genesis 16:8 ; Exodus 2:15 ; Psalms 68:1 ; Revelation 6:16). To "provoke God to his face" (Isaiah 65:3) is to sin against him openly.

Face – of God

2 The Jews prayed with their faces toward the temple and Jerusalem (1 Kings 8:38 1 Kings 8:44 1 Kings 8:48 ; Daniel 6:10). To "see God's face" is to have access to him and to enjoy his favour (Psalms 17:15 ; 27:8). This is the privilege of holy angels (Matthew 18:10 ; Luke 1:19). The "face of Jesus Christ" (2 Corinthians 4:6) is the office and person of Christ, the reveller of the glory of God (John 1:14 John 1:18).

3 Whichever way one tries to see the *face* of the Lord, is through one way – obedience which Samuel indicated is better than Sacrifice as in (1 Samuel 15:22) "But Samuel replied: "Does the LORD delight in burnt offerings and sacrifices as much as in obeying the LORD? To obey is better than sacrifice, and to heed is better than the fat of rams". Note when His face goes with you, you move as a conquer-ship. Joyous all the time because of the confidence of His Grace. Glory to Jesus. How can one see His Face. This done through constant prayer, the word, and fellowship.

Face – of God:

A term used to refer to the character of God, especially his favour towards his people. For God to turn his face to his people is to offer them his grace and help; for God to turn his face against his people is to withhold his favour and blessing. To seek the face of God is to seek his favour.

Faith:

This is the Christian practice of possessing, or confirming the unseen to reality which through confidence in God must come to fruition in the physical or as expected. It is the fruit of confidential relationship with God or a trust worthy fellow - as in (Hebrew 11:1) "Now faith is being sure of what we hope for and certain of what we do not see".

2 It is belief that is not based on proof. It can also be defined as confidence or trust in a person, thing, deity, view, or in the doctrines or teachings of a religion, as well as confidence based on some degree of warrant. The word faith is often used as a synonym for irrevocable hope, trust, or belief as in (1 Peter 1:5-9) "who through faith are shielded by God's power until the coming of the salvation that is ready to be revealed in the last time. In this you greatly rejoice, though now for a little while you may have had to suffer grief in all kinds of trials. These have come so that your faith--of greater worth than gold, which perishes even though refined by fire--may be proved genuine and may result in praise, glory and honor when Jesus Christ is revealed. Though you have not seen him, you love him; and even though you do not see him now, you believe in him and are filled with an inexpressible and glorious joy, for you are receiving the goal of your faith, the salvation of your soul"s. Again, "Yea, a man may say, Thou hast faith, and I have works: shew me thy faith

without thy works, and I will shew thee my faith by my works" (James 2:18 9)

Faith in Christ: A central notion taught by Jesus Christ himself in reference to the Good News (Mark 1:15). In the understanding of Jesus it was an act of trust and of self-abandonment by which people no longer rely on their own strength and policies but commit themselves to the power and guiding word of him in whom they believe (Mathew 21:25,32; Luke 1:20,45). Since the Protestant Reformation the meaning of this term has been an object of major theological disagreement in Western Christianity. Most of the definitions in the history of Christian theology have followed biblical formulation in the Letter to the (Hebrews 11:1):describing *faith* as the assurance of things hoped for, the conviction of things not seen. As in other Abrahamic religions, it includes a belief in God, a belief in the reality of a transcendent domain that God administers as His Kingdom from His Throne and in the benevolence of God's will or plan for humankind and the World to Come. Christianity differs from other Abrahamic religions in that it focuses on the ministry of Jesus, and on his place as the prophesied Christ. It also includes a belief in the New Covenant. According to most Christian traditions, Christian faith requires a belief in Jesus' resurrection from the dead by God the Father through The Holy Spirit.

The precise understanding of the term FAITH differs among the various Christian traditions. Despite these differences, Christians generally agree that faith in Jesus lies at the core of the Christian tradition, and that such faith is required in order to be a Christian. The Christian tradition is sometimes called "the faith", since faith in Jesus is so central to the tradition. Faith and the word "belief" are often treated synonymously, which has led to Christians being called 'believers'.

(1 Corinthians 15:14-17) "And if Christ has not been raised, our preaching is useless and so is your faith. More than that, we are then found to be false witnesses about God, for we have testified about God that he raised Christ from the dead. But he did not raise him if in fact the dead are not raised. For if the dead are not raised, then Christ has not been raised either. And if Christ has not been raised, your faith is futile; you are still in your sins".

Faith, Violent: This demonstrates aggression in faithful process to attain the expected or a destined result. It is not a religious theory but a spiritual force (Matthew 17:20) that gives motion to every destiny rules the world of impossibilities (Mark 9:23) by breaking certain natural boundaries and negative situations (Job 14:7). It is impacted as it's not gentle but violent (Matthew 11:12). It does not wait for things to come; faith goes to things that should come to it because most waiters are wast-

Fail

ers (Hebrews 11:33). Violent faith is characterised by attacking and very offensive with righteous anger.

2 Violent faith attacks whatever confronts you, (Judges 15:14-15). Men of faith like King David run towards giants, they don't run away from giants. Every record breaker and pacesetter is a 'challenge confronter'. It is not faith unless there is an attack (1 Timothy 6:12, Numbers 13:30). Those who attack, enlarge their coast. Your coast is only proportionate to your aggression. Violent faith is Resolute. It does not give up (Hebrews 10:38). When you say, 'I'm finished', it is most probable that you are out of faith. Someone said, 'Most failures in life are people who didn't know how close they were to success before they gave up'. You must never give up in Jesus name! You need to stir up violent faith by getting intoxicated with spiritual wine as in (Genesis 49:8-12). "Judah, your brothers will praise you; your hand will be on the neck of your enemies. your father's sons will bow down to you. You are a lion's cub, Judah; you return from the prey, my so. Like a lion he crouches and lies down, like a lioness—who dares to rouse him? The sceptre will not depart from Judah, nor the ruler's staff from between his feet, until he to whom it belongs shall come and the obedience of the nations shall be his He will tether his donkey to a vine, his colt to the choicest branch; he will wash his garments in wine, his robes in the blood of grapes. His eyes will be darker than wine, his teeth whiter than milk." They are manifestations of the effect of God's Spirit. Some of these wines are the wine of vision and the wine of love, work and so forth.

Fail: (verb) To be unsuccessful in achieving one's goal as in (Psalm 73:26) "My flesh and my heart may fail, but God is the strength of my heart and my portion forever". There are several ways the fail could apply in the gospel as opposed to it everyday usage. 2 unsuccessful in, not pass; More (of a person or a commodity) be unable to meet the standards set by (a test of quality or eligibility). For instance "a Christian has failed to pray" judge (a candidate in an examination or test) not to have passed. "the criteria used to pass or fail the candidate" 3 neglect to do something. "the Pastor failed to teach correct doctrines" behave in a way contrary to expectations by not doing something. 3 synonyms: let down, disappoint, break one's promise to, dash someone's hopes, fall short of someone's expectations; 4 cease to work properly; break down. break down, break, stop working, cease to function, cut out, stop, stall, crash, give out; More antonyms: w o r k , be in working order become weaker or of poorer quality. "the light began to fail" synonyms: f a d e , grow less, grow dim, dim, die away, dwindle, wane, disappear, vanish, peter out, dissolve More (of rain or a crop or supply) be insufficient when needed or expected. "the drought means crops have failed" synonyms: be deficient, be wanting, be lacking, fall short, be insufficient, be inadequate; More (of a business or a person) cease trading because of lack of funds. "he lost his savings when the store failed" synonyms: be unsuccessful, not succeed, lack success, fall through, fall flat, break down, abort, miscarry, be defeated, suffer defeat, be in vain, be frustrated, collapse, founder, misfire, backfire, not come up to scratch, meet with disaster, come to grief, come to nothing, come to naught, miss the mark, run aground, go astray; More noun noun: fail; plural noun: fails a mark which is not high enough to pass an examination or test. "a fail grade" 2. Informal mistake, failure, or instance of poor performance. "their customer service is a massive fail" Whichever way the word fail or failure is used, a study of gospel characters in the bible reveals that most of those who made history were men who failed at some point, and some of them drastically, but who refused to continue lying in the dust. Their very failure and repentance secured for them a more ample conception of the grace of God. They learned to know Him as the God of the second chance to His children who had failed Him—and third chance, too. Because the only man who never makes a mistake is the man who never does anything.

That is why Paul declared in (Romans 8: 35-39) "Who will separate us from the love of Christ? Will trouble, or distress, or persecution, or famine, or nakedness, or danger, or death? As it is written, "For your sake we encounter death all day long; we were considered as sheep to be slaughtered." No, in all these things we have complete victory through him who loved us. For I am convinced that neither death nor life, nor angels, nor rulers, nor things that are present, nor things to come, nor powers, nor height, nor depth, nor anything else in creation will be able to separate us from the love of God in Christ Jesus our Lord. Whatever will be the failure in your life as a mature Christian, note that God is adequate for all kinds of failure. Some failures may not be our fault, but they serve as reminders that we must live with eternal priorities in mind. Other failures are directly the result of our own sinful choices. So wake up from your slumber as a sleeper is waking up.

Fast: (adj. faster, fastest, fasting): There are so many meaning of the word *fast* in the ordinary usage. But our focus or concern in the Gospel is how the word relates to our everyday Christian life. 2 Fast as in high speed or velocity, may be used with anything that has a speed. 3 Fasting, abstaining from food, Acting, moving, or capable of acting or moving quickly; swift. Accomplished in relatively little time: a fast visit, Acquired quickly

Fast

with little effort and sometimes unscrupulously: made a fast buck scalping tickets. Quick to understand or learn; mentally agile: a class for the faster students, Indicating a time somewhat ahead of the actual time: The clock is fast. Allowing rapid movement or action: a fast running track, Designed for or compatible with a short exposure time: fast film. Above is just to avail you with the many meanings of the word *fast*. Fast or Fasting for the purpose of the gospel has to do with setting yourself aside and praying to dedicate yourself and purpose to the trinity – Our Heavenly father.

4 Note: the combination of fasting and praying is not a fad or a novelty approach to spiritual discipline. Fasting and praying are not part of a human-engineered method or plan. They are not the means to manipulate a situation or to create a circumstance. Fasting and praying are Bible-based disciplines that are appropriate for all believers of all ages throughout all centuries in all parts of the world. In (Matthew 6:16-18) "And when you *fast*, do not look gloomy like the hypocrites, for they disfigure their faces that their *fasting* may be seen by others. Truly, I say to you, they have received their reward. But when you fast, anoint your head and wash your face, that your *fasting* may not be seen by others but by your Father who is in secret. And your Father who sees in secret will reward you".Also,

5 Fasting in the gospel is going without food. The noun translated "fast" or "a fasting" is *tsom* in the Hebrew and *nesteia* in the Greek language. It means the voluntary abstinence from food. The literal Hebrew translation would be "not to eat." The literal Greek means "no food. To avail yourself with the reason why we fast see (Isaiah 58:3-7)

'Why have we fasted, and you see it not? Why have we humbled ourselves, and you take no knowledge of it?' Behold, in the day of your fast you seek your own pleasure, and oppress all your workers. Behold, you fast only to quarrel and to fight and to hit with a wicked fist. Fasting like yours this day will not make your voice to be heard on high. Is such the fast that I choose, a day for a person to humble himself? Is it to bow down his head like a reed, and to spread sackcloth and ashes under him? Will you call this a fast, and a day acceptable to the Lord? "Is not this the fast that I choose: to loose the bonds of wickedness, to undo the straps of the yoke, to let the oppressed go free, and to break every yoke? Is it not to share your bread with the hungry and bring the homeless poor into your house; when you see the naked, to cover him, and not to hide yourself from your own flesh?

No wonder Jesus fasted and prayed. Jesus' disciples fasted and prayed after the Resurrection. Many of the Old Testament heroes and heroines of the faith fasted and prayed. The followers of John the Baptist fasted and prayed. Many people in the early church fasted and prayed. What the Scriptures have taught us directly and by the examples of the saints is surely something we are to do for spiritual enhancement, empowerment and breakthroughs in all areas of life. Glory to Jesus!

Father: A male Parent, who has raised a child, supplied the sperm through sexual intercourse or sperm donation which grew into a child, and/or donated a body cell which resulted in a clone. The adjective "paternal" refers to a father and comparatively to "maternal" for a mother. A father delights in the son or children as in (Proverbs 3:11-12) "My son, do not despise the LORD's discipline and do not resent his rebuke, because the LORD disciplines those he loves, as a father the son he delights in". 2 A father have compassion on the Children as commanded by God. (Psalm 103:13) "As a father has compassion on his children, so the LORD has compassion on those who fear him";

Father, To: (verb) To procreate or to sire a child from which also derives the noun "fathering". Fathers determine the sex of their child through a sperm cell which either contains an X chromosome (female), or Y chromosome (male). Related terms of endearment are dad, daddy, pa, papa, poppa, pop, and pops. A male role-model that children can look up to is sometimes referred to as a father-figure. 2 To father also means to love, cherished, provides, adore, joy with, mourn with, console, chastised, prune, see (Proverbs 23:24) The father of the righteous will greatly rejoice; he who fathers a wise son will be glad in him.

Father, Adopted or Adoptive: (a·dopt·ed, a·dopt·ing, a·dopts) 1 To take into one's family through legal means and raise as one's own child. 2 To take and follow (a course of action, for example) by choice or assent: adopt a new technique. b. To take up and make one's own: adopt a new idea. 3 To take on or assume: adopted an air of importance. 4 To vote to accept: adopt a resolution.

Father, My: *See father*

Father, Our: Our father in Heaven or our heavenly father – Christ. The Lord's Prayer, also called the *Our Father* which is a venerated Christian prayer that, according to the New Testament, was taught by Jesus to his disciples. Two forms of it are recorded in the New Testament: a longer form in the Gospel of (Matthew 6:5–13) as part of the Sermon on the Mount, and a shorter form in the Gospel of (Luke[11:1–4) as a response by Jesus to a request by "one of his disciples" to teach them "to pray as John taught his disciples". The prayer concludes with "deliver us from evil" in Matthew, and with "lead us not into temptation" in

Luke. The first three of the seven petitions in Matthew address God; the other four are related to our needs and concerns. The liturgical form is the Matthean. Some Christians, particularly Protestants, conclude the prayer with a doxology, a later addendum appearing in some manuscripts of Matthew. The prayer as it occurs in (Matthew 6:9–13) Our Father in heaven, hallowed be your name. Your kingdom come, your will be done, on earth, as it is in heaven. Give us this day our daily bread, and forgive us our debts, as we also have forgiven our debtors. And lead us not into temptation, but deliver us from evil". Again, (Luke 11:2–4) Father, hallowed be your name. Your kingdom come. Give us each day our daily bread, and forgive us our sinsfor we ourselves forgive everyone who is indebted to us. And lead us not into temptation'. Also see (2 Thessalonians 1:2) "To the church of the Thessalonians in God *our Father* and the Lord Jesus Christ: 2 Grace to you and peace from God the Father and the Lord Jesus Christ".

Father, Spiritual: Father in the Lord (often as a title or form of address) a priest. "pray for me, father" synonyms: priest, pastor, parson, clergyman, father confessor, churchman, man of the cloth, man of God, cleric, minister, preacher;

Father, your: A standard set by Jesus as a condition of a Childs responsibility to the parent as a pre – condition for long life and every favours. (Ephesians 6:2) "Honour *your father* and mother"--which is the first commandment with a promise—Father is singled out here as the Head of the House hold as Jesus is the Head of the Church. It is the responsibility of the sons and daughters to claim, own and be proud or someone else to infer to the perents as "Your father or mother.

Fear: An emotion induced by a threat perceived by living entities, which causes a change in brain and organ function and ultimately a change in behaviour, such as running away, hiding or freezing from traumatic events. Fear may occur in response to a specific stimulus happening in the present, or to a future situation, which is perceived as risk to health or life, status, power, security, or in the case of humans wealth or anything held valuable. The fear response arises from the perception of danger leading to confrontation with or escape from/avoiding the threat (also known as the fight-or-flight response), which in extreme cases of fear (horror and terror) can be a freeze response or paralysis. In humans and animals, fear is modulated by the process of cognition and learning. Thus fear is judged as rational or appropriate and irrational or inappropriate. An irrational fear is called a phobia. This hypothesized set includes such emotions as joy, sadness, fright, dread, horror, panic, anxiety, acute stress reaction and anger.

Fear should be distinguished from, but is closely related to, the emotion anxiety, which occurs as the result of threats which are perceived to be uncontrollable or unavoidable. The fear response serves survival by generating appropriate behavioural responses, as it has been preserved throughout evolution.

Fear of the Lord, The: The whole idea of living in respect, awe, and submission to a deity or Holy Spirit. Christianity Roman Catholics count this fear as one of the Seven gifts of the Holy Spirit. In (Proverbs 1:7) and (Proverbs 9:10), the fear of the Lord is called the beginning or foundation of wisdom.

2 The Fear of the Lord (God) is felt because one understands the "fearful expectation of judgement" (Hebrews 10:27). Still, this is not a fear that leads one to despair, rather it must be coupled with trust, and most importantly, love. In Psalms 130:3-4, it is said, "If you, O Lord, kept a record of sins, O Lord, who could stand? But with you there is forgiveness; therefore you are feared." The first mention of the fear of God in the Hebrew Bible is in (Genesis 22:12), where Abraham is commended for putting his trust in God. The New Testament book of Hebrews comments on this event by explaining, "Abraham, when he was tested, offered up Isaac, and he who had received the promises was in the act of offering up his only son, of whom it was said, 'Through Isaac shall your offspring be named.' He considered that God was able even to raise him from the dead, from which he did receive him back." (Hebrew 11:17-19). Because of this many Christians conclude that Abraham's fear of God was an act of trust in God, that God would give Isaac back to Abraham. Others believe that Abraham's fear of the Lord (God) was his willingness to obey Him, even though it would mean losing his Son. Many Jews and Christians believe the fear of the Lord (God) to be devotion itself, rather than a sense of being frightened of God. It can also mean fear of God's judgment. The fear of God is described in (Proverbs 8:13) as "the hatred of evil." Throughout the Bible it is said to bring many rewards. Conversely, not fearing God is said to result in Divine retribution. Some translations of the Bible, such as the New International Version, sometimes replace the word "fear" with "reverence". This is because the Fear of the Lord incorporates more than simple fear. "There is the convergence of awe, reverence, adoration, honour, worship, confidence, thankfulness, love, and, yes, fear."

3 The main Hebrew and Greek words translated fear in the Bible can have several shades of meaning, but in the context of the fear of the Lord, they convey a positive reverence. The Hebrew verb yare

Feast

can mean "to fear, to respect, to reverence" and the Hebrew noun yirah "usually refers to the fear of God and is viewed as a positive quality. This fear acknowledges God's good intentions (Exodus. 20:20). ... This fear is produced by God's Word (Psalm. 119:38; Proverbs. 2:5) and makes a person receptive to wisdom and knowledge (Proverbs. 1:7; 9:10)" The Greek noun 'phobos' can mean "reverential fear" of God, "not a mere 'fear' of His power and righteous retribution, but a wholesome dread of displeasing Him", "Fear, Fearful, Fearfulness"). This is the type of positive, productive fear Luke describes in the early New Testament Church: "Then the churches throughout all Judea, Galilee, and Samaria had peace and were edified. And walking in the fear of the Lord and in the comfort of the Holy Spirit, they were multiplied" (Acts 9:31, emphasis added) one resource includes this helpful summary: "The fear of God is an attitude of respect, a response of reverence and wonder. It is the only appropriate response to our Creator and Redeemer" (Psalm 128:1).

Feast: A day or days specially set apart for religious observances, an ancient practice common to all religions (including Christianity though not a religion like others). The number of feast in the Roman Catholic and Greek Churches is extensive but after the Reformation, the Church of England retain only a limited number of feast days. 2 The feast in the Christian Calendar have been divided in various ways, one of which is to group them as movable or immovable. Simply, all Sundays are feast days. The four quarter days represent the chief immovable feasts days. – Namely, the Annunciation of Lady Day, (25 March) the Nativity Day of Saint John the Baptist (24 June) Michael mass Day (29 September) Christmas (25 December) followed also with the Naming of Jesus. Formerly known as the Circumcision (1 January), Epiphany (6 January), All Hallows Day (1 November), There exists also the various Apostles Days and the anniversaries of martyrs and saints. 3 The movable feast are those that depend on Easter Day. Also among them are the Sundays after the Epiphany, Septuagesima Sunday, the Sunday of Lent, Rogation Sunday, Ascension Day, Pentecost or Whitsunday, Trinity Sunday and The Sundays after Trinity. The main Christian biblical feast identified in the gospel of Christ includes the Feast of Passover, Unleavened bread, First Fruits, The Shavout (Pentecost), Feast of Trumpets, The Yom Kippur (Day of Atonement) and the Succoth (Feast of the Tabernacle)

Feast of Passover: This originated from the Liberation from the slavery in Egypt. (Exodus 12-23) "The blood of the lamb protects against the destroyer, the Angel of Death. „He will see the blood on the top and sides of the door frame and will pass over that doorway, and he will not permit the destroyer to enter your houses and strike you down." (Exodus 12:23) A flawless male lamb, one year old. (Exodus 12,5) A male lamb (sheep or goat), one year old: Not a helpless little lamb No bone of the lamb may be broken. (Exodus 12:46) Other characteristics of the feast of Passover are; Done on the fourteenth day of the first month (Nisan) in the afternoon, the Seder (a special meal) is prepared. In the evening, it will be eaten: A lamb, bitter herbs and unleavened bread (matzoth). (Exodus 12:8) Note Since the destruction of the temple 70 AD, the lamb is left out. (Exodus. 12,21-51, Numbers 28,16-25, Joshua 3,5-7 and 5,2-6)

Passover (Hebrew - Pesah) means „to pass over, to skip" matzoth are served. The middle one will be broken in two, and one half hidden. After the meal, the children are sent out to find it. Then, every member of the family eats a small piece. This half of the middle matzoth is called **AFIKOMEN**. Rabbinical tradition has two different explanations: 3 Matzoth: Priests, Levites and Israelites the people) or Abraham, Isaac and Jacob The fulfilment of the feast of Passover is recorded in the Liberation from the slavery of Satan, of sin. So if the Son sets you free, you will be free indeed. (John 8:36) Through the blood of Jesus, we have eternal life. Whoever hears my word and believes him who sent me has eternal life and will not be condemned; he has crossed over from death to life. (John 5,24) For you know that it was not with perishable things such as silver or gold that you were redeemed from the empty way of life handed down to you from your forefathers, but with the precious blood of Christ, a lamb without blemish or defect. (1 Peter 1:18-19) Jesus was without fault: or God made him who had no sin to be sin for us, so that in him we might become the righteousness of God. (2.Cor 5,21) No bone of Jesus has been broken. (John 19,31-36) The trinity of God — 3 matzoth: Father, Son and Holy Spirit The Messiah — the middle matzoth Jesus body is broken for us all (Lord supper) **AFIKOMEN** can be traced back to the Greek word *afikomen*. It is the 1. person plural aorist active of *afikneomai* and means **We Came**

NOTE:. Jesus body is covered with stripes and is pierced. (1Peter 2:24 and John 19:34). He says: I am the bread of life. (John 6:48) If anyone eats of this bread, he will live for ever. (John 6:51) He has been born in the house of bread (Bethlehem) and was put in a vessel, which is designed to eat out of it (manger).

Feast of Unleavened Bread:
This means; For seven days you are to eat bread made without yeast. On the first day remove the yeast from your houses. (Exodus 12:15) Also, on the night before Passover eve, the house is searched for yeast (or leaven), and all which is found will be burnt. Each day

Feast of First Fruit

(Psalm 113 – 118) are recited: This is known in Hebrew as **HALLEL On** starting the 15 day. of Nissan, exclusively unleavened bread is eaten for 7 days. Yeast, a symbol for sin is eliminated! *Jesus body is buried (put into the ground): Unleavened bread (he was without sin).* I tell you the truth, unless a grain of wheat falls to the ground and dies, it remains only a single seed. But if it dies, it produces many seeds. (John 12,24)

Feast of First Fruit: When you enter the land I am going to give you and you reap its harvest, bring to the priest a sheaf of the first grain you harvest. He is to wave the sheaf before the LORD so it will be accepted on your behalf; the priest is to wave it on the day after the Sabbath. (Leviticus 23,10-11) In biblical times and today again, on the first day after Passover - Holiday (Sabbath), the feast of First fruits is celebrated. This is fulfilled in Jesus resurrection as the First fruit. Indeed He is the First Fruit. But Christ has indeed been raised from the dead, the first fruits of those who have fallen asleep. (1. Corinthians 15:20)

> The word „Easter" goes back to a Teutonic or Germanic or Anglo-Sax godhead Eostera". Behind this is the Babylonian goddess „Ishtar.

Feast of Shavout: (Penticost) Feast of Trumpets: The first time, Moses received the ten commandments on stone tablets and the whole law about 7 Weeks after the death of the Passover lambs in Egypt (Exodus 19). When Moses approached the camp and saw the calf and the dancing, his anger burned and he threw the tablets out of his hands, breaking them to pieces at the foot of the mountain. The Levites did as Moses commanded, and that day about **three** thousand of the people died. (Exodus 32:19-28) Israel has been born as a nation through the gift of the law

rom the day after the Sabbath, the day you brought the sheaf of the wave offering, count off seven full weeks. Count off fifty days up to the day after the seventh Sabbath, and then present an offering of new grain to the LORD. (Leviticus 23,15-16) From wherever you live, bring **two loaves** made of two tenths of an ephah of fine flour, baked with **yeast**, as a wave offering of first fruits to the LORD. (Leviticus 23,17) From wherever you live, bring two loaves made of two tenths of an ephah of fine flour, baked with **yeast**, as a wave offering of first fruits to the LORD. (Leviticus 23:17) Celebrate the Feast of Harvest with the first fruits of the crops you sow in your field. (Exodus 23:16) Sivan: Commemoration of the giving of the law Exodus 19:1 – 20:23 and Ezekiel 1:1-28 and 3:12. "I looked, and I saw a windstorm coming out of the north-- an immense cloud with flashing lightning and surrounded by brilliant light. The centre of the fire looked like glowing metal". (Ezekiel 1:4) Shavuot (Hebrew) means „weeks": The Feast of Weeks. Pentecost goes back to the Greek pentecont „fifty". (The Jews start counting „Omer" the 16. Nissan. They count the 50 days.) With many other words he warned them; and he pleaded with them, "Save yourselves from this corrupt generation." Those who accepted his message were baptised, and about three thousand were added to their number that day. (Acts 2:40-41) Because through Christ Jesus the law of the Spirit of life set me free from the law of sin and death. (Romans 8:2) 3000 Men came to true life!

The disciples received the Holy Spirit (Acts 2) - The law of life in your heart The Church of Jesus has been born through the gift of the Holy Spirit. Suddenly a sound like the blowing of a violent wind came from heaven and filled the whole house where they were sitting. They saw what seemed to be tongues of fire that separated and came to rest on each of them. All of them were filled with the Holy Spirit and began to speak in other tongues as the Spirit enabled them. (Acts 2,2-4) Trough the gift of the Holy Spirit, the Church has been created. It does not consist of people, who are without sin, but they are all „baked with yeast". Nobody but Jesus alone was without sin! Two loaves: Gentiles and Jews!? Harvest of first fruits: The Church of Jesus Christ is emerging!

Feast of Yom Kippur (Day of Atonement):

(Leviticus 16:29) mandates establishment of this holy day on the 10th day of the 7th month as the day of atonement for sins. It calls it the Sabbath of Sabbaths and a day upon which one must afflict one's soul. Thus "This is to be a lasting ordinance for you: On the tenth day of the seventh month you must deny yourselves and not do any work—whether native-born or a foreigner residing among you".(Leviticus 23:27) decrees that Yom Kippur is a strict day of rest. 2This is the holiest day of the year for the Jewish people. Its central themes are atonement and repentance. Jewish people traditionally observe this holy day with an approximate 25-hour period of fasting and intensive prayer, often spending most of the day in synagogue services. It must be done within the context of God's commandments to Moses. Thus, The LORD spoke to Moses, saying, "On exactly the tenth day of this seventh month is the day of atonement; it shall be a holy convocation for you, and you shall humble your souls and present an offering by fire to the LORD".

Feast of Succoth (Feast of Tabernacles, Feast of Dedication, Festival of Lights, or The Hanukkah): This is the seventh and final feast given to Israel. Sukkot is observed in the fall from 15th to 22nd of Tishi. It is one of the Three Pilgrimage Festivals *(shalosh regalim)* on which the Israelites would make a pilgrimage to the Temple in Jerusalem.

2 The holiday lasts seven days in Israel and eight in the diaspora. The first day (and second day in the diaspora) is a Shabbat-like holiday when work is forbidden, followed by intermediate days called (Chol Hamoed). The festival is closed with another Shabbat-like holiday called (Shemini Atzeret) (two days in the diaspora, where the second day is called (Simchat Torah). Note: The Hebrew word sukkot is the plural of sukkah, "booth" or "tabernacle", which is a walled structure covered with s'chach (plant material such as overgrowth or palm leaves). The sukkah is intended as a reminiscence of the type of fragile dwellings in which, according to the Torah, the Israelites dwelt during their 40 years of travel in the desert after the Exodus from slavery in Egypt. Throughout the holiday, meals are eaten inside the sukkah and some people sleep there as well.

On each day of the holiday it is mandatory to perform a waving ceremony with the Four Species.

A sukkah is also for the temporary dwelling in which agricultural workers would live during harvesting.

Fellowship: Friendliness and companionship based on shared interest. 2 A group of people meeting to pursue a shared interest or aim – According to the context, a group of Christians meeting to pray together in order to dismantle the works of Satan and attain expected victory. As (Ecclesiastes 4:9-12) declared thus "Two are better than one, because they have a good reward for their toil. For if they fall, one will lift up his fellow. But woe to him who is alone when he falls and has not another to lift him up! Again, if two lie together, they keep warm, but how can one keep warm alone? And though a man might prevail against one who is alone, two will withstand him—a threefold cord is not quickly broke" Also (1 John 1:3) has this to say about *fellowship* "That which we have seen and heard we proclaim also to you, so that you too may have *fellowship* with us; and indeed our *fellowship* is with the Father and with his Son Jesus Christ."

Fight: (*"Fight" and "Fighting"*) This is an act of Combat or fighting which also is a purposeful violent conflict meant to weaken, establish dominance over, or kill the opposition, or to drive the opposition away from a location where it is not wanted or needed. The term *combat* (French for *fight*) typically refers to armed conflict between opposing military forces in warfare, whereas the more general term "fighting" can refer to any violent conflict between individuals or nations. Combat violence can be unilateral, whereas fighting implies at least a defensive reaction. However, the terms are often used synonymously along with the term "Battle Ready". A large-scale fight is known as a battle. (Galatians 5:19-24) Now the works of the flesh are evident: sexual immorality, impurity, sensuality idolatry, sorcery, enmity, strife, jealousy, fits of anger, rivalries, dissensions, divisions, envy drunkenness, orgies, and things like these. I warn you, as I warned you before, that those who do such things will not inherit the kingdom of God. But the fruit of the Spirit is love, joy, peace, patience, kindness, goodness, faithfulness, gentleness, self control; against such things there is no law. And those who belong to Christ Jesus have crucified the flesh with its passions and desires.

Firebrands, Smoldering stumps of: (Isaiah 7:4) – Be careful, be quiet, do not fear and do not let your heart be faint because of these two stumps of firebrands at the fierce anger of Razin and Syria and the son of Remaliah.

Firmament: The sky as conceived as a solid dome. According to Genesis, God created the firmament to separate the "waters above" the earth from those below. And God said, "Let there be a vault between the waters to separate water from water." The word is anglicized from Latin *firmamentum*, which appears in the Vulgate.

The word "firmament" is first recorded in a Middle English narrative based on scripture dated 1250. It later appeared in the King James Bible. The word is anglicised from Latin *firmamentum*, used in the Vulgate (4th century). This in turn is derived from the Latin root *firmus*, a cognate with "firm The word is a' Latinization' of the Greek *'stereoma'*, which appears in the Septuagint (c. 200 BC). In the translation edition, the word "firmament" is used to translate *raqia*, or *raqiya,`* used commonly in Biblical Hebrew. The connotation of firmness conveyed by the Vulgate's *firmamentum* is consistent with that of *stereoma*, the Greek word used in the Septuagint, an earlier translation. The notion of solidity is advanced explicitly in several biblical passages The original word *raqia* is derived from the root *raqa* , meaning "to beat or spread out", e.g., the process of making a dish by hammering thin a lump of metal. *Raqa* adopted the meaning "to make firm or solid" in Syriac, a major dialect of Aramaic (the vernacular of Jesus) and close cognate of Hebrew.

Conservatives and fundamentalists tend to favour translations that allow gospel to be harmonized with scientific knowledge, for example "expanse". This translation is used by the New International Version and by the English Standard Version. The New Revised Standard Version uses "dome", as in the Celestial dome. Then God said, "Let there be a *firmament* in the midst of the waters, and let it divide the waters from the waters." Thus God made the *firmament*, and divided the waters which were under the *firmament* from the waters which were above the *firmament;* and it was so. And God called the firmament Heaven. So the evening and the morning were the second day. (Genesis 1:6-7)

"Then God said, "Let there be an expanse in the midst of the waters, and let it separate the waters from the waters." God made the expanse, and separated the waters which were below the expanse from the waters which were above the expanse; and it was so...."

2 It please God if you appreciate the work of His hands when you reference the work of His Hands in your prayers - like David who acknowledges the *firmament* in (Psalm 19:1) "The heavens declare the glory of God; the skies proclaim the work of his hands" and. (Psalm 33:6) 'By the word of the LORD the heavens were made, their starry host by the breath of his mouth'.

First and the Last, The:
(phrase) Popularly as the Alpha and Omega – the beginning and the end – showing Jesus as our only Eternal Father, His uniqueness, His Sovereign creation and as our Eternal Saviour. Without Him, there is no other God. Note that the phrase is expanded later in the book. As Revelation is concluded, the Lord affirms: "I am the Alpha and the Omega, *the first and the last,* the beginning and the end" (Revelation 22:13; Also 21:6). This is a clear declaration of the eternal nature of Christ, hence, his deity. We are complete "in Christ" (Colosian. 2:10). We have no need for the mediation of angels or "saints," and no refinement from councils or popes is required. Everything to sustain us is in the gospel package. "Thanks be to God for his unspeakable gift" (2 Corinthians. 9:15), who is the first and the last.

Firstborn: primogeniture, the concept that the first-born child inherits their parent's property. First born has priority over the fathers heritage. The term firstborn therefore has two main meanings. The first is more literal, referring to the fact that this son is the first son to be born of his father. The second meaning refers to the

First fruits

rights and authority of a person, because they are the firstborn. Our Lord is the "firstborn" in several ways,. But most of all He is the One who has been appointed by God to be in authority over all things (Colossians 1:13-23; especially verses 15, 18).Closely related is the expression "son" (which you see in (2 Samuel 7:14; Psalm 2:7-9 compare Psalm 110:1-3]; Hebrews 1:5-14). I understand the expressions, "Thou art My Son, Today I have begotten Thee" (Hebrews 1:5a) and "I will be a Father to Him, And He shall be a Son to Me" (Hebrews 5b) to be synonymous. This speaks not of the birth of our Lord (as though this were when He came into existence - for He is eternal as (John 1:1-3) indicate, but of His installation as King of the earth by His Father.

T he predication of christ as firstborn in the New Testament offers a challenge to christology's ancient and modern. One cannot help being impressed by the scope of this title. At his incarnation (Luke 2:7) Jesus is designated as mary's firstborn, an appellative connoting his consecration to God and possibly his rightful claim to the davidic throne. By his glorious resurrection, in which he was victorious over sin and death, he has become the "firstborn from among the dead" (Colossians 1:18) and now exercises sovereign sway over his redeemed people as the "firstborn from the dead" (Revelation 1:5). As the head of a new, redeemed humanity destined in the eschatological transfiguration to bear the impress of his image, he is the "firstborn among many brothers" (Romans 8:29). But the conception moves not only forward toward consummation but also, in the thought of Paul, backward into the realm of proctology (Colossians). In Paul's view all creation finds its reference point with respect to the "firstborn over all creation," "the heir of all things" (Hebrew 1:2, 6). Indeed, in the eschaton Christ is the integration point for all things (Ephesians 1:10). A Christology that falls short of this all- encompassing account. Praise the Lord of Host!

First fruits: These are a religious offering of the first agricultural produce of the harvest. In classical Greek, Roman, Hebrew and Christian religions, the first fruits were given to priests to offer to God. First Fruits were often a primary source of income to maintain the religious leaders and the facility. Beginning in 1966 a unique "First Fruits" celebration brought the Ancient African harvest festivals that became the African American Holiday, Kwanza. This reminded them that God will provide for their every need. 2 First fruits – an Episcopal tradition commanded by God to the Israelites in (Leviticus 23:10-14) "Speak to the people of Israel and say to them, When you come into the land that I give you and reap its harvest, you shall bring the sheaf of the first fruits of your harvest to the priest, and he shall wave the sheaf before the Lord, so that you may be accepted. On the day after the Sabbath the priest shall wave it. And on the day when you wave the sheaf, you shall offer a male lamb a year old without blemish as a burnt offering to the Lord. And the grain offering with it shall be two tenths of an ephah of fine flour mixed with oil, a food offering to the Lord with a pleasing aroma, and the drink offering with it shall be of wine, a fourth of a hin. And you shall eat neither bread nor grain parched or fresh until this same day, until you have brought the offering of your God: it is a statute forever throughout your generations in all your dwellings. 3 First fruits – (Greek - *apache*): In Classical Athens the First Fruits were called an offering of *apache*. Except during times of war, this would be a major source of funds for the temples of the Eleusinian goddesses, Demeter and Kore. Much of the agricultural offering was sold by the temple with the proceeds being used to pay for the daily upkeep of the temple complex. Under Pericles' rule, it became a way of extending Athens' power. The *Demos* or voting citizens would control the operation of the temple by elected boards. During times of war or for other necessity the Demos would borrow money from the treasury of the temple. Neighbouring cities under Athens' control were required to give offerings from their harvests. This served to enrich Athens and extend her power. Much of this was shown in the temple reports which were carved in stone when the governing body (called the *epistatai*) of the temple changed hands. In the stone age 386-387 it can be seen how the finances of the Eleusinian temples worked. Doctor Maureen B. Cavanaugh who translated stone IG I^3 386-387, argues that there were heavy implications of the funding realized from the First Fruits donations to the temple, in particular that it brought significant impact on Athenian power. This is noted in a loan cited in the stone record, of over 20,000 silver drachmas to the city. The Eleusinian temple complex was more than just a temple to Demeter; there were living quarters, storage, workshops, administration as well as public spaces. It was a major institution, functioning almost like a city within a city.

First Fruits in Israel: In Ancient Israel, First Fruits were a type of terumah that was akin to, but distinct from, terumah gedolah. While terumah gedolah was an agricultural tithe, *Bikkurim* (discussed in the Bikkurim tractate of the Talmud) were a sacrificial gift brought up to the altar. (Bikkurim 3:12). The major obligation to bring First Fruits (Hebrew. *Bikkurim*) to the Temple began at the festival of Shavuot and continued until the festival of Sukkot. (Bikkurim 1:6). This tithe was limited to the traditional seven agricultural products (wheat, barley, grapes in the form of wine, figs, pomegranates, olives in the form of oil, and dates) grown in Israel. This tithe, and the associated festival of Shavuot, is legislated by the Torah. Textual critics speculate that these regulations were imposed long after the offerings and festival had developed.

Flesh: The soft substance of a human or other animal body that consists of muscle and fat; for vertebrate, this especially includes muscle tissue (skeletal muscle), as opposed to bones and viscera. *Flesh* may be used as food, in which case it is commonly called meat. For the purpose of the gospel in (Galatians 5:16-17) Christians must live by the spirit as oppose to *flesh*. "But I say, walk by the Spirit, and you will not carry out the desire of the *flesh*. For the *flesh* sets its desire against the Spirit, and the Spirit against the *flesh*; for these are in opposition to one another, so that you may not do the things that you please". Ensure all your desire please God. Because God is spirit and not flesh. As a worshipper of God, you must worship Him in Spirit and Truth. 2 In real gospel sense, fresh brings about the conflict in human experience between the sinful nature and the Spirit of God (Galatians 5:17) also in (Romans 8:4-9); (Galatians 5:19-25) 3 Fresh signifies the physical aspect of human beings, which distinguishes them from God and is therefore frequently used in the New Testament as a symbol of human sinful nature in contrast with God's perfection. (The Greek word for "flesh" is sometimes translated by other words and phrases in the gospel/biblical passages cited in many themes.)

Flesh **as the bodily substance of human beings:.** As individuals or in relation to others (Psalm 84:2) as in (Genesis 2:23-24); (Genesis 29:14); (1Corinthians 15:39) The following two examples from Paul, where the normal word for *"flesh"* underlies the translation "body", make clear that to live "in the flesh" is normal human experience; the phrase does not necessarily imply that human nature is sinful, even though in many other instances a specific connection between "flesh" and "sin" is intended: (Galatians 2:20); (Philippi 1:22-24) As the means by which Jesus Christ identified with the human race to bring salvation (John 1:14) See also (Ephesians 2:15); (Hebrew 10:20); (1John 4:2)

Flood, The: (noun) this represent an overflow of a large amount of water beyond its normal limits, especially over what is normally dry land." the villagers had been cut off by floods and landslides" synonyms: inundation, swamping, deluge; 2 Our focus point here is the biblical *flood* brought by God upon the earth because of the wickedness of the human race

Fool

(Genesis 6-9). In the narrative, one of many flood myths found in human cultures, indicates that God intended to return the Earth to its pre-Creation state of watery chaos by flooding the Earth because of humanity's misdeeds and then remake it using the microcosm of Noah's ark. Thus, the flood was no ordinary overflow but a reversal of creation. The narrative discusses the evil of mankind that moved God to destroy the world by the way of the flood, the preparation of the ark for certain animals, Noah, and his family, and God's guarantee (the Noah's Covenant) for the continued existence of life under the promise that he would never send another *flooded*. Significantly, the action by God re-affirms the supremacy of the Almighty God as the only one who can do more exceedingly beyond human expectation. He can destroy and build or build to destroy according to His desire. So God is 'God of divine Model and Transformation'.

Fool: One who is deficient in judgment, sense, or understanding? 2 One who acts unwisely on a given occasion: I was a fool to have quit my job. 3 One who has been tricked or made to appear ridiculous; a dupe: They made a fool of me by pretending I had won. 4 Informal A person with a talent or enthusiasm for a certain activity: a dancing fool; a fool for skiing. 5 A member of a royal or noble household who provided entertainment, as with jokes or antics; a jester. 6 One who subverts convention or orthodoxy or varies from social conformity in order to reveal spiritual or moral truth: a holy fool. 7 A dessert made of stewed or puréed fruit mixed with cream or custard and served cold. 8 Archaic A mentally deficient person; an idiot. (Note also: fooled, fooling, fools). In the gospel, fool regarded as "a senseless fellow, a dullard." The biblical definition has the added dimension of "someone who disregards God's Word." The Bible lists many characteristics of such a person, often contrasting him with one who is wise. (Ecclesiastes 10:2) says, "The heart of the wise inclines to the right, but the heart of the *fool* to the left." A *fool* is one whose wayward heart turns continually toward foolishness. "Fools speak foolishness and make evil plans" (Isaiah 32:6). (Proverbs 26:11) says, "As a dog returns to its vomit, so fools repeat their folly." Fools do not learn their lessons from the mistakes they make. They continue doing the same foolish things over and over again, to their own destruction (Proverbs 18:7).

The following is a partial list of some characteristics of a fool from the book of Proverbs: a fool hates knowledge (Proverbs 1:22), takes no pleasure in understanding (Proverbs 18:2), enjoys wicked schemes (Proverbs 10:23), proclaims folly (Proverbs 12:23), spurns a parent's discipline (Proverbs 15:5), speaks perversity (Proverbs 19:1), is quick-tempered

(Proverbs 12:16), gets himself in trouble with his proud speech (Proverbs 14:3), mocks at sin (Proverbs 14:9), is deceitful (Proverbs 14:8), and despises his mother (Proverbs 15:20). A foolish child brings grief to his or her parents (Proverbs 17:25; 19:13). A foolish man commits sexual immorality (Proverbs 6:32; 7:7–12). A foolish woman tears.

Foolish: *(adjective)* lacking good sense or judgement; unwise. "he was foolish enough to ignore the word of God" synonyms: stupid, silly, idiotic, half-witted, witless, brainless, mindless, thoughtless, imprudent, incautious, irresponsible, injudicious, indiscreet, unwise, unintelligent, unreasonable;

The Old Testament. Several Hebrew words are rendered "fool, " with nuances ranging all the way from the naive but teachable person (Proverbs 14:15, derived from the Hebrew root meaning "open, " hence impressionable) to the hopelessly incorrigible person who deserves no corrective efforts since such will be in vain (Proverbs 26:3). 2 The heaviest concentration of the Hebrew words referring to foolishness is in the Wisdom literature, where the fool is constantly contrasted with the wise. The fool is not so much stupid (except when the context demands such a meaning) as immoral and pernicious. The fool's problem is not so much intellectual as practical and spiritual. In fact, the terms "wise" and "fool" are used by the sages to designate respectively the faithful and the sinners. This characterization is well depicted in the competition between Wisdom and Folly for the attention and loyalty of the young man. Folly is a seductress who seeks to allure the young man away from the wife of his youth (Proverb 5:18). She personifies more than stupidity. She is immorality and adultery (Proverb 6:23-35 ; 7:6-27 ; 9:13-18). A foolish is the naive person who succumbs to amorous overtures. *(See fool above)*

Forgive: (verb) to stop feeling angry or resentful towards (someone) for an offence, flaw, or mistake. "I'll never forgive Mark for the way he ignore the pastor" synonyms: pardon, excuse, exonerate, absolve, acquit, let off, grant an amnesty to, amnesty; antonyms: blame, convict, resent no longer feel angry about or wish to punish (an offence, flaw, or mistake). "I was willing to forgive all her faults for the sake of our friendship and God" cancel (a debt). "he proposed that their debts should be forgiven" 2 Significantly, this is the centre of the Gospel of Salvation and deliverance. You cannot be delivered until you forgive someone you put in your heart as enemy. 3 Also, one of the purposes Jesus Christ submitted to the death on the Cross.

Christians do have questions about forgiveness. The act of forgiving does not come easy for most of

Fountain

us. Our natural instinct is to recoil in self-protection when we've been injured. We don't naturally overflow with mercy, grace and understanding when we've been wronged. To forgive therefore, means, to release the wrongdoer from the wrong, cut the malignant tumour out of your inner life, set a prisoner free, and discover that the real prisoner was yourself because you were a prisoner in your conscience during your vexation. Knowing that (Colossians 3:13) advised you to "Bear with each other and forgive whatever grievances you may have against one another. Forgive as the Lord forgave you". The following gospels will help you to forgive: (Mark 2:7-11) "Why does this man use such words?" they said; "He is blaspheming. Who can pardon sins but One-- that is, God?"... Jesus asked them, "Which is easier?--to say to this paralytic, 'Your sins are pardoned,' or to say, 'Rise, take up your mat, and walk?' But that you may know that the Son of Man has authority on earth to pardon sins"--He turned to the paralytic, and said, "To you I say, 'Rise, take up your mat and go home.'" Also Conditional Forgiveness as in (Mathew 6:12) "Forgive us the wrongs that we have done, as we forgive the wrongs others have done us." And (Luke 6:37) "...Forgive, and you will be forgiven." (Mathew 6:14-15) "For if you forgive men when they sin against you, your heavenly Father will also forgive you. But, if you do not forgive men their sins, your Father will not forgive your sins." In fancying all these conditions. You must forgive to be forgiven.

Fountain: A source or spring) is a piece of architecture which pours water into a basin or jets it into the air to supply drinking water and or for a decorative or dramatic effect. 2 Fountains were originally purely functional, connected to springs or aqueducts and used to provide drinking water and water for bathing and washing to the residents of cities, towns and villages. Until the late 19th century most fountains operated by gravity, and needed a source of water higher than the fountain, such as a reservoir or aqueduct, to make the water flow or jet into the air. In addition to providing drinking water, fountains were used for decoration and to celebrate their builders. Roman fountains were decorated with bronze or stone masks of animals or heroes. The baroque decorative *fountains* of Rome in the 17th and 18th centuries marked the arrival point of restored Roman aqueducts and glorified the Popes who built. In Psalm 36:9 David assert "For with You is the fountain of life; In Your light we see light." Here, David's portray (Hebrew. 'ain; i.e., "eye" of the water desert), a natural source of living water. Palestine was a "land of brooks of water, of *fountains*, and depths that spring out of valleys and hills" (Deuteronomy 8:7 ; 11:11). These *fountains*, bright sparkling "eyes" of the desert, are remarkable for their abundance and their beauty, especially on the west of Jordan. All the perennial rivers and streams of the country are supplied from *fountains,* and depend comparatively little on surface water. "Palestine is a country of mountains and hills, and it abounds in fountains of water. The murmur of these waters is heard in every dell, and the luxuriant foliage which surrounds them is seen in every plain." Besides its rain-water, its cisterns and *fountains*, Jerusalem had also an abundant supply of water in the magnificent reservoir called "Solomon's Pools" , at the head of the Urtas valley, whence it was conveyed to the city by subterrean channels some 10 miles in length. These have all been long ago destroyed, so that no water from the "Pools" now reaches Jerusalem. Only one *fountain* has been discovered at Jerusalem, the so-called "Virgins's *Fountain*s," in the valley of Kidron; and only one well (Hebrew beer), the Bir Eyub, also in the valley of Kidron, south of the King's Gardens, which has been dug through the solid rock. The inhabitants of Jerusalem are now mainly dependent on the winter rains, which they store in cisterns.

Foul: (adjective) offensive to the senses, especially through having a disgusting smell or taste or being dirty. "a foul odour" synonyms: disgusting, revolting, repellent, repulsive, repugnant, abhorrent, loathsome, offensive, detestable, awful, dreadful, horrible, terrible, horrendous, hideous, appalling, atrocious, vile, abominable, frightful, sickening, nauseating, nauseous, stomach-churning, stomach-turning, off-putting, uninviting, unpalatable, unappetizing, unsavoury, distasteful, nasty, obnoxious, objectionable, odious; and much more antonyms: fragrant informal very disagreeable or unpleasant. "the news had put Michelle in a foul mood" synonyms:unkind, unfriendly, disagreeable, inconsiderate, uncharitable, rude, churlish, spiteful, malicious, mean, mean-spirited, ill-tempered, ill-natured, ill-humoured, bad-tempered, hostile, vicious, malevolent, evil-minded, surly, obnoxious, poisonous, venomous, vindictive, malign, malignant, cantankerous, hateful, hurtful, cruel, wounding, abusive; and much More 2 wicked or immoral. "Murder most foul" The gospel/bible warns in (Ephesians 5:4) "Let there be no filthiness nor foolish talk nor crude joking, which are out of place, but instead let there be thanksgiving". And in (Ephesians 4:29) the bible say "Let no corrupting talk come out of your mouths, but only such as is good for building up, as fits the occasion, that it may give grace to those who hear". Moreso (Colossians 3:8-10) But now you must put them all away: anger, wrath, malice, slander, and obscene talk from your mouth. Do not lie to one another, seeing that you have put off the old self with its practices and have put on the new self, which is being renewed in knowledge after the image of its creator.

Frankincense

Every foul sayings should not occasioned in the speech of a Christian as it is warned against in (Colossians 4:6) "Let your speech always be gracious, seasoned with salt, so that you may know how you ought to answer each person". This does not show the sign of perfection since no man is perfect except God. But just to keep the rapport with God through faith. In short be faithful to His word.

Frankincense: Also called olibanum, is an aromatic resin obtained from trees of the genus Boswellia, particularly Boswellia sacra, B. carteri, B. thurifera, B. frereana and B. bhaw-dajiana (Burseraceae). There are four main species of Boswellia that produce true frankincense and resin from each of the four is available in various grades. The grades depend on the time of harvesting. The resin is hand-sorted for quality. Frankincense is mentioned in the Bible as one of the three types of gifts the wise men gave to the young child Jesus. The following reading from the gospels/bible are in support of frankincense. (Leviticus 24:7)
And thou shalt put pure frankincense upon each row, that it may be on the bread for a memorial, even an offering made by fire unto the LORD. (Numbers 5:15)
Then shall the man bring his wife unto the priest, and he shall bring her offering for her, the tenth part of an ephah of barley meal; he shall pour no oil upon it, nor put frankincense thereon; for it is an offering of jealousy, an offering of memorial, bringing iniquity to remembrance. (1 Chronicles 9:29)
Some of them also were appointed to oversee the vessels, and all the instruments of the sanctuary, and the fine flour, and the wine, and the oil, and the frankincense, and the spices.

Fraternity: In gospel organizations, this might be referred to a group of people sharing the same profession or interest, faith in worship; sharing support in groups. Members of the body of Christ. Christians are members of the fraternity of Christ. 2. This could also be divinely referred to the saints belonging to the same union with Christ values of sharing in the kingdom of God. Thus he (Christ is in you and you in him).

Fraternity of the God-kind: *(Phr)* Act of being in vital union with the Godhead. This is Christianity! That God bring man into his own class of being! No wander the Bible declares... "ye are gods and all of you are children of the most High." *(Psalm 82:6)* This means that true Christians are in vital union with the Godhead. You can clearly see and appreciate why you are superior to Satan, principalities, forces of darkness, sin, different forms of sicknesses, failure and death. All these are as a result of your fraternity with Deity. 2. In another biblical pantheon – An assembly of gods, thus 'ye are gods' – meaning in Hebrew 'Elohim' –*(Psalms 82:1)* and all of you are the children of the Most High. Christ divined initiative through his knowledge that 'human souls are in him just as He is in them. Acknowledging their position when they judge the people wrongfully as humans. Apparently they often mis-judged not as God's good judgement. The Hebrew word for "gods" (elohim) is literally "mighty ones" such as judges. They were called "gods" not because they represented God when they judged the people. They were only men not deities. But if they were to judge the people by the power of God they will assume the position of the "children of the Most High". As Christ (God alone possesses the power to judge. In this context, when divine power is given to true Christians, they form an assembly of "gods", headed by the Lord Jesus Christ. The Apostle Peter talk about it (2 Peter 1:4) 'Whereby are given unto us exceeding great and precious promises: that by this ye might be partakers of the divine nature, having escaped the corruption that is in the world through lust'. Note: The phrase "Partakers of the divine nature' here describes the believers in Christ as being in fraternal union with divinity. *(See Divine Nature)*

Friend (s): (Friendship) Simply a relationship of mutual affection between two or more people. Friendship is a stronger form of interpersonal bond than an association. Friendship has been studied in academic fields such as sociology, social psychology, anthropology, and philosophy. Various academic theories of friendship have been proposed, including social exchange theory, equity theory, relational dialectics, and attachment styles. A World Happiness Database study found that people with close friendships are happier. Note: (Proverbs 17:17) "A friend loves at all times, and a brother is born for adversity". Although there are many forms of friendship, some of which may vary from place to place, certain characteristics are present in many types of friendship. Such characteristics include affection, sympathy, empathy, honesty, altruism, mutual understanding and compassion, enjoyment of each other's company, trust, and the ability to be oneself, express one's feelings, and make mistakes without fear of judgment from the friend. While there is no practical limit on what types of people can form a friendship, friends tend to share common backgrounds, occupations, or interests, and have similar demographics. Christ has the highest number of friends in the whole universe, the only friend that can be trusted. (John 15:12-15) "My command is this: Love each other as I have loved you. Greater love has no one than this, that he lay down his life for his friends. You are my *friends* if you do what I command. I no longer call you servants, because a servant does. not know his master's business. Instead, I have called you *friends*, for everything that I learned from my

Furniture

Father I have made known to you". Since Christianity is a relationship, friendliness is building a strong relationship with members of the God Head – the trinity through faith in Christ Jesus as the Holy Spirit direct. Hallelujah!

Furniture: (Nahum 2:9) "Take ye the spoil of silver, take the spoil of gold: for there is none end of the store and glory out of all the pleasant furniture". *Furniture* (noun) the movable articles that are used to make a room or building suitable for living or working in, such as tables, chairs, or desks. synonyms: furnishings, house fittings, fittings, fitments, movables, fixtures, appointments, appliances, effects, chattels, amenities, units, equipment, paraphernalia; More 2 the small accessories or fittings that are required for a particular task or function. "the more sophisticated Mac furniture—number wheels, colour pickers, and so on" synonyms: furnishings, house fittings, fittings, fitments, movables, fixtures, appointments, appliances, effects, chattels, amenities, units, equipment, paraphernalia; In short, furniture represent Equipment in a home used for rest, beautification, storage, and work space. We take for granted the many objects of furniture all around us in our homes, offices, and churches. We associate them with basic human activities such as sleeping, sitting, eating, and socializing.

2 They serve our practical needs at almost any given moment in our daily lives. Often, they gratify our sense of beauty as well. The common people of biblical times had no such luxuries, and very few "necessities." Their homes would seem almost empty to us.

The gospel concern about furniture is the sense of sacredly. Those things consecrated or dedicated for the worship of God as when the Ark of covenant was set aside in the tabernacle for the will of God to manifest particularly when the Israelites goes to war (Exodus 31:7) "The tabernacle of the congregation, and the ark of the testimony, and the mercy seat that is thereupon, and all the furniture of the tabernacle". All the images, candle sticks - in terms of the Roman Catholic, incense, lights, lamps in the House of God are all furniture and must be kept sacred as in the following biblical verses (Genesis 31:34) Now Rachel had taken the images, and put them in the camel's *furniture,* and sat upon them. And Laban searched all the tent, but found *them not.* (Exodus 31:8) "And the table and his *furniture*, and the pure candlestick with all his furniture, and the altar of incense", (Exodus 31:9) "And the altar of burnt offering with all his *furniture*, and the laver and his foot", Exodus 35:14 "The candlestick also for the light, and his *furniture*, and his lamps, with the oil for the light",

Gg

Gabriel: (*Hebrew –gavri'el*) meaning-Man of God. One of the Arch-Angels, sometimes regarded as the Angel of death, the prince of fire and thunder, but more frequently as one of God's chief messengers and traditionally said to be the only angel who can speak Syriac and Chaldean. He is regarded as the Chief of the angelic guard place over Paradise.

Gad: There are two people in the bible named Gad. Gad the son of Jacob and Gad the prophet. Gad was the seventh son of Jacob. His mother was Zipah who was Leah's maid. He was the founder of the tribe of Gad. He made the journey with Jacob and family from Padan Aram to Canaan, and later to Egypt, in the census taken in the second year after the Exodus, the tribe of Gad alone numbered 46,550 (Numbers 2: 14-15) 2 At the time of the second census, there were 40,500 (Numbers 26:18). In the blessing of Jacob (Genesis 49:19) it is said "Gad a troop shall tramp upon him, but it shall triumph at last". 3 In the blessing of Moses (Deuteronomy 33:20), it is said "Blessed is he who enlarges Gad" and in (Revelation 7:1-8) Gad is among the tribes who are promised the Seal of God for 12,000 of its members. 4 The other Gad- the prophet- first appears in the Bible to persuade David to leave his place of safety in Moab and return to Judah, where the insanely jealous King Saul awaited him, later on, after David had a census taken of Israel, Gad gave David a choice of punishments from the Lord for carrying out the rash act. David chose the three day plague. During the plague which took 70,000 lives, Gad, the prophet, told David to build an altar to the Lord on the threshing floor of Araunah the Jebusites (2 Samuel 24:18) The burnt offerings from this altar, caused the Lord to stop the plague. The threshing floor, later, became the site of King Solomon's Temple. 5 In 2 Chronicles 29:25, Gad along with David and the prophet Nathan, 'stationed the Levite's in the Lord House with cymbals, harp and lyres, according to the prescriptions 'from the Lord through His prophets'. Gad is described as David's seer in 1 Chroni-

Galilee

cle 21:9. In short the true meaning of the name Gad is 'Good Fortune'.

Galilee: A Chapel or porch at the west end of some churches where penitent waited before admission to the body of the church and where clergy receive women who had business with them. Examples are at Durham, Ely and Lincoln Cathedrals. 2 The name has a biblical origin. Notably the land of Zebulon, and the land of Nephthalim, by the way of the sea, beyond Jordan Galilee of the Gentiles as in (Mathew 4:15 – 16) Thus "This was to fulfil what was spoken through Isaiah the prophet: "THE LAND OF ZEBULUN AND THE LAND OF NAPHTALI, BY THE WAY OF THE SEA, BEYOND THE JORDAN, GALILEE OF THE GENTILES-- "THE PEOPLE WHO WERE SITTING IN DARKNESS SAW A GREAT LIGHT, AND THOSE WHO WERE SITTING IN THE LAND AND SHADOW OF DEATH, UPON THEM A LIGHT DAWNED."...

Galilean: An inhabitant of Galilee, and specifically Jesus Christ who was called 'the Galilean'. 2 The term was also applied to Christians as His followers. 3 The dying words attributed to the Roman Emperor Julian the Apostate were *vicisti, O Galilaee* ('Thou hast conquered, O Galilean')

Gall of bitterness, The: (Acts 8:23) "For I perceive that thou art in *the gall of bitterness*, and *in* the bond of iniquity". The real bitterness, grief, extreme affliction. The ancient thought that grief and joy were subject to the gall, as affection was to the heart and knowledge was to the kidneys. 'The gall of bitterness' which means the bitter center of bitterness as the 'heart of heart' means the innermost recesses of the heart or affections. In Acts it is used to signify the 'sinfulness of sin' which leads to the bitterest grief.

Galilee, The Sea of: "The Sea of Galilee is indeed the cradle of the gospel. The subterranean fires of nature prepared a lake basin, through which a river afterwards ran, keeping its waters always fresh. In this basin a vast quantity of shell-fish swarmed, and multiplied to such an extent that they formed the food of an extraordinary profusion of fish. The great variety and abundance of the fish in the lake attracted to its shores a larger and more varied population than existed elsewhere in Israel, whereby this secluded district was brought into contact with all parts of the world. And this large and varied population, with access to all nations and countries, attracted the Lord Jesus, and induced him to make this spot the center of his public ministry."

2 This sea is chiefly of interest as associated with the public ministry of our Lord. Capernaum, "his own city" (Matt. 9:1), stood on its shores. From among the fish-

ermen who plied their calling on its waters he chose Peter and his brother Andrew, and James and John, to be disciples, and sent them forth to be "fishers of men" (Matt. 4:18,22; Mark 1:16-20; Luke 5:1-11). He stilled its tempest, saying to the storm that swept over it, "Peace, be still" (Matt. 8:23-27; Mark 7:31-35); and here also he showed himself after his resurrection to his disciples. 3 The Sea of Galilee is situated in northeast Israel, between the Golan Heights and the Galilee region, in the Jordan Rift Valley, the valley caused by the separation of the African and Arabian Plates. Consequently the area is subject to earthquakes, and in the past, volcanic activity. This is evident by the abundant basalt and other igneous rocks that define the geology of the Galilee. 4 According to the gospels, Jesus' earthly ministry centered around the Sea of Galilee. While important events occurred in Jerusalem, the Lord spent most of the three years of His ministry along the shore of this freshwater lake. Here He gave more than half of His parables and here He performed most of his miracles... Capernaum, on the north western shore, became Jesus' "hometown" throughout His ministry. Three of His disciples hailed from Bethsaida, a few miles distant from Capernaum. These two cities, together with Chorazin 3 km (2 mi) inland from Capernaum, were condemned by Jesus for receiving much but believing little. A famous follower of Christ was Mary of Magdala, a town on the lake's western shore. Early Christians hallowed the lakeside, building churches commemorating the feeding of the five thousand, the Sermon on the Mount, the primacy of Peter, and the house of Peter. It is Known in the Hebrew Bible as Chinnereth, Josephus used the Hellenized form of this name, Gennesar or Gennesaritis, most frequently in his writings. Luke uses this term, but the more common New Testament designation is the familiar "Sea of Galilee." John twice refers to it as the "Sea of Tiberias." Pliny notes that some called it Tarichaeae after the name of ano**ther** town along its shore. *The Sea of Galilee* is the lowest freshwater lake on earth.

Gate: (Psalm 24:7-10 KJV) "Lift up your heads, O ye *gates*; and be ye lift up, ye everlasting doors; and the King of glory shall come in. Who is this King of glory? The Lord strong and mighty, the Lord mighty in battle. Lift up your heads, O ye *gates*; even lift them up, ye everlasting doors; and the King of glory shall come in. Who is this King of glory? The Lord of hosts, he is the King of glory". Selah. In ordinary meaning, a gate is a point of entry to a space enclosed by walls, or a moderately sized opening in some sort of fence. Gates may prevent or control the entry or exit of individuals, or they may be merely decorative. Other terms

Gate

for *gate* include yett and port. The word derives from the old Norse "gata", meaning road or path, and originally referred to the gap in the wall or fence, rather than the barrier which closed it. The moving part or parts of a gateway may be called "doors", but used for the whole point of entry door usually refers to the entry to a building, or an internal opening between different rooms. A *gate* may have a latch to keep it from swinging and a lock for security. Larger gates can be used for a whole building, such as a castle or fortified town, or the actual doors that block entry through the gatehouse. Today, many gate doors are opened by an automated gate operator. 2 Many forms of gates are designed for entry and exits. But the gospel clearly speaks about the song so sang by the choir; as originated by David in the, Psalm, calling upon the gates to throw themselves wide open to their full height, that free entrance might he given to the approaching sacred fabric. And be ye lift up, ye everlasting doors. Pleonastic, But giving the emphasis of repetition, and adding the epithet "everlasting," because the tabernacle was viewed as about to be continued in the temple, and the temple was designed to be God's house "for ever" (1 Kings 8:13). And the King of glory shall come in. God was regarded as dwelling between the cherubim on the mercy-seat, where the Shekinah from time to time made its appearance. The entrance of the ark into the tabernacle was thus the "coming in of the King of glory." 3 Apart from other meanings to the *gate* of the physical temple, this implies the Spiritual temple in the body of every Christian – the 'Hearts'. It is a mighty *gate* because it is the dwelling place of good and evil. But as a Christian you need to through your heart widely open for the King of Glory to come in and dwell with you so that evil thought will vanish giving way for His Glory to dwell and continue living with you till eternity. His historical manifestation here upon earth and His Incarnation, which is the true dwelling of Deity amongst men, are not enough. They have left something more than a memory to the world. He is as ready to abide as really within our spirits as He was to tabernacle upon earth amongst men. And the very central message of that Gospel which Is proclaimed to us all is this, that if we will open the *gates* of our hearts He will come in, in all the plenitude of His victorious power, and dwell in our hearts, their Conqueror and their King.

4 What a strange contrast, and yet what a close analogy there is between the victorious tones and martial air of the gospel message. 'Lift up your heads, O ye *gates*! that the King of Glory may come in,' and the gentle words of the Apocalypse: as in (Revelation 3:20) 'Behold, I stand at the door and knock; if any man hear My voice and open the door, I will come in to him.' But He that in the

Old Covenant arrayed in warrior arms, summoned the rebels to surrender, is the same as He who, in the New, with the night-dews in His hair, and patience on His face, and gentleness in the touch of His hand upon the door, waits to enter in. Brethren! Open your hearts, note: your heart is the *gate* of your body 'and the King of Glory shall come in.'

The Jewish interpreters understand the phrase of the *gates* of the temple, which David prophetically speaks of as to be opened, when it should be built and dedicated by Solomon, and when the ark, the symbol of Jehovah's presence, was brought into it, and the glory of the Lord filled the house; so the Tar gum interprets this first clause of "the gates of the house of the sanctuary"; though the next of "the gates of the garden of Eden"; but the words are better interpreted, in a mystical and spiritual sense, of the church of God, the temple of the living God, which is said to have gates, (Isaiah 60:11); and is itself called a door, (Songs of Solomon 8:8-9) "We have a little sister, And she has no breasts; What shall we do for our sister On the day when she is spoken for? "If she is a wall, We will build on her a battlement of silver; But if she is a door, We will barricade her with planks of cedar." Here the open door of the Gospel is set, or an opportunity of preaching the Gospel given, and a door of utterance to the ministers of the word, and the doors of men's hearts are opened to attend to it; and indeed the hearts of particular believers, individual members of the church, may be intended, or at least included in the sense of the passage; see (Revelation 3:20); and it may be observed, that the new Jerusalem is said to have gates of pearl, through which Christ, when he makes his glorious appearance, will enter in his own glory, and in his father's, and in the glory of the holy angels;

The answer to the summons comes from the choir within. 'Who is this King of Glory?' the question represents ignorance and possible hesitation, as if the pagan inhabitants of the recently conquered city knew nothing of the God of Israel, and recognised no authority in His name. Of course, the dramatic form of question and answer is intended to give additional force to the proclamation as by God Himself of the Covenant name, the proper name of Israel's God, as Baal was the name of the Canaanite's God, 'the Lord strong and mighty; the Lord mighty in battle,' by whose warrior power David had conquered the city, which now was summoned to receive its conqueror. Therefore the summons is again rung out, 'Lift up your heads, O ye gates! and the King of Glory shall come in.' And once more, to express the lingering reluctance, ignorance not yet dispelled, suspicion and unwilling surrender, the dramatic question is repeated, 'Who is this King of Glory?' The answer is sharp and

Gennesaret

authoritative in its brevity, and we may fancy it shouted with a full-throated burst-'The Lord of Hosts,' who, as Captain, commands all the embattled energies of earth and heaven conceived as a disciplined army. That great name, like a charge of dynamite, bursts the gates of brass asunder, and with triumphant music the procession sweeps into the conquered city. The what next? The Lord sit in His Holy Temple. Then the whole earth of the body, mind soul and Spirits, remained silence for Him and only Him alone as all Glory to His name is given to His Honour, and Power in His Majesty! Amen

Gennesaret: Otherwise known as "a garden of riches" was a town allotted to the tribe of Naphtali, called "Kinnereth" (Joshua 19:35), sometimes in the plural form "Kinneroth" (Joshua 11:2). In later times the name was gradually changed to Genezareth, Genezar and Gennesaret (Luke 5:1). No trace of the Gennesaret city remains. A city on the north western shore of the lake to which it gave its name: Lake of Gennesaret. It was perhaps half way between Capernaum and Mandala. The name is the Grecized form of "Chinnereth." The equivalent names are the Sea of Galilee or Lake Tiberias. The name is also used for the "Plain of Gennesaret". For beauty and fertility it is called "the Paradise of Galilee." Its modern name is el-Ghuweir because of its beautiful and fertile soil. This city or area is also a place where Jesus visited and performed healing according to the Gospel of (Matthew 14 34-36) "And having passed the water, they came into the country of Genesar. And when the men of that place had knowledge of him, they sent into all that country, and brought to him all that were diseased. And they besought him that they might touch but the hem of his garment. And as many as touched, were made whole".

Gethsemane: (Greek: Gethsēmanē; Hebrew: Gat-Šmânim;) Meaning 'oil press. ' Gethsemane is a garden at the foot of the Mount of Olives in Jerusalem most famous as the place where, according to the gospels, Jesus prayed and his disciples slept at *Gethsemane* the night before Jesus' crucifixion . 2 Gethsemane appears in the Greek of the Gospels of Matthew and Mark as (Gethsēmanē). The name is derived from the Aramaic (Ga☐-Šmānê), meaning "oil press". (Matthew 26:36-38) "Then Jesus went with his disciples to a place called Gethsemane, and he said to them, "Sit here while I go over there and pray." He took Peter and the two sons of Zebedee along with him, and he began to be sorrowful and troubled. Then he said to them, "My soul is overwhelmed with sorrow to the point of death. Stay here and keep watch with me."and

Gethsemane, Event at: Here the betrayer handed Jesus or delivers Jesus to sinners so that they may crucify Him as in (Mark 14:32 – 42) They went to a place called Gethsemane, and Jesus said to his disciples, "Sit here while I pray." He took Peter, James and John along with him, and he began to be deeply distressed and troubled. "My soul is overwhelmed with sorrow to the point of death," he said to them. "Stay here and keep watch." Going a little farther, he fell to the ground and prayed that if possible the hour might pass from him. "Abba,(a) Father," he said, "everything is possible for you. Take this cup from me. Yet not what I will, but what you will." Then he returned to his disciples and found them sleeping. "Simon," he said to Peter, "are you asleep? Couldn't you keep watch for one hour? 38 Watch and pray so that you will not fall into temptation. The spirit is willing, but the flesh is weak." Once more he went away and prayed the same thing. When he came back, he again found them sleeping, because their eyes were heavy. They did not know what to say to him. Returning the third time, he said to them, "Are you still sleeping and resting? Enough! The hour has come. Look, the Son of Man is delivered into the hands of sinners. Rise! Let us go! Here comes my betrayer!" In (Mark 18:1), Gethsemane is called a place or estate. The Gospel of John says Jesus entered a garden with his disciples. What Christians should note here is that without Jesus being in Gethsemane, the Gospel story would not fulfilled as the important aspect of submission, obedience, crucifixion and death on the cross which all were the complement of the passion of Christ to eternal Glory was carried out. So *Event at Gethsemane* really forms root to Christianity.

Ghost, Holy: Also known as the Holy Spirit or is the third person (hypostasis) of the Trinity: the "Triune God" manifested as Father, Son, and Holy Spirit; each person itself being God. The New Testament includes over 90 references to the Holy Spirit. The sacredness of the Holy Spirit is affirmed in all three Synoptic Gospels which proclaim blasphemy against the Holy Spirit as the unforgivable sin. The Holy Spirit plays a key role in the Pauline epistles. In the Johannine writings, three separate terms, "Holy Spirit", "Spirit of Truth", and "Paraclete" are used. The New Testament details a close relationship between the Holy Spirit and Jesus during his earthly life and ministry. The Gospels of Luke and Matthew and the Nicene Creed state that Jesus was "conceived by the Holy Spirit, born of the Virgin Mary". The Holy Spirit descended on Jesus as a dove during his baptism, and in his Farewell Discourse after the Last Supper Jesus promised to send the Holy Spirit to his disciples after his departure. Many practice today in most Christian Churches have deviated greatly to use the sign of a dove to represent Holy Spirit. That the Bible explain that the Holy Spirit or Holy Ghost descended in a the form of a dove on Jesus Head while He was Baptise

Gideon

is symbolic of the power and Glory – the Beauty of Holiness with pressure and fastness that came from above to the Head of Jesus. Though the pressured image must have resemble the image of a dove but was not really a dove but the spirit from the trinity.

2 The theology of the Holy Spirit is called pneumatology. The Holy Spirit is referred to as the Lord and Giver of Life in the Nicene Creed. The participation of the Holy Spirit in the tripartite nature of conversion is apparent in Jesus' final post-Resurrection instruction to his disciples at the end of the Gospel of (Matthew (28:19): "make disciples of all the nations, baptizing them into the name of the Father and of the Son and of the Holy Spirit". Since the first century, Christians have also called upon God with the name "Father, Son and Holy Spirit" in prayer, absolution and benediction.

3 Today, no one can see God nor have communion with the father without the Holy Ghost. Another comforter which Christ promised and have long send Him to dwell with us. Hallelujah! There are numerous Bible verses that stressed the importance of Holy Ghost in our life as Christians but only a few are presented here for your spirit you can read up your Bible to discover more.

(Acts 2:38) - Then Peter said unto them, Repent, and be baptized every one of you in the name of Jesus Christ for the remission of sins, and ye shall receive the gift of the Holy Ghost. (Acts 19:6) - And when Paul had laid [his] hands upon them, the Holy Ghost came on them; and they spake with tongues, and prophesied. (Acts 2:4) - And they were all filled with the Holy Ghost, and began to speak with other tongues, as the Spirit gave them utterance. (Acts 1:5) - For John truly baptized with water; but ye shall be baptized with the Holy Ghost not many days hence. (Luke 11:13) - If ye then, being evil, know how to give good gifts unto your children: how much more shall [your] heavenly Father give the Holy Spirit to them that ask him? (John 3:5) - Jesus answered, Verily, verily, I say unto thee, Except a man be born of water and [of] the Spirit, he cannot enter into the kingdom of God. (Ephesians 1:13) - In whom ye also [trusted], after that ye heard the word of truth, the gospel of your salvation: in whom also after that ye believed, ye were sealed with that holy Spirit of promise, (Acts 2:1-47) - And when the day of Pentecost was fully come, they were all with one accord in one place. (Acts 1:8) - But ye shall receive power, after that the Holy Ghost is come upon you: and ye shall be witnesses unto me both in Jerusalem, and in all Judaea, and in Samaria, and unto the uttermost part of the earth.

Gideon: (Hebrew: Giḏʻeôn), *meaning* "Destroyer," "Mighty warrior," or "Gideon was a Feller (of trees)" was, according to the

Gilgal

gospel as contained in the Hebrew Bible, a judge of the Israelites. His story is recorded in Judges 6 to 8.. He is also named in Hebrew 11 as a man of faith to show example to believers.

Gilead: (Hebrew – Gil ad) Hill of testimony. It is derived from galyed, which in turn comes from gal (heap, mound, hill) and ?êd (witness, testimony). There also exists an alternative theory that it means rocky region.

2 *Gilead* is also used as the name for a location in various parts of the Bible. The first time it is used in the Bible is called "the mountain of Gilead." Later it is just called "Gilead," or the "land of Gilead." all three of these expressions refer to a region in Transjordan, approximately 20 by 60 miles in area. The cities of Gilead, according to (Numbers 32), were inhabited by the tribes of Gad and Reuben after the Israelite invasion of Transjordan, after the expulsion of the native Amorites. Also, it can be regarded as a "land" or "mountain," Gilead is called a city in (Hosea 6:8): Thus "Gilead is a city of those who work iniquity; it is stained with blood."

Gilgal: A place where the Israelites first encamp after the Exodus after having crossed the Jordan River (Joshua 4:19 - 5:12). After setting up camp, Joshua orders the Israelites to take twelve stones from the river, one for each tribe, and place them in memory at *Gilgal*. Otherwise described by some gospel story writers as Gibeath Haaraloth – otherwise known as "Hill of foreskins" where Joshua orders all new birth during the Exodus to be circumcised. Research is still going on to reveal more facts.

2 Gilgal, is mentioned in 39 verses in the Bible. One of those verses is(2 Kings 2:1)—the start of a story about the prophet Elijah being taken up to heaven in a whirlwind while the prophet Elisha, his apprentice, looks on (2 Kings 2). The name Gilgal has been associated by Gospel or Bible scholars with at least five different possible locations in and around the Holy Land, all with great uncertainty. But as we will see, it seems likely that "Gilgal" is not a town name at all. Instead, it is likely a word for a particular type of human-made site. In recent decades archeologists have made some exciting new discoveries of ancient "Gilgal" sites!

3 *Gilgal* is first mentioned in (Deuteronomy 11:30) "As you know, these mountains are across the Jordan, westward, toward the setting sun, near the great trees of Moreh, in the territory of those Canaanites living in the Arabah in the vicinity of *Gilgal*". It gains its primary meaning and significance in the book of Joshua as the first camp of the Israelites after they crossed the Jordan into the Holy Land. This camp served as their base of operations during the initial conquest of the Holy Land

Give

under Joshua. Several other important events in the Bible take place either at this *Gilgal* or at a different one. Eventually, though, Gilgal became corrupt, and two of the prophets railed against it later in Israel's history.

Give: *(gave – past tense, given, giving – present cont.,)* Many definition of the verb *give* is identified, but for the purpose of the gospel dictionary, we shall evaluate the meaning principally in two category – gospel usage and ordinary application.

1 In the gospel and even in ordinary sense, *give* is to freely transfer the possession of (something) to (someone). You can give someone material things or kindness. Give God the Glory that belongs to Him! "she gave him presents and clothes" synonyms: present with, provide with, supply with, furnish with, gift with;

(John 3:16) "For God so loved the world that he *gave* his one and only Son, that whoever believes in him shall not perish but have eternal life". This is one of the most widely quoted gospel verses from the Christian Bible and has been called the most famous Bible verse. It has also been called the "Gospel in a nutshell", because it is considered a summary of the central theme of traditional Christianity. In everything given, a purpose or fulfilment is expected. If you give food to someone, the aim is to stop hunger. You give water to someone , it is to stop thirst and so forth.

2 God having so loved the world gave His one and only son or His only begotten son that who so ever believeth in Him shall not perish but have eternal life! The purpose of giving His son therefore is fulfilled when you as a Christian receive and maintain life in eternity. God take delight in good and obedient Children who ultimately pursues eternal life through every principles of righteousness and obedience to the living word as in Proverbs 28:27 "He who gives to the poor will not want, but he who hides his eyes [from their want] will have many a curse". As an act of encouragement to the practice of gift, the gospel as contained in the Amplified Bible in (Luke 6:38) reiterate "Give, and [gifts] will be given to you; good measure, pressed down, shaken together, and running over, will they pour into [the pouch formed by] the bosom [of your robe and used as a bag]. For with the measure you deal out [with the measure you use when you confer benefits on others], it will be measured back to you". As another big giving text, (Malachi 3:10) states "Bring all the tithes (the whole tenth of your income) into the storehouse, that there may be food in My house, and prove Me now by it, says the Lord of hosts, if I will not open the windows of heaven for you and pour you out a blessing, that there shall not be room enough to re-

ceive it".

3 There are many gospel verses from the Bible that the subject of 'give' is treated. But a few is cited hereunder for your edification:

Honor the Lord with your capital and sufficiency [from righteous labors] and with the firstfruits of all your income. (Proverbs 3: 9) [Remember] this: he who sows sparingly and grudgingly will also reap sparingly and grudgingly, and he who sows generously [that blessings may come to someone] will also reap generously and with blessings. (2 Corinthians 9: 6) Let each one [give] as he has made up his own mind and purposed in his heart, not reluctantly or sorrowfully or under compulsion, for God loves (He takes pleasure in, prizes above other things, and is unwilling to abandon or to do without) a cheerful (joyous, "prompt to do it") giver [whose heart is in his giving]. (2 Corinthians 9: 7) Every man shall give as he is able, according to the blessing of the Lord your God which He has given you. (Deuteronomy 16: 17) Give to him who keeps on begging from you, and do not turn away from him who would borrow [at interest] from you. (Matthew 5: 42) If you then, evil as you are, know how to give good and advantageous gifts to your children, how much more will your Father Who is in heaven [perfect as He is] give good and advantageous things to those who keep on asking Him! (Matthew 7: 11) Cure the sick, raise the dead, cleanse the lepers, drive out demons. Freely (without pay) you have received, freely (without charge) give. (Matthew 10: 8) And my God will liberally supply (fill to the full) your every need according to His riches in glory in Christ Jesus. (Philippians 4: 19) In everything I have pointed out to you [by example] that, by working diligently in this manner, we ought to assist the weak, being mindful of the words of the Lord Jesus, how He Himself said, It is more blessed (makes one happier and more to be envied) to give than to receive. (Acts 20: 35)

In ordinary usage, the correspondence to giving are several antonyms: receive, accept, take, withhold hand over (an amount) in payment; pay. "how much did you give for that?" used hyperbolically to express how greatly one wants to have or do something. "I'd give anything for a cup of tea" synonyms: sacrifice, give up, relinquish; commit or entrust. "a baby given into their care by the accident of her birth" synonyms: entrust, commit, put into someone's hands, consign, assign, render; formal commend "a baby given into their care" freely set aside or devote for a purpose. "all who have given thought to the matter agree" dated (of a man) sanction the marriage of (his daughter) to someone. "he gave her in marriage to a noble" dated (of a woman) consent to have sexual intercourse with (a man). "she was

Give

a woman who would not give herself to a man lightly" 2. cause or allow (someone or something) to have or experience (something); provide with. "you gave me such a fright" synonyms:allow, permit, let have, grant, accord; More provide (love or other emotional support) to. "his parents gave him the encouragement he needed" allow (someone) to have (a specified amount of time) for an activity or undertaking. "give me a second to bring the car around" pass on (an illness or infection) to (someone). "I hope I don't give you my cold" pass (a message) to (someone). "give my love to all the girls" synonyms: convey, pass on, impart, communicate, transmit, transfer; More make a connection to allow (someone) to speak to (someone else) on the telephone. "give me the police" 3. carry out or perform (a specified action). "I gave a bow" synonyms: perform, execute, carry out; More produce (a sound). "he gave a gasp" synonyms: utter, let out, emit; More present (an appearance or impression). "he gave no sign of life" provide (a party or social meal) as host or hostess. "a dinner given in honour of an American diplomat" synonyms: organize, arrange, lay on, provide, be responsible for; More 4.yield as a product or result. "milk is sometimes added to give a richer cheese" synonyms: produce, yield, afford, result in; More emit odour, vapour, or similar substances. "some solvents give off toxic fumes" synonyms: e m i t, produce, send out, send forth, pour out, throw out; More 5.concede (something) as valid or deserved in respect of (someone). "give him his due" allot (a score) to. "I gave it five out often"place a specified value on (something). "he never gave anything for French painting" sentence (someone) to (a specified penalty). "for the first offence I was given a fine" (of an umpire or referee) declare whether or not (a player) is out or offside. "Gooch was given out, caught behind" adjudicate that (a goal) has been legitimately scored. "the referee gave the goal" 6. state or put forward (information or argument). "he did not give his name" pledge or offer as a guarantee. "I give you my word" say to (someone) as an excuse or inappropriate answer. "don't give me any of your backchat" synonyms: administer, deliver, deal; More deliver (a judgement) authoritatively. "I gave my verdict" informal predict that (an activity or relationship) will last no longer than (a specified time). "this is a place that will not improve with time—I give it three weeks" informal tell what one knows. "okay, give—what's that all about?" 7. alter in shape under pressure rather than resist or break. "that chair doesn't give" yield or give way to pressure. "the heavy door didn't give until the fifth push" synonyms: g i v e way, cave in, collapse, break, fall apart, come apart; More NORTH AMERICANinformal concede defeat; surrender."I give!"

Giver: (noun) Simply, a person who gives something. "a giver of advice" synonyms: donor, contributor, donator, benefactor, benefactress, provider; God is a giver of life. As God's people, we should be *givers,* not only at the Christmas season, but as a way of life. *Givers* are blessed because they are freed from greed, they are being conformed to Jesus, they have enduring relationships with others, and they will reap eternal rewards. Givers are Blessed as in (Acts 20:33-38) " I coveted no one's silver or gold or apparel. You yourselves know that these hands ministered to my necessities and to those who were with me. 35 In all things I have shown you that by working hard in this way we must help the weak and remember the words of the Lord Jesus, how he himself said, 'It is more blessed to give than to receive.'" And when he had said these things, he knelt down and prayed with them all. And there was much weeping on the part of all; they embraced Paul and kissed him, being sorrowful most of all because of the word he had spoken, that they would not see his face again. And they accompanied him to the ship".

Glad Tidings: Happy news. I'm not sure I'd use the phrase glad tidings in your example at all, to be honest. I wouldn't be giving good news to people who strive, but some kind of reward or praise. The birth of a Child is glad tidings to the hearer. The Saviour is born in Bethlehem is glad tidings to all true Christians as in (Luke 2: 11-12) "But the angel said to them, "Do not be afraid; for behold, I bring you good news of great joy which will be for all the people; 11for today in the city of David there has been born for you a Saviour, who is Christ the Lord. "This will be a sign for you: you will find a baby wrapped in cloths and lying in a manger."... inside glad tidings or good news is the ingredient of salvation, redemption, victory, relief, liberty, power, glory, wisdom, might love, affection, harmony and everlasting life.

Gloria in Excelsis Deo: (Latin) Meaning "Glory to God in the highest") is a hymn known also as the Greater Doxology (as distinguished from the "Minor Doxology" or Gloria Patri) and the Angelic Hymn. The name is often abbreviated to 'Gloria in Excelsis' or simply Gloria. The hymn begins with the words that the angels sang when the birth of Christ was announced to shepherds in (Luke 2:14). "Glory to God in the highest heaven, and on earth peace to those on whom his favour rests." Other verses were added very early, forming a doxology, 2 In today's Greek text the song or *Gloria in Excelsis Deo* is translated thus: 'Glory to you who has shown us the light. Glory to God in the highest and on earth peace, goodwill to all people. We praise you, we bless you, we worship you, we glorify you, we give thanks to you for your great glory. Lord, King, heavenly God, Father,

Glory

almighty; Lord, the only-begotten Son, Jesus Christ, and Holy Spirit. Lord God, Lamb of God, Son of the Father who take away the sin of the world, have mercy on us, you who take away the sins of the world. Receive our prayer, you who sit at the right hand of the Father, and have mercy on us. For you only are holy, only you are Lord Jesus Christ, to the glory of God the Father. Amen. Each day we bless you, and we praise your name forever and to the ages of ages'.

Glory: (noun, *Hebrew – Kabod*) There are many meanings to the word Glory. In ordinary meaning, it is high renown or honour won by notable achievements. "to fight and die for the glory of one's nation" synonyms: renown, fame, prestige, honour, distinction, kudos, eminence, pre-eminence, acclaim, acclamation, celebrity, praise, accolades, laurels, recognition, note, notability, credit, repute, reputation, name, illustriousness, lustre; More antonyms: shame, obscurity magnificence or great beauty. "the train has been restored to all its former glory" synonyms: magnificence, splendour, resplendence, grandeur, majesty, greatness, impressiveness, gloriousness, nobility, pomp, stateliness, sumptuousness, opulence, beauty, elegance, brilliance, gorgeousness, splendidness "a late 17th century house restored to its former glory" antonyms: lowliness, modesty a thing that is beautiful, impressive, or worthy of praise plural noun: glories "the glories of Paris" synonyms: or 2 Gospel wise, wonder, beauty, delight, wonderful thing, glorious thing, marvel, phenomenon; the splendour and bliss of heaven. "images of Christ in glory" praise, worship, and thanksgiving offered to God. synonyms: praise, worship, glorification, adoration, veneration, honour, reverence, exaltation, extolment, homage, tribute, thanksgiving, thanks, blessing; More 4. a luminous ring or halo, especially as depicted around the head of Christ or a saint. Verb The idea of "glory" and the "glory of God" occurs throughout the Bible, so we might do well to reflect on this datum of revelation for a few moments.

3 In the Hebrew Bible the word for "glory" (kabod) originally meant weightlessness. If something was heavy and large it was important, like a mountain, and so it inspired respect. The basis of glory could be riches. Abraham was said to be "very glorious" because he possessed cattle, silver and gold (Genesis 13:2)."And Abram was very rich in cattle, in silver, and in gold".

Glory of the Lord: This is synonymous with the Glory of God. The phrase *"glory of the Lord"* occurs 38 times in the New Advance Standard Bible and 36 times in the King James Version. Glory is synonymous with splendour,

Glory of the Lord

honour, praise, worthiness, etc. The phrase is used to describe the manifestation of God's greatness (Exodus. 16:10) and is seen as a consuming fire (Exodus. 24:17), a cloud (1Kings 8:11), radiance (Ezekiel 1:26-28), and brightness (Ezekiel. 10:4). It fills the tabernacle (Exodus. 40:34) and can be seen (Numbers. 16:42), and can bring fear (Luke 2:9). See also Glory of God. Also in (Isaiah 40:5) And the glory of the LORD will be revealed, and all people will see it together. For the mouth of the LORD has spoken." Again in (Ezekiel 43: 1-5) "Then he led me to the gate, the gate facing east. And behold, the *glory of the God* of Israel was coming from the east. And the sound of his coming was like the sound of many waters, and the earth shone with his glory. And the vision I saw was just like the vision that I had seen when he[a] came to destroy the city, and just like the vision that I had seen by the Chebar canal. And I fell on my face. As the glory of the Lord entered the temple by the gate facing east, the Spirit lifted me up and brought me into the inner court; and behold, the glory of the Lord filled the temple".

2 The Expression *"the glory of the Lord"* means God himself insofar as he is revealed in his majesty, his power and his holiness. He manifests himself in two ways: in his lofty deeds and by his appearances to Abraham, Moses and the prophets of old. God showed his glory especially in the miracle of the Red Sea (Exodus 14:18) and also the manna and the quail (Exodus 16:7). The divine appearances are normally accompanied with disturbances of nature, such as thunder, lightning, fire, earthquakes, clouds. These phenomena manifest the glory of God; the cloud that surrounds the glory is there for the protection of man, for no man can see God and still live (Exodus 33:20). *The glory of God*, in the form of a cloud, filled the Tent of Meeting where Moses spoke with the Lord (Exodus 33:9). It also filled "the house of the Lord" that Solomon built (1 Kings 8:10-11). As time went on the idea of God's glory developed in the prophets from clouds and fire to the notion of illumination. We find this in Ezekiel 1 and Isaiah 60.

3 After the Exile (537 B.C.), the Jews came more and more to realize that the power of the Lord extended over the whole world. Thus his glory is shown in his dominion over all nations and all creatures. The Psalms often called upon all creatures to praise the glory of the Lord . But the one passage in the Old Testament to which the "coming in glory" of the Creed refers, more than to all others, is the description of the "son of man" in the prophet (Daniel 7:13-14): "I saw one like a son of man coming on the clouds of heaven... He received dominion, glory and kingship; nations and peoples of every language serve him." This passage is commonly interpreted as referring to Jesus Christ who will "come in glory to judge the living and the dead".

Gnat

4 Glory in the sense of majesty, power, dominion, illumination, holiness belongs primarily to God. Men like Moses or the saints can share in the *glory of God* by doing his will and by growing in virtue. Isaiah says that "all the earth is filled with his glory" (Isaiah 6:3). *The glory of God* in this sense can mean: the divine protection, and the praise that creatures give to God because of his glory. The sense of this text from Isaiah is that all creatures reflect the wisdom and perfection of God. And by their very existence, as a reflection of God's perfection, they give praise to their Creator. Man alone among all creatures on earth gives praise to *the glory of God* not only by his physical existence, but also by consciously acknowledging the goodness and the love of God.

Gnat: A gnat is any of many species of tiny flying insects in the Dipteral suborder Nematocera, especially those in the families Mycetophilidae, Anisopodidae and Sciaridae. In British English, the term applies particularly to Nematocerans of the family Culicidae (mosquitoes). The common gnat is the species Culex pipiens. Male gnats often assemble in large mating swarms or ghosts, particularly at dusk. Gnat larvae are mostly free-living and some are aquatic. Many feed on plants, though some are carnivorous. Larval plant feeders (such as the Hessian fly larva) cause root, stem, or leaf galls to be formed by the host plant. Some species of fungus gnats (families Mycetophilidae and Sciaridae) are pests of mushrooms and roots of potted plants in homes and greenhouses. Gnat is used in the scripture to describe the action of Scribe and Pharisees in (Mathew 23:23-25) "Woe to you, scribes and Pharisees, hypocrites! For you tithe the mint and dill and cumin, and have neglZ\ected the weightier provisions of the law: justice and mercy and faithfulness; but these are the things you should have done without neglecting the others. "You blind guides, who strain out a gnat and swallow a camel! "Woe to you, scribes and Pharisees, hypocrites! For you clean the outside of the cup and of the dish, but inside they are full of robbery and self-indulgence. Here, the phrase of "straining a gnat and swallowing a camel" can linguistically be thought of as, "You bother straining a gnat from your water, but you still swallow a camel anyway". Which means what it sounds like. "You bother to be all neat and clean about what you like, but what you don't pay attention to you will take by the heap."

2 Jesus is criticizing the Pharisees for obsessing over small details of their laws while ignoring the big and important matters. In the same passage, he says that they "tithe mint and dill and cumin, and have neglected the weightier matters of the law, justice and mercy and faith." They made a big show out of observing all of the holy days, giving to the temple, etc., but then they were unjust, treated

other people badly, and ignored God in many parts of their lives. As we can see, majority of Christians today have forgotten the basic ingredients of the gospel. Love is no more being practiced to the fullest and the joy of salvation through repentance of sin have been ignored as many preaching dwells solely on the so called comfort gospel were iniquity and repentance from sins are ignored. Souls are not won because the preaching centralised from the Christians to the Christians alone. People from other religions whose religions are not Christianity are not loved, preached for, converted to conversion and baptised. Therefore neighbours are not love as Christians loved themselves. Churches discriminates against members outside the same ministry. Those who practice these things are like the Pharisees and Scribes who embraced minor laws and forget the main or big issues affecting the poor and the oppress. Remember these were some of the reasons Christ came to save.

God: A Spirit being that could be seen and worshipped only in the Spirit and in truth vide the words of Jesus to the Samaritan woman as in (John 4:24) "God is spirit, and those who worship Him must worship in spirit and truth." In the Christian point of view, this imply that God is the creator, owner of what He created and supreme ruler of the universe. (Jeremiah 23:24); (Psalm 102:25-27); (Revelation 22:13) The Heavenly father to all believers in the Gospel of Christ – True Christians. That is why in Christianity and other monotheistic religions) God is known as the creator, ruler of the universe and source of all moral authority; He is the supreme being.

2 *God* is self-sufficient and self-existent: God does not expect anything to from anyone to complement His fullness and does not depend His existence on anyone else rather all thing, all people, all race depends upon Him. as in (Exodus 3:13-14); "Moses said to God, "Suppose I go to the Israelites and say to them, 'The God of your fathers has sent me to you,' and they ask me, 'What is his name?' Then what shall I tell them?" God said to Moses, "I am who I am.[a] This is what you are to say to the Israelites: 'I am has sent me to you.'" Also read (Psalm 50:10-12; Colossians 1:16)

3 God is omnipresent: He is present everywhere as in (Psalm 139:7-12) "Where can I go from your Spirit? Where can I flee from your presence If I go up to the heavens, you are there; if I make my bed in the depths, you are there. If I rise on the wings of the dawn, if I settle on the far side of the sea, even there your hand will guide me, your right hand will hold me fast. If I say, "Surely the darkness will hide me and the light become night around me," even the darkness will not be dark to you;

God is omnipotent

the night will shine like the day, for darkness is as light to you". Also, in (Jeremiah 23:24); Thus "Can any hide himself in secret places that I shall not see him? saith the Lord If a man should hide himself in the most secret and hidden places of the earth, and do his works in the most private manner, so that no human eye can see him, he cannot hide himself or his actions from the Lord, who can see from heaven to earth, and through the darkest and thickest clouds, and into the very bowels of the earth, and the most hidden and secret recesses and caverns of it. The darkness and the light are both alike to him; and also near and distant, open and secret places: do not I fill heaven and earth? saith the Lord; not only with inhabitants, and with other effects of his power and providence; but with his essence, which is everywhere, and is infinite and immense, and cannot be contained in either, or be limited and circumscribed by space and place; .

4 God is omnipotent: This adjective could be used for the description of a deity meaning having unlimited power. "God is described as omnipotent and benevolent" which is synonymous to all-powerful, almighty, supreme, most high, pre-eminent; having great power and influence. "an omnipotent sovereign". This is the quality of having unlimited power. Monotheistic religions generally attribute omnipotence to only the deity of their faith. In the monotheistic philosophies of Abrahamic religions, omnipotence is often listed as one of a deity's characteristics among many, including omniscience, omnipresence, and Omni benevolence. The presence of all these properties in a single entity has given rise to considerable theological debate, prominently including the problem of theodicy, the question of why such a deity would permit the manifestation of evil. Also, the term omnipotent has been used to connote a number of different positions. These positions include, but are not limited to, the following: A deity is able to do anything that it chooses to do. A deity is able to do anything that is in accord with its own nature (thus, for instance, if it is a logical consequence of a deity's nature that what it speaks is truth, then it is not able to lie). Hold that it is part of a deity's nature to be consistent and that it would be inconsistent for a deity to go against its own laws unless there was a reason to do so. More so, a deity can bring about any state of affairs which is logically possible for anyone to bring about in that situation. A deity is able to do anything that corresponds with its omniscience and therefore with its world plan. Every action performed in the world is 'actually' being performed by the deity, either due to omni-immanence, or because all actions must be 'supported' or 'permitted' by the deity. Indeed. He is all powerful as in His promise to Sarah (Genesis 18:14) "Is anything too hard for the LORD? I will return to you at the appointed time next year, and Sarah will have a son." (Luke 18:27) "Jesus replied, "What is impossible with man is possible with God." Also in (Revelation 19:6) "And I heard as it were the voice of a great multitude, and as the voice of many waters, and as the voice of mighty thunderings, saying, Alleluia: for the Lord God omnipotent reigneth".

5 God is Omniscient: (All knowing).

God has the capacity to know everything that there is to know. In particular, Christianity, and other religions) believe that there is a divine being who is omniscient. An omniscient point-of-view, in the gospel, is to know everything that can be known about a character, including past history, thoughts, feelings, etc. In Latin, omnis means "all" and sciens means "knowing". Although, there is a distinction between inherent omniscience —which is the ability to know anything that one chooses to know and can be known and total omniscience —that is actually knowing everything that can be known.

Some modern Christian theologians argue that God's omniscience is inherent rather than total, and that God chooses to limit his omniscience in order to preserve the freewill and dignity of his creatures. Many 16th century theologians are comfortable with the definition of God as being omniscient in the total sense, in order for worthy beings' abilities to choose freely in order to embrace the doctrine of predestination as in (Psalm 139:2-6) "You know when I sit down and when I rise up; you discern my thoughts from afar.

You search out my path and my lying down and are acquainted with all my ways. Even before a word is on my tongue, behold, O Lord, you know it altogether You hem me in, behind and before, and lay your hand upon me. Such knowledge is too wonderful for me; it is high; I cannot attain it. (Isaiah 40:13-14) thus' "Who can fathom the Spirit[a] of the Lord, or instruct the Lord as his counsellor? Whom did the Lord consult to enlighten him, and who taught him the right way?

Who was it that taught him knowledge, or showed him the path of understanding? No one can instruct the Lord. He is the God of all encompassing and overwhelming knowledge.

6 God is Eternal.

(Deuteronomy 33:27; thus "The eternal God is your shelter, and his everlasting arms support you. He will force your enemies out of your way and tell you to destroy them". (GW) (Jeremiah 10:10); added "But the LORD is the true God; he is the living God, the eternal King. When he is angry, the earth trembles; the nations cannot endure his

God is infinite

wrath". And Psalm 90:2) states "Before the mountains were born or you brought forth the whole world, from everlasting to everlasting you are God". The adjective eternal is something or Being without beginning or end; existing outside of time. See Synonyms at infinite. Continuing without interruption; perpetual. Forever true or changeless: eternal truths. Seemingly endless; interminable. See Synonyms at ageless, continual. Of or relating to spiritual communion with God, especially in the afterlife. Something timeless, uninterrupted, or endless. The Eternal God.

7 God is infinite, *as in* (1 Kings 8:22-27; " And Solomon stood before the altar of the LORD in the presence of all the congregation of Israel, and spread forth his hands toward heaven: And he said, LORD God of Israel, there is no God like thee, in heaven above, or on earth beneath, who keepest covenant and mercy with thy servants that walk before thee with all their heart: Who hast kept with thy servant David my father that thou promisedst him: thou spakest also with thy mouth, and hast fulfilled it with thine hand, as it is this day. Therefore now, LORD God of Israel, keep with thy servant David my father that thou promisedst him, saying, There shall not fail thee a man in my sight to sit on the throne of Israel; so that thy children take heed to their way, that they walk before me as thou hast walked before me. And now, O God of Israel, let thy word, I pray thee, be verified, which thou spakest unto thy servant David my father. But will God indeed dwell on the earth? *behold, the heaven and heaven of heavens* cannot contain thee; how much less this house that I have buildeth?" . Also infinity is anything - Having no boundaries or limits. Immeasurably great or large; boundless: infinite patience; a discovery of infinite importance. Mathematics Existing beyond or being greater than any arbitrarily large value. Unlimited in spatial extent: a line of infinite length. Of or relating to a set capable of being put into one-to-one correspondence with a proper subset of itself.

The Targums is the (Aramaic – "interpretations – meaning the name given to the various (Chaldean) interpretations and translations of the Old Testament made in Babylon and Palestine when Hebrew was ceasing to be the everyday speech of the Jews. They were transmitted orally and the oldest, that of Onkelos of the Pentateuch is probably of the 2nd Century AD. So God was described to have boundless might.

``does not my glory fill heaven and earth? saith the Lord;'' both of them are full of his glory; and every person and thing in either must be seen and known by him; and so the false prophets and their lies; in order to convince of the truth of which, all this is said, as appears by the following words".

8 God is unchanging or immutable: "God is unchanging in his character, will, and covenant promises." The Westminster Shorter Catechism says, 'God is a spirit, whose being, wisdom power, holiness, justice, goodness, and truth are infinite, eternal, and unchangeable." Those things do not change. A number of Scriptures attest to this idea (Numbers. 23:19; 1 Samuel. 15:29; Psalm. 102:26; Malachi. 3:6; 2 Timothy. 2:13; Hebrew. 6:17–18; James. 1:17) God's immutability defines all his other attributes: he is immutably wise, he cannot but be merciful, good, and gracious. The same may be said about his knowledge: God does not need to gain knowledge; he knows all things, eternally and immutably so. Infiniteness and immutability in God are mutually supportive and imply each other. An infinite and changing God is inconceivable; indeed it is a contradiction in definition as in (Psalm 102:25-27; Hebrews 1:10-12; 13:8)

9 God is Sovereign: The word Sovereign simply means "superior," "greatest," "supreme in power and authority," "ruler," and "independent of all others" in its definition. But gospel dictionary explanation of God's sovereignty is simply to say, " God has been in control and must always be in control." There is absolutely nothing that happens in the universe that is outside of God's influence and authority. As King of kings and Lord of lords, God has no limitations. Consider just a few of the claims the Bible makes about God:

God is above all things and before all things. He is the alpha and the omega, the beginning and the end. He is immortal, and He is present everywhere so that everyone can know Him (Revelation 21:6).

God created all things and holds all things together, both in heaven and on earth, both visible and invisible (Colossians 1:16). "For in him all things were created: things in heaven and on earth, visible and invisible, whether thrones or powers or rulers or authorities; all things have been created through him and for him". God knows all things past, present, and future. There is no limit to His knowledge, for God knows everything completely before it even happens (Romans 11:33). *God* can do all things and accomplish all things. Nothing is too difficult for Him, and He orchestrates and determines everything that is going to happen in your life, in my life, in, Africa, Australia, Asia, Europe, America, and throughout the world. Whatever

God is Wise

He wants to do in the universe, He does, for nothing is impossible with Him (Jeremiah 32:17).

God is in control of all things and rules over all things. He has power and authority over nature, earthly kings, history, angels, and demons. Even Satan himself has to ask God's permission before he can act (Psalm 103:18-20). "To those who keep His covenant And remember His precepts to do them. The LORD has established His throne in the heavens, And His sovereignty rules over all. Bless the LORD, you His angels, Mighty in strength, who perform His word, Obeying the voice of His word!... That's what being sovereign means. It means being the ultimate source of all power, authority, and everything that exists. Only God can make those claims; therefore, it's God's sovereignty that makes Him superior to all other gods and makes Him, and Him alone, worthy of worship. Just as peasants always bowed before their king for fear of offending the one who had the authority to take their life, God's sovereignty compels us to bow before Him. But unlike corrupt earthly kings who abuse their authority to terrorize their subjects, God rules in love. He loves you and wants the best for you. (Romans 8:28) promises that in all things God works for the good of those who love Him, who have been called according to His purpose.

That's an amazing promise not only because it demonstrates that an all-powerful God cares about us, but because it cannot be fulfilled unless the One Who gives it is all-knowing, all-wise, all-powerful, and all-loving. The promise itself is a testimony to God's sovereignty. But God makes that promise, and millions throughout history have testified to its truth because God has proven His ability to back it up time and time again.

Think about the implications of that promise. Because God is sovereign and He loves you, nothing will ever come into your life that He does not either decree or allow. Consequently, no matter what you face in life, you can take comfort in the fact that God is sovereign. (2 Samuel 7:22; Isaiah 46:9-11)

10 God is Wise: In everyday usage, wise means; Astute, star-aware, star careful, star educated, star enlightened, star experienced ,star informed, star judicious, star knowledgeable, star perceptive, star prudent, star rational, star sane, star sensible, star shrewd, star smart, star thoughtful, star wary, star well-informed, star contemplative, star cunning, star grasping, star keen, star knowing, star sage, star sensing, star sharp, star sound, star understanding, star calculating, star clever, star cogitative, star crafty, star discerning, star discreet, star erudite, star foresighted, star insightful, star intuitive, star perspicacious, star politic, star reflective, stars sagacious, star sapient, stars scholarly, star sophist, start tactful, start aught and star witty. In all these, God possesses the ability to discern or judge what is true, right, or lasting; sagacious: a wise leader. Exhibiting common sense; prudent: a wise decision. Shrewd; crafty and having great learning; erudite. Provided with information; informed. Used with to: These words formed the blessed peculiarity of the Christian faith, that it simplifies our outlook for good, that it brings everything to the one point of possessing the one Person, beyond whom there is never any need that the heart should wander seeking after love, that the mind should depart in its search for truth, or that the will should stray in its quest after authoritative commands. There is no need to seek a multitude of goodly pearls; the gift of Christianity to men's torn and distracted hearts and lives is that all which makes them rich, and all which makes them blessed, is sphered and included in the one transcendent pearl of price, the 'only God." Which in order word positioned God as the conceiver of wisdom. Wisdom did not conceive God and does not own God but God conceived, create and own wisdom making God very indomitable by anything as He is the only one dominating everything. Without Him nothing can be conceived or created as in (Proverbs 3:19) "By wisdom the LORD laid the earth's foundations, by understanding he set the heavens in place"; Again in (Romans 16:26-27) "But now is made manifest, and by the scriptures of the prophets, according to the commandment of the everlasting God, made known to all nations for the obedience of faith: To God only *wise*, be glory through Jesus Christ for ever. Amen". See also (1 Timothy 1:17) "Now to the King eternal, immortal, invisible, the only God, be honor and glory for ever and ever. Amen".

11 God is Holy. (Leviticus 19:2) "Speak to the entire assembly of Israel and say to them: 'Be holy because I, the LORD your God, am holy". The word Holy is adjective meaning dedicated or consecrated to God or a religious purpose; sacred.

"the Holy Bible" synonyms - sacred, consecrated, hallowed, sanctified, venerated, revered, reverenced, divine, religious, blessed, blest, dedicated "it is forbidden to abuse the name of His Holy One". As opposed to certain antonyms such as unsanctified, cursed (of a person) devoted to the service of God. "saints and holy men" synonyms: saintly, godly, saint-like, pious, pietistic, religious, devout, God-fearing, spiritual, canonized, beatified, ordained, deified; morally and spiritually excellent. As a Christian you must lead a holy life" 2 Dated humorous used in exclamations of surprise or dismay.

God is Righteous and Just

"holy smoke!" – When Popes are appointed or elected in the Romans Catholic Church. God is the Most Holy in all Creation probably since no one created Him, no one ever made the Laws of Holiness but God! That is why the apostle in (Ephesians 4: 25-28) charged the Ephesians in the name and by the authority of the Lord Jesus, that having professed the gospel, they should not be as the unconverted Gentiles, who walked in vain fancies and carnal affections. Thus' "Therefore each of you must put off falsehood and speak truthfully to your neighbour, for we are all members of one body. "In your anger do not sin"[a]: Do not let the sun go down while you are still angry, and do not give the devil a foothold. Anyone who has been stealing must steal no longer, but must work, doing something useful with their own hands, that they may have something to share with those in need". Do not men, on every side, walk in the vanity of their minds? As Christians, must not we then urge the distinction between real and nominal Christians? They were void of all saving knowledge; Must we sit in darkness, and loved it rather than light. Why must many Children of God dislike and develop hatred to a life of holiness, we must abide by the way of life God requires and approves, and by which we live to him, but which has some likeness to God himself in his purity, righteousness, truth, and goodness. The truth of Christ appears in its beauty and power, when it appears as in Jesus. The corrupt nature is called a man; like the human body, it is of diver's parts, supporting and strengthening one another. Sinful desires are deceitful lusts; men are promised happiness, but many turned to render more miserable; and brought to destruction, if not subdued and mortified. These therefore must be put off, as an old garment, a filthy garment; they must be subdued and mortified. But it is not enough to shake off corrupt principles; we must have gracious ones. By the new man, is meant the new nature, the new creature, directed by a new principle, even regenerating grace, enabling a man to lead a new life of righteousness and holiness. This is created, or brought forth by the power of God. The almighty! In all these, there is a call, for you as a Christian sharing the benefit and the grace in the gospel of Christ to be Holy as in (1 Peter 1: 14-15) "As obedient children, do not be conformed to the former lusts which were yours in your ignorance, but like the Holy One who called you, be holy yourselves also in all your behaviour; because it is written, "YOU SHALL BE HOLY, FOR I AM HOLY."...

12 God is Righteous and Just:
(Hebrew – Tzadik or Tzedakah) These are important theological concept in Christianity, Judaism and other religions. It is an attri-

God is Holy

bute that implies that a person's actions are justified, and can have the connotation that the person has been "judged" or "reckoned" as leading a life that is pleasing to God who is the father of all righteousness. The Hebrew word from which we get righteousness can also be translated as just or justice. The fact that God is righteous points to the justice and fairness with which He judges all individuals. Righteousness again indicates being separated from wickedness. It illustrates that all God does is right whether or not we think it is right in our eyes. Since this quality of God carries with it a sense of justness in judgement we can know that when we do something that God says is wrong and don't repent He will judge us the same way He would anyone else. There is no favouritism with God. Some judgments may be swift others may take a while but all are judged according to the same standard regardless of circumstances, race, creed, colour, or sex.

The following and more biblical verses not stated here, present righteousness in proper gospel form to edify our spirits (Jeremiah 23:5,6) "Behold, the days come, saith the Lord, that I will raise unto David a righteous Branch, and a King shall reign and prosper, and shall execute judgement and justice in the earth. In his days Judah shall be saved, and Israel shall dwell safely: and this is his name whereby he shall be called, THE LORD – Our Righteousness" (Psalm 4:4,5) "Stand in awe, and sin not: commune with your own heart upon your bed, and be still. Offer the sacrifices of righteousness, and put your trust in the Lord". (Psalm 129:4) The Lord is righteous: he hath cut asunder the cords of the wicked. (Isaiah 45:21) Tell ye, and bring them near; yea, let them take counsel together: who hath declared this from ancient time? who hath told it from that time? have not I the Lord? and there is no God else beside me; a just God and a Saviour; there is none beside me. (Deuteronomy 32:4) "He is the Rock, his work is perfect: for all his ways are judgement: a God of truth and without iniquity, just and right is he". (Psalm 119:142,144) "Thy righteousness is an everlasting righteousness, and thy law is truth. The righteousness of testimonies is everlasting: give me understanding, and I shall live". (Psalm 97:2) Clouds and darkness are round about him: righteousness and judgement are the habitation of his throne. (Acts 3:14) "But ye denied the Holy One and the Just, and desired a murderer to be granted unto you". (Hebrews 1:8,9) "But unto the Son he saith, Thy throne, O God, is for ever and ever: a sceptre of righteousness is the sceptre of thy kingdom. Thou hast loved *righteousness*, and hated iniquity; therefore God, even thy God, hath anointed thee with the oil of gladness above thy fel-

God is faithful

lows". (Romans 6:18) Being them made free from sin, ye became the servants of righteousness. (Ephesians 4:240) And that ye put on the new man, which after God is created in *righteousness* and true holiness. God is fair and just. His actions are righteous. There is nothing wrong in God. When I sin and do wrong in the eyes of God I will confess it immediately, knowing that He will forgive and forget that wrong action or attitude. I will try to live my life *righteous* and Holy as God has commanded. (Deuteronomy :4) Psalm 11:7;and Psalm 119:137) Thus' You are righteous, Lord, and your laws are right. The statutes you have laid down are *righteous*; they are fully trustworthy. My zeal wears me out, for my enemies ignore your words. Your promises have been thoroughly tested, and your servant loves them. Though I am lowly and despised, I do not forget your precepts. Your righteousness is everlasting and your law is true. Trouble and distress have come upon me, but your commands give me delight. Your statutes are always *righteous;* give me understanding that I may live.

13 God is faithful:
(Deuteronomy 7:9) "Know therefore that the Lord your God is God; he is the *faithful* God, keeping his covenant of love to a thousand generations of those who love him and keep his commandments". This is the concept of God's unfailingly remaining loyalty to us, all our concerns and in all circumstances, to constantly available to individuals in the body of Christ, keeping His Grace sufficiently stable and putting that loyalty into consistent practice, regardless of extenuating circumstances through Christ Jesus who already have made us the righteousness of God through Him.

2 *Faithfulness* may be applied to a husband or wife relationships who, in a sexually exclusive marriage, does not engage in sexual relationships outside of the marriage, a customer at a restaurant who regularly dines there, or even to God himself with regard to his perpetual love towards his children that is not dependent on their worthiness. Literally, it is the state of being full of faith in the somewhat archaic sense of steady devotion to a person, thing or concept as in the content of the maskil (a contemplation) of Ethan – the Ezrahite in (Psalm 89:1-8) "I will sing of the Lord's great love forever; with my mouth I will make your faithfulness known through all generations. I will declare that your love stands firm forever, that you have established your *faithfulness* in heaven itself. You said, "I have made a covenant with my chosen one, I have sworn to David my servant, 'I will establish your line forever and make your throne firm through all generations.'" The heavens praise your wonders,

Lord, your *faithfulness* too, in the assembly of the holy ones. For who in the skies above can compare with the Lord? Who is like the Lord among the heavenly beings? In the council of the holy ones God is greatly feared; he is more awesome than all who surround him. Who is like you, Lord God Almighty? You, Lord, are mighty, and your *faithfulness* surrounds you.

3 The etymology of *faithfulness* is distantly related to that of fidelity; indeed, in modern electronic devices, a machine with high "fidelity" is considered "faithful" to its source material, whereas a spouse who, inside a sexually exclusive relationship, has sexual relations outside of marriage could equally be considered as being "unfaithful" as having committed "infidelity". The followings are the cross references showing the faithfulness of God   (Psalm 89:5,37) And the heavens shall praise your wonders, O LORD: your *faithfulness* ... (Psalm 119:89) For ever, O LORD, your word is settled in heaven. (Psalm 146:6) Which made heaven, and earth, the sea, and all that therein is: which ... (Numbers 23:19) God is not a man, that he should lie; neither the son of man, that ... (Matthew 24:35) Heaven and earth shall pass away, but my words shall not pass away. (Hebrews 6:18) That by two immutable things, in which it was impossible for God ...

14 **God is true and truth**: In ordinary sense, God has enormous attribute to the adjective true which means that God is real, valid; concordant with facts accurate, divinely star appropriate, star authentic, star bona fide, star correct, star genuine, star honest star legitimate, star natural, star normal, star perfect, star proper star pure, star sincere, star truthful, star typical, star direct, star exact, star fitting, star kosher, star regular, star right, star straight, star wash, Star actual, star authoritative, star dependable, star factual, star indubitable, star lawful, star legal, star on target, star precise, star rightful, star sure-enough, star trustworthy, star undeniable, star undesigning, star undoubted, star unerring, star unfaked, star unfeigned, star unquestionable, star veracious, star veridical, star veritable and star very.

While 'truth is the interrelated consistency of statements and their correspondence with the facts of reality and the facts themselves. It suggests an integration of character, and adherence of virtue, a kind of reliability, which includes and goes beyond the literal meaning to include those aspects of personal behaviour which seem to be implied by the love of truth. The concept of truth is derived from the character of God, and is the exact opposite of the concept of lying. "It is impossible for God to lie." Since it is impossible for God

God is faithful

to lie we know that everything He says about what will happen will actually take place. If we are to become perfect we need to be known as individuals who tell the truth, like God. That means when we promise something we need to keep that promise or not make it in the first place. We need to try to place ourselves in situations where we don't feel the need to lie to defend either ourselves or our behaviour.

2 There were underlying prophesies and Jesus Christ fulfilled every one of those prophecies. He is the most convincing argument for the truth of the gospel content of the Bible. Jesus Christ - the most unique individual the world has ever known. So profound is His life that the two eras of human history are divided by His coming: B.C ("Before Christ") and A.D. ("Anno Domini," which means "year of our Lord").

3 The *true and truth of God* can also be seen in the life, the death, and especially the resurrection of Jesus Christ that rocked the world and forever altered the course of civilization. Again, Jesus claimed to be the Son of God, the Messiah. The Scriptures bear witness to this in (Luke 4:16-21 –NASB) "And He came to Nazareth, where He had been brought up; and as was His custom, He entered the synagogue on the Sabbath, and stood up to read. And the book of the prophet Isaiah was handed to Him. And He opened the book and found the place where it was written, "The Spirit of the Lord is upon me, because he anointed me to preach the gospel to the poor. He has sent me to proclaim release to the captives, and recovery of sight to the blind, to set free those who are oppressed, to proclaim the favourable year of the Lord." And He closed the book, gave it back to the attendant and sat down; and the eyes of all in the synagogue were fixed on Him. And He began to say to them, "Today this Scripture has been fulfilled in your hearing."

4 See the following scriptures to certain Gods truthfulness (Deuteronomy 32:4) "He is the Rock, his work is perfect: for all his ways is judgement: a God of truth and without iniquity, just and right is he". (John 17:2 & 3) "As thou has given him power over all flesh, that he should give eternal life to as many as thou hast given him. And this is life eternal, that they might know thee the only true God, and Jesus Christ, whom thou hast sent". (Psalm 19:9) "The fear of the Lord is clean, enduring forever: the judgments of the Lord are true and righteous altogether". (Psalm 33:4) "For the word of the Lord is right; and all his works are done in truth. (Psalm 57:10) "For thy mercy is great unto the heavens, and thy truth unto the clouds". (John 8:31b-32) "If ye continue in my word, then are ye my disciples indeed; And ye shall know the truth, and the truth

shall make you free. (John 17:17) "Sanctify them through truth: thy word is truth". (John 18:37 and 38) "Pilate therefore said unto him, Art thou a king then? Jesus answered, Thou sayest that I am a king. To this end was I born, and for this cause came I into the world, that I should bear witness unto the truth. Every one that is of the truth heareth my voice. Pilate saith unto him, What is truth? And when he had said this, he went out again unto the Jews, and saith unto them, I find in him no fault at all". (II Thessalonians 2:10-13) "And with all deceivableness of unrighteousness in them that perish; because they received not the love of the truth, that they might be saved. And for this cause God shall send them strong delusion, that they should believe a lie: That they all might be damned who believed not the truth, but had pleasure in unrighteousness. But we are bound to give thanks always to God for you, brethren beloved of the Lord, because God hath from the beginning chosen you to salvation through sanctification of the Spirit and belief of the truth".

5 Indeed, whatever God says He will do, He will do. Therefore, when He says those who believe in Jesus shall have eternal life, you can rest assured that will take place. Just as sure is His providing a way out of temptation, protection from the flaming arrows of the enemy, and Satan's eventual demise by being thrown into the Lake of Fire forever.

As His Children, it is obligation to do the words as read in the Bible something which are what God wants us to do. Do it! Trust Him to comply and follow through because He must surely give us the things He promised if we obey Him. Because His truthfulness is in His message to man, He often speaks in person, even Archaeological proof confirm this, He foretells the future, show of the Himself face to face like the case with the Pontius Pilate, His testimony by the Messiah; which makes us to submit to the truth and also lived in it as even Jesus declared the word of faith on the Cross in (Psalm 31:5) "Into your hands I commit my spirit; deliver me, LORD, my faithful God". Also, see (John 14:6; John 17:3) and Paul's greetings to Titus in (Titus 1:1-3) "Paul, a bond-servant of God and an apostle of Jesus Christ, for the faith of those chosen of God and the knowledge of the truth which is according to godliness, in the hope of eternal life, which God, who cannot lie, promised long ages ago, but at the proper time manifested, even His word, in the proclamation with which I was entrusted according to the commandment of God our Saviour".

15 God is good: This means God goodness, mercies and favour joins together to make His abundance Grace available to underserve persons – sinners as in (Psalm 25:8) "Good and upright is the LORD; therefore he instructs sinners in his ways".

God is merciful

2 As a sinner, the Holy Spirit is praying for you. "[T]he Spirit himself speaks to God for us, and even begs God for us with deep feelings that words cannot explain" (Romans 8:26 NCV). God uses everything for your good. "And we know in all things God works for the good of those who love Him" (Romans 8:28 NIV). God is bigger than your enemies. He's bigger than your critics. He's bigger than your problems. And he's working it all for good in your life. God wants you to succeed. "If God is for us, who can ever be against us?" (Romans 8:31 NLT). God wants you to succeed in all those areas where you are failing. He's pulling for you. God will give you what you need. "And since God did not spare even his own Son but gave him up for us all, won't God, who gave us Christ, also give us everything else?" (Romans 8:32 NLT). God solved your biggest problem when he paid for all your sins, including the ones you haven't done yet. If God cared enough to save you and give you the gift of eternal life, don't you think he cares about the problems in your daily life? If it's big enough to worry about, it's big enough to pray about. And if you pray about it, you won't have to worry about it. Thus "And we know that in all things God works for the good of those who love Him, who've been called according to His purpose." (Romans 8:28 - NIV) See also (Psalm 34:8) and (Mark 10:18) "Why do you call me good?" Jesus answered. "No one is good—except God alone". Praise the Lord!

16 God is merciful: This is a broad term that refers to benevolence, forgiveness and kindness in a variety of ethical, religious, social and legal contexts. The concept of a "Merciful God" appears in various religions, including Christianity, and other religions. Performing acts of mercy as a component of religious beliefs is also emphasized through actions such as the giving of alms, and care for the sick and Works of Mercy as in (Deuteronomy 4:31) "For the LORD your God is a merciful God; he will not abandon or destroy you or forget the covenant with your ancestors, which he confirmed to them by oath".

2 God is forgiving, compassionate, gracious, lenient, clement, pitying, forbearing, humane, mild, soft-hearted, tender-hearted, kind, kindly, sympathetic; as opposed to antonyms: such as merciless, cruel (of an event) coming as a mercy; Many works of mercy that abound in the life of a Christian includes - bringing someone relief from something unpleasant. welcome, blessed, acceptable and much more

3 The concept of mercy from God gives us an insight into the nature of virtue. To do something virtuously is not just to do it in a higher degree, but in a better way. God is perfectly merciful in that He perfectly displays the virtue of mercy.

God is gracious

This means that he is merciful to the right people, at the right time, to the right degree, with the right motive, and in the right circumstances. It is not appropriate to forgive a person's sins when he is defiant and unrepentant. It may be appropriate to continue trying to lead him to repentance, but it is not fitting for him to be forgiven even before he has admitted he was wrong. See (Psalm 103:8-17; Daniel 9:9) and (Hebrews 2:16 - 18) "For assuredly He does not give help to angels, but He gives help to the descendant of Abraham. Therefore, He had to be made like His brethren in all things, so that He might become a *merciful* and faithful high priest in things pertaining to God, to make propitiation for the sins of the people. For since' He Himself was tempted in that which He has suffered, He is able to come to the aid of those who are tempted". Praise the Lord!

17 God is gracious: (adjective) to be gracious means 'to favour,' 'to show kindnesses' to an inferior or an undeserved person or a sinner and 'to be compassionate.' In the Old Testament of the Bible, this adjective applies to God, indicative of His favour and mercy, His long-suffering and general inclination of favour and kindness. In (Isaiah 30:18) says, "Yet the Lord longs to be gracious to you; he rises to show you compassion." God is gracious because He is love. It is His character to love even if love is not returned to Him. He will give us good things because of His goodness. He extends favour, mercy, and kindness on whoever He pleases because it's who He is.

2 God is gracious because He is our Creator. Even when we don't acknowledge Him or worship Him, He still endows us with good things because He wants to. God created mankind as good and He won't turn His back on His creatures or creation.

"Grace is another attribute that is part of the manifold of God's love. By this we mean that God deals with his people not on the basis of their merit or worthiness, what they deserve, but simply according to their need; in other words, he deals with them on the basis of his goodness and generosity." This definition makes God to be courteous, kind, and pleasant, especially towards someone of lower social status. "a gracious attribute to man kinds behaviour, making him to be courteous, polite, civil, chivalrous, well mannered, decorous, gentlemanly, ladylike, civilized, tactful, diplomatic; as opposed to antonyms: of ungracious showing the elegance and comfort brought by wealth or high social status. God grace makes man to be "graciously living" which is synonymous: to elegant, stylish, tasteful, graceful, comfortable, luxurious, sumptuous, opulent, grand, plush, high-class,

God is loved

exquisite, smart, sophisticated, fashionable, modish, chic; informal swanky "tree-lined avenues with gracious colonial buildings" 2 (in Christian belief) showing divine grace. "I am saved by God's gracious intervention on my behalf" synonyms: merciful, forgiving, compassionate, kind, kindly, lenient, clement, pitying, forbearing, humane, mild, soft-hearted, tender-hearted, sympathetic; See (Exodus 34:6) "And he passed in front of Moses, proclaiming, "The Lord, the Lord, the compassionate and gracious God, slow to anger, abounding in love and faithfulness", (Psalm 103:8) Also, the God of grace restores us to His eternal Glory as in (1 Peter 5:10) "And the God of all grace, who called you to his eternal glory in Christ, after you have suffered a little while, will himself restore you and make you strong, firm and steadfast". Praise the Lord!

18 God is loved: God is the only one who developed the act of divine grace, mercy, affection, endurance, patience, kindness, prosperity, righteous, eternal life etc. to an undeserved person as in (John 3:16) "For God so loved the world that he gave his one and only Son, that whoever believes in him shall not perish but have eternal life" - This is one of the most widely quoted verses from the Christian Bible, and has been called the most famous Bible verse. 2 It has also been called the "Gospel in a nutshell", because it is considered a summary of the central theme of traditional Christianity thus' "For God so loved the world that he gave his one and only Son, that whoever believes in him shall not perish but have eternal life". Love is a variety of different feelings, states, and attitudes that ranges from interpersonal affection for example if one say ("I love my mother") to pleasure ("I loved that meal"). It can refer to an emotion of a strong attraction and personal attachment. It can also be a virtue representing human kindness, compassion, and affection—"the unselfish loyal and benevolent concern for the good of another". It may also describe compassionate and affectionate actions towards other humans, one's self or animals.

3 Ancient Greeks identified four forms of love: kinship or familiarity (in Greek, storage), friendship (philia), sexual and or romantic desire (eros), and self-emptying or divine love (agape). Modern authors have distinguished further varieties of romantic love. Non-Western traditions have also distinguished variants or symbioses of these states. This diversity of uses and meanings combined with the complexity of the feelings involved makes love unusually difficult to consistently define, compared to other emotional states.

4 In the gospel, we can see God's love in various forms. Love in its various forms acts as a major fa-

God is loved

cilitator of interpersonal relationships and, owing to its central psychological importance, is one of the most common themes in the creative arts. Love may be understood as a function to keep human beings together against menaces and to facilitate the continuation of the species.

Indeed, the gospel makes it clear from biblical scriptures that God is the essence of love. *God is love* because "Love is patient, love is kind. It does not envy, it does not boast, it is not proud. It is not rude, it is not self-seeking, it is not easily angered, and it keeps no record of wrongs. Love does not delight in evil but rejoices with the truth. It always protects, always trusts, always hopes, and always perseveres. Love never fails" (1 Corinthians 13:4-8). This is God's description of love, and because *God is love* (1 John 4:8), this is what He is like.

Love (God) does not force Himself on anyone. Those who come to Him do so in response to His love. Love (God) shows kindness to all. Love (Jesus) went about doing well to everyone without partiality. Love (Jesus) did not covet what others had, living a humble life without complaining. Love (Jesus) did not brag about who He was in the flesh, although He could have overpowered anyone He ever came in contact with. Love (God) does not demand obedience. God did not demand obedience from His Son, but rather, Jesus willingly obeyed His Father in heaven. "The world must learn that I love the Father and that I do exactly what my Father has commanded me" (John 14:31). Love (Jesus) was/is always looking out for the interests of others.

5 The greatest expression of God's love is communicated to us in (John 3:16) "For God so loved the world that he gave his one and only Son, that whoever believes in him shall not perish but have eternal life." (Romans 5:8) proclaims the same message: "But God demonstrates his own love for us in this: While we were still sinners, Christ died for us." We can see from these verses that it is God's greatest desire that we join Him in His eternal home, heavenly home. He has made the way possible by paying the price for our sins. He loves us because He chose to as an act of His will. Love forgives. "If we confess our sins, he is faithful and just and will forgive us our sins and purify us from all unrighteousness" (1 John 1:9).

6 That *God is love*? Love is an attribute of God. Love is a core aspect of God's character, His Person. God's love is in no sense in conflict with His holiness, righteousness, justice, or even His wrath. All of God's attributes are in perfect harmony. Everything God does loves, just as everything He does is just and right. God is the perfect example of true love. Amazingly, God

God is light

has given those who receive His Son Jesus as their personal Saviour the ability to love as He does, through the power of the Holy Spirit as in (John 1:12) "Yet to all who did receive him, to those who believed in his name, he gave the right to become children of God" See (1 John 3:1, 23-24) and (Romans 5:8) " But God demonstrates his own love for us in this: While we were still sinners, Christ died for us". Praise the Lord!

19 God is light: (James 1:17) "Every good and perfect gift is from above, coming down from the Father of the heavenly *lights*, who does not change like shifting shadows".

Light is a common metaphor in the Gospel. (Proverbs 4:18) symbolizes righteousness as the "morning sun." (Philippians 2:15) likens God's children who are "blameless and pure" to shining stars in the sky. Jesus used *light* as a picture of good works: "Let your *light* shine before others, that they may see your good deeds" (Matthew 5:16). And (Psalm 76:4) says of God, "You are radiant with *light*." If light is a metaphor for righteousness and goodness, then darkness signifies evil and sin. We are told in (1 John 1:5) that "if we claim to have fellowship with him yet walk in the darkness, we lie and do not live by the truth." And (Verse 5) says, "God is light; in him there is no darkness at all."

2 Note that we are not told that God is a *light* but that He is *light*. *Light* is part of His essence, as is love (1 John 4:8).The message is that God is completely, unreservedly, absolutely holy, with no admixture of sin, no taint of iniquity, and no hint of injustice. If we do not know light, we do not know God. Those who know God, who walk with Him, are of the light and walk in the light. They are made partakers of God's divine nature, "having escaped the corruption in the world caused by evil desires" (2 Peter 1:4). Jesus said, "I am the *light* of the world. Whoever follows me will never walk in darkness, but will have the light of life" (John 8:12). To "walk" means to make progress. Therefore, we can infer from this Scripture that Christians are meant to grow in holiness and to mature in faith as they follow Jesus as in (2 Peter 3:18).

3 It is God's plan that believers become more like Christ every day. "You are all children of the light and children of the day. We do not belong to the night or to the darkness" (1 Thessalonians 5:5). He is the Creator of physical light, as well as the Giver of spiritual light, by which we can see the truth. Light exposes that which is hidden in darkness; it shows things as they really are. To walk in the light means to know God, understand the truth, and live in righteousness.

4 Christ followers must confess any darkness within themselves – their sins and transgressions – and allow God to shine His *light* through them. Christians cannot sit idly by and watch others continue in darkness, knowing that those in the darkness of sin are destined for eternal separation from God. The *Light* of the World desires to banish the darkness and bestow His wisdom everywhere (Isaiah 9:2; Habakkuk 2:14; John 1:9). In taking the *light* of the gospel to the world, we must by necessity reveal things about people that they would rather leave hidden. is uncomfortable to those accustomed to the dark (John 3:20). Jesus, the sinless Son of God, is the "true *light*" (John 1:9). As adopted sons of God, we are to reflect His *light* into a world darkened by sin. Our goal in witnessing to the unsaved as in (Acts 26:18) "to open their eyes and turn them from darkness to light, and from the power of Satan to God" so that they may receive forgiveness of sins and a place among those who are sanctified by faith in me". Hallelujah! Here Jesus spokes from Heaven to Paul in the way to Damascus. This is the absolute conclusion of the whole Christian truth found in one last clause of the verse, 'Inheritance among them which are sanctified by faith that is in Me.' Putting that into distinct propositions, we see that: Faith refers to Christ; that is the first thing. Holiness depends on faith; that is the next: 'sanctified by faith.' Heaven depends on holiness: that is the last: 'inheritance among them which are sanctified by faith that is in Me.' So there we have the whole gospel! Praise His Holy Name!

20 God is triune or trinity:

(Matthew 28:19) "Therefore go and make disciples of all nations, baptizing them in the name of the Father and of the Son and of the Holy Spirit", The adjective triune speaks of anything consisting of three in one particularly as regards to the Godhead used especially with reference to the Trinity. The Trinity known as God comprises with three essence beings and the divine name of the three is known as God. In other words, Jehovah is God, Jesus is God, Holy Spirit is God. If any of the three persons says I am who I am. It means He refers to the triune. The complicated question to the mind is always is the trinity a club of GOD'S known as God?

2 Sometimes the Personhood of the Father and Son is appreciated, but the Personhood of the Holy Spirit is neglected. Sometimes the Spirit is treated more like a "force" than a Person. But the Holy Spirit is not an it, but a He as in (John 14:26; 16:7–15; Acts 8:16). The fact that the Holy Spirit is a Person, not an impersonal force (like gravity), is also shown by the fact that He speaks (Hebrews 3:7), reasons (Acts 15:28), thinks and un-

Gods, The

derstands (1 Corinthians 2:10–11), wills (1 Corinthians 12:11), feels (Ephesians 4:30), and gives personal fellowship (2 Corinthians 13:14). These are all qualities of personhood. In addition to these texts, the others we mentioned above make clear that the Personhood of the Holy Spirit is distinct from the Personhood of the Son and the Father. They are three real persons, not three roles God plays.

3 The Trinity is first of all important because God is important. To understand more fully what God is like is a way of honouring God. Further, we should allow the fact that God is triune to deepen our worship. We exist to worship God. And God seeks people to worship Him "in spirit and truth" (John 4:24). Therefore we must always endeavour to deepen our worship of God — in truth as well as in our hearts.

4 The Trinity has a very significant application to prayer. The general pattern of prayer in the gospel according to the Bible is to pray to the Father through the Son and in the Holy Spirit (Ephesians 2:18). Our fellowship with God should be enhanced by consciously knowing that we are relating to a tri-personal God!

5 Awareness of the distinct role that each Person of the Trinity has in our salvation can especially serve to give us greater comfort and appreciation for God in our prayers, as well as helping us to be specific in directing our prayers. Nonetheless, while recognizing the distinct roles that each Person has, we should never think of their roles as so separate that the other Persons are not involved. Rather, everything that one Person is involved in; the other two are also involved in, one way or another. That is why when we pray our prayer must reflect the essence and the important functions one essence of the trinity holds to another as in (2 Corinthians 13:14) "May the grace of the Lord Jesus Christ, and the love of God, and the fellowship of the Holy Spirit be with you all". While Jesus Christ is the Grace, Jehovah is the love and Holy Spirit is the fellowship. Therefore the triune is Grace, Love and Fellowship in Jesus Christ. Amen!

Gods, The: These are gods or – gods, "a moon god" synonyms: deity, goddess, other divine beings, celestial being. 2 Idolatry - a pejorative term for the worship of an idol. "You shall not make for yourself an idol - one of the Ten Commandments. 'Statue'. Normally written as god with "g". Not pure. They have mouth but don't speak, legs but don't walk, Nose, but don't smell, Eye's but not working. No revelation, no prophecy, no vision, lasting plan, no life, and virtually no hope. Satan uses gods to deceive human race. 3 Manmade gods. In simple terms, Christians are warned against the worship of any gods other than the Lord himself. Some of these divinities took the form of images, others were mythical. Some Israelites became involved in idolatrous worship of such gods. The book of Acts records attempts to deify human beings. False gods associated with foreign nations in the Old Testament such as Amon, the chief god of Egypt See also (Jeremiah 46:25). Asherah, a Canaanite goddess (Exodus 34:13-14) Asherah was the consort of El, the chief Canaanite god. Wooden poles, perhaps carved in her image, were often set up in her honour and placed near other pagan objects of worship. See also (Deuteronomy 7:5); (Judges 6:25-30) Gideon destroys an Asherah pole; (1King 14:15,23; 1King 15:13; 1King 16:33; 1King 18:19) Elijah summons 400 prophets of Asherah to Mount Carmel. King Josiah's reforms: 2King 23:4-7,13-16, Isaiah 27:9; Jeremiah 17:2; Micah 5:14) Ashtoreth, a goddess of war and fertility (Judges 2:12-13) Ashtoreth, the consort of Baal, was associated with the evening star and was worshipped as Ishtar in Babylon and as Athtart in Aram. To the Greeks she was Astarte or Aphrodite and to the Romans, Venus. See also (Judges 10:6; 1Samuel 7:3-4; 1Samuel 12:10; 1Samuel 31:10; 1Ki ng11:5,33) Baal, a Canaanite and Phoenician god of fertility and rain (Judges 2:10-13) Baal, meaning "lord", was pictured standing on a bull, a popular symbol of fertility and strength. Baal was associated with Asherah and Ashtoreth, goddesses of fertility.

It is on record that every attempts to stop false worship proved unsuccessful (2 King 21:3) The word "Baal" was not originally a proper name but came to be used as such. See also (2Chronicle 28:1-4; Hosea 13:1-2) Every warnings against and condemnation of the worship of false gods is recorded in (Psalm 40:4) (Daniel 3:29) and Nebuchadnezzar came to realise the foolishness of worshipping false gods as recorded in Psalm 4:2; Jerimiah 13:25; Jeremiah 16:19; Amos 2:4; Zephaniah 1:4. More so, the first Christians were confronted with the worship of Greek and Roman deities Zeus and Hermes Acts 14:12 Zeus was the patron god of the city of Lystra and his temple was there. Paul was identified as the god Hermes (the Roman Mercury), Zeus' attendant and spokesman. Artemis (Acts 19:24-28) Artemis was the Greek name for the Roman goddess, Diana. There are several other gods not mentioned here. Christians have to identify gods, their meanings and characteristics in order not to worship them in error in expense of the true and Real God. For the Bible say in (1 John 4:1) "Beloved, do not believe every spirit, but test the spirits to see whether they are from God, because many false prophets have gone out into the world. By this you know the Spirit of God: every spirit that confesses

God, Kingdom of

that Jesus Christ has come in the flesh is from God;..."

God, Kingdom of: The rule of an eternal sovereign God over all creatures and things (Psalm 103:19; Daniel 4:3). The kingdom of God is also the designation for the sphere of salvation entered into at the new birth (John 3:5-7), and is synonymous with the "kingdom of heaven." The kingdom of God embraces all created intelligence, both in heaven and earth that are willingly subject to the Lord and are in fellowship with Him. *The kingdom of God is, therefore, universal in that it includes created angels and men. It is eternal, as God is eternal, and it is spiritual—found within all born-again believers.* We enter the kingdom of God when we are born again, and we are then part of that kingdom for eternity. It is a relationship "born of the spirit" (John 3:5), and we have confident assurance that it is so because the Spirit bears witness with our spirits (Romans 8:16). God is sovereign, omnipotent, omniscient and the ruler over all of His creation. However, the designation "the kingdom of God" compasses that realm which is subject to God and will be for eternity. The rest of creation will be destroyed. Only that which is part of the "kingdom of God" will remain. 2 It is the eternal reign of God as the resultant effect of the rapture into the New Heaven and New Earth where the government of God alone will be felt by all Christly souls. There will be no tears, no agony, no injustice, hatred, and sin will not be among the elect. The Kingdom of God will be feel by God's authority and ruling power and Glory, Joy and Happiness since death and sickness will be no more.

God, Kingdom of; and Kingdom of Heaven: While some believe that the Kingdom of God and Kingdom of Heaven are referring to different things, it is clear that both phrases are referring to the same thing. The phrase "kingdom of God" occurs 68 times in 10 different New Testament books, while "kingdom of heaven" occurs only 32 times, and only in the Gospel of Matthew. Based on Matthew's exclusive use of the phrase and the Jewish nature of his Gospel, some interpreters have concluded that Matthew was writing concerning the millennial kingdom while the other New Testament authors were referring to the universal kingdom. However, a closer study of the use of the phrase reveals that this interpretation is in error. For example, speaking to the rich young ruler, Christ uses "kingdom of heaven" and "kingdom of God" interchangeably. "Then Jesus said to his disciples, 'I tell you the truth, it is hard for a rich man to enter the kingdom of heaven'" (Matthew 19:23). In the very next verse, Christ proclaims, "Again I tell you, it is easier for a camel to go through the eye of a needle than for a rich man to enter the kingdom of God" (verse 24). Jesus makes no distinction between the two terms but seems to consider them synonymously.

Mark and Luke used "kingdom of God" where Matthew used "kingdom of heaven" frequently in parallel accounts of the same parable Compare (Matthew 11:11-12) with (Luke 7:28; Matthew 13:11with Mark 4:11 and Luke 8:10; Matthew 13:24 with Mark 4:26; Matthew 13:31 with Mark 4:30 and Luke 13:18; Matthew 13:33 with Luke 13:20; Matthew 18:3 with Mark 10:14 and Luke 18:16; and Matthew 22:2 with Luke 13:29). In each instance, Matthew used the phrase "kingdom of heaven" while Mark andor Luke used "kingdom of God." Clearly, the two phrases refer to the same thing.

Golden Rule, The: 'Do as you would be done by'. All things whatsoever ye would that men do to you, do ye even so to them for this is the law and the prophets. (Mathew 7:12)

Golgotha: The place outside Jerusalem where Christ was crucified. The word is Aramaic – meaning 'skull'. 2 It may have been a place of execution when bodies were picked clean by animals or was so named from the round bear contour of the site. There is no biblical evidence to support that it was a hillock. The traditional site is that discovered by Constantine. *Calvaria* is the Greek and Latin equivalent of 'Golgotha'.

Gomorrah, Sodom and: Generally, any town or towns regarded as exceptional centre of vice and immorality. 2 An allusion to cities that God destroyed for their wickedness as in (Genesis 18:19). Sodom in particular was the city whose inhabitant wanted to know the two angels staying with Lot (Genesis 19:5), but Lot offered them his two daughters instead. Hence sodomy as alternative term for buggery. And also, 'sodomite' as the word for a person who practice this, while 'sod' is a slang term for an unpleasant person or any person in general ('lucky sod') and 'sod off' as one of the several fairly crude expressions meaning 'go away'.

Good: There are many meanings of good or goodness often used in everyday communication. Meaning to be desired or approved of. "it's good that he's is a Christian" showing approval. These words often appear in a non-moral sense; a "good" or "good-of-appearance" woman is beautiful (Genesis 6:2 ; 24:16 ; 26:7 ; 2 Samuel 11:2 ; Esther 1:11 ; Esther 2:2-3 Esther 2:7) and a "good" man is handsome (1 Samuel 9:2). A land may be good (Deuteronomy 1:25 Deuteronomy 1:35) and so may gold (2 Chronicles 3:5 2 Chronicles 3:8), soil (Luke 8:8), a tree (Mathew 7:17), wine (John 2:10), or all of creation (seven times in Genesis. 1). But the most theologically important uses of these words have

Good

to do with moral qualities. God's goodness is a bedrock truth of the gospel of Christ. His goodness is praised in the (Psalms 25:8 ; 34:8 ; 86:5 ; 100:5 ; 118:1 ; 136:1 ; 145:9). Jesus affirms the Father's goodness when speaking to the rich young ruler (Mathew 19:17 ; Mark 10:18 ; Luke 18:19). In (1 Peter 2:3) Peter echoes the language of (Psalm 34:8): "Taste and see that the Lord is good!" Although we might discuss God's goodness in some abstract philosophical sense, in Scripture his goodness appears most clearly in his dealings with people. He is not only good in general, but he is good to us (Psalm 23:6 ; 68:10 ; 73:1 ; 119:65 ; 145:9 ; Lamentation 3:25 ; Luke 6:35 ; Romans 2:4 ; 11:22 ; Ephesians 2:7 ; Titus 3:4). Human goodness is modelled on divine goodness (Mathew 5:48). For human beings goodness involves right behaviour, expresses itself in kindness and other praiseworthy qualities, includes avoiding evil, and springs from the inner person. It is nearly impossible to think about goodness in the abstract. In Scripture goodness always involves particular ways of behaving. Because God is good, he is good to his people; when people are good they behave decently toward each other, based on God's goodness to them. Moses' invitation to Hobab expresses this emphasis: "Come with us and we will treat you well, for the Lord has promised good things to Israel" (Numbers 10:29). The general biblical words for "good/ goodness" include this idea of right behaviour, although the idea is often expressed by means of a more specific term like "upright or uprightness" or "righteous or righteousness."

The goodness God's people exhibit shows itself in various moral qualities, notably kindness; , translated "goodness" or "kindness, " serves as one of the major synonyms of "good, " in the Old Testament. In the New Testament many words describe the specific characteristics and behaviours of good people, including "just/justice, " "righteous/ righteousness, " "holy/holiness, " "pure/ purity, " "gentle/gentleness, " and "kind/ kindness." If "goodness" is the general term, these other specific terms show what goodness means in daily living.

In other words, if we say "the play had good reviews" having the required qualities; of a high standard. a high standard, quality, superior; as opposed to the antonyms bad. skilled at doing or dealing with a specified thing. "I'm good at crosswords" synonyms: capable, able, proficient, adept, adroit, accomplished, seasoned, skilful, skilled, gifted, talented, masterly, virtuoso, expert, knowledgeable, qualified, trained; More healthy, strong, or well. "she's not feeling too good" synonyms: healthy, fine, sound, tip-top, hale, hale and hearty, hearty, lusty, fit, robust, sturdy, strong, vigorous it means Goodness involves not only right behaviour but also avoiding its opposite, evil. The choice between good and evil has lain before people since the garden of Eden when Adam and Eve ate fruit from the "tree of the knowledge of good and evil" (Genesis 2:9). Since then God's curse has fallen on "those who call evil good and good evil, who put darkness for light and light for darkness, who put bitter for sweet and sweet for bitter" (Isaiah 5:20). A wise ruler like Solomon, or indeed anyone who wants to obey God, needs the wisdom to tell good from evil (1 Kings 3:9) ; (Hebrew 5:14). Those who serve God will "seek good, not evil, hate evil, love good" (Amos 5:14-15). For the Christian or the faithful Israelite, goodness has never been a matter of outward behaviour alone; it comes from within. An evil person is evil within (Genesis 6:5) ; (Mark 7:14-23) ; and parallels). In the same way a good person's good behaviour shows a good heart (Mathew 12:33-35). In the Old Testament God's goodness to his people and their goodness in response is based on the covenant between them. God's appeal to his people to return to the covenant relationship finds expression in a call to simple goodness (Micah 6:6-8). In the New Testament goodness is a fruit of the Spirit (Galatians 5:22), while moral excellence is one of the steps on the "ladder of virtue" as in (2 Peter 1:5)."For this very reason, make every effort to add to your faith goodness; and to goodness, knowledge";

Good Friday: A religious holiday, observed primarily by Christians, commemorating the crucifixion of Jesus Christ and his death at Calvary. The holiday is observed during Holy Week as part of the Paschal Triduum on the Friday preceding Easter Sunday, and may coincide with the Jewish observance of Passover. It is also known as Holy Friday, Great Friday, Black Friday, or Easter Friday, though the last term properly refers to the Friday in Easter week. Based on the details of the canonical gospels, the Crucifixion of Jesus was most likely to have been on a Friday (the day before the Jewish Sabbath) (John 19:42). "Because it was the Jewish day of Preparation and since the tomb was nearby, they laid Jesus there". The estimated year of the Crucifixion is AD 33, by two different groups, and originally as AD 34 by Isaac Newton via the differences between the Biblical and Julian calendars and the crescent of the moon. A third method, using a completely different astronomical approach based on a lunar Crucifixion darkness and eclipse model (consistent with Apostle Peter's reference to a "moon of blood" in (Acts 2:20) "he sun will be turned to darkness and the moon to blood before the coming of the great and glorious day of the Lord". points to Friday, 3 April AD 33. Good Friday is a widely-instituted legal holiday in many national governments

Gospel

around the world, including in most Western countries as well as in 12 U.S. states.

Gospel: ('Good news', from Ecclesiastical *Latin bonus nuntius,* literally translating latin evangelism, itself representing Greek *euaggelion)* The word is used to describe collectively the lives of Christ as told by the Evangelists in the New Testament, to signify the message of redemption set forth in those books, to denotes the entire Christian message and to apply to any doctrine or teaching set forth for some specific purposes.

2 The first four books of the New Testament, known as the Gospels, are ascribed to Mathew, Mark, Luke, and John, although their exact authorship is uncertain. The first three of these are called the Synoptic Gospel because the follow the same line and may be brought under the General view of synopsis. The forth Gospel stands apart as the work of just one mind. There are many Apocryphal Gospels as those shown below.

Gospel, Synopsis: *Synoptic,* in Greek, means "seeing or viewing together," and by that definition, Matthew, Mark, and Luke cover much the same subject matter and treat it in similar ways by putting the texts of the first three Gospels side by side so they could be compared. They are otherwise known by coining the term "Synoptic Gospels."

Because the first three accounts of Christ's life are so alike, this has produced what Bible scholars call the Synoptic Problem. Their common language, subjects, and treatment cannot be coincidental.

2 However, a couple theories try to explain what happened. Some scholars believe an oral gospel existed first, which Matthew, Mark, and Luke used in their versions. Others argue that Matthew and Luke borrowed heavily from Mark. A third theory claims an unknown or lost source once existed, providing much information on Jesus. Scholars call this lost source "Q," short for quelle, a German word meaning "source." Still another theory says Matthew and Luke copied from both Mark and Q.

3 The *Synoptics* are written in third person. Matthew, also known as Levi, was an apostle of Jesus, an eyewitness to most of the events in his text. Mark was a traveling companion of Paul, as was Luke. Mark was also an associate of Peter, another of Jesus' apostles who had firsthand experience of Jesus Christ.

Grace (noun): The free and unearned favour of God. 2. A short prayer of thanks said before or after meal. 3 Grace is an amplifying force for destiny. (Psalm 18 :36) When Grace is at work, one take a step and God amplifies it. For instance, the four Lepers in (2 Kings 7: 3-7) encountered Grace as they approached the Syrian

Green Pastures

Camp.. Grace happen when God made the enemy hear the sound of Chariots and caused the enemy to flee, leaving everything behind. The four lepers walk by Grace into plenty. Having been rejected from the city, they became celebrities overnight because God amplified their steps.. 3. Concerning the apostles, great Grace was released upon them as they were praying. That grace placed them in a unique class of their own It is not of him that willeth nor of him that runneth, but of God that showeth mercy' (Romans 9:36) .

Grace, Exceeding: *(Phr)* meaning The unspeakable, immeasurable, in-explainable, indescribable, surpassing and unfathomable gift of God. (Ephesians 2:7) affirmed the Exceeding Grace 'That in the ages to come he might show the exceeding riches of his grace in his kindness towards us through Christ Jesus. Again in (2 Corinthians 9: 14-15) "And by their prayer for you, which long after you for the exceeding grace of God in you. Glory to God for his unspeakable gift".

Green Pastures: In (Psalm 23:2) David – a man fond of boasting in the Lord declared "He makes me to lie down in *green pastures*: he leads me beside the still waters." Green pasture here means -

> Pasture: Noun, plural : pastures 1 land covered with grass and other low plants suitable for grazing animals, especially cattle or sheep. "areas of rich meadow pasture" synonyms: grazing land, grazing, grassland, grass, pasture land, pasturage, range, ley, paddock, croft; More 2 used to refer to a person's situation in life. "she left the office for pastures new" verb 3rd person present: pastures 1 put (animals) to graze in a pasture. "they pastured their cows in the water meadow"

-The Redemptive Grace. A better or more exciting opportunity or place, Areas of good vegetation, rich meadow. In ordinary usage, often, lot of scientists are seeking greener pastures abroad because of the scarcity of opportunities at home. A better situation After a successful year of labour, toiling or work. The young, ambitious coach was seeking greener pastures with another team. The survey finds many older residents are looking for greener pastures.

2 In the case of David and Christians, this indicates that as a sheep in Christ's care, "He makes me to lie down in green pastures: he leads me beside the still waters."

Green Pastures

Both the "green pastures" and "still waters" indicate a blessed abundance, further illustrating the benefits of a God-led life. There is fullness of God in green pastures. No sorrow, there is permanent joy, happiness, favours, prosperity as everything is provided by the shepherd, Flocks rest in perfect tranquillity, The shepherd in His effort often remember the crown and the blood at the "Mercy seat" and provides abounding grace in honour and glory to the trinity. Praise the Lord!

3 The Christian life has two elements in it, the contemplative and the active, and both of these are richly provided for. First, the contemplative. He maketh me to lie down in green pastures. What are these "green pastures" but the gospel of truth -- always fresh, always rich, and never exhausted? There is no fear of biting the bare ground where the grass is long enough for the flock to lie down in it. Sweet and full are the doctrines of the gospel; fit food for souls, as tender grass is natural nutriment for sheep. When by faith we are enabled to find rest in the promises, we are like the sheep that lie down in the midst of the pasture; we find at the same moment provender and peace, rest and refreshment, serenity and satisfaction. But observe: "He maketh me to lie down." It is the Lord who graciously enables us to perceive the preciousness of his truth, and to feed upon it. How grateful ought we to be for the power to appropriate the promises! There are some distracted souls who would give worlds if they could but do this. They know the blessedness of it, but they cannot say that this blessedness is theirs. They know the "green pastures", but they are not made to "lie down" in them. Those believers who have for years enjoyed a "full assurance of faith" should greatly bless their gracious God. Hallelujah!

3 The second part of a vigorous Christian's life consists in gracious activity. We not only think, but we act. We are not always lying down to feed, but are journeying onward toward perfection; hence we read, he leadeth me beside the still waters. What are these "still waters" but the influences and graces of his blessed Spirit? His Spirit attends us in various operations, like waters -- in the plural -- to cleanse, to refresh, to fertilise, to cherish. They are "still waters", for the Holy Ghost loves peace, and sounds no trumpet of ostentation in his operations. He may flow into our soul, but not into our neighbour's, and therefore our neighbour may not perceive the divine presence; and though the blessed Spirit may be pouring his floods into one heart, yet he that sitteth next to the favoured one may know nothing of it. "In sacred silence of the mind My heaven, and there my God I find." Still waters run deep. There is nothing noisy than empty drum. That silence is golden indeed in which the Holy Spirit meets with the souls of his saints. Not to rag-

ing waves of strife, but to peaceful streams of holy love does the Spirit of God conduct the chosen sheep? He is like a dove, not an eagle; the dew, not the hurricane. Our Lord leads us beside these "still waters;" we could not go there of ourselves, we need his guidance, therefore it is said, "he leadeth me." He does not drive us. Moses drives us by the law, but Jesus leads us by his example, and the gentle drawing of his love. Praise the living Jesus and crown the trinity!!

4 *Green Pasture* can also mean, the "Pastures of tender grass." The Hebrew word rendered "pastures" as usually "dwellings," or "habitations." It is applied here properly to "pastures," as places where flocks and herds lie down for repose. The word rendered in the margin "tender grass" - refers to the first shoots of vegetation from the earth - young herbage - tender grass - as clothing the meadows, and as delicate food for cattle, (Job 6:5). It differs from ripe grass ready for mowing, which is expressed by a different word. The idea is that of calmness and repose, as suggested by the image of flocks "lying down on the grass." But this is not the only idea. It is that of flocks that lie down on the grass "fully fed" or "satisfied," their wants being completely supplied. The exact point of contemplation in the mind of the poet, I apprehend, is that of a flock in young and luxuriant grass, surrounded by abundance, and, having satisfied their wants, lying down amidst this luxuriance with calm contentment. It is not merely a flock enjoying repose; it is a flock whose wants are supplied, lying down in the midst of abundance. Applied to the psalmist himself, or to the people of God generally, the idea is, that the wants of the soul are met and satisfied, and that, in the full enjoyment of this, there is the conviction of abundance - the repose of the soul at present satisfied, and feeling that in such abundance want will always be unknown and no calamity will perpetrate for you as a Christian to be wanted! Is by enemies or foe? When the Lord is your Shepherd?

Group, the people (PG):
The largest group through which the Gospel can flow without encountering significant barriers of understanding and acceptance. There are approximately 11,690 people groups worldwide.

Group, an unreached people (UPG):
A people group in which less than 2% of the population is Evangelical Christians. Globally there are approximately 6,400 UPGs.

Group, an unengaged, unreached people (UUPG):
Unengaged unreached people groups have no coordinated evangelical Christian missionary presence among them. Unengaged unreached people groups have never heard the Gospel, or they may have been exposed to the Gospel in the past, but have been forgotten. There are 5,845 UUPG worldwide.

Hh

Habakkuk: *Habakkuk* was a prophet in the Hebrew Bible. He is the author of the Book of Habakkuk, the eighth of the collected twelve minor prophets. *Habakkuk* is unique among the prophets in that he openly questions the wisdom of God.

2 Since the book of Habakkuk consists of five oracles about the Chaldeans (Babylonians), and the Chaldean rise to power is dated from (612 BC), it is assumed he was active about that time, making him an early contemporary of Jeremiah and Zephaniah. Jewish sources, however, do not group him with those two prophets, who are often placed together, so it is possible that he was slightly earlier. Because the final chapter of his book is a song, it is sometimes assumed that he was a member of the tribe of Levi which served as musicians in Solomon's Temple. 3 The name Habakkuk, or 'Habacuc' appears in the Hebrew Bible only in (Habakkuk 1:1, 3:1) This name does not occur elsewhere. The Septuagint transcribes his name into Greek as (*Hambakoum*), andthe Vulgate transcribes it into Latin as *Abacuc*.]

Habakkuk appears in Bel and the Dragon, which is part of the Additions to Daniel found in the Biblical apocrypha. (Habakkuk 1: 33–39) state that Habakkuk is in Judea and after making some stew, he's told by an angel to take the stew to Daniel, who was in Babylon in the lion's den. After proclaiming he is unaware of both the den and Babylon, Habbakuk is transported to the den with Daniel via the angel. Habakkuk gives Daniel the food to sustain him, and is immediately taken back to "his own place". 4 Habakkuk is also mentioned in Lives of the Prophets, which also notes his time in Babylon.

Haggai: (Hebrew: Ḥaggay or Hag-i, Koine – Greek): Meaning 'my holiday' Was a Hebrew prophet during the building of the Second Temple in Jerusalem, and one of the twelve minor prophets in the Hebrew Bible and the author of the Book of Haggai. He was the first of three post-exile prophets from the Neo-Babylonian Exile of the House of Judah (with Zechariah, his contemporary, and Malachi, who lived about one hundred years later), who belonged to the period of Jewish history which began after the return from captivity in Babylon. Rarely anything is known of his personal history. He may have been one of the captives taken to Babylon by Nebuchadnezzar.

Haggai Ministry: This means Haggai gospel devotion and teachings. Haggai began his ministry about sixteen years after the return of the Jews to Judah (ca. 520 BC). The work of rebuilding the temple had been put to a stop through the intrigues of the Samaritans. After having been suspended for eighteen years, the work was resumed through the efforts of Haggai and Zechariah. They exhorted the people, which roused them from their lethargy, and induced them to take advantage of a change in the policy of the Persian government under Darius the Great. The name Haggai, with various vocalizations, is also found in the Book of Esther, as a eunuch servant of the Queen. He supported the officials of his time, specifically Zerubbabel, the governor, and Joshua the High Priest. In the Book of Haggai, God refers to Zerubbabel as "my servant" as King David was, and says he will make him as a "signet ring," as King Jehoiachin was (Haggai 2:22-23) 'I will overthrow the thrones of kingdoms and destroy the power of the kingdoms of the nations; and I will overthrow the chariots and their riders, and the horses and their riders will go down, everyone by the sword of another.' On that day,' declares the LORD of hosts, 'I will take you, Zerubbabel, son of Shealtiel, My servant,' declares the LORD, 'and I will make you like a signet ring, for I have chosen you,'" declares the LORD of hosts. see also (Jerimiah 22:24) "As surely as I live," declares the Lord, "even if you, Jehoiachin [c] son of Jehoiakim king of Judah, were a signet ring on my right hand, I would still pull you off". The signet ring symbolized a ring worn on the hand of Yahweh, showing that a king held divine favour. Thus, Haggai is implicitly, but not explicitly, saying that Zerubbabel would preside over a restored Davidic kingdom. As a God servant or Prophet, do you claim the qualities exhibit by Haggai? Claim it in Jesus Name! Hallelujah.

Hallelujah: A transliteration of the Hebrew word (Modern halleluya), which is composed of two elements: (second-person imperative masculine plural form of the Hebrew verb hallal: an exhortation to "praise" addressed to several people and (Yah). A word so acknowledge as attribute to the works of the trinity. The complimentary being Amen!. Meaning "Let it be so" or Let it be! Thus'

Hallowed

"The Lord is great in His Might Heaven! Hallelujah and the Gentiles or Christians - worshippers in a Church or anyone Praising responds – Amen!

2 Most well-known English versions of the Hebrew Bible translate the Hebrew "Hallelujah" as in (Psalm 150:1 -2) Let Everything that has Breath "Praise the LORD! Praise God in His sanctuary; Praise Him in His mighty expanse. Praise Him for His mighty deeds; Praise Him according to His excellent greatness...." as two Hebrew words, generally rendered as "Praise (ye)" and "the LORD", but the second word is given as "Yah" in the Lexham English Bible and Young's Literal Translation, "Jehovah" in the American Standard Version, and "Hashem" in the Orthodox Jewish Bible. Instead of a translation, the transliteration "Hallelujah" is used by JPS Tanakh, International Standard Version, Darby Translation, God's Word Translation, Holman Christian Standard Bible, and The Message, with the spelling "Halleluyah" appearing in the Complete Jewish Bible. The Greek-influenced form "Alleluia" appears in Wycliffe's Bible, the Knox Version and the New Jerusalem Bible. In the great song of praise to God for his triumph over the Whore of Babylon in chapter 19 of the New Testament Book of Revelation, the Greek word (allēluia), a transliteration of the same Hebrew word, appears four times, as an expression of praise rather than an exhortation to praise. In English translations this is mostly rendered as "Hallelujah", but as "Alleluia" in several translations, while a few have "Praise the Lord", "Praise God", "Praise our God", or "Thanks to our God" is found 24 times in the book of Psalms, and the Greek transliteration appears in the Septuagint version of Psalms and four times in Revelation 19. The word is used in Judaism as part of the Hallel prayers, and in Christian prayer, where since the earliest times it is used in various ways in liturgies, especially those of the Catholic Church and the Eastern Orthodox Church, both of which use the form "alleluia"anslit. The Evangelicals dwells on the modern English transliteration "Hallelujah"

Hallowed: (verb) past tense: hallowed; past participle: hallowed honour as holy. "the Ganges is hallowed as a sacred, cleansing river" make holy; consecrate. "hallowed ground" synonyms: h o l y, sacred, consecrated, sanctified, blessed, blest; greatly revere and honour. Jesus advised the disciples in (Luke 11:2) "And he said unto them, When ye pray, say, Our Father which art in heaven, *Hallowed* be thy name. Thy kingdom come. Thy will be done, as in heaven, so in earth". This is to say, when we pray as Christians, we must always reverence our Heavenly Father to hallow His name as He deserve all Glory to His name. Honour Jesus in your life everyday. Consider also what Solomon did in (2 Chronicles 7:7) "Moreover

Solomon hallowed the middle of the court that was before the house of the LORD: for there he offered burnt offerings, and the fat of the peace offerings, because the brazen altar which Solomon had made was not able to receive the burnt offerings, and the meat offerings, and the fat". As a Christian, what do you hallow for the Kingdom of God (Deuteronomy 26:13) "Then thou shalt say before the LORD thy God, I have brought away the *hallowed* things out of mine house, and also have given them unto the Levite, and unto the stranger, to the fatherless, and to the widow, according to all thy commandments which thou hast commanded me: I have not transgressed thy commandments, neither have I forgotten them" Significantly, this tithe of the third year was to be spent at home, these words must signify either that every man was to make this solemn profession at home in his private addresses to God, or that the next time he went up to the place of the sanctuary he was to make this declaration before the most holy place, where God was supposed to be peculiarly present. At whichever place he made it, it was to be done as before God; that is, solemnly, seriously, and in a religious manner, with due respect to God's presence, in obedience to his command, and with an eye to his glory.

Hand: As in (Isaiah 59:1) – "Behold, the LORD'S hand is not shortened, that it cannot save; neither his ear heavy, that it cannot hear": Hand is a prehensile, multi-fingered extremity located at the end of an arm or forelimb of primates such as humans, chimpanzees, monkeys, and lemurs. The right hand of God as in (Isaiah 41:10) –" Fear thou not; for I [am] with thee: be not dismayed; for I [am] thy God: I will strengthen thee; yea, I will help thee; yea, I will uphold thee with the right *hand* of my righteousness".

2 The word hand predominates the entire gospel and can be used on a few other vertebrates such as the koala (which has two possible thumbs on each "hand" and fingerprints remarkably similar to human fingerprints) are often described as having either "*hands*" or "*paws*" on their front limbs. The gospel dictionary focuses on Hands with Fingers which are some of the densest areas of nerve endings on the body, are the richest source of tactile feedback, and have the greatest positioning capability of the body; thus the sense of touch is intimately associated with hands. Like other paired organs (eyes, feet, legs), each hand is dominantly controlled by the opposing brain hemisphere, so that handedness, or the preferred hand choice for single-handed activities such as writing with a pencil, reflects individual brain functioning. All which are the creation of God.

Hands, Laying on of

Some evolutionary anatomists use the term *hand* to refer to the appendage of digits on the forelimb generally — for example, in the context of whether the three digits of the bird hand involved the same homologous loss of two digits as in the dinosaur hand. 3 The human hand has 27 bones, not including the 'sesamoid' bone, the number of which varies between people. 14 of which are the phalanges (proximal, intermediate and distal) of the fingers. The metacarpals are the bones that connects the fingers and the wrist. Each human hand has 5 metacarpals and 8 carpal bones. Among humaghtns, the hands play an important function in body language and sign language and greater role in the communication with God in form of lifting up of hands to Heaven when praying. Or Jesus lay hand from time to time on the sick as in (Mark 7:32) - And they bring unto him one that was deaf, and had an impediment in his speech; and they beseech him to put his hand upon him. To the Christian, there is the hand of Love, hand of favour, hand of fellowship — right hand, hand of blessing, hand in marriage etc.

Hands, Laying on of:

A religious ritual that accompanies certain religious practices, which are found throughout the world in varying forms. In Christian churches, this practice is used as both a symbolic and formal method of invoking the Holy Spirit primarily during baptisms and confirmations, healing services, blessings, and ordination of priests, ministers, elders, deacons, and other church officers, along with a variety of other church sacraments and holy ceremonies. As in (Hebrew 6:1-3) Therefore let us leave the elementary doctrine of Christ and go on to maturity, not laying again a foundation of repentance from dead works and of faith toward God, and of instruction about washings, the laying on of hands, the resurrection of the dead, and eternal judgment. And this we will do if God permits. Again (1 Timothy 5:22) warns " Do not be hasty in the laying on of hands, nor take part in the sins of others; keep yourself pure". (Mark 16: 17-18) "And these signs will accompany those who believe: in my name they will cast out demons; they will speak in new tongues; they will pick up serpents with their hands; and if they drink any deadly poison, it will not hurt them; they will lay their hands on the sick, and they will recover." (Acts 13:3) Then after fasting and praying they laid their hands on them and sent them off.

Hands, Why Laying on of:

In ordaining those who serve Indicating acceptance and approval of those who have been selected by the congregation - (Acts 6:1-6); (1Timothy 5:22) Beseeching God's blessing and protection on those who serve (Acts 13:1-3) "...the imposition of hands, accompanied by fasting and prayer, was, in this case, as in that of the seven deacons (Acts 6:6), merely their formal separation to the special work to which they had been called. This, indeed, is sufficiently evident from the context. What they did was doubtless what they had been told to do by the Holy Spirit. But the Holy Spirit simply said to them, 'Separate me Barnabas and Saul to the work to which I have called them.' The fasting, prayer, and imposition of hands was then, merely their separation to this work. It was a ceremony deemed by infinite wisdom suitable to such a purpose; and, therefore, whenever a congregation has a similar purpose to accomplish, they have, in this case, the judgments and will of God, which should be their guide as in (Acts 13:1-3) "Now in the church at Antioch there were prophets and teachers: Barnabas, Simeon called Niger, Lucius of Cyrene, Manaen (who had been brought up with Herod the tetrarch) and Saul. While they were worshiping the Lord and fasting, the Holy Spirit said, "Set apart for me Barnabas and Saul for the work to which I have called them." So after they had fasted and prayed, they placed their hands on them and sent them off". Praise the Lord!

2 In praying for those who are sick as in (Jeremiah 5:14-15) Nothing is said about laying on of hands in this passage. But its practice could certainly symbolize the blessing from God for which we pray "The laying on of hands was accompanied by prayer, the imposition of hands being the outward symbol of the prayer as in (Hebrew 6:2) "Of the doctrine of baptisms, and of *laying on of hands,* and of resurrection of the dead, and of eternal judgment.

Hanukkah: *See feast of Succoth or Festival of Lights.*

Harp: (1 Chronicles 13:6-8) "David and all Israel went up to Baalah, that is, to Kiriath-jearim, which belongs to Judah, to bring up from there the ark of God, the LORD who is enthroned above the cherubim, where His name is called. They carried the ark of God on a new cart from the house of Abinadab, and Uzza and Ahio drove the cart. David and all Israel were celebrating before God with all their might, even with songs and with lyres, *harps,* tambourines, cymbals and with trumpets. A harp is multi-string musical instrument which has the plane of its strings positioned perpendicularly to the soundboard. Organ logically, it is in the general category of chordophones (stringed instruments) and has its own sub category (the harps). All harps have a neck, resonator and strings. Some, known as frame harps, also have a pillar; those without the pillar are referred to as open harps. Depending on its size, which varies, a harp may be played while held in the lap or while it stands on a

Harp

table, or on the floor. *Harp* strings may be made of nylon, gut, wire or silk. On smaller *harps*, like the folk *harp*, the core string material will typically be the same for all strings on a given harp. Larger instruments like the modern concert harp mix string materials to attain their extended ranges. A person who plays the *harp* is called a harpist or harper. Folk musicians often use the term "harper", whereas classical musicians use "harpist". Harp is a significant instrument probably in praises to God. As God is the creator of everything, He takes delight in every contribution of what He created for particularly, the Israelites were in the habit of praising the Lord with *Harp* and lyre as in (1 Chronicles 15:28) "Thus all Israel brought up the ark of the covenant of the LORD with shouting, and with sound of the horn, with trumpets, with loud-sounding cymbals, with *harps* and lyres. Here we must see that praise is fitting for the upright as in (Psalm 33:1-2)

"Sing for joy in the LORD, O you righteous ones; Praise is becoming to the upright. Give thanks to the LORD with the lyre; Sing praises to Him with a *harp* of ten strings. Sing to Him a new song; Play skilfully with a shout of joy...." The *harp* is a musical instrument invented many centuries ago. When properly strung and played upon it yields sweet music, making glad the heart. The first mention of the harp made in the gospel is in (Genesis 4:21), and the inventor's name was Jubal. He was therefore called "the father of all such as handle the harp and organ".

Various types of harps are found in Africa, Europe, North and South America and in Asia. In antiquity, harps and the closely related lyres were very prominent in nearly all cultures. The harp also was predominant with medieval bards, troubadours and mine singers throughout the Spanish Empire. Harps continued to grow in popularity due to improvements in their design and construction through the beginning of the 20th century.

2 It was 1812 years before the coming of Jesus in the flesh that God organized the twelve tribes of Israel, the descendants of Jacob, into a nation, which nation thereafter was known as the nation of Israel. It was the only nation with which God made a covenant, and he did not recognize any other nation in the same way. (Amos 3:2) The nation of Israel was used to make living pictures or types, foreshadowing better things to come; and those who study the Scriptural account of Israel's experiences

are able to approximate closely future events which will be good for mankind. — (1 Corinthians 10:1-13) (Hebrews 10:1).

3 With the nation of Israel the harp was an instrument consecrated to joy and exultation. David, who for forty years was king of Israel, was an expert player on the *harp*, and it will be noted that in the Psalms often the *harp* is used to symbolize or teach some great truth. The Jews used this instrument on occasions of joy, such as jubilees and festivals.

Hate: Strong dislike or strong aversion towards a particular thing. As Christians, we must refrain from those things that God particularly say He *hate*; notably, Seven which are abomination to Him, Haughty eyes, a lying tongue, and hands that shed innocent blood, a heart that devise wicked plans, feet that run rapidly to evil, a false witness who utters lies and one who spreads strife among brothers. *(Proverbs 6: 16-19)* 2 For I *hate* divorce says the Lord, the God of Israel, and him who covers his garment with, 'says the Lord of hosts. So take heed to your spirit, that you do not deal treacherously *(Malacai 2:16)* 3 Christians must have a very strong dislike for sin, to the extent that we abhor sin. 4 Paul emphasized in *(Romans 12:9)* 'Let love be without hypocrisy. Abhor what is evil; cling to what is good'. 5 David adumbrate, "From your precepts I get understanding; therefore I hate every false way" *(Psalm 109:104)*

Haughty: (adjective) (Proverbs 16:18) Pride goes before destruction, a *haughty* spirit before a fall. arrogantly superior and disdainful. "a look of *haughty* disdain" synonyms: proud, vain, arrogant, conceited, snobbish, stuck-up, pompous, self-important, superior, egotistical, supercilious, condescending, lofty, patronizing, smug, scornful, contemptuous, disdainful, overweening, overbearing, imperious, lordly, cavalier, high-handed, full of oneself, above oneself;

In (Proverbs 6:16-19) is a list of "six things that the Lord hates, seven that are an abomination to Him." The first one listed is "haughty eyes," followed by such things as a lying tongue, hands that shed innocent blood, a false witness, and feet quick to run to evil. Haughty eyes are said to be sin in (Proverbs 21:4), along with a proud heart. To have haughty eyes is to have an arrogant demeanour; it's an overall attitude of one's heart that causes one to scorn or "look down on" others. The haughty person sets himself above others, and ultimately above God. When we are haughty, we become the centre of our universe; everything revolves around us. There is little, if any, concern for what others think and no consideration of the will of God. Pride, haughtiness, is the trunk of the tree from which all other sins sprout. When we are

Heart

at the centre of our world, then nothing that we want is unlawful to us. God is resistant to haughtiness. Over and over in Scripture, we read that God brings down the haughty and the proud (2 Samuel 2:28; Psalm 18:27; Isaiah 2:11, 5:15; Ezekiel 16:50). Twice in Proverbs, we read that haughtiness precedes destruction (Ezekiel 16:18, 18:12). The New Testament is clear on the dangers of arrogance, warning repeatedly against it. Both James and Peter warn that God actively opposes the proud (James 4:6, 1 Peter 5:5).

None of us are immune to pride. The Bible tells us of otherwise good people who were brought down in one way or another by pride. The godly king Uzziah was struck with leprosy because, in arrogance, he tried to take the place of the priest and burn incense before the Lord (2 Chronicles 26:16). Similarly, Hezekiah's pride in his possessions eventually brought the discipline of God on him (2 Chronicles 32:25). Peter's prideful statement that he would never forsake Jesus (Matthew 26:33-35) was found to be false when he denied Him (Matthew 26:69-75). The danger of pride is the reason for the many exhortations to humility in Scripture. Meditation on some key passages can fight the tendency we all have toward pride. First Corinthians 4:7 tells us that all we have is a gift, for which we should be thankful. Both (1 Peter 5:6) and (James 4:6) encourage humility by saying that God gives grace to the humble. (Isaiah 66:2) goes so far as to say that humility in the heart of a person actually draws God's attention. Humility of heart gives us a proper perspective. A proud heart – haughty eyes, if you will – renders a person intractable. Such a person is resisted by God.

Have come at once, All one's Christmases: A form of saying, one has been especially or unusually lucky or favoured. Normally, Christmas comes but once a year' and its pleasure are thus infrequent. So, enjoy it when you see it.

Heart: *(noun)* The hollow muscular organ in the chest that pumps blood around the body. 2 The central innermost or the heart of the city. 3 Heart could not be discussed here in its ordinary sense but as it is relative to the Gospel of Christ. This tiny organ is very important to our retention of the Gospel, Christ Jesus, who is also the Holy Spirit. 4 The Bible says that the life of a person is the blood. And it is the heart which pumps this life throughout the body. If any part of our body is deprived of the blood it soon withers and dies. 4 Even in everyday life, when someone is so serious they may find themselves saying; Come on! let's get to the 'heart' of the matter!" So just what is the heart of the Gospel of Jesus Christ? Most people in the Christian world believes the true gospel is a message about Christ

Heaven

and His crucifixion, while most of our Sabbath keeping congregation teach a different message as the gospel. 5 Jesus is the Heart of the Gospel particularly as he charged, after His death and the resurrection which follow. The resurrected Jesus Christ appeared to his disciples and commissioned them to take the gospel to the whole world. "Thus, go therefore and make disciples of all the nations, baptizing them in the name of the Father and the Son and the holy spirit, teaching them to observe all that I commanded you" (Mathew 28: 19-20). 6 Another heart of the gospel is Pauls teaching in 1 Corinthians 15: 1-4. Thus I make known to you brethren, the gospel which I preached to you, which also you received and which also you stand, by which also you are saved, if you hold fast the word which I preached to you unless you believed in vain. For I delivered to you as of first importance what I also received, that Christ died for our sins according to the Scriptures, and that He was buried, and that He was raised on the third day." 7 He continued with his letter to the Philippians in Philippians 1:12, He said that the "cause of Christ" had become well-known throughout the whole praetorian guard. As a result people had far more courage to speak the gospel without fear. He also admit that some were teaching "Christ" out of selfish ambition, but said that even in this he would rejoice because "Christ was preached." Once again, we find the *heart* of gospel message was about the person Jesus Christ.

Heaven: Often described as a "higher place", the holiest place, a Paradise, in contrast to Hell or the Underworld or the "low places", and universally or conditionally accessible by earthly beings according to various standards of divinity, goodness, piety, faith, or other virtues or right beliefs or simply the will of God. Some believe in the possibility of a heaven on earth in a World to Come. 2 ideally, it is a common religious, cosmological, or transcendent place where heavenly beings such as gods, (sky deities like the King or Queen of heaven, the Heavenly Father or Mother, or the Son of Heaven), angels, jinn, saints, or venerated ancestors originate, are enthroned, or live. It is commonly believed that heavenly beings can descend to earth or incarnate and that earthly beings can ascend to heaven in the afterlife or in exceptional cases, enter heaven alive. This confirm the belief by gospel believers that Heaven is a Kingdom as in (Matthew 5:17-20) "Do not think that I have come to abolish the Law or the Prophets; I have not come to abolish them but to fulfil them. I tell you the truth, until heaven and earth disappear, not the smallest letter, not the least stroke of a pen, will by any means disappear from the Law until everything is accomplished.

Heaven, Love in

Anyone who breaks one of the least of these commandments and teaches others to do the same will be called least in the kingdom of heaven, but whoever practices and teaches these commands will be called great in the *kingdom of heaven*. For I tell you that unless your righteousness surpasses that of the Pharisees and the teachers of the law, you will certainly not enter the *kingdom of heaven*.

Heaven, Love in: This explains if there will be any social structure or socialism in glory. Thus the common question is "Will we (the elects) be greater fools there than here?" Of course we will know our loved ones. This is a divinely designed, essential part of our joy. We are not designed to be solitary mystics, lovers of God alone, but to be, like God himself, lovers of men and women as well. Just as Jesus on Earth loved each person differently and specially—he did not love John as he loved Peter, because John was not Peter—so we are designed to love people specially. There is no reason why this specialness should be removed, rather than added to, in eternity. Our family and special friends will always be our family and special friends. In this life a child begins to learn to love by loving mother, then father, then siblings, then pets. The concentric circles of love are then gradually expanded, but the beginning lessons are never abandoned. There is no reason to think God rips up this plan after death.

Fortunately, we have some solid data to build on: divine revelation. God wants us to use our reason and also our imagination (for why should we neglect any God-given faculty) to explore the treasure of tantalizing hints in the gospel. To be indifferent to it is to be like the unprofitable servant who hid his master's talent in the ground. Those who sow their talent rightfully will be crowned as in (Revelation 7:13-17) "Then one of the elders asked me, "These in white robes--who are they, and where did they come from?" I answered, "Sir, you know." And he said, "These are they who have come out of the great tribulation; they have washed their robes and made them white in the blood of the Lamb. Therefore, "they are before the throne of God and serve him day and night in his temple; and he who sits on the throne will spread his tent over them. Never again will they hunger; never again will they thirst. The sun will not beat upon them, nor any scorching heat. For the Lamb at the center of the throne will be their shepherd; he will lead them to springs of living water. And God will wipe away every tear from their eyes." In having this data, we are in a position very different from that of the unbeliever (or rather, the difference lies in our believing the data, for the whole human race has it; it is public). We are like the sighted compared to the blind, who can only speculate about things visible. We can do more than speculate about things invisible. "What do you know about Heaven, anyway? Have you ever been there?" "No, but as Christians we have a very good Friend who has. He came here and told us about it and showed it to us. He is the Way, the Truth, and the Life."

Heaven, Citizen of: Indeed God created everyone and commissioned us to take a test on earth to see our level of endurance. Thus, he who endures till the end will wear the glorious crown. No wonder we pass through diverse temptation as children of God. Despite all the tribulation and woes of this life, what can or who separate us from the love of God as in (Romans 8: 35-39) "Who shall separate us from the love of Christ? shall tribulation, or distress, or persecution, or famine, or nakedness, or peril, or sword? As it is written , For thy sake we are killed all the day long; we are accounted as sheep for the slaughter. Nay, in all these things we are more than conquerors through him that loved us. For I am persuaded, that neither death, nor life, nor angels, nor principalities, nor powers, nor things present , nor things to come , Nor height, nor depth, nor any other creature, shall be able to separate us from the love of God, which is in Christ Jesus our Lord. Love is emphasize here, because of the love we have for Christ in Grace, we can withstand and endure every tribulation to the extent nothing can separate us from Him. Because we know where we are going – our Heavenly Home as Citizens. Love and work. The two are really one, for love is a work and work is a love. Love is a work, for it is something you do, not something you just feel or fall into. And work must be a love, for if not, it is threatening and boring. What love-work will we do in Heaven, then? (Revelation 21:4-8) explain how Christ will start the same way He started loving us on earth. For He first love us and poor His blood to wipe away our sins, so that we may attain our life eternal in our Heavenly Home. Thus when He start to love us in the Kingdom of Heaven, He will wipe every tears from our eyes "He will wipe every tear from their eyes. There will be no more death or mourning or crying or pain, for the old order of things has passed away." He who was seated on the throne said, "I am making everything new!" Then he said, "Write this down, for these words are trustworthy and true." He said to me: "It is done. I am the Alpha and the Omega, the Beginning and the End. To him who is thirsty I will give to drink without cost from the spring of the water of life. He who overcomes will inherit all this, and I will be his God and he will be my son. But the cowardly, the unbelieving, the vile, the murderers, the sexually immoral, those who practice magic arts, the idolaters and all liars--their place will be in the fiery lake of burning sulphur. This is the second death." In much the same way that He loved us, 'We will complete the very love-works we are meant to do on Earth. There are only six things that never get boring on Earth, six things that never come to an end: knowing and loving yourself, your neighbour, and God. Since persons are subjects and not objects, they are not exhaustible; they are like magic cows that give fresh milk forever as in (Mathew 6:10) "your kingdom come, your will be done, on earth as it is in heaven". These along with the two great commandments that are our job description for life, in both this world and the next, express this plan: We must love God wholly and we must love our neighbour as ourselves. And in order to love we must know; get to know, as endlessly as we love endlessly. This never gets boring, even on Earth: getting to know and love more and more someone we already know and love. It is our clue and our preparation for our eternal destiny of infinite fascination in the Heavenly Kingdom as Citizens.

Heaven of Heavens: This is where God now has His heavenly throne and to which, after His resurrection, Christ "ascended up far above all heavens" (Ephesians 4:10) to be seated at the right hand of the Father. It is beyond all the stars and galaxies and presumably has no end. It may be synonymous with the third heaven as in (1 Kings 8:27) "But will God indeed dwell on the earth? behold, the heaven and heaven of heavens cannot contain thee; how much less this house that I have builded?" (1 Kings 8:27). Actually, the concept of "first heaven," "second heaven," and "third heaven" may also have another meaning, depending on context. For example, Peter speaks of "the heavens |which| were of old," "the heavens . . . which are now," and the "new heavens" which God has promised (2 Peter 3:5, 7, 13) in the ages to come. The phrase "heaven of heavens" actually occurs at least six times in the Old Testament. Someday, however, the heavenly Jerusalem will come "down from God out of heaven" (Revelation 21:2), and "the throne of God and of the Lamb shall be in it" (Revelation 22:3). The heaven of heavens will be on earth (the new earth) and we also shall be there-with our Lord--forever. Therefore, sing praises "to him that rideth upon the heavens of heavens" (Psalm 68:33).

Heaven, The Kingdom of:
See – the Kingdom of God.

Heavenly Host: (Hebrew Sabaoth "armies") refers to a large army (Luke 2:13) of good angels mentioned both in the Hebrew and Christian Bibles, as well as other Jewish and Christian texts. Most descriptions of angels in the

Heavenly Signs, The

Bible describe them in military terms, such as encampment (Genesis 32:1-2), command structure (Psalms 91:11-12; Mathew.13:41; Revelation.7:2), and combat (Judges.5:20; Job 19:12; Revelation.12:7). The heavenly host participate in the War in Heaven and, according to some interpretations, will battle Satan and Satan's own army at the End of Days and be victorious.

The nativity of our Saviour was published first by one angel, but it must be celebrated by a multitude of angels, who appear praising God upon this occasion. These are called the Lord's host, (Psalm 103:20 – 21) not only because he useth them as his arms, to destroy his enemies, but also because of the order which is amongst them. How they praised God is expressed in (Luke 2:14), they sang "Glory to God in the highest, and on earth peace, goodwill toward men. The words may be taken either judicative, as signifying that was come to pass that day, by which God would have glory, men would have peace, and the good will of God to the sons of men was unspeakably declared: or predatorily, the angels desiring God might have glory, and that peace might be on earth, and the goodwill of God published to the sons of men. But the Vulgar Latin is most corrupt, that rendereth these words, peace to men of good will. When we consider that *the heavenly host* was here praising God, it will appear very reasonable to interpret these words as judicative; the angels hereby declaring their apprehensions, and the truth concerning this act of providence, no act more declaring the glory of God's power, wisdom, or goodness; nor more declaring his good will towards men, and more conducing to peace upon the earth, whether by it we understand the union of the Jews and Gentiles, or that peace of particular souls which floweth from a justification by faith in Christ; for though the text seemeth to speak of three things, glory to God, peace on earth, and good will toward men, yet indeed they are but two; the two latter differing only as the cause and the effect; the good will of God is the cause, peace with or amongst men is the effect, as in (Romans 5:1) "Therefore, since we have been justified through faith, we[a] have peace with God through our Lord Jesus Christ"; Again, (Ephesians 2:14) state - "For he himself is our peace, who has made the two groups one and has destroyed the barrier, the dividing wall of hostility",

Heavenly: (adjective). Anything, Sublime; delightful; enchanting. Of or relating to the firmament; celestial: the sun, the moon, and other heavenly bodies Of or relating to the abode of God; divine things.

Heavenly Signs, The: In (Matthew 24), Jesus Christ prophesied some important end-time signs: "Immediately after the tribula-

Heavenly home

tion [the unprecedented time of trouble described earlier in the chapter] of those days the sun will be darkened, and the moon will not give its light; the stars will fall from heaven, and the powers of the heavens will be shaken" (verse 29). John expanded on this theme of heavenly signs under the inspiration of Jesus Christ. (Revelation:6:12-17) "I watched as he opened the sixth seal. There was a great earthquake. The sun turned black like sackcloth made of goat hair, the whole moon turned blood red, and the stars in the sky fell to earth, as figs drop from a fig tree when shaken by a strong wind. The heavens receded like a scroll being rolled up, and every mountain and island was removed from its place. Then the kings of the earth, the princes, the generals, the rich, the mighty, and everyone else, both slave and free, hid in caves and among the rocks of the mountains. They called to the mountains and the rocks, "Fall on us and hide us[a] from the face of him who sits on the throne and from the wrath of the Lamb! For the great day of their[b] wrath has come, and who can withstand it?" Through the ages mankind has been fascinated by the heavenly bodies, sometimes worshipping them, sometimes reading portents in them. Unusual events such as eclipses and comets sparked fear and were seen as signs of impending disasters. But modern man has mapped the heavens and calculated the eclipses and orbits of comets. What would it take to get people's attention today? Likely it will take the awesome spectacles Christ foretold. The heavenly signs He mentioned will be clearly supernatural, and they will fulfil numerous prophecies of the Old Testament traceable in the gospels.

Heavenly home: (2 Corinthians 5) Simply Our Home in Heaven. We know that the earthly tent we live in will be destroyed. But we have a building made by God. It is a house in heaven that lasts forever. Human hands did not build it. During our time on earth we groan. We long to put on our house in heaven as if it were clothing. 3 Then we will not be naked. While we live in this tent of ours, we groan under our heavy load. We don't want to be naked. We want to be dressed with our house in heaven. What must die will be swallowed up by life. God has made us for that very purpose. He has given us the Holy Spirit as a down payment. The Spirit makes us sure of what is still to come. So here is what we can always be certain about. As long as we are at home in our bodies, we are away from the Lord. We live by believing, not by seeing. We are certain about that. We would rather be away from our bodies and at home with the Lord. So we try our best to please him. We want to please him whether we are at home in our bodies or away from them.

Hebrews: This is an ethnonym, appearing 34 times within 32 verses of the Tanakh (Hebrew Bible). It is mostly taken as synonymous with the Semitic Israelites, especially in the pre-monarchic period when they were still nomadic, but in some instances it may also be used in a wider sense, referring to the Phoenicians, or to other ancient groups, such as the group known as Shasu of Yhw on the eve of the Bronze Age collapse. By the Roman era, Greek Hebraios could refer to the Jews in general, as Strong's Hebrew Dictionary puts it "any of the Jewish Nation" and at other times more specifically to the Jews living in Judea.

Hebron: (Hebrew: ?evron;) is a Palestinian city located in the southern West Bank, 30 km (19 mi) south of Jerusalem. Nestled in the Judean Mountains, it lies 930 meters (3,050 ft) above sea level. It is the largest city in the West Bank, and the second largest in the Palestinian territories after Gaza, and home to approximately 250,000 Palestinians, and between 500 and 850 Jewish settlers concentrated in O'Neill settlement and around the old quarter. The city is divided into two sectors: H1, controlled by the Palestinian Authority and H2, roughly 20% of the city, administered by Israel. The settlers are governed by their own municipal body, the Committee of the Jewish Community of Hebron. The city is most notable for containing the traditional burial site of the biblical Patriarchs and Matriarchs, within the Cave of the Patriarchs. It is therefore considered the second-holiest city in Judaism after Jerusalem. The city is venerated by Jews, Christians, and Muslims for its association with Abraham.] It was traditionally viewed as one of the "four holy cities of Islam."

Hebron is a busy hub of West Bank trade, responsible for roughly a third of the area's gross domestic product, largely due to the sale of marble from quarries. It is locally well known for its grapes, figs, limestone, pottery workshops and glassblowing factories, and is the location of the major dairy product manufacturer, al-Junaidi. The old city of Hebron is characterized by narrow, winding streets, flat-roofed stone houses, and old bazaars. The city is home to Hebron University and the Palestine Polytechnic University and notably has no cinemas or places of entertainment. Hebron is detached to cities of ad-Dhahiriya, Dura, Yatta, the surrounding villages with no borders. Hebron is also the largest Palestinian governorate with its population of more than half a million.

2 Hebron is noted as the place wherewith Abraham moved to live in a land called Mamre as in (Genesis 13:18) "Then Abram removed his tent, and came and dwelt in the plain of Mamre, which is in Hebron, and built there an altar unto the LORD". Also, it is a place Sarah, the wife of Abraham died and was buried – see (Genesis 23:2) "And Sarah died in

Hephzibah

Kirjatharba; the same is Hebron in the land of Canaan: and Abraham came to mourn for Sarah, and to weep for her", (Genesis 23:19) "And after this, Abraham buried Sarah his wife in the cave of the field of Machpelah before Mamre: the same is Hebron in the land of Canaan".

Hephzibah: *(Heph-zi-bah)*-My delight in her. The wife of Hezekiah and mother of king Manasseh (2 Kings 21:1) 2 A symbolic name of Zion, as representing the Lord's favour towards her (Isaiah 62:4 NKJ)

Herod: A name used of several kings belonging to the Herodias Dynasty of the Roman province of Judaea: There are several of the Herod's as: Herod the Great (c. 74–4 BC), client king of Judea who rebuilt the Second Temple (in Jerusalem) into Herod's Temple, Herod Archelaus (23 BC–c. AD 18), ethnarch of Samaria, Judea, and Idumea, Herod Antipas (20 BC–c. AD 40), tetrarch of Galilee and Peraea, called "Herod the Tetrarch" or "Herod" in the New Testament up to (Acts 4:27), and described therein as ordering John the Baptist's death and as mocking Jesus.

Others are, Herod II (c. 27 BC–33 AD), sometimes called Herod Philip I, father of Salome, Philip the Tetrarch (4 BC–AD 34), sometimes called Herod Philip II, tetrarch of Ituraea and Trachonitis, Herod Agrippa I (c. 10 BC–AD 44), client king of Judaea, called "King Herod" or "Herod" in Acts 12 of the New Testament, Herod of Chalcis, also known as Herod III, king of Chalcis (AD 41–48), Herod Agrippa II (AD 27–100), tetrarch of Chalcis who was described in Acts of the Apostles as "King Agrippa" before whom Paul of Tarsus defended himself, Herodes Atticus (AD 101–177), an unrelated Greek aristocrat who served as a Roman Senator and proponent of Sophism and many others defined accordi.ng to their influence and importance in the gospel story

Hezekiah: (Hebrew, Greek: - Ezekias, in the Septuagint; also transliterated as ?izkiyyahu or ?izkiyyah) was, the son of Ahaz and the 13th king of Judah. Archaeologist Edwin Thiele has concluded that his reign was between c. 715 and 686 BC. He is also one of the most prominent kings of Judah mentioned in the Hebrew Bible and is one of the kings mentioned in the genealogy of Jesus in the Gospel of Matthew. According to the Hebrew Bible, Hezekiah witnessed the destruction of the northern Kingdom of Israel by Sargon's Assyrians in c. 720 BC and was king of Judah during the invasion and siege of Jerusalem by Sennacherib in 701 BC. Hezekiah enacted sweeping religious reforms, including a strict mandate for the sole worship of Yahweh and a prohibition on venerating other deities within the Temple in Jerusalem. Isaiah and Micah were the prophets during his reign.

2 Hezekiah was the twelfth king of Judah, son of the apostate Ahaz and Abi or Abijah, ascended the throne at the age of 25, B.C. 726.

Hezekiah was one of the three most perfect kings of Judah. (2 Kings 18:5) His first act was to purge and repair and reopen with splendid sacrifices and perfect ceremonial the temple. He also destroyed a brazen serpent, said to have been the one used by Moses in the miraculous healing of the Israelites, (Numbers 21:9) which had become an object of adoration. When the kingdom of Israel had fallen, Hezekiah invited the scattered inhabitants to a peculiar Passover, which was continued for the unprecedented period of fourteen days. (2 Chronicles 29:30,31) At the head of a repentant and united people, Hezekiah ventured to assume the aggressive against the Philistines and in a series of victories not only rewon the cities which his father had lost, (2 Chronicles 28:18) but even dispossessed them of their own cities except Gaza, (2 Kings 18:8) and Gath. He refused to acknowledge the supremacy of Assyria. (2 Kings 18:7) Instant war was imminent and Hezekiah used every available means to strengthen himself. (2 Kings 20:20) It was probably at this dangerous crisis in his kingdom that we find him sick and sending for Isaiah, who prophesies death as the result. (2 Kings 20:1) Hezekiah's prayer for longer life is heard. The prophet had hardly left the palace when he was ordered to return and promise the king immediate recovery and fifteen years more of life. (2 Kings 20:4) An embassy coming from Babylon ostensibly to compliment Hezekiah on his convalescence, but really to form an alliance between the two powers, is favourably received by the king, who shows them the treasures which he had accumulated.

Holy Ghost, The: (Holy Spirit) The circulating man of the trinity. Charged with the divine executive functions to carry out the will or order of the trinity. Going everywhere, remaining everywhere, Having authority to embolden, empower, divinely acted and reacted to restore life and counter all agent of discomfort in the life of Christians, believers. Another comforter. The conveyer of communication and listener to every conversation whose role is channelling between Jesus and the Father as authorised messenger making complete the system of the God Head. 2 popularly regarded by Christians as the third person (hypostasis) of the Trinity: the "Triune God" manifested as Father, Son, and Holy Spirit; each person itself being God. In short, the Holy Ghost is the Third Person of the Blessed Trinity. Though really distinct, as a Person, from the Father and the Son, He is consubstantial with Them; being God like Them, He possesses with Them one and the same Divine Essence or Nature. He proceeds, not by way of generation, but by way of aspiration, from the Father and the Son together, as from a single principle. 3 Holy Ghost is the serving power of the Almighty.

Holy Ghost, Characteristics of the

As Children of the Most High, we need to be empowered with the same Spirit were with God Himself is the Spirit – No wonder we must worship Him in Spirit and in truth. When God commissioned His servants He send the power – Holy Ghost to fill the messenger as in (Acts 2:1-47) – "And when the day of Pentecost was fully come, they were all with one accord in one place... and in (Acts 1:8) – "But ye shall receive power, after that the Holy Ghost is come upon you: and ye shall be witnesses unto me both in Jerusalem, and in all Judaea, and in Samaria, and unto the uttermost part of the earth". The New Testament includes over 90 references to the Holy Spirit. The sacredness of the Holy Spirit is affirmed in all three Synoptic Gospels which proclaim blasphemy against the Holy Spirit as the unforgivable sin. The Holy Spirit plays a key role in the Pauline epistles. In the Johannine writings, three separate terms, "Holy Spirit", "Spirit of Truth", and "Paraclete" are use. Again, the New Testament details a close relationship between the Holy Spirit and Jesus during his earthly life and ministry. The Gospels of Luke and Matthew and the Nicene Creed state that Jesus was "conceived by the *Holy Spirit*, born of the Virgin Mary". The *Holy Spirit* descended on Jesus as a dove during his baptism, and in his Farewell Discourse after the Last Supper Jesus promised to send the *Holy Spirit* to his disciples after his departure. Remember, the power that descended on Jesus as a dove, deposited or remained in Him. He now have authority to advice, discharge, raise from death order, command, decree, proclaim as the Head of the administration in the right Hand of the Father. Anyone so honest, truthful and loving is His friend as the impartation enables all things to be possible and all authorities subject to His rule.

4 The Holy Spirit is thought by some to be an "essence" or "power" of God rather than a separate person, because "ruach", the Hebrew word for Spirit, also means breath, and "pneuma", the Greek word for Spirit, also means wind or air. We as Christians know He is a person.

The early Church scholar, Arias, caused division with his declaration that God the Father was the only true God, that Jesus was a created being, and the Holy Spirit was only an essence. This doctrine is known as the Arian heresy.

Holy Ghost, Characteristics of the: The Holy Spirit has the characteristics of a person (1Corinthians 2:10-11) - the Holy Spirit searches and has knowledge. (ICorinthians 12:11) - the Holy Spirit distributes gifts as He wills. (Romans 8:27) - He has a mind. (Romans 15:30) - He loves us. (John 15:26, 16:13)- He testifies of Jesus and exalts the Father and Son over

Holy Ghost, Characteristics of the

Himself. Personal pronouns are used when referring to the Holy Spirit (John 14:16-17, John 16:7-15). "Comforter" in (John 14:16) is "parakletos" which means "One who comes alongside of to help". The Holy Spirit is always with us ready to help when we ask Him to. Personal acts are ascribed to the Holy Spirit. (Acts 13:2) - the Holy Spirit speaks. (Romans 8:26) - the Holy Spirit intercedes for us. (I John 2:20-27. John 14:26) - He teaches us. (Acts 16:6-7) - the Holy Spirit guides Paul, sometimes forbidding things. (Genesis 6:3) - the Spirit strives with man. The Holy Spirit can receive treatment as a person. (Ephesians 4:30) - He can be grieved by us. (Hebrews 10:29) - We can insult Him. (Acts 5:3) - He can be lied to. (Matthew 12:31-32) - He can be blasphemed. The Holy Spirit is identified with the Father and the Son as a person. (Matthew 28:19) - He is named with the Father and Son in baptism. 2 (Corinthians 13:14) - He is named with the Father and Son in benediction. (Acts 15:28) - He is identified with the believers as a person.

The following biblical verses shows various promises and acts in Holy Ghost from the bible- good for edification. (Acts 2:38) - Then Peter said unto them, Repent, and be baptized every one of you in the name of Jesus Christ for the remission of sins, and ye shall receive the gift of the *Holy Ghost*. (Acts 19:6) - And when Paul had laid [his] hands upon them, the *Holy Ghost* came on them; and they spake with tongues, and prophesied.(Acts 2:4) - And they were all filled with the *Holy Ghost*, and began to speak with other tongues, as the Spirit gave them utterance. (Acts 1:5) - For John truly baptized with water; but ye shall be baptized with the *Holy Ghost* not many days hence. (Luke 11:13) - If ye then, being evil, know how to give good gifts unto your children: how much more shall [your] heavenly Father give the *Holy Spirit* to them that ask him? (John 3:5) - Jesus answered, Verily, verily, I say unto thee, Except a man be born of water and [of] the Spirit, he cannot enter into the kingdom of God. (Ephesians 1:13) - In whom ye also [trusted], after that ye heard the word of truth, the gospel of your salvation: in whom also after that ye believed, ye were sealed with that *holy Spirit* of promise,

The theology of the Holy Spirit is called pneumatology. The Holy Spirit is referred to as the Lord and Giver of Life in the Nicene Creed. The participation of the Holy Spirit in the tripartite nature of conversion is apparent in Jesus' final post-Resurrection instruction to his disciples at the end of the Gospel of (Matthew (28:19): "make disciples of all the nations, baptizing them into the name of the Father and of the Son and of the Holy Spirit". Since the first century, Christians have also called upon God with the name "Father, Son and Holy Spirit" in prayer, absolution and benediction.

Holy of holies

Holy of holies: The innermost apartment of the Jewish Temple in which The Ark of the Covenant was kept. 2 *The Holy of Holies* (Tiberian - Hebrew:) is a term in the Hebrew Bible which refers to the inner sanctuary of the Tabernacle and later the Temple in Jerusalem where the Ark of the Covenant was kept during the First Temple, which could be entered only by the High Priest on Yom Kippur. The Ark of the Covenant is said to have contained the Ten Commandments, which were given by God to Moses on Mount Sinai.

2 The construction "Holy of Holies" is a literal translation of a Hebrew idiom which is intended to express a superlative. Examples of similar constructions are "servant of servants" (Genesis 9:25), "Sabbath of sabbaths" (Exodus 31:15), "God of gods" (Deuteronomy 10:17), "Vanity of vanities" (Ecclesiastes 1:2), "Song of Solomon or songs" (Song of Songs 1:1), "king of kings" (Ezra 7:12), etc. In the Authorized King James Version, "Holy of Holies" is always translated as "Most Holy Place". This is in keeping with the intention of the Hebrew idiom to express the utmost degree of holiness. The King James Version of the Bible has been in existence for over four hundred years. For most of that time, it was a primary reference in much of the English speaking world for information about Judaism. Thus, the name "Most Holy Place" was used to refer to the "Holy of Holies" in many English documents.

Holy of holies – The Dressing of:

This set out rules order where with The Holy of Holies was maintained or kept. The Holy of Holies was covered by veil, and no one was permitted to enter except the High Priest, and even he could only enter once a year on the Day of Atonement, to offer the blood of sacrifice and incense before the mercy seat. In the wilderness, on the day that the tabernacle was first raised up, the cloud of the Lord covered the tabernacle. There are other times that this was recorded, and instructions were given that the Lord would appear in the cloud upon the mercy seat (*kapporet*), and at that time the priests should not enter into the tabernacle as reflected in the Law of Atonement (Leviticus 16:1-3) "Now the LORD spoke to Moses after the death of the two sons of Aaron, when they had approached the presence of the LORD and died. The LORD said to Moses: "Tell your brother Aaron that he shall not enter at any time into the holy place inside the veil, before the mercy seat which is on the ark, or he will die; for I will appear in the cloud over the mercy seat. "Aaron shall enter the holy place with this: with a bull for a sin offering and a ram for a burnt offering...." According to the Hebrew Bible, the Holy of Holies contained the Ark of the Covenant with representation of Cherubim. Upon completion of the dedication of the Tabernacle, the Voice of God spoke to Moses "from between the Cherubim". (Numbers 7:89).

"Now when Moses went into the tent of meeting to speak with Him, he heard the voice speaking to him from above the mercy seat that was on the ark of the testimony, from between the two cherubim, so He spoke to him".

Holy of Holies, The location of: The Holy of Holies, the most sacred site in traditional Judaism, is the inner sanctuary within the Tabernacle and Temple in Jerusalem when Solomon's Temple and the Second Temple were standing. The Holy of Holies was located in the westernmost end of the Temple building, being a perfect cube: 20 cubits by 20 cubits by 20 cubits. The inside was in total darkness and contained the Ark of the Covenant, gilded inside and out, in which was placed the Tablets of the Covenant. According to Hebrews 9:4 "which had the golden altar of incense and the gold-covered ark of the covenant. This ark contained the gold jar of manna, Aaron's staff that had budded, and the stone tablets of the covenant".In the New Testament, Aaron's rod and a pot of manna were also in the ark. The Ark was covered with a lid made of pure gold (Exodus 37:6), known as the "mercy seat" for the Divine Presence.

Holy of holies – Babylon after the Collapsed of: Second Temple was constructed after the collapsed of the Babylonian Empire. When the Temple was rebuilt after the Babylonian captivity, the Ark was no longer present in the Holy of Holies; instead, a portion of the floor was raised slightly to indicate the place where it had stood. Josephus records that Pompey profaned the Temple by insisting on entering the Holy of Holies.

Holy Land, The: Christians, Jews and members of other religions duped an area roughly located between the Jordan River and the Mediterranean Sea – *the Holy Land*, the land of Canaan, acquired as instructed by God to Abrahamic lineage down to the chosen Jacob who signed the title deeds as David declared in (Psalm 44: 2-4) You with Your own hand drove out the nations; Then You planted them; You afflicted the peoples, Then You spread them abroad. For by their own sword they did not possess the land, And their own arm did not save them, But Your right hand and Your arm and the light of Your presence, For You favoured them. You are my King, O God; Command victories for Jacob"

Historically, it is synonymous with both the Land of Israel and Palestine, and is thus inclusive of the 20th century concepts of both Palestine and Israel. Part of the significance of the land stems from the religious significance of Jerusalem, the holiest city to Judaism, the historical region of Jesus's ministry, and the Isra and Mi'raj event in Islam. The perceived holiness of the land to Christianity was part of the motivation for the Crusades, as European Christians sought to win the Holy Land back from the Muslim Suljuq Turks. They had taken it over after defeating the Muslim Arabs, who had in turn taken control from the Christian Byzantine Empire. Many sites in the Holy Land have long been pilgrimage destinations for adherents of the Abrahamic religions, including Jews, Christians, Muslims, and Bahá'ís. Pilgrims visit the Holy Land to touch and see physical manifestations of their faith, confirm their beliefs in the holy context with collective excitation, and connect personally to the Holy Land as recorded in (Zechariah 12:10) – "And I will pour upon the house of David, and upon the inhabitants of Jerusalem, the spirit of grace and of supplications: and they shall look upon me whom they have pierced, and they shall mourn for him, as one mourneth for [his] only [son], and shall be in bitterness for him, as one that is in bitterness for [his] firstborn" Also (Psalm 78:54) "And he brought them to the border of his sanctuary, even to this mountain, which his right hand had purchased". This psalm shows how the Lord brought them to the border of his sanctuary in the land of Canaan, which the Lord had sanctified, and set apart for them; and of Jerusalem, the holy city, the city of the great God, and of the temple where his residence was to be; so as recorded in the Targum, "to the border of the place of the house of his sanctuary:" even to this mountain, which his right hand purchased; the mount Moriah, on which the temple was built; this psalm being composed, after it was made known to David, by the prophet Gad, the place where the temple should be built; namely, on the very mountain, on part of which David had his palace; and this was obtained and possessed, not by the power nor through the merits of the Israelites, but through the power and goodness of God;

Holy Land, The title deeds to the:
The Holy Land – The promise Land belongs to God as in (Leviticus 25:23) "The land must not be sold without reclaim because the land belongs to me, for you are foreigners and residents with me." Base to understanding of the Hebrew Scriptures with respect to the Hebrews' themselves, the vital connection between a specific area of land and a specific people in covenant relationship with God. The preceding context (Leviticus: 25:8-12) of the above verse (Leviticus: 25:23) deals with the observance of the year of jubilee, while its surrounding context (Leviticus: 25:13-34) discusses the

effects of the year on the possession of property. The Israelites were to buy and sell property in view of the upcoming year of jubilee during which time all property would revert to its original tribal leases. This special year reminded the Israelites that they really didn't own the land themselves but were tenants of God, the true owner. So then one key aspect of the jubilee year is its declaration that the land was ultimately God's possession, and as such no individual had the inalienable right to sell or incorporate as they saw fit as this is the property of the incorruptible God.

2 God gave the *Holy land* to the descendants of Abraham as in (Genesis 12:7) " The LORD appeared to Abram and said, 'To your descendants I will give this land." This promise of land is one key aspect of the Abrahamic Covenant. In the gospel or scripture, the concept of covenant refers to an agreement or contract between two parties that binds one or both parties to certain obligations and commitments. In several passages the Abrahamic Covenant is expressly portrayed as eternal and therefore unconditional – see (Genesis. 13:15; 17:7, 13, 19; 48:4; 1 Chronicle. 16:17; Psalm. 105:10). This means that it is only binding on the party making the promise. In the Abrahamic covenant God alone commits Himself to a course of action through Abraham and his descendants that cannot be reversed (else God would prove untrue – you must note in (Numbers 23:19) "God is not man, that he should lie, or a son of man, that he should change his mind. Has he said, and will he not do it? Or has he spoken, and will he not fulfil it?" so it cannot be annulled by the failure of either Abraham or his descendants). However, it should also be noted that while the gift or title deed to the land is unconditional, actual enjoyment of the land is conditioned upon obedience. In (Deuteronomy 29:2-30:1), Moses prophetically spoke of Israel's coming disobedience to the Mosaic Law and subsequent scattering over the entire world. This is one reason why full restoration of Israel to its land with complete peace and security will require the second coming of Messiah—immediately prior and scripturally requisite to that great eschatological event is foretold the spiritual regeneration of Jewish physical survivors of the Tribulation resulting in a new capacity to render Spirit–empowered obedience to God.

3 Indeed, this Land was not given to the Descendants of Ishmael, but rather to the Descendants of Isaac as in (Genesis. 17:18) "Abraham said to God, 'that Ishmael might live before you!" The phrase "might live before you" can also be translated as "might live with your blessing." The point is Abraham himself considered Ishmael as a possible descendant to whom God would give this land. How-

ever, in the very next (verse . 19) "God said, 'No, Sarah your wife is going to bear you a son and you will name him Isaac. I will confirm my covenant with him as a perpetual covenant for his descendants after him." In (Genesis. 17:20) God promised to bless Ishmael and use him to create a great nation, but His covenant to Abraham, (which again prominently included the specific promise of land), was to be accomplished through his son Issac, not Ishmael (Genesis. 17:21) This Land was not given to the Descendants of Esau, but only to Jacob. As seen in the previous point, even though God promised to bless Abraham's descendants, He singled out only one branch of his family for covenant blessing. (Romans 9:10-13) stresses that God's choice Jacob over Esau are for reasons that lay within Himself, not because any human merits election. This is why in (Genesis. 28:13-15; 35:11-12) and (Genesis 48:3-4) God Himself through direct revelation is portrayed as convincing Jacob of his covenant destiny specifically in relation to the promise of land.

4 The important point to note here is that God is Restoring Jewish People to the Land; The bible predicts that Israel will initially return to the land of promise in unbelief as (Ezekiel 36:24) pointed out, "I will take you from the nations and gather you from all the countries and bring you to your land." The next two verses continued, "I will sprinkle pure water over you and you will be clean from all your uncleanness; I will purify you from all your idols. I will give you a new heart, and I will put a new spirit within you; I will remove the heart of stone from your body and give you a heart of flesh." From the sequence of events depicted in these verses it should be noted that the national restoration of the Jewish people precedes the spiritual regeneration of the Jewish people. Therefore, it should not surprise us that Israel was reborn as a secular state by secular Jews for this is a precursor of the day when the entire nation becomes faithful to Jesus as Messiah.

5 This return to the land in stages is also borne out in the vision of a valley of dry bones from (Ezekiel 37). In (verses 6-10) the bones come to life in stages. First, the sinews or tendons on the bones, then flesh, then skin, and finally the breath of life. Then in (verse 11), God tells Ezekiel that "these bones are the house of Israel," and their restoration is illustrative of the way He will bring His people back "to the land of Israel" (verse. 12). Thus, the re-gathering of Israel to its land should not be viewed as a single event but rather a process which culminates in the Jewish people receiving the breath of life by turning to their Messiah. Which means wars, tribulation and other event will scatter them and then peace will return in stages to restore the whole body of Is-

rael to Gods glory! Praise the Lord, the Most High God through Jesus Christ!!

Holy Name of Jesus, The: The name of Jesus as an object of devotion both among Roman Catholic who until 1969 celebrated it as a feast day in the first week of January and among Anglicans for whom the Book of Common Prayer has assigned it the date 7 August. Some modern Anglican liturgies use the Naming of Jesus as an alternative title for the feast of the Circumcision (1 January). The close relation between Name of Jesus and His person is manifested in the many references to the name of Jesus in the New Testament. The disciples performed miracles and exorcisms in the name of Jesus as well as baptized in it. (Philippines 2:10) "At the name of Jesus every knee should bow, of things in the heaven, and things in earth, and things under the earth" 2 It a generator or source of power and miracle when faith goes along with it possibly through the Word of God. 3 Every other power and authority are bound to obey unconditionally.

Holy Orders: The threefold division of sacred ministers (bishops, priests and deacons) prefigured in the Old Law (high priest, priests, Levites) is clearly revealed in Scripture. Yet, most so-called "bible-believing" Protestant churches do not have them. (Acts 6:3-6; Acts 13:2-3; 1 Timothy. 3:1; 1 Timothy. 3:8-9; 1 Timothy. 4:14; 1 Timothy. 4:16; 1 Timothy. 5:17-19; 1 Timothy. 5:22).

Holy Spirit: *See Holy Ghost*

Holy Trinity: This defines God as three consubstantial persons, expressions, or hypostases: the Father, the Son (Jesus Christ), and the Holy Spirit; (Another Comforter) - All "one God in three persons". The three persons are distinct, yet are one "substance, essence or nature". In this context, a "nature" is what one is, while a "person" is who one is. According to this central mystery of most Christian faiths, there is only one God in three persons: while distinct from one another in their relations of origin, "it is the Father who generates, the Son who is begotten, and the Holy Spirit who proceeds") and in their relations with one another, they are stated to be one in all else, co-equal, co-eternal and consubstantial, and "each is God, whole and entire". Accordingly, the whole work of creation and grace is seen as a single operation common to all three divine persons, in which each shows forth what is proper to him in the Trinity, so that all things are "from the Father", "through the Son" and "in the Holy Spirit".

2 While the Fathers of the Church saw even Old Testament elements such as the appearance of three men to Abraham in (Genesis 18), as fore-shadowing of the Trinity, it

was the New Testament that they saw as a basis for developing the concept of the Trinity. The most influential of the New Testament texts seen as implying the teaching of the Trinity was (Matthew 28:19), which mandated baptizing "in the name of the Father, and of the Son, and of the Holy Spirit". Reflection, proclamation and dialogue led to the formulation of the doctrine that was felt to correspond to the data in the Bible. The simplest outline of the doctrine was formulated in the 4th century, largely in terms of rejection of what was considered not to be consonant with general Christian belief. Further elaboration continued in the succeeding centuries.

3 Gospels or Scripture does not contain expressly a formulated doctrine of the Trinity. Rather, according to the Christian theology, it "bears witness to" the activity of a God who can only be understood in the Trinitarian terms. The doctrine did not take its definitive shape until late in the fourth century. During the intervening period, various tentative solutions, some more and some less satisfactory were proposed. Trinitarians contrast with non-Trinitarian positions which include Bitarianism (one deity in two persons, or two deities), Unitarianism (one deity in one person, analogous to Jewish interpretation of the Shema. A Oneness Pentecostalism or Modalism (one deity manifested in three separate aspects) in performing divine functions in reflection to their divined existence.

Holy water: Also known as Consecrated Water or Blessed Water, especially in Non-Abrahamic religions, and Wicca or Paganism. Water that has been blessed by a member of a clergy or religious figure. The use for cleansing prior to a baptism and spiritual cleansing is common in several religions, from Christianity to Sikhism. The use of holy water as a sacramental for protection against evil is common among Anglicans and Roman Catholics.

2 In Catholicism, Anglicanism, Eastern Orthodoxy, Oriental Orthodoxy and some other churches, holy water is water that has been sanctified by a priest for the purpose of baptism, the blessing of persons, places, and objects, or as a means of repelling evil.

3 The use of holy water in the earliest days of Christianity is attested to only in somewhat later practices in the Apostolic constitutions, which go back to about the year 400, attribute the precept of using *holy water* to the Apostle Matthew. It is plausible that in earliest Christian times water was used for expiatory and 'purificatory' purposes in a way analogous to its employment in Jewish Law. Yet, in many cases, the water used for the Sacrament of Baptism was flowing water, sea or river water, and it could not receive the same

blessing that as contained in the baptisteries in the view of the Roman Catholic church. However, Eastern Orthodox do perform the same blessing whether in a baptistery or an outdoor body of water. Holy water practices started far back to recall the issue of the adultery woman recorded in (Number 5: 17-27) "Then he shall take some holy water in a clay jar and put some dust from the tabernacle floor into the water. After the priest has had the woman stand before the LORD, he shall loosen her hair and place in her hands the reminder offering, the grain offering for jealousy, while he himself holds the bitter water that brings a curse. Then the priest shall put the woman under oath and say to her, "If no other man has slept with you and you have not gone astray and become impure while married to your husband, may this bitter water that brings a curse not harm you. But if you have gone astray while married to your husband and you have defiled yourself by sleeping with a man other than your husband"-- here the priest is to put the woman under this curse of the oath--"may the LORD cause your people to curse and denounce you when he causes your thigh to waste away and your abdomen to swell. May this water that brings a curse enter your body so that your abdomen swells and your thigh wastes away. " 'Then the woman is to say, "Amen. So be it." 'The priest is to write these curses on a scroll and then wash them off into the bitter water. He shall have the woman drink the bitter water that brings a curse, and this water will enter her and cause bitter suffering. The priest is to take from her hands the grain offering for jealousy, wave it before the LORD and bring it to the altar. The priest is then to take a handful of the grain offering as a memorial offering and burn it on the altar; after that, he is to have the woman drink the water. If she has defiled herself and been unfaithful to her husband, then when she is made to drink the water that brings a curse, it will go into her and cause bitter suffering; her abdomen will swell and her thigh waste away, and she will become accursed among her people".

Holy week: (Greek - Ayia Kai, Hagia kai Megale Hebdomas) "Greater week", Passion Week; "Holy and Great Week") This is the week just before Easter to all Christians. In the west, it is also the last week of Lent, and includes Palm Sunday, Holy Wednesday (Spy Wednesday), Maundy Thursday (Holy Thursday), Good Friday (Holy Friday), and Holy Saturday. It does not include Easter Sunday, which is the beginning of another liturgical week.

2 The earliest allusion to the custom of marking this week as a whole with special observances is to be found in the Apostolical-

Holy week

ly designed Constitutions dating from the latter half of the 3rd and 4th century. In this text, abstinence from flesh is commanded for all the days, while for the Friday and Sunday an absolute fast is commanded.

3 The whole period from Palm Sunday through Easter Sunday (Resurrection Sunday). Also included within Passion Week are Monday, Thursday, Good Friday, and Holy Saturday. Passion Week is so named because of the passion with which Jesus willingly went to the cross in order to pay for our sins. Passion Week is described in (Matthew 21-27); Mark chapters 11-15; (Luke chapters 19-23); and (John chapters 12-19). Passion Week begins with the triumphal entry of Jerusalem on Palm Sunday on the back of a colt as prophesied as "The Coming of Zion's King" in (Zachariah 9:9) thus' "Rejoice greatly, Daughter Zion! Shout, Daughter Jerusalem! See, your king comes to you, righteous and victorious, lowly and riding on a donkey, on a colt, the foal of a donkey.

4 *Holy Week* contained several memorable events. Jesus cleansed the Temple for the second time as in (Luke 19:45-46), "When Jesus entered the temple courts; he began to drive out those who were selling. "It is written," he said to them, "'My house will be a house of prayer' but you have made it 'a den of robbers." then disputed with the Pharisees regarding His authority. Then He gave His Olivet Discourse on the end times and taught many things, including the signs of His second coming. Jesus ate His Last Supper with His disciples in the upper room (Luke 22:7-38), then went to the garden of Gethsemane to pray as He waited for His hour to come. It was here that Jesus, having been betrayed by Judas, was arrested and taken to several sham trials before the chief priests, Pontius Pilate, and Herod (Luke 22:23:25). Following the trials, Jesus was scourged at the hands of the Roman soldiers, then was forced to carry His own instrument of execution (the Cross) through the streets of Jerusalem along what is known as the Via Dolorosa (way of sorrows). Jesus was then crucified at Golgotha on the day before the Sabbath, was buried and remained in the tomb until Sunday, the day after the Sabbath, and then gloriously resurrected. It is referred to as Passion Week because in that time, Jesus Christ truly revealed His passion for us in the suffering He willingly went through on our behalf. As Christians, What should our attitude be during Passion Week? We should be passionate in our worship of Jesus and in our proclamation of His Gospel! As He suffered for us, so should we be willing to suffer for the cause of following Him and proclaiming the message of His death and resurrection. Remember, He accom-

plishes all the above persecutions out of the covenant or agreement of love He Signed with the father and the Holy Spirit or the Board of the Trinity, when He accepted and declared "Father! I Shall go to save my people from their sins". In Holy week, we must try to show love to widows, visit Orphanages with our gifts, visit the prison and preach release to the captives and those who are kept in bondage, visit the sick and preach healing in the name of Jesus and also declare the acceptable year of the Lord in Jesus Mighty and Wonderful Name! Praise the King of Kings! Amen!!

Honour: (noun) In the gospel, *honour* should be considered as 'complete regards to the sum total of good works, trustworthiness, purposefulness, integrity, attainments, Spiritual endowment and influence through wisdom, effectiveness in love life, Godliness, divine favour, power, sound mind, growth in grace and worshipping God in Spirit and in truth. While this formed the concept of divine *honour* and recipients qualifies for eternal crown in the judgement day, so, this means divine honour is everlasting or lasting honour. Honour in the gospel perspective here means "esteem, value, or great respect." To honour someone is to value him highly or bestow value upon him in considering honourable qualities listed above. The gospel exhorts us to express honour and esteem toward certain people: our parents, the aged, and those in authority (Ephesians 6:2; Leviticus 19:32; Romans 13:1). But we must understand that all authority and honour belong to God alone (1 Chronicles 29:11; 1 Timothy 1:17; Revelation 5:13). Though He can delegate His authority to others, it still belongs to Him (Ephesians 4:11-12). Peter tells us to "honour all people, love the brotherhood, fear God, honour the king" (1 Peter 2:17). The idea of honouring others, especially those in authority (the king), comes from the fact that they represent God's ultimate authority. A classic example is the command to "submit to the governing authorities because they have been established by God" (Romans 13:1-6). Therefore, "he who rebels against the authority is rebelling against what God has instituted, and those who do so will bring judgment on themselves" (Romans 13:2). This means it is incumbent upon Christians to honour those whom God has placed over us through our obedience and demonstration of respect. To do otherwise is to dishonour God.

Upon all these, we ought to know as believers that as the heavens and all therein raise their voices in honour and praise to God, as Christians, we are to do likewise: "You are worthy, our Lord and God, to receive glory and honour and power, for You created all things, and by Your will they were created and have their being" (Revelation 4:11). There has never been, nor will there ever be, anyone in any position of power or worldly influence who can claim such an honour (1 Timothy 6:16). God alone is the Creator and finisher of all creation in all the heavens and the earth (Revelation 14:7). Therefore, all true believers are to honour God and His Son, Jesus Christ, through our acknowledgement and confession that He is the one and only God (Exodus 20:3; John 14:6; Romans 10:9). We are to honour God in our recognition that the gift of life eternal and the very salvation of our souls come through Jesus Christ and Him alone (John 11:25; Acts 4:12; 1 Timothy 2:5). Knowing this, we give honour and obeisance to our Saviour through our humble adoration and obedience to His will (John 14:23-24; 1 John 2:6). As such, He will honour us when He seats us on His throne in heaven

2 This is opposed to the layman or abstract concept entailing a perceived quality of worthiness and respectability that affects both the social standing and the self-evaluation of an individual or corporate body such as a family, school, regiment or nation. Accordingly, individuals (or corporate bodies) are assigned worth and stature based on the harmony of their actions with a specific code of honour, and the moral code of the society at large.

3 Honour can be viewed in the light of Psychological nativism as being as real to the human condition as love, and likewise deriving from the formative personal bonds that establish one's personal dignity and character. From the point of moral relativism, honour is perceived as arising from universal concerns for material circumstance and status, rather than fundamental differences in principle between those who hold different honour codes. This type of honour is short live and perished when a person dies - an irretrievable honour - honour without everlasting glory. 4 Again, Dr Samuel Johnson, in his A Dictionary of the English Language (1755), defined honour as having several senses, the first of which was "nobility of soul, magnanimity, and a scorn of meanness." This sort of honour derives from the perceived virtuous conduct and personal integrity of the person endowed with it. On the other hand, Johnson also defined honour in relationship to "reputation" and "fame"; to "privileges of rank or birth", and as "respect" of the kind which "places an individual socially and determines his right to precedence." This sort of honour is not so much a function of moral or ethical excellence, as it is a consequence of power. Finally, with respect to sexuality, honour has traditionally been associated with (or identical to) "chastity" or "virginity", or in case of married men and women,

Honour, Vain

"fidelity". Some have argued that honour should be seen more as a rhetoric, or set of possible actions, than as a code. The book of Proverbs illustrates the association of a one's behaviour with its resulting honour. For example, "He who pursues righteousness and love finds life, prosperity and honour" (Proverbs 21:21 and Proverbs 22:4; 29:23). Often, honour is conferred upon those of wisdom and intelligence, thereby earning praise and adoration (1 Kings 10:6-7). Another kind of honour pertains to those who have great wealth or fame (Joshua 6:27). Correspondingly, we also know that such worldly honour, fame and wealth, in the end, is meaningless and short-lived (Ecclesiastes 1:14; James 4:14) Honour as taught in the Scriptures is far different from the type of honour sought after by the world. Honour and awards are heaped upon those with wealth, political clout, worldly power, and celebrity status. Those who thrive on this world's fleeting honour and stature are unmindful that "God opposes the proud but gives grace to the humble" (1 Peter 5:5; see also Proverbs 16:5; Isaiah 13:11). Such were the Pharisees of Jesus' time, who sought honour and accolades from men. But in truth, Jesus rejected them. He said, "Everything they do is done for men to see" (Matthew 23:5). He not only labelled them as hypocrites, but "snakes" and "vipers," essentially condemning them to hell (Matthew 23:29-33).

Honour, Vain: This signifies the boasters, people with pompous behaviour, negligent or disobedience, those attaining vainglory etc. The secret of true worship is that we "worship in spirit and in truth" (John 4:24). Not only must the things we say and feel be true, but they must be the love of our spirits, our heart's deep desire. Unfortunately many people worship from ulterior motives, and the desires of their hearts are far from God. For example: Self-glory. Some seek their own glory and praise (Mathew 6:2-7, 16-18) Money: Some seek wealth and earthly prosperity. They seem to be serving God, but they do so because they think God will make them rich on earth. This is not true Christianity (Mathew 6:19-24) Own Inventions: Some love and follow their own tradition rather than the word of God. As we noticed earlier, this was the particular problem that Jesus was referring to when he quoted Isaiah, "In vain do they worship me, teaching for doctrines the commandments of men" (Mathew 15:7-9). The point to be made here is that the world in which we reside is corrupt (Deuteronomy 32:5; Philippians 2:15) because it does not give to God the honour He deserves. The one who honours the world and the things of it makes himself an enemy of God (James 4:4). The apostle Paul wrote, "For even though they knew God, they did not honour Him as God or give

Honour, Personal or Individual:

thanks, but they became futile in their speculations, and their foolish heart was darkened" (Romans 1:21). The Bible teaches that honour is found in God and His Son and in our being like Him (John 15:8). We are to give obeisance to Him through the fruits of our labours (Proverbs 3:9; 1 Corinthians 10:31), as well as through the care and nurture of our bodies (2 Corinthians 6:19). To esteem God as first in our lives (Matthew 22:37-38) is thereby expressed in both the total commitment of our lives and devotion of our possessions to His service and glory (Colossians 3:17). Though we are in this world, we are not of this world (John 15:18-21). This means, as we honour God through our godly character, we will reap dishonour from those of the world. In fact, the Bible teaches us that "everyone who wants to live a godly life in Christ Jesus will be persecuted" (2 Timothy 3:12).

Honour, Personal or Individual: The Bible also gives us the command to honour one another in our employer and employee relationships (1 Timothy 3:17; 6:1) (Ephesians 6:5-9), as well as in the marriage relationship with the husband and wife being in submission to and honouring one another (Hebrews 13:4; Ephesians 5:23-33). Interestingly enough, of all the commands to honour one another, the most oft-repeated pertains to that of honouring one's father and mother (Exodus 20:12; Matthew 15:4). This command was so important to God that if anyone cursed or struck his parent, he was to be put to death (Exodus 21:7).

2 The word love is also sometimes synonymous for honour. Paul commands us to "be devoted to one another in brotherly love. Honour one another above yourselves" (Romans 12:10). Honouring others, however, goes against our natural instinct, which is to honour and value ourselves. It is only by being imbued with humility by the power of the Holy Spirit that we can esteem and honour our fellow man more than ourselves (Romans 12:3; Philippians 2:3).

Honour, Double: The gospel speaks of another noteworthy group of people who are deserving of "double honour," the leadership of the church, called elders: "Let the elders who rule well be considered worthy of double honour, especially those who labour in preaching and teaching" (1 Timothy 5:17). In the first-century church, some elders laboured in word and doctrine by devoting their time to preaching and teaching, while others did so privately. However, all elders gave attention to the interests of the church and the welfare of its members. These men were entitled to double honour of both respect and deference for their position, as well as material or monetary support. This was especially significant because the New Testament was not yet available as the case today in our churches.

Horeb: This is thought to mean glowing or heat, which seems to be a reference to the Sun, while Sinai may have derived from the name of Sin, the Sumerian deity of the Moon, and thus Sinai and Horeb would be the mountains of the moon and sun, respectively. They both are mountains of great importance in the Old Testament gospel and exert significant importance to all revelations in the new testament particularly as concerns the transition from Law to Grace after the death and resurrection of Jesus Christ. See mount Horeb below.

Horeb, Mount: The mountain at which the book of Deuteronomy in the Hebrew Bible states that the Ten Commandments were given to Moses by God. It is described in two places (Exodus 3:1, 1 Kings 19:8) as the "Mountain of God". The mountain is also called the Mountain of YHWH. In other biblical passages, these events are described as having transpired at Mount Sinai. Although Sinai and Horeb are often considered to have been different names for the same place, there is a body of opinion that they may have been they are located separately.

Hosea: (Modern – Hebrew-Hoshea) meaning "Salvation"; Greek - Hosee) was the son of Beeri, a prophet in Israel in the 8th century BC and author of the book of prophecies bearing his name. He is one of the Twelve Prophets of the Jewish Hebrew Bible, also known as the Minor Prophets of the Christian Old Testament. Hosea is often seen as a "prophet of doom", but underneath his message of destruction is a promise of restoration. The Talmud (Pesachim 87a) claims that he was the greatest prophet of his generation. The period of Hosea's ministry extended to some sixty years and he was the only prophet of Israel who left any written prophecy.

Host: (Hebrew – Saboath - armies) A person responsible for guests at an event and or providing hospitality during it, or to an event's presenter or master or mistress of ceremonies. Host or hosts may also refer to Host. 2 Sacramental bread (Hostia), sometimes called the body of Christ, altar bread, the host, the Lamb or simply Communion bread, is the bread which is used in the Christian ritual of the Eucharist.

Host, Heavenly: See *Heavenly host*

Hosts, Lord of: God is first called the "LORD of hosts" in (1 Samuel 1:3). The word LORD, capitalized, refers to Yahweh, the self-existent, redemptive God. The name "LORD of hosts" occurs some 261 times in the Old Testament Scriptures.

The word hosts is a translation of the Hebrew word sabaoth, mean-

Hosts, Lord of

ing "armies"—a reference to the angelic armies of heaven. Thus, another way of saying "LORD of hosts" is "Jehovah, God of the armies of heaven." The NIV translates YHWH saboath as "LORD Almighty." This name for God first appears at the close of the period of the judges. In the same sentence as "LORD of hosts" is a reference to Shiloh, where the Ark of the Covenant was kept. The Ark symbolized Yahweh's rulership, among other things, for He sits enthroned above the cherubim (1 Samuel 4:4; Psalm 99:1). Some have suggested that "LORD of hosts" reaffirms that God is the true Leader of Israel's armies, in spite of the low spiritual condition of the nation of Israel at the time of the judges. In (1 Samuel 17:45), as part of his pre-fight verbal sparring with Goliath, David evokes this name of God.

2 The sovereign LORD of hosts has the grace to always be there for the one who comes to Him through faith in the Lord Jesus Christ. The King of glory, who commands the armies of heaven and who will eventually defeat all His enemies in this world, is none other than Jesus Christ. He is the LORD of hosts (Revelation 19:11–20). In doing so, David was claiming that God is the universal ruler over every force whether in heaven or on earth. Soon after David's defeat of Goliath, Israel would enter the international scene. It was necessary for the nation to realize that Yahweh was King even of the many other mighty nations. This kingship of the LORD of hosts is vividly expressed in (Psalm 24:10): "Who is this King of glory? The LORD of hosts, he is the King of glory!" 2 He is the glorious King of Israel, and (Zechariah 14:6) tells us that He will be King of the world, over all the kingdoms of the earth (Isaiah 37:16). Eventually, Yahweh of armies will put down all rebellion (Isaiah 24:21–23) and establish His Kingdom from Mt. Zion (Isaiah 31:4–5; 34:12). As the LORD of hosts, God is the all-powerful Ruler over the entire universe. All power and authority are His. He alone intervenes to provide victory for His people. He alone brings world peace. At the same time, He is available to hear the prayers of His people (Psalm 80:19). There is no other God like this.

House: (noun) (John 14:2) "In my Father's *house* are many mansions: if it were not so, I would have told you. I go to prepare a place for you". In common English a house is a building for human habitation, especially one that consists of a ground floor and one or more upper storeys. "a *house* of Cotswold stone" synonyms: home, place of residence, homestead, lodging place, a roof over one's head; More the people living in a house; a household. "make yourself scarce before you wake the whole house" synonyms: household, family, family circle, ménage, clan, tribe; informal brood "make yourself scarce before you wake the whole house" a noble, royal, or wealthy family or lineage; a dynasty. "the power and prestige of the *House* of Stewart" synonyms: clan, kindred, family, tribe, race, strain; More a dwelling that is one of several in a building. a building in which animals live or in which things are kept. "an animal *house*" House of God as Jesus referred in (John 14:2) "In my Father's house are many mansions: if it were not so, I would have told you. I go to prepare a place for you".

The Greek word used for "house" here is slightly different from that used of the material temple on earth in (John 2:16). The exact meaning will be at once seen from a comparison of (2Corinthians 5:1), the only other passage in the New Testament where it is used metaphorically. The Jews were accustomed to the thought of heaven as the habitation of God; and the disciples had been taught to pray, "Our Father, which art in heaven." (Comparative chapters are found in (Psalm 23:6; Isaiah 63:15; Matthew 6:9; Acts 7:49; and especially Hebrews 9) The Greek word for "mansions" occurs again in the New Testament only in (John 14:23), where it is rendered abode." or "dwellings." "with the exact meaning of the Greek, that is; "resting-places," "dwellings." the word meant no more than this, and it now means no more in French or in the English of the North. A maison or a manse, is not necessarily a modern English mansion. It should also be noted that the Greek word is the substantive answering to the verb which is rendered "dwelleth" in (John 14:10, and "abide" in (John 15:4-10). The words refer rather to the extent of the Father's *house*, in which there should be abiding-places for all. There would be no risk of that house being overcrowded like the caravanserai at Bethlehem, or like those in which the Passover pilgrims, as at this very time, found shelter at Jerusalem. Though Peter could not follow Him now, he should hereafter (John 13:36); and for all who shall follow Him there shall be homes. What is the life like in our earthly homes or Houses. Here there is joy of living, sleep, bath, play, cook, eat, dance, sing, pray, make merry, love, full security, tribulation, sickness and death and so forth – all these have mansions or rooms within the same set up. If we have these facilities in our earthly houses, how much more the giver of strength and energy for us to acquire houses like some people who possesses many houses and rent sale some for commercial wealth and profits etc.

Jesus Christ spoke in parable meaning that for all those who come to Christ and have faith in the trinity , - the one House there are many rooms or mansions as in (John 14:2 – 4, ESV) "In my Father's house are many rooms. If it were not so, would I have told you that I go to prepare a place for you?[a] And if I go and prepare a place for you, I will come again and will take you to myself, that where I am you may be also. And you know the way to where I am going." for joy, happiness, security, sickness free, death free, no more day, no more night, as, no sorrow or tears the father have already prepared all provisions beginning from His death and resurrection and ascension, now seated at the right hand of the father.

As Christians and by God Grace must we to dwell isolated in our several mansions in Heaven? Is that the way in which children in a home dwell with each other? Surely if He be the Father, and heaven be His house, the relation of the redeemed to one another must have in it more than all the sweet familiarity and unrestrained frankness which subsists in the families of earth. A solitary heaven would be but half a heaven, and would ill correspond with the hopes that inevitably spring from the representation of it as 'my Father's house.' But consider further that this great and tender name for heaven has its deepest meaning in the conception of it as a spiritual state of which the essential elements are the loving manifestation and presence of God as Father, the perfect consciousness of son ship, the happy union of all the children in one great family, and the derivation of all their blessedness from their Elder Brother - Jesus

2 A building in which people meet for a particular activity. "a house of prayer" a firm or institution. "a publishing house" synonyms: firm, business, company, corporation, enterprise, establishment, institution, concern, organization, operation; More audience, crowd, those present, listeners, spectators, viewers, gathering, assembly, assemblage, congregation; In heaven, there will be congregations of the elect – worshipping and Praising God throughout. This will be one most important feature of the new Heaven and the new Earth – Heaven of Heavens

House, My Father: Most of us have long since left behind us the sweet security, the sense of the absence of all responsibility, the assurance of defence and provision, which used to be ours when we lived as children in a father's house here. But we may all look forward to the renewal, in far nobler form, of these early days, when the father's house meant the inexpugnably fortress where no evil could befall us, the abundant home where all wants were supplied, and where the shyest and timidest child could feel at ease and secure. It is all coming again, brother, and amidst the august and unimaginable glories of that future the old feeling of being little children, nestling safe in *the Father's house*, will fill our quiet hearts once more as the promise in (John 14:2) "In my Father's house are many mansions: if it were not so, I would have told you. I go to prepare a place for you".

Ii

Idol: (noun) Christians from onset are warned about the worship of idol. An idol is image used as an object of worship. A false god. One that is adored, often blindly or excessively. Something visible but without substance. An image or other material object representing a deity to which religious worship is addressed or any person or thing regarded with admiration, adoration, or devotion. Indeed, God hate and destroys idols; He is the great iconoclast. Even good things can become idols, and while revelling and boasting seem good at the time, it is a grave disservice to idolize anything or anybody. The result is God's wrath, on you and the idol. God will not be eclipsed as in (Exodus 20:3-6) "You shall have no other gods before me. You shall not make for yourself a carved image, or any likeness of anything that is in heaven above, or that is in the earth beneath, or that is in the water under the earth. You shall not bow down to them or serve them, for I the Lord your God am a jealous God, visiting the iniquity of the fathers on the children to the third and the fourth generation of those who hate me, but showing steadfast love to thousands of those who love me and keep my commandments" See also (Colossians 3:5) "Put to death therefore what is earthly in you: sexual immorality, impurity, passion, evil desire, and covetousness, which is idolatry". (1 John 5:21) "Little children, keep yourselves from idols". (Jonah 2:8) "Those who pay regard to vain idols forsake their hope of steadfast love".

Idolatry, Worship of: "The worship of idols or excessive devotion to, or reverence for some person or thing." An idol is anything that replaces the one, true God. The most prevalent form of idolatry in Bible times was the worship of images that were thought to embody the various pagan deities.

From the beginning, God's covenant with Israel was based on exclusive worship of Him alone (Exodus 20:3; Deuteronomy 5:7). The Israelites were not even to mention the names of false gods (Exodus 23:13) because to do so would acknowledge their existence and give credence to their power and influence over the

Idolatry, Worship of

people. Israel was forbidden to intermarry with other cultures who embraced false gods, because God knew this would lead to compromise. The book of Hosea uses the imagery of adultery to describe Israel's continual chasing after other gods, like an unfaithful wife chases after other men. The history of Israel is a sad chronicle of idol worship, punishment, restoration and forgiveness, followed by a return to idolatry. The books of 1 and 2 Samuel, 1 and 2 Kings, and 1 and 2 Chronicles reveal this destructive pattern. The Old Testament prophets endlessly prophesied dire consequences for Israel if they continued in their idolatry. Mostly, they were ignored until it was too late and God's wrath against idol-worship was poured out on the nation. But ours is a merciful God, and He never failed to forgive and restore them when they repented and sought His forgiveness.

2 In reality, idols are impotent blocks of stone or wood, and their power exists only in the minds of the worshipers. The idol of the god Dagon was twice knocked to the floor by God to show the Philistines just who was God and who wasn't (1 Samuel 5:1-5). The "contest" between God and His prophet Elijah and the 450 prophets of Baal on Mount Carmel is a dramatic example of the power of the true God and the impotence of false gods (1 Kings 18:19-40). The testimony of Scripture is that God alone is worthy of worship. Idol worship robs God of the glory that is rightfully His, and that is something He will not tolerate (Isaiah 42:8).

3 Even today there are religions that bow before statues and icons, a practice forbidden by God's Word. The significance God places upon it is reflected in the fact that the first of the Ten Commandments refers to idolatry: "You shall have no other gods before me. You shall not make for yourself an idol in the form of anything in heaven above or on the earth beneath or in the waters below. You shall not bow down to them or worship them; for I, the LORD your God, am a jealous God, punishing the children for the sin of the fathers to the third and fourth generation of those who hate me" (Exodus 20:3-5). Idolatry extends beyond the worship of idols and images and false gods. Our modern idols are many and varied. Even for those who do not bow physically before a statue, idolatry is a matter of the heart—pride, self-centeredness, greed, gluttony, a love for possessions and ultimately rebellion against God. It is not surprising that God hates it the worship of idol. Because into day's world, people love themselves more than God, most places of worships are empty on Sundays because people are in their various places of work. They love work more than God and forgot the commandment in " remember the Sabbath and keep it Holy. (Exodus 20: 8-11) "the worship of idols or excessive devotion to, or reverence for some person or thing." An idol is anything that replaces the one, true God. The most prevalent form of idolatry in

Bible times was the worship of images that were thought to embody the various pagan deities.

4 Idolatry extends beyond the worship of idols and images and false gods. Our modern idols are many and varied. Even for those who do not bow physically before a statue, idolatry is a matter of the heart—pride, self-centeredness, greed, gluttony, a love for possessions and ultimately rebellion against God. Is it any wonder that God hates it? Because many have forgotten about the commandment "remember the Sabbath and keep it Holy (Exodus 20: 8-11) - meaning "Keep it holy," means set it aside from all other days as special. Specifically, as verse 10 says, keep it "to the Lord," or "for the Lord." In other words, the rest is not to be aimless rest, but God-centred rest. Attention is to be directed to God in a way that is more concentrated and steady than on ordinary days. Keep the day holy by keeping the focus on the holy God.

Image: (noun - Genesis 1:27) "So God created mankind in his own *image*, in the image of God he created them; male and female he created them".

Image is a representation of the external form of a person or thing in art. "her work juxtaposed images from serious and popular art" synonyms: likeness, resemblance; More a visible impression obtained by a camera, telescope, microscope, or other device, or displayed on a computer or video screen and many other meanings in various fields of endeavours.

Man, in his natural, but especially in his moral image, with an habitual conformity of all his powers to the will of God, his understanding clearly discerning, his judgment entirely approving, his will readily choosing, and his affections cordially embracing his chief good; without error in his knowledge, disorder in his passions, or irregularity or inordinacy in his appetites; his senses also being all inlets to wisdom and enjoyment, and all his faculties of body and mind subservient to the glory of God and his own felicity! But man being in honour did not abide, but became like the beasts that perish! What cause we have for thankfulness that this image of God may be restored to our souls, and how earnestly ought we to pray for, and how diligently to seek this most important of all attainments! Male and female created he them — Not at once, or both together, as some have unscriptural taught, but first the man out of the earth, and then the woman out of the man.

They seem both, however, to have been made on the sixth day, as is here related, and as the following words, promising they should be fruitful, manifest: but the particular history of the woman's creation is brought in afterward by way of further elucidation, and to introduce the account of the institution of marriage. God formed

Incarnation

the woman from the man, and caused the whole race of mankind to descend from one original pair, that all the families and nations of men, being made of one blood, and proceeding from one common stock, might know themselves to be brethren, and might love and assist one another to the uttermost of their power: but, alas! what a sad reverse of this do we daily see exemplified before our eyes!

2 Again *image* could be seen in the perspective of photo images sent back from the planet Neptune" synonyms: picture, facsimile, photograph, snapshot, photo; More an optical appearance or counterpart produced by light from an object reflected in a mirror or refracted through a lens. synonyms: reflection, mirror image, likeness; echo "he contemplated his image in the mirrors" MATHEMATICS a point or set formed by mapping from another point or set. COMPUTING an exact copy of a computer's hard disk, made for backing up data or setting up new machines. a mental representation or idea. "I had a sudden image of Sal bringing me breakfast in bed" synonyms: conception, impression, idea, concept, perception, notion; More a person or thing that closely resembles another. "he's the image of his father" synonyms: d o u - ble, living image, replica, lookalike, clone, copy, reproduction, twin, duplicate, exact likeness, facsimile, counterpart, mirror image; More semblance or likeness.

"made in the image of God" (in biblical use) an idol. synonyms: idol, icon, fetish, false god, golden calf, totem, talisman "a graven image" 2 the general impression that a person, organization, or product presents to the public. "she strives to project an image of youth" synonyms: public perception, public conception, public impression, persona, profile, face, identity, front, facade, mask, guise, role, part; More 3 a simile or metaphor. "he uses the image of a hole to describe emotional emptiness" synonyms: simile, metaphor, metonymy; More verb: image; 3rd person present: images; past tense: imaged; past participle: imaged; gerund or present participle: imagine make a representation of the external form of. "artworks which imaged women's bodies". Whatever meaning is attached to the word and for the purpose of the gospel dictionary, Christians must always understand that man was created or crafted in the *image* of God and build their faith solidly to take control and dominion as God can with faith.

Immanuel: *See Emmanuel*

Incarnation: This literally means, 'that embodied in flesh or taking on flesh. It refers to the conception and birth of a sentient creature that is the material manifestation of an entity, god or force whose original nature is immaterial. In its religious context the word is used to mean the descent from Heaven of a god, or divine being in human or animal form on Earth.

Iniquity

2 In the gospel, we can see that this is that act of grace whereby Christ took our human nature into union with his Divine Person, became man. Christ is both God and man. Human attributes and actions are predicated of him, and he of whom they are predicated is God. A Divine Person was united to a human nature (Acts 20:28; Rom. 8:32; 1 Corinthians. 2:8; Hebrew. 2:11-14; 1 Timothy. 3:16; Galatians. 4:4, etc.). The union is hypostatical, i.e., is personal; the two natures are not mixed or confounded, and it is perpetual.

3 To incarnate therefore, means to become flesh. The *incarnation* of Jesus is when the human nature (Jesus the man) was added to the nature of God the second person of the Trinity. It is where God became a man (John 1:1,14; Philipians. 2:5-8). It was the voluntary act of Jesus to humble himself so that he might die for our sins (1 Pet. 3:18). Thus, Jesus has two natures: Divine and human. This is known as the Hypostatic Union. The doctrine is of vital importance to the Christian. By it we understand the true nature of God, the atonement, forgiveness, grace, etc. It is only God who could pay for sins. Therefore, God became man (John 1:1-14) to die for our sins (1 Peter. 2:24) which is the atonement. Through Jesus we have forgiveness of sins. Since we are saved by grace through faith (Ephesians. 2:8-9), it is essential that our object of faith be accurate. The doctrine of the *incarnation* ensures accuracy--the knowledge that God died on the cross to atone for sin and that the God-man (Jesus) is now in heaven as a mediator (1 Timothy. 2:5) between us and God.

4 This also mean that Jesus came to reveal the Father (Mathew. 11:27; Luke 10:22), to do His will (Hebrew. 10:5-9), to fulfil prophecy (Luke 4:17-21), to reconcile the world (2 Corinthians. 5:18-21), and to become our High Priest as in (Hebrew. 7:24-28) "But because Jesus lives forever, he has a permanent priesthood. Therefore he is able to save completely[a] those who come to God through him, because he always lives to intercede for them. Such a high priest truly meets our need—one who is holy, blameless, pure, set apart from sinners, exalted above the heavens. Unlike the other high priests, he does not need to offer sacrifices day after day, first for his own sins, and then for the sins of the people. He sacrificed for their sins once for all when he offered himself. For the law appoints as high priests men in all their weakness; but the oath, which came after the law, appointed the Son, who has been made perfect forever". Praise the Lord!

Iniquity: (noun) this is the things that can happen in our human nature to hid God face from us. The Bible uses words such as iniquity, transgression, and trespass to indicate levels of disobedience to God. They are all categorized as "sin." (Micah 2:1) says, "Woe to those who plan iniquity, to those

Iniquity

who plot evil on their beds! At morning's light they carry it out because it is in their power to do it." immoral or grossly unfair behaviour. "a den of iniquity" synonyms: wickedness, sinfulness, immorality, impropriety, vice, evil, sin; and much more (Psalms 66:18 -KJV) "If I regard iniquity in my heart, the Lord will not hear me": God does not like any form of *iniquity*. As Christians, we must always flee away from the devil who is sin itself, the devil will run away from us.

2 The Hebrew word (avon) used most often for "iniquity" means "guilt worthy of punishment." Iniquity is sin at its worst. Iniquity is premeditated, continuing, and escalating. When we flirt with sin, we fall for the lie that we can control it. But like a cute baby monkey can grow to be a wild, out-of-control primate, sin that seems small and harmless at first can take control before we know it. When we give ourselves over to a sinful lifestyle, we are committing iniquity. Sin has become our god rather than the Lord (Romans 6:14). When we realize we have sinned, we have a choice. We can see it for the evil it is and repent. When we do, we find the forgiveness and cleansing of God (Jeremiah 33:8; 1 John 1:9). Or we can harden our hearts and go deeper into that sin until it defines us. Partial lists of iniquities are given in (Galatians 5:19–21 and in 1 Corinthians 6:9–10).

3 These are sins that become so consuming that a person can be identified by that lifestyle. The psalmists distinguish between sin and iniquity when they ask God to forgive both (Psalm 32:5; 38:18; 51:2; 85:2). If we continue to choose sin, our hearts harden toward God. One sin leads to another, and iniquity begins to define our lives, as it did when David sinned with Bathsheba (2 Samuel 11:3–4). His initial sin of lust resulted in a hardening of his heart, and his sin deepened. He committed adultery, then had Bathsheba's husband killed (verses 14–15). "In the morning David wrote a letter to Joab and sent it with Uriah. In it he wrote, "Put Uriah out in front where the fighting is fiercest. Then withdraw from him so he will be struck down and die." – a deliberate sin.

3 Iniquity had taken over David's life. It was only when confronted by the prophet Nathan that he repented with great sorrow. His heartfelt cry for forgiveness is detailed in (Psalm 51: 2) says, "Wash away all my iniquity and cleanse me from my sin." David is a picture of someone who clearly understood the progression of iniquity and who experienced the mercy and forgiveness of God (Psalm 103:1–5). Romans 1 outlines the progression of sin (Romans 1: 10–32). The end result for those with such hardened hearts is that God turns them over to a "reprobate mind" (verse 28, KJV), and they no longer have the desire or ability to repent. Reprobate means "thoroughly depraved, given over to evil until the conscience is

seared." The Scripture is clear that God forgives even iniquity (Micah 7:18), but if we persist in it, we will reap the wages of sin, which is eternal separation from God (Romans 6:23).

Iniquity in my Heart: This simply means indwelling sinful nature in one's life. If I regard iniquity in my heart - literally, "If I have conceived - iniquity in my heart." Meaning if I know my venture is sinful in other word, If I have indulged in a purpose of iniquity; if I have had a wicked end in view; if I have not been willing to forsake all sin; if I have cherished a purpose of pollution or wrong. The meaning is not literally, If I have "seen" any iniquity in my heart - for no one can look into his own heart, and not see that it is defiled by sin; but, If I have cherished it in my soul; if I have gloated over past sins; if I am purposing to commit sin again; if I am not willing to abandon all sin, and to be holy. The Lord will not hear me - That is, He will not regard and answer my prayer. The idea is that in order that prayer may be heard, there must be a purpose to forsake all forms of sin. This is a great and most important principle in regard to prayer. The same principle is affirmed or implied in (Psalm 18:41; Psalm 34:15; Proverbs 1:28; Proverbs 15:29; Proverbs 28:9; Isaiah 15:1-9; Jeremiah 11:11; Jeremiah 14:12; Zechariah 7:13; John 9:31). It is also especially stated in (Isaiah 58:3-7). 'Why have we fasted, and you see it not? Why have we humbled ourselves, and you take no knowledge of it?' Behold, in the day of your fast you seek your own pleasure,[a] and oppress all your workers. Behold, you fast only to quarrel and to fight and to hit with a wicked fist. Fasting like yours this day will not make your voice to be heard on high. Is such the fast that I choose, a day for a person to humble himself? Is it to bow down his head like a reed, and to spread sackcloth and ashes under him? Will you call this a fast, and a day acceptable to the Lord? "Is not this the fast that I choose: to lose the bonds of wickedness, to undo the straps of the yoke, to let the oppressed go free, and to break every yoke? Is it not to share your bread with the hungry and bring the homeless poor into your house; when you see the naked, to cover him, and not to hide yourself from your own flesh? The principle is applicable, to secret purposes of sin; to sinful desires, corrupt passions. and evil propensities; secondly to acts of sin in individuals, as when a man is pursuing a business founded on fraud, dishonesty, oppression, and wrong; and possesses or device many sinful strategies in doing so more and more".

Thirdly, to public acts of sin, as when a people fast and pray (Isaiah 58:1-14), and yet hold their fellow-men in bondage; or enact and maintain unjust and unrighteous laws; or uphold the acts of wicked rulers; or countenance and support by law that which is contrary to the law of God; and fourthly, to the feelings of an awakened and

Intercession

trembling sinner when he is professedly seeking salvation. If there is still the love of evil in his heart; if he has some cherished purpose of *iniquity* which he is not willing to abandon; if there is any one sin, however small or unimportant it may seem to be, which he is not willing to forsake, he cannot hope that God will hear his prayer; he may be assured that he will not. All prayer, to be acceptable to God, must be connected with a purpose to forsake all sin.

Intercession (Or intercessory Prayers): This shows how the gospel relates to society. It is the act of praying to God on behalf of others. In western forms of Christian worship, intercession forms a distinct form of prayer, alongside Adoration, Confession and Thanksgiving. In public worship, intercession is offered as prayer for the world beyond the immediate vicinity and friendship networks of the church community. As such, intercession constitutes part of the worshipping community's engagement with otherness, as it expresses Christians' solidarity with those who are 'other' than themselves. In doing so, a church both appeals to, and seeks to embody, God's own love for the world.

2 In the Christian (Greek) Scriptures, Apostle Paul's tailored exhortation to Timothy specified intercession prayers can be made for those of worldly authority where it benefits God's immediate family members in maintaining their current way of life, as opposed to the use of intercession prayers motivated by agape - love for worldly authorities as in (1 Timothy 2: 1-2) "I urge, then, first of all, that petitions, prayers, intercession and thanksgiving be made for all people— for kings and all those in authority, that we may live peaceful and quiet lives in all godliness and holiness. See the word also in (1 John 2:15) "Do not love the world or anything in the world. If anyone loves the world, love for the Father is not in them". In intercessory prayers the word "we" is common, especially if it is written prayer like those in various churches: such as Baptist, Roman Catholic, Church of England, Ecumenical, Emerging Church, Methodist as the person offering the prayer is offering it for everyone within that church, community, or for all Christians around the world.

Isaac: (Hebrew - Yitskhak, meaning "he will laugh"; (Greek: Isaak) ⁇ as described in the Hebrew Bible and the Qur'an, was the only son Abraham had with his wife Sarah, and was the father of Jacob and Esau. According to the Book of Genesis, Abraham was 100 years old when Isaac was born, and Sarah was past 90. According to the Genesis narrative, Abraham brought Isaac to Mount Moriah, where, at God's command, Abraham built a sacrificial altar to sacrifice Isaac. At the last moment an angel stopped him. This event served as a test of Abraham's faith. Isaac was one of the three patriarchs of the Israelites. Isaac was the only biblical patriarch whose name was not changed, and the only one who did not move out of Canaan. Compared to those of Abraham and Jacob, Isaac's story relates fewer incidents of his life. He died when he was 180 years old, making him the longest-lived of the three. Isaac was a Lover of Peace. Born in Canaan and died in Canaan. Family, Spouse was Rebecca

Isaiah, (Greek – Esaias, Modern Hebrew – Yeshayahu) meaning "Yah is salvation" was a prophet documented by the Biblical Book of Isaiah to have lived around the time of 8th-century BC Kingdom of Judah. The exact relationship between the Book of Isaiah and any such historical Isaiah remains the subject of on-going scholarly discussion. One widespread view sees parts of the first half of the book (chapters 1–39) as originating with the historical prophet, interspersed with prose commentaries written in the time of King Josiah a hundred years later; with the remainder of the book dating from immediately before and immediately after the end of the exile in Babylon, almost two centuries after the time of the original prophet. Jews and Christians consider the Book of Isaiah a part of their Biblical canon; he is the first listed (although not the earliest) of the neviim akharonim, the latter prophets.

Ishmael: Modern Hebrew - Yishma'el Greek: Ismael) is a figure in the Hebrew Bible and the Qur'an and was Abraham's first son according to Jews, Christians, and Muslims. Ishmael was born of Abraham's marriage to Sarah's handmaiden Hagar (Genesis 16:3). According to the Genesis account, he died at the age of 137 (Genesis 25:17) "Ishmael lived a hundred and thirty-seven years. He breathed his last and died, and he was gathered to his people".

2 The Book of Genesis and other traditions consider Ishmael to be the ancestor of the Ishmaelite's.

Israel: A country in Western Asia, situated at the south eastern shore of the Mediterranean Sea. It shares land borders with Lebanon to the north, Syria in the northeast, Jordan on the east, the Palestinian territories comprising the West Bank and Gaza Strip on the east and southwest, respectively, and Egypt and the Gulf of Aqaba in the Red Sea to the south. It contains geographically diverse features within its relatively small area. Israel's financial centre is Tel Aviv, while Jerusalem is the country's most populous city and its designated capital, although Israeli sovereignty over Jerusalem is not recognized internationally.

2 On 29 November 1947, the United Nations General Assembly recommended the adoption and implementation of the Partition Plan for Mandatory Palestine. The end of the British Mandate for Palestine was set for midnight on 14 May 1948. That day, David Ben-Gurion, the Executive Head

Israelites

of the Zionist Organization and president of the Jewish Agency for Palestine, declared "the establishment of a Jewish state in Eretz Israel, to be known as the State of Israel," which would start to function from the termination of the mandate. The borders of the new state were not specified. Neighbouring Arab armies invaded the former Palestinian mandate on the next day and fought the Israeli forces. Israel has since fought several wars with neighbouring Arab states, in the course of which it has occupied the West Bank, Sinai Peninsula (1956–1957, 1967–1982), part of South Lebanon (1982–2000), Gaza Strip and the Golan Heights. It annexed portions of these territories, including East Jerusalem, but the border with the West Bank is disputed. Israel has signed peace treaties with Egypt and with Jordan, but efforts to resolve the Israeli–Palestinian conflict have so far not resulted in peace.

The population of Israel, as defined by the Israel Central Bureau of Statistics, was estimated in 2014 to be 8,146,300 people. It is the world's only Jewish-majority state; 6,110,600 citizens, or 75.3% of Israelis, are Jewish. The country's second largest group of citizens are designated as Arabs, with 1,686,000 people (including the Druze and most East Jerusalem Arabs). The great majority of Israeli Arabs are settled Muslims, with smaller but significant numbers of semi-settled Negev Bedouins; the rest are Christians and Druze. Other minorities include Maronites, Samaritans, Dom people, Black Hebrew Israelites, other Sub-Saharan Africans, Armenians, Circassia's, Roma and others. Israel also hosts a significant population of non-citizen foreign workers and asylum seekers from Africa and Asia.

3 In its Basic Laws, *Israel* defines itself as a Jewish and Democratic State. Israel is a representative democracy (disputed–discuss) with a parliamentary system, proportional representation and universal suffrage. The Prime Minister serves as head of government and the Knesset serves as Israel's legislative body. Israel is a developed country and an OECD member, with the 43rd-largest economy in the world by nominal gross domestic product as of 2012. The country has the highest standard of living in the Middle East and the fifth highest in Asia, and has the fourteenth highest life expectancy in the world.

Israelites: A Semitic people of the Ancient Near East, who inhabited part of Canaan during the tribal and monarchic periods (15th to 6th centuries BCE), and lived in the region in smaller numbers after the fall of the monarchy. The term "Israelites" is the English term (derived from the ancient Greek) for the Hebrew biblical term Bnei Yisrael which properly translates as either "Sons of Israel" or "Children of Israel", and refers both to the direct descendants of the patriarch Jacob as well as to the historical populations of the United Kingdom of Israel and Judah. In the post-exilic period, beginning in the 5th century BCE, the two known remnants of the Israelite tribes came to be referred to as Jews and Samaritans, inhabiting the territories of Judea, Galilee and Samaria. Other terms sometimes used include the "Hebrews" and the "Twelve Tribes" of *Israel.*

2 The Jews, which include the tribes of Judah, Simeon, Benjamin and partially Levi, are named after the southern Israelite Kingdom of Judah. This shift of ethnonym from *"Israelites"* to "Jews", although not contained in the Torah, is made explicit in the Book of Esther (4th century BCE), a book in the Ketuvim, the third section of the Jewish Tanakh. The Samaritans, whose religious texts consists of the five books of the Samaritan Torah (but which does not contain the books comprising the Jewish Tanakh), do not refer to themselves as Jews, although they do regard themselves as Israelites, as per the Torah.

The Kingdom of Samaria contained the remaining ten tribes, but following Samaria's conquest by Assyria, these were allegedly dispersed and lost to history, and henceforth known as the Ten Lost Tribes. Jewish tradition holds that Samaria is named so because the region's mountainous terrain was used to keep "Guard" (Shamer) for incoming enemy attack. According to Samaritan tradition, however, the Samaritan ethnonym is not derived from the region of Samaria, but from the fact that they were the "Guardians" (Shamerim) of the true *Israelite* religion. Thus, according to Samaritan tradition, the region was named Samaria after them, not vice versa. In Jewish Hebrew, the Samaritans are called Shomronim, while in Samaritan Hebrew they known as the Shamerim. Also in Judaism, an *Israelite* is, broadly speaking, a lay member of the Jewish ethno religious group, as opposed to the priestly orders of Kohanim and Levites. In texts of Jewish law such as the Mishnah and Gemara, the term יהודי (Yehudi), meaning Jew, is rarely used, and instead the ethnonym (Yisraeli), or Israelite, is widely used to refer to Jews. Samaritans commonly refer to themselves and Jews collectively as *Israelites*, and describe themselves as the *Israelite* Samaritans.

Issachar: (Hebrew: meaning "reward; recompense") was, according to the Book of Genesis, a son of Jacob and Leah (the fifth son of Leah, and ninth son of Jacob), and the founder of the Israelite Tribe of Issachar; however some Biblical scholars view this as post diction, an eponymous metaphor providing an aetiology of the connectedness of the tribe to others in the Israelite confederation. The text of the Torah gives two different etymologies for the name of *Issachar,* which some textual scholars attribute to different sources - one to the Yahwist and the other to the Elohist; the first being that it derives from ish sakar, meaning man

Issachar

of hire, in reference to Leah's hire of Jacob's sexual favours for the price of some mandrakes; the second being that it derives from yesh sakar, meaning there is a reward, in reference to Leah's opinion that the birth of Issachar was a divine reward for giving her handmaid Zilpah to Jacob as a concubine. Scholars suspect the former explanation to be the more likely name for a tribe, though some scholars have proposed a third etymology - that it derives from ish Sokar, meaning man of Sokar, in reference to the tribe originally worshipping Sokar, an Egyptian deity.

Moreso, in the Biblical account, Leah's status as the first wife of Jacob is regarded by biblical scholars as indicating that the authors saw the tribe of *Issachar* as being one of the original Israelite groups; however, this may have been the result of a typographic error, as the names of *Issachar* and Naphtali appear to have changed places elsewhere in the text, and the birth narrative of Issachar and Naphtali is regarded by textual scholars as having been spliced together from its sources in a manner which has highly corrupted the narrative. A number of scholars think that the tribe of *Issachar* actually originated as the Shekelesh group of Sea Peoples - the name 'Shekelesh' can be decomposed as men of the Shekel in Hebrew, a meaning synonymous with man of hire (ish sakar); scholars believe that the memory of such non-Israelite origin would have led to the Torah's authors having given *Issachar* a handmaiden as a matriarch.

2 In classical rabbinical literature, it is stated that *Issachar* was born on the fourth of Av, and lived 122 years. According to the midrashim Book of Jasher, *Issachar* married Aridah, the younger daughter of Jobab, a son of Joktan; the Torah states that *Issachar* had four sons, who were born in Canaan and migrated with him to Egypt, with their descendants remaining there until the Exodus. The midrashim Book of Jasher portrays *Issachar* as somewhat pragmatic, due to his strong effort in being more learned, less involved with other matters which led him to such actions like taking a feeble part in military campaigns involving his brothers, and generally residing in strongly fortified cities and, depending on his brother Zebulon's financial support in return for a share in the spiritual reward he gains. 3 The Talmud argues that *Issachar*'s description in the Blessing of Jacob - *Issachar* is a strong ass lying down between two burdens: and he saw that settled life was good, and the land was pleasant; and bowed his shoulder to bear, and became a servant unto tribute - is a reference to the religious scholarship of the tribe of Issachar, though scholars feel that it may more simply be a literal interpretation of Issachar's name.

Jealous

Jj

Jealous: (adj) (Exodus 20:5) "You shall not bow down to them or serve them, for I the LORD your God am a *jealous* God, visiting the iniquity of the fathers on the children to the third and the fourth generation of those who hate me" Also in (James 3:16) For where *jealousy* and selfish ambition exist, there will be disorder and every vile practice. *Jealousy* is simply a resentful and envious, as of someone's success, advantages, etc.: to be jealous of a rich brother. Proceeding from suspicious, fears or envious resentment: a jealous rage. 3 Inclined to suspicions of rivalry, unfaithfulness, etc., as in love: a jealous husband. 4 watchful in guarding something: to be *jealous* of one's independence. 5 intolerant of unfaithfulness or rivalry: The Lord is a jealous God. Jealousy is a disloyal instinct showing a complete lack of interest or inappreciable instinct to another's — (deemed superiors) achievement or positioning. God having created Heaven and earth, positioned Himself to a Supreme Authority reigning over the Heavens and the whole Universe. He did not want any conflict brought about by any other gods or creature. He therefore warned the in (Exodus 20:5)

2 Not only has God warned against jealousy, Jealousy is an ugly word. It has overtones of selfishness, suspicion, and distrust, and implies a hideous resentment or hostility toward other people because they enjoy some advantage. It is possessive, demanding, and overbearing; and that is repulsive. It stifles freedom and individuality, it degrades and demeans, it breeds tension and discord, it destroys friendships and marriages. We view *jealousy* as a horrible trait and we hate it.

In particular, Whoremongers and adulterers God will surely judge. Though we have not now the waters of jealousy, yet we have God's word, which ought to be as great a terror. Sensual lusts will end in bitterness. God will manifest the innocence of the innocent. The same providence is for good to some, and for hurt to others. And it will answer the purposes which God intends.

Jehovah

Jehovah: The proper name of the God of Israel in the Hebrew Bible. This vocalization has been transliterated as "Yehowah", while YHWH itself has been transliterated as "Yahweh". And it appears 6,518 times in the traditional Masoretic Text, in addition to 305 instances of (Jehovih). The earliest available Latin text to use a vocalization similar to Jehovah dates from the 13th century. Most scholars believe "Jehovah" to be a late (c. 1100 CE) hybrid form derived by combining the Latin letters JHVH with the vowels of Adonai, but there is some evidence that it may already have been in use in Late Antiquity (5th century). The consensus among scholars is that the historical vocalization of the Tetragrammaton at the time of the redaction of the Torah (6th century BCE) is most likely Yahweh, however there is disagreement. The historical vocalization was lost because in Second Temple Judaism, during the 3rd to 2nd centuries BCE, the pronunciation of the Tetragrammaton came to be avoided, being substituted with Adonai ("my Lord").

2 *"Jehovah"* was popularized in the English-speaking world by William Tyndale and other pioneer English Protestant translators, but is no longer used in mainstream English translations, with Lord or LORD used instead, generally indicating that the corresponding Hebrew is Yahweh or YHWH.

Jesus: (Greek: Iesous;), The glorified Head and Ruler of the Church. Jesus is Grace at the right hand of God – the Father in the Holy Trinity otherwise known as God in flesh (John 1:1, 14). He is fully God and fully man (Colossians: 2:9); thus, He has two natures: God and man. He is not half God and half man. He is 100% God and 100% man. He never lost his divinity. He existed in the form of God; and when He became a man, He added human nature to Himself (Philippians. 2:5-11). "Therefore, there is a union in one person of a full human nature and a full divine nature. Right now in heaven there is a man, Jesus, who is Mediator between us and God the Father (1Timothy 2:5). Jesus is our advocate with the Father (1 John 2:1). He is our Saviour (Titus 2:13). He is our Lord (Romans. 10:9-10). He is not, as some cults teach, an angel who became a man (Jehovah's Witnesses) or the brother of the devil (Mormonism). He is wholly God and wholly man, the Creator, and the Redeemer. He is Jesus.

2 Also referred to as Jesus of Nazareth, is the central figure of Christianity, whom the teachings of most Christian denominations hold to be the Son of God. Christianity regards Jesus as the awaited Messiah of the Old Testament and refers to him as Jesus Christ, a name that is also used in non-Christian contexts. Virtually all modern scholars of antiquity agree that Jesus existed historically, although the quest for the historical Jesus has

produced little agreement on the historical reliability of the Gospels and on how closely the biblical Jesus reflects the historical Jesus. Most scholars agree that Jesus was a Jewish rabbi from Galilee who preached his message orally, He was baptized by John the Baptist, and was crucified in Jerusalem on the orders of the Roman prefect, Pontius Pilate. Scholars have constructed various portraits of the historical Jesus, which often depict him as having one or more of the following roles: the leader of an apocalyptic movement, Messiah, a charismatic healer, a sage and philosopher, or an egalitarian social reformer. Scholars have correlated the New Testament accounts with non-Christian historical records to arrive at an estimated chronology of Jesus' life. The most widely used calendar era in the world (abbreviated as "AD", alternatively referred to as "CE"), counts from a medieval estimate of the birth year of Jesus.

3 Christians believe that Jesus has a "unique significance" in the world. Christian doctrines include the beliefs that Jesus was conceived by the Holy Spirit, was born of a virgin, performed miracles, founded the Church, died by crucifixion as a sacrifice to achieve atonement, rose from the dead, and ascended into heaven, whence he will return. The great majority of Christians worship Jesus as the incarnation of God the Son, the second of three persons of a Divine Trinity. Thus "Let them praise the name of the LORD: for his name alone is excellent; his glory [is] above the earth and heaven."(Psalm 148:13) . Hallelujah!

4 The Bible is about Jesus (Luke 24:27, 44; John 5:39; Heb. 10:7). The prophets prophesied about Him (Acts 10:43). The Father bore witness of Him (John 5:37, 8:18). The Holy Spirit bore witness of Him (John 15:26). The works Jesus did bore witness of Him (John 5:36; 10:25). The multitudes bore witness of Him (John 12:17). And, Jesus bore witness of Himself (John 14:6, 18:6). Praise His Holy Name!!

Joy: Rejoice in the Lord – (Philippians 3:1) – is a command, be joyful always. (1 Thessalonians 5:16) Joy is divine Happiness, divine emotion Joy (given name), 2 people with the given name Joy. Joy (surname), or people with the surname Joy. 3 *Joy* is a positive human condition that can be either a feeling or an action. In this passage the Greek uses the word "joy" in the action senses. As Christians, we must always rejoice and be glad in good times or bad times.

4 The passion or emotion excited by the acquisition or expectation of good; pleasurable feelings or emotions caused by success, good fortune, and the like, or by a rational prospect of possessing what we love or desire; gladness; exhilaration of spirits; delight. That which causes joy or happiness,

Joy, exuberant

Joy (noun.) The sign or exhibition of joy; gayety; mirth; merriment; festivity. (noun.) To rejoice; to be glad; to delight; to exult. To give joy to; to congratulate. To gladden; to make joyful; to exhilarate. And to enjoy.

5 Again, the idea of joy is expressed in the Old Testament by a wealth of synonymous terms that cannot easily be differentiated. The commonest is simchah (1 Samuel 18:6, etc.), variously translated in English Versions of the Bible "joy," "gladness," "mirth"; from sameah, properly "to be bright," "to shine" (Proverbs 13:9, "The light of the righteous rejoiceth," literally, "is bright"), but generally used figuratively "to rejoice," "be glad" (Leviticus 23:40) and very frequent).

Other nouns are masos and sason, both from sus, properly "to spring," "leap," hence, "exult," "rejoice"; rinnah, "shouting." "joy"; gil, from verb gil or gul, "to go in a circle," hence, "be excited" (dancing round for joy), "rejoice." In the New Testament, far the commonest are chara, "joy," chairo, "to rejoice" (compare charis, "grace").

Joy, exuberant: (Greek – agalliasis) meaning exultation" (not used in classical Greek, but often in the Septuagint; in the New Testament, Luke 1:14, 44 Acts 2:46; Jude 1:24; Hebrews 1:9), and the corresponding verb agalliaoo (-aomai), "to exult," "rejoice exceedingly" (Matthew 5:12, etc.). In English Versions of the Bible we have sometimes "to joy" (now obsolete as a verb), used in an intransitive sense - "to rejoice" (Habakkuk 3:18 2 Corinthians 7:13, etc.).

Judgement: (2 Corinthians 5:10 ESV) "For we must all appear before the judgment seat of Christ, so that each one may receive what is due for what he has done in the body, whether good or evil".

Judgement is an act of carrying out the evaluation of evidence to make a decision. The term has four distinct uses: Informal - opinions expressed as facts. used in the concept of salvation to refer to the adjudication of God in determining Heaven or Hell for each and all human beings.

2 There are two separate judgments. Believers will be judged at the Judgment Seat of Christ (Romans 14:10-12). Every believer will give an account of himself, and the Lord will judge the decisions he made—including those concerning issues of conscience. This judgment does not determine salvation, which is by faith alone (Ephesians 2:8-9), but rather is the time when believers must give an account of their lives in service to Christ. Our position in Christ is the "foundation" spoken of in (1 Corinthians 3:11-15). That which we build upon the foundation can be the "gold, silver, and precious stones" of good works in Christ's name, obedience and fruitfulness—dedicated spiritual service to glorify God and build the church. Or what we build on the foundation may be the "wood,

hay and stubble" of worthless, frivolous, shallow activity with no spiritual value. The Judgment Seat of Christ will reveal this.

The gold, silver and precious stones in the lives of believers will survive God's refining fire (verse. 13), and believers will be rewarded based on those good works— how faithfully we served Christ (1 Corinthians 9:4-27), how well we obeyed the Great Commission (Matthew 28:18-20), how victorious we were over sin (Romans 6:1-4), how well we controlled our tongues (James 3:1-9), etc. We will have to give an account for our actions, whether they were truly indicative of our position in Christ. The fire of God's judgment will completely burn up the "wood, hay and stubble" of the words we spoke and things we did which had no eternal value. "So then, each of us will give an account of himself to God" (Romans 14:12).

3 The second judgment is that of unbelievers who will be judged at the Great White Throne Judgment (Revelation 20:11-15). This judgment does not determine salvation, either. Everyone at the Great White Throne is an unbeliever who has rejected Christ in life and is therefore already doomed to the lake of fire. (Revelation 20:12) says that unbelievers will be "judged out of those things which were written in the books, according to their works." Those who have rejected Christ as Lord and Saviour will be judged based on their works alone, and because the Bible tells us that "by the works of the Law no flesh will be justified" (Galatians 2:16), they will be condemned. No amount of good works and the keeping of God's laws can be sufficient to atone for sin. All their thoughts, words and actions will be judged against God's perfect standard and found wanting. There will be no reward for them, only eternal condemnation and punishment. As Christians, we must check ourselves and stay away from sinful act in order that we may be in consonant with Jesus in the great day of Judgement. And also stay away from judging others as cautioned in (Romans 2: 1) "You, therefore, have no excuse, you who pass judgment on someone else, for at whatever point you judge another, you are condemning yourself, because you who pass judgment do the same things".

See also the following scriptures (Romans 8:9) - But ye are not in the flesh, but in the Spirit, if so be that the Spirit of God dwell in you. Now if any man have not the Spirit of Christ, he is none of his. (Romans 8:1-39) - [There is] therefore now no condemnation to them which are in Christ Jesus, who walk not after the flesh, but after the Spirit. (Romans 6:23) - For the wages of sin [is] death; but the gift of God [is] eternal life through Jesus Christ our Lord. (Romans 5:12) - Wherefore, as by one man sin entered into the world, and death by sin; and so death passed upon all men, for that all have sinned:

Judgement day

Judgement day: The glorious day to the Elects and day of damnation to the sinners as in (Acts 2:20) "The sun will be changed into darkness, and the moon will be changed into blood, before the great and spectacular day of the Lord comes". Day of Judgment, Judgment Day, or The Day of the Lord Which is part of the eschatological world view of the Abrahamic religions and in the Frashokereti of Zoroastrianism. In Christian theology, it is the final and eternal judgment by God of every nation. The concept is found in all the Canonical gospels, particularly the Gospel of Matthew. Christian Futurists believe it will take place after the Resurrection of the Dead and the Second Coming of Christ while Full Preterists believe it has already occurred. The Last Judgment has inspired numerous artistic depictions.

2 That there will be a "judgment day" is significant for an understanding of a good deal of Scripture. In these days there are many who are ready to accept the thought of accountability but who reject the idea of judgment day. They see this as no more than a needless piece of imagery and hold that what the Bible really means is that God is constantly at work judging his people. Here is, of course, a truth here. God does watch over his people and in the happenings of every day he disciplines them. This is scriptural, but it is not the whole of the teaching of the Bible. In addition to any earlier judgments Scripture looks forward to God's judgment at the end of time. Paul tells the Romans that what the law says is written on the hearts of the Gentiles and that their response to this will determine what will happen to them on judgment day (Romans 2:15-16). It is what God has done in them and not what they have decided for themselves that forms the standard. For an understanding of judgment day it is important to bear in mind that God knows what goes on in the hearts of all people and he knows accordingly whether they are responding as they should to the leading he has given them.

3 The Judge. Very often the day is related to God or to Christ. Thus it is "the great day of God Almighty" (Revelation 16:14); it is "the day of God" (2 Peter 3:12). The earliest use of this imagery is when Amos pronounces a woe on "you who long for the day of the Lord" (Amos 5:18). Clearly the Israelites expected that day to be a day of deliverance and blessing, but Amos goes on to assure them that "That day will be darkness, not light." "The day he (God visits us") (1 Peter 2:12) means of course "the day when God visits" so it belongs here. It reminds us that God's "visitation" on judgment day will be a serious affair. So is it when we read of "the great and glorious day of the Lord" (Acts 2:20). This occurs in a quotation from Joel, so "the Lord" is clearly Yahweh. 4 The final and eternal judgment by God of every nation

Just, The: (Habakkuk 2:4) ... "Behold the proud, his soul is not upright in him; but *the just* shall live by his faith." (NKJ). The ordinary usage of the word Just is - Based on or behaving according to what is morally right and fair: a just generation fighting for a just cause synonyms: fair, fair-minded, equitable, even-handed, impartial, unbiased, objective, neutral, disinterested, unprejudiced, open-minded, non-partisan, non-discriminatory; as opposed to unjust, unfair (of treatment) deserved or appropriate in the circumstances. For example "we all get our just deserts" synonyms: deserved, well deserved, well earned, merited, earned; (of an opinion or appraisal) well founded; justifiable ."these simplistic approaches have been the subject of just criticism" synonyms: valid, sound, well founded, well grounded, justified, justifiable, warranted, warrantable, defensible, defendable, legitimate, reasonable, logical; "just criticism"

However, as Christians, we ought to be *the Just*. We should exhibit the quality of true Christians by doing always what is right as opposed to the pride of the Chaldeans. The Chaldeans faced their downfall, while the faithfulness of the righteous will be his salvation. Habakkuk says the Babylonians are self-centred and therefore doomed; the righteous are God-centred and therefore triumphant (Daniel 4:30-32; Proverbs 3:5-6). In other words, the righteous man trusts, not in himself, but in God. His faith is directed upward, not inward! Herein is faith -- the ability to accept as reality what one cannot fully understand. The one who trusts in God is not troubled by the enigmas of life. He knows that God does all things right and all things well. Running the universe is God's business, but the righteous man has a daily task to fulfil, and he will live by his faithfulness. He will trust and obey, even if he does not comprehend all of God's ways. The Just shall live by faith. Hallelujah!

Justification: The legal act where God declares the sinner to be innocent of his or her sins. It is not that the sinner is now sinless, but that he is "declared" sinless. This declaration of righteousness is being justified before God. This justification is based on the shed blood of Jesus, " . . . having now been justified by His blood . . . " (Romans. 5:9) where Jesus was crucified, died, was buried, and rose again (1 Corinthians. 15:1-4). God imputed (reckoned to our account) the righteousness of Christ at the same time our sins were imputed to Christ when he was on the cross. That is why it says in (1 Peter. 2:24), "and He Himself bore our sins in His body on the cross, that we might die to sin and live to righteousness; for by His wounds you were healed." Also, (2 Corinthians. 5:21) says, "He made Him who knew no sin to be sin on our behalf, that we might become the righteousness of God in Him." Additionally, we are justified by faith

Justify

(Romans. 5:1) apart from works of the Law (Romans. 3:28).

2 *Justification* - To be saved means that God has delivered us (saved us) from His righteous wrathful judgment due us because of our sins against Him. It means that we will not be judged for our sins and be therefore sentenced to eternal damnation. To be saved means that we are justified before God. Only Christians are saved. Only Christians are justified. The issue at hand is whether or not this salvation, this justification, is attained by faith or by faith and something else.

Justify: (verb – Justified, past tense) There are various usage of the word Justify. In ordinary usage the word means to show or prove to be right or reasonable. "the person appointed has fully justified our confidence" synonyms: give grounds for, give reasons for, give a justification for, show just cause for, explain, give an explanation for, account for, show or prove to be reasonable, provide a rationale for, rationalize; More be a good reason for. "the situation was grave enough to justify further investigation" synonyms: warrant, be good reason for, be a justification for.

2 While in the gospel the word means to declare or make righteous in the sight of God. "one of the elect, justified by faith" References (Romans. 3:22), "even the righteousness of God through faith in Jesus Christ for all those who believe; for there is no distinction." (Romams. 3:24, "being justified as a gift by His grace through the redemption which is in Christ Jesus;" (Romans. 3:26), "for the demonstration, I say, of His righteousness at the present time, that He might be just and the justifier of the one who has faith in Jesus." (Romans. 3:28-30), "For we maintain that a man is justified by faith apart from works of the Law. 29Or is God the God of Jews only? Is He not the God of Gentiles also? Yes, of Gentiles also, 30since indeed God who will justify the circumcised by faith and the uncircumcised through faith is one." (Romans). 4:3, "For what does the Scripture say? "And Abraham believed God, and it was reckoned to him as righteousness." (Romans. 4:5), "But to the one who does not work, but believes in Him who justifies the ungodly, his faith is reckoned as righteousness," (Romans. 4:11), "And he received the sign of circumcision, a seal of the righteousness of the faith which he had while still uncircumcised, that he might be the father of all those who believe, though they are uncircumcised, that righteousness might be imputed to them also,"

3 Justify means the act of God when he says that he sees us as good. He says this at the moment when we are saved . This is the moment when we trust Jesus. *See justification*

Kk

Keep: (Verb) as in Aaron's Blessing in (Numbers 6: 23-25) ..."Speak to Aaron and to his sons, saying, 'Thus you shall bless the sons of Israel. You shall say to them: The LORD bless you, and *keep* you; The LORD make His face shine on you, And be gracious to you;..." Also in (Isaiah 26:3 KJV) " Thou wilt keep him in perfect peace, whose mind is stayed on thee: because he trusteth in thee.

2 To *keep* therefore means to Bestow upon you all manner of blessings, temporal and spiritual. Keep thee — That is, continue his blessings to thee, and preserve thee in and to the use of them; keep thee from sin, and its bitter effects. Shine upon thee — alluding to the shining of the sun upon the earth, to enlighten, and warm, and renew the face of it. The Lord loves thee, and makes thee know that he loves thee. We cannot but be happy, if we have God's love; and we cannot but be easy, if we know that we have it. Lift up his countenance — That is, look upon thee with a cheerful and pleasant countenance, as one that is well pleased with thee and thy services. Peace — Peace with God, with thy own conscience, and with all men; all prosperity is comprehended under this word.

3 To keep is to have or retain possession of. Example "my father would *keep* the best for himself" retain or reserve for future use. "return one copy to me, keeping the other for your files" synonyms: retain, hold on to, keep for oneself, retain possession of, keep possession of, retain in one's possession, keep hold of, not part with, hold fast to, hold back; More put or store in a regular place. "the stand where her umbrella was kept" synonyms: store, house, stow, keep a place for, put away, place, put, deposit, stack, pile "the stand where her umbrella was kept"

4 The word *keep* is a predominant word throughout the whole gospel. Right from the time of Adam, Good appointed man to *keep* the Garden. It is the word of life, the beginning of faith in Christ Jesus, *Keep* is also the word of Love, as in when Jesus Promises the Holy Spirit in (John 14:15 -16) "If you love Me, you will *keep* My com-

Keep

mandments. "I will ask the Father, and He will give you another Helper, that He may be with you forever";

There are several Bible verses expanding the word *keep*. To keep in the true sense of the gospel means to live with it, retain it like to Keep Jesus in your life He is in me as I am in Him or I am in Him and He – Jesus is in me. See the following Biblical references for more ingredients: (Genesis 2:15) And the LORD God took the man, and put him into the garden of Eden to dress it and to keep it. (Genesis 3:24) So he drove out the man; and he placed at the east of the garden of Eden Cherubim's, and a flaming sword which turned every way, to keep the way of the tree of life.(Genesis 4:2) A n d she again bare his brother Abel. And Abel was a keeper of sheep, but Cain was a tiller of the ground. (Genesis 4:9) And the LORD said unto Cain, Where is Abel thy brother? And he said, I know not: Am I my brother's keeper? (Genesis 6:19) And of every living thing of all flesh, two of every sort shalt thou bring into the ark, to keep them alive with thee; they shall be male and female. (Genesis 6:20) Of fowls after their kind, and of cattle after their kind, of every creeping thing of the earth after his kind, two of every sort shall come unto thee, to keep them alive. (Genesis 7:3) Of fowls also of the air by sevens, the male and the female; to *keep* seed alive upon the face of all the earth. (Genesis 17:9) And God said unto Abraham, Thou shalt *keep* my covenant therefore, thou, and thy seed after thee in their generations. (Genesis 17:10) This is my covenant, which ye shall keep, between me and you and thy seed after thee; Every man child among you shall be circumcised. (Genesis 18:19) For I know him, that he will command his children and his household after him, and they shall *keep* the way of the LORD, to do justice and judgment; that the LORD may bring upon Abraham that which he hath spoken of him. (Genesis 28:15) And, behold, I am with thee, and will *keep* thee in all places whither thou goest, and will bring thee again into this land; for I will not leave thee, until I have done that which I have spoken to thee of. (Genesis 28:20) And Jacob vowed a vow, saying, If God will be with me, and will keep me in this way that I go, and will give me bread to eat, and raiment to put on, (Genesis 30:31) nd he said, What shall I give thee? And Jacob said, Thou shalt not give me any thing: if thou wilt do this thing for me, I will again feed and keep thy flock: (Genesis 33:9)And Esau said, I have enough, my brother; keep that thou hast unto thyself. As Christians we are bound to keep the faith, practice it, retain it, maintain it through, love, prayer, thanksgiving, Praise and worship, show charity, practice righteousness by staying away from sin, reference and acknowledge the love of God and know that He indeed loves us in Jesus Name!

Kenan: Son of Enosh the grandson of Adam. Kenan was the great grandson of Adam. Kenan died when he was 905 years.

King: (A monarch) the sovereign head of state, officially outranking all other individuals in the realm. The word "king" is in Scripture very generally used to denote one invested with authority, whether extensive or limited. In the New Testament, the Roman emperor is spoken of as a king (1Peter 2:13, 17), and Herod Antipas, who was only a tetrarch, is also called a king (Mathew. 14:9; Mark 6:22). Pharaoh, tetrarch There were thirty-one kings in Canaan (Joshua 12:9, 24), whom Joshua subdued. Adonibezek subdued seventy kings (Judges. 1:7).

2 A monarch may exercise the most and highest authority in the state or others may wield that power on behalf of the monarch. Typically a monarch either personally inherits the lawful right to exercise the state's sovereign rights (often referred to as the throne or the crown) or is selected by an established process from a family or cohort eligible to provide the nation's monarch. Alternatively, an individual may become monarch by conquest, acclamation or a combination of means. A monarch usually reigns for life or until abdication. Monarchs' actual powers vary from one monarchy to another and in different eras; on one extreme, they may be autocrats (absolute monarchy) wielding genuine sovereignty; on the other they may be ceremonial heads of state who exercise little or no power or only reserve powers, with actual authority vested in a parliament or other body (constitutional monarchy).

Jehovah was the sole King of the Jewish nation (1 Samuel. 8:7; Isaiah. 33:22). But there came a time in the history of that people when a king was demanded, that they might be like other nations (1 Samuel 8:5). The prophet Samuel remonstrated with them, but the people cried out, "Nay, but we will have a king over us." The misconduct of Samuel's sons was the immediate cause of this demand. The Hebrew kings did not rule in their own right, nor in name of the people who had chosen them, but partly as servants and partly as representatives of Jehovah, the true King of Israel (1 Samuel. 10:1).

Kings in Israel before its division: Saul, David, Solomon

Kings in Israel after division: Jeroboam, Nadab, Baasha, Elah, Zimri, Tibni, Omri, Ahab, Ahaziah, Jehoram, Jehu, Jehoahaz, Jehoash, Jeroboam, Zechariah, Shallum, Menahem, Pekahiah, Pekah, Hoshea,

Kings in Judah: Rehoboam, Abijah, Asa, Jehoshaphat, Jehoram, Ahaziah, Athaliah, Joash, Amaziah, Uzziah, Jotham, Ahaz,

Hezekiah, Manasseh, Amon, Josiah, Jehoahaz, Jehoiakim, Jehoiachin, Zedekiah

Kings in the Bible – alphabetical: Abijam, Abimelech, Achbor, Achish, Adoni-zedec, Adonizedek, Agag, Agrippa , Ahab, hasuerus, Ahaz, Ahaziah, Alexander the Great, Amaziah, Amon, Amraphel, Aretas, Arioch, Artaxerxes, Asa, Asnapper, Baal-hanan, Baalis, Baasha, Bela, Belshazzar, Ben-hadad, Berodach-baladan, Birsha, Chedorlaomer, Chushan-rishathaim, Cyrus, Debir, Eglon, Elah, Eliakim, Ethbaal, Evil-merodach, David, Hadad, Hadadezer, Hanun, Herod Agrippa I, Herod the Great, Hezekiah, Hiram, Hoham, Hoshea, Hur, Jabin, Japhia, Jechoniah (Jechonias), Jehoash, Jehoiachin, Jehoiakim, Jehoram, Jehoshaphat, Jehu, Jeroboam, Joash, Jobab, Josiah, Lemuel, Melchizedek, Menahem, Mesha, Nadab, Nahash, Nebuchadnezzar, Necho II, Nimrod, Og, Omri, Oshea, Osnapper, Piram, Pul, Rehoboam, Rezin, Rezon, Sargon, Saul, Sennacherib, Shallum, Shalman, Shemeber, Shinab, Shishak I, So, Solomon, Talmai, Tiglath-Pileser III, Tirhakah, Toi, Uzziah, Xerxes, Zachariah, Zedekiah, Zerahe prescribed (1 Samuel 10:25).

King of Kings: The Deity. 2 The blessed and only Potentate. The King of Kings and Lord of Lord. (1 Timothy 6:15) The One and the only True God.

Kingdom: A form of government in which sovereignty is actually or nominally embodied in a single individual (the monarch). Forms of monarchy differ widely based on the level of legal autonomy the monarch holds in governance, the method of selection of the monarch, and any predetermined limits on the length of their tenure. When the monarch has no or few legal restraints in state and political matters, it is called an absolute monarchy and is a form of autocracy. Cases in which the monarch's discretion is formally limited (most common today) are called constitutional monarchies. In hereditary monarchies, the office is passed through inheritance within a family group, whereas elective monarchies use some system of voting. Each of these has variations: in some elected monarchies only those of certain pedigrees are eligible, whereas many hereditary monarchies impose requirements regarding the religion, age, gender, mental capacity, and other factors. Occasionally this might create a situation of rival claimants whose legitimacy is subject to effective election. Finally, there have been cases where the term of a monarch's reign is either fixed in years or continues until certain goals are achieved: an invasion being repulsed, for instance. Thus there are widely divergent structures and traditions defining monarchy.

2 Richard I of England being anointed during his coronation

in Westminster Abbey, from a 13th-century chronicle. Monarchy was the most common form of government until the 19th century, but it is no longer prevalent. Where it exists, it is now usually a constitutional monarchy, in which the monarch retains a unique legal and ceremonial role, but exercises limited or no political power: under the written or unwritten constitution, others have governing authority. Currently, 44 sovereign nations in the world have monarchs acting as heads of state, 16 of which are Commonwealth realms that recognise Queen Elizabeth II as their head of state. All European monarchies are constitutional ones, with the exception of the Vatican City, but sovereigns in the smaller states exercise greater political influence than in the larger. The monarchs of Cambodia, Japan, and Malaysia "reign, but do not rule" although there is considerable variation in the degree of authority they wield. Although they reign under constitutions, the monarchs of Brunei, Oman, Qatar, Saudi Arabia and Swaziland appear to continue to exercise more political influence than any other single source of authority in their nations, either by constitutional mandate or by tradition.

3 In the gospel, the following Kingdoms were in place according to the bible; Assyria, kingdom of Babylon, Egypt, kingdom of Israel, kingdom of Judah, Persia, Rome, Chaldea, Media.

Kingdom of God: The kingship of God appears in all Abrahamic religions, where in some cases the terms Kingdom of God and Kingdom of Heaven are also used. The notion of God's kingship goes back to the Hebrew Bible, which refers to "his kingdom" but does not include the term "Kingdom of God". The "Kingdom of God" (Greek - Basileia tou Theou) and its equivalent form "Kingdom of Heaven" (, Basileia tōn Ouranōn) in the Gospel of Matthew is one of the key elements of the teachings of Jesus in the New Testament. Drawing on Old Testament teachings, the Christian characterization of the relationship between God and humanity inherently involves the notion of the "Kingship of God".

References (Exodus 15:18) "The LORD shall reign forever and ever." (1 Samuel 12:12) "When you saw that Nahash the king of the sons of Ammon came against you, you said to me, 'No, but a king shall reign over us,' although the LORD your God was your king. (1 Chronicles 16:31) "Let the heavens be glad, and let the earth rejoice; And let them say among the nations, "The LORD reigns."

Know: (Hebrew – *yada*, Greek – *Oida, ginosko*, , knew) (Genesis 4) "And Adam knew Eve his wife; and she conceived." Meaning Adam made love to his wife Eve. In other words this signifies having practical affection and cherishing someone. In terms of Adam the word "know" is used as a euphemism

Know

for sex and intercourse: Adam knew his wife Eve and she became pregnant (Genesis 4:1). Women who have "known" a man are no longer virgins (Numbers 31:17 Numbers 31:35). In his declining days David had an attractive attendant who served him but did not have sexual relationships with him (1 Kings 1:4). Even sexual perversions such as sodomy (Genesis 19:5 ; Judges 19:22) and rape (Judges 19:25)are designated by the word "know."

2 Literally, know is to be aware of through observation, inquiry, or information. synonyms: be aware, realize, be conscious, have knowledge, be informed, have information; More have knowledge or information concerning. "I would write to him if I knew his address" synonyms: have knowledge of, be aware of, be cognizant of, be informed of, be apprised of "I would write to him if I knew his address" be absolutely certain or sure about something. "I just knew it was something I wanted to do" 2 have developed a relationship with (someone) through meeting and spending time with them; be familiar or friendly with. "he knew and respected Laura" synonyms: be acquainted with, have met, be familiar with;

3 The word "know" is used also to express acquaintance with a person. Jacob questioned the shepherds of Haran, "Do you know Laban?" (Genesis 29:5). The pual-participle of the Hebrew word indicates a close friend (Job 19:14 ; Psalm 55:13), a neighbour (Psalm 31:11), a companion (Psalms 88:8 Psalms 88:18),and a relative (Ruth 2:1) Divine-human relationships are also expressed by this term. The Lord knew Moses very well— "by name" (Exodus 33:11 Exodus 33:12 Exodus 33:17) Moses sought a reciprocal acquaintance with God (Exodus 33:13). The psalmist is amazed at God's intimate knowledge (Psalm 139:6) of his personal life, his daily activities (Psalm 139:1-2), even his unuttered and unformed thoughts (Psalm 139:4 The fact that God knows often indicates divine choice. He knew Jeremiah before his birth, singling him out to be a prophet (Jeremiah 1:5). He chose Abraham to be the father of a great nation (Genesis 18:19). The statement of (Amos 3:2), "You (Israel) only have I chosen of all the families of the earth, " indicates divine selection. It is the way of the righteous that the Lord knows, endorses, and cherishes (Psalm 1:6).

4 "Know" also is used as a treaty term. To know is to acknowledge. Thus when the new king of Egypt did not *know* Joseph (Exodus 1:8) he did not recognize the agreement that had been developed between Joseph and Pharaoh at the time his family came to Egypt. While the ox and donkey know their owner, Israel does not know (Isaiah 1:3). More than instinct is intended here. Loyalty to the covenant is clearly in mind since the witnesses of that covenant are

Knowledge

invoked (Isaiah 1:2) Moses demands that those who had stood at Mount Sinai and entered into covenant with the Lord acknowledge that agreement and live by it (Deuteronomy 11:1-25).

5 In the New Testament. The above Greek and Hebrew words have the various nuances of meaning of the English word "know." They have been influenced by the Hebrew word yada such influence having been mediated through the Septuagint, but they also reflect an adaptation demanded by a pagan world ignorant of God's existence. The New Testament emphasizes that knowing God is not simply an intellectual apprehension, but a response of faith and an acceptance of Christ. It is he who has made God known (John 1:18).To know Christ is to know God (John 14:7). Eternal life is to know the true God and Jesus Christ (John 17:3). Paul desires to know Christ in his death and resurrection (Philippians 3:10). Failure to know Jesus as Lord and Messiah (Acts 2:36) resultedin his rejection and crucifixion (1 Corinthians 2:8). To know Christ is to know truth (John 8:32). While this is personal, it is also propositional. Knowledge of the truth (1 Timothy 2:4 ; 2Tim 2:25 ; 3:7 ; Titus 1:1) is both enlightenment and acceptance of the cognitive aspects of faith.

6 Paul uses the rhetorical question, "Don't you know?" several times in 1Corinthians (3:16 ; 5:6 ; 1 Corinthians 6:2 1 Corinthians 6:3 1 Corinthians 6:9 1 Corinthians 6:15 ; 1 Corinthians 9:13 1 Corinthians 9:24). This may be an appeal to common knowledge, or a reference to a corpus of teaching that the apostle had communicated. Affirmations about God's knowledge are more limited in the New Testament than in the Old Testament. He knows the human heart (Luke 16:15). He knows his children's needs such as clothing and food (Matthew 6:32). He even anticipates our petitions (Matthew 6:8). In fact, he knows everything (1John 3:20).

7 Jesus uniquely knows God (John 8:55 —here knowledge and obedience are equated). He knows the hidden designs of his questioners (Luke 11:17) He is also perceptive of humankind. Nowhere is his penetrating knowledge noted more than it is in the Fourth Gospel (Luke 2:25; 5:42; 6:64; 10:14 John 14 ; John 13:1 John 13:11 ; 18:4 ; 19:28).

Knowledge: Literally, knowledge is familiarity, awareness or understanding of someone or something, such as facts, information, descriptions, or skills, which is acquired through experience or education by perceiving, discovering, or learning. Knowledge can refer to a theoretical or practical understanding of a subject. It can be implicit (as with practical skill or expertise) or explicit (as with the theoretical understanding of a subject); it can be more or less formal or systematic. In philosophy,

Knowledge

the study of knowledge is called epistemology; the philosopher Plato famously defined knowledge as "justified true belief", though "well-justified true belief" is more complete as it accounts for the Get tier problems. However, several definitions of knowledge and theories to explain it exist.

2 Knowing or knowledge, " appears almost 950 times in the Hebrew Bible. It has a wider sweep than our English word "know," including perceiving, learning, understanding, willing, performing, and experiencing. To know is not to be intellectually informed about some abstract principle, but to apprehend and experience reality. Knowledge is not the possession of information, but rather its exercise or actualization.

3 Thus, biblically to know God is not to know about him in an abstract and impersonal manner, but rather to enter into his saving actions (Micah 6:5). To know God is not to struggle philosophically with his eternal essence, but rather to recognize and accept his claims. It is not some mystical contemplation, but dutiful obedience. The limits of human knowledge are recognized in the New Testament. It is not through wisdom that the world knows God, but rather through the divine initiative (Galatians 4:8-9). It is through the kerygma that humans can know God (1 Corinthians 1:20-25) Spiritual discernment is not the result of profane reasoning (1 Timothy 6:20). God's revelation in Christ has made *knowledge* of him possible. But at best, this *knowledge* is partial. Perfection in the area of knowledge is reserved for the age to come (1 Corinthians 13:12).

4 References (Proverbs 18:15) An intelligent heart acquires *knowledge*, and the ear of the wise seeks knowledge. (Proverbs 2:10) For wisdom will come into your heart, and knowledge will be pleasant to your soul; (Proverbs 1:7) The fear of the Lord is the beginning of *knowledge*; fools despise wisdom and instruction. (Hosea 4:6-7) My people are destroyed for lack of *knowledge*; because you have rejected knowledge, I reject you from being a priest to me. And since you have forgotten the law of your God, I also will forget your children. The more they increased, the more they sinned against me; I will change their glory into shame. (Proverbs 8:10) Take my instruction instead of silver, and *knowledge* rather than choice gold, (Proverbs 24:5) A wise man is full of strength, and a man of *knowledge* enhances his might,

Ll

Labour: (Hebrew – *Avoda Ivrit*) this could be used as noun or verb. As in (Psalm 128:2) "You will eat the fruit of your labour; blessings and prosperity will be yours". Labour is a complementary part of our faith in Christ Jesus. For the work of faith to be completed, we must labour as co-workers with Christ. That is to say, we must do good works to be blessed with eternal life, and all who have eternal life do such works. Our Saviour expects us to become co-workers with Him in our salvation, as well as the salvation of all mankind. Paul writes, "For we are His workmanship, created in Christ Jesus for good works, which God prepared beforehand that we should walk in them" (Ephesians 2:10). Note as important that faith without works is dead. This makes labour the life wire of faith. When we say the work of Faith, this implies the labour of our faith in Him. Because without labour there is no faith as faith is a spiritual tool used by Christly labourers – Christians to accomplish the will of the father. Praise the Lord!

Again, we also know that faith does not replace our doing good works. Works do not save us, but are required nevertheless as evidence of our faith. The issue is not "works or faith" but "works and faith," since "faith without works is dead" (James 2:20, 26). If "faith without works" is useless, then surely "faith with works" must have a use!

As noun labour means work, especially physical work. "the price of repairs includes labour, parts, and VAT" synonyms: work, toil, employment, exertion, industry, industriousness, toiling, hard work, hard labour, drudgery, effort, the sweat of one's brow, donkey work, menial work; as opposed to antonyms such as rest, leisure, ease, idleness. – Sometimes bringing nothing. Like the Futility of Pleasures in (Ecclesiastes 2:10-11) "...All that my eyes desired I did not refuse them. I did not withhold my heart from any pleasure, for my heart was pleased because of all my labour and this was my reward for all my labour. Thus I considered all my activities which my hands had done and the labour which I had exerted, and behold all was vanity and striving after wind and there was no profit under the sun"

The whole earth came to being by the working command of God through the power of Holy Spirit Let there be light and there was light. So where work and faith matches together the Law of God set in as in the Ten Commandment.

Labour in Christ Context: We can be tempted, however, to believe that works ended and faith began with Christ's sacrificial death and resurrection. Some may think that, with the beginning of the New Testament era, Christ in us, through the Holy Spirit, keeps the law in our stead. They believe that it is self-righteous to try to keep the Ten Commandments to ensure salvation. They feel that working to keep God's law takes credit away from Him for our salvation and that these works are just so many "filthy rags" in His sight. Are we guilty of not submitting to God's righteousness, His spirit and faith, if we try to keep His law? A good way to gain a better perspective of "works and faith," as well as "law and grace," is to understand God's definition of righteousness. He reckons some people as righteous and others He does not. He has never changed His standard of righteousness, which "endures forever" (Psalm 111:3). God imputes righteousness to those who believe Him—who do what He commands, who yearn to keep all His commandments, who have faith. Also, Paul records that the carnal Israelites established their own righteousness (Romans 10:3), because they decided what laws they would keep and how, instead of following God's definition of righteousness. They thought this kind of righteousness—really self-righteousness—would force God to give them salvation. These works, though, are vain, self-serving and faithless. The kind of works in (Ecclesiastes 2:10-11)

The Bible leaves us little room for negotiation about what God expects of us during our walk with Him. In (Matthew 19:16-17), a man asks Jesus, "'Good Teacher, what good thing shall I do that I may have eternal life?' So He said to him, '. . . If you want to enter into life, keep the commandments." Jesus tells him he must do something, not just believe, to gain salvation. By this, He also tells us what works He expects of us, if we would live forever with God. The church of God has taught that God's grace does not abolish His law. The issue is not "law or grace" but "law and grace," for the grace of God does not grant us license to transgress His law. God's spiritual law coexists with His grace. Even that He blesses us with His law is an act of His grace! David prayed, "Grant me your law graciously" (Psalm 119:29).

Labour as works of His Hands: We are the works of His hands and the same Father who calls us to work in His name also

Labour of Love

provides the necessary resources. As Paul said, the Lord makes grace abound to His children so that they have abundance for every good deed (2 Corinthians 9:8). Moreover, we are equipped by His Word and strengthened and guided by His Holy Spirit (2 Timothy 3:16–17). From these sources, Christians learn lessons about relating to others so they can help, encourage, and give to them. Let's be clear that works have nothing to do with salvation. We are saved by grace alone through Jesus Christ's sacrifice on the cross. After that happens, a believer is motivated to do well in the Lord's name in order to please Him.

Literally, Labour is to do with labourers. Comprises workers, especially manual workers, considered collectively. "non-union casual *labour*" synonyms: workers, employees, workmen, workforce, staff, working people, blue-collar workers, hands, labourers, labour force, hired hands, proletariat, wage-earners, manpower, human resources, personnel; humorous live ware "the conflict of interest between capital and labour" workers considered as a social class or political force. "the labour movement" a government department concerned with a nation's workforce. modifier noun: Labour; modifier noun: Labour "the Labour Secretary" 2 the Labour Party. "the Labour leader" 3 the process of childbirth from the start of uterine contractions to delivery. "a woman in labour" synonyms: childbirth, birth, birthing, delivery, nativity; More verb: labour; 3rd person present: labours; past tense: laboured; past participle: laboured; gerund or present participle: labouring; verb: labour; 3rd person present: labors; past tense: laboured; past participle: laboured; gerund or present participle: labouring, work hard; make great effort. "they laboured from dawn to dusk" synonyms: work (hard), toil, slave (away), grub away, plod away, grind away, sweat away, struggle, strive, exert oneself, overwork, work one's fingers to the bone, work like a Trojan, dog or slave, keep one's nose to the grindstone; sometimes is vanity as in (Ecclesiastes 2: 10 – 11) above. But when God is at the work you do, faith must come in and you will please the father not flesh, not eye service, something must happen, mountains will move, the sick will be heal, miracle signs and wonders will take place in an unimaginable way. Praise the Lord!

Labour of Love: Work undertaken for the pleasure of it or for the benefit of a loved one. We are called to act out our faith every day. God works through us to reach those who may never otherwise open the Bible or enter a church. What's more, He borrows our voice to tell His story and uses our life to demonstrate His grace and glory. Good deeds are a believer's labour of love. In the gospel, this phrase originated from the Bible and appears in Thessalonians

Lamb

and Hebrews. See (Thessalonica 1:2 and 1:3) thus "We give thanks to God always for you all, making mention of you in our prayers; Remembering without ceasing your work of faith, and *labour of love*, and patience of hope in our Lord Jesus Christ, in the sight of God and our Father"; Then (Hebrews 6:10) added "For God is not unrighteous to forget your work and *labour of love*, which ye have shewed toward his name, in that ye have ministered to the saints, and do minister". Note: Shakespeare didn't use the expression 'labour of love' in any of his works but it is possible that the writers of the KJV were familiar with his play Love's Labour's Lost, 1588, and that they adapted the expression from that title.

Lamb: (Hebrew – *Seh or Zeh*) A young sheep, Lamb and mutton, the meat of domestic sheep. In the Orthodox Church, a cube of bread offered at the Divine Liturgy, Lamb of God, and a metaphorical reference to Jesus Christ. Meant to be slaughtered for food, meat, Bread of Life . Humbling (Lamb is humbled) for the purpose of Love to underserved persons - sinners. As in (John 6:35) "Then Jesus declared, "I am the bread of life. Whoever comes to me will never go hungry, and whoever believes in me will never be thirsty". Fancy the conversation with the woman of Samaria (John 6:35). Here they have asked for "this bread," the bread which giveth life, as distinct from that which perisheth. It is now present with them. He is that bread, whose characteristic is life. He is the Word of God, revealing God to man, teaching the eternal truths which are the life of the spirit just as bread is of the body. Praise God!

Lamb of God: Hebrew – Shaddai, Latin - Agnus Dei" meaning A lamb holding a Christian banner is a typical symbol for Lamb of God. (Greek: amnos tou theou;) as in Abraham answer to His son Isaac in (Genesis 22: 8) "Abraham said, "God will provide for himself the lamb for a burnt offering, my son." Lamb of God (Latin: Agnus Dei) is one of the titles given to Jesus in the New Testament and consequently in the Christian tradition. It refers to Jesus' role as a sacrificial lamb atoning for the sins of man in Christian theology, harkening back to ancient Jewish Temple sacrifices in which a lamb was slain during the Passover (the "Paschal Lamb", Hebrew: Korban Pesach), the blood was sprinkled on the altar, and the whole of the lamb was eaten. In the original Passover in Egypt, the blood was smeared on the door posts and lintel of each household (Exodus 12:1-28). So they went both of them together". This is a title for Jesus that appears in the Gospel of John. It appears at (John 1:29), where John the Baptist sees Jesus and exclaims, "Behold the Lamb of God who takes away the sin of the world."

2 Although "Lamb of God " refers in Christian teachings to Jesus

Christ in his role of the perfect sacrificial offering, Christological arguments dissociate the term from the Old Testament concept of a "scapegoat," which is a person or animal subject to punishment for the sins of others without knowing it or willing it. Christian doctrine holds that Jesus chose to suffer at Calvary as a sign of his full obedience to the will of his Father, as an "agent and servant of God". The Lamb of God is thus related to the Paschal Lamb of Passover, which is viewed as foundational and integral to the message of Christianity.

3 When Jesus is called the *Lamb of God* in (John 1:29) and (John 1:36), it is referring to Him as the perfect and ultimate sacrifice for sin. In order to understand who Christ was and what He did, we must begin with the Old Testament, which contains prophecies concerning the coming of Christ as a "guilt offering" (Isaiah 53:10). In fact, the whole sacrificial system established by God in the Old Testament set the stage for the coming of Jesus Christ, who is the perfect sacrifice God would provide as atonement for the sins of His people (Romans 8:3; Hebrews 10). The sacrifice of lambs played a very important role in the Jewish religious life and sacrificial system. When John the Baptist referred to Jesus as the *"Lamb of God* who takes away the sin of the world" (John 1:29), the Jews who heard him might have immediately thought of any one of several important sacrifices. With the time of the Passover feast being very near, the first thought might be the sacrifice of the Passover lamb. The Passover feast was one of the main Jewish holidays and a celebration in remembrance of God's deliverance of the Israelites from bondage in Egypt. In fact, the slaying of the Passover lamb and the applying of the blood to doorposts of the houses (Exodus 12:11-13) is a beautiful picture of Christ's atoning work on the cross. Those for whom He died are covered by His blood, protecting us from the angel of (spiritual) death.

4 Another important sacrifice involving lambs was the daily sacrifice at the temple in Jerusalem. Every morning and evening, a lamb was sacrificed in the temple for the sins of the people (Exodus 29:38-42). These daily sacrifices, like all others, were simply to point people towards the perfect sacrifice of Christ on the cross. In fact, the time of Jesus' death on the cross corresponds to the time the evening sacrifice was being made in the temple. The Jews at that time would have also been familiar with the Old Testament prophets Jeremiah and Isaiah, who foretold the coming of One who would be brought "like a lamb led to the slaughter" (Jeremiah 11:19; Isaiah 53:7) and whose sufferings and sacrifice would provide redemption for Israel. Of course, that person was none other than Jesus Christ, "the Lamb of God."

Lamb of God

5 While the idea of a sacrificial system might seem strange to us today, the concept of payment or restitution is still one we can easily understand. We know that the wages of sin is death (Romans 6:23) and that our sin separates us from God. We also know the Bible teaches we are all sinners and none of us is righteous before God (Romans 3:23). Because of our sin, we are separated from God, and we stand guilty before Him. Therefore, the only hope we can have is if He provides a way for us to be reconciled to Himself, and that is what He did in sending His Son Jesus Christ to die on the cross. Christ died to make atonement for sin and to pay the penalty of the sins of all who believe in Him.

6 It is through His death on the cross as God's perfect sacrifice for sin and His resurrection three days later that we can now have eternal life if we believe in Him. The fact that God Himself has provided the offering that atones for our sin is part of the glorious good news of the gospel that is so clearly declared in (1 Peter 1:18-21): "For you know that it was not with perishable things such as silver or gold that you were redeemed from the empty way of life handed down to you from your forefathers, but with the precious blood of Christ, a lamb without blemish or defect. He was chosen before the creation of the world, but was revealed in these last times for your sake. Through him you believe in God, who raised him from the dead and glorified him, and so your faith and hope are in God."

7 A lion-like lamb that rises to deliver victory after being slain appears several times in the Book of Revelation. It is also referred to in Pauline writings in (1Corinthians 5:7) which suggests that, 'Saint Paul intends to refer to the death of Jesus, who is the Paschal Lamb. The *Lamb of God* title is widely used in Christian prayers, and the Agnus Dei is used as a standard part of the Catholic Mass, as well as the classical Western Liturgies of the Anglican and Lutheran Churches. It also is used in liturgy and as a form of contemplative prayer. The Agnus Dei also forms a part of the musical setting for the Mass. As a visual motif, the lamb has been most often represented since the Middle Ages as a standing haloed lamb with a foreleg cocked "holding" a pennant with a red cross on a white ground, though many other ways of representing it have been used.

Law: A system of rules which are enforced through social institutions to govern behaviour. Laws can be made by legislatures through legislation (resulting in statutes), the executive through decrees and regulations, or judges through binding precedents (normally in common law jurisdictions). Private individuals can create legally binding contracts, including (in some jurisdictions) arbitration agreements that may elect to accept alternative arbitration to the normal court process. The formation of laws themselves may be influenced by a constitution (written or unwritten) and the rights encoded therein. The law shapes politics, economics, and society in various ways and serves as a mediator of relations between people.

2 A general distinction can be made between (a) civil law jurisdictions (including canon and socialist law), in which the legislature or other central body codifies and consolidates their laws, and (b) common law systems, where judge-made binding precedents are accepted.

3 Historically, religious laws played a significant role even in settling of secular matters, which is still the case in some religious communities, particularly Jewish, and some countries, particularly Islamic. Islamic Sharia law is the world's most widely used religious law. The adjudication of the law is generally divided into two main areas referred to as (i) Criminal law and (ii) Civil law. Criminal law deals with conduct that is considered harmful to social order and in which the guilty party may be imprisoned or fined. Civil law (not to be confused with civil law jurisdictions above) deals with the resolution of lawsuits (disputes) between individuals or organisations. These resolutions seek to provide a legal remedy (often monetary damages) to the winning litigant. Under civil law, the following specialties, among others, exist: Contract law regulates everything from buying a bus ticket to trading on derivatives markets. Property law regulates the transfer and title of personal property and real property. Trust law applies to assets held for investment and financial security. Tort law allows claims for compensation if a person's property is harmed. Constitutional law provides a framework for the creation of law, the protection of human rights and the election of political representatives. Administrative law is used to review the decisions of government agencies. International law governs affairs between sovereign states in activities ranging from trade to military action. To implement and enforce the law and provide services to the public by public servants, a government's bureaucracy, military, and police are vital. While all these organs of the state are creatures created and bound by law, an independent legal profession and a vibrant civil society inform and support their progress.

4 Law provides a rich source of scholarly inquiry into legal history, philosophy, economic analysis and sociology. Law also raises important and complex issues concerning equality, fairness, and justice. There is an old saying that 'all are equal before the law'. The author Anatole France said in 1894, "In its majestic equality, the law forbids rich and poor alike to sleep under bridges, beg in the streets, and steal loaves of bread." Writing in 350 BC, the Greek philosopher Aristotle declared, "The rule of law is better than the rule of any individ-

ual." Mikhail Bakunin said: "All law has for its object to confirm and exalt into a system the exploitation of the workers by a ruling class". Cicero said "more law, less justice". Marxist doctrine asserts that law will not be required once the state has withered away. The church of God has taught that God's grace does not abolish His law. The issue is not "law or grace" but "law and grace," for the grace of God does not grant us license to transgress His law. God's spiritual law coexists with His grace. Even that He blesses us with His law is an act of His grace! David prayed, "Grant me your law graciously" (Psalm 119:29). See the ten commandment because every Laws practice on earth derived its natural authority there from. *References* (Luke 16:17) But it is easier for heaven and earth to pass away than for one dot of the Law to become void. (Romans 7:12) So the law is holy, and the commandment is holy and righteous and good. (1Timothy 1:8-10) Now we know that the law is good, if one uses it lawfully, understanding this, that the law is not laid down for the just but for the lawless and disobedient, for the ungodly and sinners, for the unholy and profane, for those who strike their fathers and mothers, for murderers, the sexually immoral, men who practice homosexuality, enslavers, liars, perjurers, and whatever else is contrary to sound doctrine, (Romans 7:7) What then shall we say? That the law is sin? By no means! Yet if it had not been for the law, I would not have known sin. For I would not have known what it is to covet if the law had not said, "You shall not covet." (1 John 3:4) Everyone who makes a practice of sinning also practices lawlessness; sin is lawlessness. (Romans 13:1) Let every person be subject to the governing authorities. For there is no authority except from God, and those that exist have been instituted by God. (John 1:17) For the law was given through Moses; grace and truth came through Jesus Christ.

Laws, God: Otherwise known as divine Laws - Any law that comes directly from the will of God, in contrast to man-made law. Like natural law (which may be seen as a manifestation of divine law) it is independent of the will of man, who cannot change it. However it may be revealed or not, so it may change in human perception in time through new revelation. Divine law is commonly equated with eternal law, meaning that if God is infinite, then his law must also be infinite and eternal. In Thomas Aquinas's Treatise on Law, divine law, as opposed to natural law, comes only from revelation or scripture, hence biblical law, and is necessary for human salvation. According to Aquinas, divine law must not be confused with natural law. Divine law is mainly and mostly natural law, but it can also be positive law.

The law of God contains ten commandments. It's in the Bible, (Exodus 20:1-17, NKJV). "And God spoke all these words, saying: "I am the LORD your God, who

Laws, God

brought you out of the land of Egypt, out of the house of bondage.

(1) "You shall have no other gods before Me.

(2) "You shall not make for yourself a carved image—any likeness of anything that is in heaven above, or that is in the earth beneath, or that is in the water under the earth; you shall not bow down to them nor serve them. For I, the LORD your God, am a jealous God, visiting the iniquity of the fathers upon the children to the third and fourth generations of those who hate Me, but showing mercy to thousands, to those who love Me and keep My commandments.

(3) "You shall not take the name of the LORD your God in vain, for the LORD will not hold him guiltless who takes His name in vain.

(4) " Remember the Sabbath day, to keep it holy. Six days you shall labor and do all your work, but the seventh day is the Sabbath of the LORD your God. In it you shall do no work: you, nor your son, nor your daughter, nor your male servant, nor your female servant, nor your cattle, nor your stranger who is within your gates. For in six days the LORD made the heavens and the earth, the sea, and all that is in them, and rested the seventh day. Therefore the LORD blessed the Sabbath day and hallowed it.

(5) "Honour your father and your mother, that your days may be long upon the land which the LORD your God is giving you.

(6) "You shall not murder.

(7) "You shall not commit adultery.

(8) "You shall not steal.

(9) "You shall not bear false witness against your neighbour.

(10) "You shall not covet your neighbour's house; you shall not covet your neighbour's wife, nor his male servant, nor his female servant, nor his ox, nor his donkey, nor anything that is your neighbour's."

God's law gives direction, wisdom, and joy to our lives. It's in the Bible, *References*: (Psalm 119:9-10, NKJV). "How can a young man cleanse his way? by taking heed according to Your word. With my whole heart I have sought You; Oh, let me not wander from Your commandments!" "Teach me, O LORD, the way of Your statutes, and I shall keep it to the end. Give me understanding, and I shall keep Your law; indeed, I shall observe it with my whole heart. Make me walk in the path of Your commandments, for I delight in it" Again (Psalm 119:33-35, NKJV). "Oh, how I love Your law! It is my meditation all the day. You, through Your commandments, make me wiser than my enemies; for they are ever with me. I have more understanding than all my teachers, for Your testimonies are my meditation. I understand more than the ancients, because I keep Your precepts" (Psalm 119:97-100, NKJV) "Oh, how I love Your law! It is my medi-

Lead

tation all the day. You, through Your commandments, make me wiser than my enemies; for they are ever with me. I have more understanding than all my teachers, for Your testimonies are my meditation. I understand more than the ancients, because I keep Your precepts" (Psalm 119:97-100, NKJV)

Lead: (Hebrew – *nachah*, Greek – *ago*). This scientific word is often used by a shepherd. Remember we are His Sheep. So to *lead* involved Shepherd and Sheep (Psalms 5:8) *Lead* me, O LORD, in thy righteousness because of mine enemies; make thy way straight before my face. This word could be used as verb like to cause (a person or animal) to go with one by holding them by the hand, a halter, a rope, etc. while moving forward, .be a route or means of access to a particular place or in a particular direction. 3 be in charge or command of.

4 have the advantage over competitors in a race or game. 5 have or experience (a particular way of life). As a noun - the initiative in an action; an example for others to follow. 7 a position of advantage in a contest; first place. 8 the chief part in a play or film. 9 a strap or cord for restraining and guiding a dog or other domestic animal. 10 a wire that conveys electric current from a source to an appliance, or that connects two points of a circuit together. 11 the distance advanced by a screw in one turn. 12 an artificial watercourse leading to a mill etc.

Also to instruct and make a way through precept as in (Deuteronomy 6:4-9, KJV) "Hear, O Israel: The LORD our God is one LORD: And thou shalt love the LORD thy God with all thine heart, and with all thy soul, and with all thy might. And these words, which I command thee this day, shall be in thine heart: And thou shalt teach them diligently unto thy children, and shalt talk of them when thou sittest in thine house, and when thou walkest by the way, and when thou liest down, and when thou risest up. And thou shalt bind them for a sign upon thine hand, and they shall be as frontlets between thine eyes. And thou shalt write them upon the posts of thy house, and on thy gates".

(Mathew 6:13) "*Lead* us not into temptation.—The Greek word includes the two thoughts which are represented in English by "trials," i.e., sufferings which test or try, and "temptations," allurements on the side of pleasure which tend to *lead* us into evil. Of these the former is the dominant meaning in the language of the New Testament, and is that of which we must think here. (Matthew 26:41) We are taught not to think of the temptation in which lust meets opportunity as that into which God leads us (James 1:13-14); there is therefore something that shocks us in the thought of asking Him not to *lead* us into it. But trials of another kind, persecution, spiritual conflicts, agony of body or of spirit, these may come to us as a test or as a discipline. Should we shrink from these? An ideal stoicism, a perfected faith, would say, "No, let us accept them, and leave the issue in our Father's hands." But those who are conscious of their weakness cannot shake off the thought that they might fail in the conflict, and the cry of that conscious weakness is therefore, "Lead us not into such trials," even as our Lord prayed, "If it be possible, let this cup pass away from me" (Matthew 26:39). And the answer to the prayer may come either directly in actual exemption from the trial, or in "the way to escape" as in (1Corinthians 10:13), or in strength to bear it. It is hardly possible to read the prayer without thinking of the recent experience of "temptation" through which our Lord had passed. The memory of that trial in all its terrible aspects was still present with Him, and in His tender love for His disciples He bade them pray that they might not be led into anything so awful. As Christians let us always pray the father – the Shepherd to *lead* us to the right part not to *lead* us into temptation but to *lead* us, to enable us be delivered from our enemies, hardship, poverty, sickness, shame, trouble and prepare grounds for us to abide with Him in eternity. Hallelujah!

Least: (Hebrew – *qatan*, Greek – *etachistos*); This word as used in (Mathew 25:40) shows a superlative of little with less or lesser as compared to smallest in size, amount, degree, etc.; slightest: and it demonstrate the divine self-emptying of Christ in the incarnation and its link to the gospel emphasis on the unity between Christ and the poor. The *mira* res consists in this is that Christ is in need here on earth; that the needy Christ asks men and women to help him; that, if they fail to do so, no matter how exemplary their lives otherwise are, they will be judged as barren and will not be counted among the blessed; and that the criterion for judgment will be different from what people thought judgment is, not good morals but concern for the needs of Christ's least ones, that is, for Christ himself. Eternal life is to be found in nourishing, clothing, hospitably receiving, and visiting the Christ who is so rich in goodness and the capacity to set people free that he allows himself to be served in each of his little ones. presenting Augustine's treatment of the humility of God.

2 *Least* refers to lowest in consideration, position, or something we don't attached importance to (noun) 3 something that is least; the least amount, quantity, or the lowest degree things as in the parable of the Sheep and Goat (Mathew 25:40) "The King will reply, 'Truly I tell you, whatever you did for one of the least of these brothers and sisters of mine, you did for me". Think how blessed was Zacchaeus from (Luke 19:1-10) in being able to receive Christ into his home, even to the extent is that, most Christians may sigh with joy wanting to offer similar hospitality to Christ as Zacchaeus. "Can we do like that?" we may ask,

Leviticus

but the candid answer is: "No, because Christ has already ascended into heaven." Christians, Listen to what the judge will say: "When you did it to one of the

least of mine you did it to me." Each of you expects to receive Christ seated in heaven. Turn your attention to him ... in need and a stranger... As your knowledge of Christian life grows, so may your good works increase, so that you may be selected as Sheep in the right signifying eternal life in Christ Jesus, not as goat in the left signifying eternal condemnation. Praise the Living God!.

Leviticus: This is the third book of Moses.

> It is a terrible shame that so-called Bible believing Christians take a beautiful term like "liberty" and completely redefine it in diametrical terms to the Scriptures so they may partake in their pet sins. It is ironic that these same sin seeking Christians will be the first to point out the sins of someone else while justifying their own pet lusts - Smoking and drinking are as incongruous to the Christian walk as fornicating and murder.

Liberty: (Hebrew – *darar*, Greek – *Eleftheria, or Eleutheria*) meaning to flow freely, to fly away, freedom, liberty – as in (Galatians 5:13 KJV) "For, brethren, ye have been called unto *liberty*; only use not liberty for an occasion to the flesh, but by love serve one another". (*Liberty* in the context is a noun) the state of being free within society from oppressive restrictions imposed by authority on one's behaviour or political views. 2 A right or privilege, especially a statutory one. 3 A presumptuous remark or action base on divine facts as in (Isaiah 61:1-11) "The Spirit of the Lord God is upon me, because the Lord has anointed me to bring good news to the poor; he has sent me to bind up the broken-hearted, to proclaim *liberty* to the captives, and the opening of the prison to those who are bound; to proclaim the year of the Lord's favour, and the day of vengeance of our God; to comfort all who mourn; to grant to those who mourn in Zion— to give them a beautiful headdress instead of ashes, the oil of gladness instead of mourning, the garment of praise instead of a faint spirit; that they may be called oaks of righteousness, the planting of the Lord, that he may be glorified. They shall build up the ancient ruins; they shall raise up the former devastations; they shall repair the ruined cities, the devastations of many generations. Strangers shall stand and tend your flocks; foreigners shall be your ploughmen and vinedressers";

After all, if God had granted the *liberty* to engage in sins again, then how come there are still consequences attached to those sins? Can one drink alcohol and not expect liver problems? Can one smoke and not expect oral or lung cancer? Can one gamble and not expect to go broke? Pick your sin and then try to convince yourself there are no aftereffects.

2 (James 1:25 KJV) declared "But whoso looketh into the perfect law of *liberty*, and continueth therein, he being not a forgetful hearer, but a doer of the work, this man shall be blessed in his deed". Here God is telling us that those who are truly saved will continue in the work which God has given to each believer. The idea of intentional effort to look into the law of *liberty* is conveyed. Again (James 2:12 KJV) "So speak ye, and so do, as they that shall be judged by the law of liberty. Here we are being warned to walk properly in our Christian walk or else God will judge our actions and it will bring consequences in our lives". By this, the true believer will never come into judgment for any sins because they were all atoned for by Christ but there is always divine chastisement for our misdeeds in our Christian walk. For example, when we speak of verses which say we have freedom from the law, it does not mean we are independent of the law of God rather it means that we need not fulfil the requirements of the law for salvation because the penalty for sin demanded by God's holy law was satisfied by the vicarious atonement of Christ on behalf of His elect. So far we have looked at nine verses and not one of them hinted that we have the freedom to engage in evil. (Smoking and drinking are evil!) For those Christians who feel this liberty means they can partake of the ways of the world again, here is the verse which applies to them: (Proverbs 26:11 KJV) "As a dog returneth to his vomit, so a fool returneth to his folly". Think, where did we ever get the notion that Christ went to the cross to die for our sins so we could go right back and enjoy sin again. There is no such thing as a "redeemed sinner" in the Gospel sense. Either you are redeemed by the blood of Christ and walking in His statutes or you are still a sinner on your way to hell. You can't have it both ways. Here are the basic freedoms from Liberty the Christian can enjoy; Freedom from the penalty of eternal damnation, Freedom from the fulfilment of the demands of God's holy law for salvation, Freedom not to sin and entangle ourselves in evil again

Freedom from the fear of death, Freedom from not having to face the judgment of God, Freedom from religious rituals, Freedom to be part of the Great Commission without guilt of past sins, Freedom to worship God without traditional or religious overtones and Freedom to approach the throne of grace boldly. Praise the Lord!

Life

Life: (Noun, Greek: zóé [dzo-ay'], Hebrew: Chai -[hay]); life, both of physical (present) and of spiritual (particularly future) existence. (John 6:6) "Jesus said to him, "I am the way, and the truth, and the *life*; no one comes to the Father but through Me". Chronologically to the basic ingredients of this verse is that the way and truth depends on life. Since the way is meant for the living. Without life there is no way and truth. The gospel shows that our purpose in life is to build a friendship with God. Consider some of these fundamental truths as revealed in the gospel. God is our Creator. The Bible says: "It is [God] that has made us, and not we ourselves."—(Psalm 100:3; Revelation 4:11). God has a purpose for everything he creates, including us.—(Isaiah 45:18). God created us with a "spiritual need," which includes the desire to find meaning in life. (Matthew 5:3) He wants us to satisfy that desire.—(Psalm 145:16).We fill our spiritual need by building a friendship with God. Although the idea of being God's friend might seem far-fetched to some, the Bible gives us this encouragement: "Draw close to God, and he will draw close to you."— (James 4:8; 2:23).To become God's friend, we must live in harmony with his purpose for us. The Bible states this purpose at (Ecclesiastes 12:13): "Have reverence for God, and obey his commands, because this is all that we were created for."—Good News Translation. In the future, we can experience in full God's original purpose for us when he eliminates suffering and grants everlasting life to his friends, those who worship him.— (Psalm 37:10, 11).

Life is a characteristic distinguishing physical entities having signalling and self-sustaining processes from those that do not, either because such functions have ceased (death), or because they lack such functions and are classified as inanimate. Biology is a science concerned with the study of life. The smallest contiguous unit of life is called an organism. Organisms are composed of one, or more, cells, undergo metabolism, maintain homeostasis, can grow, respond to stimuli, reproduce and, through evolution, adapt to their environment in successive generations. A diverse array of living organisms can be found in the biosphere of Earth, and the properties common to these organisms—plants, animals, fungi, protists, archaea, and bacteria—are a carbon- and water-based cellular form with complex organization and heritable genetic information.

For instance, the Earth was formed about 4.54 billion years ago. The earliest life on Earth existed at least 3.5 billion years ago. during the Eoarchean Era when sufficient crust had solidified following the molten Hade an Eon.

Though life is confirmed only on the Earth, many thinks that extra-terrestrial life is not only plausible, but probable or inevitable.

Other planets and moons in the Solar System have been examined for evidence of having once supported simple life, and projects such as SETI have attempted to detect radio transmissions from possible alien civilizations. According to the panepermia hypothesis, microscopic life exists throughout the Universe, and is distributed by meteoroids, asteroids and planetoids.

The meaning of life—its significance, origin, purpose, and ultimate fate—is a central concept and question in philosophy and religion and same is transliterated into practical gospel preachings. Both philosophy and religion have offered interpretations as to how life relates to existence and consciousness, and on related issues such as life stance, purpose, conception of a god or gods, a soul or an afterlife. The heart of the revelation has now been given in Jesus' keynote address in (John 5), in which he claims to have the divine prerogatives of life-giver and judge. These two rights will be depicted throughout the rest of the Gospel, beginning immediately with the description of Jesus as the Bread of Life--the one who not only gives life but sustains it. We also see judgment taking place as people are unable to receive this revelation. First the Jews and then most of Jesus' disciples are offended rather than enlightened. By the end of the chapter only the Twelve are left.

Life, Spiritual: As God is spirit and those who worship Him must do so in spirit and in truth. So when you know God, you know the 'what' and the 'why' of spirituality. When you know His ways, you know Him, and when you know Him and practice His precepts, you are living a spiritual life. In one hand *Spiritual life* is abiding in God and bearing more than just a few of the nine spiritual fruits mentioned in (Galatians 5:22-23) "But the fruit of the Spirit is love, joy, peace, long suffering, kindness, goodness, faithfulness, gentleness, self-control. Against such there is no law". This means that living a spiritual life must include more than simply doing spiritual things. It must go beyond self-discipline and spiritual exercises because true spirituality isn't something you "do." Instead, to live a truly spiritual life, you engage the One who created you to be a spiritual being. You have to get to know your Father, and that means knowing His ways.

2 In the other hand, *Spiritual life* embodied the practice by spiritualists – being in obeisance to strange gods and getting involved in heathen practices. Although many people claimed to be spiritual, many of them don't even believe in God, let alone Jesus. Even in the Church, we often experience a good deal of confusion regarding what is truly and deeply spiritual.

Light

References: (1 John 5:5-8) Who is it that overcomes the world except the one who believes that Jesus is the Son of God? This is he who came by water and blood—Jesus Christ; not by the water only but by the water and the blood. And the Spirit is the one who testifies, because the Spirit is the truth. For there are three that testify: the Spirit and the water and the blood; and these three agree. (James 1:22-25) But be doers of the word, and not hearers only, deceiving yourselves. For if anyone is a hearer of the word and not a doer, he is like a man who looks intently at his natural face in a mirror. For he looks at himself and goes away and at once forgets what he was like. But the one who looks into the perfect law, the law of liberty, and perseveres, being no hearer who forgets but a doer who acts, he will be blessed in his doing. (John 4:24) God is spirit, and those who worship him must worship in spirit and truth." (James 1:1-27) James, a servant of God and of the Lord Jesus Christ, to the twelve tribes in the Dispersion: Greetings. Count it all joy, my brothers, when you meet trials of various kinds, for you know that the testing of your faith produces steadfastness. And let steadfastness have its full effect, that you may be perfect and complete, lacking in nothing. If any of you lacks wisdom, let him ask God, who gives generously to all without reproach, and it will be given him. (John 14:20) In that day you will know that I am in my Father, and you in me, and I in you. (John 14:6) Jesus said to him, "I am the way, and the truth, and the life. No one comes to the Father except through me.

Light: (Hebrew – *Or*, Greek – *Phos*) Literally, an electromagnetic radiation part of which stimulates the sense of vision and the gospel meaning addresses a true and direct revelation as attribute of every true Christian. Every truth must be revealed to show the way to sinners "Your Word is a lamp for my feet and a *light* on my path" (Psalm. 119:105) Also, (Mathew 5: 14-15) "You are the light of the world. A city set on a hill cannot be hidden; nor does anyone light a lamp and put it under a basket, but on the lamp stand, and it gives light to all who are in the house. "Let your light shine before men in such a way that they may see your good works, and glorify your Father who is in heaven". Light a metaphor used by Christ to describe the sign of any true Christian first applied to John when He described him as a burning and shining *light*, is applicable also to every true minister of Christ, every such a one is not only a burning light, a person burning with love to God, and zeal for his glory, and love to mankind, and zeal for their salvation; but also a shining light, communicating his light to others, both by instruction and a holy conversation, showing the loss souls the way to salvation. Praise the Lord!

Light, the Divine: An aspect of divine presence, specifically an unknown and mysterious ability of God, angels, or human beings to express themselves communicatively through spiritual means, rather than through physical capacities.

2 The *Divine Light* was in the beginning with God. All things came into being through Him, and apart from Him nothing came into being that has come into being. In Him was life, and the life was the *Light* of men. The Light shines in the darkness, and the darkness did not overpower it. There came a man sent from God, whose name was John. He came as a witness, to testify about the Light, so that all might believe through him. He was not light, but he came to testify about the Light. There was the true Light which, coming into the world, enlightens every man – *the Divine Light* . He was in the world, and the world was made through Him, and the world did not know Him. He came to His own, and those who were His own did not receive Him. But as many as received Him, to them He gave the right to become children of God, even to those who believe in His name, who were born, not of blood nor of the will of the flesh nor of the will of man, but of God. And the Word became flesh, and dwelt among us, and we saw His glory, glory as of the only begotten from the Father, full of grace and truth." Glory to His name!

Light of the World: (Hebrew: *or ha-olam*, Greek - *Phôs tou kósmou*) is a phrase Jesus used to describe himself and his disciples in the New Testament. The phrase is recorded in the Gospel of John and again in the Gospel of Matthew. It is closely related to the parables of Salt and Light and Lamp under a bushel.

Light up: *(Phr)* Shine forth, show your effulgence like in the face of Christ. Never be intimidated by the evil and wickedness that dominate the world today. Rather, light up yourself with God's word. Mathew 5 : 14 Jesus said 'you are the light of the world; meaning that without you, those in your world (your sphere of contact) – will be in darkness. Remember to shine in order to quell the works of darkness through good works; the preaching and doing the gospel even in the midst of prevalent darkness.

Live: (Greek – *Bios*, Hebrew – *chaya*) Literally, to remain alive. 2 make one's home in a particular place or with a particular person. (adjective) not dead or inanimate; living. 2 relating to a musical performance given in concert, not on a recording.3 (of a wire or device) connected to a source of electric current. 4 (To do with a question or subject) of current or continuing interest and importance.

"Everyone who is called by My name, And whom I have creat-

Live by the sword, die by the sword

ed for My glory, Whom I have formed, even whom I have made." (Isaiah 43:7). According to the gospel, our purpose--the reason we are here--is for God's glory. In other words, our purpose is to praise God, worship him, to proclaim his greatness, and to accomplish his will. This is what glorifies him. Therefore, in this we find that God has given us a reason for our existence--a meaning for our existence. We were created by him according to his desire, and our lives are to be lived for him so that we might accomplish what he has for us to do. When we trust the one who has made us--who works all things after the counsel of his will (Ephesians 1:11), then we are able to *live* a life of purpose. How the particulars of that purpose are expressed is up to the individual.

"Live by the sword, die by the sword":

A saying derived from a saying of Jesus, quoted in the Bible, to the effect that if you use violence, or other harsh means, against other people, you can expect to have those same means used against you; "You can expect to become a victim of whatever means you use to get what you want." The saying comes from the Gospel of (Matthew 26:52), which describes a disciple (identified in the Gospel of John as Simon Peter) drawing a sword to defend against the arrest of Jesus in the Garden of Gethsemane, but was rebuked by Jesus, who tells him to sheath the weapon: Then said Jesus unto him, Put up again thy sword into his place: for all they that take the sword shall perish with the sword (Matthew 26:52)

Livelihood: Literally, this refers to the "means of securing the basic necessities - food, water, shelter and clothing- of life". Livelihood is defined as a set of activities, involving securing water, food, fodder, medicine, shelter, clothing and the capacity to acquire above necessities working either individually or as a group by using endowments (both human and material) for meeting the requirements of the self and his or her household on a sustainable basis with dignity. The activities are usually carried out repeatedly. For instance, a fisherman's livelihood depends on the availability and accessibility of fish as in (Deuteronomy 24:6) "Do not take a pair of millstones—not even the upper one—as security for a debt, because that would be taking a person's livelihood as security". The "upper" stone being concave covers the "nether" like a lid; and it has a small aperture, through which the corn is poured, as well as a handle by which it is turned. The propriety of the law was founded on the custom of grinding corn every morning for daily consumption. If either of the stones, therefore, which composed the hand mill was wanting, a person would be deprived of his necessary provision. Again (Zechariah 13:5) "Each will say, 'I am not a prophet. I am a farmer; the land has been my *livelihood* since my youth.' - Meaning that the blood of Christ, and God's pardoning mercy in that blood, made known in the new covenant, are a fountain always flowing, that never can be emptied. It is opened for all believers, who as the spiritual seed of Christ, are of the house of David, and, as living members of the church, are inhabitants of Jerusalem. Christ, by the power of his grace, takes away the dominion of sin, even of beloved sins. Those who are washed in the fountain opened, as they are justified, so they are sanctified. Souls are brought off from the world and the flesh, those two great idols, that they may cleave to God only. The thorough reformation which will take place on the conversion of Israel to Christ is here foretold. False prophets shall be convinced of their sin and folly, and return to their proper employments *(livelihood)*. As Christians, when convinced that we are gone out of the way of duty, we must show the truth of our repentance by returning to it again. It is well to acknowledge those to be friends, who by severe discipline are instrumental in bringing us to a sight of error; for faithful are the wounds of a friend, (Proverbs 27:6). And it is always well for us to recollect the wounds of our Saviour. Often has he been wounded by professed friends, nay, even by his real disciples, when they act contrary to his word.

Livelihood, sustainable: The concept of Sustainable Livelihood is an attempt to go beyond the conventional definitions and approaches to poverty eradication. These had been found to be too narrow because they focused only on certain aspects or manifestations of poverty, such as low income, or did not consider other vital aspects of poverty such as vulnerability and social exclusion. It is now recognized that more attention must be paid to the various factors and processes which either constrain or enhance poor people's ability to make a living in an economically, ecologically, and socially sustainable manner. The *Sustainable Livelihood* concept offers a more coherent and integrated approach to poverty. The sustainable livelihoods idea was first introduced by the Brundtland Commission on Environment and Development, and the 1992 United Nations Conference on Environment and Development expanded the concept, advocating for the achievement of sustainable livelihoods as abroad goal for poverty eradication. Note "a livelihood in this sense, comprises the capabilities, assets (stores, resources, claims and access) and activities required for a means of living: a livelihood is sustainable when it can cope with and recover from stress and shocks, maintain or enhance its capabilities and assets, and provide *sustainable livelihood* opportunities for the next generation; and which contributes net benefits to other livelihoods

Livelihood, sustainable

at the local and global levels and in the short and long term. The Church position is important to encourage *sustainable livelihood*, preachers of the gospel, ministers should avoid the temptation of that will through Christ followers to adverse poverty. Now, we as Christians all know the parable of the "Widow's Two Mites" which these deceivers will constantly hit you over your head with it. Always claiming this is the example you should have in giving out of your poverty and giving to their church building fund or some other project the pastor comes up with or without your consent.

2 Yet, this parable nowhere says you should give your "whole livelihood" (Mark 12:44) to some man-made church or minister. Remember, the temple of God is your body in which the Spirit of Christ and His Father in heaven resides - if you want to give to God you give to His saints in need and the poor of this world; unless, you yourself is disqualified not having the Holy Spirit in you (one of those who pretend to be a Christian). (Mark 12 : 41 – 44) - The Widow's Two Mites provides the path way: "Now Jesus sat opposite the treasury and saw how the people put money into the treasury. And many who were rich put in much. Then one poor widow came and threw in two mites, which make a quadrants. So He called His disciples to Himself and said to them, "Assuredly, I say to you that this poor widow has put in more than all those who have given to the treasury; for they all put in out of their abundance, but she out of her poverty put in all that she had, her whole livelihood." Also see (Luke 21: 1-4) "And He looked up and saw the rich putting their gifts into the treasury, and He saw also a certain poor widow putting in two mites. So He said, "Truly I say to you that this poor widow has put in more than all; 4 for all these out of their abundance have put in offerings for God, but she out of her poverty put in all the livelihood that she had."

Jesus in (Mark 12: 38-40), had just warned the disciples about the behaviour of the Pharisees and Scribes... "Then He said to them in His teaching, "Beware of the scribes, who desire to go around in long robes, love greetings in the marketplaces, the best seats in the synagogues, and the best places at feasts, who devour widows' houses, and for a pretence make long prayers. These will receive greater condemnation"... As you can see here these scribes walked around with nice "long robes" on, and like so many of the gospel peddlers today they loved to be greeted "in the marketplaces" being called "reverend" and "father" even "holy father". These gospel peddlers love to sit up front in the pulpit as they say, and they ravish getting their "props" as they say at special events. Now, notice what Christ says in (verse 40), after warning His disciples not to be like these phonies who "will receive greater condemnation" than others who sin because they know what they are doing, "they see" as they claim. This same warning is given in (Luke 20:45-47) also just before Jesus spoke concerning the widow's mites here in (Luke 21) and (Mark 12) above. In (verse 40), Jesus speaks of these scribes "who devour widows' houses, and for pretence make long prayers". Now, the same scribes should be kept in mind when Jesus is speaking the parable of the "widow's two mites"; because these scribes were devouring widows' houses by robbing them of their livelihood. These scribe required all too given to the temple even poor widows without any means of supporting themselves. This part of the story these gospel peddlers always leave out.

3 *References:* Read it again for yourself, in (Luke 21:4) it says... the Widow "out of her poverty put in all the livelihood that she had." In (Mark 12:44), it says, the Widow "put in all that she had, her whole *livelihood*". And these scribes and temple leaders had no shame in accepting this woman's last; all they were concern about was everyone putting something in the temple treasury. Now, do you see why Jesus spoke first on how these scribes behaved? For the picture of the widow putting in all her livelihood, takes on a more profound spiritual meaning than the worldly meaning these gospel peddlers love to use to get you to give more to them.

4 The Greek word translated here as "devour" means "to devour i.e. forcibly appropriate: widows' property, to strip one of his goods". Therefore, this parable speaks of the scribes "forcibly taking the *livelihood* of widows, stripping them of all their goods and money" to support the temple; something God never intended, go back and read the Scriptures about tithing. Only those with livestock and land were to tithe - not widows and the poor (who were the ones who the Levites were commanded to share the tithes with every three years). Think about it, if the Scriptures say the scribes "devour widows' houses", and we know the Scripture cannot be broken and God's word is truth; then do you think the scribes were going to widows' homes and dragging them out and taking their livelihood? Or were these money lovers preaching that these widows had to give to the temple treasury no matter how poor they are? Think about what the Scripture is saying here. Something that is very sad and ungodly about what these gospel peddlers who get your "tithes and offerings" do is this: they will tell you your tithes and offerings are for the church to preach, teach, and the building fund, etc. However, they rarely if ever say it's for the poor in your congregation, which as the Gospel preach, it should be for the poor and needy indeed. Glory to Jesus! The giver of Gospel!!

Lord

Lord: *(Greek – kurios, Hebrew – Adonai)* See Adonai

Lordship: (noun: Greek – *kurieuó*, : *(ko-ree-yoo'-o,* Hebrew – *kuriotés (koo-ree-ot'-ace)* Meaning –Overwhelm or supernatural control, domination, dignity divine or angelic lordship, domination, dignity, usually with reference to a celestial hierarchy *as* in (Romans 14: 7 – 12) "For none of us liveth to himself, and no man dieth to himself. For whether we live, we live unto the Lord; and whether we die, we die unto the Lord: whether we live therefore, or die, we are the Lord's. For to this end Christ both died, and rose, and revived, that He might be Lord both of the dead and living. But why dost thou judge thy brother? Or why dost thou set at nought thy brother? For we shall all stand before the judgment seat of Christ. For it is written, as I live, saith the Lord, every knee shall bow to Me, and every tongue shall confess to God. So then every one of us shall give account of himself to God" -

2 *Lordship* is a recognized pre-eminence of the supreme authority by a Christian. In the Church of Rome to whom Paul wrote, an outburst of criticism and judgment had begun. Paul wrote them to say, "Get off each other's backs! Cut the criticism! It is not your opinion of someone that counts, nor their opinion of you; you both belong to Jesus—and Jesus is Lord!"

In the gospel dictionary, the definition of the word 'Lord' – *Adonai,* is one with absolute power, absolute authority. We often speak of commitment, but the real question is surrender. When you're committed, you're in control; when you surrender, you relinquish control. If a robber puts a gun to your head, you don't commit your wallet; you surrender it! To understand that truth is the beginning of kingdom authority. He is called Lord no less than 747 times in the New Testament. You can't make Him Lord; He has already claimed the title. Your questions are, first, will you recognize His *Lordship*, and second, will you submit to it? He is Lord of all you have and all you do. Do you live by that *Lordship?* Let us at all times crown Him 'Lord of all' in all our actions, thoughts and deeds. Hallelujah!

Lordship, the redeeming claim of His: This means that as Christians, we are heavenly property. Jesus' claim for Lordship is simple: He died for us. In the manner of His death He was purchasing us. That truth undercuts any illusion of independence we may foster. "What! Know ye not that your body is the temple of the Holy Ghost which is in you, which ye have of God, and ye are not your own?" (1 Corinthians 6:19). This to say, you do not belong to yourself if you're a Christian. The decision to give one's heart to Jesus is the last independent legitimate decision we ever make. Is that statement unsettling? It

Lost

should be wonderful and exciting! After all, who can better manage our lives: the Lord of Creation, or we ourselves?

2 Indeed, we are the purchased possession! God bought you with a price, and put a mark or seal on you—a mark called the Holy Spirit. A seal, in New Testament times, meant a legal document. A king would create a document, put melted wax on it, and use his signet ring to make a seal. This marked it as the property of the king.

3 We do not take Christ "as Saviour"; we can only take Him as "Lord and Saviour." When we get married ... we are binding ourselves, committing and surrendering ourselves, to that bond. We don't accept Jesus with any reservations. He surrendered on Calvary without reservation. He is Lord!

Lordship, the resurrection conquest of:
As in (Romans 14:9), "To this end Christ both died, and rose..." In those two actions we see the redeeming claim and the resurrection conquest. When He died, He gave Himself for us, but when He rose, He gave Himself to us to live within us. This calls for: 1 *Total Submission* - No man can serve two masters. Jesus is no part-time king. He must be Lord of all to be Lord at all, so you are committed to Jesus Christ completely and exclusively. 2 *Absolute Ownership* - Jesus is not simply the owner of the tithe. He doesn't own ten per cent of a Christian, He owns it all. The tithe is simply a tangible expression of that. It is a symbol of all our resources. 3 *Unquestioned Obedience* - "No, Lord," is a contradiction in terms. Being Christian means obedience in our work, in our witness, in our friendships and families, in our recreation, and in every area there is. Are you afraid to surrender to that kind of obedience? Make up your mind and cleft to the rock in which ye were hewn.

Lordship, the Regal Confession of His:
(Romans 14:11) Paul goes on to say that the time will come when all will bow down and confess His name. "Every knee shall bow to me, and every tongue shall confess to God". The implication here is you don't need to wait until that great day of history's culmination because - That sincere confession seals salvation and it conquers Satan. He will do anything to keep you from saying it and meaning it. Again, it also confirms saints and will strengthen your faith. The more you confess, the greater your love will grow; and the greater your love grows, the more you will confess. More so, confessing Jesus will help your separation from the world. The more you concentrate on Jesus and His Lordship, the more the things of this world will fall away in importance. Hallelujah!

Lost:
(adjective: Greek – *apollumi*, [ap-ol'-loo-mee], Hebrew – *abedah* – [ab-ay-daw]') to destroy, to put out of the way entirely, abolish, put an end to ruin, render useless, to kill, to declare that one must be put to death, metaphor meaning to devote or give over to

Lost-man reject God

eternal misery in hell, to perish, to be lost, ruined, destroyed, to destroy, to lose unable to find one's way; not knowing one's whereabouts. 2that has been taken away or cannot be recovered.

2 Lose (*verb*) be deprived of or cease to have or retain (something). 2 become unable to find (something or someone). 3 fail to win (a game or contest). 4 earn less (money) than one is spending or has spent. 5 waste or fail to take advantage of (time or an opportunity. The gospel presents the truth that mankind is *lost*. Understanding what it means to be *lost* and how it can be fixed is the difference between eternity with God or without God; of heaven or hell. So, we will start by examining how the Bible describes man as lost.

3 This word comes from *apo* - "away" and *olethros* [ollumi] - "destruction, ruin, death" A New Shorter Lexicon of the Greek New Testament, F. Wilbur Gingrich, p.138]. Therefore it meant to "completely destroy" or to "ruin away." It is illustrated in (Matthew 2:13) Herod desired to kill the child Jesus. In (Matthew 8:25) the disciples feared they would perish in the boat. Specifically, they feared that they would drown. These are physical examples.

4 *Lost* in a spiritual sense described Israelites who needed to be saved (Matthew 10:6; 18:11). *Lost* describes those to whom the good news about Jesus Christ is hidden (2 Corinthians 4:3). Lost describes the condition of those who have not believed the good news and do not have eternal life (John 3:15, 16). Finally, it describes those people who have not loved the truth so that they should be saved (2Thessalonians 2:10). So, *lost* in a spiritual sense describes those who are not saved, who do not know the good news about Jesus Christ, and those who do not have eternal life.

5 Part of being *lost* is being dead. This is not physical death but spiritual death. We were once dead in trespasses and sins (Ephesians 2:1). God views the world of the unsaved as a graveyard full of dead people (Ephesians 5:1). The unsaved man is dead because he is alienated from God's life (Ephesians 2:18). We needed God to make us alive (Ephesians 2:5). Spiritual death is separation from God's life.

Lost-man reject God: (Psalm 53:1) "The fool has said in his heart that there is no God In contrast, the believer is one who knows God and is known by God (Galatians 4:9). Think about that last part "known by God." If you believe in Jesus Christ, God knows you! How important this is becomes plain when we read Jesus' words in (Matthew 7:23) "Depart from Me, I never knew you." "Knew" is the Greek word *ginosko* [ginwskw] and means experiential knowledge. As God, Jesus knows everything and knows who everybody is. He knows who they are but He has no relationship with them. The lost deny God or do not know God.

Lost Soul: *See lost man*

Love: (noun - from Old English – To desire, to please and to have "a strong positive emotion of regard; 2 Any object of warm affection or devotion; a beloved person; used as terms of endearment. 3 "**To Love**" (verb) is to have a great affection and liking for, to get pleasure from, to be enamoured or in love with; in (1 Corinthians13:4-7), lists some attributes and virtues of **Love**: "*Love is patient, love is kind. It does not envy, it does not boast, it is not proud. It does not dishonour others, it is not self-seeking, it is not easily angered, it keeps no record of wrongs. Love does not delight in evil but rejoices with the truth. It always protects, always trusts, always hopes, always preserves.*" The **best** example and the **greatest** lesson of *Love* is given to us by God the Father Himself who, out of His unthinkable kind of *Love* for the world (the human race) (John 3:16), sent His one and only Son Jesus Christ to die in order to save us and to redeem us from eternal damnation. His evident gesture of *Love* through the death of His Son has therefore eliminated His intended wrath against us in terms of His anger towards us after the first man, Adam, disobeyed Him and sinned against Him in the Garden of Eden. His Great-Creator's *Love* for us has compelled Him to offer His own Son as the utmost sacrifice to save us all from the consequences of the original sin (Genesis3 or Whole Chapter). By doing this, God send love (Jesus) to the world through His Righteous Anger over Sin and Satan. The kind of love Satan will not be able to convince to sin as he did to Adam and Eve. So, No wonder Christ bear our sins righteously and die sinfully and was raise victoriously to continue eternal living in us and for us Righteously. Hallelujah! – Why because the love was too strong and ever – ever – without limit or boundary. 4 As a true faithful recipe to Christians, Love is the greatest power, the most powerful force that ever exists. It drives our lives, it motivates our actions, it stimulates our passion, it shapes our thoughts, it moulds our thinking, it directs our behaviour, it justifies our reactions. **Love** determines our sacrifices, it sustains our endurance, it sharpens our choices, it dictates outcomes, it maximizes our care, it conceives our plans, it enhances our planning. **Love** always seeks to please, to protect, to defend, to nurture, to care, to court, to charm, to dream, to beautify, to attract, to preserve, to persevere, to cover, to educate, to uplift, to promote, to respect, to liberate, to elevate, to build up, to repair, to pull up, to push up, to publicize, to market, to exhibit, to advertise, to talk about, to exalt, to valorize, to brag about, to display, to show off.

Love of Agape: *See Agape, Love of*

Love of God: Refers to the dual process of love, particularly, 'that from God to man and from man to God. Can also mean either love for God or love by God. Love for God (philotheia) is associated with the concepts of piety, worship,

Lower

and devotions towards God. Love by God for human beings (philanthropia) is lauded in (Psalm 52:1): "The steadfast love of God endures all the day"; (Psalm 52:8): "I trust in the steadfast love of God forever and ever"; (Romans 8:39): "Nor height nor depth, nor anything else in all creation, will be able to separate us from the love of God"; (2 Corinthians 13:14): "The grace of the Lord Jesus Christ and the love of God and the fellowship of the Holy Spirit be with you all"; (1 John 4:9): "In this the love of God was made manifest among us, that God sent his only Son into the world, so that we might live through him"; etc.

The Greek term theophilia means the love or favour of God, and theophilos means friend of God, originally in the sense of being loved by God or loved by the gods; but is today sometimes understood in the sense of showing love for God. The Greek term agape is applied both to the love that human beings have for God and to the love that God has for man.

Lower: (adjective) less high in position. "the lower levels of the any high object" synonyms: bottom, bottommost, under, underneath, further down, beneath, nether "the curtain covers the lower half of the window" antonyms: top, upper, higher less high in status or amount. "managers lower down the hierarchy". In the gospel, opposite of Higher or Majestic in honour and excellence as in (Psalm 8:4-6) How majestic is Your Name! – thus' "What is man that You take thought of him, And the son of man that You care for him? Yet You have made him a little *lower* than God, And You crown him with glory and majesty! You make him to rule over the works of Your hands; You have put all things under his feet,"...

2 *Lower* is synonyms to subordinate, inferior, lesser, junior, minor. In (Hebrew 2: 6-8) Jesus brought Himself lower to His brothers and really He made Like His Brothers "... But one has testified somewhere, saying, "WHAT IS MAN, THAT YOU REMEMBER HIM? OR THE SON OF MAN, THAT YOU ARE CONCERNED ABOUT HIM? "YOU HAVE MADE HIM FOR A LITTLE WHILE *LOWER* THAN THE ANGELS; YOU HAVE CROWNED HIM WITH GLORY AND HONOR, AND HAVE APPOINTED HIM OVER THE WORKS OF YOUR HANDS; YOU HAVE PUT ALL THINGS IN SUBJECTION UNDER HIS FEET." For in subjecting all things to him, He left nothing that is not subject to him. But now we do not yet see all things subjected to him....

To expatiate on the above, this means a little while inferior to." The Greek may here mean a little inferior in rank, or inferior for a little time. But the probable meaning is, that it refers to inferiority of rank. Such is its obvious sense in (Psalm 8:1-9), from which this is quoted. The meaning is, that God had made man but little inferior to the angels in rank. He was inferior, but still God had exalted him almost to their rank. Feeble, and weak, and dying as he was, God had exalted him, and had given him a dominion and a rank almost like that of the angels. The wonder of the Psalmist is, that God had given to human nature so much honour - a wonder that is not at all diminished when we think of the honour done to man by his connection with the divine nature in the person of the Lord Jesus. If in contemplating the race as it appears; if when we look at the dominion of man over the lower world, we are amazed that God has bestowed so much honour on our nature, how much more should we wonder that he has honoured man by his connection with the divinity. Paul applies this to the Lord Jesus. His object is to show that he is superior to the angels. In doing this he shows that he had a nature given him in itself but little inferior to the angels, and then that that had been exalted to a rank and dominion far above theirs. That such honour should be put on "man" is what is suited to excite amazement, and well may one continue to ask why it has been done? When we survey the heavens, and contemplate their glories, and think of the exalted rank of other beings, we may well inquire why benefit has such honour been conferred on ma then? – Just for the single determination of Jesus Christ to die on the Cross to take away the sins of man who was lowered after falling away from grace in the Garden of Eden. Man was graciously lucky, that after all the inferiority through submission to sin and yet was favoured, to be inputted with sin in Christ. So that when Christ was crucified, man was crucified with Him, when He was buried, man was buried with Him and as Christ resurrected, man resurrected with Him so that from lowering Christ to the grave where man who was also lowered with Him, the Angels were not lowered, As Christ resurrected and ascended, seated at the right hand of the father and was crowned with honour and Glory, man who suppose not to experience or benefit from such crowning benefited from all the goodness. (From lowering to Migesty).

3 Thou crownedst him with glory and honour. - That is, with exalted honour. Glory and honour here are nearly synonymous. The meaning is, that elevated honour had been conferred on human nature. A most exalted and extended dominion had been given to "man," which showed that God had greatly honoured him. This appeared eminently in the person of the Lord Jesus, "the exalted Man," to whom this dominion was given in the widest extent. And didst set him over ... - "Man" has been placed over the other works of God: by the original appointment Genesis 1:26; man at large - though fallen, sinful, feeble, dying; man, eminently in the person of the Lord Jesus, in whom human nature has received its chief exaltation. This is what is particularly in the eye of the apostle - and the language of the Psalm will accurately express this exaltation.

Made

Mm

Made: (Past tense and past participle of make) as used in (Psalm 139:14) "I praise you because I am fearfully and wonderfully *made*; your works are wonderful, I know that full well". The word made means - Produced or manufactured by constructing, shaping, or forming. Often used in combination: handmade lace; ready-made suits. Produced or created artificially: bought some made goods at the local store. Having been invented; contrived: These made excuses of yours just won't wash. Assured of success: a made man. Idiom: made for Perfectly suited for: They're made for each other. Made, woman was made:

Other references in the gospel can be found in the following verses (Psalm 139: 13-16), For you formed my inward parts; you knitted me together in my mother's womb. I praise you, for I am fearfully and wonderfully made. Wonderful are your works; my soul knows it very well. My frame was not hidden from you, when I was being made in secret, intricately woven in the depths of the earth. Your eyes saw my unformed substance; in your book were written, every one of them, the days that were formed for me, when as yet there was none of them. (Psalm 139:14) I praise you, for I am fearfully and wonderfully made. Wonderful are your works; my soul knows it very well. (Jeremiah 1:5) "Before I formed you in the womb I knew you, and before you were born I consecrated you; I appointed you a prophet to the nations." (Psalm 139:13-14) "For you formed my inward parts; you knitted me together in my mother's womb. I praise you, for I am fearfully and wonderfully made. Wonderful are your works; my soul knows it very well". (Job 33:4) "The Spirit of God has made me, and the breath of the Almighty gives me life". (Ephesians 2:10) "For we are his workmanship, created in Christ Jesus for good works, which God prepared beforehand, that we should walk in them. (Jeremiah 1:4-5) "Now the word of the Lord came to me, saying, "Before I formed you in the womb I knew you, and before you were born I consecrated you; I appointed you a prophet to the nations."

Made, Fearfully and Wonderfully:
As in Psalm 139:14 I praise you because I am fearfully and wonderfully made; your works are wonderful, I know that full well. I will praise thee –That is, I will not merely admire what is so great and marvellous, but I will acknowledge thee in a public manner as wise, and holy, and good: as entitled to honour, love, and gratitude. With all truthfulness born by thy Spirit, so that the praises and honour given to you might be yours and for you alone.

For I am fearfully and wonderfully made – So that no one could imagine me as a foetus in my mother's womb, now growing to carry out the works through the graces which thou bestowed or destined for me to accomplish. The word rendered "fearfully" means properly "fearful things;" things suited to produce fear or reverence. The word rendered "wonderfully made" means properly to distinguish; Surprising things or accomplishment, to separate. The literal translation of this - as near as can be given - would be, "I am distinguished by fearful things;" that is, by things in my creation which are suited to inspire awe. I am distinguished among thy works by things which tend to exalt my ideas of God, and to fill my soul with reverent and devout feelings. The idea is, that he was "distinguished" among the works of creation, or so "separated" from other things in his endowments as to work in the mind a sense of awe. He was made different from inanimate objects, and from the brute creation; he was "so" made, in the entire structure of his frame, as to fill the mind with wonder. The more anyone contemplates his own bodily formation, and becomes acquainted with the anatomy of the human frame, and the more he understands of his mental organization, the more he will see the force and propriety of the language used by the psalmist.

2 Marvellous are thy works - Fitted are they to excite wonder and admiration. The particular reference here is to his own formation; but the same remark may be made of the works of God in general. And that my soul knoweth right well - Margin, as in Hebrew, "greatly." I am fully convinced of it. I am deeply impressed by it. We can see clearly that the works of God are "wonderful," even if we can understand nothing else about them. Hallelujah!

Maker:
(noun) a person or thing that makes or produces something. "film-makers" synonyms: creator, manufacturer, builder, constructor, producer, fabricator, author, architect, designer, framer, originator, inventor, founder, father "the maker's name is stamped on the back" 2. God. synonyms: God, Creator, Prime Mover, master of the universe; God – the maker of Heaven and Earth.

Man

God often create or make things. So that He uses what He makes to get what He want. He created man in His like image of creativity, so that at the time when money will not be there for you to buy, you can make for your self. Look at Paul in (Acts 18:3) "And because he was of the same craft, he abode with them, and wrought: for by their occupation they were tentmakers" For decades and even centuries, studies have been done on the life of the Apostle Paul. However, in most of these studies, his trade has been handled as a peripheral need because of his circumstances and lack of resources. Therefore, for many theologians and gospel teachers, his trade is not central to understanding Paul. However, as you will see in this study, we view his trade as integral to his identity. The fact that he was a tentmaker and a missionary actually penetrated to the depth of who he was and the efficacy of his ministry. Tent making was central to his ministry. Paul was a missionary, but his trade was not mutually exclusive or compartmentalized from his ministry. The two roles were intertwined, and he was a tentmaker with the intention of the "Great Commission." Just as Paul did not wander into the marketplace, he did not simply "fall" into tent making desperate to pay for his needs. So for something to happen you must make it, by making it, you conceive the idea, research, plan, organise, create as in the film industry. Make things to happen in Evangelisation, draw up sound evangelising strategy with boldness, vision able and commitment, without fear or favour, preach the gospel with sound doctrine and win soul for Jesus. Hallelujah!

Man: (Men - Plural) (Genesis 1:26) Then God said, "Let us make mankind in our image, in our likeness, so that they may rule over the fish in the sea and the birds in the sky, over the livestock and all the wild animals, and over all the creatures that move along the ground." Man - A male human. The term man is usually reserved for an adult male, with the term boy being the usual term for a male child or adolescent. However, the term man is also sometimes used to identify a male human, regardless of age, as in phrases such as "Men's basketball". Like most other male mammals, a man's genome typically inherits an X chromosome from his mother and a Y chromosome from his father. The male foetus produces larger amounts of androgens and smaller amounts of oestrogens than a female foetus. This difference in the relative amounts of these sex steroids is largely responsible for the physiological differences that distinguish men from women. During puberty, hormones which stimulate androgen production result in the development of secondary sexual characteristics, thus exhibiting greater differences between the sexes. However, there are exceptions to the above for some intersex and transgender men.

2 God went on to say: "Let us make man in our image, according to our likeness, . . . This verse explains that Jesus was there helping his Father in creating man: (Colossians 1:16) because by means of him all [other] things were created in the heavens and upon the earth, the things visible and the things invisible, no matter whether they are thrones or lordships or governments or authorities. All [other] things have been created through him and for him. Some have claimed that the "us" and "our" in this expression indicate a Trinity. But if you were to say, 'Let us make something for ourselves,' no one would normally understand this to imply that several persons are combined as one inside of you. You simply mean that two or more individuals will work together on something. So, too, when God used "us" and "our," he was simply addressing another individual, his first spirit creation, the master craftsman, the prehuman Jesus. ((John 17:4-5) . . .I have glorified you on the earth, having finished the work you have given me to do. 5 So now you, Father, glorify me alongside yourself with the glory that I had alongside you before the world was.) And in Our image is explained in the following - it is in relation to qualities that we have: (Colossians 3:10) and clothe yourselves with the new [personality], which through accurate knowledge is being made new according to the image of the One who created it, In the gospel God uses the word Man to represent 'Man and Woman' so that when He say 'Blessed is the Man... He implies man and woman particularly as Man was created and woman made from the rips of a man. So God considers 'man and woman' to be one particularly in issues of effectiveness in marriage and upholding the institution to be one manly institution recognise strongly by God as in (Psalm 1:1-6) "Blessed is the man who walks not in the counsel of the wicked, nor stands in the way of sinners, nor sits in the seat of scoffers; but his delight is in the law of the Lord, and on his law he meditates day and night. He is like a tree planted by streams of water that yields its fruit in its season, and its leaf does not wither. In all that he does, he prospers. The wicked are not so, but are like chaff that the wind drives away. Therefore the wicked will not stand in the judgment, nor sinners in the congregation of the righteous";

Manger: A feeder that is made of carved stone, wood, or metal construction and is used to hold food for animals (as in a stable). Mangers are mostly used in livestock raising. They are also used to feed wild animals, e.g., in nature reserves. The word comes from the French manger (meaning "to eat"), from Latin 'manducare' (meaning "to chew"). A manger is also a Christian symbol, associated with nativity scenes where Mary,

Maranatha

forced by necessity to stay in a stable instead of an inn, placed the baby Jesus in a manger. (Greek: phatnē) as in (Luke 2:7)."And she gave birth to her firstborn, a son. She wrapped him in cloths and placed him in a *manger*, because there was no guest room available for them.

Maranatha: (This is a two-word Aramaic formula joined together in Greek translation occurring only once in the New Testament (see Aramaic of Jesus) and also in the Did - ache, which is part of the Apostolic Fathers' collection. It is transliterated into Greek letters rather than translated and, given the nature of early manuscripts, the lexical difficulty lies in determining just which two Aramaic words comprise the single Greek expression, found at the end of Paul's First Epistle to the Corinthians (1Corinthians 16:22). If one chooses to split the two words as (maranâ thâ), a vocative concept with an imperative verb, then it can be translated as a command to the Lord to come. 2 If one decides that the two words (maran 'athâ), a possessive "Our Lord" and a perfect or preterit verb "has come," are actually more warranted, then it would be seen as a creedal expression. This interpretation, "Our Lord has come," is supported by what appears to be an equivalent of this in the early creedal acclamation found in the biblical books of (Romans 10:9) and (1 Corinthians 12:3), "Jesus is Lord."

3 The recent interpretation has been to select the command option ("Come, Lord!"), changing older decisions to follow the preterit option ("Our Lord has come") as found in the ancient Aramaic Peshitta, in the Latin *Clementine Vulgate*. As presented in the New Revised Standard Version Bible (1Corinthians 16:22) *Maranatha* is translated in the expression as: "Our Lord, come!" but notes that it could also be translated as: "Our Lord has come". For true believers, when the Lord has come, it means He has as in (Genesis 2:22-24)

"Then the LORD God made a woman from the rib he had taken out of the man, and he brought her to the man. The man said, "This is now bone of my bones and flesh of my flesh; she shall be called 'woman, ' for she was taken out of man." For this reason a man will leave his father and mother and be united to his wife, and they will become one flesh. He is with us;

3 The New International Version translates: "Come, O Lord"; the Message version puts it differently as: "Make room for the Master!" As understood here ("O Lord, come!"), it is a prayer for the early return of Christ. If the Aramaic words are divided differently (Maran atha, "Our Lord has come"), it becomes a creedal declaration. The former interpretation is supported by what appears to be a Greek equivalent of this acclamation in the Book of (Revelation

22:20) "Amen. Come, Lord Jesus!" 4 The New Jerusalem Bible translates *Maranatha* (1 Corinthians 16:22), "If there is anyone who does not love the Lord, a curse on such a one. Maran atha." In the context of 1 Corinthians, understanding the Greek *"maranatha"* as Aramaic "Maran atha" in the preterit sense would provide substantiation for the preceding anathema. That is, one who does not love the Lord is accursed because our Lord has ascended and come unto his throne (see, Daniel 7:13) and wields power to implement such a curse. It would also substantiate the following prayer for grace from the ascended Lord Jesus, who has come to his throne and then sends the Holy Spirit as a comforter who dwells in us and is with us – Christians. Glorify the Lord!

Maranatha Ministries: A Christian Church in the South West of London embracing the 'Maranathaic 'doctrine in preaching the Gospel of Christ or other similar ministries.

Marriage: A sacred vow between a man and woman and the gospel of Christ offers many verses that offer guidance for married couples, husbands, wives, newlyweds and engagement. Here we must consider marriage as a social recognized union and marriage in relation to God, Jesus Christ, and the Christian faith. Whichever conception fulfils the instincts or the basic or natural condition of the couples joined in marriage, the divined origin must be obeyed as in (Genesis 2:22-24) "Then the LORD God made a woman from the rib he had taken out of the man, and he brought her to the man. The man said, "This is now bone of my bones and flesh of my flesh; she shall be called 'woman, ' for she was taken out of man." For this reason a man will leave his father and mother and be united to his wife, and they will become one flesh".

2 In (Romans 13:1-2) is one of several passages in Scripture that refers to the importance of believers honouring governmental authority in general: "Everyone must submit himself to the governing authorities, for there is no authority except that which God has established. The authorities that exist have been established by God. Consequently, he who rebels against the authority is rebelling against what God has instituted, and those who do so will bring judgment on themselves." These gospels gives position number 2 (the couple is married in the eyes of God when the couple is legally married) a stronger gospel or biblical basis for support. The problem, however, with a legal process only is that some governments require couples to go against the laws of God in order to be legally married. Also, there were many marriages that took place in history before governmental laws were established for marriage. Even today some countries have no legal re-

Marriage, The Character of the wife in

quirements for marriage. Therefore, a more correct position in the gospel is for a couple, as believers, to submit to governmental authority and recognize the laws of the land, as long as that authority does not require them to break one of the laws of God.

3 No wonder (Hebrews 13:4-7) reminds us that "Marriage should be honoured by all, and the marriage bed kept pure, for God will judge the adulterer and all the sexually immoral. Keep your lives free from the love of money and be content with what you have, because God has said, "Never will I leave you; never will I forsake you." So we say with confidence, "The Lord is my helper; I will not be afraid. What can man do to me?" Remember your leaders, who spoke the word of God to you. Consider the outcome of their way of life and imitate their faith". Also, many blessings abound to married couples or the family as in (Proverbs 5:18-19) May your fountain be blessed, and may you rejoice in the wife of your youth. A loving doe, a graceful deer-- may her breasts satisfy you always, may you ever be captivated by her love.

Marriage, The Character of the wife in

: In (Proverbs 12:4) A wife of noble character is her husband's crown, but a disgraceful wife is like decay in his bones. This clearly defines the quality - the characteristic of a good wife. Nobility can involve coiling attitude as attribute to humility and what is good and receives od fearing (Proverbs 18:22) He who finds a wife finds what is good and receives favour from the LORD. Also see (Proverbs 19:14) Houses and wealth are inherited from parents, but a prudent wife is from the LORD., (Proverbs 20:6-7) Many a man claims to have unfailing love, but a faithful man who can find? The righteous man leads a blameless life; blessed are his children after him and (Proverbs 30:18-19) "There are three things that are too amazing for me, four that I do not understand: the way of an eagle in the sky, the way of a snake on a rock, the way of a ship on the high seas, and the way of a man with a maiden.

Marriage as Socially or Ritually Recognized Union:

Here, the fact that marriage is seen in the perspective of socially or ritually recognized union or legal contract between spouses that establishes rights and obligations between them, and between them and their children, and between them and their in-laws, does not mean that the gospel value has lost. Probably, this is what (1 Corinthians 7:1-16) attempted to fulfil. Thus' "Now for the matters you wrote about: It is good for a man not to marry. But since there is so much immorality, each man should have his own wife, and each woman her own husband. The husband should fulfil his marital duty to his wife, and likewise the wife to her husband. The wife's body does not belong to her alone but also to her husband. In the same way, the husband's body does not belong to him alone but also to his wife. Do not deprive each other except by mutual consent and for a time, so that you may devote yourselves to prayer. Then come together again so that Satan will not tempt you because of your lack of self-control. I say this as a concession, not as a command. I wish that all men were as I am. But each man has his own gift from God; one has this gift, another has that. Now to the unmarried and the widows I say: It is good for them to stay unmarried, as I am. But if they cannot control themselves, they should marry, for it is better to marry than to burn with passion. To the married I give this command (not I, but the Lord): A wife must not separate from her husband. But if she does, she must remain unmarried or else be reconciled to her husband. And a husband must not divorce his wife. To the rest I say this (I, not the Lord): If any brother has a wife who is not a believer and she is willing to live with him, he must not divorce her. And if a woman has a husband who is not a believer and he is willing to live with her, she must not divorce him. For the unbelieving husband has been sanctified through his wife, and the unbelieving wife has been sanctified through her believing husband. Otherwise your children would be unclean, but as it is, they are holy. But if the unbeliever leaves, let him do so. A believing man or woman is not bound in such circumstances; God has called us to live in peace. How do you know, wife, whether you will save your husband? Or, how do you know, husband, whether you will save your wife?"

Absolutely, the definition of marriage varies according to different cultures, but it is principally an institution in which interpersonal relationships, usually sexual, are acknowledged. In some cultures, marriage is recommended or considered to be compulsory before pursuing any sexual activity. When defined broadly, marriage is considered a cultural universal.

2 Individuals may marry for several reasons, including legal, social, libidinal, emotional, financial, spiritual, and religious purposes. Who they marry may be influenced by socially determined rules of incest, prescriptive marriage rules, parental choice and individual desire. In some areas of the world arranged marriage, child marriage, polygamy, and sometimes forced marriage, may be practiced as a cultural tradition. Conversely, such practices may be outlawed and penalized in parts of the world out of concerns for human rights and because of international law. In developed parts of the world, there has been a general trend towards ensuring equal rights within marriage for women and legally recognizing the marriages of interracial, interfaith, and same-gender couples. Oftentimes, these trends have been motivated by a desire

to establish equality and uphold human rights.

Marriage, Recognition of:

Marriage can be recognized by a state, an organization, a religious authority, a tribal group, a local community or peers. It is often viewed as a contract. Civil marriage is a marriage without religious content carried out by a government institution in accordance with marriage laws of the jurisdiction, and recognised as creating the rights and obligations intrinsic to matrimony. Marriages can be performed in a secular civil ceremony or in a religious setting via a wedding ceremony. The act of marriage usually creates normative or legal obligations between the individuals involved, and any offspring they may produce. In terms of legal recognition, most sovereign states and other jurisdictions limit marriage to opposite-sex couples and a diminishing number of these permit polygamy, child marriages, and forced marriages. Over the twentieth century, a growing number of countries and other jurisdictions have lifted bans on and have established legal recognition for interracial marriage, interfaith marriage and most lately, same-sex marriage. Some cultures allow the dissolution of marriage through divorce or annulment. In some areas, child marriages and polygamy may occur in spite of national laws against the practice.

Since the late twentieth century, major social changes in Western countries have led to changes in the demographics of marriage, with the age of first marriage increasing, fewer people marrying, and more couples choosing to cohabit rather than marry.

Marriage, Right of:

Historically, in most cultures, married women had very few rights of their own, being considered, along with the family's children, the property of the husband; as such, they could not own or inherit property, or represent themselves legally (see for example coverture). In Europe, the United States, and other places in the developed world, beginning in the late 19th century and lasting through the 21st century, marriage has undergone gradual legal changes, aimed at improving the rights of the wife. These changes included giving wives legal identities of their own, abolishing the right of husbands to physically discipline their wives, giving wives property rights, liberalizing divorce laws, providing wives with reproductive rights of their own, and requiring a wife's consent when sexual relations occur. These changes have occurred primarily in Western countries. In the 21st century, there continue to be controversies regarding the legal status of married women, legal acceptance or leniency towards violence within marriage (especially sexual violence), traditional marriage customs such as dowry and bride price, forced marriage, marriageable age, and criminalization of consensual behaviours such as premarital and extramarital sex.

Master: Let us see the word master in ordinary or everyday usage before the gospel application. Master as a (noun) is a Word denoting some kind of rank or status with several meanings and may refer to: Historical a man who has people working for him, especially servants or slaves. "he acceded to his master's wishes" synonyms: lord, overlord, lord and master, ruler, sovereign, monarch, liege, liege lord, suzerain; More antonyms: servant, underling a person who has complete control of something. "he was master of the situation" Dated male head of a household. "the master of the house" the male owner of a dog, horse, or other domesticated animal. "in many ways dogs reflect the styles of their masters" synonyms: owner, keeper "the dog's pining for his master" a machine or device directly controlling another. "a master cylinder".

Master, Servants Duties to the

: In the gospel, the bible make it clear in (Mathew 6:24) that "No one can serve two masters. Either you will hate the one and love the other, or you will be devoted to the one and despise the other. You cannot serve both God and money" while slaves are really advised in (Ephesians 6:5) "Slaves, obey your earthly masters with respect and fear, and with sincerity of heart, just as you would obey Christ". While the above two gospel verses shows services from slaves to their masters, below are the samples of responsibility of the masters to their slaves or servants

The duty of servants is summed up in one word, obedience. The servants of old were generally slaves. The apostles were to teach servants and masters their duties, in doing which evils would be lessened, till slavery should be rooted out by the influence of Christianity. Servants are to reverence those over them. They are to be sincere; not pretending obedience when they mean to disobey, but serving faithfully. And they must serve their masters not only when their master's eye is upon them; but must be strict in the discharge of their duty, when he is absent and out of the way. Steady regard to the Lord Jesus Christ will make men faithful and sincere in every station, not grudgingly or by constraint, but from a principle of love to the masters and their concerns. This makes service easy to them, pleasing to their masters, and acceptable to the Lord Christ. God will reward even the meanest drudgery done from a sense of duty, and with a view to glorify him.

Masters Duties to Servants:

By this, and as far as the gospel is concern, masters must act after the same manner like the servants by way of being just to servants, especially, as you expect they should be to you; show the like

Master your functions as a Worker of the Gospel

good-will and concern for them, and be careful herein to approve yourselves to God. Be not tyrannical and overbearing. You have a Master to obey, and you and they are but fellow-servants in respect to Christ Jesus. If masters and servants would consider their duties to God, and the account they must shortly give to him, they would be more mindful of their duty to each other, and thus will abide by the gospel as in (Colossians 4:1) "Masters, grant to your slaves justice and fairness, knowing that you too have a Master in heaven". (Ephesians 6:9) "And masters, do the same things to them, and give up threatening, knowing that both their Master and yours is in heaven, and there is no partiality with Him". ("Job 31:13-14") "If I have despised the claim of my male or female slaves When they filed a complaint against me, What then could I do when God arises? And when He calls me to account, what will I answer Him?

Master your functions as a Worker of the Gospel:

a man in charge of an organization or group, in particular: BRITISH a male Sunday schoolteacher. "the games master" synonyms: teacher, Sunday, schoolteacher, Sunday schoolmaster, tutor, instructor, pedagogue; rare preceptor "the geography master" the head of a Church or school. the presiding officer of a livery company or Masonic lodge. synonyms: g u r u , Priest, teacher, spiritual leader, guide, mentor, torch-bearer, swami, Roshi, Maharishi "they regarded him as their spiritual master" the captain of a merchant ship. synonyms: captain, skipper, commander "the master of the ship" the person in control of a pack of hounds. "the master of the Aylesbury Vale Hunt" (in England and Wales) an official of the Supreme Court. 3 a skilled practitioner of a particular art or activity. "I'm a master of disguise" synonyms: expert, adept, genius, past master, maestro, virtuoso, professional, doyen, authority, pundit, master hand, prodigy, grandmaster, champion, star; More antonyms: amateur, novice a great artist or musician.

Master over your Worries:

This shows the ability for us as Christians to master our worries, take full control of our troubles by hand or nailing it to the Cross of Christ through prayers, gain control of; overcome them. "I love to managed to master my fears" synonyms: overcome, conquer, beat, quell, quash, suppress, control, repress, restrain, overpower, triumph over, over; informal lick subdue, vanquish, subjugate, hegemonies, prevail over, govern, curb, check, bridle, tame, defeat, get the better of, get a grip on, get over, gain mastery as in (Ephesians 6: 19-24) "Pray also for me, that whenever I open my mouth, words may be given me so that I will fearlessly make known the mystery of the gospel, for which I am an ambassador in chains. Pray that I may declare it fearlessly, as

Master over your Worries

I should. (Final Greetings) Tychicus, the dear brother and faithful servant in the Lord, will tell you everything, so that you also may know how I am and what I am doing. I am sending him to you for this very purpose, that you may know how we are, and that he may encourage you. Peace to the brothers, and love with faith from God the Father and the Lord Jesus Christ. Grace to all who love our Lord Jesus Christ with an undying love". Spiritual strength and courage are needed for our spiritual warfare and suffering. Those who would prove themselves to have true grace, must aim at all grace; and put on the whole armour of God, which he prepares and bestows. The Christian armour is made to be worn; and there is no putting off our armour till we have done our warfare, and finished our course. The combat is not against human enemies, nor against our own corrupt nature only; we have to do with an enemy who has a thousand ways of beguiling unstable souls. The devils assault us in the things that belong to our souls, and labour to deface the heavenly image in our hearts. We must resolve by God's grace, not to yield to Satan. Resist him, and he will flee. If we give way, he will get ground. If we distrust either our cause, or our Leader, or our armour, we give him advantage. The different parts of the armour of heavy-armed soldiers, who had to sustain the fiercest assaults of the enemy, are here described. There is none for the back; nothing to defend those who turn back in the Christian warfare. Truth, or sincerity, is the girdle. This girds on all the other pieces of our armour, and is first mentioned. There can be no religion without sincerity. The righteousness of Christ, imputed to us, is a breastplate against the arrows of Divine wrath. The righteousness of Christ implanted in us, fortifies the heart against the attacks of Satan. Resolution must be as greaves, or armour to our legs; and to stand their ground or to march forward in rugged paths, the feet must be shod with the preparation of the gospel of peace. Motives to obedience, amidst trials, must be drawn from a clear knowledge of the gospel. Faith is all in all in an hour of temptation. Faith, as relying on unseen objects, receiving Christ and the benefits of redemption, and so deriving grace from him, is like a shield, a defence every way. The devil is the wicked one. Violent temptations, by which the soul is set on fire of hell, are darts Satan shoots at us. Also, hard thoughts of God, and as to ourselves. Faith applying the word of God and the grace of Christ, quenches the darts of temptation. Salvation must be our helmet. A good hope of salvation, a Scriptural expectation of victory, will purify the soul, and keep it from being defiled by Satan. To the Christian armed for defence in battle, the apostle recommends only one weapon of attack; but it is enough, the sword of the Spirit, which is the word of God. It subdues and mortifies evil de-

Matrimony

sires and blasphemous thoughts as they rise within; and answers unbelief and error as they assault from without. A single text, well understood, and rightly applied, at once destroys a temptation or an objection, and subdues the most formidable adversary. Prayer must fasten all the other parts of our Christian armour. There are other duties of religion, and of our stations in the world, but we must keep up times of prayer. Though set and solemn prayer may not be seasonable when other duties are to be done, yet short pious prayers darted out, always are so. We must use holy thoughts in our ordinary course. A vain heart will be vain in prayer. We must pray with all kinds of prayer, public, private, and secret; social and solitary; solemn and sudden: with all the parts of prayer; confession of sin, petition for mercy, and thanksgiving for favours received. And we must do it by the grace of God the Holy Spirit, in dependence on, and according to, his teaching. We must preserve in particular requests, notwithstanding discouragements. We must pray, not for ourselves only, but for all saints. Our enemies are mighty, and we are without strength, but our Redeemer is almighty, and in the power of His might we may overcome. Wherefore we must stir up ourselves. Have not we, when God has called, often neglected to answer? Let us think upon these things, and continue our prayers with patience.

Matrimony: Marriage is, as St. Paul states, a mystery (mysterion). The Latin word used to translate mysterion is "sacramentum". The sacraments are mysteries (as Eastern Christians still call them), for one thing is visible and something else is known by faith. By faith, matrimony is a sign of Christ and the Church, as well as a special calling. (Mathew. 19:10-11; Ephesians. 5:31-32).

Mediation: Very often on the human plane, mediation takes place in the gospel, as it has in many cultures throughout history, both in innocent circumstances and when people are at odds with one another. People use interpreters to mediate the metaphorical distance between them created by a foreign language (Genesis 42:23) and envoys to mediate the real distance created by the geography of the region (2 Chronicle 32:31). They also use mediators to argue a case or to negotiate terms of peace with a hostile party, as Moses did with Pharaoh on behalf of Israel (Exodus 6:28-12:32) and Joab did with David on behalf of Absalom (2 Sam 14:1-24). Both kinds of mediation are sometimes intertwined in the Bible, as when Moses used Aaron to mediate between himself and Pharaoh (Exodus 7:1-2) and Joab used the wise woman of Tekoa to mediate his message about Absalom to David (2 Sam 14:2-20). So what the real meaning of mediation then? Mediation is a form of alternative dispute resolution (ADR), a way of

Mediator

resolving disputes between two or more parties with concrete effects. Typically, a third party, the mediator, assists the parties to negotiate a settlement. Disputants may mediate disputes in a variety of domains, such as commercial, legal, diplomatic, workplace, community and family matters. The term "mediation" broadly refers to any instance in which a third party helps others reach agreement. More specifically, mediation has a structure, timetable and dynamics that "ordinary" negotiation lacks. The process is private and confidential, possibly enforced by law. Participation is typically voluntary. The mediator acts as a neutral third party and facilitates rather than directs the process.

2 God's dealings with his people throughout Scripture also incorporate these two kinds of mediation. Some kind of mediation between God and humanity is necessary simply because God is separate from all he has created and, yet, graciously extends his fellowship to his creatures. Mediation takes on a particularly important role, however, in light of humanity's rebellion against the Creator. The situation of hostility that resulted from Adam's fall could only be remedied through the mediation of a third party. Innocent mediation, with no connotation that the mediation is necessary because of sin, takes place between God and his people in Scripture through angels, through "Wisdom, " and through ordinary people whom God uses for the purpose. The angel of the Lord frequently appears in Scripture as God's messenger and spokesperson, one who graciously extends God's help to those in need and delivers important instructions for the execution of God's saving purposes in history. In (Proverbs 8), Wisdom takes on a personal role and announces that God created her so that people might obtain "favour from the Lord" by finding her (v. 35). As a Christian be ready at all times because God can use you to mediate a cause to your friend, relatives or a fellow Christian, because People, too, serve as God's mediators. Priests served as mediators between God and his people not only when sin was at issue but also when the people of God wanted simply to make offerings of gratitude (Lev iticus 2:1-16). Similarly, the king often functioned as the channel through which God mediated his blessings to his people (2 Samuel 7:5-17) ; (Psalm 72:1-4), a role the Messiah especially was expected to perform (Isaiah 9:2-7) ; (Isaiah 11:1-9) Likewise, God graciously provided for the communication of his will to his people in special circumstances through the prophets. God used Nathan's prophetic word to tell David of his desire for a temple (2 Sam 7:2-17) and Isaiah to calm the fears of Hezekiah about Sennacherib's threatened invasion (2 Kings 19:1-37) ;(Isaiah 37:1-38).

Mediator: A professional or a divined person who mediate − A

Mediator

peace maker. The first mediator is God when He say in (Isaiah 1:18) "Come now, and let us reason together, saith the Lord: though your sins be as scarlet, they shall be as white as snow; though they be red like crimson, they shall be as wool". In the gospel, Christ Jesus is our mediator as is only Him alone can Satan obey or be afraid. He as a member of the trinity can assigned authority to anyone in the name of Jesus and at the mention of the name of Jesus, Satan authority to Moses to commensurate with broken human relations. Just as broken human relations often require the reconciling services of a mediator, however, the gospel often speaks of mediation when God and his people are at odds. Abraham mediated between Sodom and God when he pled with the Lord to spare the city for the sake of even ten righteous people who might have lived there (Genesis 18:23-33). In a similar way, Job wished for an "umpire" who would lay his hand on both Job and God to end their wrestling match long enough for Job to speak with his apparent adversary (Genesis 9:32-35). The greatest of all mediators in the Old Testament, however, is Moses. Moses not only served as a mediator in the innocent sense when, at God's gracious initiative, he communicated the terms of the Sinaitic covenant with Israel (Exodus 19:9 ; 20:19 ; 24:1-2 ; 34:27-28 ; Leviticus 26:46 ; Deuteronomy 5:5); but he served as Israel's intercessor after they had broken the covenant and stood in danger of God's righteous wrath according to the covenant's terms (Exodus 32:7-14 ; 33:12-23 ; Numbers 14:13-19). After Moses' death, and in the face of continued violation of the covenant, other figures arose to urge Israel's compliance with the law and to intercede for Israel during times of disobedience. Samuel pled with God for the people generally and for the king in particular (1Sam 12:17-18 ; 13:13-14 ; 15:10-33); the true prophets attempted to stand between God and his disobedient people to avert disaster; and the priests, when they were faithful to their appointed tasks, offered sacrifices to atone for the people's sins (Leviticus 4:1-5:19)

2 Mediators use various techniques to open, or improve, dialogue and empathy between disputants, aiming to help the parties reach an agreement. Much depends on the mediator's skill and training. As the practice gained popularity, training programs, certifications and licensing followed, producing trained, professional mediators committed to the discipline. 3 No wonder Paul echoes the new covenant language of the Old Testament when he tells us that believers have peace with God (Romans 5:1), have experienced the outpouring of God's love in their hearts through the Holy Spirit (Romans 5:5), and have been reconciled to God (Romans 5:10-11) (2 Corinthians 5:11-20). All of this, he says, has happened through faith in Christ, whose

death served as the ultimate atoning sacrifice for sin (Romans 3:21-26 ; (Romans 5:1 Romans 5:6-9). The covenant mediated through Moses was glorious, he says, but the new covenant is far more so, for unlike the old covenant that punished sin and therefore brought death, the new covenant brings life (2 Corinthians 3:4-18 ; John 1:17 ; . Galatians 3:19-22). Paul ties these concepts neatly together in (1Timothy 2:4-6) when he declares that God's desire to save all people is expressed in the "one mediator, " Christ Jesus, who gave himself as a ransom for all. Hallelujah!

Meek: (adjective, meekness - noun) A virtue of solemnity. quiet, gentle, and easily imposed on; submissive. Like in the Hymn of Charles Wesley "Gentle Jesus, meek and mild, Look upon a little child; Pity my simplicity, Suffer me to come to Thee". Synonyms: patient, long-suffering, forbearing, resigned; There are two essential components for this quality to come into play in the gospel: a conflict in which an individual is unable to control or influence circumstances. Typical human responses in such circumstances include frustration, bitterness, or anger, but the one who is guided by God's spirit accepts God's ability to direct events (Galatians 5:23 ; Ephesians 4:2 ; Colossians 3:12 ; 1 Timothy 6:11 ; Titus 3:2 ; James 1:21 ; 3:13). Meekness is therefore an active and deliberate acceptance of undesirable circumstances that are wisely seen by the individual as only part of a larger picture. Meekness is not a resignation to fate, a passive and reluctant submission to events, for there is little virtue in such a response. Nevertheless, since the two responses resignation and meekness are externally often indistinguishable, it is easy to see how what was once perceived as a virtue has become a defect in contemporary society. The patient and hopeful endurance of undesirable circumstances identifies the person as externally vulnerable and weak but inwardly resilient and strong. Meekness does not identify the weak but more precisely the strong who have been placed in a position of weakness where they persevere without giving up. The use of the Greek word when applied to animals makes this clear, for it means "tame" when applied to wild animals. In other words, such animals have not lost their strength but have learned to control the destructive instincts that prevent them from living in harmony with others. Therefore, it is quite appropriate for all people, from the poor to ancient Near Eastern kings, to describe their submission to God by the term "meek" (Moses in Numbers 12:3). On the other hand, this quality by definition cannot be predicated of God, and therefore constitutes one of the attributes of creatures that they do not share with their Creator. Nevertheless, in the incarnation Jesus is freely described as meek, a concomitant of his

Mercy

submission to suffering and to the will of the Father (Mathew 11:29 ; 21:5) The single most frequently attested context in which the meek are mentioned in the Bible is one in which they are vindicated and rewarded for their patient endurance (Psalm 22:26 ; Psalm 25:9 ; Psalm 37:11 ; 76:9 ; 147:6 ; 149:4 ; Isa 11:4 ; 29:19 ; 61:1) ; Zephaniah 2:3 ; Mathew 5:5).

Mercy: (noun, Greek – *eleos* - [elleo], Hebrew – *hesed* [d,s,j] – denoting compassion of love, not just felling of emotions as expressed in tangible ways. A concept integral to an understanding of God's dealings with humankind. It comes to expression in phrases such as "to be merciful, " "to have mercy on, " or "to show mercy toward." The corresponding term, "merciful, "describes a quality of God and one that God requires of his people. God's covenant "loving-kindness." in one form or another, but

2 *Mercy*: (particularly in the Old Testament) A Part of God's Nature. Although people have the capacity for showing mercy, especially toward those with whom they already have a special relationship (1 Kings 20:31 ; Isaiah 49:15 ; Jeremiah 31:20 ;), a lack of mercy is more natural to the human condition (Proverbs 5:9 ; 12:10 ; Isaiah 13:18 ; 47:6 ; Jeremiah 6:23 ; 50:42 ; Mercy is, however, a quality intrinsic to the nature of God. It is for this reason that in some situations "merciful" was a sufficient description of God (Psalm 116:5) . Sometimes it appears alongside other qualities as one expression of his nature that God's children particularly observe and recount (Exodus 34:6 ; Deuteronomy 4:31 ; 2 Chronicle 30:9 ; Psalm 86:15 ; Daniel 9:9 ; Jonah 4:2). The experience of God's people is that God's mercy, unlike human mercy, cannot be exhausted (2 Samuel 24:14 ; Lamentation 3:22). Yet divine mercy is not blind or dumb; although God tolerated Israel's rebellion with mercy for a very long time (Nehemiah 9:17 Nehemiah 9:19 Nehemiah 9:31 ; Jeremiah 3:12), ultimately ungodliness in Israel was met by a withdrawal of God's mercy, leading to judgment (Lamentations 2:2 Lamentations 2:21 ; Zechariah 1:12). But even in judgment and discipline God's mercy can be seen and hoped for (2 Samuel 24:14 ; Psalm 57:1 ; Isaiah 55:7 ; 60:10 ; Jeremiah 31:20 ; Habakkuk 3:2), for it is part of the basic disposition of love toward his people, and it directs his actions ultimately in ways that benefit his people.

Mercy as the Foundation of God's Covenant:

This means that God's covenant love, are integrally related. So close is the relationship that *hesed* [d,s,j] sometimes is to be viewed in terms of *mercy*. In this relationship, mercy then comes to be seen as the quality in God that directs him to forge a relationship with people who absolutely do not deserve to be in relationship with him. *Mercy* is manifested in God's activity on behalf of his people to free them from slavery; it is neither theory nor principle. As the naration taken up with the establishment of the covenant with Israel show, God's mercy is a driving force in leading him to create a relationship with Israel (Exodus 34:6 ; Deuteronomy 4:31 ; 13:17 ; Hosea 2:19); its meaning through *hesed* [d,s,j] extends to that of loyalty based on merciful love, a loyalty that maintains the covenant despite Israel's own resistance (Psalm 25:6 ; 40:11 ; 69:17 ; Isaiah 63:7 ; Jeremiah 16:5 ; 42:12 ; Hosea 2:19 ; Joel 2:13 ; Zechariah 7:9). God's mercy is mediated through the covenant, by which he becomes the God of a people promising protection, (Psalm 23:6). Because God is the initiator, the mercy he gives is gracious, unmerited, undeserved (Genesis 19:16 ; Exodus 33:19 ; Jeremiah 42:12). Within the relationship, God's mercy is thus closely linked to forgiveness (Exodus 34:9 ; Numbers 14:19 ; Jeremiah 3:12 ; Dan 9:9), a more basic disposition of compassion (Deuteronomy 13:17) leading to forgiveness, and to the steadfast love by which God sustains the covenant and repeatedly forgives his people (Psalm 25:6 ; 40:11 ; 51:1 ; 69:16 ; 103:4 ; 119:77 ; Jer 3:12 ; 16:5).

2 Salvation, membership in the covenant, and the promises of God all derive logically from the constellation of divine qualities that includes mercy. God's ability to provide, protects, and sustain a people finds its channel and direction through his gracious mercy acted out in historical contexts.

Mercy in the New Testament:

The pattern of God's dealings with people in the Old Testament, at the core of which is mercy, also provides the shape for understanding his dealings in the New Testament. God desires a relationship with humankind, but must show *mercy* to them in order for this relationship to be built. Of course, the New Testament expounds the theme of God's *mercy* in the light of Christ, the supreme expression of love, *mercy*, and grace.

Mercy in the Continuance of God's Covenant:

Meaning that, although the redemptive ministry of Christ comes to be thought of as the clearest expression of God's *mercy*, the Old Testament theme continues to be sounded as the basis for a people of God. In the "Magnificat" Mary recalls the *mercy* of God, God's (*hesed*) - love, expressed in his continuing faithfulness to Israel (Luke 1:50, Luke 1:54, Luke 1:58, Luke 1:72, Luke 1:78). Paul links this same divine commitment of *mercy* to undeserving people in the Old Testament with God's stubborn pursuit of Israel in and through Christ in the New Testament era and its extension to the Gentiles (Romans 9:15-16 Romans 9:23 ; 11:31-32 ; 15:9). This latter thought is taken up in (1 Peter 2:10 NRSV): "Once you were not

Mercy of God as displayed in the Ministry of Christ

a people; but now you are God's people; once you had not received mercy, but now you have received mercy" . Applied with special emphasis to the Gentile believers to remind them of their undeserved blessings, the fact is equally true of Gentiles and Jews: people come into relationship with God only because God shows mercy to them. Similarly, the New Testament writers echo the Old Testament belief that mercy belongs to God (2 Corinthians 1:3 ; James 5:11) and that this resource of mercy is inexhaustible (Ephesians 2:4). For this reason, people can confidently cry out to God for *mercy* in time of need – See (Luke 18:13 ; 2 Timothy 1:16 2 Timothy 1:18 ; cf. Matt 15:22 ; 17:15).

Mercy of God as displayed in the Ministry of Christ:

Meaning - The great Acts of *mercy* shown by God to the people of Israel found intimate expression in the ministry of Christ. The pattern he set, however, was not a new one, for he simply worked out the *mercy* of God at the human level. This is seen most clearly in his Acts of healing. Cleansed of the legion of demons, the healed man is told to return home and declare the *mercy* that God has shown to him (Mark 5:19). The man had received from God without even asking. Others who beseeched Jesus to heal them or people with various afflictions knew that what they requested was for God to "be merciful" (Mathew 15:22 ; 17:15 ; Mark 10:47-48 ; Luke 17:13).

And invariably he was. *Mercy* was manifested in practical help, not simply in a consoling message that God was sympathetic with their plight.

Mercy as the Foundation of Salvation:

Ultimately the mercy of God that Jesus demonstrated in individual salvific Acts becomes for the New Testament writers the illustration of the release from sin and death that God offers to the whole world through the sacrificial death and resurrection of His Son, Jesus Christ. The counterpart to the theme of the establishment of God's covenant with Israel in the Old Testament is the New Testament theme of God's gracious provision of salvation through the work of Christ. Each redemptive act of God the exodus from Egypt and Jesus' crucifixion and resurrection is interrelated. The one grounds and shapes the other, which receives clarity and development through the concept of salvation in the New Testament. What God did for Israel in rescuing them from slavery in Egypt, as He "saved" them, which was also part of the relationship he made with this people. Now in Christ the new from sin forms the basis for the relationship God desires with humankind. But the fundamental factor in each act of God is mercy: God's compassionate love for his creation that leads him to do for it what it cannot do for itself. *Mercy* thus forgives and liberates those who have no right to such blessings.

Mercy of God, Salvation thus rests on the:

Mercy as executed in and through the Christ-event. This is perhaps seen most clearly in Paul's discussion with the Roman Christians about the Gentiles' place in God's family in (Romans 9:15-18) . The point is made that salvation depends utterly on God's *mercy* and that the salvation of the Gentiles is but another display of this *mercy:* "For he (God]) says to Moses, I will have *mercy* on whom I have *mercy*, and I will have compassion on whom I have compassion'" (Romans 9:15) ; quoting (Exodus 33:19). Mercy is such a dominant concept within salvation that the heirs of salvation are called "vessels of mercy" (Romans 9:23) in contrast to those who fail to receive it and are called "vessels of wrath" (Romans 9:22 NRSV). This theme is echoed elsewhere in the New Testament. (1 Peter 1:3) reached back to the Old Testament records of God's establishment of a covenant with Israel and connected them with the new life in Christ to describe the salvation of Christians: "By his great mercy he has given us a new birth through the resurrection of Jesus Christ from the dead". (Titus 3:5 NRSV) declares: "he saved us not because of any works of righteousness that we had done, but according to his mercy". Also, (Ephesians 2:4-5) links the salvation of the Gentiles with God's richness of mercy. Throughout the New Testament it is clear that God's mercy is displayed to the world in Christ.

Mercy of God as the Response of Those to Whom Mercy Has Been Shown:

The gospel meaning to this phrase is that; Beyond viewing salvation as God's great act of *mercy*, the profound effect on the early church that God's mercy had can be seen in several other ways. Paul was conscious that his own rescue from a life as the church's and God's enemy came about because of God's *mercy* His (1 Timothy 1:13 1 Timothy 1:16). Behaviour deserved judgment, but God in his *mercy* bestowed salvation instead. Paul also regarded the right to participate in ministry as a decision of God grounded on his *mercy* (2 Corinthians 4:1). He saw with great sensitivity that even seemingly mundane events were actually manifestations of God's helping mercy (Philippians 2:27). It is this kind of imprint on the heart that made *mercy* a common wish and blessing of one believer to another (2 Timothy 1:16 2, Timothy 1:18), and in some cases the opening greetings of letters included the wish for *mercy* (1 Timothy 1:2 ; 2 Timothy 1:2 ; 2 John 3 ; Jude 2 ; cf. Galatians 6:16). In view of these examples, it is not exaggerating to say that life in Christ gives birth in believers' hearts to a consciousness not only of being recipients of God's mercy in one gift of salvation, but also of being daily recipients of fresh "mercies" of God, emblems of his ownership of us and care for us (Romans 12:1 ; 2 Corinthians 1:3 ; all of the greetings cf. (Lamentation 3:22-

23). In this awareness of God's past, present, and future (Jude 21) mercy toward us, an element of our response to God takes on a new force in the New Testament. Christians are to be channels of God's *mercy* in the church and in the world. Praise the Lord.

2 The awareness in Judaism and early Christianity of the responsibility to show *mercy* is evident in the practice of almsgiving. This practice of *mercy* in the form of charitable giving might be driven by wrong motives (Mathew 6:2-4), but in Luke's writings especially it is cited as an example of true spirituality. Thus in (Luke 11:41) the value of giving alms is placed high above religious rules about purity, which the Pharisees guarded so carefully. In (Luke 12:33) *mercy* as expressed in charitable giving is made a characteristic of discipleship. This specific way of showing *mercy* is praised in the early church (Acts 9:36 ; 10:2) and clearly regarded as an aspect of the normal Christian life (Acts 24:17). In this way Christians become living signs of God's perfect *mercy* introduced in Christ and one day to be fully realized (Acts 3:3 Acts 3:6).

Mercy of God - as a general term in Godliness:

In general terms, to show *mercy* is a characteristic of life in God's kingdom, a demonstration of kingdom power. The beatitude (an announcement of blessing) as in (Matthew 5:7) - showing mercy is one of the marks of righteousness, the gift of God associated with the in breaking of God's kingdom. God has made it possible; therefore his people must do it. In so doing, they mirror the God who has saved them (Luke 6:36) ; the opposite picture in (Mathew 18:33 ;James 2:13). To illustrate fulfilment of the half of God's law given to direct human relationships, Jesus told the parable of the good Samaritan. Thus, showing *mercy* to our "neighbours" is part of the basic response of God's people to his covenant (Luke 10:25-37 ; Leviticus 19:17-18 ; Deuteronomy 6:4-5). Compassion and merciful action on behalf of those around us are the essence of spiritual living. Note: The absence of *mercy* is a sign of unbelief and rejection of God (Romans 1:28 Romans 1:31). The Jews were reprimanded for emphasizing cultic Acts and ignoring mercy toward one another (Hosea 6:6). Jesus took up this reprimand to denounce the legalistic practices of the Pharisees as in (Mathew 9:13). True Christian faith produces genuine compassion and fruit in the form of Acts of mercy toward those in need. It was this characteristic of *mercy* that caused Christ to go among all kinds of people to help. Believers are to respond to the *mercy* shown them in the same way by allowing unending love to flow through the Grace Jesus has given unto us.

Mercy Seat:
(Greek – *hilastérion* - [hil-as-tay'-ree-on], Hebrew: *Kapporet)* Literally, the Seat of Grace. Mostly by which a sin of-

fering is offered to cover sins. (a) a sin offering, by which the wrath of the deity shall be appeased; a means of propitiation, (b) the covering of the ark, which was sprinkled with the atoning blood on the Day of Atonement. 2 A piece of atonement. Made with a lid of solid gold of the Ark of the Covenant, and was connected with the rituals of the Day of Atonement; the term also appears in later Jewish sources, and twice in the New Testament, from where it has significance in Christian theology as relates to the Feast of the Tabancle.

The tabernacle was the portable sanctuary used by the Israelites from the time of their wandering in the wilderness after the Exodus from Egypt to the building of the temple in Jerusalem (Exodus 25–27). Within the tabernacle was the ark of the covenant which included the mercy seat (Hebrews 9:3-5 NKJV). The ark of the covenant, the chest containing the two stone tablets inscribed with the Ten Commandments, was the most sacred object of the tabernacle and later in the temple in Jerusalem, where it was placed in an inner area called the Holy of Holies. Also within the ark were the golden pot of manna, such as was provided by God in the wilderness wanderings (Exodus 16:4) and Aaron's almond rod (Numbers 17:1-13). On top of the ark was a lid called the *mercy seat* on which rested the cloud or visible symbol of the divine presence. Here God was supposed to be seated, and from this place He was supposed to dispense mercy to man when the blood of the atonement was sprinkled there.

3 The *mercy seat* concealed the people of God from the ever-condemning judgment of the Law. Each year on the Day of Atonement, the high priest entered the Holy of Holies and sprinkled the blood of animals sacrificed for the atonement of the sins of God's people. This blood was sprinkled on the *mercy seat*. The point conveyed by this imagery is that it is only through the offering of blood that the condemnation of the Law could be taken away and violations of God's laws covered.

The Greek word for "mercy seat" in (Hebrews 9:5) is hilasterion, which means "that which makes expiation" or "propitiation." It carries the idea of the removal of sin. In (Ezekiel 43:14), the brazen altar of sacrifice is also called hilasterion (the propitiatory or mercy seat) because of its association with the shedding of blood for sin.

In the New Testament, Christ Himself is designated as our "propitiation." Paul explains this in his letter to the Romans: "Being justified freely by His grace through the redemption that is in Christ Jesus, whom God set forth as a propitiation by His blood, through faith, to demonstrate His righteousness, because in His forbearance God had passed over the sins that were previously committed" (Romans 3:24-25 NKJV). What Paul is teaching here is that Jesus is the cover-

Messiah

ing for sin, as shown by these Old Testament prophetic images. By means of His death, and our response to Christ through our faith in Him, all our sins are covered. Also, whenever believers sin, we may turn to Christ who continues to be the propitiation or covering for our sins (1 John 2:1, 4:10). This ties together the Old and New Testament concepts regarding the covering of sin as exemplified by the *mercy-seat* of God. Thank God for His goodness and compassion to mankind.

Messiah: (the anointed one) is a saviour or liberator of a group of people, most commonly in the Abrahamic religions. In the Hebrew Bible, a messiah (or *mashiach*) is a king or High Priest traditionally anointed with holy anointing oil. However, messiahs were not only Jewish, as the Hebrew Bible refers to Cyrus the Great, king of Persia, as a messiah for his decree to rebuild the Jerusalem Temple. The Jewish messiah is a leader anointed by God, physically descended from the Davidic line, who will rule the united tribes of Israel and herald the Messianic Age of global peace also known as the World to Come.

The translation of the Hebrew word *Mašía*▢ as (*Khristós*) in the Greek Septuagint became the accepted Christian designation and title of Jesus of Nazareth. Christians believe that prophecies in the Hebrew Bible (especially Isaiah) refer to a spiritual saviour and believe Jesus to be that Messiah. Islamic tradition holds that Jesus, the son of Mary, was the promised Prophet and *Masîḥ* (Messiah) sent to the Israelites, and that he will again return to Earth at the end of times, along with the *Mahdi*, and they will defeat *Masih ad-Dajjal*, the "false Messiah" or Antichrist. 2 It is the title of the expected leader of the Jews who shall deliver the nation from its enemies and reign in permanent triumph and peace. Equivalent to the Greek word Christ. It is applied by Christians to Jesus (John 4:25)- The woman saith unto him, I know that Messias cometh, which is called Christ: when he is come, he will tell us all things.

Mind: Greek : *nous* – [nooce], Hebrew : *leb* -[labe], meaning the heart, the mind, reasoning faculty, intellect. 2 The set of cognitive faculties that enables consciousness, perception, thinking, judgement, and memory—a characteristic of humans, but which also may apply to other life forms. In the Gospel or the entire Christian life, the mind is a test ground for good or evil, right and wrong, Life and death, Success and failure and finally Heaven or Hell. This means that as a Christian, you are perpetually in a battle–but you are not alone–for all of God's people fight this same fight (Ephesians 6:12). Make up your *mind* not to give up! According to (Colossians

3:2), set your mind on things above and keep it set! As you begin this battle, it will seem worse than ever. The reason is that the demonic powers are fighting to keep their place in your *mind* (and in your thinking). Call upon God's grace in the Name of Jesus, and He will give you the power of the Holy Spirit to overcome every evil tendency fully. Remember, regaining your *mind* is a process. We all fail at one time or another. God knows our weakness; that is why He gave us (1 John 1:9). Just ask for forgiveness and see the Blood of Jesus washing away your sin. Don't give up! Continue claiming what belongs to you (your *mind* and your thinking belong to you), and Jesus will help you overcome as in (2 Timothy 1:7) "For God did not give us a spirit of fear, but of power and of love and of a sound mind!"

Mind, peace of: Meaning rest of the spirit. The expression "peace of mind" conjures up images of Buddha-like composure wherein calm, comfort, and composure are so prevalent that nothing can disturb the one who has peace of mind. An imperturbable, placid person is said to have *peace of mind*. The only time "peace of mind" is found in the Bible is the NIV translation of (2 Corinthians 2:13) where Paul says he found no "peace of mind" because he didn't find Titus in Troas. The literal translation of this phrase is "rest of my spirit." The Bible uses the word peace in several different ways. Peace sometimes refers to a state of friendship between God and man. This peace between a holy God and sinful mankind has been effected by Christ's sacrificial death, "having made peace through the blood of his cross" (Colossians 1:20). In addition, as High Priest the Lord Jesus maintains that state of friendship on behalf of all who continue to "come to God by him, seeing he always lives to make intercession for them" (Hebrews 7:25). This state of friendship with God is a prerequisite for the second kind of peace, that which sometimes refers to a tranquil mind. It is only when "we have peace with God through our Lord Jesus Christ" (Romans 5:1) that we can experience the true peace of mind that is a fruit of the Holy Spirit, in other words, His fruit exhibited in us (Galatians 5:22).

2 Also, (Isaiah 26:3) tells us that God will keep us in "perfect peace" if our minds are "stayed" on Him, meaning our minds lean on Him, centre on Him, and trust in Him. Our tranquillity of mind is "perfect" or imperfect to the degree that the "mind is stayed on" God rather than ourselves or on our problems. Peace is experienced as we believe what the Bible says about God's nearness as in (Psalm 139:1-12), and about His goodness and power, His mercy and love for His children, and His complete sovereignty over all of

Miracle

life's circumstances. But we can't trust someone we don't know, and it is crucial, therefore, to come to know intimately the Prince of Peace, Jesus Christ.

3 Peace of mind also means that Peace is experienced as a result of prayer as in (Philippians 4: 6-7) "Be anxious for nothing, but in everything by prayer and supplication, with thanksgiving, let your requests be made known to God; and the peace of God which surpasses all understanding, will guard your hearts and minds through Christ Jesus". A peaceful mind and heart are experienced as a result of recognizing that an all-wise and loving Father has a purpose in our trials. "We know that all things work together for good to those who love God and are called according to His purpose" (Romans 8:28).

4 God can bring a variety of good things, including peace, from the afflictions that we experience. Even the discipline and chastening of the Lord will "yield the peaceable fruit of righteousness" in our lives (Hebrews 12:11). They provide a fresh opportunity for "hoping in God" and eventually "praising Him" (Psalm 43:5). They help us "comfort" others when they undergo similar trials (2 Corinthians 1:4), and they "achieve for us an eternal glory that far outweighs them all" (2 Corinthians 4:17).

5 *Peace of mind* and the tranquility of spirit that accompanies it are only available when we have true peace with God through the sacrifice of Christ on the cross in payment of our sins. Those who attempt to find peace in worldly pursuits will find themselves sadly deceived. For Christians, however, *peace of mind* is available through the intimate knowledge of, and complete trust in, the God who meets "all your needs according to his glorious riches in Christ Jesus" (Philippians 4:19).

Miracle: *See dunamis*

Miracle Baby: Blessed Child. Unexpected, unplanned, trouble free, but blessed child or birth. Child enjoying 'Hebrew Birth'. 2 Every baby is indeed a miracle, and if you struggled with infertility or health issues with your child, it really makes you appreciate the miracle of life. These baby names are unique and meaningful and perfect for your blessed baby boy or baby girl. 3 Outstanding birth filled with signs and wonders as in (Matthew 1:18-25) Now the birth of Jesus Christ took place in this way. When his mother Mary had been betrothed to Joseph, before they came together she was found to be with child from the Holy Spirit. And her husband Joseph, being a just man and unwilling to put her to shame, resolved to divorce her quietly. But as he considered these things, behold, an angel of the Lord appeared to him in a dream, saying, "Joseph, son of David, do not fear to take Mary as your wife, for that which is conceived in her is from the Holy Spirit. She will bear a son, and you shall call his name Jesus, for he will save his people from their sins." All this took place to fulfill what the Lord had spoken by the prophet: (Acts 2:22) "Men of Israel, hear these words: Jesus of Nazareth, a man attested to you by God with mighty works and wonders and signs that God did through him in your midst, as you yourselves know— (John 1:1) In the beginning was the Word, and the Word was with God, and the Word was God. (Mark 16:18) They will pick up serpents with their hands; and if they drink any deadly poison, it will not hurt them; they will lay their hands on the sick, and they will recover." (Mark 11:12-14) On the following day, when they came from Bethany, he was hungry. And seeing in the distance a fig tree in leaf, he went to see if he could find anything on it. When he came to it, he found nothing but leaves, for it was not the season for figs. And he said to it, "May no one ever eat fruit from you again." And his disciples heard it. (Isaiah 9:6) For to us a child is born, to us a son is given; and the government shall be upon his shoulder, and his name shall be called Wonderful Counselor, Mighty God, Everlasting Father, Prince of Peace.

Miracle Man: Man endowed with might, power, marvellous works, physical power, force, might, ability, efficacy, energy, meaning 2 plural: powerful deeds, deeds showing (physical) power, marvellous works. Example - Elijah who loved and served God. Everywhere he went, God used him to perform amazing miracles and warn people who did wrong. He was fed by ravens and brought a boy back to life. As you read about Elijah in (1 King 18 and 2 Kings 2) learn more about God and his purpose for our lives. 3 Note also that Jesus while on earth was also the Miracle Man ever seen on the necked eyes as narrated in the four canonical Gospels contain that contains six stores of Jesus giving sight to one or more blind people. Three of these periscopes may or may not be independent traditions, since their settings and details are very different (Mark 8:22-26; Mathew 9:27-31; John 9:1-7). The other three periscopes are clearly parallel versions of the same synoptic tradition, despite some differences in the details (Mark 10:48-52; Mathew 20:29-34; Luke 18:35-43).There are several other miracle men in the Bible that you would discover when searching the Gospel.

Miracle Woman: This does not really need to connote women filled with powers to perform miracles but has to do with women with strong faith like the "woman with an issue of blood" and other variants) is one of the miracles of Jesus in the Gospels (Mark 5:21-43, Matthew 9:18-26,

Money

Luke 8:40-56). The woman's condition, which is not clear in terms of a modern medical diagnosis, is translated as an "issue of blood" in the King James Version and a "flux of blood" in the Wycliffe Bible and some other versions. In scholarly language she is often referred to by the original New Testament Greek term as the haemorrhoissa ("bleeding woman"). In the Gospel accounts, this miracle immediately follows the exorcism at Gerasa and is combined with the miracle of the Daughter of Jairus. The incident occurred while Jesus was traveling to Jairus' house, amid a large crowd: And a woman was there who had been subject to bleeding for twelve years. She had suffered a great deal under the care of many doctors and had spent all she had, yet instead of getting better she grew worse. When she heard about Jesus, she came up behind him in the crowd and touched his cloak, because she thought, "If I just touch his clothes, I will be healed." Immediately her bleeding stopped and she felt in her body that she was freed from her suffering.

At once Jesus realized that power had gone out from him. He turned around in the crowd and asked, "Who touched my clothes?" "You see the people crowding against you," his disciples answered, "and yet you can ask, 'Who touched me?' " But Jesus kept looking around to see who had done it. Then the woman, knowing what had happened to her, came and fell at his feet and, trembling with fear, told him the whole truth. He said to her, "Daughter, your faith has healed you. Go in peace and be freed from your suffering."

Search the scripture for many other women of strong faith – the Miracle women, build your faith accordingly as a Christian to please God.

Money: (Greek: nomisma, Hebrew: Kesaph [kes-af']) Silver, or Any item or verifiable record that is generally accepted as payment for goods and services and repayment of debts in a particular country or socio-economic entity. The main functions of money are distinguished as: a medium of exchange; a unit of account; a store of value; and, perhaps, a standard of deferred payment. Any item or verifiable record that fulfils these functions can be considered money.

Note: There is no promise in the Bible that being a Christian will lead to a good job, wealth, freedom from debt, etc. One verse is sometimes cited:In (Jeremiah 29:11) For I know the plans I have for you," declares the Lord, "plans to prosper you and not to harm you, plans to give you hope and a future". In context, this verse was directed specifically to the Israelite exiles in Babylon. The original Hebrew word translated as "prosperity" can mean peace, completeness, safety, health, satisfaction or blessings. It does not imply financial prosperity. This translation probably comes closer to the intended meaning: For I know the plans I have for you," says the Lord. "They are plans for good and not for disaster, to give you a future and a hope. God's faithful people may be rich or poor (2 Chronicles 17:3-5, Job 1:1-3, Matthew 27:57, Mark 12:41-44, Luke 16:19-22, 19:2-9, Proverbs 22:2, Luke 6:20). With money one can acquire the end product and necessity for life – wealth. Jesus saw wealth as a gift from God to be used in His service (Matthew 25:14-30). Those who have been blessed with wealth must share generously with the poor (Matthew 25:31-46), and avoid the sins of arrogance (1 Timothy 6:17-19), dishonesty (Exodus 20:15, Mark 10:19, Luke 3:12-14) and greed (Luke 12:13-21).

2 Those of us who are blessed with wealth beyond our need have a responsibility to share generously with the less fortunate. We should view our wealth as a gift from God, entrusted to us, to carry out His work on earth. If anyone has material possessions and sees his brother in need but has no pity on him, how can the love of God be in him? (1 John 3:17) NIV. What God give to us is the spirit of Love, power and sound mind. See the Scripture in (1 Timothy 6:17-19) NIV, "Command those who are rich in this present world not to be arrogant nor to put their hope in wealth, which is so uncertain, but to put their hope in God, who richly provides us with everything for our enjoyment. Command them to do good, to be rich in good deeds, and to be generous and willing to share. In this way they will lay up treasure for themselves as a firm foundation for the coming age, so that they may take hold of the life that is truly life".

3 Money is historically an emergent market phenomenon establishing a commodity money, but nearly all contemporary money systems are based on fiat money. Fiat money, like any check or note of debt, is without intrinsic use value as a physical commodity talk less of eternity treasury value. Then Jesus looked around and said to his disciples, "How hard it will be for those who have wealth to enter the kingdom of God!" And the disciples were perplexed at these words. But Jesus said to them again, "Children, how hard it is to enter the kingdom of God! It is easier for a camel to go through the eye of a needle than for someone who is rich to enter the kingdom of God." They were greatly astounded and said to one another, "Then who can be saved?" Jesus looked at them and said, "For mortals it is impossible, but not for God; for God all things are possible." (NRSV, Mark 10:23-27) It is not that wealth is intrinsically evil, or that poverty is blessed. Rather, a devotion to gathering wealth is incompatible with devotion to God. God must always be the most

Money is the route of all Evils:

important thing in our lives:

"No one can serve two masters. For you will hate one and love the other, or be devoted to one and despise the other. You cannot serve both God and money." (NLT, Luke 16:13)

Money is the route of all Evils: The craving for wealth and possessions can lead us into all kinds of temptation. While we spend evenings and weekends earning extra money, we are depriving our families of our love and attention. We may take unfair advantage of our customers, employers, or employees. We may attempt to rationalize our greed by closing our minds and hearts to the needs and rights of others. In the process, we could end up being stingy, bitter and isolated. (Proverbs 23:4-5) "Do not wear yourself out to get rich; have the wisdom to show restraint. Cast but a glance at riches, and they are gone, for they will surely sprout wings and fly off to the sky like an eagle". What good will it be for a man if he gains the whole world, yet forfeits his soul? Or what can a man give in exchange for his soul? (NIV, Matthew 16:26)

2 Those who want to get rich fall into temptation and a trap and into many foolish and harmful desires that plunge people into ruin and destruction. For the love of money is a root of all kinds of evil. Some people, eager for money, have wandered from the faith and pierced themselves with many grief's. (1 Timothy 6:9-11, emphasis added) "Do not store up for yourselves treasures on earth, where moth and rust destroy, and where thieves break in and steal. But store up for yourselves treasures in heaven, where moth and rust do not destroy, and where thieves do not break in and steal. For where your treasure is, there your heart will be also. (NIV, Matthew 6:19-21)

References (Matthew 13:22, Luke 12:15, 1 Timothy 6:17-19, James 5:1-5). (Hebrews 13:5) Keep your life free from love of money, and be content with what you have, for he has said, "I will never leave you nor forsake you." (1 Timothy 6:10) For the love of money is a root of all kinds of evils. It is through this craving that some have wandered away from the faith and pierced themselves with many pangs. (Matthew 6:24) "No one can serve two masters, for either he will hate the one and love the other, or he will be devoted to the one and despise the other. You cannot serve God and money. (Proverbs 22:7) The rich rules over the poor, and the borrower is the slave of the lender. (Ecclesiastes 5:10) He who loves money will not be satisfied with money, nor he who loves wealth with his income; this also is vanity. (Matthew 6:31-33) Therefore do not be anxious, saying, 'What shall we eat?' or 'What shall we drink?' or 'What shall we wear?' For the Gentiles seek after all these things, and your heavenly Father knows that you need them all. But seek first the kingdom of God and his righteousness, and all these things will be added to you. (Proverbs 13:11) Wealth gained hastily will dwindle, but whoever gathers little by little will increase it. (Matthew 6:19-21) "Do not lay up for yourselves treasures on earth, where moth and rust destroy and where thieves break in and steal, but lay up for yourselves treasures in heaven, where neither moth nor rust destroys and where thieves do not break in and steal. For where your treasure is, there your heart will be also.

Money, Bad: This signifies unmerited gains or taking unusual advantage of other's benefits or interest. The rationalization required to obtain and keep dishonest gain can make a person cold, cynical and separated from God. It may be taking unfair advantage or misrepresenting the facts to employers, employees, customers, clients or associates. It may be stealing, fraud, inflating insurance claims, cheating on taxes, "pirating" music and movies, wilful non-payment of debts, or any form of dishonesty for personal gain. In whatever form, dishonest gain brings only fear of discovery - never peace of mind.

As warned in (Leviticus 19:13) NAS "You shall not oppress your neighbour, nor rob him. The wages of a hired man are not to remain with you all night until morning". Also, notes, "The LORD abhors dishonest scales, but accurate weights are his delight". (NIV, Proverbs 11:1)

2 He who walks righteously and speaks what is right, who rejects gain from extortion and keeps his hand from accepting bribes, who stops his ears against plots of murder and shuts his eyes against contemplating evil-- this is the man who will dwell on the heights, whose refuge will be the mountain fortress. His bread will be supplied, and water will not fail him. (NIV, Isaiah 33:15-16) (Romans 13: 1, 6-7) asserts, "Let every person be subject to the governing authorities; for there is no authority except from God, and those authorities that exist have been instituted by God... For the same reason you also pay taxes, for the authorities are God's servants, busy with this very thing. Pay to all what is due them - taxes to whom taxes are due, revenue to whom revenue is due, respect to whom respect is due, honor to whom honour is due". Glory to God!

Refernces: (Exodus 20:15, Leviticus 19:35-36, Proverbs 21:6, Amos 8:4-8, Micah 6:10-13, Mark 10:19, Luke 3:12-14).

Mother: (Greek: Mama, Hebrew: Amah) or mum/mom/mam(s)) are women who inhabit or perform the role of bearing

Mother

some relation to their children, who may or may not be their biological offspring. Thus, dependent on the context, women can be considered mothers by virtue of having given birth, by raising their child(ren), supplying their ovum for fertilization, or some combination thereof. Such conditions provide a way of delineating the concept of motherhood, or the state of being a mother. Women who meet the third and first categories usually fall under the terms 'birth mother' or 'biological mother', regardless of whether the individual in question goes on to parent their child. Accordingly, a woman who meets only the second condition may be considered an adoptive mother, and those who meet only the third a surrogacy mother.

2 Being a mother is a very important role that the Lord chooses to give to many women. A Christian mother is told to love her children (Titus 2:4-5), in part so that she does not bring reproach on the Lord and on the Saviour whose name she bears. Children are a gift from the Lord (Psalm 127:3-5). In (Titus 2:4), the Greek word *philoteknos* appears in reference to mothers loving their children. This word represents a special kind of "mother love." The idea that flows out of this word is that of caring for our children, nurturing them, affectionately embracing them, meeting their needs, and tenderly befriending each one as a unique gift from the hand of God. Several things are commanded of Christian mothers in God's Word: Availability – morning, noon, and night (Deuteronomy 6:6-7) Involvement – interacting, discussing, thinking, and processing life together (Ephesians 6:4) Teaching – the Scriptures and a biblical worldview (Psalm 78:5-6; Deuteronomy 4:10; Ephesians 6:4) Training – helping a child to develop skills and discover his or her strengths (Proverbs 22:6) and spiritual gifts (Romans 12:3-8 and 1 Corinthians 12) Discipline – teaching the fear of the Lord, drawing the line consistently, lovingly, firmly (Ephesians 6:4; Hebrews 12:5-11; Proverbs 13:24; 19:18; 22:15; 23:13-14; 29:15-17) Nurture – providing an environment of constant verbal support, freedom to fail, acceptance, affection, unconditional love (Titus 2:4; 2 Timothy 1:7; Ephesians 4:29-32; 5:1-2; Galatians 5:22; 1 Peter 3:8-9) Modeling with Integrity – living what you say, being a model from which a child can learn by "catching" the essence of godly living (Deuteronomy 4:9, 15, 23; Proverbs 10:9; 11:3; Psalm 37:18, 37).

3 The Bible never states that every woman should be a mother. However, it does say that those whom the Lord blesses to be mothers should take the responsibility seriously. Mothers have a unique and crucial role in the lives of their children. Motherhood is not a chore or unpleasant task. Just as a mother bears a child during pregnancy, and just as a

mother feeds and cares for a child during infancy, so mothers also play an on-going role in the lives of their children, whether they are adolescents, teenagers, young adults, or even adults with children of their own. While the role of motherhood must change and develop, the love, care, nurture, and encouragement a mother gives should never cease.

4 The above concepts defining the role of mother are neither exhaustive, nor universal as any definition of 'mother' may differ based on how social, cultural, and religious roles are defined. The parallel conditions and terms for males: those who are (typically biologically) fathers do not, by definition, take up the role of fatherhood. It should also be noted that mother and fatherhood are not limited to those who are or have parented. Women who are pregnant may be referred to as expectant mothers or mothers-to-be, though such applications tend to be less readily applied to (biological) fathers or adoptive parents.

Mourn: Greek: *Pentheó* [pentheh'-o] Hebrew: *abal* [aw-bal'] 1 mourn, lament, feel guilt, I grief. 2 Feel or show sorrow for the death of (someone), typically by following conventions such as the wearing of black clothes. Grief.

2 Mourning or Grief is an emotion common to the human experience, and we witness the process of grief throughout the biblical narrative. Multiple Bible characters experienced deep loss and sadness, including Job, Naomi, Hannah, and David. Even Jesus mourned (John 11:35; Matthew 23:37-39). After Lazarus died, Jesus went to the village of Bethany, where Lazarus was buried. When Jesus saw Martha and the other mourners weeping, He also wept. He was moved by their grief and also by the fact of Lazarus's death. The astounding thing is that, even though Jesus knew He was going to raise Lazarus from the dead, He chose to partake of the grief of the situation. Jesus truly is a high priest who can "sympathize with our weaknesses" (Hebrews 4:15).

Mourning or Grief, Steps on overcoming: One step in overcoming grief is having the right perspective on it. First, we recognize that grief is a natural response to pain and loss. There is nothing wrong with grieving. Second, we know that times of grief serve a purpose. Ecclesiastes 7:2 says, "It is better to go to the house of mourning than to go to the house of feasting, for this is the end of all mankind, and the living will lay it to heart." This verse implies that grief can be good because it can refresh our perspective on life. Third, we remember that feelings of grief are temporary. "Weeping may remain for a night, but rejoicing comes in the morning" (Psalm 30:5). There is an end to mourning. Grief has its purpose,

Mouth

but it also has its limit. Through it all, God is faithful. There are many Scriptures that remind us of God's faithfulness in times of mourning. He is with us even in the valley of the shadow of death (Psalm 23:4). When David sorrowed, he prayed this in (Psalm 56:8): "You have kept count of my tossing's; put my tears in your bottle. Are they not in your book?". The touching image of God catching our tears is full of meaning. He sees our grief and does not disdain it. Like Jesus entered into the grief of the mourners in Bethany, God enters into our grief. At the same time, He reassures us that all is not lost. (Psalm 46:10) reminds us to "be still" and rest in the knowledge that He is God. He is our refuge (Psalm 91:1-2). He works all things together for the good of those He has called (Romans 8:28).

2 An important part of overcoming grief is expressing it to God. The Psalms contain numerous examples of pouring out one's heart to God. Interestingly, the psalmist never ends where he began. He may start a psalm with expressions of grief, but, almost invariably, he will end it with praise (Psalm 13; Psalm 23:4; Psalm 30:11-12; Psalm 56). God understands us (Psalm 139:2). When we commune with Him, we are able to open our minds to the truth that He loves us, that He is faithful, that He is in control, and that He knows how He is going to work it out for our good.

3 Another important step in overcoming grief is to share it with others. The body of Christ is designed to ease the burdens of its individual members (Galatians 6:2), and fellow believers have the ability to "mourn with those who mourn" (Romans 12:15). Often, the grieving tend to shun others, increasing feelings of isolation and misery. It is much healthier to seek counselling, and group settings can be invaluable. Groups offer listening ears and helpful encouragement, camaraderie, and guidance in working through the grief. When we share our stories with God and others, our grief is lessened.

4 Sadly, grief is part of the human experience. Loss is part of life, and grief is a natural response to loss. But we have the hope of Christ, and we know that He is strong enough to carry our burdens (Matthew 11:30). We can give our hurt to Him because He cares for us (1 Peter 5:7). We can find solace in the Holy Spirit, our Comforter and Paraclete (John 14:16). In grief, we cast our burdens on Him, rely on the community of the church, delve into the truth of the Word, and ultimately experience hope (Hebrews 6:19-20). Be strong in the Lord. Hallelujah!

Mouth: *(noun, Greek-Stoma - [stom'-a], Hebrew: Peh [peh]; the mouth, speech, eloquence in speech, the point of a sword. The oral cavity, buccal cavity, or in Latin cavum oris, is the opening

Mouth

through which many animals take in food and issue vocal sounds. It is also the cavity lying at the upper end of the alimentary canal, bounded on the outside by the lips and inside by the pharynx and containing in higher vertebrates the tongue and teeth. This cavity is also known as the buccal cavity derived from the Latin bucca meaning a "cheek". Some animal phyla, including vertebrates, have a complete digestive system, with a mouth at one end and an anus at the other. Which end forms first in ontogeny is a criterion used to classify animals into protostome and deuterostome (Ecclesiastes 5:1-9) Solomon writes in (verse 1), "Guard your steps as you go to the house of God and draw near to listen rather than to offer the sacrifice of fools; for they do not know they are doing evil." This verse is rather meaty because it encapsulates two important issues: our preparation for worship and our participation in worship. The first emphasis is upon our preparation for worship. Since Solomon built the Old Testament temple, he was an expert on how to approach God. It took him seven years and 153,000 men to build the temple, so he knows a thing or two., Solomon's first words are a command to "guard your steps." This is a common expression in our culture. Solomon warns you to "guard your step as you go to the house of God." This seems out of the ordinary to our modern culture. We have warnings about sin, temptation, and unbelief, but a warning about how to worship seems unusual to our ears. Our problem is that we do not take worship seriously enough. We tend to think that as long as we are worshiping the Lord, it does not really matter how we worship. But the Scriptures teach otherwise. So sacred was God's house that the Lord said to Moses in (Leviticus 15:31): "Thus you shall keep the sons of Israel separated from their uncleanness, so that they will not die in their uncleanness by their defiling My tabernacle that is among them." God at times actually took the lives of those who failed to come to His house in the right way, as a warning to the whole nation that they were dealing with a holy God. So, mouth is the executor of achieving and loosing as its pronounces the content of the heart – the word.

References:(Ephesians 4:29) Let no corrupting talk come out of your mouths, but only such as is good for building up, as fits the occasion, that it may give grace to those who hear. (Jeremiah 1:9) Then the Lord put out his hand and touched my mouth. And the Lord said to me, "Behold, I have put my words in your mouth. (Matthew 15:11) It is not what goes into the mouth that defiles a person, but what comes out of the mouth; this defiles a person." (James 3:10) From the same mouth come blessing and cursing. My broth-

Mysterious

ers, these things ought not to be so. (James 3:8) But no human being can tame the tongue. It is a restless evil, full of deadly poison. (James 3:5-6) So also the tongue is a small member, yet it boasts of great things. How great a forest is set ablaze by such a small fire! And the tongue is a fire, a world of unrighteousness. The tongue is set among our members, staining the whole body, setting on fire the entire course of life, and set on fire by hell. (Hebrews 4:12) For the word of God is living and active, sharper than any two-edged sword, piercing to the division of soul and of spirit, of joints and of marrow, and discerning the thoughts and intentions of the heart.

Mysterious: Baffling, star cryptic, star curious, star dark, star enigmatic, star inexplicable, star inscrutable, star magical, star mystical, star mystifying, star obscure, star perplexing, star puzzling, star secretive, star strange, star unknown, star weird, star abstruse, star alchemistic, star arcane, star astrological, star cabalistic, star covert, star difficult, star enigmatical, star equivocal star esoteric, star furtive, star hidden, star impenetrable, star incomprehensible, star insoluble, star necromantic, star occult, star oracular, star recondite, star sphinx like, star spiritual, star subjective star symbolic, star transcendental, star uncanny, star unfathomable, star unknowable, star unnatural, star veiled, star Antonyms for mysterious. *See mystery below.*

References: (2 Peter 2:20) For if, after they have escaped the defilements of the world through the knowledge of our Lord and Saviour Jesus Christ, they are again entangled in them and overcome, the last state has become worse for them than the first. (Hebrews 1:6) And again, when he brings the firstborn into the world, he says, "Let all God's angels worship him." (Titus 2:13) Waiting for our blessed hope, the appearing of the glory of our great God and Saviour Jesus Christ, (Titus 2:12) Training us to renounce ungodliness and worldly passions, and to live self-controlled, upright, and godly lives in the present age, (2 Timothy 3:16) All Scripture is breathed out by God and profitable for teaching, for reproof, for correction, and for training in righteousness, (1 Corinthians 13:1-13) If I speak in the tongues of men and of angels, but have not love, I am a noisy gong or a clanging cymbal. And if I have prophetic powers, and understand all mysteries and all knowledge, and if I have all faith, so as to remove mountains, but have not love, I am nothing. If I give away all I have, and if I deliver up my body to be burned, but have not love, I gain nothing. Love is patient and kind; love does not envy or boast; it is not arrogant or rude. It does not insist on its own way; it is not irritable or resentful; (Acts 15:1-4) But some men came down from Judea and were teaching the brothers, "Unless you are circumcised according to the custom of Moses, you cannot be saved." And after Paul and Barnabas had no small dissension and debate with them, Paul and Barnabas and some of the others were appointed to go up to Jerusalem to the apostles and the elders about this question. So, being sent on their way by the church, they passed through both Phoenicia and Samaria, describing in detail the conversion of the Gentiles, and brought great joy to all the brothers. When they came to Jerusalem, they were welcomed by the church and the apostles and the elders, and they declared all that God had done with them. But some believers who belonged to the party of the Pharisees rose up and said, "It is necessary to circumcise them and to order them to keep the law of Moses." (Acts 2:38) And Peter said to them, "Repent and be baptized every one of you in the name of Jesus Christ for the forgiveness of your sins, and you will receive the gift of the Holy Spirit.

Mystery: (Noun, Greek: *Mustérion* - [moos-tay'-ree-on] Hebrew: *raz* - [rawz] Anything hidden, a mystery, secret, of which initiation is necessary; in the New Testament: the counsels of God, once hidden but now revealed in the Gospel or some fact thereof; the Christian revelation generally; particular truths or details of the Christian revelation. 2 the secret rites of Greek and Roman pagan religion, or of any ancient or tribal religion, to which only initiates are admitted. 3 a religious belief based on divine revelation, especially one regarded as beyond human understanding. 4 something that is difficult or impossible to understand or explain. Often times the phrases "the mystery of iniquity," "the mysteries of the kingdom," "the mystery of godliness," "the mystery of the church," and so on are spoken, "Mystery" in the Gospel refers to something that has not yet been revealed. These mysteries are revelations of new information about God's plan that has not yet been disclosed, but is disclosed in the Scriptures, especially through the writings of the apostle Paul. The church is a "mystery" in this sense, as we are told in (Ephesians 3:3-6). It was not revealed in the Old Testament. The prophets spoke about the kingdom, but they did not speak about the church, nor did they speak of the rapture of the church. The rapture is something that pertains to the church, not to Israel. The rapture was not revealed in the Old Testament.

Mystery of the catching away of the saints: Paul asserts in (I Corinthians 15:51) "Behold, I show you a *mystery*; We shall not all sleep, but we shall all be changed." Not a single text in the Old Testament speaks of this catching away. In (Romans 11:25), where Paul writes, "For I would not, brethren, that ye should be ignorant of this *mystery*...." "This mystery" has to do with Israel's spiritual blindness. It was no *mystery* that there was blindness in Israel, deep, profound, and spiritual. However, the new item of information that is being revealed here is the scheduling of the removal of Israel's blindness. Paul is addressing the question, "If Israel constitutes the covenant people of God how do you explain Israel's current blindness?" Paul explains the *mystery* of it all. This blindness will be removed when the full number of the Gentiles has been brought in, and then God will begin to work mightily among the Jews.

Mystery of Iniquity: Another important "mystery" is in (II Thessalonians 2:7), "For the *mystery* of iniquity doth already work: only he who now letteth will let, until he be taken out of the way." The apostle is speaking about the power of evil that is already at work in the world, and that the restrained is limiting this power and the scope of its influence for the present time. However, one day the, restrained will be taken away. Here the apostle is speaking about Satan's plan for the man of sin, the Antichrist, and how he will come on the scene in the Tribulation. It is a *mystery* because we would not be able to figure it out through natural and unaided human reason.

Mystery of the Kingdom: Matthew 13, Mark 4, and Luke 8 speak about the "mysteries of the Kingdom." What this mean is that; If you look at the context of these passages you will find that Jesus is teaching His disciples hidden truths concerning God's Kingdom plan in the light of Israel's rejection of her Messiah. The Kingdom had been offered to Israel, but Israel has rejected her Messiah and, consequently, the Kingdom plan as revealed in the Old Testament has been postponed. What happens to the Kingdom between His First and Second Advents? We may summarize the teaching as to the course of the age that, there will be a sowing of the Word throughout the age, which will be imitated by a false counter-sowing; the kingdom will assume huge outer proportions, but be marked by inner doctrinal corruption; yet, the Lord will gain for Himself a peculiar treasure from among Israel, and from the church; the age will end in judgment with the unrighteous excluded from the kingdom to be inaugurated and the righteous taken in to enjoy the blessing of Messiah's reign.

2 Indeed, this very one is a good designation for the *mystery*. The Kingdom, as proclaimed in the Old Testament, will be glorious. Christ will be honoured around the world, and He will rule from Jerusalem. But the form that the Kingdom takes during the Church Age is very different. It is unlike the Kingdom proclaimed in the Old Testament. It is the "mystery

form of the kingdom."

Mystery of the emerging Church: The Emerging Church and the Mega church Movement somehow fit into the mystery form of the kingdom. The Mustard Seed in (Matthew 13:31) and following depicts the kingdom growth in the present age. But it depicts growth that is unhealthy. A mustard seed grows into a monstrosity as in (Matthew 13:32) "the birds of the air come and lodge in the branches thereof." You will remember that in the Parable of the Sower, also found in (Matthew 13), birds represent Satan's agents. They devour the Word of God. Birds are never used in the Bible to indicate Christians. They are scavengers and feed off of rotting meat. In (Revelation 19:18) the fowls that fly in the midst of heaven come and eat "the flesh of kings, and the flesh of captains, and the flesh of mighty men and the flesh of horses."

And we must not neglect the fact that right after the Parable of the Mustard Seed we are told the parable of the leaven. It says, "The kingdom of heaven is like unto leaven, which a woman took and hid in three measures of meal, till the whole was leavened." Leaven is a symbol of evil and corruption. The mysteries of the kingdom is that in its mystery the form the kingdom would show itself is in a corrupted and debased form. This is what we have in the 21st century.

Mock, God is not: To mock God is to disrespect, dishonour, or ignore Him. It is a serious offense committed by those who have no fear of God or who deny His existence. The most easily recognized form of mockery is disrespect typified by verbal insults or other acts of disdain. It is associated with ridicule, scoffing, and defiance. Mockery is a dishonouring attitude that shows low estimation, contempt, or even open hostility. In the Christian Gospel as contain in the Bible, mockery is a behaviour and attitude shown by the fool (Psalm 74:22), the wicked (Psalm 1:1), the enemy (Psalm 74:10), the hater of knowledge (Proverbs 1:22; 13:1), the proud (Psalm 119:51; Isaiah 37:17), and the unteachable (Proverbs 15:12). A mocker goes beyond mere lack of judgment to making a conscious decision for evil. Mockers are without a spirit of obedience, teach ability, discernment, wisdom, worship, or faith.

2 Those who mock God will mock the people of God as well. The prophet Jeremiah "became the laughingstock of all my people" and was mocked "in song all day long" (Lamentations 3:14). Mockery of God's prophets was commonplace (2 Chronicles 36:16). Nehemiah was mocked by his enemies (Nehemiah 2:19). Elisha was mocked by the youths of Bethel (2 Kings 2:23). And of course our Lord Jesus was mocked—by Herod

Mock, God is not

and his soldiers (Luke 23:11), by the Roman soldiers (Mark 15:20; Luke 23:36), by a thief on a cross (Luke 23:39), and by the Jewish leaders who passed by the cross (Matthew 27:41).

3 It is easy for us as believers to point the finger at those outside the church who mock God. But the most subtle mockery of God, and the most dangerous, comes from those of us sitting in church. We are guilty of mockery when we behave with an outward show of spirituality or godliness without an inward engagement or change of heart.

4 Invariably, "to mock God is to pretend to love and serve him when we do not; to act in a false manner, to be insincere and hypocritical in our professions, pretending to obey him, love, serve, and worship him, when we do not. . . . Mocking God grieves the Holy Spirit, and sears the conscience; and thus the bands of sin become stronger and stronger. The heart becomes gradually hardened by such a process." God warns that mockery of what is holy will be punished. Zephaniah predicted the downfall of Moab and Ammon, saying, "This is what they will get in return for their pride, for insulting and mocking the people of the LORD Almighty" (Zephaniah 2:10, Isaiah 28:22) warns that mockery will cause the chains of Judah's sin to become stronger and that destruction will follow.

(Proverbs 3:34) says that God will mock the mocker but give favour to the humble and oppressed. (2 Kings 2:24) records the punishment that befell the youths who jeered Elisha. This is what it means that God is not mocked. There are repercussions for ignoring God's directives and wilfully choosing sin. Adam and Eve tried and brought sorrow and death into the world (Genesis 2:15–17; 3:6, 24). Ananias and Sapphira's deception brought about a swift and public judgment (Acts 5:1–11). Galatians 6:7 states a universal principle: "Do not be deceived: God cannot be mocked. A man reaps what he sows."

5 God cannot be deceived (Hebrews 4:12–13). Achan's sin (Joshua 7) and Jonah's flight (Jonah 1) were not unknown to God. Jesus' repeated words to every church in Revelation 2—3 were, "I know your works." We only deceive ourselves when we think our attitudes and actions are not seen by an all-powerful and all-knowing God. The Bible shows us the way to live a blessed life, sometimes by the good examples of godly men and women and sometimes by the negative examples of those who choose to follow another path. (Psalm 1:1–3) says, "Blessed is the one who does not walk in step with the wicked or stand in the way that sinners take or sit in the company of mockers, but whose delight is in the law of the Lord, and who meditates on his law

day and night. That person is like a tree planted by streams of water, which yields its fruit in season and whose leaf does not wither—whatever they do prospers."

6 The term to mock, in its gospel sense, means to act hypocritically; to make false pretences or professions. We sometimes speak of having our hopes mocked, that is, they are disappointed. To be a mocker is to be hypocritical, to make false pretences, representations that are not true. To mock God is to pretend to love and serve him when we do not; to act in a false manner, to be insincere and hypocritical in our professions, pretending to obey him, love, serve, and worship him, when we do not. Anything that amounts to insincerity is mockery, anything that is only pretence, and does not represent the state of the heart. The term to mock, in ordinary language, means to dishonour. In this sense it is that God is mocked by not being honoured. He is not dishonoured really, but only so far as man is concerned. When it is said in the Bible, "God is not mocked," means 'God is not dishonoured' really, although individuals do that which would dishonour him, if he could be dishonoured or be a man or the son of man which He could lie. But Glory be to His name for He is not a man nor the son of man which He could lie. So Jesus must always be honoured in our lives every moment of our time. Hallelujah!

Mountain, Faith will move:

Late 19th century proverbs, meaning that with the help of faith something naturally impossible can be achieved; in allusion to the gospel of Christ or the word of God from the Bible – as Jesus replied to His disciples when they met Him privately in (Matthew 17:20 -21) thus' "Then the disciples came to Jesus privately and said, "Why could we not drive it out?" And He said to them, "Because of the littleness of your faith; for truly I say to you, if you have faith the size of a mustard seed, you will say to this mountain, 'Move from here to there,' and it will move; and nothing will be impossible to you. "But this kind does not go out except by prayer and fasting." 2 Christians, for you to move mountain – which also means getting your problems solve or gaining victory or overcoming that horrible situation confronting you, you must do a great deal of faithful prayer and fasting praying in the name of JESUS with faith.

Name above all names

Nn

Name above all names: (Hebrew: YAHWEH) The name above all names is a powerful phrase connoting the impartation of authority. Inside the Ten Commandments contains 613 Laws. That was given to Moses (Mosheh) to teach to the Children of Israel (Known in Hebrew as Israyl). He vowed an oath saying that those who would truly obey His voice and walk in all his ways would be a "special treasure"' to Him. He also promised that He would establish these Law-abiding people as his holy people as in (Exodus 19:5-6)— "Now therefore, if you will truly obey My voice, by keeping My covenant, then you shall be a special treasure to Me above all people; for all the earth is Mine. And you shall be to Me a kingdom of priests, and a holy nation... (Deuteronomy 28:9-10) — Yahweh will establish you as His Holy People unto Himself, as He promised you on oath, if you will keep the Laws of Yahweh your Father, and walk in all His ways.

Then all the people on the earth will see that you are called by the Name of Yahweh, and they will fear you. These Scriptures show that all the people of the earth will see that Yahweh's holy people (those who walk in all of Yahweh's Ways) are known by the name of Yahweh. There has never been an inspired Scripture written in the Torah or by the prophets telling us that Yahweh's holy people would ever be called (known) by any other name. In fact, the Prophet Yahyl was inspired to write a wonderful prophecy concerning everyone who calls with the name of Yahweh.

2 While this was in the Old Testament, the Scripture became fulfilled in the New Testament as could be seen in the attitude of Christ. In (Philippians 2:9) "Being found in appearance as a man, He humbled Himself by becoming obedient to the point of death, even death on a cross. For this reason also, God highly exalted Him, and bestowed on Him the name which is *above every name*, so that at the name of Jesus EV-

ERY KNEE WILL BOW, of those who are in heaven and on earth and under the earth, this is begotten – The eternal delegation of Authority in God. Which means upon all the Old Testament people and those in the New Testament, Christ alone abides by the Law and no other Law can accursed Him any more so that it is the turn of gracious impact of exoneration through Grace. Being so exonerated, He is exalted above every condition of the Law. That is by His resurrection from the dead, Grace has taken over because the curse of the Law has been broken, taken away, Invariably, the Name YAHWEH – Name above all Names, meaning ranking with authority above every other authority, designation above every other designation, nicknaming above every other nicknaming is now called in Gracious way – Jesus. Not as YAHWEH anymore for in the old dispensation it was against the Hebrews Law to pronounce the name above all names –YAHWEH.

Again, in the days of John the Baptist and the Son of God, the preserved language of the devout Jews was Hebrew. So, when the angel Gabriel brought the good news to the Hebrew virgin, Miriam (or Mary in English), that she would give birth to the Saviour of the world, and told her what His name would be, what language do you suppose he spoke? Hebrew, of course! And certainly Miriam and Yoceph (or Joseph in English) named the child just as the angel had commanded them — Yahshua. In (Matthew 1:21), many Bible probably reads, "...and you shall call His name Jesus, for He will save His people from their sins." But the name Jesus is a modern English adaptation of the Greek name, Iesous, which is itself a corruption of the original Hebrew name Yahshua. The name Jesus or Iesous has no meaning of its own, but the Hebrew name Yahshua literally means Yahweh's Salvation,1 which makes sense out of what the angel said in (Matthew 1:21), "...you shall call His name Yahshua [Yahweh's Salvation], for He shall save His people from their sins."

Looking in an old King James Bible, we found the name Jesus in these two passages: Which also our fathers that came after brought in with Jesus into the possession of the Gentiles, whom God Drave out before the face of our fathers, unto the days of David... (Acts 7:45, KJV) For if Jesus had given them rest, then would he not afterward have spoken of another day. (Hebrews 4:8, KJV) However, if you look in any modern translation of the Bible, including the New King James, you will find that in place of the name Jesus they use the name Joshua, for in the context it is clear that it is speaking there of Moses' successor and not the Son of God. But in the Greek manuscript the name in both of these

Nation, to all

verses is Iesous. Clearly, Joshua is the popular English transliteration of the Hebrew name Yahshua. Joshua of the Old Testament had the same name as the one called Jesus in the New Testament, for Joshua was the prophetic forerunner of the Son of God, bringing Israel into the Promised Land and leading them to victory over their enemies. But since the translators obviously know this fact, why do they only translate Iesous as Joshua in these two verses, and as Jesus everywhere else? The fact is, the name of God's Son was not even pronounced as "Jesus" in English until the 1600s, simply because there was no "J" sound or letter in English until then.2 The modern letter "J" evolved from the letter "I" which began to be written with a "tail" when it appeared as the first letter in a word. So in old English the name now written as Jesus was actually written and pronounced much like the original Greek Iesous. Eventually the hard "J" sound crept into the English language to accompany the different way of writing the initial "I" in the name. You may also find it interesting that in (Acts 26:14-15), it says that the apostle Paul heard the name of the Son of God pronounced "in the Hebrew tongue" by the Son of God Himself, so he certainly didn't hear the Greek name Iesous or the English name Jesus, but rather the Hebrew name, the name above all names, Yahshua - Jesus

Nation, to all: And this gospel of the kingdom will be preached in the whole world as a testimony *to all nations*, and then the end will come." — (Matthew 24:14 NIV) The phrase "of all nations' is found throughout Scripture, but what does it actually mean? When Scripture speaks of nations, is it referring to the modern day nations-states that appear on our geo-political maps of the world? The New Testament Greek phrase is "panta ta ethne". The word ethne is very similar to our English word ethnic. So, another way to say this is that the gospel will be preached to all the ethnic peoples or people groups of the world. Ultimately, we see this Biblical reality fulfilled in (Revelation 7:9-10). As we take a look at the current status of this task we see that all people are equally lost without Jesus, but all people do not have equal access to the message of saving faith through Jesus.

Neighbour: (Greek: *plésion* [play-see'-on] Hebrew: *Rea* [ray'-ah] near, nearby, a neighbour. (Noun) Literally, A person living next door to or very near to the speaker or person referred to: 'We did speak with one of his next-door neighbours who claims to be a family friend as well who kind of defended the doctors. ''But I'd sometimes go to the next-door neighbours who had a cow called Buttercup.' 'Most Australians don't know their next-door neighbours

Neighbour

or care what becomes of them. A person or place in relation to others next or near to it: 'It had good relations with its *neighbours* and other countries, and the people were largely contented. "Maintaining friendly relations with *neighbours* and calm within the country are the big tasks ahead. "It is good politics for any country to have friendly relations with its *neighbours*. Any person in need of one's help or kindness (after biblical use): 'love thy neighbour as thyself'

'And Matthew said most important of all, is love, love thy neighbour as thyself. "What Jesus does say repeatedly is to love thy neighbour as thyself." To love thy neighbour as thyself is also a common teaching to many religions. Other people who are not related to you biologically. The famous parable of the Good Samaritan is a lesson about being a good neighbour. So let's look at it in (Matthew 22:37-40) Jesus said to him, "'You shall love the Lord your God with all your heart, with all your soul, and with all your mind.' "This is the first and great commandment. "And the second is like it: 'You shall love your neighbour as yourself.' "On these two commandments hang all the Law and the Prophets."

(Matthew 7:12) "Therefore, whatever you want men to do to you, do also to them, for this is the Law and the Prophets." (Romans 13:9-10) For the commandments, "You shall not commit adultery," "You shall not murder," "You shall not steal," "You shall not bear false witness," "You shall not covet," and if there is any other commandment, are all summed up in this saying, namely, "You shall love your neighbour as yourself." Love does no harm to a neighbour; therefore love is the fulfilment of the law as God also is Love.

2 Loving your neighbour as yourself is the second great commandment. Christ says we are to treat others the way we want to be treated. When dealing with people, we need to stop and think how we would want to be treated, then treat them that way. The last six of the Ten Commandments are summarized in this second great commandment. See (1 John 3:17) But whoever has this world's goods, and sees his brother in need, and shuts up his heart from him, how does the love of God abide in him? (Luke 10:33) But a certain Samaritan, as he journeyed, came where he was. And when he saw him, he had compassion. A person must have compassion if he or she wants to be able to genuinely help others. Human beings have a natural compassion, but too often we learn to shut our eyes and hearts to the needs around us. We should seek to reverse that trend, and we should ask God to give us His and the deeper compassion that comes through His Holy Spir-

Neighbour

it. To know who truly is our neighbour, see (Deuteronomy 10:17-19) "For the Lord your God is God of gods and Lord of lords, the great God, mighty and awesome, who shows no partiality nor takes a bribe. "He administers justice for the fatherless and the widow, and loves the stranger, giving him food and clothing. "Therefore love the stranger, for you were strangers in the land of Egypt." Also in (Matthew 5:43-48) "You have heard that it was said, 'You shall love your neighbour and hate your enemy.' "But I say to you, love your enemies, bless those who curse you, do good to those who hate you, and pray for those who spitefully use you and persecute you, that you may be sons of your Father in heaven; for He makes His sun rise on the evil and on the good, and sends rain on the just and on the unjust. "For if you love those who love you, what reward have you? Do not even the tax collectors do the same? "And if you greet your brethren only, what do you do more than others? Do not even the tax collectors do so? "Therefore you shall be perfect, just as your Father in heaven is perfect." Anyone and everyone is our neighbour. Friends, strangers and enemies alike—we are to treat them all the way we want to be treated.

3 From the parable of the "Good Samaritan" in (Luke 10:25-37) And behold, a certain lawyer stood up and tested Him, saying, "Teacher, what shall I do to inherit eternal life?" He said to him, "What is written in the law? What is your reading of it?" So he answered and said, "'You shall love the Lord your God with all your heart, with all your soul, with all your strength, and with all your mind,' and 'your neighbour as yourself.'" And He said to him, "You have answered rightly; do this and you will live." But he, wanting to justify himself, said to Jesus, "And who is my *neighbour*?"

Then Jesus answered and said: "A certain man went down from Jerusalem to Jericho, and fell among thieves, who stripped him of his clothing, wounded him, and departed, leaving him half dead. "Now by chance a certain priest came down that road. And when he saw him, he passed by on "Likewise a Levite, when he arrived at the place, came and looked, and passed by on the other side.

"But a certain Samaritan, as he journeyed, came where he was. And when he saw him, he had compassion. "So he went to him and bandaged his wounds, pouring on oil and wine; and he set him on his own animal, brought him to an inn, and took care of him. "On the next day, when he departed, he took out two denarii, gave them to the innkeeper, and said to him, 'Take care of him; and whatever more you spend, when I come again, I will repay you.' "So which of these three do you think was neighbour to him who fell among the thieves?" And he said, "He who showed mercy on him." Then Jesus said to him, "Go and do likewise."

Meaning that the Samaritan saw someone in need and had compassion. He could have easily continued on his way like the other two people did, but he stopped when he saw the man in need. Next, the Samaritan temporarily put his needs on hold so he could assist this man who needed help now. The Samaritan sacrificed his time and money to help this stranger. Finally, the Samaritan quietly departed after he helped, and made no scene about the good deed that he had done (Matthew 6:1-4).

4 The actual State of mind needed to be a good *neighbour* is in (Philippians 2:3-4) "Let nothing be done through selfish ambition or conceit, but in lowliness of mind let each esteem others better than himself. Let each of you look out not only for his own interests, but also for the interests of others. Humility is also needed to be a good neighbour. We can't be selfish. We need to think about others and their needs. If our minds are focused on others and not just ourselves, we will be able to help others when we come across something they need. Again, (Proverbs 3:28) Do not say to your neighbour, "Go, and come back, and tomorrow I will give it," when you have it with you. See (Matthew 5:14-16) "You are the light of the world. A city that is set on a hill cannot be hidden. "Nor do they light a lamp and put it under a basket, but on a lampstand, and it gives light to all who are in the house. "Let your light so shine before men, that they may see your good works and glorify your Father in heaven." Moreso, (1 John 3:18) my little children, let us not love in word or in tongue, but indeed and in truth. Meaning in (James 1:27) Pure and undefiled religion before God and the Father is this: to visit orphans and widows in their trouble, and to keep oneself unspotted from the world. In order to be a good neighbour, we must take action. We must not only see the needs of others, we must act on those needs. Perhaps the need is simply opening a door for someone whose hands are full. Maybe the need is offering an encouraging word to someone who is depressed. Perhaps a fatherless son would like to go fishing. Maybe some widow needs some company. Or maybe someone needs his car pulled out of a ditch. Whatever the need, we must show by our actions that we care about our neighbor. And in today's self-absorbed world, others will definitely take notice—and be grateful— when we take time to help and encourage them.

Neighbour

The Bible only lists a few of the hundreds upon hundreds of good works Jesus Christ did for others, and we are to follow His example as in (John 21:25; 1 John 2:6). To maintain our position as good neighbours, should abide by (Leviticus 19:18) "You shall not take vengeance, nor bear any grudge against the children of your people, but you shall love your neighbour as yourself: I am the Lord. (Proverbs 3:29) Do not devise evil against your neighbour, for he dwells by you for safety's sake. God doesn't want us to think evil about our fellow man. We're not to try to get even, hold grudges or try to cause bad things to happen to anyone. God doesn't even want us to be glad when something bad happens to our enemy (Proverbs 24:17). Remember, we would not want to be treated that way! If you love your neighbour as commanded you will reap the fruit as in (Proverbs 19:17), "Whoever is generous to the poor lends to the Lord, and he will repay him for his deed. Luke 6:38 "Give, and it will be given to you: good measure, pressed down, shaken together, and running over will be put into your bosom. For with the same measure that you use, it will be measured back to you."

5 In the New Testament, this limitation of moral obligation to fellow-countrymen is abolished. Christ gives a wider interpretation of the commandment in (Leviticus 19:18), so as to include in it those outside the tie of nation or kindred. This is definitely done in the parable of the Good Samaritan (Luke 10:25-37), where, in answer to the question, "Who is my neighbour?" Jesus shows that the relationship is a moral, not a physical one, based not on kinship but on the opportunity and capacity for mutual help. The word represents, not so much a rigid fact, but an ideal which one may or may not realize (Luke 10:36), "Which of these three, thinkest thou, proved (literally, became, not was) neighbour," etc.). This larger connotation follows naturally as a corollary to the doctrine of the universal Fatherhood of God. The commandment to love one's neighbour as one's self must not be interpreted as if it implied that we are to hate our enemy (an inference which the Jews were apt to make); human love should be like the Divine, impartial, having all men for its object (Matthew 5:43). Love to one's fellow-men in this broad sense to be placed side by side with love to God as the essence and sum of human duty (Matthew 22:35-40) parallel (Mark 12:28-31). Christ's apostles follow His example in giving a central position to the injunction to love one's neighbour as one's self (James 2:8, where is called the "royal law" i.e. the supreme or governing law; (Romans 13:9; Galatians 5:14). God takes notice of those who help others. He says that when we give to oth-

ers, we will be "repaid," though that is not our motivation for serving. Blessings won't always come immediately, but in time God will make sure good things will happen to us. The more sincere and wholehearted we are about helping others, the more blessings will follow us (2 Corinthians 9:6-8). Praise the Lord!

New: (Adjective, Greek: kainos [kahee-nos'], Hebrew: chadash [khaw-dawsh'] meaning fresh, new, unused, novel., produced, introduced, or discovered recently or now for the first time; not existing before. 2 already existing but seen, experienced, or acquired recently or now for the first time. 3 beginning anew and in a transformed way as in (2 Corinthians 2:17) "Therefore, if anyone is in Christ, the new creation has come: The old has gone, the new is here! Adverb - newly; recently. The rebirth of the human spirit, that invisible though vital part of every human being. Peter, one of Jesus' disciples, referred to the human spirit as the "hidden man of the heart."2 Paul referred to the spirit as the "inward man" when he wrote, "Though our outward man perish, yet the inward man is renewed day by day." Praise the Lord!

New Creation, the: As described in (2 Corinthians 5:17): "Therefore, if anyone is in Christ, he is a new creation; the old has gone, the new has come!" The word "therefore" refers us back to (verses 14-16) where Paul tells us that all believers have died with Christ and no longer live for themselves. Our lives are no longer worldly; they are now spiritual. Our "death" is that of the old sin nature which was nailed to the cross with Christ. It was buried with Him, and just as He was raised up by the Father, so are we raised up to "walk in newness of life" (Romans 6:4). That new person that was raised up is what Paul refers to in (2 Corinthians 5:17) as the "new creation." To understand *the new creation*, first we must grasp that it is in fact a creation, something created by God. (John 1:13) tells us that this new birth was brought about by the will of God. We did not inherit the new nature, nor did we decide to re-create ourselves anew, nor did God simply clean up our old nature; He created something entirely fresh and unique. The new creation is completely new, brought about from nothing, just as the whole universe was created by God ex nihilo, from nothing. Only the Creator could accomplish such a feat.

Secondly, As *the new creation* emerged "old things have passed away." The "old" refers to everything that is part of our old nature—natural pride, love of sin, reliance on works, and our former opinions, habits and passions.

Most significantly, what we loved has passed away, life without miracle signs and wonders, especially the supreme love of self and with it self-righteousness, self-promotion, and self-justification. The new creature looks outwardly toward Christ instead of inwardly toward self. The old things died, nailed to the cross with our sinful nature.

3 Along with the old passing away, "the new has come!" Old, dead things are replaced with new things, full of life and the glory of God. The new born soul delights in the things of God and abhors the things of the world and the flesh. Our purposes, feelings, desires, and understandings are fresh and different. We see the world differently. The Bible seems to be a new book, and though we may have read it before, there is a beauty about it which we never saw before, and which we wonder at not having perceived. The whole face of nature seems to us to be changed, and we seem to be in a new world. The heavens and the earth are filled with new wonders, and all things seem now to speak forth the praise of God. There are new feelings toward all people—a new kind of love toward family and friends, a new compassion never before felt for enemies, and a new love for all mankind. The things we once loved, we now detest. The sin we once held onto, we now desire to put away forever. We "put off the old man with his deeds" (Colossians 3:9), and put on the "new self, created to be like God in true righteousness and holiness" (Ephesians 4:24).

6 What about the Christian who continues to sin while being *newly created*? There is a difference between continuing to sin and continuing to live in sin. No one reaches sinless perfection in this life, but the redeemed Christian is being sanctified (made holy) day by day, sinning less and hating it more each time he fails. Yes, we still sin, but unwillingly and less and less frequently as we mature. Our new self-hates the sin that still has a hold on us. The difference is that the new creation is no longer a slave to sin, as we formerly were. We are now freed from sin and it no longer has power over us (Romans 6:6-7). Now we are empowered by and for righteousness. We now have the choice to "let sin reign" or to count ourselves "dead to sin but alive to God in Christ Jesus" (Romans 6:11-12). Best of all, now we have the power to choose the latter. *The new creation* is a wondrous thing, formed in the mind of God and created by His power and for His glory. Praise the Lord!

New testament, the: The new covenant. Books of the Gospels after the Old Testament - Matthew, Mark, Luke, John, Acts of the Apostles, Epistles, Romans

1Corinthians, 2Corinthians, Galatians · Ephesians, Philippians · Colossians, 1 Thessalonians 2 Thessalonians, 1 Timothy, 2 Timothy, Titus, Philemon, Hebrews · James, 1 Peter · 2 Peter, 1 John · 2 John · 3 John,Jude, Apocalypse (Revelation)

The New Testament (Koine Greek: Hebrew Καινὴ Διαθήκη, Hē Kainḕ Diathḗkē) is the second major part of the Christian biblical canon, the first part being the Old Testament, based on the Hebrew Bible. Although Christians hold different views from Jews about the Hebrew scriptures, Christians regard both the Old and New Testaments together as sacred scripture. The contents of the New Testament deal explicitly with first-century Christianity. Therefore, the New Testament (in whole or in part) has frequently accompanied the spread of Christianity around the world. It reflects and serves as a source for Christian theology and morality. Both extended readings and phrases directly from the New Testament are also incorporated (along with readings from the Old Testament) into the various Christian liturgies. The New Testament has influenced religious, philosophical, and political movements in Christendom, and left an indelible mark on its literature, art, and music.

2 The New Testament is an anthology, a collection of Christian works written in the common Greek language of the first century, at different times by various writers, who were early Jewish disciples of Jesus of Nazareth. In almost all Christian traditions today, the New Testament consists of 27 books. The original texts were written in the first and perhaps the second centuries of the Christian Era, generally believed to be in Koine Greek, which was the common language of the Eastern Mediterranean from the Conquests of Alexander the Great (335–323 BC) until the evolution of Byzantine Greek (c. 600). All of the works which would eventually be incorporated into the New Testament would seem to have been written no later than around AD 150.

3 Collections of related texts such as letters of the Apostle Paul (a major collection of which must have been made already by the early 2nd century)[2] and the Canonical Gospels of Matthew, Mark, Luke, and John (asserted by Irenaeus of Lyon in the late-2nd century as the Four Gospels) gradually were joined to other collections and single works in different combinations to form various Christian canons of Scripture. Over time, some disputed books, such as the Book of Revelation and the Minor Catholic (General) Epistles were introduced into canons in which they were originally absent. Other works earlier held to be Scripture, such as 1 Clement, the Shepherd

Nothing

of Hermas, and the Diatessaron, were excluded from the New Testament. The Old Testament canon is not completely uniform among all major Christian groups including Roman Catholics, Protestants, the Greek Orthodox Church, the Slavic Orthodox Churches, and the Armenian Orthodox Church. However, the twenty-seven-book canon of the New Testament, at least since Late Antiquity, has been almost universally recognized within Christianity (see Development of the New Testament canon).

4 *The New Testament* consists of four narratives of the life, teaching, death and resurrection of Jesus, called "gospels" (or "good news" accounts); a narrative of the Apostles' ministries in the early church, called the "Acts of the Apostles", and probably written by the same writer as the Gospel of Luke, which it continues; twenty-one letters, often called "epistles" in the biblical context, written by various authors, and consisting of Christian doctrine, counsel, instruction, and conflict resolution; and an Apocalypse, the Book of Revelation, which is a book of prophecy, containing some instructions to seven local congregations of Asia Minor, but mostly containing prophetical zymology, about the end times. Whatever is written in the Epistles, revelation and even in the Old Testament still reveals the contents of the Gospels – Christ Birth, Mission, Death and His coming back – the glorious rapture of the Church – the saints.

Nothing: (Adjective, Greek: *oudeis* and *outheis, oudemia, ouden* and *outhe* - [oo-dice'], Hebrew - *Klum* meaning no one, none, nothing. In the Gospel context, this simply means life without Christ. 2 Also a pronoun denoting the absence of anything. *Nothing* is a pronoun associated with nothingness. In nontechnical uses, nothing denotes things lacking importance, interest, value, relevance, or significance. Nothingness is the state of being nothing, the state of nonexistence of anything, or the property of having nothing. Nothing featured in diverse verses in the scriptures, expressing the need for contentment in Godliness as in (1 Timothy 6:7-8) "But godliness actually is a means of great gain when accompanied by contentment. For we have brought *nothing* into the world, so we cannot take anything out of it either. If we have food and covering, with these we shall be content....

(Philippians 4:6) (NASB) "Be anxious for *nothing*, but in everything by prayer and supplication with thanksgiving let your requests be made known to God.

Oo

Obadiah: In Modern Hebrew (*Ovadyah*) is a Gospel or Biblical theophorical name, meaning "servant of Yahweh" or "worshipper of Yahweh." It is related to "Abdel", "servant of God", which is also cognate to the Arabic name "Abdullah" or "Obaidullah". Turkish name Abdil or Abdi. The form of Obadiah's name used in the Septuagint is *Obdios*;. 2 The canonical Book of *Obadiah* is an *oracle* concerning the divine judgment of Edom and the restoration of Israel The text consists of a single chapter, divided into 21 verses, making it the shortest book in the Hebrew Bible. In Judaism and Christianity, its authorship is attributed to a prophet who lived in the *Assyrian Period* and named himself in the first verse, Obadiah. His name means "servant of Yehowah". In Christianity, the book of Obadiah is classified as a minor prophet of the Old Testament, due to its short length. In Judaism, Obadiah is considered a "later prophet" and this Masoretic Text is chronologically placed in the Tanakh under the section Nevi'im in the last category called *The Twelve Prophets*.

In some Christian traditions he is said to have been born in "Sychem" (Shechem), and to have been the third centurion sent out by Ahaziah against Elijah. The date of his ministry is unclear due to certain historical ambiguities in the book bearing his name, but is believed to be around 586 B.C. He is regarded as a saint by several Eastern churches. His feast day is celebrated on the 15th day of the Coptic Month Tobi (January 23/24) in the Coptic Orthodox Church. The Eastern Orthodox Church and those Eastern Catholic Churches which follow the Byzantine Rite celebrate his memory on November 19. (For those churches which follow the traditional Julian Calendar, November 19 currently falls on December 2 of the modern Gregorian Calendar). He is celebrated on February 28 in the Syrian and Malankara Churches, and with the other Minor prophets in the Calendar of saints of the Armenian Apostolic Church on July 31. 3 According to an old tradi-

Obey

tion, Obadiah is buried in Sebastia, at the same site as Elisha and where later the body of John the Baptist was believed to have been buried by his followers.

Obey, Simply the act of following instructions or recognizing someone's authority as stated in (Luke 11:28) But he said, "Blessed rather are those who hear the word of God and keep it!" Opening up one's mind for advise, and acting accordingly for a positive result. Christians are responsible to here and adhere to positive instructions from the authority of State, the Community and the Church as to obey is better than sacrifice, and to heed is better than the fat of rams.–(I Samuel 15:22)

Obtain: (verb: Greek lagchanó [lang-khan'-o] (Verb) (Greek - lagchano get, acquire, or secure (something). 2 be prevalent, customary, or established. Obtain by lot, cast lots (a) Obtain (receive) by lot, my lot (turn) is, (b) draw lots. Obtain wisdom – simply to acquire divine Knowledge like Solomon.

Offend: Synonymous to, insult, affront, outrage these verbs mean to cause resentment, humiliation, or hurt. To offend is to cause displeasure, wounded feelings, or repugnance in another: "He often offended men who might have been useful friends" Insult implies gross insensitivity, insolence, or contemptuous rudeness: "I . . . refused to stay any longer in the church with him, because he had insulted me" To affront is to insult openly, usually intentionally: "He continued to belabor the poor woman in a studied effort to affront his hated chieftain" Outrage implies the flagrant violation of a brother's orsister's integrity, pride, or sense of right and decency: "Agnes . . . was outraged by what seemed to her Rose's callousness" 2 commit an illegal acts ."a small hard core of young criminals who offend again and again" With all these the gospel warns in (Matthew 18:15-17) "If your brother sins against you, go and tell him his fault, between you and him alone. If he listens to you, you have gained your brother. But if he does not listen, take one or two others along with you, that every charge may be established by the evidence of two or three witnesses. If he refuses to listen to them, tell it to the church. And if he refuses to listen even to the church, let him be to you as a Gentile and a tax collector. Again, (Ephesians 4:30-32) advised us (Christians) not to offend the Holy Spirit – which is a Divined Minister to our life thus' "And do not grieve the Holy Spirit of God [do not offend or vex or sadden Him], by Whom you were sealed (marked, branded as God's own, secured) for the day of redemption (of final deliverance through Christ from evil and the consequences of sin). Let all bitterness and indignation and wrath (passion, rage, bad temper) and resentment (anger, animosity) and quarrelling (brawling, clamour, contention) and slander (evil-speaking, abusive or blasphemous language) be banished from you, with all malice (spite, ill will, or baseness of any kind). And become useful and helpful and kind to one another, tender hearted (compassionate, understanding, loving-hearted), forgiving one another [readily and freely], as God in Christ forgave you. As you read this practice forgiveness outright in your Spirit, so that the God of truth will forgive you in the name of Jesus. Amen!

Offering, Burnt: The first and the most significant offerings; offered on the bronze alter of burnt offering according to the plan for which God gave Moses in the book of Exodus. The alter of burnt offering is made of acacia wood, five cubits long and five cubit wide; square in shape, three cubits in height, with horns in four corners overlaid with bronze. The pails was for removing its ashes, while its shovels, basins, forks and fire pans were all of bronze rings at it four corners. There was a grating of network of bronze, while the net was adorned with four bronze rings at its four corners. This was put beneath, under the edges of the alter so that the net might reach halfway up the alter. Poles of acacia wood was overlaid with bronze and was inserted into the rings to be on the two sides of the alter when it is carried. It hollow was made with blanks as was shown to Moses in the mountain. Its size was 8 feets square and about four and a half feet high. A very large alter indeed. Leviticus 1 (1-17), 2 Sacrifice and burnt offering I do not desire . Psalm 51 V 16. Knowing this as the most significant offering David sing to the chief Musician when Nathan the prophet came unto him after he had gone in to Bath – sheba. "For thou desirest not sacrifice: else will I give it: thou delightest not in burnt offering. The sacrifice of God are a broken spirit. A broken and a contrite heart.

3 But Samuel replied "Does the LORD delight in burnt offerings and sacrifices as much as in obeying the Lord? To obey is better than sacrifice and to heed is better than the fat of rams (1 Samuel 15:22) 4 Jeremiah 7:22 For when I bring your ancestors out of Egypt and spoke to them, I did not just give them commands about burnt offerings and sacrifices.

Offering, Peace: (Hebrew – shelem) "to pay to God the praises due to Him" This sacrifice, therefore, would imply payment of what either has been vowed or is due to God (Psalm 14: 23; 14, 17; Jonah 2: 10; Hosea 14:3). The relation between man and God is made complete; the disparity is removed: this is "shalom" "peace." Every grace of God makes man a debtor. The offering of the first-fruits is counted among shelamim, as is also the offering of the vow, which was made not at its assumption, but at its fulfilment (Numbers 6)

Offering, Peace

2 One of the sacrifices and offerings in the Hebrew Bible (Leviticus 3; 7.11–34). The term "peace offering" is generally constructed from "slaughter offering" zevah and the plural of shelem (Hebrew zevah hashelamiym), but is sometimes found without zevah as shelamim plural alone. The term korban shelamim is also used in rabbinical "peace offering" or "offering of well-being".

3 *Peace-offerings* were usually private sacrifices, their characteristic feature being the fact that the worshipers entered into a common feast; but they were probably offered on high occasions also. Ezekiel suggests that the kings furnish animals for the assembled people as in (Ezekiel 45:16 -18) "All the people of the land shall give to this offering for the prince in Israel. "It shall be the prince's part to provide the burnt offerings, the grain offerings and the drink offerings, at the feasts, on the new moons and on the Sabbaths, at all the appointed feasts of the house of Israel; he shall provide the sin offering, the grain offering, the burnt offering and the peace offerings, to make atonement for the house of Israel." Thus says the Lord GOD, "In the first month, on the first of the month, you shall take a young bull without blemish and cleanse the sanctuary...., and regards the common meal as the centre of the entire cult; for he speaks of "eating upon the bamoth" (Deuteronomy. 12: 18, 14:26). Other instances of the public peace-sacrifice are the offering of the ram at the installation of the priests (Exodus 10) and the annual offering of two lambs along with two loaves of new wheat bread at Pentecost (Leviticus. 22: 19). These last were originally local offerings; in later times they were presented in the Temple for the whole people. Sometimes guests were invited, and the poor, the stranger, and the Levite, as well as the male and female servants, could join the domestic circle (Deuteronomy. 12: 17-18), (Deuteronomy 16: 11, Psalm. 22:27); but only 'Levitically' clean persons could participate in the meal (Leviticus. 7:19-21). The meals were in general of a joyful character, wine being freely indulged in. Meat that was unconsumed might not be profaned. That which was left over from the "praise-offering" had to be consumed on the same day, while the residue of the other communal sacrifices had to be disposed of on the second day; and all that then remained had to be disposed of outside the camp on the third day (Leviticus. 7: 16-17) "...Now as for the flesh of the sacrifice of his thanksgiving *peace offerings*, it shall be eaten on the day of his offering; he shall not leave any of it over until morning. 'But if the sacrifice of his offering is a votive or a freewill offering, it shall be eaten on the day that he offers his sacrifice, and on the next day what is left of it may be eaten; but what is left over from the flesh of the sacrifice on the third day shall be burned with fire...."

Offering, Sin

Offering, Sin: (Hebrew: korban khatta'at) is a biblical sacrifice offered to achieve atonement for the committing of an unintentional sin. This offering is brought only for those sins that had been committed unintentionally: for intentional sins, the punishment would be' kareth. See (Leviticus 4: 1-12) "The Lord said to Moses, "Say to the Israelites: 'When anyone sins unintentionally and does what is forbidden in any of the Lord's commands— "'If the anointed priest sins, bringing guilt on the people, he must bring to the Lord a young bull without defect as a sin offering[a] for the sin he has committed. He is to present the bull at the entrance to the tent of meeting before the Lord. He is to lay his hand on its head and slaughter it there before the Lord. Then the anointed priest shall take some of the bull's blood and carry it into the tent of meeting. He is to dip his finger into the blood and sprinkle some of it seven times before the Lord, in front of the curtain of the sanctuary. The priest shall then put some of the blood on the horns of the altar of fragrant incense that is before the Lord in the tent of meeting. The rest of the bull's blood he shall pour out at the base of the altar of burnt offering at the entrance to the tent of meeting. He shall remove all the fat from the bull of the sin offering—all the fat that is connected to the internal organs, 9 both kidneys with the fat on them near the loins, and the long lobe of the liver, which he will remove with the kidneys— just as the fat is removed from the ox[b] sacrificed as a fellowship offering. Then the priest shall burn them on the altar of burnt offering. But the hide of the bull and all its flesh, as well as the head and legs, the internal organs and the intestines— that is, all the rest of the bull—he must take outside the camp to a place ceremonially clean, where the ashes are thrown, and burn it there in a wood fire on the ash heap".

As a Christian, remember Christ became Sin for us. Preaching the gospel is not just about the Kingdom of God but includes many attendant features that flesh out understanding necessary for establishing communion with God. Paul goes on to say, "Therefore, we are ambassadors for Christ, as though God were pleading through us: we implore you on Christ's behalf, be reconciled to God. For He made Him who knew no sin to be sin for us, that we might become the righteousness of God in Him" (verses 20-21). As the person who offered his life for us all, Jesus brought Himself, as it were, to God's altar, and then offered Himself before God as the *sin offering*. When He did that, our sins fell on His head as His responsibility, and He became sin personified. Our sins thus caused Him— for the first time in His life—to be cut off from God. Our sins, now His sins, caused Him to be judged, rejected, and slain, for the wages of sin is death. No longer a sweet -

savour to God, He was cast out of the camp, that is, cast from God's presence. With His judgment, justice was satisfied. Because He took our sins upon Him and justice has been satisfied, God has judged us in Him, and He can now forgive us. In this manner, God can legally meet the requirements of His law: that sin can be expiated only by death. Because we are judged in Christ and He has already been judged, we are also judged already and free and clear of sin.

This is a most encouraging truth to understand: There is no death penalty hanging over us! Because our sins were transferred to Him, Christ was the One rejected and put out of the camp. This fact was acted out in the course of the ritual of the sin offering: "But the bull's hide and all its flesh, with its head and legs, its entrails and offal—the whole bull he shall carry outside the camp to a clean place, where the ashes are poured out, and burn it on wood with fire; where the ashes are poured out it shall be burned" (Leviticus 4:11-12).

At this point, it is good to consider a major aspect of Christ's life and what it means to us. From the time recorded in (Mark 1), when Jesus came into Galilee preaching the gospel, His life was three years and a half of trials of ever-increasing intensity. Though there were undoubtedly periods when He was relatively free of persecution, they nonetheless mounted toward a crescendo. It was especially so around Jerusalem, where those in power feared Him because, as they said, "Look, the world has gone after Him!" (John 12:19). John 7 shows that His own family did not believe in Him. Even of those closest to Him, the apostles, one betrayed Him outright, and the others abandoned Him out of fear for their own lives. Through it all, we find in Him a story of undaunted courage. He gave every impression of being fearless and faithful to the highest degree. He kept going forward wisely, discreetly, enduring whatever came upon Him in carrying out His mission. In the end He had to endure the taking away of his freedom; an unfair, illegal trial; conviction; scourging; and death. While being crucified, He makes a telling statement by crying out, "My God, My God, why have You forsaken Me?" (Matthew 27:46). Could it be that this provides insight into the only thing He feared—the loss of contact and communication with His Father—and that He did not know what He would do then?

We need to consider this deeply and appreciatively because this is the great gift made available to us by Christ's sacrifice. Fellowship with God, being at peace with Him, and having access to Him are admittance to the very fountain of living waters. We can safely say that, once our sins are covered by Christ's blood, access to God is the source of all spiritual strength and growth because the love of God is poured out in our hearts by the

Holy Spirit given to us (Romans 5:1-5) and (Hebrews 13:10) tells us, "We have an altar from which those who serve the tabernacle have no right to eat." This altar is God's table. We are fed spiritual food from this spiritual altar. Jesus said in (John 6:63), "The words I speak to you are spirit, and they are life." The priests were permitted to eat of the peace, sin, and trespass offerings. Thus those who serve at the altar are fed at the altar. We are now part of a spiritual priesthood. It is our responsibility to offer up spiritual sacrifices acceptable to God by Jesus Christ (I Peter 2:5).

Again (Hebrews 13:11-12) concludes, "For the bodies of those beasts, whose blood is brought into the sanctuary by the high priest for sin, are burned outside the camp. Therefore Jesus also, that He might sanctify the people with His own blood, suffered outside the gate." God will not budge one inch with His law even when the sinner is His own Creator Son. Is sin serious to us? Do we appreciate the sacrifice of Christ? Long before His actual sacrifice, God laid the groundwork of instruction in Leviticus so we would thoroughly understand and truly appreciate what has been done to provide us, so pitifully weak and undeserving, access to Him to receive forgiveness and strength. Glory to Jesus.

Offering, Sacrificial: *See* (Greek: – Holokautein, Hebrew: Korban)

Offering, Trespass: Greek: paraptóma - [par-ap'-to-mah] Hebrew: asham, plural ashamot, Synonymous with sin offering, 2 Guilt offering, a falling away, sin a falling away, lapse, slip, false step, a type of Biblical sacrifice, specifically a sacrifice made as a compensation payment for unintentional transgressions. It was distinct from the biblical sin offering

Guilt offerings or trespass offerings were mandated in (Leviticus 5 – 7), where references are made to the offering "for sin" or "for sins". In the Greek Septuagint, the phrase used is the offering *peri tes plemmeleias*. The guilt offering is to be slaughtered in the place where the burnt offering is slaughtered, and its blood is to be splashed against the sides of the altar as in (Leviticus 7:2, NIV)

2 The transgressor furnished an unblemished ram for sacrifice at the Temple in Jerusalem, as well as (in cases of sins against holy items, theft, commission of fraud or false oaths) monetary compensation to the victim for their loss, plus a mark-up of 20% of the value to cover the priest's earnings. Monetary restitution had to be given in the pre-exile version of the currency (the shekel of the sanctuary), rather than the currency of the time, giving rise to a need for currency exchange in the Temple (hence the New Testament narrative of Jesus and the Money Changers). Such compensation payments were given on

Oil, Anointing

occasion of: infringing the rights of the priests to portions of other sacrifices (referred to in the text as God's holy things, unknown potential infringement of the regulations - as these infringements were uncertain and possibly had not occurred at all, this was voluntary (just in case) and there was no restitution element in cheating a kinsman by theft, finding lost property and lying about it, false oaths etc.

Oil, Anointing: (Noun, Greek: elaion [el'-ah-yon], Hebrew: yitshar – [yits-hawr'] meaning oil, olive oil. Anointing oil is that sanctified to possess unction for protection based in the Gospel or the word of God.

2 Literally, this is any neutral, non-polar chemical substance that is a viscous liquid at ambient temperatures and is both hydrophobic (immiscible with water, literally "water fearing") and lipophilic (miscible with other oils, literally "fat loving"). Oils have a high carbon and hydrogen content and are usually flammable and slippery. The general definition of oil includes classes of chemical compounds that may be otherwise unrelated in structure, properties, and uses. Oils may be animal, vegetable, or petrochemical in origin, and may be volatile or non-volatile. They are used for food, fuel, lubrication, and the manufacture of paints, plastics, and other materials. Specially prepared oils are used in some religious ceremonies as purifying agents.

mentioned 20 times in Scripture, was used in the Old Testament for pouring on the head of the high priest and his descendants and sprinkling the tabernacle and its furnishings to mark them as holy and set apart to the Lord (Exodus 25:6; Leviticus 8:30; Numbers 4:16). Three times it is called the "holy, anointing oil," and the Jews were strictly forbidden from reproducing it for personal use (Exodus 30:32-33). The recipe for anointing oil is found in (Exodus 30:23-24); it contained myrrh, cinnamon and other natural ingredients. There is no indication that the oil or the ingredients had any supernatural power. Rather, the strictness of the guidelines for creating the oil was a test of the obedience of the Israelites and a demonstration of the absolute holiness of God.

3 Only four New Testament passages refer to the practice of anointing with oil, and none of them offer an explanation for its use. We can draw our conclusions from context. In (Mark 6:13), the disciples anoint the sick and heal them. In (Mark 14:3-9), Mary anoints Jesus' feet as an act of worship. In (James 5:14), the church elders anoint the sick with oil for healing. In (Hebrews 1:8-9), God says to Christ as He returns triumphantly to heaven, "Your throne, O God, will last for ever and ever," and God anoints Jesus "with the oil of gladness."

4 Oil is often used as a symbol for the Holy Spirit in the Bible as in

the Parable of the Wise and Foolish Virgins (Matthew 25:1-13). As such, Christians have the presence of the oil of the Spirit who leads us into all truth and anoints us continually with His grace and comfort. "But you have an anointing from the Holy One, and all of you know the truth" (1 John 2:20). Glory to Jesus.

Old Testament: This is the first section of the Christian Bible, based primarily upon the Hebrew Bible, a collection of religious writings by ancient Israelites. It is the counterpart to the New Testament, the Christian Bible's second section. The Old Testament canon varies between Christian denominations; Protestants accept only the books found in the canon of the Hebrew Bible, dividing them into 39 books, while Catholic, Eastern Orthodox, and Oriental Orthodox churches accept somewhat larger collections of writings.

2 The Old Testament consists of many distinct books written, compiled, and edited by various authors over a period of centuries. It is not entirely clear at what point the parameters of the Hebrew Bible, the basis for the Christian Old Testament, were fixed. Some scholars have opined that the canon of the Hebrew Bible was established already by about the 3rd century BC; evidence from early Judaism and early Christianity, however, would seem to undermine such an early date. The development of the various forms of the Christian Old Testament, at any rate, continued for centuries.

The books of the Old Testament can be broadly divided into several sections: the first five books or Pentateuch (Torah); the history books telling the history of the Israelites, from their conquest of Canaan to their defeat and exile in Babylon; the poetic and "Wisdom" books dealing, in various forms, with questions of good and evil in the world; and the books of the biblical prophets, warning of the consequences of turning away from God. Many prophesies in the Old Testament are fulfilled in the New testament. This makes the theme of Gospel Dictionary and Biblical Phrases interesting as it covers a wide spectrum of events in both testaments.

Olive, mount of: (Hebrew: Har HaZeitim) A mountain ridge east of and adjacent to the Jerusalem's Old City. It is named for the olive groves that once covered its slopes. The southern part of the Mount was the necropolis of the ancient Judean kingdom. The Mount has been used as a Jewish cemetery for over 3,000 years, and holds approximately 150,000 graves, making it central in the tradition of Jewish cemeteries. Several key events in the life of Jesus as related in the Gospels took place on the Mount of Olives, as in (Mathew 24: 1-51) "Jesus left the temple and was going away, when his disciples came to point out to him the buildings of the temple.

Oil, Anointing

But he answered them, "You see all these, do you not? Truly, I say to you, there will not be left here one stone upon another that will not be thrown down." As he sat on the *Mount of Olives*, the disciples came to him privately, saying, "Tell us, when will these things be, and what will be the sign of your coming and of the close of the age?" And Jesus answered them, "See that no one leads you astray. For many will come in my name, saying, 'I am the Christ,' and they will lead many astray. Also (Zechariah 14:4) "On that day his feet shall stand on the *Mount of Olives* that lies before Jerusalem on the east, and the Mount of Olives shall be split in two from east to west by a very wide valley, so that one half of the Mount shall move northward, and the other half southward.

(Matthew 24:3) As he sat on the Mount of Olives, the disciples came to him privately, saying, "Tell us, when will these things be, and what will be the sign of your coming and of the close of the age?" and in the Book of Acts it is described as the place from which Jesus ascended to heaven. Because of its association with both Jesus and Mary, the Mount has been a site of Christian worship since ancient times and is today a major site of Christian pilgrimage for Orthodox, Catholic and Protestant Christians because of the great importance and significant of the mount of Olives to Jesus teachings as the recorded in (Mark 13:1-37) "And as he came out of the temple, one of his disciples said to him, "Look, Teacher, what wonderful stones and what wonderful buildings!" And Jesus said to him, "Do you see these great buildings? There will not be left here one stone upon another that will not be thrown down." And as he sat on *the Mount of Olives* opposite the temple, Peter and James and John and Andrew asked him privately, "Tell us, when will these things be, and what will be the sign when all these things are about to be accomplished?" And Jesus began to say to them, "See that no one leads you astray".

Ordain or Ordination: (verb, Greek: *diatassó* [dee-at-as'-so] Hebrew: *Semikhah*) Give orders to, prescribe, arrange. Make (someone) a priest or minister; confer holy orders on. 2 order (something) officially. Derived from a Hebrew word which means to "rely on" or "to be authorized". It generally refers to the ordination of a rabbi within Judaism. In this sense it is the "transmission" of rabbinic authority to give advice or judgment in Jewish law. Although presently most functioning synagogue rabbis hold semikhah by some rabbinical institution or academy, this was until quite recently not always required, and in fact many Haredi rabbis may not be required to hold a "formal" semikhah even though they may occupy important rabbinical and leadership positions. Classical semikhah refers to a specific type of ordination that, according to traditional Jewish teaching, traces a line of authority back to Moses and the seventy elders. The line of classical semikhah seems to have died out in the 4th or 5th century CE but it is widely held that the line of Torah conferment remains unbroken. Some believe evidence exists that classical semicha was existent during the 12th century when semuchim from Lebanon and Syria were traveling to Israel in order to pass on semikhah to their students. Today many believe in the existence of an unbroken chain of authority dating back to the time of Moses and Joshua (See "The Unbroken Chain of Torah" below).

A third and distinct meaning of ordination – (semikhah) is the laying of hands upon an offering of a korban ("sacrifice") in the times of the Temple in Jerusalem and is still in practice in many Christian Churches and diocese of Roman Catholics and Anglicans this days.

3 The modern definition of ordination is "the investiture of clergy" or "the act of granting pastoral authority or sacerdotal power." Usually, we think of an ordination service as a ceremony in which someone is commissioned or appointed to a position within the church. Often, the ceremony involves the laying on of hands. However, the biblical definition is a little different. The word ordain in the Bible refers to a setting in place or designation; for example, Joseph was "ordained" as a ruler in Egypt (Acts 7:10); the steward in Jesus' parable was "ordained" to oversee a household (Matthew 24:45); deacons were "ordained" to serve the Jerusalem church (Acts 6:1-6); and pastors were "ordained" in each city in Crete (Titus 1:5). In none of these cases is the mode of ordination specified, nor is any ceremony detailed; the "ordinations" are simply appointments. The word can even be used negatively, as an appointment to punishment (Luke 12:46).

Ordination, ministerial: As shown in (Acts 13), this includes a good example of a ministerial appointment: "While they were worshiping the Lord and fasting, the Holy Spirit said, 'Set apart for me Barnabas and Saul for the work to which I have called them.' So after they had fasted and prayed, they placed their hands on them and sent them off. The two of them, sent on their way by the Holy Spirit, went down to Seleucia" (verse. 2-4). In this passage, we note some key facts: (1) It is God Himself who calls the men to the ministry and qualifies them with gifts (Acts 20:28; Ephesians 4:11). (2) The members of the church recognize God's clear leading and embrace it. (3) With prayer and fasting, the church lays hands on Paul and Barnabas to demonstrate their commissioning (Acts 6:6; 1 Timothy 5:22). (4) God works through the church, as both the church and the Spirit are said to "send" the missionaries.

Ordination of Pastors and Elders

Ordination of Pastors and Elders: Paul regularly *ordained pastors* for the churches he planted. He and Barnabas directed the appointment or *ordination of elders* "in each church" in Galatia (Acts 14:23). He instructed Titus to "appoint elders in every town" on Crete (Titus 1:5). Titus himself had been ordained earlier, when "he was chosen by the churches" (2 Corinthians 8:19). In the above passages, the ordination of elders involves the whole congregation, not just the apostles. The Greek word used it as in (2 Corinthians 8:19) for Titus's appointment and in (Acts 14:23) for the choosing of the Galatian elders literally means "to stretch forth the hands." It was a word normally used for the act of voting in the Athenian legislature. Thus, the ordination of church leaders involved a general consensus in the church, if not an official vote. The apostles and the congregations knew whom the Spirit had chosen, and they responded by placing those men in leadership.

2 When God calls and qualifies a man for the ministry, it will be apparent both to that man and to the rest of the church. The would-be minister will meet the qualifications set forth in (1 Timothy 3:1-16) and (Titus 1:5-9), and he will possess a consuming desire to preach (1 Corinthians 9:16). It is the duty of the church elders, together with the congregation, to recognize and accept the calling. After that, a formal commissioning ceremony—an ordination service—is appropriate, though by no means mandatory. The ordination ceremony itself does not confer any special power; it simply gives public recognition to God's choice of leadership. Praise the Lord.

Ouches: (noun) An Old English word denoting cavities or sockets in which gems were set (Exodus. 28:11). a clasp, buckle, or brooch, especially one worn for ornament. 2 the setting of a precious stone. verb (used with object) 3 to adorn with or as if with ouches. The term "ouche"—more properly "nouch"—is derived from the old French "nouche,"a buckle or clasp.

References: (Exodus 28:11) With the work of an engraver in stone, like the engravings of a signet, shalt thou engrave the two stones with the names of the children of Israel: thou shalt make them to be set in ouches of gold. (Exodus 28:13) And thou shalt make ouches of gold; (Exodus 28:14) And two chains of pure gold at the ends; of wreathen work shalt thou make them, and fasten the wreathen chains to the ouches. (Exodus 28:25) And the other two ends of the two wreathen chains thou shalt fasten in the two ouches, and put them on the shoulder pieces of the ephod before it. (Exodus 39:6) And they wrought onyx stones inclosed in ouches of gold, graven, as signets are graven, with the names of the children of Israel. (Exodus 39:13) And the fourth row, a beryl, an onyx, and a jasper: they were inclosed in ouches of gold in their in closings. (Exodus 39:16) And they made two ouches of gold, and two gold rings; and

Overcoming Temptation

put the two rings in the two ends of the breastplate. (Exodus 39:18) And the two ends of the two wreathen chains they fastened in the two ouches, and put them on the shoulder pieces of the ephod, before it. (Amos 6:4) That lie upon beds of ivory, and stretch themselves upon their couches, and eat the lambs out of the flock, and the calves out of the midst of the stall;

Overcome: o·ver·came (-km), o·ver·come, o·ver·com·ing, o·ver·comes To defeat (another) in competition or conflict; conquer. See Synonyms at defeat. 2 To prevail over; surmount: tried to overcome the obstacles of poverty. 3 To overpower, as with emotion; affect deeply. To surmount opposition; be victorious.

Overcoming Fear: This means to be victorious over the spirit of fear as in Psalms 27:1 The LORD is my light and my salvation; whom shall I fear? The LORD is the stronghold of my life; of whom shall I be afraid? (Isaiah 54:4) "Fear not, for you will not be ashamed; be not confounded, for you will not be disgraced; for you will forget the shame of your youth, and the reproach of your widowhood you will remember no more. (Matthew 10:28) And do not fear those who kill the body but cannot kill the soul. Rather fear him who can destroy both soul and body in hell. (1 Peter 3:13-14) Now who is there to harm you if you are zealous for what is good? But even if you should suffer for righteousness' sake, you will be blessed. Have no fear of them, nor be troubled,

Overcoming Temptation: Victory over the devil. Often times, we need to figure out what is holding us back and then we can move forward. (Luke 22:40) And when he came to the place, he said to them, "Pray that you may not enter into temptation."(1 Corinthians 6: 18-20) Flee from sexual immorality. Every other sin a person commits is outside the body, but the sexually immoral person sins against his own body. Or do you not know that your body is a temple of the Holy Spirit within you, whom you have from God? You are not your own, For you were bought with a price. So glorify God in your body. (1 Corinthians 10:13) No temptation has overtaken you that is not common to man. God is faithful, and he will not let you be tempted beyond your ability, but with the temptation he will also provide the way of escape, that you may be able to endure it. Galatians 5:16 But I say, walk by the Spirit, and you will not gratify the desires of the flesh. (Hebrews 2:18) For because he himself has suffered when tempted, he is able to help those who are being tempted. (James 1:14) But each person is tempted when he is lured and enticed by his own desire. (James 4:7) Submit yourselves therefore to God. Resist the devil, and he will flee from you. (James 4:17) So whoever knows the right thing to do and fails to do it, for him it is sin. (1 John 1:9) If we confess our sins, he is faithful and just to forgive us our sins and to cleanse us from all unrighteousness.

Overcoming Anger

Overcoming Anger: (Psalms 37:8) Refrain from anger, and forsake wrath! Fret not yourself; it tends only to evil. (Psalms 149:8-9) to bind their kings with chains and their nobles with fetters of iron, to execute on them the judgment written! This is honor for all his godly ones. Praise the LORD! Proverbs 14:29 Whoever is slow to anger has great understanding, but he who has a hasty temper exalts folly.(Proverbs 17:27) Whoever restrains his words has knowledge, and he who has a cool spirit is a man of understanding. (Ecclesiastes 7:9) Be not quick in your spirit to become angry, for anger lodges in the heart of fools. (2 Timothy 2:23-24) Have nothing to do with foolish, ignorant controversies; you know that they breed quarrels. And the Lord's servant must not be quarrelsome but kind to everyone, able to teach, patiently enduring evil, (James 1:19-21) Know this, my beloved brothers: let every person be quick to hear, slow to speak, slow to anger; for the anger of man does not produce the righteousness of God. Therefore put away all filthiness and rampant wickedness and receive with meekness the implanted word, which is able to save your souls.

Overcome, We shall" This a protest song that became a key anthem of the African-American Civil Rights Movement (1955–1968). It is widely believed that the title and structure of the song are derived from an early gospel song, "I'll Overcome Someday", by African-American composer Charles Albert Tindley (1851–1933) although the musical and lyrical structure of Tindley's hymn is in fact substantially different from that of We Shall Overcome. In addition, there is no mention whatsoever of Tindley in either the 1960 and 1963 copyrights of "We Shall Overcome".

2 The song "We Will Overcome" was published in the September 1948 issue of People's Songs Bulletin (a publication of People's Songs, an organization of which Pete Seeger was the director and guiding spirit). It appeared in the bulletin as a contribution of and with an introduction by Zilphia Horton, then music director of the Highlander Folk School of Monteagle, Tennessee, an adult education school that trained union organizers. In it, she wrote that she'd learned the song from members of the CIO Food and Tobacco Workers Union: "It was first sung in Charleston, S.C. ... Its strong emotional appeal and simple dignity never fails to hit people. It sort of stops them cold silent." It was her favourite song and she taught it to countless others, including Pete Seeger, who included it in his repertoire, as did many other activist singers, such as Frank Hamilton and Joe Glazer, who recorded it in 1950. The song became associated with the Civil Rights movement from 1959, when Guy Carawan stepped in as song leader at Highlander, which was then focused on

non-violent civil rights activism. It quickly became the movement's unofficial anthem. Seeger and other famous folksingers in the early 1960s, such as Joan Baez, sang the song at rallies, folk festivals, and concerts in the North and helped make it widely known. Since its rise to prominence, the song, and songs based on it, have been used in a variety of protests worldwide.

Overcoming habitual Sins: The ability to rule over indwelling sinful nature is considered habitual sin and how to overcome habitual sin is to note the change, or transformation, that takes place when a person is saved. The Bible describes the natural man as "dead in sin and trespasses" (Ephesians 2:1). As a result of Adam's fall into sin, man is born spiritually dead. In this state of spiritual death, man is unable and unwilling to follow and obey God and *habitual sin* naturally follows. Natural man sees the things of God as foolishness (1 Corinthians 2:14) and is hostile toward God (Romans 8:7). When a person is saved, a transformation takes place. The apostle Paul refers to this as the new creation (2 Corinthians 5:17). From the moment we place our faith in Christ, we are in the process of sanctification.

2 The process of sanctification is that by which those who are in Christ are confirmed by the Holy Spirit into the image of Christ (Romans 8:29). Sanctification in this life will never be fully complete, which means that believers will always struggle with remaining sin. Paul describes this battle with sin in (Romans 7:15–25). In that passage he notes that, even though he desires to do what is good in the eyes of God, he often does what is evil instead. He does the evil he doesn't want to do and fails to do the good that he wants to do. In this, he is describing every Christian's struggle with sin. James says we all sin in different ways (James 3:2), and that means each of us has what may be called "besetting" sins. Some sins are easier to overcome than others. Some struggle with anger, others with gossip, and others with lying. The point is that each of us has a sin (or some sins) with which we struggle. These besetting sins are often, but not exclusively, habits that we developed during our lives as unbelievers and require more grace and discipline to overcome.

3 Part of the process of overcoming these habitual, or besetting, sins is in recognizing the transformation that has indeed taken place within the believer. Paul writes, "So you also must consider yourselves dead to sin and alive to God in Christ Jesus" (Romans 6:11). When Paul says, "Consider yourselves dead to sin," he is telling us to remember that, in coming to Christ, the power of sin has been broken in our lives. He uses the metaphor of slavery to make this point. We were at one

Overcomer

time slaves to sin, but now we are slaves to righteousness (Romans 6:17–18). At the cross the power of sin was broken, and, in becoming Christians, we are set free from sin's mastery over us. Therefore, when a Christian sins, it is no longer out of the necessity of his nature, but because he has wilfully submitted himself to sin's dominion (Galatians 5:1).

4 The next part of the process is recognizing our inability to overcome habitual sin and our need to rely on the power of God's Holy Spirit, who dwells within us. Back to (Romans 7). Paul says, "For I know that nothing good dwells in me, that is, in my flesh. For I have the desire to do what is right, but not the ability to carry it out" (Romans 7:25). The Christian's struggle against sin is one in which our ability does not match our desire. That is why we need the power of the Holy Spirit. Paul later says, "If the Spirit of him who raised Jesus from the dead dwells in you, he who raised Christ Jesus from the dead will also give life to your mortal bodies through his Spirit who dwells in you" (Romans 8:11). The Holy Spirit, through God's Word (John 17:17), works sanctification in the people of God. Habitual sin is overcome as we submit ourselves to God and refuse the temptations of the flesh (James 4:7–8).

5 Another part of the process of overcoming habitual sin is to change the habits that facilitate it. We have to adopt the attitude of Joseph who, when tempted by Potiphar's wife to come to bed with her, left the room so quickly that he left his cloak in her hands (Genesis 39:15). We simply must make every effort to run from the things that tempt us to sin, including access to food if we are given to overeating, and access to pornography if we are tempted to sexual sin. Jesus tells us to cut off our hand or pluck out our eye if they "offend" us (Matthew 5:29–30). This means removing from our lives anything, even those things close to us, if they tempt us to sin. In short, we have to change the habits that lead to habitual sin.

Finally, we need to immerse ourselves in the truth of the gospel. The gospel is not only the means by which we are saved, but it is also the means by which we are sanctified (Romans 16:25). If we think we are saved by grace, but sanctified by our own efforts, we fall into error (Galatians 3:1–3). Sanctification is as much a work of God as justification. The promise we have from Scripture is that He who began a good work in us will complete it on the last day (Philippians 1:6).

Overcomer: Greek: Nikaó - [nik-ah'-o], Hebrew: *Sovel or Sovelet)* meaning to overwhelmed, Heroism, conquer, overcome, conquer, am victorious, overcome, prevail, subdue. Someone who overcomes and establishes ascendancy and control by force or persuasion, subdue, surmounted, controller, restrained - a person who directs and restrains.

Overcomer

2 The term overcomer is especially prominent in the book of Revelation, where Jesus encourages His people to remain steadfast through trials (Revelation 2:26; 3:21; 21:7). Also, (1 John 5:4–5) says, "For whatever is born of God overcomes the world; and this is the victory that has overcome the world—our faith. Who is the one who overcomes the world, but he who believes that Jesus is the Son of God?" *Overcomers* are followers of Christ who successfully resist the power and temptation of the world's system. An *overcomer* is not sinless, but holds fast to faith in Christ until the end. He does not turn away when times get difficult or become an apostate. Overcoming requires complete dependence upon God for direction, purpose, fulfilment, and strength to follow His plan for our lives (Proverbs 3:5–6; 2 Corinthians 12:9).

The Greek word most often translated "overcomer" stems from the word nike which, according to Strong's Concordance, means "to carry off the victory. The verb implies a battle." The Bible teaches Christians to recognize that the world is a battleground, not a playground. God does not leave us defenceless. (Ephesians 6:11–17) describes the armour of the Lord available to all believers. Scattered throughout this narrative is the admonition to "stand firm." Sometimes all it takes to *overcome* temptation is to stand firm and refused to be dragged into it as in (James 4:7), "Resist the devil and he will flee from you." An *overcomer* is one who resists sin no matter what lures Satan uses.

3 The apostle Paul wrote eloquently of overcoming in (Romans 8:35–39). He summarizes the power believers have through the Holy Spirit to overcome any attacks of the enemy. (Verse 37) says, "In all these things we are more than conquerors through him who loved us." Overcoming is often equated with enduring. Jesus encouraged those who followed Him to "endure to the end" (Matthew 24:13). A true disciple of Christ is one who endures through trials by the power of the Holy Spirit. An overcomer clings to Christ, no matter how high the cost of discipleship. (Hebrews 3:14) says, "We have come to share in Christ, if indeed we hold our original conviction firmly to the very end."

4 In the book of Revelation, Jesus promised great reward to those to overcome. *Overcomers* are promised that they will eat from the Tree of Life (Revelation 2:7), be unharmed by the second death (Revelation 2:11), eat from hidden manna and be given a new name (Revelation 2:17), have authority over the nations (Revelation 2:26), be clothed in white garments (Revelation 3:5), be made a permanent pillar in the house of God (Revelation 3:12), and sit with Jesus on His throne (Revelation 3:21). Jesus warned that holding fast to Him would not be easy, but it would be well worth it. In (Mark 13:13) He says, "You will be hated by all for my name's sake. But the one who endures to the end will

Overcometh' the world

be saved". We have the guarantee of Jesus that, if we are His, we will be able to endure to the end and His rewards will make it all worthwhile and we (True Christians) will be crown. Praise the Lord!

'Overcometh' the world:
(phr) Breakthrough through mysteries of the kingdom; Today the gospel is fulfil. 'We are heirs of the father and joint heir with the son. We are the children of the kingdom we are a family; we are one'. Jesus Christ said: Behold I overcometh the world. Favour by God Grace, The benefit through divine mercies, The affluence in the joy of the Lord. Progressing in the divine success in the spiritual issues of life or the world.

Overtake: (verb) (Genesis 44:4) "And when they were gone out of the city, and not yet far off, Joseph said unto his steward, Up, follow after the men; and when thou dost overtake them, say unto them, Wherefore have ye rewarded evil for good? The word overtake or overtook –past tense carries a solid and strong spiritual force that makes it to appear 19 instances in the bible.

2 There are various ways of applying the word overtake in the gospel. In ordinary sense the word meant to - catch up with and pass while travelling in the same direction. "the driver overtook a line of vehicles" synonyms: Children of God should pray without ceasing in order to overtake Satan his angels at all times. Overtake also means to pass, get past, go past, go by, overhaul, get or pull ahead of, leave behind, outdistance, outstrip; More become greater or more successful than. "Germany rapidly overtook Britain in industrial output" synonyms: outstrip, surpass, overshadow, eclipse, outshine, outclass; and much more 3 (especially of misfortune) come suddenly or unexpectedly upon. "disaster overtook the town in AD 303". The following biblical verses simplifies the word overtake to be more adaptable in the gospel. 3 (Deuteronomy 19:6) "Lest the avenger of the blood pursue the slayer, while his heart is hot, and overtake him, because the way is long, and slay him; whereas he was not worthy of death, inasmuch as he hated him not in time past". (Deuteronomy 28:2) "And all these blessings shall come on thee, and overtake thee, if thou shalt hearken unto the voice of the LORD thy God. (Deuteronomy 28:15) But it shall come to pass, if thou wilt not hearken unto the voice of the LORD thy God, to observe to do all his commandments and his statutes which I command thee this day; that all these curses shall come upon thee, and overtake thee: (Deuteronomy 28:45) Moreover all these curses shall come upon thee, and shall pursue thee, and overtake thee, till thou be destroyed; because thou hearkenedst not unto the voice of the LORD thy God, to keep his commandments and his statutes which he commanded thee: (Joshua 2:5) And it came to pass about the time of shutting of the gate, when it was dark, that the men went out: whither the men went I wot not:

Overtake

pursue after them quickly; for ye shall *overtake* them. (1 Samuel 30:8) And David enquired at the LORD, saying, Shall I pursue after this troop? Shall I *overtake them?* And he answered him, Pursue: for thou shalt surely overtake them, and without fail recover all. (2 Samuel 15:14) And David said unto all his servants that were with him at Jerusalem, Arise, and let us flee; for we shall not else escape from Absalom: make speed to depart, lest he *overtake* us suddenly, and bring evil upon us, and smite the city with the edge of the sword. (1 Chronicles 21:12) Either three years' famine; or three months to be destroyed before thy foes, while that the sword of thine enemies *overtaketh* thee; or else three days the sword of the LORD, even the pestilence, in the land, and the angel of the LORD destroying throughout all the coasts of Israel. Now therefore advise thyself what word I shall bring again to him that sent me. 4 The above biblical verses presents overtaking as both blessings or curse. In other word, overtaking is a spiritual force as in (Psalm 18:37) "I have pursued my enemies, and overtaken them: neither did I turn again till they were consumed". It can be a curse to your enemies if you overtook them and a blessing to you – the over taker. According to (Psalm 18: 37) above, I have pursued mine enemies, and overtaken them - He had not only routed them, but had had strength to pursue them; he had not only pursued them, but he had been enabled to come up to them. The idea is that of complete success and absolute triumph. Neither did I turn again - I was not driven back, nor was I weary and exhausted, and compelled to give over the pursuit. Till they were consumed - Until they were all either slain or made captive, so that the hostile forces vanished. None of my enemies were left. And the following verses, are the gifts of God to the spiritual warrior, whereby he is prepared for the contest, after the example of his victorious Leadership. Learn that we must seek release being made through Christ and shall be rejected. In David, the type, we behold out of trouble through Christ. The prayer put up, without reconciliation. Look at Jesus our Redeemer, In conflicting with the enemies, compassed with sorrows and with floods of ungodly men, enduring not only the pains of death, but the wrath of God for us; yet calling upon the Father with strong cries and tears; rescued from the grave; proceeding to reconcile, or to put under his feet all other enemies, till death, the last enemy, shall be destroyed. We should love the Lord in all our Strength, to maintain our Salvation; we should call on him in every trouble, and praise him for every deliverance; we should aim to walk with him in all righteousness and true holiness, keeping away from sin. If we belong to him, He gave us the ability, the spiritual force or empowerment to conquer our enemies as He conquers death and reigns for us, and we shall overtake, conquer, and reign through him, and partake of the mercy of our anointed King, which is promised to all his seed for evermore. Praise the lord!

Paradise

Pp

Paradise: A religious or metaphysical term for a place in which existence is positive, harmonious and eternal. It is conceptually a counter-image of the supposed miseries of human civilization, and in paradise there is only peace, prosperity, and happiness. 2 Paradise is a place of contentment, but it is not necessarily a land of luxury and idleness. 3 Paradise is often described as a "higher place", the holiest place, in contrast to this world, or underworlds such as Hell. Paradisiacal notions are cross-cultural, often laden with pastoral imagery, and may be cosmological or eschatological or both. 4 In eschatological contexts, paradise is imagined as an abode of the virtuous dead. In Christian and Islamic understanding, Heaven is a paradisiacal relief, evident for example in the Gospel of Luke when Jesus tells a penitent criminal crucified alongside him that they will be together in paradise. In old Egyptian beliefs, the otherworld is Aaru, the reed-fields of ideal hunting and fishing grounds where the dead lived after judgment. For the Celts, it was the Fortunate Isle of Mag Mell.

5 For the classical Greeks, the Elysian fields was a paradisiacal land of plenty where the heroic and righteous dead hoped to spend eternity. The Vedic Indians held that the physical body was destroyed by fire but recreated and reunited in the Third Heaven in a state of bliss. In the Zoroastrian Avesta, the "Best Existence" and the "House of Song" are places of the righteous dead. On the other hand, in cosmological contexts 'paradise' describes the world before it was tainted by evil. So for example, the Abrahamic faiths associate paradise with the Garden of Eden, that is, the perfect state of the world prior to the fall from grace, and the perfect state that will be restored in the World to Come. Let us read (2 Corinthians 12:4) How that he was caught up into paradise, and heard unspeakable words, which it is not lawful for a man to utter. This means that Apostle Paul was shown or was on the seat of happy Spirits., in their separate state between death and the resurrection. See

(Luke 23:43). Most of the ancients, views were of opinion that the apostle had two different raptures; because, If one rapture only were spoken of, the repetition of whether in the body, would have been needless, when speaking of his being caught up into paradise. And heard unspeakable words — Or things, words being frequently used by the Hebrews to denote matters: which it is not lawful — Or possible, as the word properly signifies, and as the apostle doubtless means; for a man to utter — Spiritual words are not spoken everywhere, those type of words can only be spoken to those who understands. So, in paradise, the word spoken are not those spoken in this canal world. Men having no terms of speech fit to express such sublime ideas as the apostle was there taught to understand: nor, probably, would it be consistent with the schemes of Providence, which require that we should be conducted by faith rather than by sight, to suffer such circumstances as these to be revealed to the inhabitants of mortal flesh. It is justly observed that since the things which he saw and heard in paradise could not, or might not, be expressed in human language, "it is plain that the purpose for which he was caught up was not to receive any revelation of the gospel doctrine, because that could have served no purpose, if the apostle could not communicate what he heard. But it was to encourage him in the difficult and dangerous work in which he was engaged. Accordingly, by taking him up into paradise, and showing him the glories of the invisible world, and making him a witness of the happiness which the righteous enjoy with Christ, even before their resurrection, his faith in the promises of the gospel must have been so exceedingly strengthened, and his hope so raised, as to enable him to bear with alacrity that heavy load of complicated evils to which he was exposed in the course of his ministry. Not to mention that this confirmation of the apostle's faith is no small confirmation of ours also." Some suppose that it was here the apostle was made acquainted with the mystery of the future state of the church, and received his orders to turn from the Jews, and go to the Gentiles. No wonder, when Holy Ghost filled the disciples, they spoke in unknown tongues – The language of Paradise that can only be understood by the Creator and the Saint in Paradise.

Pardon: (Greek: *aphesis* [af'-es-is], Hebrew: *salach* - [saw-lakh']) meaning deliverance, pardon, complete forgiveness, a sending away, a letting go, a release, pardon, completes forgiveness. (Verb) meaning to forgive, the forgiveness of sins granted freely (Isaiah 43:25), readily (Nehemiah 9:17 ; Psalms 86:5), abundantly (Isaiah 55:7 ; Romans 5:20). It is the act of a judge, and not of a sovereign, and includes pardon and, at the same time, a title to all the rewards and blessings promised in the covenant of life. 2 Pardon is an act of a sovereign, in pure sovereignty, granting simply a remission of the penalty due to sin, but securing neither honour nor reward to the pardoned. Justification. In real Gospel sense, it is a divine Amnesty. Divine favour through the Grace of our Lord Jesus Christ. Unmerited redemption. Praise the God of Grace!

Pardon as the Removal of the Sin: Nowhere do we see a more graphic picture of God's forgiveness than on Israel's day of atonement, the day God dealt with the nation's sins for another year. After the high priest offered a sacrifice for his own sins, he secured two goats, one to be sacrificed as a sin offering and the other to be used as a scapegoat. Then he slaughtered the sin-offering goat, brought its blood inside the veil of the tabernacle and sprinkled it on and in front of the mercy seat to "make atonement for the holy place, because of the impurities of the sons of Israel, and because of their transgressions" (Leviticus 16:16). The word translated "make atonement" is also translated "forgive" in the Old Testament e.g. in (Psalm 78:38). It means, basically, "to cover." The blood of that goat was not actually the basis for the Israelites' forgiveness, but it dramatically pictured the important fact that God would cover their sins. Under the mercy seat, in the ark of the covenant, were the symbols of Israel's sin—the manna about which they murmured and complained, the tables of the law which they broke, and Aaron's rod that budded when they rebelled against their divinely appointed leaders. But all those sins were covered by the blood of the goat. In like manner, when God forgives our sins, He covers them with the blood of His Son; He hides them from view. Micah said, it is as though He casts them into the depths of the sea (Micah 7:19). What a relief to know that the sins which have haunted us, burdened us, and grieved us are permanently removed from view, perfectly covered. David expressed that relief when he exclaimed in (Psalm 82:1) "How blessed is he whose transgression is forgiven, Whose sin is covered"!

2 But that is not all God did on the day of atonement. When the high priest finished making an atonement in the holy place, he laid both of his hands on the head of the live goat and confessed over it the sins of the nation, then sent it away into the wilderness as in (Leviticus 16:20-22). As he placed his hands on the goat's head, it was as though he were lifting the sins of the people and placing those sins on a substitute. Then as he let the goat go into the wilderness, it was as though those sins were being removed far away. He lifted them up, then he let them go.

Pardon as two Sides of Forgiveness: It is interesting that of the two major words translated "forgiveness" in the Old Testament, one means literally "to lift up" and the other "to let go." The most common New Testament word for forgiveness likewise means "to let go" or "to send away." When God forgives us, He lifts our sins from us and sends them far away. David said, As far as the east is from the west, So far has He removed our transgressions from us (Psalm 103:12). He chose an analogy that describes a place infinitely beyond which anybody could ever find our sins. While we know where north stops and south begins, nobody can determine precisely where east stops and west begins. Why should we bear a burden of guilt any longer when God has taken the trouble to remove our sins that far from us and cover them so thoroughly? The first great blessing of knowing a God who forgives is the complete removal of our sin from us. Praise the Lord!

Pardon as the Remission of the Debt: When somebody wrongs us, we usually consider him to be indebted to us. He owes it to us to right the wrong, or he owes us an apology. If we commit a crime and are apprehended, tried, and convicted, we must pay our debt to society. We understand that principle clearly; it permeates our culture because sin incurs a debt. When we sin against the God who made us and gave us life, we are indebted to Him. If He wants to forgive us, must cancel that debt. This facet of forgiveness is beautifully illustrated in Jesus' parable of the unmerciful servant, the man who owed his king ten thousand talents, the equivalent of approximately ten million Pounds in our money (Matthew 18:21-35). It is inconceivable that a servant could accumulate a debt of that magnitude, but Jesus chose such an extraordinary figure to emphasize how much we owe God because of our sin. Furthermore, there was no way a servant could possibly repay such a debt on a meagre salary of a few pennies a day, and that too is part of the point Jesus made. We can never repay the debt we owe God. An eternity of torment in hell will not even begin to satisfy the extent of His offended holiness.

2 Like the servant in the story, some of us think we can repay God what we owe Him. We say as he said, "Have patience with me, and I will repay you everything" (Matthew 18:26). We think that given enough time we can do enough good works and keep enough of His commandments to compensate God for all the debt of our sin. That attitude displays our gross failure to grasp the awesomeness of His holiness and the awfulness of our sin. God knows it can never be done. So in the story, the master took pity on his servant and cancelled his debt for him. That is exactly what God does for us. He cancels the debt of our sin, and that is an essential element of forgiveness.

3 But how can God do that? His infinite holiness has been violated and His justice demands that the debt be paid. He cannot simply ignore it. Who will pay it? In infinite love and grace, He decided to pay it Himself. In the story, it cost the king ten million pounds that was rightfully his in order to forgive his servant. We often overlook the inescapable fact that forgiveness always costs somebody something. If an offense has been committed, somebody has to pay. When justice is served, the one who has committed the offense pays. When forgiveness is granted, the one who has been offended pays. Guilt cannot be transferred to a third party. The Psalmist said, "No man can by any means redeem his brother, Or give to God a ransom for him (Psalm 49:7). Sometimes we think we have forgiven a person who has wronged us, but yet we are subconsciously looking for some way to reclaim from him what we have lost, whether it be our reputation, our money, our pride, or whatever else he might have taken from us. We are looking for a way to make him pay; and that is not forgiveness. When we forgive him, we pay in full for his wrong. Since God is forgiving by nature, He pays in full for our sins. That is what Jesus Christ was doing on that cross. He was not a third party trying to get God and man together. He was the offended One, God in flesh, who came to earth to pay for man's forgiveness.

As the Apostle Paul put it, "God was in Christ reconciling the world to Himself, not counting their trespasses against them" (2 Corinthians 5:19). When He bowed His head and voluntarily dismissed His Spirit, He cried, "It is finished." That statement is one word in the Greek text, a word that was used in business transactions meaning "paid in full." The obligation which our sins incurred was paid in full at Calvary's cross. God took our place and paid our debt as our substitute. It is still infinitely greater to know that the eternal debt of our sin has been cancelled. When God forgives, He not only takes away our sin, He also cancels our debt. But there is still more to His forgiveness.

Pardon as the Repeal of the Penalty: The debt of a broken law is called a penalty, so if the debt is cancelled, it is obvious that the penalty must also be revoked. While the two are related, it is essential that we understand both aspects of forgiveness. As we have seen, on the day of atonement one of the goats was killed as a sacrifice for the sins of the people. It pictured the punishment of a substitute. The goat's blood could not in itself pay for Israel's sins (Hebrews 10:4), but blood did have to be shed nevertheless. The penalty for sin is death, and only death could satisfy that requirement (Hebrews 9:22). The death of that goat portrayed to the people of Israel that God Himself would suffer

Pardon as the Release From Guilt

the penalty of their sin. That is exactly what Jesus Christ was doing on the cross. Isaiah predicted that He would be pierced for our transgressions and crushed for our iniquities, that the penalty of our sins would fall on Him (Isaiah 53:5-6). Peter described how it happened: "And He Himself bore our sins in His body on the cross" (1 Peter 2:24). He died for our sins, "the just for the unjust" (1 Peter 3:18). The basis for our eternal forgiveness is the blood of Jesus Christ, and nothing could be clearer in Scripture (Ephesians 1:7). Jesus Himself declared, "For this is My blood of the covenant, which is poured out for many for forgiveness of sins" (Matthew 26:28). So, 'Believers' never again need to fear punishment from God. The penalty for our sins has been assessed and fully satisfied by God's Son. "There is therefore now no condemnation for those who are in Christ Jesus" (Romans 8:1). No punishment! No penalty! No eternal judgment! The penalty has been paid. The case is settled and will never come up for review. There is no possibility of appeal to any higher court. We as God's children are free from sin's penalty, free from all fear of punishment. He may lovingly discipline us to help us grow in Him and so experience greater satisfaction and joy in living, but we never need to fear His retribution as indeed there is no condemnation for those who are in Christ Jesus. The penalty has been repealed.

Pardon as the Release From Guilt: Fear of punishment can be damaging to our emotional and spiritual wellbeing, but our greatest danger probably comes from guilt. Guilt can be constructive, one of the tools God uses to help us see our need for forgiveness and acknowledge our sin. But after we have seen it and have received His forgiveness by faith, the guilt is gone forever. We never need to struggle with its venomous effect again. "Come now, and let us reason together," Says the LORD, "Though your sins are as scarlet, They will be as white as snow; Though they are red like crimson, They will be like wool" (Isaiah 1:18).

2 Guilt is viewed as a red stain. That would be most appropriate if the crime were murder, as Shakespeare's character Macbeth could well attest. But it may also be a fitting description of any sin against God's holiness. It is a blot, a blemish, a taint, a flaw, a stigma, a red stain that dirties our lives and contaminates our relationships. God's forgiveness washes that ugly stain as white as snow. Before the days of air pollution, there was nothing purer or cleaner than fresh fallen snow. That is how clean we are when God forgives us. The blood of Jesus Christ washes us and cleanses us as in (1 John 1:7). It leaves us pure and blameless. What a relief! "Blessed is the man whose sin the LORD does not count against him"

Pardon as the Restoration To Fellowship

(Psalm 32:2) NIV. His nagging guilt is gone. We read that and we really may believe it. But somehow when our minds are occupied with our sins, we tend to forget it and we still feel guilty. Satan works very hard at making us feel guilty, accusing us, and condemning us, trying to convince us that God could never forgive the awful things we have done. He knows that when we wallow in guilt, we become discouraged and defeated and are of little use to God. We may begin to say things like, "I'm no good. I never will get victory over this sin, so I might as well go ahead and enjoy it." And our spiritual power plummets to new lows. Satan also knows that when we fail to accept God's forgiveness, we will not be able to forgive ourselves. And when we do not forgive ourselves, we will not be able to forgive others. We will be harsh, demanding, overbearing, intolerant, and punitive in our relationships. Remember Christ's parable of the unmerciful servant. Because the servant never grasped the reality of his forgiveness, he grabbed one of his fellow slaves by the throat and tried to choke him, demanding payment for the mere equivalent to nine pounds he was owed (Matthew 18:28-30). There have been some fierce battles precipitated by professing believers who have never learned to enjoy their freedom from guilt. Satan's advantage is to hold us in that bondage to guilt. Do not let him do it. God has forgiven you. Accept His forgiveness, and then forgive yourself. It will help you forgive others who have wronged you and treat them with kindness, patience, and tolerance. People who know a forgiving God will forgive others. If you have been experiencing conflicts, your new attitude will help to bring peace to your relationships. Praise God!

Pardon as the Restoration To Fellowship: It is difficult to look people in the eye when we know that we have wronged them. We wonder if they know what we have done, whether or not they are holding it against us, or what they might try to do to get back at us. But if we are sure they have forgiven us, the barriers are gone and we are free to enjoy an open and cordial relationship with them once again.

In like manner, sin builds a barrier that hinders our fellowship with God. Isaiah said to the people of his day, "your iniquities have made a separation between you and your God" (Isaiah 59:2). He likens those sins to a thick cloud that blocks the rays of the sun. But just as a cloud can be dispelled by the sun or the wind, so God dispels our cloud of sin when he forgives us as in (Isaiah 44:22) thus "I have wiped out your transgressions like a thick cloud, And your sins like a heavy mist. Return to Me, for I have redeemed you". With the cloud of sin removed, the debt cancelled, the penalty satisfied, and the guilt gone, we are free to come boldly into His presence and enthusiastically enjoy His fellowship.

And it will ever be so. God assures us that when He forgives our sins, He remembers them no more (Isaiah 43:25; Jeremiah 31:34; Hebrews 8:12; 10:17). He will never allow them to come between us again. Why then should we? The child of God stands forgiven for all time. Paul says we have been forgiven of all our trespasses, and that includes sins that are past, present, and future (Colossians 2:13) see also (Psalm 103:3). When we believe that, we can come joyfully and confidently into His presence.

2 Remember that while our forgiving God has provided for our eternal forgiveness, He still reserves the right to establish the condition by which we may experience that forgiveness. Peter mentioned the condition as he preached in the house of Cornelius, the Roman centurion. He was speaking about the Lord Jesus when he said, "everyone who believes in Him receives forgiveness of sins" (Acts 10:43). Belief in Christ—that is the condition. Forgiveness is offered to all, but it is only experienced by those who will turn from their sin and place their personal trust in Jesus Christ as the One who can deliver them from its guilt and penalty. Thus, 'Let the wicked forsake his way, And the unrighteous man his thoughts; And let him return to the LORD, And He will have compassion on him; And to our God, For He will abundantly pardon (Isaiah 55:7).

Abundant pardon is pardon that is multiplied over and over, pardon that has no limit. It is ours for the believing. If you have never done so before, avail yourself by faith of God's offer and the King of Glory will come into your life. Praise the Lord!

Partaker's: (Adjective: Greek: *metochos* - [met'-okh-os] Hebrew: *koinonos*, meaning a sharer, partner, associate. "share in," derived from , "with change afterward" and "have") – properly, change due to sharing, i.e. from being an "active partaker with." the sanctification process here on earth with the reward of inheritance in the Millennial Kingdom. (Colossians 1:10–13) connects this for us: "That ye might walk worthy of the Lord unto all pleasing, being fruitful in every good work, and increasing in the knowledge of God; strengthened with all might, according to His glorious power, unto all patience and longsuffering with joyfulness; Giving thanks unto the Father, which hath made us meet [qualified] to be partakers of the inheritance of the saints in light: Who hath delivered us from the power of darkness, and hath translated us into the kingdom of His dear Son". Here Paul connects the importance of "walking worthily" with the Lord and "being qualified" with becoming a partaker of the inheritance of Christ in the future Millennial Kingdom.

2 Partaker also means "to be a participant of something, (a sharer in something), or a carrier of some-

Partaker in Christ

thing." All believers are partakers of Christ's divine nature as in (2 Peter 1:3 -4) "According to His divine power hath given unto us all things that pertain unto life and godliness, through the knowledge of Him that hath called us to glory and virtue: Whereby are given unto us exceeding great and precious promises; that by these ye might be partakers of the divine nature".

Partaking of Christ's Life means not only receiving His Life in our hearts when we are born again, but also living that Life out in our souls. Partaking of His Life is what empowers us to become overcomers—the faithful ones who produce "fruit." It means that the Life of Christ is now being lived out through us. His Life has filled us and the Holy Spirit is now empowering us.

Partaker in Christ: Being a partaker in Christ, however, is not the same thing as being a partaker of Christ. The former is "positional" whereas the latter is "experiential." We are placed in Christ when we are first born again as a free gift (justification), but we become partakers of Christ when His Life begins to come forth through us (by sanctification). In other words, we continually lay our self-life down at the Cross saying, "Not my will, but 'Thine'" and thus, His Life is able to come forth through us.

Partaking of His Life results in becoming the overcomers that Revelation refers to as ruling and reigning in the Millennium. As Christians we are living Christ's overcoming Life—His Agape Love, His supernatural power, and His divine wisdom. These overcomers are simply partaking of His Life. They are loving with His Love, depending upon His strength, and making decisions through His wisdom. These are the ones who will be Christ's co-heirs in His future kingdom.

Partakers of the same life: Meaning partakers of Christ life or same life like Christ, i.e same divine nature. Partaking of Christ's Life means that our self-life (our own natural self-centred thoughts and emotions) has been set aside and God's Life freed to come forth. Matthew tells us that if we want to save our lives, we must first lose them. And only when we lose them, will we then i-ⁿnd them (Mathew 16:24–26). We must constantly go to the Cross with our self-life—and leave it there—so that Christ's Life can come forth. When our self-life is replaced with Christ's Life, it is called "the exchanged life," "the shared life," or "the imparted life." We exchange our love for His Love (Ephesians 3:19), our wisdom for His wisdom, our strength for His (Romans 3:22; Galatians 2:16), and so forth. It's Christ's eternal Life, but because we are open and cleansed vessels, we can now partake of it, share it, and live it.

2 This is the oneness and the union of spirits as in (Galatians 2:20): "I

am crucified with Christ; nevertheless I live; yet not I, but Christ liveth in me; and the life which I now live in the flesh I live by the faith of the Son of God, who loved me and gave Himself for me". This is the exchanged Life. This exchange of life, however, does not happen automatically. In order to live Christ's Life, we must not only be cleansed vessels (sanctified), we must also have childlike faith. By faith, we choose to give God our hurts, our bitterness, our insecurities, our unforgiving behaviour (any self-life that has quenched His Spirit in us) and exchange, He gives us His Life—His power and His Love. (John 12:24–25) also describes this exchange of life perfectly: "Verily, verily, I say unto you, except a corn of wheat fall into the ground and die it abideth alone; but if it die, it bringeth forth much fruit. He that loveth [holds on to] his life shall lose it; and he that hateth [lets go of] his life in this world shall keep it unto life eternal. When we make "faith choices" to do His will regardless of how we feel or what we think, His Life comes forth through our soul and body reflecting His Life to all we come in contact, bearing godly "fruit." This is what is meant to "walk by the Spirit." If, however, we quench God's Spirit in our hearts by making "emotional choices" to follow our own hurts, fears, resentment and unbelief, our own "self-life" will be shown forth in our souls, not God's Life at all. And, consequently, no "fruit" will be produced.

Partaker, purpose of a: The purpose of being a partaker of Christ's Life is that we might become those overcomers that Revelation 2 and 3 refer to, who produce the "fruit of righteousness" in their lives (Philippians 1:10–11). The Greek word for fruit is *karpos,* which means "that which is produced by the Spirit of God in us." Godly "fruit" comes from sanctification, through deliverance from a life of sin and self, and the subsequent filling and empowering of the Holy Spirit. Note, "Our work is our fruit; and our fruit is the product of our lives." By fruit, we mean "good works"—the righteous deeds and the godly actions—that are done by the Spirit of God through us (Ephesians 5:9; Philippians 1:11). Without a continual "co-death" with Christ (the crucifixion of self), there will be no exchange of Life, and thus, no fruit. You shall know them by their fruits... every good tree bringeth forth good fruit, but a corrupt tree bringeth forth bad fruit. A good tree cannot bring forth bad fruit, neither can a corrupt tree bring forth good fruit as in (Matthew 7:16–18) In other words, fruit is the visible expression of the power of God working in us. That being so, "Every branch in Me that beareth not fruit He taketh away: and every branch that beareth fruit, He purgeth it, that it may bring forth more fruit... Abide in Me, and I in you. As the branch cannot bear fruit of itself, except it abide in Me, and I in him, the

Passover

same bringeth forth much fruit: for without Me ye can do nothing. Glory to Jesus!

Passover: Hebrew: *Pesach*) Observed by Jews. (In various forms also by: Samaritans; Messianic Jews; Some groups claiming affiliation with Israelites). Type One of the Three Pilgrim Festivals

Significance Celebrates the Exodus, the freedom from slavery of the Children of Israel from ancient Egypt that followed the Ten Plagues. Beginning of the 49 days of Counting of the Omer

Celebrations In Jewish practice, one or two festive Seder meals – first two nights; in the times of the Temple in Jerusalem, the Passover sacrifice. In Samaritan practice, men gather for a religious ceremony on mount Gerizim that includes the ancient lamb Sacrifice in the 7th day.

2 Passover begins in the 15th day of Nisan and Ends 21st day of Nisan in Israel, and among some liberal Diaspora Jews; 22nd day of Nisan outside of Israel among more traditional Diaspora Jews. Its related to Shavuot ("Festival of Weeks") which follows 49 days from the second night of Passover. It is an important biblically derived Jewish festival. The Jewish people celebrate Passover as a commemoration of their liberation over 3,300 years ago by God from slavery in ancient Egypt that was ruled by the Pharaohs, and their freedom as a nation under the leadership of Moses. It commemorates the story of the Exodus as described in the Hebrew Bible especially in the Book of Exodus, in which the Israelites were freed from slavery in Egypt.

In the narrative of the Exodus, the Bible tells us that God helped the Children of Israel escape from their slavery in Egypt by inflicting ten plagues upon the ancient Egyptians before the Pharaoh would release his Israelite slaves; the tenth and worst of the plagues was the death of the Egyptian firstborn. The Israelites were instructed to mark the doorposts of their homes with the blood of a slaughtered spring lamb and, upon seeing this, the spirit of the Lord knew to pass over the first-born in these homes, hence the English name of the holiday - *Passover*

When the Pharaoh freed the Israelites, it is said that they left in such a hurry that they could not wait for bread dough to rise (leaven). In commemoration, for the duration of *Passover* no leavened bread is eaten, for which reason *Passover* was called the feast of unleavened bread in the Torah or Old Testament. Thus Matzo (flat unleavened bread) is eaten during *Passover* and it is a tradition of the holiday.

Passover for Christians today: The first of God's seven annual festivals is the Passover (Leviticus:23:5) In the fourteenth day of the first month at even is the

Passover for Christians today

LORD's *passover*.). *Passover* falls in early spring in the Holy Land and is a reminder of how God spared His people from death in Egypt. To rescue His people from slavery, God took the lives of all the firstborn Egyptian males (Exodus:12:7) "And they shall take of the blood, and strike it on the two side posts and on the upper door post of the houses, wherein they shall eat it., (Exodus 2: 26-29) but passed over the Israelites' homes that had the blood of a sacrificed lamb on their door frames. The blood of the *Passover* lamb foreshadowed the sacrifice of Jesus Christ, which passes over the sins of people who repent in order to spare them from eternal death.

2 The New Testament makes clear that Christ is the true *Passover* Lamb (compare (Exodus 12:21) "Then Moses called for all the elders of Israel, and said unto them, Draw out and take you a lamb according to your families, and kill the Passover. with (1 Corinthians:5:7) "Purge out therefore the old leaven, that ye may be a new lump, as ye are unleavened. For even Christ our *Passover* is sacrificed for us). In observing His last Passover with His disciples, Jesus explained that the symbols of bread and wine represent His body and blood offered by Him for the forgiveness (or passing over) of our sins and the death penalty our sins have earned for us (Matthew 26:26-28) "And as they were eating, Jesus took bread, and blessed it, and brake it, and gave it to the disciples, and said, Take, eat; this is my body. And he took the cup, and gave thanks, and gave it to them, saying, Drink ye all of it; For this is my blood of the new testament, which is shed for many for the remission of sins".

Also, (Mark:14:22-24) "And as they did eat, Jesus took bread, and blessed, and brake it, and gave to them, and said, Take, eat: this is my body. And he took the cup, and when he had given thanks, he gave it to them: and they all drank of it.

And he said unto them, This is my blood of the new testament, which is shed for many".

3 The death of Christ actually took place during the daylight hours that followed the Passover evening—which was still the same date according to Hebrew sunset-to-sunset reckoning. Christ was sacrificed on Passover. The New Testament *Passover* is a memorial of the suffering and death of Jesus Christ. This is also when baptized, Christians renew the agreement to come under the blood of Jesus Christ, the perfect *Passover* Lamb, for the forgiveness of sins. Often times, we approach this period of the year with deep spiritual introspection. We commemorate the Passover on the 14th day of the first month of the sacred year with a service based on the instructions of (1 Corinthians:11:23-28) For I have received of the Lord that which also I de-

Passover for Christians today

livered unto you, "That the Lord Jesus the same night in which he was betrayed took bread: And when he had given thanks, he brake it, and said, Take, eat: this is my body, which is broken for you: this do in remembrance of me. After the same manner also he took the cup, when he had supped, saying, This cup is the new testament in my blood: this do ye, as oft as ye drink it, in remembrance of me. For as often as ye eat this bread, and drink this cup, ye do show the Lord's death till he come. Wherefore whosoever shall eat this bread, and drink this cup of the Lord, unworthily, shall be guilty of the body and blood of the Lord. But let a man examine himself, and so let him eat of that bread, and drink of that cup".

This solemn service begins with a brief explanation of its purpose, followed by foot-washing (based on Christ's example and instructions in (John 13). Then the minister gives an explanation of the symbols of the *Passover*, unleavened bread and wine, which represent the body and blood of our Saviour. Each baptized member of the Church eats a small piece of the unleavened bread and drinks a small glass of the wine (Mark 14:22-24) and as they did eat, Jesus took bread, and blessed, and breaks it, and gave to them, and said, Take, eat: this is my body. And he took the cup, and when he had given thanks, he gave it to them: and they all drank of it. And he said unto them, This is my blood of the new testament, which is shed for many".

4 Christians who observe this annual memorial marking Jesus' death (1 Corinthians 11:26) For as often as ye eat this bread, and drink this cup, ye do shew the Lord's death till he come.) are reminded that eternal life is possible only through Him (John:6:47-54) Verily, verily, I say unto you, He that believeth on me hath everlasting life. I am that bread of life. Your fathers did eat manna in the wilderness, and are dead. This is the bread which cometh down from heaven, that a man may eat thereof, and not die. I am the living bread which came down from heaven: if any man eat of this bread, he shall live for ever: and the bread that I will give is my flesh, which I will give for the life of the world. The Jews therefore strove among themselves, saying, How can this man give us his flesh to eat? Then Jesus said unto them, Verily, verily, I say unto you, Except ye eat the flesh of the Son of man, and drink his blood, ye have no life in you. Whoso eateth my flesh, and drinketh my blood, hath eternal life; and I will raise him up at the last day. More so, (Acts:4:10-12) "Be it known unto you all, and to all the people of Israel, that by the name of Jesus Christ of Nazareth, whom ye crucified, whom God raised from the dead, even by him doth this man stand here before you whole. This is the stone which was set at nought of you builders, which is become the head

of the corner. Neither is there salvation in any other: for there is none other name under heaven given among men, whereby we must be saved". Jesus' sacrifice is the starting point for salvation and the foundation of the annual feast days that follow. Praise the Lord!

Patience: (Adjective, Greek: *hupomoné*, [hoop-om-on-ay'], Hebrew: *arek* –[aw-rake']) meaning endurance, steadfastness endurance, steadfastness, patient waiting for, slow

The gospel, however, praises patience as a fruit of the Spirit (Galatians 5:22) which should be produced for all followers of Christ (1 Thessalonians 5:14). Patience reveals our faith in God's timing, omnipotence, and love.

Although most people consider patience to be a passive waiting or gentle tolerance, most of the Greek words translated "patience" in the New Testament are active, robust words. Consider, for example, (Hebrews 12:1- NKJV): "Therefore since we also are surrounded with so great a cloud of witnesses, let us lay aside every weight and the sin which so easily besets us, and let us run with *patience* the race that is set before us". Does one run a race by passively waiting for slow-pokes or gently tolerating cheaters? Certainly not! The word translated "patience" in this verse means "endurance." A Christian runs the race patiently by persevering through difficulties. In the Gospel of Christ, patience is persevering towards a goal, enduring trials, or expectantly waiting for a promise to be fulfilled.

2 *Patience* does not develop overnight. God's power and goodness are crucial to the development of patience. (Colossians 1:11) tells us that we are strengthened by Him to "great endurance and patience," while (James 1:3-4) encourages us to know that trials are His way of perfecting our *patience*. Our *patience* is further developed and strengthened by resting in God's perfect will and timing, even in the face of evil men who "succeed in their ways, when they carry out their wicked schemes" (Psalm 37:7). Our *patience* is rewarded in the end "because the Lord's coming is near" (James 5:7-8). "The Lord is good to those whose hope is in him, to the one who seeks him" (Lamentations 3:25).

We see in the Bible many examples of those whose patience characterized their walk with God. James points us to the prophets "as an example of patience in the face of suffering" (James 5:10). He also refers to Job, whose perseverance was rewarded by what the "Lord finally brought about" (James 5:11). Abraham, too, waited patiently and "received what was promised" (Hebrews 6:15). Jesus is our model in all things, and He demonstrated patient endurance: "Who for the joy set before him endured the cross, scorning its shame, and sat down at the

Passover for Christians today

right hand of the throne of God" (Hebrews 12:2).

How do we display the *patience* that is characteristic of Christ? First, we thank God. A person's first reaction is usually "Why me?", but the Bible says to rejoice in God's will (Philippians 4:4, 1 Peter 1:6). Secondly, we seek His purposes. Sometimes God puts us in difficult situations so that we can be a witness. Other times, He might allow a trial for sanctification of character. Remembering that His purpose is for our growth and His glory will help us in the trial. Thirdly, we remember His promises such as in (Romans 8:28), which tells us that "all things God works for the good of those who love him, who have been called according to his purpose." The "all things" include the things that try our *patience*.

3 Practically, the next time you lacked money, stocked in a traffic jam, betrayed by a friend, or mocked for your testimony, how will you respond? The natural response is impatience which leads to stress, anger, and frustration. Praise God that, as Christians, we are no longer in bondage to a "natural response" because we are new creations in Christ Himself (2 Corinthians 5:17). Instead, we have the Lord's strength to respond with patience and in complete trust in the Father's power and purpose as in (Romans 2:7) "To those who by persistence in doing good seek glory, honour and immortality, he will give eternal life"

In the Scripture, God consistently rewards those who patiently endure suffering, wait for the fulfilment of His promises, and rest in Him during the storms of life. But patience, a fruit of the Spirit, may be one of the most difficult virtues to master.

We all struggle with "waiting on the Lord," even if we know that "good things come to those who wait." But if we do not wait, (1 Samuel) tells us that a "lack of patience" can cause us to miss a blessing. The Bible has not left us empty handed. Scripture quotes provides many solid promises for growing in *patience* and being a people who wait on God and "rise up on the wings like eagles." Many people in the Bible learned how patient expectation led to blessing (or how not waiting led to disaster), and their examples can help us grow in our walk with Christ. When we praise God in our waiting, He gives us the strength to keep going. Let these Bible verses inspire you to patiently seek Him.

References: (2 Samuel 5:4-5) David was thirty years old when he became king, and he reigned forty years. In Hebron he reigned over Judah seven years and six months, and in Jerusalem he reigned over all Israel and Judah thirty-three years. (Psalm 75:2) You say, "I choose the appointed time; it is I who judge uprightly. (Habakkuk 2:3) For the revelation awaits an appointed time; it speaks of

Peace

the end and will not prove false. Though it linger, wait for it; it will certainly come and will not delay. (Romans 5:2-4) through whom we have gained access by faith into this grace in which we now stand. And we rejoice in the hope of the glory of God. Not only so, but we also rejoice in our sufferings, because we know that suffering produces perseverance; perseverance, character; and character, hope (Revelation 6:9-11) When he opened the fifth seal, I saw under the altar the souls of those who had been slain because of the word of God and the testimony they had maintained. They called out in a loud voice, "How long, Sovereign Lord, holy and true, until you judge the inhabitants of the earth and avenge our blood?" Then each of them was given a white robe, and they were told to wait a little longer, until the number of their fellow servants and brothers who were to be killed as they had been was completed.

Peace: (Greek: *eiréné* - [i-ray'-nay], Hebrew: *Shalom* [sholom, sholem, sholoim, shulem] meaning: peace of mind; invocation of peace a common Jewish farewell, in the Hebraistic sense of the health (welfare) of an individual, completeness, prosperity, and welfare and can be used idiomatically to mean both hello and goodbye. As it does in English, it can refer to either peace between two entities (especially between man and God or between two countries), or to the well-being, welfare or safety of an individual or a group of individuals. Peace is an occurrence of harmony characterized by lack of violence, conflict behaviours and the freedom from fear of violence. Commonly understood as the absence of hostility and retribution, peace also suggests sincere attempts at reconciliation, the existence of healthy or newly healed interpersonal or international relationships, prosperity in matters of social or economic welfare, the establishment of equality, and a working political order that serves the true interests of all.

2 Peace is something everyone wants, yet few seem to find. It can be defined as "tranquillity, harmony, or security." Depending on the situation, it could mean "prosperity" or "well-being." Various forms of the word peace are found 429 times in the King James Version of the Bible. There are different types of peace, including false peace, inner peace, peace with God and peace with man.

In the Old Testament, the primary Hebrew word for "peace" is shalom, and it refers to relationships between people (Genesis 34:21), nations (1 Kings 5:12), and God with men (Psalm 85:8). Peace is a desired status in each of these arenas, and shalom is often tied to a covenant or a promise kept. A familiar friend (literally, "friend of my peace" as in (Psalm 41:9) is one with whom you would be at ease,

Peace

a trusted companion. "Peace" was the standard greeting (1 Samuel 25:6), still used in many cultures today.

3 *Peace* is directly related to the actions and attitudes of individuals; but it is ultimately a gift from God (Isaiah 45:7; Leviticus 26:6; John 14:27). The presence of peace indicates God's blessing on man's obedience (Isaiah 32:17; Malachi 2:5) and faith (Isaiah 26:3). There is no peace for the wicked (Isaiah 48:22). As valuable as *peace* is, it is not surprising to find that it is sometimes counterfeited. Empty promises of peace can be used to manipulate others. Deceitful men speak words of peace while secretly planning evil (Obadiah 1:7). The Antichrist will confirm a treaty, producing a temporary peace which he will then abruptly shatter as he reveals his true colours (Daniel 9:27). False teachers proclaim peace when God is actually proclaiming judgment (Ezekiel 13:10-16). In Jeremiah's day, the religious leaders dealt only with the symptoms of the national problems, without addressing the sinful root of the crisis. These false prophets declared everything was well between God and Israel: "Peace, peace," they said, when there was no real peace (Jeremiah 6:14).

4 In the New Testament, the primary Greek word for "peace" is eirene, and it refers to rest and tranquillity. A key focus of peace in the New Testament is the advent of Jesus Christ, as announced by the angels in (Luke 2:14) ("Peace on earth . . ."). Isaiah had predicted the Messiah would be the Prince of Peace (Isaiah 9:6), and He is called the Lord of peace in (2 Thessalonians 3:16). It is through Christ's work of justification that we can have peace with God (Romans 5:1), and that peace will keep our hearts and minds secure (Philippians 4:7).

5 God commands us to seek *peace* (Psalm 34:14; Matthew 5:9). We should "make every effort to do what leads to *peace*" (Romans 14:19). Of course, there will be some people who do not desire *peace*, but we are still to do our utmost to be at peace with them (Romans 12:18). Believers have an obligation to "let the *peace* of God rule" in their hearts (Colossians 3:15). This means we have the choice either to trust God's promises (letting His *peace* rule) or to rely on ourselves and reject the *peace* He offers. Jesus gave His disciples *peace* based on the truth that He has overcome the world (John 14:27; 16:33). *Peace* is a fruit of the Spirit, so, if we are allowing the Spirit of God to rule in our lives, we will experience His *peace*. To be spiritually minded brings life and *peace*, according to (Romans 8:6) thus' "The mind governed by the flesh is death, but the mind governed by the Spirit is life and *peace*".

6 The world will continue to have wars and interpersonal conflicts until Jesus comes to establish true, lasting *peace* as in (Isaiah 11:1-10), but God will give His *peace* to those who trust Him. Jesus took the chastisement of our *peace* (Isaiah 53:5) and has made it possible for us to have *peace* with God. Once His *peace* rules in our hearts, we are able to share that *peace* with others; we become publishers of *peace* as in (Isaiah 52:7) and ministers of reconciliation as in (2 Corinthians 5:18) "All this is from God, who reconciled us to himself through Christ and gave us the ministry of reconciliation": Praise the Lord!

People: (noun, Greek: *laos* [lah-os'], Hebrew: *Ammi* – [am-mee] a people, the crow (a) a people, characteristically of God's chosen people, first the Jews, then the Christians/Gentiles, (b) sometimes, but rarely, the people, the crowd; human beings in general or considered collectively; the members of a particular nation, community, or ethnic group., one's supporters or employees., one's parents or relatives. (verb) of a group of people who inhabit (a place). 2 (noun) .a human being regarded as an individual. 3 a category used in the classification of pronouns, possessive determiners, and verb forms, according to whether they indicate the speaker first person, the addressee second person, or a third party third person. 4 each of the three modes of being of God, namely the Father, the Son, or the Holy Ghost, who together constitute the Trinity.

People of God: This is a description that in the Old Testament or Hebrew Bible applies to the Israelites and that the New Testament applies to Christians. Within the Catholic Church, it has been given greater prominence because of its employment in documents of the Second Vatican Council (1962–1965). In the Old Testament, the Israelites are referred to as "the people of God" in (Judges 20:2) and (2 Samuel 14:13). The equivalent phrases "the people of the Lord" and "the people of the Lord your God" are also used. In those texts God is also represented as speaking of the Children of Israel as "my people". The people of God was a term first used, by God in the book of Exodus (Exodus 6:7) which carried stipulation in this covenant between man and God. God promised deliverance, in return the people owed obedient.

2 Christian views on the Old Covenant is shown in the New Testament, the expression "people of God" is found in (Hebrews 4:9 and 11:25), and the expression "his people", that is, God's people, appears in (Revelation 21:3. 2 Corinthians 6:16) mentions the same promises to the New Testament believer "I will dwell in them, and walk in them; and I will be their God, and they shall be my people" which is a parallel to (Exodus 6). Praise God!

Perfect

Perfect: (Adjective, Greek: teleios [tel'-i-os] Hebrew: tamim [taw-meem'] defect, full-grown (a) complete in all its parts, (b) full grown, of full age, (c) specially of the completeness of Christian character, having all the required or desirable elements, qualities, or characteristics; as good as it is possible to be. 2 absolute; complete (used for emphasis). 3 (of a number) equal to the sum of its positive divisors, e.g. the number 6, whose divisors (1, 2, 3) also add up to 6. (Verb) make (something) completely free from faults or defects; make as good as possible. Perfection could be seen in the story of Abraham. "Abraham believed God, and it was accounted to him for righteousness.' Now to him who WORKS, the wages are NOT counted as grace but as debt! But to him who does NOT work but BELIEVES in Him who justifies the ungodly, his faith is accounted for righteousness." (Romans. 4:3-5, NKJV) "Jesus Christ, AUTHOR AND FINISHER of OUR faith." (Hebrew. 12:2)

References: (Genesis 6:9) These are the generations of Noah: Noah was a just man and perfect in his generations, and Noah walked with God. (Genesis 17:1) And when Abram was ninety years old and nine, the LORD appeared to Abram, and said unto him, I am the Almighty God; walk before me, and be thou *perfect*. (Leviticus 22:21) And whosoever offereth a sacrifice of peace offerings unto the LORD to accomplish his vow, or a freewill offering in beeves or sheep, it shall be *perfect* to be accepted; there shall be no blemish therein. (Deuteronomy 18:13) Thou shalt be *perfect* with the LORD thy God. (Deuteronomy 25:15) But thou shalt have a *perfect* and just weight, a *perfect* and just measure shalt thou have: that thy days may be lengthened in the land which the LORD thy God giveth thee. (Deuteronomy 32:4) He is the Rock, his work is *perfect:* for all his ways are judgment: a God of truth and without iniquity, just and right is he. (1 Samuel 14:41) Therefore Saul said unto the LORD God of Israel, Give a perfect lot. And Saul and Jonathan were taken: but the people escaped.

Penance. Christ gave authority, the keys, to the apostles to forgive sin, to decide between absolving or retaining guilt. This requires "confession" of sins for this judgment not to be arbitrary, hence the popular name of the sacrament. This authority was passed on to bishops, and from them to priests, with ordination. (Matthew 16:19; John 20:21-23; Revelation 1:18).

Persecute: (verb, Greek: diókó – [dee-o'-ko], Hebrew: radaph – [raw-daf'] I pursue, persecute, to subject (someone) to hostility and ill-treatment, especially because of their race or political or religious beliefs. This is the systematic mistreatment of an individual or group by another individual or group. The most common forms are religious persecution, ethnic persecution and political persecution, though there is naturally some overlap between these terms. The inflicting of suffering, harassment, isolation, imprisonment, internment, fear, or pain are all factors that may establish persecution. Even so, not all suffering will necessarily establish persecution. The suffering experienced by the victim must be sufficiently severe. The threshold level of severity has been a source of much debate. As we live by faith, we must never forget God's loving wisdom that we are the clay and He is the Potter, shaping us according to His purpose. Four valuable fruits will be produced by fully accepting God's sovereignty: the fear of God, humility, submissiveness, and uncomplaining endurance. With these no form of persecution can overtake us as Christians. Praise the Lord!

References: (2 Timothy 3:12) Indeed, all who desire to live a godly life in Christ Jesus will be persecuted, (John 15:18) "If the world hates you, know that it has hated me before it hated you. (Matthew 5:44) But I say to you, Love your enemies and pray for those who persecute you, (1 Peter 3:17) For it is better to suffer for doing good, if that should be God's will, than for doing evil. (1 Peter 4:12-14) Beloved, do not be surprised at the fiery trial when it comes upon you to test you, as though something strange were happening to you. But rejoice insofar as you share Christ's sufferings, that you may also rejoice and be glad when his glory is revealed. If you are insulted for the name of Christ, you are blessed, because the Spirit of glory and of God rests upon you. (1 Peter 3:14) But even if you should suffer for righteousness' sake, you will be blessed. Have no fear of them, nor be troubled, (1 Peter 3:16) Having a good conscience, so that, when you are slandered, those who revile your good behavior in Christ may be put to shame. (1 John 3:13) Do not be surprised, brothers, that the world hates you. (Luke 6:22) "Blessed are you when people hate you and when they exclude you and revile you and spurn your name as evil, on account of the Son of Man! (Matthew 5:10) "Blessed are those who are persecuted for righteousness' sake, for theirs is the kingdom of heaven. (2 Corinthians 4:8-12) We are afflicted in every way, but not crushed; perplexed, but not driven to despair; persecuted, but not forsaken; struck down, but not destroyed; always carrying in the body the death of Jesus, so that the life of Jesus may also be manifested in our bodies. For we who live are always being given over to death for Jesus' sake, so that the life of Jesus also may be manifested in our mortal flesh. So death is at work in us, but life in you.

Pleasure: (noun Greek: eudokia [yoo-dok-ee'-ah], Hebrew: chephets – [khay'-fets], meaning desire good-will, favour (good-pleasure),

Pleasure

feeling of complacency of God to man, (b) good-pleasure, satisfaction, happiness, delight of men, a feeling of happy satisfaction and enjoyment.. As (adjective) it is used or intended for entertainment rather than business.

Indeed God created us with the ability to experience pleasure. Several Scriptures speak of our delight and pleasure, for example, (Psalm 16; Proverbs 17:22; and Proverbs 15:13). The beauty of creation and the diversity of humanity show us God's creative palette. Many people find pleasure in spending time out of doors or in relating with those of different personalities. This is good and proper. God wants His creation to be enjoyed.

2 In the Bible, we see God Himself take pleasure in things. (Zephaniah 3:17), for example, says that God delights in us and sings over us. God also instituted multiple celebrations and festivals in the Old Testament. To be sure, these feasts had a didactic element, but they were also celebrations in their own right. Scripture speaks of having joy — Philippians and the Psalms are two places where we see plenty of it. Jesus declares, "The thief comes only to steal and kill and destroy; I have come that they may have life, and have it to the full" (John 10:10). Life "to the full" sounds like a pleasurable experience.

3 God's design of the human body reveals that pleasure is part of His plan. Taste buds and other sensory organs are proof that God is not opposed to pleasure. A hamburger taste so good, the scent of roses pleasing, a back massage enjoyable Because God wanted it that way. Pleasure was God's idea. Sometimes we think that when Christians talk about pleasure or joy, they mean being joyful in reading their Bibles, meditating, or serving. We certainly do take pleasure in those things but not to the exclusion of other activities. God also created us for fellowship with others and for recreation. We were made to delight in being His children, in using the talents He bestows and in participating in the pleasures He offers.

4 It is also wise to distinguish between the different types of "pleasure" in this world. We live in a fallen world where God's best for us is often perverted. Just because society deems an activity pleasurable does not mean it is pleasing to God as in (Galatians 5:19-21; Colossians 3:5-10; and 1 Corinthians 6:12-17). When we consider these "pleasures" of the world, we find that they are not in fact healthy for us or conducive to long-term pleasure. The prodigal son reveled in sin until the money ran out; then he found that the pleasures of sin are fleeting (Luke 15:11-17). They are false friends that leave us empty and longing. It is also important to realize that the purpose of our lives is not pleasure. Hedonism is a false philosophy. We were created to delight in God (Psalm 37:4)

and accept with gratitude the good things He provides. More importantly, we were created to have a relationship with God.

No, God is not opposed to pleasure. He is opposed to pleasure usurping His place in our lives. Sometimes we are called to forgo the pleasure of the moment in order to invest in the greater pleasure of God's kingdom. We won't be disappointed. For those who seek Him and His righteousness, God has "eternal pleasures" in store (Psalm 16:11). So as Christians, we need to joy in the Lord and take pleasure in the power of might because God did not give us the spirit of fear, instead He has given unto us the Spirit of Love, the spirit of power and sound mind in which pleasure is also included. Praise the Lord!

Poor: (adjective, Greek: *ptóchos* - pto-khos'], Hebrew: *anav* – [aw-nawv'] meaning humble, poor, destitute, poor, destitute, spiritually poor, either in a good sense (humble devout persons) or bad. As an (adjective) it related to a state of poverty, low quality or pity. Poor may also refer to:1 lacking sufficient money to live at a standard considered comfortable or normal in a society. 2 of a low or inferior standard or quality. 3 (of a person) deserving of pity or sympathy

2 The gospel has a lot to say about being *poor*. In many places, Scripture portrays poor people as having been blessed, while many who are rich are seen in a negative light. Jesus Himself was poor, not having a home or a place "to lay his head" (Matthew 8:20). The disciples and most of Jesus' followers were poor, at least in worldly terms, but rich in spiritual wealth. The disciples even left all they had to follow Him, giving up all they owned, placing their full trust in Him to provide what they needed. Jesus said the poor will always be with us (Matthew 26:11). There is no shame in being poor. Our attitude should be that of the writer in Proverbs who said, "Give me neither poverty nor riches, but give me only my daily bread" (Proverbs 30:8).

2 The rich, on the other hand, are generally portrayed negatively in the Gospel or Bible. Wealth itself is seen as a detriment to those who desire to enter the kingdom of God. Jesus talks a lot about the woes of being rich and the blessings of being poor. For example, in the scene where He interacted with the rich young ruler, He declares: "How hard it is for the rich to enter the kingdom of God!" (Mark 10:23). In fact, He repeated this statement in the very next verse to emphasize the reality of what He just said. Why did He make such a shocking statement? Because the rich tend to trust in their "riches" more than in God. Wealth tends to pull us away from God.

3 The story of the rich man and Lazarus (Luke 16:19-31) displays

Poor

clearly the temporary nature of riches. The rich man enjoyed great luxury in life, but spent eternity in hell because of his greed and covetousness. Lazarus suffered the indignities of extreme poverty, but was comforted in heaven forever. Jesus Himself left His throne in heaven in order to take on the lowly form of a *poor* man. Paul said of Him, "For you know the grace of our Lord Jesus Christ, that though he was rich, yet for your sakes he became *poor*, so that you through his poverty might become rich" (2 Corinthians 8:9).

4 At some point, as Christians we must ask ourselves: What are we really doing here in this temporary place? Where is our heart (Luke 12:34)? Are we really denying ourselves? Are we really giving sacrificially as did the *poor* widow? To follow Jesus is to take up our cross. This means to literally give our total lives to Him, unencumbered by the riches of this world. As Jesus put it in the parable of the sower, "The one who received the seed that fell among the thorns is the man who hears the word, but the worries of this life and the deceitfulness of wealth choke it, making it unfruitful" (Matthew 13:22).

5 It is those thorns, "the worries of this life" and the "deceitfulness of wealth," the not-so-subtle tools of Satan, that lure us away from God and His Word. In essence, the Scriptures paint for us a vast contrast between those who are *poor* yet rich in Christ and those who are rich yet without God. May the Lord enable us to live a life pleasing to Him, not so rich not so *poor but* joy in Him.

Pour out: (Verb Greek: ekcheo [ek-kheh'-o,], Hebrew: shaphak - [shaw-fak'], I pour out (liquid or solid); I shed, bestow liberally, pour out your heart; to put some drink into a glass or cup from another container. to tell someone everything that you are feeling. Example, She began pouring out her fears about the future. pour your heart out: She wrote him a long letter, pouring her heart out. Most common to Christians: Christ poured out His blood to wipe off our sins. Pour out Spirit as in (Acts 2:17) "In the last days, God says, I will *pour out* my Spirit on all people. Your sons and daughters will prophesy, your young men will see visions, your old men will dream dreams". This means nothing will be hidden. Everything will be revealed by the Spirit of truth – through prophecy, dreams, visions as every content of the Spirit of truth will be poured out and be manifested.

2 Also (Psalm 62:8) "Trust in him at all times, you people; *pour out* your hearts to him, for God is our refuge". Ye people, pour out your heart before him. Ye to whom his love is revealed, reveal yourselves to him. His heart is set on you; lay bare your hearts to him. Turn the vessel of your soul upside down in his secret presence, and let your inmost thoughts, desires, sor-

rows, and sins be poured out like water. Hide nothing from him, for you can hide nothing. To the Lord unburden your soul; let him be your only father confessor, for he only can absolve you when he has heard your confession. To keep our grief's to ourselves is to hoard up wretchedness. The stream will swell and rage if you dam it up: give it a clear course, and it leaps along and creates no alarm. Sympathy we need, and if we unload our hearts at Jesus' feet, we shall obtain a sympathy as practical as it is sincere, as consolatory as it is ennobling. The writer in the Westminster Assembly's Annotations well observes that it is the tendency of our wicked nature to bite on the bridle, and hide our grief in sullenness; but the gracious soul will overcome this propensity, and utter its sorrow before the Lord through pouring out of indignation or wrath as in (Jeremiah 10:25). *Pour out* thine indignation upon the heathen, — Let thy justice be made known, by bringing an exemplary punishment upon the Chaldeans and their allies, see also (Jeremiah 1:15,) who do not acknowledge thy providence, but ascribe all their successes to their idols: for they have eaten up Jacob, note (Jeremiah 6:3). This prayer, it must be observed, did not proceed from a spirit of malice or revenge in the prophet, nor was it intended to prescribe to God on whom he should execute his judgments, or in what order; but, 1st, It is an appeal to his justice; as if he had said, Lord, we are a provoking people, but are there not other nations that are more so? And shall we only be punished? Really, it is a prediction of God's judgments upon all the impenitent enemies of his church and kingdom. If judgment begins thus at the house of God: what shall be the end of those that obey not his gospel? (1 Peter 4:17).

References: (Psalms 62:8) Prayer, Described As dependence Heart, And Holy Spirit Trusting Trust in Him at all times, O people; *Pour out* your heart before Him; God is a refuge for us. Selah. (Psalms 142:2) Complaints Resentment, Against God I *pour out* my complaint before Him; I declare my trouble before Him. (Titus 3:6) Shedding Riches Of Grace Generosity, God's Christ, Names For whom He *poured out* upon us richly through Jesus Christ our Savior, (Amos 9:6) Sea Creation Of The Seas Pouring Water The One who builds His upper chambers in the heavens And has founded His vaulted dome over the earth, He who calls for the waters of the sea And pours them out on the face of the earth, The LORD is His name. (Genesis 35:14) Ceremonies Oil Monuments Obelisks drink offering Stones As Monuments Jacob set up a pillar in the place where He had spoken with him, a pillar of stone, and he *poured out* a drink offering on it; he also poured oil on it. (Leviticus 8:15) Fingers Horns Clean Objects Next Moses slaughtered it and took the blood and with his finger put some of it

Power, Divine

around on the horns of the altar, and purified the altar. Then he *poured out* the rest of the blood at the base of the altar and consecrated it, to make atonement for it. (Psalms 22:14) Wax Human Emotion Bowels Enjoyment, Lack Of Dislocating Heart, Human Melting I am *poured out* like water, And all my bones are out of joint; My heart is like wax; It is melted within me. (Joel 2:28) Baptism, significance of Inspiration Of The Holy Spirit, Nature Of Dreams Prophetess Guidance, Receiving God's Hope For Old People daughters Sons Visions From God Girls Visions "It will come about after this That I will *pour out* My Spirit on all mankind; And your sons and daughters will prophesy, Your old men will dream dreams, Your young men will see visions.

Power: *See dunamis*

Power, Divine: (Greek: *theios* [thi'-os] divine; substitute : the Deity. Hebrew: divinity is the state of things that come from a supernatural power or deity, such as a god, or spirit beings, and are therefore regarded as sacred and holy. Such things are regarded as "divine" due to their transcendental origins, and or because their attributes or qualities are superior or supreme relative to things of the Earth. Divine things are regarded as eternal and based in truth, while material things are regarded as ephemeral and based in illusion. Such thing that may qualify as "divine" are apparitions, visions, prophecies, miracles, and in some views also the soul, or more general things like resurrection, immortality, grace, and salvation. Otherwise what is or is not divine may be loosely defined, as it is used by different belief systems. The root of the word "divine" is literally "godlike" (from the Latin deus, Dyaus, closely related to Greek zeus, but the use varies significantly depending on which deity is being discussed. In (Matthew 13:11), Jesus told the disciples, "To you it has been granted to know the mysteries of the kingdom of heaven, but to [the crowd] it has not been granted." As followers of Christ, we, too, have the privilege to know all of the truths God has chosen to reveal in Scripture. Praise the Lord!

Potters House, the: This phrase came from (Jeremiah 18:1-10) "The word which came to Jeremiah from the LORD, saying, Arise, and go down to *the potter's house*, and there I will cause thee to hear my words. Then I went down to *the potter's house*, and, behold, he wrought a work on the wheels. And the vessel that he made of clay was marred in the hand of the potter: so he made it again another vessel, as seemed good to the potter to make it. Then the word of the LORD came to me, saying, O house of Israel, cannot I do with you as this potter? saith the LORD. Behold, as the clay is in the potter's hand, so are ye in mine hand, O house of Israel. At what instant I shall speak concerning a nation, and concerning a kingdom, to pluck up, and to pull down, and to destroy it; If that nation, against whom I have pronounced, turn from their evil, I will repent of the evil that I thought to do unto them. And at what instant I shall speak concerning a nation, and concerning a kingdom, to build and to plant it; If it do evil in my sight, that it obey not my voice, then I will repent of the good, wherewith I said I would benefit them". Here, God had set up the nation of Judah, but if they did not obey Him then He could bring them down, as He later did. On the other hand, if they listened to God and obeyed Him, then God would preserve them. It was spoken specifically to the nation of Judah, but the principle applies generally. God sets up nations and brings down nations based on their obedience to Him.

2 It is interesting that there are religious groups that call themselves "the Potter's House" without really understanding what it means. Are they putting themselves in God's place, saying they can set up and bring down nations? Are they saying they can create or destroy, like God? Usually not. Yet that is the basic meaning of *the potter's house* in scripture. As the concept applies to the religious groups, it may mean bringing down strongholds. But they cannot set up the strongholds in the way God can set up and bring down nations.

Praise: (verb, Greek: *epainos* -[ep'-ahee-nos], Hebrew: *Halal*.

This is a primary Hebrew root word for praise. Our word "hallelujah" comes from this base word. It means "to be clear, to shine, to boast, show, to rave, celebrate, as in (Psalm 113:1-3) Praise (halal) ye the Lord, praise (halal) o ye servants of the Lord, praise (halal) the name of the Lord. (Psalm 150:1) Praise (halal) the Lord! Praise (halal) God in his sanctuary; Praise (halal) him in his mighty expanse. (Psalm 149:3) Let them *praise* (halal) his name in the dance: let them sing *praises* with the timbrel and harp (1 Chronicle 2), commendation, praise, approval, Also as (noun) 1 express warm approval or admiration of. 2 express one's respect and gratitude towards (a deity), especially in song. The expression of approval or admiration for someone or something. 2 the expression of respect and gratitude as an act of worship.

As Christians, each day we should remember who provided us salvation. Jesus Christ is our Savior who died for us - praising Jesus is what it's all about, isn't it? He is the reason we can live eternally in Heaven, so never stop praising the One who made it all possible! Everyone's praise is different, so don't worry about how other people praise Jesus. If you feel like standing up in front of your fellow Christians, then do it. If you feel like praying daily by yourself to *praise* and honour Christ, then do that. It doesn't matter as long as we remember and PRAISE our Lord Jesus Christ! We should eter-

Praise

nally thank Him for what he did for us. Not one of us can truly imagine what it was like for Jesus when he died. He suffered terribly for the people he loved. His sacrifice and our resulting salvation should fill us with joy! We have been saved! Praise to His Holy name now and forever!

References: (Exodus 15:2) The LORD is my strength and song, and he is become my salvation: he is my God, and I will prepare him an habitation; my father's God, and I will exalt him. (Deuteronomy 10:21) He is your praise, and he is your God, that has done for you these great and terrible things, which your eyes have seen. (Judges 5:3) Hear, O you kings; give ear, O you princes; I, even I, will sing to the LORD; I will sing praise to the LORD God of Israel. (2 Samuel 22:50) Therefore I will give thanks to you, O LORD, among the heathen, and I will sing praises to your name. (1 Chronicles 29:13) Now therefore, our God, we thank you, and praise your glorious name. (Psalms 35:18) I will give you thanks in the great congregation: I will praise you among much people. (Psalms 35:28) And my tongue shall speak of your righteousness and of your praise all the day long. (Psalms 43:4) Then will I go to the altar of God, to God my exceeding joy: yes, on the harp will I praise you, O God my God. (Psalms 92:1) IT IS A GOOD THING TO GIVE THANKS UNTO THE LORD, AND TO SING PRAISES UNTO THY NAME, O MOST HIGH: (Psalms 100:4) Enter into his gates with thanksgiving, and into his courts with praise: be thankful to him, and bless his name. (Psalms 101:1) I will sing of mercy and judgment: to you, O LORD, will I sing. (Psalms 138:1) I will praise you with my whole heart: before the gods will I sing praise to you. (Jeremiah 17:14) Heal me, O LORD, and I shall be healed; save me, and I shall be saved: for you are my praise. (Daniel 2:23) I thank you, and praise you, O you God of my fathers, who have given me wisdom and might, and have made known to me now what we desired of you: for you have now made known to us the king's matter. (Daniel 4:34) And at the end of the days I Nebuchadnezzar lifted up my eyes to heaven, and my understanding returned to me, and I blessed the most High, and I praised and honored him that lives for ever, whose dominion is an everlasting dominion, and his kingdom is from generation to generation: (Romans 4:11) And he received the sign of circumcision, a seal of the righteousness of the faith which he had yet being uncircumcised: that he might be the father of all them that believe, though they be not circumcised; that righteousness might be imputed to them also: (Ephesians 1:3) Blessed be the God and Father of our Lord Jesus Christ, who has blessed us with all spiritual blessings in heavenly places in Christ: (Hebrews 13:15) By him therefore let us offer the sacrifice of praise to God continually, that is, the fruit of our lips giving thanks to his name. (1 Peter 2:9) But you are a chosen generation, a royal priesthood, an holy nation, a peculiar people; that you should show forth the praises of him who has called you out of darkness into his marvelous light; (Revelation 5:12) Saying with a loud voice, Worthy is the Lamb that was slain to receive power, and riches, and wisdom, and strength, and honor, and glory, and blessing. (Revelation 7:12) Saying, Amen: Blessing, and glory, and wisdom, and thanksgiving, and honor, and power, and might, be to our God for ever and ever. Amen.

Prayer: (Verb, Greek: *proseuchomai* [pros-yoo'-khom-ahee], Hebrew: *Tefilah* – [te-fi- la'] meaning I pray, pray for, offer prayer. An invocation or act that seeks to activate a rapport with a deity, an object of worship, or a spiritual entity through deliberate communication. *Prayer* can be a form of religious practice, may be either individual or communal and take place in public or in private. It may involve the use of words or song. When language is used, *prayer* may take the form of a hymn, incantation, formal creed, or a spontaneous utterance in the praying person. There are different forms of prayer such as petitionary prayer, prayers of supplication, thanksgiving, and worship/praise. Prayer may be directed towards a deity, spirit, deceased person, or lofty idea, for the purpose of worshipping, requesting guidance, requesting assistance, confessing sins or to express one's thoughts and emotions. Thus, people pray for many reasons such as personal benefit or for the sake of others.

Most major religions involve prayer in one way or another. Some ritualize the act of prayer, requiring a strict sequence of actions or placing a restriction on who is permitted to pray, while others teach that prayer may be practiced spontaneously by anyone at any time.

Scientific studies regarding the use of prayer have mostly concentrated on its effect on the healing of sick or injured people. Meta-studies of the studies in this field have been performed showing evidence only for no effect or a potentially small effect. For instance, a 2006 meta-analysis on 14 studies concluded that there is "no discernable effect" while a 2007 systemic review of studies on intercessory prayer reported inconclusive results, noting that 7 of 17 studies had "small, but significant, effect sizes" but the review noted that the most methodologically rigorous studies failed to produce significant findings.] Some studies have indicated increased medical complications in groups receiving prayer over those without. The efficacy of petition in prayer for physical healing to a deity has been evaluated in numerous other studies, with contradictory results. There has been some criticism of the way the studies were conducted.

Prayer of Intercession

Prayer of Intercession: Intercessory prayer is the act of praying on behalf of others. The role of mediator in prayer was prevalent in the Old Testament, in the cases of Abraham, Moses, David, Samuel, Hezekiah, Elijah, Jeremiah, Ezekiel, and Daniel. Christ is pictured in the New Testament as the ultimate intercessor, and because of this, all Christian prayer becomes intercession since it is offered to God through and by Christ. Jesus closed the gap between us and God when He died on the cross. Because of Jesus' mediation, we can now intercede in prayer on behalf of other Christians or for the lost, asking God to grant their requests according to His will. "For there is one God and one mediator between God and men, the man Christ Jesus" (1 Timothy 2:5). "Who is he that condemns? Christ Jesus, who died—more than that, who was raised to life—is at the right hand of God and is also interceding for us" (Romans 8:34).

2 A wonderful model of intercessory prayer is found in Daniel 9. It has all the elements of true intercessory prayer. It is in response to the Word (verse. 2); characterized by fervency (verse. 3) and self-denial (verse. 4); identified unselfishly with God's people (verse. 5); strengthened by confession (verse. 5-15); dependent on God's character (verses. 4, 7, 9, 15); and has as its goal God's glory (verse. 16-19). Like Daniel, Christians are to come to God on behalf of others in a heartbroken and repentant attitude, recognizing their own unworthiness and with a sense of self-denial. Daniel does not say, "I have a right to demand this out of You, God, because I am one of your special, chosen intercessors." He says, "I'm a sinner," and, in effect, "I do not have a right to demand anything." True intercessory prayer seeks not only to know God's will and see it fulfilled, but to see it fulfilled whether or not it benefits us and regardless of what it costs us. True intercessory prayer seeks God's glory, not our own. The following is only a partial list of those for whom we are to offer intercessory prayers: all in authority (1 Timothy 2:2); ministers (Philippians 1:19); Jerusalem (Psalm 122:6); friends (Job 42:8); fellow countrymen (Romans 10:1); the sick (James 5:14); enemies (Jeremiah 29:7); those who persecute us (Matthew 5:44); those who forsake us (2 Timothy 4:16); and all men (1 Timothy 2:1).

3 There is an erroneous idea in contemporary Christianity that those who offer up intercessory prayers are a special class of "super-Christians," called by God to a specific ministry of intercession. The Bible is clear that all Christians are called to be intercessors. All Christians have the Holy Spirit in their hearts and, just as He intercedes for us in accordance with God's will (Romans 8:26-27), we are to intercede for one another. This is not a privilege limited to an exclusive Christian elite; this is the command to all. In fact, not

to intercede for others is sin. "As for me, far be it from me that I should sin against the LORD by failing to pray for you" (1 Samuel 12:23). Certainly Peter and Paul, when asking others to intercede for them, did not limit their request to those with a special calling to intercession. "So Peter was kept in prison, but the church was earnestly praying to God for him" (Acts 12:5). Notice it was the whole church that prayed for him, not just those with a gift of intercession. In (Ephesians 6:16-18), Paul exhorts the Ephesian believers—all of them—on the fundamentals of the Christian life, which includes intercession "on all occasions with all kinds of prayers and requests." Clearly, intercessory prayer is part of the Christian life for all believers.

4 Further, Paul sought prayer on his behalf from all the Roman believers in (Romans 15:30). He also urged the Colossians to intercede for him in (Colossians 4:2-3). Nowhere in any biblical request for intercession is there any indication that only a certain group of people could intercede. On the contrary, those who seek others to intercede for them can use all the help they can get! The idea that intercession is the privilege and calling of only some Christians is without biblical basis. Worse, it is a destructive idea that often leads to pride and a sense of superiority. God calls all Christians to be intercessors. It is God's desire that every believer be active in intercessory prayer. What a wonderful and exalted privilege we have in being able to come boldly before the throne of Almighty God with our prayers and requests. Praise the Lord!

Prayer, petitionary: This seems to be a prominent feature of every religion. When people pray, they attempt to communicate with special persons or entities, such as a God or gods, or dead relatives, or exemplary human beings who are believed to occupy some special status. People pray for all kinds of reasons. Sometimes people pray in order to give thanks, sometimes to praise, sometimes to apologize and seek forgiveness, and sometimes to ask for things. The focus here is petitionary prayer, namely, prayer that involves some kind of request. Historically, the most interesting philosophical puzzles concerning petitionary prayer have arisen in connection with the traditional monotheism shared by Judaism, Christianity, and other religion. According to traditional monotheism, God is omniscient (knows everything that can be known), omnibenevolent (perfectly good), omnipotent (can do everything that is compatible with the other attributes mentioned above), impassable (unable to be affected by an outside source), immutable (unchanging), and free. In this light, we will explore the philosophical puzzles that arise in connection with the idea of offering petitionary prayers to God, as understood along the lines just de-

Prayers of supplication

scribed, along with the most influential attempts to solve problems. Praise the Lord!

Prayers of supplication: We come to God in prayer for a variety of reasons—to worship Him, to confess our sins and ask for forgiveness, to thank Him for His blessings, to ask for things for ourselves, and or to pray for the needs of others. The Hebrew and Greek words most often translated "supplication" in the Bible mean literally "a request or petition," so a prayer of supplication is asking God for something. Unlike the prayer of petition, which is praying on behalf of others, the prayer of supplication is generally a request for the person praying. The Bible includes many prayers of supplication. Numerous examples are found in the Psalms. David's psalms are filled with supplication for mercy in (Psalm 4:1), for leading in (Psalm 5:8), for deliverance in (Psalm 6:4), for salvation from persecution in (Psalm 7:1), and so on. When Daniel learned that King Darius had issued an edict prohibiting prayer to any god but the king, Daniel continued to pray to God with prayers of thanksgiving as well as prayers of supplication for His help in this dire situation.

2 Also, in the New Testament, Jesus tells us to ask for our daily bread in (Matthew 6:11), which falls into the category of a prayer of supplication. In addition, in (Luke 18:1-8), Jesus teaches us not to give up praying for what we need. James says that: on the one hand we don't receive because we don't ask (James 4:2). On the other hand, we ask and don't receive because we are thinking only of our fleshly desires (James 4:3). Perhaps the best way to approach supplications is to ask God in all honesty as children talking to their kind-hearted Father, but ending with "Your will be done" (Matthew 26:39), in full surrender to His will.

After describing the need to take up the "full armour of God" (Ephesians 6:13-17), the apostle Paul exhorted the Ephesians (and us) to remain alert and to pray in the Spirit, "making supplication for all the saints" (Ephesians 6:18). Clearly, prayers of supplication are part of the spiritual battle all Christians are engaged in. Paul further exhorts the Philippian church to relieve their anxieties by remaining faithful in prayer, especially prayers of thanksgiving and supplication. This, he concludes, is the formula for ensuring that "the peace of God, which passes all understanding, will guard your hearts and your minds in Christ Jesus" (Philippians 4:6-7).

3 Here we see another crucial aspect of the *prayer of supplication*—the necessity of faith in the Lord Jesus Christ. Those who belong to Christ also have the indwelling Holy Spirit who intercedes on our behalf. Because we often don't know what or how to pray when we approach God, the

Spirit intercedes and prays for us, interpreting our supplications so that, when we are overwhelmed by trials and the cares of life, He comes alongside to lend assistance with our prayers of supplication as He sustains us before the throne of grace as in (Romans 8:26). "In the same way, the Spirit helps us in our weakness. We do not know what we ought to pray for, but the Spirit himself intercedes for us through wordless groans".

Prayer of thanksgiving:

Thanksgiving in the Bible is the giving of thanks to God for everything that we receive at his hand. We receive from him our lives and the food and drink to sustain us. Every good thing in our lives comes ultimately from God and we owe him thanks for all. (Acts 17:25)... Seeing he giveth to all life, and breath, and all things; Under the Law of Moses an offering of thanksgiving could be made to God via the priest. It is described in (Leviticus 7). (Leviticus 7:12) If ye offers it for a thanksgiving, then ye shall offer with the sacrifice of thanksgiving unleavened cakes mingled with oil, and unleavened wafers anointed with oil, and cakes mingled with oil, of fine flour, fried.

2 It was a voluntary offering as we might expect. God does not compel us to gives thanks; it is our free response to him. (Leviticus 22:29). And when ye will offer a sacrifice of thanksgiving unto the LORD, offer it at your own will. As part of the worship of God, thanksgiving is offered in both song and prayer. It is a theme which recurs in the psalms. (Psalms 69:30) I will praise the name of God with a song, and will magnify him with thanksgiving. (Psalms 95:2) Let us come before his presence with thanksgiving, and make a joyful noise unto him with psalms. (Psalms 100:4) Enter into his gates with thanksgiving, and into his courts with praise: be thankful unto him, and bless his name. (Psalms 107:1) O give thanks unto the LORD, for he is good: for his mercy endureth for ever.

It was a feature of the life of Daniel. (Daniel 6:10) Now when Daniel knew that the writing was signed, he went into his house; and his windows being open in his chamber toward Jerusalem, he kneeled upon his knees three times a day, and prayed, and gave thanks before his God, as he did foretime. It is enjoined upon Christians by Paul to be part of everyday life. (Ephesians 5:20) Giving thanks always for all things unto God and the Father in the name of our Lord Jesus Christ; (Philippians 4:6) Be careful for nothing; but in everything by prayer and supplication with thanksgiving let your requests be made known unto God. (Colossians 3:17) And whatsoever ye do in word or deed, do all in the name of the Lord Jesus, giving thanks to God and the Father by him. (1 Thessalonians 5:18) In everything give thanks: for this is the will of God in Christ Jesus concerning you. (Hebrews 13:15) By him therefore let us offer the sacrifice of praise to

Prayer of Praise and Worship

God continually, that is, the fruit of our lips giving thanks to his name. We should not eat without first giving thanks. (1 Timothy 4:4) For every creature of God is good, and nothing to be refused, if it be received with thanksgiving: Paul gave thanks before he ate. (Acts 27:35) And when he had thus spoken, he took bread, and gave thanks to God in presence of them all: and when he had broken it, he began to eat. Christ gave thanks when he fed the 5000. (Matthew 15:36) And he took the seven loaves and the fishes, and gave thanks, and breaks them, and gave to his disciples, and the disciples to the multitude. It is an important part of the Lord's supper. (Luke 22:17) And he took the cup, and gave thanks, and said, take this, and divide it among yourselves: (Luke 22:19) And he took bread, and gave thanks, and brake it, and gave unto them, saying, This is my body which is given for you: this do in remembrance of me. When we meet to remember Jesus in bread and wine we likewise give thanks. In the bread and wine remembrance is made that he lay down his life that we might have the hope of eternal life in the kingdom of God. By belief of the gospel and baptism into Christ we can be saved from sin and death. (Mark 16:16) He that believeth and is baptized shall be saved; Eternal life through Christ is the ultimate gift of God. (Colossians 1:12) Giving thanks unto the Father, which hath made us meet to be partakers of the inheritance of the saints in light:

Prayer of Praise and Worship: Prayer showing an expression of approval or admiration; acknowledging God's perfection, works, and benefits. Man can be praised, God must be praised. The focus is on the power of God's - Miracles, deeds; While prayer of worship is to bow down, to fall down, to serve, to kiss the hand, fall to the knees, touch the forehead to the ground also to pay honour, devotion, and reverence to God. Positioning ourselves in humility before God.

Preach: (Greek: kérussó – [kay-roos'-so] Hebrew: Qoheleth [ko-heh'-leth] proclaim, herald, proclaim, herald, preach. As verb to deliver a sermon or religious address to an assembled group of people, typically in church. "he preached to a large congregation" synonyms: give a sermon, deliver a sermon, sermonize, spread the gospel, evangelize, address, speak; More publicly proclaim or teach (a religious message or belief). "he preached the word of God" synonyms: proclaim, teach, spread, propagate, expound, explain, make known "a church that preaches the good news" earnestly advocate (a belief or course of action). "my parents have always preached toleration and moderation" synonyms: advocate, recommend, advise, urge, exhort, teach, counsel, champion, inculcate, instil "my parents have always preached toleration"

Prevail

2 God has ordained that only men are to serve in positions of spiritual teaching authority in the church. This is not because men are necessarily better teachers or because women are inferior or less intelligent (which is not the case). It is simply the way God designed the church to function. Men are to set the example in spiritual leadership—in their lives and through their words. Women are to take a less authoritative role. Women are encouraged to teach other women (Titus 2:3–5). The Gospel or Bible also does not restrict women from teaching children. The only activity women are restricted from is teaching or having spiritual authority over men. This precludes women from serving as pastors to men. This does not make women less important, by any means, but rather gives them a ministry focus more in agreement with God's plan and His gifting of them.

Precious: (Adjective, Greek: *timios* – [tim'-ee-os] Hebrew: *Yaqar* [yaw-kar'] of great price, precious, honoured of great price, precious, honoured. Of high cost or worth; valuable: precious jewels. 2 Highly esteemed; cherished: precious moments with the new baby. 3 Dear; beloved: a friend who is precious to me. 4 Affectedly dainty or over refined: precious mannerisms. 5 Informal Thoroughgoing; unmitigated: a precious messenger – noun, One who is dear or beloved; a darling -adverb. (Psalm 116: 15) "Precious in the sight of the LORD is the death of his faithful servants".

Prevail: (Verb, Greek: *nikaó* – [nik-ah'-o] Hebrew: *Gabar* [gawbar'] To conquer, overcome, am victorious, overcome, *prevail*, subdue (verb) prove more powerful or superior. "it is good for faith to *prevail* over the flesh" synonyms: win, win out, win through, triumph, be victorious, be the victor, gain the victory, carry the day, carry all before one, finish first, come out ahead, come out on top, succeed, prove superior, conquer, overcome, gain or achieve mastery, gain ascendancy; be widespread or current in a particular area or at a particular time. "a friendly atmosphere *prevailed* among the congregation the Church " synonyms: exist, be in existence, be present, be the case, hold, obtain, occur, be prevalent, be current, be rife, be rampant, be the order of the day, be customary, be established, be common, be widespread, be in force, be in effect; 2 persuade (someone) to do something. 3 Persuade, induce, talk someone into, coax, convince, make, get, press someone into, win someone over, sway, bring someone round, argue someone into, urge, pressure someone into, pressurize someone into, bring pressure to bear on, coerce, influence, prompt; See (Jeremiah 1:19) "They will fight against you but will not overcome you, for I am with you and will rescue you," declares the LORD". Also, "God Will Prevail (Haggai 2:20-23) If we aren't careful, we

Prevent

can easily develop the perspective that convince us the devil is winning, because looking around, it seems as if the enemy is winning. No, not the Sovereign Lord ("Lord of hosts") will prevail because God has a definite plan for history. Note the repetition of the first personal pronoun, "I": "I am going to shake the heavens and the earth..." "I will overthrow the thrones of kingdoms..." "I will overthrow the chariots and their riders..." "I will take you, Zerubbabel..." "I will make you like a signet ring..." "'I have chosen you,' declares the Lord of hosts." God is mighty to accomplish His plan,

God's plan is carried out in accordance with His choice. God's plan centres on the person of Jesus Christ, God's timing for fulfilling His plan is different than our timing. God's servants should be encouraged to trust Him and to do His will. But if God's Word is true and if Christ is raised from the dead, then let us "be steadfast, immovable, always abounding in the work of the Lord, knowing that your toil is not in vain in the Lord" (1 Corinthians. 15:58) then we shall prevail. Praise the name of the Lord!

Prevent: (Verb, Greek: *kóluó* – [ko-loo'-o] Hebrew: *qadam* – [kaw-dam'] prevent, debar, hinder; with infinty: from doing so and so. Verb keep (something) from happening. 2 (of God) go before (someone) with spiritual guidance and help as in (Malachi 3: 11) "I will prevent pests from devouring your crops, and the vines in your fields will not drop their fruit before it is ripe," says the LORD Almighty".

Pride: (Noun, Greek: *Huperéphania* -[hoop-er-ay-fan-ee'-ah] Hebrew: Gevah [gay-vaw' pride meaning, arrogance, disdain. Two kinds of prides are identified here. The kind of pride that God hates (Proverbs 8:13) and the kind of pride we feel about a job well done. The kind of pride that stems from self-righteousness is sin, and God hates it because it is a hindrance to seeking Him. (Psalm 10:4) explains that the proud are so consumed with themselves that their thoughts are far from God: "In his pride the wicked does not seek him; in all his thoughts there is no room for God." This kind of haughty pride is the opposite of the spirit of humility that God seeks: "Blessed are the poor in spirit: for theirs is the kingdom of heaven" (Matthew 5:3). The "poor in spirit" are those who recognize their utter spiritual bankruptcy and their inability to come to God aside from His divine grace. The proud, on the other hand, are so blinded by their pride that they think they have no need of God or, worse, that God should accept them as they are because they deserve His acceptance.

2 Throughout the Gospels or Scriptures we are told about the consequences of pride. (Proverbs 16:18-19) tells us that "pride goes before destruction, a haughty

Proclaim

spirit before a fall. Better to be lowly in spirit and among the oppressed than to share plunder with the proud." Satan was cast out of heaven because of pride (Isaiah 14:12-15). He had the selfish audacity to attempt to replace God Himself as the rightful ruler of the universe. But Satan will be cast down to hell in the final judgment of God. For those who rise up in defiance against God, there is nothing ahead but disaster (Isaiah 14:22).

3 *Pride* has kept many people from accepting Jesus Christ as Saviour. Admitting sin and acknowledging that in our own strength we can do nothing to inherit eternal life is a constant stumbling block for prideful people. We are not to boast about ourselves; if we want to boast, then we are to proclaim the glories of God. What we say about ourselves means nothing in God's work. It is what God says about us that makes the difference (2 Corinthians 10:13). Why is pride so sinful? Pride is giving us the credit for something that God has accomplished. Pride is taking the glory that belongs to God alone and keeping it for ourselves. *Pride* is essentially self-worship. Anything we accomplish in this world would not have been possible were it not for God enabling and sustaining us. "What do you have that you did not receive? And if you did receive it, why do you boast as though you did not?" (1 Corinthians 4:7). That is why we give God the glory—He alone deserves it. Praise the Lord!

Proclaim: (verb, Greek: *Kérussó* - [kay-roos'-so] Hebrew: qara - [kaw-raw'] Call, proclaim, herald, preach. Make known publicly. (Leviticus 23:37) These are the feasts of the LORD, which ye shall proclaim to be holy convocations, to offer an offering made by fire unto the LORD, a burnt offering, and a meat offering, a sacrifice, and drink offerings, every thing upon his day:

References: (Leviticus 25:10) And ye shall hallow the fiftieth year, and proclaim liberty throughout all the land unto all the inhabitants thereof: it shall be a jubile unto you; and ye shall return every man unto his possession, and ye shall return every man unto his family. (Deuteronomy 20:10) When thou comest nigh unto a city to fight against it, then proclaim peace unto it. (Judges 7:3) Now therefore go to, proclaim in the ears of the people, saying, Whosoever is fearful and afraid, let him return and depart early from mount Gilead. And there returned of the people twenty and two thousand; and there remained ten thousand. (1 Kings 21:12) They proclaimed a fast, and set Naboth on high among the people. (2 Kings 10:20) And Jehu said, Proclaim a solemn assembly for Baal. And they proclaimed it. (2 Kings 23:16) And as Josiah turned himself, he spied the sepulchres that were there in the mount, and sent, and took the bones out of the sepulchres, and burned them upon the altar, and polluted it, according to the word

Profit

of the LORD which the man of God proclaimed, who proclaimed these words. (2 Kings 23:17) Then he said, What title is that that I see? And the men of the city told him, It is the sepulchre of the man of God, which came from Judah, and proclaimed these things that thou hast done against the altar of Bethel. (2 Chronicles 20:3) And Jehoshaphat feared, and set himself to seek the LORD, and proclaimed a fast throughout all Judah. (Ezra 8:21) Then I proclaimed a fast there, at the river of Ahava, that we might afflict ourselves before our God, to seek of him a right way for us, and for our little ones, and for all our substance. (Nehemiah 8:15) And that they should publish and proclaim in all their cities, and in Jerusalem, saying, Go forth unto the mount, and fetch olive branches, and pine branches, and myrtle branches, and palm branches, and branches of thick trees, to make booths, as it is written. (Esther 6:9) And let this apparel and horse be delivered to the hand of one of the king's most noble princes, that they

Profit: (Greek: *Sumphero* – [soom-fer'-o] Hebrew: *yithron* - [yith-rone] advantage, I collect, am profitable to I bring together, collect; I am profitable to. (Proverbs 14: 23) All hard work brings a *profit*, but mere talk leads only to poverty Those who Labour in their spiritual lives will be profited spiritually. (II Peter. 1:5-7) There is spiritual Profit in the effort we put into prayer; reading the Word; evangelizing; ministering to the brethren; service; etc. The *profit* may not be noticed in this life, but will be rewarded in the life to come. (Hebrew.6:10-11) - God does not forget. In ALL labour there is *profit* – especially labouring in the spiritual realm... labour to enter into His rest! There is *profit* in that!

2   Those whose faith is nothing more than TALK will be exposed. That kind of faith doesn't And even true believers who TALK about walking with God and TALK about serving God and do not do what He says are building with wood, hay, and stubble... But the talk of the lips tendeth only to penury. If we only TALK about God and spiritual things, and are not doing... and Living them... we will be spiritually poor! May God help us to profit in His word! Being In Debt Being Blessed Amazing Plans Rashness Goal Setting Poverty, Causes Of diligence Active Lifestyles Diligence, Results Of Haste The plans of the diligent lead surely to advantage, But everyone who is hasty comes surely to poverty. (Proverbs 31:18) Lamps She senses that her gain is good; Her lamp does not go out at night. (Proverbs 11:24) Hoarding Poverty, Causes Of Growth In Wealth Shortages Misers Thrift There is one who scatters, and yet increases all the more, And there is one who withholds what is justly due, and yet it results only in want. (Luke 6:38) Being Blessed Abundant Life God, The Provider Giving, Of Possessions People Shaking Giving To Others Generosity, Human Plenty

Promise

Through God Acknowledging God Pressing Bad Leadership Stewardship "Give, and it will be given to you. They will pour into your lap a good measure--pressed down, shaken together, and running over. For by your standard of measure it will be measured to you in return." (Deuteronomy 8:18) Blessed Ability Property, Nature Of Money, Attitudes To Giving, Of Oneself Financial Advice Materialism, As An Aspect Of Sin Work, Divine And Human Guardians Giving, Of Talents Remembering "But you shall remember the LORD your God, for it is He who is giving you power to make wealth, that He may confirm His covenant which He swore to your fathers, as it is this day. (Deuteronomy 28:15-20) The Curse Of The Law Threats "But it shall come about, if you do not obey the LORD your God, to observe to do all His commandments and His statutes with which I charge you today, that all these curses will come upon you and overtake you: "Cursed shall you be in the city, and cursed shall you be in the country. "Cursed shall be your basket and your kneading bowl. read more. "Cursed shall be the offspring of your body and the produce of your ground, the increase of your herd and the young of your flock. "Cursed shall you be when you come in, and cursed shall you be when you go out. "The LORD will send upon you curses, confusion, and rebuke, in all you undertake to do, until you are destroyed and until you perish quickly, on account of the evil of your deeds, because you have forsaken Me. Jeremiah 12:13 Unprofitable Sins Wheat Sowing And Reaping Sin, Effects Of Thorns Harvest Not Reaping What You Sow "They have sown wheat and have reaped thorns, They have strained themselves to no profit But be ashamed of your harvest Because of the fierce anger of the LORD." (Haggai 1:9) Gathering Much God's Dwelling Little Food Unreliability Destruction Of The Temple Building Houses Poverty, Causes Of" You look for much, but behold, it comes to little; when you bring it home, I blow it away Why?" declares the LORD of hosts, "Because of My house which lies desolate, while each of you runs to his own house.

Promise: (noun, Greek: *epaggelia* - [ep-ang-el-ee'-ah], Hebrew: *omer* - [o'-mer])

A commitment by someone to do or not do something. As a noun promise means a declaration assuring that one will or will not do something. As a verb it means to commit oneself by a promise to do or give. It can also mean a capacity for good, similar to a value that is to be realized in the near future. In the law of contract, an exchange of promises is usually held to be legally enforceable, according to the Latin maxim *pacta sunt servanda*

2 The Gospel story generally is the word of God as contained in the Bible. It carries God's promises. It is a very powerful tool that can be life changing for many people

Promise

when they read it. What we read and learn in the Bible is coming directly from God. His words are very inspiring and encouraging in our lives and are full with covenanted promises as in (2 Peter 1:4) *"And because of his glory and excellence, he has given us great and precious promises. These are the promises that enable you to share his divine nature and escape the world's corruption caused by human desires".* Also in *(Philippians 4:19)* *"And this same God who takes care of me will supply all your needs from his glorious riches, which have been given to us in Christ Jesus".* In (Matthew 11:28-29) *"Come to me, all you who are weary and burdened, and I will give you rest. Take my yoke upon you and learn from me, for I am gentle and humble in heart, and you will find rest for your souls".* (Romans 10:9) *"If you confess with your mouth that Jesus is Lord and believe in your heart that God raised him from the dead, you will be saved".* See also (Isaiah 40:29-31) thus' He gives power to the weak, and strength to the powerless. Even youths will become weak and tired, and young men will fall in exhaustion. But those who trust in the Lord will find new strength. They will soar high on wings like eagles. They will run and not grow weary. They will walk and not faint.

References: (Romans 3:4) By no means! Let God be true though everyone were a liar, as it is written, "That you may be justified in your words, and prevail when you are judged." (1 Peter 2:1-25) So put away all malice and all deceit and hypocrisy and envy and all slander. Like new born infants, long for the pure spiritual milk, that by it you may grow up into salvation— if indeed you have tasted that the Lord is good. As you come to him, a living stone rejected by men but in the sight of God chosen and precious, you yourselves like living stones are being built up as a spiritual house, to be a holy priesthood, to offer spiritual sacrifices acceptable to God through Jesus Christ. (1 Peter 1:24-25) For "All flesh is like grass and all its glory like the flower of grass. The grass withers, and the flower falls, but the word of the Lord remains forever." And this word is the good news that was preached to you. (Romans 8:28) And we know that for those who love God all things work together for good, for those who are called according to his purpose. (Romans 8:1) There is therefore now no condemnation for those who are in Christ Jesus. (John 15:26) "But when the Helper comes, whom I will send to you from the Father, the Spirit of truth, who proceeds from the Father, he will bear witness about me. (Luke 22:36) He said to them, "But now let the one who has a moneybag take it, and likewise a knapsack. And let the one who has no sword sell his cloak and buy one. (Matthew 28:19) Go therefore and make disciples of all nations, baptizing them in the name of the Father and of the Son and of the Holy Spirit, (Matthew 25:31-46) "When the Son of Man comes in his glory, and all the angels with him, then he will sit on his glorious throne. Before him will be gathered all the nations, and he will separate people one from another as a shepherd separates the sheep from the goats. And he will place the sheep on his right, but the goats on the left. Then the King will say to those on his right, 'Come, you who are blessed by my Father, inherit the kingdom prepared for you from the foundation of the world. For I was hungry and you gave me food, I was thirsty and you gave me drink, I was a stranger and you welcomed me,

Prosper: (verb, Greek: *euodoó* [yoo-od-o'-o] Hebrew: *tselach* [tsel-akh'] meaning; success, cause to prosper, pass: I have a happy. ucceed in material terms; be financially successful. "his business prospered" To flourish physically; grow strong and healthy. "areas where grey squirrels cannot prosper" synonyms: do well, get on well, go well, fare well; archaic, make successful. "God has wonderfully prospered this nation"

2 In the Gospel, Biblical *prosperity* is part of the definition of wellness and wholeness that is nothing missing and nothing broken. The good news of the kingdom of God teaches that you can attain success in the here and now using the principles of Jesus. It's supernatural how these manifests as you submit to the Word of God and the leading of His Holy Spirit.

The perfect will of God is a dimension of wellness that is wholeness in every area of your life including finances. In Bible verses this is written for us to clearly see... (2 Corinthians .8:9)..."For you know the grace of our Lord Jesus Christ, that though He was rich, yet for your sakes He became poor, that you through His poverty might become rich."

Prosper, God's will is for us to:
There are great benefits in learning about Biblical *Prosperity*. Jesus Himself preached the gospel to the poor. Gospel means "good news" and good news to a poor person is... (as paraphrased)..."You don't have to be poor any more!" We don't have to wait to go to Heaven to experience this. Jesus brought the knowledge of the Kingdom of God here with Him when He came. He told us that the Kingdom of God is within us (already). And His Gospel the good news teaches us how to tap into it even now.

Prosper, According To Your Calling:
Everything you financially need to be the most effective to fulfil Gods purpose in your life is included in Biblical Prosperity. At the very least you can believe according to "your calling" needs. You may not believe that this includes ten homes, ten cars, three airplanes and a world class luxury ship. But don't limit God. Surely you can believe that a God who owns the Universe can supply

Prosperity Bring the spirit to Life

what you need.... right. You may say, "Well God won't feed your fleshly lusts". You could say that, but a loving Father loves to give good gifts to His children. And He is the richest Father I know. 'More than enough' has always been Gods way of doing things. Our needs will be met as we focus on Gods supply and not our need. In other words, eyes on God not on self.

2 You should have everything you need to be the most effective to fulfil Gods purpose in your life whatever that may be, and be a blessing to others. By Studying the Laws of prosperity and following the principles of God we can be among those who have peace and prosper even in times of famine. We can become aware of the power we possess within us even now when our faith filled words move mountains with our Christian Payers.

Prosperity Bring the spirit to Life:
This speaks of Spiritual wellness. Our spiritual wellness is vitally connected to our overall Biblical prosperity. You can't understand the things of the Spirit unless your spirit is alive. Your spirit must come alive, be born again, through your relationship with the Holy Spirit. (It only takes a simple prayer of faith to go to Him even right now and ask Him in your own words to make your spirit come alive, be born again.) as in (John 3:6-8) "That which is born of the flesh is flesh, and that which is born of the Spirit is spirit. 7 Do not marvel that I said to you, 'You must be born again.' Jesus answered and said to him, "Most assuredly, I say to you, unless one is born again, he cannot see the kingdom of God." (John 3:3)

Prospers, Just as your Soul:
There much more to Biblical Prosperity than just financial gain. Biblical prosperity encompasses a dimension of wellness and wholeness in all things. Including your health and wellness in mind body and spirit. You could call it holistic healing. You are a spirit, you live in a body and you have a soul. The soul includes mind, free will, emotional health, personality and even social relationships. Biblical Prosperity is also recorded in (3 John 1:2) "Beloved, I pray that you may *prosper* in all things and be in health, just as your soul *prospers*." Hear how Bible verses in (3 John 2) show the way, this is a key; "As your soul prospers", (as it is brought up to a higher place in your understanding of the kingdom of God,) so too will you prosper in all things and be in health. 'Shalom', Peace, a Hebrew Blessing. May God Bless you with wellness and wholeness that is nothing missing and nothing broken. .

Prosperity as a Treasure of Knowledge:
Within Bible verses themselves God's will for you is found, a treasure of knowledge written to you personally. It's available for you to take full advantage of. Jesus provided it for you and His Holy Spirit will guide you into all truth. You practical understand-

ing of how emotions like anger and forgiveness can dramatically affect your health. You will find the ways God breaks generational curses over your life and He gives you understanding and victory over strongholds that keep you in bondage. The Word of God is filled with *prosperity* affirmations and it includes supernatural economic *prosperity*. More than enough abundance and *prosperity* is a rule in the Kingdom of God. The definition of *prosperity* is to go to a higher place in something desirable: the state of succeeding or flourishing, especially. financially.

All of these things and so much more is available Christians. You don't have to be a theologian to understand your Father, He gives you His Holy Spirit to teach you. As Jesus said, (John 14:26-27) "But the Helper, the Holy Spirit, whom the Father will send in My name, He will teach you all things, and bring to your remembrance all things that I said to you".

God Himself wants You to experience Biblical *prosperity*. Continue to study His Word and be Blessed. For more information follow links below. Prosper in all things and be in health, just as your soul prospers.

Purchase: (Verb, Greek: ayopa, Hebrew: qanah - [kaw-naw'], meaning to acquire (something) by paying for it; buy as Jeremiah's Land Purchase in (Jeremiah 32: 6 – 12) Jeremiah replied, "The word of the Lord came to me: Watch! Hanamel, the son of your uncle Shallum, is coming to you to say, 'Buy my field in Anathoth for yourself, for you own the right of redemption to buy it.' "Then my cousin Hanamel came to the guard's courtyard as the Lord had said and urged me, 'Please buy my field in Anathoth in the land of Benjamin, for you own the right of inheritance and redemption. Buy it for yourself.' Then I knew that this was the word of the Lord. So I bought the field in Anathoth from my cousin Hanamel, and I weighed out to him the money—17 shekels of silver. I recorded it on a scroll, sealed it, called in witnesses, and weighed out the silver in the scales. I took the *purchase* agreement—the sealed copy with its terms and conditions and the open copy — and gave the *purchase* agreement to Baruch son of Neriah, son of Mahseiah. I did this in the sight of my cousin Hanamel, the witnesses who were signing the *purchase* agreement, and all the Judeans sitting in the guard's courtyard.

2 As a (Noun); it means the action of buying something from decision, choosing, payment, receipting, and griping, owning or belonging. Firm contact or grip. Jesus repurchase us – Christians with His blood, He decided – Father I shall go to save my people, He paid the price heavily with His blood, the receipt was delivered when His blood was laid as a witness at the 'Mercy seat'. He gripped us to Himself, He owns us so, we belong

Pure

to Him and Him alone; Sin, sickness, poverty, the enemy cannot see us nor have us because we are not their property as we don't own ourselves anymore as in (Revelation 5:9) "And they sung a new song, saying, Thou art worthy to take the book, and to open the seals thereof: for thou wast slain, and hast redeemed us to God by thy blood out of every kindred, and tongue, and people, and nation; and (Acts 20:28) "Keep watch over yourselves and all the flock of which the Holy Spirit has made you overseers. Be shepherds of the church of God, which he bought with his own blood". Praise the Lord!

Pure: Adjective, Greek: *katharos* - [kath-ar-os'], Hebrew: bar [bar]

Meaning, clean, pure, unstained, either literally or ceremonially or spiritually; guiltless, innocent, upright. not mixed or adulterated with any other substance or material. 2 (of a sound) perfectly in tune and with a clear tone. 3 wholesome and untainted by immorality, especially that of a sexual nature. (of a subject of study) dealing with abstract concepts and not practical application. 5 involving or containing nothing else but; sheer (used for emphasis). 6 (of a vowel) not joined with another to form a diphthong.

2 *Pure* or purity, has to do with sanctification as in (1 Thessalonians 4: 3-8) "For this is God's will, your sanctification: that you abstain from sexual immorality, so that each of you knows how to possess his own vessel in sanctification and honor, not with lustful desires, like the Gentiles who don't know God. This means one must not transgress against and defraud his brother in this matter, because the Lord is an avenger of all these offenses, as we also previously told and warned you. For God has not called us to impurity, but to sanctification. Therefore, the person who rejects this does not reject man, but God, who also gives you His Holy Spirit".

The word "sanctification" comes from the same root word as the word "holy." Both of them convey the idea of separation from that which is ungodly and attachment to that which is *pure*. Notice that this is not just something negative. There is a positive aspect to sanctification. Without the attachment to something positive, people would be left to live in a vacuum. See (Leviticus. 15:31; Numbers. 6:2; 1 Chronicle: 23:13; Romans: 1:1; 2 Corinthians: 6:17; 1 Peter: 2:9;) We can avoid sexual immorality by learning to control our bodies (verse 4). Paul points out three aspects of this: (1) controlling our bodies in a holy way, (2) controlling our bodies in an honourable way, and (3) not giving in to passionate lust. See (Galatians 5:16) "So I say, walk by the Spirit, and you will not gratify the desires of the flesh" Also, (Philippians 4:8) states, "Finally, brothers and sisters, whatever is true, whatever is noble, whatever is right, whatever is *pure*, whatever is lovely, whatever is admirable—if anything is excellent or praiseworthy—think about such things". Praise the Lord!

Pure in Heart: This simply means living by the rule of God, living a life that is pleasing to God and Living for the purpose of God, having a single-minded devotion to God.

See the beatitude "Blessed are the *pure* in heart, for they shall see God" (Matthew 5:8). That's it! That's the goal of the Christian life! That's what we are living for – that we may live our life in such a way that we see God. If we see God, that will open up the treasure trove of all the blessings, not only for eternity, but also for life here and now. And the key to open that treasure trove is a *pure heart*! This is the most central and the most significant of all the beatitudes. You cannot be poor in spirit without having a *pure* heart. You cannot mourn for the things that displease God without having a *pure heart*. You cannot be meek, you cannot hunger and thirst for righteousness, you cannot be merciful; you cannot be a peacemaker or be prepared to stand persecution for the name of Christ without having a *pure heart*. Actually, this is one of the most central principles of the Christian life that we see in the whole Bible. The heart of the matter is the matter of the heart.

2 The initial use of the word "pure" in the Bible was in the sense of "clean" as opposed to "unclean" – clean or unclean animals, clean or unclean foods, the clean or unclean condition of a person. What do you think the basis was for determining what (or who) was "clean" or "unclean"? It was God's arbitrary decision. In some instance, we may be able to see a logical reason. For example, crows are unclean because they eat dead, rotten flesh. A person with leprosy is unclean because leprosy is an infectious disease. However, there is not always a logical reason why the flesh of some animals was considered clean and others unclean. If man was commanded to be fruitful and multiply and if sex was a gift from God, we do not know why semen discharge made a person unclean. If childbirth is an occasion of great joy, we do not know why it made the mother unclean. And if there was something medically bad in eating pork, the Department of Agriculture of most countries would have long ago prohibited raising pigs for food, and the Food and Drug Administration in most countries would have banned the sale of this meat.

That this was God's arbitrary decision is also seen from the fact that what was at one time considered unclean, God can declare clean at another time, as He does in Peter's vision (Acts 10), where Peter is asked to eat some of the things that were considered unclean. "Do not call anything impure that God has made clean" (Acts 10:15). Paul also declared, "As one who is in the Lord Jesus, I am fully convinced that no food [or thing] is unclean in itself" as in (Romans 14:14). Glory to Jesus.

Qq

Quail: (noun) a small short-tailed Old World game bird resembling a tiny partridge, typically having brown camouflaged plumage. 2 A small or medium-sized New World game bird, the male of which has distinctive facial markings. 3 A collective name for several genera of mid-sized birds generally considered in the order Galliformes Manna and Quail from Heaven as in (Exodus 16:12-14) I have heard the grumblings of the sons of Israel; speak to them, saying, 'At twilight you shall eat meat, and in the morning you shall be filled with bread; and you shall know that I am the LORD your God.'" So it came about at evening that the *quails* came up and covered the camp, and in the morning there was a layer of dew around the camp. When the layer of dew evaporated, behold, on the surface of the wilderness there was a fine flake-like thing, fine as the frost on the ground...." Old World *quail* are found in the family Phasianidae, and New World *quail* are found in the family Odontophoridae. The buttonquail are named more for their superficial resemblance to *quail*, and are members of the Turnicidae family in the Charadriiformes order. The king *quail*, one of the Old World *quail*, is often sold in the pet trade; and within this trade is commonly, though mistakenly, referred to as a "button *quail*". Many of the common larger species are farm-raised for table food or egg consumption, and are hunted on game farms or in the wild, where they may be released to supplement the wild population, or extend into areas outside their natural range. At evening the quails came up, and the people caught with ease as many as they needed. The manna came down in dew. They called it to Manna, Manhu, to which means, to What is this? to It is a portion; it is that which our God has allotted us, and we will take it, and be thankful. to It was pleasant food; it was wholesome food. The manna was rained from heaven; it appeared, when the dew was gone, as a small round thing, as small as the hoar frost, like coriander seed, in colour like pearls.

Queen: (noun, Greek - *anassa*, [*ánassa; from* wánassa**,** Hebrew - *malka* or *malkah* [mal-kaw'] meaning the female ruler of an independent state, especially one who inherits the position by right of birth. a male homosexual, typically one regarded as ostentatiously effeminate. As verb (of a woman) behave in an unpleasantly superior way towards (someone). 2 convert (a pawn) into a queen when it reaches the opponent's back rank on the board.

References: (Esther 1:9) Queen Vashti also gave a feast for the women in the palace that belonged to King Ahasuerus. (1 Peter 5:8) Be sober-minded; be watchful. Your adversary the devil prowls around like a roaring lion, seeking someone to devour. (Romans 10:9) Because, if you confess with your mouth that Jesus is Lord and believe in your heart that God raised him from the dead, you will be saved. (Jeremiah 44:25) Thus says the Lord of hosts, the God of Israel: You and your wives have declared with your mouths, and have fulfilled it with your hands, saying, 'We will surely perform our vows that we have made, to make offerings to the queen of heaven and to pour out drink offerings to her.' Then confirm your vows and perform your vows!

Queen of Sheba: The queen who appears in the Bible. The tale of her visit to King Solomon has undergone extensive Jewish, Arabian and Ethiopian elaborations, and has become the subject of one of the most widespread and fertile cycles of legends in the Orient. See (1 King 10)

2 According to narrative in the gospel, she was a woman of great wealth, beauty, and power. Sheba, believed to be either in Ethiopia or Yemen by most biblical scholars, was a well-established city, and, although there is little evidence outside the Bible as to the nature of the monarchy and how it was established, it is clear that the Queen of Sheba ruled alone and was not enamoured with the religions in her own land. The Queen of Sheba travelled to Jerusalem as she had "heard about the fame of Solomon and his relationship to the LORD, and came to test Solomon with hard questions" (1 Kings 10:1). As God had granted Solomon the gift of wisdom (1 Kings 3:5–12), "nothing was too hard for the king to explain to her" (1 Kings 10:3). After a meal together, the Queen of Sheba declares how impressed she is with Solomon's answers, hospitality, and the reputation that preceded him. The story ends with an exchange of resources and the Queen of Sheba returning "with her retinue to her own country" (1 Kings 10:13).

3 Probably, the nameless woman in the Song of Solomon is the *Queen of Sheba* (with the man being King Solomon). Both are speculative and, while interesting, cannot be declared factual. Whether she has any relation to the "Sheba" mentioned in (Genesis 10:7 and 28), or if she was the ancestor of "Candace, queen of the Ethiopians" (Acts 8:27), is, again, open to speculation.

Quench

4 The Queen of Sheba is mentioned again in the New Testament, by an alternative title, the Queen of the South (Matthew 12:42; Luke 11:31). Jesus refers to her, reaffirming her historical personage, as a means to illustrate the point that, despite being originally pagan in belief and Gentile in race, the Queen of Sheba recognized the truth and reality of God, unlike the religious leaders who opposed Jesus. As such, they would be condemned for their ignorant and defiant nature.

5 Two lessons can be learned from the story of the Queen of Sheba. First, like King Solomon, believers are to show evidence of God's favour in their lives, whatever their role, profession, or environment. Second, the reputation of believers should precede them by their godly words and actions, for we are "Christ's ambassadors" (2 Corinthians 5:20).

Quench: (Verb, Greek: *sbennumi* [sben'-noo-mee], Hebrew: *kabah* - [kaw-baw'] to extinguish, quench, (2) I suppress, thwart, 3 satisfy (one's thirst) by drinking. 4 rapidly cool (red-hot metal or other material), especially in cold water or oil.(Noun) an act of *quenching* a very hot substance. So, when the word "quench" is used in Scripture, it is speaking of suppressing fire. When believers put on the shield of faith, as part of their armour of God (Ephesians 6:16), they are extinguishing the power of the fiery darts from Satan. Christ described hell as a place where the fire would not be "quenched" (Mark 9:44, 46, 48). Likewise, the Holy Spirit is a fire dwelling in each believer. He wants to express Himself in our actions and attitudes. When believers do not allow the Spirit to be seen in our actions, when we do what we know is wrong, we suppress or *quench* the Spirit (1 Thessalonians 5:19). We do not allow the Spirit to reveal Himself the way that He wants to.

2 To understand what it means to grieve the Spirit, we must first understand that this indicates the Spirit possesses personality. Only a person can be grieved; therefore, the Spirit must be a divine person in order to have this emotion. Once we understand this, we can better understand how He is grieved, mainly because we too are grieved. (Ephesians 4:30) tells us that we should not grieve the Spirit. We grieve the Spirit by living like the pagans (Ephesians 4:17-19), by lying (Ephesians 4:25), by being angry (Ephesians 4:26-27), by stealing (Ephesians 4:28), by cursing (Ephesians 4:29), by being bitter (Ephesians 4:31), by being unforgiving (Ephesians 4:32), and by being sexually immoral (Ephesians 5:3-5). To grieve the Spirit is to act out in a sinful manner, whether it is in thought only or in both thought and deed.

Both *quenching* and grieving the Spirit are similar in their effects. Both hinder a godly lifestyle. Both happen when a believer sins against God and follows his or her own worldly desires. The only correct road to follow is the road that leads the believer closer to God and purity, and farther away from the world and sin. Just as we do not like to be grieved, and just as we do not seek to quench what is good—so we should not grieve or *quench* the Holy Spirit by refusing to follow His directives. Praise the Lord!

References: (Numbers 11:2) And the people cried unto Moses; and when Moses prayed unto the LORD, the fire was quenched. (2 Samuel 14:7) And, behold, the whole family is risen against thine handmaid, and they said, Deliver him that smote his brother, that we may kill him, for the life of his brother whom he slew; and we will destroy the heir also: and so they shall *quench* my coal which is left, and shall not leave to my husband neither name nor remainder upon the earth. (2 Samuel 21:17) But Abishai the son of Zeruiah succoured him, and smote the Philistine, and killed him. Then the men of David sware unto him, saying, Thou shalt go no more out with us to battle, that thou quench not the light of Israel. (2 Kings 22:17) Because they have forsaken me, and have burned incense unto other gods, that they might provoke me to anger with all the works of their hands; therefore my wrath shall be kindled against this place, and shall not be *quenched*. (2 Chronicles 34:25) Because they have forsaken me, and have burned incense unto other gods, that they might provoke me to anger with all the works of their hands; therefore my wrath shall be poured out upon this place, and shall not be *quenched*. (Psalms 104:11) They give drink to every beast of the field: the wild asses *quench* their thirst.

Quick: (Quickly,Quicken: Adjective, Greek: *tachus* [takh-oos'], Hebrew: (Noun) Meherah - [meh-hay-raw'] meaning - quick, swift, speedy, ready, prompt 1 moving fast or doing something in a short time. 2 prompt to understand, think, or learn; intelligent. (Adverb) at a fast rate; quickly. (noun) the soft tender flesh below the growing part of a fingernail or toenail. 2 those who are living. 3 a fast bowler.

(Hebrews 4:12) For the word of God is *quick*, and powerful, and sharper than any two edged sword, piercing even to the dividing asunder of soul and spirit, and of the joints and marrow, and is a discerner of the thoughts and intents of the heart. Also, Christians are warned from get rich quick schemes – see (Proverbs 13:11-13) "Wealth from get-rich-quick schemes quickly disappears; wealth from hard work grows over time".

Quick and the Dead, the: A phrase originating in the Christian Bible and popularized by the Apostles' Creed, one of the earliest statements of faith in the Christian religion and still one of the most widely used in worship.

Rr

Raise: (Verb, Greek: *egeiró* [eg-i'-ro] Hebrew: *qum* [koom] wake, arouse, (b) raise up as in (Matthew 10:8) "Heal the sick, *raise* the dead, cleanse those who have leprosy,[a] drive out demons. Freely you have received; freely give" (Proverbs 22:6)Train up a child in the way he should go; even when he is old he will not depart from it. (Ephesians 6:4) Fathers, do not provoke your children to anger, but bring them up in the discipline and instruction of the Lord. (Proverbs 29:15) The rod and reproof give wisdom, but a child left to himself brings shame to his mother. (Proverbs 23:13) Do not withhold discipline from a child; if you strike him with a rod, he will not die. (Deuteronomy 6:7) You shall teach them diligently to your children, and shall talk of them when you sit in your house, and when you walk by the way, and when you lie down, and when you rise.

Reap: (Verb, Greek: *therizó* [ther-id'-zo] Hebrew: *qatsar* -[kaw-tsar'] reap, gather, harvest, to get (something, such as a reward) as a result of something that you have done, 2 Harvest, the process of gathering mature crops from the field

We *reap* in kind to what we sow. Those who plant apple seeds should expect to harvest apples. Those who sow anger should expect to receive what anger naturally produces. (Galatians 6:8) says, "Whoever sows to please their flesh, from the flesh will reap destruction; whoever sows to please the Spirit, from the Spirit will reap eternal life." Living a life of carnality and sin and expecting to inherit heaven is akin to planting cockle burrs and waiting for roses. This principle works both positively and negatively. "The one who sows righteousness *reaps* a sure reward" (Proverbs 11:18b), but "whoever sows injustice *reaps* calamity" (Proverbs 22:8a).

2 We *reap* proportionately to what we sow. The rule is, the more seed planted, the more fruit harvested. The Bible applies this law to our giving. Those who show generosity will be blessed more than

those who don't. "Whoever sows sparingly will also *reap* sparingly, and whoever sows generously will also *reap* generously" (2 Corinthians 9:6). This principle is not concerned with the amount of the gift but with the spirit in which it is given. God loves a cheerful giver (2 Corinthians 9:7), and even the widow's mites are noticed by our Lord (Luke 21:2-3).

3 We reap more than what we sow. In other words, the law of sowing and reaping is related to the law of multiplication. Jesus spoke of seed that brought forth "a hundred, sixty or thirty times what was sown" (Matthew 13:8). One grain of wheat produces a whole head of grain. In the same way, one little fib can produce an out-of-control frenzy of falsehoods, fallacies, and fictions. Sow the wind and *reap* the whirlwind (Hosea 8:7). Positively, one kind deed can result in a blessing to last a lifetime. Praise the Lord!

Receive: (Verb, Greek: *dechomai* [dekh'-om-ahee], Hebrew: *qabal* - [kaw-bal'] to take, receive, accept, welcome

References: (Acts 20:35) In all things I have shown you that by working hard in this way we must help the weak and remember the words of the Lord Jesus, how he himself said, 'It is more blessed to give than to receive.'" (2 Corinthians 9:7) Each one must give as he has decided in his heart, not reluctantly or under compulsion, for God loves a cheerful giver. (James 1:17) Every good gift and every perfect gift is from above, coming down from the Father of lights with whom there is no variation or shadow due to change. (Hebrews 13:16) Do not neglect to do good and to share what you have, for such sacrifices are pleasing to God. (Matthew 6:1-34) "Beware of practicing your righteousness before other people in order to be seen by them, for then you will have no reward from your Father who is in heaven. "Thus, when you give to the needy, sound no trumpet before you, as the hypocrites do in the synagogues and in the streets, that they may be praised by others. Truly, I say to you, they have received their reward. But when you give to the needy, do not let your left hand know what your right hand is doing, so that your giving may be in secret. And your Father who sees in secret will reward you. "And when you pray, you must not be like the hypocrites. For they love to stand and pray in the synagogues and at the street corners, that they may be seen by others. Truly, I say to you, they have received their reward

Redeem: (Verb, Greek - *Exagorazó* - [ex-ag-or-ad'-zo] Hebrew: gaal [gaw-al'] buy out, buy away from, ransom; mid: to purchase out, buy, redeem, choose. 1 compensate for the faults or bad aspects of. 2 gain or regain possession of (something) in exchange for payment. 3 fulfil or carry out (a pledge or promise).

Redeemer

2 Everyone is in need of redemption. Our natural condition was characterized by guilt: "all have sinned and fall short of the glory of God" (Romans 3:23). Christ's redemption has freed us from guilt, being "justified freely by His grace through the redemption that is in Christ Jesus" (Romans 3:24). The benefits of redemption include eternal life (Revelation 5:9-10), forgiveness of sins (Ephesians 1:7), righteousness (Romans 5:17), freedom from the law's curse (Galatians 3:13), adoption into God's family (Galatians 4:5), deliverance from sin's bondage (Titus 2:14; 1 Peter 1:14-18), peace with God (Colossians 1:18-20), and the indwelling of the Holy Spirit (1 Corinthians 6:19-20). To be redeemed, then, is to be forgiven, holy, justified, free, adopted, and reconciled. See also (Psalm 130:7-8; Luke 2:38; and Acts 20:28.

The word redeem means "to buy out." The term was used specifically in reference to the purchase of a slave's freedom. The application of this term to Christ's death on the cross is quite telling. If we are "redeemed," then our prior condition was one of slavery. God has purchased our freedom, and we are no longer in bondage to sin or to the Old Testament law. This metaphorical use of "redemption" is the teaching of (Galatians 3:13 and 4:5).

3 Related to the Christian concept of redemption is the word ransom. Jesus paid the price for our release from sin and its consequences (Matthew 20:28; 1 Timothy 2:6). His death was in exchange for our life. In fact, Scripture is quite clear that redemption is only possible "through His blood," that is, by His death (Colossians 1:14). The streets of heaven will be filled with former captives who, through no merit of their own, find themselves redeemed, forgiven, and free. Slaves to sin have become saints. No wonder we will sing a new song—a song of praise to the Redeemer who was slain (Revelation 5:9). We were slaves to sin, condemned to eternal separation from God. Jesus paid the price to redeem us, resulting in our freedom from slavery to sin and our rescue from the eternal consequences of that sin.

Redeemer: He who redeems – Jesus Christ.

Refuge: (Greek: *Katapheugó* [kat-af-yoo'-go] Hebrew: machaseh or machseh - [makh-as-eh'] To flee for refuge (implying that the refuge is reached); aor. indicates moment of arrival. Refuge is a place or state of safety. It may also refer to a more specific meaning: Area of refuge, a location in a building that may be used by occupants in the event of a fire Mountain hut, a shelter for travellers in mountainous areas, often remote

2 In a layman's language, the word refuge implies an imposing building with locks on the doors, maybe a thick-walled fortress, or

Refuge

perhaps something as simple as a canopy to keep you dry in a rainstorm. Whatever picture comes to mind, it can be agreed that a refuge is a safe place. When the Bible describes God as our refuge, it is saying that God is our safe place when we need protection from something. Knowing God as our refuge enables us to trust Him more freely. We need not fear situations or people who threaten our well-being, whether in a physical or spiritual sense. There is no situation we will ever face that is out of God's control, so the best place to be, always, is right with Him. "The name of the LORD is a fortified tower; the righteous run to it and are safe" (Proverbs 18:10).

3 The best way to make God our refuge is to lean on Him like David. David is a great example of someone who knew God as his *refuge*. At different points in his life, David was on the run from people who literally wanted to kill him, but he always found safety in God. "My salvation and my honour depend on God; he is my mighty rock, my *refuge*. Trust in him at all times, you people; pour out your hearts to him, for God is our *refuge*" (Psalm 62:7–8). An easy way to make God our *refuge* is to simply ask Him to be. David said, "Pour out your hearts to him"; that's what David did all the time. He poured out his heart to God about what was going on in his life and asked God to intervene on his behalf. When we turn to God for help or protection, we begin to know Him as our *refuge*.

4 In contrast to David's faith, the leaders of Israel in Isaiah's day tried to find security in things other than God. In (Isaiah 28:15), the Lord rebukes them for making "a lie our *refuge* and falsehood our hiding place." God's then offers them a true *refuge*: "See I lay a stone in Zion, a tested stone, a precious cornerstone for a sure foundation; the one who relies on it will never be stricken with panic. I will make justice the measuring line; hail will sweep away your *refuge*, the lie, and water will overflow your hiding place" (Isaiah 28:16–18). We may be tempted to look for safety in things other than God, but such things can only provide a false sense of security. God is the only real *refuge* we'll ever find.

God is our *refuge*. However, that does not mean He will never lead us into difficult or dangerous situations. Jesus led the disciples into a boat, knowing full well that a violent storm was brewing; the disciples were terrified, but Jesus, their *refuge*, calmed the storm (Matthew 8:23–27). When we are in God's will, we can face even the most dangerous situations with confidence, because God is with us.

6 Countless times, God led the Israelites into battles against armies much more powerful than they, yet

Rejoice

when they trusted God and obeyed Him, they always came out victorious - see (Joshua 6 and 8) for some examples. Jesus told us, "In me you may have peace. In this world you will have trouble. But take heart! I have overcome the world" (John 16:33). No matter what our circumstance, the safest place to be is always in the centre of God's will. He promises to be our *refuge*: "'Never will I leave you; never will I forsake you.' So we say with confidence, 'The Lord is my helper; I will not be afraid. What can man do to me?'" (Hebrews 13:5–6).

References: (Psalms 91:2) God, The Rock Optimism Refuge God Being Our Fortress Fortifications I will say to the LORD, "My refuge and my fortress, My God, in whom I trust!" (Deuteronomy 33:27) God Battles Sustaining Providence Loneliness Security Arms Everlasting Arms Refuge enemies, of Israel and Judah God's Omnipotence God, The Eternal Eternally With God Refugees enemies, of believers Afflictions, Consolation During God, The Provider Destruction Of Satan's Worksest, Physical dependence Immortality, In OT Things Under Sanctuary defence, divine" The eternal God is a dwelling place, And underneath are the everlasting arms; And He drove out the enemy from before you, And said, 'Destroy!' (Exodus 33:22) God's Handand it will come about, while My glory is passing by, that I will put you in the cleft of the rock and cover you with My hand until I have passed by. (Psalms 27:5) Stones For Protection Rocks God Hiding People God Being Our Hiding Place Comfort In Affliction Trouble, God's Help In God Lifting People defence, divine For in the day of trouble He will conceal me in His tabernacle; In the secret place of His tent He will hide me; He will lift me up on a rock. (Psalms 31:20) God Being Our Hiding Place God Hiding People defence, divine Safety Sanctuary You hide them in the secret place of Your presence from the conspiracies of man; You keep them secretly in a shelter from the strife of tongues. (Psalms 46:1) Comforting Adversity Protection, From God defence, divine Rich, The Trouble, God's Help In God, Titles And Names Of Sanctuary enemies, of believers Protection Security Being Betrayed Refuge Fortifications Trouble dependence Reliability God is our refuge and strength, A very present help in trouble. (Psalms 71:3) Rocks Fortifications defence, divine God, The Rock Refuge Be to me a rock of habitation to which I may continually come; You have given commandment to save me, For You are my rock and my fortress. (Proverbs 14:26) Being Confident Reverence To God defence, divine Spiritual Adoption, Benefits Of Solutions To Insecurity Fortresses Reverence, And Blessing Fortifications Bravery In the fear of the LORD there is strong confidence, And his children will have refuge

Rejoice: (Verb, Greek: *katapheugó* [kat-af-yoo'-go] Hebrew: *gil* - [gheel] flee for refuge (implying

Rejoice

that the refuge is reached); aor. indicates moment oRejoicing is a spiritual weapon to fight off attacks on our mind. Rejoicing is a spiritual weapon given to us from God. It's like anti-venom from a poisonous snake bite. Truly - It can be a spiritual life-saver, especially when you're being strongly tempted to tell God at a subconscious level, "Go take a hike, God. You could have prevented this pain I'm experiencing, but you didn't!"

2 Rejoicing is not about trying to pretend you're not in pain. It's believing that through the focused discipline of rejoicing ... the peace of God which surpasses all understanding may visit you when it might not otherwise. See: (Philippians. 4:7). Rejoicing may also impart to you the supernatural ability to deal EASIER with your pain ... as the Holy Spirit through the Apostle Paul declared: "I can do all things through Christ who strengthens me." - (Philippians 4:13)

3 Rejoicing may also impart trust (faith) in God (which includes His promises in the Bible) that you may not receive otherwise. Rejoicing may also motivate God to shower you with greater blessing -- or withhold blessing from you -- if you choose not to engage in rejoicing. Bottom line: To the wise Christian, purposing to *rejoice* always is not an option. No soldier refuses to use a weapon if odds increase it will help him/her stay alive, and increase one's well-being. Once you realize "rejoicing" is the powerful spiritual weapon that it IS ... you'll want to use it on a daily basis. arrival. Feel or show great joy or delight. **References:** (Philippians 4:4) Rejoice in the Lord always; again I will say, Rejoice. (Psalm 5:11) But let all who take refuge in you rejoice; let them ever sing for joy, and spread your protection over them, that those who love your name may exult in you. (1 John 4:18) There is no fear in love, but perfect love casts out fear. For fear has to do with punishment, and whoever fears has not been perfected in love. (Psalm 91:1-16) He who dwells in the shelter of the Most High will abide in the shadow of the Almighty. I will say to the Lord, "My refuge and my fortress, my God, in whom I trust." For he will deliver you from the snare of the fowler and from the deadly pestilence. He will cover you with his pinions, and under his wings you will find refuge; his faithfulness is a shield and buckler. You will not fear the terror of the night, nor the arrow that flies by day, (Philippians 4:4-7) Rejoice in the Lord always; again I will say, Rejoice. Let your reasonableness be known to everyone. The Lord is at hand; do not be anxious about anything, but in everything by prayer and supplication with thanksgiving let your requests be made known to God. And the peace of God, which surpasses all understanding, will guard your hearts and your minds in Christ Jesus.

Remission: (Greek: *aphesis* - [af'-es-is] Hebrews: *hemittah* - [shem-it-taw'] a sending away, a letting go, a release, pardon, complete forgiveness. Remission (law), also known as remand, the proceedings by which a case is sent back to a lower court from which it was appealed, with instructions as to what further proceedings should be had. Remission (medicine), the state of absence of disease activity in patients with a chronic illness, with the possibility of return of disease activity. Remission (spectroscopy), the reflection or scattering of light by a material. Remission (theology), the absence of the power and penalty of sin, as in (Hebrews 9:22), Remission (EP), a 1984 EP by Skinny Puppy, Remission (Mastodon album), the debut album by American metal band Mastodon, Remission (Catholicism), the forgiveness of sin, particularly after the Sacrament of Penance. Clemency, the reduction of a prison sentence

2 *Remission:* To remit is to forgive. Remission is a related word, and it means "forgiveness." The "remission of sin," then, is simply the "forgiveness" of sin. The phrase used in eight places in the King James Version of the Bible. In the Gospel of (Matthew 26:28), for example, says, "For this is my blood of the new testament, which is shed for many for the *remission* of sins." Modern translations such as the English Standard Version render the phrase "for the forgiveness of sins."

3 Luke has three examples of this phrase. (Luke 1:77) says, "To give knowledge of salvation unto his people by the remission of their sins." John the Baptist "came into all the country about Jordan, preaching the baptism of repentance for the remission of sins" (Luke 3:3). When Jesus appeared to His disciples after His resurrection, He said that "repentance and remission of sins should be preached in his name among all nations, beginning at Jerusalem" (Luke 24:47).

4 In Acts, Peter tells a Roman named Cornelius that "whosoever believeth in [Christ] shall receive remission of sins" (Acts 10:43). Cornelius and those in his home did believe, and they received forgiveness in Christ. God remits sin on the basis of Jesus' sacrifice on the cross (Romans 3:24-25). The teaching of Scripture is that remission only comes by grace through faith (Ephesians 2:8-9). Praise the Lord!

Renew: The Old and New Testaments use terms such as "restore" and "renew" to image God's control of history and the believer's spiritual life. Both terms, represented by a variety of Hebrew and Greek words, are used in literal and figurative contexts. It is the extension of the literal meaning into a figure for explaining God's program or the nature of spiritual living that presents challenges for interpretation.

2 The literal meaning of these terms is clear and needs little comment. The usage pattern for the words translated "restore" is mostly a literal meaning. Life, land, property, health, and other tangible items are the subject of restoration (Genesis 42:25 ; 1 Kings 20:34 ; Job 20:10 ; Ezekiel 18:7 ; Mark 3:5 ; Luke 19:8). On the other hand, the "renew" pattern is predominantly figurative. Passages on literal renewal (to take something up again), such as kingdom renewal at Gilgal (1Samuel 11:14), are rare (2 Chronicle 15:8 ; Job 10:17 ; 29:20 ; Psalm 103:5) The New Testament usage is exclusively figurative.

3 The figurative usage of "restore" falls into three areas with only about six passages to consider. First, there is personal spiritual restoration. In (Psalm 23:3) the psalmist pleads for strength in trials. In (Psalm 51:12) David is seeking a sense of restoration in light of grievous sin against God. Second, (Galatians 6:1) calls for mature believers to identify their areas of strength and to mentor back to spiritual health another ailing believer. Third, there are references (Mathew 17:11 ; Mark 9:12 ; Mathew 19:28 ; Acts 1:6 ; 3:21) to an eschatological restoration. This latter category is the focus of much theological discussion and will be examined below.

4 The figurative usage of "renew" occurs in over two-thirds of the passages. There is a renewal that is the regaining of inner strength and resolve in our pursuit of God (Isaiah 40:31 ; 41:1 ; Lamentation 5:21 ; 2 Corinthians 4:16). Some contexts stress the acquisition of knowledge as a means of providing mental renewal (Romans 12:2 ; Ephesians 4:23 ; Colossians 3:10). This mental alignment to God's truth is the foundation of the value clarification the believer begins to pursue at conversion (Romans 12:2). Two references view renewal from the perspective of repentance (Psalm 51:10 ; Hebrew 6:6). The use of *palingenesia* [paliggenesiva] and *anakainosis* [ajnakaivnwsi"] in (Titus 3:5) provides metaphors for rebirth (NIV; "regeneration" KJV) and renewal. Paul finishes the sentence of (Titus 3:5) in (Titus3:7) with the crescend of justification.

5 Both renewal and restoration illustrates two important issues for the new comers into the Gospel or Bible Students: (1) no theological concept can be treated by merely looking up a key word or two (i.e., theological concepts are often conveyed by a variety of terms); (2) the reader of English versions should beware. The King James Version translated *palingenesia* [paliggenesiva] as "regeneration" while more recent versions translate this term as "renewal" (Mathew 19:28 ; NIV). But compare the New International Version on (Titus 3:5), where the same Greek term is translated "rebirth, " a translational necessity since a more direct term for "renew" follows in this verse. Glory to Jesus!

Repent or Repentance

Repent or Repentance: (Verb; Greek: *metanoeó* - [met-an-o-eh'-o], Hebrew: *Yom Kippur*) To repent, change my mind, change the inner man (particularly with reference to acceptance of the will of God), repent.

2 The activity of reviewing one's actions and feeling contrition or regret for past wrongs. It generally[citation needed] involves a commitment to personal change and resolving to live a more responsible and humane life. The practice of repentance plays an important role in the soteriological doctrines of the world's major religions where it is considered necessary for the attainment of salvation. In religious contexts it often involves an act of confession to a spiritual elder (such as a pastor or priest). This typically includes an admission of guilt, a promise or resolve not to repeat the offense; an attempt to make restitution for the wrong, or in some way to reverse the harmful effects of the wrong where possible. Jesus died on the cross and gave us the free gift of salvation for anyone willing to accept it. However, our salvation needs to be accepted, we have to embrace Jesus Christ as our Lord and Saviour. Not only that, but repenting of your sins is part of accepting that special gift.

To repent of our sins, every Christian must realize their sins and feel sorry for them - we have to feel remorse for our past conduct or else our salvation won't mean anything to us. We must continually turn away from sin to honour our Lord and to live a Christian life. Though, it's hard to stay away from sin because our world is simply filled with it. However, if we keep our Heavenly Father and everlasting life on our minds, that sin is much easier to avoid. So turn away from sin! Repent! That way, you will be able to feel the joy and love of Jesus Christ!

Within a secular context repentance may form part of the process of psychological healing that takes place during a course of psychotherapy.

According to (Acts 17:30), "In the past God overlooked ..ignorance, but now he commands all people everywhere to *repent*". Also in (Luke 24:47) "And that repentance and release from bondage of sins should be preached in his name among all nations, beginning at Jerusalem". The original Greek word for release from bondage of sin could be translated as release from bondage, forgiveness, or remission, of sin. Release from bondage of sin is far more accurate, and perfectly describes the purification necessary to avoid being banned from heaven. The cleansing of the Word, the cleansing in the Light, both attained by waiting on the Lord, listening, hearing, watching, and obeying - such cleansing is a release from the bondage of sin. But the poor souls, who were trying to translate the Bible, had not experienced release from bondage of sin within them, and so obviously chose to emphasize forgiveness instead. Yet release from captivity, from the prison house, from the oppression, is what Christ said he came to do: Thus in (Luke 4: 18-19), "The Spirit of the Lord is upon me, because he has anointed me to preach the gospel to the poor; he has sent me to heal the broken hearted, to preach release to the captives [of sin], and recovery of sight to the blind, to deliver [free] those who are oppressed [by sin] and (Isaiah 61: 1-2) "The Spirit of the Lord GOD is upon me because the LORD has anointed me to preach good tidings to the poor; he has sent me to heal the broken-hearted, to proclaim deliverance to the captives, and the opening of the prison to those who are bound" and for what Paul said Jesus sent him to the Gentiles to accomplish: Note: (Acts 26:18) 'To open their eyes, and to turn them from darkness to light, and from the power of Satan to God, that they may receive forgiveness of sins, release from sin's slavery, and an inheritance among those who are sanctified and purified by faith in me'. With the above verses, forgiveness is not deliverance, recovery, healing, opening the prison, release, turned from power of Satan, - while release from the bondage of sin accurately describes all. In (John 8:11) Jesus told the adulteress: I do not condemn you either. Go on your way and sin no more, least a worse thing come upon you. The worse thing is to be banned from heaven for still sinning, and sent to Hell, until you have paid the last farthing. He would not have commanded her to sin no more, unless it were possible. Repentance is the way.

According (Luke 13: 3 – 5) Jesus being the way often show nus the way to eternal life and divine pleasure as He often warned us: "Unless you repent you will all likewise perish". Jesus requires us to be holy, pure, and perfect, which work he does for us by grace, as we carry the inward cross of self-denial, repenting from what he shows us as the sins in our heart, and obeying his commands that we hear him speak to us from Jesus, the word, in our heart. Sanctify yourselves for His Love; Glory to His Name!

References: (Ezekiel 33:11) Say to them: 'As I live,' says the Lord GOD, 'I have no pleasure in the death of the wicked, but that the wicked turn from his way and live. Turn, turn from your evil ways! For why should you die, O house of Israel?' (Ezekiel 18:30-32) *"Repent!* And turn from all your transgressions, so iniquity will not be your ruin. Cast away from you all your transgressions, by which you have transgressed; and get a new heart and a new spirit. For why will you die. For I have no pleasure in the death of him who dies," says the Lord GOD. "Therefore turn [from you evil ways] and live!" (2 Kings 17:13) Yet the LORD warned Israel and Judah through all the proph-

Resist

ets and all the seers, saying, "Turn from your evil ways and keep my commands and my statutes, according to all the law that I commanded your forefathers and sent to you by my servants the prophets." (Zechariah 1:4) Thus said the LORD of hosts: "Turn now from your evil ways and from your evil doings;" but they did not hear or listen to me, says the LORD. (2 Peter 3:9) The Lord is not slow in keeping his promise, as some understand slowness. He is patient with you, not wanting anyone to perish, but everyone to come to repentance. (Matthew 3:2) And saying, Repent (think differently; change your mind, regretting your sins and changing your conduct), for the kingdom of heaven is at hand. (Luke 3:11-14) Share from your excess with those who are without the necessities of life. Be honest in all your dealings, never exaggerating or overreaching anyone. Don't oppress people or frighten anyone, don't lie, don't want more, don't complain. (Matthew 3:8) Produce fruit in keeping with repentance.

Resist: (Verb, Greek: *anthistémi* -[anth-is'-tay-mee] Hebrew: *anthistemi* set against; To withstand, resist, oppose. to set one' s self against, to withstand, resist, oppose (2) to set against withstand the action or effect of. As a (Noun) a resistant substance applied as a coating to protect a surface during a process, for example to prevent dye or glaze adhering.

References: (1 Peter 4:12) Dear friends, do not be surprised at the painful trial you are suffering, as though something strange were happening to you. (2 Peter 2:9) if this is so, then the Lord knows how to rescue godly men from trials and to hold the unrighteous for the day of judgment, while continuing their punishment. (Galatians 4:14) Even though my illness was a trial to you, you did not treat me with contempt or scorn. Instead, you welcomed me as if I were an angel of God, as if I were Christ Jesus himself. (1 Thessalonians 3:5) For this reason, when I could stand it no longer, I sent to find out about your faith. I was afraid that in some way the tempter might have tempted you and our efforts might have been useless.

Resist the devil: The phrase "resist the devil" is found in (James 4:7) where the apostle James exhorts believers to *resist the devil* in order to cause him to flee or "run away" from us. To resist means to withstand, strive against, or oppose in some manner. Resistance can be a defensive manoeuvre on our part, such as resisting or withstanding the temptation to sin. Or, it can be an action we take to use the only offensive weapon in the full armor of God (Ephesians 6:13-18), the sword of the Spirit which is the Word of God. Using the Scriptures to expose Satan's lies and temptations is the most effective way to strive against and defeat them.

Resist the devil

2 Apostle John records Jesus saying about Satan, "The thief comes only to steal and kill and destroy; I have come that they may have life, and have it to the full" (John 10:10). As Christians, we have full life when we are aware of the reality of the presence of evil. As we struggle to stand firm in our faith, we must realize that the enemies we are up against are not merely human ideas, but real forces that come from the powers of darkness. The Bible says in (Ephesians 6:12) "For our struggle is not against flesh and blood, but against the rulers, against the powers, against the world forces of this darkness, against the spiritual forces of wickedness in the heavenly places" .

3 Resistance will cause the devil to flee because he knows he cannot have victory over us if we are prepared to do battle against him. As mentioned before, the Gospel as recorded in the Bible assures us that we need only put on the full armour of God to be fully protected from evil and to actively resist it. There is nothing more frightening to Satan than a believer who is fully equipped with spiritual armour, beginning with the "helmet of salvation," which protects our minds and the "breastplate of righteousness," which protects our hearts because it is the righteousness of Christ (2 Corinthians 5:21). Only a true believer wears these because only those who have received God's forgiveness by grace through faith have eternal salvation and the righteousness of Christ imputed to them.

4 Once fitted with the helmet and breastplate (literally "chest protector"), we are then to take up other defensive weapons with which to battle Satan: truth, the readiness to proclaim the gospel, and the faith that shields us from all the flaming arrows of the evil one. The final piece of armour is prayer. We pray for strength to resist evil and to actively battle against it. We pray for wisdom in the conflict and most of all, we remain steadfast in our prayers, both for the ability to resist the devil and also for other believers who struggle in the same battle. When the church, the body of Christ, stands united against evil, fully-equipped with the armour of God, we present a formidable foe to the evil one and we will see God get the glory for the victory.

> Note as important: Throughout the whole Gospel of Christ; the Bible never gives Christians the authority to "rebuke" the devil, only to resist him. (Zechariah 3:2) tells us that it is the Lord who rebukes Satan. Even Michael, one of the most powerful of the angels, did not dare to accuse Satan, but rather said, "The Lord rebuke you" (Jude 1:9).

Rest

In response to Satan's attacks as Christians, we should redouble efforts to clothe ourselves in the spiritual armours, wield the Word of God, and rely on His power through prayer. Instead of focusing on "rebuking" the devil, we should focus on resisting him with the full armour of God. Praise the Lord of Host!

Rest: (Verb, Greek: *anapauó* - [an-ap-ow'-o], Hebrew: *nuach* - [noo'-akh] *Rest*. To make to rest, give rest to; mid. and pass: I rest, take my ease.

2 "Rest" is defined as "peace, ease or refreshment." "Relax" means "to become loose or less firm, to have a milder manner, to be less stiff." The Bible speaks quite highly of *rest*. It is a repeated theme throughout Scripture, beginning with the creation week (Genesis 2:2-3). God created for six days; then He *rested*, not because He was tired but to set the standard for mankind to follow. The Ten Commandments made resting on the Sabbath a requirement of the Law (Exodus 20:8-11). Notice that God said, "Remember the Sabbath." It wasn't something new; it had been around since creation. All God's people and their servants and the animals were to have one day in seven to rest. The command to rest was not an excuse to be lazy. You had to work for six days to get to the Sabbath. The land also needed to rest (Leviticus 25:4, 8-12). God is very serious about *rest*.

3 God desires *rest* for us because it does not come naturally to us. To *rest*, we have to trust that God will take care of things for us. We have to trust that, if we take a day off, the world will not stop turning on its axis. From the beginning (Genesis 3), when we decided that we would start making all the decisions, mankind has become more tense and less able to relax. It was disobedience in the Garden that started the problem, but obedience now will bring the rest that God so desires for us (Hebrews 3:7 - 4:11). If one of the definitions of "relax" is "to become less firm," then relaxing our grip on our own lives, careers, families, etc., and giving them over to God in faith is the best way to relax.

4 For the Christian, the ultimate *rest* is found in Christ. He invites all who are "weary and burdened" to come to Him and cast our cares on Him (Matthew 11:28; 1 Peter 5:7). It is only in Him that we find our complete rest—from the cares of the world, from the sorrows that plague us, and from the need to work to make ourselves acceptable to Him. We no longer observe the Jewish Sabbath because Jesus is our Sabbath *rest*. In Him we find complete *rest* from the labours of our self-effort, because He alone is holy and righteous. "God made him who had no sin to be sin for us, so that in him we might become the righteousness of God" (2 Corinthians 5:21). We can now cease from our spiritual labours and rest in Him, not just one day a week, but always. Praise the Lord!

References: (Exodus 33:14) And he said, "My presence will go with you, and I will give you rest." (Matthew 11:28-30) Come to me, all who labour and are heavy laden, and I will give you rest. Take my yoke upon you, and learn from me, for I am gentle and lowly in heart, and you will find rest for your souls. For my yoke is easy, and my burden is light." (Matthew 11:29) Take my yoke upon you, and learn from me, for I am gentle and lowly in heart, and you will find rest for your souls. (Psalm 127:2) ESV, It is in vain that you rise up early and go late to *rest*, eating the bread of anxious toil; for he gives to his beloved sleep. (Exodus 34:21) "Six days you shall work, but on the seventh day you shall *rest*. In plowing time and in harvest you shall rest. (Mark 6:31) And he said to them, "Come away by yourselves to a desolate place and rest a while." For many were coming and going, and they had no leisure even to eat. (Psalm 46:10) "Be still, and know that I am God. I will be exalted among the nations, I will be exalted in the earth!"

Restore: (Verb, Greek: *katartizó* [kat-ar-tid'-zo], Hebrew: *arukah* - [ar-oo-kaw'] health (a) To fit (join) together; met: To compact together, (b) act. and mid: to prepare, perfect, for his (its) full destination or use, bring into its proper condition (whether for the first time, or after a lapse). *Please see Renew above*

Resurrection: (Verb, Greek: *anastasis* - [an-as' tas-is] a rising again, resurrection. Resurrection means a 'raising up', or 'rising up' from the Greek word ANASTASIS. In the verb form it means 'to cause to stand or rise up; to raise from sleep or from the dead'. The word 'rapture' is a term not found in scripture and represents an erroneous doctrine. Rapture comes from the word Raptus which is found in the Latin Vulgate and it is the Latin form of the Greek word Harpazo which means "caught up" (1 Thessalonians 4:16-18) is the doctrine of the Rapture. When Christ comes again, there will be a *resurrection* of all the dead. Both those who are saved and the wicked will be resurrected at some point in time. Those who are saved will receive new glorified bodies and take their place with God in heaven, but the wicked will be cast into hell (Matthew 5:29-30, 10:28, 18:8-9, 25:31-46, Mark 9:43-47, John 5:28-29, Acts 24:15, Revelation 20:12-15). Jesus said, "Do not be amazed at this, for a time is coming when all who are in their graves will hear his [Christ's] voice and come out - those who have done good will rise to live, and those who have done evil will rise to be condemned. (John 5:28-29) Our new glorified bodies will be different from our old earthly bodies, but will in some ways be similar (1 Corinthians 15:50-55, 2 Corinthians 5:1-5, Philippians 3:21-22).

Resurrection from the death

Resurrection from the death: Death is not a state of non-existence, nor is it annihilation, but in its scriptural sense it is a separation from the Source of life. Our present existence is actually a state of death as in (Luke 16:19-31; Isaiah 14:9-11; 1 Peter 3:18-20) Death affects man in three levels. (1) Spiritually (2) Physically (3) Eternally - 'to the ages of the ages'

1 **Spiritual Death:** This is the separation of the soul of man from God through sin. Adam as a living soul died spiritually in the literal day that he sinned. He became severed from the life that is in Yahweh God. "the soul who sins will die" (Ezekiel 18:20) "The wages of sin is death" (Romans 6:23) - death (separation from the true and living God) is the repayment you receive from being your own 'god'. "To be carnally minded is death, but to be spiritually minded is life and peace" (Romans 8: 6). 'Carnal' as used here is 'fleshly' - i.e. thinking according to the flesh, or allowing the flesh to dominate your life. That brings death (James 1:12-15). So although physically alive, you can be spiritually 'dead'. (1 Timothy 5: 6; Revelation 3: 1)

2 **Physical Death:** Physical death is the separation of the soul and spirit from the body. Man was not meant to die, Adam died physically 930 years after he sinned, which was in the typical 'day' that Yahweh predicted (2 Peter 3:8, Romans 5:12,14,21, Hebrews 9:27).

Our bodies were formed to regenerate - the cells renew themselves and medical science cannot determine why man dies. It is the principle of sin outworking in our bodies, in death as a process - "dying you shall die". Weakness, sickness and disease.

3 **Eternal Death:** This is the judgment determined on all those who reject the atonement for sin purchased by the Saviour. It is called in scripture, the 'second death' which is effected through the 'lake of fire'. (Revelation 20:11-15) Of this all the prophets warned "to flee from the wrath to come" where He will "burn up the chaff with unquenchable fire" (Matthew 3: 7 - 12) This is the 'worm' that never dies and the fire that is not quenched as in (Isaiah 66:24; Mark 9:43-48) Those who overcome the 'flesh' are assured that they will not be hurt by the 'second death' recorded in (Revelation 2:11; 20:6). Also (Revelation 21:8) asserts "But, "...the cowardly, unbelieving, abominable, murderers, sexually immoral, sorcerers, idolaters, and all liars shall have their part in the lake which burns with fire and brimstone, which is the second death."

Again; Y'shua, the second man, the substitute Adam tasted death in every form for man. As the 'last Adam', He overcame death on our behalf. He tasted death spiritually in His separation from the Father, physically by being put to death in the flesh, and when He went into

Sheol or Hades, He experienced eternal death on our behalf. (Hebrews 2:9; 1 Corinthians 15:45-47)

2 Because of His Holiness, death could not hold him in its clutches, when the sentence was completed that He took on our behalf, the Spirit of Yahweh raised Him from the grave triumphant over all the powers of darkness that had sought to hold Him in their grip. As in (Psalm 22: 6-8,14-18) of the Saviour's suffering. He arose! He arose the victor, triumphant over death and now as a life-giving Spirit He imparts His victorious life to us. Praise His Holy Name!

Resurrection, the process of: Death is not a state of non-existence, nor is it annihilation, but in its scriptural sense it is a separation from the Source of life. Our present existence is actually a state of death. See (Luke 16:19-31; Isaiah 14:9-11; 1 Peter 3:18-20) Death affects man in three levels. 1. Spiritually 2. Physically 3. Eternally - 'to the ages of the ages'

Resurrection, First: "There will be a resurrection of the dead, both of the just and the unjust" (Acts 24:15) "The hour is coming, in which all that are in the graves shall hear His voice, and shall come forth, they that have done good, unto the resurrection of life, and they that have done evil, unto the resurrection of judgment." (John 5:28,29) *First Resurrection* is a resurrection to life in the flesh for all those who have died in Messiah and have no need of judgment in their lives. They will live with Him during the Messianic age on earth as a first fruits of His creation that come to perfection. "we also who have the first fruits of the Spirit, even we ourselves groan within ourselves, eagerly awaiting the adoption, the redemption of our body. For we were saved in this hope .. .. .." "Likewise the Spirit helps us in our infirmities .. .. .. because He makes intercession for the saints according to the will of Yahweh. .. .. "For whom He foreknew, He also predestined to be conformed to the image of His Son, that He might be the firstborn among many brethren." (Romans 8:23,26a,27b,29). The redemption of our bodies is dependent upon us being conformed to His image by the working of His Spirit in our lives. From the initial deposit of the Spirit in our lives (the 'firs fruits') to the outworking of His image in us, we are called to be holy. The operation of His Spirit is to produce a Bride without spot or wrinkle. (Ephesians 5:25) This is what He is coming for! "Blessed and holy is he who has part in the first resurrection." (Revelation 20: 6; 19:7-9)

Resurrection, Second: This is a resurrection to judgment. Sometimes called the Great White Throne judgment. The books are opened and all who are raised in this *resurrection* are judged according to their works as in (Revelation 20:12,13)

Reveal

The book of Life is also opened and whoever is not found written in this book is cast into the Lake of Fire. (Revelation 20:15) Death and the place of the dead, Sheol or Hades are cast into the Lake of Fire. Death is abolished and the grave emptied.

2 Y'shua gave many parables regarding unfaithfulness and its rewards. Faithful and wise stewards of our Masters goods will receive dominion to rule and reign with Him (i.e. the first resurrection), but the unwise shall receive their portion with the unbelievers, which means they will be raised in the second resurrection to judgment as in (Luke 12:35-50). "The Lord knows how to keep the unrighteous under punishment for the Day of Judgment." (2 Peter 2:9) Also, the unprofitable servant who knew His master's will and didn't do it, is cast into outer darkness where there will be weeping and wailing and gnashing of teeth. (Matthew 25:30; 8:11,12) "Therefore, brethren, be even more diligent to make your call and election sure, for if you do these things you will never stumble; for so an entrance will be supplied to you abundantly into the everlasting kingdom of our King and Savior Messiah Y'shua." (2 Peter 1:2-11)

Note as important: Y'shua (Jesus) was raised to life by the power of Yahweh God. (Acts 4:10, Romans 6:4) He was subsequently seen by over 500 witnesses. (Acts 2:32, 1 Corinthians 15:6) The Bible clearly teaches the resurrection of the dead as a foundational teaching. (1 Corinthians 15:20-23) There are two general resurrections: The first, the Resurrection to Life, will take place at the return of Messiah. (1 Thessalonians 4:16-17, John 5:29), The second, the Resurrection to Judgment, will occur a thousand years after the first resurrection. (Revelation 20: 5-6) Resurrected believers who rise at the first resurrection will come forth with glorified and immortal bodies, similar to the body Y'shua possessed when He rose from the grave. (1 Corinthians 15:42-44, 1 John 3:2)

Reveal: (Verb, Greek: *apokaluptó* - [ap-ok-al-oop'-to] Hebrew: *Galah* [gaw-law'] To uncover, bring to light, reveal.

A true understanding of God comes from only one source - God's revelation to mankind, the Bible. What does it reveal about God the Father and Jesus Christ? "For this reason I bow my knees to the Father of our Lord Jesus Christ, from whom the whole family in heaven and earth is named" (Ephesians:3:14-15) For this cause I bow my knees unto the Father of our Lord Jesus Christ, Of whom the whole family in heaven and earth is named,). Most people have their own distinctive opinions of a Supreme Being. But where do these impressions come from? Many are simply reflections of how people perceive God—based on what they've heard from others and their own reasoning. As a consequence the word God has come to embody a range of meanings, many of them quite foreign to the Bible. So which meaning is the true one? How does the Creator reveal Himself to man?

2 God *reveals* Himself in His Word, the Bible. The Bible is a book about God and His relationship with human beings. The Scriptures contain a long history of God's *revelation* of Himself to man—from the first man Adam to the prophet and lawgiver Moses down through the apostles of Jesus Christ and the early Church. In contrast to many human assumptions, the Bible communicates a true picture of God. This remarkable book reveals what He is like, what He has done and what He expects of us. It tells us why we are here and reveals His little-understood plan for His creation. This handbook of basic knowledge is fundamentally different from any other source of information. It is genuinely unique because it contains, in many ways, the very signature of the Almighty. The Creator tells us in His Word, "I am God, and there is no other; I am God, and there is none like Me, declaring the end from the beginning, and from ancient times things that are not yet done, saying, 'My counsel shall stand . . .'" (Isaiah:46:9-10) Remember the former things of old: for I am God, and there is none else; I am God, and there is none like me, Declaring the end from the beginning, and from ancient times the things that are not yet done, saying, My counsel shall stand, and I will do all my pleasure: He tells us that He alone not only foretells the future but can bring it to pass. What a powerful testimony to the mighty God of the Bible declared I the Gospel of Grace!

But, great as He is, God is not unapproachable. He is not beyond our reach. We can come to know our magnificent Creator!

3 The real key to understanding God as inspired by God Himself, as the Bible gives us the master key to knowing Him: "Scripture speaks of 'things beyond our seeing, things beyond our hearing, things beyond our imagining, all prepared by God for those who love him'; and these are what God has revealed to us through the Spirit. For the Spirit explores everything, even the depths of God's own nature" (1 Corinthians:2:9-10) But as it is written, Eye hath not seen, nor ear heard, neither have entered into the heart of man, the things which God hath prepared for them that love him. But God hath revealed them unto us by his Spirit: for the Spirit searcheth all things, yea, the deep things of God. Praise the Lord! Can we then apply a bit of the macro - economic theory in describing the revelation of Christ wherewith we can described Him as a Macro reveller where every other micro-revelation emanate?

Reward

Reward: (Noun, Greek: misthos [mis-thos'], Hebrew: sakar - [saw-kawr'] Wages (a) pay, wages, salary, (b) reward, recompense, punishment. a thing given in recognition of service, effort, or achievement. As a (verb) give something to (someone) in recognition of their services, efforts, or achievements. A reward is "something given or received for service, merit, hardship, etc." A reward is something you earn.

References: (Colossians 3:23-24) whatever you do, work heartily, as for the Lord and not for men, knowing that from the Lord you will receive the inheritance as your reward. You are serving the Lord Christ. (Hebrews 11:6) And without faith it is impossible to please him, for whoever would draw near to God must believe that he exists and that he rewards those who seek him. (Galatians 6:9) And let us not grow weary of doing good, for in due season we will reap, if we do not give up. (1 Timothy 6:17-19) As for the rich in this present age, charge them not to be haughty, nor to set their hopes on the uncertainty of riches, but on God, who richly provides us with everything to enjoy. They are to do good, to be rich in good works, to be generous and ready to share, thus storing up treasure for themselves as a good foundation for the future, so that they may take hold of that which is truly life. (Matthew 6:1-34) "Beware of practicing your righteousness before other people in order to be seen by them, for then you will have no reward from your Father who is in heaven. "Thus, when you give to the needy, sound no trumpet before you, as the hypocrites do in the synagogues and in the streets, that they may be praised by others. Truly, I say to you, they have received their reward. But when you give to the needy, do not let your left hand know what your right hand is doing, so that your giving may be in secret. And your Father who sees in secret will reward you. "And when you pray, you must not be like the hypocrites. For they love to stand and pray in the synagogues and at the street corners, that they may be seen by others. Truly, I say to you, they have received their reward

Righteous: Also called rectitude, is an important theological concept in Hinduism, Christianity, Judaism and Islam. It is an attribute that implies that a person's actions are justified, and can have the connotation that the person has been "judged" or "reckoned" as leading a life that is pleasing to God. Many Dictionaries define "righteousness" as behaviour that is morally justifiable or right. Such behaviour is characterized by accepted standards of morality, justice, virtue, or uprightness. The Bible's standard of human righteousness is God's own perfection in every attribute, every attitude, every behaviour, and every word. Thus, God's laws, as given in the Bible, both describe His own character, and constitute the plumb line by which He measures human righteousness.

2 The Greek New Testament word for righteousness primarily describes conduct in relation to others, especially with regards to the rights of others in business, in legal matters, and beginning with relationship to God. It is contrasted with wickedness, the conduct of the one who, out of gross self-centeredness, neither reveres God nor respects man. The Bible describes the righteous person as just or right, holding to God and trusting in Him as in (Psalm 33:18-22).

3 The bad news is that true and perfect righteousness is not possible for man to attain on his own; the standard is simply too high. The good news is that true righteousness is possible for mankind, but only through the cleansing of sin by Jesus Christ and the indwelling of the Holy Spirit. We have no ability to achieve righteousness in and of ourselves. But Christians possess the righteousness of Christ, because "God made him who had no sin to be sin for us, so that in him we might become the righteousness of God" (2 Corinthians 5:21). This is an amazing truth. On the cross, Jesus exchanged our sin for His perfect righteousness so that we can one day stand before God and He will see not our sin, but the holy righteousness of the Lord Jesus. This means that we are made righteous in the sight of God; that is, that we are accepted as *righteous*, and treated as *righteous* by God on account of what the Lord Jesus has done. He was made sin; we are made righteousness. On the cross, Jesus was treated as if he were a sinner, though he was perfectly holy and pure, and we are treated as if we were righteous, though we are defiled and depraved. On account of what the Lord Jesus has endured on our behalf, we are treated as if we had entirely fulfilled the Law of God, and had never become exposed to its penalty. We have received this precious gift of righteousness from the God of all mercy and grace. To Him be the glory!

Righteousness, breast plate of:
Part of amour of God as described by Paul. A lesson from ancient Israel provides an ironic example of just how important armour can be. Perhaps you recall the cowardly and capricious life of King Ahab, but how did this evil king's life come to an end? This selfish leader who allowed a man to be killed just so he could have his vineyard (1 Kings 21). This king of Israel "who did evil in the sight of the Lord more than all who were before him" (1 Kings 16:30). God had prophesied that Ahab would die in the battle described in (1 Kings 22). So Ahab decided to disguise himself, while his ally King Jehoshaphat of Judah wore his own kingly robes. Their enemy had ordered his captains, "'Fight with no one small or great, but only with the king of Israel.' When the captains of the chariots saw Jehoshaphat, they said, 'It is

Righteousness, breast plate of

surely the king of Israel.' So they turned to fight against him; and Jehoshaphat cried out. When the captains of the chariots saw that it was not the king of Israel, they turned back from pursuing him.

2 "But a certain man drew his bow and unknowingly struck the king of Israel between the scale armour and the breastplate...at evening he died; the blood from the wound had flowed into the bottom of the chariot" (1 Kings 22:31-35), NRSV. Is it perhaps poetic justice that this unrighteous king lost his life due to an opening in his armour?

The *breastplate* was a central part of the Roman soldier's armour—it provided protection for the torso, which contains vital organs like the heart, lungs and so on. Without a breastplate, a soldier would be asking for death, as any attack could instantly become fatal. With a sturdy *breastplate*, the very same attacks become ineffective and useless, as blows glance off the armour. As Christians, we need to take some time for introspection. What laws of God do you find yourself most likely to compromise? We can't expect the *breastplate* to stay securely fastened unless we remain true to His commands. Once you identify your weaker areas, resolve to keep from compromising in them. Pick one area at a time to pay special attention to: When you do compromise, what prompts it? Is it because of certain conditions, environments, company, etc.? Try to decrease your chances of being tempted to compromise, right away.

3 Righteousness associates with protective armour like a breastplate as in (Proverbs 11:4) "Riches do not profit in the day of wrath, but righteousness delivers from death". Obviously, without righteousness, we leave ourselves open to almost certain death. With righteousness—just as with a *breastplate*—the otherwise fatal attacks of our enemy are thwarted. Righteousness is described in (Psalm 119:172) like this; "My tongue shall speak of Your word, for all Your commandments are righteousness". Also (1 John 3:4) "Whoever commits sin also commits lawlessness, and sin is lawlessness". Again, (1 Corinthians 15:34) "Awake to righteousness, and do not sin; for some do not have the knowledge of God. I speak this to your shame". To be righteous is to do what is right in God's eyes. God's commandments are righteousness. In contrast, lawlessness is sin, and sin is the opposite of righteousness. So to be righteous is to obey God's laws of love so that we may not be separated from God, causing Him to withhold His protection as in (Isaiah 59:1-2) "Behold, the Lord's hand is not shortened, that it cannot save; nor His ear heavy, that it cannot hear. But your iniquities have separated you from your God; and your sins have hidden His face from you, so that He will not hear". Iniquities and sins are actions and thoughts that go

against God's laws. Since they are in conflict with God's way of living and are harmful to ourselves and others, our perfect and just God will not associate with us if we go down the path of sin and evil. We cut ourselves off from God and His protection!

4 It is interesting to note that in this same chapter Isaiah mentions that God Himself puts on righteousness as a breastplate (Isaiah 59:17), which may be part of what inspired Paul to use this analogy. For us to wear correct righteousness, let see (Isaiah 64:6) "But we are all like an unclean thing, and all our righteousness's are like filthy rags; we all fade as a leaf, and our iniquities, like the wind, have taken us away. Righteousness may deliver from death, but whose righteousness are we talking about? The above scripture makes it clear that our individual level of righteousness is on par with "filthy rags"— and when you're looking to protect yourself from death, filthy rags make for a lousy *breastplate*. So in His days declare in (Jeremiah 23:6) In His days Judah will be saved, and Israel will dwell safely; now this is His name by which He will be called: THE LORD OUR RIGHTEOUSNESS. Also consider scriptures such as (Job 36:3; Psalm 5:8; 23:3; 24:5; and Psalm 71:16), which show that true righteousness comes from God. It is God's righteousness, and not our own, which must serve as our *breastplate* and defence against Satan.

Paul also compares other characteristics with a breastplate as in (1 Thessalonians 5:8) "But let us who are of the day be sober, putting on the breastplate of faith and love, and as a helmet the hope of salvation". Indeed, Faith and love also protect our hearts. It's interesting to study how faith and love relate to righteousness. Faith works "through love" (Galatians 5:6) and Abraham's faith (which was shown by his doing what God said to do) was "accounted to him for righteousness" (Romans 4:3; Genesis 26:5).

Righteousness, wearing the breastplate of:

(Ephesians 6:13) "Therefore take up the whole armour of God, that you may be able to withstand in the evil day, and having done all, to stand. So now we know what the breastplate of righteousness is. Paul gives us the command to "take up the whole armour of God"—the obvious question is, "How?" By an in-depth concordance study of all the scriptures concerning righteousness (there are 301 in the New King James Version!) that reveals servants of God in the Bible who had righteousness all had it because they followed God's way. Though it may seem a sweeping statement, it is through a continuing and dedicated adherence to both the letter and spirit of God's law that we can defend ourselves with His righteousness. As a Christian, you must study the word of God theoretical digested and practically apply it to every of your sit-

Rock

uation daily. Once we have put on the *breastplate of righteousness*, we must be sure not to remove it. (Ezekiel 33:13) shows that wearing righteousness is not a one-time event; rather, it requires a lifetime of action. One day, the war we're fighting will be over. And when it is, we are promised, "The work of righteousness will be peace, and the effect of righteousness, quietness and assurance forever" (Isaiah 32:17). By faithfully living God's way and staying clear of Satan's, we will find this peace, quietness and assurance—forever. Praise the Lord!

Rock: Noun, Greek: *petra* - [pet'-ra] Hebrew: *tsur* - [tsoor], a rock, ledge, cliff, cave, stony ground. Rock is a naturally occurring solid aggregate of one or more minerals or mineraloids. For example, the common rock granite is a combination of the quartz, feldspar and biotite minerals. The Earth's outer solid layer, the lithosphere, is made of rock. Rocks have been used by mankind throughout history. From the Stone Age rocks have been used for tools. The minerals and metals found in rocks have been essential to human civilization. Three major groups of rocks are defined: igneous, sedimentary, and metamorphic. The scientific study of rocks is called petrology, which is an essential component of geology.

What concerns our attention here is Christ declaration, "Upon this rock I will build my church"

The name Peter (Greek., Petros) means "rock" or "rock-man." In the next phrase Christ used petra (upon this rock), a feminine form for "rock," not a name. Christ used a play on words. He does not say "upon you, Peter" or "upon your successors," but "upon this rock"—upon this divine revelation and profession of faith in Christ.

(Peter 16:17-20). Peter's words brought a word of commendation from the Lord. Peter was blessed because he had come to a correct conclusion about the person of Christ and because great blessing would be brought into his life. The Lord added, however, this was not a conclusion Peter had determined by his own or others' ability. God, the Father in heaven, had revealed it to him. Peter was living up to his name (it means "rock") for he was demonstrating himself to be a rock. When the Lord and Peter first met, Jesus had said Simon would be named Cephas (Aram. for "rock") or Peter (Greek: for "rock"; (John 1:41-42).

But his declaration about Messiah's person led to a declaration of Messiah's program. Peter (Petros, masc.) was strong like a rock, but Jesus added that on this rock (petra, fem.) He would build His church. Because of this change in Greek words, many conservative scholars believe that Jesus is now building His church on Himself. Others hold that the church is built on Peter and the other apostles as the building's foundation stones

(Ephesians. 2:20; Revelation. 21:14). Still other scholars say that the church is built on Peter's testimony. It seems best to understand that Jesus was praising Peter for his accurate statement about Him, and was introducing His work of building the church on Himself (1 Corinthians. 3:11).

(Psalm 18:2) The Lord is my *rock* and my fortress and my deliverer, my God, my rock, in whom I take refuge, my shield, and the horn of my salvation, my stronghold. (Psalm 144:1) Of David. Blessed be the Lord, my *rock*, who trains my hands for war, and my fingers for battle; (2 Samuel 22:32) "For who is God, but the Lord? And who is a *rock*, except our God? (1 Samuel 2:2) "There is none holy like the Lord; there is none besides you; there is no *rock* like our God. (Matthew 16:18) And I tell you, you are Peter, and on this rock I will build my church, and the gates of hell shall not prevail against it. (Luke 8:13) And the ones on the *rock* are those who, when they hear the word, receive it with joy. But these have no root; they believe for a while, and in time of testing fall away.

Run: (Verb, Greek: *trechó* [trekh'-o], Hebrew: *ruts* -[roots] meaning to run, exercise myself, make progress. Apostle Paul declare in (1 Corinthians 9:24-27) Do you not know that in a race all the runners *run*, but only one receives the prize? So *run* that you may obtain it. Every athlete exercises self-control in all things. They do it to receive a perishable wreath, but we van imperishable. So I do not *run* aimlessly; I do not box as one beating the air. But I discipline my body and keep it under control, lest after preaching to others I myself should be disqualified.

Here Paul sort of stimulates the Evangelism by using the sporting term *run* showing competition feeling and spirit in the process to show the difference between the Evangelists and non - Evangelists. The evangelist ignore all the hazards that abound in the process of winning a race, all the odds, barriers, tribulation, persecution and negative conditions, run the race to a finishing line because they expect a crown when winning at the end while non - Christians don't care and have no goal to evangelise and receive no crown at the end. Look at the Parable of the Vineyard Workers in (Mathew 20: 15 -16) "Is it not lawful for me to do what I wish with what is my own? Or is your eye envious because I am generous?' "So the last shall be first, and the first last." This shows a clear determinant of race result, sometimes, whereby the last can suddenly overtakes the first runner. As Christians, we need to take our position so that those who are still in the world may not over – run us and become first in the last day and attain a higher or first position thereby erupting our first position to earn a higher crown in the Lord's day.

Ss

Sabbath: (Hebrew – *Shabath* – to rest) The seventh day of the week enjoined on the ancient Hebrews by the forth commandment (Exodus 20:8-11) as a day of rest and worship. Thus' "Remember the *Sabbath* day, to keep it holy. Six days shalt thou labour, and do all thy work: But the seventh day is the *Sabbath* of the LORD thy God: in it thou shalt not do any work, thou, nor thy son, nor thy daughter, thy manservant, nor thy maidservant, nor thy cattle, nor thy stranger that is within thy gates: For in six days the LORD made heaven and earth, the sea, and all that in them is, and rested the seventh day: wherefore the LORD blessed the *Sabbath* day, and hallowed it". NKJ 2 *Sabbath* – the Christian Sunday otherwise known positas 'the Lords Day' – the first day of the week of course is often referred to as the *Sabbath* to Christians as opposed to other religious 'rest days'.

Sackcloth (Hebrew - *sak̠*) is a term originally denoting a coarsely woven fabric, usually made of goat's hair. It later came to mean also a garment made from such cloth, which was chiefly worn as a token of mourning by the Israelites. It was furthermore a sign of submission (I Kings 20:30), and was occasionally worn by the Prophets. 2 In short, the Old Testament gives no exact description of the garment, so its shape must be a matter of conjecture and according to a number of gospel Preachers, the sak̠cloth was like a corn-bag with an opening for the head, and another for each arm, an opening being made in the garment from top to bottom. 3 Many gospel teachers concludes that it originally was simply the loin-cloth, bases his opinion on the fact that the word "ḥagar" (to gird) is used in describing the mode of putting on the garment (see Joshua 1:8; Isaiah 3:24, 15: 8, 22:12; Jerimiah 6:26,). One fastens the sak̠ around the hips ("sim be-motnayim," (Genesis. 37:34); "he'elah 'al motnayim," (Amos 8: 10), while, in describing the doffing of the sak̠, the words "pittea☐ me-'al motnayim" are used (Isaiah. 20:2). According to (I Kings 21: 37) and (II Kings 6 30), it was worn next the skin. 4 In prehistoric times the loin-cloth was the usual and sole garment worn by the Israelites. In historic times it came to be worn for religious purposes only, on extraordinary occasions, or at mourning ceremonies. It is natural that, under certain circumstances, the Prophets also should have worn the Sackcloth, as in the case of Isaiah, who wore nothing else, and was commanded by God to do it (Isaiah. 20:2). NOTE: Old traditions easily assume a holy character.

Sacrament: This is the "efficacious signs of grace, instituted by Christ and entrusted to the Church, by which divine life is dispensed to us. The visible rites by which the sacraments are celebrated signify and make present the graces proper to each sacrament. It is a Christian rite recognized as of particular importance and significance. There are various views on the existence and meaning of such rites. The Catechism of the Catholic Church defines the sacraments as They bear fruit in those who receive them with the required dispositions."[1] The catechism included in the Anglican Book of Common Prayer defines a sacrament as "an outward and visible sign of an inward and spiritual grace given unto us, ordained by Christ himself, as a means whereby we receive the same, and a pledge to assure us thereof".

2 Many times in Scripture God's action, presence, or the working out of His plan in history is said to be a mystery. The "mystery" is known to Him alone and those to whom He reveals it (Ephesians. 1:9, 3:3, 3:9). Only by faith in Divine Revelation can the spiritual truth behind actions and events be discerned. The Incarnation is such a mystery, since only by faith do we believe that the man Jesus Christ whom we see, read about, or have preached to us, is God. Further, Jesus is a mystery concealing not just His divinity but His Father. As he told Philip, "whoever has seen me has seen the Father" (John 14:9). Thus, we can say that Christ is a sacrament of His Father. The Church is a mystery, since it is the mystical Christ, Head and members. Vatican II speaks of the Church as the sacrament of Christ. Finally, the seven sacraments are mysteries which unfold in our souls and in our lives the working of Christ and His grace.

3 The Catholic Church and Oriental Orthodoxy teach that there are seven sacraments. In each of the sacraments we can see that there is an outward sign of the mystery taking place, a sign in matter or deed and in word (Ephesians. 5:26), and that the sign bears a relationship to the spiritual grace or reality conferred by the Holy Spirit's action. In Baptism, for example, the individual is baptized in

Sacred

water, since water cleans, effecting an interior cleansing and renewal by God's gift of Himself (John 3:5, Acts 2:38). It also symbolizes dying and rising with Christ (Romans. 6:3-4), especially when performed by immersion. While the action of baptism is performed the word which Christ commanded is spoken (Mathew. 28:19), completing the sign. Catholic teaching speaks of these two elements of the sign as matter (water) and form ("I baptize you in the name of the Father, and of the Son, and of the holy Spirit"). The Eastern Orthodox Church also believes that there are seven major sacraments, but applies the corresponding Greek word, (mysterion) also to rites that in the Western tradition are called sacramental and to other realities, such as the Church itself. Similarly, the Catholic Church understands the word "*sacrament*" as referring not only to the seven sacraments considered here, but also to Christ and the Church. Most Protestant denominations identify two sacraments instituted by Christ; the Eucharist (Holy Communion) and Baptism. However some traditions avoid the word "sacrament". Reaction against the 19th-century Oxford Movement led Baptists to prefer instead the word "ordinance", practices ordained by Christ to be permanently observed by the church. Anglican teaching is that "there are two Sacraments ordained of Christ our Lord in the Gospel, that is to say, Baptism and the Supper of the Lord", and that "those five commonly called Sacraments, that is to say, Confirmation, Penance, Orders, Matrimony, and Extreme Unction, are not to be counted for Sacraments of the Gospel"

Sacred: (Latin – sacrare: To consecrate): That which is consecrated or dedicated to religious use. 2 Connected with God or a god and treated as Holy or maintained in state of sanctity. 3 A religious rather than secular. 4 Too valuable to be tempered carelessly. Keep in high esteemed for spiritual offerings.

Sacrifice: This is the offering of food, objects or the lives of animals to a higher purpose, in particular divine beings, as an act of propitiation or worship. While sacrifice often implies ritual killing, the term offering (Latin oblatio) can be used for bloodless sacrifices of cereal food or artefacts.

God became incarnate in Jesus Christ, sacrificing his son to accomplish the reconciliation of God and humanity, which had separated itself from God through sin (see the concept of original sin). According to a view that has featured prominently in Western theology since early in the 2nd millennium, God's justice required atonement for sin from humanity if human beings were to be restored to their place in creation and saved from damnation. However, God knew limited human beings could not make sufficient atonement, for humanity's offense to God was infinite, so God created a covenant with Abraham, which he fulfilled when he sent his only Son to become the sacrifice for the broken covenant. In Christian theology, this sacrifice replaced the insufficient animal sacrifice of the Old Covenant; Christ the "Lamb of God" replaced the lambs' sacrifice of the ancient Korban Todah (the Rite of Thanksgiving), chief of which is the Passover in the Mosaic law.

3 The complete identification of the Mass with the sacrifice of the cross is found in Christ's words at the last supper over the bread and wine: "This is my body, which is given up for you," and "This is my blood of the new covenant, which is shed...unto the forgiveness of sins." The bread and wine, offered by Melchizedek in sacrifice in the old covenant (Genesis 14:18; Psalm 110:4), are transformed through the Mass into the body and blood of Christ (see transubstantiation; note: the Orthodox Church does not hold as dogma, as do Catholics, the doctrine of transubstantiation, preferring rather to not make an assertion regarding the "how" of the sacraments), and the offering becomes one with that of Christ on the cross. In the Mass as on the cross, Christ is both priest (offering the sacrifice) and victim (the sacrifice he offers is himself), though in the Mass in the former capacity he works through a solely human priest who is joined to him through the sacrament of Holy Orders and thus shares in Christ's priesthood as do all who are baptized into the death and resurrection of Jesus, the Christ. Through the Mass, the merits of the one sacrifice of the cross can be applied to the redemption of those present, to their specific intentions and prayers, and to the release of the souls from purgatory.

4 The concept of self-sacrifice and martyrs are central to Christianity. Often found in Roman Catholicism is the idea of joining one's own sufferings to the sacrifice of Christ on the cross. Thus one can offer up involuntary suffering, such as illness, or purposefully embrace suffering in acts of penance. Some Protestants criticize this as a denial of the all-sufficiency of Christ's sacrifice, but it finds support in St. Paul: "Now I rejoice in my sufferings for your sake, and in my flesh I complete what is lacking in Christ's afflictions for the sake of his body, that is, the church" (Colosians 1:24). Pope John Paul II explained in his Apostolic Letter Salvifici Doloris (11 February 1984): "In the Cross of Christ not only is the Redemption accomplished through suffering, but also human suffering itself has been redeemed... Every man has his own share in the Redemption. Each one is also called to share in that suffering through which the Redemption was accomplished...In bringing about the Redemption through suffering, Christ has also raised

Sacristan

human suffering to the level of the Redemption. Thus each man, in his suffering, can also become a sharer in the redemptive suffering of Christ...The sufferings of Christ created the good of the world's redemption. This good in itself is inexhaustible and infinite. No man can add anything to it. But at the same time, in the mystery of the Church as his Body, Christ has in a sense opened his own redemptive suffering to all human suffering"

Sacristan: A person in charge of a church sacristy.

'Scaring Bell': (From the obsolete verb 'to sacre', 'to consecrate'). Scaring bell is usually used by Bishops and sovereigns. It is the bell rung in churches to draw attention to the most solemn part of the Mass. 2 In medieval times it served to announce to those outside that the Mass was in progress, and for this purpose a hand bell was often rung out of a side window. 3 It is more usually called the Sanctus bell because it was rung at the saying of Sanctus at the beginning of the Canons of The Mass, and also at the Consecration and Elevation and other moment. It is still used in the Roman Catholic Church and several other Churches and places of worship.

Sadducees: Simply a Jewish party opposed to the Pharisees. 2 Sadducees did not accept oral tradition, but dwells on the written law, denied the existence of angels and spirits. They also rejected the idea of future punishment in an afterlife as well as the resurrection of the body. 3 They were major opponent of Christ (antichrist) and disciples and actively participated in the crucifixion. Evidently, they represented the interests and attitudes of the privileged and wealthy, and nothing more is heard of them after the destruction of Jerusalem in (AD 70). 4 Probably the Sadducees are the descendants of Zadok – who was the high priest at the time of Solomon and who was also named among David Officers . "Joab the son of Zeruiah was over the army, and Jehoshaphat the son of Ahilud was recorder. Zadok the son of Ahitub and Ahimelech the son of Abiathar were priests, and Seraiah was secretary. Benaiah the son of Jehoiada was over the Cherethites and the Pelethites; and David's sons were chief ministers (2 Samuel 8:16-18))

Salvation: (Noun, Greek: *sótéria* [so-tay-ree'-ah] Hebrew: *yesha* [yeh' – shuah]; welfare, prosperity, deliverance, preservation, salvation, safety. It is being saved or protected from harm or being saved or delivered from some dire situation. 2 In religion, salvation is stated as the saving of the soul from sin and its consequences. 3 The academic study of salvation is called soteriology. It concerns itself with the comparative study of how different religious traditions conceive salvation (a concept existing across a wide range of cultural traditions), and how they believe it is obtained.

2 Deliverance from danger or suffering. To save is to deliver or protect. The word carries the idea of victory, health, or preservation. Sometimes, the Bible uses the words saved or salvation to refer to temporal, physical deliverance, such as Paul's deliverance from prison (Philippians 1:19). More often, the word "salvation" concerns an eternal, spiritual deliverance. When Paul told the Philippian jailer what he must do to be saved, he was referring to the jailer's eternal destiny (Acts 16:30-31). Jesus equated being saved with entering the kingdom of God (Matthew 19:24-25).

3 In the Christian doctrine of salvation, we are saved from "wrath," that is, from God's judgment of sin (Romans 5:9; 1 Thessalonians 5:9). Our sin has separated us from God, and the consequence of sin is death (Romans 6:23). Biblical salvation refers to our deliverance from the consequence of sin and therefore involves the removal of sin done only by God who can remove sin and deliver us from sin's penalty (2 Timothy 1:9; Titus 3:5).

In the Christian doctrine of *salvation,* God has rescued us through Christ (John 3:17). Specifically, it was Jesus' death on the cross and subsequent resurrection that achieved our salvation (Romans 5:10; Ephesians 1:7). Scripture is clear that salvation is the gracious, undeserved gift of God (Ephesians 2:5 - 8) and is only available through faith in Jesus Christ (Acts 4:12).

4 As Christians, we are saved by faith. First, we must hear the gospel—the good news of Jesus' death and resurrection (Ephesians 1:13). Then, we must believe—fully trust the Lord Jesus (Romans 1:16). This involves repentance, a changing of mind about sin and Christ (Acts 3:19), and calling on the name of the Lord (Romans 10:9-10, 13). A definition of the Christian doctrine of *salvation* would be "The deliverance, by the grace of God, from eternal punishment for sin which is granted to those who accept by faith God's conditions of repentance and faith in the Lord Jesus." *Salvation* is available in Jesus alone (John 14:6; Acts 4:12) and is dependent on God alone for provision, assurance, and security. Praise the Lord!

Salvation, the helmet of:

This is the fifth piece of God's armour. It is represented by the Roman soldier's helmet, without which he would never enter battle. Some of the *helmets* were made of thick leather covered with metal plates, and others were of heavy moulded or beaten metal. They usually had cheek pieces to protect the face. The purpose of the *helmet,* of course, was to protect the head from injury, particularly from the dangerous broadsword commonly used in the warfare of that day. That was not the much smaller sword mentioned later in this verse, but was a large two-handed, double-edged sword (rhomphaia, see (Revelation. 1:16; 2:12; 6:8) that measured three to

Salvation, the helmet of

four feet in length. It was often carried by cavalrymen, who would swing at the heads of enemy soldiers to split their skulls or decapitate them.

2 The fact that the helmet is related to salvation indicates that Satan's blows are directed at the believer's security and assurance in Christ. The two dangerous edges of Satan's spiritual broadsword are discouragement and doubt. To discourage us he points to our failures, our sins, our unresolved problems, our poor health, or to whatever else seems negative in our lives in order to make us lose confidence in the love and care of our heavenly Father. Since Paul is addressing believers, putting on the *helmet of salvation* cannot refer to receiving Christ as Saviour. The only ones who can take up any piece of God's armour, and the only ones who are involved in this supernatural struggle against Satan and his demon forces, are those who are already saved. Praise God!

3 Trusting in Jesus Christ, immediately saves from the penalty of sin. For believers, this first aspect of salvation, which is justification, is past. It was accomplished the moment we trusted in Christ, and that particular act of faith need never be repeated, because we are secure in our Father's hands—from whom, as we have just seen, we can never be snatched (John 10:28–29). We are forever saved from condemnation (Romans 8:1).

4 The second aspect of salvation, which is sanctification, involves our life on earth, during which time we experience a measure of freedom from the dominating power of sin. Being now under God's grace, sin no longer has mastery or dominion over us; we are no longer sin's slave but God's (Romans. 6:14, 18–22). Paul shows these first two aspects of salvation side by side in the previous chapter of Romans: "For if while we were enemies, we were reconciled to God through the death of His Son, much more, having been reconciled, we shall be saved by His life" (Romans 5:10). Christ's death saved us once and for all from sin's penalty, and His life within us now is saving us day to day from sin's power and mastery.

5 The third aspect of salvation is future, the aspect of glorification, when we shall one day be saved altogether and forever from sin's presence. Looking forward to that glorious time, John says, "Beloved, now we are children of God, and it has not appeared as yet what we shall be. We know that, when He appears, we shall be like Him, because we shall see Him just as He is" (1 John 3:2). To be like God is to be without sin. We rejoice that this aspect of our salvation "is nearer than when we believed" (Romans. 13:11).

It is this final aspect of salvation that is the real strength of the believer's *helmet*. If we lose hope in the future promise of salvation, there can be no security in the present. This, no doubt, is why Paul calls this same piece of armour "the helmet" which is "the hope of salvation" (1 Thessalonians. 5:8). "Having the first fruits of the Spirit," Paul explains in Romans, "even we ourselves groan within ourselves, waiting eagerly for our adoption as sons, the redemption of our body. For in hope we have been saved" (Romans 8:23–24).

6 *The helmet of salvation* is that great hope of final salvation that gives us confidence and assurance that our present struggle with Satan will not last forever and we will be victorious in the end. We know the battle is only for this life, and even a long earthly life is no more than a split second compared to eternity with our Lord in heaven. We are not in a race we can lose. We have no purgatory to face, no uncertain hope that our own continued efforts or those of our loved ones and friends will perhaps someday finally make us acceptable to God. We know that whom God "predestined, these He also called; and whom He called, these He also justified; and whom He justified, these He also glorified" (Romans. 8:30). There is not the loss of a single soul from predestination to justification to sanctification to glorification. That is God's unbroken and unbreakable chain of salvation (John 6:39–40; 10:27–30).

We have a certain hope, "a living hope," as Peter calls it. "Blessed be the God and Father of our Lord Jesus Christ," he exults in his first epistle, "who according to His great mercy has caused us to be born again to a living hope through the resurrection of Jesus Christ from the dead, to obtain an inheritance which is imperishable and undefiled and will not fade away, reserved in heaven for you, who are protected by the power of God through faith for a salvation ready to be revealed in the last time" (1 Peter 1:3–5). When the helmet of that hope is in place, we can "greatly rejoice, even though now for a little while, if necessary, [we] have been distressed by various trials, that the proof of [our] faith, being more precious than gold which is perishable, even though tested by fire, may be found to result in praise and glory and honour at the revelation of Jesus Christ; and though [we] have not seen Him, [we] love Him, and though [we] do not see Him now, but believe in Him, [we] greatly rejoice with joy inexpressible and full of glory, obtaining as the outcome of [our] faith the salvation of [our] souls" (1 Peter 6–9). That is the *salvation* which is our *helmet*. Our *helmet* is the certain prospect of heaven, our ultimate salvation, which "we have as an anchor of the soul" (Hebrew. 6:19).

7 Often when a runner is on the home stretch of a race he suddenly "hits the wall," as the expression goes. His legs wobble and refuse to go any farther. The only hope

Salvation, the helmet of

for the runner is to keep his mind on the goal, on the victory to be won for himself and his team. It is that hope that keeps him going when every other part of his being wants to give up. To the persecuted and discouraged believers at Thessalonica, Paul wrote words parallel to the thought here in Ephesians: "Since we are of the day, let us be sober, having put on the breastplate of faith and love, and as a helmet, the hope of salvation. For God has not destined us for wrath, but for obtaining salvation through our Lord Jesus Christ, who died for us, that whether we are awake or asleep, we may live together with Him. Therefore encourage one another, and build up one another, just as you also are doing" (1 Thessalonians. 5:8–11).

8 To the worldly, fleshly Corinthians who were self–centred, divisive, and confused about the resurrection, Paul said, "If from human motives I fought with wild beasts at Ephesus, what does it profit Me? If the dead are not raised, let us eat and drink, for tomorrow we die" (1 Corinthians. 15:32). If the Christian has no future element of salvation to look forward to, if, as the apostle had said a few verses earlier, "we have hoped in Christ in this life only," then "we are of all men most to be pitied" (verse 19). Paul's own spiritual helmet was his firm hope in the completion of his salvation. "Momentary, light affliction is producing for us an eternal weight of glory far beyond all comparison, while we look not at the things which are seen, but at the things which are not seen; for the things which are seen are temporal, but the things which are not seen are eternal" (2 Corinthians. 4:17–18). The faithful believer does not "lose heart in doing good," because he knows that "in due time we shall reap if we do not grow weary" (Galatians. 6:9).

To the persecuted and beleaguered Christians to whom he wrote, Jude gave sobering warnings about false teachers, "ungodly persons who turn the grace of our God into licentiousness and deny our only Master and Lord, Jesus Christ" (verse 4). But he began the letter by addressing believers as "those who are the called, beloved in God the Father, and kept for Jesus Christ" (verse 1). *Tereo* (the verb behind "kept") means to guard, keep watch over, and protect. God Himself guards, watches over, and protects every person who belongs to Him. Jude ended the letter by assuring believers that He "is able to keep you from stumbling, and to make you stand in the presence of His glory blameless with great joy" (verse 24; 1 Thessalonians. 5:23). The word behind "keep" in this verse is not *tereo*, as in (verse 1), but *phulasso*, which has the basic idea of securing in the midst of an attack. No matter what our spiritual enemies may throw against us, we are secured by God's own power. Praise His Holy Name!

Sanctify (Sanctification):

(verb, Greek: *hagiazó* - [hag-ee-ad'-zo], Hebrew: *Qadash* [kaw-dash'] make holy, treat as holy, set apart as holy, sanctify set apart as or declare holy; consecrate. The same Greek word as holiness, "hagios," meaning a separation. First, a once-for-all positional separation unto Christ at our salvation. Second, a practical progressive holiness in a believer's life while awaiting the return of Christ. Third, we will be changed into His perfect likeness—holy, sanctified, and completely separated from the presence of evil.

2 *Sanctification* also refers to the practical experience of this separation unto God, being the effect of obedience to the Word of God in one's life, and is to be pursued by the believer earnestly (1 Peter 1:15; Hebrews 12:14). Just as the Lord prayed in (John 17), it has in view the setting apart of believers for the purpose for which they are sent into the world: "As Thou didst send Me into the world, even so send I them into the world. And for their sakes I sanctify Myself, that they themselves also may be sanctified in truth" (verse. 18, 19). That He set Himself apart for the purpose for which He was sent is both the basis and the condition of our being set apart for that for which we are sent (John 10:36). His *sanctification* is the pattern of, and the power for, ours. The sending and the *sanctifying* are inseparable. On this account they are called saints, *hagioi* in the Greek; "sanctified ones." Whereas previously their behaviour bore witness to their standing in the world in separation from God, now their behaviour should bear witness to their standing before God in separation from the world.

3 Jesus had a lot to say about *sanctification* as in the (John 17:16) "They are not of the world, even as I am not of the world," and this is before His request: "*Sanctify* them in the truth: Thy word is truth." *Sanctification* is a state of separation unto God; all believers enter into this state when they are born of God: "But of Him you are in Christ Jesus, who became for us wisdom from God—and righteousness and *sanctification* and redemption" (1 Corinthians 1:30). This is a once-for-ever separation, eternally unto God. It is an intricate part of our salvation, our connection with Christ (Hebrews 10:10).

4 There is one more sense that the word *sanctification* is referred to in Scripture. Paul prayed in (1 Thessalonians 5:23), "The God of peace Himself sanctify you wholly; and may your spirit and soul and body be preserved entire, without blame at the coming of our Lord Jesus Christ." Paul also wrote in Colossians of "the hope which is laid up for you in the heavens, whereof ye heard before in the word of the truth of the Gospel" (Colossians 1:5). He later speaks

Satan

of Christ Himself as "the hope of glory" (Colossians 1:27) and then mentions the fact of that hope when he says, "When Christ, who is our Life, shall be manifested, then shall ye also with Him be manifested in glory" (Colossians 3:4). This glorified state will be our ultimate separation from sin, total *sanctification* in every aspect. "Beloved, now we are children of God; and it has not yet been revealed what we shall be, but we know that when He is revealed, we shall be like Him, for we shall see Him as He is" (1 John 3:2).

Satan: Like the cute little cherubim you can buy for your garden or bookshelf. Satan himself is described as being "perfect in beauty," being adorned with all kinds of precious stones.

Satan, The fall of: Satan was created as a perfect being. He is described as originally being wise and completely righteous. 2 However, pride caused Satan to fall, ("your heart was lifted up because of your beauty"), since he wanted to receive the worship due to God alone. 3 At that point there was rebellion in heaven, when Satan convinced one third of the angels to rebel against God. 4 Michael, an archangel of God, fought with God's angels against Satan and his angels, with Satan losing the battle and being cast from heaven down to earth. 5 It isn't certain when Satan rebelled against God, but a passage from the book of Job (Job 38:4-7) suggests it occurred between the creation of the earth and the creation of Adam and Eve. In describing the creation of the earth to Job and his friends, God said that "all the sons of God shouted for joy." 6 Presumably, "all the sons of God" would have included *Satan* as well, suggesting he hadn't rebelled at the point the earth was created. However, Satan wasn't finished in his rebellion against God. Satan took on the form of a snake in the Garden of Eden to tempt Eve. 7 He managed to convince Eve that God's instructions against eating from the tree of the knowledge of good and evil were done as a way of keeping something good from her. She believed Satan's lie that she would "become like God." 8 We don't know where Adam was at the time of Satan's temptation, but he followed his wife's lead and also disobeyed God's instructions.

Satan's continued rebellion: Satan continues in his rebellion today, since he hates God and His plans. He wants people to worship him and follow his evil ways. He opposes Jesus. 2 The Bible says that Satan will continue in his rebellion against God until the very end. Near the end, a "beast" (world ruler) will arise from the "sea" (the gentile nations), having been given power by Satan to perform signs and wonders for the world. In addition, a false prophet, a religious leader empowered by Satan will deceive people into worshipping him. 3 The beast and the false prophet will convince the leaders of the earth to follow them into war against God and His people. However, the armies of the leaders of the world will be destroyed at the battle of Armageddon and the beast and false prophet will be thrown into the Lake of Fire. 4 At this point, Satan will be locked up for 1,000 years, while Jesus Christ rules the earth with His saints .5 At the end of that period, Satan is released for a short period of time, deceives the leaders of the world again, and convinces them to attack Jesus and His rule on the earth. 6 The battle is short as fire from heaven consumes the rebels. Satan is then thrown into the Lake of Fire (hell) to "be tormented day and night for ever and ever." 7 Following Satan's demise, the saints of Jesus Christ will judge the angels who joined him in rebellion.

Satan, Overcoming: The apostle John says that believers can overcome Satan when "the word of God abides in you." 2 When Jesus was tempted by Satan, He cited scripture to him (Matthew 4:1-1037). In addition, Paul tells us that the sword of the spirit, which is the word of God, is our only offensive weapon against the Satan (Ephesians 6:13-1738). In the parable of the sower, Jesus said that there were those who heard the word of God, but failed to take it in, and so were led astray by the devil (the seed that fell by the side of the road). 39 So Christians resist the devil by knowing and memorizing scripture so that we cannot be deceived by the lies of Satan. 3 The Bible gives believers the following instructions about resisting the devil: Submit therefore to God. Resist the devil and he will flee from you. (James **4:7**) "In your anger do not sin": Do not let the sun go down while you are still angry, and do not give the devil a foothold. (Ephesians 4:26-27) In addition to all this, take up the shield of faith, with which you can extinguish all the flaming arrows of the evil one. (Ephesians 6:16) Be of sober spirit, be on the alert. Your adversary, the devil, prowls around like a roaring lion, seeking someone to devour. But resist him, firm in your faith, knowing that the same experiences of suffering are being accomplished by your brethren who are in the world. (1 Peter 5:8-9)

Save: (Verb; Greek – sózó - [sode'-zo] Hebrew: yasha - [yaw-shah'] save, heal, preserve, rescue 2 As a verb, to keep safe or rescue (someone or something) from harm or danger. 3 keep and store up (something, especially money) for future use.4 keep (data) by moving a copy to a storage location. 5 avoid, lessen, or guard against. 6 prevent an opponent from scoring (a goal or point) in a game or from winning (the game). As a noun, 7 an act of preventing an opponent scoring. 9 An act of saving data to a storage location.

10 Incessant prayers has saved someone or something from being killed, injured, or destroyed as in

Saving money

(Ephesians 2:8) "For it is by grace you have been *saved*, through faith--and this is not from yourselves, it is the gift of God".

11 In ordinary English usage, Wearing seat belts has *saved* many lives. He fell in the river but his friend saved him from drowning. He had to borrow money to save his business. He was desperately trying to *save* their failing marriage. We all need to do our bit to save the planet. The former tennis champion was now serving to *save* the match (= to win the next point so that the other player did not win this part of the competition).

References: (Romans 10:13) For "everyone who calls on the name of the Lord will be saved." (Ephesians 2:8-10) For by grace you have been saved through faith. And this is not your own doing; it is the gift of God, not a result of works, so that no one may boast. For we are his workmanship, created in Christ Jesus for good works, which God prepared beforehand, that we should walk in them. (Romans 10:9-10) Because, if you confess with your mouth that Jesus is Lord and believe in your heart that God raised him from the dead, you will be saved. For with the heart one believes and is justified, and with the mouth one confesses and is saved. (John 3:5) Jesus answered, "Truly, truly, I say to you, unless one is born of water and the Spirit, he cannot enter the kingdom of God. (John 3:16) "For God so loved the world, that he gave his only Son, that whoever believes in him should not perish but have eternal life. (1 John 5:13) I write these things to you who believe in the name of the Son of God that you may know that you have eternal life. (1 Peter 3:18-22) For Christ also suffered once for sins, the righteous for the unrighteous, that he might bring us to God, being put to death in the flesh but made alive in the spirit, in which he went and proclaimed to the spirits in prison, because they formerly did not obey, when God's patience waited in the days of Noah, while the ark was being prepared, in which a few, that is, eight persons, were brought safely through water. Baptism, which corresponds to this, now saves you, not as a removal of dirt from the body but as an appeal to God for a good conscience, through the resurrection of Jesus Christ, who has gone into heaven and is at the right hand of God, with angels, authorities, and powers having been subjected to him. (Romans 3:23) For all have sinned and fall short of the glory of God, (Acts 22:16) - ESV "And now why do you wait? Rise and be baptized and wash away your sins, calling on his name." (Romans 6:23) For the wages of sin is death, but the free gift of God is eternal life in Christ Jesus our Lord.

Saving money: A wise practice for many different reasons. God is our source and provider for everything we need. "And my God will meet all your needs according to the riches of his glory in Christ

Saviour

Jesus" (Philippians 4:19). One of the main ways God provides for us is through money, and it is our job to steward that money well (Matthew 25:14–27). We are accountable to God for how we use everything He gives us in this life, including money. Saving money demonstrates good stewardship of the resources God gives us. Saving money allows us to be prepared for the future, and being prepared for the future is good. Example; (Proverbs 6:6–8) shows us that this principle is lived out even in nature: "Go to the ant, you sluggard; consider its ways and be wise! It has no commander, no overseer or ruler, yet it stores its provisions in summer and its food at harvest." Planning ahead and saving money makes it easier to accomplish goals and allows us to be more effective in ministry see also (1 Corinthians 16:2). When we don't plan ahead and save money, we are more prone to go into debt, which the Bible tells us is unwise (Proverbs 22:7).

2 Of course, there are plenty of wrong motives for saving money. If we're saving money out of fear of the future, it shows we're not really trusting God to provide as in (Luke 12:7; 2 Timothy 1:7). Miserliness is sin, and it's foolish and arrogant to make money our security. "The wealth of the rich is their fortified city; they imagine it a wall too high to scale" (Proverbs 18:11), yet riches "will surely sprout wings and fly off to the sky like an eagle" (Proverbs 23:5). (1 Timothy 6:10) warns against greed, saying, "The love of money is a root of all kinds of evil. Some people, eager for money, have wandered from the faith and pierced themselves with many grief's." 3 Tois fully understand the value of saving money, we must remember what the Bible says about giving. God desires His people to be cheerful givers (2 Corinthians 9:7). It's impossible to out-give God! "Give and it will be given to you. A good measure, pressed down, shaken together and running over, will be poured into your lap. For the measure you use, it will be measured to you" (Luke 6:38). Sometimes when God gives us things, be it money or something else, it's intended for us to give away. Other times, He gives us things that are meant for us to keep for our selves and use in His service and for His glory. It's wise to hold everything God gives us loosely so that we can give it away if He asks us to. Glory to Jesus.

Saviour: (noun, Greek: sótér - [so-tare'], Hebrew: yasha - [yaw-shah'] a saviour, deliverer, preserver. This clearly explain the concept of God our Saviour as in (Psalm 106:21), "They forgot God their saviour, which had done great things in Egypt." It was Almighty God that brought the children of Israel out of the bondage of Egypt. As in this (Psalm 106:21), we see that Almighty God the Father is clearly shown as being their saviour the saviour of God's people Israel. Also, (Isaiah 45:21)

Saviour

says, "Tell you, and bring them near; yea, let them take counsel together: who has declared this from ancient time? Who has told it from that time? Have not I the Lord? And there is no God else beside me; a just God and a Saviour; there is none beside me." This verse plainly shows that Almighty God is the Saviour. Let us now read two more verses that clearly show God to be our Saviour from the New Testament. (I Timothy 2:3) "For this is good and acceptable in the sight of God our Saviour." (Jude verse 25). "To the ONLY wise God our Saviour, be the glory and majesty, and dominion and power, both now and forever, Amen."

 and Christ – the Author and finisher of our faith. In consideration, God conceived the idea of bringing a Saviour to the world after the fall of Adam. Since no man can see God who is uniquely Spirit. God decide to allow His Saving impact to be felt by mankind by turning the word into flesh in order that the sin of human kind may be imputed. The divine or spiritual conception in the womb of Virgin Mary equipped Jesus with divine Characteristic of endurance which fills Jesus with TRIUME Capabilities to endure death on the Cross as the sin of the entire Human race was imputed. Then the curse of death was abolished as in (2 Timothy 1:10) says, "But is now made manifest by the appearing of our Saviour Jesus Christ, who has abolished death, and has brought life and immortality to light through the gospel."

Then in (Philippians 3:20), "For our conversation in heaven; from whence also we look for the Saviour, the Lord Jesus Christ." Now these verses clearly show us that Jesus Christ is our Saviour, so we can see how one could conclude that since Jesus Christ is shown to be our Saviour, and Almighty God the Father is shown to be our Saviour, then therefore either Jesus is God, as in, ONE and the same as Almighty God.

So then, we can CLEARLY see from these verses of scripture that Almighty God the Father PROMISED unto us a Saviour meaning the father is the source of the saving Grace of the world, that the Lord God Almighty HIMSELF GAVE to us as his Saviour to save all who believe and trust in his Saving Grace, his SON Jesus. Again we also see that this Saviour is his only begotten SON Jesus, which Almighty God HIMSELF sent to be the Saviour of the world. Almighty God the Father then RAISED UP and EXALTED his Son Jesus to be a Saviour AFTER his Son Jesus became obedient unto death on the cross.

References: (Luke 1:47) And my spirit rejoices in God my Savior, (1 John 4:14) And we have seen and testify that the Father has sent his Son to be the Savior of the world. (Acts 4:12) And there is salvation in no one else, for there is no other name under heaven given among men by which we must be saved." (Romans 8:38-39) For I am sure that neither death nor life, nor angels nor rulers, nor things present nor things to come, nor powers, nor height nor depth, nor anything else in all creation, will be able to separate us from the love of God in Christ Jesus our Lord. (Romans 6:23) For the wages of sin is death, but the free gift of God is eternal life in Christ Jesus our Lord. (1 John 2:2) He is the propitiation for our sins, and not for ours only but also for the sins of the whole world. (Ephesians 2:8-9) For by grace you have been saved through faith. And this is not your own doing; it is the gift of God, not a result of works, so that no one may boast. (John 3:16) "For God so loved the world, that he gave his only Son, that whoever believes in him should not perish but have eternal life. (2 Timothy 2:19) But God's firm foundation stands, bearing this seal: "The Lord knows those who are his," and, "Let everyone who names the name of the Lord depart from iniquity." (Romans 15:13) May the God of hope fill you with all joy and peace in believing, so that by the power of the Holy Spirit you may abound in hope

Scripture: (Noun, Greek: *graphé* - [graf-ay'], Hebrew: *Tanackh* (a) a writing, (b) a passage of scripture; plural: the scriptures. A sacred writing or book, A passage from such a writing or book. Often *Scripture* or *Scriptures*. The writings collected as the Bible. A statement regarded as authoritative. Like in Pauls charge to Timothy (2 Timothy 3:10–17) "You, however, know all about my teaching, my way of life, my purpose, faith, patience, love, endurance, persecutions, sufferings—what kinds of things happened to me in Antioch, Iconium and Lystra, the persecutions I endured. Yet the Lord rescued me from all of them. In fact, everyone who wants to live a godly life in Christ Jesus will be persecuted, while evil men and impostors will go from bad to worse, deceiving and being deceived. But as for you, continue in what you have learned and have become convinced of, because you know those from whom you learned it, and how from infancy you have known the holy *Scriptures*, which are able to make you wise for salvation through faith in Christ Jesus. All *Scripture* is God-breathed and is useful for teaching, rebuking, correcting and training in righteousness, so that the man of God may be thoroughly equipped for every good work" . Praise the Lord.

Search: (verb) Try to find something by looking or otherwise seeking carefully and thoroughly. (noun) an act of searching for someone or something. Search the Gospel.

Secret: (Noun, Greek: *mustérion* - [moos-tay'-ree-on], Hebrew: *mistar* -[mis-tawr'] Places, a mystery, secret, of which initiation is necessary; in the New Testament: the counsels of God, once hidden but now revealed in the Gospel or some fact thereof; the Christian

Saviour

revelation generally; particular truths or details of the Christian revelation.

2 As (adjective) Something not known or seen or not meant to be known or seen by others. "how did you guess I'd got a secret plan?" synonyms: confidential, strictly confidential, top secret, classified, restricted, unrevealed, undisclosed, unpublished, untold, unknown, uncommunicated, behind someone's back, under wraps, unofficial, off the record, not for publication/circulation, not to be made public, not to be disclosed; More (antonyms): known, public, visible, overt, open, known about not meant to be known as such by others. "a secret drinker" – committing secret sins

3 synonyms: clandestine, covert, undercover, underground, hidden, shrouded, conspiratorial, surreptitious, stealthy, cloak-and-dagger, hole-and-corner, closet; fond of or good at keeping things about oneself unknown. "he can be the most secret man" synonyms: uncommunicative, secretive, unforthcoming, reticent, taciturn, silent, non-communicative, quiet, tight-lipped, close-mouthed, close, playing one's cards close to one's chest, clam-like, reserved, introvert, introverted, self-contained, discreet

"he's a very secret person" noun: secret; plural noun: secrets

1 something that is kept or meant to be kept unknown or unseen by others. 2 "The state secret of Isreal" synonyms: confidential matter, confidence, private affair, skeleton in the cupboard. For nothing is hidden that will not be made manifest, nor is anything secret that will not be known and come to light.

References: (Ecclesiastes 12:14) For God will bring every deed into judgment, with every secret thing, whether good or evil. (Mark 4:22) For nothing is hidden except to be made manifest; nor is anything secret except to come to light. (Luke 12:3) Therefore whatever you have said in the dark shall be heard in the light, and what you have whispered in private rooms shall be proclaimed on the housetops. (Hebrews 4:13) And no creature is hidden from his sight, but all are naked and exposed to the eyes of him to whom we must give account. (Proverbs 25:9) Argue your case with your neighbor himself, and do not reveal another's secret, (Psalm 44:21) Would not God discover this? For he knows the secrets of the heart. (Romans 2:16) On that day when, according to my gospel, God judges the secrets of men by Christ Jesus. (Proverbs 25:2) It is the glory of God to conceal things, but the glory of kings is to search things out. (1 Corinthians 4:5) Therefore do not pronounce judgment before the time, before the Lord comes, who will bring to light the things now hidden in darkness and will disclose the purposes of the heart. Then each one will receive his commendation from God. (Matthew 18:15) "If your brother sins against you, go and tell him his fault, between you and him alone. If he listens to you, you have gained your brother. (Psalm 139:13-16) For you formed my inward parts; you knitted me together in my mother's womb. I praise you, for I am fearfully and wonderfully made. Wonderful are your works; my soul knows it very well. My frame was not hidden from you, when I was being made in secret, intricately woven in the depths of the earth. Your eyes saw my unformed substance; in your book were written, every one of them, the days that were formed for me, when as yet there was none of them

Secret, Keeping: A secret can be difficult to keep and equally difficult to share. Yet life seems to run on secrets, from concealing birthday presents to obscuring a difficult past to protecting the whereabouts of an important political figure. The Bible teaches, indirectly, that secrets can be either good or bad, but it does not clearly delineate the right and wrong uses of secrets. Throughout the history of Israel, political and military secrets are mentioned without pronouncing any moral judgments for or against them. Example, (2 Samuel 15:35-36). "Are not Zadok and Abiathar the priests with you there? So it shall be that whatever you hear from the king's house, you shall report to Zadok and Abiathar the priests. Behold their two sons are with them there, Ahimaaz, Zadok's son and Jonathan, Abiathar's son; and by them you shall send me everything that you hear." However, in the story of Samson and Delilah (Judges 16:4-22), Samson reveals the source of his strength, an act which, based on the aftermath of his admission, indeed, he was awfully stupid. It was a secret he should have kept.

2 Esther's story provides a positive example of someone who kept a secret. Her decision to hide her nationality (Esther 2:20) became an integral part of God's plan to save His people (Esther 4:13; 7:3-6). The same story also supports the morality of revealing a secret that, if kept hidden, would cause great wrong or serious harm (Esther 2:21-23).

3 Proverbs, the central book among the "wisdom literature" of the Bible, is the most explicit about secrets. (Proverbs 11) says that "a man of understanding holds his tongue. A gossip betrays a confidence, but a trustworthy man keeps a secret" (Proverbs 11: 12-13). So, *keeping a secret* can be noble. But secrets kept for the wrong reason earn a person the title of "wicked," for "a wicked man accepts a bribe in secret to pervert the course of justice" (Proverbs 17:23), and "whoever slanders his neighbour in secret, him will I put to silence" (Psalm 101:5).

4 One type of secret is always wrong: trying to hide sin. "He who conceals his sins does not prosper,

Seek

but whoever confesses and renounces them finds mercy" (Proverbs 28:13). When it comes to our sin, God wants full disclosure, and He grants full forgiveness (Isaiah 1:18). Of course, there's no use trying to hide our sin from God. Nothing can be kept from Him. He is "the God of gods . . . and a reveller of secrets" (Daniel 2:47, NKJV). Even our "secret sins" are exposed in His light (Psalm 90:8). "For nothing is secret that will not be revealed, nor anything hidden that will not be known and come to light" (Luke 8:17).

5 God Himself keeps some things—probably many things—hidden from us: "The secret things belong to the LORD our God" (Deuteronomy 29:29). Jesus asked several people to keep miracles He had done secret. For example, Jesus healed two blind men and told them to "see that no one knows about this" (Matthew 9:30). When Job realized the immensity of God's knowledge, he spoke of "things too wonderful for me to know" (Job 42:3). In conclusion, God does not consider *keeping a secret* to be sinful in and of it. There are some things that people should know and some things they should not. God's concern is how secrets are used, whether to protect or to hurt or use encourage a cohort for the devil. In that case God is always there for us as Christians. Praise the Lord!

Seek: (Verb, Greek: zéteó – [dz-ay-teh'-o], Hebrew: baqash – [baw-kash'], I seek, search for, desire, require, demand.

Literally, attempt to find (something)."they came here to seek shelter from biting winter winds" synonyms: search for, try to find, look for, look about or around/round for, cast about or around or round for, be on the lookout for, be after, hunt for, be in quest of, quest (after), be in pursuit of

"six bombers took off and flew southwards to seek the enemy" attempt or desire to obtain or achieve (something). "the new regime sought his extradition" synonyms: try to obtain, pursue, go after, strive for, go for, push towards, work towards, be intent on, aim at/for, have as a goal, have as an objective More ask for (something) from someone - "he sought help from the police"

synonyms: ask for, request, solicit, call on, invite, entreat, beg for, petition for, appeal for, apply for, put in for "you may need to seek the advice of a specialist"

References: (Deuteronomy 4:29) But from there you will seek the Lord your God and you will find him, if you search after him with all your heart and with all your soul. (Proverbs 8:17) I love those who love me, and those who seek me diligently find me. (Jeremiah 29:12-14) Then you will call upon me and come and pray to me, and I will hear you. You will seek me and find me, when you seek me with all your heart. I will be found by you, declares the Lord, and I will restore your fortunes and gather you from all the nations and all the places where I have driven you, declares the Lord, and I will bring you back to the place from which I sent you into exile "Ask, and it will be given to you; seek, and you will find; knock, and it will be opened to you. For everyone who asks receives, and the one who seeks finds, and to the one who knocks it will be opened. (1 Chronicles 16:11) Seek the Lord and his strength; seek his presence continually! (Lamentations 3:25) The Lord is good to those who wait for him, to the soul who seeks him. (Isaiah 55:6-7) "Seek the Lord while he may be found; call upon him while he is near; let the wicked forsake his way, and the unrighteous man his thoughts; let him return to the Lord, that he may have compassion on him, and to our God, for he will abundantly pardon. (Psalm 119:10) With my whole heart I seek you; let me not wander from your commandments!

Septuagint, The: (noun) The Greek version of the Hebrew Bible (or Old Testament), including the Apocrypha, made for Greek-speaking Jews in Egypt in the 3rd and 2nd centuries BC and adopted by the early Christian Churches.

Servant: (Noun, Greek: diakonos – [dee-ak'-on-os], Hebrew: ebed – [eh'-bed], a waiter, servant; then of any one who performs any service, an administrator. The central theme of the Bible is the Servant of all—Jesus Christ. "For even the Son of Man did not come to be served, but to serve, and to give His life a ransom for many" (Mark 10:45). When we give Jesus Christ His rightful place as Lord of our lives, His lordship will be expressed in the way we serve others (Mark 9:35; 1 Peter 4:10; John 15:12-13). How can we demonstrate love for God? Our love for God will be expressed in our love for others. "For what we preach is not ourselves, but Jesus Christ as Lord, with ourselves as your servants for Jesus' sake" (2 Corinthians 4:5).

2 True leadership is servant-hood, and the greatest leader of all time is Jesus Christ. Servant-hood is an attitude exemplified by Christ "who, though he was in the form of God, did not count equality with God a thing to be grasped, but emptied himself, taking the form of a *servant*" (Philippians 2:6-7). The five words in the New Testament translated "ministry" generally refer to servant-hood or service given in love. Serving others is the very essence of ministry. All believers are called to ministry (Matthew 28:18-20), and, therefore, we are all called to be servants for the glory of God. Living is giving; all else is selfishness and boredom.

3 It has been rightly stated, "Rank is given you to enable you to better serve those above and below you. It is not given for you to

Serve

practice your idiosyncrasies. Let's serve others by serving Christ (Colossians 3:23-24). God the Father has served us by sacrificing Christ on the cross for our sins, and we should serve others by giving the gospel and our lives to them (1 Thessalonians 1:5-6). Those who desire to be great in God's kingdom must be the servant of all as in (Matthew 20:26), "Not so with you. Instead, whoever wants to become great among you must be your servant". Praise God!

References: If anyone serves me, he must follow me; and where I am, there will my servant be also. If anyone serves me, the Father will honour him. (Galatians 5:13) For you were called to freedom, brothers. Only do not use your freedom as an opportunity for the flesh, but through love serve one another. (Mark 10:42-45) And Jesus called them to him and said to them, "You know that those who are considered rulers of the Gentiles lord it over them, and their great ones exercise authority over them. But it shall not be so among you. But whoever would be great among you must be your servant, and whoever would be first among you must be slave of all. For even the Son of Man came not to be served but to serve, and to give his life as a ransom for many." (Colossians 3:12) Put on then, as God's chosen ones, holy and beloved, compassionate hearts, kindness, humility, meekness, and patience, (John 13:16) Truly, truly, I say to you, a servant is not greater than his master, nor is a messenger greater than the one who sent him. (1 Corinthians 4:1-2) This is how one should regard us, as servants of Christ and stewards of the mysteries of God. Moreover, it is required of stewards that they be found trustworthy. (Mark 10:45) For even the Son of Man came not to be served but to serve, and to give his life as a ransom for many." (Ephesians 2:10) For we are his workmanship, created in Christ Jesus for good works, which God prepared beforehand, that we should walk in them. (2 Timothy 2:15) Do your best to present yourself to God as one approved, a worker who has no need to be ashamed, rightly handling the word of truth.

Serve: (Verb, Greek: *diakoneó* - [dee-ak-on-eh'-o], Hebrew: *abad* – [(aw-bad'] wait at table (particularly of a slave who waits on guests); I serve (generally).

Jesus serves as a Servant as in (Mark 10:45) "For even the Son of Man came not to be *served* but to *serve*, and to give his life as a ransom for many." When Jesus speaks about serving, we should listen to Him. Here is the very God of the universe who came as a Man to *serve*. The word He uses for servant is the Greek word "diakoneō" which is where we get the name "deacon" and diakoneō means "to be a servant of, to *serve*, wait upon, or minister to." That is what every believer is called to do, not to be a deacon but to be a servant of the members of Christ's Body, the church. He *served* to the uttermost, giving His very "life as a ransom for many." Since He gave His life as a ransom for many we must shoot down the false teaching of universalism. He didn't say He gave His life as a ransom for all but for many and those "many" are those who freely choose to repent, confess their sins, and trust in Him as Redeemer.

2 To *serve* as Slaves for Christ, as shown in (Philippians 2) "Have this mind among yourselves, which is yours in Christ Jesus, who, though he was in the form of God, did not count equality with God a thing to be grasped, but emptied himself, by taking the form of a servant, being born in the likeness of men." – explains how Paul uses a different form of the word for servant here and the fact is that almost in every place where the word servant is used in the New Testament it is the Greek word "doulos" which means a "slave, bondman, man of servile condition." Jesus had all glory with the Father in heaven yet emptied Himself of His glory and took "the form of a servant." Even though He is equally God He didn't count it as something to grasp or hold on too but for our sake gave His life. To be a servant of Christ means we must be His slave and do all that He asks us to do (Mathew 28:18-10; Acts 1:8). This means we should also "have this mind among" us. This is so easy to say, hard so very difficult to do.

3 Paul demonstrated himself as the Slave of Christ as in (2 Corinthians 4:5) "For what we proclaim is not ourselves, but Jesus Christ as Lord, with ourselves as your servants for Jesus' sake." Paul had the apostolic authority, yet very infrequently did he use it. Paul became a "bond servant" (dulous or slave) for Jesus' sake. Paul, having the great commission from Jesus Christ did not "proclaim" himself but Jesus Christ as Lord and humbled himself in the sense that he too was a servant for Jesus' sake. If Paul saw himself as a slave to Christ, how much more do everyday believers have to see themselves as the same - a slave for the Great Master and Lord, Jesus Christ.

4 To *serve* also implied to be Servants of All as in (Mark 9:35) "And he sat down and called the twelve. And he said to them, "If anyone would be first, he must be last of all and servant of all." Just like most of Jesus' teachings, this goes against the grain of the world's thinking. To be first we must put ourselves last. The one who would be first must be the servant of all and this is certainly not the way of the world. Isn't it like God that His ways are in direct conflict with the ways most people think even in the church? I am a pastor but really, I *serve* the church. Since the foot of the cross is level ground I am no better or no worse than anyone else in the church. I must *serve* Christ and by serving Christ I must *serve* others. Praise the Lord.

Serve

5 To serve also means to be Servants of One Another as in (Galatians 5:13) "For you were called to freedom, brothers. Only do not use your freedom as an opportunity for the flesh, but through love serve one another." Some people come to church only to be *served*. They don't get it. They should come to *serve* others and not only expecting to be *served*. We are commanded "through love to *serve* one another." Love is a verb. It is action oriented, not so much a feeling but it's what you do and what we are to do is to *serve* others and do this serving in love, not grudgingly or expecting anything in return.

6 To serve we must also be the Servants of the Lord as in (Colossians 3:23-24) "Whatever you do, work heartily, as for the Lord and not for men, knowing that from the Lord you will receive the inheritance as your reward. You are serving the Lord Christ." Indeed! Whatever we are doing we should be doing it "for the Lord and not for men" because" our "inheritance" will ultimately be from Jesus Christ and not from men. That is who we really *serve* and when we *serve* others we are actually serving Christ. Jesus said "if anyone gives even a cup of cold water to one of these little ones who is my disciple, truly I tell you, that person will certainly not lose their reward" (Mathew 10:42) so even though we are not giving a cold drink to Jesus (or helping out someone financially, giving them food, our time, or our attention) when we *serve* others it's like giving Jesus a cold drink of water for when we do it for others, Jesus sees it as doing it for Him.

7 To serve makes us God's Servants in Society as in (Romans 13): "Let every person be subject to the governing authorities. For there is no authority except from God, and those that exist have been instituted by God. Therefore whoever resists the authorities resists what God has appointed, and those who resist will incur judgment. For rulers are not a terror to good conduct, but to bad. Would you have no fear of the one who is in authority? Then do what is good, and you will receive his approval, for he is God's servant for your good. But if you do wrong, be afraid, for he does not bear the sword in vain. For he is the servant of God, an avenger who carries out God's wrath on the wrongdoer. Therefore one must be in subjection, not only to avoid God's wrath but also for the sake of conscience." When we disobey the laws we are really resisting God for God has sovereignly placed those in authority over us and those who are in authority are God's representatives on earth. Just as (Romans 12) shows how Christians should relate to one another (Romans 13) shows how Christians should relate to those who are in authority in the world - whether they are in the church or not. These "rulers are not a terror to good conduct, but to bad" so if we are obedient to the laws of the land we have no reason to fear them but if we dis-

obey them and break the law we have every reason to fear because not only are we disobeying them, we are indirectly disobeying God.

Finally, Paul asked the church at Rome, "Don't you know that when you offer yourselves to someone as obedient slaves, you are slaves of the one you obey-whether you are slaves to sin, which leads to death, or to obedience, which leads to righteousness" (Romans 6:16)? You are a slave or a servant to the desires of your heart - whether it is to sin or whether it's to Christ. You are a slave either way. You must ether *serve* God or money but you can't *serve* both at the same time (Mathew 6:24). Who are you serving: Yourself or God? If you haven't repented and trusted in Christ then you are still a slave to sin and your future is grim (Revelation 20:11-15; Daniel 12:3) but if you are now serving Christ, you will hear these precious words someday: "Well done, thou good and faithful servant: thou hast been faithful over a few things, I will make thee ruler over many" (Mathew 25:21). Glory to Jesus Christ!

Seth: First son of Adam or son of first human being.

Sheep: (Noun; Greek: *probaton* - [prob'-at-on], Hebrew: *seh* [seh] a sheep. are quadrupedal, ruminant mammals typically kept as livestock. Like all ruminants, sheep are members of the order Artiodactyla, the even-toed ungulates. Although the name "sheep" applies to many species in the genus Ovis, in everyday usage it almost always refers to Ovis aries. Numbering a little over one billion, domestic sheep are also the most numerous species of sheep. An adult female sheep is referred to as a ewe, an intact male as a ram or occasionally a tup, a castrated male as a wether, and a younger sheep as a lamb. Sheep raising has a large lexicon of unique terms which vary considerably by region and dialect. Use of the word sheep began in Middle English as a derivation of the Old English word scēap; it is both the singular and plural name for the animal. A group of sheep is called a flock - used prominently in the gospel, herd or mob.

2 *Sheep* are mentioned in the gospel more than 500 times, more than any other animal. The prominence of sheep in the Bible grows out of two realities. Sheep were important to the nomads and agricultural life of the Hebrews and similarly peoples. Secondly, *sheep* are used throughout the Bible to symbolically refer to God's people.

3 *Sheep* are most likely descended from the wild mouflon of Europe and Asia. One of the earliest animals to be domesticated for agricultural purposes, sheep is raised for fleece, meat (lamb, hogget or mutton) and milk. A sheep's wool is the most widely used animal fibre, and is usually harvested by shearing. Ovine meat is called lamb when from younger animals and mutton when from older

Sheep

ones. Sheep continue to be important for wool and meat today, and are also occasionally raised for pelts, as dairy animals, or as model organisms for science. Sheep husbandry is practised throughout the majority of the inhabited world, and has been fundamental to many civilizations. In the modern era.

4. Many other specific terms for the various life stages of sheep exist, generally related to lambing, shearing, and age. Being a key animal in the history of farming, sheep have a deeply entrenched place in human culture, and find representation in much modern language and symbology. As livestock, *sheep* are most often associated with pastoral, Arcadian imagery. *Sheep* figure in many mythologies—such as the Golden Fleece—and major religions, especially the Abrahamic traditions. In both ancient and modern religious ritual, *sheep* are used as sacrificial animals. Dozens of times in the Bible, the people of God are referred to as *sheep*. A few of the more notable passages that come to mind are (Psalm 23, Isaiah. 53:6 and John 10). There are a couple of good reasons why we are called *sheep* in the Bible and one of them is because of the nature of the *sheep*.

5 By nature, *sheep* have three strikes against them. (a) *Sheep* are Dumb - In other words, they are not the smartest animals in the world. As a result, they are constantly getting into terrible situations. People are the same way! People who are away from the Lord live lives that are often just plain dumb as in (Jeremiah. 5:4)! Unfortunately, even after a person is saved, there is still a definite lack of understanding among most of the Lord's 3. (b) *Sheep* are Directionless - If a *sheep* wanders off from the rest of the herd, it will have a hard, if not impossible time, finding its way back. They have no sense of direction. So it is with those outside the Lord, there is simply no sense of spiritual direction in their lives. They cannot find their way to the Lord by themselves. (c) *Sheep* are Defenceless - Lions have teeth and claws, bears have the same. Snakes have fangs; even the fowls of the air have some type of defensive mechanism. Not so with *sheep*. They have absolutely no means of protecting themselves from danger. If they are /attacked, they are simply helpless! Again, people are the same way. There is no way that anyone can protect his or her self against the attacks of the evil one. We need someone else to protect us. God is the protector of His people as Vengeance belongs to Him and only Him alone. By their very nature, *sheep* need a shepherd and I suppose this is another reason why the figure of *sheep* is used to describe the people of God. Because in the person of the shepherd, we see many characteristics that speak of the Lord Jesus Christ. Therefore, it becomes clear that this idea of the shepherd and

his *sheep* is a good way to describe the relationship between the Lord and His people.

6 Sheep are basically helpless creatures who cannot survive long without a shepherd, upon whose care they are totally dependent. Likewise, like sheep, we are totally dependent upon the Lord to shepherd, protect, and care for us. Sheep are essentially dumb animals that do not learn well and are extremely difficult to train. They do not have good eyesight, nor do they hear well. They are very slow animals who cannot escape predators; they have no camouflage and no weapons for defence such as claws, sharp hooves, or powerful jaws.

Sheep as a Sacrificial lamb: This refer to an act of divine authority executed by Abraham as he looked up and there in a thicket he saw a ram caught by its horns. He went over and took the ram and sacrificed it as a burnt offering instead of his son. (Genesis 22:1-18). It is well-known to Christians and others, that Abraham was asked to sacrifice his son. He was willing to do so, but God gave him a *sheep* (ram) to sacrifice instead of his son Christians and Jews believe that the life of Isaac was saved, while the rest religions believed otherwise.

Sheep as the Lamb of God: Christians traditionally refer to Jesus as the "Lamb of God." Many Christians serve lamb as part of their Easter dinner. In many homes, a lamb-shaped cake decorates the table. Many Eastern Orthodox Christians hang pictures of the Easter lamb in their homes.

Sheep, Spotted: This has to do with sheep with patches on the body as in (Genesis 30:35) "So that very day, Laban went out and formed a flock for Jacob. He took from his herds all the male goats that were ringed and spotted. He also included the females that were speckled and spotted with any white patches, and all of the black sheep". Jacob *sheep* were named for the Biblical story of Jacob who selected spotted *sheep* for his flock. It tells how Jacob took every speckled and spotted *sheep* as his own from Laban's flock. Some claim that Jacobs of today descend directly from the *sheep* raised by Jacob that travelled from Palestine to Egypt and to Spain via the coast of North Africa and Morocco.

Sheep from the goats, separating the: Explaining impending judgement day scenario where Jesus Christ – the shepherd of all saints will select the sheep – the saints subject for eternal life from the goats – sinners bound for eternal condemnation – the goats as in (Mathew 25:33) "He shall set the *sheep* on His right hand, but the goats on the left". With regards to "judgement day," sheep and goats are used as metaphors in the Bible. Sheep are the followers of Christ, while goats chose not to follow

Shepherd

Christ. The parable is based on the differences in behaviour between sheep and goats. Sheep are gentle, quiet, innocent animals. They do not give their shepherds a lot of problems. They are easily led. Sheep are grazers, unlike the goat, which likes to browse. Goats are rebellious. In the Bible, goats are sometimes used to symbolize evil.

Shepherd: (Noun, Greek: *poimén* - [poy-mane'], Hebrew: (Verb, *roi* [ro-ee'] shepherd, a shepherd; hence met: of the feeder, protector, and ruler of a flock of men. A person who tends, herds, feeds, or guards herds of sheep. The word stems from an amalgam of sheep herder.

Shepherds, Biblical: This refers to shepherds in the gospel – from Old Testament times to the New Testament. The very first shepherd was Abel as in (Genesis 4: 3-4). He was also humanity's first murder victim, slain by his brother Cain. Abraham and Moses were shepherds. King David was the best known shepherd of Bible history. He wrote the beloved (Psalm 23). Shepherds were the first people to see the new-born Jesus Christ. Shepherds in Bible times faced incredible dangers in caring for their sheep, putting their own lives at risk by battling wild animals such as wolves and lions who threatened the flock. David was just such a shepherd (1 Samuel 17:34–35). In order to be good shepherds,

Shepherd and flocks, A close relationship between: "My sheep listen to my voice; I know them, and they follow me". (John 10:27) The Bible describes close relationships between shepherds and their flocks. The sheep recognize the voice of the shepherd. They follow him (or her). The shepherd protects his flock and would give his life for them. It is known that animals can instantly recognize the voice of a familiar trusted person. Sheep have excellent memories for faces. They remember their handler. They also remember people who inflict abuse upon them.

Shepherd, the Lord is my: Phrase from one of the most beloved of all passages of Scripture, the (Psalm 23). In this passage and throughout the New Testament we learn that the Lord is our Shepherd in two ways. First, as the Good Shepherd, He laid down His life for His sheep and, second, His sheep know His voice and follow Him as in (John 10:11, 14). God is using the analogy of sheep and their nature to describe us. Sheep have a natural tendency to wander off and get lost. As believers, we tend to do the same thing. It's as Isaiah has said: "We all, like sheep, have gone astray, each of us has turned to his own way" (Isaiah 53:6). When sheep go astray, they are in danger of getting lost, being attacked, even killing themselves by drowning or falling off cliffs. Likewise, within our own nature there is a strong tendency to go astray (Romans 7:5; 8:8), following the lusts of our flesh and eyes and pursuing the pride of life (1 John 2:16). As such, we are like sheep wandering away from the Shepherd through our own futile self-remedies and attempts at self-righteousness. It is our nature to drift away (Hebrews 2:1), to reject God, and to break His commandments. When we do this, we run the risk of getting lost, even forgetting the way back to God. Furthermore, when we turn away from the Lord, we soon find ourselves confronting one enemy after another who will attack us in numerous ways.

2 Sheep are basically helpless creatures who cannot survive long without a *shepherd*, upon whose care they are totally dependent. Likewise, like sheep, we are totally dependent upon the Lord to *shepherd*, protect, and care for us. Sheep are essentially dumb animals that do not learn well and are extremely difficult to train. They do not have good eyesight, nor do they hear well. They are very slow animals who cannot escape predators; they have no camouflage and no weapons for defence such as claws, sharp hooves, or powerful jaws.

Furthermore, sheep are easily frightened and become easily confused. In fact, they have been known to plunge blindly off a cliff following one after another. they had to be willing to lay down their lives for the sheep.

3 Jesus declared that He is our Shepherd and demonstrated it by giving His life for us. "The Son of Man did not come to be served, but to serve, and to give His life a ransom for many" (Matthew 20:28). Through His willing sacrifice, the Lord made salvation possible for all who come to Him in faith (John 3:16). In proclaiming that He is the good shepherd, Jesus speaks of "laying down" His life for His sheep (John 10:15, 17–18).

4 Like sheep, we, too, need a shepherd. Men are spiritually blind and lost in their sin. This is why Jesus spoke of the parable of the lost sheep (Luke 15:4–6). He is the Good Shepherd who lay down His life for us. He searches for us when we're lost, to save us and to show us the way to eternal life (Luke 19:10). We tend to be like sheep, consumed with worry and fear, following after one another. By not following or listening to the Shepherd's voice (John 10:27), we can be easily led astray by others to our own destruction. Jesus, the Good Shepherd, warns those who do not believe and listen to Him: "I did tell you, but you do not believe . . . you do not believe because you are not my sheep. My sheep listen to my voice; I know them, and they follow me. I give them eternal life, and they shall never perish; no one can snatch them out of my hand" (John 10:25–28).

5 Also, (Psalm 23:1–3) tells us that the shepherd meets the sheep's

every need: food, water, rest, safety, and direction. When we as believers follow our *Shepherd*, we, too, know that we will have all we need. We will not lack the necessities of life, for He knows exactly what we need (Luke 12:22–30). Sheep will not lie down when they are hungry, nor will they drink from fast-flowing streams. Sometimes the *shepherd* will temporarily dam up a stream so the sheep can quench their thirst. (Psalm 23:2) speaks of leading the sheep "beside the quiet or stilled waters." The shepherd must lead his sheep because they cannot be driven. Instead, the sheep hear the voice of their shepherd and follow him—just as we listen to our Shepherd, Jesus Christ—in His Word and follow Him (John 10:3–5, 16, 27). And if a sheep does wander off, the shepherd will leave the flock in charge of his helpers and search for the lost animal (Matthew 9:36; 18:12–14; Luke 15:3–7).

6 In (Psalm 23:3), the Hebrew word translated "paths" means "well-worn paths or ruts." In other words, when sheep wander onto a new path, they start to explore it, which invariably leads them into trouble. This passage is closely akin to the warning in (Hebrews 13:9): "Do not be carried away by all kinds of strange teachings." The apostle Paul also alludes to this idea in (Ephesians 4:14). Finally, the shepherd cares for the sheep because he loves them and wants to maintain his own good reputation as a faithful shepherd.

As we've seen in (Psalm 23), the analogy of the Lord as the Good Shepherd was also applied by Jesus in (John 10). In declaring that He is the shepherd of the sheep, Jesus is confirming that He is God. The Eternal God is our Shepherd. And we would not want it any other way.

Shepherd's personal Possession, a: The sheep belonged to the shepherd, he had paid a personal price to own it and wasn't going to stand idly by while it was lost. (The price Jesus paid for the sheep on Calvary – (1 Corinthians. 6:19-20)

Shepherd's as a Prized Possession: Meaning one sheep may have been no different from any other ordinary sheep, but special to the shepherd. To the shepherd, it is a prized possession. (All are special to the Lord! He died for the individual! He died for you. Had you been the only one who would have responded in faith in Christ, Jesus would still have gone to Calvary just for you!) Praise the Lord!

Shepherd as a precious Possession: Wherefore, to the shepherd, there are no big sheep and little sheep. Every sheep is precious in his eyes. So the Lord loves all His sheep equally. All are precious in His sight. You and I can never begin to understand the value of the human soul. We are so precious to the Lord that He willingly gave up His Son Jesus to die on the cross for our sins. We are precious in His sight.

Shepherd's search, the:
The shepherd's first motive is not in anger to punish, but in love to rescue. The shepherd doesn't go after the sheep in an effort to punish it for going astray. His motive is to find the sheep and restore it to its proper place in the fold. So it is with the Lord. He doesn't go after the lost ones so that He can punish them for their sins. He pursues them in order that He might prove His love for them and that they might be restored to a right relationship with the Lord. His motive is to deliver them from punishment not inflict punishment upon them. This is the way Jesus demonstrate His Love towards us.

Shepherd's Method, the:
He Initiates The Search - The sheep is powerless to find its way back to the flocks or to the shepherd. If the shepherd waits on the sheep to return of its own accord, then it would die in the wilderness. Instead of waiting, the shepherd goes after the sheep. He is the One who begins the process. (It is the same in salvation! The lost ones do not make the first moves toward God. They cannot, because they are dead, (Ephesians. 2:1). It is the Good Shepherd who makes the first move toward the sinner, (John 6:44). In fact, no one can ever be saved unless they are first approached by the Lord. He comes looking for us, it is never the other way around!) (He finds us, not we Him.)

2 Shepherd intensifies the Search:
As (John 6:44) says, 'the shepherd searches until he finds the sheep'. He doesn't give up after just a few minutes or hours of searching, but he stays on the job until the sheep has been recovered. So it is with the Lord. He never gives up on the lost sheep. He keeps calling and knocking and waiting, hoping that they will come to Him before it is too late. (Thankfully and gratefully that the Lord didn't give up on us! Rather, He kept knocking and kept calling until we answered – (Revelation. 3:20) We shouldn't be surprised though, after all, that is the Shepherd's business as in (Luke 19:10) "For the Son of Man came to seek and to save the lost."

3 Shepherd's success, the:
He locates the Sheep - He finds the sheep. (God already knows where every lost sheep is. He doesn't have to seek; He knows where you are right now!)

4 Shepherd lay hands on the sheep:
The shepherd reaches out to the sheep in its need. He doesn't turn away from it and leave it to languish in it dangerous place. He lovingly lays his hands upon it bringing comfort and hope to the wayward sheep. (When the Lord comes to a lost sheep, He too lays His hands upon it. He reach-

Shepherd lifts the sheep

es right into the midst of the mess we find ourselves in and by doing so shows us that there is hope and that there is a God in Heaven who loves us. Thank God that He doesn't condemn us when He comes alongside us. I am grateful that He comes to us in grace and mercy offering hope, forgiveness and a new beginning to everyone who will place their faith in the shed blood of Christ.

5 Shepherd lifts the sheep:

This means that shepherd doesn't stop with a mere touch. He reaches down and lifts the sheep out of the place where he finds it. He removes it from the place of danger. (Ill. The Good Shepherd does the same for those He finds wandering the dark hills of sin. He comes alongside them, reaches out to them and when they respond to His touch, He lifts them out of their sin and removes them from the danger they were in. Thank God, when Jesus comes into a heart and life, He delivers us from all danger, as in (Romans. 5:9) "Since we have now been justified by his blood, how much more shall we be saved from God's wrath through him!"

6 Shepherd Lugs the Sheep home:

The gospel declare that the shepherd lifts the sheep and lays it upon his shoulders. Certainly, we can picture him taking the front feet in one hand and the hind feet in another. By so doing, the sheep is draped around the neck of the shepherd and is absolutely safe and secure! Next, the Bible teaches us that the shepherd carries the sheep home. Notice that the sheep is not required to get there under its own power, but it goes there under the power of the shepherd. (This implies real picture of our salvation. When Jesus comes to where we are and finds us in our sins, He places us securely in Himself and carries us home – (Colosians 3:3; 1 Peter. 1:5; John 10:28). None of us are going to Heaven in our own power, but if we go, we will go through Jesus and Him alone! (for Salvation isn't like a bicycle) Praise the Lord!

Shepherd's satisfaction, the:

There Is Rejoicing - When the shepherd returns home, he calls all the neighbours together and they all rejoice in the fact that the shepherd has had his sheep restored to the fold. (Again, this is a picture of what happens when a lost sheep comes into the fold of the Lord. According to (Luke 10:10), there is rejoicing in the presence of the angels. Apparently, God the Father gets excited when a lost sheep is rescued. There is rejoicing in Heaven an there ought to be rejoicing in the earth. If there was ever anything to get excited over it is the redemption of souls - Luke 10:20.)

2 Shepherd has reason to be satisfied:

The Sheep has been saved from: (i) Disuse - As long as it was lost; it was of no benefit to the shepherd. (for the Lord cannot use a wayward life. He demands holy vessels.) (ii) Danger - Unless the shepherd had intervened the sheep would have remained in serious danger. It could never have defended itself or rescued itself. (For as long as men are apart from the Lord Jesus Christ, they are in serious danger. Hell and judgment are out there in front of them and they need desperately to be delivered. Only the blood of the Lord Jesus Christ saved from the penalty of sin)

(iii) Death - If the shepherd had not come looking for the sheep, it would have most certainly died out there in the wilderness. But now, it lives all because the shepherd came looking to save a wayward sheep. (For the Bible tells us that "the wages of sin is death." (Romans 6:23). Without the intervention of the Good Shepherd the lost sinner has no hope and will eventually wind up in Hell. We need to understand very clearly that there is only one means of salvation for all men and that is the blood of the Lord Jesus Christ. Any other religion, any other method, any other system of belief, no mater how good, is doomed to fail. Only Jesus saves the human soul – (Acts 4:12; John 14:6; Acts 16:31; John 3:16.) Praise the God of Grace fom Everlating to Everlasting!!

Shield of faith, the: The fourth piece of armour Paul mentions in (Ephesians 6) is "the shield of faith." Meaning standing firm, not weaver with the word and God's promise. The Roman soldiers use their shields effectively. Spiritual shield serve a protective purpose for us.

The Bible, in (Daniel 3), records the story of the burning fiery furnace: The three young men stood looking at the very site where they were to be put to death. The edict had gone out—they were to be thrown, alive and bound, into a furnace heated to seven times its usual fervor. Everyone watching understood: This was an execution. This was what happened when you disobeyed the king. Just moments ago, the three men had been given the chance to circumvent this ugly fate. With little more than a few motions on their part, they could have saved their own lives. But they refused. Why?

2 The king had previously set up a 90-foot-high golden statue. At various times throughout the day, which were to be prompted by music, he commanded that his people fall down and worship this statue. Out of the entire nation, we are given the names of only three men who had the courage to stand against this royal decree. And for that courage, Shadrach, Meshach and Abed-Nego were going to die.

3 When King Nebuchadnezzar became aware of their insubordination, he summoned the rebels and gave them an ultimatum: Worship the statue or be thrown into a fiery furnace. Their response is preserved for us in (Daniel 3:16-18). "Shadrach, Meshach, and

Shout

Abed-Nego answered and said to the king, 'O Nebuchadnezzar, we have no need to answer you in this matter. If that is the case, our God whom we serve is able to deliver us from the burning fiery furnace, and He will deliver us from your hand, O king. But if not, let it be known to you, O king, that we do not serve your gods, nor will we worship the gold image which you have set up.'" The faith of these three men in God allowed them to stand up to the world's most powerful man and refuse to follow his blasphemous orders. They were then thrown into the furnace and miraculously delivered unharmed by God. But perhaps the most amazing thing about their story is their unwavering dedication to God in the face of an unknown outcome. Their faith was strong enough to accept giving their lives!

4 Up until now, Paul's description of the armor of God has been limited to items we wear. We put on the belt, the breastplate and the shoes, and they essentially hold themselves up. The shield is different. Paul tells us that the shield is something we must take up, something we are required to raise. Just strapping it to our arm won't do any good at all if we don't make the effort to hold it aloft and use it.

5 Armor of God: The Shield of Faith. The Roman shield—the *scutum*—was not the standard "medieval-esque" shield most picture in their minds upon hearing the word. It was instead a very large, slightly curved rectangular shield featuring at its center a large metal knob (called a boss). The *scutum* was an impressive line of defence. Because of its sheer size (some were three and a half feet tall and almost three feet wide), soldiers were afforded a great deal of protection from enemies. Because of its slight curve, it was able to deflect attacks without transferring the full force of the assault to the man holding the shield. Because of its boss, it was able to deflect even the more vicious blows and function in a limited offensive capacity as a means of knocking an opponent backwards.

Shout: (Noun, Greek: *keleusma* - [kel'-yoo-mah]; Hebrew (verb) - *rua* - [roo-ah'], shout, a word of command, a call, an arousing outcry as in (Psalms 5:11) "But let all those that put their trust in thee rejoice: let them ever shout for joy, because thou defendest them: let them also that love thy name be joyful in thee".

Shout of joy, a: This can take different forms of utterances. It can be a song sung loudly, an acclamation or a proclamation, or simply an ecstatic crying out. "Hosanna!" and "Hallelujah!" were expressed as shouts in the Bible. They are occasionally heard in conventional worship services today, but usually in hymns and songs. I take as a model the apostle Paul, who added one of the greatest New Testament books to the Bible when he wrote to the Christians of Galatia. In it he asked this loaded question: "What has happened to all your joy?" At the close of the book of Psalms *a shout of joy* is raised that is worth repeating as in (Psalm 150): "Praise the Lord! . . .Praise him with the sounding of the trumpet, Praise him with the harp and lyre, Praise him with tambourine and dancing, Praise him with the strings and flutePraise him with the clash of cymbals, Praise him with resounding cymbals. Let everything that has breath praise the Lord. Praise the Lord!

Shout of initial consecration: As in (Leviticus 9:24) The Jews shouted when God lit the altar on fire for the first time. Whenever a person gets saved there is a reason for shouts of joy.

Shout of a King, the: As in (Numbers 23:21) the shout of confidence that comes from a redeemed people when they know their king is in their midst.

Shout of Faith, the: As in (Joshua 6:20) Anybody can shout after the walls come down it takes faith to shout before the walls come down.

Shout of the Philistines, the: As in (Judges 15:14) an attempt at intimidation by the enemy. Don't fear any racket the devil may be making.

Shout of the empty religious formalism: As in (1 Samuel 4:5-6). Several times in scripture God told people to stop praying. He told Moses to stop praying over Israel, He told Joshua to get up off his face and quit praying because of the sin of Achan. He told Samuel to stop praying for Saul, and David records that when once praying for his enemies his prayer returned to his bosom. (God was telling him to shut up.) In this story the Jews made a lot of noise but God was not in it. In (Mathew. 17:14-21) "And when they had come to the multitude, a man came to Him, kneeling down to Him and saying, "Lord, have mercy on my son, for he is an epileptic and suffers severely; for he often falls into the fire and often into the water. So I brought him to Your disciples, but they could not cure him." Then Jesus answered and said, "O faithless and perverse generation, how long shall I be with you? How long shall I bear with you? Bring him here to Me." And Jesus rebuked the demon, and it came out of him; and the child was cured from that very hour. Then the disciples came to Jesus privately and said, "Why could we not cast it out?" So Jesus said to them, "Because of your unbelief; for assuredly, I say to you, if you have faith as a mustard seed, you will say to this mountain, 'Move from here to there,' and it will move; and nothing will be impossible for you. However, this kind does not go out except by prayer and fasting". The disciples could not cast out a devil, Jesus said it was because of a lack of prayer and fasting on their part. Imagine the ruckus they made trying to cast the devil out! Fleshly shouting will never get God's work done.

Shout of faith awakened, the:
As in (1 Samuel 17:52) "Then the men of Israel and Judah surged forward with a shout and pursued the Philistines to the entrance of Gath and to the gates of Ekron. Their dead were strewn along the Shaaraim road to Gath and Ekron". David's actions awakened the slumbering faith of the rest of Israel. It only took a spark to get a fire going.

Shout of joy in the works of God, the:
As in (Ezra 3:11) "With praise and thanksgiving they sang to the Lord: "He is good; his love toward Israel endures forever." And all the people gave a great shout of praise to the Lord, because the foundation of the house of the Lord was laid. We should always shout when we see the Kingdom of God going forward. Praise the Lord!

Shout, God went up with a:
As in (Psalms 47:5) God is gone up with a shout, the LORD with the sound of a trumpet. Imagine Jesus' homecoming after Calvary! The saints and angels lined the streets and the angel of the Lord blew trumpets.

Shout, God comes back with a:
As in (1 Thessalonians 4:16) For the Lord himself shall descend from heaven with a shout, with the voice of the archangel, and with the trump of God: and the dead in Christ shall rise first: What a day that will be, when my Jesus I shall see...

Shouting is the desire of God for His children:
As in (Psalms 132:9) "Let thy priests be clothed with righteousness; and let thy saints shout for joy".

Sick, Anointing of the:
Anointing prepares the person for death, and only incidentally may produce physical healing. The salvation and resurrection spoken of in James are in the first place spiritual. (James 5:14-15)

Sign:
(Noun, Greek: *sémeion* - [say-mi'-on], Hebrew: *oth* [oth] a sign, miracle, indication, mark, token, portent, mighty power, wonder etc.

2 Literally, an object, quality, or event whose presence or occurrence indicates the probable presence or occurrence of something else, a gesture or action used to convey information or an instruction, a notice on public display that gives information or instructions in a written or symbolic form, each of the twelve equal sections into which the zodiac is divided, named from the constellations formerly situated in each, and associated with successive periods of the year according to the position of the sun on the ecliptic,

Sign

the positiveness or negativeness of a quantity.

3 Events which unmistakeably involve an immediate and powerful action of God designed to reveal His character or purposes. Words used in the Gospel, the Bible and Scriptures to describe the miraculous include sign, wonder, work, mighty work, portent, power. These points out the inspired authors' sense of God's pervasive activity in nature, history, and people.

In Old Testament; The two Hebrew words most frequently used for "miracle" are translated "sign" (*oth*) and "wonder" (*mopheth*). They are synonyms and often occur together in the same text as in (Exodus 7:3; Deuteronomy 4:34; Deuteronomy 6:22; Deuteronomy 7:19; Deuteronomy 13:1; Deuteronomy 26:8; Deuteronomy 28:46; Deuteronomy 34:11; Nehemiah 9:10; Psalm 105:27; Isaiah 8:18; Jeremiah 32:20; Daniel 6:27).

4 "Sign" may be an object or daily activity as well as an unexpected divine action (Genesis 1:14; Exodus 12:13 , RSV; Joshua 4:6 Ezekiel 24:24). The basic nature of a sign is that it points people to God. Wonders can serve as a sign of a future event. Signs seek to bring belief (Exodus 4:5; compare Exodus 10:2), but they do not compel a person to believe (Exodus 4:9).

5 At times God invites people to ask for *signs* (Isaiah 7:11). The signs He has done should make all peoples on earth stand in awe (Psalm 65:8). They should join the Psalmist in confessing that the God of Israel "alone works wonders" (Psalm 72:18 NAS).

6 In the New Testament, the phrase *signs* and wonders" is often used in the same sense as it is found in the Old Testament and also in Hellenistic literature. (Matthew 24:24; Mark 13:22; John 4:48; Acts 2:43; Acts 4:30; Acts 5:12; Acts 6:8; Acts 7:36; Acts 14:3; Acts 15:12; Romans 15:19; 2 Corinthians 12:12; 2 Thessalonians 2:9; Hebrews 2:4). Accordingly, *Sign* in the New Testament is used of miracles taken as evidence of divine authority. Sometimes it is translated as "miracle" (Luke 23:8 NIV; Acts 4:16, Acts 4:16,4:22 NAS,). John was particularly fond of using *sign* to denote miraculous activity as in (John 2:11 ,John 2:11,2:18 ,John 2:18,2:23; John 3:2; John 4:54; John 6:2 ,John 6:2,6:14 ,John 6:14,6:26; John 7:31; John 9:16; John 10:41; John 11:47; John 12:18; John 37:1; John 20:30; Revelation 12:1 ,Revelation 12:1,12:3 ,; Revelation 13:13-14; Revelation 15:1; Revelation 16:14; Revelation 19:20)

As a (verb) this means to write one's name on (a letter, card, document, etc.) to identify oneself as the writer or sender, use gestures to convey information or instructions, indicate with signposts or other markers, .mark or consecrate with the sign of the cross.

Signs and wonders

Signs and wonders: Supernatural manifestations brought on by the Holy Spirit (such as prophecy and healing). 2 *Sign and wonders* is a phrase used often by leaders of the Charismatic movement from late 1980s. It is closely associated with the ministry of John Wimber and the Vineyard Movement. One of the major emphases of the belief is that the Gospel can be communicated more effectively to unbelievers if accompanied by supernatural manifestations brought on by the Holy Spirit (such as prophecy and healing).

3 The origin of the phrase is in (Deuteronomy 26:8), which describes the commandment to tithe first fruits as linked to God's having brought the Israelites out of Egypt "with a strong hand and an outstretched arm, and with signs and wonders". This passage is read with emphasis in the Passover Haggadah and Seder. A key verse in scripture that is understood by Christian ministries which allow God to move in *signs and wonders* is (Mark 16:20), which states "Then the disciples went out and preached everywhere, and the Lord worked with them and confirmed his word by the signs that accompanied it."

Sign and wonders, reasons why people seek: Considering the facts that our God is a God of wonders (Psalm 136:3-4). As the Creator and Sustainer of all that is, God has the power to suspend natural laws in order to fulfill His purposes. Miracles were a part of the ministries of Moses, Elijah and Elisha, and of course Jesus and the apostles, and their miracles primarily served the purpose of confirming their message as being from God (Hebrews 2:3-4). Today, many people still seek to experience the miraculous, and some will go to great lengths to have that experience. There may be many reasons for such a desire, and Scripture gives us at least five. (1) Some people seek after signs and wonders because they want confirmation of the truth of God. There is nothing inherently wrong with this desire. In fact, God willingly gave signs to Moses (Exodus 4:1-9) and Gideon (Judges 6:11-22) to confirm His word. Miracles can aid a person's coming to faith, as in (John 2:23), "Many people saw the miraculous signs he was doing and believed in his name."

However, there comes a time when enough miracles have been performed—the truth has been proved—and it is time to exercise faith. When Moses hesitated to obey after a series of miracles at the burning bush, "the LORD's anger burned" (Exodus 4:14). Also, it is nobler in God's sight to believe without needing a miracle. Jesus visited the Samaritans, and "because of his words many more became believers" (John 4:41) for more emphasis. Just a few verses later, Jesus rebukes the Galileans: "Unless you people see miraculous *signs and wonders . . .* you will never believe" (John 4:48). Unlike the Samaritans, the people of Galilee required signs and wonders.

2 Some people seek after *signs and wonders* because they do not believe the signs and wonders which have already been performed. The Pharisees in (Matthew 12) were just such a lot. Jesus had been performing miracles for quite some time when a group of scribes and Pharisees came to Him with an insolent demand to see another sign. In response, Jesus condemned them as "wicked and adulterous" as in (Matthew 12:38-39).

In the issue of the Sign of Jonah: "Then some of the Pharisees and teachers of the law said to him, "Teacher, we want to see a sign from you." He answered, "A wicked and adulterous generation asks for a sign! But none will be given it except the sign of the prophet Jonah". They were "wicked" in that they refused to believe the signs and wonders Christ had already performed. "In spite of his wonders, they did not believe" (Psalm 78:32). Their hearts were hardened towards the truth, even after numerous public miracles. Nothing would make them believe; their hearts were as pharaoh's, hardened after witnessing so many of Moses' miracles in Egypt (Exodus 9:34-35). They were "adulterous" in the spiritual sense, having left the true worship of God to follow a man-made set of rules and traditions. Not satisfied with the miracles Jesus was doing, they demanded something even greater. They looked for signs at their own devising. So entrenched was their rejection of Christ that, when later presented with the "sign of the prophet Jonah" (Christ's resurrection, (Matthew 12:39-40), they still would not believe.

3. *Some people seek after signs and wonders* because they seek an occasion to excuse their unbelief. There were people in Jesus' day who "tested" Him by seeking a sign (Matthew 16:1; Luke 11:16). Since they specified that the sign be "from heaven," they most likely wanted something spectacular, similar to Elijah's calling down fire from the sky (1 Kings 18:38) or Isaiah's causing the sun to reverse course (Isaiah 38:8). Probably, their "test" was designed to be something "too big" for Jesus to accomplish—they simply hoped He would attempt it and fail in the attempt.

4. Again, some people seek after signs and wonders because they are curious thrill-seekers. Like the crowds in (John 6:2) and King Herod in Luke 23:8, they want to see something sensational, but they have no real desire to know the truth of Christ.

5. *Some people seek after signs and wonders* because they hope to get something for themselves. After Jesus fed the multitudes, a large crowd followed Him to the other side of Galilee. Jesus saw their true motivation, however, and rebuked it: "I tell you the truth, you

Sin

are looking for me, not because you saw miraculous signs but because you ate the loaves and had your fill" (John 6:26). The crowd's desire was not to know Christ or even to see more miracles; it was simply to fill their stomachs again. Better than seeking after a new miracle is taking God at His Word. Simple faith is more pleasing to the Lord than a reliance on a dazzling sensory experience. "Jesus told him, 'Because you have seen me, you have believed; blessed are those who have not seen and yet have believed'" – full text in (John 20:29). Praise the living God.

Sin: (Noun, Greek: *hamartia* [ham-ar-tee'-ah], Verb, Hebrew: *chata* [khaw-taw'] Proposition: missing the mark; hence: (a) guilt, sin, (b) a fault, failure (in an ethical sense), sinful deed.

2 Every human whoever existed, except Jesus, has sinned. We were born with Original Sin... We live in such a sinful world that it almost seems impossible that we will avoid sin for the rest of our lives. Fear not, praying to God and meditating on the Gospel or the bible can help you with sin. If you ask for the Holy Spirit to be within you and help guide you, you can avoid sin. You will receive the wisdom and guidance you seek if you just ask for it. Remember, sin is WORDLY and temporary. In the end, greed, sex, money and the rest will mean nothing. What will be important is your love for God and what good things you did in your life. To embrace our salvation, we must turn away from sin. Repentance is hard, but it is necessary. Don't be scared, because God is here for you. None of us are perfect, so we shoul always turn to God for help.

3 From the very beginning, God told man what was right and wrong. To Adam in the Garden, God said, "You are free to eat from any tree in the garden; but you must not eat from the tree of the knowledge of good and evil, for when you eat of it you will surely die" (Genesis 2:16-17). When the children of Israel came out of Egypt, God established His Law with them at Mount Sinai. The Ten Commandments (Exodus 20:1-17) were not the whole law, but a summary of all that God had to tell them. The entire books of Leviticus and Deuteronomy are devoted to revealing to the Israelites God's laws. Jewish rabbis say that there are 613 laws in the Torah (Books of Moses). Of those, 365 are in the "thou shalt not..." category.

4 From the Ten Commandments we have false worship, idolatry, misusing God's name, violating the Sabbath, dishonoring parents, murder, adultery, stealing, lying/libel, and coveting. In the Sermon on the Mount (Matthew 5–7), Jesus took some of these same sins to a new level. Regarding murder, Jesus said, "Anyone who is angry with his brother will be subject to judgment.... But anyone who says, 'You fool!' will be in danger of the

fire of hell" (Matthew 5:22). Regarding adultery, Jesus said, "Anyone who looks at a woman lustfully has already committed adultery with her in his heart" (Matthew 5:28). In (Galatians 5:19-21), we are told, "The acts of the sinful nature are obvious: sexual immorality, impurity and debauchery; idolatry and witchcraft; hatred, discord, jealousy, fits of rage, selfish ambition, dissensions, factions and envy; drunkenness, orgies, and the like. I warn you, as I did before, that those who live like this will not inherit the kingdom of God." Just these brief lists will give most people plenty of things to work on for a lifetime. In addition to the various lists that can be found in Scripture, we are told in 1 (John 5:17) that "all wrongdoing is sin." Not only does the Bible tell us the things not to do, but in (James 4:17), we are informed that anyone "who knows the good he ought to do and doesn't do it, *sins*."

5 When we try to compile a list of *sins*, we find ourselves buried under the guilt of our own failures because we discover that we have *sinned* far more than we realized. The Scriptures inform us, "All who rely on observing the law are under a curse, for it is written: 'Cursed is everyone who does not continue to do everything written in the Book of the Law'" (Galatians 3:10). While that statement might seem self-defeating, it is actually the best news possible. Since we can never fully keep God's Law, there must be another answer, and it is found in the very next verses: "Christ redeemed us from the curse of the law by becoming a curse for us, for it is written: 'Cursed is everyone who is hung on a tree.' "He redeemed us in order that the blessing given to Abraham might come to the Gentiles through Christ Jesus, so that by faith we might receive the promise of the Spirit" (Galatians 3:13-14). The Law of God, or the lists of sins that we find in the Bible, serve as a tutor to "lead us to Christ that we might be justified by faith" (Galatians 3:24).

6 The Bible has all sorts of words to describe sin. The most striking of these is Hebrew. mešubah (infidelity); the covenant people Israel was chasing after other lovers, as the prophets described it. In the Hebrew Scriptures, other words include 'ahar (transgression, law-breaking), ma'al (trespass), 'awon (straying, wandering), tum'ah (becoming unclean), beged (disloyalty, treason), and peša (revolt, rebellion). The image of sin which the New Testament most picked up on was the idea of an archer missing his mark (Heb. chatta't, Gk hamartia). Anyone who does these is in some sense a 'sinner'. The origin of hamartia is the reward from competition; due to missing the mark badly or often, the archer has no (ha-) share in the allotment (mer-) or prize.

Refernces: (Psalms 69:5) O God, you know my foolishness; and my

Sinner

sins are not hid from you. (Proverbs 28:13) He that covers his sins shall not prosper: but whoever confesses and forsakes them shall have mercy, (Isaiah 55:7) Let the wicked forsake his way, and the unrighteous man his thoughts: and let him return to the LORD, and he will have mercy on him; and to our God, for he will abundantly pardon. (Luke 13:3) I tell you, No: but, except you repent, you shall all likewise perish. (Romans 3:23) For all have sinned, and come short of the glory of God; (Romans 6:10) For in that he died, he died to sin once: but in that he lives, he lives to God. (Ephesians 4:22) That you put off concerning the former conversation the old man, which is corrupt according to the deceitful lusts; (Colossians 3:5) Mortify therefore your members which are on the earth; fornication, uncleanness, inordinate affection, evil concupiscence, and covetousness, which is idolatry: (Colossians 3:6) For which things' sake the wrath of God comes on the children of disobedience: (Hebrews 9:22) And almost all things are by the law purged with blood; and without shedding of blood is no remission. (Hebrews 12:1) Why seeing we also are compassed about with so great a cloud of witnesses, let us lay aside every weight, and the sin which does so easily beset us, and let us run with patience the race that is set before us, (Hebrews 12:3) For consider him that endured such contradiction of sinners against himself, lest you be wearied and faint in your minds. (Hebrews 12:4) You have not yet resisted to blood, striving against sin. (James 4:17) Therefore to him that knows to do good, and does it not, to him it is sin. (1 John 1:9) If we confess our sins, he is faithful and just to forgive us our sins, and to cleanse us from all unrighteousness.

Sinner: (Adjective; Greek: *hamartólos* [ham-ar-to-los']**;** Hebrew: *chatta* [khat-taw'] Sinners, sinning, sinful, depraved, detestable. The soul that sin. A transgressor.

2 Someone who is deeply depraved, evil, bad. However, that's not what the Christian faith means by the word. In Christian belief, 'sinner' is not a moral description, but a relational one. Sin is the broken state of our relationship with God. There's a distance, a gap between us (with the rest of the created universe) and God, a distance far too wide for us to cross over, a distance bridged only by God's act of coming over onto our side of the gap through Jesus Christ (God-with-us) and the Spirit that Jesus sent in His place. The nicest, kindest, most spiritual, and most virtuous of us is a sinner. The vilest, darthest, crookedest, most evil of us is a sinner. Everyone in between is a sinner. Each and all of these sinners are loved by God. Praise the God of Grace!

Sleep: (Noun, Greek: hupnos - [hoop'-nos], Hebrew: (verb) yashen - [yaw-shane']); fig: spiritual sleep. Used literally when the state of the body is in normal unconscious repose. On one occasion when Jesus and his disciples were crossing the Sea of Galilee, the Lord was sleeping on a cushion in the stern of the boat (Markk. 4:38). This is but one of the many evidences which argue for the true humanity of the Saviour.

2 It is interesting that the Scriptures refer to different levels of *sleep*. At Troas, Eutychus, in a late-night church service, was borne down with "deep *sleep*," and fell from an upstairs window to the ground (Acts 20:9). Science makes a distinction between a lighter *sleep* (REM = Rapid Eye Movement, i.e., the dream stage) and a deeper *sleep* (non-REM). This is determined by the measurement of brain waves on an electroencephalograph (EEG). In adults, deep slumber represents about 75% of one's sleeping time.

Sleep as a Symbol: The term *sleep* is used symbolically in several different senses in the Gospel or Bible. A consideration of these makes a fascinating study.

Sleep, God cannot: The concept of *sleeping* is biblically employed with figurative language to stress certain truths about God. In emphasizing the fact that the Lord is ever watchful of our needs, a psalmist wrote: "He will not allow your foot to slip; he who keeps you will not slumber. Behold, he who keeps Israel, will neither slumber nor *sleep*" (Psalm 121:3-4). As a result of the Lord's providential care, the faithful saint takes consolation. "In peace will I both lay me down and *sleep*; for you, Jehovah, alone make me dwell in safety" (Psalm. 4:8). On the other hand, when the Hebrew people drifted into sin, and the Lord allowed them to suffer the consequences of their rebellion, it was as if he was asleep (i.e., he did not intervene to deliver them from certain calamities). They exclaimed: "Awake. Why do you *sleep*, O Lord? Arise; do not cast us off forever" (Psalm. 44:23).

Sleep as symbol of laziness: Sometimes sleep is used as the equivalent of being lazy. "Do not give sleep to your eyes, nor slumber to your eyelids …. Go to the ant, O sluggard. Observe her ways and be wise …. How long will you lie down, O sluggard? When will you arise from your sleep? A little sleep, a little slumber, a little folding of the hands to rest. And your poverty will come in like a vagabond, and your need like an armed man" (Proverb. 6:4-11).

Sleep as the destruction of the wicked: *Sleep* can portray the utter and final punishment of a wicked power that has stood in opposition to God. The prophet Jeremiah foretold the complete destruction of the evil Babylonian regime. "Babylon shall become heaps, a dwelling-place for jackals, an astonishment, and a hissing, without inhabitant …. When they are heated, I will make their feast, and I will make them drunken, that they may rejoice, and sleep a perpetual sleep, and not wake, saith Jehovah" (Jeremiah 51:37-39).

Sleep as Spiritual apathy:
Sometimes spiritual lethargy is represented as a sleep. To the brethren in Rome Paul wrote: "And this, knowing the season, that already it is time for you to awake out of sleep: for now is salvation nearer to us than when we first believed" (Roman. 13:11). The apostle subsequently amplifies the significance of the figure by suggesting that the pursuit of an ungodly lifestyle is tantamount to a spiritual coma (v. 13). A similar thought is suggested in Paul's letter to the Ephesians: "Awake, you who are sleeping, and arise from the dead, and Christ shall shine on you" (Ephesian. 5:14).

Sleep as being unprepared:
Sleep can suggest the notion of being unprepared to meet the Lord at the time of his return. Jesus warned: "Watch therefore: for you do not know when the lord of the house is coming … lest he come suddenly and find you *sleeping*" (Mark. 13:35-36). When Paul corresponded with the brothers in Thessalonica, he warned about a false sense of security. Folks will be relaxing in a delusional state of "peace and safety," when suddenly destruction will come upon them. And so he admonished: "let us not sleep, as do the rest, but let us watch and be sober" (1 Thessalonica. 5:3-6). To be awake is thus to be vigilant, ever prepared.

Sleep in the case where the dead are asleep:
Sleep is commonly used as a designation for death, both in the Old Testament and in the New Testament. David petitioned the Creator: "Consider and answer me, O Jehovah my God: Lighten my eyes, lest I *sleep* the sleep of death" (Psalm. 13:3). When Lazarus of Bethany died, Jesus informed the disciples: "Our friend Lazarus has fallen *asleep*…." The Master's men did not comprehend the nature of his language. They initially thought that Christ spoke of natural sleep; he therefore had to tell them plainly: "Lazarus is dead" (John. 11:14).

Sleep as figuratively depicted as death:
First, there is a common appearance between a sleeping body and a corpse. The analogy is thus quite natural.

Second, just as the soul of a sleeping person still exists but is oblivious to its material surroundings, even so, in death the soul of man is not extinct; rather, it is only unaware of earth's environment. Solomon asserted that the dead have neither knowledge of, nor reward for, anything transpiring "under the sun," i.e., on earth (Ecclesistes. 9:5-6).

Third, as the sleeping person awakes and rises from his bed. Even so, the dead will rise from their graves at the time of the Lord's return. We must briefly pause and comment further about these final two points. It is not the case, as alleged by some, that the dead are unconscious, i.e., they are in a state of mindless *sleep*, awaiting the day of judgment. There is ample evidence that the dead are entirely conscious in their own realm of existence. Both the rich man and Lazarus were cognizant (Luke: 16:23-25), and so were the martyred souls in John's heavenly vision (Revelation. 6:9-11). Whenever the Bible describes death as a *sleep*, it is only the body that is under consideration. For example, Daniel referred to those who "*sleep* in the dust of the earth" (Daniel 12:2). Note that the part of man which sleeps is that part which is planted in the dust. A common Greek word for the *sleep* of death is *koimaomai* (Mathew. 27:52), a kindred term to koimeterion, from which derives our word "cemetery," the abode of dead bodies.

In the end, the term "sleep" implies the future resurrection of the human body. In spite of the fact that there are some who say, "there is no resurrection of the dead" (1 Corinthians. 15:12), ' Paul argues that Christ "is the firstfruits of them that are asleep" (1 Cointhiansr. 15:20). This is a clear affirmation that Christ's bodily resurrection is Heaven's pledge that we shall be raised similarly—the firstfruits being the initial harvest (Exodus. 23:16), and the guarantee of that which is to follow. As the Lord awoke from the dead, so shall we. In short *Sleep* is an intriguing study—both from the literal and figurative perspectives.

Slumber: The state of consciousness between being awake and being asleep. As recorded in the Holy Scriptures, the LORD frequently appeared "In a dream, in a vision of the night, when deep sleep falleth upon men, in *slumberings* upon the bed" see also (Appearances of the Lord God). "That he may withdraw man from his purpose, and hide pride from man" i.e. The "humble" and "slumber" connection - that extends to the original languages of the Bible, as written in (Job 33:14) For God speaketh once, yea twice, yet man perceiveth it not. (Job 33:15) In a dream, in a vision of the night, when deep sleep falleth upon men, in slumberings upon the bed;(Job 33:16) Then he openeth the ears of men, and sealeth their instruction, (Job 33:17) That he may withdraw man from his purpose, and hide pride from man. 33:18 He keepeth back his soul [see What Does The Bible Really Say About Your Soul?] from the pit, and his life from perishing by the sword." (Job 33:14-18 KJV). One of the most well-known incidents was when the LORD warned both the Magi and Joseph about Herod while they were in a state of slumber at night.

Son

Son: (Noun, Greek: *Huios* - [hwee-os'] Hebrew: *Ben* [bane] a son, descendent. a boy or man in relation to either or both of his parents. synonyms: male child, boy, son and heir; More, a male offspring of an animal. a male descendant.

2 Most important meaning of the word "Son" in the Gospel is the 'Believer in Jesus' as in (John 3:16) "For God so loved the world, that he gave his only begotten Son, that whosoever believeth in him should not perish, but have everlasting life". (KJV). This is one of the most widely quoted verses from the Christian Bible and has been called the most famous Bible verse. It has also been called the "Gospel in a nutshell", because it is considered a summary of the central theme of traditional Christianity. Note: The Child – Son believed on the father. By so believing, does not beg, but ask, and the father gives, When the son knocks, the father open without hesitation; etc.

Sonship, the eternal: This simply affirms that the second Person of the triune Godhead has eternally existed as the Son. In other words, there was never a time when He was not the Son of God, and there has always been a Father and *Son* relationship within the Godhead. This doctrine recognizes that the idea of *Sonship* is not merely a title or role that Christ assumed at some specific point in history, but that it is the essential identity of the second Person of the Godhead. According to this doctrine, Christ is and always has been the Son of God.

Yes, the eternal *Sonship* is biblical and is a view that is widely held among Christians and has been throughout church history. This is not to say that this is not an important doctrine, because it is; it simply acknowledges the fact that there are orthodox or evangelical Christians that hold or have held both views. Those that deny the doctrine of eternal *Sonship* are not denying the triune nature of God or the deity or eternality of Christ, and those that embrace the eternal *Sonship* of Christ are not inferring that Jesus Christ was anything less than fully God.

2 Throughout Gospel history the doctrine of eternal *Sonship* has been widely held, with most Christians believing that Jesus existed as God's eternal *Son* before creation. It is affirmed in the Nicene Creed (325 A.D.) which states: "We believe in one God, the Father, the Almighty, maker of heaven and earth, of all that is, seen and unseen. We believe in one Lord, Jesus Christ, the only Son of God, eternally begotten of the Father, God from God, Light from Light, true God from true God, begotten, not made, of one Being with the Father. Through him all things were made. For us and for our salvation he came down from heaven: by the power of the Holy Spirit

he became incarnate from the Virgin Mary, and was made man. For our sake he was crucified under Pontius Pilate; he suffered death and was buried. On the third day he rose again in accordance with the Scriptures; he ascended into heaven and is seated at the right hand of the Father. He will come again in glory to judge the living and the dead, and his kingdom will have no end." It was also later reaffirmed in the fifth century in the Athanasian Creed.

3 There is considerable biblical evidence to support the eternal *Sonship* of Christ. First of all, there are many passages that clearly identify that it was "the Son" who created all things as in (Colossians 1:13-16; Hebrews 1:2), thereby strongly implying that Christ was the *Son* of God at the time of creation. When one considers these passages, it seems clear that the most normal and natural meaning of the passages is that at the time of creation Jesus was the *Son* of God, the second Person of the Triune Godhead, thus supporting the doctrine of eternal *Sonship*.

4 Also, there are numerous verses that speak of God the Father sending the Son into the world to redeem sinful man (John 20:21; Galatians 4:4; 1 John 4:14; 1 John 4:10) and giving His Son as a sacrifice for sin (John 3:16). Clearly implied in all the passages that deal with the Father sendingor giving the *Son* is the fact that He was the Son before He was sent into the world. This is even more clearly seen in (Galatians 4:4-6), where the term "sent forth" is used both of the *Son* and the Spirit. Just as the Holy Spirit did not become the Holy Spirit when He was sent to empower the believers at Pentecost, neither did the *Son* become the *Son* at the moment of His incarnation. All three Persons of the Triune Godhead have existed for all eternity, and their names reveal that they are, not simply what their title or function is.

5 Again, (1 John 3:8) speaks of the appearance or manifestation of the Son of God: "the one who practices sin is of the devil; for the devil has sinned from the beginning. The Son of God appeared for this purpose, that He might destroy the works of the devil." The verb "to make manifest" or "appeared" means to make visible or to bring to light something that was previously hidden. The idea communicated in this verse is not that the second Person of the trinity became the *Son* of God, but that the already existing *Son* of God was made manifest or appeared in order to fulfill God's predetermined purpose. This idea is also seen in other verses such as (John 11:27) and (1 John 5:20).

6 Accordingly, (Hebrews 13:8) declare that "Jesus Christ is the same yesterday and today, and forever." This verse again seems to support the doctrine of eternal *Sonship*. The fact that Jesus' divine nature is unchanging would seem to in-

Soul, the

dicate that He was always the *Son* of God because that is an essential part of His Person. At the incarnation Jesus took on human flesh, but His divine nature did not change, nor did His relationship with the Father. This same truth is also implied in (John 20:31), where we see John's purpose in writing his gospel was so that we might "believe that Jesus is the Christ, the *Son* of God; and that believing you may have life in His name." It does not say that He became the *Son* of God but that He is the *Son* of God. The fact that Jesus was and is the *Son* of God is an essential aspect of Who He is and His work in redemptive Grace.

7 Importantly, one of the strongest evidences for the eternal *Sonship* of Christ is the triune nature of God and the eternal relationship that exists among the Father, *Son*, and Holy Spirit. Particularly important is the unique 'Father and Son' relationship that can only be understood from the aspect of Christ's eternal *Sonship*. This relationship is key to understanding the full measure of God's love for those whom He redeems through the blood of Christ. The fact that God the Father took His *Son*, the very *Son* He loved from before the foundation of the world, and sent Him to be a sacrifice for our sins is an amazing act of grace and love that is best understood from the doctrine of eternal *Sonship* as in (John 16:28). "I came forth from the Father, and have come into the world; I am leaving the world again, and going to the Father." Implied in this verse is again the fact that the 'Father and Son' relationship between God the Father and God the *Son* is one that always has and always will exist. At His incarnation the *Son* "came from the Father" in the same sense as upon His resurrection He returned "to the Father." Implied in this verse is the fact that if Jesus was the *Son* after the resurrection, then He was also the *Son* prior to His incarnation. Other verses that support the eternal Sonship of Christ would include (John 17:5) and (John 17:24), which speak of the Father's love for the Son from "before the foundation of the world." Praise the Lord!

Soul, the: In many religious, philosophical, and several other traditions, soul is the incorporeal and, in many conceptions, immortal essence of a person or living thing. According to the Abrahamic religions in most of their forms, souls—or at least immortal souls—belong only to human beings. For example, the Catholic theologian Thomas Aquinas attributed "soul" (*anima*) to all organisms but taught that only human souls are immortal. Other religions (most notably Jainism and Hinduism) teach that all biological organisms have souls, and others teach that even non-biological entities (such as rivers and mountains) possess souls. This latter belief is called animism. Greek philosophers such as Socrates, Plato and Aristotle understood the *psyche* to be crowned with the logical faculty, the exercise of which was the most divine of human actions. At his defence trial, Socrates even summarized his teachings as nothing other than an exhortation for his fellow Athenians to firstly excel in matters of the psyche since all bodily goods are dependent on such excellence. 2 Christians must note that "The life of a human being came more directly from God, and it is also evident that when someone dies, the breath, e.g., (Psalm 104:28-29) - showing the greatness of God. Thus "O Lord, My God, You are Very Great: ...You give to them, they gather it up; You open Your hand, they are satisfied with good You hide Your face, they are dismayed; You take away their spirit, they expire And return to their dust.30You send forth Your Spirit, they are created; And You renew the face of the ground".or the life (nepeš), e.g., Genesis 35:17-18) disappears and returns to the God who is (rûaḥ) being the words of the midwife's to Rachel when she dies in Labour for delivering Benjamin. Thus: "Do not fear, for now you have another son." It came about as her soul was departing (for she died), that she named him Ben-oni; but his father called him Benjamin. So Rachel died and was buried on the way to Ephrath (that is, Bethlehem)....

Soul, Immortality of the: The concept of an immaterial soul separate from and surviving the body is common today but according to modern scholars, it was not found in ancient Hebrew beliefs. The word *nephesh* never means an immortal or an incorporeal part of the human being that can survive death of the body as the spirit of dead, an addition (Ecclesiastes 9:5) states " For the living know that they shall die: but the dead know not anything, neither have they any more a reward; for the memory of them is forgotten. "(King James)

Soul in the traditional Christianity: Christians have adapted to the word Soul one important component of Human being. The other two being The body and the Spirit. In Patristic thought, towards the end of the 2nd century, ad begun to be understood in a more Greek than a Hebrew way, contrasted with the body. By the 3rd century, with the influence of Origin, there was the establishing of the Roman Catholic tradition of the inherent immortality of the soul and its divine nature. Inherent immortality of the soul was accepted among western and eastern theologians throughout the middle ages, and after the Reformation, as evidenced by the Westminster Confession. In the last six decades, Eastern Orthodox theologians have also widely accepted conditional immortality, or "immortality by grace" (Greek - *kata charin athanasia*), of the soul, returning to the views of the late 2nd century, where im-

Speak

mortality was still considered as a gift granted with the value of Jesus' death and resurrection. Many modern theologians reject the view that the gospel teaches the doctrine of the immortal soul.

Speak: (Verb, Greek: *Logos* - [log'-os], Hebrew: *dabar* [daw-bar'],a word, speech, divine utterance, analogy. To speak is the first acts of faith. Speaking the word makes hearing easy. Then faith by hearing and understanding and acting on the word as in (Romans 10:17) "So then faith cometh by hearing, and hearing by the word of God". This means that real Christianity is Speaking the word of God and keeping oneself to enable God to speak back to us.

2 The Bible records God speaking audibly to people many times (Exodus 3:14; Joshua 1:1; Judges 6:18; 1 Samuel 3:11; 2 Samuel 2:1;Job 40:1; Isaiah 7:3; Jeremiah 1:7 ;Acts 8:26; 9:15)—this is just a small sampling). There is no biblical reason why God could not speak to a person audibly today. With the hundreds of times the Bible records God speaking, we have to remember that they occur over the course of 4,000 years of human history. God speaking audibly is the exception, not the rule. Even in the biblically recorded instances of God speaking in various Gospel, it is not always clear whether it was an audible voice, an inner voice, or a mental impression.

Indeed, God does speak to people today. First, God speaks to us through His Word (2 Timothy 3:16–17). Also, (Isaiah 55:11) tells us, "So is my word that goes out from my mouth: it will not return to me empty, but will accomplish what I desire and achieve the purpose for which I sent it." The Bible is God's Word, everything we need to know in order to be saved and live the Christian life. (2 Peter 1:3) declares, "His divine power has given us everything we need for life and godliness through our knowledge of Him who called us by his own glory and goodness."

3 God can also *speak* to us through events—i.e., He can guide us through arranging our circumstances. And God helps us to discern right from wrong through our consciences (1 Timothy 1:5; 1Peter 3:16). God is in the process of conforming our minds to think His thoughts (Romans 12:2). God allows events to occur in our lives to direct us, change us, and help us to grow spiritually (James 1:2–5; Hebrews 12:5–11). Again, (1 Peter 1:6–7) reminds us, "In this you greatly rejoice, though now for a little while you may have had to suffer grief in all kinds of trials. These have come so that your faith—of greater worth than gold, which perishes even though refined by fire—may be proved genuine and may result in praise, glory and honor when Jesus Christ is revealed."

4 God sometimes speak audibly

to people. It is highly doubtful, though, that this occurs as often as some people claim it does. Again, even in the Bible, God speaking audibly is the exception, not the ordinary. If anyone claims that God has spoken to him or her, always compare what is said with what the Bible says. If God were to speak today, His words would be in full agreement with what He has said in the Bible (2 Timothy 3:16–17). God does not contradict Himself.

Above all, (1 Peter 4:11) remind us "If anyone *speaks*, they should do so as one who *speaks* the very words of God. If anyone serves, they should do so with the strength God provides, so that in all things God may be praised through Jesus Christ. To him be the glory and the power for ever and ever. Amen.

Speaking in tongues: Utterances in an unknown or unfamiliar language. In (1 Corinthians 12:8-11) "kinds of tongues" and "the interpretation of tongues" are said to be sovereignly bestowed gifts of the Holy Spirit. In (1 Corinthians 12:28-30) "tongues" appears in the list of gifts. We call them "spiritual gifts" from the Greek word charisma, suggesting that the gift is a bestowment of God's grace. It is not a natural ability that one might develop, but rather a special gift as those appearing in the above mentioned passages in First Corinthians. The Holy Spirit is sovereign in the distribution of these gifts. Following the listing of the gifts, Paul adds, "But all these worketh that one and the selfsame Spirit, dividing to every man severally as He will" (1 Corinthians 12:11). No one person has all the gifts, nor are we to seek the gifts. We must be careful that we do not confuse the Spirit as a gift to the believer with the gifts the Spirit gives to believers. Every believer has received the gift of the Spirit, but not every believer has received the gifts which the Spirit bestows.

2 The term that is used to identify the tongues movement is "glossolalia," made up of two Greek words, glossa (language or tongue) and lalia (speech). It therefore means speaking in languages or tongues. Glossology is that department of anthropology which has to do with the study and classification of languages and dialects. The word glossa appears in the Greek New Testament not less than fifty times. It is used to refer to the physical organ of the tongue as in (James 3:5); once in reference to the flames of fire shaped like tongues (Acts 2:3); at least once in a metaphorical sense when referring to speech as in the statement, "my tongue (speech) was glad (joyous)" (Acts 2:26). As far as I understand the remaining usages of the word it always means a language.

When our Lord predicted the gift of tongues (the only mention of tongues in the four Gospel records) He said, "And these signs

Speaking in tongues

shall follow them that believe; In my name they shall cast out devils; they shall speak with new tongues" (Mark 16:17). The adjective "new" (Greek. kainos) can only mean they were going to speak in languages new to them, that is, languages they had not learned or used until that time.

In (Acts 2:4) Luke uses a different adjective when he says, "they began to speak with other tongues." The word "other" (Greek; *heteros*) simply means that they spoke in languages different from the normal language they were used to. The context substantiates this. Notice the surprised reaction on the part of the hearers—"And they were all amazed and marveled, saying one to another, Behold, are not all these which speak Galileans? And how hear we every man in our own tongue, wherein we were born?" (Acts 2:7,8). Every man heard them speak in his own language (Acts 2:6). Here the word "language" is the translation of dialekto from which our word "dialect" comes. The two words glossa (tongue) and dialektos (language) are used synonymously, making it obvious that the disciples were speaking in known languages other than the language native to them. In (Luke 2: 9-11) the languages are then identified. It was a miraculous phenomenon which enabled the disciples to speak in languages which they had never learned. Here in this Acts passage we have tongues-speaking in its pure and unperverted form as God gave it.

3 The following verses in the Book of the Revelation should be examined carefully (Revelation 5:9; 7:9; 10:11; 11:9; 13:7; 14:6; 17:15). In each passage where the word "tongue" is mentioned it means one of the languages associated with the various nationalities and races.

But the more serious problems arise in the interpretation of the twenty-one references to tongues in (1 Corinthian 12-14). There are those who tell us that the tongues in First Corinthians are ecstatic utterances not known in any country on earth. They base their conclusion on the term "unknown" which appears in (1 Corinthians 14:2, 4, 13, 14, 19, and 27). But the reader of this chapter in God's Word must not fail to observe that the word "unknown" in every place where it appears is in italicized letters, which means that it does not occur in any Greek manuscript but was inserted by translators. In short, the Holy Spirit did not direct Paul to write that the tongue is unknown. In every other place where the word is used it means languages. All the usages of tongues in Paul's treatment of the subject refer to foreign languages. "So likewise ye, except ye utter by the tongue words easy to be understood, how shall it be known what is spoken? for ye shall speak into air" (1 Corinthians 14:9).

4 There is no reason for anyone to speak except to converse intelligibly. The Greek word *laleo* means

"I speak." The word is never used for mere sound or noise. Nor is it used for a mere mumbling or muttering of unintelligible gibberish. The tongues-speaking in the New Testament was in the native languages of hearing people. The supernatural phenomenon which took place at Pentecost was the exercise of a gift whereby many people from many countries, gathered at Jerusalem, heard God's message in their own language. This was indeed a miracle of God.

It would be an arbitrary and strange interpretation of Scripture that would make tongues-speaking in the New Testament anything other than known languages. There is no trace of Scriptural evidence that tongues were ever heard by anyone as incoherent, incomprehensible babbling.

Speaking in tongues, the Ministry of: God gave the gift of speaking in tongues to communicate the Gospel message. With unmistakable clarity Paul says, "Wherefore tongues are for a sign, not to them that believe, but to them that believe not . . . " (1 Corinthians 14:22). The word "sign" (Greek. *semeion*) in the New Testament is often associated with the conveying of a Divinely-given message to unbelievers. This is the emphasis in (John 20:30 -31) where we read, "And many other signs truly did Jesus in the presence of His disciples, which are not written in this book: But these are written, that ye might believe that Jesus is the Christ, the Son of God; and that believing ye might have life through His name." The signs (miracles) were never performed without purpose, but because of the message they communicated.

2 The true function of the gift of tongues is "for a sign . . . to them that believe not." To exercise the gift when unbelievers were not present would be exercising the gift above the purpose for which it was given. The gifts were never given for the self-satisfaction or self-glory of the recipients. The one upon whom the gift was bestowed was merely an instrument through whom God wanted to communicate His message.

Because of the abuse and misuse of tongues in the Corinthian Assembly Paul states its purpose. The spiritual immaturity of the saints in Corinth called for instruction, so in the middle of his discourse on tongues he writes, "Brethren, be not children in understanding: howbeit in malice be ye children, but in understanding be men" (1 Corinthians 14:20). The Greek word for "men" (teleios) means mature. In their misuse of speaking in tongues they were showing their immaturity, a behaviour pattern which characterized the believers at Corinth. The Apostle reminded them that they remained "babes in Christ" (1 Corinthians 3:1).

Note: Their failure to grow up spiritually resulted from their neglected study of the Scriptures.

The Epistle to the Hebrews stresses this point. "For when for the time ye ought to be teachers, ye have need that one teach you again which be the first principles of the oracles of God; and are become such as have need of milk, and not of strong meat. For every one that useth milk is unskillful in the word of righteousness; for he is a babe. But strong meat belongeth to them that are of full age, even those who by reason of use have their senses exercised to discern both good and evil" (Hebrews 5:12-14). Peter wrote, "As newborn babes, desire the sincere milk of the Word that ye may grow thereby"

3 Again, to confirm the Gospel message, it was not merely a communicating sign but a confirmatory sign as well. When the Apostles used the gift of tongues it was because they did not have what we have today, the completed Word of God, God's full and final revelation to man. When they went about preaching the Gospel, their message was confirmed by the exercise of the sign gifts. Tongues-speaking vindicated both the message and the messenger. "Truly the signs of an apostle were wrought among you in all patience, in signs, and wonders, and mighty deeds" (2 Corinthians 12:12). If one could find an Apostle living today who saw the bodily-resurrected Lord Jesus, he would not be exercising the sign gifts because he would have what we have today.

4 The baptizing work of the Spirit is not an experience in the believer subsequent to salvation. Rather it is that act of the Holy Spirit which joins the believing sinner to the Body of Christ. More emphatically, there is no other means whereby one can become a member of the Church which is Christ's Body. All saved persons have been baptized by the Holy Spirit, but not all saved persons speak in tongues. The baptizing work of the Spirit places the believer in the Body positionally. Be careful that you do not confuse the baptism of the Spirit with the command to be "filled with the Spirit" (Ephesians 5:18). All believers share equally in this position in Christ and thus share equally in union with Him. There is only one experience of baptism by the Holy Spirit but there can be many experiences of being filled with Spirit. Paul said that not all of the Corinthian Christians spoke in tongues (1 Corinthians 14:5), and yet he stated clearly that all had been baptized with the Holy Spirit (1 Corinthians 12:13).

(2) It is a mistake to assume that speaking in tongues is an evidence of being filled with the Spirit. All believers are commanded to "be filled with (controlled by) the Spirit" (Ephesians 5:18), but nowhere in Scripture are believers commanded to speak in tongues. A Christian can be under the influence and control of the Holy Spirit and not speak in tongues. There are numerous instances when the disciples were filled with the Spirit

but did not speak in tongues. See Acts 4:31 and 13:9-11. To be Spirit-filled is to be Spirit-controlled. Are we to believe that the thousands of mightily used men and women of God who were among the world's best missionaries of Christ's Gospel and Bible teachers were never filled with the Holy Spirit because they never spoke in tongues? Perish the thought! Can one know if he is filled with the Spirit? Look at one verse in the Bible where the command to be filled with the Spirit is recorded. "And be not drunk with wine, wherein is excess; but be filled with the Spirit; Speaking to yourselves in psalms and hymns and spiritual songs, singing and making melody in your heart to the Lord; Giving thanks always for all things unto God and the Father in the name of our Lord Jesus Christ; Submitting yourselves one to another in the fear of God" (Ephesians 5:18-21). Three things are mentioned as evidence of being Spirit-filled; a joyful heart, a thankful heart and a submissive heart. Nothing is said about speaking in tongues. To sum it up in one word, Christlikeness is the manifestation of being filled with the Spirit, and the Scriptures do not tell us that our Lord ever spoke in tongues.

(3) It is a mistake to assume that speaking in tongues is the fruit of the Spirit. The fruit of the Spirit results from being filled with the Spirit. The fruit of the Spirit is mentioned in (Galatians 5:22-23) and includes nine characteristics. "But the fruit of the Spirit is love, joy, peace, longsuffering, gentleness, goodness, faith, meekness, temperance." None of the sign-gifts are included in this nine-fold cluster of fruit. The Christian who is filled with the Spirit will manifest the fruit of the Spirit apart from ever having spoken in tongues. As a matter of fact, in Ephesians and Galatians, where the fullness and fruit of the Spirit are discussed tongues-speaking is not mentioned once. Moreover, in the list of gifts mentioned by Paul, gifts that the ascended Lord bestowed upon His Church, the sign gifts are omitted. "And He gave some, apostles; and some, prophets; and some, evangelists; and some, pastors and teachers" (Ephesians 4:11). All Christians should be filled with the Spirit and all are to exhibit the fruit of the Spirit, but not every Christian has all the gifts. Spirituality does not depend on speaking in tongues. God's goal for every child of His is to be Spirit-controlled, but that goal does not include speaking in tongues. No Christian need ever feel that he is lacking in spirituality because he has not spoken in tongues. Quality of life is the best evidence of the fullness and fruit of the Holy Spirit. John the Baptizer was filled with the Spirit from his mother's womb (Luke 1:15), yet this Spirit-filled man did no miracles and never spoke in tongues (John 10:41). But he was so Christ-like that people who were looking for the Messiah were led to ask of him, "Art thou the Christ?"

Speaking in tongues, the Ministry of

(4) It is a mistake to assume that speaking in tongues is an evidence of one's faith. To the contrary, the persons who seek signs and sign-gifts show their lack of faith. It is a sin for any Christian to seek for signs before he will believe God's Word. As was pointed out earlier in this study, "tongues are for a sign, not to them that believe, but to them that believe not" (1 Corinthians 14:22). So you see, the Christians at Corinth were showing that they were weak in faith, and possibly some who identified themselves with the believer had never been saved. The person who seeks any sign, whether it be speaking in tongues or any other sign-gift, is either a babe in Christ or an unbeliever. Thomas is an illustration of a disciple weak in faith who would not believe without seeing. After our Lord arose from death, He appeared to the disciples. "But Thomas, one of the twelve, called Didymus, was not with them when Jesus came. The other disciples therefore said unto him, We have seen the Lord. But he said unto them, Except I shall see in His hands the print of the nails, and put my finger into the print of the nails, and thrust my hand into His side, I will not believe" (John 20:24 - 25). Thomas was like the Corinthians, weak in faith, demanding to see the sign (miracle) before he would believe.

Eight days later the Lord appeared again. "Then saith He to Thomas, Reach hither thy finger, and behold my hands; and reach hither thy hand, and thrust it into my side:and be not faithless but believing." (John 20:27). The doubting Thomas needed a sign, so the Lord appeared to him so that he would not continue without faith. And then He said to Thomas, "Thomas, because thou hast seen me, thou hast believed; blessed are they that have not seen, and yet have believed" (John 20:29). The Christian who will study the Bible and believe what it says will walk by faith, not by sight or sound.

(6) It is a mistake to seek the gift of speaking in tongues. It is clear that not all in the church at Corinth spoke in tongues. Why didn't they? The Apostle says, "Now there are diversities of gifts, but the same Spirit . . . for to one is given by the Spirit the word of wisdom; to another the word of knowledge by the same Spirit; To another faith by the same Spirit; to another the gifts of healing by the same Spirit; To another the working of miracles; to another prophecy, to another discerning of spirits; to another divers kinds of tongues, to another the interpretation of tongues: But all these worketh that one and the selfsame Spirit, dividing to every man severally as He will" (1 Corinthians 12:4-11). Please note that the gifts were given "as He (the Holy Spirit) will," not as we will, "as it hath pleased Him" (vs. 18), not us. The reason why all the Christians did not have the gift of tongues is because all of the gifts are divinely

bestowed. The Spirit divides and distributes to each believer his own gift. Not one of us is capable of choosing his own gift. The Spirit will not give a gift according to our desire and the way we pray. Don't try to tell God which gift He should give to you. We are but members of the Body, and no one member has any right to tell the Head what to do. Corinthians erred in overemphasizing the gift of tongues as the most coveted gift of all. To them tongues was the prestige gift, hence its misuse and abuse at Corinth.

(7) It is a mistake for a woman to speak in tongues. "Let your women keep silence in the churches: for it is not permitted unto them to speak . . ." (1 Corinthians 14:34). The prohibition here has a direct relation to the problem with which the Apostle is dealing, namely, speaking in tongues. Earlier in the same Epistle he told the women how to dress when they prayed or prophesied in the church (1 Corinthians 11:3-10), therefore he would not forbid them here in Chapter 14 that privilege which is countenanced in Chapter 11. The setting of (1 Corinthians 14:34) has reference primarily to women speaking in tongues. It is clear and unmistakable that speaking in tongues was a gift limited to men and is never to be exercised by women. Now he is not saying that women may not teach or testify or pray, but that they may not speak in tongues. Elsewhere Paul writes, "But I suffer not a woman to teach, nor to usurp authority over the man, but to be in silence" (I Timothy 2:12). The point of this passage is that a woman's ministry must not usurp authority over the man. She may teach women or children, but not men. If this admonition were heeded today much of the present tongues movement would be eliminated. Women are the worst offenders in the modern confusion of tongues. The word "speak" in (1 Corinthians 14:34) is the same word used in verse 28, therefore it cannot mean mere "chatter" that would disturb a service in the church. The purpose of this entire section on speaking in tongues is to curb the wrong use of the gift. Verses 27-33 give instruction for men in the matter of speaking in tongues. "If any man speak in an unknown tongue . . ." (1 Corinthians 14:27); verses 34-36 are directed to "women" exercising the gift of tongues. And if any women wanted to take issue with Paul, he would ask them one question, "Which book in all the inspired Scriptures was written as the result of the Holy Spirit revealing the woman?" (Verse 36). It is a mistake for a woman to speak in tongues.

(8) It is a mistake to assume that the sign-gifts are given to believers today. Now I am not arbitrarily closing the door on miracles. God does intervene in supernatural ways performing miracles when and wherever He pleases to do so. The matter before us now is

whether or not the Bible teaches that certain gifts were temporarily given. The evidence of God's Word must be the final source of authority. I am stressing this because there are many persons who are not students of the Bible, therefore their only source of knowledge and understanding is subjective, namely, reason or experience. Whatever appeals to their reason, or whatever experiences they have had, settle a matter for them once and for all time.

In (1 Corinthians 13). Now keep in mind the fact that the subject in Chapters 12-14 is spiritual gifts with the main emphasis on tongues, because tongues was the one gift that the Corinthians were abusing. Chapter 12 concludes with "tongues" (12:30) and Chapter 13 begins with "tongues" (13:1). Obviously from the behavior of the Corinthians they were lacking in the fruit of the Spirit, namely, love. And so in Chapter 13 the Apostle dwells upon the essential ingredient of love which supercedes the gifts, and without which the Christian is nothing at all. Among the Corinthians there were quarreling and division, but the needed fruit of the Spirit, love, was missing, so Paul writes, "Though I speak with the tongues of men and of angels, and have not charity (or love), I am become as sounding brass, or a tinkling cymbal" (13 :1). In Corinth the tongues-speaking amounted to so much noise because carnality had invaded their exercise of the gift. Even today there is a kind of spiritual prestige associated with tongues-speaking. For a Christian to show off any gift that God has given manifests pride that is lacking in love. Where love is lacking, the exercise of any gift is worthless.

If Christians would take seriously, within context, all of the teaching about tongues in 1 Corinthians, they could not fail to see that tongues-speaking would cease. Paul writes, "Charity (love) never faileth: but whether there be prophecies, they shall fail; whether there be tongues, they shall cease; whether there be knowledge, it shall vanish away" (1 Corinthians 13:8). There will always be the need for love, therefore love will never drop off. But when the canon of Scripture is made "perfect" (or complete), there will be no further revelation from God, neither in predictive prophecy nor in divinely revealed knowledge other than prophecy. The gifts of "prophecy" and "knowledge" will be entirely unnecessary with the completion of the Scriptures. And "if any man shall add unto these things, God shall add unto him the plagues that are written in this book" (Revelation 22:18).

Spirit: (Noun, Greek: *pneuma* [pnyoo'-mah], Hebrew: *ruach* - [roo'-akh]; wind, breath, spirit. 2

The non-physical part of a person which is the seat of emotions and character; the soul., the prevailing or typical quality, mood, or attitude of a person, group, or period of time, the real meaning or the intention behind something as opposed to its strict verbal interpretation. 3 An important attribute of God that brings liberty or freedom as in (2 Corinthians 3:17) "Now the Lord is the *Spirit*, and where the *Spirit* of the Lord is, there is freedom".

4 As (verb) anything that convey rapidly and secretly. The *Spirit* receives impressions of outward and material things through the soul. The spiritual faculties of the 'Spirit' are 'Faith,' 'Hope,' 'Reverence,' 'Prayer' and 'Worship.' 5 In his unfallen state the *Spirit* of man was illuminated from Heaven, but when the human race fell in Adam, sin closed the window of the *Spirit*, pulled down the curtain, and the chamber of the *spirit* became a death chamber and remains so in every unregenerate heart, until the Life and Light giving power of the Holy *Spirit* floods that chamber with the Life and Light giving power of the new life in Christ Jesus.

Spirit, holy: *See Holy Ghost*

***Spirit* of man, the:** This is the sphere of God-consciousness, which also is the inner or private office of man where the work of regeneration takes place. 2 The Apostle Paul gives us the Word of God on this, a passage that is sadly neglected. According to (Isaiah 64), Paul wrote: "But as it is written, Eye hath not seen, nor ear heard, neither have entered into the heart of man, the things which God hath prepared for them that love Him". A great many people stop here, content to remain in ignorance. However, Paul continues: "But God hath revealed them unto us by His *Spirit*; for the *Spirit* searcheth all things, yea, the deep things of God. For what man knoweth the things of a man, save the *spirit* of man which is in him? Even so the things of God knoweth no man, but the *Spirit* of God (1 Corinthians 2:9-11).

Man in his unregenerate state comes to know the things of man by the operator of "the spirit of man" which is in him. If man have a will to know certain scientific facts, by his human spirit he will be able to investigate, think, and weigh evidence. If he set himself to the task, he may become a scientist of world-renown and of great accomplishments. However, his human spirit is "limited to the things of man." If he want to know about the things of God, his dead and dormant spirit is not able to know them.

Stand

Stand: (Verb, Greek: *stékó* [stay'-ko], Hebrew: *qum [koom], arose,* stand fast, stand firm, persevere as in (1 Corinthians 16:13) "Be on your guard; stand firm in the faith; be courageous; be strong".

Steadfast: (Adjective, Greek: hedraios - [hed-rah'-yos], Hebrew: hedraios [hed-rah'-yos]; sitting, seated; steadfast, firm. 2 resolutely or dutifully firm and unwavering as in (1 Corinthians 15:58) "Therefore, my beloved brothers, be steadfast, immovable, always abounding in the work of the Lord, knowing that in the Lord your labor is not in vain" ESV. This verse concludes a chapter that details the future resurrection of our earthly bodies. Paul encouraged the Corinthian church to remain faithful to everything he had taught them. When we see the word therefore in Scripture, we should always back up to see why it is there: what is the "therefore" there for? The word usually indicates a summation of what was previously stated. In this case, Paul addresses those who had fallen away from his original teaching on the resurrection. They were embracing heresy and introducing destructive ideas contrary to the gospel. Paul restates the truth of Jesus' death for sin and bodily resurrection and then exhorts them to remain firm in that teaching.

3 To be steadfast and unmovable is to be spiritually grounded. A steadfast person knows what he believes and cannot be "tossed back and forth by the waves, and blown here and there by every wind of teaching" - See (Ephesians 4:14). An unmovable person can hear false teaching, engage doubters, and defend truth without it shaking his own faith. In his other epistle to Corinth, Paul expresses his concern for this church: "I am afraid that just as Eve was deceived by the serpent's cunning, your minds may somehow be led astray from your sincere and pure devotion to Christ" (2 Corinthians 11:3). Even believers who had been personally taught by the apostle Paul were victims of deception. How much more other Christians who are vulnerable to temptation and vices of the devil?

4 In other to remain steadfast and unmovable, we have to know the Word of God. (2 Timothy 2:15) says, "Be diligent to present yourself approved to God as a workman who does not need to be ashamed, accurately handling the word of truth" (NASB). To accurately handle the word of truth, we must not only read the Bible, but we must allow it to become part of us. Its truth should so penetrate our minds and hearts that it shapes our thinking and our actions. It should so fill our minds that we can detect error when we hear it.

> Satan uses Scripture for his own purposes, twisting it to sound as though it says something it doesn't say (Luke 4:9–11). If we have not been diligent in our study and meditation on truth, we are vulnerable to error. The false religions of the world can be persuasive when they quote Bible verses to support their error. Even Christians can be duped by smooth-sounding heresy if they do not have a solid grounding in the "whole counsel of God" (Acts 20:27).

It is God's desire that we grow daily in our understanding of Him and His Word so that we will remain faithful to the end (John 8:31; 2 Peter 1:2; 3:18; 1 John 2:24). Praise the Lord!

Soul: (Noun, Greek: *psuché* – [psoo-khay'], Hebrew: *nephesh* - [neh'-fesh]; (a) the vital breath, breath of life, (b) the human soul, (c) the soul as the seat of affections and will, (d) the self, (e) a human person, an individual.

2 The term "soul" expresses two main ideas. Firstly, humans are by nature creatures of desires and ongings. Secondly, humans are living beings who eagerly seek to live but are unable to acquire or preserve life by themselves. "Soul" refers to the whole person in need of God, who is the only one who can preserve a human being or extinguish the self forever as in (Mathew. 10:28). Therefore, nephesh and psuche refers to the totality of the person as a center of life, emotions, feelings, and longings that can be fully realized only in union with God.

3 Concerning the grammatical used of the *soul*: *Soul* is used to refer to the person as a self, the term came to be used as a pronoun to designate a person. Abram asked Sarai to say that she was his sister in order that "my life [literally, "my soul,"] will be spared" (Genesis. 12:13). The Hebrew way of saying "Let me live" (1 Kings 20:32) is "Let my *soul* live." The phrase "that my soul may bless you before I die" (Genesis. 27:4, NKJV) simply means "that I may bless you."

Sow: (verb, Greek: *speiró* - [spi'-ro], Hebrew: *zara* spread, scatter. plant (seed) by scattering it on or in the earth. Literally, to fill a pot with compost and *sow* a thin layer of seeds on top. synonyms:scatter, spread, broadcast, disperse, strew, disseminate, distribute; plant the seeds of (a plant or crop). "Catch crops should be *sown* after minimal cultivation", plant (a piece of land) with seed. "the field used to be *sown* with oats", synonyms:

plant, seed, reseed "large fields were *sown* with only cabbages or asparagus" be thickly covered with. "the night sky was *sown*

Sowing and Ripping

with stars" lay or plant (an explosive mine) or cover (territory) with mines.

disseminate or introduce (something undesirable). "the new policy has *sown* confusion and doubt" synonyms: cause, bring about, occasion, create, give rise to, lead to, produce, engender, generate, induce, invite, implant, plant, lodge, prompt, evoke, elicit, initiate, precipitate, instigate, trigger, spark off, provoke.

2 To *sow* is one part of the law of nature. Most of the Bible was originally written to those living in an agrarian society, people familiar with working the land, managing livestock, and raising crops. Many of Jesus' parables involve the farming life. God's blessing comes generally to the whole world as He sends sun and rain to the just and the unjust (Matthew 5:45). In some cases His blessing comes more specially to those of His choosing, such as Isaac. (Genesis 26:12) says that Isaac *sowed* a crop and received a hundredfold in one season because the Lord targeted him for blessing. Praise the Lord!

Sowing and Ripping This is the law of the natural world. On the third day of creation, God commanded the earth to bring forth living plants "bearing seed" and fruit "with seed in it" (Genesis 1:12). These plants were then given to man for food (verse 29). Ever since the beginning, man has understood the process of sowing and reaping and has applied it to his benefit.

2 God uses the law of *sowing and reaping* to bestow His blessing. God's blessing comes generally to the whole world as He sends sun and rain to the just and the unjust (Matthew 5:45). In some cases His blessing comes more specially to those of His choosing, such as Isaac. (Genesis 26:12) says that Isaac sowed a crop and received a hundredfold in one season because the Lord targeted him for blessing. As a Christian, you must be targeted for your blessing in Jesus Name!

3 Israel's gratefulness for God's yearly blessing was expressed in the Feast of First fruits, when the first of the harvest was brought to the Lord as an offering (Exodus 23:19a; Leviticus 23:10). God warned Israel that, if they forsook Him and pursued idols, the law of sowing and reaping would be suspended and their crops would fail (Leviticus 26:16b). This happened to disobedient Judah on a couple occasions (Jeremiah 12:13; Micah 6:15).

4 *Sowing and reaping* are used as a metaphor for death and resurrection. When Paul discusses the doctrine of the resurrection of the body, he uses the analogy of planting a seed to illustrate physical death. "The body that is sown is perishable, it is raised imperishable; it is sown in dishonour,

it is raised in glory; it is sown in weakness, it is raised in power; it is sown a natural body, it is raised a spiritual body" (1 Corinthians 15:42b-44a). A seed may "die" when it falls to the ground, but that is not the end of its life (John 12:24). Praise God!

Speak: (verb, Spoke, Speaking, Spoke) – To say something. Talk to someone in order to pass information. Speak in tongues.

Speak in tongues: This is the New Testament phenomena where a person speaks in a language that is unknown to him. This language is either the language of angels or other earthly languages (1 Corinthians 13:1). It occurred in (Acts 2) at Pentecost and also in the Corinthian church as is described in (1 Corinthians 14). This New Testament gift was given by the Holy Spirit to the Christian church and is for the purpose of the edification of the Body of Christ as well as for glorifying the Lord. There seems to be three divisions in the use of tongues: First, a private prayer language that is not interpreted; second, a language that is interpreted--this defines proper usage in the Christian congregation; and third, missionary context--that is, it appears in the context of evangelism where people (in the New Testament) are presenting the gospel.

Today there is much debate as to the validity of speaking in tongues, especially since there is so much misuse of it in Christian circles. Nevertheless, some Christian churches teach that all the charismatic gifts (speaking in tongues, word of knowledge, prophecy, etc.,) have ceased with the completion of the New Testament (1 Corinthians. 13:8-12). Others maintain that the charismatic gifts are still for the church today (1 Corinthians. 1:7). It is not the purpose of this paper to take sides on this issue since it is so divisive and believing or not believing in them does not affect one's salvation. Nevertheless, there are good arguments on both sides; and the Christian church needs to be as gracious as possible to those with opposing views.

2 The first occurrence of speaking in tongues occurred on the day of Pentecost in (Acts 2:1-4). The apostles went out and shared the gospel with the crowds, speaking to them in their own languages: "We hear them declaring the wonders of God in our own tongues!" (Acts 2:11). The Greek word translated tongues literally means "languages." Therefore, the gift of tongues is speaking in a language a person does not know in order to minister to someone who does speak that language. In (1 Corinthians 12–14), Paul discusses miraculous gifts, saying, "Now, brothers, if I come to you and speak in tongues, what good will I be to you, unless I bring you some revelation or knowledge or prophecy or word of instruction?" (1 Corinthians 14:6). According to the apostle

Speak in tongues

Paul, and in agreement with the tongues described in Acts, speaking in tongues is valuable to the one hearing God's message in his or her own language, but it is useless to everyone else unless it is interpreted or translated.

A person with the gift of interpreting tongues (1 Corinthians 12:30) could understand what a tongues-speaker was saying even though he did not know the language that was being spoken. The tongues interpreter would then communicate the message of the tongues speaker to everyone else, so all could understand. "For this reason anyone who speaks in a tongue should pray that he may interpret what he says" (1 Corinthians 14:13). Paul's conclusion regarding tongues that were not interpreted is powerful: "But in the church I would rather speak five intelligible words to instruct others than ten thousand words in a tongue" (1 Corinthians 14:19).

3 In today Gospel life, (1 Corinthians 13:8) mentions the gift of tongues ceasing, although it connects the ceasing with the arrival of the "perfect" in (1 Corinthians 13:10). Some point to a difference in the tense of the Greek verbs referring to prophecy and knowledge "ceasing" and that of tongues "being ceased" as evidence for tongues ceasing before the arrival of the "perfect." While possible, this is not explicitly clear from the text. Some also point to passages such as (Isaiah 28:11) and (Joel 2:28-29) as evidence that speaking in tongues was a sign of God's oncoming judgment. (1Corinthians 14:22) describes tongues as a "sign to unbelievers." According to this argument, the gift of tongues was a warning to the Jews that God was going to judge Israel for rejecting Jesus Christ as Messiah. Therefore, when God did in fact judge Israel (with the destruction of Jerusalem by the Romans in A.D. 70), the gift of tongues would no longer serve its intended purpose. While this view is possible, the primary purpose of tongues being fulfilled does not necessarily demand its cessation. Scripture does not conclusively assert that the gift of speaking in tongues has ceased.

At the same time, if the gift of speaking in tongues were active in the church today, it would be performed in agreement with Scripture. It would be a real and intelligible language (1 Corinthians 14:10). It would be for the purpose of communicating God's Word with a person of another language (Acts 2:6-12). It would be in agreement with the command God gave through the apostle Paul, "If anyone speaks in a tongue, two—or at the most three—should speak, one at a time, and someone must interpret. If there is no interpreter, the speaker should keep quiet in the church and speak to himself and God" (1 Corinthians 14:27-28). It would also be in accordance with (1 Corinthians 14:33), "For God is not the author of confu-

Speak in tongues

sion, but of peace, as in all churches of the saints." God most definitely can give a person the gift of speaking in tongues to enable him or her to communicate with a person who speaks another language. The Holy Spirit is sovereign in the dispersion of the spiritual gifts (1 Corinthians 12:11). Just imagine how much more productive missionaries could be if they did not have to go to language school, and were instantly able to speak to people in their own language. However, God does not seem to be doing this. Tongues does not seem to occur today in the manner it did in the New Testament, despite the fact that it would be immensely useful. The vast majority of believers who claim to practice the gift of speaking in tongues do not do so in agreement with the Scriptures mentioned above. These facts lead to the conclusion that the gift of tongues has ceased or is at least a rarity in God's plan for the church today.

4 Some churches erringly maintain that you must speak in tongues in order to be saved. This is a grave mistake since not all people speak in tongues because not all people are gifted by the Holy Spirit this way. In (1 Corinthians. 12:7-11,28-31), "But to each one is given the manifestation of the Spirit for the common good. For to one is given the word of wisdom through the Spirit, and to another the word of knowledge according to the same Spirit; to another faith by the same Spirit, and to another gifts of healing by the one Spirit, and to another the effecting of miracles, and to another prophecy, and to another the distinguishing of spirits, to another various kinds of tongues, and to another the interpretation of tongues. But one and the same Spirit works all these things, distributing to each one individually just as He wills . . . (1 Corinthians 12: 28 - 31) And God has appointed in the church, first apostles, second prophets, third teachers, then miracles, then gifts of healing, helps, administrations, various kinds of tongues. All are not apostles, are they? All are not prophets, are they? All are not teachers, are they? All are not workers of miracles, are they? All do not have gifts of healing, do they? All do not speak with tongues, do they? All do not interpret, do they? But earnestly desire the greater gifts."

5 So, the gifts of the Spirit are varied, and they are for the edification of the body of Christ. *Speaking in tongues* is not necessary for salvation, and it is not a prerequisite proof of Baptism in the Holy Spirit. We must remember the words of Paul in (1 Corinthians 13:1-2,13) "If I speak with the tongues of men and of angels, but do not have love, I have become a noisy gong or a clanging cymbal. And if I have the gift of prophecy, and know all mysteries and all knowledge; and if I have all faith, so as to remove mountains,

Spirit

but do not have love, I am nothing . . . 13 But now abide faith, hope, love, these three; but the greatest of these is love." Praise the Lord!

Spirit: (Noun, Greek: *pneuma* [pnyoo'-mah], Hebrew: *Ruach* - [roo'-akh], wind, breath, spirit. This has many differing meanings and connotations, most of them relating to a non-corporeal substance contrasted with the material body. The word spirit is often used metaphysically to refer to the consciousness or personality. The notions of a person's spirit and soul often also overlap, as both contrast with body and both are understood as surviving the bodily death in religion and occultism, and "spirit" can also have the sense of "ghost", i.e. a manifestation of the spirit of a deceased person. The term may also refer to any incorporeal or immaterial being, such as demons or deities. In the Bible "the Spirit" (with a capital "S") specifically denotes the Holy Spirit.

Spirit of the Lord, The: *(Phr)* The third person in the trinity; So called to distinguish him from all other spirits. . 2 The only one every other spirit must obey, bow down, fear, afraid of, flee from and be subdued. The spirit of the Lord –the only pre-requisite to seeing or communicating with the Almighty God. For God is the spirit and those who worship God, must worship Him in spirit and in truth. to revelation and destiny. 3 The comforter, who is the messenger given to Christ without measure or limit of ability or capability to do more, abundantly and exceedingly above all things and in every situation to the Glory of the Father-God. Everyone in the Trinity are the Spirit. Since the Spirit formed the integral part of the Trinity.

Stand: (Verb, Greek: stékó [stay'-ko], Hebrew: qum [koom], stand fast, stand firm, persevere.To have or maintain an upright position, supported by one's feet; (of an object, building, or settlement) be situated in a particular place or position. To be in a specified state or condition.To withstand (an experience or test) without being damaged. As a noun; to have an attitude towards a particular issue. 2.a rack, base, or piece of furniture for holding, supporting, or displaying something. 3 the place where someone typically stands or sits. 4 a large raised tiered structure for spectators, typically at a sporting venue. 5 a cessation from motion or progress. 6 a group of growing plants of a specified kind, especially trees.

(Ephesians 6:10-11) "Finally" means, "for the rest," and shows that this section is built on what precedes. Paul is saying, "Based upon your glorious position in Christ (Ephesians 1-3) and in light of the worthy walk to which you are called (Ephesians 4-5, and 6:1-9), I want to conclude by explaining to you the serious conflict in which your faith necessarily en-

Steadfast

gages you." Because you are fighting in the Lord's army…

1. You must be strong in the Lord as Paul piles up words for strength in verse 10, using three of the four words that he employed in (Ephesians 1:19-20). There he mentioned "the surpassing greatness of His power toward us who believe. These are in accordance with the working of the strength of His might which He brought about in Christ, when He raised Him from the dead and seated Him at His right hand in the heavenly places." Also, in (Ephesians 3:16) Paul prayed that God would grant you … "to be strengthened with power through His Spirit in the inner man." As in that verse, the verb in (Ephesians 6:10) is probably passive, meaning, "be strengthened in the Lord".

Steadfast: (Adjective; Greek: *hedraios* - [hed-rah'-yos], Hebrew: *hedraios* [hed-rah'-yos] sitting, seated; steadfast, firm and unmovable, as in (1 Corinthians 15:58 ESV) "Therefore, my beloved brothers, be *steadfast*, immovable, always abounding in the work of the Lord, knowing that in the Lord your labor is not in vain". This verse concludes a chapter that details the future resurrection of our earthly bodies. Paul encouraged the Corinthian church to remain faithful to everything he had taught them. When we see the word therefore in Scripture, we should always back up to see why it is there: as the word usually indicates a summation of what was previously stated. In this case, Paul addresses those who had fallen away from his original teaching on the resurrection or Grace. They were embracing heresy and introducing destructive ideas contrary to the gospel. Paul restates the truth of Jesus' death for sin and bodily resurrection and then exhorts them to remain firm in that teaching.

2 To be *steadfast* and unmovable is to be spiritually grounded. A steadfast person knows what he believes and cannot be "tossed back and forth by the waves, and blown here and there by every wind of teaching" (Ephesians 4:14). An unmovable person can hear false teaching, engage doubters, and defend truth without it shaking his own faith. In his other epistle to Corinth, Paul expresses his concern for this church: "I am afraid that just as Eve was deceived by the serpent's cunning, your minds may somehow be led astray from your sincere and pure devotion to Christ" (2 Corinthians 11:3). Even believers who had been personally taught by the apostle Paul were victims of deception. How much more vulnerable are we?

3 To remain *steadfast* and unmovable we have to know the Word of God as in (2 Timothy 2:15), "Be diligent to present yourself approved to God as a workman who does not need to be ashamed, accurately handling the word of truth" - To accurately handle the word of

Stone

truth, we must not only read the Bible, but we must allow it to become part of us. Its truth should so penetrate our minds and hearts that it shapes our thinking and our actions. It should so fill our minds that we can detect error when we hear it.

4 Note: Satan uses Scripture for his own purposes, twisting it to sound as though it says something it doesn't say (Luke 4:9–11). If we have not been diligent in our study and meditation on truth, we are vulnerable to error. The false religions of the world can be persuasive when they quote Bible verses to support their error. Even Christians can be duped by smooth-sounding heresy if they do not have a solid grounding in the "whole counsel of God" as in (Acts 20:27).

It is God's desire that we grow daily in our understanding of Him and His Word so that we will remain faithful to the end (John 8:31; 2 Peter 1:2; 3:18; 1 John 2:24). Hallelujah!

Stone: (Noun, Greek: Petros - [pet'-ros], Hebrew: eben - [eh'-ben], stone Peter, a Greek name meaning rock. In (Matthew 24:2) Jesus said "There shall not be left here one *stone* upon another, that shall not be thrown down," when speaking of the temple (which refers to our spiritual temple in progress), so it is important for us to make sure that once the winds and the rains have torn down our fortress and nothing is left but the foundation, that we begin building with a new and more permanent one.

Just as God wrote the ten commandments "in stone" in the heart of Moses, Isaiah prophesied that the true laws of God would also be written upon our own hearts today. The Father hears the crys of the ones who are, like Lazarus, ready to heed the call of Christ as he commands us to "Awaken, and arise from your sleep." To best explain this, smooth polished *stones* are sometimes sold in various Christian novelty stores that have scriptures or some other message written on them. Now imagine writing on those stones your thoughts, your opinions, AND most importantly, your perceptions of what you believe to be the truth (your beliefs, which are many times heavily indoctrinated). These are the stones we build with, and it is up to each individual to choose carefully what types of stones they build with.

2 Now we all know what a rock looks like. For the most part, the edges are jagged and ugly, and no one builds a house with a bunch of unshaped rocks. *Stones*, however, are nothing more than rocks that have been made smooth by the continuous action of water flowing over them. The smoothness of the *stone* depends upon how much time and also how much force or pressure has been in con-

tact with the rock. Spiritual rocks and spiritual *stones* are the same way to the soul.

3 In the Bible, spirit is likened to water. Rocks are made smooth by the continuous flow of water over them. Our thoughts (the things we contemplate the most) are the spiritual water that polishes our *stones* and building blocks within the soul. Like water, the spirit within a soul can be contaminated and harmful to the self, or it can be pure and sustain the self. Jesus said, "Where your heart is, there also will be your treasure." This means that where your attention is placed, there also will be the type of temple you are building, as you are always choosing and polishing *stones* for your eternal home.

4 There is another way that *stones* are used in the Gospel or Bible and that is to cause death to another person. Remember, *stones* aren't always polished smooth by the spirit of truth. Many times they are polished by deception, and when we hastily and insistently throw our own perceptions and deceptions into the soul of another, it can cause permanent damage to another soul, even stoning them to death (spiritually speaking). Have you ever ran up on someone who insisted that they kill the truth within you and replace it with their own version, such as a persistent religious fanatic preaching "the truth?" This is why it is written that the tongue is a fire. Our words are spirit, so we must be careful what manner of spirit we are instilling in another.

- Jesus said that his words were spirit

- Water is symbolic of spirit, and one form of spirit is our "thoughts"

- Flows of spirit (continuous attention and thought) eventually turn rocks into stones

- Stones formed by man's spirit (the ignorance of ego) are deceptive and can cause a soul to be "*stoned* to death," and they build temples that will not stand the test of time.

- *Stones* formed by God's Spirit are used to build strong foundations and temples (your eternal spiritual temple)

- *Stones* are used in the Gospel or Bible, to block the flow of water (spirit) in rivers (heavy flows of spirit, which tells us to be careful what *stones* we place that may prevent the flow of true wisdom).

- *Stone* walls protect us all, just like stone walls protect the residents of cities in the Bible. Have you ever met someone with walls so thick that it was almost impossible to penetrate them? In the Bible, a city is only as safe as the stone walls that protect it. See Tearing Down the Walls of Jericho ~

Stone, Precious

The Symbolic Interpretation of this is that the Bible says that the Pharisees picked up *stones* to throw at Jesus (John 8:59). Also, (John 18:28-32) carefully declare that the Jews did not have permission to put anyone to death by any means including *stoning*, which would have been the penalty for the crimes they were accusing Jesus of under the Mosaic Law. When interpreting the scriptures, in many cases, it is the words that are not written that we must pay the most attention to, and this is why John tells us nothing more than the fact that "Jesus hid himself" from them. The words on paper should only be enough to lead us within our soul to contemplate the truth that is hidden within us all. The words never give the truth. Truth is only always perceived through meditation and contemplation.

Stone, Precious: Stones remarkable for their colour, brilliancy, or rarity. Such stones have at all times been held in high esteem everywhere, particularly in the East where their use and adornment have served ceremonial, ritualistic and stylistic purposes. Sacred Scripture illustrates that very early on the Eastern civilizations appropriated them for diverse ornamental uses: rings, bracelets, collars and necklaces. The crowns of kings, their garments and those of their officers and of the priests were all set with precious stones, often as engraved gems, a major art form throughout the ancient Near East.

Straight: (Adjective, Greek: *orthos* - [or-thos']; Hebrew: yashar - [yaw-shawr'], upright, straight, direct. See (Isaiah 42: 16)"I will lead them in paths that they have not known: I will make darkness light before them, and crooked things *straight*"

2 *Straight* is the shortest route between any two points. The shortest route between physical life and eternal life is also a *straight* line. Moreover, the road to Salvation is both *straight* (not crooked) and strait (not wide open). Again (Mathew 7: 13 – 14) states "Enter ye in at the strait gate: for wide is the gate, and broad is the way, that leadeth to destruction, and many there be which go in thereat 7:14 Because strait is the gate, and narrow is the way, which leadeth unto life, and few there be that find it." (KJV)

On the other hand, those who travel a crooked path (like a *serpent*), not only expend far more effort to go their greater distance, they may never arrive because, by definition, a crooked path will end up anywhere but the right place, even if one was aiming at it (the result of living life with a "bent sight"). That was the lesson of why the adult Israelites of the Exodus didn't make it to the promised land. The LORD led them *straight* out of Egypt, *straight* down to Mount Sinai, and then *straight* up to enter the land of Israel from the south. But when they became crooked in their obedience to Him, He turned the rebels around and let them wander their crooked path to no where It was their children and grandchildren, forty years later, who crossed the Jordan. As a Christian, may the Lord help to make your path *straight* as the context of John the Baptist Gospel, 'the voice crying in the Wilderness'. See."The beginning of the gospel of Jesus Christ, the Son of God. As it is written by Isaiah the prophet, "Behold, I send My messenger before Your face, who will prepare Your way; 3The voice of one crying in the wilderness, 'Make ready the way of the Lord, make His paths *straight*.'" (Mark 1:1-3). Praise the Lord!

Stranger: (noun, Greek: *Xenos* [xénos], Hebrew: *ger* [gare];alien, new, novel; noun: a guest, stranger, foreigner.

2 A foreigner, who is not a native of the land in which he resides, (Genesis 23:4). The Mosaic Law enjoined a generous hospitality towards foreign residents, saying, "Thou shalt love him as thyself," (Leviticus 19:33 – 34, Deuteronomy 10:18 - 19 24:17 27:19. They were subject to the law, Exodus 20:10 Leviticus 16:20) and were admitted to many of the privileges of the chosen people of God, as in (Numbers 9:14, 15:14).

3 The strangers whom David collected to aid in building the temple, (1 Chronicles 22:2), probably comprised many of the remnants of the Canaanite tribes, (1 Kings 9:20,21). Hospitality to strangers, including all travellers, was the duty of all good citizens, (Job 31:32 Hebrews 13:2).

References:(Hebrews 13:2) Do not neglect to show hospitality to strangers, for thereby some have entertained angels unawares. (Galatians 5:14) For the whole law is fulfilled in one word: "You shall love your neighbor as yourself." (Leviticus 25:35-38) "If your brother becomes poor and cannot maintain himself with you, you shall support him as though he were a stranger and a sojourner, and he shall live with you. Take no interest from him or profit, but fear your God, that your brother may live beside you. You shall not lend him your money at interest, nor give him your food for profit. I am the Lord your God, who brought you out of the land of Egypt to give you the land of Canaan, and to be your God. (Galatians 3:28) There is neither Jew nor Greek, there is neither slave nor free, there is no male and female, for you are all one in Christ Jesus. (Jeremiah 22:3) Thus says the Lord: Do justice and righteousness, and deliver from the hand of the oppressor him who has been robbed. And do no wrong or violence to the resi-

Strength

dent alien, the fatherless, and the widow, nor shed innocent blood in this place. (Romans 14:1-23) As for the one who is weak in faith, welcome him, but not to quarrel over opinions. One person believes he may eat anything, while the weak person eats only vegetables. Let not the one who eats despise the one who abstains, and let not the one who abstains pass judgment on the one who eats, for God has welcomed him. Who are you to pass judgment on the servant of another? It is before his own master that he stands or falls. And he will be upheld, for the Lord is able to make him stand. One person esteems one day as better than another, while another esteems all days alike. Each one should be fully convinced in his own mind. ... (Ezekiel 22:29) The people of the land have practiced extortion and committed robbery. They have oppressed the poor and needy, and have extorted from the sojourner without justice. (Exodus 12:49) There shall be one law for the native and for the stranger who sojourns among you." (Matthew 25:35) For I was hungry and you gave me food, I was thirsty and you gave me drink, I was a stranger and you welcomed me, (Leviticus 24:22) You shall have the same rule for the sojourner and for the native, for I am the Lord your God." (Romans 13:8-10) Owe no one anything, except to love each other, for the one who loves another has fulfilled the law. For the commandments, "You shall not commit adultery, You shall not murder, You shall not steal, You shall not covet," and any other commandment, are summed up in this word: "You shall love your neighbor as yourself." Love does no wrong to a neighbor; therefore love is the fulfilling of the law.

Strength: *(See dunamis)*

Subject: (Verb, Greek: *hupotassó* - [hoop-ot-as'-so], place under, subject to; mid, pass: I submit, put myself into subjection as in (Romans 13: 1-2) (KJV) "Let every soul be *subject* unto the higher powers. For there is no power but of God: the powers that be are ordained of God. Whosoever therefore resisteth the power, resisteth the ordinance of God: and they that resist shall receive to themselves damnation".

Submit: (Verb, Greek: *hupotassó* -[hoop-ot-as'-so] place under, subject to; mid, pass: I submit, put myself into subjection. To arrange under, to subordinate, to subject, put in subjection, to subject one's self, obey, to submit to one's control, to yield to one's admonition or advice, to obey, be subjected.

2 *Submit* – A Greek military term meaning "to arrange [troop divisions] in amilitary fashion under the command of giving in, cooperating, assuming responsibility.

3 Wives *submit* yourselves to

your husband. The word submission is not limited to wives alone. For example, Christians are to *submit* themselves to each other (Ephesians 5:21), to government (Romans 13:1), and unto God (James 4:7). This is a frequent concept in the Gospel. Self-sacrifice is required in each circumstance. *Submission* is never glossed over to be seen as easy or always convenient. Instead, it is viewed as service unto God.

By following the Greek word *hupotasso*, "to subordinate...put under..." God exhorts women to voluntarily follow their husband's leadership (Ephesians 5:22, 1 Peter 3:1). A woman is actively doing this -- choosing to put herself under leadership, choosing to be subordinate in a circumstance or relationship. This is not forced upon her by the recipient. A wife shows *submission* unto her husband when she allows him to take leadership in the relationship. His position as leader is biblical (1 Corinthians 11:3). Abraham's wife, Sarah, is an example of a woman following her husband's lead (1 Peter 3:6). Sarah has never been confused with being a woman who was a frail doormat. Peter notes that she was not afraid in life. *Submission* should not be confused with a person being weak.

4 Women are not commanded to *submit* to their husband's because God insures that men will be just or loving. When a woman submits unto her husband, she is actually submitting unto God (Ephesians 5:22). A woman therefore does not *submit* because her husband deserves it in his own merit- she *submits* because she knows it is pleasing to her Lord. There will be times when a woman needs to *submit*, and her husband does not deserve it from a human perspective. But by divine right, God set the man as leader and a woman can trust that God is good. She can also know that nothing escapes God's notice, and a wicked man will be held accountable for his actions.

5 When a wife *submits* to her husband, she does not try to take leadership from him. From the beginning of time, woman has tried to take leadership from the man - and man has often gladly given it away (Genesis 3). Some scholars believe that (Genesis 3:16) refers to Eve's new sin drive to override her husband's headship, which has continued down the line of women. Women use many tactics to try taking control of leadership, including nagging, deception, and manipulation. This always results in sin and often, sorrowful consequences (Genesis 27). When a woman resorts to these tactics, she is trying to usurp God's good design of relationship roles. A *submissive* wife must first learn to trust God's goodness and His sovereignty.

Suffer

6 However, a *submissive* wife is not relegated to idly sitting by while her husband makes all the family decisions. In a healthy marriage, husband and wife work as a team. When a decision cannot be jointly agreed upon, the leader makes it, knowing he is responsible foremost unto God for that decision. In these circumstances or in a decision that the husband must make alone, a *submissive* wife is not overstepping her boundaries by offering counsel. She must learn to do it in a way that shows respect for his God-given position as head of the family. A *submissive* woman also offers abundant encouragement, understanding that making decisions is a heavy responsibility on a man's shoulders.

7 Nevertheless, some women are not satisfied with this. They want to be in charge. But realistically, marriage cannot work this way. Unity requires relational structure. We see this pattern in other relationships. But *submission* is never a sign of value. Jesus *submitted* to the will of His Father (Matthew 26:39). It would be heresy to say that Jesus is of lesser value than the Father. They are One, and Jesus cannot be of lesser value. His submission had nothing to do with His value—it had to do with God-ordained structure. It is the same with husband and wife.

Simply, *submission* takes humility. It also takes a lot of prayer and relying on the Holy Spirit. But so does Godly leadership. Women can look unto Jesus as an example, and reflect His love and Self-sacrifice as they lovingly choose to *submit* unto the husband God has placed in their life. Praise the Lord!

Suffer: (Verb, Greek: paschó - [pas'-kho], Hebrew: *nasa or nasah* - [naw-saw']; lifted, I am acted upon in a certain way, either good or bad; I experience ill treatment. Simply, suffering is anything which hurts or irritates. In the design of God, it is also something to make us think. It is a tool God uses to get our attention and to accomplish His purposes in our lives in a way that would never occur without the trial or irritation

2 Suffer or *Suffering* is a tool God uses to get our attention and to accomplish His purposes in our lives. It is designed to build our trust in the Almighty, but *suffering* requires the right response if it is to be successful in accomplishing God's purposes. *Suffering* forces us to turn from trust in our own resources to living by faith in God's resources. Hallelujah!

3 *Suffering* is not in itself virtuous, nor is it a sign of holiness. It is also not a means of gaining points with God, nor of subduing the flesh (as in asceticism). When possible, rather, *suffering* is to be avoided. Christ avoided *suffering* unless it meant acting in disobedience to the Father's will. That is

why, (Ecclesiastes 7:14) "In the day of prosperity be happy, But in the day of adversity consider-God has made the one as well as the other so that man may not discover anything that will be after him".

Whatever the suffering in your life is as a Christian, your survival depends on your response to the problem, lessons learned, the faith demonstrated, love for God and for others, your ability to show Christ-like character, values, commitment, priorities, and the usefulness by God in your life.

Suffering, General Causes of: We suffer because we live in a fallen world where sin reigns in the hearts of men. 2 We suffer because of our own foolishness. We reap what we sow (Galatians 6:7-9). 3 We sometimes suffer because it is God's discipline. "For those whom the Lord loves He disciplines, and He scourges every son He receives." (Hebrew. 12:6).

(4) We may suffer persecution because of our faith-especially when we take a stand on biblical issues, i.e., suffering for righteousness sake (2 Timothy. 3:12). Of course, all of these do not apply at the same time. All *suffering* is not, for instance, a product of our own foolishness, self-induced misery, or sin. It is true, however, that rarely does *suffering* not reveal areas of need, weaknesses, and wrong attitudes that need to be removed like dross in the gold refining process - See (1 Pet. 1:6-7).

Suffering, the nature of: Indeed, *suffering* is Painful - *Suffering* is hard. It is never easy. Regardless of what we know and how hard we apply the principles, it is going to hurt (1 Peter. 1:6) -"distressed" is lupeo meaning "to cause pain, sorrow, grief").

2 Suffering is Perplexing — This means that suffering is somewhat mysterious. We may know some of the theological reasons for suffering from Scripture, yet when it hits, there is still a certain mystery. Why now? What is God doing? In this, it is designed to build our trust in the Almighty God; Praise the Lord!

Suffering is Purposeful — meaning suffering is not without meaning in spite of its mystery. It has as its chief purpose the formation of Christ-like character (Romans. 8:28-29). Hallelujah!

Sun: (Noun), the star round which the earth orbits."the sun shone from a cloudless sky" the light or-sunshine, sunlight, daylight, light, warmth; Literary, a person or thing regarded as a source of glory, inspiration, etc."the rhetoric faded before the sun of reality". Literary, used with reference to someone's success or prosperity. "the sun of the Plantagenets went down in clouds"

Supplication: (Noun, Greek: hiketéria - [hik-et-ay-ree'-ah], Hebrew: techinnah [tekh-in-naw'],

Sword

(originally: the olive branch held in the hand of the suppliant), supplication, entreaty *(See prayer of supplication)*

Sword: This is a blade weapon used primarily for cutting or thrusting. The precise definition of the term varies with the historical epoch or the geographical region under consideration. A sword in the narrowest sense consists of a straight blade with two edges and a hilt. However, in nearly every case, the term may also be used to refer to weapons with a single edge (backsword).

The word sword comes from the Old English sweord, cognate to swert, Old Norse sverð, from a Proto-Indo-European root *swer- "to wound, to cut". Non-European weapons called "sword" include single-edged weapons such as the Middle Eastern saif, the Chinese dao and the related Japanese katana. The Chinese jian is an example of a non-European double-edged sword, like the European models derived from the double-edged Iron Age sword. Historically, the sword developed in the Bronze Age, evolving from the dagger; the earliest specimens date to ca. 1600 BC. The Iron Age sword remained fairly short and without a crossguard. The spatha as it developed in the Late Roman army became the predecessor of the European sword of the Middle Ages, at first adopted as the Migration period sword, and only in the High Middle Ages developed into the classical arming sword with cross guard. The use of a sword is known as swordsmanship or (in an early modern or modern context) as fencing. In the Early Modern period, the sword developed into the rapier and eventually the small sword, surviving into the 18th century only in the role of duelling weapon. By the 19th century, swords were reduced to the status of either ceremonial weapon or sport equipment in modern fencing.

The sword is said to be the emblem of military honour and should incite the bearer to a just and generous pursuit of honour and virtue. It is symbolic of liberty and strength. In the Middle Ages, the sword was often used as a symbol of the word of God. The names given to many swords in mythology, literature, and history reflect the high prestige of the weapon and the wealth of the owner

Tt

Tabitha: Commonly spelled as Tabetha, or Tabatha, is an English language feminine given name, derived from an Aramaic word ☐ablta meaning gazelle. It is a biblical name from (Acts 9:36), in which *Tabitha* is a woman raised from the dead by Saint Peter. Other alternate spellings include Tabytha, Tabathina and Tabea. Nicknames include Tab, Tabby and Tibby.

2 *Tabitha* was common in 18th century New England, and of those born between 1718 and 1745, ranked about 31st as most common female given names, about 0.56% of the population.

The name gained resurgence in the United States in the 1970s and 1980s, when it was ranked among the 200 most popular names for girls. The character *Tabitha* Stephens, a child witch on the 1960s television situation comedy Bewitched, raised the profile of the name. It has since declined in popularity. In 2009 it was the 647th most popular name for girls in the United States. The name was the 209th most popular name for girls in England and Wales in 2007. Tabitha is rare as a surname.

Tabitha, Cumi: This refers to the Miraculous Resurrection of Dorcas. Meaning Tabitha arise! The miracle credited to Jesus Christ by Peter.

Tabitha, Cumi's – Background of: In the Greek the name "Tabitha" is "Dorcas," which means "gazelle," or "beautiful." This young girl was very beautiful, not only physically but also morally. The text tells us Tabitha was full of good works and almsgiving.

2 She was a single Christian woman of some means who distributed her wealth for the welfare of the poor, especially the poor widows of the church of Joppa, spending her time and resources making clothing for them. As stated in the book of Acts about the apostles being full of the Holy Ghost, full of faith, full of wisdom, and full of grace. Here we are told about someone who was full of good works and almsgiving.

3 *Tabitha's* good works demonstrated that her faith was saving faith, not temporal faith or the faith of the devil - that merely believes in the existence of God. James said, "Faith without works is dead," but *Tabitha* was full of good works. Those with temporal faith will have no good works. A believer who is truly regenerate is a new creation, created in Christ Jesus unto good works. A Christian who is disobedient to Jesus Christ is a contradiction in terms. If you are a converted person, you will be full of good works done in obedience to the Lord.

4 In fact, *Tabitha* was like the Thessalonians of whom Paul spoke when he said, "We continually remember before our God and Father your work produced by faith, your labour prompted by love, and your endurance inspired by hope in our Lord Jesus Christ" (1 Thessalonica. 1:3). This girl was fruitful. *Tabitha* was abiding in her master, the Lord Jesus Christ, and as such she was loaded with fruit.

5 *Tabitha* was not a lazy woman who lived only for pleasure. She was like the woman described in (Proverbs 31:17, 20) who "sets about her work vigorously; her arms are strong for her tasks," and "opens her arms to the poor and extends her hands to the needy."

6 *Tabitha* was a great blessing to the church of Joppa. She probably was not married, as nothing is known of a husband, parents, or children. Like the four daughters of the evangelist Philip, *Tabitha* totally immersed herself in serving the Lord, spending and being spent for his service. In her desire to be rich toward God in good works, she invested her riches and her life in the kingdom of God and found complete and true happiness in her service to the Lord Jesus Christ.

Tabitha, the death and restoration to Live of: According to (Acts 9:37) tells us Tabitha became ill and died. This was a great loss to the church, and probably a great surprise.

Tabitha was ready to die. Like Paul, Tabitha would say, "To me to live is Christ and to die is gain." Like Paul, she desired to depart and be with Christ. Why do we know she was ready? She had lived to please the Lord and was rich in good works.

Tabitha died, but she was not anointed and wrapped in clothes for burial. Instead, the disciples washed her body and put her in an upper room. Because these saints in the church of Joppa had heard about the mighty ministry of the apostle Peter in the nearby town of Lydda and thought maybe God could perform a miracle for them as he had in Lydda. They wanted the apostle to come and comfort them, and were probably hoping he could raise Tabitha from the dead. So they sent two people to bring Peter from Lydda to Joppa.

But, unlike Jesus, Peter came immediately to Joppa and went to the upper room where he saw the widows who had benefited so much from Tabitha's labours. They were all weeping, and they said to Peter, "Look at all these clothes Tabitha made for us. She loved us and helped us so much, spending her time and money for us. We benefited so much from this sister, and now she is no longer with us. Peter, can you comfort us?" Peter sent all the people out of the room, closed the door and knelt to pray, alone with the dead body. Peter remembered when he, together with the other apostles, was sent by the Lord Jesus Christ with authority to heal the sick and to raise the dead, as in (Matthew 10)

The door was closed, there was a dead body, and Peter was alone on his knees. But he was not really alone. Peter saw God Almighty and prayed to him. And the Spirit of God gave him the confidence that it was God's will to raise this young woman from the dead. So Peter turned, looked at the dead body and spoke to it: "Tabitha, cumi!" or "Tabitha, arise!" We are told that when Peter spoke, *Tabitha* opened her eyes, saw Peter and sat up. Peter gave her his hand, lifted her up, and she stood. Praise the Lord!

Talitha, Cumi: The miracle Jesus performed when he raised Jairus's daughter. The twelve-year-old girl had just died when Jesus came, so she was not washed, anointed or wrapped in clothes. Jesus came in and said to her, "Talitha, cumi!" meaning "My child, arise!" and she got up.

Take God's name in vain:
To use God's name profanely, thoughtlessly or irreverently. (Exodus 20:7) "Thou shall not take the name of the Lord they God in vain". Among traditional societies as well as ancient Hebrews, the name of a deity is regarded as his manifestation and is treated with the greatest respect and veneration. Among savage tribes there is a reluctance in disclosing one's name because this might enable by magic to work one some deadly injury. The Greek were particularly careful to disguise uncomplimentary names.

Teach: (Verb, Greek: didaskó - [did-as'-ko], Hebrew: Alaph; teach, direct, admonish. Note:

(Verb) impart knowledge to or instruct (someone) as to how to do something. "she taught him to read the Bible". Synonyms: educate, instruct, school, tutor, give lessons to, coach, train, upskill, ground, enlighten, illuminate, verse, edify, prepare, din something into, indoctrinate, brainwash to accept the Gospel.

2 To give information about or instruction in (a subject or skill). "he came one day each week to teach preaching". synonyms: give lessons in, lecture in, give instructions in, inform someone about, familiarize someone with, ac-

quaint someone with, instil, inculcate, explicate, explain, expound. work as a teacher. "she teaches at the local Church Sunday school"

3 To cause (someone) to learn or understand something by example or experience. "she'd been taught that it paid to be a Christian", Also, to encourage someone to accept (something) as a fact or principle. "the philosophy teaches self-control"

"A disciple is not above his teacher, but everyone when he is fully trained will be like his teacher." [Luke 6:40 -ESV] "Therefore whoever relaxes one of the least of these commandments and *teaches* others to do the same will be called least in the kingdom of heaven, but whoever does them and *teaches* them will be called great in the kingdom of heaven." [Matthew 5:19]

Temple: (noun, Greek: *Tho naós*; Hebrew: *hekal* [hay-kal'] - meaning "dwelling", semantically distinct from Latin templum "temple") were structures built to house deity statues within Greek sanctuaries in ancient Greek religion. The temple interiors did not serve as meeting places, since the sacrifices and rituals dedicated to the respective deity took place outside them. Temples were frequently used to store votive offerings. They are the most important and most widespread building type in Greek architecture. In the Hellenistic kingdoms of Southwest Asia and of North Africa, buildings erected to fulfill the functions of a temple often continued to follow the local traditions. Even where a Greek influence is visible, such structures are not normally considered as Greek temples. This applies, for example, to the Graeco-Parthian and Bactrian temples, or to the Ptolemaic examples, which follow Egyptian tradition. Most Greek temples were oriented astronomically.

2 The symbols appeal to the senses, but not simply as "visual aids." The ark, cherubim, and the tent of the meeting become the institutional representations of the Lord's presence among his people. Here, in this place, Yahweh appears and makes his will known (Exodus 33:7-11).

The tent of the meeting in the Pentateuch, and the priestly tabernacle, is not, however, a projection (or retrojection!) of the temple, but an independent dwelling reflecting the life of Israel prior to settlement and the centralization of worship. The tent is a "portable temple" of sorts, but not provisional nor simply a pattern; rather, the tent is a unique "dwelling." With the ritual performances in the tabernacle or temple complex, and the personnel and attendant appurtenances, we come to a theologically significant point about temple practice: coming into the presence of a holy God. In each change of location, vestment, instrument, or ritual act, with their various gradations of importance, the "needs" of the people and the holiness of God come together: I am holy, it is holy, you are (to be) holy.

The extensions and the symbolic associations began early in the canonical literature. As a commentary on the Torah, Deuteronomy expresses the presence of Yahweh in the cult devoid of some simplistic equation of Yahweh's presence constrained by the natural order of cause and effect by utilizing his alter ego, his "name, " as the manifestation of his transcendent reality. Even the ark itself is divested of its throne-like setting by its role as the "container" of the tablets of the law (Deuteronomy 10:1-5). Yahweh is not seated on a throne like some dowager duchess.

Temple, the construction of the: The construction of the temple began with David to serve as, at least on sociopolitical grounds, a "media event" of divine support and favour. David, however, was deterred from completing the task. No doubt sociopolitical forces played their usual role in this. The biblical authors were not oblivious to these explanations (1 Kings 5:13-18), but characteristically pass theological judgment (1 Chronicle 22:8-9), or, more important, God himself divulges his feelings on the matter: "Did I ever say Why have you not built me a house of cedar'?" (2 Samuel 7:7). God does not require an immutable dwelling, but the metaphoric associations are kept open, even those of monarchal justification (i.e., a "house" like the house in which the monarch resides).

2 The "cedar house" is ultimately built. And in Solomon's great prayer of dedication the paradox of this dwelling is acknowledged once again by his classic statement: "But will God really dwell on earth? The heavens, even the highest heaven, cannot contain you. How much less this temple I have built!" (1 Kings 8:27). The paradox is softened by "quoting" the Deuteronomic "name" formula: "My Name shall be [in this place]" (1 king 8: 29). -This terminology underscores the point that the correspondence between God's presence and his "dwelling"tabernacle or templeis more "textual" than physical) But what does the Lord think of this structure? Solomon, like Bezalel before him with the building of the tabernacle, is described as having "wisdom." Unlike Bezalel, however, Solomon sends straightaway for supplies and instructions from Phoenician artisans. Moreover, a labour force is needed to complete the project, a force not unlike what the Israelites experienced in Egypt. Finally, Solomon is portrayed as the central figure in the planning and implementation of the project: "As for this temple that you are building " (1 Kings 6:12

The equivocal nature of the project is supported by the Lord's response to it in (1 Kings 9:3-5). The

Lord does hallow the place, but it is still Solomon's doing: "I have consecrated this temple which you have built" as in (verse. 3). A clear stipulation is also attached: "if you walk before me" (verse. 4); the sanctity of the place must be preserved, at the very least).

Temple, Responses to the:

What responses do we find in Scripture to the building of the temple beyond those found in the immediate context of it being built?

Rather than "going up" to the mountain of the house of the Lord to hear the word of the Lord, as in the eschatological visions of Isaiah and Micah (Micah 4:1-2), the Babylonians "descend" upon the temple to break down its wall and carry off the temple treasures. After centuries of covenant disloyalty, the Lord withdraws his presence from this place (Ezekiel 10:18); in fact, he is driven from the temple because of the abominations of the people (Ezekiel 8:6). This destruction could be seen as one of the contingencies of history except for the interpretations put upon it; the theologian of Lamentations states the destruction of the temple in unequivocal terms: "The Lord determined to tear down the wall of the Daughter of Zion" (Lamentation 2:8). The destruction is purposed by God because the people failed to live before him.

Temple, Reconstruction:

High on the agenda of the postexilic community was the rebuilding of the temple. Indeed, it was not long before all their troubles which were many and were attributed to the disrepair, the virtual absence, of the dwelling of God (Haggai 1:3-9). The Lord commands its construction (Ezra 1:2). The means for rebuilding temple theology are present in the preexilic theology itself, the selfsame theology that so thoroughly critiqued an overly literal-minded approach to the presence of God.

2 The temple was always symbolic, "textual" even before (and as much as) it was physical. To the extent that the metaphoric associations speak to the reality of our experience(s) before God, the symbol retains its power as a symbol. Although Jeremiah held little esteem for the ark and the temple, he nevertheless prophesied that God's throne would be Jerusalem itself (Jeremiah 3:17), and Torah would be written in their hearts (Jeremiah 31:31-34). These extensions of the symbol are developed further in the New Testament (Revelation 21:22-27) : "I did not see a temple in the city, because the Lord God Almighty and the Lamb are its temple Nothing impure will ever enter it.". The relativizing of the temple and moral earnestness that we see in Jeremiah were precisely the points of the Deuteronomic theology that influenced the short-lived reforms of Josiah.

3 The most extensive view of the new temple comes from Ezekiel. The construction of the temple is once again more ideal than real. In Ezekiel's new temple a remarkable event takes place: water flows from the temple (in Jerusalem) with such abundance that it calls to mind the rivers of paradise see also (Psalm 46:4 ; Revelation 21:6).

4 The Songs of Zion in the Psalter are particularly rich in their celebration of the *temple*. With all their "sensuality"the Christian is instructed to "behold" the beauty of the temple; walk about it; clap and shout; smell; bow down; and other sense-oriented activitiesthe Songs show that one is not to ponder the temple simply as a theological abstraction. The one who enters the temple not only receives spiritual blessings but material ones as well (Psalm 36:7-9). While we do not find much by way of extensions of this symbol, its paradoxical and metaphoric nature are everywhere testified to in what takes place in the life of the communicant. The most powerful statement of this sort comes in (Psalm 73), where the psalmist cries out because his inherited beliefs are at odds with his personal experiences. Everything is "oppressive" (Psalm 73: 16). "Till I entered the sanctuary of God " and what unfolds is a transformation of his character and his understanding of God. What happens in the sanctuary? It is, as it should be, unspecified. We are simply told at the end of the psalm that "as for me, it is good to be near God I will tell of all your deeds." Really, by building the *temple* and by extending the metaphoric associations with the *temple*, a continuity between the pre- and post-exilic community was established as in (Ezra 1:7 ; Haggai 2:9). For all the critique of the temple, in the final analysis, Yahweh takes pleasure in this place and it is a source of delight for those who assemble there (Psalm 43:3-4 ; 65:4 ; 84:1).

Temple in Believing: (Jesus, Paul, and Judaism). In Judaism the *temple* was the religious, cultural, and national center; indeed, the *temple* was a microcosm of the universe. The power of the *temple* as a symbol is especially seen in its ability to continue long after the *temple* building itself was destroyed in a.d. 70.

2 According to the Gospels, Jesus participated fully in the practices and ethos of the *temple*. Jesus' birth was announced in the temple (Luke 1:17 ; 2:27-32), where he was also circumcised and studied with the rabbis as a lad (Luke 2:46). Later, of course, Jesus taught in the temple himself (John 7:14). It is not without significance that while Jesus is teaching in the temple precincts, he says, "If anyone is thirsty, let him come to me" (John 7:37), and the next day offers forgiveness to the woman taken in adultery (John 8:1-11). Blessing and forgiveness, priestly functions, are pronounced by Jesus in the shadow of the *temple*.

Temple theology

3 Jesus is not only a communicant and priest of sorts; he is also a prophet. Thus, when the temple practices are compromised, Jesus assails those who jeopardize the sanctity of the temple: "My house will be called a house of prayer But you have made it a den of robbers" (Mark 11:17). They were not living before God. Jesus, while teaching in its precincts, preserves the sanctity of the temple by his ethical admonitions. Even the forgiven woman is told to sin no more (John 8:11 ; see also (John 4:23).

4 In the cleansing of the *temple* we also find a development and extension of the metaphoric associations of *temple*. Jesus employs a word play equivocating on the term "body" to break the parochial thinking of his audience (John 2:19). John characteristically points out the error of their literal-mindedness: "But the temple he had spoken of was his body" (John 2:21). Thus, in Jesus' acts and words we see the temple once again as a place of holiness, of danger (words of judgment; Jesus's own death) as well as blessing, and further extensions of the symbol are generated.

5 Paul also makes the correspondence between the *temple* and body: "Do you not know that your body is a temple of the Holy Spirit?" (1 Corinthians 6:19 ; see also (Romans 12:1-2). Of course, the believer can be called the t*emple* of God only because Christ himself is the temple and the believer participates in Christ (1 Corinthians 3:9-17). The believer, like Paul himself, must be (cultically) pure in order to live in God's presence (2 Corinthians 2:17). If God can dwell in a holy place, by extension, He could dwell in a holy person! – Such as a true Christian! Praise the Lord!!

Temple theology: This shows a high degree of theological sophistication holding ambivalent attitudes and doctrines in tension, part of the mystery of faith, of paradox. Temple theology is most fruitful when it is functioning as a powerful symbol, with the ability to be fully grounded in (sacred) space and yet generate new metaphoric associations which is a vision of life in the presence of the Lord. Even though the temple is both protological and eschatological, it is always grounded in the realities of our lives: it is a mere edifice, yet, Behold! Thy God.

Temple, Solomon's: The First Temple, was the Holy Temple (Hebrew: *Bet HaMikdash*) in ancient Jerusalem, on the Temple Mount (also known as Mount Zion), before its destruction by Nebuchadnezzar II after the Siege of Jerusalem of 587 BCE. There is no archaeological evidence for the existence of Solomon's Temple, and no mention of it in the surviving contemporary extra-biblical literature.

Testify

2 The Hebrew Bible states that the temple was constructed under Solomon, King of the United Kingdom of Israel and Judah and that during the kingdom of Judah, the temple was dedicated to Yahweh (God), and is said to have housed the Ark of the Covenant. Josephus claims that "the temple was burnt four hundred and seventy years, six months, and ten days after it was built," though Rabbinic sources state that the First Temple stood for 410 years and, based on the 2nd-century work Seder Olam Rabbah, place construction in 832 BCE and destruction in 422 BCE (3338 AM), 165 years later than secular estimates.

3 Because of the religious sensitivities involved, and the politically volatile situation in Jerusalem, only limited archaeological surveys of the Temple Mount have been conducted. No excavations have been allowed on the Temple Mount during modern times. An Ivory pomegranate mentions priests in the house of Yahweh, and an inscription recording the Temple's restoration under Jehoash have appeared on the antiquities market, but the authenticity of both has been challenged and they remain the subject of controversy.

4 After the destruction of the *temple* in a.d. 70, *temple* theology loses none of its living and healing power since the *temple* was always "beyond" its physical presence. A theology of *temple* answers the problem of how God's presence is mediated. Specifically, *temple theology* recognizes the importance of "sacred space." Its analogue is sacred time Sabbath, festivals, and appointed times of prayer. Humankind is oriented in time and space, thus Sabbath and *temple* testify to "eternity" beyond the confines of our usual orientation. Sabbath and *temple* redeem time and space. Praise the Lord!

Testament: (Noun, Greek: diathéké – [dee-ath-ay'-kay], Hebrew: Tanakh, meaning (a) a covenant between two parties, (b) (the ordinary, everyday sense [found a countless number of times in papyri]) a will, testament.

Testify: (Noun, Greek: *marturia* - [mar-too-ree'-ah], (Verb, Hebrew: *uwd* [ood], Admonish, witness, evidence, testimony, reputation. It is testifying to the world, the faithfulness of God in our fears ,trials and temptations as in (Luke 21: 12), says,' but you shall be tested, tried and afflicted. But (Luke 21: 13) says, it shall turn to your testimony In the Gospel, the Bible don't say you shall overcome by prayer or fasting but by the word of your testimony. Indeed, people may not know what you are going through, you might be called all sort of names, you might be treated in a bad way, but keep testifying, that is what would make you to overcome. However, if you know how to testify in your fear, trial and teestmptation, then you would have a big testimony. Some Christians, complain, murmur and grumble,these things prolong our stay in (Luke 21:12), but praise, worship, testifying, rejoicing speed us towards (Luke 21: 13). Other aspects of testimonies are:

2 To make a solemn declaration, verbal or written, to establish some fact; to give testimony for the purpose of communicating to others a knowledge of something not known to them or to make a solemn declaration under oath or affirmation, for the purpose of establishing, or making proof of, some fact to a court; to give testimony in a cause depending before a tribunal. 3 To declare a charge; to protest; to give information; to bear witness; -- with against or to bear witness to; to support the truth of by testimony; to affirm or declare solemnly. 4 To affirm or declare under oath or affirmation before a tribunal, in order to prove some fact. Also as adverb to be in a testy manner; fretfully; peevishly; with petulance.

Testifying the goodness of God, Keep:

Meaning, testimony is not just, i buy a new car, i have a new job, new birth and many more. Ofcourse, we can celebrate theses achievements, but they are not testimony. Even unbelievers get such blessings from God. But your testimony is what you say when you are in the mist of your challenges, like the three Hebrew children going into the furnace, like Daniel in the lions den, Job, Joseph ,Paul and Silas, and many more.

Their testimony was not what they said after the challenges, rather, it was what they said while they were in that situation. Words like ,' I know my redeemer liveth', 'we know that our God would save us...','even if He slays me yet will I trust Him', what shall separate me from the love of Christ........', 'greater is He that is in me, than he that is in the world',.. For those that feel like they are failures, or they are about to, they must testify.' I am more that a conqueror '. However, Christians should remember that, the bible says 'you shall have whatever you say'. Not what you say, after your challenges, but rather what you say during your challenges.

2 Abraham was found faithful in the midst of his challenges. and God called him righteous while he had not gotten the promises of God (not after he had Isaac).

Many things people call testimony today are just testiphonies, people trumpeting their own achievements, saying them with pride as if they have deserve the result of their own labour. No wonder soon after these, more challenges come back, and they claim its the pastor, its the church members or some witches & wizards.

But you must understand that anything that gives glory to you and not to God is only setting you up for more danger. May God take Glory always in our testimonies.

Thanksgiving: Thanksgiving has its historical roots in religious and cultural traditions and has long been celebrated in a secular manner as well.

2 In 1621, the Plymouth colonists and Wampanoag Indians shared an autumn harvest feast that is acknowledged today as one of the first Thanksgiving celebrations in the colonies. For more than two centuries, days of thanksgiving were celebrated by individual colonies and states. It wasn't until 1863, in the midst of the Civil War, that President Abraham Lincoln proclaimed a national Thanksgiving Day to be held each November.

Thanksgiving Day: This is a national holiday celebrated primarily in the United States and Canada as a day of giving thanks to God for the blessing of the harvest and of the preceding year. It is celebrated on the fourth Thursday of November in the United States and on the second Monday of October in Canada. Several other places around the world observe similar celebrations.

Think: (Verb, Greek: *phroneó* - [fron-eh'-o], Hebrew: ho-shev' [you, he] think, (b) *think*, judge, (c) direct the mind to, seek for, (d) I observe, (e)I care for, .have a particular belief or idea., direct one's mind towards someone or something; use one's mind actively to form connected ideas., have a specified opinion of. As a (noun) an act of thinking

References:(Philippians 4:8) Finally, brothers, whatever is true, whatever is honorable, whatever is just, whatever is pure, whatever is lovely, whatever is commendable, if there is any excellence, if there is anything worthy of praise, think about these things. (1 Corinthians 3:18) Let no one deceive himself. If anyone among you *thinks* that he is wise in this age, let him become a fool that he may become wise. (Proverbs 15:28) The heart of the righteous ponders how to answer, but the mouth of the wicked pours out evil things. (Romans 8:5-6)For those who live according to the flesh set their minds on the things of the flesh, but those who live according to the Spirit set their minds on the things of the Spirit. For to set the mind on the flesh is death, but to set the mind on the Spirit is life and peace. (Romans 12:2) Do not be conformed to this world, but be transformed by the renewal of your mind, that by testing you may discern what is the will of God, what is good and acceptable and perfect. (Colossians 3:2) Set your minds on things that are above, not on things that are on earth. (2 Timothy 2:7) *Think* over what I say, for the Lord will give you understanding in every-

Thirst

thing. (Jeremiah 29:11) For I know the plans I have for you, declares the Lord, plans for welfare and not for evil, to give you a future and a hope. (2 Timothy 4:7) I have fought the good fight, I have finished the race, I have kept the faith.

Thirst: (Verb, Greek: *dipsaó* [dip-sah'-o]: I thirst for, desire earnestly. Hebrew: Noun - *tsama* [tsaw-maw'] (noun, a feeling of needing or wanting to drink something. Verb have a strong desire for something. 2 feel a need to drink something.

3 The Bible says, "Come, everyone who *thirsts*, come to the waters; and he who has no money, come, buy and eat" (Isaiah 55:1). And "let the one who is *thirsty* come; let the one who desires take the water of life without price" (Revelation 22:16-17). Yes, come and buy; it's without price. Some of you are thirsting for this—a personal relationship with Christ. Come to the water! Drink of the living water! Become excited about Christ! "With joy you will draw water from the wells of salvation" (Isaiah 12:3). The wells of salvation are being offered to you. Come and draw the water with joy!

Time: (Noun, Greek: *kairos* – [kahee-ros'], Hebrew: *moed* – [mo-ade'], fitting season, season, opportunity, occasion, time. Meeting. Simply *time* is "the divinely created sphere of God's preserving and redemptive work, and the arena of man's decision on his way to an eternal destiny.

2 The right or opportune moment (the supreme moment). The ancient Greeks had two words for time, chronos and kairos. While the former refers to chronological or sequential time, the latter signifies a time lapse, a moment of indeterminate time in which everything happens. What is happening when referring to kairos depends on who is using the word. While chronos is quantitative, kairos has a qualitative, permanent nature. Kairos also means weather in both ancient and modern Greek. The plural, καιροί (kairoi (Ancient Greek and Modern Greek.) means the *times*. (Ecclesiastes 3:1-8) For everything there is a season, and a time for every matter under heaven: a time to be born, and a time to die; a time to plant, and a time to pluck up what is planted; a time to kill, and a time to heal; a time to break down, and a time to build up; a time to weep, and a time to laugh; a time to mourn, and a time to dance; a time to cast away stones, and a time to gather stones together; a time to embrace, and a time to refrain from embracing; ...

3 *Time* - There are different ways of looking at time that are consistent with biblical revelation. It is, for instance, advantageous to divide pre-Christian history into periods that are marked by significant events. Paul spoke of the *times* that preceded the redemp-

tive mission of Jesus (Ephesians. 1:10). The apostle employs the term kairos (frequently rendered "seasons" – KJV), which generally denotes an era characterized by certain features. There was, for example, a "period of beginnings" that featured the early centuries of earth's history, during which significant events like the creation, the fall of man, the great flood, etc. occurred. There was a span that might be characterized as "the Hebrew family," in which the lives of certain prominent patriarchs were chronicled. The Hebrews passed through a stage known as "Egyptian bondage," followed by "the wilderness wandering," and then the "conquest of Canaan," etc. There was the era of the united kingdom, and subsequently that of Israel and Judah. And so, Old Testament history was delineated by distinct *times*.

On the other hand, it is also possible to view human history in terms of "phases." There are three distinct phases that may be considered.

Time, the preparatory phase of:

There first was a phase that may be described as the preparatory period of history. This embraces all of that time before the first advent of Christ, during which God was working out those providential events which would facilitate the Saviour's mission. Example is Paul's point in (Galatians 3). When he affirms: "But before faith came, we were kept in ward under the law, shut up unto the faith which should afterwards be revealed. So that the law is become our tutor (schoolmaster – KJV) to bring us unto Christ, that we might be justified by faith. But now that faith is come, we are no longer under a tutor" (Galatians 3: 23-25). The word "tutor" translates the Greek term *paidagogos*, and neither "tutor" nor "schoolmaster" does justice to the significance of the original word. The Greek literally means "a servant leader," and it signifies the role of a slave who functioned as the "custodian" of the child, being responsible for the moral and physical well-being of the youngster until he reached the age of maturity.

The Old Testament regime, with its hundreds of prophecies and its great collection of "types," i.e., pictorial aids (1 Corinthian 10:6; Hebrew. 9:1-10) wonderfully prepared the ancient world for the arrival of the Saviour. The explosive growth of the early church was no accident.

Time, the Fulfillment phase of:

Following the preparatory phase of human history, there was the *fulfillment* era. This was a time when the divine plan of salvation was set into motion. The early portion of Mark's Gospel account affirms that Jesus came into Galilee preaching the "gospel of God, and saying, The *time* is fulfilled" (Mark 1:14-15). Paul described the culmination of Jehovah's redemptive system in the following way: ". . . [But when the fulness of *time* came, God sent forth his Son . . ." (Galatians. 4:4). The apostle has a more elaborate statement in (Ephesians 1:9-10). There he argues that God has made known to us the mystery of his will. The term "mystery" denotes the more obscure suggestions of the divine plan in Old Testament *times*, as compared with the full revelation of that system under the New Testament economy.

In short, the heavenly plan was focused "in him" (i.e., in Christ), in anticipation of a forthcoming "dispensation." "Dispensation," as here used, refers to a "plan of salvation". The divine "plan of salvation" was to become effective when the "fulness of the times" was realized, at which point "all things" were to be "summed up" in the work of Christ.

That is why the book of Hebrews asserted that Christ, "at the end of the ages," was manifested to put away sin by the sacrifice of himself (Hebrew 9:26). With the death and resurrection of Jesus, God's great system of deliverance from sin was implemented. It only remains for honest human beings to submit to the conditions imposed. Glory to Jesus.

Time, the Consummation phase of:

This means that the consummation of the divine purpose for history will occur. *Time* is moving towards a goal which will be realized at the time of Christ's return. In that connection, Paul affirms: "Then comes the end when he shall deliver up the kingdom to God . " (1 Corinthians. 15:24). What is "the end" here contemplated? It is the end of the world, the consummation of the work of redemption.

The Lord's return will signal the end of: (1) Time (as that term is used with reference to earth's history) – Jesus spoke repeatedly about the coming "last day" (John. 6:39-40, 44,54; 12:48). (2) The Universe – The created universe will "perish" (Hebrew. 1:11). The elements will be "dissolved" (2 Peter. 3:10-11) and "pass away" (Mathew. 24:35; Revelation. 21:1). (3) Earthly Suffering – All the ravages associated with this sinful environment will be eliminated (Revelation. 7:16-17; 21:4). (4) Physical Death – Death, as man's final enemy, will be destroyed (1 Corinthians. 15:26). (5) Deceptive Teaching – The deceptive doctrines that have confused and destroyed souls will be vanquished (Revelation. 20:3). (6) Opportunity for Salvation – The door of opportunity for spiritual reconciliation with the Creator will be closed (Mathew. 25:10; Hebrew. 9:27).

4 One thing is certain, the Scriptures make a distinction between the "temporal" and the "eternal." Paul says that the things that are seen are "temporal" but the things not seen are "eternal" (2 Corinthians. 4:18). In describing God, the psalmist declares: ". . . from ever-

lasting to everlasting, you are God . . ." (Psalm. 90:2). Yet, in the same context, of man it is said: "The days of our years are threescore years and ten . . ." (Psalm 90: 10). "Time" clearly does not relate to God and man in the same way. Eternity is endless, but time is measured by a "beginning" and an "end." The Bible commences with these words: "In the beginning God created the heavens and the earth" (Genesis. 1:1). Jesus once said: "But from the beginning of the creation, Male and female made he them" (Mark. 10:6).

Also, by way of contrast, in some sense there will be an end. In the Parable of the Tares, Christ said that the "harvest" represented the "end of the world" (Mathew 13:39). Elsewhere the Lord announced: "He that rejects me, and receives not my sayings, has one that judges him: the word that I spoke, the same shall judge him in the last day" (John12:48).

In an epistle to the saints at Corinth, Paul discussed the concept of the future resurrection of the body, which, he affirmed, will occur at the time of the Lord's "coming" (1Corinthians. 15:23). In that connection the apostle writes: "Then comes the end, when he shall deliver the kingdom to God . ." (verse. 24). Clearly there is a span, an era, between the "beginning" and the "end".

References: (2 Peter 3:8) But do not overlook this one fact, beloved, that with the Lord one day is as a thousand years, and a thousand years as one day. (Proverbs 16:9) The heart of man plans his way, but the Lord establishes his steps. (Psalm 90:12) So teach us to number our days that we may get a heart of wisdom. (Jeremiah 29:11) For I know the plans I have for you, declares the Lord, plans for welfare and not for evil, to give you a future and a hope. (James 4:13-15) Come now, you who say, "Today or tomorrow we will go into such and such a town and spend a year there and trade and make a profit"— yet you do not know what tomorrow will bring. What is your life? For you are a mist that appears for a little time and then vanishes. Instead you ought to say, "If the Lord wills, we will live and do this or that."

Tongue: (Noun, Greek: glóssa - [gloce-sah']; Hebrew: lashon – [law-shone'], the tongue, a language, a nation (usually distinguished by their speech)

2 Literally, *tongue* is a muscular hydrostat on the floor of the mouth of most vertebrates which manipulates food for mastication. It is the primary organ of taste (gustation), as much of its upper surface is covered in taste buds. The tongue's upper surface is also covered in numerous lingual papillae. It is sensitive and kept moist by saliva, and is richly supplied with nerves and blood vessels. In humans a secondary function of the tongue is phonetic articulation. The tongue also serves as a

Tongue, the Lying

natural means of cleaning one's teeth. The ability to perceive different tastes is not localised in different parts of the tongue, as is widely believed.

"Speech is the index of the mind." Jesus said that "out of the abundance of the heart the mouth speaketh." (Mathew 12:34) According to (Proverbs 18:21), "Death and life are in the power of the tongue: and they that love it shall eat the fruit thereof." In (James 3:6), the Bible says that the tongue is "a fire, a world of iniquity", and (James 3:8) calls the tongue a "deadly poison."

As a fool would carelessly play and prank with a loaded gun, so many Christians today do likewise with their deadly tongue. If only we could fully realize the untold damage that we are doing to the body of Christ! If only we could see the full effect of the words we use! Then Christians would not only used the Gospel dictionary and Biblical phrases effectively but mind what word is uttered by their tongue. Perhaps a closer look into the Bible can help. God made man, and God made man's tongue, so surely God should be qualified to comment on the subject. Surely God should have some good counsel concerning the use and misuse of the human tongue. Let us consider some sins of the tongue as revealed in God's word.

Tongue, the Lying: According to (Proverbs 25:18), "A man that beareth false witness against his neighbour is a maul, and a sword, and a sharp arrow." So a *lying tongue* is a misuse of a deadly weapon. It can be used to harm others near at hand (a maul), a few feet away (a sword), or a great distance away (an arrow). Satan is the father of lies (John 8:44), and God said that he hates a lying tongue (Proverb. 6:17). All liars will have their part in the lake of fire, according to (Revelation 21:8).

Tongue, the Flattering: Meaning and act of gratifying with praise; pleasing by applause; wheedling; coaxing. 2 A Pleasing to pride or vanity; gratifying to self-love; as a flattering eulogy. The minister gives a flattering account of his reception at court. 3 Pleasing; favorable; encouraging hope. We have a flattering prospect of an abundant harvest. The symptoms of the disease are flattering. 4 Practicing adulation; uttering false praise; as a flattering tongue.

2 Flattery is also a sin of the tongue. The Bible speaks of *flattery* as a characteristic of the wicked, not the righteous: "For there is no faithfulness in their mouth; their inward part is very wickedness; their throat is an open sepulchre; they *flatter* with their tongue." (Psalm 5:9) Imagine the improvements which could be made in our nation if voters elected leaders on the basis of the record rather than on the basis of the flattering

speeches! *Flattery* is just a form of lying, and it has no place in the life of a Christian.

Tongue, the Proud: The quality or state of being proud, is an adherence to pride which is an inordinate self-esteem, an unreasonable conceit of superiority(as in talents, beauty, rank, or wealth); such pride is personified as one of the seven deadly sins; 2 A sense of one's own worth and abhorrence of what is beneath or unworthy of oneself; lofty self-respect; 3 proud or disdainful treatment: insolence or arrogance of demeanor: disdain.

4 The Bible also speaks of *the proud tongue* as in (Psalm 12:3-4), "The LORD shall cut off all flattering lips, and the tongue that speaketh proud things: Who have said, With our tongue will we prevail; our lips are our own: who is lord over us?" The most annoying Christians in the world are those with *proud tongues* because a *proud tongue* usually comes with two closed ears! Proud- tongued Christians are generally so full of themselves that they learn very little from anyone else. A *proud-tongued* Christian will talk much of his knowledge and service, but very little about the Lord.

In a church, a *proud-tongued* Christian will make all sorts of suggestions about how the church should function, yet his suggestions, if received, will place burdens on everyone but himself. A *proud- tongued* Christian is hard to teach or reason with because he thinks he knows everything.

God hates a *proud tongue*. Allow the Holy Spirit to use your *tongue* in the way of humility and kindness because pride will only quench God's Spirit and damage your testimony.

Tongue, the Overused: Some people sin by simply overusing their tongue. (Ecclesiastes 5:3) says that "a fool's voice is known by multitude of words." People think they appear smart by much talking, but the Bible states just the opposite. (Ecclesiastes 5:2) says, "Be not rash with thy mouth, and let not thine heart be hasty to utter any thing before God: for God is in heaven, and thou upon earth: therefore let thy words be few." God doesn't like a blabber mouth. You can say, "Well, that's just the way I am!" Then Repent! Confess your sin and repent. Stop justifying your wickedness and ask God to help you repent. In the name of Jesus!

Tongue, the Swift: Some people are guilty of speaking too swiftly when they really need to wait before saying anything. God's word says the following in (Proverbs 18:13): "He that answereth a matter before he heareth it, it is folly and shame unto him." How many times have you had to "eat" your words because you spoke too swiftly? (James 1:19) warns us to be swift to HEAR and SLOW to speak. Why do you suppose God gave us two ears but only one mouth?

Tongue, the Backbiting:

In (Proverbs 25:23) and (Romans 1:30) make mention of a backbiting tongue. A backbiter is someone who uses their tongue against you when you aren't present, yet they will not face you with their charges when you are present. This is a cowardly backbiter who would rather stir up problems than solve problems.

A backbiter would much rather talk about the preacher than talk to the preacher. A backbiter would much rather talk about some weak Christian in the church than offer some words of encouragement to them. A backbiter is of no use to anyone, and no one has ever been strengthened or edified through backbiting. Beware of the backbiters, especially the ones who sow discord among brethren as in (Proverbs. 6:19)!

Tongue, the Talebearing:

(Proverbs 18:8) says, "The words of a talebearer are as wounds, and they go down into the innermost parts of the belly." (Leviticus 19:16) says, "Thou shalt not go up and down as a talebearer among thy people. . ." Every Christian has the duty to deny his own desires and seek to edify other Christians (Romans 14:19; Philip. 2:3). *Talebearing* runs wholly contrary to Christian edification. *Talebearing* (carrying and telling tales) spreads all sorts of hurtful information around, and Satan uses such information to hinder and tear down God's work. A victim of *talebearing*, according to Proverbs, is a "wounded" person. God forbid that a Christian should wound another Christian, but it does happen all the time! Some Christians live as though they think God has "called" them to bear tales on other Christians. Many "Christian" newsletters are dedicated to informing the body of Christ on the latest news about someone's ministry or personal life. There are many nice words and phrases used to justify such conduct, but the Bible word is Talebearing.

Tongue, the Cursing:

Some people, Christians included, have a nasty habit of using their tongue for cursing. (Romans 3:13-14) says, "Their throat is an open sepulchre; with their tongues they have used deceit; the poison of asps is under their lips: Whose mouth is full of *cursing* and bitterness." This passage deals strictly with unsaved people and their ungodly ways, yet there are a great many professing Christians who *curse* regularly. Friend, why would you want to identify yourself with someone whom God describes as being dead, deceitful, and poison? This does not make you an 'Heavenly bound Soul'

"As he loved cursing, so let it come unto him: as he delighted not in blessing, so let it be far from him.

As he clothed himself with cursing like as with his garment, so let it come into his bowels like water, and like oil into his bones."(Psalm 109:17-18) Many people curse because their life is miserable. They are unhappy so they make it known with their degenerate speech. This text says that God keeps them unhappy BECAUSE of their speech! God curses those who curse! Christian, don't expect God's blessings when your mouth is filled with *cursing.*

Tongue, the Piercing: Another sinful tongue is the *piercing tongue.* (Proverbs 12:18) speaks of this tongue by saying, "There is that speaketh like the *piercings* of a sword: but the tongue of the wise is health." Some people have a sharp *piercing tongue* which Satan uses to offend and insult others. The Bible commands Christians to have their speech dominated by GRACE (Colosians. 4:6), yet most churches have a few people who use their tongue like a sword to pierce their brethren in Christ.

It was Teddy Roosevelt who said, "Speak softly and carry a big stick," but the truth is that if you speak softly you won't need a big stick! (Titus 2:8) commands us to use sound speech which cannot be condemned. Every Christian's prayer should be, "Lord, make my words gracious and tender, for tomorrow I may have to eat them." In Jesus Name!

Tongue, the Silent: A *silent tongue* is also a sinful tongue because we have been commanded to speak up and witness for the Lord Jesus Christ. In (Acts 1:8), Jesus said, "But ye shall receive power, after that the Holy Ghost is come upon you: and ye shall be witnesses unto me both in Jerusalem, and in all Judaea, and in Samaria, and unto the uttermost part of the earth." We, as Christians, have an obligation to tell others about the saving grace of Jesus. To be silent about Christ is to sin against Christ. Jesus said, "Whosoever therefore shall be ashamed of me and of my words in this adulterous and sinful generation; of him also shall the Son of man be ashamed, when he cometh in the glory of his Father with the holy angels." (Mark 8:38); Christian-friend, if you do not want to be ashamed of yourself when the Lord returns, then don't be ashamed of Jesus today. Pray for opportunities to speak up for your Saviour. Don't be found guilty of having a *silent tongue.* All Glory to His Name be given! Amen!

Transgression: (noun: Greek: *paraptóma* - [par-ap'-to-mah], Hebrew: *pasha* – [peh'-shah]; a falling away, lapse, slip, false step, trespass, sin; an act that goes against a law, rule, or code of conduct; an offence. Wrong-doing; a violation of a law.

Surely thou hast spoken in mine hearing, and I have heard the voice of thy words, saying, I am clean

Trespass

without Transgression, I am innocent; neither is there iniquity in me. (Job 33:8-9) 2 "I'll be keeping an eye out for further transgressions" synonyms: offence, crime, sin, wrong, wrongdoing, misdemeanour, felony, misdeed, lawbreaking, vice, evil-doing, indiscretion, peccadillo, mischief, mischievousness, wickedness, misbehaviour, bad behaviour; Travail:

3 *Transgression* refers to presumptuous sin. It means "to choose to intentionally disobey; willful trespassing." Samson intentionally broke his Nazirite vow by touching a dead lion (Numbers 6:1–5; Judges 14:8–9) and allowing his hair to be cut (Judges 16:17); in doing so he was committing a *transgression*. David was referring to this kind of sin when he wrote, "Blessed is the one whose *transgressions* are forgiven, whose sins are covered" (Psalm 32:1). When we knowingly run a stop sign, tell a lie, or blatantly disregard an authority, we are *transgressing*.

Trespass: (Noun, Greek: *paraptóma* [par-ap'-to-mah], Hebrew: *maal* [mah'-al], a falling away, lapse, slip, false step, trespass, sin. (Also, tres·passed, tres··pass·ing, tres·pass·es) 1. Law To commit an unlawful injury to the person, property, or rights of another, with actual or implied force or violence, especially to enter onto another's land wrongfully.2. To infringe on the privacy, time, or attention of another: "I must ... not trespass too far on the patience of a good-natured critic" (Henry Fielding).3. To commit an offense or a sin; transgress or err.n. (trĕs'păs') 1. Law; a. The act of trespassing. b. A suit brought for trespassing.2 An intrusion or infringement on another.3 The transgression of a moral or social law, code, or duty. See Synonyms at breach

References: (Luke 11:2-4) And he said to them, "When you pray, say: "Father, hallowed be your name. Your kingdom come. Give us each day our daily bread, and forgive us our sins, for we ourselves forgive everyone who is indebted to us. And lead us not into temptation." (Matthew 18:15-17) "If your brother sins against you, go and tell him his fault, between you and him alone. If he listens to you, you have gained your brother. But if he does not listen, take one or two others along with you, that every charge may be established by the evidence of two or three witnesses. If he refuses to listen to them, tell it to the church. And if he refuses to listen even to the church, let him be to you as a Gentile and a tax collector. (Psalm 91:3) For he will deliver you from the snare of the fowler and from the deadly pestilence. (1 Corinthians 10:13) No temptation has overtaken you that is not common to man. God is faithful, and he will not let you be tempted beyond your ability, but with the temptation he will also provide the way of escape, that you may be able to endure it. (Romans 8:1) There is therefore now no condemnation for those who are in Christ Jesus. (1 John 1:9) If we confess our sins, he is faithful and just to forgive us our sins and to cleanse us from all unrighteousness.

(John 1:1-51) In the beginning was the Word, and the Word was with God, and the Word was God. He was in the beginning with God. All things were made through him, and without him was not any thing made that was made. In him was life, and the life was the light of men. The light shines in the darkness, and the darkness has not overcome it. ... (Luke 23:34) And Jesus said, "Father, forgive them, for they know not what they do." And they cast lots to divide his garments. (Genesis 1:1-31) In the beginning, God created the heavens and the earth. The earth was without form and void, and darkness was over the face of the deep. And the Spirit of God was hovering over the face of the waters. And God said, "Let there be light," and there was light. And God saw that the light was good. And God separated the light from the darkness. God called the light Day, and the darkness he called Night. And there was evening and there was morning, the first day. ... (Revelation 22:1-21) Then the angel showed me the river of the water of life, bright as crystal, flowing from the throne of God and of the Lamb through the middle of the street of the city; also, on either side of the river, the tree of life with its twelve kinds of fruit, yielding its fruit each month. The leaves of the tree were for the healing of the nations. No longer will there be anything accursed, but the throne of God and of the Lamb will be in it, and his servants will worship him. They will see his face, and his name will be on their foreheads. And night will be no more. They will need no light of lamp or sun, for the Lord God will be their light, and they will reign forever and ever. ... (Revelation 21:1-27)

Tribulation: (Noun, Greek: thlipsis [thlip'-sis] Hebrew: tsarah [tsaw-raw'], persecution, affliction, distress, tribulation.

2 The *Tribulation* is a future time period when the Lord will accomplish at least two aspects of His plan: He will complete His discipline of the nation Israel (Daniel 9:24), and He will judge the unbelieving, godless inhabitants of the earth (Revelation 6 - 18). The length of the Tribulation is seven years. This is determined by an understanding of the seventy weeks of Daniel (Daniel 9:24-27); also see the article on the Tribulation). The Great Tribulation is the last half of the Tribulation period, three and one-half years in length. It is distinguished from the Tribulation period because the Beast, or Antichrist, will be revealed, and the wrath of God will greatly intensify during this time. Thus, it is important at this point to emphasize that the Tribulation and the Great

Tribulation, the great

Tribulation are not synonymous terms. Within eschatology (the study of future things), the Tribulation refers to the full seven-year period while the "Great Tribulation" refers to the second half of the Tribulation

Tribulation, the great: This refers to the second half of the tribulation   It is Christ Himself who used the phrase Great Tribulation with reference to the last half of the Tribulation. In (Matthew 24:21), Jesus says, "For then there will be a great tribulation, such as has not occurred since the beginning of the world until now, nor ever shall." In this verse Jesus is referring to the event of (Matthew 24:15), which describes the revealing of the abomination of desolation, the man also known as the Antichrist. Also, Jesus in (Matthew 24:29-30) states, "Immediately after the tribulation of those days . . . the Son of Man will appear in the sky, and then all the tribes of the earth will mourn, and they will see the Son of Man coming on the clouds of the sky with power and great glory." In this passage, Jesus defines the Great Tribulation (verse.21) as beginning with the revealing of the abomination of desolation (verse.15) and ending with Christ's second coming (verse.30). Other passages that refer to the Great Tribulation are (Daniel 12:1b), which says, "And there will be a time of distress such as never occurred since there was a nation until that time." Here, it seems that Jesus was quoting this verse when He spoke the words recorded in (Matthew 24:21). Also referring to the Great Tribulation is (Jeremiah 30:7), "Alas! for that day is great, There is none like it; And it is the time of Jacob's distress, But he will be saved from it." The phrase "Jacob's distress" refers to the nation of Israel, which will experience persecution and natural disasters such as have never before been seen.

2 Considering the information Christ gave us in (Matthew 24:15-30), it is easy to conclude that the beginning of the Great Tribulation has much to do with the abomination of desolation, an action of the Antichrist. In (Daniel 9:26-27), we find that this man will make a "covenant" (a peace pact) with the world for seven years. Halfway through the seven-year period—"in the middle of the week"—we are told this man will break the covenant he made, stopping sacrifice and grain offering, which specifically refers to his actions in the rebuilt temple of the future. (Revelation 13:1-10) gives even more detail concerning the Beast's actions, and just as important, it also verifies the length of time he will be in power. (Revelation 13:5) says he will be in power for 42 months, which is three and one-half years, the length of *the Great Tribulation*.

3 Revelation offers us the most information about *the Great Tribulation*. From (Revelation 13) when the Beast is revealed until Christ returns in (Revelation 19), we are

given a picture of God's wrath on the earth because of unbelief and rebellion (Revelation 16-18). It is also a picture of how God disciplines and at the same time protects His people Israel (Revelation 14:1-5) until He keeps His promise to Israel by establishing an earthly kingdom (Revelation 20:4-6)."And I saw thrones, and they sat upon them, and judgment was given unto them: and I saw the souls of them that were beheaded for the witness of Jesus, and for the word of God, and which had not worshipped the beast, neither his image, neither had received his mark upon their foreheads, or in their hands; and they lived and reigned with Christ a thousand years. But the rest of the dead lived not again until the thousand years were finished. This is the first resurrection. Blessed and holy is he that hath part in the first resurrection: on such the second death hath no power, but they shall be priests of God and of Christ, and shall reign with him a thousand years" Hallelujah!

Trouble: (Verb, Greek: tarassó - [tar-as'-so], Hebrew: akar [aw-kar'] disturb, agitate, stir up, trouble. Everyone has troubles. We face problems, affliction, suffering, and hardship. We need strength, endurance, and patience

"Man who is born of woman is of few days and full of *trouble*" (Job 14:1). We can especially appreciate these words when we think of the suffering endured by the one who spoke them. Different people deal with different problems and afflictions, and it seems that some suffer more hardships than others do. But we all know by personal experience and from the experiences of those we know, that Job's statement is true. *Troubles* concern us, not just because hardship itself is a burden, but also because affliction can lead to spiritual temptations. We may be tempted to feel that our trials justify committing sin. We may become so discouraged that we blame God for our troubles, lose faith in Him, or begin to doubt His goodness and mercy. As Job's wife said, "Curse God and die" (Job 2:9).

2 Literally as (noun) difficulty or problems.synonyms:problems, difficulty, issues, bother, inconvenience, worry, anxiety, distress, concern, disquiet, unease, irritation, vexation, annoyance, stress, agitation, harassment, unpleasantness; More the malfunction of something such as a machine or a part of the body., synonyms: disease, illness, sickness, ailment, complaint, problem; effort or exertion made to do something, especially when inconvenient., "I wouldn't want to put you to any trouble"synonyms: bother, inconvenience, fuss, effort, exertion, work, labour; a cause of worry or inconvenience., "the kid had been no trouble up to now" synonyms: nuisance, bother, inconvenience, irritation, irritant, problem, trial, pest, cause

True

of annoyance, source of difficulty, thorn in someone's flesh or side; More a particular aspect of something regarded as unsatisfactory or as a source of difficulty. "that's the trouble with capitalism" synonyms: shortcoming, weakness, weak point, failing, fault, imperfection, defect, blemish; More

a situation in which one is liable to incur punishment or blame. "he's been in trouble with the police" informal dated used to refer to the condition of a pregnant unmarried woman.

3. Public unrest or disorder."there was crowd trouble before and during the match" synonyms: disturbance, disorder, unrest, bother, fighting, scuffling, conflict, tumult, commotion, turbulence, uproar, ructions, fracas, rumpus, brouhaha, furore, breach of the peace; any of various periods of civil war or unrest in Ireland, especially in 1919–23 and (in Northern Ireland) since 1968.

plural proper noun: Troubles; plural noun: the Troubles "he was not troubled by doubts" synonyms: worry, bother, cause concern to, concern, disturb, upset, make anxious, make uncomfortable, make uneasy, agitate, distress, grieve, alarm, perturb, annoy, irritate, vex, irk, torment, plague, nag, niggle, gnaw at, prey on someone's mind, weigh/lie heavy on someone's mind, oppress, weigh down, burden, afflict; More

True: (Adjective, Greek: *aléthinos* [al-ay-thee-nos'], Hebrew: *Emet*, (literally: made of truth), real, genuine. *See* (*truth*) below.

Truth: (Noun, Greek: *alétheia* – [al-ay'-thi-a]; Hebrew: *emeth* [eh'-meth], *truth*, but not merely *truth* as spoken; *truth* of idea, reality, sincerity, *truth* in the moral sphere, divine *truth* revealed to man, straightforwardness. Truth is "the true or actual state of a matter ...; conformity with fact or reality ...; a verified or indisputable fact uniquely revealed in the Gospel as the character of Christ, His teachings and His promises. Anything that does not agree with the Bible is false, error, deception or heresy.

2 In the night before His crucifixion, Jesus offered a heartfelt prayer to His Father on behalf of His disciples—not only those of that day, but also those who would follow Him in the future. Within the context of that prayer, He said, "Sanctify (set apart) them by Your *truth*. Your word is *truth* (John 17:17). Here, Christ is saying one should be able to examine the pages of God's Word—the Holy Bible—to learn the *truth* on any subject of major importance or significance. The Bible contains the answers to questions about why we were born, our purpose in life, whether God exists and the potential of mankind—to name only a few of the subjects covered within the Gospel.

3 The Psalmist wrote similarly: "The entirety of Your word is *truth*" (Psalm 119:160). Interestingly, the word *truth* can be found more than 200 times in Scripture. Also, in an interesting twist on the above, Jesus said to Thomas, "I am the way, the *truth*, and the life" (John 14:6).

4 Paul said to the Ephesians, "If indeed you have heard Him and have been taught by Him, as the *truth* is in Jesus" (Ephesians 4:21). Christ, as God, is the personification of *truth*. He embodies *truth*. Again, Paul, in the introductory comments in his epistle to Titus, said, "Paul, a bondservant of God and an apostle of Jesus Christ, according to the faith of God's elect and the acknowledgement of the *truth* which accords with godliness, in hope of eternal life which God, who cannot lie, promised before time began" (Titus 1:1-2).

5 Jesus said to those Jews who believed Him, "If you abide in My word, you are My disciples indeed and you shall know the *truth*, and the *truth* shall make you free" (John 8:31-32). Knowing the *truth* freed the disciples from deceptions, errors and heresies.

6 Moreover, Christ said that Satan, who as Lucifer had known the *truth*, did not abide in the *truth*. Rebuking the Pharisees who did not believe in Him, Jesus told them they were of their father the devil. He went on to say, "He [the devil] was a murderer from the beginning, and does not stand in the *truth*, because there is no *truth* in him. When he speaks a lie, he speaks from his own resources, for he is a liar and the father of it" (John 8:44).

Truth, Spiritual force against: Significantly, this is monumental revelation for God is the source of *truth* through His Word. Jesus embodied *truth*. And an evil being who is dedicated to falsifying *truth* is at work in our world! People should be wary of their belief that "truth is not absolute." Where did that concept originate? It came from Satan, "the father of lies." Satan lies now and he has throughout history, literally deceiving the entire human race (Revelation 12:9). Countless people think they have "discovered" an idea that he simply plants in their minds.

2 Notice the warning Paul gave in the concluding comments of his first letter to Timothy, "O Timothy! Guard what was committed to your trust, avoiding the profane and idle babblings and contradictions of what is falsely called knowledge—by professing it some have strayed concerning the faith" (1 Timothy 6:20-21).

Truth, Science not the source of: Many people believe that science can reveal truth. But Kathy Sykes, a British physicist and professor at the University of

Bristol, explains, "Science is not about truth, but is about trying to get closer to the truth. This is important, because, too often, people look to scientists as having the 'truth.' What we have is wrapped in uncertainties, caveats and simplifications."

Truth, absolute: Absolute is defined as "free from imperfection; complete; perfect." The word truth is defined as "the true or actual state of a matter ...; conformity with fact or reality ...; a verified or indisputable fact." Philosophers and scientists have debated the issue of absolute truth for centuries. Moreover, many others have chosen to accept another philosophy, called situation ethics. Situation ethics is defined as "a theory of ethics according to which moral rules are not absolutely binding but may be modified in the light of specific situations",

Ironically, if one were to say, "There is no such thing as absolute truth," he or she might be asked, "Are you absolutely sure that no absolute truth exists?" To make such a statement is itself the claim of an absolute truth and, therefore, self-contradictory! For example, just because one may choose not to believe in the law of gravity does not mean that gravity does not exist. The same can be said of God's existence. What one person believes about God's existence has nothing to do with the fact that He indeed exists! Indeed, people would have to admit that they don't know whether there is absolute truth about a specific subject. Yet God, through the pages of the Bible, states that absolute truth truly does exist.

Truth, Worship must be in: Knowledge of "the *truth*" is essential for worship. Notice what Jesus said to a Samaritan woman He met by Jacob's well. "But the hour is coming, and now is, when the true worshipers will worship the Father in spirit and truth; for the Father is seeking such to worship Him. God is Spirit, and those who worship Him must worship in spirit and truth" (John 4:23-24).

On one occasion, even Christ's enemies, the Pharisees, admitted to Him, "Teacher, we know that You are true, and teach the way of God in truth" (Matthew 22:16). Although they likely said this tongue in cheek—for they were trying to trick Christ in this situation—their description of Him was true. God speaks of His Holy Spirit as a Spirit of *truth* that would eventually guide those who believed in Him into all *truth* (John 16:13).

By looking at David and Paul's example, we notice the examples of a few faithful people of God who understood that God had absolute *truth*. David prayed, "Lead me in Your *truth* and teach me" (Psalm 25:5). Speaking to the Ephesians, Paul reminded them that "in Him [God] you also trusted, after you heard the word of *truth*, the gospel of your salvation" (Ephesians 1:13).

To members of the Church of God in Colossae, Paul wrote, "Because of the hope which is laid up for you in heaven, of which you heard before in the word of the truth of the gospel" (Colossians 1:5). The gospel Christ and the apostles preached was the *truth* of the coming Kingdom of God.

Furthermore, Paul reminded Timothy to be diligent and accurate in explaining and expounding the Word of God. "Be diligent to present yourself approved to God, a worker who does not need to be ashamed, rightly dividing [correctly presenting] the word of truth" (2 Timothy 2:15). The "word of truth" is the Bible beie Gospel of ng preached throughout the Gospel of Christ. Paul also told Timothy, "I write so that you may know how you ought to conduct yourself in the house of God, which is the church of the living God, the pillar and ground [foundation] of the *truth*" (1Timothy 3:15). Paul is saying that there is also a "true Church" and that the *truth* can be found in it.

Truth, Act on the: Jesus said God's Word, the Bible, is truth (John 17:17).•Christ, as God, is the personification of truth (John 14:6; Ephesians 4:21). •God cannot lie (Titus 1:1-2). •Satan does lie unabashedly! And we have to be on guard against his attacks on the truth (Revelation 12:9). •Jesus promised His disciples that they would know the truth (John 8:31-32). •Truth is revealed in God's Word—not through science. •God will only accept worship of Him "in spirit and truth" (John 4:24).

2 Knowing the *truth* is wonderful, but it is not enough! God expects us to act on the *truth* as He helps us learn it. More important than knowing the *truth* is living the *truth*—walking in *truth*. Wisdom, knowledge, understanding and *truth* are all attributes of God. You can know the *truth* if you diligently and prayerfully seek for it. "Yes, if you cry out for discernment, and lift up your voice for understanding, if you seek her as silver, and search for her as for hidden treasures; then you will understand the fear of the LORD, and find the knowledge [truth] of God. For the LORD gives wisdom; from His mouth comes knowledge and understanding" (Proverbs 2:3-6). This is the absolute *truth*! Praise the God of truth! Hallelujah!!

Uu

Unbelief: (Greek and Hebrew: *apistia*, [ap-is-tee'-ah]) meaning unfaithfulness, distrust. Unbelief took the form of a doubt of the divine veracity, or a mistrust of God's power as in (2 Kings 7:19)

"And that lord answered the man of God, and said, Now, behold, if the Lord should make windows in heaven, might such a thing be? And he said, Behold, thou shalt see it with thine eyes but shalt not eat thereof"

The king was a sinner of the blackest dye, his iniquity was glaring and infamous. Jehoram walked in the ways of his father Ahab, and made unto himself false gods. The people of Samaria were fallen like their monarch: they had gone astray from Jehovah; they had forsaken the God of Israel; they remembered not the watchword of Jacob, "The Lord thy God is one God;" and in wicked idolatry they bowed before the idols of the heathens, and therefore the Lord of Hosts suffered their enemies to oppress them until the curse of Ebal was fulfilled in the streets of Samaria, for "the tender and delicate woman who would not adventure to set the sole of her foot upon the ground for delicateness," had an evil eye to her own children, and devoured her offspring by reason of fierce hunger (Deuteronomy 28:56-58). In this awful extremity the one holy man was the medium of salvation. The one grain of salt preserved the entire city; the one warrior for God was the means of the deliverance of the whole beleaguered multitude. For Elisha's sake the Lord sent the promise that the next day, food which could not be obtained at any price, should be had at the cheapest possible rate—at the very gates of Samaria. We may picture the joy of the multitude when first the seer uttered this prediction. They knew him to be a prophet of the Lord; he had divine credentials; all his past prophecies had been fulfilled. They knew that he was a man sent of God, and uttering Jehovah's message. Surely the monarch's eyes would glisten with delight, and the emaciated multitude would leap for joy at the prospects of so speedy a release from famine. "To-morrow," would they shout, "to-morrow our hunger shall be over, and we shall feast to the full." Hallelujah!

However, the lord on whom the king leaned expressed his disbelief. We hear not that any of the common people, the plebeians, ever did so; but an aristocrat did it. Strange it is, that God has seldom chosen the great men of this world. High places and faith in Christ do seldom well agree. This great man said, "Impossible!" and, with an insult to the prophet, he added, "If the Lord should make windows in heaven, might such a thing be." His sin lay in the fact, that after repeated seals of Elisha's ministry, he yet disbelieved the assurances uttered by the prophet on God's behalf. He had, doubtless, seen the marvellous defeat of Moab; he had been startled at tidings of the resurrection of the Shunamite's son; he knew that Elisha had revealed Benhadad's secrets and smitten his marauding hosts with blindness; he had seen the bands of Syria decoyed into the heart of Samaria; and he probably knew the story of the widow, whose oil filled all the vessels, and redeemed her sons; at all events the cure of Naaman was common conversation at court; and yet, in the face of all this accumulated evidence, in the teeth of all these credentials of the prophet's mission, he yet doubted, and insultingly told him that heaven must become an open casement, ere the promise could be performed. Whereupon God pronounced his doom by the mouth of the man who had just now proclaimed the promise: "thou shalt see it with thine eyes, but shalt not eat thereof." And providence—which always fulfils prophecy, just as the paper takes the stamp of the type—destroyed the man. Trodden down in the streets of Samaria, he perished at its gates, beholding the plenty, but tasting not of it. Perhaps his carriage was haughty and insulting to the people; or he tried to restrain their eager rush; or, as we would say, it might have been by mere accident that he was crushed to death; so that he saw the prophecy fulfilled, but never lived to enjoy it. In his case, seeing believed, but it was not enjoying. Always belief in God evermore!

Referrences (Mark 9:24) "And Jesus said to him, "'If You can?' All things are possible to him who believes." Immediately the boy's father cried out and said, "I do believe; help my unbelief." When Jesus saw that a crowd was rapidly gathering, He rebuked the unclean spirit, saying to it, "You deaf and mute spirit, I command you, come out of him and do not enter him again."... which the LORD had commanded them not to do like them. Nehemiah 9:16 Self Will Pride, Results Of Forgetting God Necks Stubbornness Self-Justification "But they, our fathers, acted arrogantly; They became stubborn and would not listen to Your commandments. (Psalms 78:17-19) Yet they still continued

Unbelief

to sin against Him, To rebel against the Most High in the desert. And in their heart they put God to the test By asking food according to their desire. Then they spoke against God; They said, "Can God prepare a table in the wilderness? (Psalms 95:8-11) Stiff necked People Do not harden your hearts, as at Meribah, As in the day of Massah in the wilderness, "When your fathers tested Me, They tried Me, though they had seen My work. "For forty years I loathed that generation, And said they are a people who err in their heart, And they do not know My ways. read more. "Therefore I swore in My anger, Truly they shall not enter into My rest." (Mark 6:1-6) Preaching, Effects Of Resentment, Against God denial of Jesus Christ Jesus went out from there and came into His hometown; and His disciples followed Him. When the Sabbath came, He began to teach in the synagogue; and the many listeners were astonished, saying, "Where did this man get these things, and what is this wisdom given to Him, and such miracles as these performed by His hands? "Is not this the carpenter, the son of Mary, and brother of James and Joses and Judas and Simon? Are not His sisters here with us?" And they took offense at Him. read more.Jesus said to them, "A prophet is not without honor except in his hometown and among his own relatives and in his own household." And He could do no miracle there except that He laid His hands on a few sick people and healed them. And He wondered at their unbelief. And He was going around the villages teaching. (Luke 4:14-30) And Jesus returned to Galilee in the power of the Spirit, and news about Him spread through all the surrounding district. And He began teaching in their synagogues and was praised by all. And He came to Nazareth, where He had been brought up; and as was His custom, He entered the synagogue on the Sabbath, and stood up to read. read more.And the book of the prophet Isaiah was handed to Him. And He opened the book and found the place where it was written, "the spirit of the lord is upon me, because he anointed me to preach the gospel to the poor. he has sent me to proclaim release to the captives, and recovery of sight to the blind, to set free those who are oppressed, to proclaim the favorable year of the Lord." And He closed the book, gave it back to the attendant and sat down; and the eyes of all in the synagogue were fixed on Him. And He began to say to them, "Today this Scripture has been fulfilled in your hearing." And all were speaking well of Him, and wondering at the gracious words which were falling from His lips; and they were saying, "Is this not Joseph's son?" And He said to them, "No doubt you will quote this proverb to Me, 'Physician, heal yourself! Whatever we heard was done at Capernaum, do here in your hometown as well.'" And He said, "Truly I say to you, no prophet is welcome in his hometown. "But I say to you in truth, there were many widows in Israel in the days of Elijah, when the sky was shut up for three years and six months, when a great famine came over all the land; and yet Elijah was sent to none of them, but only to Zarephath, in the land of Sidon, to a woman who was a widow. "And there were many lepers in Israel in the time of Elisha the prophet; and none of them was cleansed, but only Naaman the Syrian." And all the people in the synagogue were filled with rage as they heard these things; and they got up and drove Him out of the city, and led Him to the brow of the hill on which their city had been built, in order to throw Him down the cliff. But passing through their midst, He went His way. (Matthew 12:22-24) Pharisees, Attitudes To Jesus Christ. Then a demon-possessed man who was blind and mute was brought to Jesus, and He healed him, so that the mute man spoke and saw. All the crowds were amazed, and were saying, "This man cannot be the Son of David, can he?" But when the Pharisees heard this, they said, "This man casts out demons only by Beelzebul the ruler of the demons." (Mark 3:22) Confusion Pharisees, Attitudes To Jesus ChristFalse Gods Satan, Kingdom Of Beelzebub Blasphemy, Against The Holy Spirit Jesus Casting Out Demons Princes Unforgivable Sin False Accusations, Examples Of The scribes who came down from Jerusalem were saying, "He is possessed by Beelzebul," and "He casts out the demons by the ruler of the demons." (Luke 11:14-16) And He was casting out a demon, and it was mute; when the demon had gone out, the mute man spoke; and the crowds were amazed. But some of them said, "He casts out demons by Beelzebul, the ruler of the demons." Others, to test Him, were demanding of Him a sign from heaven. (Acts 19:9) Unbelief, Results Of Being Guilty Obstinate Individuals Way, The evangelism, kinds of Discussions Unbelief, Sourced In Schools Unbelief, Examples Of But when some were becoming hardened and disobedient, speaking evil of the Way before the people, he withdrew from them and took away the disciples, reasoning daily in the school of Tyrannus. (Acts 28:24) Not Believing The Gospel Faithlessness, As Disobedience Some were being persuaded by the things spoken, but others would not believe. (Titus 1:15) Fall Of Man, Consequences Of Sex Within Marriage Imagination, Evil Scheming Not Believing The Gospel Evil Hearts The Carnal Mind Purity, Moral And Spiritual To the pure, all things are pure; but to those who are defiled and unbelieving, nothing is pure, but both their mind and their conscience are defiled. (Romans 1:18) Godlessness Unbelief, Nature

Understand

And Effects Of Unrighteousness Ungodliness Those Against Truth Malice Absolute Truth Hiding Sins Astrology Propitiation Impiety Divine Displeasure Punishment, By God Sin, And God's Character Agnosticism God's Intolerance Of Evil Honesty For the wrath of God is revealed from heaven against all ungodliness and unrighteousness of men who suppress the truth in unrighteousness, (2 Thessalonians 2:12) Love, Abuse Of Not Believing The Gospel Sin, Love Of Faith, Necessity Of Pleasure Unbelief, Nature And Effects Of Delighting, Wrong Kinds Of Faithlessness, As Disobedience Unbelief, Results Of Being Guilty in order that they all may be judged who did not believe the truth, but took pleasure in wickedness. (2 Thessalonians 3:2) Spiritual Warfare, As Conflict Faithlessness, As Disobedience and that we will be rescued from perverse and evil men; for not all have faith. (1 Timothy 1:1) Unbelief, Examples Of God's Mercy, Example Of Moral Bankruptcy Faithlessness, As Disobedience Blasphemy, Examples Of Ignorance Of Evil Persecution, Forms Of Unbelievers Not Believing The Gospel Ignorance Towards God, Examples Of Sin, Nature Of even though I was formerly a blasphemer and a persecutor and a violent aggressor Yet I was shown mercy because I acted ignorantly in unbelief; (Nehemiah 9:16-17) Forgiveness, Divine Stubbornness, Consequences Of Forgetting God, Patience Of doubt, results of" But they, our fathers, acted arrogantly; They became stubborn and would not listen to Your commandments. "They refused to listen, And did not remember Your wondrous deeds which You had performed among them; So they became stubborn and appointed a leader to return to their slavery in Egypt But You are a God of forgiveness, Gracious and compassionate, Slow to anger and abounding in loving kindness; And You did not forsake them.

Understand (Understanding) (Greek – *nous* - [nooce] Hebrew - *Binah* – [bee-naw'] meaning the mind, reasoning faculty, intellect) the ability to understand something; comprehension. sympathetic awareness or tolerance. an informal or unspoken agreement or arrangement. Adjective sympathetically aware of other people's feelings; tolerant and forgiving, having insight or good judgement. (Psalms 119:127) - Therefore I love thy commandments above gold; yea, above fine gold. (Job 28:12-13) - But where shall wisdom be found? and where [is] the place of understanding? (Read More...) (Proverbs 3:1-35) - My son, forget not my law; but let thine heart keep my commandments: (Read More...) (Proverbs 19:21) - [There are] many devices in a man's heart; nevertheless the counsel of the LORD, that shall stand. (Proverbs 3:3-10) - Let not mercy and truth forsake thee: bind them about thy neck; write them upon the table of

Ungodly

thine heart: (Read More...) (Proverbs 2:1-11) - My son, if thou wilt receive my words, and hide my commandments with thee; (Read More...) Ephesians 1:18 - The eyes of your understanding being enlightened; that ye may know what is the hope of his calling, and what the riches of the glory of his inheritance in the saints, Hebrews 11:3 - Through faith we understand that the worlds were framed by the word of God, so that things which are seen were not made of things which do appear. Luke 6:22-31 - Blessed are ye, when men shall hate you, and when they shall separate you [from their company], and shall reproach [you], and cast out your name as evil, for the Son of man's sake. (Read More...) (James 3:13-18) - Who [is] a wise man and endued with knowledge among you? let him shew out of a good conversation his works with meekness of wisdom. (Read More...) (Ecclesiastes 3:1-12) - To every [thing there is] a season, and a time to every purpose under the heaven: (Proverbs 3:5) - Trust in the LORD with all thine heart; and lean

Ungodly: (adjective, Greek - asebés [as-eb-ace'] Hebrew – *avil* [av-eel'] - meaning ruffians impious, ungodly, wicked, Ruffians, 1 irreligious or immoral. 2 unreasonably early or inconvenient as in (Psalm 1:1), "Blessed is the man that walketh not in the counsel of the *ungodly*, nor standeth in the way of sinners, nor sitteth in the seat of the scornful." It is inevitable that we will be given *ungodly* advice at times in our life, but we ought not walk in that direction. Often times, everyone've had some ungodly advice given to us at times in our life, but thankful that we didn't walk in that advice. Ungodly counsel abounds everywhere.

3 bad, evil - tall - thin - vile – weak, awful - frail - nasty - rough – thick, absurd - adamic - carnal - cursed - erring - fallen - impure - infirm - lapsed - sinful - ungood - unholy - wanton – wicked, beastly - corrupt - demonic - dubious - fleshly - godless - heinous - hellish - immoral - impious - profane - satanic - suspect - unclean - ungodly – wayward, a bit thin - damnable - demoniac - depraved - devilish - diabolic - doubtful - dreadful - fiendish - ghoulish - improper - indecent - infernal - peccable - prodigal - shocking - terrible - unchaste - unseemly – untoward, a bit thick - appalling - atheistic - barbarous - doubtable - dubitable - execrable - frightful - heretical - monstrous - unangelic - unearthly - unsaintly demoniacal - diabolical - flagitious - incredible - indecorous - indelicate - iniquitous - irreverent - malodorous - outrageous - recidivist - ridiculous - suspicious - un-christly - unbecoming - undecorous - unhallowed - unvirtuous - villainous – virtueless, backsliding - blasphemous - implausible - irreligious - open to doubt - problematic - unchristian - uncivilised - uncivilized

Ungodly, the counsel of

- unrighteous – unthinkable, beyond belief - hard of belief - iconoclastic - of easy virtue - preposterous - questionable - recidivistic - sacrilegious - unbelievable - unconvincing - unimaginable hard to believe - inconceivable - passing belief - postlapsarian - problematical unconscionable, not to be believed - open to suspicion, staggering belief - unworthy of belief, not deserving belief.

Ungodly, the counsel of:
The "counsel of the *ungodly*" is *ungodly* advice coming from ungodly people. Those people who defend homosexuality are ungodly people. Anyone who says "gay is ok" is giving ungodly advice. God hates homosexuality. (Romans 1:18), "For the wrath of God is revealed from Heaven against all ungodliness and unrighteousness of men, who hold the truth in unrighteousness." Anyone who recommends a divorce is *ungodly*, and is giving ungodly advice. God hates divorce (Malachi 2:16; Jeremiah 3:20; Matthew 19:8; Mark 10:9; Matthew 18:22). Only an *ungodly* person would break apart a marriage. Divorce is a sin and so is remarriage for the one who quit. The Bible warns us not to walk in *the counsel of the ungodly*. Unforgiveness, breaking one's lifetime vows and quitting are always the *ungodly* thing to do in a marriage. The world nations now become an ungodly nation of liars, quitters and self-righteous hypocrites. No one has a God-given right to divorce. Just as homosexuals and abortionists pervert the Scriptures to justify their sins, so do quitters twist the Bible to justify divorce.

2 Getting an abortion is *ungodly* advice. The biggest misnomer in the world is the bogus phrase "Planned Parenthood." Where does the "planning" part fit in with an abortion? How is getting an abortion planning to be a mother? What a bunch of deceitful liars. They talk about planning to be a parent, when that is not the goal at all. The plan is to kill the child, curb the world's population and convince the ungodly mother that she did the right thing. Planned Parenthood is the leading provider of abortion services in the Western World. They are an ungodly organization, who give ungodly advice, and only ungodly people walk in the counsel of the ungodly.

3 The bogus teachings of Evolution are *the counsel of the ungodly*. You cannot hold to a literal Biblical view while also believing the nonsense of Evolution. There is not one shred of evidence in support of Evolution. Try as they may, the world's top scientists have never been able to validate the theories of Evolution. The Missing Link will always be missing, because it doesn't exist in reality. To teach impressionable children that they evolved from slime is a sin. God spoke the universe into existence; but he formed mankind with His own hands from the dust

of the earth (Genesis 2:7). Instead of teaching children that they are the object of God's love, lovingly designed by a divine God; they are robbed of God and truth in their life. The theories of Evolution are *ungodly counsel.*

4 Feminism is ungodly counsel. Feminism is rebellion. The gospel teaches the word in the Bible in (1 Samuel 15:23) that "rebellion is as the sin of witchcraft, and stubbornness is as iniquity and idolatry." Rebellion is the same as witchcraft. There are several other forms of ungodly counsel not mentioned herein. Clubs and dancers of Rock 'n Roll, the lying media, worldly dressing, Clients of a Psychics, etc. Without the knowledge of sin there can be no healing of the soul, for to get right with God, one must first acknowledge their debt of sin before God. Modern psychology attempts to repair the human soul without addressing the reality of sin, like a foolhardy lion-tamer who sticks his head in a hungry lion's mouth. The human sin-nature cannot be tamed. Men do not need education, reformation, nor rehabilitation; but rather, regeneration by the Holy Spirit of the Lord Jesus Christ (Romans 8:9; 2nd Corinthians 5:17).

Unrighteousness: Not righteous; wicked. 2 Not right or fair; unjust abomination, star baseness, star crime, star evildoing, star heinousness, star immorality, star infamy, star injustice, star misdeed, star offense, star, sinfulness, star unfairness, star wickedness, star wrong, star wrongdoing, star discrepancy.

References: (Exodus 23:1) Thou shalt not raise a false report: put not thine hand with the wicked to be an unrighteous witness. (Leviticus 19:15) Ye shall do no unrighteousness in judgment: thou shalt not respect the person of the poor, nor honour the person of the mighty: but in righteousness shalt thou judge thy neighbour. (Leviticus 19:35) Ye shall do no unrighteousness in judgment, in met yard, in weight, or in measure. (Deuteronomy 25:16) For all that do such things, and all that do unrighteously, are an abomination unto the LORD thy God. (Job 27:7) Let mine enemy be as the wicked, and he that riseth up against me as the unrighteous. (Psalms 71:4) Deliver me, O my God, out of the hand of the wicked, out of the hand of the unrighteous and cruel man. (Psalms 92:15) To shew that the LORD is upright: he is my rock, and there is no unrighteousness in him. (Isaiah 10:1) Woe unto them that decree unrighteous decrees, and that write grievousness which they have prescribed; (Isaiah 55:7) Let the wicked forsake his way, and the unrighteous man his thoughts: and let him return unto the LORD, and he will have mercy upon him; and to our God, for he will abundantly pardon.

Vv

Vail or Veil: A veil is an article of clothing or cloth hanging that is intended to cover some part of the head or face, or an object of some significance. It is especially associated with women and sacred objects. One view is that as a religious item, it is intended to show honour to an object or space. The actual sociocultural, psychological, and socio-sexual functions of veils have not been studied extensively but most likely include the maintenance of social distance and the communication of social status and cultural identity. As in (2 Corinthians 3:13 – 15) the Glory of the New Covenant in Christ Jesus. "...and are not like Moses, who used to put a veil over his face so that the sons of Israel would not look intently at the end of what was fading away. But their minds were hardened; for until this very day at the reading of the old covenant the same veil remains unlifted, because it is removed in Christ. But to this day whenever Moses is read, a veil lies over their heart;...)

Elisha's servant had risen early in the morning and gone outside. In the light of the rising sun, he saw the enemy's army surrounding them and with great alarm informed his master. Unruffled, Elisha told his servant, "Do not fear, for those who are with us are more than those who are with them" (2 Kings 6:16). Elisha then prayed for the eyes of his servant to be opened, so that he could see the unseen realities of the spiritual realm. The servant saw the heavenly forces, the horses and chariots of fire surrounding Elisha. When Elisha prayed again, the eyes of the enemy forces were blinded, and the prophet was able to lead this enemy army into the city of Samaria. At times, the *veil* is lifted in the gospel allowing the Christian to see the unseen. At the birth and baptism of our Lord, the *veil* concealing the glory of our Lord was lifted, and the heavens opened revealing the angelic hosts. At our Lord's transfiguration, once again the *veil* is lifted, allowing three of His disciples to see a preview of the kingdom of God. Hallelujah!

Vail or Veil

Vain: (adjective: vain; comparative adjective: vainer; superlative adjective: vainest) (Philippians 2 : 3) 'Do nothing out of selfish ambition or *vain* conceit. Rather, in humility value others above yourselves, having or showing an excessively high opinion of one's appearance, abilities, or worth." their flattery made him vain" synonyms: conceited, narcissistic, self-loving, in love with oneself, self-admiring, self-regarding, wrapped up in oneself, self-absorbed, self-obsessed, self-centred, egotistic, egotistical, egoistic, egocentric, egomaniac; More antonyms: modest producing no result; useless. "a vain attempt to tidy up the room" synonyms: futile, useless, pointless, worthless, nugatory, to no purpose, in vain; More antonyms: successful, productive having no likelihood of fulfilment; empty. "a vain boast" synonyms: futile, useless, pointless, to no purpose, worthless, nugatory; More antonyms: successful, productive What ever description is attached to vain the gospel provide guidance and warned in (Exodus 20:7) "Thou shalt not take the name of the LORD thy God in vain; for the LORD will not hold him guiltless that taketh his name in vain."

2 Although many people believe taking the Lord's name in vain refers to using the Lord's name as a swear word, there is much more involved with a *vain* use of God's name. To understand the severity of taking the Lord's name in *vain*, we must first see the Lord's name from His perspective as outlined in the gospel or Scripture. The God of Israel was known by many names and titles, but the concept embodied in God's name plays an important and unique role in the Gospel. God's nature and attributes, the totality of His being, and especially His glory are reflected in His name (Psalm 8:1). (Psalm 111:9) tells us His name is "holy and awesome," and the Lord's prayer begins by addressing God with the phrase "hallowed be your name" (Matthew 6:9), an indication that a reverence for God and His name should be foremost in our prayers. Too often we barge into God's presence with presumptuous "to-do lists" for Him, without being mindful of His holiness, His awesomeness, and the vast chasm that separates our nature from His. "That we are even allowed to come before His throne is due only to His gracious, merciful love for His own" (Hebrews 4:16). We must never take that grace for granted.

3 Because of the greatness of the name of God, any use of God's name that brings dishonour on Him or on His character is taking His name in *vain*. The third of the Ten Commandments forbids taking or using the Lord's name in an irreverent manner because that would indicate a lack of respect for God Himself and automatically result in using the name of the Lord in *vain*. A person who misuses

Vail or Veil

God's name will not be held "guiltless" by the Lord (Exodus 20:7). In the Old Testament, bringing dishonour on God's name was done by failing to perform an oath or vow taken in His name (Leviticus 19:12). The man who used God's name to legitimize his oath, and then broke his promise, would indicate his lack of reverence for God as well as a lack of fear of His holy retribution. It was essentially the same as denying God's existence. For believers, however, there is no need to use God's name to legitimize an oath as we are not to take oaths in the first place, letting our "yes be yes" and our "no be no" (Matthew 5:33-37).

4 There is a larger sense in which people today take the Lord's name in *vain*. Those who name the name of Christ, who pray in His name, and who take His name as part of their identity, but who deliberately and continually disobey His commands, are taking His name in *vain*. Jesus Christ has been given the name above all names, at which every knee shall bow (Philippians 2:9-10), and when we take the name "Christian" upon ourselves, we must do so with an understanding of all that signifies. If we profess to be Christians, but act, think, and speak in a worldly or profane manner, we take His name in *vain*. When we misrepresent Christ, either intentionally or through ignorance of the Christian faith as proclaimed in the gospel, we take the Lord's name in *vain*. When we say we love Him, but do not do what He commands (Luke 6:46), we take His name in *vain* and are in danger of hearing Him say to us, "I never knew you. Away from me" in the day of judgment (Matthew 7:21-23). The name of the Lord is holy, as He is holy. The name of the Lord is a representation of His glory, His majesty, and His supreme deity. We are to esteem and honour His name as we revere and glorify God Himself. To do any less is to take His name in *vain*. Since this is a commandment, the Second Temple Judaism by the Hellenistic period developed a taboo of (not) pronouncing the name of God at all, resulting in the replacement of the Tetragrammatons' by "Adonai" (literally "my lords" – see Adonai) in pronunciation. Modern violations of this commandment consist of saying things such as "God damn it" and swearing on the Lords name and bearing false witness or lying.

5 In the Hebrew Bible itself, the commandment is directed against abuse of the name of God, not against any use; there are numerous examples in the Hebrew Bible and a few in the New Testament gospels - where God's name is called upon in oaths to tell the truth or to support the truth of the statement being sworn to, and the books of Daniel and Revelation include instances where an angel sent by God invokes the name of God to support the truth of apocalyptic revelations. God himself is presented as swearing by his own name ("As surely as I live ...") to

guarantee the certainty of various events foretold through the prophets.

Vainglory: (noun, Vain glories – plural) - This is a very dangerous vice in the life of any person or a Christian. meaning excessive elation or pride over one's own achievements, abilities, etc.; boastful vanity. 2 empty pomp or show. Unwarranted pride in one's accomplishments or qualities. 3 Vain, ostentatious display. A boastful man of God in earthly achievement or miraculous power when actually not so equipped. Do you worry over what others think of you? Do you sometimes say or do things to draw attention to yourself? Do you replay conversations in your mind, wondering if you left the right impression? If so, you might be struggling with the vice known as vainglory. "glory" denotes someone's excellence being known and approved by others. There is nothing wrong with others recognizing our good qualities and deeds. In fact, seeking to live in a way that inspires others to give glory to God and to pursue a more virtuous life is good. Jesus Himself said (Mathew 5:16) "Let your light so shine before men, that they may see your good works and give glory to your Father who is in heaven"

However, seeking human praise for its own sake is sinful. Such a person wants glory for himself more than he wants glory for God. He wants to receive the praise of men, which is a vain glory that is empty, fickle, and often off the mark. Aquinas explains that the glory we seek can be vain in one of three ways.

Vainglory as a Capital Vice: This is a strong weakness that gives birth to many other vices. When our hearts are set on gaining the praise of men, we are likely to develop several other faults along the way. For example, we may seek to win people's attention through self-promotion in our words. In conversation, we might drop certain people's names, point out our achievements, or exaggerate our successes with the hopes of having others esteem us highly ("He must be important"). This vice is boasting. We also might tend to throw ourselves into the centre of attention through eccentric behaviour, or by being "in the know" about the latest news or gossip, or by having the latest technology. Indeed, this fruit is termed love of novelties.

2 What about hypocrisy? Hypocrisy also is a great danger for the vain person. The Greek word translated "hypocrite" to mean "actor" or "pretender." It is used in the New Testament to describe someone who, like an actor on stage, is concerned about projecting a certain character to his audience and pretending to be something he is not. Driven by his desire to receive praise from men, the hypocrite is more worried about giving the impression that he does good deeds than actually doing good deeds for

their own sake. The vain person also is more likely to fall into divisive actions in his attempt to show he is not inferior to others. Divisiveness could breed due to one's intellect, unwillingness, speech, and deeds. First is the intellectual vice of obstinacy: "by which a man is too much attached to his own opinion," such that he is unwilling to accept another opinion that might be better. Second is a vice related to the will called discord, which is an unwillingness to give up one's own will and concur with others? The third vice is related to speech and is called contention, whereby a man likes to be argumentative, or "quarrels noisily with another." Fourth is disobedience: by which "a man refuses to carry out the command of his superiors." Each of these smaller vices flows from the capital vice of vainglory. They support a man's vain drive to have others think that he is superior to others. As Christians, let this thought be in you. Do not think you are superior to others because the moment you do, you introduce the vice of creed into your life.

3 Since the vain person is concerned about the praise of men, Magnanimity and vainglory are directly opposed to each other. The vain person is more concerned about receiving the praise of men than he is about living a truly praiseworthy life, whereas the magnanimous person seeks to do good and live an honourable life, even if he is never noticed. Such a virtuous man can be confident that even if no one on earth notices his righteous deeds, his heavenly Father sees and will reward him as in (Mathew. 6:4).

Vainglory in taking God's glory to one's own glory:

Again, if we perform righteous deeds in order to receive human recognition, we spoil the gift or glory we could have given to God. Hired, seeking glory is sinful if in one's heart, one desires human praise more than God's praise. Do we do virtuous deeds out of love for God and neighbour? Or is there a part of us wanting to be noticed and esteemed by others? For example, a parish catechist might pour her heart into her ministry partly because she loves the praise she receives from the pastor and her fellow parishioners for her good work. Similarly, Catholic parents might arrive at Mass early and train their kids to behave well during the liturgy, not just for the good of their children's spiritual development, but also because they like the attention they receive ("What a beautiful Catholic family!"). To the extent that we do good deeds in order to draw attention to ourselves and not to God, to that extent we suffer from vainglory.

Similarly, when it comes to devotional practices, Jesus said, "Beware of practicing your piety before men in order to be seen by them; for then you will have no reward from your Father who is in heaven" (Mat. 6:1). If we perform righteous deeds in order to receive human recognition, we spoil the gift we could have given to God.

This teaching challenges us to examine how pure our motives are when we practice our faith. Do we worship God and serve the Church purely out of selfless love for God, or is there a part of us selfishly seeking to receive attention and praise from men? Often, our motives are quite mixed. We may give time and money to the parish, but is there something within us hoping that others will notice our generosity? We may take time for prayer because we love the Lord, but is there a part of us also hoping our friends, our spiritual director, or the people we serve will notice and think better of us? We may practice mortifications such as fasting, but is there a part of us wanting to appear more devout than others? If we perform righteous deeds in order to receive human recognition, we spoil the gift we could have given to God. We might receive applause here on earth, but Jesus says we will not receive a reward in heaven. On the other hand, the soul that desires to keep his piety hidden is the one who draws down the praise of the angels and saints. The soul that prays, fasts, and makes charitable contributions out of pure love of God-without seeking human praise-is the one who will be rewarded by the heavenly Father.

Vainglory as a symptoms of Vanity: It is vain to seek praise for something that is not truly praiseworthy. Of course, this would include seeking praise for sinful acts. The college student, for example, who hopes to gain respect from his peers for his drunkenness, his sexual exploits, or his cheating on an exam is pursuing not true, but vain glory. Yet even devout Christians are susceptible to this vice when they plan their lives around the standards of happiness and success set up by the world. For example, a part of us might hope to gain respect from old friends and family members for having a successful career, wearing the latest fashions, having children succeed in school, living in a nice home, etc. These are not evil pursuits in themselves, but they can distract us from pursuing Christian ideals such as charity, generosity, simplicity, and humility. If these worldly pursuits hinder us from living a truly praiseworthy life-a life of virtue and holiness-then we may be seeking the vain glory of this world more than the glory of God.

Second, it is sinful to seek glory from people whose judgment is not sound. Most of us desire the approval of our bosses, parents, spouses, or friends. And this is natural. If, however, these people do not truly understand what a good, virtuous life is, we likely will be disappointed, frustrated, or misled. To seek their recognition would be pursuing vainglory, for

Valley

they are not able to judge what is truly praiseworthy. They sometimes will praise the wrong things, and they will fail to recognize what is most noble in life. They might even look down upon aspects of our Christian life. Therefore, instead of seeking the approval of worldly men, we should seek the praise of Christ-and by extension, His faithful followers who judge by His standards, not the world's. See (Galatians 5:26) "Let us not be desirous of vain glory, provoking one another, envying one another".

Valley: (noun, Greek – *Gehenna* or *geenna* - [gheh'-en-nah], Hebrew - *biqah* - [bik-aw'] Gehenna, and originally the name of a valley or cavity near Jerusalem, a place underneath the earth, a place of punishment for evil. 2 depression that is longer than it is wide. The terms U-shaped and V-shaped are descriptive terms of geography to characterize the form of valleys. Most valleys belong to one of these two main types or a mixture of them, (at least) with respect of the cross section of the slopes or hillsides. See (Ezekiel 39:11 and 15) "I will give to Gog a place for burial in Israel, the *valley* of them that pass through, and there shall they bury Gog and all his multitude whence they shall call it, The *valley* of the multitude of Gog". Here, Gog denotes those who are in external worship without internal, whence his burial place is called the *valley* of them that pass through, and the *valley* of the multitude of Gog. In David: Yea, when I walk through the *valley* of shadow I will fear no evil (Psalm. 23:4); where the v*alley* of shadow denotes lower things, which are relatively in shade. Also, as valleys were between mountains and hills, and below them, therefore by *valleys* are signified the lower or exterior things of the church, because by hills and mountains are signified its higher or interior things, by higher things which are of charity, and by mountains those which are of love to the Lord; and as by the land of Canaan is signified the Lord's kingdom and His church, therefore it is called a land of mountains and *valley*s, that drinketh water of the rain of heaven (Deuteronomy. 11:11). That Joseph is here said to have been sent out of the valley of Hebron is because the mission was to those who taught concerning faith; for those who are in faith, and not in' charity, are in lower things; because with them faith is only in the memory and thence in the mouth, but not in the heart and thence in the work.

Valley of Siddim, the: This is the valley of the slime pits. Why? The valley of Siddim is on the very spot where the cities of Sodom and Gomorrah were. You recall the awful story in the Bible of the destruction of Sodom and Gomorrah. God looked down and saw the wickedness of those wicked and vile cities and said, "I am going to rain fire and brimstone on them." This is a valley where sin abounded. This represents a valley in our lives, the valley of sin as in (Genesis 14) Siddim is thought to be located on the southern end of the Dead Sea where modern bitumen deposits have been found in respect to the tar pits (asphalt, slime pits) mentioned in (Genesis 14:10). This scripture indicates that the valley was filled with many of these pits that the armies of Sodom and Gomorrah fell into during their retreat from Mesopotamian forces. It has been suggested by theologians that the destruction of the cities of the Jordan Plain by divine fire and brimstone may have caused Siddim to become a salt sea, what is now the Dead Sea.

2 Do you know that when you go out to the nightclubs and the pubs and go into the depths of sin, God still loves you and God is still there? Do you know that when you go down to the very bottom of sin and taste the last drop in the cup of the dregs of sin, God is there? Do you know that when you have gone to the bottom and no one

It does not matter where you are or how deep in sin you have gone; He is there. Are you in the valley of Siddim? Are you in the city of Sodom? Are you in the city of Gomorrah in deep awful sin? Have you gone to the bottom? Is your life empty and friendless? Are you without anybody who seems to care? He says, "I am there."

Valley of Eschol, the: This locates just inside the Promised Land. Christians, do you recall the grapes of Eschol? The Israelites came to the door of the Promised Land at Kadesh-Barnea and they appointed twelve spies. Those twelve spies went over into the Promised Land. They said it was a land that flowed with milk and honey. They brought back some grapes that were so big that it took two men to carry one bunch. Those were the grapes of Eschol. They were gotten in the valley of Eschol, one of the seven great valleys featuring in the gospel.

2 Eschol is where the Jews made the decision of their life. It was at Eschol where they had to decide, "Shall we go forward or shall we go backward?" It was in the valley of Eschol where they decided, "Shall we obey God, or shall we go back into the wilderness?" It was at Eschol that they decided, "Shall we be at our fullest or shall we be less than we ought to be?" The Valley of Eschol is the valley of decision. Yea, though you walk through the valley of Eschol, He is there in that valley of decision!

3 Whenever you come to *the valley of Eschol*, the valley of decision, always do what God wants you to do. Ask God to help you and He must surely help in Jesus Name!

Valley of Kidron, the: (Hebrew - *Cedron*, from Naḥal Qidron; also Qidron Valley) is the valley on the

Valley of Kidron, the

eastern side of The Old City of Jerusalem, separating the Temple Mount from the Mount of Olives as in (Jeremiah 30:41). "The whole valley where dead bodies and ashes are thrown, and all the terraces out to the Kidron Valley on the east as far as the corner of the Horse Gate, will be holy to the LORD. The city will never again be uprooted or demolished." Otherwise called the valley of Jehoshophat. It is the valley just outside the east wall of the city of Jerusalem. The Valley Of Kidron is located along the eastern side of Jerusalem, between the Temple Mount (see Mount Moriah) and the Mount of Olives. Many important events of Bible History have occurred, and many tremendous events of Bible Prophecy will occur, in or very near *the Valley Of Kidron*. Jesus Christ travelled through *the Kidron Valley* many times to and from Jerusalem, including on His way to visit Lazarus at Bethany, the Triumphal Entry in which He rode a Donkey from the Mount of Olives to the city, or crossing the valley from the "Last Supper" to the Garden of Gethsemane where He was arrested That Fateful Night. Also, the Pool of Gihon is located in the *Kidron Valley*. The Brook Kidron runs through the valley during the wet season, but remains dry much of the year.

2 To the south of the city the Kidron joins the Valley Of Hinnom. King David crossed the *Kidron Valley* to escape his rebellious son Absalom (2 Samuel 15:23,30). King Asa (see Kings of Israel and Judah) burned his grandmother's pagan Asherah pole in the Kidron Valley (1 Kings 15:13), and the evil Athaliah was executed there (2 Kings 11:16). It became for some time a dumping place for destroyed pagan items (2 Chronicles 29:16, 30:14). By the time of King Josiah, *the Kidron Valley* had become the city cemetery (2 Kings 23:6, Jeremiah 26:23). For this reason, the valley has been of much interest to archaeologists.

3 It is the valley between Jerusalem and the Mount of Olives. *The valley of Kidron* is a big, deep valley. There is a cemetery there. Ever since the time of Josiah, it has been a cemetery. Samson is buried there. Samuel, I think, is buried there. James is buried there. Absalom is buried there. Many others are buried there in this cemetery in the valley of Kidron. This is the valley of suffering. The shadow of death is there. David says, "Yea, though I walk through the valley of the shadow of death, I will fear no evil: for Thou are with me." God is in the valley of Siddim, the valley of sin. God is in the valley of Eschol, the valley of decision. He is also there in the valley of suffering.

4 As a Christian, have you come to the place in your life where you are at the bottom of sin? If you face a decision, if you are in the valley of decision, God is there. If you face suffering and heartache, our Lord is there.

Valley of Elah, the: "The valley of the terebinth" (Hebrew:⬜ *Emek HaElah*) so called after the large and shady terebinth trees (Pistacia atlantica) which are indigenous to its parts, and best known as the place described in the Bible where the Israelites were encamped when David fought Goliath (1 Samuel. 17:2, 19). It was near Azekah and Socho (1 Samuel 17:1). On the west side of the valley, near Socho, there is a very large and ancient tree of this kind, 55 feet in height, its trunk 17 feet in circumference, and the breadth of its shade no less than 75 feet. It marks the upper end of the valley, and forms a noted object, being one of the largest terebinths in the area. Rising up from the valley on its extreme south-east end lies the hilltop ruin, Adullam. Elah Valley on its south-eastern side The Valley of Elah has gained new importance as a point of support for the argument that Israel was more than a tribal chiefdom in the time of King David. Others are sceptical, and suggest it might represent either a Judahite or Canaanite fortress.

2 Elah Valley, spring of 2010. Today the valley is threatened by shale oil extraction through the CCR ground-heating process, with the Green Zionist Alliance and the grassroots group Save Adullam, among others, working to stop shale oil extraction in the region

3 This is a place where David looked out and heard Goliath shout his challenges across the valley. David with his slingshot met Goliath in the valley of Elah. There he felled Goliath. Known as the valley of battle. In the valley of Elah, the valley of battle, God is there. In the valley of decision, God is there. In the valley of suffering, He is there. In the valley of battle, He is there.

2 Is some battle or some sin about to conquer you? Is there one temptation you feel you cannot resist? God is there as in (1Corinthians 10:13) "There hath no temptation taken you but such as is common to man: but God is faithful, Who will not suffer you to be tempted above that ye are able; but will with the temptation also make a way of escape, that ye may be able to bear it." Lean heavy upon God. In the valley of battle, He is there!

Valley of Achor, the: The valley of trouble or punishment. Achor is the valley where Achan was stoned to death. The Lord said, "Do not take anything that is in Jericho." (Joshua 7), relates the story from which the valley's name comes. After the problems the Israelites had as a result of Achan's immoral theft of items commanded to be destroyed, the Israelite community stoned Achan and his household. Liberal scholars and archaeologists regard the narrative about Achan as an aeti-

Valley of Gehenna, the

ological myth, and instead suspect that it gained this name for another reason.

Due to the horrific nature of this narrative, the phrase *valley of trouble* became eminently proverbial and occurs elsewhere in the Hebrew bible. The Book of Isaiah and Book of Hosea use the term - the valley of trouble, a place for herds to lie down in (Isaiah 65:10), the valley of trouble for a door of hope (Hosea 2:15) as a way of describing the redemption promised by God.

Achan saw a coat and said, "My wife sure would like to have that coat." The Lord said not to take anything. He knew he shouldn't. Achan saw amount equivalent to approximately, £120 or $185 and said, "I sure could use that." Achan took the money and the coat, and sin came into the camp. Then the battle of Ai was lost. Joshua called all the people and cast lots. The lot fell on Achan. God said, "Take him out to the valley and stone him to death." They stoned Achan and his wife and his children. They named that place the valley of Achor (the valley of chastening).

As a Christians,we shall not fear any evil because even in the valley of chastening, the Lord is still there. He has to spank us. He has to take the rod of chastening and put it across our backs, but even when God has had to put us in the valley of chastening, spank us, put is in the hospital, cause us to lose a job, put us in the middle of a road in an automobile accident, or knock us down and spank us, it is always blessed because even in the valley of chastening, valley of Siddim or sin, He is there. In the valley of Eschol or decision, He is there. In the valley of Kidron or suffering, He is there. In the valley of Elah or battle, He is there.

Valley of Gehenna, the: Gehenna, the garbage dump of Jerusalem. Iinitially where apostate Israelites and followers of various Ba'als and other Canaanite gods, including Moloch (or Molech), sacrificed their children by fire (2 Chronicle. 28:3, 33:6). Thereafter it was deemed to be cursed (Jeremiah. 7:31, 19:2-6). In Jewish, Christian, and Islamic scripture, Gehenna is a destination of the wicked. This is different from the more neutral Sheol or Hades, the abode of the dead, though the King James version of the Bible translates both usually with the Anglo-Saxon word Hell.

There was a fire going on there all the time. When our Lord spoke about hell, He said there shall be "eternal Gehenna." In other words, there is going to be eternal fire there. That is the way it will be forever. For those of you who will die without God, I am calling this the valley of death. You have to die someday. "Yea, though I walk through the valley of the shadow of death, I will fear no evil: for Thou are there."

Valley of Jezreel, the: (Hebrew: *Emek Yizra'el*), is a large fertile plain and inland valley south of the Lower Galilee region in Israel. The Samarian highlands and Mount Gilboa border the valley from the south and to the north lie the Israeli cities Afula and Tiberias. To the west is the Mount Carmel range, and to the east is the Jordan Valley. As recounted in (2 Kings 9:1–10), after Jehu kills King Jehoram, he confronts Jezebel in Jezreel and urges her eunuchs to kill Jezebel by throwing her out of a window. They comply, tossing her out the window and leaving her in the street to be eaten by dogs. Only Jezebel's skull, feet, and hands remained.

2 The end time battle field. The valley of Jezreel is important in the gospel as written in the Bible because in that valley the great end-time battle shall be fought. Russia will come on the valley of Jezreel and fight against Palestine. Egypt will come from the south to the valley of Jezreel and fight against Palestine. China will come from the east to the valley of Jezreel and fight against Palestine. There the armies of the world will be gathered together in the great end-time battle. Russia and her horses, a great cavalry, and the nations of the East and the North shall be gathered together in the valley of Jezreel against Palestine. All of a sudden, the Western powers, the United States, England and the revived Roman Empire will come and fight against Russia in the valley of Jezreel.

3 It is in *the valley of Jezreel* where there is found Mount Megiddo, from which comes the word "Armageddon." It is in the valley of Jezreel where the battle shall be fought. It is in the valley of Jezreel where the Antichrist shall rise up as the victor and conqueror of the entire world. The man of sin shall be king of the whole world. The valley of Jezreel is where our Lord shall descend from Heaven and shall come back with His own people, coming back riding on white horses. He shall come back as King of Kings and Lord of Lords, and forever we shall be with Him. Even in the valley of Jezreel He is there. "Yea, though I walk through the valley of the shadow of death, I will fear no evil: for Thou art with me." Isn't that wonderful!

2 God is calling, beloved children, which ever valley you are; is it in the valley of sin, come to Christ; trust Him as your Saviour. Somebody who is in the valley of decision, obey Him; do His will. Somebody who is in the valley of suffering, depend on Him. Somebody who is in the valley of chastening, just say, "Thank God. If He is spanking me, He must be there." Somebody who is facing death, realize that He is there. Realize, too, that He is coming! When He shall come with trumpet sound, O may I then in Him be found, Dressed in His righteousness alone, Faultless to stand before the throne! As long as there be a Heaven, as long

as God lives, as long as the eternal God Who was and is and shall be forever, as long as God lives, He'll be with thee. In the valley or on the mountain top, He is there.

Valley of the shadow of death: Earthly troubles, Cares, Sicknesses, Crisis, Sorrows, Tears, discomforts, 'Agonies' and all forms of worries. Clearly, this psalm and phrase therein demonstrate the redemptive power and care of Jehovah towards mankind. Particularly – the believers in the heart of all tribulations and yearnings of life causing mankind to sin. 'The wages of sin is death' This Psalm portrays God as a good shepherd, feeding (verse 1) and leading (verse 3) his flock. The "rod and staff" (verse 4) are also the implements of a shepherd. Most Christians see the shepherd imagery pervading the entire psalm. It is known that the shepherd is to know each sheep by name, thus when God is given the analogy of a shepherd, he is not only a protector but also the caretaker. God, as the caretaker, leads the sheep to green pasture (verse 2) and still waters (verse 2) because he knows that each of his sheep must be personally led to be fed cared for and be protected in a rough world. Thus, without its Shepherd, the sheep would enter into wrong path, sin and pay the wages of sin which is death either by a predator or of starvation, since sheep are known for their stupidity. verse 5 ("Thou preparest a table before me") refers to the "old oriental shepherding practice" of using little raised tables to feed sheep Similarly, "Thou anointest my head with oil" may refer to an ancient form of back liner – the oil is poured on wounds, and repels flies. Also, verse 6 ("Goodness and mercy shall follow me") represents two loyal sheepdogs coming behind the flock

Vanity: (Greek – *mataiotés* - [mat-ah-yot'-ace], Hebrew - *Hebel* - [heh'bel]) meaning purposelessness, emptiness, unreality, purposelessness, ineffectiveness, instability, frailty; false religion

2 The excessive belief in one's own abilities or attractiveness to others. Prior to the 14th century it did not have such narcissistic undertones, and merely meant futility. The related term vainglory is now often seen as an archaic synonym for vanity, but originally meant boasting in vain, i.e. unjustified boasting; although glory is now seen as having an exclusively positive meaning, the Latin term gloria (from which it derives) roughly means boasting, and was often used as a negative criticism.

3 The words "vanity" and "vain" apply to conceited persons with exaggerated self-opinions. While the gospel usage includes this nuance, it describes the world as having as no ultimate meaning, a concept shared with some philosophies. The meanings of emptiness and lacking in reality are already present in the Latin vanitas, from which the English word "vanity" is derived.

4 *Vanity* approaches the chief Old Testament understanding that human life apart from God, even at its best, has no ultimate significance and consequently is valueless. This theme characterizes the Book of Ecclesiastes, which begins with "Vanity of vanities! All is vanity" (Ecclesiastes 1:2 NRSV), the Hebrew for vanity, as its Arabic cognate, suggests a wind or vapor. Man's life is like a breath (Psalm 39:5). The development of vanity as reflecting the despair of human life in Ecclesiastes revealed the fact that its author was a sceptic, an agnostic, or a rationalist, as its message seemed to contradict the prophetic message that Israel place its hope in God. The tension between hope and hopelessness can be resolved in realizing that the inspired writer is expressing his emotions apart from his life as a believer. It does not suggest that he has gone after other gods, but rather he views life apart from God. Searching for wisdom is no more productive than striving after the wind (Ecclesiastes 1:14 Ecclesiastes 1:17). All work (Ecclesiastes 4:8), wealth (Ecclesiastes 2:1-17), and varied experiences (Ecclesiastes 4:7) add nothing to life's meaning. Human life is of equal value with that of animals (Ecclesiastes 3:19-20).

5 Though *vanity* is the theme of Ecclesiastes, the idea is found elsewhere. It is the despair and frustration in seeing that projected goals are unrealized as with Job in (Job 7:3), David in (2 Sam 18:31-33), and with Elijah in (1 Kings 19:4). Despair is lacking in Jesus, who in the forsakenness of death places his confidence in God (Mathew 27:46). In the 'Sermon on the Mount' he uses the transience of life to engender the Christians confidence as God's children ((Mathew 6:25-33). The other biblical usage of vanity condemns idolatrous religions and philosophies as useless. Gentiles or pagans failing to recognize the true God live in the vanity of their minds. Their unbelief is caused by ignorance and hardness of heart (Ephesians 4:17-24). The vanity of false worship is of no value, as it fails to see that other religions and philosophies lead only to damnation. Vanity as a despair of value of human life thus destroying confidence in self, abilities, and possessions can be of value if faith is allowed to focus on him with whom true joys are to be found. We should also note that the rebirth in all Christians experience is pictured as a washing and renewal by the Holy Spirit as in (Titus 3:5). So it's clear that inward washing and cleansing are important themes in the gospel. Praise the Lord!

References: (Proverbs 31:30 ESV) Charm is deceitful, and beauty is vain, but a woman who fears the Lord is to be praised. (Psalm 119:37 ESV) Turn my eyes from looking at worthless things; and give me life in your ways. (1 Samuel 16:7 ESV) But the Lord said to Samuel, "Do not look on his appearance or on the height of his stature, because I have rejected him. For the Lord sees not as man sees: man looks on the outward appearance, but the Lord looks on the heart." (Jeremiah 4:30 ESV) And you, O desolate one, what do you mean that you dress in scarlet, that you adorn yourself with ornaments of gold, that you enlarge your eyes with paint? In vain you beautify yourself. Your lovers despise you; they seek your life. (Matthew 6:1-7 ESV) "Beware of practicing your righteousness before other people in order to be seen by them, for then you will have no reward from your Father who is in heaven. "Thus, when you give to the needy, sound no trumpet before you, as the hypocrites do in the synagogues and in the streets, that they may be praised by others. Truly, I say to you, they have received their reward. But when you give to the needy, do not let your left hand know what your right hand is doing, so that your giving may be in secret. And your Father who sees in secret will reward you. "And when you pray, you must not be like the hypocrites. For they love to stand and pray in the synagogues and at the street corners, that they may be seen by others. Truly, I say to you, they have received their reward. (1 Timothy 4:8 ESV) For while bodily training is of some value, godliness is of value in every way, as it holds promise for the present life and also for the life to come. (Ecclesiastes 5:10 ESV) He who loves money will not be satisfied with money, nor he who loves wealth with his income; this also is vanity. (Hebrews 13:5 ESV) Keep your life free from love of money, and be content with what you have, for he has said, "I will never leave you nor forsake you."

Vanity, Excessive Hygiene as: This has to do with body image and health which are huge topics of discussion in our culture, and it can be difficult to know how to care for our bodies without allowing them to become our idols. The most important thing to remember is that the body of a Christian is God's temple; His Holy Spirit dwells within us. Paul writes, "Do you not know that your body is a temple of the Holy Spirit, who is in you, whom you have received from God? You are not your own; you were bought at a price. Therefore honour God with your body" (1 Corinthians 6:19–20). Earlier, he wrote, "Don't you know that you yourselves are God's temple and that God's Spirit lives in you? If anyone destroys God's temple, God will destroy him; for God's temple is sacred, and you are that temple" (1 Corinthians 3:16).

2 Clearly, we are called to care for our physical bodies. We were physically created by God and called to honour Him physically. That being said, our hygiene is important to God. The Old Testament is filled with references to hand-washing and foot-washing, washing clothing, washing before eating, etc. Ritual washings were to remind the people that they

were not to come into God's presence without washing the dust and dirt of the world from their bodies. The tabernacle in the wilderness included a basin for the priests to wash themselves before serving the Lord (Exodus 30:18). Even Jesus washed the disciples' feet at the Last Supper, although this was more a comment on servant hood than on cleanliness.

3 Washing is used in the New Testament to signify a spiritual cleansing of sin available only through Christ. (Ephesians 5:26) tells us that Christ cleansed the church—all those who believe in Him for salvation—by "washing with water through the word." Here we see the picture of the internal spiritual cleansing the Word of God provides for us. The rebirth all Christians experience is pictured as a washing and renewal by the Holy Spirit (Titus 3:5). So it's clear that inward washing and cleansing are important themes in the Christian gospel.

But what about washing and hygiene as a physical, rather than spiritual, act? There is a line between hygiene and vanity that can be easily blurred, especially in a culture so motivated by visual beauty. How do we steward our bodies as temples of the Holy Spirit without becoming vain? The most important thing is to monitor the condition of the heart. If we see our value in terms of physical beauty, we are missing the point. Our value lies in what God has done for us, cleansing us inwardly from sin, not in how much we clean and wash our outer selves. Our hearts reflect the person we have become—new creations in Christ (2 Corinthians 5:17). It's important to remember that man looks at the outward appearance, but God looks at the heart (1 Samuel 16:7). (Proverbs 31:30) says, "Charm is deceptive and beauty is fleeting; but a woman who fears the Lord is to be praised." God is not condemning beauty or caring for the body but simply saying that the body (or worldly beauty) is not the most important thing. We are to care for our bodies to keep them in good shape so we can be of value to God and His people, and this certainly includes hygiene. But (1 Timothy 4:8) reminds us, "Physical training is of some value, but godliness has value for all things, holding promise for both the present life and the life to come."

4 As with many things in life, practicing hygiene while avoiding vanity is something that requires prayer and perhaps daily conscious effort. If our hearts are focused on God, we can't go wrong. We should seek Him; trust Him for our needs; delight in the inward beauty He has given us; and steward our bodies as His servants, not as if they were our own. When we seek God first and abide in Him, we will learn to listen to Him and obey Him. In doing this, we will care for the bodies He has given us without allowing our bodies to rule over us. Body can rule over us

Vengeance

when we pay attention to the art of tattooing and beastlike appearances.

Vengeance: Greek – *ekdikésis* [ek-dik'-ay-sis], Hebrew – *naqam* - [naw-kawm] Meaning a defense, vengeance, full punishment, a defense, avenging, vindication, vengeance, (b) full (complete) punishment. Literally,

This means a harmful action against a person or group in response to a grievance. To avenge. God said, "It is mine to avenge; I will repay. In due time their foot will slip; their day of disaster is near and their doom rushes upon them" (Deuteronomy 32:35; Romans 12:19; Hebrews 10:30). In Deuteronomy, God is speaking of the stiff-necked, rebellious, idolatrous Israelites who rejected Him and incurred His wrath with their wickedness. He promised to avenge Himself upon them in His own timing and according to His own perfect and pure motives. The two New Testament passages concern the behaviour of the Christian, who is not to usurp God's authority. Rather, we are to allow Him to judge rightly and pour out His divine retribution against His enemies as He sees fit.

2 Unlike us, God never takes *vengeance* from impure motives. His *vengeance* is for the purpose of punishing those who have offended and rejected Him. We can, however, pray for God to avenge Himself in perfection and holiness against His enemies and to avenge those who are oppressed by evil. In (Psalm 94:1), the psalmist prays for God to avenge the righteous, not out of a sense of uncontrolled vindictiveness, but out of just retribution from the eternal Judge whose judgments are perfect. Even when the innocent suffer and the wicked appear to prosper; it is for God alone to punish. "The LORD is a jealous and avenging God; the LORD takes vengeance and is filled with wrath. The LORD takes vengeance on his foes and maintains his wrath against his enemies" (Nahum 1:2).

3 There are only two times in the Bible when God gives men permission to avenge in His name. First, after the Midianites committed hideous, violent acts against the Israelites, the cup of God's wrath against the Midianites was full, and He commanded Moses to lead the people in a holy war against them. "The LORD said to Moses, 'Take vengeance on the Midianites for the Israelites. After that, you will be gathered to your people'" (Numbers 31:1-2). Here, again, Moses did not act on his own; he was merely an instrument to carry out God's perfect plan under His guidance and instruction. Second, Christians are to be in submission to the rulers God has set over us because they are His instruments for "vengeance on evildoers" (1 Peter 2:13-14). As in Moses' case, these rulers are not to act on their own, but are to carry out God's willed for the punishment of the wicked.

Vengeance as the role of God: It is tempting to try to take on the role of God and seek to punish those who we feel deserve it. But because we are sinful creatures, it is impossible for us to take revenge with pure motives. This is why the Mosaic Law contains the command "Do not seek revenge or bear a grudge against one of your people, but love your neighbour as yourself. I am the LORD" (Leviticus. 19:18). Even David, a "man after God's own heart" (1 Samuel 13:14), refused to take revenge on Saul, even though David was the innocent party being wronged. David submitted to God's command to forego *vengeance* and trust in Him: "May the LORD Judge between you and me. And may the LORD avenge the wrongs you have done to me, but my hand will not touch you (1 Samuel 24:12). 2 As Christians, we are to follow the Lord Jesus' command to "love our enemies and pray for those who persecute us" (Matthew 5:44) "But I tell you, love your enemies and pray for those who persecute you", leaving the *vengeance* to God. Praise His Holy Name!

Virgin: (Greek – *parthenos* [parthen'-os] Hebrew – *almah* or *Bethulah*) meaning a maiden, virgin; extended to men who have not known women. As in (Isaiah 7:14) "Therefore the Lord Himself will give you a sign: Behold, a virgin will be with child and bear a son, and she will call His name Immanuel." This means that a virgin will bear a son. The problem is dealing with the Hebrew word for virgin, which is "almah." According to the Strong's Concordance it means, "virgin, young woman or of marriageable age, maid or newly married." Therefore, the word "almah" does not always mean virgin. The word occurs elsewhere in the Old Testament only in (Genesis 24:43) "maiden"; (Exodus 2:8) "girl"; (Psalm 68:25) "maidens"; (Proverbs 30:19) "maiden"; (Song of Songs 1:3) "maidens"; (Song of Songs 6:8) ("virgins").[1] Additionally, there is a Hebrew word for virgin: bethulah. According to A Greek-English Lexicon of the New Testament and Other Early Christian Literature, parthenos means "virgin." This word is used in the New Testament of the Virgin Mary (Mathew. 1:23; Luke 1:27) and of the ten virgins in the parable (Mathew. 25:1, 7, 11). If the Hebrews translated the Hebrew word "alma" into the Greek word for virgin, then they understood what the Hebrew text meant here. The Gospel meaning of a virgin has to do with the purity of the Church. Our body the Bible is the temple of the living God. As Christians, we are married to Christ. We must therefore be sanctified, holy, not committed to other gods or vain things. Those who come to Christ after engaging in premarital sexual relationships are not virgins; however, they are fully cleansed by Christ at the moment they are saved. God can redeem anyone, and He can heal those who have indulged their fleshly lusts. And, in the horrible case of a woman vic-

Virgin

timized by sexual abuse or rape, who may feel that she, through no fault of her own, no longer measures up to the ideal standard of "virginity," Christ is able to restore us spirit, heal our brokenness, and grant her wholeness.

2 Marriage is to model the relationship between the church and Christ. A married couple is to serve God in a strong, unified partnership. Sex, along with procreation, was designed by God to strengthen that partnership. Sex outside of marriage creates bonds that tear apart people's hearts instead of joining them together. Note, if two people make a conscious, deliberate choice to commit to each other in marriage, and then allow the intimacy that releases these chemicals, the body can reaffirm the connection the mind has made. The physiological feelings of trust and attachment are reinforced by the reality of the relationship. In this way, two people become one physically, and that reflects what God has done spiritually. To be Christly means to stay refrain from sin to provoke a sweet smelling savour to Christ. A sum total of holy manners of lives move Christ to work signs and wonders in our life, strengthen our faith, open our eyes to see Jesus at all times, attend His ears to our prayers, make His light pointing to show us the way so long as we continue to be Holy before Him.

3 When the Bible uses the word *virgin*, it refers to an unmarried person who has not had sexual relations *see* (Esther 2:2) and (Revelation 14:4). In today's culture, many people use the word virginity to express sexual purity; however, many others use a technical definition to find loopholes in moral standards, limiting the word to mean only "the condition of never having gone all the way"—thus, a couple can do anything and everything short of sexual intercourse and still technically call themselves "virgins." This is an unprofitable word game. Chastity should affect the heart, mind, and soul, not just certain body parts.

4 The Bible's emphasis is not so much on a technical or medical definition of virginity as it is on the condition of a person's heart. The morality we espouse and the actions we choose give evidence of our heart's condition. The Bible's standard is clear: celibacy before marriage and monogamy after marriage. There are three serious reasons to save sex for marriage. First, as believers, we are to obey what God tells us to do. First (Corinthians 6:18–20) "Flee from sexual immorality. All other sins a person commits are outside the body, but whoever sins sexually, sins against their own body. Do you not know that your bodies are temples of the Holy Spirit, who is in you, whom you have received from God? You are not your own; you were bought at a price. Therefore honour God with your bodies." If we are in Christ, He has purchased us with the sacrifice of

His life. He calls the shots, and we are to honour Him.

5 The second reason is that we are to fight our spiritual battles wearing the breastplate of righteousness (Ephesians 6:14). We are in a contest between our new nature in Christ and our fleshly desires. (1Thessalonians 4:3–7) says, "It is God's will that you should be sanctified: that you should avoid sexual immorality; that each of you should learn to control your own body in a way that is holy and honourable, not in passionate lust like the pagans, who do not know God; and that in this matter no one should wrong or take advantage of a brother or sister. The Lord will punish all those who commit such sins, as we told you and warned you before. For God did not call us to be impure, but to live a holy life." Allowing your body (rather than the Spirit) to control your actions is an act of defiance against God. Godly, loving sex between a husband and wife is giving and unselfish. Using someone to fulfil a desire of the flesh is self-centred and abusive. Even if the partner is willing, you are still helping him or her to sin and negatively altering that person's relationship with God and others.

6 The final reason involves the "mystery" of marriage (Ephesians 5:31). When God spoke of two people being joined as one, He was referring to something we're only beginning to understand in a real, physiological way. When two people are intimate, the hypothalamus in the brain releases chemicals that induce feelings of attachment and trust. Having sex outside of marriage results in a person forming an attachment and trusting someone with whom he or she does not have a committed relationship. The definition of trust in the mind deteriorates. To have that kind of link with someone without the security of working together toward God is dangerous. Two individuals who are—even mildly—physiologically obsessed with each other but not committed to growing in God as a couple can be torn from God and His plans for them.

References (Leviticus 21:13-14) Widows 'He shall take a wife in her virginity. 'A widow, or a divorced woman, or one who is profaned by harlotry, these he may not take; but rather he is to marry a virgin of his own people, (Deuteronomy 22:13-19) Gates Domestic Violence divorce, in OT Male And Female Parents Slander "If any man takes a wife and goes in to her and then turns against her, and charges her with shameful deeds and publicly defames her, and says, 'I took this woman, but when I came near her, I did not find her a virgin,' then the girl's father and her mother shall take and bring out the evidence of the girl's virginity to the elders of the city at the gate. read more. "The girl's father shall say to the elders, 'I gave my daughter to this man   he has charged her with shameful deeds, saying,

Voice

"I did not find your daughter a virgin." But this is the evidence of my daughter's *virginity*.' And they shall spread the garment before the elders of the city. "So the elders of that city shall take the man and chastise him, and they shall fine him a hundred shekels of silver and give it to the girl's father, because he publicly defamed a *virgin* of Israel. And she shall remain his wife; he cannot divorce her all his days. (Isaiah 62:5) Wives Weddings Knowing God, Effects Of Marriage, The Bridegroom Brides Love, In Relationships Intimacy Marriage, Customs Concerning Bridegroom Youth For as a young man marries a *virgin*, So your sons will marry you; And as the bridegroom rejoices over the bride, So your God will rejoice over you. (Ezekiel 44:22) Priests, Function In OT Times divorce, in OT Widows" And they shall not marry a widow or a divorced woman but shall take *virgins* from the offspring of the house of Israel, or a widow who is the widow of a priest. (2 Corinthians 11:2) Courting Fellowship With Christ God, Jealous Perfection, Human Christ, Names For Purity, Moral And Spiritual Husbands Betrothal Engagement Love, In Relationships Cherishing Marriage, Between God And His People Restored In Jesus Christ. For I am jealous for you with a godly jealousy; for I betrothed you to one husband, so that to Christ I might present you as a pure *virgin*.

Voice: (Greek - *Phone* – [fo-nay'] Hebrew [*Qol* - [kole]) meaning a sound, noise, voice a sound, noise, voice, language, dialect. Voice is sound through which creation story begin.of It forms the the base to all creation and destiny. As a (noun) the sound produced in a person's larynx and uttered through the mouth, as speech or song. a particular opinion or attitude expressed. the range of pitch or type of tone with which a person sings, such as soprano or tenor. sound uttered with resonance of the vocal cords (used in the pronunciation of vowels and certain consonants). a form or set of forms of a verb showing the relation of the subject to the action. As a verb express in words. utter (a speech sound) with resonance of the vocal cords (e.g. b, d, g, v, z) regulate the tone quality of (organ pipes)**.** The *voice* of the Lord is upon the waters; the God of glory thunders; the Lord is upon many (great) waters. (Psalm 29: 3) The *voice* of the Lord makes the hinds bring forth their young, and His *voice* strips bare the forests, while in His temple everyone is saying, Glory! While God could speak audibly to people today, He speaks primarily through His written Word. Sometimes God's leading can come through the Holy Spirit, through our consciences, through circumstances, and through the exhortations of other people. By comparing what we hear to the truth of Scripture, we can learn to recognize God's *voice*.

2 To hear God's voice we must be-

long to God. Jesus said, "My sheep listen to my voice; I know them, and they follow me" (John 10:27). Those who hear God's voice are those who belong to Him—those who have been saved by His grace through faith in the Lord Jesus. These are the sheep that hear and recognize His voice, because they know Him as their Shepherd. If we are to recognize God's voice, we must belong to Him.

3 We hear His *voice* when we spend time in Bible study and quiet contemplation of His Word. The more time we spend intimately with God and His Word, the easier it is to recognize His *voice* and His leading in our lives. Employees at a bank are trained to recognize counterfeits by studying genuine money so closely that it is easy to spot a fake. We should be so familiar with God's Word that when someone speaks error to us, it is clear that it is not of God. Samuel heard the voice of God, but did not recognize it until he was instructed by Eli (1 Samuel 3:1–10). Gideon had a physical revelation from God, and he still doubted what he had heard to the point of asking for a sign, not once, but three times (Judges 6:17–22,36–40). When we are listening for God's *voice*, how can we know that He is the one speaking? First of all, we have something that Gideon and Samuel did not. We have the complete Bible, the inspired Word of God, to read, study, and meditate on. "All Scripture is God-breathed and is useful for teaching, rebuking, correcting and training in righteousness, so that the man of God may be thoroughly equipped for every good work" (2 Timothy 3:16–17). When we have a question about a certain topic or decision in our lives, we should see what the Bible has to say about it. God will never lead us contrary to what He has taught in His Word (Titus 1:2).

References (Psalm 29: 9) [God's *voice* may be heard by man when] he is chastened with pain upon his bed and with continual strife in his bones or while all his bones are firmly set. (Job 33: 19) [God's *voice* may be heard] if there is for the hearer a messenger or an angel, an interpreter, one among a thousand, to show to man what is right for him [how to be upright and in right standing with God]. (Job 33: 23) And the Lord utters His voice before His army, for His host is very great, and [they are] strong and powerful who execute [God's] word. For the day of the Lord is great and very terrible, and who can endure it? (Joel 2: 11) When you are in tribulation and all these things come upon you, in the latter days you will turn to the Lord your God and be obedient to His *voice*. (Deuteronomy 4: 30) If only you carefully listen to the *voice* of the Lord your God, to do watchfully all these commandments which I command you this day. (Deuteronomy 15: 5)

Wages

Ww

Wages: A **wage** is monetary compensation (or remuneration) paid by an employer to an employee in exchange for work done. Payment may be calculated as a fixed amount for each task completed (a *task wage* or piece rate), or at an hourly or daily rate, or based on an easily measured quantity of work done. Payment by wage contrasts with salaried work, in which the employer pays an arranged amount at steady intervals (such as a week or month) regardless of hours worked, with commission which conditions pay on individual performance, and with compensation based on the performance of the company as a whole. Waged employees may also receive tips or gratuity paid directly by clients and employee benefits which are non-monetary forms of compensation. Since wage labour is the predominant form of work, the term "wage" sometimes refers to all forms (or all monetary forms) of employee compensation. 2 Ultimately, the gospel makes it clear that the wages of sin is death while the wages of righteousness is eternal life in Christ Jesus. (Deuteronomy 24:15) "You are to pay him his wages the day he earns them, before sunset; for he is poor and looks forward to being paid. Otherwise he will cry out against you to ADONAI, and it will be your sin". Bad wages like those James and Paul warns in their epistles – Letters to Christians. The apostle James warned people who did not pay their workers good wages: James 5:1-6 " Now, you rich people, weep and cry aloud. There are terrible troubles that will soon be coming to you. Your riches have lost their value. Your beautiful clothes are as if moths had eaten them. Your gold and your silver have become dirty and stained. The dirt and stains will be evidence against you in the judgement. They are like poison that will eat up your bodies as with fire. That is because you have heaped up a lot of riches in these last days. Listen! You have not paid the wages of those who worked in your fields. The money you kept from them cries out to God against you. The Lord of all power has heard the cries of the workers. You have lived on earth in luxury. And you have had all that you wanted. You lived to please yourselves. You have made yourself fat, like animals ready for men to kill. You have accused. And you have caused the death of those who were innocent." The apostle Paul also wrote to Christian slave masters: in (Ephesians 6:9) "Those of you who are masters must also be fair to your slaves. You must not frighten them by saying that you will hurt them. Remember that you and your slaves have the same master in heaven. God is fair and you are all his slaves. He does not think that masters in this world are more important than their slaves."

Wages of Sin, the: Wages in Greek – *misthos* -[mis-thos'] Hebrew – sakar [saw-kawr'] meaning wages, reward (a) pay, wages, salary, (b) reward, recompense, punishment. (Romans 6:23) "For *the wages of sin* is death, but the gift of God is eternal life in Christ Jesus our Lord" This refers to a payment. When a person works, the person receives a wage or payment for the work. For example, James wrote of "the wages of the labourers who mowed your fields" (James 5:4) and (1Corinthians 3:8) adds, "each will receive his wages according to his labour." Invariably, there are righteous works and there also are sinful works. The phrase is not speaking of physical death, but is contrasting spiritual death with eternal life all representing sinful works and righteous works. Wages of sin is therefore define as benefit or reward for all sinful works a person does and the wage is spiritual death or eternal condemnation. This is to say, sinners are the kind of people who still suffers under the curse of the Law. Except one accepts Jesus Christ as the only Lord and Saviour the curse of the Law will still have effect on the sinful one.

2 *Wages of Sin* means that those whose "work" is sin will receive a payment of spiritual death, which is ultimately eternal separation from God in hell. While this is a dreadful situation, the gospel immediately includes an answer to this problem. Through faith in Jesus Christ as Lord, the gift of eternal life is given. It is not earned through human effort (Ephesians 2:8-9), but is instead freely given through God's grace because of what Jesus did on the cross, dying as a substitute for our sin.

3 Earlier in (Romans 6: 20-21), the apostle Paul wrote, "For when you were slaves of sin, you were free in regard to righteousness. But what fruit were you getting at that time from the things of which you are now ashamed? For the end of those things is death". In other words, prior to faith in Christ, we are slaves to sin, but the outcome is death – signifying curse of the Law, (punishment). Often the death is experienced both in the present and for eternity. The sins

Wait

of the moment may seem fun or liberating, but they are ultimately unfulfilling and do not result in the eternal outcome we desire. The solution is faith in Christ.

4 Understand this: After we have put our faith in Christ, it is still possible to experience the symptoms of spiritual death. Our eternity is secure and we will not be separated from God in hell. However, when we live out of our old natures rather than out of our new natures (2 Corinthians 5:17), we experience a sense of separation from God. This is very similar to what occurs when a child disobeys a parent. The child's status as a family member and the parent's love for the child do not change. However, the vitality of their relationship is damaged. Thankfully, this relationship can be restored. All we need do is confess our sins and turn back to God as in (1 John 1:9). We may still experience the natural consequences of our sins, but our fellowship with God can be restored through the comfort provided to us by the Holy Spirit – the Carrier of the executive function of Grace and Love in completion of the works of the trinity.

5 To avoid the *wages of sin*, first, we must place our faith in Christ. Only He can save us as in (John 14:16).Then, out of our trust in Him and our love for Him (in response to His love for us; (1 John 4:19), we obey Him (John 14:15; John 15:1-11). Our obedience leads us to a more vibrant experience of true life (John 10:10). Paul wrote in (Romans 6:22), "But now that you have been set free from sin and have become slaves of God, the fruit you get leads to sanctification and its end, eternal life." As Christ-followers, we are free to live in obedience to God and undergo the process of sanctification. As part of that sanctification, we begin to experience eternal life even while on this earth (John 10:10; John 15:11). And, ultimately, we will spend eternity with God. Praise the Lord!

Wait: (verb - Hebrew - Qavah [kaw-vaw],, 'perimenó [per-ee-men'-o] meaning to "remain, abide") – properly, remain all-around, i.e. steady (regardless of the obstacles involved); to "endure, putting up with surrounding difficulty") – note the force of the intensifying prefix, peri (used only in (Acts 1:4). 2 Stay where one is or delay action until a particular time or event. remain in readiness for a purpose .used to indicate that one is eagerly impatient to do something or for something to happen. 4 act as a waiter or waitress, serving food and drink. Wait as (noun) a period of waiting.2 street singers of Christmas carols. (Psalm 37:7) "Be still before the LORD and *wait* patiently for him; do not fret when people succeed in their ways, when they carry out their wicked schemes". Waiting is a great part of life's discipline, and therefore God often exercises the grace of waiting. Waiting has four purposes. It practises the patience

Walk

of faith. It gives time for preparation for the coming gift. It makes the blessing the sweeter when it arrives. And it shows the sovereignty of God, -- to give just when and just as he pleases. It may be difficult to define exactly what the Psalmist had in his mind when he said, "I wait for the Lord, my soul doth wait, and in his word do I hope. My soul waiteth for the Lord more than they that watch for the morning." It may have been the Messiah, whose coming was a thing close at hand to the mind of the ancient Jews, just as the Second Advent is to us. Praise the Lord!

Walk: (noun, Greek - *peripateó* -[per-ee-pat-eh'-o] Hebrew - *mahalak* - [mah-hal-awk'] To move over a surface by taking steps with the feet at a pace slower than a run: a baby learning to walk; a horse walking around a riding ring. (Verb) move at a regular pace by lifting and setting down each foot in turn, never having both feet off the ground at once. 2 guide, accompany, or escort (someone) on foot. 3 (of a thing) go missing or be stolen. 4.abandon or suddenly withdraw from a job or commitment. 5 (of a ghost) be visible; appear. 6 (of a batsman) leave the field without waiting to be given out by the umpire. 7reach first base automatically after not hitting at four balls pitched outside the strike zone. 8 live or behave in a particular way. More meanings in the (noun) form: 1 an act of travelling or an outing on foot. 2 a route recommended or marked out for recreational walking. 3 an unhurried rate of movement on foot. 4 a part of a forest under one keeper. 5 a farm where a hound puppy is trained. References (Matthew 14:25-26) Walking On Water And in the fourth watch of the night He came to them, walking on the sea. When the disciples saw Him walking on the sea, they were terrified, and said, "It is a ghost!" And they cried out in fear.(Acts 3:6-8) Healing But Peter said, "I do not possess silver and gold, but what I do have I give to you: In the name of Jesus Christ the Nazarene--walk!" And seizing him by the right hand, he raised him up; and immediately his feet and his ankles were strengthened. With a leap he stood upright and began to walk; and he entered the temple with them, walking and leaping and praising God. (Acts 14:10) Miracles Of Paul The Healed Walking Individuals Shouting said with a loud voice, "Stand upright on your feet." And he leaped up and began to walk. (Leviticus 26:12) Relationships Lordship, Human And Divine Walking With God, Human Descriptions Of God, Present Everywhere Fellowship, With God' I will also walk among you and be your God, and you shall be My people. (Genesis 3:8) Concealment, Of Sin Hearing God's Voice Hiding From God Unity, God's Goal Of Adam, Sin Of The Cool Of The Day Garden Of Eden, The God, Human Descriptions Of Suffering, Emotional Aspects Of Guilty Fear God Walking Quietness God, Presence Of They

Walk in the Light

heard the sound of the LORD God walking in the garden in the cool of the day, and the man and his wife hid themselves from the presence of the LORD God among the trees of the garden. (1 Kings 15:26) He did evil in the sight of the LORD, and walked in the way of his father and in his sin which he made Israel sin. (Proverbs 2:12-13) To deliver you from the way of evil, From the man who speaks perverse things; From those who leave the paths of uprightness To walk in the ways of darkness; strike zone.

Walk in the Light: This means obeying, resembling or being like, relationship – with Jesus by learning and leaning on him, to get Knowledge, Purity, Examination, Revelation, Freedom, Fullness of life, love and the Gospel message. See (1 John: 2:9-10) "Anyone who claims to be in the light but hates a brother or sister[a] is still in the darkness. Anyone who loves their brother and sister[b] lives in the light, and there is nothing in them to make them stumble". Note: the Greek word for brother or sister (adelphos) refers here to a believer, whether man or woman, as part of God's family; also in verse 11; and in 3:15, 17; 4:20; 5:16. Also (1 John 2:10) The Greek word for brother and sister (adelphos) refers here to a believer, whether man or woman, as part of God's family; also in (1 John 3:10; 4:20, 21.)

2 God is light; in him there is no darkness at all. If we claim to have fellowship with him yet walk in the darkness, we lie and do not live by the truth. But if we walk in the light, as he is in the light, we have fellowship with one another, and the blood of Jesus, his Son, purifies us from all sin. If we claim to be without sin, we deceive ourselves and the truth is not in us. If we confess our sins, he is faithful and just and will forgive us our sins and purify us from all unrighteousness.

3 This believe is a common metaphor within Christian culture. It is often taken to mean "acting correctly" or even "living openly." Gospel, however, the phrase has the idea of relinquishing sin by following Jesus.

The only Old Testament occurrence of this precise phrase is in (Isaiah 2:5), "O house of Jacob, come and let us walk in the light of the Lord." The Psalms contain similar phrases (Psalm 56:13; 89:15), as does (Isaiah 9:2; 50:10-11; 59:9).

5 In the New Testament, "walking in the light" is directly related to following Jesus, who said, "I am the light of the world. He who follows me shall not walk in darkness, but have the light of life" (John 8:12). While this verse does not directly say, "Walk in the light, i.e., Jesus," it does pointedly warn of doing the opposite; therefore, those who follow Jesus are "walking in the light."

To "walk" is, in short, to live one's

life. One's lifestyle or way of life can be considered a "walk." The word also indicates progress. Walking is related to growth; it is taking steps toward maturity. "Light" in the Bible can be a metaphor for life, happiness, righteousness, or understanding. The Bible is clear that light comes from the Lord God, the "Father of the heavenly lights" (James 1:17). He is the opposite of evil. Putting it all together, "walking in the light" means "growing in holiness and maturing in the faith as we follow Jesus."

The apostle John repeatedly used the "light" metaphor in relation to the Messiah. For example, he writes that Jesus is "the true light that gives light to every man" (John 1:9). In (1 John 1:7) he says, "If we walk in the light as He [God] is in the light, we have fellowship with one another, and the blood of Jesus Christ His Son cleanses us from all sin." In verse 5, John says that God's very nature is light. Jesus, then, is the conduit or provider of light to the world. Our Christian duty is to live in the light God gives: "Now you are light in the Lord. Walk as children of light" (Ephesians 5:8). When we walk in the light, we cannot walk in darkness. Sin is left in the shadows as we let our light "shine before men" (Matthew 5:16). It is God's plan for us to become more like Christ (1 Thessalonians 4:3).

6 "Walking in the light" means we consider Jesus as "the light" in this world, and we "walk" in that light by following His precepts, living in His power, and growing in His grace. Praise the Lord!

Walk in the Spirit: This means allowing oneself to an incredibly detailed direction, power over demonic interference, worry-free dependence on the Lord, freedom from fearing men. Each of these blessings is a by-product of a higher *walk in the Spirit* that goes beyond all these things! See (1 Samuel 9). The Gospel makes it clear that, Saul was sent by his father to find some runaway donkeys. Taking a servant with him, Saul searched throughout the lands of Ephraim, Shalim, Benjamin and Zuph. Finally, he got discouraged and was ready to give up the hunt. But then his servant told him about Samuel, a seer; maybe he could tell him where to find the donkeys. On this occasion, one can see Saul as a type of believer who seeks direction only. All he had in mind was: "Where are my donkeys? Where should I go? I'm at my wits' end!"

Meanwhile, God had already told Samuel a young man was going to come to him, and that he was to anoint him. Samuel here is a type of the Holy Spirit, who knows the mind of God; he has more on his mind than just direction. He knows Saul has been chosen by God to play a part in heaven's eternal purposes! The first thing Samuel did when Saul arrived was to call for a feast: "...go up before me unto the high place; for ye shall eat with

Want, I shall not

me to day, and to morrow I will let thee go, and will tell thee all that is in thine heart" (1 Samuel 9:19).

This is exactly what the Holy Spirit desires of us: to sit at the Lord's Table and minister to Him -- having quality time alone, hearing His heart. Samuel asked Saul to clear his mind so they could commune together: "And as for thine asses that were lost three days ago, set not thy mind on them; for they are found..." (verse 20). Samuel was saying, "Don't focus on getting direction now -- that's all settled. There's something more important at hand. You've got to know God's heart -- His eternal purposes!"

2 Samuel laid a whole shoulder of meat before Saul, and they spent time communing: "And...Samuel communed with Saul upon the top of the house" (verse 25). After that night of communion, Samuel asked Saul to send his servant out of the room, so they could have an intimate, face-to-face session: "...Bid the servant passes on before us... but stand thou still a while, that I may show thee the word of God. Then Samuel took a vial of oil, and poured it upon his head, and kissed him, and said, is it not because the Lord hath anointed thee to be captain over his inheritance?" (1 Samuel 9:27; 10:1).

Do you see what God is saying here? Today as a Christian "If you really want to walk in the Spirit -- if you really want the anointing of God -- you need to seek more than direction from Him. You need to enter into His presence and get to know His heart, His desires! You see, He *want* to anoint you -- to use you in His kingdom!"

3 Beloved in Christ, forget direction -- forget everything else for now! Allow the Holy Spirit to teach you the deep, hidden things of God. Stand still in His presence, and let Him show you the very heart of the Lord. That is the walk of the Spirit in its highest form! When you do this, direction will come -- and you won't even have to ask! As Saul was leaving, Samuel said, "By the way -- go to Rachel's sepulchre and you'll get the information you need about your donkeys" (1 Samuel 10:2).

4 Then Saul received some of the most incredibly detailed instructions in all of God's Word! God has a precious oil of anointing He wants to pour on you. He wants you to come out of His presence with the aroma of His anointing on you. And as you're leaving, He will whisper "Oh, by the way -- here's what you wanted to know...." He promises as in (Isaiah 30:30) "And the Lord shall cause his glorious voice to be heard...." And don't forget those who believe in the Lord will not lack any good thing.

Want, I shall not: As in a Psalm of David (Psalm 23:1) "The LORD is my shepherd, *I shall not want*". Meaning lacking nothing. If we stop the phrase here, it may be incomplete. To complete the verb,

Want, I shall not

the past tense of want – wanted must also be considered. As Christians, when the Lord is our Shepherd, we shall not 'want' or be 'wanted'. This means we shall not lack any of our needs nor be wanted or chased by our enemies. Though the enemies can try to pursue us but one thing is sure, the Lord whom all the benefit of freedom, security, protection, prosperity and pastures are in His hands, is shepherding or fathering us. Base on the above ingredients I or we shall not lack as individual, the Church of true Christians shall lack nothing base on this true psychology of believing.

David declared this having understood or possesses the knowledge of who is shepherding him. He presented himself as a Sheep needing the capable hand of a Shepherd - Not just out of ordinary lips. He knows that God took him out from the mouth of lion, save him from the hands of Goliath and even hide him from the hand of Saul. This means in the hand of the Shepherd, there has never been and will never be any disappointment. Glory to Jesus!

2 The true psychology of a believer in God is bounded on security or protection and prosperity. To literally understand the verb 'want' 'means having a desire to possess or do (something); wish for. 3 "I want an apple" synonyms: desire, wish for, hope for, fancy, have a fancy for, take a fancy to, have an inclination for, care for, like, set one's heart on; and much more wish to speak to (someone). "Tony wants me in the studio"

4 A suspected criminal is wanted - sought by the police for questioning. "He is 'wanted' by the police in connection with an arms theft". He is wanted by his enemies.

5 Wanted could also be used to express sinful desire, desire (someone) sexually. "I've wanted you since the first moment I saw you" NORTH AMERICAN informal

6 *Want* or wanted could also be used to express desire to be in or out of a particular place or situation. "if anyone wants out, there's the door" 2 informal should or need to do something. "you don't *want* to believe everything you hear" synonyms: should, ought, need, must "you *want* to be more careful"

7 In the British usage, want is for a thing required to be attended to in a specified way. "The wheel wants greasing" synonyms: need, be or stand in need of, require, demand, cry out for "his toaster wants repairing" 8 literary lack something desirable or essential. "You shall want for nothing while you are with Jesus".

9 As opposed to archaic which is chiefly used in expressions of time, lack or be short of (a specified amount of time or thing), absence, non-existence, unavailability; and anything to opposed

War

to abundance, that is the state of being poor and in need of essentials; poverty. "Freedom from want" synonyms: need, neediness, austerity, privation, deprivation, poverty, impoverishment, impecuniousness, impecuniosity, pennilessness, or pauperism, penury, destitution, famine, drought, indigence "a time of want" a desire for something. "the expression of our wants and desires"

10 synonyms: wish, desire, demand, longing, yearning, fancy, craving, hankering; and so forth.

"*I shall not want,*" in David's context indicates here that as a sheep in Christ's care, he was confident that he would lack nothing. This sentiment is repeated in (Psalms 34:9-10) thus' "Fear the Lord, you his holy people, for those who fear him lack nothing. The lions may grow weak and hungry, but those who seek the Lord lack no good thing. " – NIV and this clearly indicates David's understanding in regards to putting God and God's way first in his life see also (Matthew 6:25-34). Continue to make the Lord your Shepherd and remain or leave all your life like a 'conquer-ship' in Jesus name. Hallelujah!

War: The intentional, premeditated killing of another person with malice; murder or an organized and often prolonged conflict that is carried out by states or non-state actors. It is generally characterised by extreme violence, social disruption and an attempt at economic destruction. War should be understood as an actual, intentional and widespread armed conflict between political communities, and therefore is defined as a form of (collective) political violence or intervention. The set of techniques used by a group to carry out war is known as warfare. An absence of war is usually called peace. Oftentimes, many people make the mistake of reading what the Bible says in (Exodus 20:13), "You shall not kill," and then seeking to apply this command to war. God often ordered the Israelites to go to war with other nations (1 Samuel 15:3; Joshua 4:13). God ordered the death penalty for numerous crimes (Exodus 21:12, 15; 22:19; Leviticus 20:11). So, God is not against killing in all circumstances, but only murder. War is never a good thing, but sometimes it is a necessary thing. In a world filled with sinful people (Romans 3:10-18), war is inevitable. Sometimes the only way to keep sinful people from doing great harm to the innocent is by going to war.

2 In the Old Testament, God ordered the Israelites to "take vengeance on the Midianites for the Israelites" (Numbers 31:2, Deuteronomy 20:16-17) declares, "However, in the cities of the nations the LORD your God is giving you as an inheritance, do not leave alive anything that breathes. Completely destroy them...as the LORD your God has commanded you." Also,

(1 Samuel 15:18) says, "Go and completely destroy those wicked people, the Amalekites; make *war* on them until you have wiped them out." Obviously God is not against all *war*. Jesus is always in perfect agreement with the Father (John 10:30), so we cannot argue that war was only God's will in the Old Testament. God does not change (Malachi 3:6; James 1:17).

3 Jesus' second coming will be exceedingly violent. (Revelation 19:11-21) describes the ultimate war with Christ, the conquering commander who judges and makes war "with justice" (verse. 11). It's going to be bloody (verse. 13) and gory. The birds will eat the flesh of all those who oppose Him (verse. 17-18). He has no compassion upon His enemies, whom He will conquer completely and consign to a "fiery lake of burning sulphur" (verse. 20). It is an error to say that God never supports a war. Jesus is not a pacifist. In a world filled with evil people, sometimes war is necessary to prevent even greater evil. If Hitler had not been defeated by World War II, how many more millions would have been killed? If the American Civil War had not been fought, how much longer would African-Americans have had to suffer as slaves?

4 *War* is a terrible thing. Some wars are more "just" than others, but *war* is always the result of sin (Romans 3:10-18). At the same time, (Ecclesiastes 3:8) declares, "There is...a time to love and a time to hate, a time for war and a time for peace." Christians should not desire war, but neither are Christians to oppose the government God has placed in authority over them (Romans 13:1-4; 1 Peter 2:17). The most important thing we can be doing in a time of war is to be praying for godly wisdom for our leaders, praying for the safety of our military, praying for quick resolution to conflicts, and praying for a minimum of casualties among civilians on both sides (Philippians 4:6-7). "Do not be anxious about anything, but in every situation, by prayer and petition, with thanksgiving, present your requests to God. And the peace of God, which transcends all understanding, will guard your hearts and your minds in Christ Jesus". Amen!

Warfare, spiritual: (Ephesians 6:10-12) declares, "Finally, be strong in the Lord and in his mighty power. Put on the full armour of God so that you can take your stand against the devil's schemes. For our struggle is not against flesh and blood, but against the rulers, against the authorities, against the powers of this dark world and against the spiritual forces of evil in the heavenly realms." This text teaches some crucial truths: we can only be strong in the Lord's power, it is God's armour that protects us, and our battle is against spiritual forces of evil in the world". Spiritual warfare is therefore, the Christian version of the concept of taking a stand against

Warfare, spiritual

supernatural evil forces. The foundation for this ideology is having a belief in evil spirits which are able to intervene in human affairs. Various Christian groups have adopted practices to repel such forces, as based on their doctrine of Christian demonology. A common form of spiritual warfare among Christians is prayer in Christianity. Other practices may include exorcisms, laying-on of hands, fasting, or anointing with oil.

2 There are two primary errors when it comes to *spiritual warfare*—over-emphasis and under-emphasis. Some blame every sin, every conflict, and every problem on demons that need to be cast out. Others completely ignore the spiritual realm and the fact that the Gospel tells us our battle is against spiritual powers. The key to successful spiritual warfare is finding the biblical balance. Jesus sometimes cast demons out of people and sometimes healed people with no mention of the demonic. The apostle Paul instructs Christians to wage war against the sin in themselves (Romans 6) and to wage war against the evil one. Example of someone strong in the Lord's power is Michael, the archangel, in (Jude 9). Michael, likely the most powerful of all of God's angels, did not rebuke Satan in his own power, but said, "The Lord rebuke you!" (Revelation 12:7-8) records that in the end times Michael will defeat Satan. Still, when it came to his conflict with Satan, Michael rebuked Satan in God's name and authority, not his own. It is only through our relationship with Jesus Christ that Christians have any authority over Satan and his demons. It is only in His Name that our rebuke has any power.

3 (Ephesians 6:13-18) gives a description of the spiritual armour given to us by God. We are to stand firm with the belt of truth, the breastplate of righteousness, the gospel of peace, the shield of faith, the helmet of salvation, the sword of the Spirit, and by praying in the Spirit. What do these pieces of spiritual armour represent in spiritual warfare? We are to speak the truth against Satan's lies. We are to rest in the fact that we are declared righteous because of Christ's sacrifice for us. We are to proclaim the gospel no matter how much resistance we receive. We are not to waver in our faith, no matter how strongly we are attacked. Our ultimate defence is the assurance we have of our salvation, an assurance that no spiritual force can take away. Our offensive weapon is the Word of God, not our own opinions and feelings. We are to follow Jesus' example in recognizing that some spiritual victories are only possible through prayer.

4 Jesus is our ultimate example for *spiritual warfare*. Observe how Jesus handled direct attacks from Satan when He was tempted by him in the wilderness (Matthew 4:1-11). Each temptation was answered the same way—with the

words "It is written." Jesus knew the Word of the living God is the most powerful weapon against the temptations of the devil. If Jesus Himself used the Word to counter the devil, do we dare to use anything less?

5 The ultimate example of how not to engage in *spiritual warfare* is the seven sons of Sceva. "Some Jews who went around driving out evil spirits tried to invoke the name of the Lord Jesus over those who were demon-possessed. They would say, 'In the name of Jesus, whom Paul preaches, I command you to come out.' Seven sons of Sceva, a Jewish chief priest, were doing this. One day the evil spirit answered them, 'Jesus I know, and I know about Paul, but who are you?' Then the man who had the evil spirit jumped on them and overpowered them all. He gave them such a beating that they ran out of the house naked and bleeding" (Acts 19:13-16). The seven sons of Sceva were using Jesus' name. That is not enough. The seven sons of Sceva did not have a relationship with Jesus; therefore, their words were void of any power or authority. The seven sons of Sceva were relying on a methodology. They were not relying on Jesus as their Lord and Saviour, and they were not employing the Word of God in their spiritual warfare. As a result, they received a humiliating beating. May we learn from their bad example and conduct *spiritual warfare* as the Gospel instructs. The first key in waging spiritual warfare is, we rely on God's power, not our own. Second, we rebuke in Jesus' Name, not our own. Third, we protect ourselves with the full armour of God. Fourth, we wage warfare with the sword of the Spirit—the Word of God. Finally, we remember that while we wage *spiritual warfare* against Satan and his demons or cohorts, not every sin or problem is a demon that needs to be rebuked to avoid the temptation of inviting demons to take control. The name of Jesus is powerful!

Watch: (verb –Greek – grégoreó [gray-gor-yoo'-o] Hebrew – shamar – [shaw-mar] (Mathew 26:41) "Watch and pray, that ye enter not into temptation: the spirit indeed is willing, but the flesh is weak". Meaning to be awake I am awake, am vigilant, watch (a) I am awake (in the night), watch, (b) I am watchful, on the alert, vigilant, look at or observe attentively over a period of time. 2.exercise care, caution, or restraint about. 3 remain awake for the purpose of religious observance. (Noun) 1 a small timepiece worn typically on a strap on one's wrist. 2 an act or instance of carefully observing someone or something over a period of time. 3 a film or programme considered in terms of its appeal to the public

Jesus told His disciples to "watch and pray" several times. This phrase occurs only three times in the New Testament. Here are the other two, in (Mark 13:33) Take

Water

ye heed, watch and pray: for ye know not when the time is". And in (Mark 14:38) Watch and pray, that ye enter not into temptation: the spirit indeed is willing, but the flesh is weak. The Greek word for "watch" in (Mathew 26:41) and (Mark 14:38) is the same. It is GREGOPEO. It has the sense of being "vigilant," "to keep awake," "to be on the alert," and "to keep one's eyes open." In (Mark 13:33) a different Greek word, AGRYPNEO, is used for "watch." This word means "to be sleepless," or "to keep oneself awake for the purpose of watching." The two Greek words are similar but different, the later one having an emphasis on not sleeping. All of these passages deal with moments of crisis. In Matthew, Jesus warned His disciples to remain spiritually awake for the purpose of not falling into sin. This is a great reminder for us to be watchful in order to flee sin and trust in Him.

Water: (noun Greek – *hudór* [hoo'-dore]- Hebrew - *mayim* - [mah'-yim] Water symbolizes Gods Word in many places throughout the gospel. In both Psalms and Ephesians water is a symbol of God's word. Water is a colourless, transparent, odourless, liquid which forms the seas, lakes, rivers, and rain and is the basis of the fluids of living organisms. 2 a stretch or area of water, such as a river, sea, or lake. 3 urine. 4 the amniotic fluid surrounding a fetus in the womb, especially as discharged in a flow shortly before birth. 5 the quality of transparency and brilliance shown by a diamond or other gem. 6 capital stock which represents a book value greater than the true assets of a company. (*Verb)* pour or sprinkle water over (a plant or area) in order to encourage plant growth. 2 (of a person's eyes) fill with tears. 3 dilute or adulterate (a drink, typically an alcoholic one) with water. 4 (of a river) flow through (an area of land). 5 increase (a company's debt, or nominal capital) by the issue of new shares without a corresponding addition to assets.

Indeed the natural explains the spiritual? In day five of creation we find in (Genesis 1:20) God said "Let the waters bring forth abundantly the moving creature that have life..." This passage shows us that life comes out of the water. In the natural birth process that is true also. After conception we continue to develop and grow in what is essentially a sack of water inside the womb. When a woman is in labour and the baby is about to be born, we wait for that 'water to break' so that the baby can come forth into life. Also physical birth (water birth) must come before Spiritual birth as we see in (John 3) when Nicodemus, a ruler of the Jews, is asking questions of Jesus.

In (John 3: 1-5) "Now there was a man of the Pharisees named Nicodemus, a member of the Jewish ruling council. He came to Jesus at night and said, "Rabbi, we know you are a teacher who has come from God. For no one could perform the miraculous signs you are doing if God were not with him." In reply Jesus declared, "I tell you the truth, no one can see the kingdom of God unless he is born again." "How can a man be born when he is old?" Nicodemus asked. "Surely he cannot enter a second time into his mother's womb to be born!" Jesus answered, "I tell you the truth, no one can enter the kingdom of God unless he is born of water and the Spirit.

Water, The Anointing: See the anointing water

Way: (Greek – hodos [hod-os'] Hebrew – Derek [deh'-rek])meaning a way, road, journey or a way, road, journey, path as in (John 3:3) "This is he who was spoken of through the prophet Isaiah: "A voice of one calling in the wilderness, 'Prepare the way for the Lord, make straight paths for him.'" Jesus Christ said He is "the way" to the Father as in (John 14:6) "Jesus said to him, 'I am the way, the truth, and the life. No one comes to the Father except through Me". "The way" God has called us to is challenging. It is not just a hobby, but a total way of life. "Because narrow is the gate and difficult is the way which leads to life, and there are few who find it" (Matthew 7:14).

2 "The Way" was a title for followers of Jesus—the name of followers of Jesus before the term "Christian" was used. "And asked letters from him to the synagogues of Damascus, so that if he found any who were of the Way, whether men or women, he might bring them bound to Jerusalem" (Acts 9:2; see Acts 11:26) for the first reference to Christians). Also the Nelson Study Bible says, "Originally, the church called themselves 'The Way.' But later they began to refer to themselves as Christians, despite the fact that the name most likely was originally used to ridicule the believers."

3 Whatever the case may be, the way means only through Jesus Christ can a person be saved. It is written ,(Mathew 7:13)- ENTER YE IN AT THE STRAIT GATE: FOR WIDE IS THE GATE, AND BROAD IS THE WAY, THAT LEADETH TO DESTRUCTION, AND MANY THERE BE WHICH GO IN THEREAT. The Strait Gate and Narrow...Way is a total commitment to Jesus Christ. It is not just saying, Lord, Lord. It is not just saying you have accepted Jesus as your Saviour. Many name the name of Jesus, but they perish. The STRAIT GATE and NARROW...WAY is: BE YE DOERS OF THE WORD, AND NOT HEARERS ONLY, DECEIVING YOUR OWN SELVES- (James 1:22). As Jesus tells us, AND WHY CALL YE ME, LORD, LORD, AND DO NOT THE THINGS WHICH I SAY?- (Luke 6:46). It is doing THE WILL OF MY FATHER WHICH IS IN HEAVEN – see (Mathew 7:15 -23) Understand, it is not a matter of, if you know

Water

Jesus. It is a matter of, does Jesus know you?- as in (Mathew 25:12). Jesus shall say to many that are absolutely positive they are saved, "I KNOW YOU NOT"- (Luke 13:25). Ponder "How can this be?" It is because people base their belief that they are saved on emotions, or what someone tells them, or on lying thoughts in their mind from the devil, or on a lack of understanding of God's Word, or on other things. One can say, "I feel I am saved! I can feel the Holy Spirit inside me! God is my Father! God has answered my prayer! Jesus has done this or that for me! I have suffered for Jesus! I serve the Lord! The Spirit of God leads me! I sing in the church! I teach a Sunday school class." These type of thoughts or feelings mean nothing at the judgment day. The Word of God (the in the Gospel as contained in the Bible) shall judge. As it is written (John 12:48). "He that rejecteth me, and receiveth not my words, hath one that judgeth him: the word that I have spoken, the same shall judge him in the last day". See also (Mathew 7:24-27)

4 To say that the way is narrow implies that once you are saved, the battle has started –strong men even the devil will be on your *way* to block you: This is known as the Spiritual Warfare. Yet despite Satan's vast arsenal of devices and deceptions, a few by the grace of God come to Jesus when "He" calls. They come by faith and surrender all to Jesus. They follow Him. They have overcome the many devices and deceptions of the devil, by the mercy of God, through faith. Now there is a new battle. Satan can be expected to attack the new Christian in ways that do not even come to his mind as in (Peter 4:12-14) "Dear friends, do not be surprised at the fiery ordeal that has come on you to test you, as though something strange were happening to you. But rejoice inasmuch as you participate in the sufferings of Christ, so that you may be overjoyed when his glory is revealed. If you are insulted because of the name of Christ, you are blessed, for the Spirit of glory and of God rests on you". This fiery trial or battle that a person goes through is called "spiritual warfare."

5 Today in the Church System in which we live, the masses of professing Christians are almost totally ignorant of or indifferent to these truths. Others openly criticize and oppose them. The church of today is getting further and further away from the strait gate and the narrow *way* of the Bible. New ideas and doctrines are coming into most churches at what seems to be an ever increasing rate. People are being tossed to and fro with the winds of all kinds of misleading doctrines. The God-fearing, born-again, love-filled, fruit-bearing, obedient, Bible-reading, and discerning Christian, who understands spiritual warfare, who demonstrates his

Way in the Laodicean Church

love for God by obeying His commandments, who reveals his faith by serving God and taking a stand for truth, and who is watching and ready for Jesus to return, seems to be a disappearing figure in this generation. Most churches today are places where make-believe, or comfort Christians gather on Sundays to feel comfortable and be entertained. They leave church confident and reassured that all is right in their life. Then they die and are shocked, as they find themselves in a place called "hell."

Again, many Christians are the same way. They make light of sin. The strait gate and the narrow way is seldom taught. Many so-called Christians today also have a golden calf. Their money, pride, selfishness, television, job, house, automobile, the things of this world, astrology, drinking, drugs, sex, the government, or their own desires are their "golden calf." Jesus is to be your LORD and Saviour. He is to come "first." Most Christians today, as then, have not known God's ways. Many call upon the name of the Lord, but they will not follow "Him." Many commit abominations and are not ashamed. They are NOT VALIANT FOR THE TRUTH- as in (Jeremiah 9:3). Their MOLTEN IMAGE IS FALSEHOOD - (Jeremiah 10:14). God is IN THEIR MOUTH, but FAR FROM THEIR REINS- (Jeremiah 12:2). THEY HAVE BURNED INCENSE TO VANITY-(Jeremiah 18:15). Jesus described the Laodicean church as lukewarm.

Way in the Laodicean Church: (Jeremiah 18:15). Jesus described the Laodicean church as lukewarm. "Does the snow of Lebanon forsake the rock of the open country? Or is the cold flowing water from a foreign land ever snatched away? 'For My people have forgotten Me, They burn incense to worthless gods And they have stumbled from their ways, From the ancient paths, To walk in bypaths, Not on a highway, To make their land a desolation, An object of perpetual hissing; Everyone who passes by it will be astonished And shake his head....

2 The lukewarm are confident they are correct and righteous. Their confidence is so deeply rooted that it is nearly impossible to reach them with the truth. Lukewarmness comes from mixing both hot and cold. They are not cold toward the things of God, but neither are they hot. They are content, apathetic, and indifferent. They are not truly concerned with what is right and wrong or what is good and evil. Within the Laodicean church is the prevailing attitude of "live and let live; don't rock the boat; don't cause waves; it will all turn out O.K." - the *way* is narrow. They are taking a neutral position. They are trying to serve God, but are also trying to please men. They are serving two masters and justify their position. They are serving God, and they are serving "self." They are serving God, and they are serving the world. This is totally unacceptable

with God. Remember, the name "Laodicea" means "the rights of the people." Their knowledge and understanding of God, His Word, and of these things is, at best, only lukewarm. Their obedience, love, fruits of the Spirit, and works are, at best, only lukewarm. Their daily conversation may be centred on both the things of the world and the things of God. They are like a wave. They are carnal and have not denied themselves. They are not fully following Jesus, though they are usually sure they are. Jesus is in their life, but He is not the centre of their life. Their life revolves around things of the world and worldly circumstances; Jesus is only a part. They have need of milk (basic doctrines) and not meat (perfection). They are not ready for the doctrine of perfection and holiness. Their thoughts are divided between Jesus and the things of the world. Laodiceans want to maintain a level of control over their lives; they will trust Jesus only to a point. They do not have the understanding that Jesus is in control when very difficult situations come against them; their knowledge is lukewarm.

3 At best, their understanding of who is saved, by the grace of God, and who is not saved is only lukewarm. It may be said, they do not fully comprehend the strait gate and narrow *way*. Their teaching may consist of some sound doctrine mixed with confusion, false doctrine, deceit, doctrines of men and denominations, new fads, or other distortions of Scripture that come along. They may have a great church complex, a magnificent choir, large attendance, much money coming in, a vast radio and television ministry, an extensive mailing list reaching multitudes with a monthly magazine, and many letters and telephone calls coming in. They may be claiming to have won many souls, but if the message proclaimed is only lukewarm, then that is all they are.

3 The following should be considered. Sound doctrine is disappearing; most people will not tolerate it. One might ask, "What would happen if sound doctrine was being taught?" The answer is found in the Scriptures. In the days of the apostles, sound doctrine was being taught in Laodicea; however, it was rejected. The Laodicean church was only lukewarm; this is unacceptable to God. For those who may wonder if lukewarm is really so bad, Jesus gives the following warning. I will spew – meaning spit, through away. Thee out of my mouth. This mean s that the entire Laodicean church will be spit out and perish. There will be such a small number from this church that will repent, not even the word "few" is used as it was in the "dead" church of Sardis. The lukewarm will not be taken when the Rapture comes. But thanks be to God because of His everlasting mercies towards us. Praise His Name!

Weak: (verb, Greek - *astheneó* [as-then-eh'-o] Hebrew – *rapheh* - [raw-feh']) To a person, meaning I am weak, sick or I am weak (physically: then morally), I am sick. A verb used metaphorically to describe those who lack clarity and are unsure of how they are supposed to use their freedom in Christ. Knowledge alone cannot determine our use of Christian liberty; rather, the love of God in Christ must be the guiding factor in how we seek to realize the kingdom of God on earth.

Weak and Strong: This phrase serves as operative terms that combine such concepts as the kingdom of God, knowledge, love, conscience, freedom, and judgment. Paul's special use of the terms provides a theological context that informs and clarifies them. Those who have an accurate understanding of God and his kingdom and are able to actualize their Christian freedom without a conflict in conscience are "strong." Those who lack clarity and are unsure of how they are supposed to use their freedom in Christ are "weak." The words "strong" and "weak" are often found in conjunction in Paul's writings. The parallelism of the two terms is used to communicate two central principles. First, human weakness allows the power of God to be most pre-eminently manifested. As Paul says, "For when I am weak, then I am strong" (2 Corinthians 12:10b). Second, the two words are used metaphorically to describe the degree of spiritual development in the life of the believer (Romans 14:1-23; 15:1-8 ; 1 Corinthians 8:7-13 ; 1 Corinthians 10:23 1 Corinthians 10:32).

2 Paul specifically identifies two areas of concern when addressing the strong and the weak: food and holy days. Some have the strength to eat meat; others, "whose faith is weak" (Romans 14:1), feel that they should eat only vegetables (verse. 2). Similarly, the weak are very concerned about observing special holy days, while the strong consider each day alike (verse. 5). The weak consider issues like this extremely important in regards to God's kingdom, while the strong do not. The beliefs and customs of the weak influence their understanding of Christian liberty. Their scrupulosity over sensitizes their consciences. When they look at the antithetical conduct of the strong, they end up in great moral torment (Romans 14:14-15). Some weak people start emulating the practices of the strong, yet do so out of fear and doubt (verse. 23). This experience of confusion and doubt has serious consequences for the weak. The strong have caused the weak to stumble, and have possibly even destroyed them (verse. 20).

3 A similar situation can be seen centring around meat offered to idols (1Corinthians 8:1-13 ; 10:23-33). The strong have knowledge that an idol is nothing (verses.

Weary

4-6). They have adopted a libertarian approach and believe that "everything is permissible" (1 Corinthians 10:23). The weak possess no such knowledge, and experience a great moral conflict because of the actions of the strong (1 Corinthians 8:7-13).

4 The *weak* judge the freedom of the strong as impiety; the strong scoff at the convictions of the weak. Such tensions between believers threaten the very unity of the church. Paul addresses the issue as follows. Because God is the Creator of all things, nothing is unclean in and of itself (Romans 14:14 Romans 14:20 ; 1 Corinthians 8:8 ; 10:26). Food and observance of holy days have nothing at all to do with salvation they are adiaphorous, of no spiritual consequence. We are no better off for partaking or abstaining, because these things are of no significance to the kingdom of God. It is for this reason that Paul identifies with the strong - See (Romans 14:14 ; 1 Corinthians 8:4-6 ; 1 Corinthians 10:25-27 1 Corinthians 10:29-31).

Weary: (adjective, Greek: *ekkakeó* - [ek-kak-eh'-o] Hebrew: *ayeph* -[paw-yafe'] meaningI am faint, am weary I am faint, am *weary*. Physically or mentally fatigued. 2 Expressive of or prompted by fatigue: a weary smile. 3 Having one's interest, forbearance, or indulgence worn out: weary of delays. 4 Causing fatigue; tiresome: a weary wait. There are many meanings to the word *weary*. People are tired when they labour all day long or carry heavy loads or burden. That is why Jesus having look at the overall human condition, He called in (Mathew 11:28) "Come to me, all you who are *weary* and burdened, and I will give you rest. For my yoke is easy and my burden is light. Jesus was speaking to a group of people who had been trying to carry an impossible load, namely the Jewish law and other standards imposed upon them by the religious leaders of the day. In the language of the New Testament, the word "labour" carried the idea of working to the point of utter exhaustion. The term "heavy laden" indicated that, at some time in the past, a great load had been dumped on a person and the individual was continuing to bear the load. Together, the terms described a person who was exhausted from trying to carry a burden assumed in the past. Jesus' listeners were exhausted from trying to measure up to the expectations of the law.

Refer the gospels in (Matthew 11:30) My soul finds rest in God alone; my salvation comes from him. (Psalm 62:1) He gives strength to the weary, and increases the power of the weak. (Isaiah 40:29) Never tire of doing what is right. (2 Thessalonians 3:13) Let us not become weary in doing good, for at the proper time we will reap a harvest if we do not give up .(Galatians 6:9) Never be lacking in zeal, but keep your spiritual fervour, serving the LORD. (Romans

Weep

12:11) Consider him who endured such opposition from sinful men, so that you will not grow weary and lose heart. (Hebrews 12:3) To this end I labour, struggling with all His energy, which so powerfully works in me. (Colossians 1:29) Refresh my heart in Christ. (Philemon 1:20)

Weep: (Greek: *Klaió* - [klah'-yo], Hebrew: *Bakah* [baw-kaw'] meaning to shed tears. 2.used in names of tree and shrub varieties with drooping branches, e.g. weeping cherry. 3 exude liquid I weep, weep for, mourn, I weep, weep for, mourn, lament. In the Gospels our Lord wept as He looked on man's misery, and both instances demonstrate our Lord's (loving) human nature, His compassion for people, and the life He offers to those who believe. When Jesus wept, He showed all these things. Two passages in the Gospels and one in the Epistles (Hebrews 5:7) teach that Jesus wept.

2 In (John 11:1–45) which concerns the death and resurrection of Lazarus, the brother of Mary and Martha and a friend of our Lord. Jesus wept (John 11:35) when He gathered with the sisters and others mourning Lazarus's death. Jesus did not weep over the death itself since He knew Lazarus would soon be raised and ultimately spend eternity with Him in heaven. Yet He could not help but weep when confronted with the wailing and sobbing of Mary, Martha, and the other mourners (John 11:33). The original language indicates that our Lord wept "silent tears" or tears of compassion for His friends (Romans 12:15). If Jesus had been present when Lazarus was dying, His compassion would have caused Him to heal His friend (John 11:14–15). But preventing a death might be considered by some to be a chance circumstance or just a "minor" miracle, and this was not a time for any doubt. So Lazarus spent four days in death's grave before Jesus publicly called him back to life. The Father wanted these witnesses to know that Jesus was the Son of God, that Jesus was sent by God, and that Jesus and the Father had the same will in everything (John 11:4, 40–42). Only the one true God could have performed such an awesome and breath-taking miracle, and through this miracle the Father and the Son were glorified, and many believed (John 11:4, 45).

3 Also in (Luke 19:41–44) the Lord is taking His last trip to Jerusalem shortly before He was crucified at the insistence of His own people, the people He came to save. Earlier, the Lord had said, "O Jerusalem, Jerusalem, the city that kills the prophets and stones those sent to her! How often I wanted to gather your children together, just as a hen gathers her brood under her wings, and you would not have it" (Luke 13:34). As our Lord approached Jerusalem and thought of all those lost souls, "He saw the city and wept over

White

it" (Luke 19:41). Here, wept (*past-tense*) is the same word used to describe the weeping of Mary and the others in (John 11:33), so we know that Jesus cried aloud in anguish over the future of the city. That future was less than 40 years distant; in AD 70 more than 1,000,000 residents of Jerusalem died in one of the most gruesome sieges in recorded history.

4 As we can see, our Lord wept differently in these two instances because the eternal outcomes were entirely different. Martha, Mary, and Lazarus had eternal life because they believed in the Lord Jesus Christ, but most in Jerusalem did not believe and therefore did not have life. The same is true today: "Jesus said to her, 'I am the resurrection and the life; he who believes in Me will live even if he dies'" (John 11:25). In (Luke 6:21b) "Blessed are you who *weep* now, for you will laugh." Without this being mere emotions "Blessed are those who are burdened with the suffering of the world... even to the point of tears... Blessed are you because you find the condition so unbearable that you HAVE to do something... Blessed are you because you have seen the heart of God... you have found in all of the crap that's going on... a sense of hope... and you laugh... Blessed are you because you have realized that your prayers for God to do something about this crap of a world that we live in... meaning you... are God's answer to a world wondering where he is. Christians are the answer to any good thing in this world. Praise the Lord!

White: (adjective: Greek *aspros* - [AHS-bros], Hebrew: *Laban* [law-bawn'] Whiter, Whitest) White is a colour of purity and righteousness. It is also used to describe things in nature. Sometimes it is used when describing the body, primarily when healthy and beautiful but also when sick. It also have the following direct meanings animals – (Genesis 30:35, Judges 5:10, Zechariah 1:8; 6:3;6, Revelation 6:2; 19:11;14) plant flesh - Genesis (30:37, Joel 1:7) baskets – (Genesis 40:16) teeth – (Genesis 49:12) Manna –(Exodus 16:31) leprosy or plague – (Leviticus 13:4;10;19;42, etc., Numbers 12:10, II Kings 5:27), linen – (II Chronicles 5:12, Revelation 15:6; 19:8;14), garments or raiment - Esther 8:15, Ecclesiastes 9:8, Daniel 7:9, Matthew 17:2; 28:3, Mark 9:3; 16:5, Luke 9:29, John 20:12, Acts 1:10, Revelation 3:4-5;18; 4:4; 6:11; 7:9;13-14; 19:14 compared as snow – (Psalm 51:7, Isaiah 1:18, Daniel 7:9, Mark 9:3) compared as milk – (Lamentations 4:7) hair – (Matthew 5:36, Revelation 1:14) painted – (Matthew 23:27, Acts 23:3), fields – (John 4:35) a stone – (Revelation 2:17) a cloud – (Revelation 14:14) a throne - Revelation 20:11, white colour symbolism - purity, refinement, unblemished, righteousness, heavenly – (Psalm 51:7, Ecclesiastes 9:8, Daniel 7:9; 11:35; 12:10, Matthew 17:2, Mark 9:3,

Luke 9:29, John 20:12, Acts 1:10, Revelation 3:4-5;18; 4:4; 6:11; 7:9;13-14) victory – (Revelation 6:2; 19:11;14) false righteousness (when only outward) – Matthew 23:27, Acts 23:3) Associated Symbols: baskets - food (Genesis 40:17, Exodus 29:23, Leviticus 8:26, Numbers 6:15, Jeremiah 24:2, Amos 8:1, Matthew 14:20, Mark 8:8), escape (Exodus 2:3, Acts 9:25, II Corinthians 11:33), days (Genesis 40:18) teeth - devouring destruction (Deuteronomy 32:24, Psalm 124:6, Proverbs 30:14, Isaiah 41:15, Daniel 7:7;19), terror (Job 41:14, Daniel 7:7;19) milk - first teachings (Isaiah 28:9, I Corinthians 3:1-2, Hebrews 5:12-14, I Peter 2:2)

White Lies: Lying is a sin (Leviticus 19:11; Proverbs 12:22). "little white lies" are lies that involve an ever-so-slight stretching of the truth? Literally, lying is defined as "making an untrue statement with the intent to deceive." A white lie is an untrue statement, but it is usually considered unimportant because it does not cover up a serious wrongdoing. A *white lie* is deceptive, but it may also be polite or diplomatic at the same time. It could be a "tactful" lie told to keep the peace in a relationship; it could be a "helpful" lie to ostensibly benefit someone else; it could be a "minor" lie to make one look better in some area.

2 Some *white lies* are common: lying about one's age, for example, or the size of the fish that got away. We live in a society that conditions us to lie by telling us that, in many situations, lies are justified. The secretary "covers" for the boss who doesn't want to be disturbed; the salesman exaggerates the qualities of his product; the job applicant pads his résumé. The reasoning is, as long as no one is hurt or the result is good, little lies are fine.

3 It is true that some sins bring about worse consequences than others. And it is true that telling a *white lie* will not have the same serious effect as, say, murdering someone. But all sins are equally offensive to God (Romans 6:23a), and there are good reasons to avoid telling *white lies*. First, the belief that a *white lie* is "helpful" is rooted in the idea that the end justifies the means. If the lie results in a perceived "good," then the lie was justified. However, God's condemnation of lying in (Proverbs 6:16–19) contains no exception clause. Also, who defines the "good" that results from the lie? A salesman telling *white lies* may sell his product—a "good" thing for him—but what about the customer who was taken advantage of?

4 Telling a *white lie* to be "tactful" or to spare someone's feelings is also a foolish thing to do. A person who consistently lies to make people feel good will eventually be seen for what he is: a liar. Those who traffic in *white lies* will damage their credibility.

Whore

White lies have a way of propagating themselves. Telling more lies to cover up the original lie is standard procedure, and the lies get progressively less "white." Trying to remember what lies were told to what person also complicates relationships and makes further lying even more likely.

5 Telling a *white lie* to benefit oneself is nothing but selfishness. When our words are motivated by the pride of life, we are falling into temptation (1 John 2:16).

6 Little *white lies* are often told to preserve the peace, as if telling the truth would in some way destroy peace. Yet the Bible presents truth and peace as existing together: "Love truth and peace" (Zechariah 8:19). Tellers of white lies believe they are speaking lies out of "love"; however, the gospel tells us to speak "the truth in love" (Ephesians 4:15). Sometimes telling the truth is not easy; in fact, it can be downright unpleasant. But we are called to be truth-tellers. Being truthful is precious to God (Proverbs 12:22); it demonstrates the fear of Lord. Furthermore, to tell the truth is not a suggestion, it is a command (Psalm 15:2; Zechariah 8:16; Ephesians 4:25). Being truthful flies in the face of Satan, the "father of lies" (John 8:44). Being truthful honours the Lord, who is the "God of truth" (Psalm 31:5, ISV). Jesus must be honour in our lives as Christians – Praise His Holy Name!

Whore: (noun, Hebrew – *qedeshah* - [ked-ay-shaw'] a prostitute. Verb (of a woman) work as a prostitute. Whore: Metaphorically used to denote the worship of idol and strange gods in the Bible. *See* (Leviticus 19:29) Do not prostitute thy daughter, to cause her to be a whore; lest the land fall to whoredom, and the land become full of wickedness. (Leviticus 20:5) Then I will set my face against that man, and against his family, and will cut him off, and all that go a whoring after him, to commit whoredom with Molech, from among their people. (Leviticus 21:7) They shall not take a wife that is a whore, or profane; neither shall they take a woman put away from her husband: for he is holy unto his God. (Leviticus 21:9) And the daughter of any priest, if she profane herself by playing the whore, she profaneth her father: she shall be burnt with fire. (Numbers 14:33) And your children shall wander in the wilderness forty years, and bear your whoredoms, until your carcases be wasted in the wilderness. (Numbers 25:1) And Israel abode in Shittim, and the people began to commit whoredom with the daughters of Moab. (Deuteronomy 22:21) Then they shall bring out the damsel to the door of her father's house, and the men of her city shall stone her with stones that she die: because she hath wrought folly in Israel, to play the whore in her father's house: so shalt thou put evil away from among you. (Deuteronomy 23:17) There shall be no whore of the daughters of Israel, nor a sodomite of the sons of Israel.

Whore of Babylon: Whore of Babylon or Babylon the Great is a Christian figure of evil mentioned in the Book of (Revelation 17 and 18) in the Bible. Her full title is given as "Babylon the Great, the Mother of Prostitutes and Abominations of the Earth." And there came one of the seven angels which had the seven vials, and talked with me, saying unto me, Come hither; I will shew unto thee the judgment of the great whore that sitteth upon many waters: With whom the kings of the earth have committed fornication, and the inhabitants of the earth have been made drunk with the wine of her fornication. ["Fornication" is interpreted or translated as "idolatry" in the Amplified Bible (AMP), the New American Bible mentions "harlotry"] So he carried me away in the spirit into the wilderness: and I saw a woman sit upon a scarlet coloured beast, full of names of blasphemy, having seven heads and ten horns. And the woman was arrayed in purple and scarlet colour, and decked with gold and precious stones and pearls, having a golden cup in her hand full of abominations and filthiness of her fornication:

And upon her forehead was a name written, MYSTERY, BABYLON THE GREAT, THE MOTHER OF HARLOTS AND ABOMINATIONS OF THE EARTH. [King James Version; the New International Version uses "prostitutes" instead of "harlots"].

And I saw the woman drunken with the blood of the saints, and with the blood of the martyrs of Jesus: and when I saw her, I wondered with great admiration. And here is the mind which hath wisdom. The seven heads are seven mountains, on which the woman sitteth. [King James Version; the New International Version Bible and the New American Bible use "hills" instead of "mountains"]. And there are seven kings: five are fallen, and one is, and the other is not yet come; and when he comes, he must continue a short space. And the beast that was, and is not, even he is the eighth, and is of the seven, and goes into perdition. And the ten horns which thou saw are ten kings, which have received no kingdom as yet; but receive power as kings one hour with the beast. And he said unto me, The waters which thou sawest, where the whore sitteth, are peoples, and multitudes, and nations, and tongues. And the woman which thou sawest is that great city, which reigns over the kings of the earth.

Wicked: (Wickedness: Greek - pon-ay-ros, Hebrew – raw-shaw) meaning to be wrong by making trouble, or twisting things with wicked works. This originated from the old Anglo-Saxon word wiker (or "wicker" in the present-day spelling) which meant to twist i.e. a candle "wick" is called that because it is twisted (and

Wicked

ironically, it burns, as the wicked are also going to do if they don't repent). The twisted definition of wicked was formed from an earlier word meaning weak i.e. not strong enough to resist being twisted (the English words wicked, wick and weak all originated from the same word). Just as string is weak enough to be twisted into wicks, people can allow themselves to be weak enough to be "twisted" into a state of wickedness (although wickedness takes many forms, the word for witchcraft, Wicca, is also based on the same root word as weak, wick and wicked).

Wickedness means to be hurtful by degeneracy i.e. the practice of "twisting" what is good into something that is demoralized psychologically and perverted physically. As with the Hebrew word, it is done by "wicked works" - sick, satanic behaviour.

2 Evil by nature and in practice: "this wicked man Hitler, the repository and embodiment of many forms of soul destroying hatred" 3 Playfully malicious or mischievous: a wicked prank; a critic's wicked wit. 4 Severe and distressing: a wicked cough; a wicked gash; wicked driving conditions. 5 Highly offensive; obnoxious: a wicked stench. 6 Slang Strikingly good, effective, or skillful: a wicked curve ball; a wicked imitation. Christians be focus because those ignorance's to members of your households or family can result to wickedness. See the gospel according to (1 Timothy 5: 8) "But if anyone does not provide for his relatives, and especially for members of his household, he has denied the faith and is worse than an unbeliever"

(Psalm 141:4) "Incline not my heart to any evil thing, to practice wicked works with men that work iniquity: and let me not eat of their dainties."

7 Notice carefully however that the "wicked" can become "untwisted" by repentance and obedience to God's Law as in (Colossians 1:21 -KJV) "And you, that were sometime alienated and enemies in your mind by wicked works, yet now hath he reconciled" "Repent therefore of this thy wickedness, and pray God, if perhaps the thought of thine heart may be forgiven thee"

Simon the sorcerer (see Simon Magus) was a prime example of how people often twist true Christianity into self-serving (i.e. selfish) wickedness (see Weapons of Mass Deception). He was rebuked by another Simon, more popularly known as Peter as in (Acts 8:18 – 22 KJV) "And when Simon saw that through laying on of the apostles' hands the Holy Ghost was given, he offered them money, Saying, Give me also this power, that on whomsoever I lay hands, he may receive the Holy Ghost. But Peter said unto him, Thy money perishes with thee, because thou hast thought that the gift of God may be purchased with money. Thou

Wife

hast neither part nor lot in this matter: for thy heart is not right in the sight of God. Repent therefore of this thy wickedness, and pray God, if perhaps the thought of thine heart may be forgiven thee."

8 Often times, when confronted by the wicked religionists who attempted to "twist" the Messiah's Words, He defined "wickedness" with another word - "hypocrites." Very often, the wicked will seek to "twist" others while maintaining an untwisted or righteous (i.e. "right") appearance for themselves (as in fact Satan does himself.

In (Mathew 22:15 – 22 KJV) Then went the Pharisees, and took counsel how they might entangle him in his talk. And they sent out unto him their disciples with the Herodias, saying, Master, we know that thou art true, and teachest the way of God in truth, neither carest thou for any man: for thou regardest not the person of men. Tell us therefore, What thinkest thou? Is it lawful to give tribute unto Caesar, or not? But Jesus perceived their *wickedness*, and said, why tempt ye me, ye hypocrites? Show me the tribute money. And they brought unto him a penny. And he saith unto them, Whose is this image and superscription? They say unto him, Caesar's. Then saith he unto them, Render therefore unto Caesar the things which are Caesar's; and unto God the things that are God's. When they had heard these words, they marvelled, and left him, and went their way."

In the end, all of the wicked will be given their warning to repent and obey God's Sacred Law. The wicked who do not repent, will become "wicks" in the fire to come (They Shall Be Ashes) as in (Malachi 4:1-6) For, behold, the day cometh, that shall burn as an oven; and all the proud, yea, and all that do wickedly, shall be stubble: and the day that cometh shall burn them up, saith the LORD of hosts, that it shall leave them neither root nor branch. But unto you that fear my name shall the Sun of righteousness arise with healing in his wings; and ye shall go forth, and grow up as calves of the stall. And ye shall tread down the wicked; for they shall be ashes under the soles of your feet in the day that I shall do this, saith the LORD of hosts. Remember ye the Law of Moses my servant, which I commanded unto him in Horeb for all Israel, with the statutes and judgments. Behold, I will send you Elijah the prophet before the coming of the great and dreadful day of the LORD: And he shall turn the heart of the fathers to the children, and the heart of the children to their fathers, lest I come and smite the earth with a curse."

Wife: One favourable goodness to man from God as in "He who finds a wife finds a good thing, And obtains favour from the Lord" as in (Proverbs 18: 22). A wife is therefore a female partner in a

Wife

continuing marital relationship. A wife may also be referred to as a spouse. The term continues to be applied to a woman who has separated from her husband and ceases to be applied to such a woman only when her marriage has come to an end following a legally recognised divorce or the death of her spouse. On the death of her husband, a wife is referred to as a widow, but not after she is divorced from her husband. The rights and obligations of the wife in relation to her husband, and others, and her status in the community and in law, varies between cultures and has varied over time. But in Christendom, God has Plan for the Wife and is clearly described in the gospel or Bible. Although males and females are equal in relationship to Christ, the Bible gives specific roles to both the husband and the wife in marriage. Wives are mentors as in (Titus 2:4-5), "Then they can train the younger women to love their husbands and children, to be self-controlled and pure, to be busy at home, to be kind, and to be subject to their husbands, so that no one will malign the word of God." 2 Wives are Witnesses – as in (1 Peter 3:1) "Wives, in the same way be submissive to your husband's so that, if any of them do not believe the word, they may be won over without words by the behaviour of their wives." They must set examples - 1 Timothy 3:11 says, "In the same way, their wives are to be women worthy of respect, not malicious talkers but temperate and trustworthy in everything." Above all

4 We also learn that a wife is a blessing to her husband. She is worth more than rubies! Wives can follow her example by living in the wisdom of God as in (Proverbs 31: 10 – 31) "A wife of noble character who can find? She is worth far more than rubies. Her husband has full confidence in her and lacks nothing of value. She brings him good, not harm, all the days of her life. She selects wool and flax and works with eager hands. She is like the merchant ships, bringing her food from afar. She gets up while it is still dark; she provides food for her family and portions for her servant girls. She considers a field and buys it; out of her earnings she plants a vineyard. She sets about her work vigorously; her arms are strong for her tasks. She sees that her trading is profitable, and her lamp does not go out at night. In her hand she holds the distaff and grasps the spindle with her fingers. She opens her arms to the poor and extends her hands to the needy. When it snows, she has no fear for her household; for all of them are clothed in scarlet. She makes coverings for her bed; she is clothed in fine linen and purple. Her husband is respected at the city gate, where he takes his seat among the elders of the land. She makes linen garments and sells them, and supplies the merchants with sashes. She is clothed with strength and digni-

ty; she can laugh at the days to come. She speaks with wisdom, and faithful instruction is on her tongue. She watches over the affairs of her household and does not eat the bread of idleness. Her children arise and call her blessed; her husband also, and he praises her: 'Many women do noble things, but you surpass them all.' Charm is deceptive, and beauty is fleeting; but a woman who fears the LORD is to be praised. Give her the reward she has earned, and let her works bring her praise at the city gate"

Will: Simply the auxiliary verb, present singular 1st person will, 2nd will or(*Archaic*) wilt, 3rd will, present plural will; past singular 1stperson would, 2nd would or (*Archaic*) wouldst, 3rd would, past-plural would; past participle (*Obsolete*) wold or would; *imperative,infinitive, and present. participle lacking.* Will could not be expressed without a noun or an article to qualify the intention or expression. 2 Often times we say as an act to acknowledge good works or gesture "God will bless you or God bless you" or we pray "Lord let thy 'will' be done" Will in this sense is a noun.. Christians are generally concern about the 'Will' of the father – God (1 (Thessalonians 5:18) Give thanks in all circumstances; for this is the *will* of God in Christ Jesus for you (Romans 12:2) Do not be conformed to this world, but be transformed by the renewal of your mind, that by testing you may discern what is the *will* of God, what is good and acceptable and perfect. (1 Thessalonians 4:3) For this is the *will* of God, your sanctification: that you abstain from sexual immorality; **(Jeremiah 29:11-13)** For I know the plans I have for you, declares the Lord, plans for welfare and not for evil, to give you a future and a hope. Then you will call upon me and come and pray to me, and I will hear you. You will seek me and find me, when you seek me with all your heart. (Hebrews 13:20-21) Now may the God of peace who brought again from the dead our Lord Jesus, the great shepherd of the sheep, by the blood of the eternal covenant, equip you with everything good that you may do his *will*, working in us that which is pleasing in his sight, through Jesus Christ, to whom be glory forever and ever. Amen. **(1 John 2:16-17)** For all that is in the world—the desires of the flesh and the desires of the eyes and pride in possessions—is not from the Father but is from the world. And the world is passing away along with its desires, but whoever does the will of God abides forever.

(Matthew 7:21-23) "Not everyone who says to me, 'Lord, Lord,' *will* enter the kingdom of heaven, but the one who does the *will* of my Father who is in heaven. On that day many *will* say to me, 'Lord, Lord, did we not prophesy in your name, and cast out demons in your name, and do many mighty works in your name?' And then *will* I declare to them, 'I never knew you; depart from me, you workers of lawlessness.'

Wind: One wonder in God's creation. This is the flow of gases on a large scale. On the surface of the Earth, wind consists of the bulk movement of air. In outer space, solar wind is the movement of gases or charged particles from the sun through space, while planetary wind is the out gassing of light chemical elements from a planet's atmosphere into space. Winds are commonly classified by their spatial scale, their speed, the types of forces that cause them, the regions in which they occur, and their effect. The strongest observed winds on a planet in our solar system occur on Neptune and Saturn. Winds have various aspect, one important aspect is its velocity; another the density of the gas involved; another is the energy content or wind energy of a wind.

2 In meteorology, winds are often referred to according to their strength, and the direction from which the wind is blowing. Short bursts of high speed wind are termed gusts. Strong winds of intermediate duration (around one minute) are termed squalls. Long-duration winds have various names associated with their average strength, such as breeze, gale, storm, hurricane, and typhoon. Wind occurs on a range of scales, from thunderstorm flows lasting tens of minutes, to local breezes generated by heating of land surfaces and lasting a few hours, to global winds resulting from the difference in absorption of solar energy between the climate zones on Earth. The two main causes of large-scale atmospheric circulation are the differential heating between the equator and the poles, and the rotation of the planet (Coriolis effect). Within the tropics, thermal low circulations over terrain and high plateaus can drive monsoon circulations. In coastal areas the sea breeze/land breeze cycle can define local winds; in areas that have variable terrain, mountain and valley breezes can dominate local winds.

In human civilization, wind has inspired mythology, influenced the events of history, expanded the range of transport and warfare, and provided a power source for mechanical work, electricity and recreation. Wind powers the voyages of sailing ships across Earth's oceans. Hot air balloons use the wind to take short trips, and powered flight uses it to increase lift and reduce fuel consumption. Areas of wind shear caused by various weather-phenomena can lead to dangerous situations for aircraft. When winds become strong, trees and man-made structures are damaged or destroyed.

Winds can shape landforms, via a variety of Aeolian processes such as the formation of fertile soils, such as loess, and by erosion. Dust from large deserts can be moved great distances from its source region by the prevailing winds; winds that are accelerated by rough topography and associated with dust outbreaks have been assigned regional names in various parts of the world because of their significant effects on those regions. Wind affects the spread of wildfires. Winds disperse seeds from various plants, enabling the survival and dispersal of those plant species, as well as flying insect populations. When combined with cold temperatures, wind has a negative impact on livestock. Wind affects animals' food stores, as well as their hunting and defensive strategies. In (John 3: 7 – 9) Jesus use wind to demonstrate to Nicodemus concerning the new birth (To be born again or rebirth) thus "Do not be amazed that I said to you, 'You must be born again.'"The wind blows where it wishes and you hear the sound of it, but do not know where it comes from and where it is going; so is everyone who is born of the Spirit." Nicodemus said to Him, "How can these things be?"...

Whirring wings, The Land of:
A close study of the gospel in (Isaiah 18:1 - 3) shows Messengers Come From Beyond the Rivers of Cush. "Ah, land of whirring wings which is beyond ! When a trumpet is blown, hear! the rivers of Ethiopia; which sends ambassadors by the Nile, in vessels of papyrus upon the waters! Go,you swift messengers, to a nation, tall and smooth, to a people feared near and far, a nation mighty and conquering, whose land the rivers divide. All you inhabitants of the world, you who dwell on the earth, when a signal is raised on the mountains, look

The "land shadowing with wings" or whirring wings is not the focal point of the chapter. It is an un-named nation "which is beyond the rivers of Cush". As mentioned earlier, in the chapter the third country is not the focus of destruction. Instead, it is a nation that sends its ambassadors to the fourth country mentioned in verse two of Isaiah 18: below *Woe to the land shadowing with wings, which is beyond the* rivers of Ethiopia: Christians find the mention of "Ethiopia" in verse 1 and assume that the gospel is about it. The passage is not about "Ethiopia". The real name here is "Cush". The real identity of Cush does not change the reference to America later in the chapter. Cush is a nation that helps identify another nation which is the "land shadowing with

Wisdom

wings". The *"land shadowing with wings"* is not the focal point of this chapter either. Instead, it is a nation that sends its ambassadors to the nation in verse two. The land of whirring wings would be the land beyond the rivers of Cush from the perspective of the people of Israel who were the first intended listeners. In verse 1 "beyond" must mean on the other side of the rivers of Cush or Iraq with respect to Israel; that is, the land east of Iraq. There are two countries that are mentioned in the Bible east of the Tigris and Euphrates: Persia, known today as Iran (mentioned 25 times) and India (Esther 1:1) "This is what happened during the time of Xerxes the Xerxes who ruled over 127 provinces stretching from India to Cush"and (Esther 8:9). "The king's scribes were summoned at that time, in the third month, which is the month of Sivan, on the twenty-third day. And an edict was written, according to all that Mordecai commanded concerning the Jews, to the satraps and the governors and the officials of the provinces from India to Ethiopia, 127 provinces, to each province in its own script and to each people in its own language, and also to the Jews in their script and their language" Here we can see that the country just beyond Cush is Iran. Other countries that are beyond the rivers of Cush are Pakistan, Afghanistan, India at least a dozen more.

Wisdom: (noun) Simply the ability to discern or judge what is true, right, or lasting; insight. 2 Common sense; good judgment: "It is a characteristic of wisdom not to do desperate things" 3.a. The sum of learning through the ages; knowledge: "In those homely sayings was couched the collective wisdom of generations" b. Wise teachings of the ancient sages. 4. A wise outlook, plan, or course of action. 5 Wisdom Bible Wisdom of Solomon. As Christians we can gain knowledge and *wisdom* through the study of God's word. As in (Psalm 37:30) "The mouth of the righteous man utters wisdom, and his tongue speaks what is just" To be endowed with wisdom we must fear the Lord in all aspects of our life as stated in (Proverbs 1:7) "The fear of the LORD is the beginning of knowledge, but fools despise *wisdom* and discipline". When we please God, He gives us wisdom (Ecclesiastes 2:26)"To the man who pleases him, God gives wisdom, knowledge and happiness, but to the sinner he gives the task of gathering and storing up wealth to hand it over to the one who pleases God. This too is meaningless, a chasing after the wind". Particularly as all treasures of wisdom is hidden in Christ as Apostles Paul asserted in (Colossians 2:2-3) "My purpose is that they may be encouraged in heart and united in love, so that they may have the full riches of complete understanding, in order that they may know the mystery of God, namely, Christ, in whom are hidden all the treasures of *wisdom* and knowledge." 6 Note that *Wisdom* comes with age, according to Job. Wisdom is something that the writer of Proverbs said that we should "get" and not forget. He said it is the principal thing. He even says while you're at it, get understanding too. He says *wisdom* and understanding are better than gold and silver. There are some great words of wisdom for life set to an upbeat, fun song. Etc. In short, there are many gems of wisdom and knowledge throughout the gospel of Christ, all stated in the bible. The above quoted verses are just a few examples of the words of wisdom which can be found in God's word. If someone wanted to study the concept of *wisdom* in-depth in the Bible, then starting with the book of Proverbs is recommended. Proverbs was mostly written by Solomon, the man to whom the Bible says God gave great *wisdom*. 7 In other words, by means of wisdom you can make your way into a hope-filled future. It is the key to lasting happiness. (Proverbs 19:8) says, "He who gets wisdom loves himself." In other words, do yourself a favour: Get wisdom! Get wisdom! (Proverbs 8:32–36) sums it all up beautifully. Here wisdom herself is speaking and she says, "And now, my sons, listen to me: happy are those who keep my ways . . . Happy is the man who listens to me, watching daily at my gates, waiting beside my doors. For he who finds me finds life and obtains favour from the Lord; but he who misses me injures himself; all who hate me love death." If we do not make it our aim to "get wisdom," we will suffer injury and finally death. Therefore, the command, "Get wisdom; get insight," is very important. As (Proverbs 16:16) puts it, "To get wisdom is better than gold; to get understanding is to be chosen rather than silver." It is a matter of life and death. The ultimate, eternal happiness that all people long for will only be found by those who first "get wisdom."

Wise: (noun) This means to be civilized and star knowledgeable, star literate, star open minded, star reasonable, star sophisticated, star cultivated, star instructed, star learned, star liberal, star refined, star savvy, star sharp, star aware, star broad-minded, star hip to, star in the picture, star, knowing what's what, star plugged in, star tuned in, star wised up, informed star contemplative, star cunning, star grasping, star keen, star knowing, star sage, star sensing, star sharp, star sound, star understanding, star calculating, star clever, star cogitative, star crafty, star discerning, star discreet, star erudite, star foresighted, star insightful star intuitive, star perspicacious, star politic, star reflective, star sagacious, star sapient, stars scholarly, strophic, star tactful, star taught and star witty. All this makes the meaning of wise to be strong as describes in (Proverbs 29:11) thus "A fool gives full vent

Witness

to his spirit, but a *wise* man quietly holds it back" Also see the saying of the wise in (Proverbs 22: 17-21) "Pay attention and turn your ear to the sayings of the wise; apply your heart to what I teach, for it is pleasing when you keep them in your heart and have all of them ready on your lips So that your trust may be in the Lord, I teach you today, even you. Have I not written thirty sayings for you, sayings of counsel and knowledge, teaching you to be honest and to speak the truth, so that you bring back truthful reports to those you serve? You can read beyond to know more saying of the *wise* for your knowledge.

Witness: A witness is someone who has, who claims to have, or is thought, by someone with authority to compel testimony, to have knowledge relevant to an event or other matter of interest. In law a witness is someone who, either voluntarily or under compulsion, provides testimonial evidence, either oral or written, of what he or she knows or claims to know about the matter before some official authorized to take such testimony. As Christians, we are bound to be witnesses to Christ Jesus that God has raised Him from the death, and before He died we died with Him, When He resurrected we also resurrected with Him! And as He is now seated at the right hand of the Father we also are there with Him. Because He has made us the Righteousness of God through Him (Christ Jesus) as in (2 Corinthians 5:21) - For he hath made him [to be] sin for us, who knew no sin; that we might be made the righteousness of God in him. The phrase, might be made, comes from the Greek word ginomai which means to cause to be. Check out what the Strong Hebrew and Greek Dictionary says about this word: G1096 γίνομαι ginomai (ghin'-om-ahee) A prolonged and middle form of a primary verb; to cause to be (gen -erate), that is, (reflexively) to become (come into being), used with great latitude (literally, figuratively, intensively, etc.) Also, we should be witnesses to Him because He says to the twelve and us that we shall receive power in (Acts 1:8) – "But ye shall receive power, after that the Holy Ghost is come upon you: and ye shall be witnesses unto me both in Jerusalem, and in all Judaea, and in Samaria, and unto the uttermost part of the earth". And in (1 Peter 3:15) - But sanctify the Lord God in your hearts: and [be] ready always to [give] an answer to every man that asketh you a reason of the hope that is in you with meekness and fear: Hallelujah!

Witness, Percipient: A percipient witness or eyewitness is one who testifies what they perceived through his or her senses (e.g. seeing, hearing, smelling, touching). That perception might be either with the unaided human sense or with the aid of an instrument, e.g., microscope or stethoscope, or by other scientific means, e.g.,a chemical reagent which changes colour in the presence of a particular substance.

Witness, Hearsay: A hearsay witness is one who testifies what someone else said or wrote. In most court proceedings there are many limitations on when hearsay evidence is admissible. Such limitations do not apply to grand jury investigations, many administrative proceedings, and may not apply to declarations used in support of an arrest or search warrant. Also some types of statements are not deemed to be hearsay and are not subject to such limitations.

Witness, Expert: An expert witness is one who allegedly has specialized knowledge relevant to the matter of interest, which knowledge purportedly helps to either make sense of other evidence, including other testimony, documentary evidence or physical evidence (e.g., a fingerprint). An expert witness may or may not also be a percipient witness, as in a doctor or may or may not have treated the victim of an accident or crime.

Witness, A Reputation: A reputation witness is one who testifies about the reputation of a person or business entity, when reputation is material to the dispute at issue.

Witness, Principal: The key witness who knows the whole story, event or incident to foretell the whole ingredients. The ring leader in crime. For example Judas Iscariot was the Key witness in the betrayal of Jesus. He is notoriously known for his kiss and betrayal of Jesus to the hands of the chief Sanhedrin priests in exchange for a payment of thirty silver coins. His name is often invoked to accuse someone of betrayal, and is sometimes confused with Jude Thaddeus. See(Mark 14:43-45) "And immediately, while he was still speaking, Judas came, one of the twelve, and with him a crowd with swords and clubs, from the chief priests and the scribes and the elders. Now the betrayer had given them a sign, saying, "The one I will kiss is the man. Seize him and lead him away under guard." And when he came, he went up to him at once and said, "Rabbi!" And he kissed him". In law a witness might be compelled to provide testimony in court, before a grand jury, before an administrative tribunal, before a deposition officer, or in a variety of other proceedings (e.g., judgment debtor examination). Sometimes the testimony is provided in public or in a confidential setting (e.g., grand jury or closed court proceeding).

Although informally a witness includes whoever perceived the event, in law, a witness is different from an informant. A confidential informant is someone who claimed to have witnessed an event or have hearsay information, but whose identity is being withheld from at least one party

Woman

(typically the criminal defendant). The information from the confidential informant may have been used by a police officer or other official acting as a hearsay witness to obtain a search warrant. A subpoena commands a person to appear. It is used to compel the testimony of a witness in a trial. Usually, it can be issued by a judge or by the lawyer representing the plaintiff or the defendant in a civil trial or by the prosecutor or the defense attorney in a criminal proceeding. In many jurisdictions, it is compulsory to comply, to take an oath, and to tell the truth, under penalty of perjury.

Woman: (*Plural* – women) A female human. The term woman is usually reserved for an adult, with the term girl being the usual term for a female child or adolescent. However, the term woman is also sometimes used to identify a female human, regardless of age, as in phrases such as "women's rights". "Woman" may also refer to a person's gender instead of their sex. Women are typically capable of giving birth from puberty until menopause, although some sterile, intersex and/or transgender women cannot. Throughout history women have assumed various social roles. 2 For centuries they've inspired, enlightened, and empowered us. With their unadorned faith, the women of the Bible continue to teach us how to live authentic, God-touched lives. No matter what our spiritual traditions are, we can find ourselves in their stories. The gospel in the book of (1 Timothy 2:11-15) provides guidance as to the way a woman must conduct herself thus "Let a woman learn quietly with all submissiveness. I do not permit a woman to teach or to exercise authority over a man; rather, she is to remain quiet. For Adam was formed first, then Eve; and Adam was not deceived, but the woman was deceived and became a transgressor. Yet she will be saved through childbearing—if they continue in faith and love and holiness, with self-control". Also in (Titus 2:3-5) Older women likewise are to be reverent in behaviour, not slanderers or slaves to much wine. They are to teach what is good, and so train the young women to love their husbands and children, to be self-controlled, pure, working at home, kind, and submissive to their own husbands, that the word of God may not be reviled. There are several other bible verses that instruct the conduct of a woman that is beneficial to all God's loving women.

Women Pastors and Preachers: There is perhaps no more hotly debated issue in the church today than the issue of women serving as pastors and or preachers. As a result, it is very important to not see this issue as men versus women. There are women who believe women should not serve as pastors and that the Bible places restrictions on the ministry of women, and there are men

Women Pastors and Preachers

who believe women can serve as preachers and that there are no restrictions on women in ministry. This is not an issue of chauvinism or discrimination. It is an issue of biblical interpretation. The Word of God proclaims, "A woman should learn in quietness and full submission. I do not permit a woman to teach or to have authority over a man; she must be silent" (1 Timothy 2:11–12). In the church, God assigns different roles to men and women. This is a result of the way mankind was created and the way in which sin entered the world (1 Timothy 2:13–14). God, through the apostle Paul, restricts women from serving in roles of teaching and or having spiritual authority over men. This precludes women from serving as pastors over men, which definitely includes preaching to them, teaching them publicly, and exercising spiritual authority over them.

2 There are many objections to this view of women in pastoral ministry. A common one is that Paul restricts women from teaching because in the first century, women were typically uneducated. However, (1 Timothy 2:11–14) nowhere mentions educational status. If education were a qualification for ministry, then the majority of Jesus' disciples would not have been qualified. A second common objection is that Paul only restricted the women of Ephesus from teaching men (1 Timothy was written to Timothy, the pastor of the church in Ephesus). Ephesus was known for its temple to Artemis, and women were the authorities in that branch of paganism—therefore, the theory goes, Paul was only reacting against the female-led customs of the Ephesian idolaters, and the church needed to be different. However, the book of 1 Timothy nowhere mentions Artemis, nor does Paul mention the standard practice of Artemis worshipers as a reason for the restrictions in (1 Timothy 2:11–12).

3 A third objection is that Paul is only referring to husbands and wives, not men and women in general. The Greek words for "woman" and "man" in 1 Timothy 2 could refer to husbands and wives; however, the basic meaning of the words is broader than that. Further, the same Greek words are used in (verses 8–10). Are only husbands to lift up holy hands in prayer without anger and disputing (verse 8)? Are only wives to dress modestly, have good deeds, and worship God (verses 9–10)? Of course not. (Verses 8–10) clearly refer to all men and women, not just husbands and wives. There is nothing in the context that would indicate a narrowing to husbands and wives in (verses 11–14). Yet another objection to this interpretation of women in pastoral ministry is in relation to women who held positions of leadership in the Bible, specifically Miriam, Deborah, and Huldah in the Old Testament. It is true that these women were chosen by God for special service to Him and that they stand

as models of faith, courage, and, yes, leadership. However, the authority of women in the Old Testament is not relevant to the issue of pastors in the church. The New Testament Epistles present a new paradigm for God's people—the church, the body of Christ—and that paradigm involves an authority structure unique to the church, not for the nation of Israel or any other Old Testament entity.

4 Similar arguments are made using Priscilla and Phoebe in the New Testament. In (Acts 18), Priscilla and Aquila are presented as faithful ministers for Christ. Priscilla's name is mentioned first, perhaps indicating that she was more prominent in ministry than her husband. Did Priscilla and her husband teach the gospel of Jesus Christ to Apollos? Yes, in their home they "explained to him the way of God more adequately" (Acts 18:26). Does the Bible ever say that Priscilla pastored a church or taught publicly or became the spiritual leader of a congregation of saints? No. As far as we know, Priscilla was not involved in ministry activity in contradiction to (1 Timothy 2:11–14).

5 In (Romans 16:1), Phoebe is called a "deacon" (or "servant") in the church and is highly commended by Paul. But, as with Priscilla, there is nothing in Scripture to indicate that Phoebe was a pastor or a teacher of men in the church. "Able to teach" is given as a qualification for elders, but not for deacons (1 Timothy 3:1–13); (Titus 1:6–9). The structure of (1 Timothy 2:11–14) makes the reason why women cannot be pastors perfectly clear. Verse 13 begins with "for," giving the "cause" of Paul's statement in (verses 11–12). Why should women not teach or have authority over men? Because "Adam was created first, then Eve. And Adam was not the one deceived; it was the woman who was deceived" (verses 13–14). God created Adam first and then created Eve to be a "helper" for Adam. The order of creation has universal application in the family (Ephesians 5:22–33) and in the church.

6 The fact that Eve was deceived is also given in (1 Timothy 2:14) as a reason for women not serving as pastors or having spiritual authority over men. This does not mean that women are gullible or that they are all more easily deceived than men. If all women are more easily deceived, why would they be allowed to teach children (who are easily deceived) and other women (who are supposedly more easily deceived)? The text simply says that women are not to teach men or have spiritual authority over men because Eve was deceived. God has chosen to give men the primary teaching authority in the church. Many women excel in gifts of hospitality, mercy, teaching, evangelism, and helps. Much of the ministry of the local church depends on women. Women in the church are not restricted from public praying or prophesy-

ing (1 Corinthians 11:5), only from having spiritual teaching authority over men. The Bible nowhere restricts women from exercising the gifts of the Holy Spirit (1 Corinthians 12). Women, just as much as men, are called to minister to others, to demonstrate the fruit of the Spirit (Galatians 5:22–23), and to proclaim the gospel to the lost (Matthew 28:18–20; Acts 1:8; 1 Peter 3:15). Praise the Lord.

Wonders: (Greek:: *Teras*; Hebrew: *Mophets*) These describes God's supernatural activity, a special manifestation of His power (Exodus 7:3), but false prophets can perform actions people perceive as signs and *wonders*. (Deuteronomy 13:1-3). *Wonders* can serve as a sign of a future event. Signs seek to bring belief (Exodus 4:5; compare Exodus 10:2), but they do not compel a person to believe (Exodus 4:9).

2 "Wonders" translates a Greek word from which the word terror comes. It denotes something unusual that causes the beholder to marvel. Although it usually follows "signs," it sometimes precedes it (Acts 2:22 ,Acts 2:22,2:43; Acts 6:8) or occurs alone (as in Acts 2:19). Whereas a sign appeals to the understanding, a wonder appeals to the imagination. "Wonders" are usually presented as God's activity (Acts 2:19; Acts 4:30; Acts 5:12; Acts 6:8; Acts 7:36; Acts 14:3; Acts 15:12), though sometimes they refer to the work of Satan through human instruments (Matthew 24:24; Mark 13:22; 2 Thessalonians 2:9; Revelation 13:11-13).

Word, The: The Gospels, Scriptures, Christ as the logos of the word of God, i.e. His revelation or His meaning as in (John 1:1) "In the beginning was *the word* and *the word* was with God and *the word* was God. This implies that when we speak the word 'we speak God'. As Christians, we should gird and guide our lips as the word we speaks being God releases power through faith and righteousness. It is clear that in the translation "the Word was God," the term God is being used to denote his nature or essence, and not his person. But in normal English usage "God" is a proper noun, referring to the person of the Father or corporately to the three persons of the Godhead. Moreover, "the Word was God" suggests that "the Word" and "God" are convertible terms, that the proposition is reciprocating. But the Word is neither the Father nor the Trinity... *but divine."*

Work: (Hebrew: *ergon*) this simply means human labour and there are various references to *work* in the scriptures. Certain energy are applied to make things happen. This could be in form of project management, the effort applied to produce a deliverable or accomplish a task, Work life or Employment, a contract between two parties, one being the employer and the other being the employee, Creative work, a manifestation of creative effort,

Work

in copyright law, House work, management of a home, Manual work, physical work done by people, Paid work, relationship in which a worker sells labour and an employer buys it, Job, a regular activity performed in exchange for payment. What ever definition chosen, work can be fulfilling, but it can also be the cause of great frustration. The gospel helps put those bad times in perspective. Work is honourable, Scripture says, no matter what kind of occupation you have. Honest toil, done in a joyful spirit, is like a prayer to God. Draw strength from these Bible verses about work as in (Deuteronomy 15:10) Give generously to them and do so without a grudging heart; then because of this the LORD your God will bless you in all your work and in everything you put your hand to. Also, (Deuteronomy 24:14) cautioned "Do not take advantage of a hired worker who is poor and needy, whether that worker is a fellow Israelite or a foreigner residing in one of your towns". And (Psalm 90:17) May the favour of the Lord our God rest on us; establish the *work* of our hands for us-yes, establish the *work* of our hands. (Psalm 128:2) You will eat the fruit of your labour; blessings and prosperity will be yours. (Proverbs 12:11) "Those who work their land will have abundant food, but those who chase fantasies have no sense".

Work is also employed in the New Testament in the sense of "miracle." John the Baptist heard of the "works" of Jesus while he was in prison (Matthew 11:2). The apostle John used the term frequently (Matthew 5:20 Matthew 5:20,5:36; Matthew 7:3; Matthew 10:38; Matthew 14:11-12; Matthew 15:24).

2 By working, one must not be alone. So, *work* require relationship – whether master or servant, Hirer and labourer, in modern usage, Employer and Employees, or in situations working out from bad situation to good situation etc. In all these all things must work together for good result as in the gospel according to (Romans 8:28) "And we know that all things *work* together for good to them that love God, to them who are the called according to his purpose".

These things we, true believers in Christ and his gospel, know, — but on what ground? First, On the ground of the divine perfections, particularly God's infinite wisdom, power, and love, which are all engaged for the good of his people. For as these dispensations do not happen to us by chance, but by the permission or appointment of Him who numbers the hairs of our head, and without whom a sparrow falleth not to the ground, his wisdom cannot but know what is best for us, his love must have our good in view; and what his wisdom sees will be for our good, and his love designs, his power permits or appoints to happen to us.

Secondly, Thirdly, on the ground of the relations in which he stands to us; not only as our Creator, Preserver, and Redeemer, but as our Friend, Father, and Husband, in Christ Jesus; all which relations lay a solid foundation for our expecting good, and only good at his hand, though sometimes afflictive good. Fourthly, On the ground of his faithful declarations and promises, particularly this by his inspired apostle. Fifthly, on that of the nature of things; the providential dispensations which are painful and distressing to us, being evidently calculated to mortify our inordinate attachment to things visible and temporal, to crucify our corrupt inclinations, and raise our thoughts and affections to another and a better state of existence. Sixthly, On the ground of observation and experience: we have seen trials, troubles, and afflictions of various kinds, to have a good effect upon others, and if we be the true disciples of Jesus, we have proved their salutary influence upon our own souls. Like the case of Martha and Mary - (Luke 10:40) "But Martha was distracted by all the preparations that had to be made. She came to him and asked, "Lord, don't you care that my sister has left me to do the *work* by myself? Tell her to help me!" and in (John 5:17) "In his defence Jesus said to them, "My Father is always at his *work* to this very day, and I too am working." More so Jesus warned in (John 6:27) "Do not work for food that spoils, but for food that endures to eternal life, which the Son of Man will give you. For on him God the Father has placed his seal of approval". (Acts 20:35) "In everything I did, I showed you that by this kind of hard *work* we must help the weak, remembering the words the Lord Jesus himself said: 'It is more blessed to give than to receive.'

World: Jesus Christ warned all believers in -(1 John 2: 15) "Do not love the *world* or anything in the *world*. If anyone loves the world, love for the Father is not in them". World is a common name for the whole of human civilization, specifically human experience, history, or the human condition in general, worldwide, i.e. anywhere on Earth or pertaining to anywhere on earth. In a philosophical context it may refer to: the whole of the physical Universe, or an ontological world (see world disclosure). In a theological context, world usually refers to the material or the profane sphere, as opposed to the celestial, spiritual, transcendent or sacred. The "end of the world" refers to scenarios of the final end of human history, often in religious contexts. World history is commonly understood as spanning the major geopolitical developments of about five millennia, from the first civilizations to the present. World population is the sum of all human populations at any time; similarly, world economy is the sum of the economies of all societies (all countries), especially in the context of globalization. Terms like world cham-

World

pionship, gross world product, world flags etc. also imply the sum or combination of all current-day sovereign states. In terms such as world religion, world language, world government, and world war, world suggests international or intercontinental scope without necessarily implying participation of the entire world. In terms such as *world* map and world climate, world is used in the sense detached from human culture or civilization, referring to the planet Earth physically. In all these definition of the world, Christ warned in (Romans 12:2) "Do not be conformed to this world, but be transformed by the renewal of your mind, that by testing you may discern what is the will of God, what is good and acceptable and perfect". Rather know that – as a Christian, you are the light of the world – to direct the people of the world, teach, preach the gospel of Christ, control, prosper, remain as agent of grace etc . Hence (Matthew 5:14) "You are the light of the world. A city that is set on an hill cannot be hid".

The effect of light being to make things manifest, (Ephesians 5:13), and to direct us in the way in which we are to walk; the import of this metaphor is, that Christ had appointed his disciples in general, and his apostles and the other ministers of his gospel in particular, to enlighten and reform the world, immersed in ignorance, sin, and misery, by their doctrine and example; and so to direct their feet into the way leading to life and salvation. Christ, it must be observed, is in the highest sense the light of the world; the original light, the great light, who, like the sun, hath light in and from himself; but the ministers of his gospel are, in an inferior sense, lights of the world also, for the angels of the churches are said to be stars, (Revelation 1:20); and holy persons are children of the light, (1 Thessalonians 5:5). A city that is set on a hill cannot be hid — As if he had said, If you do not hide this light from mankind, but cause it to shine forth in your doctrine and practice, it will be so clear and resplendent as not possibly to be hid, any more than a city set on a hill. The Church of Christ is often called the city of God, and it must be here observed, that his people are not here merely compared to a city, but to a city upon a hill; so that all our Saviour has in view in mentioning a city here, is the conspicuousness of one so built. It is as much as if our Saviour had said, You had need be wise and holy, for your conversation can no more be hid than a city that is built upon a hill, and is obvious to every eye. Neither do men light a candle — Or lamp rather, as, signifies. Indeed, candles were not used at that time in Judea for lighting their houses; consequently, the word here and elsewhere in the New Testament, translated candlestick, means a lamp stand. The purport of this verse is, you, my apostles and disciples, ought to consider for what end I have communicated my light to you. In the other hand, in (1 John 2:15-17) Do not love the world or the things in the world. If anyone loves the world, the love of the Father is not in him. For all that is in the world—the desires of the flesh and the desires of the eyes and pride in possessions—is not from the Father but is from the world. And the world is passing away along with its desires, but whoever does the will of God abides forever" Again, (James 4:4) reminds sinners: "You adulterous people! Do you not know that friendship with the *world* is enmity with God? Therefore whoever wishes to be a friend of the world makes himself an enemy of God. So be attentive with your eyes open, be wise as in (Colossians 2:8) "See to it that no one takes you captive by philosophy and empty deceit, according to human tradition, according to the elemental spirits of the *world*, and not according to Christ". Praise the Lord!

Worship: An act of religious devotion usually directed towards a deity. In the Christianity manner of *worship*, true *worship* is based on the inexhaustible excellences of God. To *worship* God is to affirm His supreme worth, for He alone is worthy. *Worship* involves awareness of God, awe in His presence, adoration of Him because of His excellences and acts, and an affirmation of praise in all He is and does. Perhaps the greatest need in all of Christendom is the clear understanding of the gospel teachings about worship. That consuming, selfless desire to give to God is the essence and the heart of *worship*. Genuine worship takes place only when God is worshipped for His own sake. The greatest achievement of the human soul is to be able to commune with God. The most significant activity of any group of people is to come into His presence and to magnify and *worship* His holy name. An act of *worship* may be performed individually, in an informal or formal group, or by a designated leader. "Let us come boldly to the throne of grace that we may obtain mercy and find grace to help in the time of need." And we read that in heaven those before Your throne fall down and worship You; may that really happen in our hearts.

In (Revelation 4: 1-11) "After these things I looked, and behold, a door standing open in heaven. And the first voice which I heard was like a trumpet speaking with me, saying, "Come up here, and I will show you things which must take place after this." Immediately I was in the Spirit; and behold, a throne set in heaven, and One sat on the throne. And He who sat there was like a jasper and a sardius stone in appearance; and there was a rainbow around the throne, in appearance like an emerald. Around the throne were twenty-four thrones, and on the thrones I saw twenty-four elders sitting, clothed in white robes; and they had crowns of gold on their heads.

And from the throne proceed-

Worship

ed lightning's, thundering's, and voices. Seven lamps of fire were burning before the throne, which are the seven Spirits of God. Before the throne there was a sea of glass, like crystal. And in the midst of the throne, and around the throne, were four living creatures full of eyes in front and in back. The first living creature was like a lion, the second living creature like a calf, the third living creature had a face like a man, and the fourth living creature was like a flying eagle. The four living creatures, each having six wings, were full of eyes around and within. And they do not rest day or night, saying: "Holy, holy, holy, Lord God Almighty, Who was and is and is to come!" Whenever the living creatures give glory and honour and thanks to Him who sits on the throne, who lives forever and ever, the twenty-four elders [who we believe represent the church of Jesus Christ in heaven, the twenty-four elders] fall down before Him who sits on the throne and worship Him who lives forever and ever, and cast their crowns before the throne, saying:" You are worthy, O Lord, To receive glory and honour and power; For You created all things, And by Your will they exist and were created."

Here, the scene is heaven-the centre of what is known as the throne of God. *Worship* asserts the reality of its object and defines its meaning by reference to it. For instance, you can assert "I love to think about how I am the same as God. That helps me. I think because God thinks. I feel because I have emotions-because God does. I have volitional choice and rational thought because God does. I am made in His image, after His likeness, but I am not God. And even in the sense in which I am the same, I am so inadequate, imperfect, and so insufficient to even compare me with the eternal God who is perfect in His personality. Worship the Lord and praise His Holy Name even as the Cherubim's and Seraphim's fell down and worship Him (God). Tap other ingredients from (John 4:24) "God is spirit, and those who worship him must worship in spirit and truth." (Psalm 95:6) "Oh come, let us worship and bow down; let us kneel before the Lord, our Maker! (Colossians 3:14-17) "And above all these put on love, which binds everything together in perfect harmony. And let the peace of Christ rule in your hearts, to which indeed you were called in one body. And be thankful. Let the word of Christ dwell in you richly, teaching and admonishing one another in all wisdom, singing psalms and hymns and spiritual songs, with thankfulness in your hearts to God. And whatever you do, in word or deed, do everything in the name of the Lord Jesus, giving thanks to God the Father through him. (Isaiah 12:5) "Sing praises to the Lord, for he has done gloriously; let this be made known in all the earth. (Romans 12:1) I appeal to you therefore, brothers, by the mercies of God, to present your bodies as a living sacrifice, holy and acceptable to God, which is your spiritual *worship and* many other biblical verses when worshipping. Praise the Lord.

Wrath: Several meanings are attached to the definition of wrath. Extreme anger. "he hid his pipe for fear of incurring his father's (God's) wrath". *Wrath* is defined as "the emotional response to perceived wrong and injustice," often translated as "anger," "indignation," "vexation," or "irritation." Both humans and God express wrath. But there is vast difference between the wrath of God and the wrath of man. God's wrath is holy and always justified; man's is never holy and rarely justified. Wrath is synonymous to anger, rage, fury, annoyance, indignation, outrage, pique, spleen, chagrin, vexation, exasperation, dudgeon, high dudgeon, temper, bad temper, badmood, illhumour, irritation, irritability, crossness, displeasure, discontentment, disgruntlement, irascibility, cantankerousness, peevishness, querulousness, crabbiness, testiness, tetchiness, snappishness; an so forth.

Wrath of God, The: In the Old Testament, *the wrath of God* is a divine response to human sin and disobedience. Idolatry was most often the occasion for divine wrath. (Psalm 78:56-66) describes Israel's idolatry. The wrath of God is consistently directed towards those who do not follow His will (Deuteronomy 1:26-46); (Joshua 7:1); (Psalm 2:1-6). The Old Testament prophets often wrote of a day in the future, the "day of wrath" (Zephaniah 1:14-15). God's wrath against sin and disobedience is perfectly justified because His plan for mankind is holy and perfect, just as God Himself is holy and perfect. God provided a way to gain divine favour—repentance—which turns God's wrath away from the sinner. To reject that perfect plan is to reject God's love, mercy, grace and favour and incur His righteous wrath. In the New Testament, Jesus' teachings support the concept of God as a God of wrath who judges sin. The story of the rich man and Lazarus speaks of the judgment of God and serious consequences for the unrepentant sinner (Luke 16:19-31). There was a rich man who was dressed in purple and fine linen and lived in luxury every day. At his gate was laid a beggar named Lazarus, covered with sores and longing to eat what fell from the rich man's table. Even the dogs came and licked his sores. "The time came when the beggar died and the angels carried him to Abraham's side. The rich man also died and was buried. [23] In Hades, where he was in torment, he looked up and saw Abraham far away, with Lazarus by his side. So he called to him, 'Father Abraham, have pity on me and send Lazarus to dip the tip of his finger in water and cool my tongue, because I am in agony in this fire.'

"But Abraham replied, 'Son, remember that in your lifetime you received your good things, while Lazarus received bad things, but now he is comforted here and you are in agony. And besides all this, between us and you a great chasm has been set in place, so that those who want to go from here to you cannot, nor can anyone cross over from there to us.' "He answered, 'Then I beg you, father, send Lazarus to my family, for I have five brothers. Let him warn them, so that they will not also come to this place of torment.' "Abraham replied, 'They have Moses and the Prophets; let them listen to them.' "'No, father Abraham,' he said, 'but if someone from the dead goes to them, they will repent.' "He said to him, 'If they do not listen to Moses and the Prophets, they will not be convinced even if someone rises from the dead.'"

Jesus said in John 3:36, "Whoever believes in the Son has eternal life, but whoever rejects the Son will not see life, for *God's wrath* remains on Him." The one who believes in the Son will not suffer God's wrath for his sin, because the Son took God's wrath when He died in our place on the cross (Romans 5:6-11). Those who do not believe in the Son, who do not receive Him as Savior, will be judged on the day of wrath (Romans 2:5-6). Conversely, human wrath is warned against in (Romans 12:19,Ephesians 4:26) and (Colossians 3:8-10). God alone is able to avenge because His vengeance is perfect and holy, whereas man's wrath is sinful, opening him up to demonic influence. For the Christian, anger and wrath are inconsistent with our new nature, which is the nature of Christ Himself (2 Corinthians 5:17). To realize freedom from the domination of wrath, the believer needs the Holy Spirit to sanctify and cleanse his heart of feelings of wrath and anger. (Romans 8) shows victory over sin in the life of one who is living in the Spirit (Romans 8:5-8).(Philippians 4:4-7) tells us that the mind controlled by the Spirit is filled with peace. The wrath of God is a fearsome and terrifying thing. Only those who have been covered by the blood of Christ, shed for us on the cross, can be assured that God's wrath will never fall on them. "Since we have now been justified by His blood, how much more shall we be saved from God's wrath through Him!" (Romans 5:9).

Writers of Biblical Books:

The Bible was written by approximately 40 men of diverse backgrounds over the course of 1500 years. Isaiah was a prophet, Ezra was a priest, Matthew was a tax-collector, John was a fisherman, Paul was a tentmaker, Moses was a shepherd, Luke was a physician. Despite being penned by different authors over 15 centuries, the Bible does not contradict itself and does not contain any errors. The authors all present different perspectives, but they all proclaim the same one true God, and the same one way of salvation—Jesus Christ (John 14:6; Acts 4:12). Few of the books of the Bible specifically name their author. Here are the books of the Bible along with the name of who is most assumed by biblical scholars to be the author, along with the approximate date of authorship:

Genesis, Exodus, Leviticus, Numbers, Deuteronomy = Moses - 1400 B.C, Joshua = Joshua - 1350 B.C, Judges, Ruth, 1 Samuel, 2 Samuel = Samuel, Nathan, Gad - 1000 - 900 B.C, 1 Kings, 2 Kings = Jeremiah - 600 B.C 1 Chronicles, 2 Chronicles, Ezra, Nehemiah = Ezra - 450 B.C, Esther = Mordecai - 400 B.C, Job = Moses - 1400 B.C, Psalms = several different authors, mostly David - 1000 - 400 B.C, Proverbs, Ecclesiastes, Song of Solomon = Solomon - 900 B.C, Isaiah = Isaiah - 700 B.C, Jeremiah, Lamentations = Jeremiah - 600 B.C, Ezekiel = Ezekiel - 550 B.C, Daniel = Daniel - 550 B.C, Hosea = Hosea - 750 B.C, Joel = Joel - 850 B.C, Amos = Amos - 750 B.C, Obadiah = Obadiah - 600 B.C, Jonah = Jonah - 700 B.C, Micah = Micah - 700 B.C, Nahum = Nahum - 650 B.C, Habakkuk = Habakkuk - 600 B.C, Zephaniah = Zephaniah - 650 B.C, Haggai = Haggai - 520 B.C Zechariah = Zechariah - 500 B.C Malachi =Malachi - 430 B.C, Matthew = Matthew - A.D. 55, Mark = John Mark - A.D. 50, Luke = Luke - A.D. 60, John = John - A.D. 90, Acts = Luke - A.D. 65, Romans, 1 Corinthians, 2 Corinthians, Galatians, Ephesians, Philippians, Colossians, 1 Thessalonians, 2 Thessalonians, 1 Timothy, 2 Timothy, Titus, Philemon = Paul - A.D. 50-70, Hebrews = unknown, mostly likely Paul, Luke, Barnabas, or Apollos - A.D. 65, James = James - A.D. 45, 1 Peter, 2 Peter = Peter - A.D. 60, 1 John, 2 John, 3 John = John - A.D. 90, Jude = Jude - A.D. 60 and Revelation = John - A.D. 90

Xmas: *kriss-muhas, eks-muhas/* noun-informal Christmas

Xylophone: A musical instrument played by striking, a row of wooden bars of graduated length with small hammers originated from Greek *zulon* 'wood'

Yy

Yahweh: [*yaueh*] Form of Hebrew name for God. Jehovah Yahweh. The covenant God of Isreal YHWH. In the original Hebrew. According to Jewish custom and because of reverence the divine name was not to be spoken, so the Hebrew words for Lord and God were substituted. Whenever the words Lord and God appear in large and small capital letters, the original Hebrew reads YHWH.

Youth: Literally, this signifies the period between childhood and adult age. 2 The state or quality of being young, energetic, and immature Like in (Proverbs 20:29) – "The glory of young men is their strength, And the honor of old men is their gray hair". 3 The age of rejoicing as a young man as recorded in (Ecclesiastes 11:9-10) ... Rejoice, O young man, in your **youth**, and let your heart cheer you in the days of your **youth**. Walk in the ways of your heart and the and sight of your eyes ..." meaning, do as you like, be buoyantly and cheerfully follow the inclinations and the desire which are stamped upon your nature as prevailing in your time of life. 1 Timothy 4:12 Don't let anyone look down on you..._because "Today's **youth** are the leaders of tomorrow". 4 So "Let no one despise you for your **youth**, but set the believers an example in speech, conduct, love, faith and in purity... (1 Timothy 4:12) " and above all "Remember thy Creator in the days of thy youth , before the days of trouble and the years approach when you will say, "I find no pleasure in them" (Ecclesiastes 12:1 NKJ). The **Bible** has lots to say about **youth**

Zz

Zacchaeus: In the New Testament account in (Luke Chapter 19)- A tax collector who being 'little of stature' climbed a tree to see Jesus and with whom Jesus stays despite complaints that he is a sinner. He is redeemed by the experience.

Zacharias: Two Zacharias appear in the New Testament. In Mathew 23:35 and Luke 11: 51 Zacharias is mentioned as a prophet stoned between the temple and the altar for his prophecies. He is probably the same as the Zachariah of 2 Chronicles 24:20-23 described as being slain in this way as distinct from the identically named 'Zechariah' The Zacharias of Luke is better known particularly his account in Luke 1 as the father of John the Baptist.

Zeal, Zeel (noun)/: Origin: Greek zelos: Great energy or enthusiasm for a cause or aim. Active interest, loving and admirable quality. My zeal, your zeal. My zeal for the Lord, My zeal for the Gospel. Zeal for prayers; active love for prayer; prayerfully inclined. Zeal of God: Have *zeal* of God. Permanently protected by God. God's mercy and kindness to a person. To have great zeal for someone or a thing. Divine zeal; Supernaturally covered, protected, favoured and belonging. For instance, the zeal of GOD to protect His Prophets. *'Touch not my anointed and do my prophets no harm'.* - A form of zeal from God to His prophets.

Zealous: Having or showing zeal. "the church council was extremely zealous in the application of the regulations" synonyms:
fervent, ardent, fervid, fiery, passionate, impassioned, devout, devoted; Having passionate energy for a belief or purpose. An example of zealous is a preacher in an energetic church. 2 Someone who is zealous spends a lot of time or energy in supporting something that they believe in very strongly. Zealous of good works like Christ in (Titus 2:14) "He gave Himself for us, that He might redeem us from all iniquity, and purify us for Himself, a people of His own, zealous of good works"' Also see: (Revelation 3:19) Those whom I love, I reprove and discipline, so be zealous and repent. (Romans 10:2) For I bear them witness that they have a zeal for God, but not according to knowledge. (Romans 12:11) Do not be slothful in zeal, be fervent in spirit, serve the Lord (Isaiah 59:17) He put on righ-

teousness as a breastplate, and a helmet of salvation on his head; he put on garments of vengeance for clothing, and wrapped himself in zeal as a cloak. (Psalm 119:139) My zeal consumes me, because my foes forget your words. (Philippians 1:27) Only let your manner of life be worthy of the gospel of Christ, so that whether I come and see you or am absent, I may hear of you that you are standing firm in one spirit, with one mind striving side by side for the faith of the gospel,

3 In these words we have two truths -- what Christ has done to make us His own, and what He expects of us. In the former we have a rich and beautiful summary of Christ's work for us: He gave Himself for us, He redeemed us from all iniquity, He cleansed us for Himself, He took us for a people, for His own possession. And all with the one object, that we should be a people zealous of good works. The doctrinal half of this wonderful passage has had much attention bestowed on it; let us devote our attention to its practical part -- we are to be a people zealous of good works. Christ expects of us that we shall be zealots for good works -- ardently, enthusiastically devoted to their performance. This cannot be said to be the feeling with which most Christians regard good works. What can be things that wakens zeal in work is a great and urgent sense of need. A great need wakens strong desire, stirs the heart and the will, rouses all the energies of our being. It was this sense of need that roused many to be *zealous* of the law; they hoped their works would save them. The Gospel has robbed this motive of its power. Has it taken away entirely the need of good works? No, indeed, it has given that urgent need a higher place than before. Christ needs, needs urgently, our good works. We are His servants, the members of His body, without whom He cannot possibly carry on His work on earth. The work is so great -- with the hundreds of millions of the unsaved -- the work is so great, that not one worker can be spared. There are thousands of Christians to-day who feel that their own business is urgent, and must be attended to, and have no conception of the urgency of Christ's work committed to them. The Church must waken up to teach each believer this.

4 A second great element of zeal in work is delight in it. An apprentice or a student mostly begins his work under a sense of duty. As he learns to understand and enjoy it, he does it with pleasure, and becomes *zealous* in its performance. The Church must train Christians to believe that when once we give our hearts to it, and seek for the training that makes us in some degree skilled workmen, there is no greater joy than that of sharing in Christ's work of mercy and beneficence. As physical and mental activity give pleasure, and call for the devotion and zeal of millions,

the spiritual service of Christ can waken our highest enthusiasm.

Zealots: A Jewish sect founded by Judas of Gamala in the early years of the 1st century AD, who fiercely opposed Roman domination. They fought fanatically during the great rebellion, which ended in the destruction of Jerusalem in AD 70.

Zebedee: (Zebedaios, Greek word in Strong's; Hebrew - Zvad'yah), according to all four Canonical gospels, was the father of James and John, two disciples of Jesus. The gospels also suggest that he was the husband of Salome: whereas Mark 15:40 names the women present at the crucifixion as "Mary Magdalene and Mary the mother of James the Less and of Joses, and Salome", the parallel passage in Matthew 27:56 has "Mary Magdalene, and Mary the mother of James and Joses, and the mother of Zebedee's children." Gospel sources concludes that the Salome of Mark 15:40 is probably identical with the mother of the sons of Zebedee in Matthew Zebedee was a fisherman, "probably of some means." 2 Although named several times in the gospels, the only times he actually appears are in (Matthew 4:21-22) "Going on from there, he saw two other brothers, James son of Zebedee and his brother John. They were in a boat with their father Zebedee, preparing their nets. Jesus called them, 22 and immediately they left the boat and their father and followed him. and (Mark 1:19-20) also states, when Jesus calls His First Disciples "...Going on a little farther, He saw James the son of Zebedee, and John his brother, who were also in the boat mending the nets. Immediately He called them; and they left their father Zebedee in the boat with the hired servants, and went away to follow Him. Note: where he is left in the boat after Jesus called James and John. Mark notes that e: Zebedee was left with the "hired men". Zebedee lived at or near Bethsaida.

Zebulun: (also **Zebulon, Zabulon** or **Zaboules**; Hebrew: (Tiberian Hebrew *Zəḇūlūn*, Standard Hebrew *Zevulun/Zvulun*)) was, according to the Books of Genesis and Numbers, the sixth and last son of Jacob and Leah, and the founder of the Israelite Tribe of Zebulun. Some gospel scholars believe this to be an eponymous metaphor providing an aetiology of the connectedness of the tribe to others in the Israelite confederation. With Leah as a matriarch, gospel scholars believe the tribe to have been regarded by the text's authors as a part of the original Israelite confederation. The name is derived from the Northwest Semitic root *zebulun*, common in 2nd millennium BC Ugaritic texts as an epithet (title) of the god Baal, as well as in Phoenician and (frequently) in Biblical Hebrew in personal names. The text of the Torah gives two dif-

Zebulun, The tomb of

ferent etymologies for the name *Zebulun*, which contextual scholars attribute to different sources – one to the 'Yahwist' and the other to the Elohist; the first being that it derives from *zebed*, the word for *gift*, in reference to Leah's view that her gaining of six sons was a *gift* from God; the second being that it derives from *yizbeleni*, meaning *honour*, in reference to Leah's hope that Jacob would give her honour now that she had given birth to six sons. In Deuteronomy, however an allusion is made to a third potential etymology, that it may be connected with *zibhe*, literally meaning *sacrifice*, in reference to commercial activities of the tribe of Zebulun – a commercial agreement made at Mount Tabor between the tribe of Zebulun and a group of non-Israelites was referred to as *zibhe-tzedek*, literally meaning *sacrifice to justice* or *sacrifice to Tzedek*. The Torah states that Zebulun had three sons – Sered, Elon, and Jahleel – each the eponymous founder of a clan. Beyond this, there is little other reference to Zebulun.

Zebulun, The tomb of:

The Tomb of Zebulun is located in Sidon, Lebanon. In the past, towards the end of Iyyar, Jews from the most distant parts of Palestine would make a pilgrimage to this tomb.

Some believe the depopulated village of Sabalan in the District of Safad was named after Zebulun

Zechariah; Zecher; Zacharias: An Old Testament prophet who had visions of a new world order and of a nameless 'Messaiah' who would bring universal peace. The book named after him contains many less conventional prophecies and some strange imagery. (Zachariah 1:10 - 11) "And I took my staff, even Beauty and cut it asunder that I might break the covenant which I had made with the people" - *And I took my staff, even Beauty* — Or, *pleasantness,* or *delight.* See (Zechariah 11:7) : emblematical, as of God's favour, gentleness, or kindness to his people, and of the honour and privilege which they possessed in his oracles, instituted worship, and temple; so especially of God's covenant with them, and all the blessings of it. *And cut it asunder* — To signify that, as they had rejected God and his favour, and refused to comply with the terms of his covenant, so that God had now annulled it, and rendered it utterly void. *That I might break my covenant* — This, in some measure, illustrates what is meant by the staff *Beauty.* While it was unbroken, the covenant between God and the Jews was whole and unbroken. And it is to be observed, Christ calls it *his* covenant, for he was the mediator of it: namely, to bring us to God in repentance, faith, and holy obedience; and to reconcile God to us in mercy and grace. *Which I had made with all the people* — Hebrew, , literally, *all* *people,* that is, all the tribes of Israel; and all other people that, by being proselyte to their religion, were incorporated into their nation. The Jewish Church is thus represented as being now stripped of all its glory, its crown profaned and cast to the ground, and all its honour laid in the dust, God being departed from it, and resolved no more to own it for his church. When Christ told the Jews that the kingdom of God should be taken from them, and given to another people, then he broke the staff of *Beauty,* (Matthew 21:43). And it was broken in that day, though Jerusalem and the Jewish people were spared yet forty years longer; and though the great men did not, or would not, understand Christ's words uttered on that occasion as a divine sentence, but thought to put it by with a cold, *God forbid,* (Luke 20:16). Yet *the poor of the flock, that waited upon him* — Namely, who knew the Messiah, believed in him, observed his doctrine, miracles, and life, and obeyed him; who understood with what authority he spoke, and could distinguish the voice of their shepherd from that of a stranger; *knew that he was the word of the Lord* — Saw and acknowledged God in all this, trembled at his word, and were confident that it would not fall to the ground.

Zedekiah: (Hebrew - Tsidkiyyahu (Tiberian) "My righteousness is Yahweh"; Greek - Zedekías; Latin - Sedecias), also written Tzidkiyahu), was a biblical character, said to be the last king of Judah before the destruction of the kingdom by Babylon. Zedekiah had been installed as king of Judah by Nebuchadnezzar II, king of Babylon, after a siege of Jerusalem in 597 BCE, to succeed his nephew, Jeconiah, who was overthrown as king after a reign of only three months and ten days. Zedekiah was born in c. 627 BCE or 618 BCE, being twenty-one on becoming king. Zedekiah's reign ended with the siege and fall of Jerusalem to Nebuchadnezzar II, which took place in 586 BCE, though more recent evidence dates the fall of Jerusalem to 587 BCE. The prophet Jeremiah was his counsellor, yet his epitaph is "he did evil in the sight of the Lord". (2 Kings 24:19-20) - "He did evil in the eyes of the Lord, just as Jehoiakim had done. 20 It was because of the Lord's anger that all this happened to Jerusalem and Judah, and in the end he thrust them from his presence". Accounted also is (Jeremiah 52:2-3) "He did evil in the eyes of the Lord, just as Jehoiakim had done. It was because of the Lord's anger that all this happened to Jerusalem and Judah, and in the end he thrust them from his presence".

Zeitgeist: The spirit of the time. The zeitgeist spirit is which has to do with individual or moral tendency. The characteristic of a period – as in the 'Christmas spirit.'

Zephaniah

Zephaniah: (Hebrew: "Concealed of or is Lord") is the name of several people in the Bible Old Testament and Jewish Tanakh. His name is commonly transliterated Sophonias in bibles translated from the Latin Vulgate or Septuagint. The name might mean "Yah(weh) has concealed", "[he whom] Yah(weh) has hidden", or ""Yah(weh) lies in wait"

Zephaniah, The Prophet: The most well-known Biblical figure bearing the name Zephaniah is the son of Cushi, and great-grandson of King Hezekiah, ninth in the literary order of the minor prophets. He prophesied in the days of Josiah, king of Judah (B.C. 641-610), and was contemporary with Jeremiah, with whom he had much in common. The only primary source from which we obtain our scanty knowledge of the personality and the rhetorical and literary qualities of this individual is the short book of the Old Testament which bears his name. The scene of his activity was the city of Jerusalem. (Zephaniah 1:4-10; 3:1, 14)

Ziggurat: A large stepped pyramid with a shrine on the top, of a type built in ancient Mesopotamia as a temple tower. 2 It is thought that the idea of the tower of Babel may have been base on a ziggurat.

Zillion: As in the church, cardinal number informal – a very large number of people or things. The form of most progressive evangelical churches of modern times.

Zodiac: The imaginary belt or zone of the heavens extended about eight degrees each side of the Ecliptic which the sun traverses annually. 2 The zodiac was divided by the ancient into 12 equal parts, proceeding from west to east, each part of 30 degrees and distinguished by a sign. This originally corresponded to the zodiacal constellations bearing the same names.

Zion: *(Tziyyon)* 1 An ancient Hebrew word-meaning a place of refuge or a Sanctuary. Also, the name of the hill in Jerusalem on which the city of David was built. 2 An alternative etymology holds that Zion is from the Aramaic word meaning "pure". Because a man had to be pure to enter the tent where the Ark of the Covenant was kept, this tent became known as Zion. When the Ark was brought by the Israelites into the Promised Land, the Land itself was known as Zion—pure and holy, because it contained the Ark. When the Israelites were captives in Babylon and cried for Zion, it wasn't only for their homeland, but for the Ark itself, for the state of being pure, holy, chosen. 3 ----the name of the "last free city" in the Matrix trilogy. 4 Zion:/zy-uhn/ (also sion /sy-uhn/) noun: the Jewish people or religion (In Christian thought/faith) the heavenly city or the Kingdom of Heaven.

Zionism: (*noun*) A movement for the development and protection of a Jewish nation in Israel.

Zoroastrianism: (noun) Religion of ancient Persia based on the worship of single god founded by the prophet Zoroaster (also called Zarathustra) in the 6th century BC.

Gospel Notes

Gospel Notes